CONVERSATIONS

> "... all learning involves conversation. That conversation may be with ourselves, between ourselves and an author's words on the page, with a colleague, with a mentor, with an apprentice, with a student."

"Always, conversations play a major role in
my thinking, learning, teaching, and changing."

Regie Routman
CONVERSATIONS

**Strategies
for Teaching,
Learning,
and Evaluating**

HEINEMANN
Portsmouth, NH

Heinemann
A division of Reed Elsevier Inc.
361 Hanover Street
Portsmouth, NH 03801–3912
www. heinemann.com

Offices and agents throughout the world

The author and publisher thank those who generously gave permission to reprint borrowed material:

"Bumble," "Knights, Armor, Castle," and "June" are from the book *Kids' Poems: Teaching Kindergartners to Love Writing Poetry* by Regie Routman, published by Scholastic Professional Books. © Copyright 2000 by Regie Routman. Used by permission of the publisher.

"My Friend" is from the book *Kids' Poems: Teaching First Graders to Love Writing Poetry* by Regie Routman, published by Scholastic Professional Books. © Copyright 2000 by Regie Routman. Used by permission of the publisher.

"Bees," "Violin (Nervous)," and "Piano Recital" are from the book *Kids' Poems: Teaching Second Graders to Love Writing Poetry* by Regie Routman, published by Scholastic Professional Books. © Copyright 2000 by Regie Routman. Used by permission of the publisher.

"Mix-Up," "Guitar," and "My Pencil" are from the book *Kids' Poems: Teaching Third and Fourth Graders to Love Writing Poetry* by Regie Routman, published by Scholastic Professional Books. © Copyright 2000 by Regie Routman. Used by permission of the publisher.

Figures 11-4 and 11-5 from *Time for Kids*. Reprinted by permission of the editor.

Appendixes C-1, C-2, and C-3 reprinted with permission of NCTE. May be reprinted for educational purposes. See Web site: *www.ncte.org/resolution/* for other resolutions on topics of interest to teachers of English and language arts.

Appendix C-4 adopted June 1999 © American Association of School Librarians, a division of the American Library Association.

Appendix E-1 from *Teachers as Readers Books Groups: Exploring Your Own Literacy* from the *Teachers as Readers Starter Kit* (1996), developed by the International Reading Association Teachers as Readers Committee. Copyright © 1996 by the International Reading Association. All rights reserved. Reprinted with permission. The kit includes a video, bookmarks, and brochures and can be ordered by calling the IRA at 800-336-READ, ext. 265. Ask for publication number 9103.

Library of Congress Cataloging-in-Publication Data
CIP data is on file with the Library of Congress.
ISBN: 0-325-00109-X

Editor: Lois Bridges
Production: Melissa L. Inglis and Renée Le Verrier
Cover design: Catherine Hawkes/Cat and Mouse
Text design: Darci Mehall/Aureo Design
Manufacturing: Louise Richardson

Cover photo by Donna Terek:
Working on *WACK*, monthly newsmagazine for parents, in Julie Beers' grade four class, March 1998

Printed in the United States of America on acid-free paper
03 02 01 00 99   RRD   1 2 3 4 5

For Frank

Contents

4   Teaching Children to Read   92

6   Quality Writing: Principles, Problems, and Goals   **205**

7 Journal Writing   233

8 Organizing for Writing: Procedures, Processes, and Perspectives   283

11 Reading Nonfiction   **440**

14   Developing Collaborative Communities: Creation, Organization, and Sustenance   520

15   Evaluation as Part of Teaching   557

THE BLUE PAGES: RESOURCES FOR TEACHERS

xxii *Contents*

A Note on the Use of Pronouns

To maintain a personal and objective tone, the use of he/she and him/her has been alternated and balanced throughout this book.

A Note About References

To keep the text unencumbered, complete references and bibliographic information are listed alphabetically by author at the end of the white pages, in the "Works Cited" section.

A Note About Professional Resources

Annotated professional resources are organized in The Blue Pages to align with chapters in *Conversations*. See The Blue Pages section in the Contents for the specific delineation and location.

ACKNOWLEDGMENTS

While I penned the words for *Conversations*, much of my thinking has been influenced by others. I collaborated with teachers in their classrooms, explored new ideas with authors as I read their works, dialogued with teachers and parents across the country, listened to educators speak at conferences, and engaged in lively discussion and debate with other authors, editors, and educators through e-mail, faxes, letters, and phone calls. So it is, in both theory and practice, that this book is a collaboration. It could never have been completed without the assistance and generosity of many people.

First of all, I am grateful to my talented colleagues in Shaker Heights, Ohio City School District where I worked from 1971–1998. Their ongoing support enabled me to work successfully as both a teacher and writer. Stimulating conversations with my colleagues shaped, and continue to shape, my thinking and my practice. In particular, I appreciate all the teachers who welcomed me into their classrooms each week. Also, superintendent of schools, Mark Freeman; director of elementary education, Bernice Stokes; principals George Cannon, Pat Heilbron, Rebecca Kimberly, Larry Svec, Rosemary Weltman, and Barbara Whitaker; and staff assistants Marianne Bursi, Lynn Cowen, and Sharron Williams all provided ongoing leadership, collegiality, and support. Wonderful building secretaries Bonnie Bolton, Lizbeth Coyne, Karen Dribben, Darlene Frantz, Judy Kalan, Linda Mendelsohn, Pat Neville, Lorene Rider, Beverly Scoby, Donna Segesdy, Lisa Toth, and Betsy Woodring cheerfully and efficiently provided me whatever I needed to do my job well.

The following people assisted me by sharing ideas and materials, providing or verifying information, and/or fulfilling a specific request and lending support: Karen Anderson, Leslie Bakkila, Christine Banks, Patsy Bannon, Ellen Battle, Josh Berger, Lori Bianchini, Brennan Bird, Fred Bolden, Louise Borden, Jane Braunger, Debbie Brighton, Denise Brown, Dana Bulan, Jim Burke, Cissy Burns, Cindy Campbell, Charee Cantrell, Marlene Cohn, Joanna Connors, Cathy Corrado, Amy Correa, Liz Crider, Gary Davidian, Joan Di Dio, Lori Jane Dowell-Hantelmann, Mary Downey, Stephanie Eagleton, Bill Eastman, Harryette Eaton, Marilyn Eppich, Lisa Farmer, Alan Farstrup, Robyn Feinstein, Amy Fingerhut, Toni Gibson, Stephanie Green, Delores Groves, Vanessa Hancock, Savannah Harbison, Lisa Hardiman, Pat Henderson, Jim Henry, Ana Hernandez, Bonnie Campbell Hill, Kevin Hill, Sherri Jarvie, Judy Jindra, Nancy J. Johnson, Rudy Kalafus, Vi Kante, Tammy Kastner, Perry Klass, Ed Kmitt, Leslie Landreth, Patricia Lease, Marsha Lilly, Karen Lum, Bonnie McCants, Mary Macchiusi, Miriam Maracek, Ruth Mardell, Louisa Matthias, Carlton Moody, Margaret Moustafa, Dana Noble, Katherine Schlick Noe, Gloria Norton, Lori Oczkus, Mike Oliver, Norris Ross, Thommie Piercy, Jody Brown Podl, Joyce Pope, Louise Pope, Peg Rimedio, Richard Routman, Ellen Rubin, Linda Schlein, Elizabeth Schutter, Drake Sharp, Anika Simpson, Karen Smith, David Stewart, Hallie Stewart, Beverly Sullivan, Mimi Testen, Andrew Thomas, Ken Wallis, Elaine Weiner, Vickie Weinland, Peg Welch, Christine Wilson, Antonia Wylie, Lauren Wohl, Kathy Wolfe, and Danny Young.

Trusted colleagues graciously reviewed one or more sections, partial drafts, and/or chapters. Their thoughtful insights are woven into this text: Veronica Allen, Mark Austin, Christine Cachat, Cathy Grieshop, Pat Heilbron, Carol Hochman, Chris Hayward, Nancy

Johnston, Rebecca Kimberly, Diane Levin, Donna Maxim, Jennie Nader, Kathy O'Neal, Jeannine Perry, Neal Robinson, Nancy Schubert, Joan Servis, Jennifer Shoda, Barbara Speer, Tara Strachan, Elisabeth Tuttle, and Linda Wold.

Five outstanding colleagues read and responded to most or all of the text. English teacher Holly Burgess carefully read the entire manuscript. Holly greatly appreciates what elementary teachers do and always sees connections to her high school classroom. Again and again she inspired me to rethink and rewrite, making the text stronger. I love her wide vision, her keen insights, her wonderful generosity, and her unflinching honesty.

Karen Sher, whose talents as a teacher shine in her kindergarten classroom, read my evolving text and responded with thoughtful queries and affirmations. This book is much richer for her knowledge, experiences, and insights.

Linda Cooper, gifted grade four teacher, read and responded with candor, enthusiasm, and helpful suggestions. Linda's close friendship and collegiality continue to enrich my teaching and all aspects of my life.

Julie Beers, grade four teacher, responded with intelligence and care. She is a gifted teacher of writing and many of my insights on writing emanate from our continuing work together. Julie's own terrific work permeates this book. I appreciate her energy, openness, generosity, and our warm friendship.

Second-grade teacher Loretta Martin continues to be an intellectual lifeline. In addition to thoughtfully reading and responding to most of this text, Loretta and I enjoy ongoing conversations about teaching and literacy. I treasure our friendship and collegiality.

For their kind assistance in consolidating my thoughts about spelling development and related research, I am grateful to spelling experts Sandra Wilde and Richard Gentry. I am also indebted to talented teacher Cindy Marten for carefully reading, rereading, and adding immeasurably to the spelling chapter.

My deep appreciation to Richard Allington and Jeff McQuillan for their thoughtful comments regarding reading research. And I extend my sincere thanks to Michael Artale for his skillful graphic rendition of teachers' room plans that appear in Chapter 14.

I am indebted to Kathy O'Neal, who understands the importance and implementation of a flexible library program, for her keen insights (I savor our ongoing conversations over coffee at Starbucks). My appreciation to Jo Ann Everett for all her expertise and generosity, and to Ann Van Duesen who graciously responded to a last minute request for information.

The Blue Pages, Resources for Teachers, have been an enormous undertaking and benefited from the generosity and efforts of several talented educators. Once again, I was blessed to work with gifted educator Susan Hepler who wrote all the annotations for both the literature and supplemental lists. Susan's wide knowledge as a children's literature specialist and her flair for writing yielded succinct yet detailed and engaging annotations that provide essential information and more. Susan also masterfully critiqued several chapter drafts. I value her enormous talents, our thought-provoking conversations about literature, and our continuing friendship.

Long ago, Judy Wallis won my great respect, admiration, and deepest appreciation. When I was literally drowning—trying to keep up with reading and selecting current professional books and articles and, then, writing corresponding annotations for The Blue Pages—Judy graciously stepped in and assumed a partnership role. With enthusiasm and unflagging energy, she also tracked down books and articles, contacted publishers, and paid meticulous attention to the myriad details as she oversaw the entire project.

Our conversations about literature and literacy, and our continuing friendship, have been a high point in writing this book.

Several other educators added their considerable talents to The Blue Pages. Libby Larrabee, stellar Reading Recovery teacher leader, carefully evaluated and annotated many "little books" for developing readers and selected the most useful for The Blue Pages. Fourth–fifth grade teacher Annie Gordon (with expert guidance from Toby Gordon, Leigh Peake, and Susan Ohanian) skillfully selected, evaluated, and annotated practical resources for teaching mathematics. Danny Miller, social studies expert, deftly selected and annotated useful resources in that discipline.

Wendy Saul deserves special mention. She has been wonderfully generous in our conversations on the page and over the phone. Her enlightened thinking added clarity and depth to the chapters on nonfiction and curriculum inquiry. Her contributions to The Blue Pages, regarding science and inquiry resources, are first rate. I am in awe of her knowledge and talents.

Lee Sattelmeyer, third-grade teacher and computer expert, gets special commendation. At my invitation, Lee wrote an extensive section on technology in the classroom as well as compiled and annotated useful technology terms and resources for The Blue Pages. Lee's knowledge, enthusiasm, friendship, and gentle spirit are a continuing gift.

I am indebted to kindergarten teacher Christine Hoegler for always welcoming me into her classroom and generously sharing her knowledge, students, and materials. Susan Mears, kindergarten teacher, has been similarly kind and has pushed my thinking forward.

Wonderful friends sustained me during the long writing days and forgave my unavailability for many months at a time. Harriet Cooper has been a cherished friend for almost forty years. I treasure our weekly phone calls and her unfailing love and support. Judie Thelen remains a dear friend and colleague. I rely on her devoted friendship, good humor, and enthusiasm for learning. Esteemed friend Diane Levin never fails to boost me with her contagious enthusiasm, generous support, and cutting-edge knowledge. Dear friend Tena Rosner understood the work pressures and valued my friendship even when the best we could do was talk by phone. Juliette Hamelecourt continues to inspire and nurture me with her wisdom, friendship, and love. Sung-a and Chanho Park are dear and generous friends. Vincent and Adele Monnier are equally gracious and understanding. Joan Servis inspires me with her energy, good sense, and superlative teaching skills. Our deep and continuing friendship and collegiality mean the world to me. Jim Servis, also, has been a dear friend who has performed many kindnesses. Also near and dear and ever-supportive are my friends Toby Gordon, Lois Kalafus, Rebecca Kimberly, Judy Levin, Susan Michelson, Carol Weinstock, and Rosemary Weltman.

A special thanks to Don Graves for his continuing friendship, for thoughtfully responding to a chapter draft, for reminding me on days of self-doubt that I knew enough, and for uplifting me with: "Any day with even bad writing is a good day writing" (personal communication).

I would be remiss not to mention and honor Bonnie Chambers who lived her life valiantly and who contributed mightily to our profession. Bonnie inspired me—and so many others with her passion, knowledge, humor, and deep commitment to literacy. Bonnie raised the level of our educational conversations.

Heinemann, my publishing company, has been splendid in its efforts to produce this huge book. My editor Lois Bridges has been magnificent in every way, a joy to work with.

Lois is amazingly responsive and insightful. She knows exactly where and when to intervene to strengthen the text while being totally respectful of the author's voice and intention. An added bonus is that we have become close and trusted friends.

Mike Gibbons continues to lead Heinemann with skill and grace. I am grateful for his dedication to excellence, willingness to go "the extra mile," and multiple talents. My affection and admiration for Mike is deep and enduring.

I am thankful for Leigh Peake, multi-talented director of editorial. It was Leigh who suggested writing about what it means to be "professional," which became Chapter 1 of this book. I have enjoyed our special conversations together and look forward to more of them.

Once again, I was extremely fortunate to have the copyediting talents of Alan Huisman. Alan is a rare and gifted copyeditor, able to strengthen and tighten the text, all the while maintaining the author's tone and voice. I am also grateful to copyeditor Melissa Dobson for her diligence and skill.

Janine Duggan, editorial assistant, provided extraordinary support of exceptional quality. With the assistance of Bill Varner, Christine Monahan, Lynne Mehley, and Brenda Manix, Janine efficiently answered all my queries regarding information and research I was seeking. She supervised the acquisition of more than a hundred professional resources through the generosity of leading publishers and helped update information on professional journals and resources. Thanks, too, to Karen Chabot, who promptly and graciously responded to urgent requests.

The production staff, under the leadership of Renée Le Verrier, did a marvelous job in carrying the book to publication in a beautiful and timely fashion. Renée worked tirelessly attending to endless details and overseeing the cover and interior design. For her unfailing efforts, I am very grateful.

Melissa Inglis, my production editor, ever-efficient and good-humored as she shoulders the enormous challenge of taking an author's manuscript and bringing it to publication, manages to make it all look effortless. For her terrific efforts, talents, and meticulous attention to myriad details, I am most appreciative.

Others working for Heinemann were also integral to getting the book successfully published. Production Supervisor Abigail Heim oversaw schedules and skillfully supervised the entire production editing process. Louise Richardson, manufacturing supervisor, carefully chose the paper for the book and attended to the actual production of the book. Contract and Permissions Supervisor Roberta Lew dealt masterfully with permissions. I am also grateful to Cape Cod Compositors for the fine work they did with typesetting and page composition, to John Brotzman for his outstanding work creating an index, and to Cindy Black for the careful proofreading work. And thanks to Catherine Hawkes for the beautiful cover design, and to Darci Mehall of Aureo Design for her lively, opening photo essay.

Beyond book publication, a team of able people at Heinemann continue to help me organize speaking engagements and workshops and support me professionally. Karen Hiller has been first rate in organizing my speaking engagements. Susie Stroud, Cherie Lebel, Kristine Gallant, and Pat Goodman work diligently to ensure that workshops run smoothly. Grateful thanks also go to others at Heinemann for their excellent efforts: Lori Lampert, sales manager who also graciously arranges author signings and receptions at conferences; Maxine Graves, business manager and financial wizard; Deanna Richardson who overseas reprints; and Maura Sullivan for all her terrific marketing and behind-the-scenes efforts. A heartfelt thanks to Kevlynn Annandale, who heads the First Steps program and who has become a dear friend and colleague. Sincere thanks, too, to all the representatives who work diligently to sell my—and other authors'—books. In particular, I have appreciated my warm, long-term relationship with Pat Eastman, Greg Michaels, Nancy O' Connor, and Peggy Sherman.

I am especially thankful for my family. First and foremost, I could never have written this book without the loving support of Frank, my dear husband of thirty-five years. His daily understanding, generous love, and willingness to set aside our everyday life together for more than a year was an unselfish gift of love. My son Peter and his wife Claudine are close to my heart and always supportive. I love them dearly. My father, Manny Leventhal, is loving and proud. I am also grateful to all members of my family who have offered their love and support.

My acknowledgments would not be complete without mention of my Macintosh Powerbook on which I did all my writing. I lived in fear of a freeze or imminent disaster, and it never happened.

In closing, while I accept responsibility for the book's flaws, I have extended my best effort—an effort I was able to make through the rich and varied conversations I shared with many fine educators, valued colleagues, dear friends, and my wonderful family. For all their kindness, generosity, and understanding, I am humbled and thankful.

Regie Routman, July 1999

The question came out of the blue at the end of a two-hour workshop at the Colorado Council of the International Reading Association in February 1992: "Are you going to write a follow-up to *Invitations*?" The woman might as well have asked, *Will you be climbing Mount Everest?*

Only a year had gone by since I had completed *Invitations*. I was still exhausted and believed that I would never write another education book. It was too hard, too time-consuming, and I had said everything I wanted to. Now I wanted to balance my life. I remember my response. "No. Absolutely not. There are other things I want to do. For example, I want to stay married." The audience laughed, but I meant it.

I had written *Invitations* while I was working full time. It had taken two years. I wrote in every spare moment—evenings, weekends, vacations. I wasn't prepared to make such a sacrifice again. Yet the question from the Colorado teacher stayed with me. A follow-up book? No. Never. Well, maybe. Perhaps. I started thinking about it in bits and pieces. A third book—*Conversations*—would bring full circle the writing I had started with *Transitions* and *Invitations*, would complete the trilogy. It would examine and explain the multiple dimensions of language learning, teaching, and evaluating that we teachers must know and understand. And it would draw from the rich professional conversations that we educators need to guide, nurture, and sustain us.

Then, in the fall of 1995, just as I was about to begin writing this book, the political climate sent me on a detour. The "reading wars" were going strong, and politics was dictating educational policy. I wrote *Literacy at the Crossroads: Crucial Talk About Reading, Writing, and Other Teaching Dilemmas* to clarify all the issues, not just the grievous public misunderstanding that pitched whole language against phonics. My goal was to examine the research and reality around reading and writing practices, the process of change, and what we teachers must do to counteract the continuing media blitz decrying the inadequacy of our schools and our teaching methods.

Since that time, I have been increasingly concerned that we are stepping backward, that we are embracing "scientific" research based on a deficit, medical model, that teachers' voices are absent from curricular decisions on local, state, and national levels, that we are running scared. Pressured by the demand—and the desire—for high test scores, we have looked for simple solutions to complex literacy issues. Instead of functioning as informed and influential professionals, we have been cowed by what we read in the media, by special-interest groups with narrow agendas, by our collective lack of self-confidence as a profession. As in the past, we have become overfocused on methodology, relying on programs and packages instead of our knowledgeable professional judgment. Only by becoming teachers who know and can articulate what we do and how and why we do it and who stand up for what we know and hold dear can we make our schools viable for our most precious natural resources, our students.

I write with the hope that our continuing dialogue will move our practices, principles, and participation in professional life forward. The writing life and the teaching life are similar. The demands, the immersion, the total commitment necessary to do a good job, the ongoing thoughts about ways to do "it" better, do not end at the close of the workday. Pondering over teaching—and writing—is all consuming. Much of my composing takes the form of conversations with myself. Should I say it this way or that way? What should I leave out? How much detail is necessary? Is this clear? How should I organize? Where should I begin? Should I try this another way?

While writing this book, and thinking about the title, it struck me that all learning involves conversation. The ongoing dialogue, internal and external, that occurs as we read, write, listen, view, compose, observe, refine, interpret, and analyze is how we learn. That conversation may be with ourselves, between ourselves and an author's words on the page, with a colleague, with a mentor, with an apprentice, with a student. We need many opportunities to explore, expand, and develop our thinking and teaching:

- Ongoing interior dialogue
- Conversations with authors on the page (or screen)
- Discussions with colleagues
- Interactions with our students in the various roles we take with them: mentor, guide, facilitator, collaborator, listener, encourager
- Conversations with community members (parents and other stakeholders)

These conversations also need to occur in many contexts: discussions about strategies, reading with a partner, spelling, journal writing, literature, research, collaborative reading and writing—in short, all aspects of teaching, learning, and evaluating.

Conversations need to be relevant, inviting, purposeful, respectful, and thought provoking. As Arthur Applebee states in his exceptionally thoughtful *Curriculum as Conversation* (1996):

> Rather than beginning with an exhaustive inventory of the structure of the subject matter, we begin with a consideration of the conversations that matter. . . . The question then becomes, how can we orchestrate these conversations so that students can enter into them? (52)

I would add that we teachers need to initiate and participate in the conversations that must take place for "best practice" to flourish and for our students to thrive.

Much of what I know, I know because I have questioned and thought about ideas with others, tried things out, modified stances, talked with colleagues. Always, conversations play a major role in my thinking, learning, teaching, and changing. So it is with all learners. I would argue that when no conversations are going on, as in whole-class "skill and drill," it's not learning that's taking place but rather rote memorization.

Conversations denote engaged listening, a keen interest in others' ideas and opinions. For example, one day I happened to be talking by phone with my friend Diane Levin, language arts consultant at the California Department of Education. She asked me what I was working on and thinking about. Sharing my current thinking on integrated learning and hearing her reaction helped me solidify my ideas. Speaking my thoughts aloud and responding to her queries and comments helped me clarify and confirm the direction I was heading.

WHY WE NEED CONTINUING, OPEN DIALOGUE

One of my worries continues to be that there are too few conversations in too few places—no active listening or compromising, no exchanges, no discussion of curriculum, no taking seriously the feedback from teachers. Yet the connections, interactions, reflections, and new thinking that evolve from rich conversations are the means for defining what we know. I trust, as I believe we all must, that dialogue and debate, accompanied by flexibility and openness, will lead to new insights and substantive learning, not just for our students but for us as teachers, too.

Jargon and labels, in particular, seem to bring conversation to a halt; they divide people and box them in. Confusion and devastation often result. Labels such as *whole language, phonics,* and *direct instruction* shut down conversation. Those terms and others like them became so emotionally charged in the nineties that give-and-take became impossible. Are you whole language or phonics? It's yes–no, either–or. Under what conditions and in what circumstances does not arise.

Because labels don't describe, the label's meaning is different for each person based on past experiences, personal ideologies, and specific contexts. Just about every educational term offends someone or other. Parents become flustered and disconcerted and have no idea what we're talking about. Labels such as *emergent, invented spelling, standards,* and even *literacy* are charged terms that carry different, often unclear, meanings for parents, teachers, politicians, and community members. For example, no matter how much time I spent explaining *whole language,* I found most people didn't understand the term: "Isn't that where they don't teach them how to spell, they can spell however they want, and it's not corrected?" So I stopped using the label publicly and went right to explaining clearly what I do as a teacher. It was a painful lesson that took a long time to learn.

Take a recent school conference initiated by two very upset parents of two different first graders. A narrative section on the first-grade report card described their respective children as "emerging readers." Since their kindergarten teacher had used the same term on their final report card the year before, these parents assumed their children had made no growth in reading. Two hours later, after the principal and I had tried to explain the term as well as our philosophy of teaching, they were still confused. That confusion would have been avoided if the children's reading behaviors had been clearly described, without a label.

Or take my nine-month experience writing a short article for *Parents* magazine on teaching meaning-based reading and writing in first grade ("Ready to Read," 1997). The executive editor with whom I worked was smart, articulate, well informed, and open minded. Yet she had no idea what I was talking about in my early drafts. She kept telling me, "Regie, I've heard the language, but I don't understand what actually takes place when you teach reading. Show us exactly what happens, what it looks like." She had gotten bogged down in the labels I'd used: *centers, choice, reading groups, shared reading.* These terms have no meaning for people outside education. Until we not only explain the meaning of the terms we use but also describe how they relate to the teaching and learning we do in the classroom, we will continue to confuse and incite parents and the general public. (Interestingly enough, even though my position was holistic, the published article generated few letters of protest. Because the teaching detailed in the article was rigorous and explicit, it made sense.)

Now another set of labels is causing consternation: *balance, the basics, explicit instruction, phonemic awareness, guided reading,* to name a few. Once again, we must explain and demonstrate what the term or practice looks like, how it functions in the classroom, what our purposes for teaching and learning are. All of this I attempt to do in the chapters that follow.

CHANGE AND REFORM

One cannot be a professional teacher without being part of reform and change—in the classroom, the school, and the district, as well as at state and national levels. Though we might wish it to be otherwise, there is no endpoint in teaching at which we finally have the knowledge and the tools to do the job perfectly. What works today gets reexamined tomorrow. We encounter new research or make new observations. We rethink our approach. We have a conversation with colleagues that makes us question something we've been doing. We suddenly see a student's work in a new light. Learning is always fluid, never static.

I am always distressed when I overhear a teacher ask a colleague, "Why are you going to hear so-and-so (a well-known author or some other literacy notable) again? You heard him speak a few years ago." The questioner has failed to realize that learning is not just about getting new information; it's about starting new conversations with yourself and others and reflecting on how that information fits with what you believe. Just as rereading a text is never the same, because you bring different expectations and experiences to it, so hearing a speaker again becomes a new learning experience, because both you and the speaker have changed.

I always feel successful when a participant in my workshop says, "Today reconfirmed what I know. I feel validated for what I believe and do." Or, "I get it now." Or, as one middle school teacher at a recent workshop commented, "This workshop has made me think about how to focus on teaching the strategies students need to apply on their own in other situations. Sometimes I float from activity to activity, and it is so clear now." Confirmation, reconsideration, questioning what you already know and do, and making new connections are what learning is all about.

Some Realities About Change

Change is much more difficult than most of us ever imagine. We're idealistic at first, believing that our colleagues will "come along" if given enough time and opportunity. We learn that some teachers choose not to move forward, prefer to stick with the "tried and true." And it's not just teachers. Parents resist. So do students. Eventually we find out that significant change and conflict go hand in hand and that all voices—students, parents, teachers, and administrators—need to be heard and respected throughout the process if meaningful change is to occur.

There is no shortcut to schoolwide reform. Each of us, individually and collectively, must go through the process. Someone else's checklist, developmental continuum, evaluation forms, or curriculum framework can spur our thinking and get our own conversations going. But another's reform documents and process can only guide us, not direct us. What happens in the process of creating our own curriculum, framework, standards, is far more important than any document. It is the conversations around curriculum that push us to change, not the documents themselves. I am reminded of the insightful comment by a teacher who was part of our district's multiyear process of creating a K–12 language arts framework: "Curriculum is not a document; it's a dialogue." Successful reform depends on competent, knowledgeable, courageous teachers.

Visitors to a classroom get a glimpse of the thinking behind the student work and collaborative groups. Participants in a workshop get activities and ideas to use in the classroom. Readers of a textbook on literacy get a feel for what goes on in a classroom. But for ideas to transfer into thoughtful classroom practice and for meaningful change to occur, ongoing conversation and reflection are necessary. Teachers new to a district and teachers who were not on the committee that created new documents must have time to talk about the curriculum, procedures, philosophy. Teachers who attend a workshop or a conference or read a great professional book must keep the ideas alive and out front by talking about them, sharing them, trying them out.

We must create and insist on inviolate time for teachers to talk and work together. More important than computers and any new technology, the best educational tool we have is the human mind given the time to ponder, inquire, analyze, debate, suggest, plan, share, reason. Our exchange of ideas and our working through problems related to all areas of the curriculum and learning must be ongoing and collaborative. And that collaboration must not be merely teacher to teacher but must include administrators, directors, supervisors, and parents. Unless the power base is truly a shared partnership, a few key people will continue to lead the way in schools and districts, and when they leave, reform efforts will be derailed.

> The flawed belief that reforms can simply be replicated elsewhere once they have been developed in demonstration sites is one key to the unhappy history of curriculum change. The process of change is inherently constructivist. Any reform that is merely implemented will eventually recede rather than taking root. Each school community must struggle with new ideas for itself if it is to develop the deep understanding and commitment needed to engage in the continual problem solving demanded by major changes in practice. (Darling-Hammond 1997, 217)

The process of reform is exhausting, frustrating, and enormously time-consuming. Nonetheless, most of us who have engaged in conversations leading to change feel we are serving our students better. We feel more knowledgeable and professional. We collaborate more. We are more personally involved with our colleagues and our students. We continue to ask questions and feel invigorated by our teaching, which is always growing and changing. My hope in writing this book is to be your supportive partner in your own changing and teaching process.

WHAT IS THIS BOOK ABOUT?

Conversations: Strategies for Teaching, Learning, and Evaluating reflects my current thinking as a daily observer of and participant in the literacy landscape. It is not a book about whole language or phonics or a particular methodology. It is about effective teaching and what it means to be a professional. I write as a learner, a teacher, an apprentice, and an expert. I write for first-year teachers and for thirty-year veterans. I write for any teacher interested in thinking about his or her practice. I write because I want schools and classrooms to be more relevant, challenging, humane, and collaborative places for ourselves and our students. I write because I need to go on learning.

In this book I tackle issues and strategies that I believe are most critical for us and our students in the daily life of the classroom. Detailed chapters focus on issues and strategies connected with learning and teaching literature, reading, writing, spelling, curriculum inquiry, and evaluation, as well as on establishing the supports that make effective teaching possible. In the process of discussing theory and practice supported by current research and experience, I share many demonstrations and useful resources. I write narratives, essays, explanations, anecdotes, lists, stories, examples, questions, lesson plans—all of it meant as an invitation to lively discussion and thinking about your own teaching.

Because effective teaching—and successful reform—depend on knowing and applying relevant research, I back up my beliefs and practices with research that is both naturalistic (classroom based) and experimental (scientific). Sometimes, at a workshop, a teacher will say, "Don't give me all that research, I just want the practical activities"—in other words, *Tell me what to do.* Ah, if it only were that simple. Teaching is a complex business, and as professionals we must thoughtfully support our practices with theory and beliefs based on solid research. When we communicate with parents, administrators, and community members, we must be able to say, *This is what I do and why I do it, and here is the research that supports my thinking and my teaching practices.*

Along with relevant research and "best practice," I also discuss literacy problems and pitfalls. We can't move forward in our teaching until we have analyzed what hasn't worked well and why. If we are to be thoughtful decision makers, we must continually question and actively push our professional thinking forward.

An analogy involving a situation we all face at some time in our life brings home the point. When a relationship between two people is not working, all the self-help books in the world have little effect until we have some understanding of the problems and their causes. Without such analysis, the changes we make will be superficial and temporary. We must examine and understand our failures and shortcomings before we can improve our situation.

So it is with teaching. It is not enough to say, *Here is what writing workshop looks like,* or, *This is how a guided reading group functions.* There is no formula, no one best way, no step-by-step recipe. Too often we have put procedures in place while missing the heart and soul of the endeavor. We must look carefully at what works and what doesn't and learn from our experiences. Problem solving, rethinking, and reflecting are at the heart of our work as effective teachers. To this end, I conclude every chapter with a section I call "Continuing the Conversation" that helps you do just that.

HOW IS THIS BOOK ORGANIZED?

As I did in *Invitations,* I write for specific grades, but I also write across grade levels. We teachers tend to be bound to grade levels, when in fact, the learning/teaching processes are similar, regardless of the student's age. Many of the richest conversations we have in our schools are across grade levels. Kindergarten issues apply to all grades, even to high school students and teachers. Don't look at a first- or second-grade writing sample and think, *This doesn't apply to me.* Widen your lens. Look at the process. Ask yourself, *What's going on here? What is the student trying to accomplish? How is the teacher supporting and scaffolding this effort? What meaning does this have for my teaching and my classroom?*

Knowing how little time teachers have, I have struggled with the length of this book. It is long because I include a lot of demonstrations and examples: *This is how I do it. This is what it looks like and sounds like. Here is one way to organize. Here's what the students' work looks like, and here's how it came to be.* My goal is for you, the reader, to feel, *Yes, I can do this too.* While the book is meant to be read consecutively, from beginning to end, and the order of the chapters is based on logic and flow, this in no way signifies a hierarchy of importance. I am also respectful of how little time we all have. Because each of the chapters is complete within itself, they can be read in any order or grouping that makes sense.

Because this is already a big book, I have not taken on the issues surrounding the push for charter schools, second language learners, inclusion, multiage grouping, or students with learning disabilities. However, I believe that all students need the same challenging curriculum and excellent teaching. Struggling students and second language learners require more support, more demonstrations, and in some cases, specialized materials and methods. But the practices and resources that serve our highest achieving students well are the same practices all students need and are entitled to.

A NOTE ABOUT THE BLUE PAGES AND FAVORITE RESOURCES

I wrestled with how detailed to make the resources section. *Transitions* and *Invitations* have extensive Blue Pages. So many new books, publications, and articles have appeared since I completed *The Blue Pages* and the updated *Invitations: Changing as Teachers and Learners K–12.* Additionally, the Internet has made this and so many other kinds of information easily accessible.

Rather than include all the excellent resources published since 1994 (and one or two published earlier if they are particularly noteworthy and were previously overlooked), language arts coordinator Judy Wallis and I have selected and annotated those that we have found particularly helpful to the classroom teacher and that are easily accessible. Our "free" time as teachers is so limited that what we choose to read, view, and think about must be supportive and useful and worth our time.

These are the books and resources that have particularly impacted my colleagues and my teaching and learning, have helped us understand concepts more clearly and deeply, and caused us not only to reflect on teaching but also to try out new ideas and improve our practice. If we teachers are to be scholars and decision makers, we must constantly update our knowledge and challenge our thinking. Reading, viewing, and reflecting on professional resources are some of the best ways to do that.

Because the resource lists are necessarily limited, many excellent ones have been omitted. You will want to keep up to date by checking the latest professional books from Heinemann (Portsmouth, NH), Stenhouse (York, ME), Christopher-Gordon (Norwood, MA), Scholastic Professional Books (New York), Teachers College Press (New York), Peguis (Winnipeg, Manitoba), Jossey-Bass (San Francisco), and other reputable publishers.

Also check out the following excellent journals and see whether your school can subscribe to several of them: *Educational Leadership, The Reading Teacher, Language Arts, Phi Delta Kappan, Teaching K–8, The New Advocate, Primary Voices,* and *Voices from the Middle.* Professional conversations that result from such reading help us become wiser decision makers and contribute to our intelligent public conversation with parents and other community members.

For easy access, resources referred to in each chapter are organized by chapter in The Blue Pages, which opens with a detailed table of contents. In addition to professional resources, there are extensive literature lists and supplemental lists that have been compiled and annotated by noted children's literature specialist Susan Hepler. These excellent lists are full of ideas and information and are meant to support your guided reading and literature conversations program. The lists are preceded by commentary on selecting and using literature, series fiction, and related topics. There is also a comprehensive annotated list of recommended "little books" for developing readers, author/illustrator studies, and many books for encouraging children to write. In addition to appendixes that support your daily teaching practice, I have also included "Books I Have Loved," my favorites from my personal reading log.

WELCOME TO CONVERSATIONS

My hope with this book is to inspire continuing conversations with you, my valued reader. My intention is that you not just *learn about* teaching but *participate in* teaching through conversations with yourself, with me on the page as you are read, with your colleagues, and with the larger professional community—experts in the field encountered through journal articles, books, and professional conferences. My hope is that your conversations will lead to questioning, inquiring, trying out, modifying, confirming, rethinking, challenging, revising, and validating your learning, teaching, and evaluating and, in so doing, move your practice forward.

Try not to be overwhelmed by what you don't know and what you're confused about. The struggle in teaching is inherent; it is part of the professional teacher's life. However, just as we focus on only one or two major teaching points to move a student forward in reading or writing, so too we must be reasonable and gentle with ourselves. You can't struggle with everything. Choose what you want to focus on this year and then become a learner, risk taker, experimenter, collaborator, reader, writer, and thinker in that area.

Seek out supportive peers and resources. Teaching is too tough to go it alone. Also, it's hard to change old habits without support. Find a colleague or friend, even in another grade level or school, and talk things over. Talking about teaching and the process of change is a necessity for our intellectual and social well-being. When John Dewey was ninety, he is reported to have said, "Democracy begins in conversation." Let the conversations begin.

CHAPTER 1

Teacher as Professional

How are we doing? Teachers meeting to assess writing quality across the school district.

■ As teachers, we must take responsibility for our own ongoing professional development. While the district's curriculum provides specific objectives and desired outcomes, my effective day-to-day instruction is informed and guided by reading and reflecting on current research and practice, collaborating with my colleagues, observing my students, and attending workshops and seminars.

—*Loretta Martin, grade 2 teacher*

I am proud to call myself a teacher. There is no other profession that excites and empowers me the way that teaching does. I love the intellectual challenge, the opportunities for ongoing collegiality and learning, and the chance to positively influence the lives of students and teachers.

I believe that I am part of the most worthy profession in the world. Yet when most people hear the word *professional*, they think of doctors, lawyers, and architects before they think of teachers. Unfortunately, in the eyes of the public, the relatively low pay of teachers is often equated with low status. Perhaps, too, in some cases, our behavior as teachers does not foster a public view of us as "professional." But we must be professional in every way. We have the awesome responsibility of educating today's children—our best hope for a humane, productive, and thoughtful society. Surely there is no job more noble or significant.

To do our job well means being professional in the highest sense of the word. But what does this mean? For me, being professional encompasses the following roles:

- Learner
- Scholar
- Mentor
- Communicator

- Leader
- Political activist
- Researcher
- Role model for kindness

In each of these dimensions, we serve as important role models for our students as well as for other educators.

TEACHER AS LEARNER

It is far more important that we demonstrate ourselves as "model learners" than as "model knowers" (Bissex 1996, 12). Being able to listen, question, explore, and discover are more important than having all the "right answers."

I used to call myself a teacher-learner. These days I say I am a learner-teacher. The more I learn, the more questions I have. The more I know, the humbler I become in all that I don't know. As a learner, I am open and eager to wonder, inquire, discover, observe, try out, reflect, rethink, and revise my thinking and teaching. The main ways I learn are through reading and thinking, observing and questioning, risk taking and trying out, self-evaluating and reteaching, talking and collaborating with colleagues, listening and synthesizing, attending conferences and rethinking.

As learner-teachers, we must be well read and well informed so that we can exercise our best judgment in daily teaching. Otherwise, we are prone to accept without question every new teaching tactic that comes along. Lacking a firm knowledge and theory base, too many of us are unsure of which approach, materials, and methods to use.

As continual learners, we must take charge of our professional development. As fully informed professionals, we can, and need to, trust our instincts and experience and adjust our teaching for the individual needs of the students in our classrooms. As learner-teachers, we can be, and need to be, responsive and responsible and value what we know works. Effective teachers have always done this. Unaffected by swings of the pendulum, we use a variety of approaches to maximize teaching and learning.

A huge part of my learning process is collaborative. Like the rest of us, I don't learn in a vacuum. Even when I read, the text guides me as I think along with the author. Some of my richest and most supportive educational experiences have been collegial ones. I value learning through our weekly language arts support groups (see page 524), through working in classrooms with other teachers, through stimulating conversations with educators at conferences, as well as through ongoing correspondence.

The most successful learners self-motivate, self-direct, and self-evaluate. No one directs us to read a certain article, attend a conference, or improve or change a teaching practice. We are dedicated to ongoing, professional growth because learning is the fabric and sustenance of our literacy lives.

TEACHER AS SCHOLAR

I deliberately choose the word *scholar* in delineating the primary roles of teachers because the term elevates us to professionals of the highest order. One can be a learner but not a scholar. We can glean much from authors, experts, and colleagues, but to be scholarly about our learning, we have to reflect upon it, challenge it, and "push the envelope."

A scholar is a learned person, one who has "profound knowledge" and who continues to seek knowledge. A scholar is intellectual about her subject matter, not just because she knows her subject well and intricately but because her rich foundation enables her to continue learning, integrating new knowledge, forming new conclusions, and delving into further inquiry. A scholar is open to new ideas and interpretations and flexible in her thinking. A scholar is also able to communicate her deep knowledge and understanding to others.

If we are to encourage a scholarly life in our students, we must lead that life ourselves. A scholarly life includes being an avid reader, writer, and thinker, as well as a questioner of research, theory, and practice. To be fully professional, we must be able to articulate the latest theory, research, and current thinking in education and have enough background knowledge and experience to intelligently distill what is important from our reading and research. Being a scholar means looking at research the way scientists do—continuing to experiment, hypothesize, investigate, keep records, and perhaps come to new conclusions. As scholars, we must take a questioning stance to research, learning, and teaching, continually asking "Why not?" "How come?" "What if?" "Are the research findings consistent with what I know? If not, why not?" "What difference does it make?" "What action, if any, should I take?"

Perhaps most important, a scholar loves to learn. The thirst for learning and knowledge, the unending curiosity, and the passion for inquiry into both simple and complex issues are all part of the scholar's life. Teacher as scholar is far too rare in our profession.

TEACHER AS MENTOR

A school's faculty is only as strong as the total community of teachers. I believe that even when we are not paid to do so, we must mentor our colleagues. Mentoring encompasses coaching, supporting, hand holding, actively listening, gently suggesting, sharing materials, dialoguing with empathy and understanding, and much more. Mentoring and coaching have been my main jobs these last twelve years. (See "The Role of the Language Arts Coach," page 527.)

Teacher as mentor includes being a literacy role model, a reader, writer, and thinker, a learner who continually strives to become more literate and who shares her literacy with her colleagues and students. Teacher as mentor means being a demonstrator for our colleagues and students: "This is how I do it"; "This is one way to be successful at this task"; "Let me show you how." As mentors, we demonstrate how we plan and teach lessons and units of study as well as how we set up routines, procedures, and classroom rituals. Being a mentor includes being on hand to assist teachers and students as they practice what we have demonstrated for them, and taking the time and patience to do further demonstrations when necessary.

Mentoring also includes modeling how we present ourselves, how we speak, communicate, and dress. Mentor teachers not only share teaching practices; they model interpersonal behaviors such as treating all teachers and students courteously and with respect. When we behave with dignity and present ourselves—through our actions and appearance—as though teaching is the most important job in the world, we are sending the message to colleagues, students, and parents that we are proud of, and value, who we are and what we do.

Ideally, all new teachers, and experienced ones too, should be apprenticed to a mentor—a masterful teacher—for a sustained period of time. It is foolhardy to assume that teachers fresh out of school can be effective or successful without a period of apprenticeship and ongoing mentorship. Yet this is exactly what happens far too often in our profession. Should we be surprised, then, that many fail and leave the profession out of frustration and exhaustion? One study found the following: "More than 30 percent of beginning teachers leave in their first five years on the job. That proportion is even higher in some urban districts" (Bradley 1997, 9). One wonders if this rate would be so high if more beginning teachers had the guidance and encouragement that only a mentor can provide.

An example of an excellent mentoring program is Partners in Education, which involves the University of Colorado at Boulder and five local school districts. First-year teachers are privileged to have a master teacher/mentor who spends three hours each week in their classrooms. Participating first-year teachers take a cut in pay and receive university credit in exchange for this wonderful cognitive coaching model. Second-year teachers Hollyanna Haskin and Allyson Sudborough acknowledged their indebtedness to the PIE program when they stated that they would have been "lost without the help of our fabulous mentor."

TEACHER AS COMMUNICATOR

Being a clear communicator to our students' families, our students, our colleagues, and our extended school community is one of our most important professional roles. When I was doing research for *Literacy at the Crossroads: Crucial Talk About Reading, Writing, and Other Teaching Dilemmas* (1996), the overwhelming insight that emerged from my efforts was that in every case in which trust in a school community was shattered (and "back to basics" board members often elected), communication between educators and parents had broken down. Most often, parents had not been informed about change— for example, a new practice being implemented—until *after* the change was already in process or firmly in place. At the same time, parents frequently didn't understand or see the need for the change or what the new practices entailed, largely because we educators had failed to adequately communicate with them. Because parents had little or no opportunity to be a part of, or understand, the change process, they resisted it. The critical lesson I learned is that we cannot take the trust and support of the school community for granted. Our clear and effective dialogue with community members must be ongoing, especially in areas related to curriculum.

Being an effective communicator includes such endeavors as writing clear and accurate newsletters, giving assignments that students understand and can manage, letting your principal know what's going on in your classroom, setting clear and reasonable expectations that are understood, and making evaluation procedures known before the task is completed.

Our written messages must be excellent models of writing. We are judged by how we "look." If you are not a good speller, or if correct grammar is sometimes a problem for you, make sure a colleague, the school secretary, or your principal proofreads your newsletters and written communications before they go out.

Being able to speak coherently and with conviction is also a necessity for educators. So much of communication in life and in school is oral. Yet, few of us have had practice in public speaking, and many of us find talking in front of a group difficult if not impossible. I have sat in more meetings in which I have been amazed at teachers' complete silence. Teachers who are normally articulate and outspoken become mute in a room full of their colleagues and principal. When we let others take over because we are fearful of speaking up, we are being poor role models for our colleagues and for our students.

Based on my own experience, I can tell you that speaking in front of a group gets easier. I have no training whatsoever as a public speaker, and it has taken me years and years to overcome my absolute terror of speaking in front of groups. Repeated practice alone has made it possible for me to speak with growing ease and assurance.

TEACHER AS LEADER

Teacher as leader sounds easy, but it's hard for most of us to do. For whatever the reasons, my experience has been that we teachers shy away from leadership roles. It's the "tall poppy" syndrome: we're afraid that if we rise above the group in any way, we will be seen by our colleagues as pompous or all-knowing. I have literally had to beg teachers (and promise to support them in the process) to share their excellent ideas and take leadership roles with their colleagues.

So what is a leader? A leader is a team player who recognizes and utilizes the talents of colleagues. A leader is not a boss, but a masterful facilitator. Like the conductor of an orchestra, a good leader makes it possible for both key players and minor players to perform effectively, to be heard both individually and collectively. The conductor doesn't make the music, he makes it possible for beautiful music to be made. Through his knowledge and respect for others' talents, the conductor helps determine the quality of the piece, how it's interpreted, the pacing. Such leadership means demonstrating as necessary, speaking up respectfully for what you believe, listening actively and nonjudgmentally to other opinions, considering all points of view respectfully, working collaboratively, trusting others to do their job, and providing supportive human and material resources as necessary. Being a leader also requires courage.

A story comes to mind. A few years ago after a workshop, as I was autographing copies of *Literacy at the Crossroads*, a teacher said to me, "Thank you for being brave for all of us." Her comment surprised me. And then she began to explain how heartsick she was about some of the changes taking place in her district, changes that did not benefit children—for example, thousands of dollars going for phonics workbooks instead of children's books. "What are you doing about it?" I asked her. She was silent. When I autographed her book, I wrote, "You are also brave. Let your voice be heard." She started to quietly sob. Months later she wrote to me saying that she had gotten together with teachers in her school and written a letter to the school board protesting recent actions. She had taken on the role of leader.

Leaders are brave, but not necessarily because they face danger or are fearless. Bravery is also about showing courage and speaking out in ordinary circumstances that demand someone try to steer the course in order to set things right.

TEACHER AS POLITICAL ACTIVIST

Becoming political must become part of regular teacher education at the university level. Getting political cannot be an add-on or an option. It's a necessity. Education is political, and whether we like it or not we must learn how to deal with and influence the politics of literacy. We need to learn how to ask the key questions and challenge when necessary.

Until I became politically active myself, I didn't know what the term political meant or how vital and interconnected it was to teaching. I didn't know that being political isn't a dirty word. Over the past few years, many teachers have written me and said, in effect, "I didn't know that you could be political and not get nasty." In the introduction to *Literacy at the Crossroads*, I defined what it means to be political:

> I believe becoming political means actively and thoughtfully entering the educational conversation in order to make a positive difference for children, their families, and ourselves. It means having the language and the knowledge to move beyond our classrooms and schools into the wider public arena to state our case. It means carefully listening with an open mind and being responsive to the public's concerns and questions. It means knowing how and when to communicate and who to seek out for support. Becoming political means using research and reason instead of emotion and extremist views. It means being professional in the highest sense, so that our voices are listened to and respected. Becoming political means honoring diversity and using conflict as an opportunity for thoughtful dialogue, not confrontation. And it means all of us, as educators, not just a few brave souls, raising our voices and our pens with integrity, to make sure that what we know, value, and believe about teaching and learning and democratic principles is taken seriously and acted upon.

Information and communication remain our most powerful tools, but only if we use them. The media continue to bombard the public with the message that our schools are inadequate, implying that we teachers are neither competent nor trustworthy. Special interest groups outside the teaching profession continue to work to control how and what we teach. And we teachers have been mostly quiet and passive. Yet, without our overt intervention and leadership, public education will continue to be a political minefield, and public trust will continue to erode.

As political activists, we must be advocates and risk takers who are willing to write and speak publicly. We must be public relations people who testify, write letters, pen editorials, and communicate clearly with all educational stakeholders. This is a new role for most of us. The public is not used to seeing teachers on the front lines of the profession. Parents and community members are accustomed to getting news of the profession through the media. We must change that so that we are viewed and respected as the experts.

We also become important role models for our students when we are politically active in a responsible manner. When I write an editorial to the newspaper, I share it with my students with this introduction: "Look, here's what you can do in a democracy when you want your voice to be heard." Kids need to know that, like us, they have the opportunity and the ability to influence public opinion. (See letters to the editor written by second graders protesting editorials extolling phonics, page 338.)

Students need to be encouraged by us and by our own involvement to enter the political arena. As one high school student who organized a lobby to protest proposed budget cuts in his school district said, "We can't pass bills ourselves, but we can bring attention to problems." In an endeavor to involve students in school reform, some states such as Maryland and Oregon sponsor programs that teach students leadership skills including how to lobby and how to network (Coles 1998, 22, 28).

We teachers must be brave, informed, and outspoken. And we need to be heroes—ordinary people who take risks for what we strongly believe in and hold dear.

TEACHER AS RESEARCHER

Most of us, myself included, are intimidated by the words *teacher researcher*. Yet we need to feel comfortable with both the term and the role. The professional teacher is a teacher researcher every day. That is, we wonder, record our wonderings, keep track of what happens when we try something new, and note our students' reactions. The teacher researcher acts upon those observations and that new learning.

A teacher researcher is an observer and learner, who looks and looks again, questions assumptions, reconsiders practice, and continues to question what happens in the classroom (Bissex 1996, 161–162). Based on the information she gains from this process, the teacher makes decisions and takes new action.

Teacher research is valid because it is based on the very contexts that matter: our students and our classrooms. We are the ones who know the conditions and the kids. Yet our research is often devalued by "traditional" and "experimental" researchers as not being scientific, since statistics and control groups are rarely involved.

A prominent example of how little teacher research is regarded is the documentation for the highly acclaimed study *Preventing Reading Difficulties in Young Children*, released by the National Research Council in 1998. Of the more than four hundred periodical references cited to support the council's recommendations, approximately 5 percent came from journals such as *Language Arts, The Reading Teacher, Educational Leadership*, and similar journals that teachers rely on. Most research cited was "scientific," psychological, and medical, and came from journals that teachers rarely read. The message is clear: classroom-based research is not typically viewed as relevant for how reading should be taught.

Sadly, the public—and most teachers as well—accept this. Partly, it's because we don't even know that it is happening. It's also because we're not sufficiently informed about what's going on. Most important, because we don't see ourselves as teacher researchers, we don't champion our successes or speak and write about them, even in the schools where we teach. This must change. There must be far more articles and books by teachers and more teachers as spokespersons. Otherwise, the media and special interest groups will continue to have wide influence over how and what we teach, further damaging and limiting our professional status, credibility, and influence.

TEACHER AS ROLE MODEL FOR KINDNESS

How we lead our lives and conduct ourselves with others is one of the most important marks of the professional teacher. One could have all the aforementioned characteristics, yet without kindness, respect, and consideration the rest won't matter much. How we treat each other, our students, and their families greatly impacts our effectiveness as teachers.

Daily Acts of Kindness

When you get right down to it, we humans are a fragile lot. It doesn't take much—a critical comment, a feeling of being ignored, a disdainful look—to wound us. Teaching is so demanding and all encompassing that we must go out of our way to be kind, respectful, and compassionate to one another. Our accepting and nonthreatening tone of voice, our affectionateness, our refusal to participate in mean gossip, our willingness to be supportive to our colleagues and school community, and our sincerity are all necessary dimensions of the professional teacher. We are not only literacy role models for our students; we are also, always, models of human behavior.

I know a teacher who has more knowledge about her subject matter than anyone I've ever met. While I have great respect for her accomplishments, no one can work with her. Her condescending tone of voice, rude comments, and demands on teachers make her vast store of knowledge inaccessible to most of the teachers in her district.

On the other hand, another teacher I know draws colleagues to her like a magnet. She is always willing to share, never pompous about what she knows, quick to compliment a colleague on a job well done, and ready with a smile and warm greeting for whomever she encounters. She may "know" less than her brilliant colleague, but this kind and generous teacher is able to teach far more.

Daily acts of kindness make our lives more pleasurable and make coming to work easier. Granted, none of us has sufficient time during the day to do all that we want and need to do. Life's pressures can sometimes be overwhelming. Still, our load seems more manageable when someone takes the time to perform some small kindness. Some examples of acts of kindness include:

- Taking a colleague's class for fifteen minutes to give him a needed break (Either use some of your planning time, or combine your two classes.)
- Offering to make photocopies for a colleague when you've got photocopying of your own to do
- Writing a brief note to a teacher, secretary, custodian, student, or family member acknowledging or congratulating them for something they did well or something about them that you appreciate
- Leaving treats in the office or teacher's lounge
- Remembering birthdays and special occasions with a card or a congratulatory comment
- Stopping in to classrooms to give a personal greeting, welcome, encouragement, or affirmation
- Sincerely and generously complimenting teachers verbally or in writing for something they've done well

I don't know what it is about us teachers, but we are a pretty insecure lot. My thirty years of experience in and out of classrooms has led me to believe that we are starved for recognition. Most of us go about our work diligently and effectively, but we give and receive very little positive feedback. It's not that we are overly critical or negative; it's just that it is far too rare that we openly compliment one another on a job well done. Not just a "good job" comment, but "I liked the way you . . . " Specific, honest compliments let us know that what we did was noticed. When we feel appreciated, we all want to work harder. That's human nature, and it's true for our students too.

FINAL REFLECTIONS

In order for us teachers to be knowledgeable decision makers, we must embrace all of the dimensions of what it means to be professional. When we are well informed, learned, articulate, and politically and professionally active and responsible, we can decide—within the parameters of state and local guidelines—what the curriculum and climate of our classrooms and schools will be.

Until we are fully informed and professional, we will continue to use our new materials with our old mentality, to be victims of "innovation without change." We will continue to be swept up in program mania, with the business and "scientific research" sectors dictating what and how we should teach. And we will continue to doubt our ability to make informed decisions based on our own professional expertise and intimate knowledge of our students. As informed and confident professionals, we can decide what part of the required text to use, what materials and activities are worth our students' time, what strategies we must demonstrate to students, what the test scores really mean, what goals we need to set. As professionals, we are decision makers who take complete responsibility for our actions, our work, and its effects, and for our successes and failures.

Being fully professional means that our commitment to new challenges extends to our personal lives. A life beyond the classroom is a necessity for our intellectual and emotional well being. Without interests and time spent in activities and endeavors we love, our focus becomes pretty narrow. For me such interests include reading outstanding fiction and nonfiction, shopping at the local farmers' market, creating wonderful meals, making preserves, going to the theater, picking wildflowers, swimming, frequenting art museums and exhibits, dining with friends, taking long walks, writing poetry, and traveling. I don't want to be a one-dimensional person whose only topic of conversation is education. Our interests must reflect the broad spectrum that life offers.

It is true that our lives are too hectic and our schedules are too busy. More and more stuff gets crammed into an already too full curriculum. We run on overload much of the time. Yet, if we are to be life role models for our students, not just literacy role models, they need to see us not just as educators, planners, and evaluators but as fascinating people who lead interesting lives. Perhaps that is our greatest challenge of all.

Literacy Conversation *by Regie Routman*

If you are like me
You are weary,
Weary of tests and test scores
Weary of "scientific research,"
Weary of "stuff"
Stuffed into our curriculum

Our weariness
drags us down
like a dead weight
And we fail to question
what we are told to do
Even when we know
It's not right
for our children

We trust materials
but not ourselves
We believe the media
but not ourselves
And if it's "research"
We embrace it
and quickly doubt
all we know

These are tough times
in which we teach
We need courage and energy,
Compassion and skill,
Knowledge and insights
and time together
To collaborate and reflect
and renew ourselves.

Trust your own literacy—
What you do
in your life and in your classroom,
What you know
in your mind and heart and bones,
What you believe
And what you've researched and observed.

Take charge
Of your own literacy and teaching
Shape it
by your own hand and vision
Do not be swayed
by loud, insistent voices
Listen to and value your own voice
You are the teacher.

CONTINUING THE CONVERSATION

While some of the roles discussed here may already be part of your professional repertoire, others may require further development. Becoming and remaining a professional
teacher is a lifelong journey. The following are some specific suggestions:

• *Actively work at being a teacher researcher.*   After a lesson or unit of study, ask your students questions such as the following:

- What worked well for you?
- What was difficult?
- How do you think this unit or lesson could be improved?

Then, write down what your students tell you. Record their statements as they make them so that none of their ideas are lost. (I keep a spiral notebook for all of my observations, students' comments, and reflections.) Later in the day, or at another appropriate time, read your notes, reflect, and think about what changes you can and want to make.

- Jot down your own thoughts and questions. How do you think you might explore your questions as inquiry? (See my recent wonderings, page 463.)
- Get together with your colleagues, and become teacher researchers in an area you are all interested in. For example, through our weekly language arts support group, we explored—over almost a decade—the uses, benefits, possibilities, and realities of portfolios. Through our professional reading, trial and error, student and parent feedback, and ongoing collegial conversations, we made changes in our practice districtwide.

• *Set aside time each week for professional reading.*   Take stock of recent reading you have done to inform your teaching. I keep a monthly, written record of all books I read, many of which are professional. Seeing what I am reading or not reading pushes me to increase and balance my professional reading (as well as my reading in other genres).

   For all of us, it is difficult to find the time to read. Be resourceful. Use sustained silent reading time in class to catch up on your own reading. Do a shared reading of a professional article during a study group or at a faculty meeting devoted to "professional reading."

   Check the list of journals on pages 68b–70b and make sure that you have access to one or more of these, either by subscribing yourself, sharing a subscription with a colleague, or by having your school or library subscribe. Do alert colleagues to excellent articles and books, and initiate study groups to dialogue about these.

   If I were involved in hiring a new teacher, I would be sure to ask candidates, "What are you reading professionally and/or what have you read recently? How has that reading impacted you as a learner?" Any teacher who could not answer those questions would not have my vote.

• *Get involved in mentoring.*   Start by offering to share a successful lesson plan, strategy, or resource with a colleague. If you are a new teacher without an assigned mentor, try to apprentice yourself to a teacher you admire. Your mentor does not need to be on the same grade level, although that is advantageous. What is more important is that the person you seek out is someone you trust and admire.

• *Speak up at a meeting or gathering at which you are usually silent.*   Plan this act consciously. Practice at home by speaking aloud in front of a mirror. Sit next to a colleague you trust.

• *Become politically active.*   Get together with your colleagues and take a stand on something you feel strongly about. Use the suggestions in "Resources and Support for Political Action" in The Blue Pages to support your efforts and stay informed on what's happening on the national education scene. Read and discuss these resources with your colleagues.

Attend a local school board meeting and become informed on local issues. Discuss these issues with friends and neighbors and write letters to the editor showing your support for the schools. Do what you can to become an advocate for your school.

Examine the work of contemporary political activists such as Gerry Coles, Linda Darling-Hammond, Michael Fullan, Howard Gardner, Alfie Kohn, Stephen Krashen, Susan Ohanian, Patrick Shannon, Ted Sizer, Grant Wiggins, and others who challenge assumptions and make us take a second look at society's messages regarding educational practices.

Become involved in your teachers' union. Make sure policies being advocated focus on improving instruction, learning, and professional development and not just on traditional labor-management issues.

• ***Be proactive.***   Remember, the overwhelming majority of Americans do not have children in public schools, so most of what the public knows about education comes from the media. Therefore, it becomes our responsibility to effectively communicate what is going on inside our schools and classrooms.

Invite local and state politicians and media representatives into your schools. (See page 526 for more information.)

• ***Become involved in professional organizations at all levels.***   Stay informed about the teaching profession and educational issues by becoming a member of national organizations such as ASCD (Association for Supervision and Curriculum Development), IRA (International Reading Association), and NCTE (National Council of Teachers of English), and by reading their journals. (See annotations, page 68b.)

• ***Attend a state or national conference.***   Many principals will allocate funds for teachers to attend educational conferences. Often it's a matter of finding out what conferences are taking place and where. Try to go with a colleague. Talking over what you hear and learn helps clarify issues. If you have never been to a national conference such as the IRA or the NCTE, make an effort to go. It can change your professional life. While one-day local workshops can be valuable, there is nothing to compare with a state or national conference that lasts for several days or longer and offers a myriad of opportunities to learn about cutting-edge research and practice and to interact with other professionals.

First-grade teacher Chris Hayward was so excited and professionally stimulated by his first national conference, the annual meeting of NCTE, that he was determined to return the following year. With several colleagues, he submitted a proposal to speak and was thrilled to be accepted. He commented about his first national convention: "It was invigorating to be with so many people focused on education and learning, and to be inspired by people that I'd read about but never heard speak. I came away with so many new ideas. I felt totally empowered, that I could change my instruction and make a difference for my students."

When we accept the challenge to become professional teachers in the fullest sense of that term, we become empowered as individuals and as educators. It is then that we are positioned to have the most profound impact on our students, our schools, and our world.

CHAPTER 2

A Comprehensive Literacy Program

Independent reading in second grade

■ There are, in the end, only two main ways human beings learn, by observing others (directly or vicariously) and by trying things out for themselves. Novices learn from experts and from experience. That's all there is to it. Everything else is in the details.

—Deborah Meier

Recently I spent a week working with teachers and students in a large, diverse elementary school. Before I arrived, I was told how "far along" the teachers were, how much staff development they previously had, and how much money had been spent on materials. As I began working in classrooms and listening to teachers' concerns, it was clear that they were looking for "experts" to show them "how to do it." In spite of all the time that had been spent on staff development, these teachers lacked the connection between theory and practice that underpins all effective instruction. Instead of learning how to make decisions that were responsive to the children that they were teaching, most were still searching for the "right" activities and programs.

Most of us, myself included, have been in a similar situation at one time or another. We think that if someone would just tell us what to do, our teaching will improve. This Band-Aid approach never works for the long run. The history of reform in our schools makes it clear that without deep understanding and commitment of why we are doing what we are doing, things don't change very much.

Before any of us can become professional, we need to examine and articulate our beliefs about learning and what those beliefs mean for teaching in the classroom. I used to think that first you had the theory and then the practice followed, but through years of teaching, I learned that theory and practice go hand in hand. Each continues to inform the other.

Being an effective teacher is not about having the right program and activities in place. Effective teachers lay a foundation of "the basics" and integrate a variety of approaches while being constantly responsive to students they are teaching. By "the basics" I mean language and thinking. We model language—all aspects of speaking, listening, reading, and writing as well as other expressive modes such as drawing and dramatizing. We model thinking—as wondering, questioning, hypothesizing, analyzing, reflecting, and constantly inquiring.

WHAT'S BASIC?

I believe that questioning and investigation are at the heart of meaningful curriculum and learning. (See Chapter 12, "Curriculum Inquiry.") A question-centered curriculum includes question-posing, exploring, negotiating, clarifying, extending, seeking, answering, all leading to more questions as students engage in authentic literacy activities—real work, not practicing skills in isolation. I believe it means we teach the essential basics to enable students to be able to move to exploring essential concepts and questions across disciplines.

Learning results from the interaction between what students already know and what we help them know. For instance, students need to know only a few letters and sounds to begin learning how to read and write. We don't wait to give them real stories until they have learned all their "skills": we give them real stories from the start so that learning the skills is part of meaningful reading and writing and makes sense to them. Unless we teach for understanding from day one, students are merely amassing skills in isolation.

An inquiry-based classroom does not mean that the teacher does no explicit teaching. Quite the contrary. In inquiry-based classrooms, students and teachers are clear about purposes, desired outcomes, and necessary skills, and direct teaching is part of making that all happen. As effective teachers, we thoughtfully demonstrate reading, writing, and thinking as we support our students in becoming highly engaged in challenging, relevant, interesting work.

The real "basics" go way beyond skills, although the skills are fundamental. Today's "basics" also go beyond content and strategies. Our information age is ever expanding, and the definition of literacy expands with it. We must teach our students how to interpret, evaluate, analyze, and apply new knowledge and go on learning—starting in kindergarten.

How do we accomplish this? By thoughtfully applying beliefs and practices that are supported by research as well as by our own teaching practices and life experiences. While this chapter lays the groundwork by talking about the "basic" components of a comprehensive literacy program, these components can only be taught successfully based on a framework of beliefs and approaches that empower learners. Effective classroom management and the necessary social and emotional aspects of learning must also be present. These latter critical aspects of effective teaching and learning are addressed in Chapter 14, "Developing Collaborative Communities."

WHAT ABOUT BALANCE?

In *Invitations* I wrote about a "balanced" reading and writing program, and I stand by what I wrote. I described a literacy program that included basic components and contexts for teaching and learning. By *balanced* I meant that all aspects of reading and writing received appropriate emphasis and that guided contexts were used to help readers and writers become critical thinkers, independent problem solvers, self-monitors, self-evaluators, and goal setters. The knowledgeable teacher was the decision maker who, based on students' needs, interests, and experiences, determined when, how, and how much to intervene.

However, in the late 1990s, the word *balance* began to take on a curious and disturbing meaning. While the original intention of a balanced program—to provide a flexible and complete literacy framework—was a good one, in too many places, *balance* is being misinterpreted and misused. Instead of denoting a state of equilibrium between all the parts (a common definition), *balance* is now often synonymous with the belief that learning proceeds in a skills-based hierarchy (usually determined by a published program), a view not supported by research. Hand in hand with this disturbing interpretation, the teacher's role as knowledgeable decision maker has been drastically reduced. Policy mandates at state and local levels often emanate from groups and individuals outside the classroom. Additionally, huge amounts of money are being spent on "teacher training" related to expensive programmed materials instead of on ongoing professional development for effective teaching—a situation that further constrains teacher decision making and teaching for meaning.

Therefore, in place of *balance*, I now speak about a *comprehensive* literacy program. Effective teaching draws on current research and practice and depends on the teacher as professional to provide learners the balance of skills, strategies, materials, and social and emotional support they need. Instructing, demonstrating, discussing, coaching, and discovering are all part of this model. In addition, teaching for understanding is integral to everything we do, beginning with our youngest learners.

Respected educator and psychologist Gerald Coles (1998) reminds us that any question of best is the wrong question. Instead of asking, *What is the best way to teach reading?*—which focuses narrowly on methodology—we should be asking, *What needs to be done to ensure that children learn to read?*—which includes methodology but also the critical emotional, political, economic, and social influences that exist inside and outside the classroom.

If we extend Coles's thinking to all learning, the essential question becomes, *What needs to be done to ensure that children become literate?* Focusing on basic skills barely touches the surface. Teachers need to be intentional and knowledgeable as well as nurturing. We need to provide collaborative learning environments in which students are challenged to take risks (and feel comfortable doing so), follow their own questions, and explore rich literature on their journey to lifelong literacy. We need to respect students' developmental levels while also maintaining high expectations. It is teachers as knowledgeable practitioners who determine the balance and basics of literacy.

My dear colleague and friend, kindergarten teacher Karen Sher, recently changed her thinking along these lines while reading *Leo the Late Bloomer* (Kraus 1971) to parents, as she does every year during open house. I'll let her describe the experience in her own words:

> I read [the book] in past years as a message to parents not to push, to let children develop their skills in their own time. As the book says, "A watched flower never blooms." This year, when I was going over the story, I felt uneasy. Neither watching passively nor overwatering a plant will nurture it. A flower grows when it is well nurtured by appropriate amounts of

water, sunshine, weeding, etc. Educators, parents, and children need to be knowledgeable about the actions that will help children thrive and those that won't.

USING OUR OWN LITERACY TO INFORM OUR TEACHING

My beliefs and practices about teaching and learning are greatly influenced and supported by my own literacy. That is, my own behavior—my thoughts, goals, and practices—as a reader, writer, listener, speaker, inquirer, user of technology, evaluator, all impact how and what I teach. It has taken me years to value and trust my own literacy and see myself as both an expert and a learner. In order to trust my own literacy, it is necessary for me to be highly literate. My literacy grows in relation to what I read; the professional development I undertake; my collaboration with colleagues, students, and parents; and the things I observe, evaluate, and modify in my classroom as I think about teaching and learning.

I share my reading and writing practices as a way for you to begin to think about and value your own literacy practices and to use them to inform your teaching: *If this is what I do as a reader and writer (or thinker, user of technology, evaluator), what does this mean for the classroom?* Or, put another way: *How can I make my classroom practices more authentic, that is, more like literacy practices and events in the world?* We are, after all, preparing our students to succeed in life, not just in our classrooms.

Research confirms that our personal literacy habits and the strategies we use impact what we do in the classroom. For example, teachers who do more personal reading use the library more often with their students, use lots of trade books in their reading program, promote more book talks, and value and implement daily sustained silent reading (Morrison, Jacobs, and Swinyard 1999).

The list below summarizes my reading and writing practices. Use them to trigger your thinking about your own practices and what they mean for your teaching.

- I read every day.
- I read what interests me.
- I read in many genres, but nonfiction predominates.
- I read a number of books and articles concurrently.
- I read for pleasure, stimulation, information, and relaxation.
- I rely on recommendations from colleagues and friends.
- I keep a record of what I read.
- I have a personal library that I value.
- I often browse in libraries and bookstores.
- I talk about books and belong to a book club.
- I monitor my comprehension.
- I write every day.
- I write about what interests me.
- I write in various genres.

- I write for a purpose and audience that matters.
- I write to think, discover, and communicate.
- I organize before I write and as I go along.
- I revise and proofread.
- I solicit responses to what I write.
- I work on more than one piece of writing at a time.
- I write lots of letters.
- I write poetry for myself and others.
- I keep a writer's notebook.

As teachers we tend to devalue our own literacy practices. The pressures on educators have never been greater. It takes courage and knowledge as well as professional know-how to teach in a way that respects our own literacy practices, current research and educational theory, our own classroom experiences, and the students we work with.

MY ASSUMPTIONS AND BELIEFS ABOUT LEARNING

Our beliefs about teaching and learning directly affect how and why we teach the way we do, even when we do not or cannot verbalize these beliefs. Therefore, it is important to articulate our beliefs and match them with our practice: *If this is what I believe, how does that influence what I do in the classroom?*

My instruction, including how I set up the classroom both physically and emotionally, is determined by my beliefs, my observations and experiences, how well I evaluate and know my students, my knowledge of relevant research and curriculum, and my ability to apply what I know and believe so that every student will achieve to the best of her or his ability. How I translate my beliefs into practice is what this book is all about. (*Invitations*, pages 8–22, sets forth my detailed beliefs about language learning.) I share these beliefs with you as catalysts for you to think about your own beliefs and how they impact your practice. (And even as I write about these beliefs, I continue to refine and rethink them.)

My Beliefs

- Teaching for understanding underpins all effective teaching.
- Skills must be taught as part of relevant and meaningful literacy events.
- Low-achieving students need the same meaning-based instruction as high achievers.
- Conversation, collaboration, and learning through others are integral to learning.
- Children's oral language is the basis for beginning instruction.
- Effective teachers demonstrate, guide, share, celebrate, and evaluate.
- Effective teachers negotiate the curriculum with their students.
- Approximations and errors are a necessary part of all learning.
- Learners need a variety of engaging books and resources.

Teaching for Understanding
Underpins All Effective Teaching

Teaching for understanding means analyzing and interpreting information, applying learning to new contexts, evaluating what we're doing, and setting goals. Teaching for understanding goes far beyond imparting the "basic skills." Gordon Wells (1998) advises, "Our emphasis on knowledge puts the cart before the horse: what we should be concerned about is knowing and coming to know." Our emphasis on possessing knowledge undervalues how we learn with understanding—through inquiring, discussing, doing, actively participating.

With regard to everything we teach, we must analyze and question:

- *Why am I doing this?* (curriculum requirements? student needs and interests?)
- *What difference does it make?* (How will this impact learning? So what?)
- *How does this fit with what I believe about learning and teaching?* (amount and quality of collaboration? guidance? support? feedback?)
- *Are the purposes clear and relevant* (to teachers, students, parents, administrators, and the community)?
- *How will I know students have understood?* (observation? monitoring? ongoing assessment?)

When I work with students, I am often amazed that they have no idea why they are doing what they are doing. Here's a typical example. I am in a third-grade class, and the kids are creating story maps. The teacher has done a wonderful job demonstrating the process. On a big chart is a story map the teacher and class have done together. Kids are working well collaboratively. But when I ask students in their small groups why they are doing these story maps, they have no idea: it's the teacher's agenda. They say, "So we'll know how to do them next year," and "Because our teacher said to." I'm sure the teacher's intention is clear: she wants her students to have a greater understanding of how stories work so they can read and write stories with more understanding. But the kids don't know this, so the activity becomes an exercise that is mostly a waste of time.

It is no accident that after more than thirty years and more than one hundred billion dollars, our federally funded Title I programs have been shown to have little impact on long-range achievement for our nation's poor children (Rees 1998). The primary goal, as I witness it in Title I classrooms, has been increased test scores, not increased understanding. So the test scores go up, as students learn how to manipulate pieces of information in isolation, but teaching for understanding—through inquiry, dialogue—is not a major program emphasis.

[handwritten marginal note: Flaws of Title one and Assessment MSR in general]

Skills Must Be Taught as Part of
Relevant and Meaningful Literacy Events

So much of what we read and debate today about our schools revolves around basic skills—reading and writing words correctly and automatically, being able to duplicate a simple schema, recalling facts, using conventions accurately—all of which are absolutely necessary. However, the "basics" don't make sense to kids without a strong foundation of meaning. Without the latter, the former are useless. "Learning is not a linear process—with 'basic' skills preceding thinking skills—but, rather, proceeds in a cyclical manner, with facts and skills accrued in the course of developing concepts and higher-order thinking" (Falk 1998, 58). Kids need to know how the facts and skills fit into the context of their lives. Unfortunately, focus on thinking, understanding, and applying new information has gotten short shrift.

Literacy is not an amassing of skills. Literacy is developed by engaging children in meaningful literacy events (reading and discussing favorite books, writing letters for relevant purposes and audiences) and in so doing helping them (through demonstrations, support, practice, celebration, and evaluation) become better readers, writers, speakers, and thinkers. Minimum basic skills are taught to enable students to engage in meaningful learning. At the risk of misinterpretation, I do not mean that we teach minimum skills but that we teach just enough appropriate skills and strategies to propel children into real reading and writing.

My concern here is the growing trend to teach the basic skills first and then get to comprehension. Learning doesn't work that way. The most effective teachers teach skills and strategies "in the service of acquiring content knowledge" (Pressley, Allington, Morrow, et al. 1999, 36). The basics and teaching for understanding must always go hand in hand. "Skill lessons apart from students' work are useless, as shown by the extensive research on the effects of traditional instruction" (McIntyre, 1995, 232).

"Basic skills" are being used as a cure-all for reading ills. And, unfortunately, in the name of "basic skills," we continue to put many of our struggling readers at a terrible disadvantage. Noted reading researcher David Pearson (1993) comments:

> Minority students suffer from what might be called, in the spirit of . . . good intentions, a "basic skills" conspiracy—"First, you have to get the words right and the facts straight before you can get to the *what ifs* or *I wonders*." Children of diversity are also quite likely to fall victim to what some have labeled the "extra help" conspiracy. . . . Ironically, many of them get a more intensive, almost caricaturized, version of the instruction that has already proved unsuccessful in the classroom. (505)

Low-Achieving Students Need the Same Meaning-Based Instruction as High Achievers

Evidence indicates that on average all students achieve more in reading, writing, and math when teachers emphasize meaning. The first large-scale study of instruction aimed at increasing challenging instruction for low-income students in grades 1–6 found that "low-performing children increase their grasp of advanced skills at least as much as their high-achieving counterparts when both groups experience instruction aimed at meaning" (Knapp et al. 1995, 770–776). An interesting hypothesis for future research might be whether these findings also apply to second-language learners.

Conversation, Collaboration, and Learning Through Others Are Integral to Learning

We need to set up our classrooms in ways that encourage collaboration and social interaction. Meaningful conversations (which must extend to our students' families) are critical to all learning. Such conversations challenge and extend knowledge and ideas, promote inquiry, introduce different points of view, allow collaborative decision making, support learning, and show respect for individual voices.

The types and depth of conversations and who's doing the talking speak volumes about what's going on in our classrooms. Historically, teachers have dominated conversations by telling. Instead, we need to restructure our classrooms to promote real discourse:

> The essence of conversation is that it must allow interaction: among teacher and students and the texts they read or watch or listen to. If there is too much material to cover . . . dialogue is almost of necessity supplanted by monologue, in which the teacher reverts to telling students what they need to know. . . .
>
> If we do not structure the curricular domain so that students can actively enter the discourse, the knowledge they gain will remain decontextualized and unproductive. They may succeed on a limited spectrum of school tasks that require knowledge-out-of-context, but they will not gain the knowledge-in-action that will allow them to become active participants in the discourse of the field. (Applebee 1996, 56–57)

Children's Oral Language Is the Basis for Beginning Instruction

We need to respect the diversity, culture, and language of our students' families. By valuing students' language, experiences, and background—for example, by encouraging them to tell the stories of their lives, whether through dictation, writing, illustration, or dramatization—we blur the boundaries between home and school and make school part of life as a place for relevant learning.

Effective Teachers Demonstrate, Guide, Share, Celebrate, and Evaluate

These actions are part of the model of effective teaching and learning (see pages 22–25), which also includes self-regulation, self-reflection, and self-evaluation. Such a model builds on the learners' strengths to instill in them independence, a desire to continue learning, and a lifelong love of learning.

Effective Teachers Negotiate the Curriculum with Their Students

We all learn better when we have some real choice and input with regard to the curriculum, the learning approach (both process and product), and the setup of the learning environment. There is no one best way or approach that works for everyone. Just as the best teachers tend to be eclectic in their teaching style and approaches, the best students employ a whole range of strategies and materials.

Negotiating the curriculum means that within required parameters—local and state standards, required subjects, obligatory evaluative measures—teachers and students collaboratively make responsible choices and decisions about what to read, write, view, study, create; how to question and learn; and how to show what they know. For students to engage in learning fully, they must actively be part of the creation, selection, and evaluation process. They must have genuine choices (that is, other than from a teacher-created selection) in constructing meaning. Negotiating the curriculum is best defined by educator Garth Boomer (Boomer et al. 1992):

> Negotiating the curriculum means deliberately planning to invite students to contribute to, and to modify, the educational program, so that they will have a real investment both in the learning journey and in the outcomes. Negotiation also means making explicit, and then confronting, the constraints of the learning context and the non-negotiable requirements that apply.
>
> Once teachers act on their belief that students should share with them a commitment to the curriculum, negotiation will follow naturally, whether the set curriculum is traditional or progressive, and whether the classroom is architecturally open or closed. (14)

Approximations and Errors Are a Necessary Part of All Learning

Students require a safe, comfortable environment in which they feel free to take risks—pose questions, invent spellings, work things out for themselves. Intrinsic to this belief is enough time, firm support, and gentle feedback—which sometimes includes "nudging" them forward—to let learners know they are, or are not, on the right track. If there are no errors, the learner already knew how to do the task and didn't need to learn it. Think about anything new you have tried to learn. Trial and error has been inherent.

Learners Need a Variety of Engaging Books and Resources

These include but are not limited to well-stocked libraries overseen by knowledgeable librarians, all types of excellent fiction and nonfiction, useful technology and multimedia texts, and other adults and students to demonstrate, encourage, and support learning.

PUTTING MY BELIEFS INTO PRACTICE

Teaching Responsively

Effective teaching is responsive teaching: we plan our instruction in response to what the child is actually doing and attempting to do. This instructional vision (of where we want the child to go) is in turn based on our knowledge of language and learning as well as the required curriculum and standards. Judy Wallis, a K–12 language arts coordinator, notes that only recently has she realized "how much kids teach us when we don't just watch them but when we pay attention to what they're telling us." This is a key insight. (The lesson I describe on pages 27 and 29, by a highly skilled kindergarten teacher, is a fine example of responsive teaching grounded in solid theory and beliefs about how children learn.)

A Model for Effective Teaching and Learning

The best teachers make tasks explicit through demonstration, shared demonstration, guided practice, independent practice, response and feedback, more demonstrations, and ongoing assessment. This cyclical model, which I use for all my teaching and which I continue to refine, is based on a model originally proposed by Don Holdaway. It gradually decreases teacher intervention and support while guiding the learner toward independence. Because the model is cyclical, not linear, the delineated stages intersect and interrelate; see Figure 2-1.

• **_Demonstration_**   The teacher or other expert (a peer, an adult, a book, a movie, a video, a CD-ROM) performs the task (which must be relevant and purposeful to the learner)—thinking aloud, modeling, explaining, showing learners how to "do it" by making the thinking/doing process explicit. (For example, a teacher reads an article aloud, figuring out vocabulary, thinking aloud, predicting, summarizing, questioning, all in full view of his students.)

• **_Shared demonstration_** (**optional**)   The teacher or expert works through the task interactively with the students, taking the lead and guiding the process. (For example, as the teacher reads an article aloud, he asks for and guides students' thinking: *How could I figure out what this word means?*)

• **_Guided practice_**   "Hand-holding" as needed, giving support and encouragement while the learners attempt the task, either in pairs or small groups. When students are skilled, the teacher may guide one group while other groups work on their own as they document their thinking (a short summary, difficulties encountered, etc.).

• **_Independent practice_**   The learner works on her or his own, with the teacher or expert close by to offer affirmation and support. (This is the trial-and-error stage: the learner has enough knowledge to solve problems independently.) This stage is essential if students are to take responsibility for their learning.

• **_Response and feedback_**   The teacher or expert celebrates what's been done well and analyzes what needs more work, conferring with students about what's been learned, problem solving what went wrong, setting goals.

• **_More demonstration,_** if necessary.

• **_Ongoing assessment_**

Teaching and Learning Approaches

Teaching generally boils down to one of two major approaches: teacher-centered or learner-centered. "Essentially, there is the *behaviorist approach* (call it the teacher

Figure 2–1 A Model for Effective Teaching and Learning

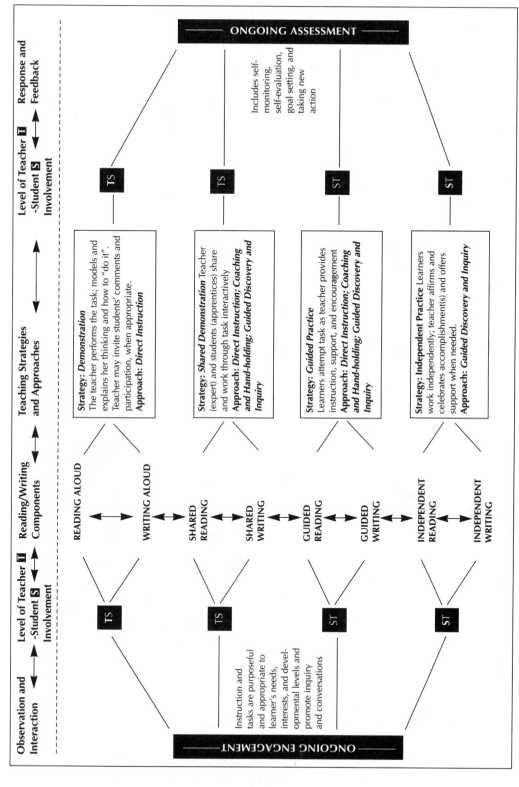

As the learner gains more control over the task and is able to assume more responsibility, the teacher, though still present, gradually releases support. The model is cyclical; that is, response and feedback are continuous and determine the necessity—or not—of reteaching strategies within a curricular framework. Teaching components, strategies, and approaches intersect and apply across the curriculum. The model also assumes a well-organized, safe, risk-taking environment as well as a caring relationship between students and teachers.

©2000 by Regie Routman from *Conversations*, Portsmouth, NH: Heinemann 'chalk-and-talk' model, 'jug to mug,' 'traditional,' 'teacher-centered') and the *constructivist approach* (the 'workshop' model, interactive and dynamic, learner-centered, exploratory)" (Boomer et al. 1992, 222).

However, these approaches need not be in conflict, and in fact, both are necessary for optimal learning. While it is our job to teach directly and explicitly—and doing so involves teacher demonstration and explanation—at the same time, project-based inquiries provide the necessary "hands on" involvement learners require. Neither approach to teaching and learning is superior: without a clearly defined purpose that is understood and relevant to students, both the best lecture and the best "hands on" learning can be equally ineffective. And without feedback and support, neither approach will be successful.

Teaching for understanding, therefore, encompasses (1) direct instruction and demonstration, (2) coaching, hand-holding, and providing feedback, and (3) guided discovery and inquiry. Knowing when and how to incorporate and foster all three types of teaching, interactively, is key (Wiggins and McTighe 1998, 163). It is up to us as knowledgeable professionals to determine which approach or combination of approaches to use for particular students and particular contexts.

Direct Instruction and Demonstration

It has always been our job to teach directly and explicitly in response to students' needs—carefully demonstrating, specifically showing how, clearly explaining. Whatever we want our students to do well, we first have to show them how. Of all the changes I have made in my teaching, adding explicit demonstration to everything I teach has been the single most important factor in increasing students' literacy. But here, as in everything we do when we teach, we must define our terms very carefully. By direct instruction I *do not mean* having all students systematically follow a scripted program in which skills are taught in a hierarchical sequence. There is strong evidence that such "basic skills" approaches may produce short-term gains but fail in the long run to produce students who can think and problem-solve independently and who can work well with others (Weikart 1998).

It is simplistic to believe that any sort of direct teaching leads to learning. There must be a match between what we teach and the child's needs, interests, engagement, and readiness to learn. It takes a knowledgeable teacher, not a program from a publisher, to determine and assess what needs to be directly taught and how and when to teach it. Even then, we don't really know whether our teaching was explicit *for the learner* until she demonstrates that she can apply what we've taught. Until a learner can apply what has been learned to a new context, we cannot be sure understanding has occurred.

Coaching, Hand-Holding, and Providing Feedback

Offering appropriate and selective assistance and support are part of effective teaching. It is our job to make sure that teaching is in the "zone of proximal development" (Vygotsky 1978): that is, with a scaffold (literally, a temporary but necessary support without which a task cannot be accomplished), the task becomes doable for the student. This means that we provide the temporary assistance, the hand-holding, students need to accomplish an activity or task they cannot yet do on their own.

The trick is knowing how and when—and for how long—to provide just the right amount of support that allows the learner to assume increasing control of the task. Effective teachers and experts give just enough support so students will experience success and feel confident but not so much support that they take over and disempower the learner. It's a gentle dance that requires careful leading, following, and (occasionally) sidestepping.

This does not mean that we see to it that our students avoid complex tasks. On the contrary. A task can be challenging without being overwhelming. By intervening and breaking up a relevant task; by demonstrating, sharing, and guiding; and by providing specific materials, information, and feedback, the teacher helps the learner meet with success. Gradually, as students become more competent, we reduce the amount of support we offer. As the learners' need for assistance decreases, the teacher "hands over" to them more responsibility for structuring their learning (Smith and Elley 1994, 83, describing the "handover principle," a term coined by Jerome Bruner).

Guided Discovery and Inquiry

When students uncover and discover patterns and relationships themselves, they remember them. One of the misconceptions surrounding learning through discovery, however, is that anything goes, that students work things out on their own. Not so. The expectations and goals of inquiry-based teaching are clear. Once we explicitly show students how to do something, we support them as they learn through practice, hypothesis, and discovery. We do not leave our students without structure.

Self-discovery and explicit teaching are not at odds. Students construct their own generalizations about how something works at the same time their teachers directly and systematically explain, demonstrate, and clarify. For example: students work out rules of phonics through invented spelling; at the same time their teachers, based on observation and past experience, teach the students what they will need to know to be successful. In a guided collaboration, educators, students, and parents all work together toward a common goal. Sometimes, the teacher leads and students follow. Other times, the teaching/learning responsibility is shared. But none of this works without student engagement. "Learners will work harder and learn better, and what they learn will mean more to them, if they are discovering their own ideas, asking their own questions and fighting hard to answer them for themselves" (Boomer et al. 1992, 16).

BASIC COMPONENTS OF A
COMPREHENSIVE LITERACY PROGRAM

We integrate our beliefs and teaching approaches every time we teach. In creating a comprehensive literacy program, we work to:

- Establish a safe, caring, well-organized, risk-taking, collaborative classroom
- Demonstrate reading, writing, and thinking processes

- Promote and inspire inquiry across the curriculum
- Discuss outstanding literature in many genres
- Use resources—books, technology, librarians, colleagues, peers
- Provide useful feedback, response, and evaluation to students and all stakeholders
- Extend literature and curriculum through oral and written responses as well as through the arts
- Share, celebrate, and publish meaningful work
- Guide and support students in becoming independent, joyful, lifelong learners

To make these practices a reality, we rely on effective teaching within a comprehensive literacy program, which includes reading and writing aloud, shared reading and writing, guided reading and writing, independent reading and writing, and opportunities to respond critically and thoughtfully to texts and learning (see Figure 2-1 on page 23, and Appendixes B-1 and B-2). These components are the foundation for everything we teach, and we gradually decrease our support as our students become increasingly competent. The amount of teacher guidance and support is therefore greatest at the top of the continuum, but independent readers and writers still require *some* support.

Since reading and writing, speaking and listening, and thinking underpin all we do, regardless of the age of our students or the subject we are teaching, begin by demonstrating these "basics." Therefore, the rest of this chapter will focus on and describe the following reading-writing components that go across the curriculum:

- Reading aloud
- Writing aloud
- Shared reading
- Shared writing
- Independent reading

These first four elements that rely on teacher demonstration—plus a fifth, a well-monitored independent reading program—are great starting points for our teaching canvas. Our own enthusiasm while demonstrating is contagious and promotes a love of reading and writing. Also, since these components are usually whole class activities, management is easier than for the small group work and conferencing required for guided reading (Chapter 3) and guided writing (Chapters 6 and 10).

Perhaps, most important, when we teachers intentionally demonstrate and teach concepts and conventions about all types of texts, we are modeling reading, writing, thinking, speaking, and listening strategies and responses that will be supported and practiced in guided reading and writing as well as applied later in independent reading and writing. In all of these contexts, we are demonstrating not only the strategies students are ready for; we are also showing them what they will be ready for soon. By exposing students to strategies that may be just outside their reach, we are demonstrating, suggesting, challenging, and practicing possibilities for future use on their own.

For each of these components, we value and model our own literacy, incorporate and integrate multiple teaching approaches, negotiate the parameters with our students, teach for understanding, and constantly monitor and assess as we teach.

Connecting Writing with Reading:
Integrating Teaching Approaches

Effective teachers integrate approaches and strategies as they intentionally build on what learners already know, extend their students' skills and knowledge, and encourage inquiry, problem solving, self-monitoring, and independent thinking. Literacy contexts are functional, social, contextualized, and purposeful to the learner. Let's look at how this works in a specific classroom.

It is a Monday morning in late spring, and kindergarten teacher Karen Sher has written the following "morning message" on the chalkboard in her classroom: *Hooray! Our chicks hatched. We might be able to see the last one come out of the egg.* Her students, who have been reading, writing, and talking about chicks and chickens for weeks, gather around the board before school begins, pointing to letters and words, talking with one another, questioning, approximating, trying to read the words. The bell rings, students take their seats, and Karen guides her class in deciphering the message (she credits "What Can You Show Us" [in Richgels et al. 1996] for this adaptation):

KAREN: What do you see that you know?

SARA: *Morning message.*

KAREN: Show us where that is. (*Sara comes up and points to the words. Karen writes over the words in colored chalk as she says them aloud*) *Morning message.* Tell me something else you know.

ADAM: *To.* (*Karen traces over the word with colored chalk as Adam reads it.*)

SARA: *Hatched.*

KAREN: How did you know that?

SARA: I know *c-h* says *ch*, and then I put the *hat* on *ch*. I put *hat* and *ch* together with *ed*, and it says *hatched*.

KAREN: That's terrific! (*Going over the word with pink chalk*) Who sees something else they know?

CURTIS: *Might.*

KAREN: How did you know that?

CURTIS: If you put an *l* in front, you'd have *light*.

KAREN: You used rhyming words to help you. Good for you.

MOLLY: *Hooray.*

KAREN: How did you figure out *hooray*? Come up and show us where that word is.

MOLLY (*pointing to parts of the word as she talks*): I knew *o-o* makes the *oo* sound, like in *too*. I know *ay* in *day*, and I kept looking at it and thinking in my mind, and I put it together to say *hooray*.

KAREN: Wow, good for you. Everyone, let's clap the word. (*Students clap twice.*) How many parts does it have?

CLASS: Two.

KAREN: Yes, that's right. Who sees something else?

KYLA: *Chicks.*

KAREN: Come up and show us where *chicks* is. (*Kyla comes up and points to the word and reads it)* Where does the word start? *(Kyla points to the beginning of the word)* Where does it end? *(Kyla points)* Yes, that's right. *(Reading the message that's been deciphered so far)* Hooray, chicks, hatched, might, to. It doesn't make sense yet.

SHERRELL *(raising her hand)*: We.

KAREN: Come show me. *(Sherrell does)* Good. Who else sees something they know?

ASHA: R *(says letter* name*)*.

KAREN: Very good. *(Highlights* r *in* our*)* I wonder what word that could be.

DAVID: *Our.*

KAREN *(reading the message so far while pointing to each word)*: Hooray! Our chicks hatched, might, to.

BRIDGET: *See.*

KAREN: *Hooray! Our chicks hatched, might, to, see.* Who knows something else?

TIARA: *The.*

KAREN: I see a couple of them. Come show me.

TIARA: Here's two. *(She points and says* the, the, *as Karen highlights the words)*

TYLER: *Egg.*

KAREN: How did you figure it out?

TYLER: I know how to spell it. *(He stands up)* E-g-g.

KAREN: Let's all spell it.

CLASS: *E-g-g.*

TORIANO: *Be. (Karen highlights the word with colored chalk)*

JAMAICA: *Able.*

KAREN: How did you know that?

JAMAICA: When I see the message, I look at the letters and sound stuff out. If it doesn't make sense, I say it faster, all together. I try it again. Like with *able*, I'd never seen it before. I said *a-b-l*, and I didn't get it. So I pushed the sounds together fast, *abl*, and then I got it.

BRANDON *(spontaneously chiming in)*: If you put *t* in front of *able*, it's *table*. *(He goes on to make the words* sable, cable, *and* stable*)*

KAREN: Good for you, Brandon. Now, let's see if this all makes sense. *Hooray! Our chicks hatched. We might be able to see the, the egg.*

CHARLES *(raising his hand)*: F *(says letter* name*)*.

KAREN: Good. Does anyone know what *o-f* says? *(She draws a circle around* of*)*

TANGELA: *If.*

KAREN: *If* is close. Let's see what *if* looks like. *(She writes* if *on the chalkboard)*

CHASE: *Of.*

KAREN: *F* says *V (says letter* sound*)* in this word because English is a crazy language.

CLASS *(chanting)*: English is a crazy language!

EAMONN: *One. (Karen highlights it)*

KAREN *(reading the message so far)*: Hooray! Our chicks hatched. We might be able to see the, one, of the egg. *(Three words are left unhighlighted:* last, come, *and* out*)*

RHYS: I see a *c*. (*Karen highlights the* c *in* come)

KAREN: Rhys, what sound does *c* make? (*Rhys makes the correct sound*)

NICOLE: *Come*.

KAREN: What's the sound at the end of *come*?

ASHA: *Me*.

KAREN: It looks like *me*, but sometimes *e* at the end of a word doesn't say anything.

CHARLES: *L* (*says letter* sound).

KAREN: Try the word.

CHARLES: *Last*.

KAREN: How did you figure it out?

CHARLES: It has *l* and *st*.

KAREN: What does *a* say? (*Charles makes the correct sound*) We're missing one word. What could it be? (*Highlighting* out) What's this word?

ADAM: *Out* makes sense.

KAREN: Good for you. Lets see if we can read the whole sentence now. (*The class joins in*) Hooray! Our chicks hatched. We might be able to see the last one come out of the egg. Does it make sense?

CLASS (*loudly*): YES!

Morning message, as it has been conducted in this classroom, involves inquiry, confirmation, and affirmation of new, applied learning. The children's attention never lags as they try to figure out the words and read the message. These young students know that words in a text must go together to make sense. Everyone has been engrossed and involved, and the whole lesson has taken just over five minutes. Each student has been successful at his or her own level, from the new student who recognizes one lowercase letter, to the student who can read most of the message's words. I am amazed at how much these children know and how much Karen has been teaching them.

Karen notes that since she has made a bigger effort to capitalize on teaching skills in context—morning message, shared reading, shared writing—she has gotten the best literacy results ever. "My kids are so aware of sounds and letters and language." Karen's findings are supported by important research that examined the practices of the most effective primary teachers. Such teachers teach and practice skills—both explicitly and opportunistically—as part of real reading and writing, and one great benefit is that lower achievers demonstrate dramatically improved performance (Pressley, Allington, Morrow, et al. 1999).

READING ALOUD

Having been read aloud to by teachers, parents, and other experts has long been viewed as a critical factor in a child's becoming a successful reader. Being read to helps a child:

- Enjoy reading
- Develop a sense of how stories work
- Build a rich vocabulary
- Predict

- Comprehend and know
- Understand literary language
- Acquire grammar
- Notice how authors write
- Listen better
- Read more

These benefits are true for students of any age, for second-language learners, and for reluctant readers. Yet, in general, reading aloud at school and at home decreases as children get older.

It is wonderful—even enthralling—to be read aloud to by an enthusiastic reader. The joy of literature and the fun of being hooked by a good book know no age limits. (My grandmother still read aloud to me when I was a teenager.) In addition to exposing us to the pleasure of reading, being read aloud to brings us in contact with books and genres we might otherwise miss as well as with rich, complex lives outside our own experience. Children, too, can listen to and understand books, concepts, and vocabulary they are not yet able to read on their own.

We must continue to be role models with regard to this crucial activity. At the very least, devote fifteen minutes a day to reading aloud. (In secondary classrooms, where only a few minutes at the beginning of a period may be available, poems and excerpts are a good compromise.) Don't miss a day. The payoff is huge for you and your students. The time spent is pleasurable, little preparation is necessary, discipline is rarely a problem, and students are cementing positive attitudes toward reading.

Communicating the Ongoing Value of Reading Aloud

Research confirms that reading aloud positively impacts overall academic achievement as well as reading skills and interest in reading. Fifth-grade teacher Fred Bolden agrees: "My highest-achieving students are still read to by their parents." Yet we cannot assume that parents are reading aloud to their children or that they understand the continuing value of reading aloud.

A parent called second-grade teacher Ed Kmitt to say, "Reading aloud in class is a waste of time." In response, Ed shared the thoughts one of his students beautifully captured in his journal early in the school year (see Figure 2-2). Now Ed makes it a point to let the parents of his students know that their children love to be read to and that it increases their passion for reading on their own.

When second-grade teacher Loretta Martin and I asked her students how often their parents read to them, we were surprised how rarely they did, even though the students said they still loved being read to. Many parents stop reading to their kids once the children can read on their own. Sobered by this information, Loretta encouraged parents to read aloud to their children one night a week. Several weeks later, student after student mentioned how wonderful it was to be read to again "just like when I was little": "It felt good and cozy." "It felt like I was four years old again when my dad used to read me a story every night." "It was an interesting story that I would like to read to my children."

Appendix A-1, "Why I Read Aloud to My Children," can be sent home as a gentle re-

Figure 2–2   A second grader's journal entry about reading aloud

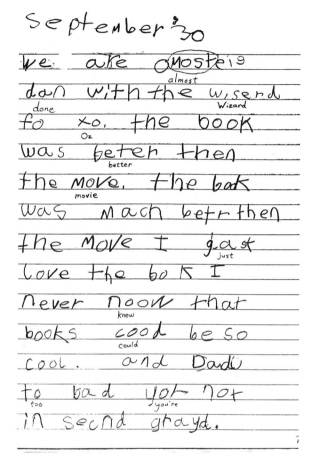

minder of the importance and joy of reading aloud. Daniel Pennac, in his eloquent book *Better Than Life* (1999), demonstrates how reading great literature aloud can motivate even our most reluctant readers. It's a great book to share with the parents of "turned off" older readers.

Reading Aloud as an Opportunity to Demonstrate and Value Reading

Best of all, reading aloud is a perfect way to demonstrate the joy of a good book. I also use reading aloud to demonstrate thinking aloud—predicting, summarizing as you go, working through tough spots. When reading aloud, I may also point out pacing, rereading for clarification, connecting to known information, and confirming or disproving predictions. (See pages 452–454 for a "think aloud" demonstration with a news magazine.)

There is no best way to read aloud. Be sure that you love the book, have read the material in advance, and read with expression. Often, I will set the stage by talking about the author, the genre, the topic or theme, and the audience. Sometimes I will read a story all the way through. Other times I will stop at logical junctures and ask for predictions. With picture books, I am careful to show and value the illustrations.

Our students cherish the books we read aloud. Therefore, our daily read-alouds need to include various genres, not just fiction. (It's a good time to make connections with other areas of the curriculum: see "Reading Nonfiction Aloud," pages 445–448, for specific guidelines, most of which also apply to fiction.) Reading series books aloud (see pages 75b–78b) can turn kids—especially developing readers—on to reading. Repeated readings of favorite books and poems encourage students to seek these materials out to read on their own. Also, consider offering students a choice: briefly describe several titles, and let the class vote on which one they want to hear. Some teachers also have students keep track of books read aloud as part of their total reading record (see pages 54–55).

Students are never too old to be read aloud to. Many of Holly Burgess's high school students tell her literature "makes more sense" when she reads it aloud—especially when the literature is challenging and she is dramatic and interpretive.

Interactive Reading Aloud

Sometimes, the book is so good that just reading aloud and savoring the moment is enough. Our silence is our appreciation. Many times, however, the conversation and interaction around the book are what make reading aloud powerful. And it is important for some of this talk to occur while the book is being read aloud, not just afterward:

> By allowing children to talk during read-alouds, teachers can assist children in their making of meaning as that meaning is in the process of being constructed. They can also observe how the children assist each other in making meaning. If children invariably understand read-alouds as a time to sit quietly and listen to the story, discussion afterward may be less rich. (Sipe 1998, 60)

Before, during, and after the reading, students may explore patterns, themes, illustrations, predictions, what they noticed; compare what's been read with other books and authors; talk about the reading with a friend; or write or do a drawing about it in their journal.

Opening Up the Possibilities for Who Reads Aloud

While books are most often read aloud by teachers, other adults and students can also do the job well. Mike Oliver is a principal in Mesa, Arizona. The first week of school he spends the entire week reading aloud to every class. His purpose is to set the tone for the school, to model for teachers, and to get to know the kids. In other schools, school board members, superintendents, administrators, special teachers, retired teachers, secretaries, and custodians are invited to come into the classroom to read aloud. Not only do students see these people in a new light, savvy teachers use this opportunity to showcase what's going on in their classrooms.

Some teachers let parents know how much they value reading aloud by inviting parents to come in and read a favorite book to the class. When second-grade teacher Loretta

Martin issued a read-aloud invitation to her students' families, every family was represented by a parent, grandparent, or other relative (see Appendix A-4). What a great way to make parents feel welcome in the school and classroom! Other schools establish a formal read-aloud program for parents and train them to read aloud interactively.

In many schools, community volunteers also read aloud to kids, especially students in kindergarten and first grade who don't have a rich literature background and don't know how stories work. Reach Out and Read is a national program in which volunteers read to children in clinic waiting rooms. Children are given free books, and the pediatricians urge parents to read to their children. (See "Home-School Connections," page 60b, for complete information.)

Often, older students can read to younger students effectively. Many of the fourth graders in my district are paired for the year with a kindergarten buddy. Once a week, at a set time, the older students read aloud to the kindergartners and interactively engage them in the story. (Upper-grade teachers first model the process, coach the fourth graders, and conduct rehearsals.) In some schools, upper-grade students volunteer to read—usually first thing in the morning, just before school starts—to first and second graders who struggle with reading. Or, as part of their weekly community service, secondary students may read to younger students. The reading-buddy relationship is a nurturing one, and reading attitudes and the library's circulation rates improve to boot.

WRITING ALOUD

When writing aloud the teacher makes her thinking visible while composing and scribing in front of students. Students see a demonstration of how writing works—planning, thinking, drafting, organizing, selecting words, forming letters, spelling, punctuating, revising, editing, and formatting.

Every time we write in front of students is an opportunity to display the thinking that lies behind the process. Writing aloud doesn't require much teacher preparation. In fact, overplanning is counterproductive: we want to model what writers do *as* they write.

The "morning message" is a quick and excellent way to demonstrate writing (*Invitations*, pages 51–52). The teacher thinks aloud while correctly writing a short message in front of her students. Students follow along visually and may also read aloud with the teacher. After the message is written, the teacher asks questions that focus on one or several conventions of writing or features of text, whatever the students need and are ready to learn or need to have reinforced. As we saw earlier in this chapter (pages 27–29), a "morning message" can also be a wonderful way to focus on figuring out letters, sounds, and words in the early grades.

SHARED READING

In shared reading, a learner—or group of learners—sees the text, observes an expert (usually the teacher) reading it with fluency and expression, and is invited to read along (see *Invitations*, pages 33–38 for specifics). Renowned New Zealand educator Don Holdaway "invented" the big book (with its oversized dimensions and enlarged type and illustrations), taking his cue from how stories are read at home at bedtime—in a relaxed setting, favorites being read again and again, the child able to see the text clearly and invited to join in. His goal was to make the sharing of stories, poems, and songs central to literacy instruction. His book *The Foundations of Literacy* (1979) is timeless; read it if you are new to shared reading or want a refresher course in specific goals, procedures, teaching strategies, and follow-up activities.

Shared reading is terrific way for students of all ages to enjoy reading and improve their reading skills. In addition to the teacher, the expert reader may be a peer, an older student, an adult volunteer, a taped voice (often the teacher's or a volunteer's), or a CD-ROM. Most often, students chime in orally, but as long as they are following along visually, I do not insist they speak the words. While shared reading is usually done with the whole class, it may also be used with a smaller group or even a single child. Shared reading is an excellent opportunity to hear text read aloud. While shared reading is often relegated to the primary grades, it is an excellent technique for all grades.

For students to reap the benefits of shared reading, they must be engaged with the text. Therefore, we need to be sure everyone is really following along. Make sure students whose attention wanders easily are sitting up front where you can quickly signal them back to attention.

Benefits of Shared Reading

I love shared reading because it is easy to do, makes reading pleasurable, and takes the pressure off having to read alone. Students who are not yet able to read the text on their own can understand it. Investigative studies show that students learning to read in a second language do better with "book floods" and an emphasis on shared reading (Elley 1998, 14). Shared reading:

- Provides an enjoyable and supportive context for reading
- Provides access to interesting, lively, and attractive texts
- Models reading in a natural, expressive voice with appropriate pacing
- Exposes children to the language and structure of stories and books
- Teaches multiple reading strategies
- Shows children how to preview a book
- Helps all children participate as readers
- Encourages close examination of the concepts of print (spaces between words, punctuation, dedication, title page, table of contents, index)
- Demonstrates one-to-one matching between spoken and written words
- Provides a meaningful context for learning and applying phonics and spelling—using what children already know about letters, sounds, letter patterns, and words to figure out new words
- Encourages and persuades students to try the book (or parts of it) on their own later
- Increases reading fluency
- Models reader response (prediction, discussion)
- Builds and supports children's confidence and positive attitudes about reading

- Helps develop a joyful community of readers
- Promotes guided reading

Much of what we teach and reinforce in guided reading (pages 140–161) can first be demonstrated in shared reading. Then, in small-group guided reading, students can practice and apply what they have already attempted with teacher support. Shared reading is particularly beneficial to struggling readers and students for whom English is their second language.

Some Shared Reading Basics

Choosing Texts

The primary purpose of shared reading is to delight and engage the reader. Therefore, choose books your students will be interested in, both old favorites and new titles. In kindergarten and first grade, I make it a point to use one or two "predictable" books, ones that include natural language, rhyme, repetition, and illustrations that support the text. Whenever students can chant or sing texts, enjoyment and learning are heightened. Students also love to read texts they have authored: class stories, news items, poems, and chants they have written during shared writing (see pages 37–43).

Be sure all your readers can see the print easily. Enlarged print—big books, poems, and stories recopied onto chart paper—is recommended in the early grades, but individual copies or projected transparencies also work well.

Organizing for Shared Reading

In the upper grades, shared reading need take only five or ten minutes. With younger students, especially in kindergarten and first grade, shared reading is often the primary context for teaching reading. Daily whole-class shared reading may thus last thirty minutes or more and include several poems and big books, some of which are read more than once.

Combining shared and silent reading lets students decode the sections of the story that are too difficult for them to read on their own while encouraging them to read the easy parts by themselves. Shared reading can also be combined with reading aloud and oral cloze (page 130). I sometimes begin a guided reading group by reading a chapter aloud while the students follow along visually. Occasionally I'll pause and let the students fill in the next word or phrase, monitoring their ability to "track" the print and read or anticipate specific words. Some teachers have students read out loud along with them but lower their own voice in the easier parts the students can handle on their own. Another option is to read a very familiar text as Readers Theatre (pages 74–75).

Teaching Skills and Strategies

The point of shared reading is for students to enjoy reading in a nonpressured, social setting. However, it is also a great way to teach children how texts work and to help them develop reading strategies. To that end, during the first reading, concentrate on being sure students enjoy and understand the story. Then, in subsequent rereadings, make one or two teaching points—you can introduce and reinforce any of the strategies students practice in small-group guided reading (see page 68):

- Noticing textual elements
- Learning the role of punctuation
- Noticing and using letters, phonemes, onsets, and rimes
- Using illustrations along with print to determine words
- Using meaning to figure out text
- Combining meaning, structure, and visual cues to figure out words
- Recognizing frequently encountered words
- Predicting
- Summarizing

Reading big books for enjoyment is a perfect and very natural opportunity to focus on features of print. Kindergarten and first-grade teachers need to be sure to point out words and aspects of print as they go along. Many teachers fail to focus on features of print when they read big books for enjoyment and a natural teaching time is lost.

Shared Poetry Reading

Shared reading of poetry, particularly when it includes rhythm and rhyme, is one of the best ways I know for promoting confidence and competency in developing readers of any age. Poems are fun to read again and again and provide the repetition struggling readers require. Language play, oral cloze, and words with common rimes can be highlighted. I often use a sliding mask (*Invitations*, page 190b) to highlight particular words and text features.

It is easy to find poems for shared reading. Poetry anthologies include many old and new favorites. Students often have favorite poems they are eager to share, some of which they may have written themselves. (Pages 364–382 discuss teaching poetry writing.)

Poetry Notebooks

Some of the teachers in my school district copy favorite poems onto transparencies, insert the transparencies into three-ring plastic envelopes, and file them, along with cover sheets bearing the poems' titles, alphabetically in a large binder. This poetry book becomes a resource for the "poet of the day" (page 37) and for literacy centers containing an overhead projector (page 165), and is a source of material to read during sustained silent reading. Adding, removing, and returning a poem to the notebook are natural ways to teach alphabetizing.

Poems can also be placed into individual notebooks that students use during shared reading in school and when they practice reading at home. Several years ago I ran into a former first-grade student. I was delighted when this sixteen-year-old proudly told me that he still had his poetry notebook!

Second graders in Ed Kmitt's class each maintain a three-ring binder filled with rhythmic poems that have cadence and rhyme and lend themselves to chanting. At least two new poems, chosen jointly by Ed and the students, are added each week. He photocopies the poems on paper of various colors so students are able to distinguish the poems easily. For fifteen minutes two or three times a week, Ed uses these poems during whole-class shared reading. His kids love these sessions: "I can't get them to stop," Ed says. The kids love to perform their poems for visitors, and they recite some of them spontaneously on the playground or on the bus during a field trip. Ed has also noticed that words from the poems are more easily decoded in other contexts and turn up in the students' writing.

Poet of the Day

I came up with "poet of the day" when I was working as a second-grade reading specialist (see *Invitations*, page 35). I was working with one group of struggling readers in particular, but I used daily shared reading of poetry as an icebreaker and community builder for the whole class. Here's how it works.

Each day one or more students, who have signed up a day or two in advance, lead the class in a shared reading of a favorite poem. (While you'll find that almost all students sign up voluntarily, you can assign a day to the few who don't.) The designated poet or poets of the day choose a transparency from the classroom poetry binder and lead the whole class in a shared reading of the poem. All readers are expected to practice reading their chosen poem until they can read it fluently.

The reader stands next to the overhead projector (on a securely positioned stool or chair if necessary) and leads the shared reading by moving a line marker down the transparency, one line at a time. (You'll need to demonstrate this process initially, but within a few weeks you'll be able to stand back and observe, coaching those readers who need additional support.)

One good thing about this activity is that all students can do it successfully. Independent readers are free to choose more difficult poems, and developing readers are able to choose short, familiar poems that they can already read or that require very little practice. It also doesn't require a lot of time, just a minute or two for each student.

SHARED WRITING

In shared writing, the teacher and students compose collaboratively, the teacher acting as expert and scribe for her apprentices as she demonstrates, guides, and negotiates the creation of meaningful text, focusing on the craft of writing as well as the conventions. (See *Invitations*, pages 59–66, for procedures and sample lessons.)

Shared writing builds on what the teacher has already been modeling through writing aloud. It is an excellent way to model quality writing and a very effective way to teach concepts of print. It's also a great way to get developing readers and writers and second-language learners to concentrate on words. Shared writing can be done in pairs, in groups, or as a whole class. Texts can be short and completed in one session or long and written over several weeks.

Composing and revising in this shared context makes the interrelationship among reading, writing, speaking, and listening very clear. Students hear sounds in words, recognize common words, and constantly reread text. Because the language is familiar and the students have helped create it, shared writing is great for practicing and improving reading: shared writing often becomes the text for shared reading.

I regularly use shared writing to demonstrate techniques I then expect students to use on their own. For example, before I encourage students to write poetry, we'll first write a poem together (see page 374). Or when students are learning to write fiction, we may develop a realistic character together (pages 358–359). Or when I'm teaching students how to write a summary, we'll compose one together first. In any shared writing I do, I start with a topic or story I know will be interesting. I brainstorm possible directions the writing could take, I sculpt the piece so it is well written, I teach conventions and spelling as I go along.

This guided writing is the scaffold writers need in order to attempt a new genre or project. After repeated exposure to this kind of modeling, students write longer and more interesting sentences, pick better topics, and improve their grammar, punctuation, and spelling.

Shared Writing Contexts

I use whole-class shared writing for a variety of purposes and audiences:

- Writing a class thank-you letter, invitation, or request for information instead of having each student write a separate but similar one
- Composing a class newsletter to parents (see Appendix A-8)
- Retelling a familiar story and/or creating a new version
- Formalizing classroom procedures, jobs, behavior (see pages 540–541)
- Reviewing a field trip or other class experience (this often becomes a booklet)
- Keeping a class record of important learning experiences (see pages 267–268)
- Entering observations of a class pet, plant, or experiment in a class journal
- Preparing a visitor's guide—for parents, teachers, administrators, congressmen— explaining what to look for in the reading/writing classroom (see page 389)
- Creating rubrics (evaluation standards) for classroom projects and assignments (see page 202)
- Making signs and charts that list school rules related to safety and decorum
- Writing continuing nonfiction or fiction
- Writing poetry (see page 364)
- Writing book reviews (see page 339)
- Establishing editing expectations (see pages 288–289)
- Determining guidelines for literacy tasks—selecting books, giving book talks, etc. (see pages 58–59)
- Preparing a story map (characters, setting, problem, main events, resolution)
- Writing a keepsake memory book of the school year (see Figure 2-3)

Figure 2–3   *Writing a keepsake memory book of the school year*

The resulting texts are often used for shared reading, and students often keep individual copies to read silently and share with their family.

Some questions/prompts I use to guide (not dominate) shared writing are:

- Who has a good beginning sentence?
- How else can we say that? How about if we say it this way?
- How can we combine those two thoughts?
- Who has another idea?
- What do you think about . . . ?
- Is there anything else you think we should include here?
- Where do you think we should add that?

Until such prompts come naturally to you, you may want to have them close by for reference.

Examples of Shared Writing Lessons

An Example of Shared Fiction Writing with First Graders

Teachers Margaret Villari and Kathy Sharkoff, who jointly teach first grade in a job-sharing arrangement, often use shared writing. Margaret says the payoff has been "enormous," and she now writes in front of the children every day. When Margaret and Kathy noticed the children were writing primarily about real happenings, they started writing a shared piece of fiction on a large, lined tablet displayed on the easel.

First, they brainstormed ideas and charted the characters and the plot (that is, an overall problem and its resolution). Then, each day they added to the story. At least part of the time, the children were expected to help with the spelling. ("How do I spell *er* at the end of a word?" "*Ladder* is in our story over and over. We know how to spell it." "If the word is on our word wall, I expect you to spell it correctly.")

Because they were in the classroom on alternate days, each teacher left a Post-it note on the tablet telling where the story was headed. (This is great modeling for what writers do: I constantly write myself notes about what I want to add, what I want to say next.) They continued writing the story for weeks, and the children's enthusiasm never lagged. When the story was finally finished, the class reread it, revised it slightly, and made it into a big book. Margaret wrote the story out by hand, and the students illustrated it. A copy was made for each student and for the classroom library.

An Example of Shared Nonfiction Writing with First Graders

Christine Cachet's first graders are enchanted with their daily recounting of the class hamster's adventures. Each day, they reread the story from the beginning, often making some revisions before continuing. After several weeks the story is finished, and the class publishes it both as a big book and as booklet-size individual copies that each student illustrates for him- or herself. Parts of the piece are copied onto transparencies and used for shared and cloze reading and to exemplify textual features. This is the writing/reading connection at its best. (Figure 2-4 is one page of a student booklet; Figure 2-5 on page 42 shows one of the transparencies.)

Christine comments, "I was surprised by how much they loved it and how long they stayed interested in the story. They're so proud of it because they can read it themselves. I never thought they could be so interested in a topic."

An Example of Shared Poetry Writing with First Graders

Students love sharing interesting information. Writing a poem together on a common research topic is a powerful motivation for reading and research, and it's a fun way to

Figure 2–4   The first page of a first grader's booklet from a shared nonfiction writing

A few days ago our hamster escaped. Ms. Cachat found out the hamster ran away. When Ms. Cachat walked in the room she saw the cage was open! "Oh no!", Ms. Cachat cried. "Where is the hamster?"

record, remember, and enjoy the new information. Every year Nancy Johnston's class creates a poem to go along with their research on animals, each student contributing a unique fact about the animal they investigated. Titles of past poems have included: "What Do the Animals Do All Day?" "Can You Believe . . . ?" "Did You Know That. . . ." (See page 381 for a complete poem that Nancy and one of her classes created through shared writing.)

Shared Writing in a Second-Grade Classroom

Lisa, a first-year teacher of second graders, is eager to help her students improve their writing. I suggest she try shared writing. We decide to write a story about Jason Thele (J. T., as he was affectionately called), the class' pet guinea pig, who recently died. The story

Figure 2–5   A first grade class' transparency from a shared nonfiction writing

A few days ago our hamster escap<u>ed</u>. Ms. Cachat found out the hamster ran away. When Ms. Cachat walk<u>ed</u> in the room she saw the cage was open!

"Oh no!", Ms. Cachat cried. "Where is the hamster?". Ms. Cachat told us about the hamster. The hamster knocked down Jamal's mailbox. Joe thought the hamster was by the mailbox. He said, "Ms. Cachat, I heard some kind of noise." Ms. Cachat said, "<u>Keep</u> your eyes <u>peel</u>ed!"

e e
e q
e - e

"<u>Please</u> stay quiet so we can <u>hear</u> the hamster" said Ms. Cachat. There were some shavings in the coatroom and Ms. Cachat said we <u>need</u> to pick <u>these</u> up before the hamster eats them.

We looked everywhere even in the trash can, the radiator, the coatroom and behind the flannelboard.

Early one morning Ms. Cachat went in the coatroom to hang up her stuff. The hamster jumped out of the closet and scared Ms. Cachat. "Ah!", Ms. Cachat screamed and she picked up the hamster. He crawled up her sleeve and then flopped on the floor. "Thump!" went the hamster's head!

goes on for days and days. (Before each day's addition, the class rereads the story and occasionally makes small changes. Shared writing and shared reading go hand in hand. See Photo 2-1.)

Modeling shared writing for Lisa, I stretch out the sounds as I write the words the class and I have agreed on. I am strict about not allowing students to call out spellings when I want to assess what a particular child knows or solicit contributions from children who are reluctant to volunteer. However, for a word I expect everyone to know how to spell, I'll say, *Okay, everyone, spell* but [or *was*, whatever] *for me.*

When I ask Kevin how to spell *when*, he gives me *w* and *e*. I write these letters down, leaving room for the missing ones. Because it is the second semester and this is a word he should know, I take a moment to focus with him. "What do you hear at the end of *when*?" I say the word slowly. He says *t*. "Listen again." He says *n*. Then I concentrate on the *h*. "There's a letter after *w* that also sometimes comes after *w* in words like *what* and *where*." When he doesn't know, I call on a volunteer and write in the *h*. After we finish

Photo 2–1   Beginning of shared writing in second grade

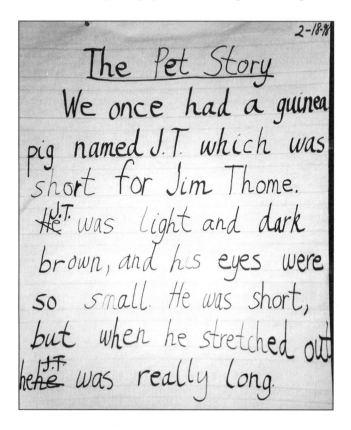

our shared writing for the day, I ask Kevin, "What was the tricky part for you?" He says *h*. Before I leave, I ask him to spell *when*, which he does easily.

Lisa continues shared writing for about ten minutes each morning (though later in the year, she switches to every other day), noting that kids who have difficulty writing by themselves are able to contribute. Shared writing gives them a voice. Lisa also mentions a significant improvement in the content, spelling, and punctuation of the students' own writing. Crossover to student work is evident; they have seen her thinking about how to word a sentence, sounding out words, pausing and putting in punctuation, rereading.

A WORD ABOUT INTERACTIVE WRITING

Interactive writing is shared writing with the addition that students also serve as scribes: they take turns holding the pen and writing the letters and words of the message. Young students love to write letters and words on large chart paper, and the advantage to having them do so is that the writing is more child centered. Developing readers and writers are jointly able to focus on and explore sounds, letters, and words. Students have the opportunity (with teacher guidance) to say the words slowly; stretch out the sounds; analyze what they hear in terms of the appropriate letters to use; and write with directionality, spacing, capitalization, and punctuation. Sometimes, the teacher holds the pen with the student, the student writing the letters she knows and the teacher filling in the remaining letters.

I find that interactive writing works very well in small groups or one-on-one. Its main disadvantage is the amount of time it takes. When children are gathered in a large group, their switching places at the easel and their often slow, laborious letter formations can disrupt the group's attention and engagement. Also, children who know their letters and sounds can be easily bored.

Another drawback for me is the stress placed on conventional spelling and overall correctness, which many students may not be ready for. I do not use the white correction tape prescribed for keeping the writing perfectly correct (Button, Johnson, and Furgeson 1996, 450, building on the work of Pinnell and McCarrier 1994). When a student misspells, the teacher is supposed to tear off a piece of tape and cover up the error. Either the child or teacher then writes the correct letter(s). I worry that the wrong message may be sent to developing writers, that is, that their approximations are not good enough. Therefore, whenever I use interactive writing, I ask students to tell me what letters they are about to write. If the letters are incorrect, we talk about the problem before they write them down. Alternately, I may write down the letters for the student. Also, while I remind students to use lowercase letters, when a young writer uses the correct letter in the middle of the word but forms it as a capital letter, I say, *Good for you. You knew that letter was* t, and let it go for the moment.

INDEPENDENT READING

Having time to read books and materials of your own choosing is absolutely necessary to becoming a reader. Recreational reading promotes comprehension, vocabulary, conventional spelling, a sense of grammar, writing competency, and a positive attitude toward the written word. Yet reading like this continues to be undervalued by some parents, teachers, and administrators. In addition, the higher the grade level, the less time seems to be devoted to independent reading.

Teachers who do devote lots of time to reading are sometimes forced to defend their position. A second-grade teacher I know tells me he is being questioned by parents about why he reads aloud every day and allows so much time for students to read independently. A fourth-grade teacher worries because her principal questions her repeatedly about beginning each day with WEB (the acronym for Wonderfully Exciting Books, which is what many teachers call our independent reading program). We need to clearly communicate to families and administrators why this activity is a daily necessity, not a frill. Then we must set up our classrooms to include lots of time and opportunity for independent reading.

The research is firmly behind us. A landmark study, often quoted, has shown that time spent reading books is the best predictor of reading achievement and growth in students in second through fifth grade (Anderson, Wilson, and Fielding 1988). In addition, students in grades 4, 8, and 12 who reported doing more daily reading at school and at home had higher average scores than their peers who reported doing less daily reading (National Center for Education Statistics 1999). Finally, "saturation reading programs," in which older students reading below grade level read in class for extended periods, dramatically improve reading scores. Still, "few administrators, or teachers, have the courage to open up their curriculums and make developing avid readers the priority" (Leonhardt 1997). We need to find that courage.

Basic Principles for Independent Reading

• *A sustained period of time is set aside each day for independent reading.* Some teachers begin the morning or afternoon with independent reading and love the settling effect it has on the students. Time set aside varies from ten or fifteen minutes at the beginning of the year to as much as forty-five minutes at the end.

• *Everyone reads, including the teacher.*   The only model for reading enjoyment some students will ever see is their teacher.

• *Students choose their own reading materials.*   They must therefore have access to materials they can read and that interest them.

• *The reading environment is quiet, relaxed, and comfortable.*   Depending on your and your students' preferences, it need not be silent, but it does need to be peaceful.

• *The focus is on enjoyment.*   Although this is a time for students to practice reading strategies and learn new information, the main purpose is reading for pleasure.

• *Students keep a record of books and genres read* as soon as they are able to do so. I base what I ask students to do on my own reading record. Asking them to include genres as well as titles and authors helps keep me, the students, and their families aware of reading preferences and lets me know when I may need to encourage students to "balance" their reading diets. Students can also rate the books, based on their own or some other agreed-on rating scale. (Figures 2-8 and 2-10, pages 53 and 55, are examples of student reading records.)

• *Written responses are rarely required.*   Knowing you will have to write a report on what you've read makes reading far less enjoyable.

• *There is time for sharing and recommending books.*   Hearing about books others love makes us want to read them too. (See "Book Talks," page 58.)

• *Students must have books with them at all times.*   Students in our WEB program are expected to carry books back and forth between school and home. I problem solve with the perpetual forgetters. We negotiate strategies to help them remember: writing a reminder note, putting the book in their backpack before bedtime, placing the book next to their lunch box (lunch is harder to forget!).

Of these, reading for pleasure is the most important. Unless they enjoy what they're reading, students will be disengaged and uncommitted.

Reading for Pleasure

In classroom after classroom I ask students why they think their teachers want them to read every night. Without exception, they respond: *To do well in school. To learn stuff. To learn new words. To find out information. To get smarter. To get ready for the next grade.* I probe a little: *Yes, all this is true, but Sunday I spent all afternoon reading a book. Why do you think I did that?* Then, finally, it dawns on them: reading is enjoyable! Students never mention the pleasure factor first, and this worries me. We have to be careful that in our zeal to turn kids on to reading, it doesn't become an assignment they dread.

Some years ago the parent of a third grader told me her son felt he *had* to read for at least thirty minutes each night: one day his teacher had told him he hadn't read enough pages the night before. So Tommy, who used to like reading on his own, was now watching the clock and counting pages. Worried that we might be mandating reading rather than encouraging it, I wrote a piece on WEB reading (Routman 1996, 188).

Ask this question of your students: *Why are we devoting sustained time in school and at home to independent reading?* Use their responses to gauge the messages they are receiving about reading. Perhaps reading for pleasure does not come to mind immediately because they are not finding enough materials they can read that interest them, they see too few role models (see page 555), or too much emphasis is being placed on "checking" their reading.

Making a Commitment to Independent Reading

When educators value and model free reading and take the time to ensure that all students are engaged with interesting books, the dividends are rewarding for everyone involved.

On the first day of school this past year, Mike Oliver, the principal of an elementary school in Mesa, Arizona, gave each of his teachers $400. In place of the usual first-day faculty meeting, he sent the teachers to the local bookstore, where they were able to purchase books at a 40 percent discount. Then they displayed the books they bought by lining them up in rain gutters (Jim Trelease's idea) so the front covers were in full view. These book displays overpowered anyone who entered any classroom in the school.

Second-grade teacher Bev Sullivan and I are talking in the hall. She tells me she thinks all her students will reach our district reading benchmark (see Appendices I-5 and I-9), that all her students are successful readers. When I ask how she accounts for that success, she says she makes sure her students read and read some more. She prompts reluctant readers to take part in WEB by having them sit with her and handpicking their books. She says her students also spend a lot of time partner-reading. We both agree that it's the amount of reading students do that's made the difference. And in mid May, Bev confirms her students' success. "They all met the benchmark! I know it's the amount of daily reading they did."

Providing Access to Interesting Reading Materials

There is a strong relationship between the amount of reading students do and reading achievement: the students who read most are the best readers (National Center for Education Statistics 1999, 134). If students are to read a lot, reading materials must be readily available. It is well documented that access to books and libraries influences how much children read (Krashen 1993; McQuillan 1998).

We can improve the reading achievement of students from lower socioeconomic backgrounds who may not have access to lots of reading materials "by improving their access to print" (Krashen 1998, 85). We need to provide these students—and all students—with lots of materials they can read and want to read. (See pages 81 and 87–88 for advice on how to establish classroom and school libraries that meet your students' interests and needs.)

In elementary school, the rate of progress for children from high and low socioeconomic backgrounds "is virtually identical"; it is during nonschool time that low-SES children fall behind (Snow et al. 1998, 31, citing a research study by Alexander and Entwisle 1996). While the cited research does not state or imply why these students fall behind in the time they are not in school, it seems fairly obvious; they are not reading. These are the students who do not frequent the library as often as their middle-class counterparts, who do not have the same access to books and preferred reading materials.

After I became aware of this research finding, I made a bigger effort to make sure that all students had lots of books to read over the summer and during other vacations. Teachers have long known that those students who do not read over the summer lose ground. I handpicked books, put them into the hands of readers I was concerned about, and sent home a letter to parents explaining the importance of independent reading for maintaining and promoting gains in reading ability. Principals may want to think about allocating funds just for giving books to students to read during vacations, especially over the summer. One teacher I know got books for students by facilitating a schoolwide book drive to which families donated books their children had outgrown.

Students of all ages will choose to read if they have materials that interest them. Reluctant middle school students will read "lighter" fare like the popular series books, scary books, magazines, comic books, and sports books. Let them. Light reading like this will help them make the transition to more complex reading (Worthy et al. 1999). I know this from experience. While my mother was signing out "classics" from the library to coax her reluctant daughters to read, my sister and I were reading teen romance comic books under the covers. This nightly reading-by-flashlight continued, quite happily, for several years.

Being a Role Model for Reading and Talking About Books

On the first day of school, Cindy, Marlene, and I are talking in the hallway, catching up. "Have you read *She's Come Undone?*" Cindy asks, and we are off and running on an enthusiastic discussion of newly discovered authors, favorite books, writing styles. It turns out we've all read Wally Lamb's book and agree it was a great summer read but not great literature. As we talk, I make notes of books I want to read: *Midnight in the Garden of Good and Evil*, by John Berendt, and *What We Keep*, by Elizabeth Berg. I tell my friends about the most extraordinary book I've read in years, *The God of Small Things*, by Arundhati Roy, and about another incredible book, Jean-Dominique Bauby's *The Diving Bell and the Butterfly*, which deeply touched me. It hits me that this beginning-of-the-school-year talk about books is exactly what we should be doing in our classrooms the first week of school.

If our goal is for students to become lifelong readers, we must model that way of living. Even if we don't like to read ourselves, we must find a book that engages us. "To teach reading without the fervor of your last novel, journal, story at the top of your heart is to false lead your children to literacy" (Nia 1998).

An intermediate-grade teacher I have been working with reluctantly admits she doesn't like to read. She tells me, "Teaching was easy. I followed the manuals. I did what I was told.

I never thought about my own literacy or being a literacy role model." I loan her *Durable Goods*, by Elizabeth Berg, a favorite book of mine and one I think she may enjoy. She winds up liking the short chapters and feeling successful, but at first she is put off because it is an easy read: "In first grade, I was reading hard books, fifth-grade level. I was always pushed to move ahead and do hard books. I read everything phonetically. I didn't enjoy reading. Reading was for answering the questions the teacher asked." Much later she confesses to me, "You told me to read during sustained silent reading. This is the first book I've read. I was embarrassed to tell you." She also tells me that now that she is reading and enjoying it ("I couldn't put the book down"), she allots more time to independent reading. Her own excitement about reading has made her a more effective teaching of reading.

The best time to start your daily independent reading program is the first day of school. (Some teachers even write to students over the summer and tell them to bring favorite books to share during their first week back.) Talk about yourself as a reader and share the things you like to read. Build community by encouraging and valuing conversations about favorite books and reading materials. Use the time set aside for independent reading for your own recreational as well as professional reading.

Many teachers of first and second grade find they cannot read silently themselves until procedures and appropriate behavior are firmly established. These teachers let students know they read by talking about and showing favorite books but initially spend their own time during independent reading ensuring that students are properly matched with books they can and want to read.

What About Reading Incentives and Rewards?

Some teachers offer pizzas or similar rewards for reading, but I'm not in favor of it. "None of the studies on incentives show any clearly positive effect on reading that can be attributed solely to the use of rewards" (Krashen and McQuillan 1998, 418). I vividly remember several first graders who were still heartbroken in second grade because they hadn't read enough books to earn a private lunch with their teacher. With rewards, the focus shifts from the joy of reading to the number of books read; reading becomes competitive. Independent readers of long chapter books are at a disadvantage, and motivation often decreases. One parent told me, "My son was so disappointed at not getting the reward that he stopped reading for a while."

Recent brain research tells us that children do not need immediate rewards. Students are intrinsically motivated when goals and tasks are clear and relevant, when they feel positive about themselves and their learning, when feedback is positive and helpful, and when stress and threat are eliminated (Jensen 1998).

Organizing for Independent Reading

Clever names for designating independent reading abound: WEB (Wonderfully Exciting Books), SSR (Sustained Silent Reading or Student Selected Reading), SQUIRT (Sustained Quiet Uninterrupted Independent Reading Time), DIRT (Daily Independent Reading Time), or DEAR (Drop Everything and Read). (Some kindergarten teachers, among themselves, refer to the time as SNR—Sustained Noisy Reading.)

The WEB program in our district goes beyond daily sustained silent reading in class and also includes:

• *Nightly reading* (between twenty and forty minutes)

• *Keeping a reading record* (WEB log)

• *Interviews on completed books* (conducted by classmates and teacher)

• *Book talks and sharing*

• *One-on-one student-teacher conferences* (at least once a month for independent readers and as often as daily for developing readers) to discuss book selection, authors, and genres read; check reading record; set goals

• *Communicating with parents*

See also *Invitations*, pages 42–49, for a description of WEB reading and Servis 1999 for an excellent description of a daily WEB program and sustained silent reading.

Whatever you call your daily independent reading and however you organize it, I recommend including the following practices:

• *Find out your students' reading preferences* (through oral or written interviews), and make their preferred materials readily available.

• *Organize the classroom library, with your students' help, so reading materials are interesting, varied, attractively displayed, and easily accessible.*   Organized baskets or crates of related books, leveled books, or magazines let students make choices more easily (see pages 85–88). Be sure to include students' published materials.

• *Make sure students are matched with books they can read.*

• *Provide time each day for students to select books on their own.*

• *Establish a procedure for carrying books between home and school.*

• *Negotiate record keeping, and carefully model this process.*

• *Monitor students' understanding of what they are reading.*   (See page 114 for one-on-one formal and informal reading conferences.)

• *Help students set goals* (trying a new genre or author, increasing amount of nightly reading, self-monitoring for comprehension).

• *Let students of any age read or browse through anything*—magazines, picture books, catalogues, even comics. Remember that light reading often helps turn reluctant readers on to reading.

Matching Kids with Books

Students need to be able to enjoy and understand reading material in a number of genres. For students to make steady progress in reading, the things they read, whether instructionally or independently, must match their interests, experiences, and reading ability. If students have a steady diet of books that are too hard for them and/or in which they have no interest, their reading actually regresses.

One of the easiest and most useful ways to ensure that a student is reading appropriate material is to conduct an individual, informal assessment (see pages 114–118 for procedures). And it's not just the struggling readers we need to monitor. Many strong readers continue to read only very easy books and need to be nudged to challenge themselves a bit.

We also need to be sure the books we choose for instructional reading offer just enough challenge that students can problem solve the trouble spots without too much guidance. A careful introduction and some explicit teaching may be necessary. (See guided reading, pages 140–161.)

Sharon Taberski (2000) spends the first month of school conferring with her first and second graders one-on-one and suggesting books to them. She also makes sure each child has a book bag of between five and ten books he or she can read independently. Second-grade teacher Loretta Martin teaches her kids how to select books from her well-stocked and organized classroom library and monitors their selections carefully. Each student selects five books and keeps them in a freezer bag. After all the books have been read, the student goes "book shopping" for five new books.

Primary-grade teachers often find that housing books in baskets or tubs rather than on shelves makes the books more appealing and accessible. Teachers make sure there are baskets of books—often grouped by topic, author, difficulty, series—on students' tables. It's amazing how well kids can focus on independent reading once they have lots of easy, interesting books readily available. For struggling readers, who typically have difficulty selecting books they can read independently, it's perhaps best to preselect and organize a basket (or group) of books at the appropriate interest and reading level and then allow the students to choose among those books. Rereading familiar books plays an important role here. Repetition helps developing readers focus on meaning and become more confident as they gain increasing control of reading strategies. Often, a reader will return to the comfort of an easy favorite after he has taken a risk with a more challenging book.

Choosing "Just Right" Books

A book is at a student's independent reading level if he can problem solve the trouble spots mostly on his own using familiar, well established strategies. That means the student should be able to read and understand almost all the words and concepts on a page and be able to discuss and explain what he has read. This holds true for independent reading at home as well as in school. Books students take home should be ones they can read mostly on their own. We can't assume parents will read these books to or with their children.

In helping a child select a book, ask yourself:

- Will she be interested in the book?
- Does she have the background knowledge to understand the ideas and the vocabulary?
- Are the amount, size, and placement of text appropriate?
- Are there illustrations that support the text?

While you may want to use book-level guidelines for developing readers (see page 84) be sure you take the individual student into account, not just the book's difficulty. Sometimes a book we think is easy may actually be hard for a student if he lacks the background or interest. Likewise, a book we decide is too hard for a student may turn out to be readable because of the student's keen interest in and familiarity with the topic. Remember, too, that readers sometimes need to read several pages before they get the gist of what's going on: once meaning kicks in, word recognition improves dramatically.

Students may choose to read familiar favorites, easy books, "just right" books, and challenging books. My own reading, while it includes all of these categories, falls mostly at the "just right" level, so I encourage students to read books they can handle without much difficulty. Figure 2-6 shows a second-grade class' guidelines for selecting a "just right" book, prepared through shared writing. The "Goldilocks" strategy for selecting books (Ohlhausen and Jepsen 1992) is explained in *Invitations* on page 189b. You can also teach developing readers and their families to use the "five-finger test": The student reads from one page in a new book she has selected. Every time she comes to a word she can't read or doesn't understand, she puts one finger up. If all five fingers go up, the book is too difficult for her.

Many teachers feel uncomfortable telling a student, *This book is too hard for you*. There is no one best solution here, and you have to trust your instincts and what you know about the child. Some students will want to read a book so badly that they will persist and triumph, often asking a "buddy" to help them. My position is that most struggling readers know they are experiencing difficulty, so why not be honest with them. They will not become readers without massive amounts of practice: in other words, the books they read independently need to be easy enough so they can actually read them. I usually say something like this: *I can tell you really want to read this book. It's a bit hard for you right now, but I'll bet you'll be able to read it on your own in several months. Why don't you have your mom or dad read this book to you? For now, please choose another book you can read on your own so you can practice your reading.* Then I jot a quick note to the parents telling them their child really wants to read the book but is as yet unable to do so independently and asking them to read it aloud.

It's important that parents understand how necessary it is for children to read "just right" books to become readers. Many parents—and some teachers, too—have the mistaken notion that the way to become a good reader is to read hard books. Our communication to parents needs to be clear on this point (see Appendix A-3). In some cases, we

Figure 2–6 A second grade class' guidelines for selecting a "just right" book; from a shared writing

1. It's on your reading level. When you read a page you can read most of the words. You understand the book and can tell what it's about.
2. You can use your strategies to figure out words and to understand the book.
3. You know a little bit about the subject or what the book is about.
4. It's not always the same kind of book—you choose among fiction, nonfiction, biographies, poetry, historical fiction, autobiographies.
5. It's not too long for you.
6. It's part of a favorite series.

also need to readjust our own attitude. As one intermediate-grade teacher told me recently, "This year I learned how important it is to match kids with books for them to grow as readers. I was always pushed into books that were too hard for me, so I never felt successful as a reader. It's still hard for me to read easy books. I feel that if the book's not a challenge I shouldn't be reading it."

Keeping a Reading Record

When I go into classrooms, I share my ongoing reading record and tell why and how I keep one. I've been keeping a monthly reading record since 1993, and it's become a cherished ritual. Each month, I start a new page, on which I record the title, author, and genre of every book I read, placing an asterisk next to the ones I find "outstanding." Seeing what I have actually read (or not read) pushes me to read more, vary genres (I used to talk about wanting to read more fiction, but I didn't realize that goal until I started keeping track of my reading), and set goals. Seeing that the page is still blank in the middle of the month nudges me to begin reading a book. (Figure 2-7 is my reading record for June, 1999.)

Figure 2–7 My reading record for June 1999

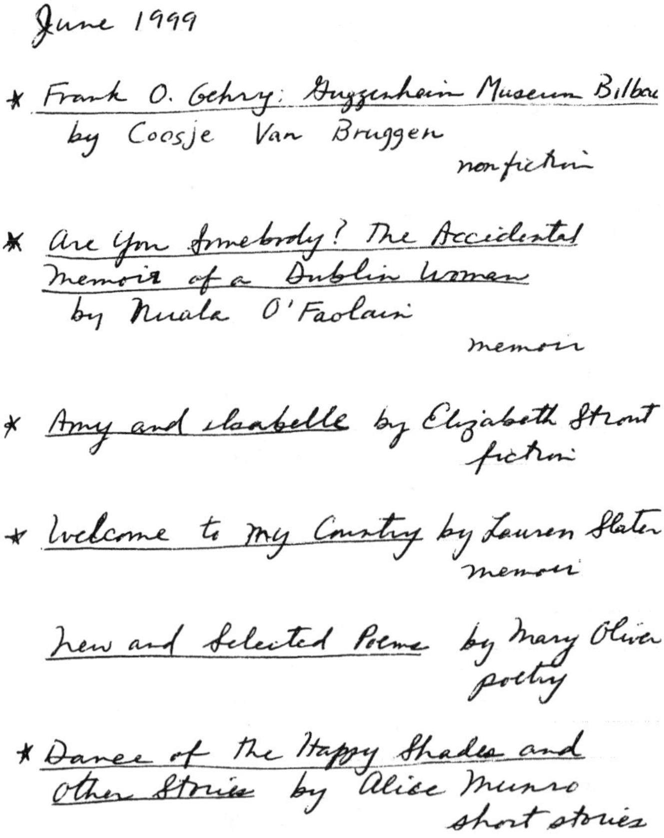

June 1999

* Frank O. Gehry: Guggenheim Museum Bilbao
   by Coosje Van Bruggen
                              nonfiction

* Are You Somebody? The Accidental
   Memoir of a Dublin Woman
   by Nuala O'Faolain
                              memoir

* Amy and Isabelle by Elizabeth Strout
                              fiction

* Welcome to My Country by Lauren Slater
                              memoir

   New and Selected Poems by Mary Oliver
                              poetry

* Dance of the Happy Shades and
   Other Stories by Alice Munro
                              short stories

I used to require students to record the number of pages they read each day. Then it hit me: I don't do that as a reader, why should they? But without a page count, how will we know they've read the book? We trust them. There will always be several students who try to beat the system no matter what, but we don't need to penalize the whole class for those few. Fourth-grade teacher Joan Servis and I found no difference in students' honesty in recording when we simplified the system. In fact, because they could decide what they recorded and when, they took the task more seriously. Fourth-grade teacher Julie Beers agrees: "I can check daily, and kids can still lie about their reading. Teachers need to teach kids how important reading is, model the pleasure of reading by sharing what they read, and read with them. We're not police."

A fourth-grade class I worked with came up with these recording criteria:

- Read at least thirty minutes at home each day.
- Write down the title and author of all books you start, and if you finish the book, make some kind of sign.
- Keep a separate monthly listing of completed books. (See Figure 2-8 for a fourth grader's and Appendix B-5 for an alternative form.)
- Have WEB log pages for the whole school year bound together.

Figure 2–8** **A fourth grader's monthly reading record

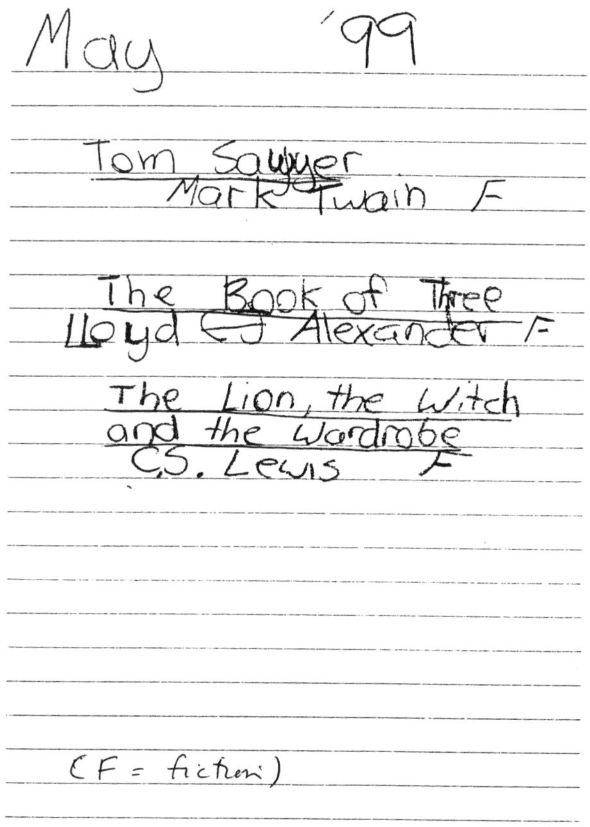
May '99

Tom Sawyer
Mark Twain F

The Book of Three
Lloyd Alexander F

The Lion, the Witch and the Wardrobe
C.S. Lewis F

(F = fiction)

- List the genre of each book you finish. (See Figure 2-9.)
- Rate books. An asterisk (*) means you recommend this book to others. Or design your own rating system: 1 (excellent), 2 (okay), 3 (not very good).

Students should keep some kind of reading record as soon as they are able. Beginning the second half of the school year, kindergarten teacher Karen Sher has her students write down (on an index card, as best they can) the titles of the books they read during independent reading. When the front and back of the card are filled up, the student takes it home to show his parents and gets a new card.

The time you take to demonstrate format and neatness will pay dividends later. Even a seemingly simple task like recording titles and authors may need to be demonstrated repeatedly before students understand and take seriously what is required—capitalizing important words in the book title and underlining it, including the author's first and last name, spelling all words correctly (referring to book to be sure), writing legibly, skipping lines, and doing whatever else you and the students determine. I am amazed at the sloppiness teachers accept. Students will do an excellent job when we refuse to accept messy work. A bonus is that students always take more pride in work that is well done.

I demonstrate on a projected transparency, verbalizing as I go along. I note that I am forming my letters carefully so my handwriting is good, that I am checking my spelling of the title and author by referring to the book's cover. Then I ask students to record their book, and as they do, I walk around and provide necessary assistance. Sometimes I appoint student monitors.

Loretta Martin, a second-grade teacher, also has students record all her daily read-alouds. Before school each morning, she places the previous day's read-alouds—the ac-

Figure 2–9   A fourth grader's genre key

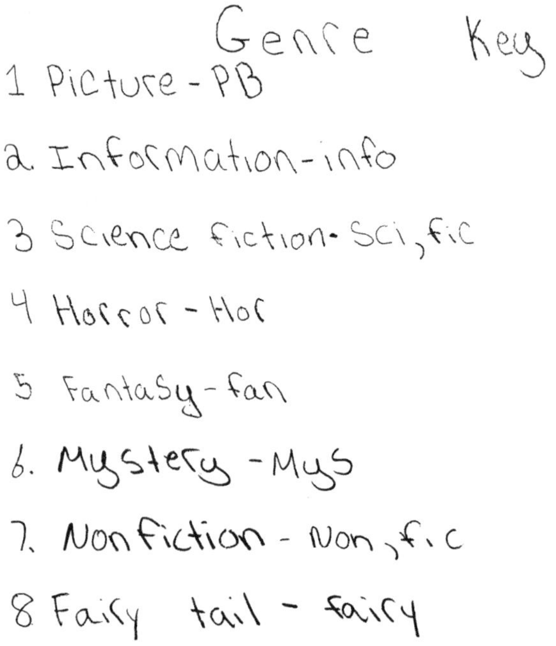

Genre   Key

1 Picture - PB

2. Information - info

3 Science fiction - Sci, fic

4 Horror - Hor

5 Fantasy - fan

6. Mystery - Mys

7. Nonfiction - Non, fic

8 Fairy tail - fairy

tual books—on the overhead projector. As students get settled, the first thing they do is record yesterday's reading, both in and out of school. A student scribe carefully copies down the titles and authors of the read-alouds onto an overhead transparency. Students add these titles to their reading record (denoting RA for read-aloud), along with their personal reading and books read in guided reading groups, indicating whether the book was easy (E), medium (M), "just-right" (JR), or hard (H). Figure 2-10 is a page from one student's record.

Monitoring Reading Through Brief Interviews

In *Invitations*, on pages 43–50, I describe what I call a WEB check, a quick comprehension check once students have finished reading a book. While I still use these procedures, I have made some refinements as I've continued to work with teachers and students.

Students, generally first thing in the morning, sign their names on a designated space on the chalkboard once they have completed a book and are ready for an interview.

Figure 2–10 *A page from a second grader's reading record*

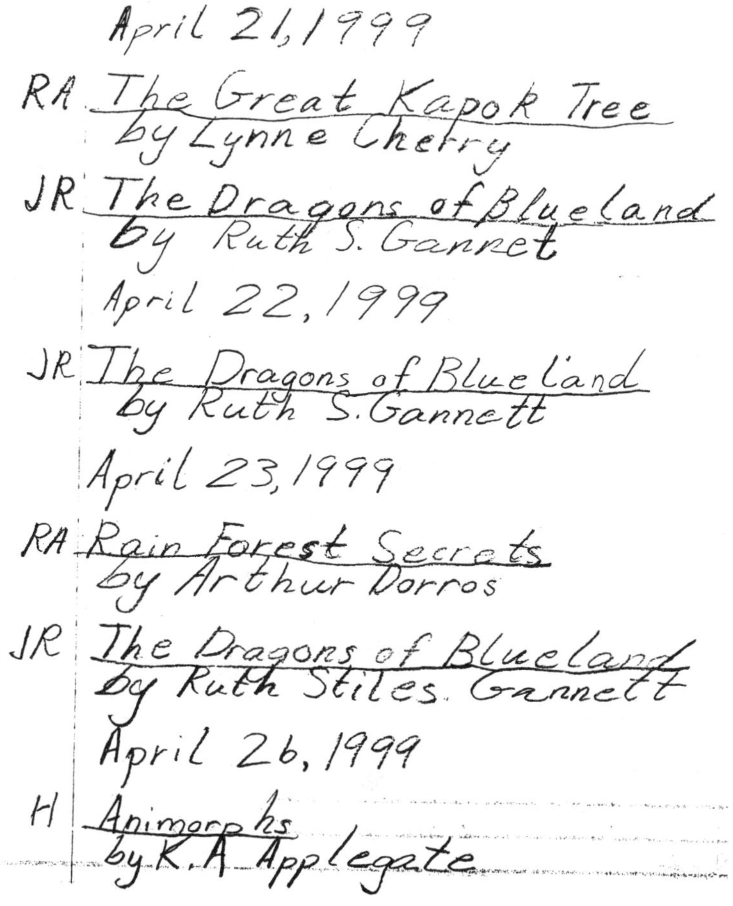

April 21, 1999

RA *The Great Kapok Tree*
by Lynne Cherry

JR *The Dragons of Blueland*
by Ruth S. Gannet

April 22, 1999

JR *The Dragons of Blueland*
by Ruth S. Gannett

April 23, 1999

RA *Rain Forest Secrets*
by Arthur Dorros

JR *The Dragons of Blueland*
by Ruth Stiles Gannett

April 26, 1999

H *Animorphs*
by K. A. Applegate

Then, just as WEB is about to begin, the teacher asks which students are willing to interview someone who has finished a book. Usually the student interviewer has also read the book, but this is not a requirement. (When I model an interview I look through the book and read the blurb on the back cover, demonstrating how to get the gist of the story.) The students choose their interview questions from a list generated by the whole class during shared writing. (See Figure 2-11 for sample questions.)

Students are paired for interviews, which follow these agreed-on procedures:

- The interviewer and interviewee go to a quiet corner of the room and speak in soft voices.
- The interviewer has her questions in front of her.
- No interview takes place without the book, which the interviewer holds.
- If there is a problem or a question about whether or not the interviewee has read and understood the book, the teacher reinterviews. (This is rarely necessary.)
- After a successful interview, the interviewee enters the book on his monthly record.

When I am teaching students how to interview, I place two chairs facing each other at the front of the classroom and ask for a student volunteer. Then I conduct the interview. Students see how manageable and rapid the process is (it usually takes about three minutes) and how easy it is to assess from the student's comments whether she has read and understood the book. After the demonstration, I ask, *How many of you*

Figure 2–11   *A fourth grade class' sample questions for a WEB interview*

WEB Interview Questions

Ask these required questions:

Title of book and author of book (Illustrator of book)

Genre

Why did you choose this book?

What was one main problem, but don't say how it was solved?

Describe the setting.

Choose one or two main charcters and describe them.

Did you learn anything new while reading this book?

Would you read another book by this author? Why or why not?

Choose several optional questions:

Why do you think the author wrote this story?

What was the most exciting part?

What do you think the message is that the author was trying to get across?

Was the book fun to read? Why or why not?

Is this book like any other you have read? Why or why not?

Are you like any of the characters in the book? How or how not?

If you could change one part of this book, what would it be? Why would you change this part?

Think of your own question.

think [student's name] read and understood the book? Almost always, this is an easy call in the affirmative. Next, I coach a pair of volunteers, an interviewer and interviewee, as the class observes. We repeat this process several times over the next few days. Students from late second grade on can easily manage this process once it has been well modeled and practiced.

Joan Servis notes that after many years of WEB, her interviews have evolved into conversational "book chats." That is, the focus is no longer on checking comprehension but on recommending a book to a peer—just as we adults do. "I no longer do reinterviews, as students just don't talk about books they have not read."

Additionally, self-evaluation of independent reading is part of our district's "common tools" (see pages 576–578) for reading. See Figure 2-12 and Appendix B-6 for a blank form.

Figure 2–12   A fourth grader's self-evaluation: "Thinking About Your Reading"

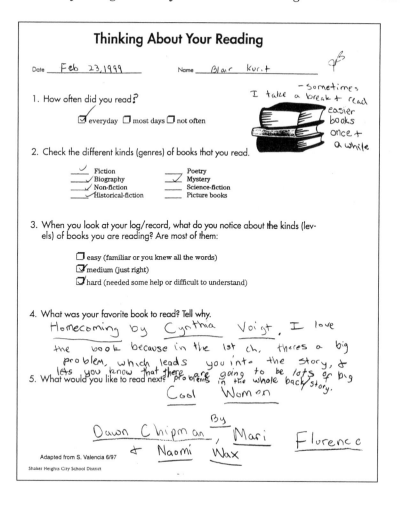

Book Talks

Most of the books I read have been recommended by friends. It makes sense, then, to give students that same opportunity. A friend's enthusiasm about a book often "sells" it. It is not unusual for a whole class of students to read books by an author one of their classmates has recommended.

Weekly student book talks are an excellent forum for recommending particular titles (see *Invitations*, "Critic's Corner," page 50). Organized book talks (see Figure 2–13 for some guidelines for students) provide important opportunities for students to speak in front of their peers and to talk up favorite books. Children are never too young to begin giving these talks.

Many kindergarten teachers have regularly scheduled times for students to give a book talk on a favorite book. To be sure students are prepared for these book talks, teachers first send home guidelines to families. The guidelines include:

- Selecting an appropriate book
- Reading and talking about the book
- Stating the title, author, and illustrator
- Briefly retelling the story
- Sharing a favorite part

When students have heard and read a book over and over again and practiced retelling the story at home, they are always successful. When necessary, teachers offer support by asking questions like:

- What else happens?
- What happened when . . . ?
- How does the story end?
- What's your favorite part?
- Why do you like this page the best?

Figure 2–13   A book talk guide sheet for students

- Choose a book you have enjoyed a lot.
- Practice your book talk ahead of time. Use markers such as Post-its for particular pages you will be referring to so you can find them easily. Plan to complete your talk in about three minutes.
- Have the book with you.
- Give the title, author, and genre.
- Tell why you chose to read this book.
- Tell what the book is about without giving away the ending.
- You may want to talk about the characters, the problem, the setting.
- Share a favorite part—show illustrations, read aloud a paragraph or two, tell about an exciting event.
- Tell why you recommend this book and what kind of readers might enjoy it.

Tara Strachan leads her second graders in a shared writing on things to include in a book talk and posts the results. Here's her class' most recent list of suggestions (the first five are required, the others are optional):

1. State the title and author.
2. Tell what kind of book it is.
3. Point out the first sentence "grabber."
4. Tell what the book is about.
5. Describe a main character.
6. Share what you like about the book.
7. Say what you can learn from the book.
8. Compare the book to something your audience already knows.
9. Rate the book's difficulty.
10. Tell where to find the book.
11. Read a favorite sentence or paragraph.
12. Show a favorite illustration.

Working Through Problems

After I've demonstrated how to work independent reading into a daily classroom schedule, teachers sometimes tell me, *But you made it look so easy. I tried it, and it didn't work.* Because independent reading is so critical to reading success, let's take a look at two classrooms that are having difficulty and notice what the problems are and how we worked them through.

Carrie Jordan faithfully schedules WEB for her fourth graders the first half hour of every day but is not happy with how it's going. She asks for my help, and I observe a session. I am impressed with the book sign-out procedures, which Carrie has modeled on another teacher's approach (see pages 89–90). However, too much is going on. Anyone who wants to give a book talk comes up to the front of the room, sits on a stool, and talks about the book. The other students can listen or not listen. Meanwhile, Carrie is monitoring everyone, not reading herself. Her eyes dart around the room. She is clearly not enjoying herself, and many of the kids aren't having a good time either. When I ask them, they mention particularly disliking the required daily comments and recording of pages read (at home and school).

I agree to oversee a few sessions. I begin by modeling the WEB-check interviews so the kids can do them by themselves. Carrie is surprised by how quickly and well it goes. After I interview two students in succession, two students model in front of the class. The next time I am back in the classroom, seven students have their name on the board for an interview (a week's accumulation). Three interview pairs stay in the room, one pair go into the coat area, one pair go into the hall. I interview one of the remaining students, and Carrie interviews the other. All the interviews are completed within five minutes.

I begin another session by passing around my own WEB log. I tell the students how keeping a reading record pushes me to read more and more-varied kinds of books. I am surprised by how interested these fourth graders are in my reading and record keeping. I show them the books I've read most recently—*Brothers and Sisters*, by Bebe Moore Campbell, and *Who Owns Learning? Questions of Autonomy, Choice, and Control*, by Curt Dudley-Marling and Dennis Searle. I tell them why I chose these books: *Brothers and Sisters* was given to me by Loretta Martin, a colleague and close friend, and *Who Owns Learning?* had a fascinating title and table of contents. I tell the kids I've been thinking a lot about control in schools and that I'd like them to come up with their own WEB interview questions. We talk about the questions I've been using, and then they brainstorm their own.

When I walk into Carrie's room first thing in the morning a week later, I smile. The room is silent (book talks have been dropped for the time being, at my suggestion), and the kids are reading in cozy areas all over the classroom. Carrie, who used to sit at the head of her kidney shaped table at the front of the room, is sitting on the floor, reading. I feel guilty interrupting this magical time, but we need to negotiate the questions we'll be using for WEB and decide on the format for the WEB log.

The kids decide to do monthly entries like mine—title, author, and genre—and that things like listing favorite authors and rating the books will be optional. We break into groups of four, and each student is given a copy of the list of WEB questions we brainstormed the week before as well as a copy of my list of questions. They negotiate what to add, delete, and change. Carrie meets later with the class and through shared writing they come up with their final list of questions (see Figure 2-11, page 56).

Another time Tara Strachan asks whether I will talk with her second graders. She is concerned that too many of them are not excited about independent reading. When I come to class, Tara and I tell her students that she and I belong to the same book club and are about to read *Paradise*, by Toni Morrison. I mention that most of the books I read have been recommended by my friends or are ones I've read reviews of in *The New York Times Book Review* (I've brought the *Times* review of *Paradise* with me and hold it up.) I show them my reading record and talk about how important it is to me and how it helps me balance what I read.

I ask students to tell me about their reading habits. Several mention how they stay up late to read—sometimes with a flashlight—when their parents think they're asleep. A few mention going to the library or the bookstore with their parents. Many are in the Junior Great Books reading club for the first time and say how much fun it is.

"So, what *don't* you like about reading?" I ask. Max says he doesn't know what to read next, that it's hard to find a book that interests him. Tara and I talk about how we always pretty much know what we're going to read next, even though we may not have decided definitely. I always have several professional books and at least one or two novels in mind, often piled up and waiting. I realize that this planning, which I haven't thought about before, is something we need to teach kids how to do.

Jason says it disturbs him when kids move about the room during independent reading. Others agree. Rachel says talking and pencil sharpening are a distraction. Several others mention being disturbed when a student interrupts with a question. I make the following recommendations:

- Once independent reading begins, stay in the reading space you have selected.
- Have with you as many books as you might need. (If you're about to finish one book, have another ready to begin.)
- Remember, absolutely no talking.

- Fill in your reading log when you come in the morning, instead of after independent reading.
- Instead of reading different books at home and in school, carry the same books back and forth.
- If you don't know what to read next, either choose from the bin of preselected books or have your teacher accompany you to the library.

Several weeks later, Tara's students are transformed. "What's changed?" I ask. The teacher-researcher in me can hardly wait to hear what they have to say. They can hardly wait to tell me:

SCOTT: I feel like the only thing that concerns me in life is reading. Everything is silent, and all I hear are the characters in my book talking.

ASHLEY: The computer people aren't on the computer making noise anymore.

BRANDON: There's not too much moving around. It's so quiet I can just enjoy my books. And I'm choosing "just right" books from the teaching basket.

NATALIE: I feel like when I'm reading, the quietness pushes me into my books.

JOSHUA: I feel like I'm at home lying in my bed reading a book.

BISHOP: Even if someone has to leave the room, they leave quietly now, so no one is disturbed.

MAX: I feel like I can find more books that I like. I went to the library and got about five books. The quiet is helping me enjoy books more.

GERALD: I'm so into my book because my neighbors are so into their books, and that helps me.

PATRICK: I feel like I'm into my book. It's made me able to read harder books because now it's quiet, and I can concentrate on chapter books.

SAMANTHA: It's more quiet, and I can really hear myself think.

GLENN: It feels like all the characters in the book are crowding around me, and I'm with them.

BISHOP: I like seeing my teacher reading because I like to do what my teacher does.

BRANDON: I look up and see [my teacher] reading, and it helps me to keep reading.

PATRICK: I know everyone is reading, even the teacher.

After lunch, I come back to observe and participate. There is absolute silence. I don't hear so much as a cough. The only sound is pages turning. Students are comfortably situated all over the room, spread out on the floor, on pillows and cushions, and at their desks. When the half hour is up, nobody, including me, wants this peaceful time to end.

FINAL REFLECTIONS ON INDEPENDENT READING

There are so many competing influences for kids' time today. Indeed, just because our students can read, doesn't mean they will read—deeply, thoughtfully, and extensively. We can no longer assume they will become readers; that is, citizens who choose to read for pleasure and information. The growth of the Internet, cable television, entertaining computer programs, and increasingly adultlike movies for children all contribute to the acceleration of childhood and the demand for ultra-sophisticated stories. If books are to continue as the lifeline for future generations, we teachers must provide the uninterrupted time and quality resources that foster the motivation to read. Imagination begins with the ability to picture stories in the mind's eye. Reading sparks the imagination of the mind and spirit. As school may well be the last place where books are valued and promoted, we teachers must do everything we can to keep the magic and beauty of books alive for our students.

CONTINUING THE CONVERSATION

• *Articulate your own theory of learning.*   Think about putting your beliefs in writing so you can reflect on them. What do you believe about how children learn? How do your beliefs translate into practice? Are your theory and practice compatible, and are they based on research and experience? How can you minimize the discrepancies between your beliefs and practices so they go hand in hand?

• *Take stock of your own reading and writing.*   How do you use what you do in your life to inform your teaching? How do you model and share your own literacy with your students? What else do you need and want to do to increase your own literacy?

• *Become familiar with how the brain learns and apply that knowledge to how you teach and organize your classroom.*   See resources on brain-based learning, page 10b.

• *Take note of your teaching approaches.*   Be sure you are not overrelying on any one of them. Are you teaching, supporting, and guiding students to make their own discoveries and confirmations? Are your approaches a combination of directed, shared, guided, and independent, that is, doing to and for students, with students, and by students? Are you gradually and appropriately releasing support and encouraging students to become independent?

• *Revisit the classroom scenarios presented on pages 27–29, 40–43, and 59–61.* What can you take away for setting up your own successful program?

• *Examine how and how often you demonstrate reading and writing processes.* Do you demonstrate before you assign? Do students understand the purposes of what they are being asked to do?

CHAPTER 3

The Literature Program

Partner reading in first grade

■ Writing, in itself, is like the sound of one hand clapping—incomplete, silent, and without impact. Only when the writer as the one hand, and the reader as the other, confront each other is there that clap, that spark of communication which makes literature alive.

—*Minfong Ho, Singaporean journalist and writer*

Since the late 1980s, our school district has been using quality trade books to teach reading in the elementary grades. Our goal in replacing basal readers with trade books has been to produce students who not only can read with understanding but who choose to read for pleasure and information, and who go on to become critical thinkers and active participants in our society.

Despite the fact that we live in a multimedia age, an age in which there exists a continuing explosion of information, there is no substitute for books. For durability, cost, portability, ease of use, and life expectancy, the book can't be beat. For turning kids on to reading, there is no substitute. Librarians talk frequently about "bringing out the reader" in people, which "speaks to a central belief about the nature of human need—of the need, timeless and immutable, for narrative; the compelling hunger to make sense of experience through the words spun out in a story; the thinking that nothing but a book can deliver" (Gornick 1998, B40). If your school continues to use basal texts as the mainstay of its reading program, you will want to enrich your literature program by supplementing it with the best of children's books.

This chapter will discuss the use of select trade books, or what we call "anchor" books, and supplemental reading material in our literature program, ways of reading the literature and possibilities for reader response, author/illustrator study, and organization strategies for the literature collection and classroom libraries. (See Chapters 4, 5, 9, and 11 for specifics on teaching reading, reading and writing nonfiction, and small-group literature conversations.)

FROM CORE BOOKS TO ANCHOR BOOKS

In the mid-1980s, our school district's elementary reading program shifted from the use of basal texts and workbooks to noteworthy children's literature trade books ("core books") and authentic response. The selected core books became the center of our reading program. They were used for whole-class, small-group, and/or independent reading. The transformation of our literature program is detailed in *Transitions*, and in Chapters 5 and 6 of *Invitations*.

Core titles were determined by a committee of teachers, with representation and input from each grade level. The reading committee also created teacher-resource folders to accompany each core book. Information in these folders included such things as ideas on how to teach and respond to the book, relevant questions and activities, or "extensions," and information about the author.

We began with about six core titles per grade level as well as supplemental titles. These core books were selected for their literary quality and were "stand alone" books. That is, we did not select them for cross-curricular connections. Each student was expected to be "exposed" to the core books, and that exposure was interpreted variously by teachers.

Problems with the Literature Program

As has been common in school districts around the country, we encountered difficulties when we moved to a literature emphasis in reading. The most pronounced problem, which we shared with many other school districts, was that core books were above the reading level of some students, and teachers needed more guidance for the kids who couldn't read these texts. As one visiting educator told me, "We used core book lists from all over the country. We thought we were making informed choices. But some of the books were too hard for the students." Other problems included the following:

- Suggested activities and questions had the effect of "basalizing" the literature.
- Because of the number of suggested activities, too much time was spent on response.
- Teachers spent far too long teaching one title, sometimes as long as two months.
- Very little small-group teaching occurred. Most reading was done in whole-class format.
- Classroom management became an issue as teachers struggled with what to do with kids not in reading group.
- Teachers above grade two expected students to come to them knowing how to read. When they didn't, some teachers were at a loss as to how to teach them and what materials to use.
- Teachers experienced problems with core book availability.
- There was not enough variety in supplemental titles.
- Parents new to the district did not understand our literature program, and often, we did not inform them sufficiently.

The Need for Parent Education

Typically in education, teachers and administrators make changes and inform parents afterward. Then we are surprised when parents are unhappy with our decisions. The following scenario could probably have been avoided had we been more conscientious in explaining to family members how our literature program works.

A distressed upper-grade elementary teacher calls me at home. The parents of one of her "gifted students" are pressuring her to remove the student from our literature program because the books are "too easy." Even when the teacher explains that the student is being challenged by the reading material, the parents are uncompromising. They view reading as reading the words, and, in their opinion, the words in these books are no challenge for their son. What has not been adequately communicated to these parents is that we choose trade books for their depth and possibilities of enriching us as humans—for the opportunities they offer us to make connections, see things through different perspectives, reexamine our view of the world, and learn from one another. While certain titles may be used to teach reading strategies and story elements, books are selected only if they meet rigorous literary criteria (see pages 66–67).

I encourage the teacher not to back down, to explain that the discussion of literature is not an option, that it is part of our course of study and our district curriculum for all students. Eventually the parents come around, but not without a struggle.

It is easy to see why these parents would want to have their child in a different program. The media has done an excellent job of defining literacy as merely the ability to read and write words. Without our clear explanation of how and why we teach as we do, parents are left to rely on the media and their own experiences of schooling.

In one school, we worked for months in our language arts support group creating a brochure for parents that explained our school's reading-writing program (see Appendix A-2). The brochure was so well received by parents that other schools in the district adapted similar brochures.

Anchor Books and Literature Units

While the use of core books proved a viable way to begin our literature program, reliance on these books proved limiting. "Confining the study of literature to one core book restricts the level of generalizations the students can make. Therefore, it is important to provide students with extended works dealing with related concepts for students to arrive at universal generalizations" (Silva and Delgado-Larocco 1993, 472).

We needed and wanted multicultural books that would work for our diverse student body, that were centered around broad generalizations and themes, that would deepen understanding, and that connected with our curriculum. We felt that anchor books, as we came to call them, would help promote in-depth study and broader perspectives on issues and themes. The books were both fiction and nonfiction, including biographies and popular science. We were aware that we needed to choose titles that were consistent with the reading abilities of our students but that would engage all students, including our highest achievers.

When our reading committee met over the summer in the mid-1990s, we selected anchor books that would be supported by conceptually related supplemental books. All students would be exposed to the anchor books through one, or a combination, of the following approaches: reading aloud, shared reading, partner reading, independent reading, guided reading, and books on tape.

Supplemental books would be used to expand key concepts as well as to provide instructional reading material at a student's reading level. In that way, all students in any particular grade level would be discussing similar concepts and themes, but they would be reading a variety of books. Incorporating into our program relevant supplemental books of varying levels of difficulty made it possible for us to serve those students who were less proficient readers.

Supplemental books have given each student an opportunity to receive reading instruction at his level. Equally important, students have the opportunity and choice to further explore concepts and experience reading success and enjoyment. Supplemental books enhance classroom libraries and also provide resources for cross-curricular study.

Charlotte's Web, with its theme of friendship, is one of our second-grade anchor books. Though our second graders read the text with varying levels of success, all students are able to experience and discuss the book through shared reading, reading aloud, partner reading, or a combination of these approaches. However, simultaneous with their exposure to *Charlotte's Web*, every student will read and learn to read books dealing with friendship *that are at his or her reading level*. Supplemental books for this text have included such titles as *Me and Neesie*; *Rosie and Michael*; the Frog and Toad and Henry and Mudge series; *Baseball Saved Us*; *Sam, Bangs, and Moonshine*; *Teammates*; and *Jamaica Tag-Along*.

Criteria for Choosing Anchor Books

Among the major criteria we rely on in the selection of anchor books are the following:

- Literary excellence (includes writing style, visual presentation, organization, and content)
- Depth of subject matter (teacher guidance required for full appreciation and understanding)
- Reading level and interest level appropriateness
- Age appropriateness

Anchor books, which ground the literature program at each grade level, are also texts that

- Display exceptional literary (and artistic) merit
- Reflect the diverse population of our district as well as our multicultural world
- Connect to students' lives and values
- Comprise mostly current literature (published within the last decade) as well as "classics"
- Challenge the reader to think deeply about important concepts
- Support thoughtful discussion, analysis, and understanding
- Can be used to teach students how to read (as long as the book is at students' instructional level)

- Can be utilized to highlight literary elements, such as setting, point of view, theme, and character development
- Can be used for examining an author's style and as a model for writing
- Connect to district objectives across the curriculum

All students are expected to experience and discuss anchor books. While it is expected that anchor books (about six or seven for grade two and above and more for kindergarten and grade one) are reserved for use at the designated grade level, teachers may borrow titles from previous grade levels for reading instruction. (See also pages 442–443 for criteria for choosing nonfiction and "The Literature Program" and "Literature Resources for Choosing Fiction and Nonfiction" in The Blue Pages.)

Guides for Anchor Books

Our reading committee met in early summer and developed written guides for anchor books, and also developed frameworks for webs (visual brainstorming maps). See Norton 1993, page 16b for ideas on webbing. Our guides were based on prototypes presented by Huck, Hepler, Hickman, and Kiefer (1997). Our expectation was that the guides would be continually refined and updated as teachers used and modified them. Our present book guides are more concise and less burdened with activities than the guides that accompanied core books. Anchor book guides contain the following components:

- Brief summary of the book
- Possible questions for discussion—before reading, during reading, and after reading
- Ideas for activities
- Related books

(See Figure 3-1 for a sample book guide and web of possibilities.)

While guides developed by others are a good reference and starting point, you and your colleagues will want to develop your own, with input from your students. It is the thoughtful conversations that take place with colleagues in the planning stage and with students in the implementation stage that enrich our teaching and move it forward.

READING THE LITERATURE

Anchor and supplemental books are read in a variety of ways, including:

- Small-group reading (guided reading and literature conversation groups—teacher or student led)
- Partner reading (reading with peer, older student, volunteer, or teacher)
- Independent reading
- Whole-class reading
- Reading aloud
- Shared reading

Figure 3–1a   A second grade book guide

A GUIDE FOR *THE SMALLEST COW IN WORLD* **Working Draft**
by Katherine Paterson
Illustrated by Jane Clark Brown

Summary: Though Rosie is the meanest cow in the herd, five-year old Marvin is inconsolable when she is sold and he and his family move to another dairy farm.

Before Reading: What can you tell about the story from the cover and from the title page? Look at the pictures. What can you tell about the setting and the characters?

Guided Reading Purpose: To discuss and make inferences.

Possible Questions:

1. What do you think about this story?
2. What do we know about Marvin? What do we know about Marvin's family? What in the story makes you think that? Give me a page or example.
3. How does Marvin feel about Rosie?
4. Tell me about the ending.
5. Have you ever had to move? How did you feel about moving?
6. Have you ever had an imaginary friend? (after discussion)
7. What do you do when you get angry?
8. Does Marvin change? If so, how?

Ideas for Activities:

1. Web—book web, theme web, character web
2. Readers Theatre
3. Write to the prompt . . . "When I had to leave my _____, I . . .".
4. Read a related book. (supplemental literature)

Reading may be accomplished through one or a combination of these formats. (In kindergarten, most literature is presented by the teacher to the whole class.) For example, students might begin a book by following along in their own copy as the teacher reads aloud, and then finish the book in a small-group guided reading. (See Chapter 4, "Teaching Children to Read," for specifics on guided reading, and Chapter 2, "A Comprehensive Literacy Program," for specifics on reading aloud and shared reading.)

Small-Group Reading

Most small-group reading consists of teacher-led guided reading groups, the heart of the instructional reading program. (See pages 142–153 in Chapter 4.) Small-group reading material includes fiction and nonfiction that crosses the curriculum. For developing readers, these groups focus on both word-solving and text-solving strategies. As students become more independent, in-depth discussion and analysis take priority.

Some of these discussion groups are student-led, collaborative groups in which students support one another during the first reading of a text (similar to the approach described in Chapter 11, "Reading Nonfiction," pages 454–455, and in "Literature Conversations").

Figure 3–1b   A book guide: a web of possibilities

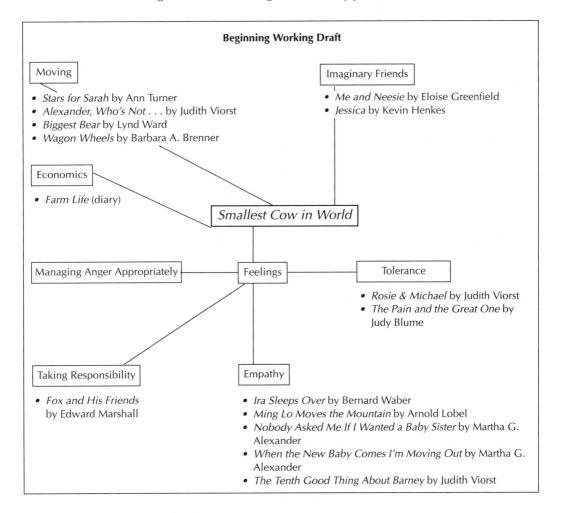

Beginning Working Draft

Moving
- *Stars for Sarah* by Ann Turner
- *Alexander, Who's Not . . .* by Judith Viorst
- *Biggest Bear* by Lynd Ward
- *Wagon Wheels* by Barbara A. Brenner

Imaginary Friends
- *Me and Neesie* by Eloise Greenfield
- *Jessica* by Kevin Henkes

Economics
- *Farm Life* (diary)

Smallest Cow in World

Managing Anger Appropriately — Feelings — Tolerance

Tolerance
- *Rosie & Michael* by Judith Viorst
- *The Pain and the Great One* by Judy Blume

Taking Responsibility
- *Fox and His Friends* by Edward Marshall

Empathy
- *Ira Sleeps Over* by Bernard Waber
- *Ming Lo Moves the Mountain* by Arnold Lobel
- *Nobody Asked Me If I Wanted a Baby Sister* by Martha G. Alexander
- *When the New Baby Comes I'm Moving Out* by Martha G. Alexander
- *The Tenth Good Thing About Barney* by Judith Viorst

Students read aloud together, summarize what they've read, make predictions about where the text is leading them, raise questions and attempt to answer them, clarify confusing elements, and define difficult vocabulary words. The teacher usually joins one group as guide or facilitator, depending on the ability of the group to self-direct and self-monitor.

Partner Reading

Partner reading is a powerful tool. In classrooms in which individuals are frequently teamed with peers, reading improvement and motivation are high. In Elisabeth Tuttle's first-grade classroom, partner reading is the activity most employed for management when small-group guided reading is in progress. After a group meets, their main assignment is to reread or continue reading with a buddy. All students in this classroom not only love to read, they are great readers. I am convinced that the daily partner reading these students do contributes greatly to their fluency, comprehension, and achievement.

Guidelines for Partner Reading

Depending on the reading purpose, students can be given the opportunity to choose their own partners or the teacher can decide who will be paired with whom. Even kindergarten students can partner informally during independent reading time. Students take turns reading aloud (or, in kindergarten, role-play reading) and discussing the book as they go along. When necessary, one partner acts as a peer tutor, modeling the reading process, suggesting strategies, and encouraging the reader to "have a go."

From my experience, partnering two low-performing readers works very well as long as the book is at the students' reading level. Evenly matched students experience success in practicing strategies and achieving fluency. This type of coupling works particularly well with respect to materials that have already been read and discussed in small guided reading groups. Likewise, two high-achieving readers can benefit from being partnered. Some of us have found that partnering a high-performing reader with a low-performing reader does not work well, especially if the teacher has not modeled the roles. Too many times, the better reader does all the reading work.

Whatever the combination, partner reading works best when it is modeled. Usually, I model the partnership first, with the help of a student, in front of the entire class. I then have two volunteers model a partnership as the class observes. We record our observations on a chart, which enables us to formulate specific guidelines for partner reading. Typical guidelines include the following points:

- Take turns reading. Decide ahead of time how much each person will read.
- Sit side by side.
- Follow along and listen carefully as your partner reads.
- Give your partner thinking time and time to self-correct.
- Offer suggestions and strategies if your partner has difficulty.
- Supply the word (if you can) when your suggestions have not helped your partner.
- Stop after a few pages and summarize the story, or talk about the main points covered so far. Or do alternate retelling, in which one person starts to tell the story and the other person describes what comes next.
- Jot down any confusion or problems you cannot work out yourselves and bring these to the teacher's attention.

In all partnerships, students need to show respect, courtesy, and kindness. Partner reading works best in caring classrooms that have already established community.

Veronica Allen's third graders gave the following reasons for why they like partner reading:

- If you don't understand or can't read a word, your partner can help you out.
- You can talk about the book and how you feel about it.
- You help yourself when you help your partner.
- You can't discuss a book with yourself. With a partner, you get to give your opinion and thoughts.

See *Buddy Reading* by Samway, Whang, and Pippit in The Blue Pages, page 13b, for many helpful suggestions for partner (buddy) reading.

Independent Reading

When a book is carefully aligned to the student's instructional level and a proper introduction has been given, he can be asked to read the book silently, in manageable chunks, on his own. As students read independently, we encourage them to jot down questions, difficult vocabulary words, and insights. Students are expected to bring these notes to their guided reading group, where their ideas and problems can be discussed.

Independent reading usually involves books of choice, with follow-up provided through individual conferences and/or small-group discussion (see Chapter 2).

Whole-Class Reading

Some teachers like to begin the year with whole-class reading of a text. Each student is given a copy of the book and then the class reads it and discusses it as a group. Whole class reading is a pleasant way to set the tone of the reading classroom and enjoy a book together. However, in whole-class reading, teachers are largely unable to monitor their students' reading and get to know their individual strengths and weaknesses as readers. Typically, the same "stars" tend to dominate class discussion of the book. It is very important that whole-class reading not take the place of small-group guided reading. In classrooms where whole-class reading predominates, individual reading problems can easily be overlooked. Kids can come out of such classrooms not knowing how to read.

Reading Aloud

Reading books aloud can take the following forms (see also Chapter 2):

- Teacher reads the text to the whole class; students listen to and discuss the text at various intervals.
- Teacher reads aloud and thinks aloud as a demonstration of how readers make meaning as they read.
- Teacher reads aloud and thinks aloud in a small group—offering explanations, defining difficult words, modeling the reading process.

Shared Reading

Shared reading of a book can take the following forms (see also Chapter 2):

- Teacher reads aloud while students follow along in shared or individual copies.
- Teacher reads aloud while students follow text on an overhead projector. Teacher may track line by line to keep all students with her.
- Skillful student reads text while peers follow along in their own copies.

LITERATURE RESPONSE

In too many classrooms, students don't read during reading time; they respond to reading. Many of us, myself included, spent years focused on extensions, or activities accompanying books. The result was that we often wound up spending more time on supplemental activities than we did reading the book itself.

The myriad extensions that have sprung up commercially and noncommercially around children's literature have gotten out of control. While fewer teachers rely on worksheets, we have come to overrely on "doing" something, often something insignificant, to correspond with every book students read. Many of us feel that we haven't properly "taught" a book unless we have lots of paper-and-pencil work to show for it. While written response to literature can deepen understanding, often the best response to a book is silent and thoughtful appreciation, conversation, or more reading. *The main focus in literature must remain on getting meaning and enjoyment from the reading.*

Years ago, Natalie Babbitt, author of *Tuck Everlasting,* wrote about her concern that activities were taking books and readers down winding paths authors never intended. She reminded us teachers to focus on the joy stories bring:

> A good story is sufficient unto the day. It is complete as it stands. If it has something to teach, let it teach in its own sufficiency. Let it keep its magic and fulfill its purpose. In other words, let it be. (Babbitt 1990, 703)

Evaluating Literature Extensions

If we keep in mind that most of students' time with books should be spent reading them, we will do a better job teaching our students to read and savor literature. Literature extensions, when we do employ them, must be worthwhile (not merely busywork) and expand students' meaningful involvement with the text.

Meaningful literature extensions:

- Develop naturally from the literature
- Thoughtfully encourage students to reexamine and reconsider the text
- Demonstrate what the reader has gleaned from the text
- Deepen students' understanding of the literary piece
- Foster connections between texts
- Promote connections between the text and students' lives
- Are secondary to reading for meaning and pleasure

We must be careful to limit elaborate, time-consuming projects such as dioramas and complex constructions. We always need to be asking:

- Is this a worthwhile use of the student's time?
- Will this enterprise deepen the student's understanding and/or enjoyment of the text?
- Would the time be better spent with more reading?

A word of caution is warranted here about graphic and visual organizers, such as Venn diagrams, literature webs, comparison charts, and various kinds of mapping. While such devices can be very effective for comparing tales or characters, their usefulness to students is dependent on teacher guidance. Visual organizers are difficult for students to do independently, and should first be modeled and then undertaken as a shared experience. Too often, such projects are assigned as independent work or overassigned, taking away from valuable reading time.

Effective Extensions

Worthwhile responses to literature can involve supplementary reading, conversations about the book (see Chapter 5), writing, retellings (see pages 595–598), art and mixed media projects, and dramatic interpretations. The following are some examples of meaningful extension activities:

- Create a dramatic interpretation (Readers Theatre) of a favorite part or parts of a book, or write an original, related script. Readers Theatre remains one of my favorite extensions. It is easy to do, encourages rereading, builds fluency, and aids comprehension through repetition and dramatization. Also, kids love dramatic, oral reading in front of an audience, especially when they've rehearsed well. (For more information, see pages 74–75.)
- Create a sequel to a book or chapter, an alternate ending, an adaptation, or an original version of a tale (prose, drama, or artistic interpretation).
- Retitle or title the chapters of a book.
- Visualize a historical experience and express it artistically. Or create a favorite scene based on the text's description. (Artistic expression can be an alternative to written assessment.)
- Write a journal entry from the point of view of a character.
- Write a book review, blurb, or endorsement for the book.
- Use a writing form presented in the book, such as an advertisement or diary, as a model, and extend the form. (For example, in their reading of *Sarah, Plain and Tall*, students can be asked to write an ad similar to the one Jacob Witting places while looking for a mate in the 1880s. You could vary the activity by asking students to advertise for a friend [Morley and Russell 1995, 257]).

In your literature response, do include and value children's illustrations and explorations of other media, which give insight into readers' understanding and appreciation of text. If you are fortunate enough to have an art and/or music teacher in your building, coordinate efforts. Before children are readers, literature extensions rely heavily on art, music, and drama.

Drama, in particular, is wonderful for helping young children understand story. I recently observed a kindergarten class "performing" a version of the *Three Billy Goats Gruff*. As the teacher read the story aloud, students took on the roles, actions, and voices of the billy goats and the troll. Over a period of several days, the book was reread enough times so that each student had a chance to play a character. Not only was attention high for every reading and dramatization, every student knew and comprehended the story.

See *Invitations* (pages 88–102), for detailed descriptions of and directions for many "tried and true" literature-extension enterprises. See also *Literature Circles and Response,* by Hill, Johnson, and Schlick-Noe (1995, 142–148) for examples of other extension projects.

Once again, keep in mind that extension exercises are but a minor focus in the comprehensive literature/reading program. If students are to become fluent, comprehending, engaged readers, the major focus must remain on reading, not on activities surrounding reading.

Readers Theatre

In Readers Theatre, students take a narrative text or part of a text and treat it as or transform it into a script to be read and performed orally for an audience, turning a well-loved story that has several or more characters and lots of dialogue into "theatre" (see *Invitations,* page 98, for creating a script). Or, students can read the text as is, while taking note of characters and their conversations. Props, if they are employed, are minimal, and scripts are visible. Students enjoy performing a play without having to memorize parts.

I often use Readers Theatre as an extension that develops from guided reading. Kids express their enjoyment of a particular story or chapter, and we decide to perform it for the class. Often, we save the scripts that they make for the performance so that other classmates can use them. Low-performing readers get a boost when they see their classmates rushing to read their scripts. One of the things I love about Readers Theatre is that students don't realize they're rereading because they're so involved in the "play."

Fourth-grade teacher Linda Cooper tells of using a chapter in *Sarah, Plain and Tall* as Readers Theatre with her fourth graders. She made photocopies of a chapter and distributed them among her students. Then, students worked in small groups deciding who would play which parts, including narrator for the passages without conversation. Most students found it helpful to highlight the parts that they would be reading. Linda noted that in the course of this exercise, her struggling readers shone. By reading their parts over and over again during practice, they read confidently while performing for their peers.

When I was working as a reading specialist with low-performing second-grade readers in a pull-in classroom model, I often employed Readers Theatre at the beginning of the year as a way to build community in the classroom. Sometimes, I combined shared reading with Readers Theatre. For example, students loved reading and performing the delightful *Possum Come A-Knockin* by Nancy Van Lann. After I read the book aloud several times and we enjoyed and discussed the rhythm and antics of the story, I put the text on overhead transparencies and gave students individual copies. There were enough character parts for about half the class. While one half read the verses, the other half performed them. Kids begged to read and perform the story over and over again, and my struggling readers were willing and able to successfully join in.

Readers Theatre is also an effective way for students to learn how conventions such as quotation marks operate in stories. One first-grade group who did not understand the mechanics of dialogue began to grasp the use of "said," "asked," and "questioned" when we practiced reading with assigned parts.

Like everything else that we teach, you will first want to demonstrate Readers Theatre for your students—how to prepare scripts (individually, with a partner, or in a small group), how to highlight or label individual character and narrator parts, and how to coordinate with the other "players" and read with dramatic expression.

Some teachers have extended Readers Theatre to the content areas as an alternate format for understanding and presenting information related to science, conflict resolution, and other units of study. Science specialist Carol Hochman has had students use Readers Theatre to personify scientific concepts such as properties of matter and weather. For example, students have taken on the roles of molecules or warm and cold weather fronts to explain their functions. As students write their scripts, reread their parts, and then perform for classmates, their understanding of important concepts is reinforced and expanded.

Creating Literature Extensions for Management

Let's face it. A lot of activities get created as management for us teachers so we can meet with small guided reading groups. To create meaningful opportunities to enhance comprehension and appreciation for literature is a challenge. In working with teachers, one of the things I often demonstrate is how to create a meaningful project "on the spot," with minimal time and effort. Too often, I see teachers spending hours of time creating "seat work" for kids, time that could be better spent on professional reading or "having a life." I'm a great believer in simplifying what we ask kids to do and creating projects and assignments that take little teacher time and preparation (see pages 166–168). For example, one very effective activity for a class of young readers, which requires a minimum of teacher preparation, is to write a book together, and then have students illustrate it and practice reading the text on their own (see page 166). Or, students may come up with an idea. Some of the best ideas and extensions have come from the students (see page 167).

What we ask students to do should not be taken lightly by us teachers. Daily tasks convey how and what we think about literacy and impact students' attitudes and motivation. When students have open-ended, challenging opportunities to construct new meanings, they participate more actively and value and enjoy literacy more than when tasks are "closed"; that is, when one correct answer is being sought and there is little opportunity for individual choice and exploration (Turner and Paris 1995).

Reading Response Logs

Many of our teachers have students above grade one keep reading response logs, also called literature-response logs or reading journals, to monitor and assess students' reactions to and understanding of texts. In the reading response log, students record personal reactions and reflections as they read and after reading. The log becomes one way readers organize their thinking and record their ideas and questions. Such logs can be used by readers to promote introspection, deep thinking, and awareness of individual thought processes. Nancie Atwell (1998) has suggested that keeping a reading response log sensitizes students to become more actively engaged as readers and writers.

Teachers and students organize their logs in various ways. When used as part of the guided reading program, logs can take the form of a spiral notebook divided into sections for each book. Students can staple or paste a photocopy of the books' cover onto a blank page at the beginning of each new section. All responses to the book are kept in the notebook. Parents, teachers, and students then have a well-organized record of what books have been read and what responses each book elicited.

Some teachers have students make their own response logs. Students can be asked to fold a designated number of sheets of 8½" × 11" paper and then staple them together at the fold. The pamphlet covers can then be individually decorated.

Students are encouraged to go beyond summaries and fact in their responses. Emphasis is on both content and meaning. While students are expected to write in complete sentences and proofread their work, the focus is not on mechanics and spelling. Often, the page numbers (from the part of the book the response involves) are recorded. Responses can be as long as three or four pages or as short as several lines.

We use these response logs in many different ways. Some are used for note taking to support literature conversations (see pages 187–189). Others are used to record personal reactions in independent reading. Some are used by teachers to monitor students' comprehension while reading. Some are used to recall important "highlights" (page 168). Still others are used for classroom management during guided reading groups.

Responses may be personal (relating the text to one's life), or literary (commenting on elements such as character, theme, setting, author's style), or a combination of both. Responses can be directed or undirected. Some teachers will ask students to make a prediction, discuss how and why characters are behaving, or jot down difficult vocabulary. Others will encourage open-ended responses such as jottings and thoughts going through the reader's mind during and after reading. (See Figure 3-2 for an open-ended response.)

However the response logs are used, we must always first model our expectations. Such demonstrating means that students observe us think aloud as we compose our own response to a text. After modeling, it is also important that we monitor the response-log

Figure 3–2   *An intermediate-grade student's response to literature*

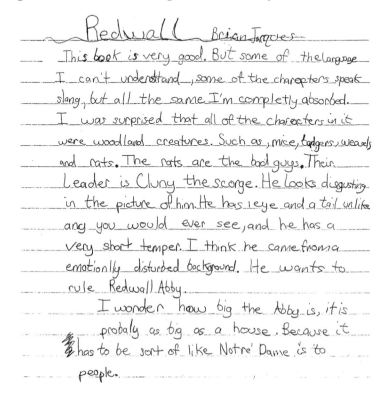

Redwall   Brian Jacques

This book is very good. But some of the language I can't understand, some of the characters speak slang, but all the same I'm completly absorbed.
I was surprised that all of the characters in it were woodland creatures. Such as, mice, badgers, weasels and rats. The rats are the bad guys. Their Leader is Cluny the scorge. He looks disgusting in the picture of him. He has 1 eye and a tail unlike any you would ever see, and he has a very short temper. I think he came from a emotionlly disturbed background. He wants to rule Redwall Abby.
  I wonder how big the Abby is, it is probaly as big as a house. Because it has to be sort of like Notre' Dame is to people.

process. Teachers collect the logs on a regular basis to make sure that goals are being met. Sometimes teachers respond in depth to students and get a dialogue going. Other times, teachers write brief comments in the margins of the logs. Sometimes, teachers just check to see that students are successfully recording their thinking in preparation for literature conversations. When I check student logs, I initial the top of the page so that students and parents know the response has been read. If there is a problem with the student's work, I will write a comment in the margin directing the student to take some specific action. For example, I might write, "Notes are incomplete for literature discussion. Reread and add at least two more thoughts," or "Check spelling of high-frequency words on this page." Then, when I recheck the log, I only have to look at my written comment to see what needs to be gone over.

Once you have some finished samples, use notable student logs as exemplars. With students' permission, make copies and file them for use with future classes. Use these samples in small-group and whole-class discussion to help set criteria for response logs.

Possibilities for Response

Numerous possibilities exist for reader response. Students could be asked, for example, to:

- Connect with a character's life. (Describe similarities and differences between reader and character.)
- Relate text to personal experience. (Show how event[s] or character[s] remind reader of his own life.)
- Write as if the reader were a character in the book. (Take on a particular voice and point of view.)
- Make a prediction about what will happen (and then alter or confirm the prediction).
- Express the central problem in the story.
- Describe a scene or scenes.
- Discuss the theme of the book and major issues it raises.
- Raise questions about what's unclear or puzzling.
- Analyze a character's behavior.
- Retell the story.
- Comment on what the text makes the reader think about.
- Reflect on feelings and thoughts while reading.
- Praise or criticize the book.
- Offer opinions on what the reader liked or disliked or wished happened differently.
- Summarize key points of the story.
- Compare the book with previously read text(s) or movie(s).
- Discuss author's writing style.
- Make literary judgments.
- Record turning points in the book.
- Make inferences about characters and/or story episodes.
- Draw conclusions about theme and/or author's purpose.

Prompts for Getting Started with Response Logs

Until students are used to responding in their logs, it works well to post a chart, written as a shared writing, of the language that can lead to response possibilities such as those listed above. While you don't want to overstructure the logs, which may have the unintended effect of obstructing students' thought processes, students just getting started with response logs often find these prompts helpful.

Make sure that the prompts are easily accessible to students, either posted on a chart in the classroom or pasted into the logs themselves. An example of a prompt list follows.

- This part reminds me of when . . .
- I predict . . .
- I wish the author . . .
- If I could change one part . . .
- I think . . .
- I was surprised . . .
- I wonder why . . . or what . . .
- I couldn't believe . . .
- I didn't understand . . .
- My favorite . . .
- I noticed . . .
- I liked (or disliked, or was bothered by) the part . . .
- I think (a character) will . . .
- If I were (a character) I would . . .
- This is a favorite passage because . . .
- The setting . . .
- As I was reading, I was thinking about . . .

Teaching Literary Elements and Literary Terms

Students need to know and understand literary elements in order to understand how literature works and to become critical readers and writers. However, such teaching occurs best in the context of literature discussion. Components of literature—theme, character, setting, author's style and tone, genre, plot, structure, point of view—as well as figurative language and literary terms, such as alliteration, simile and metaphor, personification, and imagery are best taught in the context of guided literature conversations, shared-reading discussions, and reading-aloud time. Once students are familiar with literary elements, we can expect them to include these elements in their written responses.

AUTHOR/ILLUSTRATOR STUDY

As part of our literature program, we study notable authors and illustrators. Author and illustrator study involves in-depth study of the works, background, literary and artistic style, and creative life of exemplary writers and illustrators. With teacher guidance, students read, analyze, discuss, compare, contrast, and observe all aspects of what authors and illustrators do.

Author study helps students make personal connections to texts, as many authors weave their own family stories into their work. In addition, in-depth study of an author promotes discussion of that author's writing style and choice of content, progression as a writer, and recurring themes. Such study has the power to greatly impact the quality of students' writing—their style, organization, vocabulary, and sentence structure—because favorite authors become mentors to students and their works become powerful models. For students to become successful authors and illustrators, it makes sense to apprentice them to literary and artistic masters.

Several summers ago, in addition to selecting anchor books, our district reading committee—with input from all teachers—selected subjects of author study for grades kindergarten through four. Up until that time, many teachers had been creating author studies on their own, but there was no coordinated effort to consolidate and share information. Likewise, author study was optional for teachers, so some students did not participate in the program. Author/illustrator study has since become part of our required literature curriculum.

Planning for Author/Illustrator Study

The first and hardest step in implementing an author study focus was to come to agreement on which authors to study at each grade level, since particular authors work well across several grades. We agreed on the following loose criteria for making selection decisions:

- Texts are accessible to most students with minimal teacher support (except for kindergarten and grade 1).
- Titles are readily available in paperback.
- Works connect to students' ages, interests, cultures, and values.
- Writing and/or artistic style is exemplary and promotes thoughtful discussion.
- Author/illustrator is still producing.
- Author/illustrator's life is revealed through the texts.
- Texts work across disciplines. (For example, our grade 4 author study is Jean Craighead George [see page 124b], and we use her books about biomes as part of our science curriculum.)

Once the authors are chosen, we expose students to multiple titles by the author along with useful resources.

Librarian Kathy O'Neal suggested that we create a box for each author studied, which could be moved among classrooms. These boxes would include:

- Titles by the author (mostly single copies, some pairs for partner reading, and some multiples for guided discussion)
- Video
- Biographical information about the author

- Publicity materials from publisher
- Bulletin board ideas and photos
- Any other teacher-useful material that enhances meaningful and pleasurable study

Kathy also provided us with Web site information for some of the authors we study. Today, a wealth of information is available on the Internet, most of it easily accessible by typing in a particular author, illustrator's name, or children's publisher. (See "Some Excellent Web Sites" in The Blue Pages.) You and your students can also write to the school and library marketing department of an author's publisher and request pertinent material about the author.

Once materials are assembled, the class can take any number of approaches. What follows are some general suggestions/activities for author study:

- Discuss similarities and differences that exist among an author's books and/or between the works of different authors. Use charts, Venn diagrams, webs, attribute charts, graphs.
- Make a classroom graph denoting favorite books by an author.
- Have students select and partner read a number of titles by an author and take notes on significant elements they have in common. Share responses in small groups and whole class.
- Use small-group literature conversations to respond to the text and illustrations in one or more books by an author.
- Write reviews (see pages 339–345) of an author's books.
- With teacher demonstration and coaching, have students write in the style of an author after discussing how and what the author does as a writer.
- Dramatize favorite parts of a well-loved book.
- Make a chart titled "What We Know About the Author and His/Her Book."

As much as possible, involve art and music in your author study.

See The Blue Pages for sample author studies written by Susan Hepler, for suggested author/illustrator studies at various grade levels, and for "Resources That Support Author/Illustrator Study."

ORGANIZING THE LITERATURE COLLECTION

In addition to our school library collections, each of our K–4 elementary buildings has a separately housed literature collection that is used by teachers as an extension of their classroom libraries. More than 90 percent of these collections are paperback books. We average about fifty copies of each anchor book and ten copies of each supplemental title. At Mercer School, our collection (after twelve years) encompasses about eighteen hundred titles and fourteen thousand books. Multiple copies allow for guided reading, individual and partner reading, and simultaneous use of the same titles in several classrooms.

Our school and classroom literature collections reflect the cultural diversity of both our local population and our global society. Because our school population is about 50 percent African American, we strive to ensure that new purchases—for guided reading, free-choice reading, and benchmark books used for assessment—fairly reflect that diversity.

Working Out a Schoolwide Organization System

If literature is your primary vehicle for teaching reading, you will want to devise some sort of manageable system for organizing your school and district collection. Decisions need to be made regarding purchasing, housing, organizing, maintaining, borrowing, and inventorying books.

I can't overstate the importance of housing the literature collection in a central location and utilizing a consistent, easy-to-use sign-out system. Otherwise, some teachers are short-changed. In one building, teachers became angry that they could never find the books they needed. At another school, teachers hoarded specific titles in their classrooms because there was no working organization system. Then, because some teachers have lots of books and others have few (especially teachers new to the school or grade level), the collegial climate of a school is negatively impacted.

Deciding how to organize and monitor the central literature collection continues to be a problem in our school district despite much effort on the part of many. While we know the ideal system would be computer based, using bar codes and scanners as our school and public libraries do, such a system is too costly for us to consider at this time.

At one district school, teachers stopped signing books out because the established procedure was so cumbersome and time-consuming. Many teachers never returned books that they had taken from the central location for classroom use. Nobody monitored the process. Inequity reigned. New teachers became desperate for books. Bad feelings pervaded the school, and it always seemed like teachers were short of resources—despite the fact that books were ordered on a districtwide basis and distributed equitably to each of the buildings.

At still another school, a sign-out system that relied on teacher compliance posed a dilemma. The teachers who faithfully signed out books were the same teachers who consistently returned them. Teachers who neglected to sign out books were the same teachers who habitually failed to return them. The "honest" teachers felt that they were being punished for their diligence. When the school discarded the sign-out system and implemented an across-the-board honor system, it lost three times the number of books (the average yearly loss was about 3 percent). The next year, a new system was put in place in which teachers removed cards placed in the back of books and placed those cards in a pocket labeled with their name. Returned books were refiled by volunteers.

At one of our buildings, Reading Recovery teacher Liz Schutter took the lead. Supported by the guidelines in *Guided Reading* (Fountas and Pinnell 1996), Schutter, first-grade teacher Cathy Grieshop and other primary-grade teachers, plus several parent volunteers, categorized books according to level of difficulty (see "Leveling Books," pages 82–84), moved books into boxes, put an honor system into place, and simplified the sign-out system. (See Photo 3-1 and Appendix D-4 for a letter to staff regarding leveled books.)

The Importance of Volunteers

We absolutely could not run our literature program without the assistance of our wonderful volunteers. Mimi Testen, parent volunteer coordinator for the Wonderfully Exciting Books (WEB) room at Mercer School since the fall of 1996, says, "It's an ideal job for compulsive people who love children's books." Testen donates about three hundred

*Photo 3–1   Reading Recovery teacher Liz Schutter and first-grade
teacher Cathy Grieshop organize the book collection by levels of difficulty*

hours of her time to the program each school year. Her efforts are supported by about ten volunteers who work several hours each week reshelving and repairing books as needed. Mimi notes that parents love working in the WEB. In contrast to committee work, with its typical jockeying for power, in the WEB volunteers work quietly and independently, surrounded by delightful books.

Mercer School's WEB volunteers organize the room that houses the literature collection. Books are arranged by genre—biography, poetry, folk/fairy tales, big books—and filed alphabetically in designated sections. Except for anchor books, which are reserved for grade-level reading, the books in the room are available to everyone.

WEB volunteers file new and returned books, reinforce the spines of new paperback books, stamp all books with the identifier "Mercer School Literature Program," categorize books by genre for proper placement, and carry out end-of-year inventory and repair.

Leveling Books

We "level" or categorize books for beginning readers (through grade two) based on their degree of difficulty. Readability is determined not according to an arbitrary formula but by teachers examining critical features of the text against agreed-upon criteria, and then making a judgment about where the book "fits" relative to other levels.

For developing readers, such a system ensures that students have access to texts that offer both appropriate support and challenge. The most difficult aspect about teaching with literature in the early grades is matching books with students' instructional levels. Without an informed and consistent process for book leveling, teachers run the risk of choosing books that overwhelm and frustrate students, or that do not sufficiently engage them. The best systems judge books based on gradually increasing gradients of difficulty, building on readers' growing competency and problem-solving abilities.

It is a monumentally difficult task for new and early-grade teachers to sort through literally hundreds of titles in search of appropriate instructional materials for their classes. For this reason, many of our books for beginning readers—especially for grade one—have been leveled by teachers as a guide to the book selection process. Our leveling organization makes it easier for teachers to move students to the appropriate level of reading challenge. These books are judiciously arranged for easy access in our WEB room and/or the classroom library.

We began leveling books in the late 1980s. I included a list of leveled storybooks in *Transitions*, and that list became our starting place. Most of our judgments in leveling books are based on approximations according to how well books work with different groups of children. In collaborative discussions, we compare similar books and look closely at various features of the text, including story line and concept load. Certain books eventually become benchmarks for a particular level. For example, in a discussion on first-grade books, we might ask ourselves something like, "Is this book similar to the *Little Bear* books, or is it a bit more challenging?"

Sometimes books turn out to be harder or easier for students than they at first appear to us teachers. Trial and error is important. If a book doesn't work well at one level (based on teacher feedback), we move it to another. Our leveling has never been a scientific process, nor has it needed to be. After a while, teachers get pretty good at getting a "feel" for a book's level.

Leveled books now accompany some newer reading texts and are also included in publishers' lists. While these lists can be a great help in getting started with your own collection, they often focus on books associated with particular programs or published series. To determine the level of many storybooks by well-known authors and illustrators, you may need to level them yourselves. Keep in mind, also, that someone else's standards may not meet your needs, that "what is easy or difficult will vary from district to district, from school to school, and from child to child" (Clay 1991, 201).

We have found it best to give the job of leveling books to a small committee of teachers. In our district, several teacher volunteers meet periodically after school to keep up with new books entering the collection. See "Leveling Books" in The Blue Pages for resources that provide guidance on book leveling.

Considerations for Leveling Texts

When leveling texts for developing readers, it is important to keep in mind the following:

• *Size and placement of print, and spacing between words and lines*   (Is the size of print large enough? Are there adequate spaces between words?)

• *Page format*   (Is the layout and format consistent? Are the number of words per line, lines of print per page, and text length appropriate?)

- *Sentence patterns and language structure*   (Is there adequate repetition to support the reader? Are the language patterns simple and familiar? Are many high-frequency words present? Is the description easy to follow?)

- *Predictability*   (Are the words and pattern predictable?)

- *Type of text (genre) and content*   (If it is a nonfiction book, does the author provide adequate background knowledge?)

- *Illustrations*   (Do the illustrations support and match the text?)

- *Vocabulary and concept load*   (Are the concepts familiar?)

Keep in mind that our goal is to confidently move students from books that require more support to books that they can read with less support. As students gradually read more challenging texts, our criteria for leveling changes. Be sure to consult the resources for leveling books in The Blue Pages for explicit guidelines.

A Caution About Levels

Some schools have witnessed a leveling craze that has extended through grades three through five. Some teachers have grown accustomed to selecting books based on leveling guidance, and feel that they cannot conduct guided reading groups without it. But leveling books in these grades is neither a good nor appropriate use of teacher time. Once kids are readers, it is simply not necessary to determine finite skill gradients. This doesn't mean that we stop selecting texts based on instructional level. There are notable differences between books intended for a mid-second-grade and a mid-fourth-grade level. But what is most important for selecting books for middle-elementary-grade students is that the content and story line are developmentally appropriate, interesting, and relevant as well as accessible. Additionally, consider that complexity of plot, time sequence, character development, and the author's writing style all play a role in determining a book's difficulty.

Once the child is reading well, by about beginning to mid-second grade, levels can actually be limiting factors, because they don't take into account students' varying interests, background knowledge, and motivation. These elements, along with a strong teacher introduction, may contribute to a student's successful reading of a text. In fact, a book that seems too hard for a student may be accessible to that student when the aforementioned factors are present.

CLASSROOM LIBRARIES

A comprehensive study in the early 1990s found that "effective reading programs are usually supported by large classroom libraries" (International Association for the Evaluation of Educational Achievement 1992). Research has shown that "better libraries are related to better reading, as measured by standardized tests" (Krashen 1998). Access to books increases the amount of reading children do (McQuillan 1998), and the easiest way to ensure student access to books is through a well-designed and organized classroom library (Fractor, Woodruff, Martinez, and Teale 1993). It is clear that environments that support a large amount of reading materials dramatically impact reading achievement.

Additionally, the September 1997 NAEP Trends in Academic Progress report, which analyzes achievement of U.S. students at ages nine, thirteen, and seventeen, found "a clear pattern across all three age groups: more types of reading materials in the home was associated with higher average reading scores" (U.S. Department of Education 1997, 140). We can infer from that information that a well-designed, well-organized, and well-utilized classroom library—along with lots of time for free reading—will also have a positive effect on students' reading achievement.

Designing and Organizing the Classroom Library

The first thing I look for when I walk into a classroom is the library and reading area. When I can't find it, and I happen to be working as a coach with the classroom teacher, I gently urge him to think about creating this important space. Often, I will bring in photos of wonderful classroom libraries to inspire him. The way the book area predominates (or does not) and is organized sets the tone for the literature classroom. I do most of my reading in a comfortable, cozy space (not at a desk); our students, too, should be given an environment conducive to reading enjoyment. (See Photo 3-2 and Photo 3-3.)

Photo 3–2   A classroom library in second grade

Photo 3–3   Organizing the book collection in the classroom

I deliberately choose the word *design* in heading this section because how the classroom library looks and feels—its design—impacts its use. Make your library space as comfortable and attractive as possible. Comfortable seating and colorful displays of books promote reading by inviting easy, relaxed participation.

We work hard to make the library space as attractive, appealing, and well-organized as possible. Open shelves, book tubs, and book spinners display reading materials so that students can easily find what they want. (With the aid of a library supply catalog, try to budget for and order a book spinner. Spinners take up little space and display and organize books in a pleasing, easy-to-use manner.)

Many of our classroom reading corners feature sofas, cozy chairs, bean bags, throw pillows, lamps, and rugs—all contributing a homey atmosphere that invites reader participation. Most often, many of these items have been donated by parents after teachers have requested them in the weekly newsletter.

I like using students to help structure the organization and layout of the classroom library. Some teachers invite students to submit designs for a library/reading space. Then, in small groups and whole class, students and teachers negotiate how they want the space to look. Even if you already have a well-established system, try to give each new crop of students some say in how the space is laid out. Whatever arrangement you decide on, provide room in your reading/library area for individual, paired, and collaborative experiences. Try to arrange the area so that there is room for at least five to six readers.

Organizing Books

When setting up the library each year, student input regarding the book collection is crucial. To ensure that the classroom library has books that interest all students, find out at the beginning of the year (and throughout the year) what types of books and materials students like to read. Then, honor those choices and be sure your library collection has many favorite genres, such as picture books, magazines, poetry, reference books, series books, mysteries, science fiction, biography, fairy tales, and other categories of fiction and nonfiction. At a minimum, try to have at least five to six books per student, and aim for a collection of at least several hundred titles. For younger children, include favorite storybooks, titles with predictable structures, and counting and concept books. For all children, be sure lots of informational books are included. (See pages 442–443 for criteria for selecting informational books.) And don't forget to have lots of picture books! For students of all ages, picture books are great read-alouds, perfect for partner reading, ideal for discussions of varied topics, and fine models for writing and illustrating. In addition, keep in mind that for students who cannot afford to purchase books, the library may be their only means of obtaining reading materials.

With teacher guidance, students can sort, label, and shelve books by genre and a general level of difficulty. Some teachers in grades one and two, often with student input, code books according to reading levels. For example, second-grade teacher Ed Kmitt reads aloud short excerpts from new books and asks, "What bin should we put this in, easy, medium, or hard?" I like having a small committee of students make these decisions during sustained silent reading time. Student librarians can also be responsible for book sign-out (see pages 89–90), as well as regrouping and refiling books as needed.

It helps to regularly rotate book displays and highlight new additions to the collection. Some teachers supplement the classroom library with a changing laundry basket or two of books from the school library. Changing displays and new additions keep student interest in the book collection high. Also, do include students' own publications and published books as part of the classroom library.

Be sure to have lots of books on hand for your struggling readers. Classrooms frequently lack reading materials at their interest and readability levels, further stunting their growth as readers. Additionally, there are often too few books that struggling readers can locate easily and read independently (Allington et al. 1996, 84). Most slow-achieving readers will read more if materials that appeal to them, such as series fiction, comic books, and other high-interest materials are readily available (Worthy 1996; Krashen 1999). Handpicked selections of appropriate materials organized in small tubs, boxes, or bags ensure that these readers will be amply accommodated.

Also, try to set aside a special place for series books. Some teachers will have all the copies of a particular series housed in one spot, for example, in a small plastic tub. Series books, both fiction and nonfiction, are important because they "hook" students and promote the reading of subsequent books. This is helpful especially for those students who are taking longer learning to read. (See pages 75b–78b for the benefits of using series books as well as recommended series.)

Supplying the Classroom Book Collection

My experience has been that few districts allocate funds for classroom libraries. I believe this is because, unfortunately, in-class libraries are still not seen as a literacy necessity. We teachers need to get aggressive in formally requesting budget allocations for classroom libraries. In the absence of such funds, however, we need to be creative and resourceful in supplying our classrooms with ample books.

Resources for obtaining trade books include:

• *Garage sales*   (Make sure that the texts are relevant and in good condition.)

• *Classroom book clubs*   (Bonus points from book-club orders often lead to free books.)

• *Public library book sales*

• *Sale tables at bookstores*   (Major booksellers such as Borders, Half-Price Books, and Scholastic also have discount outlets. Check what's available in your area.)

• *Donations from families or teachers whose kids have outgrown certain books* (Some teachers request books in their newsletters, as a way to commemorate a special occasion such as a child's birthday or a holiday.)

• *Loans from students' home collections*   (When second-grade teacher Ed Kmitt found his classroom library lacking, he invited willing students to bring in personal collections for short-term and long-term loans. These books were organized separately to ensure that they would not be misplaced.)

• *School and public library loans*   (Most school librarians are generous about loaning books to the classroom, and many will allow each student to choose several books for the library collection. Some librarians are willing to rotate sets of fifty or more titles to help establish classroom libraries. Fourth-grade teacher Norris Ross has each of her students sign out three "wonderful books" for the classroom library. Books are signed out in her name and kept in the classroom for four to six weeks, whereupon students are able to make a fresh selection. Also, upon special request, public libraries will often loan large numbers of books beyond the usual loan period.)

• *Administration funds*   (Some schools will reallocate funds that formerly went toward the purchase of workbooks to buy trade books.)

• *Parent-teacher organizations*   (Money for books can be raised through fund drives and donations. One year, our Parent Teacher Organization gave each classroom $600.00 for books. Second-grade teachers invested in series books.)

Book Circulation

Teachers use all kinds of sign-out systems, from simple to complex, for borrowing from the classroom library. Some teachers have students write down the title of the book and the date it is signed out in a notebook; they then check the entry off when the book is returned. Some create a system that can be managed by designated student librarians. Other teachers do the record keeping themselves, using a notebook or card file with a section for each student. Finally, some teachers reject any sign-out program as too cumbersome, and keep their students on the honor system. Second-grade teacher Loretta Martin says she knows she loses some books (most of which she has purchased herself) with this system, but the large majority come back—granted, sometimes a year later when a student returns a pile of books he has "found."

My favorite in-class library system is one that many of our elementary teachers use because it is so easily and efficiently managed by student librarians. First-grade teacher Jim Henry created this system, in which students share responsibility for book circulation; two students are put in charge of the lending process each week.

Jim orders library checkout cards and gummed adhesive pockets from a library supply catalog. Parent volunteers attach a pocket on the inside back cover of each book, and then cards labeled with the specific book titles are put into the respective book pockets. Using a large piece of finished plywood (about 20" × 40"), Jim creates a sign-out board by mounting additional pockets—one for each student, and labeled with the students' photographs and names—onto the board (see Photo 3-4). He also places three plastic tubs—

Photo 3–4   Book check-out board in a first-grade class

labeled separately for book return, supplies (consisting of gallon-size Zip-loc bags), and repairs—on a table in front of the plywood board.

After modeling the book-lending and sign-out process for the whole class, Jim designates the first two students to serve as class librarians. The librarians stand behind the sign-out table as the students file past with their book or books. The librarian takes the card from the back of the chosen book and slips it into the borrowing student's pocket on the plywood chart. Next, the librarian puts the book in a resealable plastic bag and reminds the student to put the book in his back pack.

Each morning, students put their reading bags in the "return" tub, and the librarians locate the sign-out cards on the plywood chart, return the cards to the books, and restock the bookshelves. Any books needing repair go into the "repair" tub, and Jim or a parent volunteer reinforce the books with sturdy book tape.

To minimize repair and ensure long life for your book collection, teach kids why and how to care for books. It's not the reading that ages them, but rather what happens in transport. When our students look after their books and transport them between school and home in waterproof bags, books (and they are almost all paperbacks) have lasted up to ten years.

FINAL REFLECTIONS

Regardless of the reading program used in your district, you will want to be knowledgeable about children's literature—in order to augment your reading program, to match children with appropriate books, and to equip your classroom library with wonderful titles in various genres.

Literature remains the heart and soul of the literacy program. Schools and classrooms must have an ample supply of quality books, and all students must have access to them. For developing readers in the early grades especially, large numbers of books must be available. It is then up to us teachers to make sure that books are used so that our students learn to read and learn to love reading.

CONTINUING THE CONVERSATION

• *Reflect on your classroom and school literature program.*   What aspects of the program need rethinking and/or modification? What common practices need revisiting? Is your program meeting both your needs and the students? Teacher/school reflection-research can be powerful for improving instruction.

• *Evaluate your classroom library.*   Be sure that your library is attractive, well stocked with many books and materials that represent students' interests and reading levels, and easily accessible to all students.

• *Take a close look at the materials you are using to teach reading.*   Make sure they meet the needs and interests of your students, not just for teaching reading but for enjoying and promoting lifelong reading. Be sure quality nonfiction materials are plentiful.

• *Carefully examine how your students are responding to literature.* Are they revisiting texts in a meaningful way?

• *Become proactive in the literature selection process.* Whatever reading program your school or district chooses to use, be sure that you order all books and materials based on their proven quality. You and your colleagues will need to take the time to examine programs and books and give input before purchasing decisions are made. Invite various publishers to demonstrate and explain their materials. Demand that high standards are maintained. Be choosy. (Use the resources in The Blue Pages, "Literature Resources for Choosing Fiction and Nonfiction" and "Little Books That Support Developing Readers" to help guide your selections.)

CHAPTER 4

Teaching Children to Read

Reading while the teacher is meeting with a small guided reading group

Those who think of language as simply a self-contained set of signs linked to sounds ignore the essential third element, the human being who must make the linkage between them if there is indeed to be a meaningful word. Language is socially evolved, but it is always constituted by individuals, with their particular histories.

—*Louise Rosenblatt*

A decade ago, in my book *Transitions*, I wrote that "reading for meaning should underlie all encounters with print." I still hold fast to that belief. With all the talk about how to teach children to read and the continuing discussion on how, when, and how much phonemic awareness and phonics are necessary, meaning often gets left out of the conversation. I wrote *Transitions* because I believed that years and years of overreliance on phonics—to the exclusion of other strategies—had produced students who failed to learn to read, students who were unable to read with understanding and who did not choose to read for enjoyment. I sometimes hear teachers say, "He can read but he can't understand," to which I always respond: "Then he's not reading."

Reading for meaning and understanding how stories work comes before attention to every word. Reading regularly to my neighbor's child Chessie when she was between the ages of two and four reminded me that story enjoyment and discussion, taking favorite tales to heart and retelling them, is a prerequisite for becoming a reader. An overfocus on getting words right at the beginning-reader stage runs contrary to the reading process. We must recognize the need for role-play reading (where young children "play read" a familiar book page by page and tell the story in their own words), not give the message to teachers, parents, and students that reading is simply "decoding" words.

Teaching students to decode is, in fact, the easy part. Teaching students to *understand* is where the real challenge lies. Ask upper-grade teachers about reading problems they encounter with their students and they rarely mention decoding. "They don't understand what they read" is the common cry. Despite the entrenchment of a "phonics-first" approach to teaching reading, my thirty years of experience as a reading teacher confirms that those students who are overly dependent on phonics are not our best readers. Decoding and meaning must go hand in hand.

As we move into the twenty-first century, the issue of teaching beginning reading continues to incite and inflame emotions, provoking debate and controversy. In the media, in colleges and universities, and at local, state, and national levels, discussion is ongoing. Sadly, the teaching of reading beyond beginning levels continues to receive short shrift. And reading for understanding takes a backseat to decoding and word recognition. As professionals, we need to be sure that we are knowledgeable reading teachers who value and teach comprehension along with decoding strategies.

I wrote *Literacy at the Crossroads* to deal with the problems and misunderstandings surrounding the teaching of reading, especially the controversy over whole language and phonics. It is not my intention to revisit those issues here. This chapter will focus on the effective teaching of reading and deal with current issues, relevant research, phonemic awareness and phonics, setting up a quality reading program, conducting informal reading evaluations, working with struggling readers, teaching for strategies, guided reading, and classroom management during small-group guided reading time.

WHAT'S GONE WRONG IN THE TEACHING OF READING?

It often strikes me, when I enter classrooms, how little reading is being taught. Excellent literature is present, but the old model of reading is still in place. Often, reading is done whole class. The teacher reads the book aloud, the students follow along in their own or shared copies, and the discussion is dominated by the teacher and several students. When there are small reading groups, the process employed is still primarily the traditional "round robin" reading, with students taking turns reading aloud.

I recently worked in a school in which the superintendent had mandated whole-class reading instruction, even for first grade. The rationale was that "tracking" was bad for kids. And teachers persisted in using this method, even though they knew that whole-class reading wasn't working, that they weren't meeting the needs of students, and that lots of kids were struggling with the material in their basal readers. While they felt uneasy about what they knew intuitively was bad practice, these teachers didn't have enough knowledge or confidence to adjust their teaching. When I questioned them about why there was no small-group reading instruction, they seemed relieved: here was an outside expert who valued small-group reading. Since they had gotten reinforcement for such practice from an "expert," they could finally push for it with school administrators. The fallacy here is that advocates for "best practice" come from outside a school or district's community of teachers. We teachers must be the experts. We must speak up and take a stand on what is best practice for the students we teach.

Another unfortunate practice in reading classrooms, in addition to the overuse of whole-class reading, is instructional reading time being used as "activity" time. Typical was my observation of one first-grade teacher who had a group of high-progress readers take turns reading aloud, after which, believing that she needed to "do something" with the book, she spent fifteen of the twenty minutes of group time having students do "seat work." She spent this time focusing on contractions. Students were expected to find and write down all the contractions in the story they were reading. This, mistakenly, was thought to be "teaching skills in context." These students already knew how to read and write these words, so both her "instructional" time and the students' time were not well spent.

Further complicating the issue is that, above grades two and three, teachers often expect students to come to them having already learned how to read. When they don't, far too many teachers are at a loss as to how to teach them. Many upper-grade teachers tell me that they are unsure what to do about reading instruction. They have sustained, silent reading daily and may do some shared reading, but they frequently ask, "What should I be teaching?" Often, their "instruction" consists of supervising whole-class reading, assigning reading, and asking students to write summaries, retellings, or answers to questions. But this is not teaching. Good intentions cannot take the place of instruction.

Many knowledgeable teachers, of course, never abandoned teaching skills and continued to serve as experts for their apprentice readers. However, a good number of those same teachers who went about their work teaching needed strategies and emphasizing literature and response to literature failed to communicate adequately with parents about the principles underlying their teaching practice.

METHODOLOGY IS SECONDARY TO THE INFORMED PROFESSIONAL TEACHER

We teachers—when we are informed, observant, and professional—remain the most critical element in a child's success in learning to read. Despite swings of the pendulum and pressure from media, politicians, and school boards, knowledgeable teachers remain practical and eclectic in their approach to teaching reading (Baumann, Hoffman, Moon, and Duffy-Hester 1998). That is, we consider current research, but we don't discard what we know works with our students. We value our own classroom research—our thoughtful observations and evaluations based on years of experience and day-to-day teaching with students we know well. Or, as inexperienced teachers, we apprentice ourselves to colleagues we respect. We study, we read professionally, we observe our students carefully. We teach what they need; we reflect on our practice. Effective teachers have always done this. This is our job as professionals.

Today, more than ever, teachers are feeling overwhelmed and exhausted. As more and more gets added to the curriculum, including a growing (and sometimes alarming) emphasis on preparing for high-stakes tests, teachers have less and less time and energy to stay informed and engaged in ongoing professional conversations. However, those professional conversations are a necessity. They renew us, connect us to our colleagues, and make it possible for us to make informed decisions. Especially with the teaching of reading, which remains a highly charged and political issue, we must be knowledgeable and skillful. Only then can our day-to-day decisions be solidly based on current and relevant theory, research, experience, observation, and evaluation. Otherwise, we are at the mercy of the latest political shift, pendulum swing, or publisher's program.

Unfortunately, too many of us are running scared. Without a solid knowledge and theory base, we are prone to shift positions and programs every time a new national report is released. Pressured by parents, administrators, and other stakeholders, we fail to study the issues and the research on our own or with our colleagues. Under attack, we aim to please our demanding public regardless of the consequences. Unable to explain what and why we teach, we rely on scripted programs. Lacking confidence and knowledge to teach effectively, we place our trust in commercial programs to the exclusion of our own best instincts and judgment.

Becoming More Knowledgeable

In our weekly language arts support groups (see pages 524–527), it took six years before a fourth-grade teacher finally said what many others had been thinking all along: "I don't know how to teach reading." The sigh of relief from the group was audible.

A student teacher named Cissy Burns approached me one morning and asked if we could talk. "I'm graduating as a reading specialist," she began, "and I'm scared to death. If I get into a first- or second-grade classroom, I'll be lost. I have no idea how to teach beginning reading. I'm overwhelmed and simply not ready."

Cissy went on to explain that she didn't know how to teach phonics or skills and never learned anything about shared reading or shared writing. She had four reading courses that focused on meaning strategies, such as KWL (see page 477), how to read different texts, and how to predict and confirm, retell, and do DRTA (directed reading thinking activities). I loaned her several books on phonics, and we talked about them after she was through reading them. Several other student teachers with the same concerns joined our discussions. Although it is painful for us to admit, teachers like Cissy, who have received a selective and incomplete education in reading instruction, are not uncommon.

Every time I give a workshop, and I narrate vignettes like those above, several teachers courageously, if a bit sheepishly, approach me afterward and say, "I don't know how to teach reading. What should I read?" I tell them that except for my Reading Recovery training—which finally made me a highly skilled reading teacher—all my learning about how to teach reading was self-taught. I relied on current journal articles and texts, discussions with colleagues, observations of teachers I respected, and careful observations and evaluations of my students. In particular, Connie Weaver's book *Reading Process and Practice* (1994), which I carefully read and studied, served as an excellent reading course, enabling me to move beyond the isolated skills and phonics teaching I had come to overrely on.

KNOWING AND INTERPRETING THE RESEARCH

To be excellent teachers of reading, we must first of all know the research and its implications for our teaching. This is no easy matter. Much recent research that has been publicized in the media is experimental, scientific analysis focused at the word level in reading. Classroom-based research by teachers is given little credence and is largely underreported, if published at all.

What have we learned to date about teaching reading? It depends on what body of research you read and value. In all cases, it is critical that we as teachers look at research with a critical eye. Here are some questions to consider as we assess research findings:

1. What population was used?
2. Is the study replicable? That is, was the study done in a manner and described in sufficient detail that you or I or anyone else could carry out another version of it and get similar results?
3. Were the social contexts of learning to read considered?

This last point is a major, often ignored, factor. We teachers know that shared reading, partner reading, and small-group reading—guided contexts in which students interact and converse with one another—play a major role in learning to read. Yet, because these contexts do not lend themselves to quantifiable analysis, they are often ignored by experimental researchers.

Criteria for Evaluating Research

Richard Allington, respected reading researcher and prolific author on literacy, suggested during the annual conference of the 1997 New England Reading Association in Hartford, Connecticut, that we look at the following criteria when evaluating research claims:

- *Convergence:* Does the study encompass multiple sites and multiple investigators (some of which are independent, to reduce experimenter bias)?

- *If a study is replicated and similar results are obtained*, then we can talk of "convergence evidence" or "successful replication of the study and the original effects."

- *Comparability:* Are the conditions and students dealt with in the study comparable to those in your school and community?

- *Quality:* Has the research been published in a reputable journal? (The handful of established educational publications related to reading include such journals as *Reading Research Quarterly* and *Educational Researcher.*)

- *Compellingness:* When you weigh all the criteria, do the results make sense? Are the study's conclusions convincing?

If we combine the above criteria with the following "habits of mind," the five essential questions asked of all learning at Central Park East Secondary School (the exemplary high school in East Harlem founded by Deborah Meier), we have a solid framework for evaluating research.

- How do you know what you know?
- What's your evidence?
- How and where does what you've learned "fit in"?
- Could things have been otherwise?
- Who cares; what difference does it make? (Meier 1995, 156)

Especially when the latest research is driving what goes on in our classrooms, we teachers need to keep the aforementioned criteria and questions in mind. In particular, we must make our own assessments about how compelling we regard any research to be.

The Reading/Language Arts Framework for California Public Schools (1999)—which contains suggested guidelines for how reading should be taught in California—and has influence in classrooms across the nation—purportedly drew upon research findings for its recommended practices. These findings included the following:

> For early decoding in the first grade, students read stories in which there is a high percentage of words composed of taught letter-sound correspondences and a few previously taught sight words. (24)

My experience as a longtime reading teacher is in conflict with this research. While some severely disabled readers may benefit from the use of decodable text during particular stages of development, the overwhelming majority of children can best learn to read using predictable, natural language texts as provided by excellent children's literature.

Decodable texts are texts in which a large percentage of the words employed conform to predictable phonics patterns that the reader has had previous experience in or exposure to. These are texts that are specifically created to teach particular phonics skills. Texas defines decodable texts as those containing 51 percent or more pronounceable words given phonics skills taught; California defines them as made up of 75 to 85 percent of pronounceable words; children's literature generally weighs in at the 25 percent level (Allington 1998).

It has been my experience that the tediousness and contrived nature of decodable texts turn many students off to reading, thus thwarting their development as readers. "There is also research showing that use of decodable texts produces students who make more nonsense word miscues, do less self-corrections, and read less fluently" (Allington 1998). In contrast, the use of excellent children's literature in teaching children to read has the added benefit of producing readers who enjoy books and who choose to read independently.

In making its recommendations for practice, the Framework also used the following finding:

> If students in grades four through eight are unable to comprehend the complexities of narrative and expository text, a highly probable source of the problem is inability to decode words accurately and fluently. (97)

Once again this statement, which was presented in italics (atypical for the Framework), I assume to underscore its importance, does not align with my experience. What I and many middle- and upper-grade teachers find is that most struggling readers can recognize and read words; their difficulty lies in understanding them. Consistent with the National Assessment of Educational Progress (NAEP) findings since 1971, almost all students can decode and understand words at rudimentary levels. However, a majority are unable to interpret complex information or make meaningful inferences from what they read.

Exercising Professional Judgment

So what are we teachers to do? We must first of all concern ourselves with becoming fully informed and knowledgeable about current research. We must look critically at how that research is being interpreted and used. And when that research is in conflict with our knowledge as professional teachers and our years of daily experience working successfully with children in our own classrooms, we must speak out. We must refuse to be led down the primrose path by those who do not know our children, their needs, and how they should best be taught. We must take charge of our classrooms and instruct our students as best as we know how. Sometimes, that will mean taking a strong stand.

Recent media focus related to reading research has centered almost exclusively on how children acquire phonics knowledge and phonemic awareness. Independent reading of self-selected books, reading for understanding across the curriculum, and the impact of writing on reading have received scant attention despite large federally funded studies that confirm their critical importance in the development of skilled readers. Just as important, current focus on the reading process rarely considers classroom contexts, teaching styles, and the social and emotional nature of learning—all critical to learning. Therefore, we teachers must step in to restore the balance.

Responding to the June 1998 draft of the California Reading/Language Arts Framework, Martha Rapp Ruddell, president of the National Reading Conference, cautions that "we must not confuse knowledge gained from research about reading process with knowledge about reading instruction" (Ruddell 1998, 4). A critical point. Research that may or may not be related to instruction is being used to change instruction nationwide.

Sometimes you just have to close your doors and do what you know is right and best for children. When the policies we are being asked to implement are so constrained and prescriptive that we cannot effectively teach our students, we must hold fast to ways that we know lead to understanding. According to Linda Darling-Hammond, eminent educator and researcher on teacher quality, "The evidence suggests that highly prescriptive curricular mandates do not improve student learning, especially if they effectively control teaching" (1997, 53). In a comprehensive study of teachers and their practices and beliefs, Darling-Hammond found the following:

> Most teachers tried to accommodate district requirements, at least superficially, but preserved what they felt was important for students even when that seemed an act of defiance. (1997, 90)

Of course, in order to become "creative saboteurs," we must be highly knowledgeable and professional, and that includes knowing and being conversant in the latest research.

Being a creative saboteur includes being an effective teacher of phonics. In 1993 my state—Ohio—became the first state to mandate the daily teaching of phonics. For teachers who felt that they did not have the knowledge to incorporate this subject into their practice, the state provided workshops, but these were exclusively focused on direct instruction and phonics in isolation and carried the implicit message that teaching phonics in a literature context was unacceptable. Nonetheless, while the law mandated fifteen minutes of phonics teaching each day in the primary grades, it did not specify how that teaching was to be carried out. Many of us who taught phonics all day long—through shared reading, shared writing, modeled writing, interactive writing, morning message, journal writing, individual and group conferencing, small-group guided reading, whole-group lessons, and so on—continued to do what we had always done. Our students were learning to read and write well. They were applying phonics strategies to their reading and writing. Adding fifteen minutes of isolated phonics drill would have taken fifteen minutes away from reading. We chose to hold onto our reading time.

Knowing Significant Research Findings

Because research is being used and misused to change and dictate teaching practices, we must be conversant in that research and be knowledgeable enough to judge whether or not it applies to our students and our teaching. Unless we can talk logically, clearly, and knowledgeably with parents and politicians, we are vulnerable to groups who want to control how we teach. Being both informed about and conversant in research is no easy matter, but to be professional, it's a necessity. There are several studies in particular that you will want to acquaint yourselves with.

While scientific researchers from the National Institute of Child Health and Development (NICHD) champion a large body of research from the past thirty years that places first emphasis on knowing the alphabetic principle, these studies are based mostly on students with major reading problems, that is, the special education population and, in particular, those with learning disabilities. While I have no problem with that research being applied to the small percentage of students with severe reading problems (less than 5 percent), regrettably, the research has been generalized for all student populations and has been used to pass laws at state levels mandating isolated phonics as the primary reading method.

Be sure to read and discuss with your colleagues "Decodable Text in Beginning Reading: Are Mandates and Policy Based on Research?" an article by Richard Allington and Haley Woodside-Jiron (1998) that critically examines and challenges the NICHD research claims. Allington and Woodside-Jiron contend that there is no research to support NICHD's recommendation for the use of decodable texts in beginning reading.

The fall 1997 issue of *Reading Research Quarterly*, the scholarly journal published by the International Reading Association, revisited with Guy Bond and Robert Dykstra the "First-Grade Studies" originally published by Bond and Dykstra thirty years earlier. The study was unique because it was a cooperative and collaborative research study involving twenty-seven individual projects across the country. One major purpose was to determine whether certain beginning-reading approaches were more effective than others. Among the important findings:

> To improve reading instruction, it is necessary to train better teachers of reading rather than to expect a panacea in the form of materials. (416)

> No one approach is so distinctly better in all situations and respects than the others that it should be considered the one best method and the one to be used exclusively. (416)

> A teacher who is successful with a given instructional program will probably be successful with that approach for pupils of varying degrees of readiness and capability. (417)

The most comprehensive and rational article I've read on approaches to teaching phonics appeared in a 1998 issue of *Reading Research Quarterly*. "Theory and Research into Practice: Everything You Wanted to Know About Phonics (But Were Afraid to Ask)" (Stahl, Duffy-Hester, and Dougherty Stahl 1998), reported, among other findings, that there is no one best way to teach phonics and that "the differences in quality between phonics approaches are small" (344). As long as phonics teaching occurs early and is direct and systematic, students can become successful readers.

Finally, the November 1998 issue of *The Reading Teacher* includes an article by Linda Allen, "An Integrated Strategies Approach: Making Word Identification Instruction

Work for Beginning Readers," which reports that urban primary-grade children (many of whom were "at risk") learn to read best with an approach that combines direct instruction of word recognition with real literature. I was gratified to read this research because it confirmed what I believe and know to be true from years of experience, that is, instruction can be explicit and systematic within a literature framework. (See the "Teaching Reading" resources in The Blue Pages for additional information on articles cited above.)

PHONEMIC AWARENESS AND PHONICS: WHAT'S ESSENTIAL

It is not the purpose of this book to take up the phonics/phonemic awareness debate or to go into detail on how phonics should be taught. It is my intention here to stress how important it is that students understand how sounds and letters are related, and the sooner the better.

Phonemic awareness is concerned only with sounds, not letters, and is the ability to hear, sequence, segment, and blend together the smallest units of sounds in a spoken word. Phonics is knowing the connection between those spoken sounds and the corresponding written letters and letter combinations—often called sound-symbol relationships.

Despite some media claims to the contrary, almost all teachers teach phonics (Cunningham and Allington 1999; Pressley, Rankin, and Yokoi 1996, 375) and most also teach phonemic awareness even if they don't know what the term means. As Richard Allington stated in the presentation "Balanced Reading Instruction," delivered to the annual meeting of the International Reading Association in 1997, "85 percent of our kids develop phonemic awareness without special training even if teachers never heard of the term 'phonemic awareness.' For the 15–20 percent who need it, we can provide instruction."

In *Literacy at the Crossroads*, I wrote about phonics research, commonsense views about phonics, the push for intensive systematic phonics, and the politics surrounding phonics teaching. Here I want to explore how key beliefs about phonemic awareness and phonics translate to "best" classroom practice.

Beliefs and Practices

My beliefs and practices relating to teaching phonemic awareness and phonics have been shaped as much by my thirty years of teaching as by the comprehensive body of available research. I have come to trust my experiences with children and to question research when it does not apply to actual classroom contexts.

Most young children do not need special instruction and assessment to develop phonemic awareness.

You will need to be well informed and vocal in this high-pressure area in order to maintain sensible practice. Phonemic awareness has attained considerable status (warranted or not). In an annual survey examining key topics in reading research and practice, phonemic awareness was reported to be the "hottest" literacy topic in 1999 (Cassidy and Cassidy 1998/1999s 1, 28). In fact, some states have recently mandated phonemic awareness testing, and more are likely to follow. Such attention to phonemic awareness is quite remarkable given the fact that most teachers, myself included, had been teaching reading successfully for years without knowing or hearing anything about phonemic awareness. The importance of phonemic awareness for learning to read came to national attention as late as the 1990s (Adams 1990).

It has been my experience that children easily develop phonemic awareness in literacy-rich environments through experimenting with and enjoying rhymes, poems, chants, and songs, and through such activities as "clapping" syllables, exposure to alliteration, frequent repetition of classmates' names, and regular talk about words (Allington 1997; Yopp 1995). Knowledgeable teachers deliberately encourage students' engagement in such activities. The overwhelming majority of students have developed phonemic awareness by the middle of first grade, a result of typical experiences at home as well as at school (Allington, in Braunger and Lewis 1997, 42).

The most effective kindergarten and first-grade teachers demonstrate and promote daily writing as well as verbal play, including stretching out the sounds of words—all of which develops phonemic awareness along with other needed literacy skills. Confirming the influence of wordplay, many kindergarten teachers note that knowledge of nursery rhymes is a very good indicator that a child will be a successful reader.

While it is well accepted that phonemic awareness is a strong predictor of reading achievement in first grade, what is less clear is whether phonemic awareness develops as a forerunner to (prerequisite) or corollary of (consequence) learning to read. It is highly likely that phonemic awareness develops along with learning to read and write (Coles 1998). There does seem to be a reciprocal relationship between phonemic awareness and invented spelling. According to Donald Richgels, "inventive spellers' playing with sounds and letters helps them to consolidate their phoneme awareness" (1995, 107). Therefore, special training in phoneme awareness is not a good use of time for most kids, time that would be better spent in authentic reading and writing activities.

Additionally, phonemic awareness ability is readily assessed by taking a look at your students' writing. "Phonological analysis, segmenting the syllable into its parts, and mastering the (spelling) pattern of a word are natural parts of early writing tasks" (Clay 1998, 169). Invented spelling indicates growing levels of phonemic awareness before the child fully achieves it, and we can use invented spelling as an assessment tool to track the development of phonemic awareness. For example, if students are writing words with consonants and vowels, in correct letter combinations and sequence, then they have phonemic awareness. It's that simple.

Phonics knowledge is necessary for learning to read.

It is indisputable that kids need phonics knowledge in order to read successfully. What is open to debate is how that knowledge is best acquired and taught. As a longtime reading specialist working with all kinds of readers over many years, I have seen both sides of the coin—kids who couldn't read because they had insufficient phonics knowledge and kids who couldn't read because all they could utilize was phonics.

For children to become capable readers, they must have a large core of words that they recognize and understand instantly and automatically so that they are then able to focus on meaning. Many of these "sight" words conform to regular patterns that can be taught phonetically—both for the specific word and as analogies for figuring out new, related words. (See Chapter 10.)

For most young children, it seems to be easier for them to segment and learn words by chunks (onsets and rimes) rather than letter by letter (Gunning 1995; Moustafa 1997). The onset is the part of the syllable that comes before the vowel; it is made up of one or more consonants. The rime is the rest of the unit. For example, in the word *stake,* "st" is the onset and "ake" is the rime. Nearly five hundred common words can be derived from only thirty-seven rimes. (See page 424.)

My experience as a reading teacher confirms that students find it easiest to read and learn words by pattern and analogy. Although many "scientific researchers" tell us that young children need to segment one letter at a time to become competent readers and spellers, classroom teachers know that onsets and rimes (what some used to call "word families") are much easier for children to analyze. According to Margaret Moustafa (1997):

> Children are able to analyze spoken words into onsets and rimes before they are able to analyze spoken words into phonemes when onsets and rimes consist of more than one phoneme; e.g., they can analyze *smiles* into /sm/ + /ilz/ before they analyze *smiles* into /s/, /m/, /i/, /l/, /z/.

At the beginning, when readers are developing, emphasis on graphophonic cues is necessarily strongest. As young readers attempt to read text, much energy goes into decoding. However, that decoding work must always occur in tandem with sense making. Otherwise, kids' focus is on recognizing and understanding discrete words rather than making sense of the text as a whole.

Some students need more phonics work than others. We have found that a quick, intensive, focused phonics emphasis early in first grade enables some kids to move into reading storybooks more quickly. Most enter first grade with enough phonics knowledge (much of it gleaned from working out invented spellings in their writing) that they are able to move easily into literature. A few others, however, will need intensive one-on-one instruction.

Reading comprehension does not necessarily follow from phonemic awareness and mastery of phonics skills.

There is no research that shows that competency in phonemic awareness and phonics automatically leads to understanding in reading. The visual-perceptual training exercises we put kids through in the 1970s were eventually found to lead only to improvement in visual perception (but not reading), and my prediction is that the same will prove true for phonics-first teaching. That is, many students who have received an early overemphasis on phonics to the exclusion of learning and applying meaning-based strategies will not learn to read satisfactorily. While these students will do well on tests that measure phonics skills and literal reading, it remains to be seen whether those skills will transfer to an understanding of more complex reading texts in the middle grades.

"Drilling in Texas," an article by Kathleen Kennedy Manzo (1998), focused on the benefits of intensive phonics drills as the core of reading programs. While the piece acknowledges the difficulties students encountered with reading comprehension, it was reserved for the final paragraphs of the article:

> When they begin to answer more substantial questions about why characters took certain actions, or what particular words or phrases mean, some of the students appear perplexed.
>
> One group, which read *Walk Two Moons* by Sharon Creech, cannot express what the title of the book means or why one of the story's protagonists is considered brave. The children hesitate before giving the meaning of basic vocabulary words, and they guess at explaining figures of speech. (37)

What is troubling about such media reporting is the implied message that lockstep instruction is the answer *even when students are not getting the meaning.* Yet the clear inference one can make from the article is that a heavy emphasis on direct instruction of reading skills does not necessarily lead to comprehension.

Phonics can be taught systematically and explicitly without a commercial program.

There is no research showing that there is one best way or best sequence for teaching phonics (Stahl, Duffy-Hester, and Stahl 1998). This statement also applies to the use of decodable texts, the scripted little books that many districts use as early readers to focus students' attention on phonics. According to Richard Allington (1997), "There is no research on the benefits of decodable texts. If we start with decodable texts, some kids can't get out of the habit of decoding every word."

The well-informed teacher can teach phonemic awareness and phonics as part of her comprehensive literacy program rather than as a separate "subject." Such phonics in context does not mean that we never do isolated word work. It just means that the word work has a meaningful context, that is, it is related to the authentic reading and writing students are doing—as opposed to following a publisher's sequence. Phonics in context takes place in the broad context of meaning but it may well be a separate word work focus.

The finest teachers I know teach phonics in reading-writing-speaking-listening-viewing contexts throughout the day. Using every opportunity that presents itself (some preplanned and some "teachable moments"), they use authentic language to teach phonemic awareness and phonics. Many such contexts and specific examples are presented throughout this text and include, but are not limited to, shared reading, shared writing, teacher-modeled writing, journal writing, writing in multiple genres, repeated reading, guided reading, reading and writing conferences, and spelling and word study.

These teachers do not use direct instruction programs, although they teach directly and explicitly. Their planned instruction is not dependent on scripted package programs that can turn students off to learning. Scripted lessons assume that students everywhere require the same set of skills in the same order, an assumption that is demeaning, time consuming, and thoughtless to both teachers and children. Worse yet, kids who know phonics don't need the lessons or worksheets (so are wasting valuable instructional time) while the ones who can't "do phonics" only become more frustrated.

Phonics teaching, like all good teaching, must be responsive—based on students' needs, experiences, and readiness levels as determined by teacher observations and assessment as well as curriculum requirements. We teachers must determine what skills are needed and in what order they should be taught.

One principal I know said that when her first-grade teachers came to her asking for phonics workbooks, she told them, "I will not buy them for you. I will support you and buy you resources [she subsequently purchased some of the phonics resources listed in The Blue Pages] but I cannot condone phonics sheets for seat work." She also told them, "Don't undervalue what you know. You are all successful, knowledgeable teachers." By listening to them and affirming them in both their concerns and their strengths, she supported their professionalism while validating their need for more structure.

If you do not know how to teach phonics, use the resources in The Blue Pages as a starting point to educating yourself. Become knowledgeable. Be confident about the sound practices you are already employing. Invite people in. Keep a record of phonics you have taught, and share it with your principal and your students' parents.

An overemphasis on phonics works against developing successful readers.

Most phonics instruction should be completed in the early grades (Snow, Burns, and Giffin 1998). While word study (vocabulary, etymology, syllabication, roots, prefixes, and suffixes) continues through all the grades, most students do not need heavy attention to sound-symbol relationships once they are readers. Good readers use phonics—along with other strategies—when meaning breaks down, but they do not overrely on phonics.

Ironically, we continue to see phonics as the panacea despite the fact that the most recent report of the NAEP (National Assessment of Educational Progress), a funded test that is mandated by the U.S. Congress and reported through the U.S. Department of Education, shows conclusively that almost all students at ages nine, thirteen, and seventeen can decode and read at a basic literal level. What students lack and need is instruction in reading for understanding—domains such as making inferences, summarizing, explaining, and synthesizing. What is striking here is that this data remains virtually unchanged since 1971 (U.S. Department of Education 1997).

Yet our national focus remains on phonics. Common sense tells us that if phonics alone could teach kids to read with understanding, we would not have large numbers of students who cannot read satisfactorily. I believe this stems from a lack of understanding of how children learn to read. I have seen many upper-grade teachers (sometimes at their administrator's request) resort to phonics with struggling readers because they don't know what other strategies to teach. In one school, a group of fourth-grade teachers began teaching daily whole-class phonics until the principal put a stop to it. In another, a Reading Recovery teacher gave running records (see page 112) to all fourth graders in the school (over one hundred students) and expressed surprise when the results determined that 90 percent to 95 percent were proficient decoders and "had phonics." She acknowledged that prior to administering the records, her expectations about students' phonics knowledge were low because her experience was primarily with struggling readers.

Kindergarten teacher Karen Sher tells the story of a student who arrived at school able to "sound out" words because his mother had "taught him to read." Karen soon found out that his total phonics approach had put him at a tremendous disadvantage:

> I could not move him beyond phonics. It was so awful to listen to him try to read. There was no comprehension. He was just sounding out words without paying attention to meaning. It was so difficult to get him to use other strategies such as picture cues, semantics, paying attention to patterns in words. He actually left kindergarten in a worse state than when he began. I learned that just pure phonics is not enough.

Karen went on to say, "When I have a student who reads with fluency and comprehension, I see a seamless overlapping of strategies."

Put most of your efforts into developing a rich literacy program.

Students who lack rich literature and literacy experiences don't need to be immersed first in skills work. What they need are the wealth of integrated language experiences that will help them develop as language users; only then will accompanying lessons in skills make sense to them and be perceived as useful.

I know an exemplary kindergarten teacher who pulled her "at risk" students out of a "pull-out" phonics/ phonemic awareness training program in early fall because she recognized that her students needed to develop spoken language and listening abilities as well as knowledge of how stories work *before* work in phonemic awareness and phonics would make any sense to them. Furthermore, the teacher believed—and research supports—that her classroom storybook reading would promote phonological awareness through attention to written language (Coles 1998, 65).

The decision to focus on overall literacy first is in alignment with research that suggests that children make more lasting phonemic awareness gains if they have a strong grounding in literature and literacy.

> Direct instruction seems to be most effective when it is delivered during the second portion of the year, after a variety of kindergarten experiences with literature have been experienced by the children. (Ayres 1998, quoted in Weaver 1998, 244)

Pure common sense should tell us that when we view our students as intelligent and capable, they learn more and learn more easily. A literacy story related to phonics brings home the point. Principal Becky Kimberly notes that after our school district instituted a kindergarten enrichment program, her first-grade teachers began to see their incoming students as more capable learners. Becky insightfully wondered if the subsequent improvement in student performance was due to the fact that the children entered first grade with phonemic awareness and letter-sound knowledge, or to the altered perception of teachers, who went from viewing these students as "low" in terms of their skills to viewing them as knowledgeable. Was this an example, Becky wondered, of a self-fulfilling prophecy? We expect these kids to learn well and at a good rate (because they present themselves as "knowing their letters") and so they do. Teachers treat them and teach them as if they are competent. Kids feel their teacher's appreciation of their "smartness," and they meet that expectation.

Becky Kimberly tells another interesting literacy story. The four kindergarten teachers in her building all have different teaching styles and somewhat different philosophies, but each is an exemplary teacher and has a rich literacy classroom. All the children are involved in authentic listening, speaking, reading, and writing activities throughout the day. Two of the four teachers work hard to ensure that their children know all their individual letters and sounds, while the other two teach phonics mostly in the context of reading and writing. Every spring, as she has done for years, Becky listens to every first grader read aloud. She has not noticed a correlation between the students' reading abilities and the different instruction they receive in each of their four respective kindergarten classes. In other words, even though as entering first graders, some of these students are initially able to identify more letters and sounds, their letter-sound knowledge does not lead to higher reading achievement. This is important information, as kindergarten teachers are under increasing pressure to have their students master specific letter and sound skills in order to assure that their students are "ready" for first grade.

Finally, I believe that we need to shift the prevailing emphasis from phonics first, meaning second, to a model that respects and maximizes optimal learning and human potential. That is, skills and meaning must go hand in hand, right from the start. Opportunities to learn letters and sounds must be embedded in a meaningful context of rich language and literature experiences. Such activities as analyzing and comparing stories, author studies, reading in multiple genres, informational reading, and using research and technology must begin in kindergarten. Most important, at all grade levels, we need to value and give uninterrupted daily attention to our students' voluntary reading of appropriate, self-selected books. Otherwise, we will continue to turn out students who can read words but who cannot understand and interpret texts. Perhaps most consequential, if we want to educate students who are critical thinkers and problem solvers—a necessity for a working democracy—we need to refocus our emphasis to teaching for thinking and understanding, beginning the first day of school.

SOME KEY CONSIDERATIONS IN DETERMINING YOUR READING PROGRAM

Everything presented in this chapter is meant to be a helpful guide for your own thinking, planning, and conversations with colleagues. As a professional, it is you as knowledgeable teacher—not a commercial program—that determines your reading program. How useful any materials or strategies are depends on how judicious and knowledgeable you are in determining what, how, and why these materials and strategies are being used.

What should your reading program encompass? There is no prescription for answering this question, no "best way" to proceed. While there are many factors to consider, it is you, the professional teacher, who must determine the "balance." Use the following factors (described here and throughout this book), plus your own considerations, to guide your planning. Reflect upon your teaching, talk with your colleagues, and use the resources in The Blue Pages to help determine your program.

- Choose an instructional style and materials that meet student and teacher interests and needs.
- Teach and monitor reading every day.
- Conduct regular reading conferences and evaluations, both planned and impromptu, so that you know what and how your students are reading and how best to guide them.

- Set aside an uninterrupted block of time for reading every day.
- Spend most of reading time providing and promoting opportunities for reading.
- Be sure your students are matched with books, both for guided and independent reading.
- Use small-group guided reading (optional in kindergarten) to develop and teach oral and silent reading fluency, multiple strategies for both code and meaning, and how to read for understanding in different genres.
- Include collaborative, supportive reading experiences such as shared reading, partner reading, choral reading, and Readers Theatre.
- Incorporate literature conversations around excellent literature.
- Read aloud excellent literature each day and involve students in interpretive discussion.
- Promote and monitor free-choice, independent reading every day.
- Value and demonstrate your own reading processes.
- Communicate to parents and other stakeholders in jargon-free language.

Choosing Materials for Teaching Reading

The majority of teachers in the United States teach reading using a commercial reading series from a major "basal" publisher. While these publishers are using more and more "little books" and unabridged stories, they are accompanied by detailed teachers' guides and activities that, if strictly followed, take up excessive and unproductive amounts of teacher and class time. I found it disconcerting that while *Preventing Reading Difficulties in Young Children,* the respected report published by the National Academy of Sciences (1998) was critical of current basal readers, stating that some "ignore necessary instructional components" (207), nowhere was it suggested that knowledgeable teachers and administrators could design their own reading programs. Instead, the report recommends improving basal readers. The clearly implied message is that the experts on teaching reading reside outside the classroom.

Yet since 1987, my school district has used children's literature to successfully teach reading (see *Transitions* and *Invitations*). Our standardized reading test scores have remained stable. And what is not measurable by the tests is the positive attitude and love of reading most students develop that promotes continued reading throughout the grades.

Teaching reading without a basal is most challenging in first grade, due to the number of texts required to meet the needs of readers at various levels of competence. Our reading program relies on hundreds of titles in multiple copies, many of which come from published series. (See pages 75b–78b in The Blue Pages for recommendations.) Some of these books come packaged by increasing levels of difficulty. Others, such as storybooks by well-known authors and illustrators, we level ourselves. (See pages 82–84 for leveling guidelines.)

In my experience working with both new and veteran teachers, only a handful could not teach reading well using excellent trade books as the mainstay of their reading program. For these teachers, a structured basal program that lays out the roles and rules of phonics as well as the use of language structure and context is preferable. Because these teachers lack the knowledge to become fully professional in the teaching of reading, a basal program can offer the organization, content, and strategies that they would otherwise be unable to provide. However, in my experience, these are the rare exceptions. Most teachers become very effective reading teachers, and their students become readers.

Whatever reading materials your school or district is considering for purchase, be sure you become involved, vocal, and choosy. Especially when your school district is getting ready to purchase a new basal program or reading series, which can cost many thousands of dollars, you must make the time to examine possibilities and make recommendations. (See suggestions on pages 82b–83b.) Although I am not against published programs to teach reading as a part of a comprehensive reading program (see *Literacy at the Crossroads*, 125–126), I do have a problem with their value relative to their high cost.

A case in point. In one elementary school that had been successfully using a literature approach, a program relying on "little books" (page 82b) was recently purchased to add more structure to the reading program. The cost of the program for the four first grades was twelve thousand dollars. Sadly, some of the funds used to purchase the program came out of the school's library budget. While teachers got more structure, the quality of the "little books" varied greatly. I believe that the money would have been better spent on staff development with respect to teaching beginning reading, release time so that teachers could level and reacquaint themselves with the many terrific books in their existing collection, and on the purchase of culturally diverse literature for use in all grades in the school.

Finally, if you are using a basal or commercial little books to teach reading, be sure that you also incorporate into your program children's literature books by outstanding authors and illustrators. First-grade teacher Cathy Grieshop, who uses some publishers' little books, comments that when she uses "true children's literature" in small guided reading groups, children:

- Use the context better to help decode unknown words
- Talk about story structure more easily
- Talk about more meaningful topics and learn from the story (fiction or nonfiction)
- Are proud of themselves for being able to read children's literature
- Develop a love for literature and an appreciation for the art of writing and illustrating

Dealing with Terminology and Reading Stages

I find the terminology used to describe readers and the developmental stages they go through very confusing. Oftentimes, it depends on the particular text or developmental continuum you are working with. Words such as *emergent, experimental, developing, early,* and *beginning* can have similar meanings. So can *transitional, expanding,* and *self-extending.* As well, *fluent, independent, advanced,* and *proficient* can carry comparable meanings. It all depends on who is using the term, what continuum is being utilized, and what context is being described.

Part of the problem, as I see it, is that readers don't fit into neat categories that can be described by a single word. Continuums and developmental charts do provide a useful overview, common patterns, typical behaviors, recommended teaching focuses, and a helpful language for thinking about groups of readers. However, at best these frameworks can only serve as a guide for our teaching. As professionals, we must focus on the real readers in front of us and respond to the actual behaviors we observe. Given the different tasks and texts, interests and backgrounds, and strategies employed or neglected, it is up to us as knowledgeable teachers to decide how best to teach and support the readers in our care.

Whatever term you choose to use, be sure you plainly define it and describe it with clear examples. Make sure that the language you employ and its meaning are shared among all the stakeholders involved: parents, administrators, teachers, and community members. My experience has been that parents are even more confused by the array of terms used in reading than we are and can't make heads nor tails of all the terms.

For example, while *emergent* is generally used to describe prereading behaviors—learning the conventions of written language and how books work—some continuums use "emergent" to mean early reading behaviors—learning high-frequency words and how to read simple and familiar texts. Further confusing the issue, a reader often "fits" into more than one level or classification. As an example, a reader can be "beginning" with respect to one type of text and "fluent" with respect to another. A second grader could be an "early" reader of informational books but a "proficient" reader of easy chapter books. I am a "beginning" reader of computer manuals because my lack of interest and background experience limits my understanding, while at the same time I am a "fluent" reader of adult fiction.

It is what we do, not how we label, that matters. Therefore, in this text, for purposes of clarity and simplicity, I will primarily refer to beginning readers as "developing" and to strong, self-reliant readers as "independent." Keep in mind that a reader is always developing in some areas and that even an independent reader may need minimal support at times. Similarly, a first grader may well be "independent" with respect to familiar texts but "developing" with respect to more challenging texts that are just being introduced. The same statement could also be true for a middle school reader.

Use the issues addressed in this chapter as well as the recommended reading resources (pages 22b–28b) to inform your teaching, and become familiar with reading stages and behaviors, recommended supports, teaching strategies, and guided reading. But most of all, carefully observe the reader beside you. Note and value what he or she is doing as your best guide to responsive teaching. Just as there is no formula for the best writing minilessons or conferences, the same is true for working with readers.

The Interest Factor

While the interest factor has long been viewed as important in learning to read and in the enjoyment of reading, I think we often underestimate its power with respect to a child's motivation, engagement, and understanding. It is my belief that children can and will learn to read when

- They find the material interesting.
- They are given enough instruction and support so that they are able to problem solve their way through challenging parts of texts.

- They are provided with sufficient time and opportunities for both guided and independent practice.
- They receive ongoing and supportive feedback.

I am just about illiterate when it comes to reading computer manuals. It's not just that the language and directions in such texts are difficult for me to understand. In emergency situations, having had no other choice but to resort to a manual in my attempt to fix a problem, I've sometimes managed to plod along and make some sense of things. But other than that, I have no interest in reading about how computers and software work. Because I lack the stick-to-it quality that comes from interest in the material, I have great difficulty understanding.

On the other hand, a dear friend of mine is a self-taught reader of guides, catalogs, and manuals having to do with cameras. Several years ago when he became captivated with photography, he could make little sense of what he read. The language was technical, full of jargon that was alien to him. He did not have the background that was necessary for understanding the material. But—and this is a big *but*—because he was so passionate about photography and cameras, he persisted for hours—day after day—poring through the photos, the descriptions, the captions, the advertisements, the difficult terminology. When he didn't understand something, he read it over and over until it made some sense, approximated meanings, sometimes stopped by a camera shop and asked for expert help, and kept on reading and studying. The end result is that my friend is a fluent reader of photography manuals. I observed the whole process and found it fascinating. It was his great interest that fueled concentration, persistence, and willingness to reread and question, and that eventually led to understanding. Without that interest, he would have remained as illiterate as I am with computer manuals.

So what does this mean for our teaching children to read? Some kids (and adults) just give up when the material does not grab their attention. Without interest, it is nearly impossible to bring motivation and effort to our tasks. Therefore, we must make sure that the books for independent reading in our rooms and the texts we use for teaching reading represent our students' interests, especially for our struggling students. (See pages 46 and 47.) Kids will work unfailingly at reading a recipe, game directions, guide, or text if it's something they really want to know, make, or do.

When I work with struggling readers, we often write our own texts, on the spot, based on their interests (see pages 123–124). These books are always a great hit, and students willingly reread them and illustrate them. Series fiction also serves as a great motivator for turning kids into readers (see pages 75b–88b). Knowing how important the interest factor is for understanding, we have built choice into our benchmark reading assessments (see Appendix I-9).

Even severely dyslexic students can become proficient readers if their interest in a subject is great enough. Rosalie Fink (1998) interviewed twelve such readers who became highly successful adults in their chosen disciplines. Although their decoding difficulties persisted, they became "highly skilled," "avid readers," who enjoyed reading.

> All of them read materials that are highly difficult, specialized, technical, and abstract. . . .
> Of the twelve dyslexics, 9 have written and published creative scholarly works. . . .
>
> They seem to have used the repetition in narrow, discipline-specific text to promote their skill development. . . . Furthermore, the high interest value of their reading materials seems to have increased the amount of reading they engaged in. The sheer volume of reading apparently provided greater practice of skills. . . .

These learners, hampered by nagging and persistent deficiencies in basic skills, nevertheless effectively constructed meaning in a single high interest domain.

One overarching implication is clear: Teachers should provide captivating materials based on each student's strengths, prior knowledge, skills, and interests. (401–403)

The Practice Factor

Most critical for success in anything we are learning how to do is repeated practice and the receiving of guided feedback. No matter how wonderful the instruction, kids will not become readers without massive amounts of experience reading independently, both at school and at home.

Think about taking piano or tennis lessons. You have the best teacher and coach in the world. The lessons are right on target; that is, they offer you just enough challenge to be successful, but not so much that you are working at frustration level. You are being taught the skills and strategies you need to move forward, and you are receiving helpful feedback on how to improve your playing. But without systematic, diligent, and regular practice on your own, you will never amount to much as a player. Accompanied by support, encouragement, modeling, and explicit teaching, it is the practice that follows the lesson that is most critical for sustained improvement, growth, and eventual proficiency.

So it is with becoming a reader. Especially for our struggling readers who learn at a slower pace, daily practice reading accessible books is absolutely essential for developing confidence and success. In fact, once poor readers can read well enough to take up full-length novels, their progress accelerates if they are provided with interesting texts (Krashen and McQuillan 1996).

Therefore, while guided reading lessons serve to move students forward in their reading, most of students' reading time must be spent practicing; that is, independently reading books at their level of interest, experience, and skill.

The Critical Role of Writing in Learning to Read

When I was co-teaching first grade, I was constantly amazed by students who could not yet read storybooks but who had no trouble reading what they themselves had written. We took advantage of that fact by establishing a parent-run publishing program. For some children, their first successful reading experiences are with their own written stories (see *Transitions*). I have found this to be especially true for struggling readers, which is why I often write with them the first books that they read. I start with two or three words that they know well plus the sounds and letters in their names. I find that writing right in front of them—for them and with them—with the expectation that they will then read the writing forces them to look carefully at print. (See "Creating 'Just Right' Books," pages 123–124.)

The influence of writing on learning to read and improved reading achievement is well documented (Braunger and Lewis 1997; Clay 1998; Dickinson and DiGisi 1998; Tierney and Shanahan 1991). When writing—with a focus on creating meaning—is taught reciprocally with reading, all children benefit. Such activities as shared writing, teacher-modeled writing, and journal writing impact both students' growth in phonemic awareness and phonics' knowledge and their ability to read for meaning, think on a higher level, and see reading as a composing process.

I was particularly struck by the power of writing to influence reading development when I spoke recently with a teacher whose students are unable, because of disability, to utilize phonics. Cathy Corrado teaches a multiage class of second- through fifth-grade children, most of whom are profoundly deaf. While she teaches students consonant awareness, they cannot utilize the sounds of the consonants, so Cathy has to employ other strategies besides phonics in her teaching of reading. In particular, she teaches reading through daily writing on self-selected topics and literature response. Each day, Cathy demonstrates writing in front of her students by first revealing her thought process through signing, and then writing in English. Then as students write, she confers with them and keeps her expectations high. She has found that the more her kids write, the better they read—and the higher their enjoyment of both activities. "My fifth graders are all reading on a fifth-grade level, which is virtually unheard of for deaf kids."

Writing and reading naturally complement each other. Writing down thoughts and questions while reading increases comprehension. For instance, when I read nonfiction material, such as research and practice related to literacy, I often underline, write in the margins of the text, and take notes to help me recall key ideas. This enhances my comprehension, because when I reread, I can focus on the key ideas I've noted (as opposed to the whole text), which makes it more likely that I will recall important content. We need to show students how to do this.

Written retellings and summaries of texts, when they are first well demonstrated and attempted by and with the teacher, can also extend and deepen the meaning students take away from their reading of texts.

OBSERVING AND EVALUATING YOUR READERS

Before you decide how and what to teach your readers, you will want to carefully observe them and do some evaluation. From the insights you gain on how students process text and understand it, you can determine what strategies you need to reinforce and teach.

Incorporating Running Records and Miscue Analysis

One of the best ways to observe a reader and analyze his reading process is through running records and/or miscue analysis. Both are standardized procedures you will want to be familiar with for examining the strategies the reader employs in reading orally. Text used may be familiar or unfamiliar, depending on your purposes.

Running records were developed by Marie Clay as part of Reading Recovery, a successful early-intervention program for first graders (Clay 1985). In a running record, the teacher has the student read aloud from a passage of several hundred words or less (but not less than one hundred words). The teacher then checks off each word of the text that the student reads correctly, and also notes the specific errors and self-corrections that the reader makes. (High-progress readers may make a lot of errors, but their tendency to self-correct is also high [Clay 1991, 307].) After the session, the teacher marks whether each error was visual (phonics), structural (grammar), or meaning (semantics), to determine the student's strengths and weaknesses and future teaching directions. The number of errors are tallied, and a score is given for text accuracy. The resulting percentage is used to determine if the text is at the student's instructional level (90 percent or higher), independent level (95 percent or higher), or frustration level (below 90 percent accuracy).

Even if you are an intermediate-grade teacher, you will want to know how to take a running record in order to evaluate the severely struggling reader or nonreader in your class. Once you know how to take a running record for your struggling readers, you can easily adapt the method for use with more proficient readers. I have been doing modified running records for years, noting only students' miscues relative to the text (see pages 116–120).

If you know a Reading Recovery teacher, see if she will teach you how to take and analyze a running record. Most Reading Recovery teachers are very willing to help. If not, read several sources on how to take running records. Consult *An Observation Survey* by Marie Clay (1993) and "Interpreting Oral Reading Records," co-authored by Clay, in *Knowing Literacy: Constructive Literacy Assessment* by Peter Johnston (1997). Write down the coding for taking running records, and keep these notations in front of you. Don't get discouraged. Taking and analyzing a running record is not difficult, but it does take time, practice, and feedback to get proficient at the process.

You will also want to be familiar with miscue analysis, which is often employed for more fluent and older readers. The term *miscue* was coined by reading researcher Ken Goodman (1970) and refers to any unexpected response a reader makes while reading a text, for example, an omission or substitution. Miscue analysis generally requires longer texts, and the *quality* of the miscues—not the number of miscues—is emphasized.

> Single miscues do not yield conclusions about a reader's proficiency; twenty-five miscues are the minimum to produce a pattern of miscue responses. (Martens, Goodman, and Flurkey 1995, 3)

All readers miscue. In fact, a high-quality substitution that does not change the text's meaning may indicate that the reader is comprehending. Analysis of miscues allows for better instruction. By noting where meaning has broken down, the teacher can plan appropriate strategy instruction. Miscue analysis also generally includes more student involvement than running records, as the former process requires students to do a retelling following their oral reading. "The pattern of miscues throughout a reading, including the retelling, provides a fairly complete profile of a reader's abilities" (Yetta Goodman, in Martens, Goodman, and Flurkey 1995, 7).

Regardless of which procedure or adaptation you use, take the time to observe such behaviors as reading speed, rereading, subvocalizing, and vocabulary and conceptual understanding. Also, take the time to make the student conscious of the strategies he is using and/or neglecting.

A final note about running records. While running records are a great tool for developing readers, they are being increasingly misused for older, fluent readers. Such use was never intended, is unnecessary, and is not a good use of student or teacher time. Running records are intended to be used on students through Reading Recovery's reading book level twenty, which is equivalent to the level of a typical student beginning second grade.

Once a student is beyond level twenty, there is insufficient information to be gained from a running record.

Tape-Recording Oral Reading

Many sources recommend periodically taping children's oral reading as a way to record progress. Along with other teachers in my district, I used tape-recording as part of reading assessment for years. However, most of us abandoned it because it was too time consuming and generally not worth the effort it took. Teachers and students had difficulty timing the recordings to pick up where a subsequent recording left off, and keeping track of more than twenty-five tapes eventually proved burdensome.

The exception for me was when I worked with struggling readers. I sometimes tape recorded their one-on-one reading conference, which included both the child's oral reading and my follow-up teaching. When I sent the tape home, parents commented that hearing my teaching-for-strategies language—for example, "Try that again"; "I noticed you said————." "Look how the word starts." "Could it be————?"; "Put in a word that makes sense"—was helpful to them in learning how to prompt their child beyond the usual "Sound it out." Another positive use of tape recording with struggling readers is to have them tape themselves reading, listen to the tape as they follow along in the text, practice rereading, and then tape themselves again. Hearing incremental progress seems to be a motivating factor for some children.

Informal Reading Conferences

Teacher-student reading conferences are ideal for assessing comprehension, application of reading strategies, and the appropriateness of selected texts. These one-on-one conferences provide an excellent opportunity for teaching, student self-evaluation, and mutual goal setting.

Two to three days a week, as students are reading silently and independently, you can use this sustained reading time to work one-on-one with students. You will need to meet frequently with students you are concerned about and infrequently with proficient readers. While most of these conferences will be quick "checkups," aim for a complete informal reading evaluation two to three times a year for each of your students.

Informal reading conferences utilizing books that students have chosen to read independently offer a quick, easy way to gain useful information about the student as a reader. These conferences provide opportunities to take a running record, modified running record, or miscue analysis, analyze progress and problem areas with the student, conduct direct teaching, and set goals. In our district, we also use reading conferences more formally, as part of our required "common tools" assessment in grades one through four. (See pages 595–598 in Chapter 15, "Evaluation as Part of Teaching," and Appendix I for information as well as for procedures for oral retellings.)

While many teachers across the country use commercial reading inventories in informal assessment, the selected passages often lack relevance and contextual meaning for students. By using the book the student is actually reading to evaluate progress, we are more likely to get an optimal, accurate assessment.

Procedures for an Informal Reading Conference

Ask the child:

• **<u>*Bring me a book you can read pretty well.*</u>**   This helps you determine if the child is choosing and can choose "just right" books to read independently. Since the majority of reading students do is done independently, it is critical they choose appropriate books they can read and understand. Students who continually read books that are too difficult for them regress in their reading.

• **<u>*Why did you choose this book?*</u>**   This gives insight into the self-selection process. I want to know if the student can self-select a book that he can read independently and what his attitude is about the book. Is this a favorite author or series? Did a peer or parent recommend it? Did he look through the book and choose it because of the pictures, cover, hard words, length of story? Sometimes, a student might say, "I chose this book because it's hard, and my mom wants me to read hard books."

• **<u>*What's the reading level of this book for you?*</u>**   Ask also: Is this book easy, "just right," or hard for you? How do you know? What does it mean if a book is "just right?" What kinds of books do good readers mostly read? Why is this a good book for you?

• **<u>*Tell me what the book is about so far.*</u>**   Does the child understand the text? Can he state the problem in the story? (If you are unfamiliar with the book, look through it as the child is talking. Read the blurb and back cover and skim.)

• **<u>*Read this part of the book for me.*</u>**
  • **ual*Take notes as the child is reading orally or silently.*** Oral reading is desirable for developing readers and readers we know little about. If the child is reading orally, note miscues: Did the miscue make sense in the context? Did it change the meaning? Did the student self-correct? What is causing the miscues? If it is apparent the book is too hard, discuss this with the student and guide her in choosing a more appropriate book.

  Silent reading is often used, especially with more independent and older readers, because most of the reading we do in life is silent reading. Also, some students understand more when they read silently. If the child is reading silently, read along silently with her. Observe what the student does: Does she subvocalize, reread, point to words, read slowly?

  If you are having difficulty keeping up with the reader as you are writing your observations, say something like, "Stop reading for just a minute. I need to make some notes. I will share with you later what I write down."

  Note what strategies the student is using to make sense of text. Is he self-monitoring? For example, does he stop when something doesn't make sense? Does he reread? Does he attempt to figure out unknown vocabulary?

- *Take a formal running record or a modified running record.* If you are taking formal running records, the text used is often one that the child has read previously in guided reading. Because the child is somewhat familiar with the text, he can focus on "orchestrating" strategies to problem solve. Note patterns of behavior as the reader processes and problem solves while reading aloud. Again, formal running records are most appropriate for use with developing readers.

  Since it is not always clear if the student has understood what he has read from analyzing a formal running record, once students are reading well, modified running records can be used. A modified running record notes important miscues and observations. A modified running record on unfamiliar text—along with a retelling—can provide an informal, yet in depth, comprehension check. Assessing a student's reading through analyzing the miscues and the retelling of the text is known as miscue analysis.

- **_Tell me what you remember about what you just read._**   Can the student talk about what he has read and tell the most important information? Sometimes students can decode the words accurately but can't say what the text was about. A retelling is one way to check for comprehension.

  A retelling is an oral or written reconstruction of text (that has been read orally, silently, or listened to) that can be used to check the reader's understanding and creation of meaning. The reader retells information that is directly stated, and possibly inferred, from the text. Retellings may be prompted or unprompted, simple or detailed, informal or standardized. Before asking students to do a retelling, they need to have had practice in the procedure. (See pages 595–598 in Chapter 15, "Evaluation as Part of Teaching," for information and procedures regarding retelling.)

  As an alternative, fourth-grade teacher Linda Cooper finds an easy comprehension check is to ask, "If you were to draw a picture of what's happening in the book right now, what would it look like?" (She also uses this question in small guided reading groups.)

- **_Let's look at how you did—what your strengths are and what you need to work on._**   Discuss your observations/notes with the student. Be sure to state what the student has done well. Together with the student, analyze the miscues and guide the student toward self-evaluation and self-correction where possible. For example, you might say to the student: "Did it make sense when you said . . .?" or "Could it be. . .?" or "Do you know this part or chunk? Yes, that's right, now, try this part you know in this word you had trouble with," or "Reread this part and tell me what happened."

  Emphasize a few major teaching points. Set goals together for future reading. See "Teaching During the Reading Conference" that follows.

- **_How long should it take you to complete this book?_**   This gives you insight into child's daily goal setting. Often students are unrealistic about how long it should take to complete a book and need guidance.

Reviewing the Language of an Informal Reading Evaluation

Until you are familiar with the language, you may want to have questions and prompts such as the following in front of you. Also, see the "Informal Reading Conference" example and form to guide you (Appendixes D-5 and D-6).

- Why did you choose this book?
- What's the reading level for you?
- What's your prediction for what will happen next?
- What happened on those pages? Tell me what you just read.
- Was there anything you didn't understand?
- How did you figure that out? How did you know that?
- What strategy/strategies did you use?
- What goals do you have for yourself?

For nonfiction, add:

- Do you do anything different when you read nonfiction? What do you do?
- How does the author convey information?
- Can you tell me some interesting facts?

Teaching During the Reading Conference

While I have done informal reading conferences for years, it is only recently that I fully capitalized on that one-on-one time by connecting the evaluation with teaching. Believing strongly that any time you are with a child is an opportunity to teach, I now make sure I make some teaching points and do some goal setting as part of the conference. I write down and/or ask the student to verbalize and record the goals we set so that she is more likely to follow through. The following are some suggestions for teaching that you will want to adapt to your own contexts.

Book Selection

For students having difficulty selecting appropriate books, help them choose "just right" books—those that are at their interest, experience, and independent-reading level. Teach them the "five finger test" (see page 51) and the "Goldilocks Strategy" (*Invitations*, page 189b) for choosing easy books, "just right" books, and hard books.

For struggling students, it is helpful to supply a collection of preselected books with a range of choices. We arrange books in baskets, providing one basket that contains books that are familiar to students from guided reading group or other contexts. Otherwise, students may waste a lot of time wandering the room searching for a book, or they may choose a book that is too difficult for them.

Strategies

Struggling readers tend to overrely on "sounding out" difficult words. Since good readers use multiple strategies to make sense of text, we need to teach all readers to also:

- Use known onsets and rimes to connect to familiar chunks in unknown words
- Break words into parts
- Reread paragraphs or sections that don't make sense
- Read on and then come back to the difficult word or part
- Substitute another name for names that are too difficult to read

- Connect to what is already known
- Predict and ask questions during reading

Vocabulary

Many students skip difficult words or fail to stop to figure out what they mean. Teach them to:

- Read the rest of the sentence and come back to the difficult word
- Substitute another word that makes sense in the context
- Use what they already know about the topic/text/word
- Use the dictionary

Goal Setting

Ask the student, "What will you do to help yourself the next time you read?" Make sure that the student can verbalize what has been discussed and taught during reading conference. Writing the goals down can be a helpful reminder. Monitor the student to check that she is applying agreed-upon strategies.

Examples of Informal Reading Conferences

A Student Who Needs to Learn and Apply Phonics

A second-grade teacher approaches me about a student who was reading "okay" in the fall but hasn't progressed very far since then. The teacher is not sure what the problem is and has concerns that the student will not be ready to enter grade three. I agree to conference with the student, and I ask her to bring to our meeting a book she thinks she can "read pretty well." The student, named Mandy, brings *Arthur's Tooth* by Marc Brown to the conference. When I ask her what she thinks the book's reading level is for her, she says that it is "in between easy and hard. I can read most of the words." This turns out to be true. (See Figure 4-1 for my conference notes.)

I ask her to read aloud from the text, and Mandy starts off reading fluently and with expression. She self-corrects her errors, and her phrasing indicates that she is reading for meaning. She has a strong sight vocabulary of common words, but as soon as she hits a two- or three-syllable word, she has difficulty. For example, she stumbles over "complained," "persuaded," "peanut," "waiting," "investment," and "announcer." She does not slow down, self-monitor, or self-correct for these words. When I try to connect the known to the unknown for her—"ade" to "made" to "persuade"; "ain" to "rain" to "complain"—it is clear that Mandy does not know basic rimes. She doesn't know "ai" so she can't read *waiting*. She is confused when I attempt to connect the "ou" in *round*, a word she knows, to that in *announcer*, a word she doesn't.

At my suggestion, Mandy's teacher forms a group of students who, with Mandy, need help understanding basic rimes and applying phonics strategies to multisyllable words. This is an example where directed phonics instruction will benefit students, because they are already readers and comprehension is not a problem. These students may have had lots of previous phonics instruction but, for some reason, it hasn't "clicked." Direct and explicit instruction is therefore necessary to move them toward independence.

Figure 4–1 *My notes from an informal reading conference*

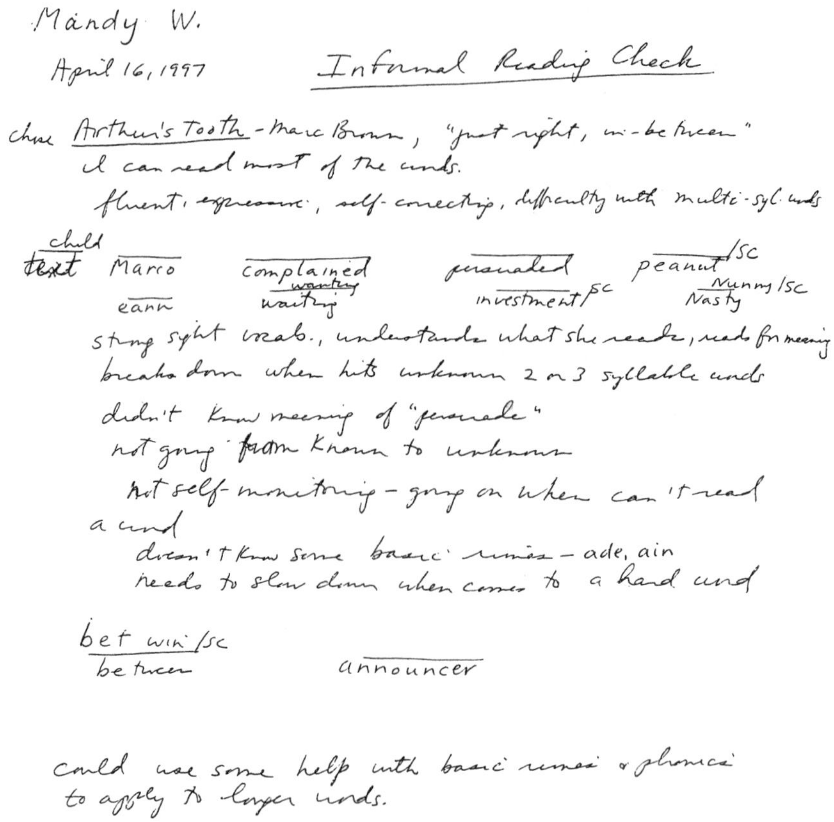

Mandy W.
April 16, 1997   Informal Reading Check

chose <u>Arthur's Tooth</u> – Marc Brown, "just right, in-between"
I can read most of the words.
fluent, expressive, self-correcting, difficulty with multi-syl. words

<u>child</u>
<s>text</s> <u>Marco</u>   <u>complained</u>   <u>persuaded</u>   <u>peanut</u>/sc
     earn   wanting/waiting   investment/sc   Nummy/sc
                                                        Nasty

strong sight vocab., understands what she reads, reads for meaning
breaks down when hits unknown 2 or 3 syllable words
didn't know meaning of "persuade"
not going from known to unknown
      not self-monitoring – going on when can't read
a word
      doesn't know some basic rules – ade, ain
      needs to slow down when comes to a hard word

<u>bet win</u>/sc   <u>announcer</u>
betwee

could use some help with basic rules & phonics
to apply to longer words.

A Student Who Needs to Self-Monitor for Meaning

A principal asks me to meet with a third grader whose parents have contacted the school because of concerns that their son is not understanding what he reads. The classroom teacher tells me, "I've got others just like him. He's not unusual."

I meet with Marcus midmorning and ask him to bring me the book he is reading for SQUIRT (Sustained Quiet Uninterrupted Reading Time). He shows me *Horrible Harry and the Green Slime* by Suzy Kline. It is a high-interest, easy chapter book that many of our second graders read. It is just right for him, convincing me that this student knows how to select books that are appropriate for him. He retells part of the book and seems to have the gist of the story. I ask him to read two pages aloud to me. He is at the part of the story that deals with a demonstration that Harry is doing for his class, which involves a microscope and slide.

Marcus reads the two pages fluently, except for the word *microscope*. Initially, he can't get passed the first consonant. He skips over the word after verbalizing the "m" sound. The second time the word appears, he verbalizes it as "macaron sop." In retelling the story, Marcus says, "Harry is going to demonstrate something to the class. He is bringing 'macaron sop.'" When I say, "That doesn't make sense," he smiles and says, "I know." Yet he never

self-monitors, rereads, or tries to figure out the word. He also supplies the wrong meaning for "slide"—visualizing playground equipment—because he missed the laboratory context provided by "microscope."

I show him how to break the word apart, and I teach him about open and closed syllables (see pages 437–438). I use his last name, "Simon," to demonstrate: "Si mon" or "Sim on." He knows his long and short vowels and catches on quickly. Eventually he is able to read the word *microscope* and get the intended meaning for "slide." I ask him to reread the two pages silently and tell me what the text describes. He now does so easily. Marcus and I then set some goals for his reading, and I put these on a bookmark for him and make several copies, so that he can keep one of the bookmarks at home. (See Figure 4-2 for conference notes and Figure 4-3 for bookmark.)

Figure 4–2 *My notes from an informal reading conference with Marcus*

<u>Informal Reading Evaluation</u>
Marcus S.   grade 3   10/16/97

<u>Horrible Harry and the Green Slime</u> by Suzy Kline
reading independently, book is his choice, says
it's "just right"
pp. 45-46, reading fluently except for multi-syllable word below.

¯¯¯   macaroon sop
microscope   microscope

• Did not get meaning of "slide" in relation to "microscope."
  Did not self monitor and say, "I can't read this word," or
  "I don't understand." In retelling, he said, "Harry is
  bringing "macaroon sop": didn't make sense

• After I showed him how to divide "microscope" into
  syllables and the rules for open and closed syllables,
  he understood "slide." After rereading pp. 45-46 silently
  he did a detailed retelling with no problem.

<u>Goals</u>:
• When something doesn't make sense, ~~stop~~ and figure it out:
     "Chunk" the word
     divide it into syllables
     Reread till it makes sense
     Ask someone
• Ask yourself, what's happening? It has to make
  sense. If it doesn't, go back and reread

Regie Routman

Figure 4–3 A bookmark for reading, based on
goals set at informal reading conference with Marcus

> As you are reading, ask your-self, "What's happening?" If you don't know, go back and reread.
>
> When you don't know a word, **stop** and figure it out:
>
> - "Chunk" the word.
> - Divide it into syllables (try open syllables—ends in a vowel and the vowel says its own name, as in "**Si** mon," or try closed sylla-bles—ends in a consonant and the vowel is always short as in "**Sim** on").
> - Reread till it makes sense;
> - Ask someone.

I have found that making a bookmark for a student (which only takes a minute or so on computer) serves several purposes. It is a visible reminder to the student, teacher, and parent of important reading goals. The bookmark also lets parents know what strategies to reinforce at home. Because parents can receive this information without the teacher necessarily having to make contact, the bookmark can be a timesaver for communicating to parents.

I especially like using bookmarks after students have a good understanding of reading strategies that promote understanding (see Appendix D-2). See Figure 4-4 on page 122 for strategies that resulted from a shared writing in a grade three class.

WORKING WITH STRUGGLING READERS

They are in every classroom, and they challenge our teaching every day. These are the students who have failed to learn to read satisfactorily, for a host of reasons. Many hate to read and avoid it at all costs. Almost all of them do not properly self-monitor for mean-ing. Most use "sounding out" as their only strategy for figuring out unknown words; oth-ers overrely on context and fail to look at print closely enough. These low-achieving students need to work on overall literacy development (not just word work)—hearing, talking about, and writing stories and texts as well as playing around with language. These students also need more instruction and learning time, but it must be instruction and time that actively engages them in strategic reading of appropriate, interesting mate-rial. Most struggling readers can be helped with early intervention (a goal of Reading Re-covery in grade one). It is usually a lot easier to remediate at grade one than at grade two or above.

Figure 4–4   A bookmark for reading, from a shared writing

A Bookmark for **when** you are reading

Ask questions
Ask questions about the story as you are reading.

Summarize
Tell the most important ideas.

Predict
Make a smart guess based on what you already know.

Clarify
Clear up confusions, such as, what a word means.
Put in a word that makes sense.
Look at the surrounding words.
Break word into chunks. Look for parts you know.
Say the first sound of the word, skip it, read on, and come back to it.

Connect to what you know

Visualize
Make a picture in your mind.

Mrs. Brown's grade 3 class
December 1997

Use Appropriate Books

A second-grade teacher invites me to observe her guided reading group and give her feedback. The teacher is supplying many of the unknown words which does not help the children become successful problem solvers or improve as readers. "This is too hard, isn't it?" I ask the students. They all nod in agreement. When we collect the books, there is an audible sigh of relief.

It is a common practice in the teaching of slow-achieving readers: we supply books that are too hard for students and then feel compelled to do most of the word work for them. In sustained silent reading time, these are the students who wander the room looking for books that they can actually read. Often, there are very few books in the classroom that are accessible to them. Learning how to match these children with books that they can successfully read and are interested in is our biggest challenge. (See pages 49 and 50.) If we continually give our struggling readers books that are too hard for them, they will regress—rather than progress—as readers. For help in finding books suitable for developing readers, see The Blue Pages, page 83b.

Regression in reading is not restricted to elementary school students. Many high schools still place much emphasis on "traditional" and "classic" literature but give little emphasis to YA (young adult) fiction or to nonfiction. Reluctant readers who choose the latter—because it seems more readable and appealing—are often given the message that they don't measure up as readers, which further deters them from reading.

Creating "Just Right" Books

I have sometimes found it so difficult to find quality literature relevant to kids that it's often easier and more efficient to create our own texts that are tailor-made to students' developmental and interest levels. I create these texts right at the reading table with the student. They are easy and can be done "on the spot." We teachers do not need additional "take home" work. (See also *Invitations*, pages 378–382.)

Angie entered first grade having been in a series of foster homes. She came in late fall not knowing any letters or sounds. By the end of first grade she could read about ten sight words and very simple pattern books. In grade two, her teacher—new to second grade—did not know how to teach her as she did not "fit" into the other reading groups, and her teacher was having a great deal of difficulty finding enough easy books that Angie could read. The teacher had her join the group reading *Frog and Toad* by Arnold Lobel. In first grade, Angie had a good memory for text and memorized the books. When I assessed her informally, I was therefore surprised she could read so few words in an unfamiliar text.

In modeling for the teacher, I sat down with Angie and told her that I knew reading was hard for her but that this would be a great year. I reminded her of how far she had come, from not knowing any letters and sounds to learning them all last year plus some sight words. I told her that we would begin to keep a list of all the words that she could read and write. I then suggested that we write a book together, and after some discussion and suggestions, she opted for the title "All About Me."

I had her choose the size of the paper, how the book would be folded or stapled, how many pages it would be, and where the print should go. Then I had her watch me as I scribed the title. "Do you know how to write *All*?" I asked. She shook her head. I wrote down the letter *A*, repeated the word, and asked her what sound she heard at the end of it. She said, "l." "Good!" I said. "There are two of them," and I finished writing the word. I next scribed "About" as I verbalized the word slowly, and then I asked her how to spell *me*. When she spelled it correctly, I praised her efforts and added *me* to a sheet titled "Words I Can Read and Write."

The first page of her story read, "I can ride my bike." After we had written four pages and practiced reading them, we did some work with the rimes "all" and "an." I had her write and read "all," then guided her as she wrote "ball," "tall," "wall," "mall," and "small." (This came after a whole-class shared reading in which we had worked with rimes and talked about why it is important to know rimes. We did the same with "an" words—building from "can," she wrote "man," "pan," "ran," and "tan" easily. Angie seemed very pleased with her progress. Another teacher who was observing the lesson commented, "She seemed two feet taller." After the conference, Angie went back to her seat and beautifully illustrated the first page of her book with colored pencil and lots of detail. (See Figure 4-5 on page 124 for how her story and word work progressed.)

Figure 4–5 Creating a "just right" book: Angie's "All About Me" and the beginning of accompanying word work

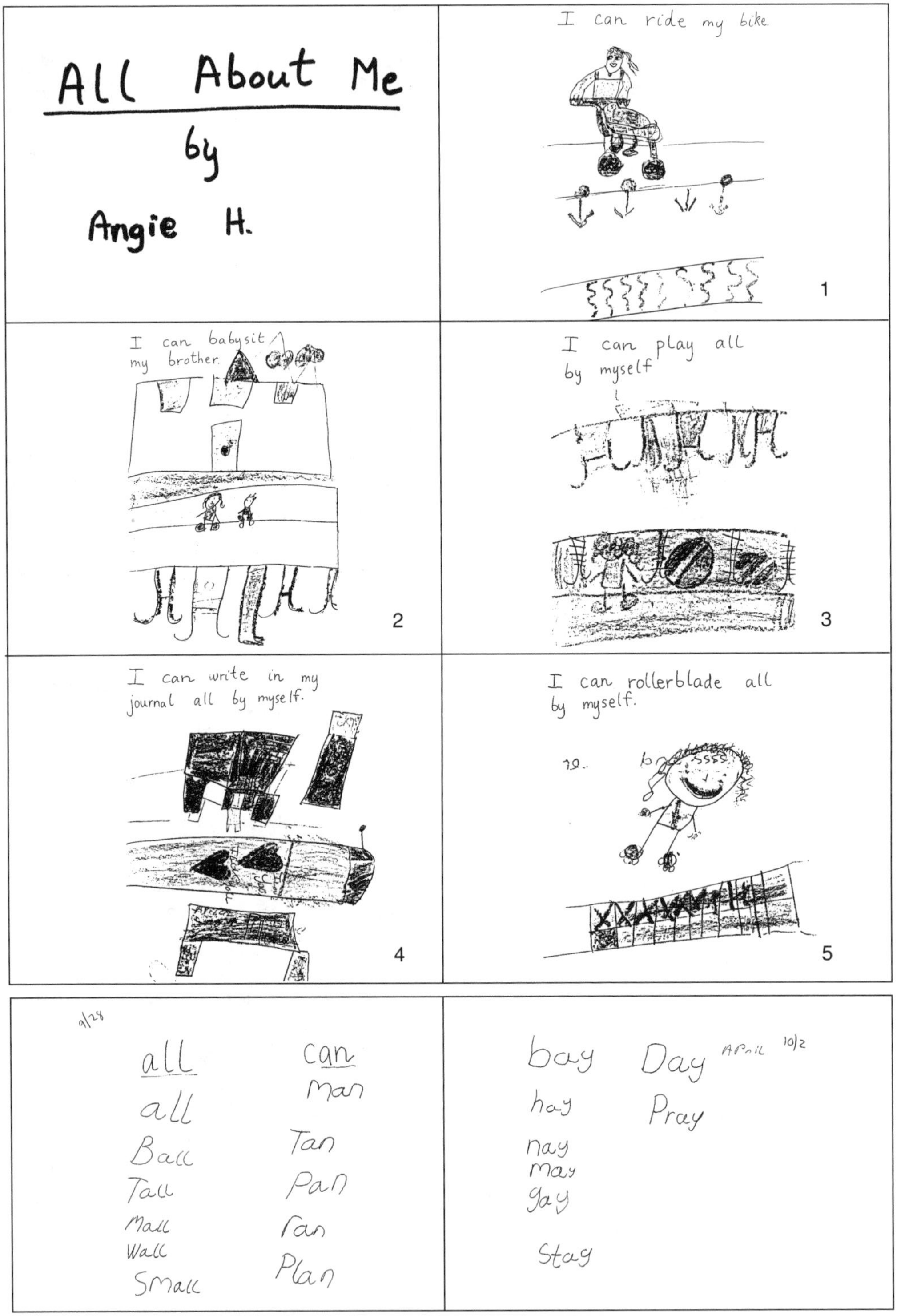

All About Me
by
Angie H.

I can ride my bike.

1

I can babysit my brother.

2

I can play all by myself

3

I can write in my journal all by myself.

4

I can rollerblade all by myself.

5

9/28

all	can
all	Man
Ball	Tan
Tall	Pan
Mall	ran
Wall	Plan
Small	

bay Day APRIL 10/2
hay Pray
nay
may
gay

Stay

Watch for Overattention to Decoding

Another problem I have noticed repeatedly is that struggling readers often lose the meaning of what they are reading because of overattention to decoding. When we overemphasize that reading is getting the words right and focus solely at the word level—students read the words, but not necessarily with the expectation that the text has to make sense. While accuracy and automaticity in word reading are critical, without understanding, such reading is just word calling:

> Low-achieving students are often stifled in their reading development by an overemphasis on phonics.
>
> These students tend to receive a heavy dose of phonics instruction at all grade levels and very little of the "print awareness" focus that is characteristic of the emergent literacy tradition. (Pearson 1993, 505)

Struggling readers don't always know that the text is supposed to make sense. Liz Schutter tells the story of a boy named Jacob, who entered first grade midyear using a phonics-first approach. In reading, he used only a sounding-out strategy. In writing, he worked word by word, choosing words that didn't relate to each other. He couldn't remember what he'd written because it didn't make sense. He wrote sentences only because the teacher asked him to. Until he realized that the text had to make sense, and until he connected meaning with decoding, he struggled as a reader and was unable to write a meaningful sentence.

I once observed a group of struggling readers who were reading a *Clifford* book by Norman Bridwell. They were completely missing the meaning. When I suggested that the book was intended to be humorous, I quickly realized that these students did not know what "humor" meant. They were so focused on getting the words right that they had no idea what the story was about and were unable to enjoy it.

In addition to decoding, we need to teach kids how to focus on meaning—how to slow down and monitor themselves by continually asking, "What's going on?," how to reread when the text is confusing, and how to use context and other strategies to help figure out words and text that are unclear.

Teach Self-Monitoring

I am coaching Neal Robinson as he teaches a guided reading group with four of his most struggling readers. It is late spring in second grade, and the students are reading *Nate the Great*, part of a popular series by Marjorie Weinman Sharmat. We are working on self-monitoring with the goal of enabling these students to become more independent in their reading.

Neal does a complete book introduction and reads and discusses the opening pages with the students. (See "Guided Silent Reading," page 147.) The students' assignment is to read to page 15, write down any words or concepts that they can't read or don't understand (and to cross out any they subsequently figure out), and to write a few sentences explaining what happened in the story.

Jacqueline has difficulty with some key words (see Figure 4-6) and this limits her understanding. However, when I encourage her to use multiple strategies—especially

Figure 4–6   A developing reader notes difficult words when reading silently

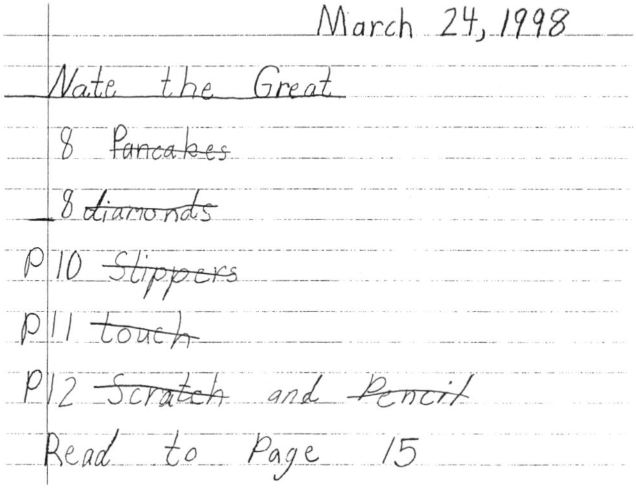

```
                            March 24, 1998
    Nate the Great
    8 Pancakes
    8 diamonds
P 10 Slippers
P 11 touch
P 12 Scratch and Pencil
Read to Page 15
```

meaning, structure, pictures, and her own experiences—not just phonics, she is able to figure out each word (and then she crosses out each word as she can read it). For example, with the word *pancakes,* I review what she knows about the word by breaking it down into "pan" and "cake" using a sliding mask to gradually reveal the word parts. The word "clicks in" for her as soon as I ask what Nate the Great was doing at this point in the text. "He was eating breakfast," she tells me, and then she has it; she immediately says "pancakes." With the word *slippers,* I ask her to make the beginning sounds of the word, say the rime "ip," which she is familiar with, and look at the accompanying illustration (of a pair of slippers). She is then able to self-correct. I guide her to figure out the word *scratch* by asking her to read the preceding sentence, which is ' "My foot itches,' Annie said." She does so easily. "What do you do when your foot itches?" I ask her. "Scratch it," she says—which is exactly what Nate the Great tells Annie to do.

Jacqueline is typical of developing readers who have enough strategies to read well but who lack the confidence, practice, and know-how to put everything together. Once she could self-monitor her reading and integrate all her strategies—which took a few months of lessons like the preceding one and lots of guided practice—she was on her way to becoming an independent reader. Neal Robinson, her teacher, commented, "It was a big turning point for her. She knew phonics but wasn't thinking about what makes sense. Once she started doing that, she took off as a reader." Because self-monitoring and self-correcting are critical skills for becoming a reader, we need to teach these right from the start.

Use Authentic Literature

I am invited to observe Barbara Speer's group of third graders, all of whom have learning disabilities. These are students who were still reading poorly at the end of second grade in spite of excellent instruction in an inclusion model. To provide the intensive reading instruction these four students needed, Barbara—a highly skilled teacher of children with learning disabilities—had decided a "pull-out" model was necessary. After forty minutes of daily instruction each day since September, they are reading fluently and with understanding.

The day I observe, in early May, they are reading *Trumpet of the Swan* by E. B. White. Barb is thrilled at their progress, and I too am very impressed. Barbara has just had them read aloud, taking on the parts of the characters, as in Readers Theatre. The text that is not conversation is read by a "narrator." To do this activity well, the students must understand "who's talking" and be able to follow the quotation marks. Not only are they reading aloud fluently, they are also having a lively dialogue about the story.

Barbara likes the pull-out model because it has allowed her to go at a slower pace. Last year she thought the pace was too fast for these kids. We both agree that inclusion can be very helpful, but for the most severely low-achieving students, pull-outs can be advantageous. In grade four, these readers will be ready to be mainstreamed because of their current level of reading achievement.

I wonder aloud if Barb has relied on other strategies besides phonics to get these students to their current reading level. She invites me to interview the four students—Jessica, Taylor, Orlandis, and Dwayne. I begin by praising the students' reading fluency and expression and the level of their conversation about the book. I tell them that I am impressed with how well they read and ask them what they are reading independently. Several have read *The War with Grandpa* by Robert Kimmel Smith. They tell me that they were reading beginning chapter book series like *Cam Jansen* by David Adler and *Horrible Harry* by Suzy Klien at the beginning of the year.

I ask them, "What strategies do you use when you're reading and you come to a hard word?" Here are their responses, in their own words:

• ***Tapping out***   "If you're at a hard word, like *wonderful,* you tap out the syllables with your finger. Or you pound it out with your fist while saying the word. Then, you blend the parts together."

• ***Blanking out the word***   "You cover the word, read on to the period, and think of what the word means. Then try to sound out the word. Like, I read 'speaking out' when the book said 'sneaking up.' I used the meaning to self-correct."

• ***Splitting the word apart***   "You take off the suffix or prefix. Put a line between the consonants, or use your finger to break the word into parts. Say the part you know. For example in *amputate,* we know "am" and "tate." [Barb had divided this word on the board—am/pu/tate.]

• ***Inserting a word that makes sense***   "You put in a word that fits the meaning when there is no one around to help you."

Barbara tells me that she now teaches phonics as the need arises, since the students already have the basics. I suggest that these students are ready to move into silent guided reading, and Barbara agrees. We do not want them focused at the word level.

Since students with learning disabilities and students who struggle as readers are part of every classroom, we must be informed about how best to teach them. (See "Selected Reading-Writing Strategies for L.D. and Other At-Risk Students" in *Invitations*, pages 390–402, or reprinted in Weaver 1998, pages 377–393. See also other resources in The Blue Pages.)

Promote Fluency

It is no secret that our struggling readers frequently stumble over their words when reading aloud and usually lack fluency. Fluency refers to reading easily and smoothly, and with expression when reading aloud. When students read fluently, aloud or silently, the reading appears automatic and effortless. Most fluent readers also read with better comprehension. However, we all have experience with the reader who can decode all the words in a text easily but who fails to comprehend the text's meaning.

It is important to remember that reading out loud is a performance. Some children stumble over words while reading aloud simply because they feel self-conscious about reading in front of others. Therefore, before we jump to conclusions about their reading ability, we must listen carefully to their miscues and engage them in a careful retelling. If their miscues and retelling reveal strong comprehension, their lack of fluency may have more to do with shyness and a lack of confidence about "performing" than a true indication of a reading difficulty.

A curriculum-based assessment coordinated by Bonnie Jasiunus, one of our school psychologists, formally evaluated one hundred of our second graders for fluency in oral reading. Teachers noted that the most fluent readers were also the best comprehenders. Without exception, our poorest-functioning readers also had the lowest fluency scores. Since fluency is usually a good marker of the successful reader, we need to make fluency a goal for all readers.

Poor readers read with less fluency for a variety of reasons. It is possible that they

- May not have been read to at home
- Have fewer opportunities to read in context
- Find the text too difficult
- Have fewer opportunities to read silently
- Focus too much on accuracy
- Have received instruction overfocused on words, sounds, and letters (Tancock 1994, 135)

There are many techniques (all of which are discussed in this text) that teachers can use to help students improve fluency. These include

- *__Repeated reading__*   Rereading of predictable texts, easy books, and familiar books is a powerful tool to improve fluency. So is Readers Theatre (page 74), which can also include puppet shows and drama. Additionally, shared reading of favorite poems, big books, and stories (pages 35–36), partner reading, and shared writing are all activities that utilize repeated reading.

- *__Modeled reading__*   This includes shared reading, reading aloud (by teacher or fluent reader), choral reading, cross-age reading, listening to a tape, echo reading (where the child follows the teacher's voice), oral cloze (see page 130).

- *__Retellings__*   (See page 595.)

- *__Guided practice__*   This could include reading with a partner who provides feedback or tape recording as one reads, listening to the tape, and then retaping.

The Power of Repeated Reading

In "Five Successful Reading Programs for At-Risk Students," an article by John Pikulski (1994), I was struck by the fact that the one strategy that all the cited programs had in common was repeated reading. There is no doubt that being familiar with a text makes it easier to read. That's one of the reasons series fiction works so well for struggling readers. So many of the elements are known—characters, how the story works, predictable format, typical vocabulary.

I am convinced that repeated reading of familiar texts caused a breakthrough for two of my students—Lonnie, a third grader, and Ashley, a second grader. Lonnie was in constant motion, had great difficulty settling down to work, and experienced continuing frustration learning to read. Early in the school year, I suggested to his teacher, Danny Young, that he monitor Lonnie's nightly reading by checking him daily and teaching him the strategies he needed to read independently.

In October, Lonnie selected the book *Freckle Juice* by Judy Blume. When I heard him read from the text aloud, we both agreed that the book was too hard for him, but Lonnie insisted that he wanted to stick with it, and he did. In December he told me that he had read *Freckle Juice* "about thirty times." Through his persistence in repeated readings of the text, he had become a fluent reader of the book, and this was the breakthrough that convinced him he was a reader. After that success he became an avid reader who often told others, "My reading is better because I read and write all the time."

Just as dramatic a breakthrough was experienced by Ashley, whose teacher Elaine Weiner and I worried about a lot. All the other students I was working with in reading were coming along well, but Ashley was struggling mightily. In fact, after much discussion, we had recommended she be evaluated for learning disabilities, and Elaine had called her mother with our concerns. Ashley's writing was illegible—she was often unable to decipher it—and she could not hear vowel sounds correctly. But in mid-January, something happened that amazed and delighted us. I had begun *The Story of Martin Luther King Day* with the group, and on the second day of reading, Ashley totally surprised me by fluently reading a page I would have thought too difficult for her.

I then made one major change as her reading teacher; I did not interrupt her miscues as long as the meaning was basically intact. In the past, I interrupted her often, trying to get Ashley to focus less on phonics and more on meaning. Whenever she got bogged down, she resorted to word-by-word reading and would forget to think about sense, but now she was reading for meaning and maintaining the flow.

What had happened? In mid-December, she had signed out *A New Dress for Maya* as her WEB (independent reading) book, after we had completed reading it in group. She loved the story, and I encouraged her to keep the book and continue reading it for fluency. She kept it for three weeks, and each day she proudly showed me more pages she could read easily. For the first time, I saw her using strategies on her own. For example, she independently figured out the word *called* by breaking the word down to "all," then adding "c" and "ed." She was able to read the whole word without prompting, a first for her. She reread a page twice, at my suggestion, and I asked her, "What do you notice about your second reading?" She said, "My first reading was like a rough draft." She kept her next WEB book, *I Wish I Was Sick Too,* for many days, telling me, "I still want to work on it." After she was able to read it pretty well, she would sign it out again, along with a new book.

I was so flabbergasted by the progress Ashley had made, literally overnight, that I asked her, "Ashley, how do you account for your great leap in reading?" She confidently told me, "I get home and read the book; then I read it again. I read it once more before I go to bed. I get up early so I can read it again before school. Then when you ask me to read, I read it real well."

Ashley and Lonnie taught me that repeated reading of familiar books is one of the most powerful strategies for helping struggling readers become successful readers. Within the comfortable territory of a well-known text, developing readers can practice multiple strategies and experience the success of reading with growing fluency and comprehension.

Incorporating Oral Cloze

A technique that works well with all readers—and particularly with struggling readers—is oral cloze, a form of assisted reading that can be used across the curriculum. Using this method, the teacher reads aloud (with students following the text visually) and periodically pauses, a signal for students to say the upcoming word aloud.

Oral cloze avoids word-bound reading, the focus of which is "getting the words" right. The technique helps students focus immediately on meaning by hearing whole parts of text read fluently. Another advantage of oral cloze is that the procedure helps the group stay focused. Since the story is read at the pace at which it was intended, those tracking the text visually typically remain engaged.

Sometimes a book is just slightly out of reach for students. With a thorough introduction and lots of beginning support, oral cloze can be a useful technique for helping students get the gist of a story before expecting them to read silently on their own. For some students, having the beginning framework of the story in their heads enables them to then problem solve the rest of the text more effectively.

I use this strategy often, especially when part of a text is too difficult and I want to get through pages quickly and to leave more time for discussion and follow-up reading. I do not have a formula for when and where to stop. Most often, I pause every few paragraphs, and at the end of a sentence when there is a word I expect students to be able to read or figure out. First-grade teacher Elisabeth Tuttle comments, "I do this with my young readers using big books. I take Post-it notes and cover several words throughout the text. It is a powerful lesson showing how context and surrounding words can give you clues to the unknown words."

TEACHING FOR STRATEGIES

Strategies are the thinking, problem-solving mental processes that the learner deliberately initiates, incorporates, and applies to construct meaning. Because we cannot see children's thinking and reasoning, we infer it by closely observing reading behaviors. While we teach for specific strategies and demonstrate how to integrate multiple strategies, good readers also employ their own "in the head" strategies as they read.

When teaching for strategies, we build on the child's existing foundation of what he knows and show how him how to connect that knowledge to new situations. We explicitly demonstrate how to use specific strategies in order to move meaningful text reading forward. While traditional skill instruction relies on isolated drill and practice leading to automaticity, strategic instruction goes much further. Students are shown how to integrate skills with strategies. Such integration requires planning, reasoning, and coordination on the part of the learner—all of which must be explicitly demonstrated (and often repeated again and again) by the knowledgeable teacher. As noted reading researcher Marie Clay (1998) writes,

> Learner-centered instruction is less about interest and motivation than it is about starting where the learner already is and helping that learner to move toward a new degree of control over novel tasks, teaching so that learners are successful and able to say, "I am in control of this." From there they go on to extend their own learning. (3–4)

Low-achieving readers must receive strategic instruction if they are to learn to read with understanding and independence. Isolated skills instruction often does not transfer well to the reading of texts. Yet, to teach reading strategically, there is no single program to follow. You must be responsive and responsible to students' needs. One research study found:

> Teachers . . . began succeeding only when they stopped looking for prescriptions to follow and began relying on their own judgment to help low achievers develop a conceptual model of what it means to be strategic. (Duffy 1993, 244)

Still, in our district, many teachers felt frustrated not knowing what skills and strategies to teach and when to teach them. We worked for months in one of our language arts support groups, at grade levels and across grade levels, identifying the skills and strategies we believed we should be teaching. We found the progression of word recognition and reading skills listed in Don Holdaway's *Independence in Reading* (1980, 157–204) a helpful starting point.

Promoting Strategic Behavior

It is very important to have students verbalize the strategic work they do. By asking questions about their reading strategies, by attempting to make their thinking visible, and by thinking aloud and demonstrating for them, we are encouraging them to think strategically in future reading situations. We are also modeling reading as an inquiry process in which the reader self-questions, monitors, reflects, and revises in order to make sense of text.

Ask questions such as the following to confirm and promote strategic reading behaviors. Until the language, or similar scaffolded language, is automatic to you, you may want to keep a list of questions in front of you.

• ***What did you do to figure that out? Or, Tell me what you just did***.   When students have difficulty responding to this question, I will say something like, "I saw you do [or I think you may have done] such and such (look at the picture, reread the sentence, run your finger under the word)." Verbalizing strategies that you think readers may have employed encourages future strategic behavior.

• *What did you do that worked?* (confirms and reinforces successful strategic behavior so that it will reoccur)

• *What do you know about that word? Do you see a chunk you know?* (makes the link from known to unknown)

• *What else can you try?* (encourages students to think independently and use what they know)

• *How did you know that?* (makes thinking visible; encourages students to repeat successful behavior on subsequent readings)

• *What can you do when it doesn't make sense?* (reminds the reader that reading is about getting meaning)

• *What do you already know about what you've read that would make sense there?* (lets the reader know that he has some tools to figure it out)

• *Where does it say that?* (makes the reader check the text to confirm or invalidate his response)

Word-Solving Strategies

Strategies are employed at the word-solving as well as text-solving level. Word-solving strategies, however, are always part of understanding the complete text and are intended to carry over to new texts. At times, utilizing phonics skills may be enough to move on, especially if the word and its meaning are familiar to the reader. At other times, the reader may need to combine phonics with grammar, surrounding context, visuals, and/or what is already known about the story or content.

Encourage multiple strategies for word recognition. Too often we only give phonics cues, such as, "What does it start with?" "Look at the ending." We also need to refer to the context and say "Look at the picture." "What makes sense? "What would sound right?" "Say the sound of the first letter, read on to the end of the sentence and come back to it. Try that again now."

The following are some word analysis strategies to teach along with phonics.

• <u>*Self-monitor and self-correct*</u>. The word has to make sense in the context. When it does not, students need to employ other "fix up" strategies, such as rereading, trying a word again, reading on and returning to the trouble spot, using prior knowledge, making sure it "sounds right." Be sure to allow enough wait time (up to about ten seconds) for the student to do the work, as careful monitoring often leads to self-correction.

• <u>*Use picture cues*</u>. Picture cues are often ignored as a strategy. Yet, notice how ignoring picture cues affected meaning in the following vignette.

A group of second graders are reading *Play Ball, Amelia Bedelia* by Peggy Parish (New York: Harper and Row, 1972), part of a great "I Can Read" series for focusing on multiple meanings. We review the silly things Amelia Bedelia does while playing baseball. We use the picture, use meaning, talk about what humor is (a new word for the group). I ask students to read pages 22–23 of the text silently. On these pages, Amelia

Bedelia is told to "tag Jack before he gets to second base." Her resulting action is conveyed by the picture, but the kids miss it because they are looking only at the words. After our discussion, I ask them, "What will you do to be sure you understand when you read?" Students now say, "Use the pictures and reread."

• ***Apply known to unknown***. Teach students how to apply rimes they know in one word to a new word. For struggling readers, mnemonic devices (page 438) and key words are useful. For example, to recall "ar," students visualize—"call up"—a picture of a "car" with the word written inside. While in guided reading group, it is helpful to have a small wipe-off board or chalk board to use when a child comes to a word he can't figure out. Write down the rime they know, and then turn back to the text to figure out the new word. (See example, page 424.)

• ***Cross-check information***. Teach students to interactively use phonics, grammar, pictures, textual meaning, and known information to self-check an attempted word.

Prompts to Encourage Word Solving

Our goal is for students to read strategically without teacher prompting. However, until students are independent, teacher prompts for word solving, such as the following, can be helpful:

• ***Sound it out.*** (Use for a word that is easily decodable so that student can continue on quickly with text.)

• ***Start that word again. Say the beginning sound and read the rest of the sentence.*** (This prompt tells student that he may be able to figure out the word if he combines the beginning sound with meaning.)

• ***I will start the word for you to help you figure it out.*** (The student has been unable to begin a word the teacher believes he knows or can figure out. The teacher gives the first sound of the problematic word and continues reading till the end of the sentence. The teacher is demonstrating how to combine meaning with structure. The student is then encouraged to try the word again.)

• ***Read the word without the vowel.*** (This statement lets student know that he can figure out a word by just using the beginning and ending consonant sounds and thinking about the word in context. He is able to keep going even if he can't decode all the parts.)

• ***Here's a word you already know.*** (This guides the student to make a connection to a new, unknown word and reinforces that what is known can be applied to new contexts.)

• ***Try reading that again.*** (This statement encourages students to reread, a valuable strategy for recapturing meaning.)

• ***The word is . . .*** (Provide student with the word only as a last resort—avoids frustration when word is beyond student's knowledge, or she has already made several attempts at solving it.)

Remember to give students sufficient time to respond to your suggestions. Our silence (about ten to fifteen seconds) lets students know we expect them to initiate the problem solving process.

After students have made problem-solving attempts, teacher comments such as the following encourage independent reading work:

- "I liked the way you tried to help yourself."
- "I noticed you tried . . . when you had trouble. Good for you. That's what good readers do."
- "You worked out the hard part. I saw you checking . . ."

For specific word work and word study, see Chapter 10, "Spelling and Word Study in the Reading-Writing Classroom" pages 417–432.

Text-Solving Strategies

When I go into classrooms and work with students, I read and think aloud. I verbalize strategies I am using and explicitly show and tell what I am doing to make sense of the text (see pages 457–458). My experience has been that students are overfocused at the word-solving level. (See page 452 for a typical fourth grader's list of what good readers do and page 454 for additions to the list after I have demonstrated my own strategic reading process.) Note "Strategies for Understanding When You Read" from a class that has been working on understanding strategic reading. (See Appendix D-2.)

While we teachers spend lots of time in prereading and postreading activities, we often fail to give adequate attention to what happens while students read. My reading of *Mosaic of Thought: Teaching Comprehension in a Reader's Workshop* (Keene and Zimmermann 1997) made me more aware that we do not really teach students how to comprehend *as they read*. Most of us assign reading and check for comprehension afterward. I am as guilty of this as the next teacher.

Teaching for understanding must become a major focus during a child's reading process. One of the best ways to determine important text-solving strategies and how to teach them is to examine our own processes while reading various texts.

Valuing Our Own Text-Solving Strategies

At one of our language arts support meetings, I take the group through a guided reading process, believing that in order to understand and teach any particular literacy process, it is important that we teachers go through it ourselves. This occurs after a fourth-grade teacher breaks the silence about reading instruction by saying, "I don't know what guided reading is or how to teach it."

In picking a text for this activity, I try to select a high-interest piece that will be on the teachers' instructional and interest level. I want a reading selection that will provide a little challenge while being both engaging and useful to teachers. I choose one page from the beginning of "Thirty Years of Research . . . : The Adequacy and Use of a Research Summary" (Allington and Woodside-Jiron 1997). This piece contains valuable information about what is happening in the field of education and how research can be misused.

I begin with a brief introduction and supply the context of the piece, explaining that an acronym used in the text, NICHD, stands for National Institute of Child Health and Development. We form small groups. I serve as facilitator for one and ask for volunteer facilitators to keep the other four groups on task. I then pass out the article and give teachers the following instructions:

1. Read silently (ten minutes). Write down any questions you have—words or concepts you don't understand. Write a one-sentence summary or inference.
2. With the facilitator, clarify questions, discuss the article, and note the reading strategies you used (seven minutes).

After each group has talked about what they read and helped each other through their questions, we come together as a whole group again. I ask participants what strategies they used when reading. These are the teachers' responses:

- Read the last paragraph first
- Went back and reread directions
- Skimmed first to "get the gist," then reread
- Underlined important parts
- Skipped a part and read on
- Omitted a difficult word
- Substituted a word
- Read slowly
- Predicted, revised predictions
- Connected to known information
- Reread difficult parts and important parts
- Bulleted sections
- Skimmed, circled important information
- Read in chunks, scanned quickly and reread
- Jotted down notes in margin
- Paraphrased on paper
- Read aloud under my breath
- Talked to myself and paraphrased aloud
- Used context and connected to something I knew

We acknowledge among ourselves that, although the research jargon has posed some difficulties for readers, it is not necessary for us to know all of the words in order to get the text's meaning. One teacher explains that she was able to work out the meaning of one unfamiliar word, *pseudoword*, by breaking it into its parts. Her knowledge of "pseudo" in other contexts aided her in supplying a definition here. Similarly, one reader was able to gain meaning for an unfamiliar concept, "add-on instruction," by looking at the text's context. We talk about the importance of practice in reading a particular genre. Teachers who were unaccustomed to reading research found the selection more difficult to read than those who read research articles often.

We also note the importance of format and interest on engagement. The page I gave them to read had small print. Because I am fascinated by the subject matter, I am undeterred. However, several teachers who are not especially interested in research literally stop reading because of the print size. That surprises me and reminds me, once again, how important interest and format are. English teacher Holly Burgess notes that high school students react similarly: "For many years, the 'classics' were usually tiny print books—which high achievers are willing to put up with but less capable readers stop on page 1!"

We also talk about only preteaching the vocabulary that readers will not be able to figure out on their own and that they must have for text understanding. I comment that nobody said they "sounded out words." Decoding was automatic.

I bring up the social/emotional nature of the experience by asking teachers, "How would you have felt if I asked you to read the piece aloud?" Several participants said that they had thought that I might and that they had felt "major panic" over the possibility. One teacher spoke of living in dread of memories of Jewish Passover seders in her family in which she was expected to read aloud. We talk about the fact that it was easier for them to risk in a small group rather than in front of the whole class. Yet several participants admit that even in a small group, feelings of inadequacy can be acute: some teachers bravely acknowledge that they didn't write down some questions they had or words they were unsure of out of fear of not measuring up.

Several teachers note discomforting feelings stemming from comparing themselves with their peers. One teacher notes, "I was aware of others finishing the piece before I did. That made me feel bad. I didn't want to be the last one to finish, or not get done on time."

Another teacher confesses, "I was self-conscious about reading some of the article under my breath. When text is difficult, I have to talk to myself and paraphrase aloud to understand it. I felt anxiety because I didn't want to disturb anyone in their reading, and also because everyone around me seemed to be having an easier time reading the piece." One teacher admits that she had gotten stuck on one part of the text and simply stopped reading.

Many teachers say that the experience has helped sensitize them to the problems that students have in reading unfamiliar material, and that they can see the need for small group work for maximizing participation and instruction in reading. One comments, "I've never understood how to teach my kids when to reread. Focusing on how I used rereading to understand will help me in my future teaching." We agree as a group that our natural focus on meaning and the strategies we ourselves employed are what we need to demonstrate and teach to our students. Use the strategies generated above, along with your own, to teach for understanding *while* reading text.

Knowing When We Understand

Another strategic way to help students read thoughtfully is to get them focused on their own thinking as they read. "Proficient readers know what and when they are comprehending and when they are not comprehending" (Keene and Zimmermann 1997, 22, citing Duffy et al. 1987).

I recently read an article in which the author interviewed several college students, asking them "how they knew when they comprehended what they read" (Hanseen 1998, 357).

This question kept going through my mind, because it was not a question I had previously asked myself or my students. How do we and our students *know* when we understand? Thinking about my own reading, I decided that I know I understand when:

- I can retell the text orally or in writing so that another person can understand what I've read.
- I am able to take clear notes that demonstrate my insights and learnings.
- I am able to use my notes (a list of a book's characters, for example, and something important about them) to help me as I read.
- I can summarize what I've read.
- I can connect or relate what I'm reading to something I know or have read.
- I can use what I've read to think about other contexts.
- I am aware of gaps in my understanding.
- I recognize connections to other texts.
- I reconsider and am open to other meanings.
- I am aware of the characteristics of the genre and use them to help me understand. (For example, when reading the newspaper, I depend on the lead sentence and first paragraph to give me the main idea.)
- I reread when something is unclear.
- I seek to converse with others to clear up ambiguities.
- I evaluate the work.
- I consider comments of other readers.
- I stick with the text even when it is difficult.
- I am aware of my own responses, thoughts, and feelings as I read.

Take time to examine your own criteria for understanding. Share your findings with your students, and begin to explore ways to make them more aware of thinking about their own processes for understanding.

Demonstrate a wide range of strategies, such as thinking and problem solving aloud as you read and write aloud, shared reading, shared writing, repeated reading, and reciprocal teaching (see below). Begin to have students read with these questions in mind:

- What will I do to be sure I understand?
- How will I know when I have understood?

Reciprocal Teaching

Reciprocal teaching is interactive, scaffolded instruction in which the teacher (or peer, older student, or parent) leads a group of students as they dialogue their way through a text to understand it. As they read together, group members monitor their understanding by stopping at regular intervals to ask questions, summarize, predict, and clarify. According to Annemarie Sullivan Palincsar (1986), "Reciprocal teaching is best represented as a dialogue between teachers and students in which participants take turns assuming the role of teacher" (77).

The dialoging technique was developed by Palincsar and Ann L. Brown and found to be successful for improving understanding with students of all ages, including first graders responding to text read aloud. The initial research was conducted with middle school students "who were adequate decoders but poor comprehenders" (Palinscar 1986, 76). This terrific technique has also been found to be instrumental for increasing reading achievement of low-performing students in an urban school district as measured by standardized tests (Carter 1997).

As explained by Palincsar and Brown, students are taught each of the following strategies to promote interaction and improve understanding of text (Palinscar 1986, 77):

• ***Generating a question***   Students identify key information in the text, frame that information in the form of a question, and self-test for understanding and recall.

• ***Clarifying***   Students note when they have experienced a failure in comprehension, identify the source of that breakdown, and take appropriate steps (e.g., rereading, reading ahead, or asking for assistance) to restore meaning.

• ***Predicting***   Students predict what will happen in the text, a strategy that provides the opportunity for them to activate relevant background knowledge or schemata.

• ***Summarizing***   Summarizing the text focuses attention on integrating information across sentences, paragraphs, and pages of text.

To teach students the procedure, I first explain and repeatedly demonstrate reciprocal teaching by thinking aloud and stopping to ask questions, summarize, predict, and clarify. Then, I have students form small, heterogeneous groups to try the procedure. I format a bookmark that highlights the components of reciprocal teaching to remind students to use these strategies whenever they read. As I work guiding one group, the others work independently, and a designated scribe keeps track of their group process on a worksheet (see Figure 4-7). Afterward, we do a whole-class evaluation, similar to what we do after literature conversations (see pages 198–199).

What follows is the beginning of a reciprocal teaching lesson in a third-grade class. I start the lesson by having the class open to the first chapter in *The Comeback Dog* by Jane Resh Thomas, one of our third-grade anchor books. I tell the students that I will be stopping occasionally and thinking aloud to let them in on my mental process as I read. I let them know that after my demonstration, I expect them to do the same thing in their small groups.

We first go over the four strategies that proficient readers use as they read (see above list). *Clarify* is a new word for them. I ask them what they do when they are reading and they come to a word they don't recognize or are confused by. They respond, "sound it out" and "skip the word or part, read ahead and come back to it." As they follow along in their texts, they see me stop occasionally to clarify something I've read aloud. The strategies I use are to "reread" and "put in a word that makes sense." Rereading is the strategy I use the most in my independent reading, and I tell that to the students. I emphasize that authors often "tell" us what a word means by what they say in the surrounding context.

After I have demonstrated my "in the head" thinking, I review again that they are to take turns reading in their small groups and support each other as readers. They are to stop periodically as I did and ask questions, predict, clarify, and summarize. (For younger students who are first attempting reciprocal teaching, you may want to suggest specific

*Figure 4–7　A group of intermediate students using reciprocal teaching
to read a newspaper article. (See pages 457–458 for reading a newspaper.)*

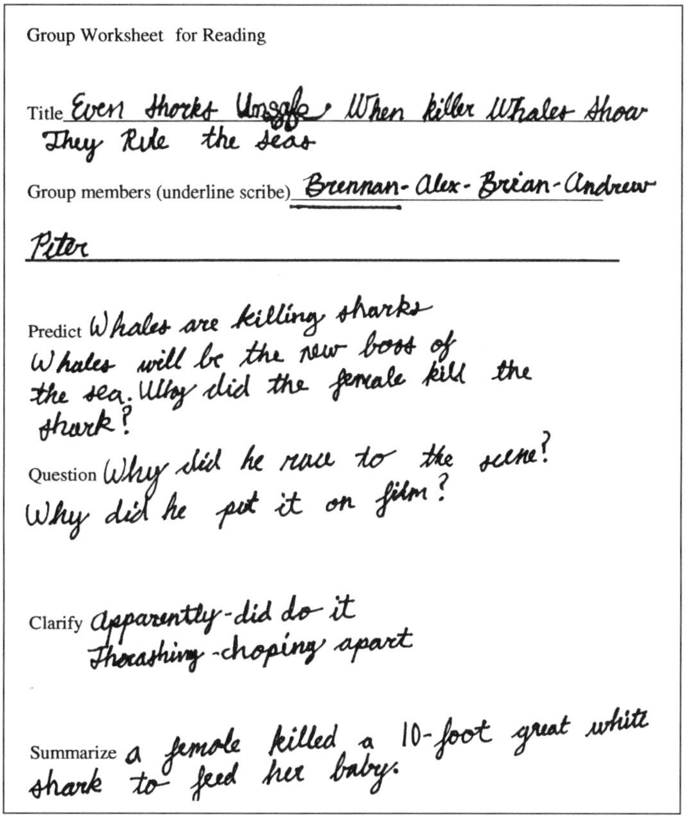

Group Worksheet for Reading

Title *Even sharks Unsafe, When killer Whales shoar*
They Rule the seas

Group members (underline scribe) *Brennan- Alex- Brian-Andrew*

Peter

Predict *Whales are killing sharks
Whales will be the new boss of
the sea. Why did the female kill the
shark?*

Question *Why did he race to the scene?
Why did he put it on film?*

Clarify *apparently- did do it
Thrashing -choping apart*

Summarize *a female killed a 10-foot great white
shark to feed her baby.*

stopping points.) I remind students that the order of these strategies is not significant. We review what *clarify* means again, and I list relevant strategies on the chalk board:

- Reread.
- Put in a word or words that make sense.
- Sound it out.
- Skip a word or part, read ahead, and come back to the trouble spot.
- Ask a peer for help.

I give them several additional pages to read. I let them know that every member of the group is expected to be able to predict, summarize, ask questions, and clarify when we come back together as a whole class. That is, no matter who I might call in the group after the reading, any member should be able to give me a summary or tell me what questions were raised in their group. I make it clear that this is a collaborative activity and that they are to help each other. Our students are used to working together. They are already seated in groups of four that are balanced by gender, race, and achievement.

Since our focus is on comprehension, I do not want students who struggle with longer words to get bogged down. For now, students in each group are to help their peers figure out words or tell them the words. If a struggling reader chooses not to take a turn reading aloud, that is fine, as long as she follows the text with her eyes and listens while a group member reads. At another time, we will work on "how to figure out hard words," either through small group work or one-on-one conferences.

Second-grade teacher Bev Sullivan tells me two weeks after we have shown her students the reciprocal teaching procedure that she notices a change in kids' understanding. She is having them partner read and ask questions and clear up confusions as they read together (assigned reading after guided reading group). They are doing it successfully and are then better able to talk about the story when Bev meets with them in guided reading group.

It seems to take several months of practice (about twenty sessions) for students to get really good at this process, but once they've got the hang of it, their application of it to independent reading is evident and lasting. I sometimes use reciprocal teaching for reading in the content areas or for the first reading of a piece of literature that we will be discussing in literature conversation groups (see pages 455–456). In this way, I can be sure that everyone—even the struggling readers—will be able to gain an understanding of what the text is about.

GUIDED READING

Guided reading is any reading instruction in which the teacher guides one or more students through any aspect of the reading process: choosing books, making sense of text, decoding and defining words, reading fluently, and so on. In guided reading, the teacher builds on what students know, provides reinforcement as well as some challenge, and supports and demonstrates strategies to help the reader move forward. Guided reading begins the day students walk into our classrooms, and we show them how reading works—through reading aloud (which may include thinking aloud and interactive discussion), shared reading (in which strategies are shared, taught, and sometimes "discovered"), reading conferences, and planned and "teachable moments" in response to students' needs and interests. In all cases, through interactive instruction, the child is supported to problem solve and read for meaning. Guided reading can take place in any curriculum area.

Traditionally, guided reading has referred to small group reading with the teacher scaffolding and instructing students in problem solving, applying strategies and skills, and whatever else is necessary to promote students' understanding. While such small-group work is at the heart of guided reading, it must not be seen as an end in itself. Too often I hear comments such as "We haven't started teaching reading yet because we don't have our guided reading groups in place," or "We can't begin teaching reading until we level our books for small-group guided reading." Small-group guided reading, as powerful a tool as it is, must be understood as but one part of a comprehensive literacy program (as described in Chapter 2).

Guided Reading in Kindergarten

Most teachers I know find it problematic, for reasons of classroom management, to conduct small-group guided reading in kindergarten, preferring to assess students one-on-

one as they move about the class. My feeling is that if you can manage small groups in kindergarten, fine. If not, kids will do just as well without groups, as long as there are lots of opportunities, both guided and independent, to interact with print throughout the day. (See story on page 105–106.)

Kindergarten teacher Rob Fellinger decides to try guided reading about mid-year since he has an aide part of the day. We talk together about the importance of book selection and focusing on one or two main teaching points. For example, he might model one-to-one matching, in which the reader crisply points to each word that is verbalized, or he might teach kids how to figure out words by matching beginning consonants with picture cues. Every afternoon, during free-choice reading time, Rob meets with one group or observes partners working together.

At the end of the school year, Rob noted great improvement in his lowest-achieving readers. Several of his students who entered school already reading now enjoyed conversing about chapter books such as *The Littles,* and some of these conversations successfully took place without the teacher present once the students understood what it meant to talk about a book.

Organizing for Guided Reading

Every time that we are with children is an opportunity to teach. If we keep in mind that teaching means showing how something is done, instructing, appropriately challenging, and enabling students to move forward, we will use our small-group time wisely. Make the time together count. Choose a book that enables you to best teach the students you are working with. Then, make sure you reinforce strategies for word solving and/or text solving each time you meet with them. Continue to ask yourself:

- What am I teaching?
- Have I chosen an appropriate book?
- Is this time being well spent?
- Am I teaching for understanding?
- How am I fostering independence?

I believe small group guided reading is a necessity for teaching all aspects of reading, not just individual reading strategies but group processes for discussing, enjoying, understanding, and benefiting from the social nature of learning. How, and how often, such small groups take place depends on many variables—time allotted for reading, students' needs and interests, teacher know-how, and personal preferences. For most teachers, I recommend small-group guided reading as the mainstay of the instructional reading program.

Individualized Guided Reading

A few teachers I know are so skilled as teachers of reading, so familiar with choosing and using literature, and such good assessors and classroom managers that they can successfully carry out an individualized guided reading program and meet the needs of all students every day. That is, most teaching of reading is one-on-one with most small group work connected to literature conversations once students are readers. But these teachers are not typical.

Second-grade teacher Loretta Martin, who is also a cherished friend and colleague, is one such teacher. She has been teaching for over twenty-five years. Through extensive professional reading, attending conferences, dialoguing with colleagues, and keen observations and evaluations of her students, she makes note of what she wants and needs to change in her teaching. As she incorporates new strategies and materials, she is constantly evaluating and modifying her practice.

Loretta meets with every student every day during the one hour (at least) of class time that is set aside for reading. Most of these meetings are brief "check-ins," intended "to help a student maintain interest and focus in order to continue reading" (Allen and Gonzalez 1998, 66). Most often, she moves to where the student is sitting in the classroom and checks the student on the book she is reading (either independently or in a guided reading group). Loretta wants to be sure that the student has a book she can both read and understand. Her students know that they must be able to read the whole book fluently (not just to have memorized it). If the student is ready, she guides him in choosing an appropriate new selection. She may also take a minute or two to teach or reinforce needed strategies "on the run," which is part of her daily "conversations" with her students.

Several conferences with students will be longer and more in-depth, such as those described on pages 115–121. During these conferences, she will take running records or modified running records, make anecdotal notes about what she observes, and make one or two major teaching points to support the reader. She might also devise future minilessons for whole-class instruction, from the needs that arise from her conferences with kids.

Small-group guided reading does occur in Loretta's class, but not every day. It is mostly used to support her developing readers—to help them firm up strategies so that they can read independently. (Struggling readers also receive additional support from tutors and L.D. resource personnel.) Small groups also meet in literature conversations once students are reading well independently. (See Chapter 5 for guidelines.)

Guided Reading Groups: What to Teach

Focus in guided reading is always on meaning, even when individual skills and strategies are being taught. The text, which is carefully selected and introduced, has just a little bit of a challenge so that students have the opportunity to problem solve and apply strategies with minimal support from the teacher. Teachers guide students during reading as well as before and after reading.

Once students can read well independently (often by the spring of first grade), most reading in group is done silently with the teacher observing, monitoring, assessing, and teaching according to demonstrated needs. Oral reading is used to promote fluency, and for enjoyment and assessment purposes. "Round robin reading," when students spend most of group time taking turns reading aloud, does not occur. (See Opitz and Rasinski 1998, for information on when and how oral reading is effective and appropriate.)

Teachers of students above grades two and three often ask what a guided reading group looks like for older readers. Once kids are reading well, guided reading groups typ-

Photo 4–1 A small guided reading group in second grade with teacher Jennifer Shoda

ically focus on literature conversations, in-depth comprehension and analysis, and authors' craft.

The following examples are teaching focuses that can occur individually or in combination in a guided reading group. Again, reading for understanding underpins everything we do, and there is no formula for this teaching.

• ***Figuring out unknown words—decoding and vocabulary*** Students are guided to pronounce new words using multiple strategies: phonics ("sounding out"), structure (syntax), context (textual meaning; illustrations), rereading, and self-correcting. Determining the meaning of new words is accomplished by analyzing surrounding text, applying prior knowledge about topic, substituting synonyms, looking at the prefixes and suffixes as well as etymology of words, and consulting a dictionary.

• ***Understanding text*** Students are supported in their use of such strategies as:

- Activating prior knowledge
- Reciprocal teaching (predicting, asking questions, summarizing, clarifying, as explained on pages 137–140)
- Determining the most important ideas and information
- Creating mental and visual images
- Making inferences
- Retelling (see pages 595–598)
- Skimming and scanning

- Thinking aloud
- Reading nonfiction and other genres (see pages 448–461)
- Understanding "story" through story maps and graphic organizers
- Writing and sharing summaries and responses to text

See additional strategies listed on page 135.

- **_Responding to and/or interpreting text_** (See Chapters 5 and 11.) Students are encouraged to:

  - Analyze texts—story structure, literary elements.
  - Compare texts by theme.
  - Connect texts to life and other texts.
  - Use response logs.
  - Incorporate Readers Theatre.
  - Generate questions on "literary" level.
  - Conduct literature conversations with and without the teacher.
  - Study and compare authors and illustrators.
  - Recommend books (via written or oral book talks).

- **_Self-monitoring and self-evaluating_** Teacher scaffolding enables students to:

  - Choose books to read independently.
  - Apply skills and strategies independently.
  - Have successful conferences (teacher/student and with peers).
  - Maintain a reading log and/or reading record.
  - Know when understanding is taking place.
  - Seek help (self-help and/or outside assistance) when comprehension breaks down.

- **_Reading orally_** Many teachers ask, "How much oral reading is appropriate?" Most kids love to read orally. And reading aloud is a good way for teachers to check fluency and note if the reader self-corrects when something doesn't make sense. In general, though, I think we ask kids to read aloud too much. We always need to be asking ourselves, "What's the purpose of this oral reading?" It can be for pleasure, to determine if a text is at the appropriate level for a student, to work on fluency, or to focus on what an author has done particularly well, such as asking students to "Practice reading a passage where the author has described a character so you can picture him (or her)."

Grouping for Guided Reading

The debate about the best way to group students for guided reading continues. Teachers struggle with how many groups they can manage, how often they should be meeting with each group, and if the groups should be homogeneous, heterogeneous, or "flexible" (i.e., having frequently changing participants and purposes). There is no one best way. Look carefully at your program, as well as current research, to examine how you are grouping and dealing with students' needs, experiences, levels, and interests.

While size generally varies from three to eight members per group, most of us have found four to six members to be ideal. When working with struggling readers, any more than five in a group seems to be counterproductive. I would make sure that you meet with your low-achieving readers every day, and as often as you can for your other readers. Be sure that you use ongoing assessment (informal is fine) so that you can regroup children according to their development as readers.

Most teachers find that they can meet comfortably with three guided reading groups a day, which results in their meeting with most groups three times a week at a minimum. However, newer teachers need to give themselves permission to meet with one or two reading groups a day when getting started. With time, much practice, good pacing, and effective management techniques, meeting with three or even four groups a day becomes more realistic and commonplace.

In addition to guided reading time in small groups, one-on-one conferencing is also terrific when you can manage it. I recommend a quick, daily monitoring of independent reading for all students. Once students are reading fluently and for understanding in various genres, guided reading moves into literature conversations.

Another important point. I find, in general, that reading groups go on too long. You can do a lot of teaching in ten to fifteen minutes and then have kids "practice" what you've taught by having them read independently or with a partner. As well, shorter group time increases how many groups you can see each day and also makes management easier. With three or four guided reading groups that last approximately fifteen minutes each, students are not working independently for more than thirty to forty-five minutes.

The Importance of Heterogeneous Grouping

I believe all students should have opportunities to participate in heterogeneous groups. My beliefs about homogeneous and heterogeneous grouping in reading solidified this past year, especially in regard to struggling readers above grade two. I recently read an article in *The Elementary School Journal* that confirms what I already knew in my heart: students need and want to be in mixed-ability groups.

The article describes a study that examined student's perceptions of the makeup or composition of reading groups. More than five hundred third-, fourth-, and fifth-grade urban, mostly minority students, including some students with learning disabilities, participated. By an overwhelming majority, students preferred mixed-ability grouping to whole class, paired reading, or working alone. Students perceived that mixed-ability grouping is not only fairer but that students receive more help and make more progress. In other words, elementary students view working with a partner or small group as helpful only if a range of abilities is present. "Notably, no student expressed the view that mixed-ability groups are unfair to better readers" (Elbaum, Schumm, and Vaughn 1997, 487). The only exception was for nonreaders, who students perceived learn best in same-ability groups.

These findings are consistent with the massive amount of literature on the impact of ability grouping across the curriculum.

> On average, the achievement effect of ability grouping is quite small, equaling less than one-fifth of a standard deviation in student achievement. (Jaeger and Hattie 1995, 219)

After I read the former article, I rethought my own grouping practices. Little by little, I had been doing more and more ability grouping with struggling readers, especially in third and fourth grades. Based on the study, which clearly showed that only nonreaders needed to be in same-ability groups, I revised my practice. In the past, when upper-grade teachers would approach me for help with struggling readers, I would work with them as a homogeneous group in the classroom. Now, I do only mixed-ability grouping as long as the kids can read. (I use independent reading time or WEB [page 44] and reading conferences to teach the word-recognition strategies specific to each student.)

For example, when third-grade teacher Veronica Allen requested that I work with her struggling readers on how to figure out multisyllable words and difficult vocabulary, I worked with those readers in a mixed-ability group. I began by reading and thinking aloud using a news article on an overhead transparency, with the class following along on individual copies (see page 457). After the demonstration, when we broke up into mixed-ability groups to continue reading and problem solving independently, I said, "Anyone who wants to get good at figuring out hard words can meet with me up at the front table."

What I have found in issuing this invitation is that most of the kids who actually need the help willingly come forward. I always get a few high achievers who join the group because they want to get better at everything. And then I invite the one or two struggling readers who haven't voluntarily stepped forward. More often than not, however, such students join the group unprompted. Veronica Allen comments, "What was fascinating was seeing the kids who would never say 'I don't understand' in front of the whole class freely asking questions and volunteering a response in the small group. I was also surprised at some of the good readers who elected to be there and who also seemed to benefit from the lesson."

When I interviewed Veronica's third graders at the end of the year, I asked them what they thought about the way students were grouped. Their thoughts parallel the results of the study (Elbaum, Schumm, and Vaughn 1997). Every student says that mixed-ability grouping is better, or in their own words:

- The not-so-good readers can learn easier.
- The poor readers don't feel bad.
- If all the not-so-good readers are all together, it would be hard for them to learn because we learn from each other.
- With mixed groups, we can all help each other.

When Homogeneous Grouping Is Appropriate

While we teachers must always be sensitive to how we teach children, it's just common sense to group young, developing readers. You can't teach much in a group in which one student is working on one-to-one matching and another is reading simple chapter books. Outsiders ask, "Don't your students and parents complain about 'ability grouping?'" No, they don't, since this particular group time comprises such a small chunk of reading time. These guided reading groups in the early grades last approximately fifteen minutes, so almost the entire day is spent in flexible, dynamic groups in which students of varying abilities work collaboratively and learn from each other, sharing literary experiences. Students work with partners, small groups formed by interest, whole class as in shared reading and shared writing, independently, as well as individually with the teacher. Once students become readers, there are more and more opportunities for grouping according to interests. For example, once a big book is introduced, the teacher might invite a group of volunteers to enjoy the small copies with her.

For the most severe readers, one-on-one may be the only option to meet their instructional needs. Anthony was a first grader who was meeting with a group of three other struggling readers. However, he was working at his frustration level, and by spring he had made no substantial reading progress. When he moved to working one-on-one with his teacher using easy readers having about two words on each page, his excitement and engagement gave him his first reading success, and for the first time he asked, "Can I read these books some more?"

While I have long been comfortable grouping developing first- and second-grade readers with similar needs for guided reading—not just for word-attack skills but for teaching multiple strategies and reading for meaning—these students are not grouped arbitrarily. First, I take the time to carefully observe them, record observational data, and evaluate their strengths and needs.

A Pull-In Model in Second Grade

After working for four years as a Reading Recovery teacher, I worked for the five years in classrooms (in a "pull-in" or "push-in" model) teaching reading every day to low-achieving readers. Believing from experience that "pull-out" models did not work well except for the most severe nonreaders, I applied what I had learned as a Reading Recovery teacher to small-group, guided reading sessions. (See *Invitations*, pages 144–146.) Working in the classroom had the added benefit of allowing for natural collaboration, observing another teacher teach, and daily planning together "on the run."

I typically worked with students during their second reading period of the day, which took place early each afternoon while the classroom teacher was also teaching reading—either conferring individually with students as they were reading independently or meeting with a small guided reading group.

Even here, however, I tried to be sensitive to the grouping-by-needs that was taking place by serving as a resource for the whole class. I took several weeks to work with all students in reading and writing before I met with my targeted group for the first time. Then, although I had a thirty-minute time slot with these students, I usually used the first five to seven minutes to facilitate a whole-class shared reading of poetry (see page 36). As well, I extended an invitation to the entire class, asking anyone who would like to join our group to do so. So, in addition to "my students" (four to five), typically two other students would join us. Sometimes, one would be a student with learning disabilities. Often, it was one or two of the best readers in the class.

One year, the parents of a student named Stefan sought me out at an open house curriculum night. It turned out that their son talked about me and the reading group often at home, and they were puzzled about my role in the classroom. What amused and satisfied me was that Stefan, one of our brightest students, had not realized that the group he'd been joining so enthusiastically was actually the "slow achievers."

Guided Silent Reading: What Happens in a Group Lesson

The goal in guided reading is for students to gain enough strategies and confidence to read independently. Since most of the reading we do in the real world is silent, most of our reading instruction in guided reading relates to silent reading.

Once students are readers, that is, they can read some text independently with understanding, I move them into guided silent reading. Typically, such independence occurs for most students in the spring of first grade. Up to that point—in the context of reading for meaning—we have been focusing on oral reading, word-solving strategies, automatic word recognition, and fluency in our small guided reading groups.

As well, we continue to model reading strategies throughout the day in other reading and writing contexts such as reading and writing aloud and shared reading and writing. The early stages of small-group guided reading then provide assisted practice on the strategies we have already been demonstrating in small and large groups.

As a result of reading and discussing *Learning to Read in New Zealand* (Smith and Elley 1994) in one of our language arts support groups, it became clear to us that even though we had been using literature to teach reading for ten years, even the most skilled teachers still relied mostly on "round-robin" reading, in which students take turns reading aloud. As one teacher finally told me, "I always felt inadequate with round-robin reading. I think I knew I wasn't teaching anything." Several teachers began to move into guided silent reading as a direct result of our open discussion.

One of the major advantages of guided silent reading is that you can check for understanding of everyone in the group. With round-robin reading, students take turns reading orally and the teacher asks questions. Once one student has answered correctly, we have no idea if the others could have arrived at a similar answer on their own. By contrast, when I am checking for comprehension using silent reading, I usually ask students to read several pages for a purpose (such as to find out why something happened) and to then write down a very brief response. In that way, I can check for understanding for each student by reading each individual response.

Notice, in the following vignette, how guided silent reading helps move the focus to reading for meaning for a group of slow-achieving second graders.

A Guided Silent Reading Group with Struggling Second Graders

Sarah Curtis approaches me, concerned because her group of struggling readers is showing little progress. We begin working together at her request. Sarah's typical small-group reading experience involved round-robin oral reading, with Sarah supplying most of the difficult words. It was my opinion that the books she was choosing for her five low-achieving students were too difficult, and we spoke about choosing a book that would allow the children to begin to do some silent reading and problem solving, both independently and with limited teacher support. Sarah chose *The Gingerbread Man* (pictures by Karen Schmidt), a book that I agreed would work well for our purposes.

I introduce the book to the students and we look through the pages. We talk about what they already know about this familiar story, who the characters are and what the pictures on the beginning pages suggest is happening in the story. Then I ask them to read the first several pages silently and to write a phrase or sentence that answers the question, "What did the woman tell the boy?" (to which the correct response would be, "Not to open the oven"). I also direct them to write down any words that they can't figure out and to cross out those that they eventually understand. I tell them that if I see that they have no words written down, I may call on them as an "expert" to help another student. I want them to be clear that I expected them to self-monitor as they read.

As the students read, I observe their behaviors. A student who is able to read all of the words has to reread the text in order to answer the question. (I compliment him on using that strategy.) Another writes down *pan* as a word he can't read, even though he knows the words *man* and *can.* Using a small chalk board, I show this student how he can use the word *man*—the word he knows—to figure out *pan*—the word he doesn't. I tell the two students who finish the assignment early to write down as many rhyming words as they can for the words *pan* and *bake.*

When I am sure that all have comprehended the text, we go over the word *watch,* which two students have written down as troublesome. One of these students later crossed the word out. When I ask her how she figured it out, she says that she "sounded it out." This is unlikely, since sounding this word out would have led to "w-at-ch." I have found that when students don't know how to articulate a strategy, they often resort to "I sounded it out." When they use the context to word solve as this student obviously did, we need to guide them to understand and verbalize the explanation "Because it makes sense." If students are unable to demonstrate and/or articulate what they have done, then we need to model and name the strategy for them. Second-grade teacher Loretta Martin reinforces any teaching she has done by reminding students to use the new strategy during independent reading.

At the end of group time, we review the strategies we used: rereading, using the context to put in a word that makes sense, and checking the word visually and using what you know in one word to figure out another. I make a note to start the next session by reinforcing the rime "an." (See Chapter 10 for specific procedures for such word work.)

Framework for a Guided Silent Reading Lesson

Use the following steps as a suggested format for implementing guided silent reading.

• ***Plan the lesson.*** It helps to have an overall written plan based on curriculum guidelines, student needs as determined by previous response and observation, and what the text offers. However, remember that much of what will be demonstrated, scaffolded, and taught arises directly—moment to moment during the lesson—from students' needs and involvement with the text being read. Observe your kids and use common sense. One new teacher told me, "It was ingrained in me to 'stick to the lesson plan,' whether students needed it or not. It took me a long time to have the confidence to teach to the kids' needs."

• ***Form a group.*** Have three to eight students meet with the teacher for about ten to fifteen minutes. (For struggling readers, five seems to be the maximum number of group participants for effective instruction.) For developing readers, typically in grade one and beginning grade two, the group will likely be homogeneous. For more fluent readers, and for reading situations focused on students' interest, groups are flexible, that is, the members and purposes of the groups change often. (See "Grouping for Guided Reading," pages 144–147.)

• ***Select a book.*** Again, it is important that you choose a text that is at the students' interest and instructional level. Try to have a copy of the book for each member of the group. Except for early developing readers who may have some experience with the book through shared reading or hearing it read it aloud, choose mostly books that are unfamiliar to students. Perhaps do a quick check with oral reading to be sure it's on their level by having students read the first few pages aloud. When a student reads orally, make sure you give him time to self-correct if he makes an error.

First-grade teacher Jim Henry notes that when he's chosen the "right book," that is, one with just a little bit of a challenge and at kids' interest level, all goes well. "When I don't choose the right book, I don't have confidence that they can read it successfully."

Learning to select appropriate books takes practice. If you choose a book that is too difficult (and we all occasionally do), don't hesitate to tell the children that you've made a mistake. Continuing to read a book that is above the students' reading level will only lead to frustration—for you as well as the students. Therefore, it's a good idea to have several sets of books on hand as possibilities while you're learning how to select books.

• ***Preview the book.*** Give students time to peruse the book before you provide an introduction. Ask questions about

- What they notice (drawing attention to important features—cover, illustrations, author information)
- How the book is organized (pointing out format and visuals)
- What they think the book may be about (making predictions)

• ***Provide a thorough introduction.*** Focus on story meaning and understanding, not just getting the words right. If appropriate, link to similar stories or content. Give just enough of an introduction and background so that children can problem solve on their own, but don't tell so much that there is no work for the child to do. More independent readers will need a short introduction or, perhaps, no introduction. Developing readers may need a detailed introduction, "walking through the text" with them, sometimes page by page, with the teacher pointing out particular words, concepts, and illustrations and putting the difficult words "in their ear." According to Marie Clay (1998), "The teacher anticipates what might trip the children as they read the story; yet *the overview of the story is like a conversational exchange, and the attention to detail should not dismember the flow of the story*" (175; italics in original).

For detailed procedures on a story introduction, see Clay's "Introducing Storybooks to Young Readers" (see the Resources for Teaching Reading in The Blue Pages for annotation).

• ***Set the framework for silent reading.*** Choose a natural breaking point in the text, and set purposes for reading. I say something like, "Read pages (usually, one to three pages) to find out what the problem is." Or, "Read pages . . . to find out what's happening." And, "Reread if you need to or don't understand." Usually, I also ask students to jot down their response to what's happening (phrases are fine) so I can quickly check for understanding.

• ***Ask students to read silently.*** (For developing readers, some may still be reading softly and quietly saying the words.) As they read, have students note difficult words by writing them down. (We often use small spiral notebooks. Some students also like to jot down words they are proud to have been able to figure out on their own.) In that way, if you are helping one student problem solve a "tough spot," the other group members can continue their reading knowing that they are in line to receive help.

Give another task to students who finish early, such as, "Find the sentence that tells . . . ," or send students who are reading with understanding back to their seats to continue reading while you work with students who are having difficulty.

• ***Observe whether and how students are monitoring themselves as they read.*** As students read one or several pages silently from the text, observe their behaviors to glean what strategies they are using or not using so you know how to support them further. Watch for such behaviors as subvocalizing, finger pointing, rereading, reading rate, hesitations, examining pictures, smiles or laughter in response to humorous material, and crossing out words that were initially troublesome.

On some days, teachers may use this time to take a running record of a child's oral reading (see page 116) or make anecdotal notes about one or more readers' behaviors.

• ***Support and scaffold as students are reading.*** Continually provide guidance to move students forward in their reading. For example, for a student who is subvocalizing, I might say, "I see that you're moving your lips and saying all the words as you're reading. Put your lips together and try reading in your mind. You'll be able to read faster that way."

Or with a student who has reread for meaning, I might say, "I saw you looking at that word carefully, checking it with the picture, and going back to another page where you had seen the same word. Good for you. That's what good readers do."

When a student gives a response that shows he has not understood, I will say, "Where does it say that? Go back and reread and find the place where it says that." If the student does not realize he has not understood, I will have him read orally in an attempt to find out where and why the breakdown is occurring. I look for the following:

- Is the text too difficult?
- Is the print size or page format distracting?
- Are there problems with decoding words?
- Is the concept load too heavy?
- Is the student skipping over "hard" words without trying to figure them out?
- Does the student lack the background or interest to understand the story?
- Is the student decoding the words without thinking about the story?
- Is the student reading too fast?

For example, when working with a group of third graders reading a book about Martin Luther King, I can tell by looking at the one-sentence summaries that I asked them to write after reading several pages silently that three have understood the material. I work closely with the two whose summaries reveal a lack of understanding to clear up confusion. To determine where their comprehension has broken down, we read orally, discuss as we go along, and I teach the strategies they need to read for understanding. If the text is still too difficult, we drop back to an easier level. (See "Teaching for Strategies," pages 130–140 for strategy instruction. See additional examples of support and scaffolding at the word level on pages 423–425.)

• ***Check for meaning first.*** When we check for meaning first (as opposed to going straight to word work), we give the message that reading for meaning is the purpose of all reading. I ask questions such as:

- Were our predictions right?
- What was the story about?
- Tell me what you just read.
- What do you think is going to happen next. Why do you think so?

Often I begin a guided reading group by checking for understanding on the previous day's assigned reading (independent classroom work). This checking can be a group oral retelling or reviewing individual written summaries or comments in the reading log. Checking for understanding takes place before we analyze the text critically. If students have not understood, we go back to the text to find out where and why the breakdown occurred.

• ***Do needed word work.*** After we have focused on overall meaning, I will ask students what words they had difficulty with, and we will work through these together. Our word work may be extensive—perhaps involving individual chalk boards, writing, making word cards (see pages 417–432 in Chapter 10, "Spelling and Word Study in the Reading-Writing Classroom")—or brief, aimed at clearing up confusions about decoding a word or understanding a word's meaning.

• ***Enjoy talking about the story.*** Once I am confident students have understood the gist of the story, I invite personal response and viewpoints, comparison to other stories, revisiting favorite parts, and any comments students feel are relevant and important. (See Chapter 5, "Literature Conversations," for information about posing and discussing high-level questions.)

Sometimes students will suggest we do an activity such as Readers Theatre, dramatization, or sequel writing, either as something they want to do in group or independently, as a follow-up activity.

• ***Use oral reading judiciously.*** Most kids enjoy reading aloud. But, except for developing readers, it's not necessary for students to read the entire text aloud. As stated previously, sometimes I will have students read a favorite page aloud to check for fluency. Or, if a student finishes his silent reading quickly and I have checked him for understanding, I may ask him to find a specific paragraph and practice reading that to himself so he can later read it to the group.

• ***Assign further reading.*** Set purposes for continued reading for after group. Make sure most of students' time is spent reading and not in activities related to reading. Students can read on in the text with a partner or individually. For example, students may be assigned to read several pages or several chapters, depending on their skill level and your purposes. Or, students may be asked to reread familiar text to increase fluency or to create and perform a Readers Theatre.

I ask students to keep track of words or concepts they don't understand so that I can monitor their understanding when I meet with them next (see page 125). To avoid having students get distracted by jotting down long lists of words (with the corresponding page numbers), second-grade teacher Loretta Martin emphasizes that they write down only those words that make them stop reading or prevent them from understanding the story.

For students who have been assigned chapters to read—or to finish reading a picture book—I usually ask them to come prepared with written thoughts. Sometimes their teacher or I direct them to write down "how the story ended" as a comprehension check (see Figure 4-8 for a first grader's response to *Dr. DeSoto* by William Steig). Sometimes,

Figure 4–8   A first grader's understanding of how Dr. DeSoto
ends after reading the last part of the book independently

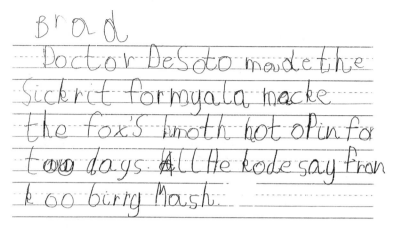

Dr. DeSoto made the secret formula. It made the fox's mouth not open for two days. All he could say, "Frank Koo burry mush."

I pose open-ended questions; other times, they jot down what strikes them as important and interesting to talk about.

• ***Evaluate and plan.***   Often before I call the next group I jot down plans for the next day—teaching points I want to make, what needs to be reinforced or checked, students I need to check or monitor for particulars. Sometimes, the plan might be to begin the next session by rereading a familiar book (to build fluency) or to have students do a retelling of an assigned reading. This planning takes only a minute or two, supplements the predetermined weekly plan, and is based on what happened in guided reading group.

Self-evaluation questions, such as the following, can help guide your planning:

- Did the students enjoy and understand what they read?
- Is the text appropriate?
- Did students problem solve effectively?
- Did they use strategies previously taught and practiced?
- Did everyone contribute to discussion?
- What do I need to teach to increase students' independence in reading?

See Figure 4-9 on page 154 for a summary of the reading framework just presented.

Guided Reading:
The Literacy Club in a First-Grade Classroom

This section describes guided reading groups in action in a first-grade class. For older students, see guided reading lessons on pages 450–458. While the text used on those pages is nonfiction, focus is on understanding, and strategies apply to fiction reading as well.

Elisabeth Tuttle has twenty-three first graders, and she meets with four guided

Figure 4–9   Framework for a guided silent reading lesson

Framework for a Guided Silent Reading Lesson

- Plan the lesson.
- Form a group.
- Select a book at students' interest and instructional level.
- Preview the book.
- Give a thorough introduction.
- Set the framework for silent reading.
- Ask students to read silently.
- Observe how and if students are monitoring themselves as they read.
- Support and scaffold as students are reading.
- Check for meaning first.
- Do needed word work.
- Enjoy talking about the story.
- Use oral reading judiciously.
- Assign further reading.
- Evaluate and plan.

Adjust the framework to suit your needs and purposes.

---

reading groups within a one-hour time slot every day. Everything moves like clockwork in this classroom where excitement about reading is high. Students know exactly what they are expected and required to do, and what their choices are while they are working independently. If a student interrupts her while a group is in session (which is rare), Elisabeth gently reminds the student that she cannot be disturbed. Her teaching is intentional, direct, explicit, and systematic, although it does not follow a hierarchical sequence. It follows the requirements and interests of her students and the district curriculum.

This is Elisabeth's second year teaching. There are no commercial materials on her walls, and the environment is lively, print-rich, and full of wonderful books—books garnered from garage sales, her childhood collection, libraries, book stores, and the building collection. (See room plan, page 546.)

Elisabeth feels that most of her learning about how to teach reading came not from her college instruction but from her own professional reading and self-study and her experience working with a cooperating teacher when she was a student teacher. Most important, she has learned how to teach reading by observing and talking with other first-grade teachers in her school. My coaching of Elisabeth has focused on her movement toward more guided silent reading in her classroom.

It is early May, and all of Elisabeth's students are readers. In addition to her daily guided reading groups, all kinds of reading activities go on throughout the day and across the curriculum—reading aloud, shared reading, partner reading, listening to books on tape, teacher-modeled reading, independent reading, repeated reading of familiar poems and stories, reading of big books, and sustained silent reading.

Setting the Tone for Independent Reading

Before she begins her reading groups, Elisabeth walks around the room to make sure that everyone is reading. Some students are reading student-authored books (published from journal stories, see pages 322 and 575), some are partner reading, some are reading big books in the reading center, some are reading individually. Most impressive, all read as the main activity during reading time. There is a quiet hum in the room as students subvocalize as they read and talk about their books. For today, students know if they finish their reading work, they can write letters to two students who are out with the chicken pox.

Elisabeth comments, "My kids are reading a huge amount of material compared to last year, when I did a lot of busywork. Partner reading, especially, has been so powerful. Whenever we finish a book in group, I expect them to find someone in class to read it to."

Providing "Just Right" Books

During the first week of school, Elisabeth's students choose whatever they want to read, and she observes their selections. The second week, she talks about how students become better readers and relates reading to riding a bike. "You can't get on your dad's bike and learn to ride. You need a bike that's just right for you. Well it's the same with books." A lively discussion encompasses how important practice and "just right" books are. In the beginning, until students are able to choose books they can actually read, she carefully monitors each of their book choices. (For guidelines on setting up a classroom library and helping students choose books, see pages 49–52 and 84–90.)

Meeting with the First Guided Reading Group

Elisabeth calls the first group, five students, up to the round table at a front corner of the room, and she sits where she can see the rest of the class. This group, like her others, are grouped according to strategic needs (see pages 146–147) and are reading "Bees and Mud" in *Mouse Soup* by Arnold Lobel (New York: Harper and Row, 1986). They take turns reading and discussing the first two pages orally. Because yesterday's reading indicated some confusion, for her teaching today, she begins by focusing on structure and checking to see that all understand what a sentence is. Each group member has been given a photocopy of one page from the text.

> TEACHER: Find the beginning and end of the first sentence. (*Students point to the proper places in the text.*) Why do we have periods?
>
> STUDENT: To take a breather.
>
> T: That's right. It's important to know when to pause when you're reading. Now, circle the first sentence. (*All do this.*) Okay, you have it. I was just checking, because sometimes when you read you forget to stop at the ending punctuation.
>
> T: What do you see here? (*Points to dialogue.*)
>
> S: Voice marks.
>
> S: Talking marks.

s: Quotation marks.

т: Yes, that's right. So, who's talking here? (*She points, and students respond correctly.*)

Elisabeth then assigns the group pages 14 and 15 to read silently. As they do so, she observes and assists individual students as needed.

s: I'm having trouble with a word. (*The student points to the word* whiskers.)

т: You can figure it out. What do you know? (*Student quietly rereads the sentence and runs his fingers under the word, stopping at the chunks he knows, "is" and "er."*) Good. You've got it now.

s: I can't read this (*points to the word* upset).

т: You can do it. Think about what you know. There's two little words in it you already know.

s: (*Reads.*) Up set.

т: Good. What does that mean?

s: Mad.

s: (*Obviously having difficulty with the word* muddy.)

т: (*Reaches over and covers up "-dy" with her fingers.*) Now what is it?

s: Mud. (*Student then reads "muddy" on her own but gets stuck on the next word,* swamp.)

т: Look how it starts. What would make sense?

s: Muddy swamp!

While Elizabeth guides one reader who is not quite finished, she instructs the others to make a prediction about what will happen next in the text. She gives them a minute or so to do this.

т: Okay, let's hear a few predictions.

s: He'll get stung.

s: He'll fall in.

s: He'll fall in the swamp, and the bees will sting him.

s: He'll get stuck, like in quicksand.

т: Okay, good thinking. When you go back to your seat, read to the end of the story with your partner. See if your prediction was right. Write down how the story ends.

Total group time has encompassed twelve minutes, and Elisabeth has done much teaching and reinforcing. (Notice how she has effectively used open-ended questioning, rather than asking questions that provoke a yes/no response.)

Meeting with the Second Guided Reading Group

Elisabeth introduces *Daniel's Duck* by Clyde Robert Bulla (New York: Harper and Row, 1982). Notice how interactive her introduction is and that the focus is on meaning throughout the lesson.

T: Look at the front cover and make a prediction. Tell me what you think the setting is.

S: It's about a little boy who's in a cabin. He might be poor.

T: Why do you say that?

S: The floor is old.

T: Could he live here in our city? When do you think this takes place?

S: I think in the olden times.

T: Look what's in the fire.

S: A kettle.

T: Do they have a kitchen and microwave?

S: No, they have to do everything by hand.

T: They cook in that fire, and that fire also . . .

S: Warms them up.

T: Look through the book and make some other predictions.

S: He has a house.

T: Is it a house like yours?

S: They live on a farm.

S: They have a nice house. There's a kitten.

T: They have some animals don't they?

T: Does Daniel have a bathtub?

S: No, it's like a basket.

T: Where would they get water?

S: They have a stream and they would have to warm up the water by the fire.

T: It might take a long time.

T: Let's start reading. (*Each student reads a page orally to get the story going and as a check for Elisabeth to ensure book is at their level.*)

T: (*Supplies the word* Pettigrew *as student reads aloud.*) Who might Henry Pettigrew be?

S: Maybe the best carver.

T: Okay, Ryan, keep going.

S: (*Reads.*) But animals are herd to do.

T: Does that make sense? (*Student self-corrects "hard" for "herd."*)

Elisabeth then pairs up students to read pages 10 through 25. Students who prefer to read alone can do so. She asks them to follow their reading with a written response answering a specific question she has posed about what happens in the story. The reading group has lasted ten minutes.

Meeting with the Third Guided Reading Group

This group of six has completed the informational book *Hungry Hungry Sharks* by Joanna Cole (New York: Random House, 1988). The students had been assigned to finish reading the book on their own the day before (after guided silent reading in group) and to write down their favorite facts contained in the book (Figure 4-10). Elisabeth begins

Figure 4–10   Response to nonfiction reading: a first grader's favorite facts

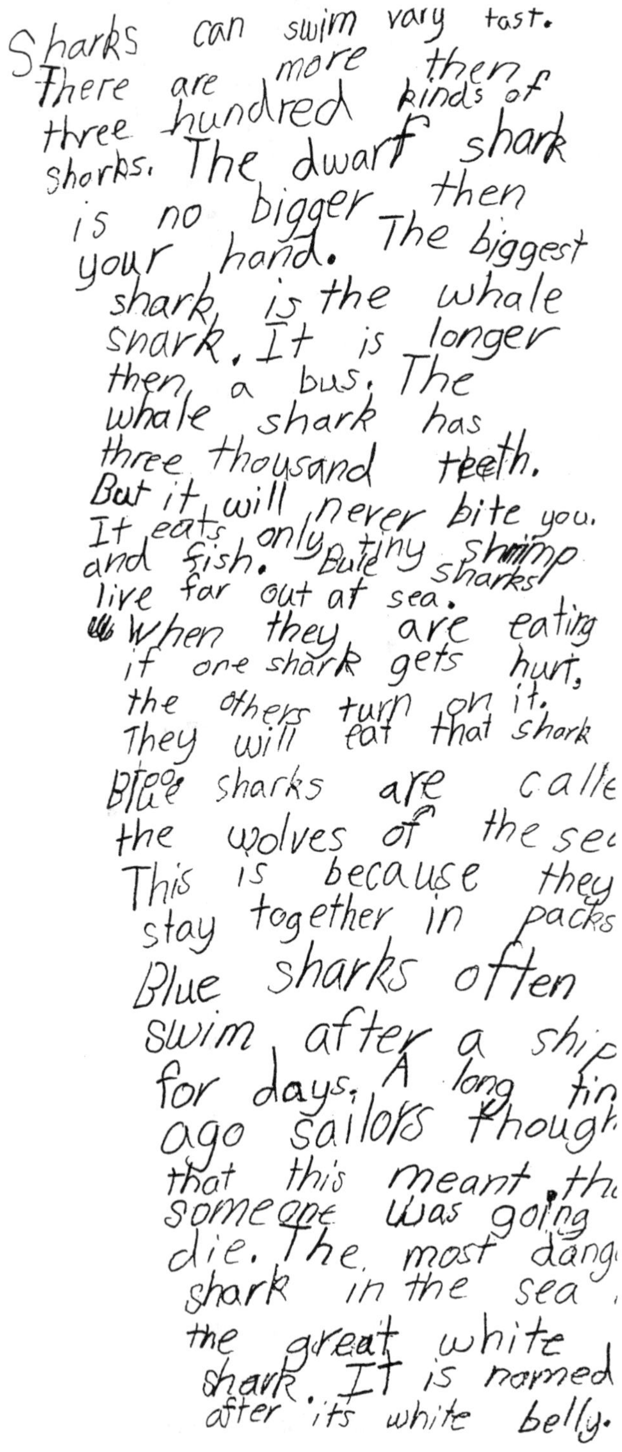

Sharks can swim vary fast.
There are more then
three hundred kinds of
sharks. The dwarf shark
is no bigger then
your hand. The biggest
shark is the whale
shark. It is longer
then a bus. The
whale shark has
three thousand teeth.
But it will never bite you.
It eats only tiny shrimp
and fish. Bule sharks
live far out at sea.
When they are eating
if one shark gets hurt,
the others turn on it.
They will eat that shark
Blue sharks are calle
the wolves of the sea
This is because they
stay together in packs
Blue sharks often
swim after a ship
for days. A long tin
ago sailors thougt
that this meant the
someone was going
die. The most dang
shark in the sea
the great white
shark. It is named
after its white belly.

the group by having each student share their responses. Students talk interactively about what they've learned.

S: I didn't know dolphins can kill sharks.

S: Dolphins are smart and can take in air.

S. Their brains are the size of peanuts. Sharks are not so smart.

Elisabeth and I had been talking about how important it is to use guided reading time for nonfiction as well as fiction. (See Chapter 11, "Reading Nonfiction.") She decides to try the primary edition of the news magazine *Time for Kids*, even though it is geared for second grade. She had given students copies of the news magazine the day before so they'd already looked through them. Notice how she talks them through the cover story "A New Deal for Ireland" and how, once again, the focus is on meaning.

T: I knew you'd be interested in this story because of St. Patrick's Day, and because of what I told you about my own visit to Ireland. (*Begins to read orally.*) Northern Ireland has had problems for years and years. (*Continues reading orally.*) Let's stop for a moment and look at the map. (*They talk about where Ireland is located.*) They were trying to bring peace to the country. Did it work?

S: No. There were bombs. That shows it didn't work.

T: What's a bomb?

S: It's something black and has a string.

T: There's different kinds of bombs.

S: Atomic bombs, time bombs.

T: Remember at the Olympics a bomb went off. Laura, in this story, is afraid a bomb will hit her school.

S: (*Reading orally.*) Violence has divided Northern Ireland for years.

T: What does that mean?

S: Families are arguing over different beliefs.

T: People are splitting into different groups.

S: Protestant religion . . .

T: What does that mean?

S: It's a kind of religion.

T: So, who's arguing?

S: Two religions.

T: So the Protestants and the Catholics are enemies.

S: Just like when Lincoln was president and the North and the South were enemies.

T: Good thinking. Who rules Northern Ireland?

S: The British.

The interactive reading continues with Elizabeth frequently asking, "What does that mean?" and then filling in what students don't understand.

S: They want to be free.

T: Yes, they want to have their own country and be free of British rule.

s: Like when the Pilgrims came here to be free.

t: Yes. And, can you believe over three thousand people have died because of the fighting?

They finish the article with Elisabeth guiding them through it. All take a short turn reading aloud from the text, but the primary focus is on discussion and meaning.

t: If you're done with *Hungry Sharks*, put it here. If you want to look for more facts, keep it. Read *Time for Kids* on your own or with a partner. Read any articles you like.

The group has lasted twelve minutes.

Meeting with the Fourth Guided Reading Group

This group is in the middle of reading *The Three Billy Goats Gruff* by Ellen Appleby (New York: Scholastic, 1984) and, although these might be considered the "struggling" readers—relative to the rest of the class—all can proudly read.

t: What's happened so far? Who can remember?

s: The billy goats came across the bridge.

t: Yes, what did the troll always say?

s: (*All together*) Now I'm going to gobble you up!

The students continue reading, mostly orally to firm up strategies but with an occasional page read silently to promote independent problem solving. Some use line markers to help them keep their place. Focus is on discussing the story.

s: (*Stumbles over the word* second.)

t: Think who's on the bridge. (*The student self-corrects.*)

s: (*Having trouble with the word* voice)

t: Can you read on? Remember how the first billy goat was talking in a high, squeaky . . .

s: Voice

t: Read it the way the troll would say it.

s: (*Reads with expression*) Now I'm coming to gobble you up!

t: What does "Be off with you" mean?

s: It means "go away."

Elisabeth noticed that a few children had trouble with the word *trap* in the story. She pulls out the small chalkboards and asks the children to try writing the word *tap*, which she knew most would know. She then asks them to share what they had written with the students around them and change the spelling if needed. Next, she asks them to try writing the word *trap*. Then she directs them back to the book to check their spelling. Students are encouraged to change their spelling if needed and then to check their final spelling with each other. Next, Elisabeth asks them to write the word *cap* under the other words they have written and to underline the "ap" rime in each of the words. After that, she tells them each to say and write a word that contains the rime "ap." Other words they say and write are *chap, lap, flap, gap, nap, map,* and *rap.*

Finally, students are asked to read the story to someone else in the room. Elisabeth asks each one who they will share the story with to make certain they pick someone who can support their reading in the event help is needed. This reading group has lasted fourteen minutes.

MANAGEMENT TECHNIQUES AND ACTIVITIES

Many teachers tell me that they overrely on whole-class reading because they can't manage multiple reading groups. Translated, that means "What would the rest of the class be doing while I'm teaching a guided reading group?" To ease that anxiety, some teachers who do use reading groups in their classrooms spend hours each week creating "seat work," busywork activities and projects designed specifically for management. Sometimes the only purpose of these activities is to keep students occupied while the teacher is engaged with the small group. As one teacher told me, "I know I'm doing too much, but I'm so worried about management." My advice is to keep written response to a minimum, especially in the early grades when what kids need most is time to enjoy and practice reading.

Excellent management is essential for effective teaching. Poor management often keeps teachers and students on one book way too long. Lara was a new primary grades teacher. Because management was such a problem (she was constantly interrupted so group went on for forty minutes instead of fifteen to twenty), she was only able to meet with two groups a day. She also had a hard time figuring out what to have kids doing that would hold their attention and keep them from interrupting her.

It usually takes teachers lots of trial-and-error time to devise a management system that they are comfortable with. Several first-grade teachers I know worked out elaborate management systems involving displays—wall boards, for example, with movable cards that explained what everyone in the class was to do outside of group. Most abandoned the system after a few months as the "management" of it was so burdensome and time consuming. One lamented, "Managing the system drove me crazy." Cathy Grieshop, who pioneered such a system, found that when she had sufficient numbers of books that kids could read, she no longer needed to manage the class around special activities. Each of her students now has his own bag of "just right" books that stays in the classroom. Most of these have been previously read in the guided reading group; some have been selected by Cathy, and others by the students.

Her management system now has kids:

- Read with a buddy (two books)
- Read independently (four to five books)
- Work on chart words
- Write a book, poem, letter, or journal entry

Indeed, when I am in her classroom, just about everyone is reading, and there is a quiet hum in the room as she works with small groups. Cathy structures the above activities more in the beginning of the school year; as the year goes on and kids can handle more on their own, they are given more independence and choice.

The important thing to remember is to have kids spend most of reading time reading, not doing activities related to reading. Again, kids become readers by reading lots of material at their interest, experience, and independent reading level.

Procedures That Promote Effective Management

During guided reading group time, students need to know exactly what is expected of them. For me that means I cannot be interrupted (both from inside and outside the guided reading group), students may not wander around the room, the noise level must be low, and all students must be engaged in reading or a reading-related activity. So how does this happen?

The following are some procedures that have been effective for me and for teachers I have worked with. Adapt and add to them based on your own and students' needs.

• ***Make expectations clear.*** Negotiate with students what behaviors are desirable and acceptable while you are working with a group. Listing expected and allowable behaviors through a class shared writing—initially posted as a draft, tried out for effectiveness, and revised until you and your students reach agreement on a final version—is a good way to begin. Typically, such guidelines for working independently include acceptable voice level, what to do if a question arises, where in the room it is acceptable to work, completing assignments, and what to do if all work is finished. Some teachers will also include procedures for such things as bathroom use and pencil sharpening, if these have not yet been firmly established.

• ***Model everything.*** Just because you've suggested a behavior or listed it as a guideline, do not expect that students will "do it." Every expected behavior needs to be modeled—often repeatedly. One teacher told me, "I never realized how nitty-gritty I would have to get in setting up rules for small-group time—modeling everything from what students need to do when they have a problem to when and how to move about the room. The behaviors I expected did not occur until I modeled them with the children over and over again."

I demonstrate such things as how students should ask another person for assistance (whisper to someone in close proximity). After I model the behavior myself, I have two students demonstrate it while the class looks on. Next, I have small groups attempt it. After each demonstration, I ask, "How did we do?" and possibly, "What do we need to do better?" I also demonstrate how students should come up to the reading table for guided reading group (push chair in quietly, bring book and any other required materials, walk quietly). Similarly, I demonstrate what it looks like and sounds like when two students are partner reading.

• ***Place responsibility for expected behaviors on the students.*** When I am working with a group and the noise level distracts us, I say something to the class like, "We're having a problem working in group. Can someone tell me what the problem is and what you can do to fix it?" Then, I expect students to suggest what needs to be done. If they cannot, I scaffold for them. This is very different from having the teacher take over and tell a particular student or group of students to be quiet. When we continue to assume responsibility for student behavior, students have little motivation to monitor their own actions.

Some teachers find that it works well to have a table monitor (when students are seated in groups) gently remind peers of expected behaviors. Again, teachers will first have to model this role, showing students how, as group monitors, they can best offer behavioral reminders to other students.

• **_Provide choice._**　When first-grade teacher Jim Henry abandoned required "seat work" activities, in which all students worked on the same assignment, in favor of "invitational" activities, in which students chose what they wanted to participate in, his management during reading time improved dramatically. He acknowledges that initially it was difficult to give up teacher control and trust students to responsibly manage their chosen activities, but the payoff for doing so was huge: "To my surprise I found that by providing options there were fewer discipline problems. Children had a greater interest in their work. That meant I was then better able to focus on the readers I was working with."

See *Invitations*, pages 87–102 and 437–445, for possible invitational activities, literature extensions, and plans for independent work in grades one through four.

• **_Get students focused quickly._**　Second-grade teacher Neal Robinson found that when he invited students to group by quietly and individually walking up to each student—rather than calling out their names—transitions between groups were a lot smoother.

First-grade teacher Cathy Grieshop uses a great management technique at the beginning of each guided reading group. As kids join the group, they pick a book from a box on the table that houses recently completed reading-group books. As the children read these books independently, she takes notes and observes them as readers. Not only does she gain information about these students that helps focus that day's reading, she is also able to use that brief time—three to five minutes—to help focus those several students in the room who have not yet settled into their reading book or activity.

• **_Have books readily available._**　Many teachers make sure that there are baskets or tubs of books at students' interest level and independent-reading level placed on desks and tables at which students are seated. Others make sure that each student has an individual bag of at least five books that can be read without teacher help.

• **_Post the assignment._**　Many teachers will post what each group of students are to do at the beginning of group time. Neal Robinson writes what each group is to do on an overhead transparency, which he leaves up during group time. Assignments usually include reading a chunk of text individually or with a partner and responding to the reading. Usually there is a guiding question, such as, "What's the problem?" or "What do you think of the story so far?"

I like to give the reading assignment at the end of our small-group reading time. I write it on a small chalkboard in front of the students, make sure everyone copies it into their reading response log, and check to be sure students understand what is expected. Some teachers have three or four such small boards (one for each reading group) and leave them visible so that students can copy at their own pace and everyone can refer back to the assignment—on the following day and when the group meets next. Keeping the assignment posted is also helpful for students who were absent.

• **_Assign More Reading._**　Our students know that the primary and first assignment is always reading. Second-grade teacher Ed Kmitt says, "Everything the kids do when I'm with a group stems from what they're reading. Kids know what to do, and that if everything is done, you read. We have books in every corner of the room." (See the photo on page 85 in Chapter 3 for Ed's reading corner.)

• ***Have students jot down difficult and interesting words and questions.*** Ask students to jot down words and concepts that are difficult/interesting and note page numbers so that words can be easily located. Teach students to use phonics plus context to figure out words. (Jennifer Shoda notes that until she showed kids how to figure out words using both strategies—phonics and meaning—students were writing down all words they couldn't "sound out." The number of words written decreased significantly after her demonstrations.)

Students enjoy having a small spiral notebook especially for writing these words, or they could use Post-it Notes for the same purpose. (See Figure 4–11.) Some teachers have students write words in their reading response logs.

• ***Encourage partner reading.*** Elisabeth Tuttle uses partner reading daily as a management strategy in first grade. She groups students of mixed ability and expects at least one partner-read book to be completed each week. Additionally, when students complete a book in group, they are expected to read it to someone in the classroom after group.

Second-grade teacher Loretta Martin uses partner reading as a management tool and to promote enjoyable, successful reading. She has partners choose a corner or place in the room, which becomes their permanent reading spot. Partners need not be reading the same book or be on the same reading level. However, if one gets "stuck," the other helps problem solve. That arrangement allows Loretta to confer with students individually or meet with a guided reading group without interruption. Loretta also encourages

Figure 4–11   Jotting down words, questions, and page numbers while reading: a second-grade developing reader in early fall (A), and a second-grade independent reader (B).

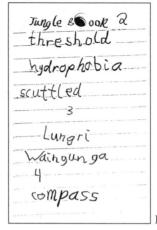

partners to do a book talk with each other about their respective books and first models exactly how that is done. (See pages 58 and 59 for book-talk guidelines.)

• **_Set up a listening center._** Listening to a book on tape is a terrific management strategy. Especially for struggling readers who may be having difficulty focusing, simultaneously hearing and seeing the text seems to help them concentrate. Such listening and viewing also promotes story enjoyment and fluency. (See Photo 4-2.) Because books for older readers can be too time-consuming to tape, teachers sometimes locate a professionally prepared tape or elicit the recording services of a competent volunteer or former student.

First-grade teacher Elisabeth Tuttle sometimes puts her actual small-group guided reading lesson of a book on tape and finds it wonderfully reinforcing for developing readers, especially at the beginning of the year. She notes, "They meet with me, then go to the listening station and, in a way, meet with me again."

• **_Make the overhead projector accessible to students._** Place an overhead projector on the floor and use a part of the wall or white paper as a backdrop. Then, a student or group of students can enjoy reading poems and picture books (which have been photocopied as transparencies for classroom use only) on the overhead projector. Developing readers can sequence pages, illustrate them with washable magic markers, find and circle rhyming words, add an original ending, and more. Some teachers also prepare word work such as word sorts (see page 428) on cut up, blank transparencies.

• **_Consider having multiple self-directed groups operating simultaneously._** As described in Chapter 11, this arrangement works very well (especially above grade two) after it has been modeled and practiced. Students work collaboratively discussing a text in

Photo 4–2 *Listening to a book on tape while the teacher*
is meeting with a small guided reading group

literature conversation groups, reading a news article or nonfiction piece (see pages 450–458), or doing a first reading of a chapter or section in preparation for literature conversations. The teacher then takes one group for guided reading.

Fourth-grade teacher Linda Cooper frequently has five simultaneous reading groups, often using literature related to the science or social studies curriculum. While she guides one heterogeneous group, the other groups help each other, using strategies they have learned through reciprocal teaching (pages 137–140), literature conversations (see Chapter 5), and other reading contexts throughout the day. To encourage the use of strategies—for example, what to do when meaning is lost or when a word needs to be pronounced or defined—each student has a bookmark noting important strategies that have been determined in a whole-class shared writing (Appendix D-2). Modeling their teacher, each group also uses a small white board to help decode hard words. Linda notes, "Unlike me, who jumps right in, the kids say, 'Would you like help?' Readers usually say, 'Yes,' 'Give me ten seconds,' or 'Let me have a try first.'"

Possible Activities

The more I teach with literature, the less crazed I become about "doing stuff" related to books. However, for management purposes during guided reading group time, some reading activities will need to be in place. Several effective management activities are mentioned below. See *Invitations*, pages 88–89, and pages 73–78 in this text, for more on worthwhile enterprises related to reading.

Readers Theatre

Readers Theatre is second-grade teacher Ed Kmitt's favorite management activity. For kids unfamiliar with the practice, Ed creates a script that the kids will then "perform," using dialogue and narration from familiar books. With modeling, students eventually learn how to dramatize texts themselves. Once he helps organize who will play the narrator(s) and characters, students work well independently reading and rereading their parts.

When I was in his classroom in late fall, a group was happily rehearsing *Fox in Love* by Edward Marshall. They had read through the script at least fifteen times and showed no signs of tiring of it. Because of this constant rereading, every student in the room could read the script fluently. (See pages 74 and 75 for procedures and additional information on Readers Theatre.)

Book-Related Projects

First-grade teachers Ruth Mardell and Elisabeth Tuttle create a "Book of the Week" project, with simple variations, using booklets made from folding an $8\frac{1}{2} \times 11$". (See Figure 4-12 for examples of two booklets.)

I sometimes write our own reading text with students in group (as I did for Angie, page 124, photocopy it, and have students illustrate the story and practice reading it. I use $8\frac{1}{2} \times 11$" copy paper (as opposed to folded paper) because it's easier to assemble pages quickly.

Figure 4–12   Two variations of a Book of the Week project
(folded 8 1/2 × 11-inch sheet of paper)

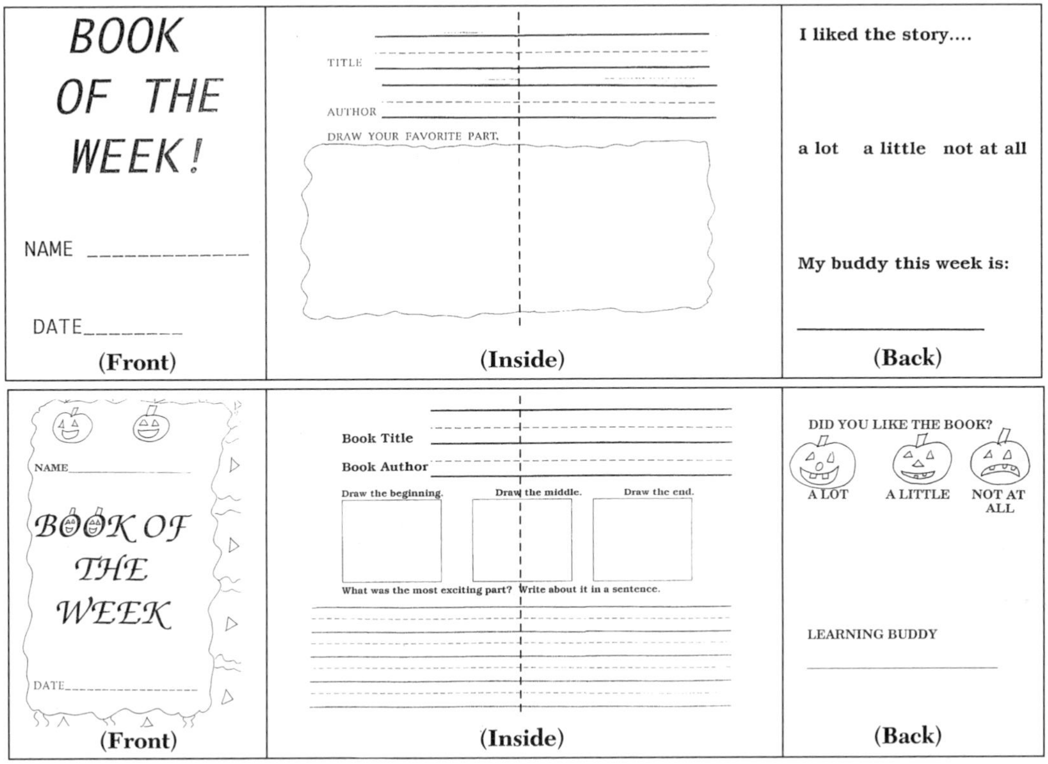

Student-Designed Group or Individual Activities

Although I am careful to limit projects that take time away from reading, once in a while murals and other involved projects can be terrific. Some students shine through the visual and creative arts, and best remember salient features of text through "doing." Additionally, group planning and collaboration can expand text understanding.

I once asked a small group to suggest their own activity for *The Mouse and the Motorcycle* by Beverly Cleary. After reading a chapter in the book that features a maze, they decided to build their own maze. They devised a plan, assembled materials, and using class time and lunch recess built a complex cardboard maze that became a favorite with the class pygmy gerbil.

Reading Response Logs

While reading response logs can be a vehicle for fostering deeper understanding of literature, this is often not the case. As one principal said to me, "We're killing reading response logs." Often reading response assignments amount to nothing more than "Read this chapter, answer these questions, and look up these vocabulary words." We must guard against the "workbook" model when using reading response logs.

For about one out of every three to five books his students read, second-grade teacher Ed Kmitt requires students to complete a response that is similar to a retelling but open to student choice. His kids love Ed's "Highlights and Responses," done in blank books, because the possibilities for response are so open-ended.

"Highlights" is modeled after sports replays. Ed uses baseball, which both girls and boys enthusiastically embrace in our city, as an analogy when explaining his expectations to students. First, Ed explains that at the end of an inning, the cameraman highlights the best pitches and most important happenings. Ed models a reading highlight—giving the book's most important and/or enjoyable scenes—by writing one himself; as he receives quality responses from students, he uses these as models.

In their writing of Highlights and Responses, Ed also requires students to make a personal connection to their own lives: Does this chapter remind you of something else you know or have read? How did you feel while reading it? How do you feel about the character? Do you know someone like this character?

Word Work

Dry erase boards, individual chalkboards, chart paper, Play-doh, magnetic letters, and alphabetic letters can be organized for word work. For example, students can generate words that go along with a spelling pattern being studied. Word sorts and word hunts (pages 428 and 429) also work well. See Chapter 10, "Spelling and Word Study in the Reading-Writing Classroom," for specific examples of word work.

Painting, Puppets, and Block Corners

I have never understood why creative response involving painting easels, block corners, felt boards, and puppets seem to vanish after kindergarten. Children continue to love opportunities to create and respond to literature through artistic expression, dramatic play, and structures they create. First-grade teacher Elisabeth Tuttle notes that "including these [materials] in my room helps to keep learning to read exciting and motivating. In fact, whenever I find a group frustrated or bored, I ask if they want to do a Readers Theatre or puppet show. It brings back all the excitement and keeps them going!"

High school English teacher Holly Burgess concurs, noting that her students love artistic and dramatic response and that such activities can "level the playing field." She says, "I have one student who is very reluctant to write, but his drawings show imagination and attention to detail that surpasses many written responses. While I've used 'art' responses for a long time, I realized that I 'value' them less than written responses in terms of credit given. Now I am careful to value artistic responses as much as written assessments."

The Well-Managed Classroom

Effective management systems are in place when books and interesting reading materials are readily available to students, lessons reflect ongoing assessment of students' needs and interests, and busywork is not in evidence because children are "busy" reading. Second-grade teacher Neal Robinson shares his initial struggles with management and where he is now, as a third-year teacher:

> As a new teacher, I felt guilty not giving my students seat work, because other teachers were giving seat work, and I thought it might be part of what "good teachers" did to teach reading. Of course, I wanted to be a "good teacher." So I literally spent hours coming up with meaningless activities for my kids to do while they weren't in group.
>
> From a management standpoint, the seat work worked; it kept the students busy while I met with the various groups. But as time went on, I began feeling even guiltier because the seat work I was giving was essentially busywork, keeping my students from engaging in quality reading time.
>
> Since dropping seat work (aside from an occasional reading response) and making uninterrupted reading the focus of reading time, I feel much more confident in my reading program. To me it just makes sense: If I want my students to be better readers, I need to provide daily opportunities for them to practice reading.

FINAL REFLECTIONS ON TEACHING CHILDREN TO READ

While observing a young child learn to read is undeniably magical, becoming an effective teacher of reading has little to do with magic and a lot to do with professional dedication and hard work. What do effective teachers of reading know and do? To begin with, they understand the key, relevant research about reading. As we've discussed in this chapter, the process of reading extends far beyond the visible print on the page. Reading is a language and thinking process that brings together the reader's knowledge, values, and experiences with those of the author; author and reader engage in a conversation that is—first and foremost—meaningful. Successful reading entails the skillful orchestration of multiple strategies that enable the reader to construct meaning from the printed page—it's not about using an eclectic mix of skills "to get the words."

Secondly, effective teachers of reading are sensitive, careful observers of their own students. They understand how to temper their instruction to meet the unique challenges and needs of each and every student. Finally, effective teachers understand their own reading processes. As readers themselves, they understand what it means to live a rich reading life and they draw on that life for inspiration in their own teaching. Accordingly, they consider coherent texts, reader interest, students' experiences, and the physical classroom setting that invites students to browse, read, and enjoy books.

Our ultimate goal, of course, is to foster a love of reading—to help our students discover and revel in the magic of reading. In this way, we know that they will choose to read and to go on reading over the course of a lifetime.

CONTINUING THE CONVERSATION

• *Read and discuss current research studies on reading.* Form a study group. Use resources listed in The Blue Pages, pages 22b–26b, as a beginning. Be sure you know how to teach reading, can articulate the research to support your practices, and that you are communicating clearly with parents.

• *Make sure you have enough books for your struggling readers.* Do these readers know where to look? For some, you may need to have a handpicked basket or box of appropriate books readily available. If you are not familiar with titles, seek out your librarian or teachers at an earlier grade level for book and series recommendations. You also may want to meet with your grade-level colleagues and put a list of easy books together for loan or purchase. Check the literature lists, "Little Books," and series books in The Blue Pages.

• *Take a critical look at your guided reading program.* Are you meeting individually and/or in small groups with your students at least several times a week? Are you teaching or reinforcing important strategies each time you meet? Are you seeing your struggling readers every day? Are you giving your struggling readers time to practice reading independently? Are you evaluating students as part of your daily reading program and using that evaluation to move your teaching (and their learning) forward?

• *Review your activities for response to literature and independent work.* Are you just keeping kids busy, or is the work meaningful and related to the literature in a way that extends students' understanding and enjoyment? Be sure students are spending more time reading than responding to reading.

• *Apprentice yourself to a teacher who has excellent management.* Use your planning time or a half-day release to observe and converse with a skillful colleague. After you try some of her techniques, see if she will coach you and help with fine-tuning. Without good management, it's impossible to teach reading well.

• *Pool resources to create scripts for Readers Theatre.* Share with colleagues scripts you've made of favorite texts. Jim Servis has put his undergraduate students' Readers Theatre scripts—poems, parts of books, picture books, fairy tales—on a computer disk, which he shares with teachers. Because he continually adds to this collection, he now has hundreds of scripts on disk. Without exception, all student teachers use and enjoy the benefits of Readers Theatre in the classroom, and many report that they have introduced this strategy to their cooperating teachers.

• *Begin to examine your own reading processes.* How do interest, format, and genre affect what you read and how well you read? Jot down the strategies you use to make sense of text. Share these with students.

• *Ask your students, "What do good readers do?"* Use their responses to evaluate what they understand about reading, what you need to reinforce and teach, and to develop criteria for students to use when self-evaluating themselves as readers. (See Appendix B-2 for a response from a grade four class.)

• *Become knowledgeable about phonics.* Use the resources in The Blue Pages to educate yourself. See also the NCTE position statement, "On Phonics as a Part of Reading Instruction," Appendix C-2.

Literature Conversations

A student-led literature conversation in fourth grade

■ Disagreement in the democratic literature classroom fosters reflection, just as the sharing of responses generates new questions, rather than merely confirming previously held beliefs.

—Gordon Pradl

A second grader stopped me in the hall one spring day. "Mrs. Routman, when can we have our literature conversation group?" I had been working in her classroom helping the teacher and students conduct discussion groups about the books they were reading. *Literature conversation groups.* That's exactly what our informal discussions in small groups were. I liked the name, and it has stuck.

When we teachers demonstrate how to explore literature and guide students in doing so, readers of all ages can and do construct their own meaning, raise important questions, learn to think critically, and talk intelligently about a book—all important life skills. Additionally, students who participate in book clubs or literature discussions recall many more titles, authors, and stories than students in a commercial textbook program (Raphael and McMahon 1994, 115).

There are many ways to talk about literature: "We do not believe it is possible to set down a definitive guide for undertaking literature studies—'first you do this, then you do that.' . . . All that is needed is a book worth talking about, a group of people who have read it, and a receptivity to what the text is saying to us" (Eeds and Peterson 1997, 55).

WHY LITERATURE CONVERSATIONS?

Literature conversations are the best way I know to get students excited about literature and talking on a deep and personal level. With guidance and modeling, students of all ages are capable of understanding literature on multiple levels and responding to it thoughtfully. Once they are able to work independently, even kindergartners can form groups in which they discuss a book they have heard and enjoyed and want to talk more about. Students explore illustrations; talk about the story, characters, and their favorite parts; perhaps dramatize the story (Parker 1997, 20–21). Literature conversations encourage and promote a number of important skills.

Making Personal Connections

I read about other lives so I can make sense of my own. It's not just reading for pleasure and information. It's a way out of my own life and into others' lives and cultures. It's a privileged look at characters in times and places I know little about. It's a connection to humanity outside of my narrow world. Perhaps, most important, it's inspiration and sustenance for my imagination, my heart, and my soul.

Connecting with literature has the power to humanize us—to help us understand the viewpoints, perspectives, hopes, sufferings, and longings of others. As teachers of literature, we have the power "more directly than most teachers" to impact students' ideas about human nature, morality, and society (Rosenblatt 1995, 4).

Along that line, approximately a third of American medical schools now have a literature program whereby medical students can reflect on the human side of medicine "to remind students there is more to people than their symptoms and to make students better, more empathetic observers" (Association of American Medical Colleges 1996). Effective doctors respond to the whole individual, just as effective teachers do.

Hearing and Appreciating Many Voices

One of the reasons students love literature conversations is because students get to be heard. When we teachers do most of the talking, we silence the voices of our students. In typical whole-class teacher-led discussions, the same "stars" (and the teacher) dominate. In student-led literature conversations, the "stars" (including the teacher) learn to take their turn talking and to listen more to others. The "quiet" students begin to discover their voices.

At first, discussions tend to be superficial: kids are getting used to the format, learning to speak and listen to one another, learning to trust their own voice. Students who have been mostly silent in the classroom still say very little. It takes some of them months to believe they have something important to contribute. But once they come to see that everyone's voice is respected and important, they, too, begin to speak.

Every year a teacher who has begun using literature conversations for the first time tells me about a student who usually doesn't speak much who begins to make insightful comments. Aaron was a struggling student who remained silent during whole-class literature discussions led by his teacher. He also remained silent the first few months of small-group literature conversations. But one day, encouraged by the student facilitator ("Aaron, we need to know what you think"), he joined in. His voice was low and tentative, but he was finally becoming a group member. When his statement prompted comments by both another student and the teacher, he visibly beamed.

Fostering Independence

Shared conversations provide lots of experience in collaborative problem solving because the students know they are responsible for the effective social and intellectual functioning of their group. Usually, there is total participation and engagement, and everyone is successful. Students listen to and respect divergent thinking. Observers are always surprised that students are so engaged, responsible, and independent.

Students also tend to behave more maturely. Fourth-grade teacher Nancy Schubert, after introducing literature conversations in her classroom, commented: "This is an immature class, but they behave as adults in these conversation groups." Once groups are running well, behavior problems dissolve: students love being in charge of their own learning and group process.

Setting a Positive Classroom Tone

Successfully functioning literature conversations can change the climate and community of the classroom. Here's an example. While working in one upper elementary classroom, I noticed the students were extremely rude to one another. There were a lot of put-downs and arguments. The climate was so argumentative I told the class, honestly, that I had never before been in a room where kids got along so poorly. Once they had learned how to speak to one another respectfully in conversation groups, that behavior began to extend to the rest of classroom life as well. Their teacher told me that their participation in literature conversations had fostered more democratic and respectful behavior throughout the day.

Raising Thoughtful Questions and Thinking Critically

Critical questioning is necessary to keep on learning. Asking questions that clarify confusions, confront stereotypes, challenge assumptions and opinions, and provoke new thought is the hallmark of a well-educated person as well as a necessary skill for being a critical, intellectual thinker in a democratic society. Yet many high-achieving students—especially at the secondary level—are reluctant to ask questions. They see asking questions as a sign of ignorance rather than as thoughtful behavior. The habit of careful questioning is fostered through literature conversations.

Literature that deals with strong issues and life struggles can help students develop their own thinking. After listening to the very first literature conversations in her classroom, Nancy Schubert said, "I'm thrilled. I saw unexpected, deep thinking in a number of students. Some just blossomed."

Providing a Framework for
Learning Across the Curriculum

Successful literature conversations are not exclusive to language arts. These kinds of conversations can and do occur across the curriculum.

Once students can manage the group process with literature, the same process of reading, questioning, thinking, inquiring, and discussing can be used in science, social studies, math, any content area. (See pages 451–458, for an example of literature conversations applied to social studies.)

Establishing Book Groups Outside School

Some students have been inspired to have literature conversations outside the school setting. Julie Beers's fourth graders set up a monthly book club modeled both on my adult book club and another fourth-grade book group (see Figures 5-1 and 5-2).

The books to be discussed are chosen by recommendation and consensus. Class members meet voluntarily one evening a month, at a student's home, from 7 to 8:30 P.M. Julie arranges transportation for students who need it. The host serves as facilitator and provides light refreshments (see Photo 5-1).

In an evaluation of one meeting, several students mentioned they read the book twice, took notes, and were more focused than for the previous meeting. Mike said, "I want to congratulate myself. Last time I goofed around and hadn't read the book. This time I was serious and prepared. I'm proud of myself."

Julie videotaped one of the group's meetings to show to her students in future years. She also applied for and received a grant to purchase books so that all the members of the book club could have their own copy.

Figure 5–1   "About the Kids' Book Club"

About the Kids' Bookclub
by Anna Hutt

Fourteen fourth-grade girls (including me) have formed a bookclub. Here is how a normal meeting would go:

The hostess chooses any book that she thinks would be good for discussion. She lets everyone else know what the book is and when the meeting is. Usually it lasts for two hours and we meet mostly on the weekends (about once a month).

After we get seated, the hostess will ask a question about the book (a literary question). As we begin to go around answering, our answers usually lead to more discussion. If the discussion ends, the host will be ready with another question. We always make sure that everyone participates.

Sometimes there are crackers or cheese to nibble on, but we've made a rule that you can't stand up to get food when someone else is talking.

Usually we then do an activity of some sort, most likely a skit. We are divided into small groups of four or five. Then we get a bag of props provided by the hostess. We have a little while to organize a skit taking place before, after, or during the book. Then we perform for everyone else.

Before we leave, the hostess has a bag that was prepared before the meeting. It has little papers inside but one is different from the rest. We close our eyes and we each pick one. The person who gets the different one gets to have the bookclub at their house next. If they already hosted one, we all pick again.

A parent will peek in every so often, but other than that, we have no parent help.

I hope from this you get an idea of what our bookclub is like.

*Figure 5–2   A fourth grader's notes from a talk about my
book group. The notes served as model for the class' out-of-school book club*

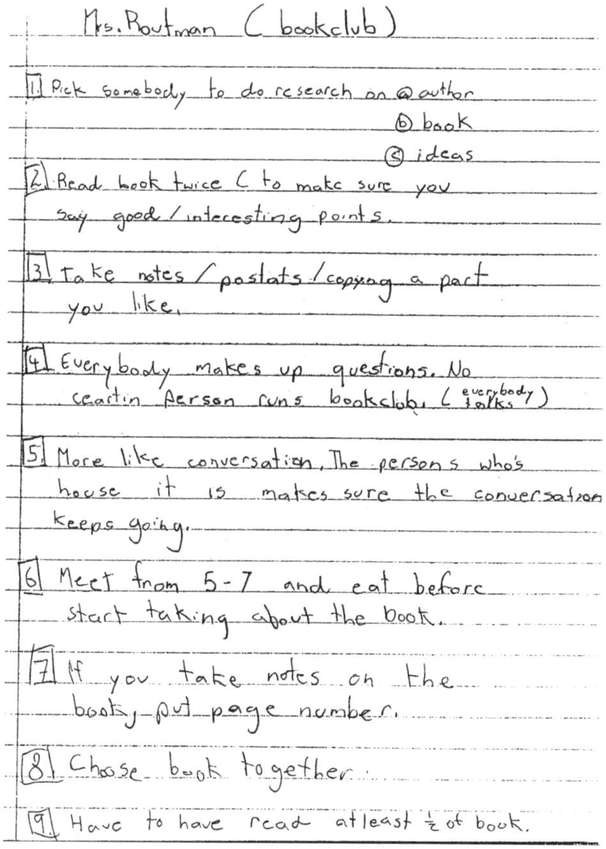

Mrs. Routman (bookclub)

1] Pick somebody to do research on ⓐ author
                                  ⓑ book
                                  ⓒ ideas

2] Read book twice (to make sure you
say good / interesting points.

3] Take notes / postats / copying a part
you like.

4] Everybody makes up questions. No
ceartin Person runs bookclub. (ᵉᵛᵉʳʸᵇᵒᵈʸ talks?)

5] More like conversation. The persons who's
house it is makes sure the conversation
keeps going.

6] Meet from 5-7 and eat before
start taking about the book.

7] If you take notes on the
book, put page number.

8] Choose book together.

9] Have to have read atleast ½ of book.

Photo 5–1   Julie Beers' fourth-grade class: monthly book club at a student's home

MAKING THE TRANSITION TO
LITERATURE CONVERSATIONS

Literature conversations—where students talk together in small, self-sustaining groups, listen actively and respectfully to one another, develop new understanding, and uncover layers of meaning—are a major shift from the teacher-in-control doing most of the talking and setting the agenda and outcome for discussion.

However, even in classrooms in which lots of time is given to independent reading of self-chosen books, it is still uncommon for students to spend time talking about books in small groups. Working with a fourth-grade teacher in my district helped me understand some teachers' reluctance.

Mark Austin had been using literature in teaching reading for several years, and all teaching had been whole class. His memories of more than fifteen years of ability grouping with the basal—and the accompanying negative impact on students—were so painful that he just assumed grouping with literature meant ability grouping of some sort. He wanted no part of it.

When I offered to collaborate with Mark and demonstrate the possibilities of literature conversation groups, he was skeptical but willing to try. Mark found (after reading two articles by Eeds and Peterson, see page 26b) this way of teaching a radical shift after eighteen years of being a responsible teacher-in-charge asking such questions as "Who's the main character?" and "What's the setting and the plot?"

Understanding "Reader Response"

Traditional response to literature has been driven by "right" answers to a teacher's structured questions. It's the way most of us were schooled and the way most schooling continues. As one student recently said when his parents asked him about his new school, "It's a question-and-answer place. The teacher questions, and we answer." Literature conversations, on the other hand, are pinned on a different model. Students are encouraged to raise their own questions about and interpretations of the text. The multiple meanings they determine and discuss are often connected not only to the particular story and related stories but also to their lives and cultures.

"Reader response" theory and practice grew out of the work of Louise Rosenblatt. In the late 1930s, she wrote of the ongoing transaction between the reader and the text on both a cognitive level (nonliterary, verifiable) and affective level (personal, experiential). She named the former "*efferent* reading, from the Latin *efferre* 'to carry away'" and the latter "*aesthetic* reading." Both stances transact continually and reciprocally and determine the meaning of the "poem" the reader creates. Whereas the efferent, or factual, meaning of the text could technically be summarized by someone else, the personal interaction with the text can be done only by the reader, who creates a "poem" as he or she reads. Such "reader response" focuses on the reader (instead of the teacher) and allows multiple interpretations of a text. In this transactional view of reading, "literature provides a *living through*, not simply *knowledge about*" (Rosenblatt 1995, 38).

Reader response has traditionally been seen as the domain of older readers, while reading in the elementary grades continues to be dominated by decoding and comprehension activities. Yet it is through considering the broad societal themes literature presents that we can better understand literature, as well as our own lives and lives in other cultures, in new and insightful ways. Such understanding can and does develop with younger readers. Second-grade teacher Loretta Martin explains,

> Once my students can read, we move to small group literature conversations. With guidance, second graders become proficient at interpreting books and making connections to their own lives.

Nancy Schubert comments:

> It helped me enormously, I always did a lot of different things—buddy reading, my reading and their following along, but I'd never done anything like this before. I used to do whole-class discussion, but I was never happy with it because it was so teacher directed. I tended to have them do a lot of writing in response to literature. This is more effective—thinking about and answering their own questions. And I have no problem throwing in my own questions too.

Teachers as Readers

One of the best ways for teachers to make the transition to student-led conversation groups in the classroom is by participating in adult book groups. My book group experience includes both occasional conversations about professional books in my school's language arts support group and a book club comprising fellow teachers that meets every few months in a member's home.

I use my own literacy practices to inform my teaching practice. Just as for adult readers, it is important for students that a book be carefully selected and that students come prepared to talk about the book. The quality and depth of the book as well as the preparedness of the readers greatly impacts discussion quality.

If we want our students to think critically about literature or, indeed, any subject at all, we need to model that thinking for them. We have to demonstrate the kinds of questions and comments we expect. There is no better way to do that than going through the experience ourselves. Experiencing literature conversations as adults gives us the opportunity to listen to our colleagues without judgment and examine texts deliberately. In considering other interpretations, we see beyond our own meaning, sort out our own beliefs, and get to know our colleagues on a deeper level.

Starting a Teachers-as-Readers Group

If you have never been part of an adult book group but welcome the opportunity to discuss literature with colleagues, you may want to think about starting such a group at your school. Some schools use these book groups as a way to ensure that teachers take time not only to read but to read in a variety of genres.

Many faculties form teachers-as-readers groups to discuss current professional literature as well as notable fiction and nonfiction for both children and adults. Linda Wold, a primary literacy researcher at the University of Chicago, who has spearheaded and sponsored teachers-as-readers groups, says that in forming these groups we are doing more than serving as models for our students: "More important, we are honoring ourselves as intrinsic learners, capable of discovering sheer joy from the pleasure of reading." Appendix E-1 presents guidelines from the International Reading Association for forming a TAR group. Figure 5-3 shows how Linda Wold structured discussion preparation for a TAR group that was reading a book on balanced literacy instruction. Notice that the way teachers are being asked to respond can easily be adapted for classroom discussions.

When my school's language arts support group decided to focus on literature conversations, we began by discussing "Literature Studies Revisited" (Eeds and Peterson 1997). We dealt particularly with the focus on productive talk, as opposed to activities, and with how a good story can raise questions that stimulate conversation.

The following week we discussed the short story "Papa's Parrot," from *Every Living Thing*, by Cynthia Rylant. I chose that story because it's from one of our anchor books in fourth grade and because it's a poignant story about a father and son's changing relationship. Additionally, I find short stories work well for those with busy schedules. See Figure 5-4 for my memo to the staff in the weekly bulletin (which included a format and model

Figure 5–3   Structuring preparation for a TAR
(Teacher as Readers) group: discussing a book on balanced literacy instruction

---

Teachers as Readers, Fall 1997
Balanced Reading Instruction: Teachers' Visions and Voices (Johns & Elish-Piper, Eds.)
Balanced Instruction: Strategies and Skills in Whole Language (McIntyre & Pressley, Eds.)

Overarching ideas to consider:

1. How is "balance" a lens for instruction?
2. What areas would you consider in a balanced reading program?
3. What in "balanced reading instruction" is essential and enduring?
4. Is balance just a current term that will soon fall by the wayside?

Debriefing ideas:

1. Rate your book on a scale of 1 (low) to 10 (high). Consider a one-minute rationale to share with the group.

2. Write down something you feel is critically important.

3. Note how this book relates to your personal life or educational work place.

4. Reveal other personal reactions and applications.

5. Mark a favorite passage to share.

6. Questions generated from this reading:

Developed by Linda Wold

*Figure 5–4   One teacher's notes for modeling
and practicing a literature conversation with teachers*

Lang. Arts Support Group- 1/30/97

We will be modeling a literature conversation
group using the attached short story, "Papa's Parrot."
Please read the story & take notes (for discussion)
using the following format (example given).
Take notes as you read. Keep them brief.   Regie

"Papa's Parrot"

Page no.	I Think...	Book says ...
20	Mr. T misses son, lonely	got a parrot- "Rocky was good company ..."
p 23-24	The parrot repeats "where's Harry" because he hears that and it means his father truly misses him.	"where's Harry" over and over "Miss Him"
p 24-25	Harry feels sad and guilty for ignoring his dad	Harry sobbed, "I'm here." The tears were coming.

for taking notes) and one teacher's notes. The format for note taking I suggested is the same one I use when I teach students to take notes and jot down what they feel is important to discuss.

GETTING STARTED WITH LITERATURE CONVERSATIONS: WHAT DO PEOPLE IN A BOOK GROUP DO?

The model for literature conversations that has evolved includes:

- Reading the book and thinking of questions related to big ideas
- Meeting in small conversation groups and agreeing on topics for discussion
- Rereading and taking notes on questions/topics raised
- Discussing the text (one or more times) in conversation groups
- Evaluating how the conversations went and setting goals for improvement

Since the groups are student led, roles and procedures must be very clear.

When I demonstrate how to get literature conversations going in the classroom, I begin by asking, "How many of you know someone in a book group?" Several students usually raise their hand and talk about their mom, aunt, or, very occasionally, a male relative who belongs to such a group. Sometimes someone will also mention Junior Great Books, a book discussion program led by a trained parent or teacher.

Next, I ask how the person they know prepares for the book group. The response is usually, "They read the book," or "They read the book, discuss it, and have dinner."

Then I suggest that the students ask the book club member, "Do you do anything to prepare for book club? What do you do?" and report back to the class. The students usually return with a statement like, "They reread, take notes, and mark certain pages."

"Why would they do that?" I ask.

"So they are prepared to talk about the book."

"Well, we're going to do the same thing that people do in the world when they talk about a book." I tell the students that I am in a book group with other teachers and that we meet regularly to talk about a book we have chosen to read. I describe how I read the book carefully and mark passages that I find significant, that I think are beautifully written, or that raise questions for me. I tell them how one member of our group usually finds and shares information about the author and serves as informal facilitator to keep the conversation on track and at a high level.

I then explain how our classroom conversation groups will work. "You know how when you have a conversation with your friends or family, you don't raise your hand. You listen to what the other person is saying and you join the conversation when you have something to say. Well, that's what we're going to be doing with the book we're reading. That's what people do in the world when they talk about books."

PLANNING FOR DISCUSSION

Choosing the Book

While many teachers allow students to choose from several titles, I usually begin by having everyone discuss one of the anchor books in our curriculum. These are books that the teachers have determined all children should read and discuss at a particular grade level. (See pages 65–67 for more about anchor books.) Most of us have found that starting with one title that all students read is easier than managing multiple titles.

Not having total choice is also realistic. In my adult book club of about ten members, I do not get to make the final decision about which book we will read. We all make suggestions and recommendations. Then we arrive at a consensus based on information about the author, the genre, group interests, what we have already read, book reviews, and anything else that seems pertinent.

Once classroom groups are established and running well, teachers give more choices to students. They may choose from several related titles or suggest titles themselves. After a short book talk about each title, students sign up for the book of their choice, and each group determines how much of the book to read for each meeting, when they will meet, the questions for discussion, who the facilitator will be for each session, how they will evaluate their work together, and possible follow-ups.

Criteria for Book Selection

In order to have deep conversations about literature, students need to read a book or short story that is thoughtful and provocative. When students discuss a book that doesn't raise interesting questions or that is formulaic or highly predictable, the discussions are usually boring.

I encourage teachers to choose books that engage students but that also, with guidance, can challenge their "view of the world" and trigger deeper understanding. Many of these books are ones students might not ordinarily seek out for independent reading. They include those that deal with broad themes, historical periods, or science as part of life; those written by notable authors; and those that are beautifully written. It's important that the reading level be appropriate for most of the students and that most of them will have the required background information. (See The Blue Pages, "Literature Resources for Choosing Fiction and Nonfiction" and the K–8 literature lists for recommended titles.)

"It is not enough merely to consider what the students *ought* to read. Choices must reflect a sense of the possible links between the material and the students' past experience and present level of emotional maturity" (Rosenblatt 1995, 41–42, author's italics). Also very important, the book must be a pleasure to read. Just as we adults are carried away by a marvelous story, we want students to delight in literature so they will choose to go on reading.

However, a delightful story is not enough. Our fourth graders used to read and discuss *James and the Giant Peach,* by Roald Dahl. While students love this fanciful adventure, there's not much to discuss that the students can't figure out on their own. By contrast, when we read and discuss Cynthia Rylant's *Every Living Thing* (thoughtful short stories that raise a lot of questions) or Mildred Taylor's *Song of the Trees*, the depth of discussion is quite different. Rylant's stories deal with loneliness, survival, love for animals, and change. Taylor's book deals with racism, courage, integrity, and family. These are societal themes that impact everyone's life.

Forming Groups

Our groups are always heterogeneous, that is teachers balance each group in terms of ability, gender, ethnicity, and personality/social skills. Students who have difficulty reading the text can buddy-read or, in some cases, listen to the book on tape.

Four to seven students per group seems to work best. With more than seven, not everyone gets enough chances to talk. Discussions usually last between ten and twenty minutes. It's surprising how much conversation can take place in that time. My colleagues and I have found it works well to keep the same group together for at least a month or more so they learn how to work together.

Reading the Book

Because literature conversations are just one part of a comprehensive literacy program, the focus here is not on learning to read but rather on reading to learn—to experience, enjoy, question, and interpret the text. If a student needs support reading the words, we provide it, thus enabling all students, even those who are "struggling" or "learning disabled" to participate fully in the conversations. Equal participation like this still occurs far too infrequently in today's classrooms.

It works best if each student has his or her own copy of the book to be discussed.

Therefore, if everyone is discussing the same book, you'll need a set for the whole class. The assigned reading can be done in various ways and combinations:

- Individually
- With a partner
- In small groups (with or without the teacher; see pages 68–69)
- Reading aloud (students often follow along in their own copy)
- Shared reading
- Listening to an audiotape and reading along

Discussions are much richer when students reread the book. During the first reading, they get an overall sense of the story and raise important questions and issues for discussion. During the second reading (after meeting in conversation groups to determine questions/issues), they read with agreed-on questions in mind and take notes for discussion.

First-year third-grade teacher Veronica Allen notes, "Initially, most students do not reread. However, once you emphasize the importance, they come to do it naturally because the expectation has been set."

Deciding How Much to Read

How much to read before discussion is a question many teachers ask and one with which I have wrestled. Should students read the book all the way through first? How many chapters should they read at one time? Isn't it wrong to ask them to stop reading when they are caught up in a book? In general, discussion goes better when students read either a chunk of a book (usually several related chapters, not chapter by chapter) or the whole book.

While in principle I like the idea of having students read the book all the way through (after all, that's what we do as adults), in practice I find that reading in chunks works better. When the whole book is assigned, the student who misses the meaning of a major part of it is lost, and the teacher doesn't know it until it's too late to intervene. As teachers, we have the responsibility to check for understanding and maximize children's understanding of what they read as they are reading, not just hope for the best.

A specific incident helped me put this in perspective. My weekly language arts support group decided to read *Other People's Children*, by Lisa Delpit. We ordered copies of the book at the local book store and were trying to decide how much to read before we got together to talk about it. Several teachers felt very strongly about reading the book in parts. One noted, "My reading is influenced and changed by the comments of others. Discussion affects the reading stance I take." This meshes nicely with what one commentator on the work of Louise Rosenblatt has to say: "Readers are forever testing their readings in a public arena and then modifying them accordingly—the essence of a democratic process" (Pradl 1996, 12).

Our decision to read the book in three chunks helped me resolve the dilemma of how much to have students read for our classroom conversation groups. While I encourage students not to read beyond the chunk we have agreed on, if they do—and some do—I tell them they are expected to reread the portion the group is going to discuss. In my own book group, I sometimes finish the book a month before our discussion takes place. However, I always prepare a day or so beforehand by rereading certain sections and going back over my questions and the passages I have marked. I expect students to do the same thorough preparation.

Still, sometimes, dividing the book into chunks doesn't work. Mark Austin's class was reading Elvira Woodruff's *Dear Levi: Letters from the Overland Trail,* one of our fourth-grade anchor books (Knopf, 1994). It's the story of twelve-year-old Austin's difficult journey west in 1851 as told through letters to his younger brother. Mark and I asked the students to read the first four chapters, take notes, and then, in their groups, come up with one or two important questions for discussion.

When students got into their groups to discuss the book, conversations were superficial. It became apparent that this book needed to be discussed in its entirety. First of all, the book takes a while to get into because of the format and story. Talking in depth about main issues—how Austin copes with the hardships of the trip, main characters and their motivations, life then and today—required a careful reading of the whole book. So we revised our strategy. Students completed the book, then we discussed it.

Again, another class was about to read and discuss Mildred Taylor's *Song of the Trees.* After rereading the book to get a sense of possible chunks to assign, I felt strongly that it should be read in its entirety. So, while we usually read a book in several chunks, sometimes we read the whole book. It depends on the book and, also, the age group.

Asking Literary Questions

Great questions inspire lively and thoughtful conversations. While at first I frame the open-ended questions for discussion (*Invitations*, pages 105–121), I do not believe the teacher should be the sole interpreter of the text. Before students start to read the designated book, I encourage them to ask their own questions, to think about issues for discussion while reading.

When students are shown how to ask their own high-level questions, they become more involved in the discussion. However, this does not happen immediately. Fourth-grade teacher Joan Servis remembers that when she asked her students to come to discussion groups with their own questions, discussion went badly; the students told her they liked it better when she gave them the questions.

It helps if students first understand the difference between a literal and a literary question. Through discussion and trial and error, students come to see that a literal question, which often begins with *who, where,* or *when,* shuts down discussion: once the "right answer" is given, there is nothing more to say. Tyler, a struggling student, wrote down two questions about a story, then crossed out one, noting, "It's not a good one for discussion. I already know the answer."

Literary questions raise the level of discussion and often begin with *why, what do you think, how, discuss, describe.* A literary question prompts readers to consider multiple possibilities, examine the text more carefully, raise additional questions, and listen to other points of view. In other words, there's lots to think about and talk about.

Generally, we teach students to think about three types of literary questions, although most come from the first category:

- Those related to the text
- Those related to other texts
- Those connected to life

Specifically, they are often framed like these:

- Describe the relationship between. . . .
- Discuss how [the major characters] change.
- What do you learn about [a character's] life?
- How does this book connect to others we have read?

If students are expected to support their "answers" and interpretations with the text, off-the-cuff comments are few. When a student makes a comment that seems extraneous, I might say, "Show us where the book says that," or "What in the book made you think that," in an effort to understand that student's thinking.

Later, we move to a more natural format in which students informally jot down notes related to questions they keep in mind as they are reading:

- What are you thinking?
- What do you notice?
- What strikes you?
- What are your questions?
- What insights do you have?

While elements such as character, plot, structure, and setting are important, we do not focus on them in literature conversations. As Rosenblatt reminds us, "The formal elements of the work—style and structure, rhythmic flow—function only as a part of the total literary experience" (1995, 7), and again, "Knowledge of literary forms is empty without an accompanying humanity" (51).

Thinking of Discussion Questions While Reading

During the first read-through, students get a sense of the story as a whole and think about the questions and issues the text raises. In the beginning, they are asked to formulate several important questions for discussion as they are reading (see Figure 5-5). Later on, once they are more skilled at book conversations, they do just as I do in reading for my book club: they jot down anything that strikes them as important. Their own questions and issues lead to the best discussions.

Choosing Questions for Discussion

Once each student has read the book and written down several open-ended questions that could be discussed, conversation groups convene for about fifteen minutes to examine everyone's questions and choose the best ones. A "best" question is a literary one that will promote open-ended, reflective discussion and that deals with important issues or questions the book raises in the reader's mind.

Figure 5–5   One student's questions for discussion from the first reading of Song of the Trees

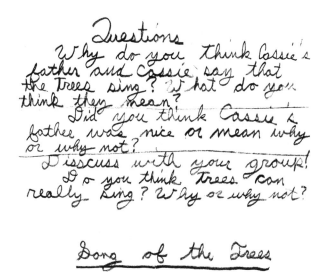

I generally ask each group to come up with several discussion questions and star the one they think is their very best one. (One student in each group serves as scribe.) When we reconvene as a whole class, a member of each group reads the questions that group selected, and I write their "best" one on large chart paper, the chalkboard, or a projected transparency. We typically end up with four or five questions—or more (sometimes a group will have two or three great questions). Then, as a class, we fine-tune questions and consolidate similar questions. If an important issue has not surfaced, we add a question or expand the wording of a question slightly to make it broader.

Then, again as a whole class, with teacher guidance, we negotiate and choose which questions for note taking and discussion will be mandatory and which optional. Usually we wind up with one or two required questions and one or two optional questions. (The questions in Figure 5-6 on page 186 are ones a class devised for *Song of the Trees,* by Mildred Taylor.) Students then read the book a second time, thinking about these questions and taking notes that respond to them.

Once students become familiar with raising questions, they no longer need teacher guidance. Often, after three or four conversation group meetings in which they select questions for discussion (combined with continuing demonstrations and individual practice), students manage quite well and raise questions that are as good as or better than any the teacher would come up with.

Teaching Students to Raise Better Questions

In preparation for discussing *Dear Levi: Letters from the Overland Trail,* one group chooses these questions:

- Why is Mr. Hickman so mean to Frank?
- Why was Rueben so interested in buttons?
- Discuss the hardships that happened on the trip.

Figure 5–6   Required questions and optional questions from Song of the Trees

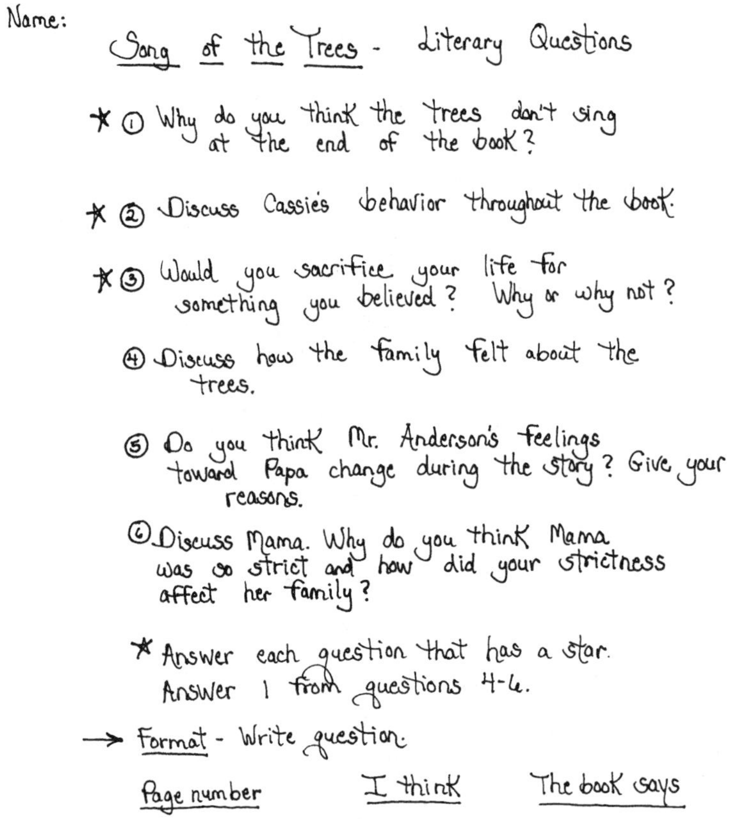

Name:

Song of the Trees - Literary Questions

✱ ① Why do you think the trees don't sing at the end of the book?

✱ ② Discuss Cassie's behavior throughout the book.

✱ ③ Would you sacrifice your life for something you believed? Why or why not?

④ Discuss how the family felt about the trees.

⑤ Do you think Mr. Anderson's feelings toward Papa change during the story? Give your reasons.

⑥ Discuss Mama. Why do you think Mama was so strict and how did your strictness affect her family?

✱ Answer each question that has a star.
Answer 1 from questions 4-6.

→ Format - Write question.

Page number   I think   The book says

During our whole-class discussion, I show them how to make the first question more open-ended by rewording it: "Discuss Mr. Hickman's behavior." We talk about how an open-ended question does not already have part of the answer in it. We also talk about the fact that the book gives no information about why Mr. Hickman treats his son so badly or why Rueben is interested in buttons and that our speculation isn't going to lead to a lively discussion or greater understanding. However, we decide that their last question (another group's version of it was, "If you were Austin and were on this trip, what would you be going through?") has lots of possibilities. Their notes on these hardships will lead to rich discussion and deeper understanding.

Here are the important questions we settle on to guide our discussions of *Dear Levi*:

- What were the hardships on the trip?
- How did Austin feel/cope over time?
- Compare life for a child in the 1850s and today.

Note that the first two questions relate specifically to the text. The final question connects to the students' lives.

Taking Notes and Rereading

After we have settled on the discussion questions, I assign a second reading of the text, and any students having difficulty reading the words are partnered with a peer. Students have both in-class time and homework assignments in which they are to reread the book and take notes on the agreed-on questions.

I expect students to come to their group prepared with adequate notes. Without good notes, the conversations go poorly. I tell students that their notes will help them "say smart things." Because we may read and take notes on a given day but not meet for discussion until several days later, our notes help us recall significant points we want to make.

Taking notes not only improves the quality of discussion, it also helps students stay focused. Taking notes "force[s] [underachieving] students to be attentive and g[ives] them a way to share ideas and information" (Ruenzel 1997, 19).

Modeling and Guiding

I model note taking in front of the students. When literature conversations are being newly implemented, this process needs to be very carefully structured. Experience has shown me that these beginning demonstrations with clear specifics and high expectations pay dividends later on. Once students understand how the quality of their notes affects their discussions, I relax the structure, and it becomes much more what I do as an adult reader.

I demonstrate note taking on a projected transparency, first writing down the title of the book, the chapters we are discussing, and the guiding question(s). (In preparation, students have had time in class to read the part of the book we will be discussing. They take their notes either in a reading response log—usually a spiral notebook—or in a blank booklet created from $8^1/_2 \times 11$" paper folded and stapled in the center, the book's cover photocopied on the cover page.)

I think out loud as I take my notes. I tell and show the students that I'll be writing in phrases, not complete sentences, since the purpose of the notes is to support future discussions. Students copy my notes into their reading logs or booklets. Then they reread and add their own insights (see Figure 5-7 on page 188). While they work, I walk around, checking how they are doing and providing guidance as necessary. Like most demonstrations, this one on note taking will need to be repeated several times. I expect each student to have several important insights in their notes before they come to group. The students understand that the notes are a way for them to organize and clarify their thoughts and that they will be able to use these notes to help start the discussion and to support their conversations. The notes are not for me, the teacher. I check only to verify that their notes are legible, thoughtful, and complete.

When modeling, I often show examples of former students' notes on books the class has already read. We talk about what makes these notes useful (or not useful) to a quality discussion.

Figure 5–7   A fourth grader's notes for Song of the Trees *following teacher modeling*

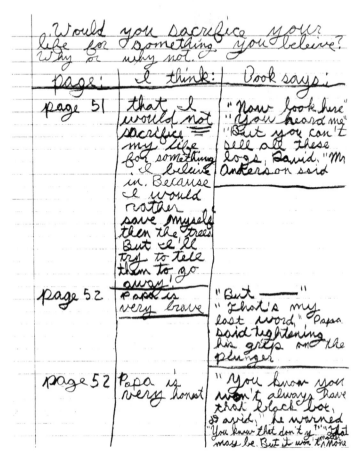

Moving Toward More Natural Note Taking

After literature conversations are successfully under way, perhaps after a few months, I model note taking in the less structured way I do it for my own adult book club. I share my actual notes, which may include jottings about character, questions I want to raise, favorite quotations (copied into my writer's notebook or flagged directly in the book, usually because they're so elegantly written), facts, inferences, ideas I want to remember. I always jot down page numbers so I can refer back to the book easily. See a fourth grader's first attempt at more natural note taking in Figure 5-8.

Young readers can learn how to do this too. A group of excellent readers in Neal Robinson's second grade are enjoying *Ramona Quimby, Age 8* by Beverly Cleary (Avon Books, 1981). They have just read the first two chapters, about Ramona's family and her first day of third grade. In preparation for our discussion, I have jotted down the big ideas in these chapters—Ramona's feelings about the first day of school; she's not sure about grownups; she thinks silent reading is the best part of the day; the unfairness of being the youngest; the changes in her life.

Figure 5–8   A fourth grader's first attempt at more natural note taking:
"What were the hardships on the trip?"

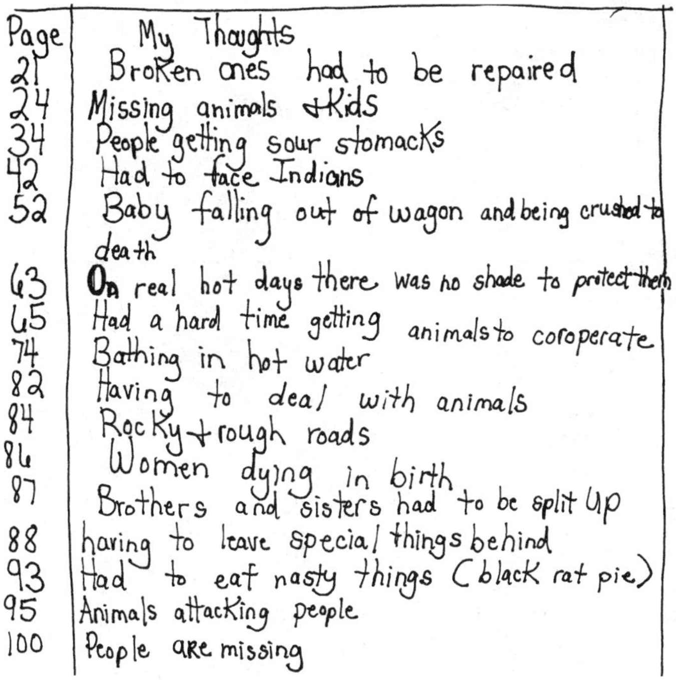

Page	My Thoughts
21	Broken ones had to be repaired
24	Missing animals + Kids
34	People getting sour stomacks
42	Had to face Indians
52	Baby falling out of wagon and being crushed to death
63	On real hot days there was no shade to pritect them
65	Had a hard time getting animals to coroperate
74	Bathing in hot water
82	Having to deal with animals
84	Rocky + rough roads
86	Women dying in birth
87	Brothers and sisters had to be split up
88	having to leave special things behind
93	Had to eat nasty things (black rat pie)
95	Animals attacking people
100	People are missing

Notes from reading *Dear Levi* by Elvira Woodruff

When I meet with the group, I give guidelines for discussion and throw out big questions about the good and bad things in Ramona's life. We have a lively discussion for about ten minutes. Kids easily make connections with being the youngest sibling or having a pesky relative. They agree to read and take notes on chapters 3 and 4 during the next several days. I show them how to jot down, in short phrases, things they think are important. Before long they have become pretty good at doing this and leading their own discussions (see Figure 5-9, page 190).

One idea for brief note taking that works well is to provide students with "idea bookmarks" for jotting page numbers and corresponding thoughts, questions, and comments (Samway and Whang 1996, 42).

ESTABLISHING DISCUSSION GUIDELINES

Conversation groups run smoothly when students know exactly what the expectations and standards are. Even in our teacher book groups at school we establish discussion guidelines ahead of time:

- Everyone must speak.
- Speakers must indicate clearly that they are speaking only for themselves.

Figure 5–9   Second grader Megan's notes from **Ramona Quimby, Age 8**

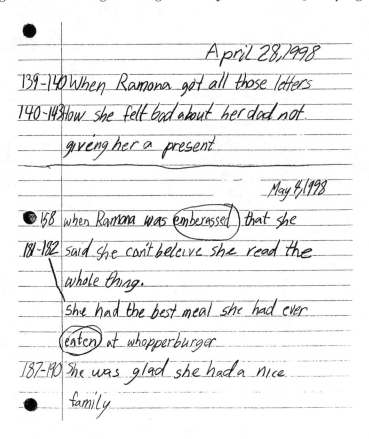

April 28,1998

139-140 When Ramona got all those letters

140-143 How she felt bad about her dad not

giveing her a present

May 4,1998

158 when Ramona was (emberassed) that she

181-182 said she can't beleive she read the

whole thing.

She had the best meal she had ever

(eaten) at whopperburger

187-190 She was glad she had a nice

family

- Speakers are not to be interrupted.
- Everyone must make eye contact with every other group member. (An African American teacher once told me she had noticed that white teachers make less frequent eye contact with African American teachers. I began to watch for this and was surprised to find out she was right.)

We review these guidelines every time before we begin, and they have helped keep our conversations respectful, more relaxed, and less judgmental.

With student groups, I go over the roles of group members and facilitator as well as what I will be doing as the teacher. After groups have met and tried out these roles, I make sure we review the roles of facilitator and group members during whole-class shared writing. These charts stay posted in the classroom for the rest of the year and are revised as necessary.

The Role of the Teacher

The teacher's job is to help students make connections and notice literary elements, pose deep questions, push their thinking. Student-led literature conversations do not give the teacher license to abandon his or her responsibility. Just the opposite. The teacher is free to take notes or join a group as a member or facilitator. The teacher is a participant, a coach, an evaluator, a demonstrator, a clarifier, and a learner.

While students are first learning how to manage their own groups, the teacher moves from group to group without speaking and takes brief notes on how the groups are functioning. Initially, we all find it hard not to intervene, especially if the group is experiencing difficulty with management or conversation. It is very difficult to leave a group to flounder. We often feel compelled to step in and "rescue" them. When we ask direct questions of our own, however, the group shuts down and lets us take over.

Keep in mind: if a group goes badly, it is only ten or fifteen minutes of one day. Also, while the group may not have been productive, the experience no doubt was. Students learn more by problem solving on their own, especially when they know they are expected to do so. A follow-up evaluation will help the group move forward and set goals for improved conversations.

Ask Questions by Making Statements

When the teacher is part of the group, as facilitator and/or participant, students need time to get accustomed to her or him being one equal voice in the conversation. Often, as soon as we ask a question, all eyes go immediately to us, we are once again in charge, and the dynamics of equality are lost. Therefore, we must learn to speak without controlling the conversation.

When I model the role of facilitator, I ask the classroom teacher to watch for the way I ask questions by making statements. For example, instead of saying, "What makes you feel that way," I say, "Tell us what you're thinking." Instead of "What do you agree with," I say "Tell us why you agree." Instead of "What is . . . ," "Why did . . . ," or "How could . . . ," I say, "Let's talk about how . . . ," "Tell me what you meant by . . . ," "Let's discuss why. . . ." This is a very subtle but very important change in approach, and it is very difficult do. Even after years of phrasing questions as statements, I find I still have to monitor myself carefully not to ask a direct question.

Some teachers initially find it helpful to have a list of statements in front of them to use as cues or prompts. Here are some other statements (not questions) to guide the conversation:

- Tell us what . . .
- Tell us why you agree.
- Let's talk about . . .
- Tell us what you meant by . . .
- Let's discuss why . . .
- So you're saying . . .
- I'm wondering . . .
- Explain what you mean.
- Let's refer back to the book.
- Talk more about that.

- Let's hear from some other people.
- Give us your proof.
- Let's turn to page so-and-so and discuss what this section means.
- Look back at your notes for other points you want to make.
- We have a few people we haven't heard from yet. Tell us what you're thinking.
- Let's piggyback (build upon another's ideas) on what so-and-so just said.

Role of Group Members

When I begin talking about literature conversations with students, we talk about how people in the world take part in a conversation. I note that astute conversationalists don't make unrelated comments, that all participants have to listen carefully. We talk about piggybacking—building on another's comments—and language to use to enter a conversation, such as: "I'd like to add something," "I disagree," "I don't understand."

We discuss how it is each group member's responsibility to participate and contribute to the successful functioning of the group. We make a list of what group members do (see Photo 5-2; see also Appendix E-2).

Photo 5–2 The role of a group member in a literature conversation

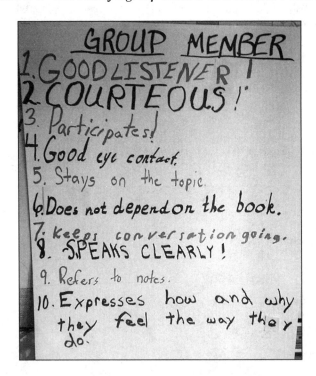

Role of Facilitator

Everyone gets a chance to be facilitator, and students love being in charge. To show my students how this role works, I tell them to watch what I do as facilitator when we have our demonstration conversation (see page 194). I explain that the facilitator is not the boss or leader but the person designated to make sure the conversation runs as smoothly as possible and that everyone participates. I tell them to notice how I look at each member of the group as I am talking and show respect for everyone's ideas. Although I do not expect or suggest that students ask questions with statements as we teachers do—students don't find questions posed by peers problematic—student facilitators wind up using much of the language I have modeled.

At first, teachers choose "top" students as facilitators but quickly find that almost all students do well in this role. It is important to keep track of who has been a facilitator so everyone gets a fair chance. Initially, the teacher designates the facilitator, but after a while the groups can easily do this themselves, deciding on their own who will be facilitator for that day.

Management Issues

Number of Books and Groups

When three or more heterogeneous conversation groups are meeting at the same time (I've had up to six), there is no "seat work" to prepare or assign, which is a great time saver. Additionally, much is accomplished in a short time. In less than a half hour, everyone participates in a literature conversation and follow-up evaluation.

Groups do not meet every day. Literature conversations are but one part of the comprehensive literacy program. Groups may meet two or three days a week for a while and then not meet for weeks while other reading work is going on daily.

Physical Setup

Groups usually sit on the floor in a close circle. That way, chairs don't have to be moved, groups can be assembled quickly, and everyone is at eye level. Once the groups are going well, a group might meet in the hallway just outside the classroom (as shown in the photo on page 171), as a lot of groups conversing at the same time can be distracting.

When we are getting started, I also talk about the posture of group members, that they sit up straight and lean into the conversation. This seems like a small detail, but when students lay on the floor some of them approach the conversations less seriously.

Voice Level

With many groups talking at once, voice level is always a problem at the beginning. With practice, students learn how to modulate their voices. Also, when groups are located strategically (in separate areas of the classroom and perhaps in adjoining spaces), conflicting voices become less of a problem. Students know it is their group's responsibility to monitor the noise level.

Unprepared Students

If a student has not finished reading the selection and/or does not have complete notes, she or he may not join her or his group. When a student is not prepared, I say something like, "I'm so disappointed you can't join the conversation today. As soon as you finish your reading and note taking, please join your group." Students hate to miss group, so unpreparedness seldom remains a problem.

Also, group members pressure one another to be prepared. One of my students once complained, "We had to say over each time what we were discussing. It made it hard to stay on the topic, and it limited our discussion." Were a teacher to make that same comment, students might not take it seriously, but they do when it comes from a peer.

Nancy Schubert sums it up this way: "If students are not prepared, they feel left out. A literature group doesn't seem like work. They don't want to miss the fun; they don't like being excluded."

DEMONSTRATING HOW LITERATURE CONVERSATIONS WORK

If we want students to participate in conversations characterized by engaged listening, a keen interest in others' ideas and opinions, and meaningful discussion of text on many levels, we first have to provide them models of what a good conversation looks and sounds like. These demonstrations need to focus on both the social and intellectual behavior that makes a conversation successful.

I frequently show a videotape we made of a literature conversation conducted by a fourth-grade group new to the process (excerpts of the conversation and the follow-up evaluation are included on pages 196–201). I ask students to take notes on what they notice (in phrases) and to focus on the positive (one student's notes are shown in Figure 5-10). I remind them that the students on the tape are new to the process and are learners. The video is powerful because students see that the students in it are "just like us" and it gives a clear picture of what I'm after.

After we have viewed the video, I ask: "What did you notice?" "Could you tell who the facilitator was?" "How could you tell?" "What was the tone of the discussions?" I am always pleased at the depth of the students' observations. Some typical comments: "they ask hard questions," "no arguing," "the conversation never stopped," "piggybacking," "no interruptions," "didn't ask the teacher," "used the dictionary," "took turns, didn't raise their hands."

Teacher as Facilitator with Student Volunteers

Don't worry if you don't get a chance to make your own video or have your neophyte class observe another class in which literature conversations are running smoothly.

Figure 5–10   A student's observation notes from viewing a video of a literature conversation

Partica pating
No interruptions
Talk at seperat times
Eye contact
Stick to the topic
Ask questions
Look back together
Look up words
Bring in personal stories if approprite
Answer questions
Have comments
Focus
Everyone has a chance to talk
Everyone has a chance to answer
Have hard & challenging questions
Ask literary questions NOT literal questions

Demonstrate the process by serving as facilitator with a group of prepared students, and your students will do very well. Here's how I go about it.

Once the classroom teacher and I are satisfied that students have read carefully and have adequate notes, I ask for volunteers for a literature conversation during which I will serve as facilitator. (With the classroom teacher's assistance, I make sure we have a representative mix of abilities—social and intellectual—genders, and cultures.) Five or six students gather with me, the book, and their notes in a circle of chairs or on the floor while the rest of the class quietly observes in an outer concentric circle.

During this initial demonstration, I am not a member of equal status. I am demonstrator, facilitator, and coach. I begin the conversation by stating one of the open-ended questions that we have agreed will frame the discussion. Often I then share some comments based on my own notes to get the conversation flowing. I show and tell students that I do not read my notes verbatim. Rather, the notes are a springboard and reminder for important comments I want to make.

Students who are observing are expected to take notes on how the discussion goes. This helps keep them focused and engaged. Often I have them do just as I do when I observe a group—divide a piece of paper in half, put a plus sign on one side and a minus sign on the other, listen carefully, and briefly note what went well and what needs improvement (see pages 199 and 200). I always say, "Be sure you have more things on the plus side and that you notice what's going well." Otherwise, some students tend to focus on the negative. I also tell them, "I want you to notice how the conversation goes as well as how the group gets along."

Excerpts from a Literature Conversation Group

Students in Mark Austin's fourth grade have been newly involved in literature conversations; they've had one discussion about the short story "Shells," from *Every Living Thing*, by Cynthia Rylant. It is the last story in the book and is about the conflict between Michael and his Aunt Esther, who began living together when Michael's parents died. One day Michael brings home a hermit crab, and as they watch and care for it, their relationship slowly begins to improve. Here is a transcript of a group of students' second discussion of the story.

REGIE: You did a really great job talking about the story "Shells" the other day. But at the end of your discussion you raised some questions that had not been answered. And so we decided as a class to continue the discussion. I know you've reread the story and taken new notes on the questions you raised and one that Mr. Austin also raised:

- Why did Aunt Esther change?
- Why is the title of the story "Shells"?
- How is this story related to other short stories in the book?

These are deep questions. Think about shells and the many possible meanings for shells. I also want you to look at the very last paragraph of the story (*"They leaned their heads over the tank and found him. The crab, finished with the old home that no longer fit, was coming out of his shell." 81*). It gave me chills when I read it. Read it together. Think about what's really going on here. Okay, I think we're ready to get into our groups.

AMANDA: Aunt Esther felt a little sorry for Michael . . .

JEROD: Yeah, that's what I put . . .

AMANDA: . . . because, after all, his parents did die. Being in Aunt Esther's house, even after six months, he was still upset.

BRIAN: On page 75 (*all turn to the page and follow along*) it says, "Even six months after their deaths, he still expected to see his parents—sitting on the couch as he walked into the living room. . . . He still smelled his father's Old Spice and his mother's talc." I think she knew how he felt.

AMANDA: She was so different from his mother.

STEPHEN: She was prejudiced. (*He stumbles over the pronunciation. Several students try out the word.*)

MALLORY: Oh, I know what that means. I heard it some place. I heard it in a book.

LESLEY: I know. It's when, it's when somebody doesn't like a person because of the color of the hair or skin or something like that. (*Stephen gets the dictionary, looks it up and confirms the meaning.*)

BRIAN: I think Aunt Esther was prejudiced, but then she changed because she feels sorry for Michael and realizes his feelings and how he still thinks about his parents.

AMANDA: After a while she sort of talked to him and she started to feel what he likes to do and stuff, and what his personality is, what he does. So she got used to what Michael does, and she changed. Then when she changed, Michael changed. Then they were happier.

MALLORY: Well, I think they had a lot in common, but they just didn't know it.

JAROD: Maybe they just got used to each other. 'Cause after a while they stopped shouting at each other and talked.

BRIAN: Yeah, at first she didn't understand him because he was all sad and everything.

AMANDA: She probably looked back at her own life when she was young, and I think she realized that she was sort of the same, lonely in a way, when she was that age.

STEPHEN: Well, why is the title "Shells"?

LESLEY: It kind of all goes together because everyone is in a shell. I think Aunt Esther changed when she realized she was in a shell.

JAROD: She was coming out of her shell a lot. She was changed at that time because, first of all, she let him keep the hermit crab.

AMANDA: Do you think the hermit crab caused them to change?

BRIAN: Like most of the stories in the book, the people change at the end 'cause of a pet. The crab helped them change.

JAROD: I'd like to add something. I think it was called "Shells" because Aunt Esther and Michael came out of their shells.

LESLEY: I think it's a moral. It's like a moral.

AMANDA: They were really changing. Like they're not shy or mean to each other any more.

LESLEY: Hermit crabs stay in their shell so much because they're afraid to come out. Aunt Esther, when she embraced him, she, well, she was kind of coming out of her shell, just like the hermit crab did.

Teacher Intervention

When conversations are not going well, it is our job to intervene, usually with additional demonstrations. Let's take an example. One day fourth-grade teacher Jennie Nader tells me that the groups are going well as far as management goes. The students know how to facilitate and participate, but the discussions are very basic and boring. They are just finishing *Every Living Thing*, a book of short stories by Cynthia Rylant.

Using a projected transparency, I raise some questions: What's the deeper meaning of the titles of these stories? What is the role of pets in the stories? What themes run through all the stories? How are the stories connected? Then I begin to reread the first story, "Slower Than the Rest," and I jot brief notes on the overhead. I ask them to reread the book looking for connections between the stories as well as for the meaning of the story titles.

The next week, the students have reread the book and noted the following connections:

- Pets and loving pets
- Feeling safe or afraid
- Not having a family
- Loneliness

- Giving up on life
- Sadness
- Poverty

Jennie and I select six students with complete notes to model a conversation while the rest of the class looks on. I barely have to say a word, their comments are so insightful. Then we divide up into five groups facilitated by members of the demonstration group. The conversations are great. Afterward I ask them if the conversations were interesting and if they learned something new. All hands go up. When I ask them what's made the difference today, they insightfully comment that they had better notes, were better prepared, and had read the book twice.

EVALUATIONS OF LITERATURE CONVERSATIONS

At the end of every literature conversation, we spend about five minutes, give or take, evaluating how the discussion went, both socially and intellectually. First, I validate and congratulate students for what they have done well so they are encouraged to continue their successful behavior. Second, we talk about what didn't go well and how those problems can be solved so groups can function more effectively in future conversations.

When students know they are accountable for their work, they take it more seriously. Each literature conversation group, with help from the teacher, is in charge of evaluating itself. (Occasionally, I'll use individual self-evaluations; see page 200). Evaluations are mostly oral or written but sometimes they are audio- or videotaped. (A videotape is an excellent self-critiquing tool as well as a model for other students and teachers.)

Evaluations are critical. When one teacher in my school decided to skip the evaluation to save time, one of her students became very upset. This student spoke to the teacher about it privately, saying things hadn't gone well in her group and she wanted to be able to talk about it, find out how to solve the problem, be able to improve. That teacher never skipped an evaluation again.

Oral Self-Evaluations by Groups

Students are expected to evaluate themselves for both group dynamics and quality of discussion after every literature conversation. At first, all our evaluations are done orally, one conversation group at a time, the whole class listening in. When students listen to each other—with teacher guidance—they learn the language of constructive evaluation. The goal, as it is for all learning, is for students to be able to evaluate themselves, solve problems, and improve without the teacher. After a few months that does happen.

I begin by saying something like,

> We need to end our conversation now so we can evaluate how we did. Think about what went well in your group, and what you still need to work on. Remember, you're evaluating as a group, so don't use individual names. I will only jump in if I have something important to add that I think you left out.

Then, one group at a time, I ask the facilitator to comment on what went well. The facilitator then calls on any group members who want to add anything the facilitator hasn't mentioned. I then add my comments (from notes I have taken while observing the groups) but only if the group has left out something significant.

After hearing positive comments, we move on to what didn't go so well, again using facilitator, group, and teacher comments. When there has been a problem, I will say something like:

- What did you do when that happened?
- What else could you as facilitator have done?
- What could you as a group member have done?
- How else could that have been handled?
- What could you say to bring that person into the conversation?
- What will you do if that happens again?

If the facilitator or group member cannot offer a solution, I demonstrate the language and behavior the group needs to use. For example, when one group member has monopolized the conversation, I suggest saying, "We've heard from you. We also need to hear from other group members." Or, if students are off topic, "Let's get back to the question we're discussing." Or, again, if the group is getting too loud, "We need to lower our voices and lean into the conversation."

Teacher Observation Notes

I recommend that while groups are meeting the teacher be a silent observer, jotting down what he or she notices about each conversation. After students in a group have given their oral observations, I refer to my notes and make additional comments, if necessary.

I usually fold a piece of paper in half and put a plus sign (+) on one side and a minus sign (–) on the other to designate strengths and weaknesses. I note behavior and statements that seem significant. I move quickly from group to group, usually staying only a few minutes with each group. The notes below (transcribed because my handwriting is so poor) are typical of the ones I take. The name listed is the facilitator for that group.

1. Woody
+ "I want to know why she wanted to die," "The book says," looked back in book when there was disagreement, asked questions,
– "Mrs. C and the dog walked farther each day"—no one built on that—just went on; went from deep comment to new topic, talking at same time, little piggybacking.

2. Mia
+ "I don't understand," "I still come back to my point that she was depressed," stayed on topic, eye contact, question was asked, "I wonder why."
– When question was asked, facilitator could have said, "We'll come back to that." Two members not prepared, came to group late, and each came at a different time. One student noted that lack of preparedness disrupted group: "We had to say over each time what we were discussing. It made it hard to stay on the topic, and it limited our discussion."

3. Chanel
+ Looked back at notes and page numbers, read important quote, stuck to topic.
Used language: "I wonder why," "I think," "I'm confused."
– More piggybacking needed, all need to talk, give each member more time to speak.
People were talking over each other.

Written Self-Evaluations

It's good to vary the evaluation process. Once groups are proficient at oral self-evaluation, I may ask them to evaluate their own behavior and set goals in writing. These written evaluations can be done individually (see Figure 5-11 and Appendix E-2) or as a group (see Figure 5-12). In the following transcript, I'm working with a group of fourth graders.

REGIE: We're going to do our evaluations a little differently today. I'm going to give each group a sheet that says, "What did we do well today?" and "What do we still need to work on and improve?" Usually we do that orally as a group. Decide in your groups who is going to be the scribe, who's going to write down what you all agree upon. I'm going to give you just five minutes to do that. So you're going to need to listen to each other carefully, and then we'll get together and listen to the

Figure 5–11   A student's written self-evaluation

Self-Evaluation
Literature Conversation Group

Name Blair Kurit   Date 5-25-99

Book/story Song of the Trees

1. What did I do well today (and/or improve on) during group discussion?

- asked a lot of questions   - I answered questions
- I was well prepared
- I participated
- I piggybacked
- used eye contact
- looked in book to answer questions
- listened to everyone

2. What do you still need to improve on during the group discussion?

- Write more notes
- Speek louder
- Helping facilitator more.

3. What questions do I still have?

- What does venomously mean?
- What does meddlesome mean?

Figure 5–12 A group's written self-evaluation on literature conversations

+	—
everybody did notes	we yelled
everybody talked	raised hands
eye contact	we did not stay
did not fight over facilitator	on topic all the time
We disagreed and agreed	not much piggybacking
We looked up book	
We mostly listened to each other	

facilitators read from the sheets. Mr. Austin and I will then only chime in if we think there is something that you missed.

RACHEL: (*after five minutes working with her group*): We all tried to say something. We had good notes. We asked good questions. We looked back in the book. We encouraged people to talk. We made eye contact. We listened to each other.

REGIE: Good. I also noticed that the facilitator, at one time said, "I agree with what you said, but we're getting a little off the subject," and then made an effort to bring everyone back. I was impressed with that. And I noticed that a couple of you said, "I have a question." And then you all tried to help each other answer those questions. Like somebody said, "What is a condo?" And you defined it.

MR. AUSTIN: When I was observing, you had a real good discussion about what the term *shells* means and whether people could be in a shell. I also was impressed with some of your notes. You really thought hard about some things and wrote your thoughts down.

REGIE: What do you think your group still needs to work on?

STEPHEN: We didn't piggyback enough. We interrupted each other. We didn't stick to the topic. Sometimes, we'd go off a little.

REGIE: Okay. And I noticed, at least when I was there, that not everyone was participating. I heard several people sort of carrying the conversation and a couple of others that were kind of trying to get into the conversation but really were not part of it. So that's something that needs to be a goal—participation of everyone. What's something you could have done?

JESSICA: We could have said, "We need to hear from so and so. Tell us what you think."

REGIE (*after hearing evaluation comments from all the group facilitators*): How many of you thought your conversation was pretty interesting? Raise your hands. How may of you found that the conversation was kind of boring? A couple. Okay. Most of you found it pretty interesting. Especially, it looks like in these two groups. Again, we talked about how that depends on how good your notes are and how good your questions are that you're raising and that we're helping you raise.

Developing a Rubric to Aid Self-Evaluation

It may be helpful to develop a rubric with your students, so that they, their parents, and you have clear objectives for what's expected in a conversation. In creating a rubric, guide students to make the criteria specific and observable. Remind them—and show them how—to use language that responds to: What does it look like? What does it sound like?

For example, if a student offers, "Be prepared," I ask her, "What would we see and hear if you're prepared?" Or again, when a student suggests, "Pay attention" or "Support group members," I guide them to refine those statements to observable behavior. We talk about the fact that you can't evaluate a behavior unless you can observe it.

Figure 5-13 is a rubric developed with an intermediate class new to literature conversations in a school where grades were required. In addition to the conversation guidelines, students gave weight to varying criteria by specifying the percentage of 100 that each item was worth. Students graded themselves, and teachers either initialed approval or negotiated with students by discussing their observable points of difference.

In general, students evaluate themselves fairly and accurately; if anything, they usually are tougher on themselves than we would be.

Written Tests

In Mark Austin's classroom, the literature groups choose four questions (one selected by each of four groups) that are then discussed in two separate conversations. For their final assessment on the book, students answer whichever one of these four questions they wish. In this open-book, notes-available test of material that has already been discussed by the groups, all students have the opportunity to do well, and they do.

Too often in school, we have cut-off points for how many students can do well. Many teachers, especially of older students, feel that if most students do well, the evaluation must not have been challenging. Not so. When students have been totally engaged in a task that they have helped structure—such as literature conversations—and when they can apply what they've learned and experienced, we have assessment that is highly relevant and valid.

Student Feedback: End-of-Year Evaluation on Literature Conversations

Close to the end of the school year, I asked the fourth graders in Mark Austin's class to give us feedback about literature conversations: what they liked, what they didn't like, what we should change. Their feedback was helpful in improving our program the following year.

• ***Choosing the book for discussion***   Many stated that it was important that the book be exciting—that is, plot centered, with lots of action. They found it hard to take notes on less exciting books.

• ***Dividing the book into sections***   Almost everyone felt it was too much to read the whole book at one time and take notes. Most felt that breaking the book into sections

Figure 5–13   A rubric developed by an intermediate class new to literature conversations

Literature Conversation Guidelines

Be Prepared

have book	5	_____
have literary questions	7	_____
have read book thoughtfully more than once	7	_____
have thoughtful notes	9	_____
sit up straight and lean into conversation	3	_____

Participate

make eye contact with speaker	5	_____
piggyback	8	_____
enter conversation at least 2–3 times	9	_____
help keep group going—stay on topic	7	_____
make connections to life and other texts	9	_____
move to new question	2	_____
encourage others to talk	5	_____
offer opinions/back them up	7	_____
ask questions/answer questions	7	_____
use helpful, respectful language	9	_____

"I agree . . ."
"I disagree . . ."
"I'd like to add . . ."
"Let's discuss . . ."
"Be more specific . . ."
"Maybe . . ."

Goals:

made it easier to take notes and concentrate on just one section at a time. However, students still preferred to talk about the book as a whole.

• ***Note taking***   Several students said they took more and better notes when the book was split into sections or when we did short stories. Almost everyone felt it was important to read the assigned section all the way through first, then reread it and take notes during the second reading.

• ***Conversation groups***   Students appreciated the opportunity to speak, be in charge, learn from their peers, and meet in small groups. Although groups usually consisted of six or seven students, the students preferred four or five in a group, stating the smaller groups allowed more opportunities to talk. "I liked discussing and telling what we think. I liked how we could share how we feel."

Appendix E-3 presents comments from another class.

FINAL REFLECTIONS

Literature conversations have the power to transform the social and intellectual life of the classroom. The free-flowing, open-ended yet focused discussions that arise from students' questions lead to new insights, critical judgments, engaged listening, and responsible, independent behavior. Conversations like this raise the bar on authenticity in learning across the curriculum.

Nancy Schubert had this to say after her first experience with literature conversations:

> In general, it amazed me and continued to amaze me, how easily the children adjusted to this. We'd never done anything of this nature, and it just fell into place. It makes so much sense. Accountability is excellent—they have the questions, formulate their own opinions, check the book. It's so high level. My sense is that everyone gains confidence from our conversations.

CONTINUING THE CONVERSATION

• *Consider taking the lead in starting a teachers-as-readers group.* If there are few outlets for professional conversations in your school or district, begin by discussing a professional book. Use The Blue Pages to guide your selection.

• *Examine the books and stories students are discussing in small group literature conversations.* Are these books rich literature and worth the students' time? Use the guidelines in Chapter 3, "The Literature Program," and the literature lists in The Blue Pages to guide your selections. Consider reading some of these books as part of a TAR group.

• *Record (audio or video) a literature discussion.* Notice who's doing the talking and asking the questions. Are students engaged in stirring dialogue or are they just completing an assignment for the teacher?

• *Monitor your own thinking processes as you are reading a noteworthy book.* What kinds of topics would you want to discuss with a friend? How can your own thinking impact your teaching of literature?

Quality Writing: Principles, Problems, and Goals

Ashley, working on revising and editing her writing

■ The biggest change [after a year of writing workshop] is the kids' attitude toward writing. I can't go a day without it, because the kids ask for it. It carries over into all subject areas. They reread everything they write now—math logs, science logs—they're more aware of what good writing is. I've even noticed my writing is getting better. My newsletters are better. I'm noticing what good writers do, too.

—Julie Beers, third-grade teacher

Vickie Weinland, a parent I know, took her daughter Madelyn, who was in fourth grade, to buy cards so Madelyn could write thank-you notes for birthday gifts. The store clerk, trying to be helpful, suggested, "If you buy these that already have a message on them, you'll have less writing to do."

"But I like to write," Madelyn said. "I want to write my own message."

The clerk seemed dumbfounded. "Well, you're the first student I've ever heard say, *I like to write*."

"I know lots of kids like me who like to write," Madelyn protested.

Vickie loves to tell this story because Madelyn not only likes to write, she writes well and wants to share her love of writing. She has spent her school years in language-rich classrooms where writing has been highly valued and taught every day.

In another vignette, professors from out of state were visiting our school one day and expressed surprise at how well our first graders were writing. I asked what they found surprising. They mentioned the variety of writing, the students' engagement, their awareness of audience *(What else do you think the reader will want to know?)*, the interesting and varied sentence structure, their sharing excitedly with one another, the sheer amount of writing, and the pride the students took in their published books.

Students who love writing and who write with voice, clarity, and accuracy for important purposes and real audiences do not just happen. Expert writers develop when their teachers value and model writing and provide the conditions that foster excellent writing.

WHY WRITE?

I care passionately about promoting literacy, supporting teachers, and making classrooms better places for children. I know firsthand how hard it is to teach well. But I know, too, that our job is easier when we collaborate. My hope in writing this book is to be your supportive collaborator and make your work both easier and more thoughtful.

When I began this book, the sheer amount of work ahead was so daunting, I was immobilized with fear for weeks. There was so much information to create, sort through, organize, delete, synthesize, that I couldn't imagine completing the project—until I slowed down and began to take a step at a time. Make an outline. Write every day, just a few pages. Reread, revise, confer. Write some more, revise some more. Little by little, day by day, month by month, a few pages became many pages. Many pages became chapters, chapters became a book, some of it easily written, most of it a struggle requiring enormous hard work and persistence.

Writing is, in fact, the hardest work I do. Sometimes I sit down to the task kicking and screaming. Other times I can't wait to begin. The discipline required is enormous. The hours are long and can be unproductive. The work is challenging, solitary, and often unrewarding.

Students need to know that writing requires hard work, discipline, and patience. But they also need to know about the payoff—that writing can be the most satisfying, important work of a lifetime. It has been for me.

Given that writing is hard to do well, difficult to teach, and time-consuming and demanding, we need to be clear about our purposes and expectations. For me it is simple: writing is the best tool I know for thinking, communicating, and discovering. Writing allows us to consider and reconsider ideas, positions, statements, and thoughts; to hypothesize, problem-solve, challenge, argue, create, summarize, ruminate, ponder; and to have a record of all this thinking and creating. Writing encourages us to question, reflect on our thinking, read about other ideas and perspectives, change our minds, reach for loftier goals. And when we write we do all these things simultaneously.

Writing as Thinking

Before I came to consider myself a writer, I was unaware of the power of writing, that writing was thinking. To me, thinking was an in-the-head process that the thinker carried on internally. Once writing became part of my daily life and sustenance, I saw that much of my best thinking occurred in the act of writing: that is, while composing—ruminating, percolating, pondering, musing, scribbling thoughts down, moving ideas around—ideas formed and got tested, changed, discarded, worked out, transformed. Rereading and rethinking were ongoing. New insights took hold. Disjointed thoughts cohered. Organization emerged from clutter. Gaps narrowed—or widened. New questions surfaced. Parts became a whole. Learning occurred.

Writing as thinking goes far beyond basic skills and has powerful implications for classroom teaching: problem solving, note taking, brainstorming, observing, reflecting, considering other points of view.

Writing as Communicating

Thoughtful writing makes it possible to communicate explicitly and profoundly, with small or large audiences, on a level not usually possible through oral conversation. The written word is permanent. The reader not only is able to digest the message at his own rate but can revisit the writing and ponder the message.

I write letters to the editor because if my letter is printed, I will be communicating my beliefs on important issues to a wide audience. There is always the hope that I may be able to spur thinking and dialogue, raise new questions in people's minds, even change action and policy. Personally, I am constantly writing to friends and colleagues to share information, thoughts, and feelings.

If we send students out into the world who, whatever the basic skills they've acquired and facts they've amassed, cannot communicate effectively, we have failed to prepare them to contribute and function both personally and professionally. Writing as communicating goes far beyond correct spelling, grammar, and other conventions, although these are absolutely necessary if the reader is to focus on the message unobstructed.

Writing as Discovering

Perhaps most of all, writing encourages us to make discoveries—whether about things we didn't realize we knew or were thinking, or new insights. I write to find out what I know and understand, to identify what I need and want to learn, to come to new understanding. Discovery writing is finding out, organizing, learning as you go. "I don't write out of what I know," says Toni Morrison. "It's what I don't know that stimulates me. I merely know enough to get started" (Murray 1990, 109).

Writing this book is largely an act of discovery. For example, when I began writing this section, I did not know I would be looking at writing as thinking, communicating, and discovering. I only knew I wanted to talk about why writing is such a critical skill and to make a case for teaching it and teaching it well. But whenever we are thinking, communicating, listening to and trusting ourselves, there is the element of surprise. We start with a premise or idea and then the writing takes over, leading us to other premises and ideas.

WHAT'S GONE WRONG IN
THE TEACHING OF WRITING?

Writing well remains elusive to too many teachers and students. Over and over again, teachers tell me their students do not take writing seriously. Translated, this means students don't revise, write neatly, invest their energies. Years after writing process is supposedly established in classrooms, there are still too few classrooms in which we find good writing. In some cases, writing is just another assignment: *Take out your journals* is the equivalent of a worksheet. My friend and mentor Don Graves confirms what I already know, that more kids are writing but that the writing isn't getting any better: "I'm still very concerned about how little writing is taught, how little time is provided for children to write. And when time is provided, I don't see children challenged by teachers who have been prepared to teach it through the teacher's own high level of literacy" (Routman 1995, 524).

The comments of a student new to our district make some of the problems with teaching writing crystal clear. In mid-November, Andrew entered Danny Young's third-grade class, where he enthusiastically participated in writing workshop for one hour each day. Writing workshop began with a minilesson presented by Danny, continued with a period of sustained writing that sometimes included peer or teacher conferences, and concluded with whole-group sharing (a public, classwide conference). I was working weekly with Danny, supporting his efforts. When Danny told me Andrew was always saying that writing was different and better at this school, I wanted to learn more:

> REGIE: Andrew, I work with a lot of teachers in writing, and I got especially interested in you when Mr. Young told me that you were asking to stay in at recess to do your writing, which is pretty unusual and pretty wonderful. Tell me why you like the writing program here better. Tell me what it was like at your other school and what the difference is here.
>
> ANDREW: At my old school, they would just let you publish any little thing you wanted. You wouldn't have to rewrite very good and you wouldn't have to be serious with conferences. [The teachers] would just go to the publishing center and sign you up and just let you publish. It wasn't serious.
>
> REGIE: And why do you think that's not a good idea?
>
> ANDREW: Because a couple of people published maybe thirteen books, but when you read them, you're thinking, *This is really, really dull. They should have worked on it more.*
>
> REGIE: Andrew, I was particularly interested when you talked with Mr. Young and me in class today, and you said you had published five books from September to November and you realized they weren't very good.
>
> ANDREW: They weren't, but the teachers kept complimenting you, just to make you work harder, but it didn't work. And you realized, *Hey, I can't do this. These aren't good books.*
>
> REGIE: You said that at the other school there was a big list of things you were supposed to do. Tell me about that.
>
> ANDREW: Oh, yeah. First, we had a list, and it said you have to write your story and then go back and put periods in and all that. And then you would have to get a friend and just have a conference. But the conferences weren't serious. After the conference, you would go back and do what they had you work on, but that didn't do much. Then you would have a conference with the teacher and then rewrite.
>
> REGIE: Um-hmm.
>
> ANDREW: And then, even though the writing wasn't good enough, they would publish it, 'cause they had a conference with you. Once the publishing people said, *Gosh, you should have worked harder on this.* I think they knew.

REGIE: Okay. And since you've been here, you've published one book, and you told me it's pretty good. Tell me about that, what you're working on now.

ANDREW: I published about my hockey experiences, and now I'm writing about my life and my hobbies.

REGIE: You seem very interested in making sure that your writing is well done. So what are you doing, or what's happening in your class to make your writing better?

ANDREW: Well, when I have a conference with you or Mr. Young, it's more serious than at my other school. Like I'm expected to have reread my writing carefully and filled out a form saying what I need. And then, at the conference I learn things, like cutting and pasting.

REGIE: Andrew, you told me that at your other school you got to choose your own writing topics. So that part's not really different. The part that's different, if I'm hearing you correctly, is that here the writing is taken more seriously.

ANDREW: Yeah.

REGIE: Over there, it was just like, take out your book and write.

ANDREW: Uh-huh, it didn't really matter what you wrote. You could even publish in a day.

REGIE: Well, sometimes you can write something short that's really excellent, but these weren't?

ANDREW: They weren't, 'cause they . . . they just weren't.

REGIE: You know, Andrew, a lot of people think that kids just want to get the stuff down and get done with it. But you're saying that's not true. You're saying you feel really good when you do quality work.

ANDREW: Yeah, you should try to take up all your time to do as much as you can and do your best.

Out of the mouths of babes. What's gone wrong? A tough question with no easy answers. However, certain factors appear to contribute strongly to the lack of quality writing in classrooms.

Lacking Knowledge

The truth is, most of us know very little about how to teach writing. To become certified as an elementary teacher in most states, courses in writing are still not required. In fact, many universities have few or no course offerings in writing (Routman 1995, 525). Furthermore, many of us fear and dislike writing ourselves. We remember writing to meet our teachers' values and purposes, we remember the red marks on our papers, some of us even remember writing as punishment.

Still, with the best of intentions, we forged ahead. Many of us read about writing process classrooms and established "writing workshops." We followed a formula without understanding the recursive, idiosyncratic nature of writing. We didn't know that we could not teach writing (or any subject) well unless we ourselves were knowledgeable and highly literate as readers and writers. We didn't realize that we could value, observe, and use our own writing processes to become better writing teachers.

Almost all the changes I have made in how I teach writing stem from trusting what

I've noticed about my own writing when I write cards, letters, notes, outlines, drafts. Observing my own process has helped me understand the importance of teaching many forms of writing; the need for correct spelling, grammar, and punctuation; and the absolute necessity of writing for a real purpose and audience. I strongly believe that students will not take writing seriously without a teacher-as-writer in the classroom. When students see how we use writing in our life, they view writing differently.

Having Unrealistic Expectations

If we are not sufficiently knowledgeable about writing, we wind up having unrealistic expectations about what students can do. Mostly, we expect too little, especially with regard to editing, spelling, and legibility. We accept unacceptable work because we don't want to "interfere" with the creative process. In the name of "invented spelling," we permit students to misspell words they are capable of spelling. We let young students scribble or write without spacing and punctuation far longer than necessary. We fail to teach and expect legible handwriting. We also expect too little in terms of how students craft their writing. Students are perfectly capable of writing with voice if we show them how. The same is true for using conversation, meaningful detail, and carefully chosen verbs—even for young writers.

Conversely, expectations can be too high. Time and time again, I observe teachers modeling and expecting writing that is beyond what young writers can do. In kindergarten classes, teachers often model writing that is beyond the ability of most of the class. At the beginning of first grade, when most of the students are appropriately writing just a few sentences, teachers model writing several paragraphs. And many teachers still expect students to write well just because the writing is assigned, never mind providing any models or guidance at all.

Students are often asked to do things as writers that real writers don't do. Some teachers expect students to complete every piece and edit it carefully before beginning a new piece. While editing is always important, we don't want to push so hard at editing that we turn students off. As students reread their drafts, I expect them to fix up common words they know how to spell and put in basic punctuation and capitalization. However, I want their main focus to be on meaningful and interesting communication. Some teachers expect all children to begin each paragraph with a topic sentence or to write using "vivid" words. When I sit down to write, I do not think about topic sentences or vivid words. I think about how I can convey meaning to my audience.

It is also unrealistic to expect young children to write well when they don't have sufficient letter-sound knowledge. Too often students are unable to stay focused, and therefore waste their time, because they need guidance and direct teaching in order to write. We need to meet with these students individually or in small groups and teach them what they need to know to be successful (see page 68). We need to look more carefully at what students are actually doing and can do in all areas of writing. Then, with high but reasonable expectations, we need to nudge them forward through demonstrations and conferences.

Doing Our Writing Behind the Scenes

"How do you become comfortable writing in front of students, especially if you don't think of yourself as a writer?" fourth-grade teacher Lisa Hardiman asked me. It's ironic that we all do lots of writing, but we haven't "come out" as writers. We write almost every day as we go about the business of living and working, but we do it behind the scenes, and our students don't know we are writers. Worse yet, most of us don't see ourselves as writers.

An exercise that helps make us aware of how much we write is to keep track of all of our writing for one month or to recall the writing we've done in the past few weeks. Taking a writing inventory (see Figure 6-1) helps me reflect on the quantity and variety of my own writing as well as set directions for my teaching. Ask your students to do this for themselves or to "shadow" a parent and record the writing he or she does. Or have your class develop a when-do-you-write survey.

The next step is to show samples of your writing and take the risk of writing in front of your students. While some educators argue that teachers don't have to write to teach writing, there's no question in my mind that we do a better job engaging and teaching students when we model for them.

Third-grade teacher Julie Beers tells how she struggled for days to compose a personal poem to the school principal, who was leaving her job after seven years. Although Julie had regularly shared her writing with her students, she'd always brought it in after she'd completed it at home. Until she heard Nancie Atwell talk about modeling personal writing in front of her students, she'd never actually done it. Julie says, "I was scared to write in front of my kids because it's so hard." So this time Julie—in front of her students—thought out loud, drafted, revised, and rewrote. Julie's students then wrote their own poems, and the principal specifically commented on their exceptional quality. Julie says it's because her students saw her write.

Figure 6–1 A one-month inventory of my writing

My Writing Record
August 1997

drafts (teaching writing)

jottings (Post-it Notes reminders)

notes (spiral notebook for writing ideas, daily happenings, talks)

writer's notebook (small notebook for memorable quotes)

lists (note pads for shopping, things to do, people to write)

outline (evolving draft for new book)

letters, greeting cards, post cards
   congratulations
   thank you
   condolence
   birthday
   anniversary
   friendship
   responses to teachers
   get well
   acknowledgment
   requests and inquiries
   business letters

e-mails and faxes

A teacher recently wrote to me, "Because of my own fears about writing, it has been difficult for me to teach my students writing." Hard as it is to do, we need to face those fears head on. Allowing students to see our process tells them we are all writers and risk takers. Without our showing the way, only a small percentage of our students will write well. Atwell encourages us: "We only have to write a *little bit better* than they do for them to take something away from our demonstrations" (Atwell 1998, 368).

Not Writing About Our Passions

Writing in front of our students is not enough. If what we write about is general, boring, and lackluster, it should be no surprise when this same kind of writing comes back at us. When we move from *this is what happened* to *this is what matters to me*, the effect on our student's writing is dramatic.

Fifth-grade teacher Janet Stringer and I are talking about journal writing. She is concerned that her students' writing is consistently mediocre and uninteresting. When I ask her whether her students have seen her write, she says this is hard for her. I suggest she take the risk and write in front of them about something that matters to her. A week later she tells me, "I did write in front of them, and their writing still didn't improve."

"What did you write about, Janet?" I ask.

"I wrote about when I was a child and my five-year-old cousin gave me a rabbit's foot. It made me realize he cared about me."

"That's an interesting story, but there's no passion. What are the issues you wrestle with, that matter most to you? Talk about those."

She tells me that the big things in her life are her new boyfriend, who is a workaholic and has trouble relaxing, and the difficulties she encounters living with her grandmother. I agree with Janet that these are not appropriate for her to write about in front of her students because they are too personal and unrelated to students' lives. But I still insist, "There must be something else significant that you could share with them."

The following week, Janet shows me the writing she's been doing in front of her students about how she felt growing up in a family where everyone was overweight. What a difference! I see and feel her passion—detail, description, and emotion permeate her writing because the subject is personally important. All her students can relate to what it's like to feel different, and several students immediately choose related topics.

Another time I am observing a primary teacher modeling writing in front of her students; she tells about getting a postcard from an uncle she likes who lives in Europe. In her conversation before she begins writing, she is animated and detailed, but what she writes is bare bones. Afterward, we talk about how her personal voice, which was so apparent when she talked about the incident, was absent when she wrote about it. She begins to slow down her writing, adding dialogue and emotion, and the improvement in the students' writing is immediate. She comments: "I didn't notice I wasn't using my own words. I was focused on what the kids could help me spell. After we talked, I realized what I was doing, and my writing became more like my conversation. That made a big difference in the quality of the students' writing."

Expecting Students to Revise Everything

How do you get kids to revise? is probably the most frequently asked question about writing. Of course, you can't *get* students to do *anything*. All you can do is set up the environment for writing so that kids want to write and do their best work.

First, in the real world lots of writing never gets revised. We create false expectations for our students if we insist that they revise everything they write. I write lots of stuff that never gets revised—notes, impromptu poems, drafts that go nowhere, letters. I only revise when my audience demands it. Then, I am relentless about "getting it right," which for me means that my writing must be clear, interesting, engaging, and easy to read.

Second, much of the stuff we ask our students to revise isn't important to them. Recently, a teacher asked me to work with her students on revising endings to Cinderella stories. "Why do you want your students to revise them?" I asked. She said she wanted to put the stories up on one of her classroom bulletin boards. "Why?" I asked again. She offered a few more reasons, but nothing she said had anything to do with the students. It was her agenda, and her students couldn't have cared less. I suggested we come up with something that would matter to the students. She liked the idea of a class log of important happenings (see pages 267–268). Because the students also liked the idea and saw a purpose for it, they took the writing seriously and did their best work (see pages 267–268).

Many times, of course, students need to write about a topic they don't love—for an assignment or a test, for example—and still be able to do their best work. That's the real world. However, even then, the purpose of the assignment or test needs to be clear.

Choosing Trivial Topics

Students have to care about their writing to write well, and they care about things in which they are interested. One of the mistakes we make is to expect writers to come up with new topics all the time—every day, in some classrooms. I've been as guilty of this as the next person. I used to expect kids to write about a new topic in their journal each day. No wonder their writing was so dull. Mem Fox set me straight: "I have about four ideas a year, and I'm a proficient, professional, published writer, yet we ask children to write story after story" (1993, 18). When I started finding out what children were interested in and what they "ache with caring about" (Fox, 22), I learned that even first graders could sustain a topic for days and weeks and write with style, voice, and descriptive detail.

Topics can be trivial even when we give students a choice. Recently, Dana Noble and I were trying to get his high school juniors to invest more in their writing. We asked them to tackle something they felt strongly about, and we discussed many possibilities. Although we both shared our real writing with them—his, a letter of complaint about a faulty oven, mine, a letter to the editor clarifying how we learn to read—overall, the content and the mechanics of the students' writing were disappointing. Only a few papers had a strong author's voice. We'd given the students a choice, but it was one without personal intention; as one student bluntly said, she chose her topic "to get the assignment done."

Devoting Too Little Time to Writing

At the beginning of a recent school year, a teacher who had up until then resisted student-initiated writing suggested I work with him: "I'm finally ready to get writing workshop going in my classroom." I was delighted. We began by planning together, talking with the students about our own writing, organizing the writing notebook, and finding out what students wanted to write about. For several months, his students wrote every day. Then, gradually, he gave less and less time to writing ("I just can't fit it in") until it dwindled to once or twice a week. Students lost interest and quality suffered. Eventually, he abandoned writing all together.

Not devoting enough time to writing is a big problem. Again and again teachers tell me they value writing but can't find the time. (See pages 291 and 292 for how two teachers *have* been able to work writing into the school day.) Without a predictable time in which to write every day, students cannot sustain interest and momentum. Learning any craft takes practice, and practice means time—time to think, mess up, experiment, share, start again, rethink, confer, imagine, and create.

Writing every day, students get an opportunity to work out the rules and patterns of spelling and grammar, to experiment with language, to try out new genres, and to explore topics and ideas. While writing regularly does not guarantee quality will improve, writing a lot does seem to help students come up with new ideas. In classrooms with knowledgeable writing teachers who schedule writing every day, topic selection ceases to be a problem.

Concentrating Too Much on Publishing

I've modified my stance on publishing. I still recommend that students in grade two and above publish a short piece, such as a letter written to a real person or persons, at least once a month. This ensures that mechanics and editing are being addressed, which in turn sends the important message to administrators, parents, and students that accuracy in spelling, capitalization, and punctuation matters.

But I've become much tougher on the big projects, the stuff kids choose to write about. I'm tired of walking into classrooms and reading "published" pieces that, even if the mechanics are passable, are incapable of holding anyone's attention. (What do *you* do when a book you've chosen to read isn't very interesting? You put it aside.) Nowadays, I tell students, we will only publish their stories and projects if they are excellent. I make the point personal: *My publisher won't publish what I write unless it's excellent. Getting it that way takes lots of hard work, lots of rewriting. I'm willing to do this hard work because I care so much about my topic and my audience. I have a responsibility to my readers to make my writing as clear and interesting and accurate as possible. I have the same expectations for your writing.*

After I had a conversation like this with a group of third graders, Dina, who had planned to publish some poems she'd written about her brother, decided they weren't good enough. She'd enjoyed writing them but didn't want to invest any more time in them. She set the drafts aside and moved on to another topic.

Not Knowing What Good Writing Is

Although many of us say we have writing process in place in our classroom, we remain focused on mechanics. Because we don't write with our students, don't share with them the writing we do in our life, we have no choice but to teach writing the old way, that is, by focusing on correctness.

Often when I go into classrooms and ask students what makes writing excellent, they talk about handwriting, spelling, capitalization, and punctuation. I have to push them: "But if I read a great piece of writing *to* you, you can't *see* any of those things. What else makes writing excellent?" Then, finally, someone will mention interesting words and content, description and detail, organization. Voice almost never comes up. Most students and teachers don't know what it is.

Students' writing doesn't improve just because we send them back to work on it. They need to know and be able to apply the criteria for excellent writing in order to write well. Together, teachers and students need to set standards for what excellent writing includes. In our school district, one way we do this is by creating specific grade-level writing rubrics: *uses lively, engaging language, writes with a logical flow and unity.* (See page 228 for one example.) With the rubric as our guide, we learn how to read what we write and set goals for improving it.

I also show students samples of excellent work from previous classes, and we talk about what makes the particular work so good. Nancie Atwell suggests giving students access to files containing excellent examples of kids' writing in various genres. That way, if a student is writing a poem, he can go directly to the poetry file for great examples; likewise for letters, stories, whatever.

HOW CAN WE FOSTER QUALITY WRITING?

If our present writing practices aren't good enough, how can we do better? Subsequent chapters deal in depth and in detail with how to teach journal writing, how to establish and manage an effective writing classroom, and how to write in many real-world genres. Here, I want to establish a framework by addressing several critical factors related to good writing: being able to choose what we write about versus writing on demand, having an audience and purpose that matter, writing with voice, teaching conventions, being exposed to powerful writing models, and having a conducive environment in which to write.

Choice

When we can write about what we value, about our passions, then what we say is more likely to be vibrant and interesting, and we're also more likely to get the spelling and punctuation right. We all invest greater effort and energy when we care deeply about a task and its outcome. However, it is not enough just to allow students to choose a topic or a genre. We need to model our expectations, offer support, allow time to practice, and provide feedback. (See pages 212 and 236–241 for teaching demonstrations geared to get students to use choice responsibly.)

Too often, writers workshop has been misinterpreted to mean students can write whatever they want, that the student always chooses. Not so. It is our job as teachers to define and negotiate the parameters. For example, require that your students respond to an essay question, but allow them to choose which of three questions to answer. Or, require that your students write a business letter, but allow them to decide to whom. (If you want everyone to write on a specific topic, try a shared writing.) It's only when we provide no choice whatsoever that the writing breaks down.

At the beginning of the year, student choices are of necessity more limited. Nevertheless, when a student wishes to write in a genre I haven't yet demonstrated, I'll let her go ahead, as long as I know she has read many examples of the genre and has a written plan for how to proceed. This is, after all, what I do myself. Before I write an editorial, an essay, a letter to the editor, or an interview, I carefully examine many examples, noting form, structure, length, tone, word choice, etc.

Writing on Demand

While being able to choose what to write is absolutely necessary, students must also be able to write "on demand": that is, they must be able to write effectively and efficiently on an assigned topic within a set time. Classroom, district, state, and national tests require writing like this, and we put our students at a disadvantage if we don't teach them how to do it. At the same time, assigned writing and exercises in isolation have no meaning for students. Once students understand and can apply the real-world behavior of good writers (and good readers), we can teach them "writing-test writing" as a separate form. Even then, we must make sure that this doesn't take over the curriculum.

Quickwrites

Quickwriting is an excellent vehicle for teaching writing on demand. In a quickwrite, we focus on getting our ideas down quickly without worrying about mechanics or revisions. It's how writers deal with writer's block. (I did this each time I started a new topic for this book—got going quickly, put the ideas down, didn't bother with revising and editing.) It's the written form of brainstorming. A quickwrite gets the energy flowing, the mind moving. No matter that the writing is dreadful; once the words are in front of us, we can move them around, think about them, make changes.

I first tried quickwrites in the classroom after I saw Linda Rief incorporate one as part of a workshop session at NCTE's national conference in 1994. The room became silent as she and the several hundred educators in the audience wrote for three minutes. (The whole exercise—including directions, writing, and sharing—took about seven minutes.) I was struck by the power of the writing that was shared and by how it made us feel like a connected group. Here's how it works:

• ***Choose a prompt students can relate to easily.*** Some good ones include *Next year, I plan to . . . , I remember when . . . , One time I . . . , Yesterday I . . . , I never knew . . . , A long time ago I . . . , I was surprised . . . , I noticed . . . , I wish that . . . , I don't understand why. . . .*

• *Give clear directions.* Check to be sure students understand the task before they begin. Let students know that the room is to be silent, that you will also be writing, that you will not be available to help them. Encourage them to do the best they can on their own.

• *Allow three to ten minutes for writing; do not intervene.* Try different time frames, depending on your purpose and the age of your students.

• *Invite students to share afterward, but do not allow additional comments by others.* What students have written needs to be acknowledged without judgment or comment. Students need to know that what they have written is accepted as is.

A focused quickwrite has a number of benefits:

• *It lets students practice timed writing and writing on demand.* Writing on demand is a real-life skill. Throughout their life, in and out of school, students will be required to write under a restricted time frame: a test, a writing sample during a job interview, a memo at work.

• *It can be completed rapidly.* Because quickwriting takes so little class time, it is an easy procedure to add to an already full curriculum.

• *It can be used to measure improvement.* Second-grade teacher Ellen Rubin uses quickwrites to monitor writing fluency, spelling, and content. She has her students do a five-minute quickwrite each month. She counts the number of words, checks the spelling, and reviews the content. She uses the results to set goals with students at individual conferences, and she shares this information with parents at formally scheduled conferences.

• *It lets students experience the surprise of writing.* The act of writing is often a complete surprise: "I write to discover what I am thinking, not what I have already thought" (Murray 1996, 46), and, "I want to discover what I know that I didn't know I knew" (47). They, and you, will be flabbergasted by what winds up on the page.

• *It increases the amount of writing students do.*

• *It helps build community.* Sharing personal stories binds people together; they risk being human and open with one another.

• *It can be used across the curriculum.*

Assigned Writing

Other kinds of assigned writing tell us what students have understood:

• <u>**Summary**</u> Writing a summary is the act of deleting nonessential information, and students need to be shown how to include only the central elements.

• <u>**Retelling**</u> An oral or written reconstruction of a story tells us what the reader or listener remembers. Retellings have more details than summaries. (For specifics and procedures for retelling, see pages 595–598.)

• <u>**Explanation**</u> When students explain their thinking, whether it be in mathematics, science, or another area of the curriculum, we—and they—get a window into their problem-solving processes. This enables us not only to evaluate their comprehension of concepts but to plan next-steps instruction. In the act of explaining our learning/doing, we clarify, modify, and refine—and in the process increase our understanding.

• ***Reflection and self-evaluation*** Writing about our attitudes and analyzing our learning experiences lets us think about the learning process, not just what was learned but how it was learned, what worked and why, what conditions promoted or inhibited learning, factors that might increase learning in related situations in the future. To improve instruction and learning, teachers ask students to reflect on a unit of study, collaborative teamwork, a field trip, a specific lesson. Questions to prompt this type of writing include, *What suggestions do you have for improving or enriching this lesson (or unit of study)? How might our groups work differently and more effectively?* (See page 200 for an example of a reflection after a literature conversation. Also see Chapter 15, "Evaluation as Part of Teaching.")

Audience and Purpose

All the writing I do is for a real purpose. I'm sure that's true for you as well. Yet, in school, we often ask children to write without a clear purpose. One of the reasons I like having students keep a writing history (see page 52) is that it shows the audience for their writing. At a glance, we, they, and their parents can see whether most of the writing has been for the teacher, for the students themselves, or for other audiences.

Even the quality of very young students' writing is impacted when they write for an audience that matters, for example, kindergarten students writing letters for real reasons (see Figure 6-2) and second graders insisting on publishing even when their teacher says it will be too much work for them (see pages 323–326).

I found it fascinating—and disconcerting—that when a group of high school students was asked to write to an audience that mattered to them (page 213), few actually did.

Figure 6–2 Requesting spiders to build a spider frame in the classroom to observe how they make their webs

Dear Mommy,
  I really need lots of spiders. Please don't be chicken. Look in the garage. Just put the spiders in a jar.

(by Heather Buffo)

Students went through the motions and appeared to write for a real purpose, but years of writing only for the teacher made it difficult for most to move beyond the teacher as audience. They made few revisions and took no pride in their work.

By contrast, when I interviewed Julie Beers' fourth graders about preparing their classroom news magazine for their parents each month, here's what they said:

- "You think more about what you're writing because there's a big audience."
- "You want to make a good impression."
- "You know your parents will read it, and you want them to say, *I love it.*"
- "It's a good type of pressure because a lot of people are reading it, so you want to do your best."

Why Do People Write? What Do People Write?

When I go into classrooms and work with students, I usually find they have little idea why we give time to writing in school, other than that it's for the teacher, to complete an assignment. They do not connect writing with life. So now I begin by saying something like this: *You've been in school for some years now, and many of you have had teachers that have given time to writing every day, so it must be pretty important. Let's talk about why people write, what they write, and how you become an excellent writer.*

We start by talking about why people write and then go on to what forms that writing takes. Often, students start out superficially by talking about writing to do well in the next grade or writing to become better spellers. Our list on chart paper builds slowly. (The first time you do this activity, the list may be meager.) I tell the students to go home, look around, talk with their parents about how they use writing in their work. Next time they have more items to add to the list (see Figure 6-3).

We follow this with, *If these are the reasons people write, what forms does the writing*

Figure 6–3   Why do people write?

Why Do People Write?

to get a job	to tell what you know and think
to communicate	to have something to do
to become authors	to persuade
to remember what you know	to explain
to entertain	to figure out what you know and don't know
to give the news	to inform parents
to identify (people, things)	to make claims
for fun	to buy something and get help
to express feelings	to sell insurance
to record events	to take messages
to specify (what to build)	to keep track of what you do (doctors' notes on patients).
to help others	
to pay bills and get paid	to review books and movies

take? We discuss possible writing formats or genres we can use when we want to express our feelings (letters, diaries, journals), when we want to share information (magazine and newspaper articles, reference books, reports), or when we want to teach someone something (guidebooks, instructional manuals). Having first focused on the purposes for writing, students easily see that there are many types of writing people do in the world (see Figure 6-4).

I have done Why Do People Write? and What Do People Write? in almost every grade; it's very freeing to think about the myriad of reasons for writing and the forms that writing can take. Students begin to connect their own writing to a real purpose and a real audience, which in turn improves their interest in writing, the topics they choose to write about, the energy with which they write, and their willingness to revise and publish.

Figure 6–4   *What do people write?*

What Do People Write?

drafts

memos

letters

books

applications

lesson plans

newsletters

report cards

assignments

exams

diary entries

journal entries

speeches

essays

summaries

tests

evaluations

poems

magazines

newspapers

word searches

comic books

jokes

riddles

stories

puzzles

biographies

autobiographies

reference books
  encyclopedias, dictionaries, almanacs, thesauri

instructions

recipes

menus

directories

outlines

"how to" manuals

charts

advertisements

displays

brochures

reflections

inventories

checks

graphs

envelopes

travel guides

signs

posters

shopping lists

grants

resumes

general correspondence
  requesting information, for/to managers,
  cancellations

invitations

legal documents
  citations, summons, contracts

reviews
  books, movies, performances

Powerful Writing Models

Early in the school year, I share myself as a writer. I want students to see that I do lots of different kinds of writing and that I write for real reasons. I bring in the beautiful art cards, colorful postcards, and favorite stationery from my desk drawer at home. I share business letters, poems, cards, drafts, directions, whatever writing I've been doing. I show the many rounds of revisions that go into a published piece and explain why I put so much time into revision. This always amazes kids, that I willingly write and rewrite to make the writing better, that I may spend an hour reworking a three-sentence paragraph. I want students to connect writing to the world, not just to school.

Our students need our example. Before you seal a letter or a card you're going to send, show it to your students. (You don't have to read it if it's personal.) Or show them the paper you are working on for the course you're taking or the draft of your article for the school newsletter you struggled with last night. Our students need to know we write and value writing.

We also have to be readers to write well. To write using rich, compelling language, we need to hear and read rich, compelling literature. Only a love of reading will promote an understanding and awareness of imagery, tone, voice, and other nuances of good writing. There is no shortcut. To write well, we have to read well and deeply. We need to make our students aware of what great authors do, how they do it, the effect they have on the reader.

Author studies are one way to make students aware of how authors work (see pages 78–80). Reading great literature aloud (including picture books, whatever the age of your audience) and talking about what the author has done to make the writing memorable—the imaginative lead that grabs the reader's attention, the lively conversation showing characters' thoughts and feelings, the vivid and precise verbs, the specific detail and imagery, the satisfying ending—is another powerful way to help students connect reading to writing. We must immerse our students in outstanding literature every day, help them notice how the author has dealt with the topic, genre, organization, setting, mood, word choice, sentence construction, more. (Pages 382–383 describe how a beautifully written picture book was able to spark quality writing in an intermediate-grade class.)

Other students' writing is the most powerful model of all. Kids think, *A kid just like me wrote this. I can do this too.* No matter what genre I am teaching, I have samples of exemplary student writing on hand to share and discuss. These samples may be the work of other students in the class (with their permission), former students, or students of a colleague. I usually enlarge these samples or make overhead transparencies so I can share them easily. Student models don't have to be peers. Exemplary teacher and author Joanne Hindley (1997) invited a fifth grader to share a memorable writing notebook entry with Joanne's third-grade class. The students noticed and discussed what worked well in the writing.

At the end of his second year of teaching, Neal Robinson told me that two things in particular helped his kids write well: finding a topic that mattered to them and being able to look at other students' work: "Those models gave kids the feeling, *Yeah, I can do this.* Once you have one or two who pick up on it, you share it with the class. That leads to four or five doing it, then eight or ten, and it just spreads. I used to just have them write but I didn't get quality."

Students also need to see examples of the criteria for quality writing and have them explained. One powerful way for students to internalize criteria for excellent writing is to put them in small groups and have them talk about several pieces of writing. Select student papers (from a previous class or another class) that have been scored high, medium, and low against a writing rubric, and make copies without the authors' names. Have the students read the papers and discuss what they notice, with one group member serving as scribe. After ten or fifteen minutes, gather the class as a whole and generate a chart depicting the criteria for quality writing in the particular genre.

Once writing criteria have been established, students can take a piece of writing, discuss what advice they would give the writer, and go to work on improving the piece. You'll first need to demonstrate how to do this:

- Find the strongest part in the piece.
- What needs deleting?
- What needs clarification?
- What more does the reader need?

Voice

I receive hundreds of letters from teachers, and it pleases me that most begin, *Dear Regie.* Often, they go on to say, *I feel like I know you.* I am convinced my correspondents choose an informal greeting because I write in a personal, conversational way. It is a deliberate stance, and one I strive to maintain.

It was during the final stages of publishing *Invitations* that the power of voice was really brought home to me. An overzealous copy editor who did not know me or my audience had gone through my text. As I was reading the first chunk of copyedited pages, I felt some discomfort. It wasn't just that lots of words had been changed and juxtaposed; the text *sounded* different. I couldn't put my finger on it until I read, ". . . just mention the word *evaluation,* and one can feel the tension." My original had read, ". . . just mention the word *evaluation,* and you can feel the tension." A one-word change, from *you* to *one,* and what was wrong became crystal clear: the text no longer sounded like me. The book was now formal and stiff, not informal and friendly. I remember the moment vividly. "My voice is gone," I wailed to my husband. "They've taken away my voice." My terrific Heinemann editor and I painstakingly went through the manuscript page by page, putting my voice back in.

Voice is hard to define, but when it's in—or missing from—a piece of writing, you sense it. Writing with voice has richness and sparkle, a distinct human spirit that makes you feel you know the writer. Ralph Fletcher says, "Voice in writing has to do with a unique personality-on-paper" (1993, 77).

Not surprisingly, voice has little to do with completeness and accuracy. A piece can have a beginning, middle, and end, be grammatically correct, have perfect spelling and punctuation, and have no voice, thereby making the writing totally uninspiring. (The still required five-paragraph essay is an example of valuing organization and form at the expense of voice. Students who follow the structure receive the message that the writing is exemplary, even when the content is dull, dull, dull.)

I see a lot of writing like this. Partly, it's because we require students to write about things they have no interest in. Second-grade teacher Loretta Martin says, "Voice is absent without choice." For example, some teachers require students to write thank-yous to classroom visitors, or assign an unknown "pen pal" to each student. It's no wonder all the letters sound the same. Why send twenty-five letters when one will do? Why not ask for a volunteer or small group to write the mandatory note of social etiquette and have all the class members sign it? Why not let students individually choose an out-of-town relative or friend for their pen pal, someone they really want to write to?

I vividly remember receiving twenty-four thank-you notes from a second-grade class for *The Magic School Bus in the Time of the Dinosaurs,* by Joanna Cole, which I had donated to their classroom library. After the first five or six, I detected a pattern. Each letter began, "Thank you for . . . ," continued with "I learned . . . ," and ended, "I liked. . . ." The teacher, excellent and conscientious in every way, had guided the students in the form the letters should take. Technically, each letter was nearly perfect, but they were all the same. They had no voice. I could have put any student's name on any letter. I lost interest, quickly skimming the rest—until I came to Mea's letter at the very end of the pile (see Figure 6-5): *Dear Mrs. Routman, I learned a lot about dinoaurs but I didn't learn a lot because I fell asleep because I was sick and my stomach hurts. And that's why I didn't learn a lot. From, your friend, Mea.* This was honest, this was real, this was Mea sounding like Mea. Her letter is the only one I remember.

We need to show our students what voice is and how to make it integral to their writing. Don Graves says, "Kids don't write with good voices unless the teacher has one" (1997). Unfortunately, many of us are intimidated by the notion of voice and don't believe we can write with voice ourselves (remember Janet's story, earlier in this chapter?).

When some of the teachers in my school district proposed adding "writes with a

Figure 6–5 Mea's letter demonstrating voice

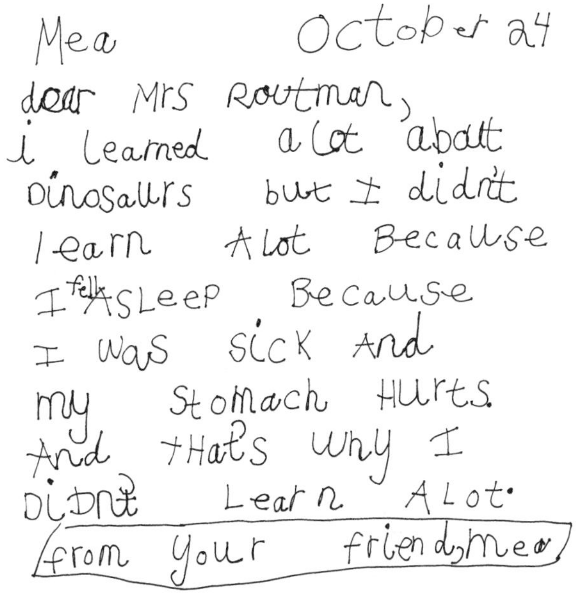
Mea October 24
dear Mrs Routman,
i learned a lot abaut
Dinosaurs but I didnt
learn A lot Because
I fell Asleep Because
I was sick And
my stomach Hurts
And that's why I
didnt Learn A lot.
from your friend, mea

personal style" or "writes with voice" to the writing section of our report card in grades one through four, many other teachers protested. Our discussions revealed that most of those who protested didn't know what voice in writing meant and therefore didn't know how to teach it. One first-grade teacher vehemently declared that it was too much to expect from first graders, who were just learning the act of transcription. (The same teacher, the following year, proudly shared a student's journal entry with me—see Figure 6-6—and proclaimed, "I've got it. First graders can write with voice.")

My experience has been that even young children can write with voice when we talk with them about what it is and show them examples. Here are a few suggestions:

- As you read aloud to students, note passages that reveal the author's voice. Use fiction, nonfiction, and poetry. Discuss words, technique, and style that make voice apparent.
- Once in a while, during independent reading, ask students to mark a passage that shows strong voice. Ask for volunteers to share their passage and talk about why they picked it.
- Save samples of student writing with strong voice and show them to your students. Ask students which lines or words show voice. Note how and what the author said and did. Encourage students: *You can do this too.*

Figure 6–6   A first grader writing with voice

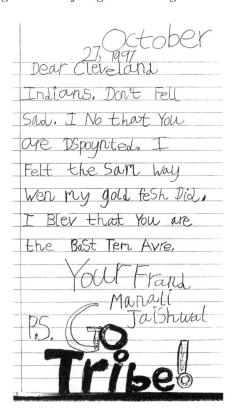

- Demonstrate your own attention to voice as you write and think out loud. Try different word choices, and discuss how changing a word affects voice.
- Point out examples of voice that occur while students are brainstorming and talking. Put those words or phrases on Post-its to remind students to use those words when they write. (See page 249 for one example.)
- Compare pieces of writing with and without voice. What's the difference? What did the author do or not do?
- Ask students to go back and read former journal entries or drafts and mark passages where they detect their own voice (or lack of it).
- Study an author with a strong, distinctive voice. Try writing in the style of this author.
- Celebrate and share the voice you find in your students' writing. High school English teacher Holly Burgess shares her students' voices with her principal. The writing isn't always "perfect" or "brilliant," but he remembers it.

Conventions

None of the aforementioned elements—choice, real audience and purpose, powerful writing models, and voice—will matter much without attention to conventions. Conventions are what the writer does with language and form to make the text readable. They are "the way we do things around here"—spelling, punctuation, capitalization, paragraphing, grammar—to render language clearly and precisely on the page. In addition, different genres (letters, plays, news articles, for example) have conventions of structure and presentation that are uniquely their own.

Conventions are essential. When they are missing, the reader becomes distracted, needs to work too hard, may eventually put the text aside. Writers learn to control conventions best "at the point of need," that is, in the context of real writing. But teachers can anticipate some of these needs and design related minilessons (see pages 298–306).

Handwriting

Time out here for a word about handwriting, another important convention. True, we are entrenched in the computer age, more deeply every day. But despite today's mania for word-processing, there continue to be occasions when students need to handwrite easily and rapidly—taking notes, writing responses on an exam. And we still expect thank-yous, invitations, and condolences to be handwritten.

Too many of us no longer value handwriting and don't teach it. While handwriting (forming letters on paper) is not writing (forming ideas), handwriting facilitates writing. When a student is not struggling with letter formation, he is freer to write fluently. Unfortunately, more and more students in our classrooms form their letters laboriously and have awkward pencil grips—perhaps because they spend too much time in front of televisions and computer games. In any case, our society values legibility and often judges content adversely when the handwriting is poor, so it is just good public relations and common sense to teach and expect good handwriting.

I am not advocating going back to the days of striving for flawless penmanship through boring daily exercises. However, ten minutes several days a week devoted to teaching handwriting is justifiable and necessary, especially in the lower grades. Not sure how to go about it? Demonstrate stroke and letter formation, size, and spacing, and have students practice on individual chalkboards and on paper. Make sure that some published pieces are handwritten, not word-processed; handwriting also reflects the individuality of the writer.

A Conducive Environment

Although the act of writing is mostly solitary, to be successful at it we need support from the various communities in which we dwell. I couldn't write without this support. While writing this book, I have been nurtured by my husband, my friends, my colleagues, my editor, and my publisher in a myriad of ways—no morning interruptions over the summer so that I would have the silence and solitude I needed, thoughtful calls and messages of support, kind critiques of work in progress, lovely late afternoon and evening meals, concerts, swims, and walks.

Establishing community in the classroom is likewise necessary if we and our students are to be able to work at our best (see Chapter 14). We need to set up our classrooms and schools, physically and emotionally, so that our students have time to write, have the necessary writing tools, are comfortable, feel encouraged to take risks, receive helpful feedback and response, and can celebrate their accomplishments proudly.

HOW ARE WE DOING?

Several years ago, the chairs of the English departments of our high school and middle school, our director of curriculum, the director of elementary education, and I met to discuss what was happening in the teaching of writing across the district. It was a very painful meeting. I heard a lot of talk about how our elementary students were coming to the upper grades as unprepared writers who couldn't spell, organize an essay, or use correct grammar. What's more, it was worse than in previous years.

I was concerned and surprised: based on what I was seeing in classrooms, I believed our students were writing well. Making an effort not be defensive, I realized that those of us around the table had different philosophies and expectations about writing. More important, none of us had any hard data to prove or disprove our perceptions and claims.

I had just finished reading *Results: The Key to Continuous School Improvement* (1996), by Mike Schmoker. On page 2, Schmoker states, "The combination of three concepts constitutes the foundation for results: meaningful teamwork; clear, measurable goals; and the regular collection and analysis of performance data." I applied these criteria to our situation. We had the teamwork and the goals in place, for the most part. We had recently completed a five-year districtwide effort to create a K–12 language arts course of study that most of us were proud of (Routman 1996). But we had no data to tell us whether we were meeting our goals. While some individual teachers were analyzing their students' writing, we had nothing formal in place as a district.

Developing a Writing Prompt

In a subsequent meeting, the district's K–4 principals and I decided to develop a standardized writing prompt. Our main purpose was to take a look at how we were doing as a district in the teaching of writing. A secondary purpose was to get students used to completing a writing prompt. Our state-mandated proficiency test for grade four (administered each spring) included such a prompt, and we all felt tremendous pressure for our students to do well. Getting students used to writing to a prompt seemed like a sensible idea.

Our first attempt was inadequate at best. Some teachers were resistant and complained about yet another demand on their time. More important, the first prompt wasn't any good. We chose *A long time ago. . .* , on the grounds that it would encourage students to write both fiction and nonfiction, that kids could write about what happened last year or thousands of years ago. Our directions were too open-ended, teachers took liberties with how they presented these directions, and many students wrote poorly.

Still, it was a beginning. The best thing to come out of it were the conversations that took place while the teachers at each grade level scored the papers. Teachers had never before met to talk about student writing across the district—to note strengths, weaknesses, and expectations; to talk about goals and staff development needs; and to see whether the grade-level writing rubrics created by the K–12 language arts committee matched our beliefs.

After school ended in June, the writing committee revised the K–4 writing prompts. A few years earlier, all students in grades one through twelve had written interesting responses to *Life Doesn't Frighten Me at All*, by Maya Angelou. The notion of a writing prompt related to a picture book appealed to many of us. We selected two different books for each grade level, one book to be used in the fall, the other in the spring. The prompts for each were identical. (See Appendix I-2 and I-3.) We also provided more specific directions for administering and scoring the prompts and refined the rubrics, balancing content with mechanics. (Figure 6-7 on page 228 is the working draft of the grade two rubric.)

Scoring Issues

While administering the prompts went better the second year and most students responded well to the topic, scoring was still problematic. A few principals devoted faculty meetings specifically to scoring, but most did not. For the most part, teachers had to meet during lunch and after school, and some of them were bitter about the amount of time it took. Still, when I suggested abandoning the prompt, one fourth-grade teacher said, "This is the only way I have a link to how other teachers think and evaluate. Scoring and talking as we worked enabled me to teach and evaluate better."

Figure 6–7   A second-grade writing rubric

WRITING RUBRIC
PHASE C (Grade 2)

Level	Indicators:
4	clearly defines topic
	includes many details to develop topic
	includes voice/writer's individual style
	organizes ideas with logical sequencing/ideas flow
	uses interesting and descriptive vocabulary
	writes clear, varied, and understandable sentences
	uses punctuation and capitals correctly
	uses mostly conventional spelling
3	stays on topic
	uses some details to develop topic
	attempts to show personal style
	organizes ideas with logical sequencing
	uses interesting vocabulary
	includes clear and understandable sentence structure
	uses punctuation and capitals correctly
	uses some conventional spelling and spells most high frequency words correctly
2	stays on topic
	uses few details to develop the topic
	presents some organization/attempts logical sequencing
	alternates between awkward and clear sentence structure
	uses some punctuation correctly
	spells some high frequency words correctly
	has limited use of conventional spelling
1	writes with some awareness of topic
	writes minimal text
	presents little organization
	uses simple sentences
	uses punctuation and capitals incorrectly
	relies on phonetic spelling
0	completely disregards the topic
	presents no understandable organization
	writes illegibly
	uses incorrect sentence structure
	uses no punctuation
	no written response

Shaker Heights City School District
8/18/98   Grade 2

Another big problem was the reliability of the scores. In some buildings, teachers at different grade levels interpreted the scoring rubrics differently. Worse, some teachers never met in grade-level groups at all, instead scoring their own students' papers subjectively high. We solved our scoring problem by creating a districtwide, cross-grade-level scoring committee consisting of at least one representative from each school and every grade level (see the photo on the first page of Chapter 1). Because we are taking a broad look at writing across the district, using our grade-level rubrics we scored each prompt holistically (one score for each student's writing) versus analytically (a separate score for each trait on the rubric).

Benefits

• If well planned and executed, a prompt can be one measure of how a district or school is doing in the teaching of writing and lead to improved instruction and learning.

• The prompt provides usable information. Most standardized tests, even those in writing proficiency, result in a numerical score. Without seeing the prompt or what their child has written in response, parents have no idea what a poor ranking really means. By contrast, our district writing assessments are kept on file so parents can see the prompt and the response. Clear comparisons between fall and spring are possible.

• The prompt gets students used to this kind of writing. Since students will undoubtedly be required to respond to a prompt on a writing test sometime in their school career, becoming familiar with this procedure in early grades makes excellent sense.

Keep in mind that while a writing prompt is a good way to get started looking at "the big picture" of writing, the most reliable and useful information comes from examining students' authentic, day-to-day writing.

PARENT EDUCATION: NEGLECTED BUT VITAL

I am constantly reminded how important it is to keep parents informed about how we teach writing. Parents, most of whom were exposed to a very different model of writing during their own school days, do not understand process writing. The home-school connection is vital.

I was recently working with upper elementary students who were writing reports about a person who had realized a dream and made a major contribution to society. In an effort to move beyond the boring reports students usually write, the classroom teacher and I had modeled how to write reports with voice, how to take factual information and reconstruct and embellish it in your own words and style.

During a conference with Amelia, a talented writer, I suggested several places in the report where adding her own voice would enliven the writing, lightly writing the word *voice* in pencil at the top of her first page. I also asked, about one sentence (as I always do whenever a student shows me something particularly well crafted), "Are those your own words?" She said yes and that was the end of that.

A few days later Amelia's mother, clearly upset, came to see me. At first, I had no idea why she was showing me Amelia's home journals and pointing out the sophisticated vocabulary her daughter used. Then it hit me. She thought that when we asked Amelia to write with voice, we were accusing her of plagiarism. *Voice* was not something we had defined for parents or communicated to them as a goal of exemplary writing. Here was a highly educated parent who had been in our school district for many years yet understood little about writing process in the elementary grades.

Amelia's teacher and I invited Amelia's mother to observe the class as the students worked on the final editing stages of their report. She watched our minilessons, came to understand our goals, and became a huge supporter who volunteered her time every week during writing workshop. As we became increasingly comfortable with each other, she spoke openly about her concerns: *Why aren't you teaching separate grammar lessons? When will you get to spelling? Why don't you teach the five-paragraph essay?* Gently, I explained that research showed that students understood grammar best after they wrote fluently and had a strong sense of language, that the best time to begin a formal study of grammar was in middle school.

Sending detailed newsletters home on the what, why, and how of teaching writing (see Appendix A) can alleviate the kind of misunderstanding we encountered with Amelia's mother. Parent-night forums are also very beneficial. In my school district, we were vigilant about offering such workshops when we first moved into process writing, but we forgot that each year there are another group of parents who are new to the school system.

Kindergarten teacher Rob Fellinger trains his parent volunteers before he has them work with his students. He gives them several articles to read and first demonstrates the writing process for them after school. Recently, he invited two students who remain at school for "after care" if they would be willing to show some parents how kindergarten students write. The kids were thrilled to show off. Rob was able to demonstrate, first-hand, the kind of support he gives his students: the language, the encouragement, the feedback, how and what he writes on the page, etc. Another kindergarten teacher, Kathy Breland, hosts an evening at a parent's home during which she explains how she teaches writing in her classroom. Both of these teachers say the parent education sessions make their jobs as teachers easier, because parents have a clearer and more realistic idea of what writing in kindergarten looks like.

Periodically, it's also a good idea to send the writing notebooks home and get feedback from family members. This is a great way for students and parents to talk together about writing and for parents to see what and how we are teaching. It is also an excellent way to find out what parents notice, value, understand, and question.

When Julie Beers sent her students' notebooks home midyear, she was surprised at how many parent questions surfaced and how thoughtful they were. Comments from family members caused her to rethink her teaching in some areas and to communicate more effectively with parents. (See Figure 6-8; see Appendixes F-4 and F-5 for a blank form and for Julie's response to parents' questions.)

FINAL REFLECTIONS

Andrew, the insightful third grader in Danny Young's classroom, reminds us how important it is to always "do your best." But understanding "our best" as writers is not always easy. Indeed, creating quality writing requires time and conscious awareness of our every "writing move." We need time to discover and understand ourselves as writers, time to share with our students the excellent models of writing alive in literature and published expository prose, and time to examine and analyze with our students why people write and what counts as first-rate writing. Over time, through reflective discussions with our colleagues and our students—and through writing ourselves—we can extend and refine

Figure 6–8   A parent's response after examining her child's writing notebook

Feedback on ___Jordan's___ Writing Notebook

Family member(s) who reviewed the notebook ___Donna Kurit___

What did you notice that impressed you? (Include strengths and weaknesses.) Jordan writes with zest and personality and humor. I especially enjoy his clever "Great Peregrine Falcon" piece which sparkles with excellent description. He uses catchy words here, such as "magnificent," "helpless," "tremendous," "grabbed," & "razor sharp." The story has a cute ending, "So, Dovs, want to walk home together + talk about cool birds? Sure. Let's find a way out..."

Another fine piece of writing is his sweet story about Joe Ontario's quest for friendship. The story has a bully, a hero + an interesting twist with the fire alarm going off. Jordan uses excellent vocabulary, such as "mumbled" & "screamed." He needs an ending for this story. Jordan recounts amusing Birthday stories, and his sports writing makes us see how much he loves baseball.

My hope is that Jordan will write more stories in the future and improve his spelling.

What are your goals for your child in writing? Our goals are for Jordan to write more. I would love for Jordan to use more dialog in his stories. I look forward to reading more pieces in the future, and I hope that Jordan tackles writing poetry, as well as science fiction and fiction stories.

Do you have any questions or comments about the writing program? Julie, You're doing an outstanding job of inspiring Jordan! He's turning into a fine writer! Thanks for everything!

Fondly,
Donna

Julie Beers, January 1998

P.S. Let me know when you need help with the next issue of "WACK."

our understanding of effective writing. Then we can teach and support our students as they come to understand how they can use writing in myriad ways: to capture their roller-coaster emotions as they welcome a new sibling into their family; to alert their state senator of their concern over a toxic waste dump near their school; or to interview a grandparent about his or her experiences in Vietnam. In time, our students will write to inform, to move, to record, to exalt—to discover all the many marvelous things writing can do—and to create writing so full and lovely and powerful that it will serve as a model of "best writing" for all who read it.

CONTINUING THE CONVERSATION

• *Ask your students, "What makes an excellent piece of writing?"* Their responses will tell you what you are actually stressing and valuing. When you begin to develop criteria for quality writing, be sure you are not overfocusing on conventions. (See Appendix B-4.)

• *Step out of your classroom and into a top-notch writing classroom.* You have to see it to believe it—what students can do and what the teacher does to foster excellent writing.

• *Read Peter Elbow's excellent* **Writing with Power** *(1998).* You'll not only get great ideas for your writing classroom (all grades), you'll learn how to become a writer yourself.

• *Start focusing on voice.* Point out voice in literature and student writing. Talk about how the author's unique voice is conveyed. Celebrate students' work in which you notice voice.

• *Use yourself as a literacy model.* Notice what you do when you write—how you organize your thoughts, compose, reread, revise, proofread, and incorporate your personality. What does this mean for how you teach writing in your classroom?

• *Reevaluate students' handwriting and how you are teaching it.* As you are conferencing with students, sit right next to them and observe how they form their letters, their efficiency and processes, and what you need to teach them.

• *Connect writing to life.* Bring in letters and cards you are about to mail. Talk about why you wrote them. Seal the envelopes in front of your students. Show your students your research papers, journals, lists, jottings, wonderings, poems—anything you are writing that is important to you. You don't have to read all these things to them; just show them that writing is a vital part of your life. Too many students see writing as something we do in school, either for the teacher or to pass a test. Until they connect writing with audience and purpose, they will fail to take it seriously, will not do their best work.

• *Write in front of your students.* Think aloud as you write. If you have never done this before, close your classroom door and risk it. It will get easier, I promise. When you write, you see firsthand the struggles, doubts, thoughts, and processes that writers (including your students) go through. When you write, you share not only your composing process but part of who you are and what matters to you. Your own insights as a writer will make you a more effective teacher of writing.

CHAPTER 7

Journal Writing

Sharing journal entries in kindergarten

I usually begin the school year with personal journal writing—writing about everyday happenings that have significance in our lives. Implementing a writing workshop can be overwhelming, and journal writing is a manageable place to begin. Most students have had some successful experience writing in a journal, and many teachers are now comfortable modeling their own journal entries in front of their students. When taught well, journal writing is a springboard to writing in all other genres: the same principles and procedures apply. Perhaps most important, journals teach children that their life is important.

Journals promote fluency in reading and writing, encourage risk taking, provide opportunities for reflection, and promote the development of written language conventions. They are also a great vehicle for recording, validating, and understanding our lives. Additionally, journal entries over a series of months can be used to note a student's progress and to set goals in writing and spelling. For all the many advantages of journal writing, however, without clear expectations and thoughtful teacher monitoring, the advantages are lost.

JOURNAL WRITING: A GOOD IDEA GONE AWRY

My former principal, Bernice Stokes, and I used to have the same conversation at least several times each year. She'd been in classrooms, looked at the journals and was not impressed. For the most part, she found the writing was sloppy, careless, had lots of easy words that were misspelled, and did not show substantial improvement over time. Of course, there were exceptions, but there were too few of them.

My own observations confirmed hers. Why was the writing so poorly done? I believe it's because in many classrooms journal writing became a homogenized time filler, the teacher's agenda—not real writing the students chose to do. Teachers used journals for daily "bell work" before school or "seat work" during reading group time.

233

Explicit, daily teacher guidance for writing was absent. Modeling and response were scarce, and expectations for quality work were often missing. Some teachers said, "Take out your journals and write" and then failed to monitor what and how students were writing. Often, even when teachers did model writing before children wrote, the writing was superficial.

Furthermore, instead of encouraging self-selection of personally important topics, topics were often assigned. A second-grade teacher had all her students journal write about what they wanted to be when they grew up. When she asked me what I thought about the idea, I responded, "Tell me why are you doing this?" She was silent. I said, "If you're using this for assessment, as a benchmark writing piece, that's fine." She then admitted that she needed something on the bulletin board for parent conferences and that she was feeling pressure because other teachers already had "stuff" up. We talked about how she could guide students in selecting a best or favorite piece of writing, with drafts attached, and put that on the bulletin board. She liked the idea and followed through with it. Because students chose the journal entry to be displayed and discussed why it was their favorite or best, it had meaning to them and their families.

Students also write better when they can choose the writing genre. Fourth-grade teacher Jennie Nader noticed that when she assigned journal writing as homework, even though students could choose their own topics, quality suffered. When some of those same students chose to do a journal entry during writing workshop, the quality of the writing was markedly improved.

Another problem with journal writing is that sloppy work with lots of misspellings and illegible handwriting became the norm in many classrooms. Pride in workmanship was often totally missing. In one classroom where I was working with a new teacher, the journals were such a mess, we had the students begin again with new spirals midyear. In addition to students not taking writing seriously, I was concerned about the message the careless, messy journals would send to parents and administrators. We set clear expectations—writing on every other line, legible handwriting, correct spelling of common words, no defacing the cover and inside pages. When students knew their teacher would no longer tolerate sloppy work, they began to take pride in their work. Over and over again, I have seen writing quality improve, as well as handwriting, when teachers refuse to accept illegible, careless work.

Moreover, teachers have separated journal writing from other forms of writing. For example, teachers tell me they do journal writing at one time of day and "writing workshop" at another. When I have suggested to teachers that they have students keep all their writing—including journal entries—in one notebook, they are often bewildered. "All writing is writing," I tell them. "Call the journal a writing notebook or writing book, and keep all the writing together." The exception for this might be in kindergarten and grade one where journals, if they are done well, can be used to teach so much about writing.

Of course, I am sympathetic to this confusion, as I used to do the same thing. In fact, I have probably contributed to the overemphasis on journal writing through writing so much about it in my previous books. At the time, I did not understand the importance of writing in many genres or value my own literacy enough. For example, I don't keep a personal journal myself. Yet, I write every day—a journal of my work in classrooms, lists, cards, letters, and more. It is only reflecting upon and trusting my own writing process, as well as my observations in classrooms and conversations with colleagues, that have enabled me to broaden my thinking and make changes in my teaching.

GREAT EXPECTATIONS

In *Invitations* I wrote about journal writing in detail (see pages 195–232). Based on my teaching experiences in the years since, I add the following specific suggestions and procedures, all of which will be discussed in depth in this and other chapters on writing:

• *Encourage students to write for several days on a topic they "ache with caring" about* (Fox 1993, 22). (After midyear, some kindergarten students can also be encouraged to continue a story. Some teachers extend the standard journal page by taping on an extension.) Some first graders stick with one topic for several months: ships that have sunk, space, my grandma, my mom's having a baby, my family.

• *Teach students, even very young students (once they are no longer struggling with transcription, usually by about mid–first grade), how to write with detail and voice.* Model this by writing yourself, by noting what authors do, and by sharing exemplary peer models. (See pages 224–225.)

• *Consider journal writing as only one type (genre) of writing students are expected to learn and do.*

• *Demonstrate rereading entries,* both while in the process of writing and when you're done. Expect frequently encountered words to be spelled correctly. Expect appropriate self-editing.

• *Do your demonstration writing on chart paper or the same kind of lined (or unlined) paper most of your students are using.* (If your students use lined paper, make sure your projected transparencies have lines—especially for developing writers.)

• *Set high standards for legibility and neatness for the writing and for the cover of the book in which the writing is done.* By midyear in first grade and thereafter, expect students to leave spaces between words, write on every other line, and cross out words or phrases with one clean line.

• *Do not allow students to withhold pages because they are "too private."* Some students abuse that privilege by writing little or nothing. Tell students they can write about private things at home in another journal.

• *Put the dictionaries away.* When students write with dictionaries on their desks, they focus on correct spelling and do not risk invented spelling of more interesting words. Bring out the dictionaries when students are proofreading and editing.

• *Teach something every day.* Use demonstrations, conferences, and sharing as opportunities to teach. View sharing as a public conference.

• *When reading and deciphering the writing in students' journals, write in only what you can't read (and need the student's help to read) or what a student is ready to spell correctly.*

• *Keep your notations few and small,* so that the child's writing predominates. (Use pencil or pen but avoid magic markers.)

• *Celebrate and reinforce the writing the students share.* Seeing and hearing what others have done and need to work on helps classmates grow and stretch.

DEMONSTRATIONS

Demonstrating what we want students to do can lead to powerful teaching and learning: "if I model, talk, show, do, write, and ask—they will go beyond anything I have imagined" (Ernst 1994, 35). First-year teacher Christine Cachat observes, "I learned not to take anything for granted. If I wanted students to be able to do it, I had to model, model, model."

Whenever I am impressed with students' writing, their teacher, in every case, has been continually providing them with excellent demonstrations, and students are writing every day. Early one April, first-grade teacher Hallie Stewart invites me into her classroom to see how well her first graders write. Just about everyone writes about two full pages in twenty minutes, and lots of frequently encountered words are spelled correctly, but the quality of the writing and the personal investment the students make in it are what really make me sit up and take notice. Jasmine is writing about a snake, Diana is recalling a thunderstorm, and DeAndre is writing about his grandmother's funeral. DeAndre's growth as a writer has been remarkable (see Figures 7-1, 7-2, and 7-3). Taking a look at Hallie's modeling that day (Figure 7-4 on page 238), I understand why her students write so well. Her writing has detail and voice, is conversational, reveals personal feelings, and offers explanations. She has dared to tell her important personal story, and the students do the same. Hallie also has a literacy-rich classroom. Her students read and write in authentic contexts all day long (Routman 1997).

Writing demonstrations can take many forms: the teacher thinking and writing aloud in front of students, shared writing, peers sharing and discussing their writing, oral brainstorming, teacher-student conversations. Initially, I write aloud in front of my students every day. Gradually, as the students become more competent and independent, I cut

Figure 7–1   DeAndre's journal writing (first week of school)

I went to Sea World.

Figure 7–2　DeAndre's journal writing (midyear)

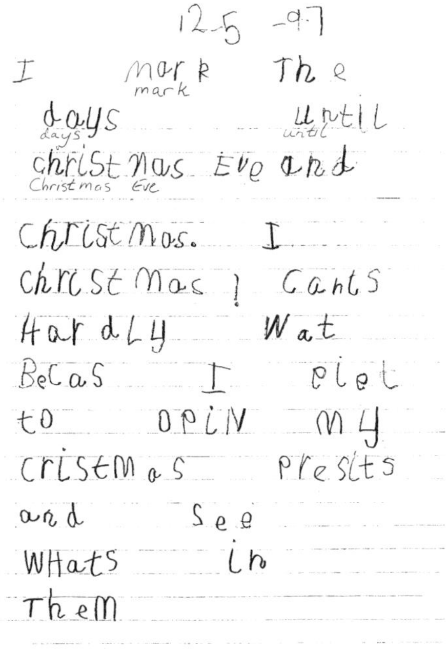

12-5 -97

I mark The days until christmas Eve and christmas. I christmas ! Cants Hardly Wat Becas I plot to Opin my crisemas presits and see whats in Them

Fig. 7-2: I mark the days until Christmas Eve and Christmas. I can hardly wait because I get to open my Christmas presents and see what's in them.

Fig. 7-3: I just came back yesterday, and I had fun except the funeral and one lady jumped up and said, "Oh Jesus" and another one could not breathe. And we got to see her and they had to hold my grandmother back and when I came back from the casket box I was crying really bad! too and everybody was sad because it was sad. And after that I went to the place where they bury her at and we did not get to see the people bury her and I asked my dad and he said because the families don't get to see and I said "Oh!" and we got back in the van.

Figure 7–3　DeAndre's journal writing (spring)

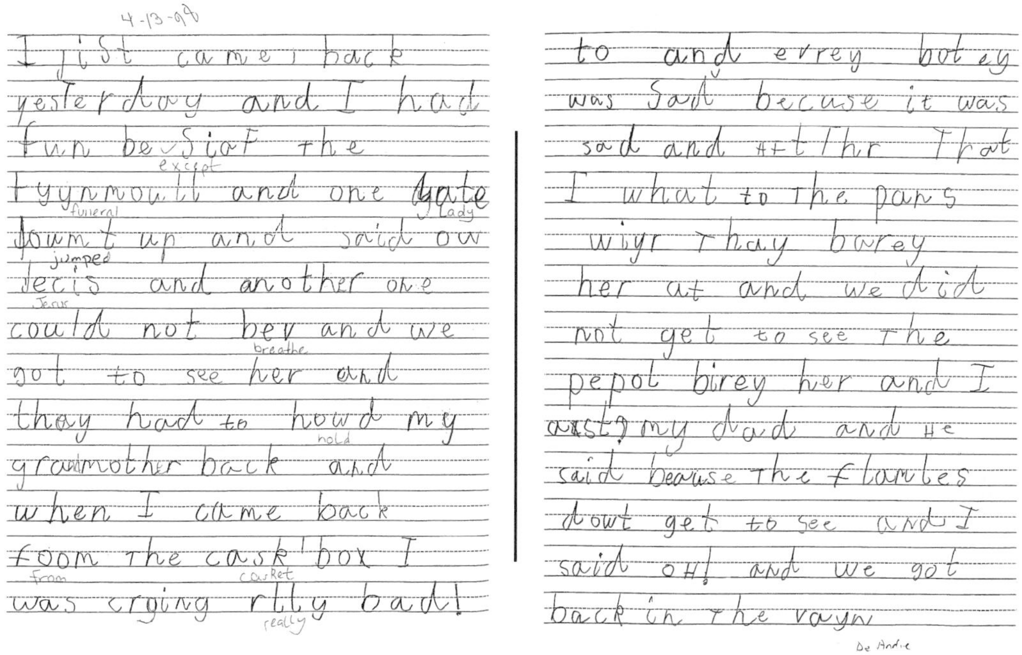

4-13-98

I jist came back yesterday and I had fun beSiof the fyynmoull and one gate (lady) down t up and said ow Jecis and another one could not bey and we got to see her and thay had to howd my gradmother back and when I came back foom The cask box I was croging rlly bad!

to and errey botey was Sad because it was sad and aftlhr That I what to the pans wiyr Thay borey her at and we did not get to see The pepol birey her and I aist my dad and He said beause The flambes dowt get to see and I said oH! and we got back in the vayn

De Andre

Figure 7–4   Hallie Stewart's writing on April 14

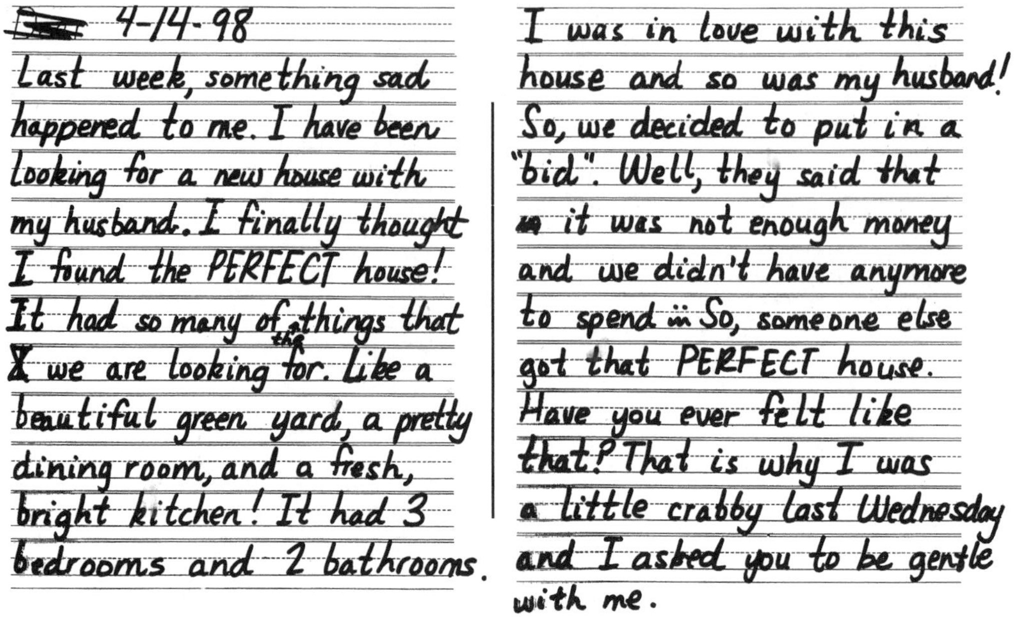

4-14-98

Last week, something sad happened to me. I have been looking for a new house with my husband. I finally thought I found the PERFECT house! It had so many of things that we are looking for. Like a beautiful green yard, a pretty dining room, and a fresh, bright kitchen! It had 3 bedrooms and 2 bathrooms. I was in love with this house and so was my husband! So, we decided to put in a "bid". Well, they said that it was not enough money and we didn't have anymore to spend in So, someone else got that PERFECT house. Have you ever felt like that? That is why I was a little crabby last Wednesday and I asked you to be gentle with me.

back on these demonstrations. However, I always talk with students before asking them to write (see pages 244–250).

The importance of demonstration and talk before writing cannot be overstated (see Figures 7-5 and 7-6). Notice what happened to Mark, a first grader who wrote in his journal every day but received little instruction. He completed each journal entry as required, but he took few risks and was clearly not invested in the writing. Notice the dramatic improvement in all aspects of his writing once effective teacher demonstration, as well as conversation before writing, become part of journal writing time. Mark, in fact, does not "look" like the same student.

Figure 7–5   Mark's typical journal entry before teacher modeling

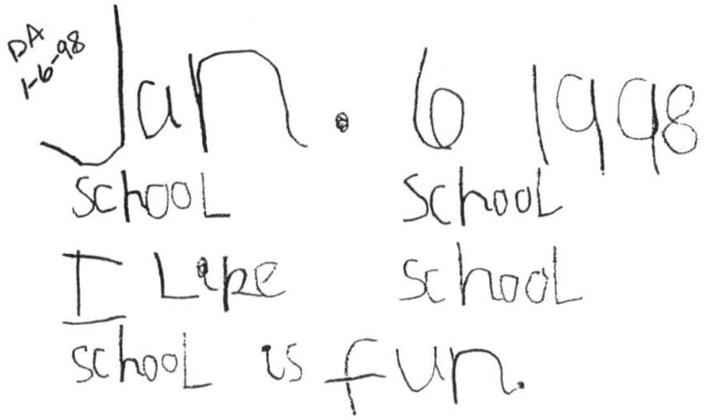

DA
1-6-98

Jan. 6 1998

School   School

I Lipe   school

school is fun.

Figure 7–6   Mark, after teacher modeling, writing about what matters to him

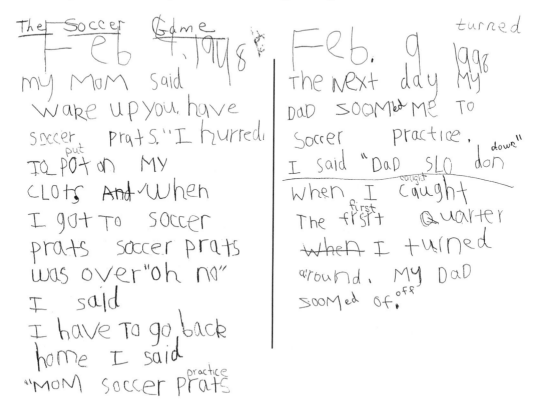

Choosing a Topic

Being able to choose what to write about is critical in journal writing. Otherwise, students are merely writing to complete an assignment, and quality suffers. However, students don't automatically choose to write about topics that are interesting or important to them. Making suitable choices, like everything else we want students to do well, has to be modeled and supported.

When I introduce journal writing, I say something like this: *I want you to think of your journal as a special place where you can write about things that really matter to you, things you want to remember always. When you look at your journal a few years from now or when you're grown up, it should show what you were thinking about when you were in this grade, what you cared about, and what was most important to you. So, we're not going to be writing about things like a trip to McDonald's and what you had for dinner unless there was something about that time that was memorable.*

Then I mention some topics I could write about, trying to pick ones students can relate to. I ask them, *How many of you have a best friend? a pet? a grandparent you love?* I talk honestly with them, telling them my personal stories about:

- My best friend
- What I'm good at
- A favorite place
- What's important to me
- A special object
- My grandmother
- My dog
- What I know a lot about
- What I love to do best

At the beginning of the school year, many teachers ask students to make lists of possible topics they might choose to write about and to tape these lists to the inside cover of their journal. Family members can help students create their list. If a child consistently has difficulty choosing topics on "journal day," kindergarten teacher Karen Sher encourages the child's parents to talk about journal writing the night before. Sometimes I give students questions to think about in choosing a writing topic (see *Invitations*, page 215b). Nancie Atwell shares her "writing territories" (topics, genres, and audiences) on overhead transparencies before students create their lists (Atwell 1998, 120–132).

While I still like to plan writing topics ahead of time, I also know that many students ignore these "prelists." When students truly understand that they can write about what matters most to them, choosing a topic is no longer an issue.

Discourage topics that involve movies, television shows, and video games: our students spend far too many hours in front of a screen. Writing about what they see there, students tend to recount one incident after another, without any depth or voice. However, if a student insists on sticking with one of these topics, I talk with him about narrowing and personalizing the focus. For example, when James persisted in writing about violent video games, I encouraged him to write about what happens when he plays these games with his brother: how they sit side by side, how Grandpa is in the next room sleeping, how they eat popcorn, and how their dog keeps interrupting them.

I also tell students that we all have things in our lives that are too private to share and that they can write about those things at home. In school, they need to be comfortable sharing their writing. In some places, teachers get into hot water if they ask children to write about their personal feelings. I can't imagine writing about something important to me without expressing my feelings and being personal. At the same time I have to be aware of what is and is not acceptable in the particular community in which I am teaching and respect those values.

Still, teachers who are uncomfortable writing about personal issues can let that discomfort keep them from encouraging students to express their feelings about things that can appropriately be shared. This is unfortunate. Until students "hear" our voice, it is difficult for their own voice to emerge. Our own writing topics need not be intensely personal; they just need to be important and true. We all have stories about our family, our hobbies, our friends, our neighborhood, adventures we have experienced, that we can share with honesty and sentiment. We need to "come out" as writers and tell those stories.

Thinking and Writing Aloud

Students need to see us think and compose in front of them, at least some of the time. If I expect students to write on the spot, I need to write the same way. My time is not well spent preparing at home what I can actually do better as part of my classroom teaching. While I usually have a rough idea of what I might write about, my only preplanning is thinking about the topic or jotting down a few notes on a Post-it. I want kids to see my thinking, my confusions, my struggles, my changes, my writing-in-progress. Sometimes I don't know what I'll be writing about until I'm ready to begin.

I want students to know that writers organize their thoughts before writing. I orally brainstorm and write down all the parts of my topic before I begin to write (see below). This also shows students that a topic has many interesting subtopics. Then I choose one of the subtopics and think and write in front of students. (See *Invitations*, pages 55, 57, and 209.)

I always write about what is important to me at that moment. My topics do not differ much by grade levels, but the depth is different. A kindergarten entry may be one sentence, while a fourth-grade entry may be several pages. Some recent topics have included:

1. My son Peter and his wife Claudine coming home to visit
2. Remembering my grandmother
3. Going to the farmer's market with my husband Frank
4. Having surgery
5. Visiting my best friend
6. Losing my glasses
7. Being scared before giving a talk to a large audience

See Figures 7-7 and 7-8 for my brainstorming and writing on overhead transparencies.

Figure 7–7   Brainstorming all the parts of my topic, "My Speech," before writing

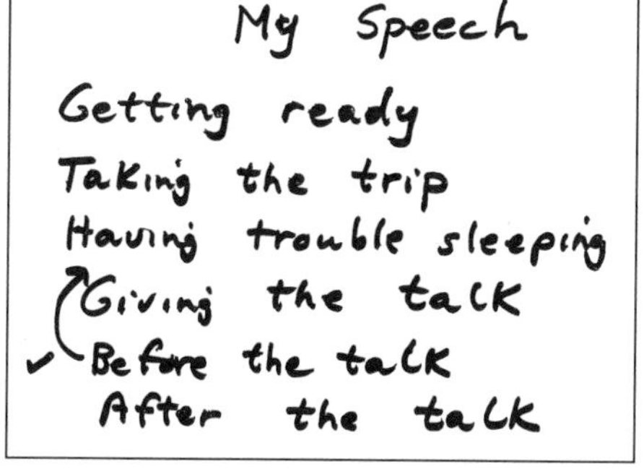

Figure 7–8   Starting to write on one subtopic from my brainstorming

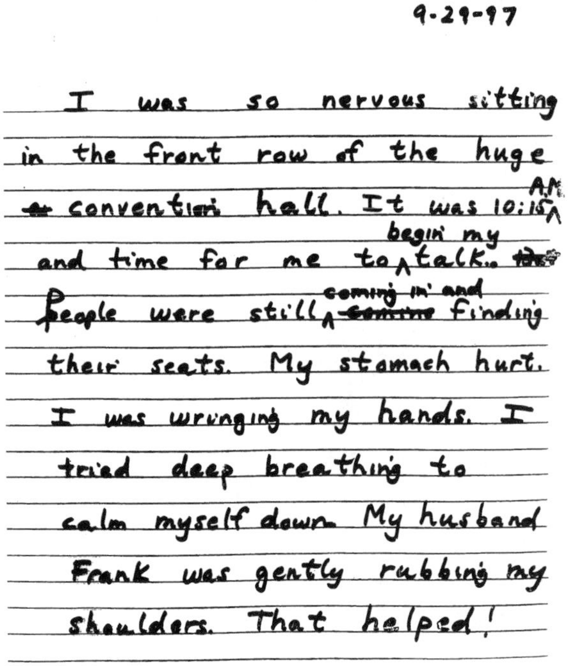

9·29·97

I was so nervous sitting
in the front row of the huge
convention hall. It was 10:15 A.M.
and time for me to begin my talk.
People were still coming in and finding
their seats. My stomach hurt.
I was wringing my hands. I
tried deep breathing to
calm myself down. My husband
Frank was gently rubbing my
shoulders. That helped!

Limiting Modeling and Emphasis

I try not to model writing for more than ten minutes and oral brainstorming for more than five minutes—and I watch the clock. When we are first learning to model, we tend to go on too long—sometimes twenty minutes or more. By that time, students are losing interest and there's not enough time left for them to write. With practice, however, and by limiting ourselves to one or two major points, we can keep our modeling sessions brief.

James, a first-year first-grade teacher I'm coaching, is modeling journal writing at the beginning of October. He limits himself to two sentences, the appropriate amount of text, since this is what most students are writing. But because, as he says later, he is "trying to get as much out of the writing as I could," his writing takes thirty minutes instead of ten as he tries to teach everything—spelling, capitals, punctuation, use of resources, skipping lines. Students bogged down with too many details are apt to remember little. I suggest he may want to buy a timer and set it for fifteen minutes—to include the writing demonstration and the oral brainstorming beforehand. I also encourage him to focus on only one or two points per demonstration.

When you model writing, it is important to observe where your students are developmentally. Remember that the invented spellings children use are "right" for their developmental level. Focus on what students can do: *Good for you; you knew so-and-so*, or, *Look how close you are.* Spending a lot of time spelling difficult words that most students are not ready for is a waste of time.

Demonstrating Accuracy

While I don't subscribe to one right or best way to teach writing, I don't believe in deliberately making errors. It's inauthentic, and our students know it. They know perfectly well that we can spell and punctuate.

If I want to know what students understand about spelling and punctuation, I ask them. I accept their invented spellings as they give them to me, celebrate what they know, and nudge them forward through inquiry and explicit teaching.

For example, when I am demonstrating in the early grades, speaking aloud as I am writing my entry, I ask students to help me spell and punctuate my story:

- Who can spell *when* for me?
- Stretch out the sounds. What do you hear?
- How did you know that?
- Look on the word wall to help you.
- What kind of punctuation mark should I put here?
- Everyone spell *my*. It's a word we know.

When I'm soliciting individual contributions like this, I don't allow a free-for-all. Because I want to determine and monitor where these students are in their learning, I call on raised hands. The class understands that their silence allows the designated student time to think and respond.

Afterward, when we are rereading the completed entry, I write the conventional spelling underneath the invented spelling with a different-color pen. I don't ordinarily comment on missing letters, because this usually means the student isn't ready to spell that word yet. My conversation focuses on what students have done well so they will do it again. For example, when a first grader offers *b-e-n* for *been*, I comment on all she knows (*Good for you; you knew the first letter, you knew there was an* e *in the middle, and you knew the ending sound and letter*) while at the same time writing *been* underneath the invented spelling.

Sometimes when I am focusing on content in a demonstration, I may write most of the words and, as in a written cloze exercise, ask students to spell only certain ones. On other occasions, when time is limited or if I have done previous modeling that day in which I have solicited their spellings—for example, during shared writing—I may write all the words as I think aloud. It depends on my purpose. Mostly, when I am soliciting spellings and conventions of print from students, I am doing it to find out what they know so I can set directions for future teaching. At the same time, I am also confirming and celebrating their knowledge of how language works.

Sustaining a Writing Topic

While some days, of course, students will want to write briefly about a topic and be done with it, I encourage students to find something they are really interested in and stick with it. My students have written extensively, for weeks at a time, on mom's having a baby, going to a magic show, cooking with Grandma, reptiles, a stamp collection, the planets and space, a pet, a family trip, a favorite keepsake, a best friend, a birthday. I model this kind of "specialization" both in my own writing and in my conversation.

THE POWER OF TALK

While I had always taken the time to find out what students were going to write about before they began writing in their journal, the process was often superficial. I would go around the room, each student would briefly say what he or she might write about, and then everyone would begin to write. The writing, in turn, was lackluster and boring—unimportant events, bare facts with little "juice," daily happenings listed in order without embellishment. When I began to take ten minutes for conversation before writing, focusing on only one or two students at a time, students began to stick with the same topic for days and weeks, and the quality of all the students' writing improved dramatically (see Chapter 6, pages 225 and 226).

Now, while I do not write in front of students every day, I always take the time for conversation before they write, because the payoff is great. I make sure that at least one of the students I call upon is a writer who continually has trouble coming up with a topic she cares about. All students have stories to tell; they just don't always know they do. Reluctant writers can take a long time to find that story and interest. But, with caring persistence and gentle, genuine questioning, a topic important to the student—and a story to go with it—usually emerges.

Brainstorming the Focus

I begin by asking students, *Who knows what you might write about, a topic you know a lot about that's important to you?*, and call on a volunteer to make a suggestion. Then the class (with my guidance) brainstorms all the possible subtopics for this main topic (dogs, snakes, family, whatever), and I record them on large chart paper or a transparency on the overhead projector. This shows students how to organize their topics into logical sections and to slow their writing down.

Second-grade teacher Neal Robinson advises: "Just like conversing with students before writing, brainstorming subtopics with students takes more time. Be prepared for this because, at first, as students are learning to organize their thoughts, little writing takes place. But later in the year, once students have brainstorming down, you'll be amazed at the detail and voice you see in your students' writing. The initial investment in time is well worth the results."

Some first graders can do this written brainstorming; just about all second graders and older students can. What usually happens is that students wind up writing about topics that never would have surfaced without this preplanning. The surprises are wonderful: detailed and interesting. In Figures 7-9 and 7-10, second graders are able to narrow their focus regarding family trips they each took. Notice that while one struggles with spelling, her sense of story and personal voice are very strong. Don't be discouraged if after you demonstrate this kind of brainstorming only a few students pick it up initially. It takes a while for most students to catch on, but they will. Notice in Figure 7-10 how (because we have been demonstrating and talking about interesting beginnings) Leah goes with a second lead.

I demonstrated written brainstorming of topics for a second-grade class one fall, and I was delighted when I went back in the spring and found many students doing this brain-

Figure 7–9 *Aja, a second grader, narrows her focus on a trip she took*

the Way Back On 10-3-97
the ainPlane

on the Way Bach hoem
my Summich Was herting
caus the Plane Was going to
Fast. I did not tall my Dad
But When I tow up my
Dad nodist He Was not
mieol He just gaev me a
Baeg If I waed tow up Sum
mor But I didit. I flet
Like I waS going to tow
up I didnot I alt
Baed I tow up on the set
and the Pilos

On the way back home my stomach was hurting 'cause the plane was going too fast. I did not tell my dad but when I threw up he noticed. He was not mad. He just gave me a bag if I would throw up some more. But I didn't. I felt like I was going to throw up. I did not. I felt bad. I threw up on the seat and the pillows.

storming/webbing independently each time they began a new topic (see Figure 7-11 on page 246). This form of outlining will serve these young writers well throughout their lives.

In another school, a first grader broke down her topic, her special blanket, this way:

- What it looks like
- What I do with it
- Why it's important to me
- How it got lost
- How I got it back

Each listed category became a chapter, and the daily journal writing evolved into a treasured, published book. (See Figures 7-12 and 7-13 on page 247 for two journal entries.)

Another student said he wanted to write about Halloween. I asked him what the possible topics were. With prodding, we came up with these categories, which I wrote on the chalkboard:

- Trick-or-treating
- Getting a costume
- Sorting the candy
- Going to a haunted house
- Carving the pumpkin

Figure 7–10   A second grader narrows her focus on a trip she took

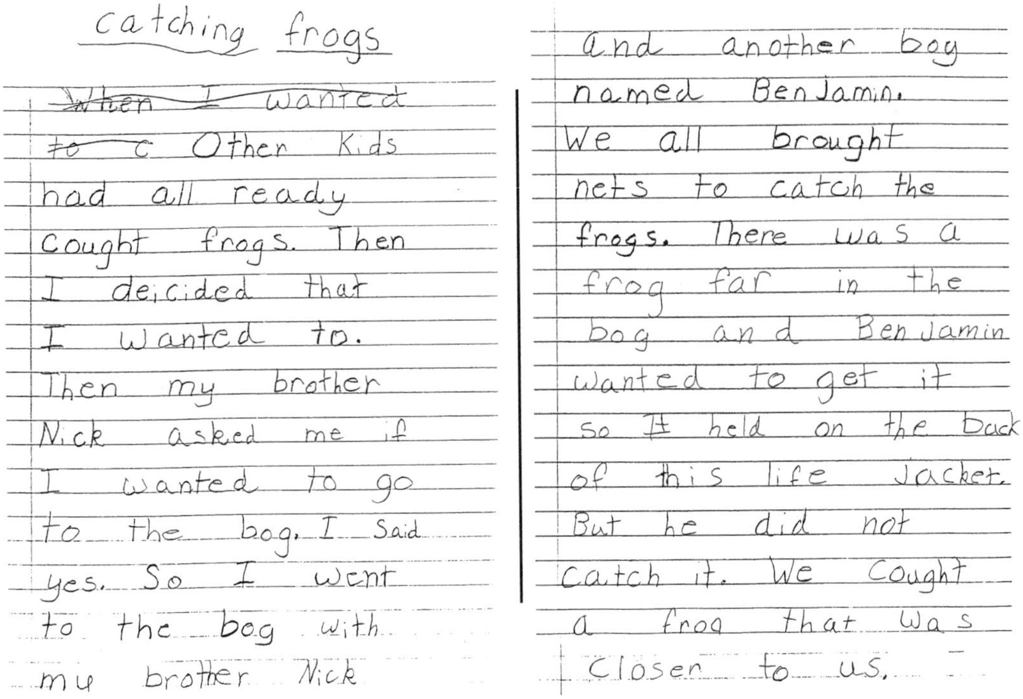

<u>catching frogs</u>

~~When~~ I wanted
~~to~~ c Other Kids
had all ready
Cought frogs. Then
I deicided that
I wanted to.
Then my brother
Nick asked me if
I wanted to go
to the bog. I said
yes. So I went
to the bog with
my brother Nick

and another boy
named BenJamin.
We all brought
nets to catch the
frogs. There was a
frog far in the
bog and BenJamin
wanted to get it
so It held on the Back
of this life Jacket.
But he did not
Catch it. We Cought
a frog that was
Closen to us.

Figure 7–11   A second grader independently brainstorms his topic before he begins to write

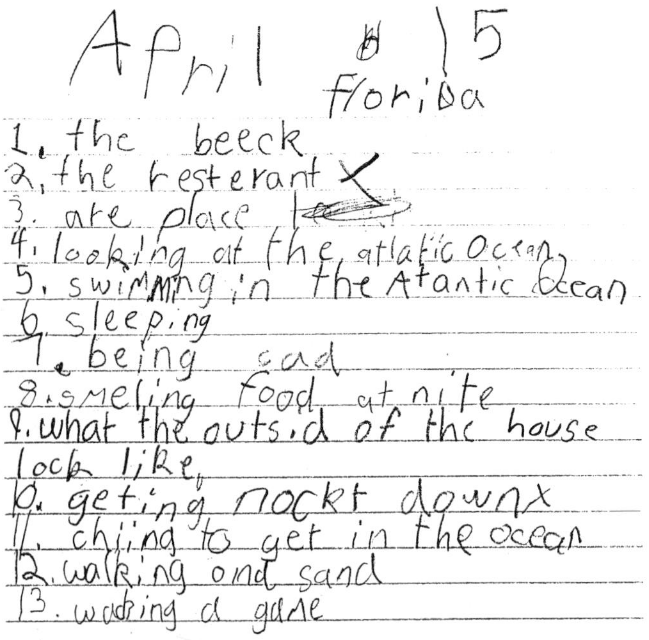

April ⌀ 15
florida
1. the beeck
2. the resterant ✗
3. ate place
4. looking at the atlatic Ocean
5. swimming in the Atantic Ocean
6. sleeping
7. being sad
8. smeling food at nite
9. what the outsid of the house
   look like,
10. geting nockt downx
11. chiing to get in the ocean
12. walking on sand
13. wacing a gane

Figure 7–12   A first grader's continuing journal story

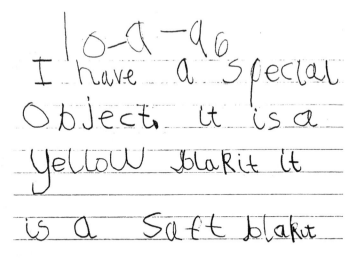

Figure 7–13   A first grader's continuing journal story

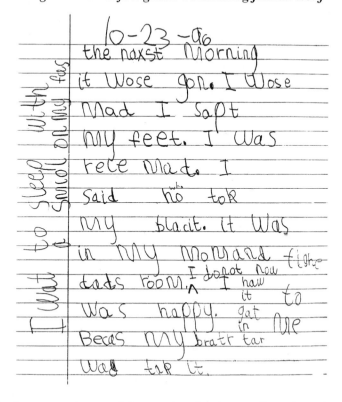

The next morning it was gone. I was mad. I stamped my feet. I was really mad. I said, "Who took my blanket?" It was in my mom and dad's room. I do not know how it got in there. I was happy because my brother wouldn't take it. I went to sleep with a smile on my face.

Getting to the Details

After we have our list of possible subtopics, I ask the student to pick one of those categories, the one she wants to begin writing about today. Then, talking naturally, I try to elicit the interesting details tucked inside.

The student writing about Halloween decided to begin with treat-or-treating, so I suggested, *Tell me what happens when you are done trick-or-treating and you come home with all that candy.* The details involved dumping the candy onto the carpet, sorting and counting, eating his favorites and saving the wrappers, and storing the rest for later.

There is no formula for this conversation. You just need to be genuinely interested in the student and the story he has to tell. I ask questions about things I really want to know. I do not, for example, routinely say *Tell me more* or *What happened next?* but am more likely to say *I'm so interested in why you did that* or *I can't picture that; what did it look like?* or *How did you feel when that happened?*

Conversation like this

- Lets the writer know she has a story to tell and that her story is valued
- Slows down the writing so interesting details and description emerge
- Provides a model for other students

All students, even high school students, benefit from guided talk before writing. Details usually emerge when we help our students "picture in their mind's eye" what happened and how they felt. For older students used to writing only for the teacher or students with special learning difficulties, this can be an ongoing struggle. However, with continual modeling of conversation before writing, even lackluster students begin writing with detail.

You can help students think back to the time they are re-creating by asking

- What do you see?
- What do you hear?
- What's going on?
- What are you thinking?
- How are you feeling?

Saving the Gems

When students discuss an event orally, they often use more descriptive words than they do if they immediately begin writing about it. When a student turns a phrase that's particularly literary or unique, I immediately jot it down on a Post-it and place the Post-it next to or at the top of the blank page on the students' desk, saying, *You just used some wonderful words to describe what you're talking about. I'm going to jot those words down for you so you don't lose them.* By writing down and singling out these verbal gems, we help students recognize and remember wonderful language. We show students we value their choice of words and encourage them to choose their words carefully and imaginatively when they write. (In Figures 7-14 and 7-15, a student incorporates the gems her teacher pointed out to him.)

Figure 7–14   *A second grader, capturing the gem in conversation before writing*

> I felt like giants were watching me.

Figure 7–15   *Applying the gem to writing*

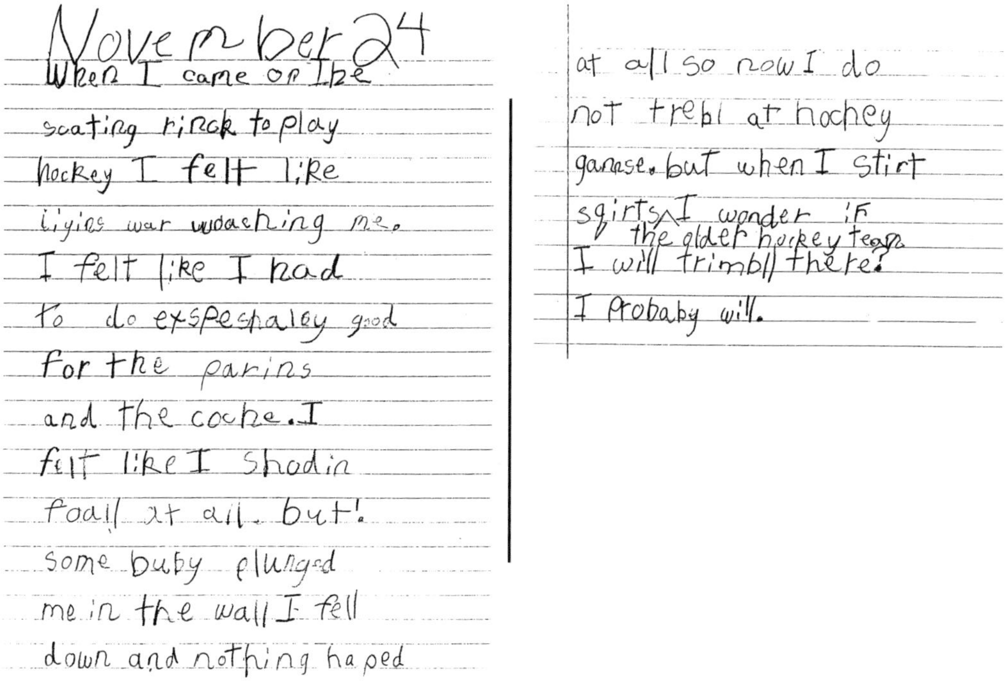

> November 24
>
> When I came on the skating rink to play hockey I felt like giants were watching me. I felt like I had to do exspechaley good for the parins and the cache. I felt like I shodin foall at all. but some buby plunged me in the wall I fell down and nothing haped at all so now I do not trebl at hockey games. but when I stirt sqirts I wonder if the older hockey team I will trimbll there? I Probaby will.

When I came on the skating rink to play hockey I felt like giants were watching me. I felt like I had to do especially good for the parents and the coach. I felt like I shouldn't fall at all. But somebody plunged me in the wall. I fell down and nothing happened at all, so now I do not tremble at hockey games. But when I start Squirts, the older hockey team, I wonder if I will tremble there? I probably will.

by Matthew Buder-Shapiro

A Sample Conversation

Here is a conversation I had with a second grader about going to her grandmother's house. The resulting story in her journal would not have emerged without our conversation.

REGIE: So what do you do there?

JESSICA: Oh, we play lots of things.

REGIE: What do you especially like to do with your grandma?

JESSICA: Play cards, watch TV, go shopping, put on makeup.

REGIE: Put on makeup. That sounds interesting. Tell me about that. What do you do?

JESSICA: Well, my brother and I put makeup on my Grandma.

REGIE: She lets you do that? Wow. What do you do? What happens?

JESSICA: We take her makeup and we put it on her.

REGIE: Tell us exactly what you do. Where is Grandma sitting? Do you put a smock on her? Does she let you put on lipstick too?

JESSICA: Grandma is in her favorite big chair in the living room. We put a big apron on her. Then we take her makeup kit and put on rouge, lots of powder, eye stuff . . .

REGIE: Eye stuff. Like what?

JESSICA: Blue and green eye shadow, mascara, an eyelash curler thing.

REGIE: Be sure to put all that in your story.

JESSICA: And then we put on the lipstick, which is hardest to do.

REGIE: What does Grandma say when you're doing all this?

JESSICA: "Can I look yet? Can I look yet?"

REGIE: And what do you say?

JESSICA: "Not yet. Not yet."

SHARING JOURNAL ENTRIES

The most powerful models for students are those created by their peers. I save examples of journal writing in which students have stayed with a personally important topic for an extended period; written an interesting beginning; used powerful verbs; incorporated conversation effectively; shown evidence of rereading and revision (moving sections around); used carets and added words; crossed out boring words or sections; demonstrated personal style and voice; and so on. I have folders of exemplary writing from each grade level, and I share these samples (usually on overhead transparencies) with students at or close to the same age and grade level. I ask, *What do you notice? What has the writer done well?* The message is, *This was written by a student just like you. You can do this too.*

Students' drawings can also be shared. Many kindergartners and first graders need to draw before they write to solidify their ideas and thinking. I share drawings to show how writers use lines, shapes, and colors; how they make sure their drawings go with the text;

and how illustrations and visuals can convey important details that are not in the writing. By mid–first grade, however, I encourage children who are writing easily to spend most of their journal time on writing and to save their illustrations for their published stories and projects.

In the early grades, informal sharing with classmates before, during, and after writing really takes off by midyear. Students love to hear and see one another's stories and illustrations and ask questions. Those conversations help writers continue, clarify, extend, and "fix up" their writing.

SUSTAINED WRITING AND WRITING CONFERENCES

Students know they are expected to write during journal writing time, and they do. Usually there is a quiet hum in the room as students talk with one another, share what they are writing about, help one another with ideas and spelling, and refer to resources in the room. In some classrooms, students write at their seats. In others, students may write anywhere in the room as long as they do not disturb anyone.

After the appropriate preparatory modeling, sharing, and talking, most students use their time well. When they don't, we need to find out what the problem is:

- Do they need help finding an engaging topic?
- Are other students at the table disturbing them?
- Do they have enough information about their topic?
- Do they know enough letters and sounds to work independently?
- Are they overrelying on the dictionary?
- Have they had breakfast?
- Did something happen at home or at school that prevents them from being "present" in today's writing assignment? (When a student is having an off day, conversing one-on-one, with kindness and concern, may need to come before talking about writing. For that student, writing may be impossible or unnecessary.)

While students are writing, you can circulate quickly from student to student, work with a small group, or have a conference. It is critical that the writing be *guided.* If you are doing something else, students lose interest, quality suffers, and the journal writing may wind up a waste of time for many students.

At the same time, students need to support each other by swapping ideas and stories and helping with spelling. Some teachers are comfortable with peer support throughout writing time. Others find some sustained quiet time is necessary for all writers to concentrate. There is no one best way. You have to find out what works best for you and your students.

Teaching Struggling Writers

Time and time again, I have observed struggling students who cannot stay focused on writing in their journal, perhaps because they don't know their letters and sounds, and who are wasting their time. These students need guidance and direct teaching in order to write.

You need to meet with these students in small groups and teach them what they need to know to be successful. In one first-grade classroom where I was working, I pulled out a group of these students for interactive writing. I had them use small white boards and dry-erase markers as we worked on developing phonemic awareness and building a sight vocabulary of such basic words as *my* and *can* (see page 149). In another first-grade classroom, I had a group of struggling writers work together on a book that began with the familiar words *We can play.* . . . We used those words, and the rimes *ay* (in *play*) and *an* (in *can*)—as well as the *all* rime in *baseball* and *football*, words that appeared in their story—to read and write a whole bunch of frequently encountered words.

To be able to teach small groups, you need to be good at managing your classroom; other students need to be able to work independently or with peers and/or volunteers. On days when you meet with a small group, you may want students to spend more time than usual sharing their work with the class, and then collect the journals of the students whose writing you didn't see or comment on.

Helping the Struggling Writer Before He Stumbles

Jermaine, a second grader, is having difficulty brainstorming his topic—My Dogs—and then narrowing his focus. Noting his difficulty, I make a point of choosing him the next day for the whole-class minilesson involving conversation before writing. When Jermaine comes up to the front of the class and stands next to the overhead projector, I ask him about his dogs, what kind they are and what they do, and he gives me three topics—"play with each other; chows [their breed]; and fight over bones"—which I list on an overhead transparency. Then, with my probing, he describes his chows, which he has decided will be his first subtopic. As he talks, I jot down his words on Post-its so he can retrieve them when writing.

Because I don't get to him immediately after everyone starts writing, he merely copies the list of his topics. However, when I kneel down next to him and guide him in getting his first sentence started, he has no trouble taking his own key words from the Post-its and putting them into several sentences (see Figure 7-16). I work with him for several

Figure 7–16   Jermaine's writing after teacher intervention and guidance

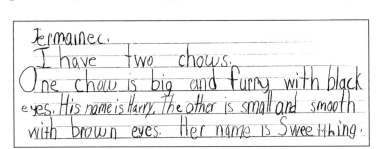

minutes, till I am confident he can write coherently on his own. His writing doesn't seem to resemble that of the child who struggled alone the previous day. Even his handwriting looks better.

I find again and again that if we can get to our struggling writers before they put pencil to paper, we can often alleviate their confusions. Of course, this is difficult to do in a class of twenty-five or more students. However, we can at least try to begin most writing sessions by conferring with one or two of those writers first.

Responding to Writing

I always talk with students at their eye level. When my knees give out, I carry a small chair with me. If the writer is engaged and the writing is going well, I may simply say, *Looks like you're moving right along,* and go on to another student. I always respond first to the content of the writing and what the writer is trying to do. I might say *Can you read me what you've written so far?* or *Tell me what you're writing about. How's it going?*

When a student is stymied and staring into space, she and I chat about the problem, and I try to find out what she is interested in and get her writing. Once in a great while, the student doesn't respond to anything I suggest. Then I say something like, *You don't have a choice not to write, so if you can't think of anything, begin with that, "I can't think of anything to write about," and use that as your topic today.* At least that gets her started.

You will want to make every effort to move quickly and get around to every student in order to cheer them on, teach and guide them as necessary, and select some students whom you will ask to share their work (because you want to celebrate their writing and/or because it is a good peer model). Because it is so easy to skip those in the "quiet middle," some teachers keep track of whom they chat with by carrying a class roster on a clipboard, which they check off and date as they go from student to student. If your students are older and can write independently and with more depth, it may not be feasible or necessary to meet with everyone.

Spelling and Conventions

After I have focused on content and any help the writer requests, I do comment on spelling and conventions. Conferring personally with students, even briefly, can produce change where written comments alone never would. For example, while it might be difficult for a student to understand the use of commas from a written comment, the convention is easy to discuss and demonstrate one-on-one. Whenever I notice that a student is ready to learn about specific punctuation or spelling, I show him, on the spot, how to move forward with that convention.

I expect my students to use the spelling, grammar, and other conventions I have taught them. Students know they are expected to reread, both as they write and after they write, to check for meaning and accuracy. If I see that a student has misspelled a word on our word wall (see pages 273–276), I remind the student, either orally or by jotting a symbol next to the word, that the word must be correctly spelled. Some teachers wisely specify that the last several minutes of journal writing time are to be spent rereading, so students get in the habit of proofreading their work.

When I cannot read an invented spelling, I lightly write the conventional spelling in pencil beneath it as the writer explains the word to me. (Because I want the student's writing to predominate, I always use pencil.) Writing the unreadable words provides a clear record when I encounter the piece again and serves as a reference for the student (see page 237). However, some teachers are uncomfortable doing this and transcribe the whole message at the bottom of the page.

If a student seems ready to spell a frequently encountered word, I may say, *I notice you're using this word a lot, so I'm going to put it here for you and on your personal word grid* (see page 276) *so you can find it easily,* or, *You're so close to spelling this word. It has an* e *on the end. I'll write the word for you here. Next time you're writing it, you can look back to this page to remind you.*

Some teachers write the correct spelling below all misspelled words. This requires too much time and effort, but more important, it discourages young writers from noticing the spelling of a few important words because there are so many "teacher marks" on the paper. In any case, a spelling notation doesn't serve any useful purpose unless the child is ready to spell the word correctly. Perhaps most important, students can become overfocused on correctness when the teacher writes in the spelling of lots of words. Some of you have probably noticed young writers who erase their "errors" and "correct" them by copying the teacher's spellings. This has convinced me that if I can read the message, I should leave it alone.

Collecting Journals

While most of your responses to the journals will take place while the students are writing, during conferences, or when they are sharing their work, it is advisable to collect all the journals periodically to check students' progress, take some notes to use when writing progress reports, and inform your future teaching. However, I also recommend that you occasionally respond to the journal in writing.

My first personal response, in writing or orally, is always a human one. I try to relate to the student and what he has attempted to say. I might begin, *I can tell this was an important time with your dad,* or, *I can remember feeling like that, too, when I was your age.* If I notice problems with conventions and spelling that the student should have caught, I might suggest, *Don't forget to check the word wall for those tricky* wh *words,* or *Try to remember not to use uppercase letters in the middle of words.*

As when checking students' reading, it is not usually necessary to read every page of a journal to see how students are progressing. Therefore, some teachers ask their students to mark one or more entries they would like the teacher to read.

Although some teachers are comfortable doing so, I do not write comments to students directly on their writing. I put my comments on a Post-it note so the writing on the page remains totally the students'. How and where you make your comments depends on your purpose. Fourth-grade teacher Linda Cooper considers it good public relations to write on the page; parents are sure to see the feedback as well as any notations from one-on-one instruction.

Your personal responses to their journal lets students know you care about them and their lives. High school English teacher Holly Burgess comments, "My responses to journals get read immediately, but my comments on papers are almost never read nor do they get results." In addition, every time you respond in writing, you are modeling writing craft and conventions.

SHARING TIME: CELEBRATING, REINFORCING, AND TEACHING

As I walk around the classroom while students are writing in their journal, conferring briefly with individuals here and there, I am on the lookout for students who have done something well or tried something new. I ask three or four of these students whether they are willing to share their work, at which time we celebrate their writing. Celebrating writing is a great way to reinforce what's been done well, to encourage other students to write similarly or take risks in their writing, and to set goals for writing through new conversations and direct teaching. While many teachers take the time to validate their students' writing by asking the class to listen respectfully to one another read from their journal—with or without comment—extending that listening to celebrating and teaching moves the writing forward.

Focusing on What the Writer Has Done Well

The first thing I do after a student has read her piece aloud, usually while she is still sitting in the author's chair, is notice what she has done well as a writer. I hold up the journal and talk about what I think is good, pointing to specific words and phrases. I also ask the student to explain what she did: *Stephanie, I see you used a caret here and put in a missing word. That shows us you reread your piece, which is what good writers do. Tell us what you did.* First grader Stephanie proudly responds, *When I was reading it over, it didn't make sense, so I put in a word, and now it sounds right. It makes sense.*

Once students have learned the language of positive response, I often begin our sharing time by asking, *What did Bob [or whoever] do well?* Then I use what the student has done well to celebrate, reinforce, and teach. Explicit comments not only celebrate the writing; they reinforce what the writer has done so he will be encouraged to do it again, and they demonstrate to other students what is expected and what is possible.

Positive response takes practice. Holly Burgess notes that it took years to develop the vocabulary. Initially, she made two copies of a list of specific kinds of "noticing" comments and kept one copy in her plan book and used the other as a bookmark so that she would "see" the vocabulary often. She comments, "It helped foster what didn't come naturally for me."

Here are some examples of things I and other students have noticed and pointed out:

- Mercedes wrote *grandmother* correctly for the first time; she copied it from my notation in a previous entry.
- Jason added a beginning to his long story on space after a one-on-one minilesson I had with him while I was circulating around the classroom. (See page 304.)
- Sara attempted to incorporate dialogue.
- Roger spaced words for the first time.

- Tara wrote a great lead.
- Justin used wonderful verbs.
- Brianna deleted a sentence after rereading her story.

One day when several first graders correctly spelled certain words I wouldn't have expected them to spell, I asked, *How did you know how to spell that?* They responded:

- I looked on the family words chart.
- I checked the word wall (see page 276) in the back of my journal.
- I looked back in my journal [to where the teacher had written the correct spelling of the word on another page].
- I asked a friend.
- I remembered it was in our chart story, so I looked there.
- It's in the title of a book I know.

By focusing on and reinforcing what students have done well, we let them know that we want to see this behavior again. If a student can't verbalize, I will assist by saying, *I saw you do . . . ,* or, *I think you may have . . . ,* or, *It looked like you were. . . .*

In general, I limit sharing to several students a day; the other students know their turn is coming. However, we shouldn't be rigid about sharing procedures. When a student has done something wonderful, ask him to share again, even if he shared recently. Some days, have everyone share with a partner. Other days, let them share in their small groups where they are seated. Sometimes, especially when you've demonstrated a new technique in a minilesson, ask a number of students to share their first attempts at using the technique. (See page 322 for one way to keep track of sharing.)

While almost all students love to share, occasionally a student declines. Then I gently ask, *Is it okay if I read what you've written?* Often students don't mind their work being shared, they just don't want to read it in front of their peers. (This is especially true for students who have difficulty reading out loud. However, once sharing becomes a way of life in the classroom, even these reluctant readers will begin to participate.) But when students truly are uncomfortable sharing, I move on to another student.

Quickshare

Sometimes, when the minilesson has taken a while or the students have been writing for a longer time than usual, I do a "quickshare": rather than gathering formally, the students stay where they are, and I call on several students who have worked hard, done something well, or tried something new.

For example, as I am walking around Christine Cachat's first-grade classroom, briefly talking with students while they are writing, I notice that Christopher is spending quite a bit of time rereading and making some changes. I mention to the class that I noticed Christopher rereading his work and then ask him why he was doing it. He says, *I was checking to see if it makes sense.* I compliment him and add, *And I see you made some changes to your writing to make it clearer.* I hold up his journal and show where he has added carets and additional words.

Next, I talk about how Keith (a struggling reader and writer) has stayed on his topic—

getting a new bike—for more than a week and how he added some details today. I hold up Keith's journal and comment on how neat today's writing is, his best ever. For the first time, his writing is legible, he has spaced between all words, and skipped lines—a big step for him.

Last, the classroom teacher and I stand next to several other students and comment on what they've done well—continuing a story with lots of detail, getting right to work, checking their spelling. This quickshare has taken about five minutes.

Students can also quickshare with one another. This often goes on surreptitiously anyway, one student passing a journal to another on the sly. So some days I make this kind of sharing legitimate. Peer sharing is a valuable way to hear others' stories, ask questions, and "fix up" one's work.

RELOOKING AT JOURNAL
WRITING IN KINDERGARTEN

I still love journal writing in kindergarten. It's a great way to note students' achievements and needs, as well as an easy way to launch the writing program. Parents like it and can see their child's progress easily. I stand by what I wrote in "Journal Writing in Kindergarten," *Invitations*, pages 216–222. But I've expanded my view of what's possible.

Two events happening close together changed and broadened my thinking. One day about halfway through a school year, Christine Banks, a skillful kindergarten teacher, showed me a journal entry: "I hate journal writing." Christine found the entry especially troubling because the child who had written it was a strong writer: she was using beginning and ending sounds independently, along with great pictures and excellent letter formation. The same week, another talented kindergarten teacher, Susan Mears, expressed her frustration and concern that journal writing was limiting her students by focusing so much on one kind of writing.

Like most of the kindergarten teachers in our district, Christine and Susan taught journal writing formally, that is, they modeled journal writing weekly and were fortunate to have parent volunteers supporting their efforts in the classroom. However, Susan, especially, was now questioning whether the procedures were too confining. She was concerned that her kids weren't writing enough and that the writing they did was too limited.

During journal writing, everyone was required to draw a picture (even though not everyone wanted to), sit at the table, write in pencil, and use the blank paper in bound journals Susan provided. Students stopped writing when they got to the bottom of the page. They never continued a story from one day to the next, nor did they choose to write in their journals during times when they were free to work as they liked.

Susan also noted that some students' writing was not indicative of what they could actually do. For example, some children were putting periods at the end of their writing because a parent volunteer directed them to. Others used correct spellings because a volunteer stretched out words and repeated the sounds in them over and over again. Instead of being gently nudged to move ahead when they were ready (which is always appropriate), some students were being pushed too soon. Additionally, some volunteers had to be reminded that students' handwriting should predominate on the page and that adult translations should be written lightly. The work of emerging writers needs to be continually encouraged and celebrated. With these well-intentioned but sometimes overinvested volunteers, that was not always happening. (Teachers also overcoach students at times: it's not a characteristic only of volunteers.)

My conversations with Susan and Christine challenged me to rethink possibilities for writing in kindergarten. Why couldn't even very young students be given more choices? Why couldn't kindergarten students be taught how to write letters, cards, poems, and book reviews as well as journal entries? Since the writing center only accommodated four students, why couldn't they write with clipboards anywhere in the room? Why couldn't they use magic markers, crayons, or colored pencils if they wanted to? Why not let them leave out the picture once in a while if they didn't want to include an illustration? And why couldn't they learn to write continuing stories? In fact, they could and would do all of those things with modeling and encouragement.

When Susan invited me to work with her, I was excited about trying to expand her students' writing possibilities. Taking the writing I do in life as my cue, I suggested that I model writing I do all the time—cards, notes, letters, lists. Our plan, which became reality, was to model and have kids try out many kinds of real-world writing (see Chapter 9, pages 396–399).

A JOURNAL WRITING LESSON IN GRADE ONE

Demonstration/Minilesson

I am in Christine Cachat's first-grade class in mid-December. I have just shared some wonderful writing samples from first graders (and a few second graders), who have written about:

- True facts about bats (see Figure 7-17)
- An airplane trip (see page 245)
- A favorite blanket (see page 247)
- A kindergarten memory (see Figure 7-18)
- Catching frogs (see page 246)
- A mom who is having a baby
- Finding chocolate on the pillow at a hotel

Even first graders can write with elaboration, detail, and voice when we teach them how to do it and expect it. I ask students, *What do you notice?* We discuss detail and description, slowing down the writing (taking time to elaborate the interesting parts of the story), the "talking marks" around conversation, sticking with an important topic, how the beginning sentence sets the tone and tells what the piece will be about, how you feel like you know the writer.

Guided Talk Before Writing

I ask for a volunteer who knows what he or she will write about. Many students raise their hand. I call on Jordan, whom I do not know.

Figure 7–17 Kenneth's true facts about bats

MI BOT BOOK
BaTS are maMis
Be CS they are mammals
WirBOID
warm-blooded.
4 Bats use their hands
to FLY NOT
their aRMS.
10-30
echo
5 BaTS i USUS e CLoCAShIn
They the at Bat Won then
ALIRING
only
OLee VanPIrBat
like LIC BLD
BaTS are IADGrD
SPeeSeS

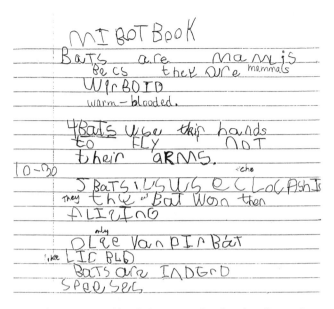

Bats are mammals because they are warm blooded. Bats use their hands to fly, not their arms. Bats use echo location when they are flying. Only vampire bats like blood. Bats are endangered species.

Figure 7–18 One kindergarten memory of many, by Anne, a second grader

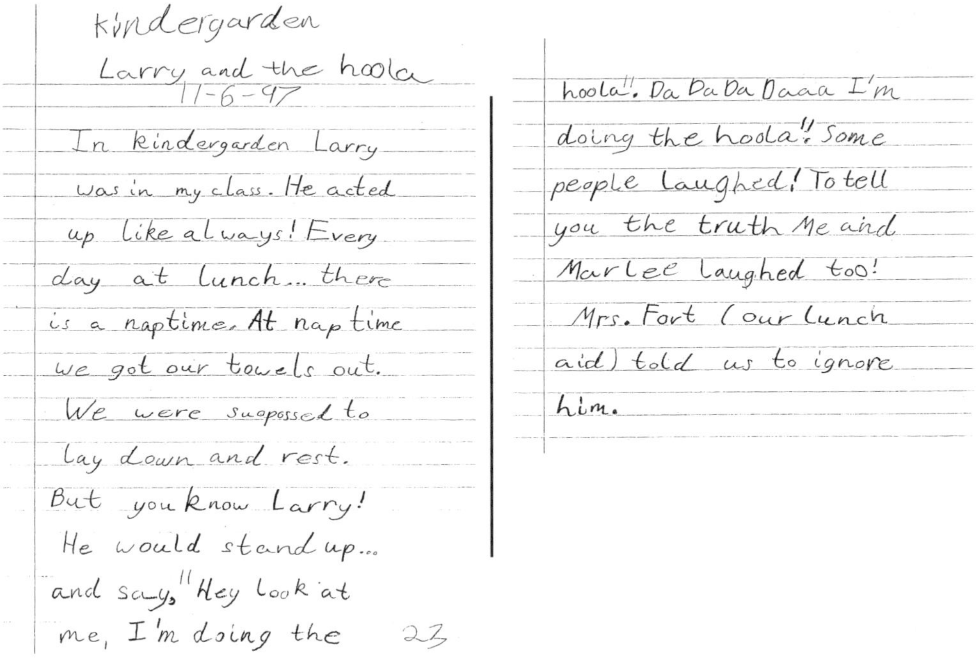

kindergarden
Larry and the hoola
11-6-97
In kindergarden Larry was in my class. He acted up like always! Every day at lunch... there is a naptime. At nap time we got our towels out. We were suopossed to lay down and rest. But you know Larry! He would stand up... and say, "Hey look at me, I'm doing the
23
hoola!! Da Da Da Daaa I'm doing the hoola!! Some people laughed! To tell you the truth Me and Marlee laughed too! Mrs. Fort (our lunch aid) told us to ignore him.

"What are you writing about?" I ask.

"Getting my new books."

"Tell me about that."

"When I came to school today, my new books were there."

"What new books?"

"The ones I ordered at the book fair."

"So how did you know they had arrived?"

"I spotted them from the doorway."

I pounce on that interesting sentence and write *spotted* on a Post-it so Jordan will think about using the word when he writes. While I do, I say to the students, "I can picture Jordan standing in the doorway and spotting the books on his desk. I can get a picture in my mind. Can you?" Then I continue. "So what did you do then?"

"I put my coat away and then sat down to look at them."

"And then?"

"I said, 'Yes!'" Jordon makes a fist and raises his arm. His excitement is evident. He talks about all four books he ordered and received. Because the earlier demonstration has been long, about fifteen minutes, I talk only with Jordon, which takes about seven minutes. Before students begin their own entries, I show Jordan, on the overhead projector—so all students can see—how to write "*Yes!*" I encourage all students to use quotation marks. (On page 262, notice how Maxwell also incorporates "*Yes!*")

Quiet Writing and Conferences

Walking around the room and conferring briefly with students, I look for students who have tried writing with more detail or have tried something we have talked about today, such as quotation marks. I ask these students if they would like to share later.

While students are writing, the room gets very noisy, an indication to me that some students may not be writing. I say, "We'll have five minutes of silent writing time so everyone can concentrate."

Before we share, I congratulate Hilary, who is writing about getting a hamster: "Tell the class what you did when you wanted to know how to spell *hamster.*"

"I got our hamster journal from next to the hamster cage, took it over to my seat, and copied the word *hamster.*"

"Good for you. When you need to spell a word, you can use what's in the room to help you, just as you did."

I also celebrate two girls I saw rereading before they started writing. I note that good writers think before they write and that one way they do that is to read over what they previously wrote to help decide what to say next.

Sharing, Celebrating, Teaching, and Goal Setting

The students who will not be sharing leave their journals and pencils at their writing tables so they can focus on listening well. We begin with Jessica in the designated author's chair. Jessica shares what she wrote today in her continuing story about going to a magic show with her mom. I note how she has taken the time to slow down her writing.

Trisha shares making Christmas decorations. I remark that I know exactly what her snowflakes look like, since she's described them so well. I reread aloud what she has written to reinforce the point.

Jordan shares his story about getting his new books, which is pretty much as he told it to us except that he has added, "I peeked in the bag" (see Figure 7-19). I celebrate his choice of *peeked* and say I can picture him "peeking" and how much more interesting *peeked* is than *looked*. I ask the students, "Can your mind's eye picture the difference between *looked* and *peeked*?" I want them to begin to notice how important verb choice is. I also say aloud, "I suspect this is the best writing Jordan has done," and Christine gives a big smile and nods in agreement. I also reread Jordan's first sentence and say, "Jordan's opening sentence tells us what his writing will be about."

Maxwell shares three pages of writing about garlands on his Christmas tree. First, he reads his entry. Then I hold it up so students can see it, and I point out what he has done well. Earlier, as I was chatting with students and encouraging them, I read his story and asked him what garlands are because I did not know. He told me, and I encouraged him to put that information in his story (see Figure 7-20 on page 262). I also notice that he has used conversation for the first time ever. We celebrate this so that he, and others, will do it again.

During the ten-minute share, I teach, celebrate, move ahead, confirm, set new goals, and do more oral brainstorming for new writing. To be sure everyone gets a fair chance, we take out the class roster and check off the names of the students who have shared today.

At the end of the day Christine, a first-year teacher, has a number of excellent student models to use later in the year and in future classes. Not only can she show examples of good spelling and mechanics, she can show the craft and art of writing as well—even to first graders.

Figure 7–19 Jordan's journal writing after conversation, grade one

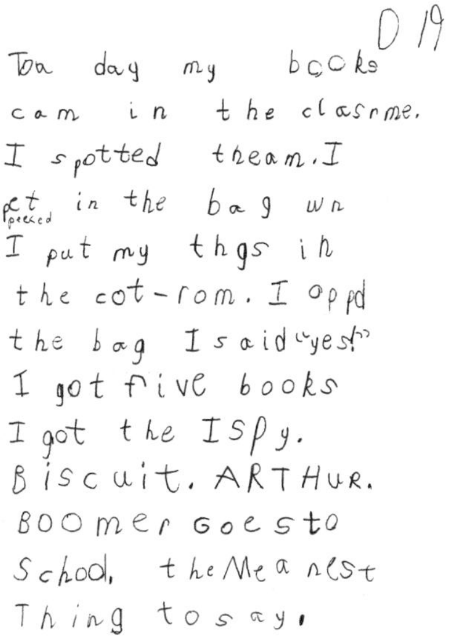
D 19
Toa day my books
cam in the clasrme.
I spotted theam. I
pt (peeked) in the bag wn
I put my thgs in
the cot-rom. I oppd
the bag I said "yes!"
I got five books
I got the ISpy.
Biscuit. ARTHUR.
BOOmer Goes to
School. the Meanest
Thing to say.

Figure 7–20   Maxwell's writing about garlands;
details that emerge because of a conference "on the run"

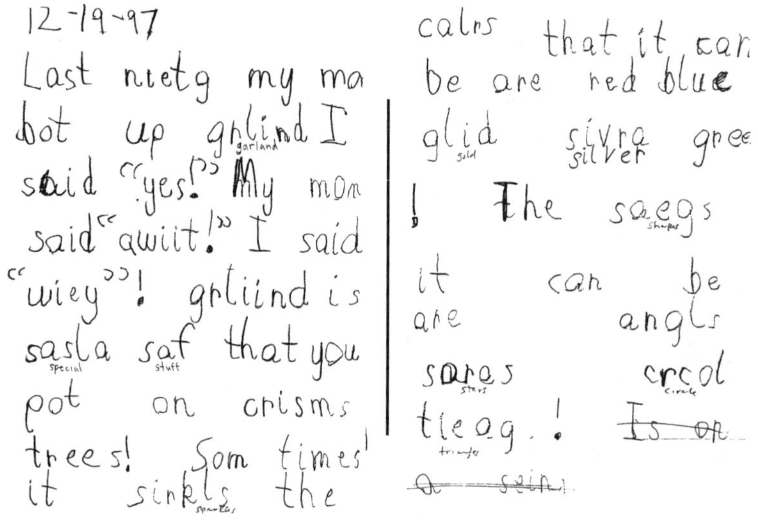

Last night my mom brought up garlands. I said, "Yes!" My mom said, "Quiet." I said, "Why?"
Garland is special stuff that you put on Christmas trees! Sometimes it sparkles. The colors that it can be are
red, blue, gold, silver, green! The shapes it can be are angels, stars, circle, triangle.

OTHER TYPES OF JOURNALS

While personal journals are the most frequently used and talked about, many teachers experiment with various journals across the curriculum:

• *Learning logs*   to record understanding about a concept, lesson, or unit of study.

• *Reflection journals*   to record learning, observations, questions, personal connections, and possible new learning directions.

• *Literary journals* (also called reading response logs)   to record personal responses and reactions to literature (see page 75).

• *Poetry journals*   to record ideas for poems, copy favorite poems, and write original poems

• *Dialogue journals*   to record written conversations between teacher-student or student-student.

• *Observation journals*   to record personal observations about science study, nature, classroom pets, trips.

Several other excellent types of journals, perhaps less well known and used, are discussed in more detail in the following pages.

Interactive Journals Between Students and Parents

Parent-child journals are a great way for parents to see and understand how writing develops and is taught in the classroom. Fourth-grade bilingual teacher Ana Hernandez uses parent-child journals to build community, foster writing for real reasons, and increase communication between parents and school. She says these journals help her plan for instruction by giving her insights into what happens in the home, the parent-child relationship, and how much parents value their child's education.

Ana also finds that asking her students to "interview" their parents like this is a way for them to deal directly with their history, language, and culture. Her students often refer to these journals to get ideas for poems, reflections, and descriptions, and to inquire into who they are. Students move away from trivial writing topics into "grand conversations."

Figures 7-21 and 7-22 are the guidelines Ana gives students and parents (in English and Spanish) for using interactive journals. Figures 7-23 and 7-24 on pages

Figure 7–21   Guidelines to parents for interactive journals

Student Directions
Instrucciones para los estudiantes

Homework—Interactive Journal

1. Write a weekly letter to someone in your family.
2. Choose the language, write the date and the person's name.
3. Write what you want to share, discuss, or ask that person.
4. Have the person in your family respond in writing in your journal. They are not to correct your errors, but instead respond in meaningful ways and model writing for you.
5. If you wish to keep the letter a secret, clip, staple, or tape the pages together.
6. If writing is difficult for your parents, you or someone else in your family can transcribe their response.
7. Bring your journal back to school at the end of the month; you should have one entry for each week in the month.

Tarea—Diario interactivo

1. Escríbele una carta a alguien en tu familia.
2. Escoge el idioma, escribe la fecha y el nombre de la persona.
3. Escribe lo que tú quieras compartir, comentar o preguntarle a esa persona.
4. Pídele a esa persona que te conteste por escrito en tu diario. La persona no debe corregir tus errores, en cambio debe responder con sentido y dar un buen ejemplo de cómo escribir.
5. Si quieres mantener la carta un secreto, engrapa o pega la páginas.
6. Si a tu familiar se le dificulta la escritura, tú o alguien más en la familia pueden transcribir sus respuestas.
7. Regresa tu diario a fin de mes a la escuela; debes de tener una carta por cada semana en el mes.

Glue this paper inside a composition booklet.
Pega esta hoja dentro de un cuaderno de composición.

Policies—Homework: Parent-Child Interactive Journals, Ana Hernandez

---

Figure 7–22   Guidelines to parents for interactive journals

Parent-Child Interactive Journal Guidelines

Dear Parents,

Once a week the students will be writing letters to you in their home journals. They may chose to write the letter in the dominant language of the home. Topics for the journals are selected by them. Family members can take turns responding in writing. This parent-child communication will continue throughout the year.

Purpose for asking parents/family to respond in child's journal:

- involvement in the child's development of writing (seeing growth over time)
- opportunity to see your child's written communication and thought processes
- acknowledgment of family members to be seen as writers by your child
- celebration to see the parents interested in their learning process
- support to strengthen the home-school collaboration
- chance to read about what is happening at school, with friends, interests, etc.
- journals can provide a wealth of ideas/topics for writer's workshop
- opportunity to weekly exchange reflective thinking in written form (sometimes we can send more meaningful messages through print rather than speech, such as poems, captions, quotes, illustrations, etc.)

Tips for responding in your child's journal:

1. The objective is to develop fluent and confident writers. Accept your child's written language as is *(this is the hardest part of all)*, do not correct spelling, grammar, or punctuation. Provide a genuine exchange of ideas, thoughts, and messages with your child. You can model correct spelling and other conventions in your response and point them out when you read the journal together.

2. Responses do not need to be lengthy. Short meaningful messages can send a powerful exchange of thoughts and ideas. If writing is difficult for you, you can have your child or another member of the family transcribe your dictation.

3. You can respond by having your child watch you model writing (hopefully in cursive writing) or respond when it is convenient to you and share it later.

4. Make sure entries are always dated. Clip, staple, or tape pages you wish to remain private between you and your child. Journals will be collected monthly.

5. Most important, make this writing exchange a wonderful experience between you and your child—it's not meant to overburden your family. I keep interactive journals with thirty-five children in class and it's a very positive and rewarding communication with my students.

Please, call me if you have questions, need help or ideas. The students are looking forward to exchanging grand conversations with you.

Sincerely,

Mrs. Hernandez

Policies—Homework: Parent-Child Interactive Journals, Ana Hernandez

---

265–266 are journal entries exchanged by Sylvia Quevado and her father. Ana says, "Both her mother and her father responded to Sylvia's journal entries throughout the year. But sadly, her father passed away midyear. This was Sylvia's favorite entry and she cherished the journal dearly."

First-grade teacher Karen Lum also has her students write to their parents, in a journal they take home at the end of each week. The students note something they learned

Figure 7–23 Journal exchanges between a student and her father

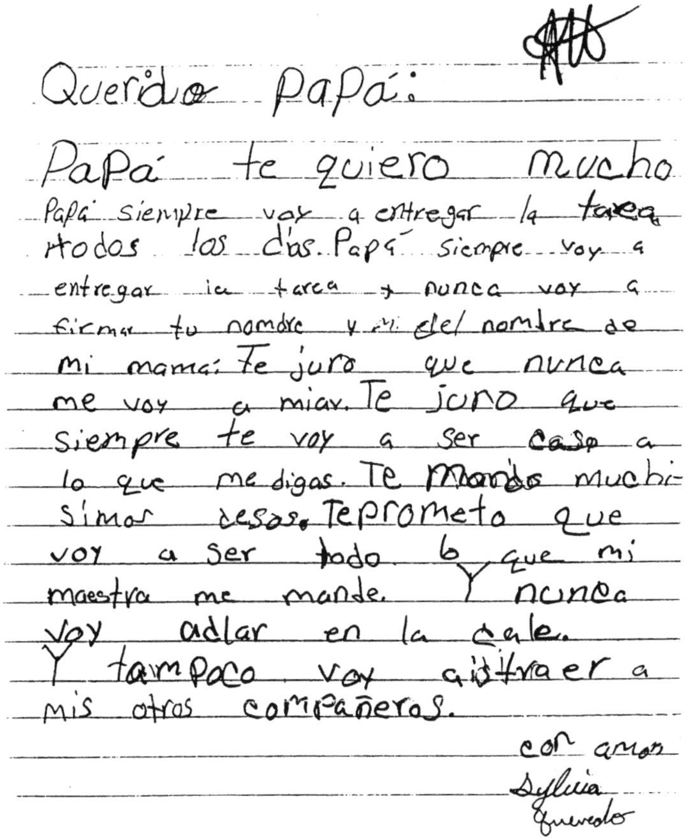

Querida Papá:

Papá te quiero mucho
Papá siempre voy a entregar la tarea
todos los días. Papá siempre voy a
entregar la tarea y nunca voy a
firma tu nombre y ni del nombre de
mi mama. Te juro que nunca
me voy a miar. Te juro que
siempre te voy a ser caso a
lo que me digas. Te mando muchi-
simas besos. Te prometo que
voy a ser todo lo que mi
maestra me mande. Y nunca
voy adlar en la cale.
Y tampoco voy a istraer a
mis otros compañeros.
                            con amor
                            Sylvia
                            Quevedo

Dear Dad,

Dad I love you very much. Dad I'm going to always turn in my homework, everyday. When I turn in my homework I won't sign your name or mom's name. I promise to always do as you like me to. I wish you the very best. I promise to do all my teacher asks of me. I'm never going to talk in class or distract my friends.

With love,
Sylvia Quevedo

and/or ask their parents a question, and the parents write back. (Figure 7-25 on page 267 is an exchange between Kalynne and her mother.) Not only do parents see their child's ongoing writing progress, the journal also serves as a memory book of first-grade happenings. (Karen gently reminds parents that their child's writing will not have been edited and to be patient with the invented spellings they see.)

Some teachers I know start a classroom journal between themselves and their students' families. The teacher writes the first entry, sharing what she did over the summer, her hobbies, her hopes for the class, stories about her family, all in a warm, detailed, personal style. Then, each Monday, the journal goes home to a different family. All family members are invited to write in the journal, and many do, grandparents and siblings

Figure 7–24   Journal exchanges between a student and her father

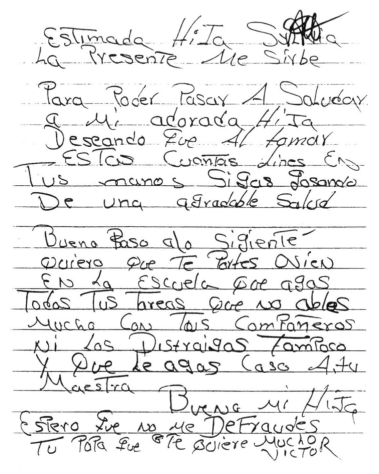

Dear Daughter Sylvia,

   At this moment I would like to say hello to my loving daughter, wishing that as you read these lines in hand you continue to enjoy such wonderful health.

   Moving on, I would like for you to behave well in school, do all your work, not talk too much with your friends, or distract them, and that you listen to your teacher.

   Well daughter, I hope you make a believer out of me.

Your father, who loves you very much,
Victor

included. Parents often comment how much they enjoy reading about other families in their child's class. One teacher who uses such a journal every year says it helps extend the community beyond the classroom and that no student ever forgets to bring it back to class on time.

   Even if you decide not to get involved with interactive family journals, you can easily give a few assignments in which a parent response must accompany the student's.

Figure 7–25   A first-grade take-home journal exchange

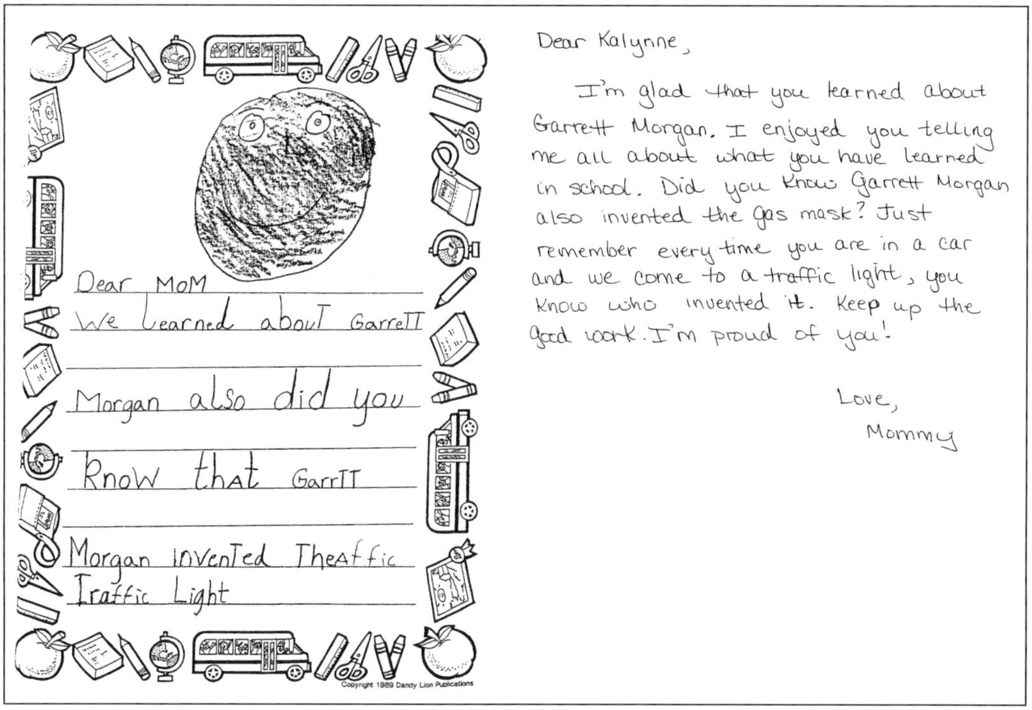

Dear Kalynne,

I'm glad that you learned about Garrett Morgan. I enjoyed you telling me all about what you have learned in school. Did you know Garrett Morgan also invented the gas mask? Just remember every time you are in a car and we come to a traffic light, you know who invented it. Keep up the good work. I'm proud of you!

Love,
Mommy

Dear MoM
We Learned abouT GarreTT
Morgan also did you
Know that GarriTT
Morgan invenTed TheAtfic
Traffic Light

Class Journals

In a class journal, teachers and students, through shared writing, keep track of important classroom happenings and lessons. These may include, but are not limited to, class trips, science observations (weather, class pets, plants) and knowledge gained during a particular curriculum focus. These journals become a class history. Entries can be kept in a large chart book, a big book, a classroom notebook, or a three-ring binder. Alternatively, each student can make an individual entry in a small journal of her own.

Some teachers use class journals to record the most significant learning or event at the end of each week. Third-grade teacher Antonie Wylie and I created a journal like this when she was looking for authentic ways to get students to revise their writing. We began by asking the students, *What happened this week in school that was memorable?* This activity started as whole-group shared writing, then was delegated to small groups after we had modeled the process repeatedly. The whole class (and later, the small group) composed together, and Antonie (or a member of the group) served as scribe. Finished pieces, copied in neat handwriting on lined notebook paper, were then added to the class journal (see Figure 7-26 on page 268). We kept the journal on the ledge at the front of the classroom, and it was informative reading not only for the class but for administrators, parents, and visitors. Students took this writing seriously because the audience and purpose were real. They revised, edited, and recopied the entries very carefully.

Figure 7–26   A page from a third-grade class journal

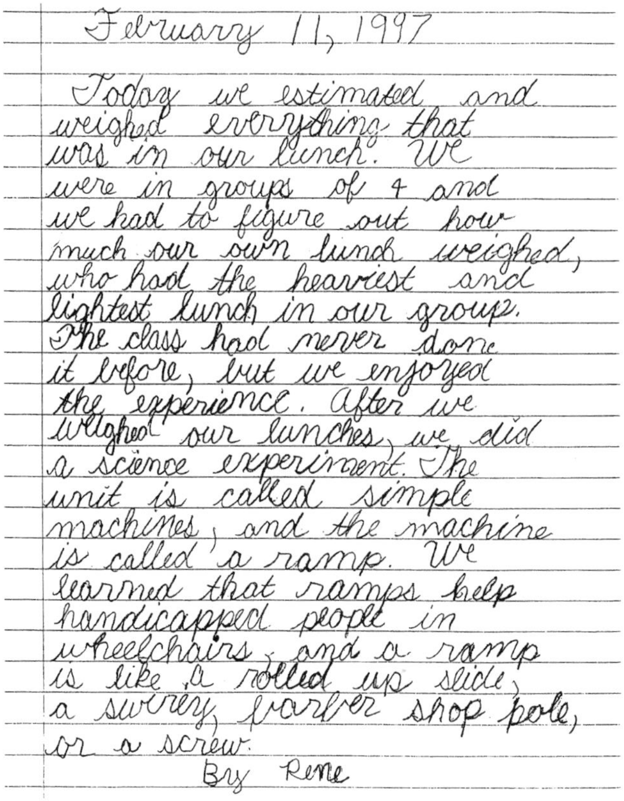

> February 11, 1997
>
> Today we estimated and weighed everything that was in our lunch. We were in groups of 4 and we had to figure out how much our own lunch weighed, who had the heaviest and lightest lunch in our group. The class had never done it before, but we enjoyed the experience. After we weighed our lunches, we did a science experiment. The unit is called simple machines, and the machine is called a ramp. We learned that ramps help handicapped people in wheelchairs, and a ramp is like a rolled up slide, a swirly barber shop pole, or a screw.
>
> By Rene

When I visited the Center for Teaching and Learning in Edgecomb, Maine, teacher and director Nancie Atwell ended the day—as she or another teacher did every day—with a whole-school share. She asked each teacher what significant learning had occurred in her classroom that day and then recorded it in a large journal. The journal was a history of the daily life of the school.

Recess Journal

Karen Sher created her "recess journal" several years ago as a way to deal with behavior problems that occurred during the lunch break. She made it a daily practice when she saw how effective it was for settling her kindergartners down for the afternoon. The added bonus is that students are focusing on letters and sounds in a meaningful context. Through the daily recess story, most of the class members have learned how to spell their classmates' names, some of which are long and difficult. (Karen also posts a daily morning message [pages 27–29], provides other daily opportunities for writing, and models journal writing once a week.)

Every day after lunch, the students gather in the reading/writing area around the easel, which holds chart paper and big books. They settle down quickly, eager for today's story. Today it is Adam's turn. He comes up and writes his name at the top of a blank piece of chart paper. Karen adds the title, "Adam's Recess Story," and then becomes the scribe.

KAREN: Who has a comment about Adam's name?

ASHA: It's good. It's on the line. It's neat.

KAREN: I like that the small letters are small and the tall letters are tall.

CHARLES: I like *a* and *m* because *a* and *m* spells *am*.

KAREN (*underlining* or *in* story): What's this little chunk?

EVERYONE (*calling out*): Or.

ADAM (*beginning to tell his story*): I played . . .

EVERYONE (*chanting the letters*): I p-l-a-y . . .

KAREN (*writing in* ed): I played.

ADAM: . . . with . . .

EVERYONE (*chanting*): . . . w-i-t-h. With.

ADAM: Brandon and David and Charlie and Toriano and Cameron. (*The students chant all the letters in the first two words correctly as Karen writes* Brandon and.)

KAREN: Adam, what kind of letter will I use to start *David*?

ADAM: A capital, because it's a name.

KAREN (*writing* David *as the students chant the letters*): D-a-v-i-d . . .

EVERYONE: . . . a-n-d. And.

KAREN (*beginning to write* Toriano): T. How do I write *or*?

EVERYONE: O-r.

KAREN (*finishing* Toriano *and* Cameron *slowly and aloud*): Tor-i-an-o and Cam-er-on . . .

ADAM: . . . and we played chicks. (*Chicks have just hatched over the weekend in the classroom, and the students have made up the game.*)

KAREN (*after writing* we played *as the children chant the letters*): Remember in morning message today, we had a word with *ch* (*she makes the sound of the* ch *digraph*).

EVERYONE: Chick.

KAREN (*after slowly writing the word as she says it*): What letter do I need at the end to make it say *chicks*?

EVERYONE: S.

KAREN: What ending should I use at the end of the sentence?

ADAM: A period.

KAREN: Good. Adam, I'm curious, how do you play chicks?

ADAM: Two people are chicks, and it's the other people's jobs to keep the chicks warm.

KAREN: Who can find a name in the story? (*As students raise their hands and call out a name, Karen circles the name in the story.*) How many students' names do we have? Let's count.

EVERYONE (*reading the names aloud and counting*): Adam, one; Brandon, two; David, three; Charlie, four; Toriano, five; Cameron, six.

KAREN: Okay, Adam, it's your turn to read the story now. Everyone read the title first.

EVERYONE (*as Karen points to each word*): "Adam's Recess Story."

ADAM (*coming up to the easel and pointing to each word as he reads*): "I played with Brandon and David and Charlie and Toriano and Cameron, and we played chicks."

I ask the class to tell me why they like the recess stories so much. Here is what students say, in the order they say it:

- "I like spelling the words."
- "I get to practice writing my name."
- "I get to learn more about people."
- "You get to read and write people's names."
- "I know other people's lives."
- "I like how we learn the words, like people's names."
- "I learned *played*."
- "I learn a lot of words."
- "We learn how to write letters because we see Mrs. Sher writing letters."
- "We learn new words."
- "We all get a turn to tell a story."

Sketch Journals

Sketch journals, which include both writing and pictures, are a great way to encourage students to observe the visual world and to validate and encourage artistic expression. Sketching is a powerful tool for many students who don't automatically "see" a picture in their mind.

Some teachers promote sketch journals exclusively as a research tool, encouraging students to employ both text and illustrations to record exploratory thinking, observations, questions, and surprising findings in science, social studies, or mathematics. Others prompt their students to include personal or reflective entries as well. As a response to informational text, written comments plus visual representation often provide a fuller and richer commentary. Other teacher-researchers have written eloquently about sketch journals. See The Blue Pages, page 29b, for particularly useful references.

ORGANIZING FOR WRITING

Some Basics

Scheduling

Having a consistent time to write every day or several days a week allows students to be able to count on writing as a way to knowledge. (See Figures 8-5 and 8-6.) Journal writing in particular lets students recap and reflect on significant happenings in their life.

Teachers whose schools lock them into an inflexible time frame for language arts sometimes schedule journal writing for full periods for several consecutive days or weeks, then shift emphasis and schedule reading/responding to literature in similar blocks.

Most often teachers schedule journal writing for about forty-five minutes to an hour, either for the whole class or for a different group of students each day. During this time they model a journal entry and talk with their students about the process, allow students to write, confer with individual students, and ask students to share what they have written. *Teacher guidance during every scheduled writing time is very important.*

In most kindergarten and grade one classes, the teacher formally models writing a journal entry at least once a week. Then, students brainstorm possible writing topics, so that everyone will have a suitable topic to write about. After that, the teacher and perhaps an aide or parent volunteer are available to guide and transcribe students' writing.

You'll need to tinker with your schedule to find the most opportune time for you and your students to write. Each group of students is different. Some kindergarten teachers prefer to schedule journal writing in the afternoon, when students are sure to have a topic. Especially for reluctant writers, being able to revisit events of the day makes writing easier. In first and second grade, scheduling journal writing in the morning seems to work best, so students can continue writing later if they wish (while you are working with small guided reading groups, for example). In grade three and above, journals are often integrated with other types of writing. Some teachers of older students always begin the writing week with journal writing.

Housing the Writing

Before you introduce journal writing, you (or you and your students together) need to decide where the entries will be written. Talk with other teachers, see what they are using, find out what works well for them: a spiral notebook, a composition book, stapled notebook paper, a three-ring binder, loose sheets kept in a folder.

Some teachers, especially in kindergarten or when students keep sketch journals, use blank books with no lines. Because these can be difficult to find, our district distributes blank spiral-bound books to teachers who request them. Some of our first-grade teachers have experimented with bound journals made with special handwriting paper. They feel using lined paper like this contributes to better handwriting in the journals.

Some students have a separate notebook for their journal writing; others do all their writing in one notebook, often a three-ring binder. Some teachers purchase spiral notebooks in bulk (often at discount stores) so that all journals will be uniform (when they are of various sizes, the smaller ones can slip out of the pile and get lost) and the pages will always stay in order, in one place (notebooks with glue bindings can come apart, particularly from the hard use journals typically receive). Other teachers have students purchase or design their own unique journal.

Dating Entries

Students need to get in the habit of dating each journal entry as a matter of record and so that they and their teachers will be able to note daily effort and progress. (Many teachers also date their written responses.)

In kindergarten, the teacher most often writes or stamps the date on the writing. Early in first grade, the teacher models how to write the date at the top of the page. It should be quick and easy for the students to do: either 9-8-99 or S.8.99 for September 8, 1999, for example. (It's a good idea to include the year.) By late first grade or second grade, students can write out the entire date in full, which is a terrific way to learn to spell the names of the months. (After they have demonstrated they can spell the name of the month correctly, you can let them use the abbreviation or the number.)

When students write on the same topic from day to day, I show them how to reread the previous day's writing, skip a line where they left off, insert today's date, skip another line, and continue.

Spacing

Writing is easier to read, revise, and edit when there are spaces between words and between lines. Constantly model how you do this as you write in front of your students. In kindergarten, many teachers supply spacers to students to use as they write (a small, colored tile that the student puts down on the page after he writes each word, for example). In first grade, by midyear, most students are ready to learn to skip lines as they write. It works well to use a lined transparency on the overhead projector when modeling how this is done or to note aloud how you are skipping lines on chart paper so you have room to make changes. If particular students tend to crowd lots of writing on a page, I put colored dots in the margin on every other line to remind them to skip lines. When I notice a student who has begun to space words or skip lines, we celebrate it: *Look how well Patrick is spacing his words now. I can read this so easily. Good for you Patrick.*

Expecting Legibility

While clearly some writers struggle with legibility because they have difficulty with fine motor control, students will write legibly if we expect it.

Neatness counts. When students are allowed to be haphazard and sloppy, the writing suffers. In the middle of one year I was so appalled by the messy, careless, graffiti-filled journals in a new teacher's classroom that we collected the journals, bought new spiral notebooks, and started again as if it were the first week of school. When students began to write legibly because it was modeled and expected, there was a huge jump in quality as well. And the students began to take pride in their work.

It's not only the students who may need this fresh start; we teachers may need it, too, in order to put the pleasure back in journal writing. (Handwriting is discussed on pages 225–226.)

Providing Resources and Demonstrating How to Use Them

Students need appropriate and readily available resources to help them move toward conventional spelling and independence in their writing. Interestingly enough, students remember and appreciate these resources. When high school English teacher Holly Burgess asks her students to describe their previous writing classrooms, they invariably refer to these resources with fondness. Print-rich environments leave a lasting impression. (See Appendix C-3.)

But it is not enough to make these resources available. We also need to demonstrate how to use them to write well.

Alphabet Aids

Many young learners have trouble recalling letter-sound associations. A picture of an object whose name begins with the sound associated with a particular letter (for example, the letters *K k* followed by a picture of a key) helps children relate the letter to its sound.

My favorite classroom alphabet charts are the ones students have made themselves. These charts also become the children's favorites. Students can make math, science, and animal alphabets, to name a few. Each year, first-grade teacher Jim Henry's students draw objects to go with the large upper- and lowercase alphabet letters he has drawn by hand on thirty-inch-wide rolls of butcher paper. He labels each picture and hangs the completed alphabet mural close to the ceiling, a very visible reference.

Many K–1 teachers give each student a small alphabet chart (often laminated for durability). The chart (sometimes purchased commercially, often handmade by the teacher) can be pasted to the journal's inside cover or made easily available in some other way.

Kindergarten and first graders need alphabet letter strips right in front of them as they write. Often, these strips will include directional arrows showing how to form the letters, very helpful clues for struggling young writers. These strips can be laminated and affixed directly to desks or tables.

Students who don't yet know their letters and sounds are frequently helped by small *letter books* that match single letters, digraphs, consonant blends, and vowel patterns with clear drawings or photographs of objects whose names begin with or contain the corresponding sound. Quality letter books are produced by several of the companies (such as Dominie Press and Sundance) who publish "little books." (See The Blue Pages.) You can also help students make their own letter books.

Word Walls

A *word wall* is a large area of a wall in your classroom, clearly visible to students from their seats, on which important words (sometimes related to a particular content area or theme study) are posted as references for writing and reading (Cunningham 1995; Wagstaff 1994).

In the earliest grades, teachers focus on frequently encountered words, usually dealing with them alphabetically. They add words one at a time, based on their observations of their students' reading and writing. While there is no one best list of frequently encountered words, published word lists can be a helpful guide (see Appenidix G-1).

When you add a word to the wall, it's best if you talk about the word and do something with it. Note strategies for remembering the word, point out any unusual features, talk about the tricky part, write the word on the chalkboard, trace over the word, use the *look, say, cover, check* technique, connect the word to other words (*If you know this word, what other words do you know?*) (Snowball 1998), highlight the rimes (d<u>ay</u>, w<u>ent</u>, b<u>all</u>) and discuss how transferring a rime makes it possible to read and write other words containing the same rime pattern.

Some teachers write words directly on the word wall, which is often covered with colored paper. Others write the word on a tagboard card (often in a contrasting color to the paper on the wall) and affix the card with pins, tape, or Velcro. (Some teachers cut closely around the letters to draw attention to the word's shape.) The words on the cards can be alphabetized as they are added, and students can take a word off the wall, copy it in their writing, and put it back (see Photo 7-1).

Always expect your students to read and write "word wall" words correctly. By the end of first grade, students can typically write (and read) about a hundred frequently encountered words. Most kindergarten teachers have a "Words We Use A Lot" list, or something similar, that includes about ten words by the end of the school year (see Photo 7-2).

Above all, the word wall must be eye-catching. There are commercial packages of words printed on tagboard, but they are bland and homogenous. It's better to come up with your own approach. That means you may choose not to use a word wall at all, but instead devise your own system of charts and resources.

Photo 7–1   *A first-grade word wall (in the spring)*

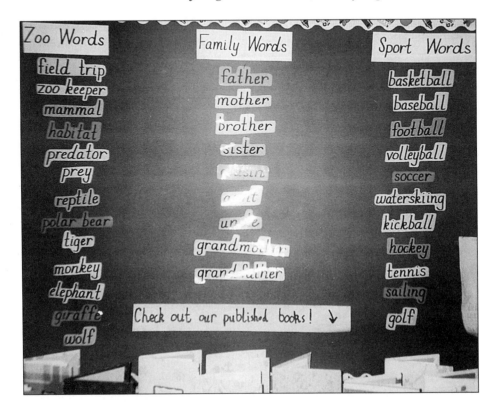

Photo 7–2   Words we can write: a resource for kindergartners

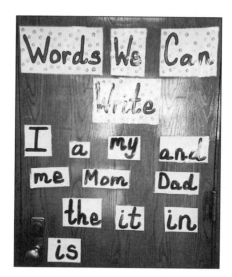

Family Words

Because children often write about their families, it's a good idea to post a "family words" chart: *grandmother, cousin, sister, brother, father, mother,* etc. Since students will use these words again and again in their writing, it makes sense for them to have a handy reference for spelling them correctly from the start.

Class Rosters

Starting in kindergarten, posting an alphabetical list of everyone's name in enlarged print helps children learn to read and spell their classmates' names. Because children are very interested in their own and their peers' names, kindergarten and grade one teachers often use the letters, sounds, and patterns in the names to teach phonics and the ABCs (Cunningham 1995, 29–32). (Revisit the story on pages 269–270.)

Personal Word "Walls"

I often paste a personal word wall at the back of students' journals (see Figure 7-27 on page 276 and Appendix G-7). This works especially well for struggling students who are not ready to spell all the words on the classroom word wall or for advanced spellers who are ready for more difficult ones. Having this handy reference, students are more likely to spell these words correctly. As many of us have experienced, when the teacher writes the correct spelling of a word on students' work, the students rarely spell the word correctly in other contexts. Having this core list of words in the journal also lets parents know what words their children are expected to spell conventionally.

Figure 7–27   Personal word wall

Jamie, gr. 2
early fall

A about	B	C come	D	E	F
G	H	I	J	K	L
MN	OP	QR	S said	T they	U V
W was wi th	X	Y	Z	Other	Other

When I'm having a conference with a student, I often add a word to his personal word wall and say, *This is a word I expect you know how to spell now, so I'm writing it for you here,* or, *You're using this word a lot and you're ready to learn how to spell it. I'm putting it here so you can find it easily when you need it.* Because these personal word walls are small to begin with and the space for each letter of the alphabet is tiny, most younger students find it too difficult to write in the words themselves. If the teacher carefully prints each word, the list remains neat, accurate, consistent in size, and easy to read.

Environmental Print

When children are surrounded by meaningful print, they use it to help them read and write. Labels, signs, calendars, charts, class rosters, and quotations that children see over and over again in school and at home are critical tools for developing readers and writers. Students also recall and seek out words in the titles of familiar books, magazines, games, and videos.

For example, in many kindergarten and first-grade classes, the terms *yesterday, today, and tomorrow* are written on cards or Post-its in large print, displayed on a large classroom calendar, and moved appropriately each day. The students then can and do refer to the calendar to use and spell these words correctly in their writing. (See "yesterday" in DeAndre's writing on page 237 and discussion of "tomorrow" on page 582.)

Dictionaries

While dictionaries, both commercial ones and those prepared by and for an individual student, are an indispensable editing resource, I do not recommend having them out on desks or tables as students are writing. When dictionaries are that close at hand, students typically spend too much time looking up words and spelling them correctly, and very little writing gets done. This is especially true for young writers who are not yet risk takers. Additionally, if a student doesn't know the first three letters of the word, the dictionary may not be helpful. (See Chapter 10, pages 416–417, for a discussion about various types of student dictionaries.)

Peers

Classmates are a great source of help for topic ideas, spelling, and editing. Peers can also listen to one another's entries and give feedback. However, teachers typically need to set guidelines on how much help students may request. Otherwise, some students get little of their own writing done because they are so busy responding to requests for help.

School Personnel

The principal, secretary, custodian, aides, and students in other grades can all take part in celebrating and sharing journal entries and other writing. In many schools, students regularly visit the principal's office with their journal in hand, or the principal stops by the classroom and listens as students share their journal entries. And your school's custodian would probably be tickled to be asked to listen to students' writing.

Kathy Wolfe's kindergartners are particularly enthusiastic about journal writing, in large part because each time they write they have a real audience. When they finish their entries, these young writers take off around the building—usually with a partner—and read to anyone who will listen: mostly older students but also teachers and volunteers.

Volunteers

In kindergarten and first grade, it is really great to have one or more volunteers to help you with the logistics of journal writing. Above grade one, volunteers are especially useful for talking with students about their topic and helping them focus. But with so many parents working these days, you may need to reach out to senior citizens, grandparents, or retired teachers in the community. Having other people in the room not only supports and eases your efforts, it gives children more security when they write. They are more comfortable asking for help and accomplish more.

What should you look for in a volunteer? Someone who accepts all children, who understands and celebrates invented spelling, and who will not take over a child's writing. Be sure volunteers have carefully observed how you work with students before you send them off on their own. Some teachers schedule a formal training session, complete with research on theory and practice and live demonstrations, as discussed on page 230.

I cannot stress enough how important the right training is, whatever the grade level. Some volunteers, because they either don't understand or don't value what we do, are never really trained by our example but go off and do their own thing. You may want to ask your volunteers either to role play helping a student with her writing or to write a paragraph or two about what they gleaned from watching you teach.

Having a competent volunteer makes it easier to coach (and with younger students, transcribe) everyone's writing and to work with individual students and small groups. For example, the teacher and the volunteer(s) can each manage a group when students are sharing their work. Kindergarten teacher Karen Sher makes a big effort each year to recruit and train four or five volunteers for just this purpose. Having a volunteer or two also makes it possible for you to work more explicitly with a small group of students who need special attention.

USING JOURNALS TO SHOW WRITING PROGRESS

Looking at past and present journal entries is an easy and effective way for students and families to note progress and for you to set goals for your teaching.

Some teachers have students go back to an earlier journal entry and edit or rewrite it. Asking students to circle and correct their misspelled words is one way to show parents how their spelling of frequently encountered words is developing. (I suggest having students work on a photocopy so that the original entry remains intact.)

Most of the kindergarten teachers in our district schedule formal journal writing once a week, and these entries become a yearlong record of writing progress: students, teachers, and parents can easily see what has been learned and what still needs to be learned. During student-led conferences (see pages 580–583), kindergartners explain their progress to their parents and write an entry (unassisted) in front of them. Guided by the teacher, parents see firsthand what their children can do and understand how far they have come and what new goals for teaching need to be set.

At the end of each month, first-grade teacher Nancy Johnston does a shared writing where she and her students remember important events that have happened—field trips, book fairs, celebrations, holidays, things learned. Then each child writes about one of these posted topics. At the end of the year, Nancy has a writing sample from each child from each month and a record of the major events that have taken place.

Second-grade teacher Tara Strachan has her students revisit a favorite early entry and publish it in final form. Figures 7-28, 7-29, and 7-30 (pages 279–281), which Ashley shared at her spring student-teacher-parent conference, show her progress in content, language, spelling, punctuation, and handwriting between September and March. (See the first page of Chapter 6 for a photo of Ashley working on her writing.) When parents see their child's writing progress firsthand like this, they understand and celebrate how young writers develop.

Figure 7–28   Revisiting an early September journal entry

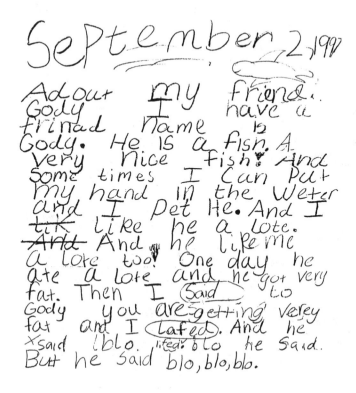

FINAL REFLECTIONS

My wise friend Holly Burgess reminds me that journal writing is a powerful teaching tool, a vehicle by which students can reflect on their life and make a personal connection with their teacher: "The very concept of a journal, that less than perfect writing is highly valued, was eye-opening for many of my students. Many believed they had nothing to say, that their words had no value, not even to them, let alone to an interested reader. They had never before perceived writing as thinking. I can't say I have instilled this idea in all my students, but every year many of them demonstrate their new understanding of the value a journal has in their life, not just in the classroom."

As I work with students across the grades, I see again and again the potential journal writing has for uniting a classroom community. Because we and our students write about what is significant in our life, we get to know one another better, which makes it possible for us to teach and listen more responsively. We learn that Keith is proud of his dad, whose job is to check that airline passengers are not carrying dangerous weapons; that Allie is excited and worried about the new baby coming into her family; that Samantha's dog chases the neighbors' cats; that Tasha's grandma just came home from a long stay in the hospital; that Malik made the winning goal on his hockey team; that Randy is fascinated with butterflies. And this is just the beginning.

The activities that surround our stories—writing them down, explaining what they mean to us, sharing and exchanging them—assure children that their life stories matter.

Figure 7–29 *Rewriting and editing a September journal entry in March, to show growth*

3-5 '10

Ashley Webb

My Best Friend Goldy

My best friend is Goldy,
~~his~~ he is a fish. I play with him
every day, because he says he
wants to play! If I (asck) ask my
Dad if I can put my hand
in the ~~water~~ aquarium Goldy will (nibole) nibble nobbler✓
on my (finger) finger. Sometimes I can
(tese) tease a Goldy, I don't (mine) mean I am ~~I'm~~
to Goldy
~~berry~~ mean, Goldy likes when
I (tese) tease him. When my Dad
cleans the (equren) aquarium✓ Goldy goes
in a (blow) bowl. And then I make

3-3-98   Ashley

(with my brother)
big   bowl (with my brother)
an (jaily) jiail (aroud) aroned ^ the (blow) bowl.
I always (asck) ask my Dad if
I can put the (blow) bowl in my
room, but he says No! Sometimes I talk to Goldy, all
blah
he says is: blo, (blo, (blo, (I think
can't
that (minss) means✓ hello!! (cannit) can't wait
untill Goldy's birthday, it's April
3, 1994! When I was in Canada
I really missed Goldy. Now
Goldy is very sick. ~~Now~~ I'm sad
feels
too, but now he (ills) fills✓ a lot better.
feels
*I'm very glad that he (fils) fills good.

O
One thing is I love him ~~and...~~
and...
*I'm glad that he is my pet!
The
End!

Figure 7–30   *The final copy, shared with parents at spring conference*

By Ashley webb

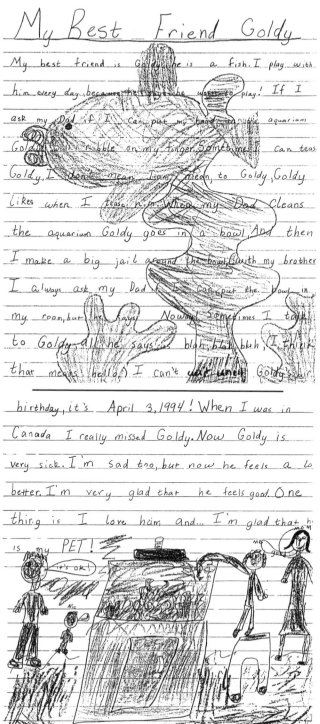

My Best Friend Goldy

My best friend is Goldy he is a fish. I play with him every day, because he says he wants to play! If I ask my Dad if I can put my hand in the aquarium Goldy will nibble on my finger. Sometimes I can teas Goldy, I don't mean I am mean to Goldy, Goldy likes when I teas him. When my Dad cleans the aquarium Goldy goes in a bowl. And then I make a big jail around the bowl with my brother I always ask my Dad if I can put the bowl in my room, but he says Now. Sometimes I talk to Goldy, all he says is blah, blah, blah, (I think that means hello.) I can't wait until Goldy's birthday, it's April 3, 1994! When I was in Canada I really missed Goldy. Now Goldy is very sick. I'm sad too, but now he feels a lo better. I'm very glad that he feels good. One thing is I love him and... I'm glad that he is my PET!

Journal writing, when done well, gives our students the vital message that what happens at home, in families, and with friends has value and relevance in school. By meaningfully connecting students' lives in and out of school, we become more effective teachers, able to teach and reach the whole child, not just the student.

CONTINUING THE CONVERSATION

• *Take a careful look at what you are modeling for students.* Be sure you are sharing what is personally important to you while focusing on both the craft and mechanics of writing.

• *Look closely at your students' journals.* Do they reflect the passion and substance of their life? Are they full of voice? Are they written legibly and with pride? If not, reevaluate your program and how you are teaching and guiding them.

• *Encourage students to publish their most meaningful stories.* Because the writing-reading connection is so strong, publishing journal stories—celebrating students' stories and validating their lives—is an integral part of a literacy program. First graders in my school publish up to eight journal stories a year through a parent-run district publishing program. (See *Invitations*, "Setting Up an In-School Publishing Process," pages 263–275.)

CHAPTER 8

Organizing for Writing

Procedures, Processes, and Perspectives

Writing on a topic that matters

Write what you need to write. Write to explore what you don't know and want to know. Write about what makes you laugh or cry, angry or happy, surprised or puzzled, worried or satisfied. And if none of that works, just write. The draft will tell you what you are interested in, what bugs you, what itches, what you need to know. Writing will reveal your subject.

—*Donald Murray*

GETTING ORGANIZED TO WRITE

It is near the end of the school year in early June and I am in my usual panic about getting ready to write. I have been spending weeks organizing my work space. This is not an act I consciously plan. A part of me takes over and makes sure it happens. My work space has a floor-to-ceiling wall of book shelves that houses my collection of professional books, children's literature including picture books, poetry, nonfiction, books for writing models and writing formats. My desk is littered with piles of papers an items that need to be sorted. Everything is in disarray from constant use and trying to cram more into an already crowded space. It takes me weeks to reorganize the shelves, give away books I no longer need to colleagues, go through piles of papers and sort, file, discard and "clean up" my space.

I have no choice in this cleanup. I absolutely cannot write in a cluttered, disorganized space. Although I am not an overly neat person, the process of writing is such messy business internally—with thoughts flying around everywhere at unpredictable times of the day and night—that a controlled, organized external environment is a necessity.

When I write, the order around me helps me to make sense of the disorder in my brain as my thoughts collide and cohere.

I cannot stress enough how important working in an organized manner is. When my home writing space is cluttered, I feel, literally, at loose ends. Sometimes, after I have begun a writing project and my piles of notes and papers have begun to take over my space, I have to break off from what I'm doing to clean up and organize. One day when I should have been writing, I took the whole afternoon off to organize papers and books. The next day, when my space was in order again, I could get back to the demanding and complex work of writing.

What does this mean for the classroom? I believe that it is absolutely essential to have in place an organization system that is easily manageable by the students and teacher. This includes a predictable daily time and space for writing and conferencing, established routines that students and teachers agree on, and systems for storage of writing and record keeping.

One of our teacher support groups concentrates on writing workshop for at least the first semester of school. We spend at minimum six meetings sharing and demonstrating how to get started in an organized manner. We talk about finding time for writing in an already packed curriculum, establishing rules during writing time, keeping track of what kids are writing, procedures for minilessons, and management and organization of student writing. We also discuss guidelines for conferencing, sharing, editing, publishing, and involving parents.

How writing workshop is organized is a matter of personal preference. Ideas presented in this chapter are not meant to be "the way," but rather are procedures and strategies that have worked for many teachers. You will want to adapt them to suit your own particular needs and contexts.

ORGANIZING STUDENT WRITING

The Writing Notebook

Most teachers experiment with various organization systems for housing student writing. What they finally settle on is based on trial and error, student and teacher needs, and the methods of colleagues. Many teachers find that a spiral notebook or folder works best for young writers.

The most efficient organization system I have seen for housing student writing is the writing notebook devised by fourth-grade teacher Julie Beers. I have used it and adaptations of it for classes in grades two and above. Some kindergarten teachers have also adapted the use of a binder notebook.

The notebook method is easy to employ. At the beginning of the year, each student receives a three-ring binder, a pack of dividers, and lined notebook paper and hole-punch reinforcements. Sheets of colored paper can be used in place of commercial dividers if cost is an issue. (In our school district, these materials are purchased by the teacher from each student's supply money, a yearly fee that families are charged.) Having the teacher purchase the materials guarantees their uniformity and quality. The notebook many teachers prefer has a plastic overlay on the front and back allowing students to personalize the book's cover. Student cover designs have included personal photographs, awards, stickers, drawings, and personal mementos—all of which are often used to "inspire" ideas for writing. Students are free to change their cover art as they desire.

Julie notes that after she moved to the three-ring binder notebook, enthusiasm for writing among her class increased. Over half of her students voluntarily take home their notebooks each day to continue writing. Second-grade teacher Jennifer Shoda says that moving to the binders made writing easier and more enjoyable for her young writers. Students particularly liked adding their own sections to their notebooks.

In deciding how to organize the notebook, we begin by talking with the students about what kinds of materials will be included in it—brainstorming notes, rough drafts, final drafts, handouts, writing forms. Sometimes, former students are asked to share with the class how their notebooks are organized. We then decide together as a group how to organize the notebook—what sections we need to have and what order they should be in.

One fourth-grade class came up with the following required sections:

- Writing records
- Handouts
- Rough drafts
- Published works

Another class came up with these divisions:

- Forms
- Minilessons (includes student notes on lessons)
- Poetry
- Nonfiction
- Fiction

While all students will have the same teacher-required sections, such as "forms," "minilessons," and "interviews," students are free to add their own optional sections. Such sections may include but are not limited to "letters," "conference notes," and sections specific to their particular topic or project, for example, "snakes" or "autobiography." This first lesson on organizing the three-ring binder takes up to one hour. Students will also need specific time and guidance each month to go through their notebooks and reorganize.

Some future lessons around organization will include how to record daily writing, keep track of minilessons, take notes during a minilesson, maintain a writing notebook, and how and when to fill out a form requesting a teacher conference.

Writing Forms

Forms I use with students include:
- Daily writing record
- Cumulative writing record
- Minilessons record

- Editing expectations form
- Revision conference form

See Appendix F for forms.

Daily Writing Record

Having students keep track of daily writing ensures that they remain focused on the task at hand. It also helps students and families see how any one piece of writing progressed over time. For years, I kept track of what students were working on. Eventually, I decided that this was something students could do for themselves. This freed me up and made students more accountable, a win-win situation. Some teachers collect these records (see Figure 8-1) weekly; others check them as they walk around the room at the end of writing period.

Some students use the record to jot reminder notes to themselves for what they want or need to do next. For example, when Andrew was working on a piece about hockey, he

Figure 8–1   Daily writing record: What did I work on today?

WRITING RECORD

What did I work on today?

Name: Laura B.

Week of: September 29–October 6, 1997

Monday	Monday
	We've both finished our notes, and I'm well into my rough draft.
Tuesday I finished interviewing Ryan Young and I started writing my rough draft of the interview.	**Tuesday** Sub (No Writing Work)
Wednesday Today I worked more on my rough draft of my interview on Ryan Young.	**Wednesday** No School
Thursday Today I started the letter to my penpal in Michigan. I've written about 2 paragraphs.	**Thursday** Mrs. Routman shares herself as a writer
Friday	**Friday** Absent

noted on his form, "Upper body equipment. Remember." This is what I do as a writer when I attach Post-it notes to drafts of my work, with notations reminding me of what needs attention.

Cumulative Writing Record

Each student also keeps a record of the title or topic of each written piece as well as its intended audience, genre, dates of beginning and completion, and eventual destination or result (see Figure 8-2). This is akin to the daily reading record our students keep, which lists the books that they have read. Keeping a writing history for the school year lets students, parents, and teachers know what genres students are focusing on, how much is being published, how many pieces have been completed, and what types of writing need to be encouraged. Not every piece included is completed or published, but every piece that a student starts is listed.

I believe it is important we include "audience" on the writing record. Even very young

**Figure 8–2   A fourth grader's cumulative writing record: Lindsay
(WACK stands for the classroom newsmagazine)**

Title/Topic	Audience	Genre	Date Started	Date Ended	What Happened to the piece?
School supply poem	class	poetry	8-28	9-2	published (class book)
growing up stone	anybody	Non-Fiction	9-10	10-2	class book
Dr.Weltman letter	Dr.Weltman	friendly letter	9-11	9-11	sent them to Dr.Weltman
WACK article	parents or friends	Article	9-24	10-1	magazine!!!
WACK article	parents	article	10-24	11-1	magazine
Bird	class	report	10-29	11-12	typed it
fiction story	anyone	fiction	10-20		never finished it
project	anyone	non-fiction	10-19		never finished it
Mrs.Jindra letter	Mrs.Jindra	letter			sent it
Business letter	Chamber of Commerce	letter	1-6	1-7	sent it
Caption	every	non-fiction	1-9	1-9	wrote in handwriting
Dear Mr.Welsburg	anyone	letter book	1-12	4-22	shared it with class
WACK	parents friends	Article	12-2	12-15	published in magazine
WACK	parents & friends	tradition	12-3	12-16	magazine
The Living Sea new	anyone	Review	1-29	2-13	WACK
WACK	parents or friends	Article	2-9	2-12	WACK
How to book	anyone	Closing	2-20	2-27	published
WACK	people	poem	3-20	3-24	WACK
WACK	people	article	3-20	3-24	WACK

students need to know we write for an audience and purpose. Some primary grade teachers use a simpler writing record form that includes *Date, Kind of Writing, My Audience, Finished, Not Finished.* Monitoring to be sure students are writing to various audiences—not just the teacher—is a good self-evaluation for us teachers as well as our students.

Minilessons Record

The term *minilesson* refers to brief (five to fifteen minutes in duration), focused instruction that usually occurs at the beginning of writing workshop. Minilessons can include complicated topics such as plagiarism and writing with voice as well as simple topics such as how to communicate quietly during writing time and how and what to record on specific forms.

While I have always kept a record of minilessons and have modeled minilesson record keeping for teachers, I didn't begin to have students keep such a record until Nancie Atwell modeled it at a 1997 conference. (See Figure 8-3 for a part of a student's record of minilessons and Figure 8-4 for notes from one minilesson, "Doing What Authors Do," a shared writing) These records remind students, parents, and the teacher what has been taught and what may need to be retaught or introduced.

Editing Expectations Form

Before I ask students to edit their own work, we do a shared writing (see pages 37–44 for a description of shared writing) to discuss what editing involves and to develop editing expectations. (See Appendixes F-6 and F-7 for examples.) I then ask them, "What can you do on your own before another editor (peer or teacher) looks at your work?" Stu-

Figure 8–3   *A fourth grader's minilessons record and notes*

MINI   LESSONS

Date	Lesson	Page #	Notes
10-13-97	Organization of writers Workshop Binder	1	Sections: Fiction, Non Fiction, Poetry, Letters, and Journal
10-14-97	Fiction. We made up character problems	2	Problems, he or she wants, and telling details
10-15-97	Fiction. Made up another character.	3	"
10-17-97	Mini Lesson Recording Sheet	4	We wrote mini lessons for the week. Learned how to fill out sheet.
10-20-97	Thank you letter to Lake County	5	I worked on details, interest words.
10-21-97	Fiction plot, ending, and opening lines	6	Characters solving problems. Plot development
10-28-97	Dialogue in opening lines	7	wrote 3 opening lines, and learned dialogue.

Figure 8–4   Notes from a minilesson

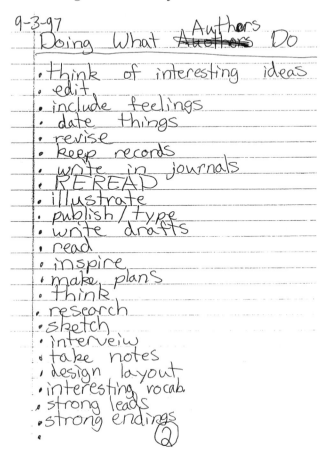

9-3-97

Doing What ~~Authors~~ Authors Do

- think of interesting ideas
- edit
- include feelings
- date things
- revise
- keep records
- write in journals
- REREAD
- illustrate
- publish/type
- write drafts
- read
- inspire
- make plans
- think
- research
- sketch
- interveiw
- take notes
- design layout
- interesting vocab.
- strong leads
- strong endings
- (2)

dents are often pretty clear about general editing procedures but confused about actual revision.

The editing expectations form serves several purposes:

- It gives students a reference for what they are expected to do on their own.
- It allows for individual expectations to be added on after conferencing.
- It enables parents and administrators to see what those expectations are.

Revision Conference Form

I have long believed that checklists work best when they are developed with ongoing student input. A form created for use with a former class cannot be as engaging or meaningful as one created with current students to suit their own needs. However, even when checklists are negotiated with students, many fill them out without much serious thought. A third grader set me straight on that account.

I required students to fill out a revision conference checklist before coming to meet with me. One day, while I was consulting with a conscientious student, she admitted (upon questioning) that she simply checked everything on the list each time she used it. A quick survey of other students revealed that they did the same thing—put check marks in all the right places in order to please the teacher. This was an eye-opener. We then spent a long time talking about revision and developing a form that would be useful to both students and teacher and would require thinking and writing (see Appendix F-3). (As with any student assessment tool, you will want to modify an existing form or develop your own with students' input so that it is relevant to your and their purposes.)

Of course, during conferences, teachers can always verify student progress by asking for an explanation or clarification. For example, if a student marks "has used interesting words" on a checklist, the teacher could say, "Show me where they are," holding the student accountable for his or her self-assessment.

MAINTAINING A PREDICTABLE SCHEDULE

When students are given a predictable schedule for sustained writing time, they come to the task prepared. I often emphasize to them the importance of preliminary thinking about a writing project. I describe my own process, how when driving to school, falling asleep at night, taking a walk, and at many other times during the day, I process my thoughts and plan my strategy. When I get an idea I am worried about forgetting, I jot it down. Because our actual writing time is short (forty-five-minute to one-hour time slots), students must think about their topics at home and throughout the day. Students develop a mind-set of planning outside of our structured class time, which maximizes their output during the writing session.

Having a predictable schedule for writing also facilitates creative momentum. In writing this book during the summer, I was most productive when I stuck to a daily schedule from early morning through midafternoon. When my schedule got interrupted—even for just a day or two—I always had a difficult time getting back the flow. It would sometimes take me days to recapture my writing fluency.

Based on my own experience, I recommend scheduling writing in the morning. Writing requires a lot of energy and mental stamina. I do best before all the distractions of the day have started to creep in, and I suspect that's true for students too. Also, teachers always ask, "How can I 'fit in' writing every day?" Take a look at Figures 8-5 and 8-6 on pages 291–292 for how two teachers fit daily writing in their schedule.

I follow, and model for teachers, the writing workshop model established by Nancie Atwell (1998), Lucy Calkins (1994), and Donald Graves (1994). We begin with a minilesson, move to sustained, quiet writing (during which individual conferencing also occurs), and conclude with whole-class sharing.

The Need for Sustained, Quiet Writing Time

My own and other teachers' experiences confirm the need for students to write in a quiet setting. After the minilesson, once writing time has begun, I insist on at least twenty min-

Figure 8–5   A teacher's daily writing schedule

SHAKER HEIGHTS CITY SCHOOL DISTRICT

Weekly Schedule

Teacher _Loretta Martin_   Grade __2__   Year _98–99_

MONDAY	TUESDAY	WEDNESDAY	THURSDAY	FRIDAY
		9:15 – 9:45 Opening / Calendar Math		
		9:45 – 12:35 Integrated Language Block Reading Workshop Writing Workshop Word study / Spelling Phonics Language Skills Assessment Computers 11:25 – 11:55 Music		9:45 – 10:15 Class Meeting
10:00 – 10:30 Mr. Mandel (Soc Studies)				
11:10 – 11:40 P.E.	11:40 – 12:10 P.E.		9:55 – 10:25 Music	11:15 – 12:05 Art
		1:25 – 1:45 Read Aloud		
		1:45 – 2:45 Math		
2:45 – 3:20 Health	2:45 – 3:15 Library	1:45 – 2:00 Math (Basic Facts) 2:00 – 2:30 P.E. 2:30 – 3:15 Science	2:45 – 3:15 Science	2:45 – 3:15 Center Time
3:20 – 3:25 Reflect	3:15 – 3:25 Reflect		3:15 – 3:25 Reflect	3:15 – 3:25 Reflect

3:25 Dismissal

utes of absolute quiet. The exceptions would be for kindergarten through grade two students, who do need to verbalize, subvocalize, and talk to their peers as they write. In those early grades, "quiet time" is often a soft buzz.

I used to allow quiet conversation during writing time, but two incidents changed my thinking. First, during a before-school meeting of our weekly language arts support group, a group of us teachers were going through the writing process to sensitize ourselves to working more effectively with students. In the course of our "quiet" writing time, we were distracted by several public-address system announcements, the ring of the telephone, and the actions of a custodian changing a fluorescent light bulb. One teacher finally remarked, "You know, in a writing course I recently took, we were told that we should let kids talk to each other, play soothing music, and get up and move around during writing workshop. But what happened here convinces me that the room has to be quiet. I haven't been able to concentrate enough to write anything at all."

Even more revealing was an experience I had while working in Julie Beers' third-grade classroom. Julie's students repeatedly complained to her that the room was too noisy during writing time (which was also student-teacher conferencing time). Initially

Figure 8–6   A teacher's daily writing schedule

SHAKER HEIGHTS CITY SCHOOL DISTRICT

Weekly Schedule

Teacher _J. Beers_   Grade __4__   Year _1997-98_

MONDAY	TUESDAY	WEDNESDAY	THURSDAY	FRIDAY
9:20 – 10:05 Reading	9:20 – 9:45 Problem Solving	9:20 – 10:10 Reading Time For Kids	9:20 – 9:45 Problem Solving	9:20 – 10:10 Art
	9:45 – 10:45 Writing		9:45 – 10:45 Writing	10:10 – 10:30 Science Experiments
10:05 – 10:55 PE		10:10 – 11:05 Writing		10:30 – 11:30 Writing
11:00 – 12:00 Writing	10:45 – 11:30 Reading		10:45 – 11:05 Reading	
				11:30 – 12:15 Reading
12:00 – 12:15 Spelling	11:30 – 12:15 Spelling	11:05 – 11:55 PE 11:55 – 12:15 Spelling	11:05 – 11:35 Music 11:35 – 12:15 Math	

12:15 – 1:05 Lunch ⟶

MONDAY	TUESDAY	WEDNESDAY	THURSDAY	FRIDAY
1:05 – 1:30 DIRT Poet	1:05 – 1:30 DIRT Poet	1:05 – 1:15 DIRT 1:15 – 1:45 Library 1:45 – 2:00 DIRT Poet	1:05 – 1:30 DIRT Poet	1:05 – 1:30 DIRT Poet
1:30 – 2:30 Math	1:30 – 2:15 Math	2:00 – 3:00 Math	1:30 – 3:00 Social Science	1:30 – 2:30 Math
2:30 – 3:20 Social Studies Read Aloud	2:15 – 2:45 Music 2:45 – 3:20 Science	3:00 Read Aloud	3:00 Read Aloud	2:30 – 3:20 Care Partners

DIRT (Daily, Independent, Reading, Time)

Julie dismissed the protests, because in her estimation the room was quiet enough. When the complaints continued, however, I suggested that we hold a class discussion to try to find out what the problem was. What we learned surprised us. Students admitted to being distracted by Julie's voice when she called out the names of students she wanted to see in conference. Also, students objected to the questions and comments—softly spoken though they may have been—of those seated beside them in their own small groups. What seemed inconsequential to us was a major distraction to the students.

Two changes immediately corrected the situation. Instead of calling out the names of students, Julie began to walk over and quietly signal to them when she wanted to meet in conference, and students agreed that there would be no talking to other students during quiet writing time.

My own need for quiet during writing greatly influenced my decision to enforce quiet in the writing classroom. My best writing time is early morning, not just because I am most alert then but also because there are no distractions—no ringing telephone, no United Parcel Service deliveries, no hustle and bustle outside my window, no people seeking my attention. As soon as the outside world intrudes, my concentration is broken and it's not easy to regain my focus.

We need to try our best, and it is often a challenge, to make sure our students have sustained, quiet writing time. I continue to be amazed, and occasionally enraged, at the number of interruptions in the daily life of the classroom that distract us from writing—indeed, from any and all learning. There are times when I wish I could make the public-address system mute or post an edict stating, "No interruptions except for emergencies."

At the Manhattan New School in New York City, where Shelley Harwayne has been principal, there are no PA announcements, and most messages are put in writing and left quietly at the door so as not to disturb the learning in progress (Harwayne 1999). Nancie Atwell says her one rule for writing workshop is: "Understand that writing is thinking, and do nothing to distract me or other writers" (Atwell 1997).

Even teachers of very young children incorporate sustained quiet time for writing into their classrooms. First-grade teacher Ruth Mardell once asked her students, "Why do you like writing in silence?" They answered as follows:

- I can concentrate (the response of a disruptive student who is low achieving).
- It is not noisy in the class.
- It is quiet so I can think.
- No one bugs me.
- No one fights; we all work.
- I can write better.

Establishing Writing Routines

In addition to students knowing when and where they will write, how much time they have, when the writing is due, and when the computer may be available for their use, they also need to know what the basic routines are when it comes to the actual work of writing. I recommend that students do the following:

- Write on every other line (allows room for making changes).
- Write only on one side of the paper (allows for cutting and pasting and easy movement of pages).
- Date everything (shows writing history and progress).
- Save everything (shows drafts and revisions).
- Cross out changes (makes changes visible; erasing removes changes permanently).
- Jot down specific feedback desired from teacher in content or editing conference (puts responsibility on student).
- Fill out daily record at end of writing workshop (monitors daily work).
- Keep writing record up to date (shows writing history and promotes goal setting).

Predictable routines also require a well-organized room layout that includes areas for writing, conferencing, and getting supplies independently. (See pages 545–547 for various layouts.) Regarding pencil sharpening, using the bathroom, and other such activities, it works well to negotiate guidelines early on. Some teachers insist that all pencils are sharpened before school; others are comfortable with students being able to sharpen their pencils as needed. I find it saves a lot of time, especially in the early grades, to have a ready supply of sharpened pencils on hand.

PLANNING FOR WRITING

Much of my writing, such as letters and greeting cards, is first draft/final copy work that I plan as I am writing. However, larger projects are always thought out ahead of time with a detailed, written plan. I begin by brainstorming, jotting down ideas as they come to me without worrying about organization. Then I look at what I have and begin to make a rough outline, listing major topics and subtopics. My planning continues throughout the writing; it is a recursive process that does not end until the project is completed. (See Figure 8-7 for a third grader's preliminary planning through brainstorming.)

In preparing to write this book, I began with an outline of several pages—enough to get me started with a sense of the whole project in mind. I use the outline to help me decide where to start writing. Then, I let the writing take me where it will. To maintain organizational flow, I continually revisit and modify the outline even as I am in the act of writing. On my outline, I jot notes of things I need to add in and don't want to forget. I refer to the outline each day to check my progress, sense of organization, and to make decisions on how to proceed. I continually revise the outline and print out a clean copy once all my notes have been incorporated.

Our students need to know that planning for writing isn't limited to prewriting, but that planning is an ongoing, necessary part of all good writing. For example, as I am composing this section and am but a small part of the way through writing this book, my initial outline has already expanded to seven pages.

Planning the Next Day's Writing

It is always easier for me to face the next writing day when I know ahead of time what I will be working on. Having a plan frees me from anxiety and saves me time. When it is getting close to the end of my writing session, I make brief notes on a Post-it or my draft, describing what I will begin working on next. I try to end the day's writing in a place where it will be easy to resume the next day, or with a topic that I'm excited about taking up. I teach students how to do this by demonstrating with a piece of my own writing. For example, I show students my notes reminding myself of exactly where I will begin the next time I write. Now when students fill out their daily writing record, they often include brief notes about what they plan to work on next. See Figure 8-8 for a student's note to himself.

Choosing the Topic

A third-grade teacher calls me aside because she is concerned that her kids aren't taking writing seriously or taking pride in their work. She can't understand it, because she feels that she is giving them flexibility in deciding what they want to write about, even though she herself chooses the overall topic. After gaining the teacher's permission to speak with her class, I hear the following complaints from the students, who admit that they "hate" writing: "The teacher gives us the topic"; "We have to begin

Figure 8–7   A third grader's preliminary planning for writing through brainstorming

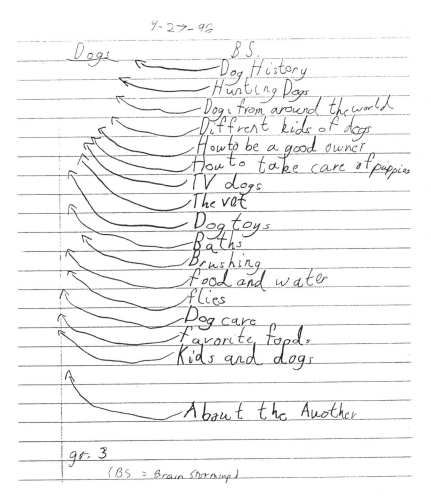

Figure 8–8   A student's reminder/planning note to self

> Make a good beggining
> so the reader will really
> want to know what is going
> to happen next.

with a topic sentence that includes who, what, and where"; "We have to write at least a page. . . ."

If we want students to write with voice, they must have real choice in their writing regarding content, organization, and form. As teachers of writing, it is our job to show students how to make responsible and gratifying decisions, as well as to negotiate possibilities with them.

Choice with Intention, Modeling, and Support

It is not enough to capitalize on students' interest and knowledge and just let them write. Choice must be accompanied by modeling and support for quality writing.

Before I encourage students to write in a particular genre such as fiction or poetry, I teach them what good writing in that genre looks like. I flood the classroom with relevant literature, read aloud from notable examples, talk with the students about their observations and perceptions, do shared writing, conduct minilessons, and ask students to make an attempt to write in the genre. They are expected to meet minimum requirements. For example, with poetry, I require students to write at least half a dozen poems and bring two to final copy. I require students to write an opening lead for a fiction story, a page of "telling details," and a scene in which dialogue moves the story forward (see page 352). Then, if students choose to continue writing in that genre, they can do so.

Choice must also include purpose. If a student is writing without a clear intention during workshop, the outcome will not likely be his best work. We need to show students, by our own and others' example, that even when writers choose their own topics, they have a reason and intended audience for their writing. Likewise, on those occasions when the purpose is not the student's—for example, during preparation for a state writing test or in satisfying a classroom requirement—the student needs to be clear about what the purpose of the writing is.

Finding a Topic That Matters

Teachers ask students to write topic after topic, but this is not how I or other writers typically work. As a writer, I do not jump from one subject to another; rather, almost all of my writing is about literacy. It's the topic I'm most passionate about. It's what I do for a living, what I read about every chance I get, what I talk about with colleagues and friends, what I think about, what I raise questions about. Yet it is only recently that I have begun sharing that passion with students when I introduce writing.

Interesting things happen when students find their passion. They read and write voraciously about the subject that has captured their attention; they stop asking about length requirements; they stay engaged for long periods of time; their handwriting improves; writing becomes their favorite subject. Just like adults, when students can spend time on what they love best, they tend to fully invest their energies and do quality work. So while some genres and topics may be required as part of writing workshop to fulfill curriculum requirements and meet district standards, there must also be lots of time for students to do free-choice writing and exploration.

Patrick, who has loved snakes since he was three, keeps a snake as a pet, makes habitual trips to the zoo, fills his home library with books about snakes, and wants to be a herpetologist (a person who studies reptiles and amphibians), wrote a detailed book about snakes. He worked diligently on the project for months. Jeremy, who is a baseball enthusiast, spent half a year writing a book about baseball for his peers—including history of the game, rules, key players, positions, leagues, and much more. Second grader Allie spent three months writing in her journal about her mom having a baby, how her life was changing, and what it all meant to her. After the baby was born, she gave the published piece to her mom, who was delighted to have such a keepsake.

Typical topics kids like to write about include, but are not limited to, pets, collections, sports, families, outings and trips, school, favorite objects, autobiographies, and stories.

When Assigning a Topic Is Appropriate

Second-grade teacher Loretta Martin reminds me that all writing is assigned, in the sense that we expect students to do it. Even when we give students freedom of choice, they have no choice not to write.

It is absolutely necessary that students know they are expected to meet certain requirements, perhaps so many journal entries and letters per month and a major project once or twice a year. Within these requirements there are guidelines and possibilities for personal choice, but students and their families must know that students are accountable. It's not just a matter of "writing whatever you please."

Giving kids choice doesn't mean that teachers stop assigning topics. Besides curriculum requirements, there are many times when specific writing assignments are appropriate and necessary. These include:

- Writing in a particular genre or format—journals, letters, poems, leads, conclusions, summaries, persuasive essays (See Chapter 9, "Writing in Multiple Genres.")
- Writing to assess—prompts, tests, self-evaluations, reflections
- Writing letters to the teacher—what students liked about a unit of study, suggestions for new school year, writing to next year's teacher
- Writing to change a situation or express an opinion—e.g., letters to the editor

There are many examples of these assignments throughout this text.

Again, even when topics are assigned, it is important that students understand the purpose of the assignment, know the expectations, and see the process modeled. Matt Jeffries, a second-grade teacher, described how he once assigned his students autobiographies but failed to model that genre properly and did not give his students adequate choice in organization and format. He wound up abandoning the project in draft form when students complained about being overwhelmed by the task and it was apparent that they were not engaged. The following year, he and his students together decided what the components of an autobiography assignment should be, including descriptions of family members and early childhood experiences, discussion of hobbies and favorite things, and so on. Matt modeled the process every step of the way by writing his own autobiography. The resulting student efforts were well organized and well written, and engagement was high.

Sometimes even the best-planned assignments fail to take hold with our students. When that happens, we need to give ourselves permission to abandon the project and start again. I have said to students, "You know what, kids? This isn't working well, so we're going to set aside what we've done so far and try this another way." It takes courage to concede defeat, but we need to embrace failure as an opportunity to learn, celebrate our self-reflection, and move forward.

Using Your Own Writing as a Guide

Reflecting on the writing I do in my life has tremendously impacted the kinds of writing I assign my students. Several years ago, in an effort to understand my writing process better, I kept track of every piece of writing I did for a month. To my surprise, the bulk of my writing included handwritten letters and greeting cards, lists, notes, memos, messages, and recipes. Almost three years later, my content isn't much different except for the addition of e-mails and faxes (see page 211). I also dash out a lot of postcards now, because they enable me to respond quickly, efficiently, and personally. What has all this meant for my classroom? I spend a lot more time teaching students of all ages (including kindergartners) how to write all kinds of letters and greeting cards. And just as I use appropriate letter paper in my personal correspondence, my students have been encouraged to forgo plain lined notebook paper in favor of real-world stationery and greeting cards in their letter writing.

Essential Minilessons

Minilessons are teacher demonstrations and interactive lessons in procedures, craft, and conventions that make the writing workshop run smoothly and help move students' writing forward. Minilessons can be conducted for the whole class or for small groups, and are based on students' needs and interests as determined by the curriculum and individual evaluation. They can be as short as several minutes or as long as fifteen to twenty minutes in duration. Their subjects are often determined on a day-to-day basis, according to student needs.

Teachers model basic organizational procedures such as pencil sharpening and line spacing as well as complex style issues such as writing with voice and authority. No desired outcome is too insignificant to be modeled. Nancie Atwell even models acceptable verbal communication, or whispering behavior, during writing workshop (Atwell 1997).

I simultaneously demonstrate the craft of writing (writing quality, including subject development and voice) and the conventions of writing (writing mechanics, including grammar, punctuation, and spelling), even for young children. That is, while I may focus on punctuation in a minilesson, I always emphasize the need for students to maintain the highest standards with respect to craft. Students learn early on that writers pay attention to mechanics as well as to style and form when they write.

While I do not have a prescribed set of minilessons, governed instead by the evolving needs of students, teachers who would appreciate such a list can consult the "Minilessons" Resources in The Blue Pages, pages 29b–30b. I do make sure that I and my students record completed minilessons on our minilessons form (see page 288). I also jot down subjects intended for future lessons. Additionally, middle-grade and older students are expected to take notes on the minilessons (Atwell 1997). In that way, the teacher, parents, and students have a detailed, organized record of what has been taught (see page 289).

Students come to depend on and value minilessons and even to request instruction in specific subjects. When I was sharing my experiences as a writer with a fourth-grade classroom, I shared letters of complaint and request I'd written, causing one student to ask her teacher, "Can we have a minilesson on how to write a business letter?" Julie Beers' fourth graders have requested minilessons on such subjects as correct word usage (for example, why we use "mine" instead of "mine's"), alternatives to the word *said* (see page 303), and how to write a letter to the editor.

Often, students are expected to experiment afterward with what has been demonstrated in the minilesson. For instance, when I conducted a lesson for fourth graders on beginning a piece of writing, I showed them the value of trying out several different beginnings and then picking the one that works best; I expected students to take this approach with their next project. When teaching upper elementary students how to create and develop a character in fictional writing, I expected them to use what they had been taught in the minilesson to create their own fictional character.

Once, a visitor to a classroom in which the teacher had given a minilesson on the use of detail and had then asked the students to try out what they had learned by describing an object in detail, asked, "Isn't it contrived to have kids do this, when they just want to write?" A fair question. I answered, "No, I don't think so, because it is our job to help students write well, not just write."

I always tell kids the intended purpose behind specific instructions. I might say: "I've noticed that you're having trouble with images and details, so we're going to concentrate on description and try out some activities that will help you." Then, during sharing time, I recognize those students who made an effort to incorporate what was taught into their writing. "Who tried writing today with images and details?" I let those kids share first.

What follows are some typical minilessons that take place every year in one form or another. Keep in mind that for students' attention, retention of information, and wise use of time, you only want to make a few major teaching points in each lesson. Many minilessons will need to be retaught.

Organizing the Writing Notebook

For every organizational form that students are expected to fill out, there is a lesson to show them how to do it. For example, in modeling how to fill out the cumulative writing record, I put a transparency of a former student's record on the overhead projector. We then go over everything students need to include on the form, column by column (see page 287). Then, using a transparency of a blank writing record form, I model how to record, and I guide students in filling out their own forms. It is very important to supervise these seemingly simple procedures; I walk around the room and check each student's work to be sure that handwriting is legible, titles are capitalized, dates are in the right places, and so on. Setting precise and strict expectations through modeling, practice, and feedback saves time in the long run by getting routines and expectations clearly established from the start.

It is important to keep in mind that just because we have modeled "how to" doesn't mean that students have "gotten it." We need to look closely at their work and, when necessary, remodel a skill, ask students to model for classmates who were absent during the instruction, and reinforce learning by starting the next day's writing with a review of the previous day's minilesson. Modeling once is rarely enough.

Rereading

Rereading is an ongoing and essential aspect of my life as a writer. I reread as I write, rewrite, revisit a piece, and prepare to continue writing. In the course of writing this chapter, I reread each day before I began writing. I probably reread this chapter-in-progress more than fifty times! When I write in front of students, even kindergarten students, I point out that I always reread as I write: to check my work and ensure that I'm making sense, to decide where I need to go next, and to gain for myself some additional thinking time. Yet, I have seen little in professional literature about the importance of rereading. We teachers need to demonstrate rereading as a vital part of all successful writing.

Often, part of what I do when I reread is to mouth the words on the page. This subvocalizing or quiet vocalizing is important in that it allows me to "hear" how the piece sounds—the rhythm, flow, meaning, organization. I do not reread in a linear fashion. Some sentences I skim over. Others I read quickly. Still others I pore over time and time again to "get them right." When I am having difficulty with a particular section of writing, speaking the words aloud seems to help me move toward clarity. I may reread one sentence ten times and fuss over word choice, the length of the sentence, the punctuation, or the flow—until it all sounds right. Then I often go back and reread the entire paragraph several times before I move on. I demonstrate this back-and-forth rereading process to students as I write aloud in front of them.

I also use rereading as a tool against getting "stuck" in a piece of writing. As I write, especially more developed pieces, it's easy to lose my way. I forget where I want to go next, or, more likely, I have no idea of what could come next. I reread to remind myself of what I have already said, and as I reread I think about possible ways to move the piece forward. Sometimes I do this rereading aloud. Once again, vocalizing the words often throws light on trouble spots.

Editing as Part of Rereading

Many students have a linear notion of writing—write first, edit later—but the natural and necessary act of rereading precludes saving essential editing for later. In actuality, I edit as I go along, and we need to teach this to students—that in our own writing we are constantly rereading and checking, and that we fix up and change our work in the process of writing, not just at the end. For example, when I am writing a letter, I do not just write the words straight down the page without interruption. I stop and reread as I go so that I can refocus, think of what I want to say next, and check my accuracy. While we do want to continue to give students the message to focus on content and do the best they can with spelling, we want to also let them know that writers maintain high standards even on drafts. Editing as you go also saves lots of time later.

We need to demonstrate editing as an integral part of rereading so students will naturally edit their writing in progress. Many students and teachers think of editing as a visual process that takes place on paper, discounting the self-correcting that goes on in the head. I am not talking about the nitty-gritty editing that takes place with the teacher and/or peers after a piece is in good form, but rather the fix-ups that we catch easily in the rereading process. When I am working on a piece of writing, on chart paper or on a transparency on the overhead projector, students often see me adding a missing word or punctuation mark, correcting a misspelling of a familiar word, or crossing out an overused word and replacing it with a more interesting one. Then, they see me rereading the section or the entire piece to make sure the change fits.

Cutting and Pasting

Young students can easily be taught to cut and paste their work using scissors and Scotch tape. This is a great way to move things around on the page and add to text without having the student waste time recopying. So that cutting and pasting can be done easily, it is important for students to double space as they write and use only one side of the page. Once I have taught a student how to cut and paste, I encourage that student to teach others.

Of course, "cutting and pasting" is easier on the computer, once students have been taught how to do it, but very few classrooms have an adequate number of computers for student use. The advantage of hand cutting and pasting is that it allows for a visible record of students' changes. (See page 385 for an example.)

Adding On

Some young students have the notion that when they reach the end of the page, their writing must also end. Even kindergartners can be shown how to tape a piece of paper onto the bottom of a page (and then fold it up to fit into the writing notebook) to gain more writing space.

I show students how to use arrows, lassos, notations, symbols, and letters to add on to a piece or section of writing without starting over or recopying (see page 304). This is exactly what I did when reading—and adding on to—the final, copyedited manuscript of this book. Of course, adding on large sections is simplest when done on a computer.

Using Interesting Words

"Miss Beers, don't you love the way William Steig paints pictures with words?" a third grader asked her teacher. Reading like a writer is a great way to help students become aware of the significance of word choice. When reading aloud, point out the lively, specific language authors use. Mark Twain said it best: "The difference between the right word and nearly the right word is the same as that between lightning and the lightning bug."

Beautifully crafted picture books are great for helping students notice energetic verbs that drive the action. After two enjoyable *Gettin' Through Thursdays* (Cooper and Bennett 1998) read-aloud sessions with a group of fourth and fifth graders, we discussed how the use of carefully chosen verbs gave the story a poignant, personal, alive feel. Several students volunteered to go through the book and jot down the powerful verbs the authors used. Making students aware of how word choice impacts the reader eventually carries over into students' writing.

Having students go through a piece of their writing and circle "interesting words" or "energetic verbs" is a valuable exercise. When students have difficulty finding such words, they get the message that they need to develop a more powerful vocabulary. Similarly, asking students to circle and replace boring words in something they've written challenges them to look critically at their work and attempt more vivid prose.

Focusing on word choice is also a great way to teach grammar. Students can't be expected to use a stronger verb or adjective until they understand those parts of speech. Grammar makes most sense to students when we teach it as part of the actual writing students are doing, rather than in isolation, with the diagramming of sentences and the like. For example, I might say to students, "I notice that many of you are overusing the verb *said* (or *play* or *walk*) in your writing. Today, as I read aloud to you, follow along and notice the different words the author uses for *said*. Then, with a partner, I want you to go back, reread this passage, and jot down all the words the author used that meant *said*. We'll display these words on a chart."

Making a class chart of alternative choices for commonly used words heightens students' awareness that every word makes a difference. Note one third and fourth graders' group of variations of *said* and other over-used words (see Figure 8-9). Energetic verbs and descriptive nouns can make a piece of writing come alive. That said, however, it's best not to encourage overuse of a thesaurus. While a thesaurus is a wonderful resource for replacing an overused or trite word, some students rely too heavily on this tool and wind up using words they don't understand or stilted language they would not ordinarily use.

To encourage her students to use interesting words, second-grade teacher Megan Sloan employs the following minilessons and activities:

- Talking about interesting words encountered during read-alouds
- Pairing interesting words found in a book with common synonyms the author could have chosen
- Creating a classroom display of interesting words
- Acting out "energetic" verbs (word-deprived students find visualization helpful)
- Brainstorming synonyms of common words
- Talking about descriptive words that poets use and painting, drawing, or clay modeling as the teacher reads poems aloud (Sloan 1996, 268–269)

Writing with Voice

According to Donald Murray, "Voice is the single most important element in attracting and holding a reader's interest" (1996, 39). Voice is essential for memorable writing. However, before we can teach students to write with voice, we have to find our own voices. (See Murray 1996, pages 38–45, for particulars on learning to write with voice, and Chapter 6, "Quality Writing: Principles, Problems, and Goals," pages 222–225, for specific ideas.)

Writing a Good Introduction or Lead

Throughout the year, we spend a great deal of time talking with students about how important beginnings are and how a good lead grabs the reader's attention. We take the time to study how authors begin books and chapters. At different times throughout the year, during independent reading time or as a minilesson, I ask students to take out the

**Figure 8–9   Third and fourth graders' more
interesting ways to say "said" and other overused words**

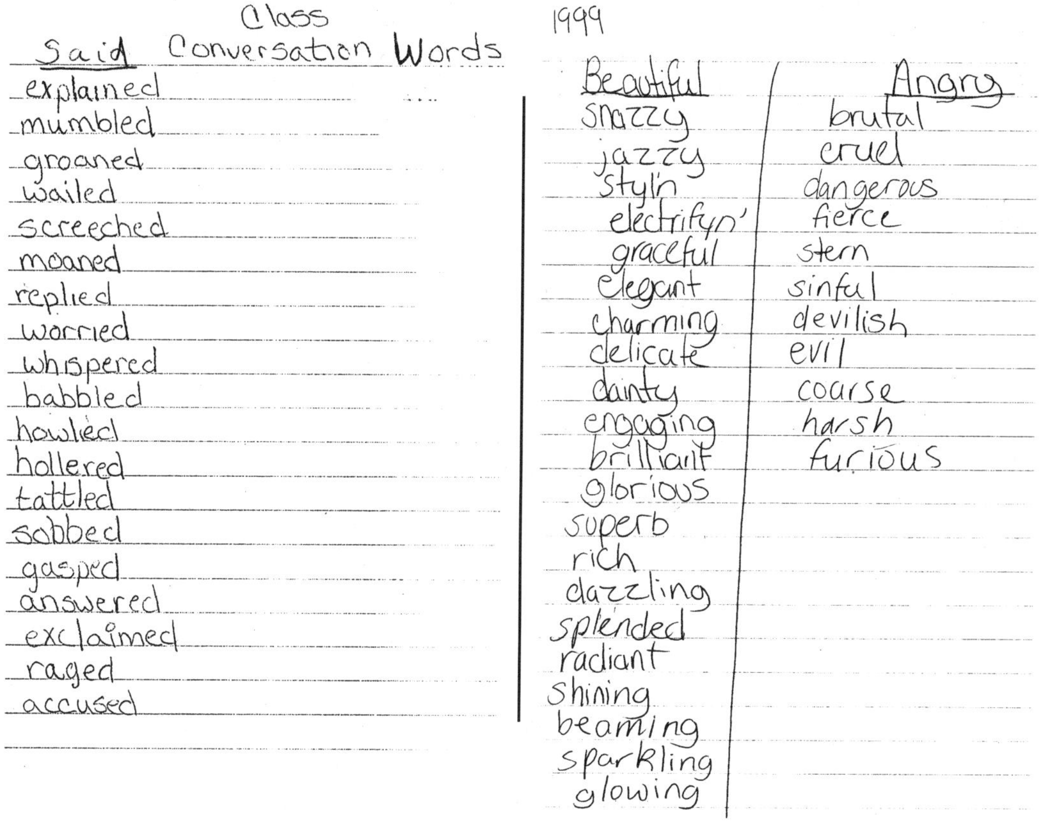

Class   1999
Said Conversation Words

Said Words	Beautiful	Angry
explained	snazzy	brutal
mumbled	jazzy	cruel
groaned	stylin'	dangerous
wailed	electrifyn'	fierce
screeched	graceful	stern
moaned	elegant	sinful
replied	charming	devilish
worried	delicate	evil
whispered	dainty	course
babbled	engaging	harsh
howled	brilliant	furious
hollered	glorious	
tattled	superb	
sobbed	rich	
gasped	dazzling	
answered	splended	
exclaimed	radiant	
raged	shining	
accused	beaming	
	sparkling	
	glowing	

book they are reading and mark a striking beginning with a Post-it. These we share with a partner, a small group, or the whole class. We discuss strategies the author used to draw in the reader. We note that interesting leads are not limited to fiction, but that it's as important to seize the reader's attention in nonfiction.

As a writer, I let students know how much attention I give opening sentences and paragraphs. In one fourth-grade classroom, I showed students my first, second, and third drafts of a letter to the editor I was working on. I told them that I had spent three hours on the opening paragraph. "Why would I do that?" I asked them. No response. I then said, "What do you do when you start a book and it's boring or poorly written?" Most admitted that they put the book down. Several students expressed surprise that I rarely got the beginning of a piece "right" the first time.

As I mentioned, I sometimes require students to write several beginnings to a piece. This exercise enables them to see firsthand that their first attempt is not usually their best. I always demonstrate first with my own writing (see page 384) and also share student efforts (see page 490). See also Figure 8-10 for a first grader who added an introduction to his continuing info-narrative about space after a demonstration and discussion about leads.

Figure 8–10   A first grader adding a lead, knowing the story will be published

I know a lot about space ships. Space ships are the hottest thing when they explode.

Writing a Satisfying Conclusion

Students often end their writing when they feel that they're done, without attempting to bring the piece full circle or to meaningful completion. Thus, student writing can often seem unfinished. We need to show students what satisfying endings look and sound like—by reading effective conclusions aloud and analyzing what makes them work and by writing successful endings with students (as in shared writing). Good models can include the writing of former students as well as known authors. We need to teach students how to write endings in multiple genres such as poetry, letters, fiction, and nonfiction.

One activity that works well is to have students look at endings (or beginnings or whatever you are focusing on) of former students' writing (with the authors' names removed). In small groups, have students work together to note why some papers work well while others don't. What has the writer done (or not done) in bringing the piece to a close? What comments and suggestions would they give the writer? As in all such activities, you will first want to demonstrate this exercise with the class by comparing several conclusions yourself and guiding students through critical features of the texts.

If you do not have papers from former students, it works well (with students' permission) to read aloud, or have students read aloud, their conclusions. Or I might ask students who think they've written a strong ending sentence or paragraph to share it with the entire class. Effective student models send the important message to other students that "I can do this too."

Writing Dialogue

Even first graders can learn to write dialogue if it is encouraged and modeled. Conversation is a powerful tool for adding voice and a sense of immediacy to writing. When I notice that a student has used conversation effectively, we celebrate it (see page 262).

When I am working in a classroom and I see a group of students who seem ready to write with conversation (as evidenced by their attempts), I gather them together as a group and show them how to do it. Another effective way to teach students to write conversation is to work with a teacher or student at the overhead projector. Using a blank transparency, each speaker records the ongoing conversation in front of the class. Emphasize that only what is spoken goes in quotation marks.

Then, put students in small groups or pairs and have them scribe their own conversations. Walk around the room and offer guidance as needed. Choose several groups that are "getting it" and have them transfer their conversation onto a blank transparency. Put the student-made transparency on the overhead projector and invite other students to take the parts of the speakers. If the conversation has been written correctly, it should be easy for students to read their "roles." If there are problems, they are readily apparent. Follow up with an evaluation. "Did you have a problem you worked out?" "What do you now understand about writing conversation?" "What else do you need to know?"

One way to encourage dialogue in student writing is to ask students to eavesdrop on a conversation and try to re-create it. Students are quick to agree that they listen attentively to conversations while tuning out monologues. Another exercise involves using a published author's work and asking students what they notice regarding placement of words on a page, white space, quotations marks, other punctuation, and use of upper- and lowercase letters. In small groups or with the whole class, ask, "What does the dialogue look like? Why does it look that way? What impact does the dialogue have on the writing?" These types of discussions encourage students to experiment with dialogue in their own writing (see page 360).

Paragraphing

While teachers model and teach paragraphing beginning in the early grades, we found—from examining hundreds of writing samples from across our school district—that the majority of students don't paragraph on their own before the beginning of fifth grade. This information was quite revealing because—until we had the data—third- and fourth-grade teachers were expecting students to paragraph as they wrote. That told us that we should continue to model paragraphing at every grade level, but not teach it formally with expectations for mastery until fifth grade, when students are ready to internalize the concept. In final copies, we still expect to see organized paragraphs, but we recognize that teacher guidance is necessary for this to occur.

Years ago I heard Frank Smith say that the purpose of the paragraph was "to give the eye a break." That made as much sense to me as anything I'd ever learned about paragraphing, and I've taken the statement to heart. When I write, I often begin a new paragraph when the one I'm writing seems adequate in length and I'm at a place where a break feels natural. I show students how I do that by writing in front of them and thinking aloud about my decision to begin a new paragraph.

Also, using a former student's work (with the name deleted) or a present student's work with his permission, I make an overhead transparency of a page or more of unparagraphed writing, and we talk about how tiresome it is to read unbroken blocks of text. Together we decide where it would make sense to insert paragraphs. Young students do understand the concept of "indenting" to make a piece easier to read.

It is important that teachers do not emphasize form over content. Several fourth-grade teachers proudly told me one fall how well their students were paragraphing. They explained that they had taught their students the "rules" of paragraphing, which included starting with a topic sentence, proceeding with several supporting details, and ending with a summary sentence.

One of the problems with formulaic writing is that once students move out of the mold, they are typically at a loss, unable to apply the rules to a different writing form. More important, that's not the way real writers work. I never say to myself, "Let's see, now I need a topic sentence." I am always thinking about meaning, cohesiveness, interest, what is logical, and who my audience is, and there is no formula for this.

Writing an "About the Author" Page

Many of our published books and projects include a short profile of the author. We model how to write lively author pages by reading those included in books, publications, and previous student writing. Have students draft and revise their author profiles just as you would any other piece of important writing (see Figure 8-11).

REVISING

Typically, students have an inadequate understanding of what revision is. Time after time, when I ask students to tell me about revision, their responses are limited to "correcting spelling and grammar"—even in schools where kids have been writing every day

Figure 8–11   A fourth grader's author profile

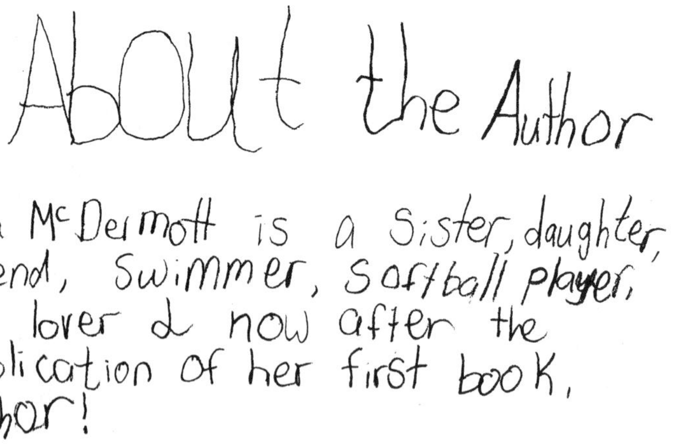

ABOUt the Author

Delia McDermott is a sister, daughter, friend, swimmer, softball player, dog lover & now after the publication of her first book, author!

for years. When that happens, I write "re vision" on the chalkboard, and ask them what "vision" is and what the prefix *re-* means. Together, we discuss the literal meaning of the word, which is "to see again." We talk about why revision matters. I ask students why they think I am willing to spend hours and hours revising even a short piece of my own writing. Eventually they answer, "Because you really care about the writing." We begin to make a list of what writers do when they revise:

- Reread carefully
- Clear up confusion
- Reorganize material—move things around, add, delete
- Rewrite for clarity and interest
- Rethink word choices
- Edit as they reread

My experience has been that even young writers will give time and effort to revision if the audience and purpose are important to them. Older students, inured by years of writing for the teacher, resist revision and will often do only a rudimentary revisit of their work. If we want students to take revision seriously and do it well, we will need to show them how, beginning with our own writing. Starting with students in the early grades, show them the communications you've drafted to parents, rough drafts of required course work, or anything you have taken time to rewrite. Also, use shared writing as an opportunity to teach revision.

Don Graves suggested to me one strategy for encouraging kids to revise their work: "Make it more of a reading exercise without the obligation to change the text. Sitting in the reader's seat creates its own unease that eventually results in changes" (1998). Because reading aloud what I've written helps me to revise my work, I also encourage students to vocalize their writing. I have observed that when students read their pieces aloud, to themselves or peers, they are often able to hear when a part lacks punch or doesn't make sense more easily than if they'd reread their work silently. Not liking the way the piece sounds often moves students to make changes. (See Photo 8-1, page 308.)

EDITING

I tell students that we need to edit carefully out of respect for our reader(s). The reader expects to be able to read through the text freely, unencumbered by poor grammar, spelling errors, or illegibility.

Students view editing as "fixing up mistakes." Editing, in fact, is doing whatever is necessary to a piece—especially once the content is set—to make it readable and understandable. This includes, but is not limited to, ensuring correct and varied sentence structure, consistent subject-verb agreement, adequate paragraphing, correct spelling and punctuation, and replacing overused or overly familiar words with varied and vibrant ones.

I believe the best way to teach editing is through writing for a real purpose. When a teacher focuses on editing by using a piece written just to teach editing skills, students don't buy in to the purpose of the exercise and quickly lose interest. I have sat in on classes with teachers who have tried to teach editing by using self-constructed examples that include

Photo 8–1   Second graders giving time and effort to revision

deliberate errors—in every case, students were squirming in their seats. In one lesson that went on for twenty-five minutes, a teacher displayed a piece of arbitrary writing and then focused on underlining the title, using capital letters at the beginning of a sentence, using exclamation marks and other punctuation, spelling words and contractions correctly, and so on. If students learned anything at all, it was that editing was a dull business.

By contrast, when we use a piece of writing that students perceive has a real purpose, or, with the child's permission, we make photocopies for the class of a piece of writing that a student has done, kids begin to see that editing is an important part of the writing process. When the writing is put up on the overhead projector so that everyone can view it and talk about it, editing is something that begins to hold student interest and be taken seriously. (You can also use pieces from a colleague's room or past year's class, as long as it is relevant to the students.) In any case, to maximize student retention, limit yourself to one or two major teaching points during any editing lesson, such as circling misspelled words and trying to correct them or putting in the necessary punctuation.

CONFERENCING

Conferencing takes place every time we meet with a student to celebrate their writing, give requested and teacher-initiated feedback on content and form, respond to revisions, and provide support for final editing. Conferencing is an opportunity to listen, appreciate, affirm, respect, reinforce, suggest, and/or teach. Whatever happens in a conference should assist the writer in what she is trying to do. Most of my conferencing strategies with students are based on what has been beneficial to me as a writer.

My editor and publisher do not see my drafts until at least several colleagues have read them and given me honest feedback. Then, after I have made revisions, I will usually give chapters to one or two additional readers. Because my teacher audience is so important to me, I want to be sure my writing is clear, coherent, and useful. Based on what has been helpful to me as a writer, I have changed how I conference with students in the classroom. Mostly this involves being more honest and direct.

When I seek response from a colleague about my writing, it is not helpful to me as a writer to hear compliment after compliment. While it's true that I would be upset to receive only critical feedback, once the responder has said something positive about the writing, I am hungry to know how I can improve it. Sure, I want to hear about the things I've done well, to be affirmed by the reader's positive response, but what I'm really after is: How can I improve this piece of writing? What's missing? What's unclear? My best readers have been critical friends who are open and honest. In a kind and constructive manner, they respond to my queries and writing with frank reactions and tactfully worded suggestions.

I think we overdid it in classrooms when we insisted that students compliment one another's writing before they made suggestions. Lots of inane comments got thrown around and a lot of time was spent making the writer feel good, but the writing didn't improve much. I used to insist that every student say something positive about a piece in whole-class share before giving another student a suggestion. However, that type of response is not helpful to me as a writer. Although it is crucial that students be respectful of one another's work and that they receive genuine support for what is good in their writing, empty compliments benefit no one.

Students will not fall apart if we speak to them honestly but gently about their writing. When students feel valued by classmates and teachers, when a kind, caring community has been established, students appreciate constructive criticism. Now, after I'm satisfied that a child has received a few genuine, positive comments, I encourage students to make suggestions or state points of confusion without giving a mandatory compliment. This has also made our sharing time more efficient.

Of course, you have to know your students. When a student who rarely takes risks and who generally has difficulty writing has a productive writing day, exclusively positive comments are in order so that the student will feel encouraged and continue to make progress. In such cases, I make a big deal about what the student has accomplished. Similarly, for low-performing students who seem only to make superficial comments during response time, it takes time, practice, and lots of modeling to elicit useful suggestions.

The other big exception to critically responding to writing is, of course, when the piece is published. Once an author has done her best work and the writing is finished, criticism is not appropriate unless the author requests it. While I am in the process of writing a book or article, I actively seek criticism and suggestions. However, once the writing is published, I only want to celebrate my efforts.

Celebrating Writing

Although we need to guard against empty compliments, two recent happenings re-minded me how important it is that teachers, in our conferences and sharing sessions with a child, acknowledge a student's accomplishments in their writing.

Susannah, a teacher I was coaching, was about to begin a sharing session in the fall of second grade. Jared, one of her students, had worked hard on a wonderful story about a camping trip and had just finished reading it in the author's chair. Susannah whispered to me that the first sentence of Jared's story was grammatically incorrect. "Should I mention that first?" she asked me. I shook my head and modeled the sharing session for her. We celebrated the writing and never mentioned the grammatical error, which would have discouraged the writer. (The grammar would be addressed later during a final editing conference.)

I had also been working with Madelyn, a new teacher. We had been modeling writing, sharing life stories, and getting incredible results from the students. Madelyn asked me to model a one-on-one writing conference. When she called up a student she was con-cerned about, I noticed comments in blue ink over and around the child's penciled writ-ing, comments such as "Check punctuation"; "Where are the capitals?"; "Fix up misspelled words." I cringed, both because the ink stood out on the draft and dwarfed the child's writing and because the emphasis of the remarks was solely on mechanics. It's true that the student's handwriting was poor, but his ideas were superb. The voice was strong. When the student read the story aloud, the spelling and grammatical mistakes were barely evident.

We must begin our response to student writing by affirming, and not immediately jump, as teachers, to "correcting." One effective way to encourage our own positive focus is to make sure we "hear" the writing first. Undistracted by "seeing" mechanical errors and illegibility, we are free to listen to what the writer is saying.

All of us need the kind of environment in which we can be free to take risks and do our best work. Don't search for what's missing. Look for what's there and build upon that.

Whole-Class Share

Before students can have an effective conference with other students, they need lots of experience with what a good conference looks and sounds like. At the end of our daily writing time, I pull the class together in the reading/writing corner or class meeting area for whole-group share. This is an efficient, effective, relaxing way for students to share their efforts and receive helpful feedback as well as to learn listen-ing and responding behaviors that support the writer's efforts. Sharing time lasts for ten to fifteen minutes, during which two to three students read aloud from their writ-ing. (See Photo 8-2.)

Sharing time provides an ideal opportunity for modeling effective conferencing strate-gies. This public forum pays big dividends. Not only do students learn firsthand how to have effective conferences, but the teacher, with the help of the students, gets to extend her individual conference time. Sharing time functions as a whole-class conference, a time not only to share and celebrate but to teach, reinforce strategies, set goals, and move students' writing forward.

Photo 8–2   Whole-class share: listening to Robert read his story

Who Shares?

During writing workshop, I am constantly on the lookout for students who have achieved something special—someone who has taken a risk, used a strategy discussed in a minilesson, written a particularly vivid description, tried something new, shown particularly high engagement with their subject, used interesting words, incorporated conversation, written an effective lead or ending, or demonstrated personal voice. Then, several minutes before sharing time, I approach these students and ask if they will share their accomplishment with the rest of the class.

Sometimes, if a student is due for a conference—either at her request or mine—she will be asked to share in front of the whole class. Or if for any reason I've been prevented from meeting with an individual student scheduled for a conference, that student may be invited to use the public conference in place of our individual one.

To keep track of students who have participated in these whole-class conferences, I recommend posting a copy of the class list, including months and days of the week, near the author's chair and making a note of when individual children shared. This ensures that all students have an opportunity to share, students know you are choosing fairly, and you can see at a glance who needs to share next (see page 322).

Preparing to Share

I never hand my writing over to a colleague for response until I am certain that my draft is easily readable and that my reader knows what kind of response I am looking for. I expect students to maintain these standards as well. Students know that if they want to receive useful feedback on their writing, they have to "prepare to share." This means, first of all, practicing reading the piece to ensure a smooth delivery. Secondly, preparation means deciding what kind of feedback they are looking to receive.

Practicing Reading

There is nothing so frustrating and distracting, not to mention time-consuming, as having a student stumbling over words because he cannot read his writing. Students must know that if they plan on sharing, they need to rehearse their piece, either quietly to themselves or to a peer. A teacher's gesture signaling the coming end of writing time reminds those who want to share (or who have been selected to share) to use these last few minutes to prepare to read aloud. For others, it is a signal to reread and proofread their work.

Determining the Desired Response

Sometimes a student just wants to share her writing with the class and is not seeking any particular response. This is fine. Mostly, however, we request that students ask for specific feedback (which is what I do as a writer when I want to improve my writing), and students need to be taught how to do that. Responses that target areas the author is concerned about can be particularly helpful. Andrew, whose interview is included in Chapter 6, "Quality Writing," reminds us of the importance of specificity in listener and reader response. In that interview, Andrew stated, "At my old school, they would just ask everyone the same questions like, 'Does your story make sense? What's it about?' And you would just answer those questions, but I mean, it wouldn't help or anything."

For at least the first several weeks of whole-class sharing, I will say to students: "Briefly tell us something about what your piece is about. What do you want us to listen for? Do you want feedback on . . . ? How can we help you?" And then I might offer some possibilities. For example, I might say, "Do you want to know if your beginning is interesting?" or, "Do you want to know if we can picture your character?" or, "Do you want us to listen for what's confusing?" After a while, students realize that it is part of their job as writers to decide what kind of response they need and want. Students initially have difficulty stating what kind of feedback would be most helpful to them, but after a few months of modeling and practice during whole-class shares, they become as expert as the teacher in doing so.

Some teachers keep a chart (composed by teacher and students) posted in the classroom with questions such as the following to guide students in eliciting class response:

- Does my beginning engage the reader?
- Is my opening clear about my intention for this piece?
- Does the order seem logical?
- Are my words interesting enough?
- Does this part make sense?
- Were you amused, or does it sound like a serious piece?
- Were you bored? Where?

Learning to Respond Helpfully

The sharing writer sits in a designated "author's chair" (most often situated in the area where the class gathers together) and reads his piece aloud. To allow time for several students to share, the writer usually reads just what he has worked on that day or the portion of his writing that he wants feedback on. Just as I do with my own writing when I am seeking response, the student authors first briefly tell the listeners (or in my case, readers) something about their topic or piece. They then state what they'd like the class to listen for.

Learning How to Listen

Before they can make helpful suggestions to writers, students must be able to actively listen. "Strategies such as watching the speaker, focusing to block distractions, visualizing, formulating questions, making mental associations, predicting while listening, summarizing, and taking notes are all useful to children as they work to improve their listening abilities" (Brent and Anderson 1993). One powerful way to foster active listening is to have students participate in literature conversation groups in which responsive listening, as well as speaking, is modeled and expected. (See Chapter 5.)

To elicit truly useful responses from students, many of us have found that it works best to have writers read their piece twice. Sometimes, if a student reads very slowly or in an especially low voice, the teacher may read it for him (with the student's permission). On the first reading, responders listen without commenting and strive to get a sense of the work as a whole. I say to students, "The first time, we're just going to listen. The second time, we'll be offering suggestions." This is what I do as an adult responder. I always read a piece in its entirety first to "hear" what the author is trying to convey. Then I go back and reread and make comments about specific aspects of the writing.

To foster good listening behaviors, only the writers who are sharing bring their work to whole-class share; the others leave their pencils and papers behind. Otherwise, many students will continue working on their own pieces rather than listening carefully, and they will not be able to give useful feedback to the writer. On rare occasions, a student who feels she must finish her writing in process is permitted to remain working at her seat.

The Writer as Listener

During whole-group share, I do not allow the writer to orally respond to comments and suggestions. The writer's job is to listen carefully and openly and to think about the comments being made. When writers are given the opportunity to comment on criticism and suggestions, they frequently feel the need to explain why they did something a certain way, and often they become defensive. Also, the writer who is given the opportunity to respond may, instead of actively listening, simply wait for his chance to speak. Not only is this time-consuming, it serves no useful purpose.

When a writer interrupts to explain himself during listener response time, I say something like the following: "This is your time to listen to suggestions and comments. When you get ready to write again, you can consider these comments. Then, as the author, you can decide what you want to do."

It can be helpful to have someone, either the teacher or an older student, take notes on the various responses. This gives the writer a record of students' comments. Most often, as I describe below, I jot down the comments on a Post-it to give to the author.

Modeling Response

In addition to listening carefully, students need to be taught how to respond to their fellow writers positively, respectfully, and specifically. After the student has read his piece, I say, "What do you think that———has done well?" The writer then calls on students who care to respond. Often, especially for developing writers, I will reread the piece aloud, showing the writing to the students clustered on the floor in front of me and celebrating the wonderful things the writer has done—written an intriguing title, written with strong voice, spelled high-frequency words correctly, slowed down the writing with lots of detail, skipped lines, described an object vividly. By focusing on what the writer has done well, the writer is encouraged to do these things again. In addition, listeners gain lots of strategies for effective writing.

The Language of Respectful Response

While I expect the first remarks responders make to focus on the positive, I don't permit students to give pat responses, such as, "I really liked your beginning," or "I liked the way you used detail." Such comments are simply not helpful to the writer. I ask the responder, "What specifically did you like about the beginning? Tell me the words you remember," or "Where did the writer use words you liked? What were some of those words?" It's easy for students who haven't listened constructively and carefully to the writing to offer bland, generic opinions. Encourage students to say, "I liked the part where you said . . ." or "I didn't understand when you said . . ." Expecting specific, relevant comments encourages students to listen more attentively.

Additionally, I often take the opportunity to help give a writer direction for the next day's writing. I might say something like, "I like how you've focused in on . . . What will you say next?" Especially when I think a writer may have difficulty continuing a piece in process, this sort of discussion helps her to start thinking and planning ahead. (See pages 244 and 250 for specifics on conversations that help students move their writing forward.)

Students need to be shown how to respond tactfully as well as honestly and to respect that the writing belongs to the writer. Comments need to be worded as suggestions, not as commands. We teachers need to model the polite language of response in offering feedback. Helpful opening phrases include:

- You might want to think about . . .
- Perhaps you could. . .
- I was wondering if you might . . .
- I suggest . . .

When I am modeling whole-class share and students are learning the language of respectful response, I will scaffold for them. For example, when a student responder starts his comments with, "You should . . ." I will intervene and say, "You might want to . . ." and request that the student restate his suggestions with that more respectful language. I have found that when response is tactful, respectful, and honest, most of us deal with it rationally and are open to making changes. If students are serious about their writing, they will think hard about suggestions that have been judiciously offered. On the other hand, if the responder takes over by telling the student what he "should" do, the writer will typically be opposed to his "suggestions."

I have had a few experiences where I sent my draft to a colleague for feedback, and she crossed out my words and sentences and replaced whole chunks with her own. There was no "Perhaps . . ." or "You might want to . . ." It made me livid, and absolutely resistant to incorporating those changes. However, when the responder makes suggestions in a way that it is clear she understands the writing to be mine and not hers, I consider every comment thoughtfully and willingly make many changes.

I have also been upset when I've given a draft to a colleague and requested substantive feedback and the draft comes back marked up with grammatical and spelling corrections and few or no remarks on content. It is demoralizing when something you've written is completely reduced to its mechanics, especially when you expected the focus to be on content. This has firmly convinced me to always attend to the content of a student's writing first.

The Gift of Post-Its

I used to insist that authors write down all the suggestions that respondents made during whole-group share. In other words, after a suggestion was offered, the student jotted that suggestion down somewhere on his writing piece. However, this was not only time-consuming and disruptive to the flow of share time, it was largely inefficient. Students wrote slowly and needed statements repeated, or they wrote so fast they couldn't read their own writing. Mostly, their having to write the suggestions down detracted from their focus on listening and enjoyment of their interaction with peers. Also, a lot of "gems" that surfaced in the sharing process were lost because students couldn't "catch" the language fast enough.

These days I give students a gift. I write the most valuable suggestions on Post-its and hand them to the writer at the end of response time (see Figure 8-12 on page 316). The student places the Post-it(s) on his paper and refers to them at the next writing time. Most students save these Post-its with their drafts in their writing notebook. Interestingly enough, without being told to do so, many students have taken up the Post-it notation idea and used it when conferencing one-on-one with peers.

Peer Conferencing

My dear friend and colleague Joan Servis teaches her fourth graders how to peer conference in small groups, and the process works beautifully (Servis 1999). In peer conferencing, classmates independently listen and give feedback to fellow student writers. While I like peer conferencing for the opportunity it affords students to share their work in progress and receive some helpful suggestions, I recognize its limitations. Students are not trained as teachers of writing. Student feedback is helpful but

Figure 8–12   Gift of a Post-it note

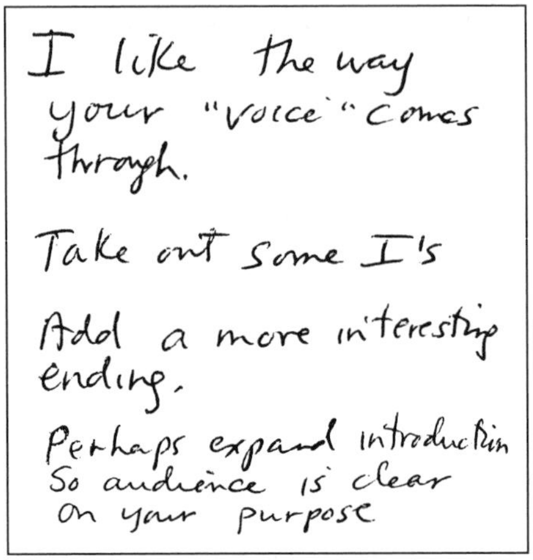

> I like the way your "voice" comes through.
>
> Take out some I's
>
> Add a more interesting ending.
>
> Perhaps expand introduction so audience is clear on your purpose

understandably limited. I believe that it is our job as teachers to conference with students one on one and provide the sophisticated feedback about organization, style, craft, and structure that writers need in order to move their writing forward.

Peer Editing

While I find the role of peers limited for improving content and craft, I have found—and research supports—that peer editing does help improve the mechanics and overall fluency of student writing. In that regard, I and other teachers have had great success partnering students for the editing process.

After I have had a content conference with the student, and she has made mutually agreed-upon revisions for a piece going to final copy (as evidenced in a follow-up conference), the student prepares for an editing conference. Using editing expectations the class has formulated in a shared writing (see Appendixes F-6 and F-7 for examples of editing expectations for grades two and three), the writer edits her piece using a colored pencil. Next, her partner edits the piece with a different-colored pencil and signs or initials the piece, usually in the upper right-hand corner. Then, when students have done their best editing work, I take over as final editor (using a different-colored pencil or pen). Holding both students equally accountable makes them take the task more seriously.

Many teachers are initially frustrated when they introduce partner editing in their classrooms. Years of having had their errors "fixed up" by teachers have made students dependent, so that, at first, they must be asked to edit their work over and over again. I will say something like, "I see some misspelled words here that I know you (and your partner) can find, circle, and correct." Or, "Check our 'editing expectations.' What does it say about commas?" It usually takes several months, especially with older students, for them to assume the major editing tasks. However, once they do, teachers are gratified by how much editing work students can do and how much easier and faster the publication process then becomes.

Individual Conferences

Being able to have a sustained one-on-one conference with students assumes excellent classroom management, that is, students can and do work quietly and independently without interrupting the teacher. For example, students who are waiting to conference know to begin a new piece or revisit previous writing without being told to do so. Classroom writing procedures and routines are well established.

Because student self-management is so critical to the success of writing workshop, for new and inexperienced teachers or teachers struggling with management, I recommend beginning with journal writing (see Chapter 7)—and perhaps continuing with journals for the duration of the school year. With this writing form, individual conferencing takes place mostly "on the run," as the teacher circulates about the classroom.

Management

In a typical writing workshop, students write quietly for about thirty minutes after the minilesson. During the writing time, I conference one-on-one with students. Students "sign up" for a conference by putting their names on the chalkboard or by filling out a conference form indicating what kind of feedback they would like. When my record keeping indicates that I have not met with a student for a while and I want to check his progress, I will initiate the conference. A conference lasts from five minutes to twenty-five minutes. Occasionally, one student will need the maximum time allotment, but this is usually when a large chunk of work has been completed. Following a long, intensive conference in which much feedback and direction have been provided, a student often doesn't need to be met with again for several weeks.

On average, I conference with two to three students each day, and I keep track of who I meet with so that no students are overlooked. In this way, in one week I can conference with ten to fifteen students. Since our whole-group shares accommodate two to three student authors daily, in a class of twenty-five students, I am able to meet with most of the class each week. Because these conferences take place during school time, there is no need for the "correcting" of papers at home, an activity that requires extensive teacher time and is often a poor use of that time. While students may take note of the comments teachers make on their papers in their absence, they typically learn little from such remarks.

While I am meeting with students, I take written notes on the conference. These notes are dated, include what the student is working on and needs feedback on, any explicit teaching that takes place, and goals that we set together. These detailed, anecdotal notes are very useful for keeping track of students' progress, determining what steps need to be taken in future conferences with students and parents, and for gathering information when writing report cards. (See Figure 8-13 on page 318.)

Before the student leaves the conference, we review my notes together, and most often, the student will be asked to write down what he has agreed to do next (see page 321). This revisiting of what took place at the conference reinforces what we have discussed and makes the conference a shared responsibility. I have always believed that students should be able to see what we teachers write about them and their work in a conference. The face-to-face, open-book nature of these meetings ensures that we teachers maintain a positive tone and emphasize what the student has done well.

Figure 8–13   My notes from a writing conference

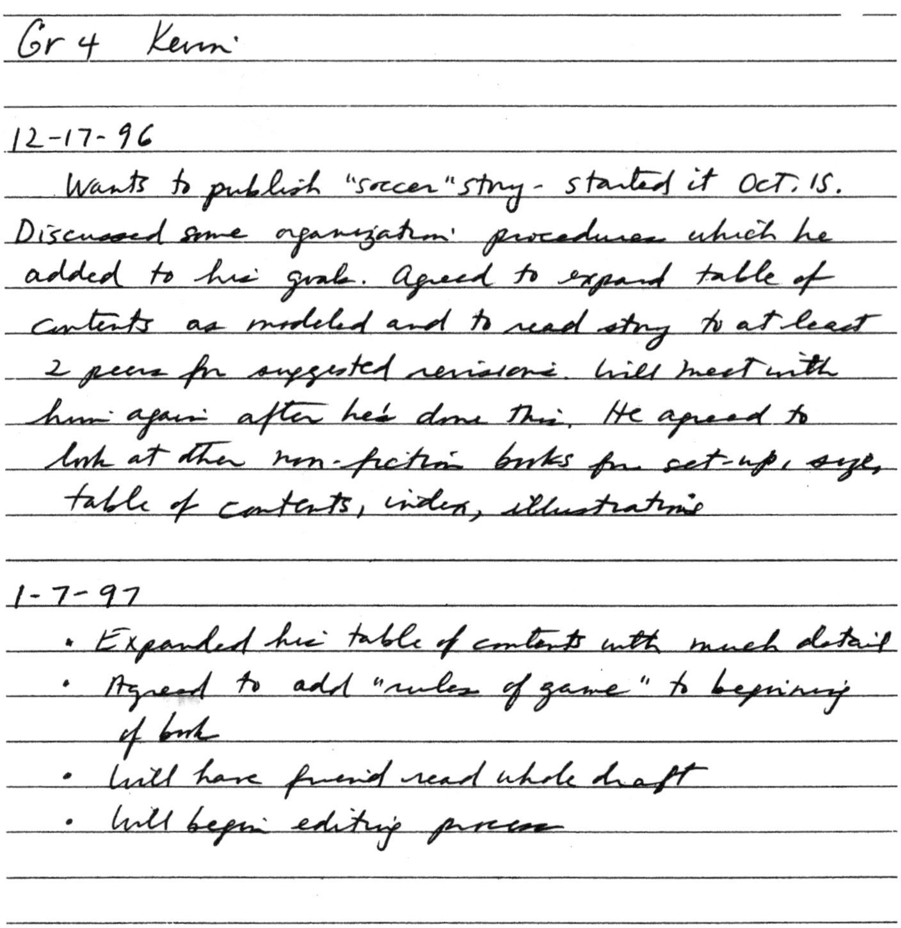

Gr 4   Kevin

12-17-96
   Wants to publish "soccer" story- started it Oct. 15.
Discussed some organizational procedures which he
added to his goals. Agreed to expand table of
contents as modeled and to read story to at least
2 peers for suggested revisions. Will meet with
him again after he's done this. He agreed to
look at other non-fiction books for set-ups, size,
table of contents, index, illustrations

1-7-97
   • Expanded his table of contents with much detail
   • Agreed to add "rules of game" to beginning
     of book
   • Will have friend read whole draft
   • Will begin editing process

A Content Conference

When I conference with students, I respond honestly and directly and focus on the substance of their writing. It is essential that we show respect for writers by listening to and supporting them in what they are attempting to say.

   The first thing I ask students is, "How can I help you?" or "What would you like feedback on?" Students learn how to request the feedback they need at a conference during our whole-class share sessions. Next, I ask the student to read her piece to me (or the part of the piece we will be working on). Having the student read the piece aloud enables teachers to focus first on the content and not get distracted by mistakes in spelling and mechanics. A piece that may "look" poor can be full of voice and originality. Sometimes, if we are pressed for time, I will read the piece silently with the student looking on. In this situation, I always attempt to look past the mechanics and grasp what the student is trying to say.

   In one second-grade classroom, Bobby reads me his piece about a time when he and his cousin made and set animal traps. It is a wonderful piece. I am incredulous at how much he knows, what he has done, and the detail in his writing. As one interested person to a fascinating human being, I ask him questions, because I am genuinely curious: "Why did you set the traps? How do you use the cage? How did you feel when you found a fawn in a trap?" These I write on Post-its for him, which I then place on a page in his spiral notebook. With his permission, we take the pages out of his notebook, and I teach him how to cut and paste so that he can add information without unnecessary and time-consuming recopying or rewriting.

When a piece is emotional, as Tiara's is when she writes about missing her late grandfather, my first response is an empathetic one: "I'm sorry your grandfather died." We might talk a few moments about what her feelings are, and then I'll turn to the writing, with comments such as, "I don't know what you mean by . . . " or "I'm confused here. Can you tell me more?"

I do not write on students' writing during these sessions, choosing to make my comments to them orally or on Post-its and expecting students to record my suggestions on their draft or revision conference form. I never write with a red pen or pencil because of my past, negative connections with teacher corrections. I tell teachers, "Sit on your hands if you have to. Let the student hold the pen."

When necessary, I do not give students a choice in what needs to be revised. For instance, I might say, "The beginning is very confusing. Let the reader know right away what this piece is about and why you're writing it." As teacher, it's my job to help the student do quality work and not accept limited efforts and outcome.

Perhaps most important, strive to provide feedback that will encourage the writer to keep writing. It's so easy to hone in on obvious "mistakes," especially with a struggling writer. It takes an effort to first think about and respond to what the writer has done well, and then comment on what he requests and/or needs to move forward.

An Editing Conference

Before I meet with students for a final edit, I expect them to have fulfilled all their obligations with respect to editing their piece. That is, they have attended to all items on our editing expectations form and they have participated in peer editing. To be certain students are take editing seriously, I often require both the writer and peer editor to attend the conference. I remind them of their role ahead of time by asking the following questions:

- What are you going to be doing when you edit?
- What are you going to do when words are misspelled?
- Does every sentence begin with a capital?
- Have you been thinking about format? (You may want to look at some other sports books to see how they are laid out.)
- Are you going to type this or handwrite it?

With young writers, it is important to focus on only one or two major areas that need work so that they will not be overwhelmed. When conferencing with Tanisha, a struggling second grader, I quickly noticed that her draft had no punctuation or capitals and was missing words that were necessary to make the intended meaning clear. It was evident that she had not reread her writing. In our conference, I focused on teaching her how to reread and how adding punctuation and missing words would aid meaning. I never mentioned the need for capitals. That would come later in another conference.

If commonplace errors are present when I have an editing conference with a student, I will often put a dot(s) or check mark(s) on a line where something needs attention, and both students are sent back to their seats to discover and correct the mistake. Some kind of notation system in the margins or on a Post-it saves time for both students and teachers. Students know exactly how much needs to be fixed and where the errors are, and when they have completed the task, the teacher can check their work quickly without having to read through the entire piece. Most important, students get the message that they are responsible for meeting the editing expectations that we have previously agreed upon.

From second grade on, students are capable of correcting most of their mechanical errors. Expecting them to do so is a huge time saver in the long run. As stated previously, an adjustment period may be required for students used to having teachers do their editing work for them; initially, teachers may spend a great deal of time looking over papers that have not been well edited. However, when students are clear about the expectations and convinced that teachers mean business, resistance gives way to cooperation and hard editing work. It's a win-win situation—more responsibility for the students and less work for us teachers.

Teachers are often surprised at how much students can do on their own. After developing editing expectations for her students, Tara Strachan, a first-year teacher of second graders, commented: "I was so impressed with how seriously students began to take the editing of their own work. I had known that they *knew* essential writing mechanics, but I was excited to find them checking for them more independently. Their pride in the written content reinforced their willingness to 'polish' their ideas and make them readable for their audience."

Teacher Documentation

It is impossible to remember, even a few days later, the details of what took place in a conference, minilesson, or share session. Therefore, careful record keeping of each student's process and progress is absolutely necessary to ensure monitoring of and goal setting for each student. You will need to find a system that works for you. I prefer using a notebook binder, where I have a divider and separate section for each student and can add pages easily, to record conference notes and minilessons.

Again, I do all record keeping and note taking while I am with students. This allows students to see everything I write (which I review with them to be sure we are in agreement) and allows me to use my time efficiently. We also set goals for the piece together.

Usually, I expect students to take notes on their own during a conference, primarily concerning what they have agreed to do based on the goals we have set together (see Figure 8-14 and page 317). As I am writing my notes, the student writes his—on the draft, on a Post-it, on a separate form, anywhere that is useful to the student. This is what I do as a writer. As I reread my draft, I write notes to myself on the draft reminding myself of the specific and general changes I intend to make. As the student writes down goals and suggestions, I record them in my writing conference notebook. The notebook is helpful not only with respect to record keeping. As Dana Bulan commented, "Writing in my spiral removes the urge for me to write on their paper."

Figure 8–14 A third grader's notes from two writing conferences

1-7-97
1. Add a Beginning chapter on Rules of the Game.
2. Have friend read soccer Book. Give sugestions.
3. Edit

WRITING CONFERENCE CHECKLIST

AUTHOR: *Kevin*

DATE:

TITLE:

_____	1. Did you reread again?
_✓_	2. Does your piece make sense?
_✓_	3. Did you use interesting words?
_✓_	4. Did you check for spelling, punctuation, and capitalization?
_✓_	5. Have you decided what kind of response you want from the conference?

12-17-96

GOALS FOR YOUR PIECE:

✓ Need to move list
✓ Add headings
✓ Expand table of contents
✓ — Read story to at least 2 people
✓ — look at Non-Ficton formats
— Find illustrator

It is very important to keep track of daily conferencing and sharing to be sure that you are meeting with all students on a regular basis. Our method, as stated previously, is to keep a class list on a clipboard near the class sharing area. I note an "S" every time a student shares in front of the class (a public conference), a "C" for those students I have conferred with individually, and a "P" when a student has published. Looking at the classroom grid, I can see at a glance if a student has been overlooked for a conference or sharing session. (See Figure 8-15 for a partial list of one class.) Most teachers also find it necessary to keep track of lessons taught and planned, student topics, and goals that have been set at conferences.

PUBLISHING

Publishing (bringing a piece of writing to finished form) for real reasons and actual audiences motivates students to do their best writing. However, publishing can be overwhelming for teachers and students. Too often, teachers of older students expect them to bring everything to final copy, which is neither practical nor realistic.

At the beginning of the year, I have a frank talk with students regarding publishing (see page 214). Regarding their free-choice writing, I ask them, "How many *major* pieces do you think it would be reasonable for you to publish this year?" Usually, we wind up deciding that two pieces is a reasonable amount. Publishing takes a lot of time and hard

Figure 8–15   *Keeping track of minilessons, conferencing, sharing, and publishing*

Class List	writing minilessons 10/13	organization of writer's note book 10/14	writing fiction—character 10/15	writing fiction—creating a character 10/16	minilesson recording sheet 10/17	writing fiction—telling details 10/20	thank-you letter 10/21	fiction plot & opening lines 10/22	dialogue in opening lines 10/23	trying more than one lead 10/24	creating a setting	Notes
Pamela Barker		S				C						
Aisha Carter			S				C					
Alex Gregory	C					S						
Antonio Lester				C				S				
Kyle Marshall					S				C			
Kelsey Silvers	S					C	P					
Brint Weber					S			C				
Tyler Wood		C				S						
Jessica Yates				C						S		
Stephanie Young	S					C						

C—Conference
S—Share
P—Publish

work by students and teachers, and what gets published must be worth the effort. (Of course, we continue to publish short, focused pieces on a regular basis, such as letters, invitations, and assignments.)

Parent Involvement

It has been my experience, as well as that of many of the teachers I work with, that parent volunteers, if you can get them, are most helpful in the final editing process. After students have done their best work, parents—who have received clear guidelines from the teacher—can do the time-consuming work of sitting down individually with students and getting the piece ready for final copy. Involving parents in earlier, substantive revision often does not work well, as some parents have a tendency to want to take over, thereby co-opting the student's voice.

We do a lot of publishing in first grade, where the reading/writing connection is strong. We depend on parents to run our district publishing program. (See *Invitations*, "Setting Up an In-School Publishing Process," pages 263–275, for procedures.)

The Importance of a Real Audience

It is the day before Thanksgiving and I am in Tara Strachan's second-grade class. I am scheduled to model one-on-one conferencing as students prepare to take their writing to final copy. The previous week, we had spoken to kids about choosing a piece for publication and determining its audience. Each student went back through their writing, putting a Post-it on the piece they wanted to publish and noting its intended audience.

Tara is overwhelmed by the effort required, and talks to me about forgoing the publishing process. She is concerned that it will be too much work for students, that some of the pieces are long, that she will be unable to manage it all. I tell her that we can have students complete their pieces and edit them without publishing. We talk, as we have before, about there not being a "best" or "right" way to do this. I suggest that we ask the kids if it's okay with them not to publish at this time. When we put this question to them, every student says that they want to publish their piece and that they are willing to do the hard work to make it happen. Tara and I are amazed at their determination, and we are also proud of these kids. Because the audience and purpose are important to them, they value this project and are willing to put major effort into revising and editing their work. (See Figure 8-16 on page 324.)

I suggest to Tara that she get parent volunteers to help with the final editing. I offer to write instructions for parents so that they are clear on their role (see Figure 8-17 on page 325). Based on past experience, we know that parents will not limit themselves to helping their children edit unless our directions and expectations are definitive. We talk about inviting parents to "fix up" spelling and other mechanics after students have done their best, to "clean up" their final papers when students miscopy from their drafts, and to word process papers when recopying by hand would involve too much labor for the young writer.

Still, Tara is apprehensive that she won't be able to complete all the individual confer-

Figure 8–16   A second grader's willingness to begin revising and editing

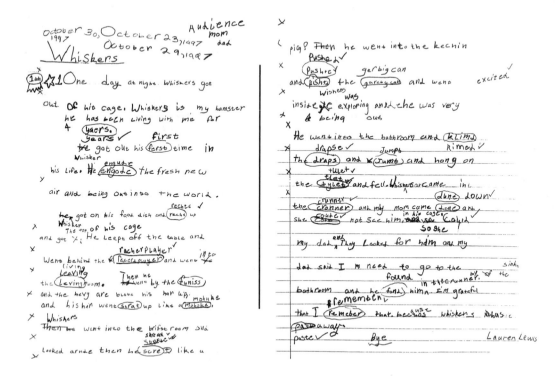

One day at night, Whiskers got out of his cage. Whiskers is my hamster. He has been living with me for four years. Whiskers got out the first time in his life. He enjoyed the fresh new air and being outside in the world. Whiskers got on his good dish and reached up and got the top of his cage. He leaped off the table and went behind the record player and went into the living room. Then he went by the furnace and the heavy air blew his hair up, and his hair went straight up like a mohawk. Whiskers went into the breakfast room and looked around. Then he screeched like a pig! Then he went into the kitchen and pushed the garbage can and went inside.

Whiskers was exploring and he was very excited being out. He went into the bathroom and climbed the drapes and jumped and hung on the toilet and fell. Whiskers came in the corner, and my mom came down and she could not see him in his cage. So she told my dad, and they looked for him and my dad said, "I need to go the bathroom" and he found him in the corner. I'm grateful that I remember that because Whiskers has passed away.

ences. I model three conferences for her. She gives me her most challenging students. Each conference lasts five minutes.

First we meet with a student who has a one-page entry from early fall about missing a pet that died. He reads it aloud. I first comment on how strong his voice is in the piece and then look for one thing we can work on for improvement. In this case, it is helping the student put in punctuation. I ask him to reread, and we practice having him put in a period when his voice naturally stops at the end of a sentence.

Next we meet with a student who wrote about cooking with her grandma. I comment on how lucky the student was to have quality time with her grandma and how I can almost pic-

Figure 8–17 Editing guidelines for parent volunteers

Guidelines for Parents for Final Editing (Grade 2)

Attend only to final editing: mechanics (spelling, capitalization, punctuation).

Only fix up what the writer is unable to do on his/her own. (See editing expectations.)

Print clearly using a colored pencil so changes stand out.

Do not change any words or move anything around. The writing belongs to the writer. If there is an apparent problem in organization, see the teacher.

If a piece seems long and would require a big effort for the student to rewrite it as a final copy, ask the student if he wants a parent volunteer to word process part or all of it.

Your help is much appreciated, as getting writing work in final copy form is labor intensive.

---

ture them together. I ask her, because I am interested, to tell me how she and her grandma made the soup she mentioned in the piece. When she explains this to me, I suggest that she add those details to her writing. I jot down on Post-its key words that she used in her description, to help her remember them. It is interesting to note that these struggling writers opted to publish a short piece, while more fluent writers are typically undaunted by length.

With the help of two parent volunteers who come in two mornings a week for two weeks, all the students are able to publish their pieces by mid-December.

On the last day of school before holiday vacation, each student uses newsprint to design their own wrapping paper. Then, each published piece is wrapped as a gift and given to its intended audience. The first day back from vacation, in early January, Tara asks her students to share their audiences' reactions. All the students describe how excited their recipients were. Some say that their parents expressed surprise at the amount of revision they had done on their own.

I asked Tara if her views on publishing have changed as a result of this experience. She states: "At first, I saw it as too much to expect from second graders just several months into the school year. But the kids pushed me because they wanted to continue. I saw they were dedicated to it. So I thought, 'All right, let's give it a try.' Once we broke it up into organizational pieces, it was doable."

I then asked Tara to delineate those elements that she found most helpful in the publishing process. She offered the following points:

- Encouraging students to publish pieces they'd already completed and cared about
- Sharing writing from other students in the class
- Observing a writing conference with a struggling student and, especially, connecting first on something positive the student has done
- Not expecting perfection, but rather emphasizing one thing that should be the child's goal and making that the goal for the piece (Tara notes this as the single most helpful element.)
- Developing written editing guidelines for parents and having parents serve as labor-intensive helpers in the editing process ("The parent helper sheet made a big, big difference. The fact that it was in writing, I could say to the parent, 'Check the sheet again.'")

- Celebrating the pride students took in their published work ("Yes, it was worth all the hard work because of the kids' excitement about their writing and the reaction of their audience.")

When second graders Rebecca and Christopher gave their finished writing as a gift to their respective moms, each mother made copies for relatives in the family—aunt, cousins, grandparents. This made a dramatic impact on the students, who saw firsthand the far-reaching power of published work.

Choosing Interesting Formats

A couple of years ago it hit me that most of the published writing in classrooms looked the same. Finished products were usually published in commercial blank books or folded colored paper booklets or books bound with wallpaper covers. Reports were mostly formal-looking projects on standard $8\frac{1}{2} \times 11$-inch paper bound together with a glitzy cover and illustrations. Even when the contents were well done, the final copies often looked bland and homogenous.

This isn't the way real books, books we love, are formatted. Many of our favorite books have bold illustrations, beautiful end pages and page borders, as well as interesting designs for organizing content. Nonfiction books have tables of contents, glossaries, indices, sidebars, maps, timelines, diagrams, and all kinds of other visuals enhancing meaning and attractiveness. The variety and possibilities are endless.

To encourage innovation in publishing projects (once students had focused on content), I began seeking out books with interesting organizational formats and designs and sharing these with students. We talked about how the unique format of certain books made the texts more appealing and artistic. Students were fascinated by all the possibilities for layout (by hand or computer), organization, spacing, shape, fonts and type size, art, graphics, end papers, front and back cover designs, and we teachers noticed an increased interest in students wanting to write and publish. We found, however, that it was not enough just to talk about format. We had to model and scaffold the possibilities for students.

One year, fourth-grade teacher Jennie Nader and I spent months working with students on a final project of their choice. The writing (introductions, body, conclusions), revising, editing, author pages, and illustrations (hand drawn and/or photographed) were all excellent, but we wound up with most reports being rendered in the old, traditional format. We realized that while we had required a written plan before students began writing, as well as multiple drafts and revisions, we had not required any plan for format. Students just went ahead and did what they wanted. The following year, in addition to a plan for the writing, all students were required to devise a mock-up of how the report would be laid out. The improvement was dramatic.

In working with younger children, project formats must be simple enough for teachers to manage on their own. When Tara Strachan had her students do research reports, she found that folding the paper into a book, deciding how many pages were needed, and laying out all the pages took too much time and planning. She simplified the format by having children keep each page separate and then putting all the pages together at the end. This also had the advantage of allowing a student to redo one page, if necessary, without messing up the entire book.

I usually teach one or more lessons on format and layout and leave my collection of uniquely formatted books on loan in the classroom. Students refer to these frequently and are inspired to think about not only their writing topics and content but what their final projects will look like. Julie Beers capitalized on her students' excitement over my book collection by scheduling a field trip to the local book store. She and her students jotted down different types of formats they saw and generated many ideas for writing and publishing. Her students' final writing projects looked a lot different from those of previous years. Some examples include: "The Amazing Baseball Book," a nonfiction book with pages formatted in the shape of a large baseball; "Everything You Want to Know About Hippos," a fact finder that fits in the pocket so that it can easily be taken to the zoo, and "Fashions of the Times Book," which opened like the doors to a mall.

Final projects in Julie's class and those of other teachers have included information presented in the form of magazines, brochures, picture books, newspapers, diaries, scrapbooks, videotapes, reference books, debates, skits, exhibitions, big books, interactive/manipulative books, speeches, and more. Within these final published forms, formats have varied. Some choices for formats have included: question and answer, interview, photo essay, pop-up, labeled diagrams, timeline, topical, alphabet book, letters, and fact/fiction.

Use the texts listed in The Blue Pages, "Good Books with Interesting Formats," page 32b, and "Nonfiction with Interesting Formatting," page 130b, as a starting place for ideas on formatting. You and your students will want to examine and discuss as many of these models—and other excellent books—as possible. Use your librarian or local book store to help you locate books and resources with interesting formats. Ask students what they notice, and begin to make a list of possibilities for publishing.

Illustrations and Design

Interesting formats are always accompanied by artwork in a variety of materials, styles, color combinations, and patterns. Illustrations and other artwork can support and extend the text, influence the tone and mood of a story, and assist in interpretation.

For many students, illustrating is easier than writing, and this is an area where they shine. As a student, well-known children's illustrator Jerry Pinkney was a poor speller and reader and relied on his drawing talent. If he could start with the picture first, he could then go on and read for more information (Pinkney 1996).

Share books about artists and illustrators, and talk about how these professionals work. Pat Cummings' *Talking with Artists* (1992, 1995, 1999) is particularly helpful. In conversations with well-known children's book illustrators (which also serve as a great model for writing interviews), Cummings compiles a good deal of information that includes how and where illustrators work, where their ideas come from, and what techniques they use for illustrating.

Also, most art teachers—if you are fortunate enough to have one in your school—will collaborate with classroom teachers in guiding and teaching students various illustration techniques to accompany their writing projects.

Technology Support

Many classrooms now have one or more computers and printers as well as access to the Internet to facilitate the writing-researching-publishing process. Many students are far ahead of teachers in the use of technology, and they often wind up teaching us.

Even very young students can word process their final drafts. Many of our schools have purchased affordable, lightweight, portable word processors that both students and teachers can easily learn to use. These portables allow the whole class to type their pieces at the same time. Students can be trained to download the writing into the computer to be printed out. Teachers have found these portable word processors wonderful for supporting reluctant writers and for whole-class publishing of documents such as classroom newspapers and magazines.

Spell checks and other computer aids facilitate a polished final product. However, we still hand write some final papers to give necessary attention to handwriting as well as to emphasize the uniqueness and personal style that a handwritten piece conveys. (See Chapter 13, pages 501–505, for more information on technology support.)

FINAL REFLECTIONS

Writing can serve as the foundation for much of the thinking and learning that our students do. As such, writing demands our attention, time, and skill. Yet, teaching writing and organizing a writing classroom are hard work—time-consuming, demanding, and requiring a highly knowledgeable teacher with well-honed classroom management skills.

In the educational literature, books about writing that are helpful to teachers' daily practice are still too few. As a professional, you will need to take it upon yourself to become a competent teacher of writing. Start with your own literacy. Look at how you use writing in your life, under what conditions you write best, and what your writing purposes and audiences are. Begin writing with your students, even if you have never done it before. Share your writing concerns with a colleague. Observe in the writing classroom of a teacher whom you admire. If you make meaningful writing central to life in your classroom, both you and your students will reap huge dividends not only in writing but in reading, thinking, and communicating.

CONTINUING THE CONVERSATION

• ***Get together with your colleagues across grade levels and share ideas about how you organize for teaching writing.*** Many of our most workable ideas have come from adapting what a respected colleague has done.

• ***Examine your record keeping.*** Do you have a system in place that gives you information on every writer? Do you know what minilessons have been taught and need to be taught? Do you know what your students' writing topics are, when they shared with the class, and when you last met in one-on-one conference? Do you have a record of your notes on each conference? Do you have enough information to evaluate students fairly?

• ***Make sure students and parents understand the expectations for revision and editing.*** Are guidelines clear and realisitic? Are your demonstrations ongoing?

• *Take a close look at your publishing program.* Are your expectations realistic? Are your students publishing for purposes and audiences that matter to them? Is there innovation and variety in the students' final products?

• *Attend a state or national writing conference.* Try to attend a meeting sponsored by the National Council of Teachers of English. Go with a colleague so that you can discuss what you saw and heard. Share information with fellow teachers when you return.

• *Check your communications to parents.* Have you been clear, explicit, and jargon-free in explaining your writing program? Have you given parents guidelines for what kind of writing help is appropriate at home? How do you know parents understand the purposes and expectations for writing?

CHAPTER 9

Writing in Multiple Genres

Third graders' book reviews on display at the local bookstore

■ Had I been blessed with even limited access to my own mind there would have been no reason to write. I write entirely to find out what I'm thinking, what I'm looking at, what I see and what it means. What I want and what I fear.

—*Joan Didion (in Murray 1996)*

Most of us write in multiple genres and formats—letters, cards, poems, instructions, messages, explanations, reports, memos, advice, plans, journal entries, and much more. Our writing forms and audiences are determined by our needs, purposes, and interests. Our students' writing should and can reflect the same authenticity, even within the bounds of required curriculum and standards.

Communicating effectively in many written forms is a necessary life skill. In many ways, clear communication demands as much from us as readers as writers. What and how we read influences how we write letters, poetry, fiction, research papers, editorials, and more. In fact, in order to become a better writer, we must study and read in the genre in which we want to write. Writing and reading go hand in hand, feeding and enriching each other.

In this chapter, I will focus on teaching students how to write with description and detail and will give guidelines for teaching real-world genres: letter writing, book reviews, fiction writing, poetry writing, and more. (For nonfiction and report writing, see Chapter 11.) Because literature appreciation and enjoyment undergirds quality writing, I will also describe how wonderful picture books can be used to spark personal narrative.

AUTHENTIC IDEAS FOR WRITING

Before we can teach our students how to write in a particular genre, we need to immerse them in the reading and writing of actual texts in that genre. This is, after all, what I do as a writer. My writing of editorials, articles, letters to the editor, interviews, and so on are always influenced by my reading of examples of these forms in the publications I hope to publish in—before I begin, I take note of structure, length, tone, word choice, and so on. Similarly, we must discuss with our students what they observe and understand about texts written in specific genres, and how they can apply that knowledge to their own writing. We must also demonstrate for them the genre's purposes and possibilities; give students opportunities to practice (with genuine audiences); and respond to their writing in ways that enable them to move forward.

In every case, students must be clear about the expectations. Though teacher demonstration is essential in teaching writing, if a student wishes to take up a genre that has not been discussed yet in class, and I'm convinced that the student is committed to the project and capable of working independently, I will usually let her proceed as long as she demonstrates a willingness to immerse herself in the genre first and shows me a written, workable plan.

Too often, writer's workshop has been misinterpreted as a forum in which students can write whatever they want. Not so. It is our job as teachers to define the parameters with our students and teach them how to write well in multiple genres. It is not enough to provide choice; we must provide choice that includes real purpose, modeling, expectations, practice, and feedback.

WRITING LETTERS

I began emphasizing letter writing when I looked at the writing I do in my life and realized that letters—personal and business—make up the bulk of my writing (see Figure 6-1, page 211). Because it is such an important component of real-world writing, we need to teach correspondence alongside major genres such as fiction and poetry.

Everyone loves to receive mail, and many classrooms feature mailboxes for each student, to encourage note and letter writing (*Transitions*, 105). Some schools also use mailboxes for writing between classrooms. More recently, e-mail—both within and outside a school—has become a popular, efficient way to exchange messages.

In my classes, I share actual letters I've written with students of all ages, and we talk about the kinds of letters and cards people write and why they write them. We then move on to discussing letters students themselves might want to write, and possible recipients.

Tapping Students' Interest in Letter Writing

A second-grade teacher approached me with her concern that students were not engaged in their writing. They were writing every day, the teacher explained, but passion for the activity was lacking. After accepting her invitation to work with her class, I talked to her students about myself as a writer, attempting to connect my writing to possibilities for them. For example, when I shared a letter I had written to Starbucks requesting that a new coffee shop in our neighborhood be kept cleaner, I asked the students, "Have you ever been somewhere where the service was poor? Have you ever bought something that didn't work? Well, when that happens you can write a letter. Most businesses take these letters seriously."

For students to be engaged in their writing, it is important that they see an actual purpose in it. Often I share with them cards that I have written to friends and I am ready to mail. I ask, "How many of you have a friend who has moved away or a special grandparent or other relative who lives out of town? Maybe you miss that person, like I miss my friends in other cities, and you want to write and tell them." Students eagerly get started writing to people they care about.

Depending on the type of letter they are writing, possible audiences for student letters can include:

- Parents and other family members
- Friends
- Pen pals
- School workers (teacher, principal, secretary, custodian, volunteer. See Figure 9-1.)
- Businesses
- News media
- Organizations
- Authors
- Publishers

Figure 9–1   Letter of request to principal requesting new equipment

October 31, 1996
Dear Dr. Stokes,

We need a new overhead projector very badly because every day we use it and there is this big brown spot on it. The spot cannot be washed off with the spot it is hard to see. So please if you can, buy a new projector right away for Mrs. Weiner's class.

Your Second Graders,

Types of Letters

Letters can be grouped into two broad categories: personal and business.

Personal Correspondence

Personal letters, greeting cards, and postcards are used to update recipients on personal events and to express such things as

- Congratulations
- Welcome
- Advice
- Condolences
- Get well
- Apology
- Thank you
- Appreciation
- Invitation

Business Letters

Business letters are formal expressions of fact, statements, and opinions to companies, organizations, public media, and individuals. They can include, but are not limited to,

- Requests
- Compliments
- Queries and inquiries
- Editorials
- Complaints
- Protests

Benefits of Letter Writing

Letter writing can be one of the most relevant of genres to students, for the following reasons:

- The audience is clear to them.
- A response is likely.

Because letters are usually short (one to two pages), they provide a good vehicle for focusing students' attention on spelling, punctuation, and grammar as well as content, and they are fairly easy to bring to final copy.

I also like letter writing because it is a genre that easily engages students. Since it is a fairly direct form of self-expression, letter writing invites voice, honesty, clarity, and brevity. Students usually take real pleasure in writing letters when the subject matter is their own life experience and they are expected to write from the heart.

English teacher Susanne Rubinstein notes that "letter writers seem to find their subjects easily, perhaps because suddenly the idea is concrete." She gives the example of two similar assignments: "Write a letter to someone to whom you owe an apology" versus "Write an essay about a time you were wrong." While the letter assignment easily connects to students' lives and invites participation, the essay, on the same topic, is interpreted as school-based and will put some students on the defensive (Rubinstein 1998, 21).

Teaching Letter Writing

We model letter writing as a real-world genre when we write to our students and their families. Christine Hoegler connects writing with purpose even before school begins. She sends each of her students a picture postcard with a personal, handwritten message, such as, "Dear Owen, Welcome to kindergarten. I am so glad you are in my class. Love, Miss Hoegler." On the last day of school, some teachers give their students a letter wishing them well over the summer and encouraging them to correspond with them during the break. Teachers provide their home or school addresses and some include postcards, writing paper, envelopes, and even stamps.

Having the format of personal and business letters readily available for students makes it more likely that the form of the letter will be correct. After the format is discussed and demonstrated in a minilesson—or perhaps, created together through a shared writing—students can file the letter-writing formats in their writing notebooks or folders for future referral.

Be sure to save samples of all types of well-written letters for topic ideas and as models. Make these accessible to students by, for example, filing them in labeled folders that they can easily refer to.

What follows are some forms of letter writing we teach students.

Pen Pal Letters

I'm not a big fan of pen pal letters, unless the students are given the opportunity to choose who they wish to write to. When a student is told to contact an unknown person in another state, many write their letters simply to fulfill the assignment, and the letters are often boring and bland, containing what I call "computer-generated" writing. They all sound the same: "My name is ———. I go to school. There are . . . people in my family. I have a dog." On the contrary, when students get to choose their pen pal—grandparents, relatives, a father in the army, a friend who moved away—engagement and quality are usually high.

Letters to Parents

Younger students regularly write to parents—inviting them to school (see Figure 9-2), summarizing their weekly progress, making requests. But older students can benefit from writing home too. Madeline Brick described middle school and high school stu-

Figure 9–2 Second grader's draft and final copy letter to parents and their response

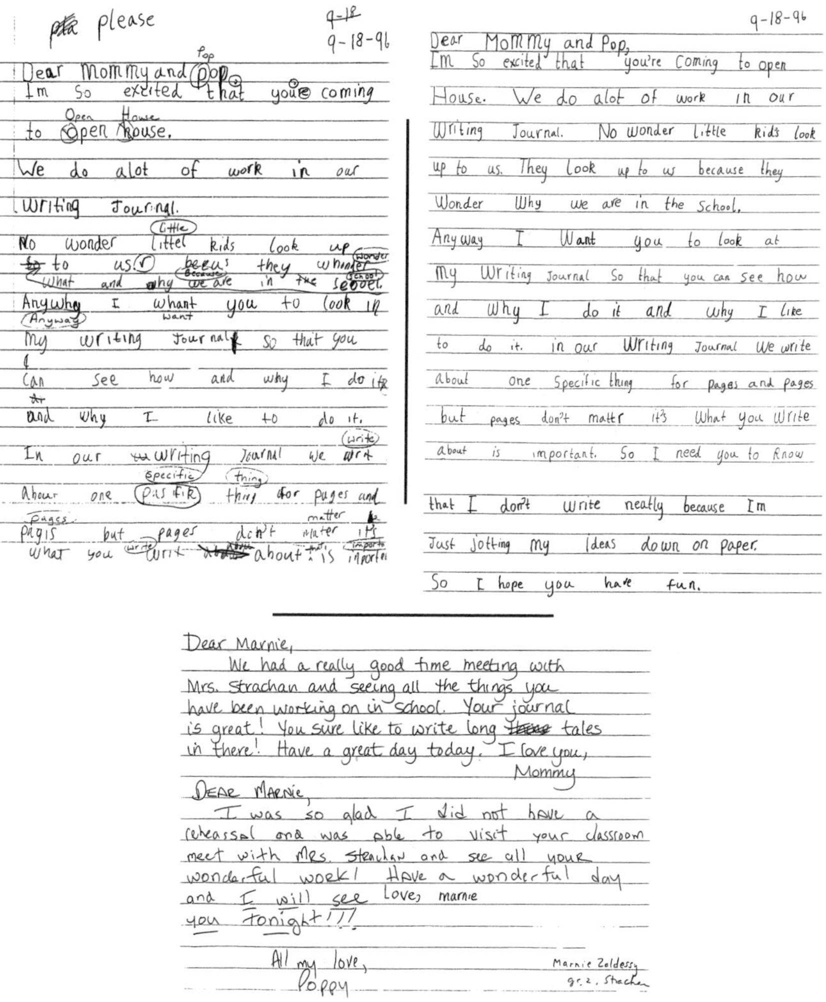
please 9-18-96
Dear Mommy and pop
Im so excited that you coming
to Open House.
We do alot of work in our
Writing Journal.
No wonder littel kids look up
to us beeus they whnder
what and why we are in the scool.
Anywhy I whant you to look in
my writing journal so that you
can see how and why I do it
and why I like to do it.
In our writing Journal we writ
about one pisfik thing for pages and
pagis but pages don't mater it's
what you writ about is importnt

9-18-96
Dear Mommy and Pop,
Im so excited that you're coming to open House. We do alot of work in our Writing Journal. No wonder little kids look up to us because they wonder why we are in the School. Anyway I want you to look at my Writing Journal So that you can see how and why I do it and why I like to do it. in our Writing Journal We write about one Specific thing for pages and pages but pages don't matter it's What you Write about is important. So I need you to know that I don't write neatly because Im Just jotting my ideas down on paper. So I hope you have fun.

Dear Marnie,
We had a really good time meeting with Mrs. Strachan and seeing all the things you have been working on in school. Your journal is great! You sure like to write long tales in there! Have a great day today. I love you,
Mommy

Dear Marnie,
I was so glad I did not have a rehearsal and was able to visit your classroom meet with Mrs. Strachan and see all your wonderful work! Have a wonderful day and I will see you tonight!!!
Love, marnie
All my love,
Poppy

Marnie Zoldessy
gr. 2, Strachan

dents who wrote letters to their parents about their progress in an English class, based on the daily/weekly reports they were keeping on such things as grades, books read, homework completion, teacher comments on papers handed back, and peer feedback. Students found it easier to be honest with parents in a letter, and, in a kind and caring manner, most parents wrote their children back (Brick 1993, 62–63).

Letters to Next Year's Teacher

As part of their permanent portfolios, our students in grades one to four write letters to their next year's teacher at the close of each school year. (See Figures 9-3 and 9-4 for samples.) Written criteria ask the students to reflect on themselves as readers, writers, and mathematicians, and as individuals with interests, goals, strengths, and

Figure 9–3   A first grader's letter to next year's teacher

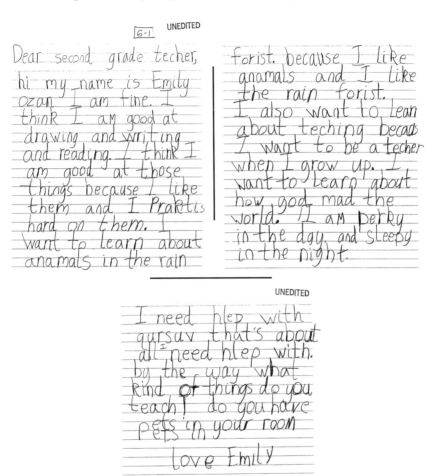

desires. All the writers are asked to focus on voice and audience, and older writers are asked to begin with an interesting first sentence (not "My name is ——— "). The guidelines for this project also include oral brainstorming and prewriting, and sharing and discussing former students' letters. Expectations include writing quality, attention to editing, choice of stationery, and handwriting. Teachers save excellent letters (and poor letters without names) from former students. With their current students, they use these letters as models for comparing, discussing, and establishing criteria for "what makes a good letter."

Since all drafts are attached to the final copy (except for those of grade one, which are marked "unedited"), students' letters can be used as an indicator of writing proficiency. Most teachers (who receive these letters from the teacher who assigned them) use the letters the first week of school as a discussion starter in beginning to establish a personal relationship with their students and set goals for the year. Because students know their letter is their teacher's first impression of them, they engage in the assignment and tend to do their best work.

Figure 9–4   A fourth grader's letter to next year's teacher

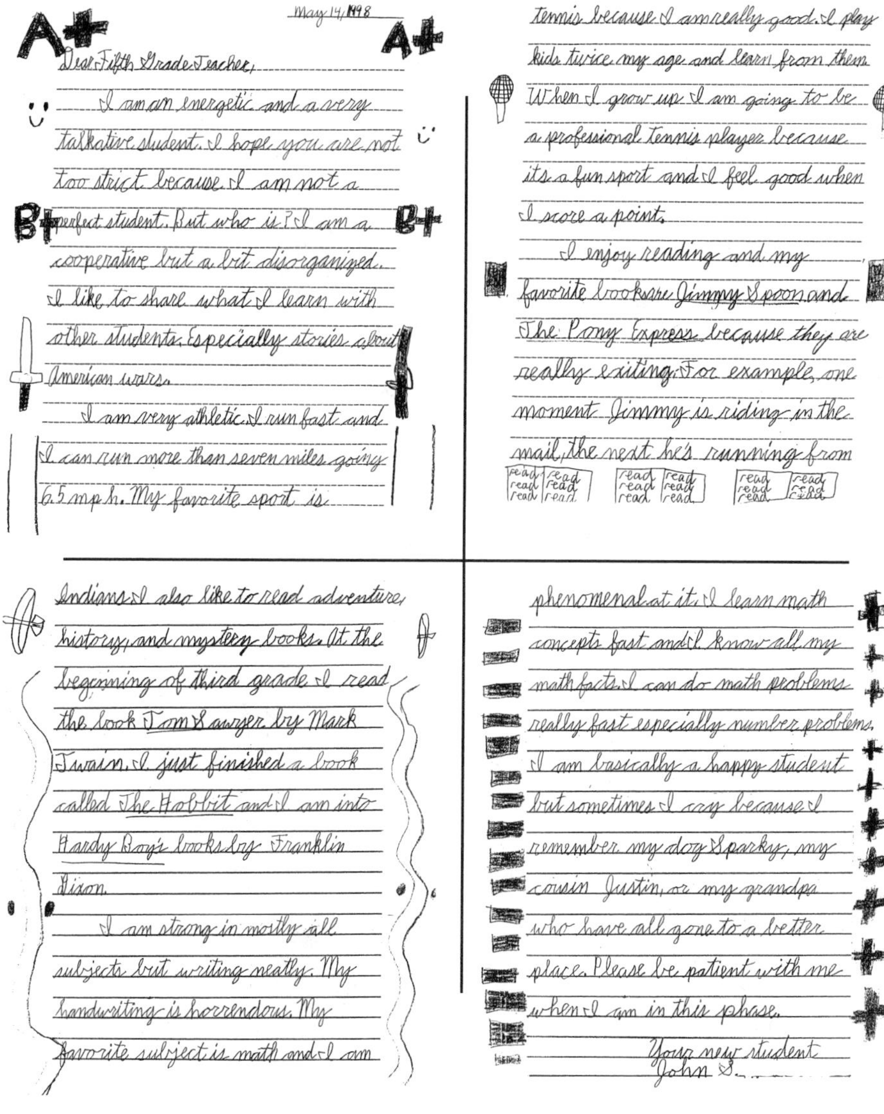

May 14, 1998

Dear Fifth Grade Teacher,

I am an energetic and a very talkative student. I hope you are not too strict because I am not a perfect student. But who is? I am a cooperative but a bit disorganized. I like to share what I learn with other students. Especially stories about American wars.

I am very athletic. I run fast and I can run more than seven miles going 6.5 m.p.h. My favorite sport is tennis because I am really good. I play kids twice my age and learn from them. When I grow up I am going to be a professional tennis player because it's a fun sport and I feel good when I score a point.

I enjoy reading and my favorite books are Jimmy Spoon and The Pony Express because they are really exiting. For example, one moment Jimmy is riding in the mail, the next he's running from Indians. I also like to read adventure, history, and mystery books. At the beginning of third grade I read the book Tom Sawyer by Mark Twain. I just finished a book called The Hobbit and I am into Hardy Boy's books by Franklin Dixon.

I am strong in mostly all subjects but writing neatly. My handwriting is horrendous. My favorite subject is math and I am phenomenal at it. I learn math concepts fast and I know all my math facts. I can do math problems really fast especially number problems.

I am basically a happy student but sometimes I cry because I remember my dog Sparky, my cousin Justin, or my grandpa who have all gone to a better place. Please be patient with me when I am in this phase.

Your new student,
John S.

Letters to the Editor

Students are well served if they know that, in a democracy, one way people express their opinions and exert influence is to write a letter or editorial to an organization or to the public media—newspaper, magazine, or television station. In teaching them about this type of letter, I always show students correspondence that I myself have written. I discuss with them why it was important for me to write the letter, what I hoped to accomplish in writing it, and how I struggled with the language and revised carefully. I also share with them any result or impact that the letter may have had.

Figure 9–5   Letter to the editor by second grader

May 26, 1998

To the Editor:

Those kids hooked on phonics books are usually kindergarten kids even presschool kids. They can read those books, but they are not challenging.

I'm not saying publishers should shut down their business, but they should make books suitable for reading so kids use their brains to read. I am learning to read by using books and comics.

From

Harold Erkins

Figure 9–6   Letter to the editor by second grader

May 26/99

To the Editor:

I don't feel comfortable with people saying use phonics only. In other letters you've published adults have said that we should use phonics books because they think phonics books teach children to read better than any other strategy.

I have never used only phonics books because I also use other strategies to help me learn to read. I still use phonics but also other strategies with it. Right now I'm reading a book called Ribsy and I'm not only using phonics but, I'm breaking the word into syllables. Sometimes I go to the end of the sentence and come back so I can figure out what the word is. I don't think its important to only use phonics.

Cameron Hellfeich

After some editorials on teaching reading and, in particular, emphasizing phonics, appeared in our city newspaper, Loretta Martin's second graders discussed the issues from their viewpoints and wrote letters in response (see Figures 9-5 and 9-6). Their letters, along with Loretta's and a parent volunteer's, were published in the Sunday "Letters to the Editor" section of the newspaper. Students learned at an early age that writing can be a powerful vehicle for expressing personal opinions to a public audience.

WRITING BOOK REVIEWS

Book reviews play a major role in my life as a reader. Every Sunday when we get the *New York Times*, I scour the *Book Review* section looking for new books. I usually cut out specific reviews or save the entire magazine to remind myself of books that I may want to read. I save and savor book reviews that are well written.

School-based book reports, on the other hand, serve no useful purpose for me. Typically, students see no point to these reports either, beyond meeting the teacher's expectations for completing an assignment. Book reviews, blurbs, endorsements, and book jackets, however, serve real-world purposes that can become a meaningful part of classroom life. Reviews of other mediums, such as movies, television programs, and CDs, are also part of most of our lives and can be used as authentic writing. For example, after reading and discussing the features of actual movie reviews, students can be asked to write reviews of movies for their peers.

My colleagues and I have used student-written book reviews to influence student reading habits and to create an ongoing resource of recommended reading. Book reviews—and other book recommendations—are an excellent way for children to learn to write succinctly and persuasively and to focus on specific, descriptive vocabulary. (See Figures 9-7 and 9-8 on pages 340–341.) Because book reviews are usually short and focused, they are an easy genre to bring to publication. Book reviews can also be compiled into a class book of recommended reading for next year's incoming class.

Getting Started with Book Reviews

I first started incorporating book reviews into my teaching several years ago when librarian Kathy O'Neal approached me about creating a closer tie-in between her weekly library time with students and what goes on in classrooms. Because book reviews impacted both of our personal and professional lives, and because I had already given some thought to trying out book reviews in classrooms, I suggested we begin with this genre.

We approach third-grade teacher Karen Horton, who embraces the proposed partnership with enthusiasm. In order to provide students with a real-world connection that would be sure to spark their interest, I contact one of our local bookstores to see if it might be interested in displaying reviews by kids. This would have the added benefit of generating good publicity for our schools. The bookstore is delighted to oblige.

Figure 9–7   Draft of book review by third grader

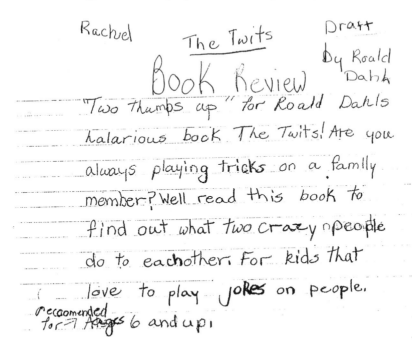

(See the photo on the first page of this chapter and also Figure 9-8 for a posted review.)

Our first lesson takes place in Karen's classroom. Kathy shares with the students children's book reviews "I wish I'd written." She asks kids to identify the book by the review, and they do so easily. She explains how she and each elementary school librarian in our school district write twenty reviews each month. Kathy tells the students how these reviews are used to help librarians decide what new books to buy for school libraries. I am struck by the fact that, up until now, students have no idea how new books come into our libraries.

Kathy shows the students different reviews that our school librarians have written about *Henry and Mudge* books by Cynthia Rylant, and she talks about the similarities and differences of these reviews. Then she describes her own process of writing a book review, noting that a review has three parts:

1. A description of the book—including what it's about and what it looks like
2. A discussion of the book—including reviewer's opinions (good or bad)
3. A recommendation for a particular audience

She tells the children that in writing reviews, she reads a book two or three times, and while she reads, she lists words that describe the book. Then she carefully writes the book review—the description, discussion, and recommendation.

In our second lesson, I bring in reviews (of both children's and adult literature) from magazines and the *New York Times*, and we look at what makes a good review. In a shared writing, we develop the following criteria for writing a review:

Figure 9–8   A third grader's book review

A BOOK REVIEW
BY: Brian Moth

Wading Through Peanut Butter
by: Pamela Curtis Swallow

Bently Barker an average fifth grader
Ha! He thinks he has the whole fifth grade
eating out of his hand. He wants kids to
go wow! They are but for the wrong reasons.
He's being stalked by the biggest, toughest 7th
grader. Will he survive the fifth grade? A great
book for experienced readers ages 7-9, grades
2-4.

- Read the book at least twice.
- Jot down words and ideas that come to mind as you are reading.
- Have the book in front of you when you write the review.
- Begin with a captivating lead.
- Don't give away the ending.
- Tell just enough of the story to capture your reader's attention.
- Use interesting vocabulary.
- Recommend the book to a particular audience.

Next, we do a shared writing of a book review using a well-loved picture book. In our third session, students begin drafting their own reviews. In subsequent sessions, we go through the writing process to produce well-written final copies. Because the purpose and audience have been clear and important to them from the outset, students beam with satisfaction and pride when their reviews are finally displayed at our local bookstore.

Writing Book Reviews in Kindergarten

I introduce book reviews in kindergarten for the first time in Susan Mear's class one mid-January. (See Photo 9-1 on page 342.) Susan and I have been experimenting with writing in many genres—lists, letters, memos, research, advice, poetry (see pages

Photo 9–1   Learning how to write book reviews:
Regie Routman working with a kindergarten class

397–398). I suggest we try book reviews and Susan readily agrees. While I usually wait until midyear to introduce young children to writing book reviews, Christine Banks introduces the genre to her kindergartners in November, with wonderful results. (See Figure 9-9.)

When I introduce book reviews into Christine Hoegler's kindergarten class in March, I begin by asking the students how they choose the books they read. They mention looking at book covers, browsing through the pictures and words in a book, seeing an interesting-looking book in their classroom, and hearing about good books through Mom or Dad or the librarian or a friend. I tell them that I choose my books in much the same way, and that most of the books I read are books that someone I know has recommended.

"But I also depend on book reviews," I tell them, holding up the *Book Review* section of the *New York Times* and explaining that it's the first thing I read every Sunday. "I am always looking for good books to read, and sometimes I find out about them by reading what someone has written about a book they have carefully read." I go on to explain how book reviews help me to decide what to read. I tell them that if a review of a book is bad, I generally won't read the book. If the review is good and I am interested in the topic, I may decide to read it. "There might be a great review of a book on ants," I say. "But since I'm not that interested in ants, I would not read the book."

I then read aloud *Badger's Bad Mood* by Hiawyn Oram, illustrated by Susan Varley

Figure 9–9   A kindergartner's book review

If you like trucks, you'll like Donald Crews.

(New York: Scholastic, 1998). This is a well-told story about a good-natured character named Badger, who is the one creature his friends most depend on. At the start of the story, Badger is in uncharacteristic low spirits and feels that he is "no good for anything." When his friends are unable to cheer him up, Mole plans an awards ceremony. Badger learns that he may be honored at this ceremony and decides to attend. After he receives recognition for all his well-loved traits, Badger feels appreciated and is happy once again. The children enjoy the book, and we talk about the possibility of having an awards ceremony to let each class member know what we most appreciate about them.

On large chart paper, I then write down the title of the book. I ask the children, "What can we tell others to let them know that this is a good book?" At first, most of their comments focus on the story. Christine and I guide them to explain why the book so appeals to them. "What can we say so that others will want to read this book?" Eventually, the class came up with the following review: "If you are in a bad mood, this book will cheer you up. For kindergarten through grade two."

After Christine models writing a book review of a familiar book, the students begin to write on their own. For their first reviews, everyone in the class uses the same book, *Chicka, Chicka, Boom, Boom,* by John Archambault. (See Figure 9-10 for one student's review.)

To get her students started with reviews, Christine Banks shared samples from several magazines. Then, with her class, she brainstormed what someone would want to know about a book and what the targeted age groups would be. After she read a familiar book to her students, she modeled writing a detailed book review, including drawing the cover and a sample picture. Her review, written on large chart paper, was of *Mousekin's Golden House,* by Edna Miller. Christine wrote as she thought aloud, "If you like mouse stories, you will love this book! Mousekins is a clever mouse."

Figure 9–10   A kindergartner's book review

chicka   chicka

Boom   Boom.

I   Lieb   Thic

Book   But

win   They

fol   ovn

My   tth

screm

I like this book but when they fall over my teeth scream.

Then, with the help of two parent volunteers, students wrote their own reviews. Christine found that the structure of reviews was a help to students who usually struggled to find writing ideas. Students understood and easily applied two criteria for reviewing a favorite book:

- Why would someone want to read this?
- Who should read it?

Parents, who saw the reviews at parent conferences the following week, were impressed that this type of writing could be accomplished in kindergarten. Christine commented, "The quality stunned me, and it was just the beginning of the year."

Writing Book Recommendations

One spring, second-grade teacher Loretta Martin and I decide to have students write recommendations of favorite books as a book selection guide for the following year's incoming second graders. First, we do a shared writing with the students to discuss what a book recommendation should include. We come up with the following elements:

- Title and author
- Type of book—fairy tale, poetry, nonfiction, picture book
- Subject of book, or problem in story
- Best features of book—favorite part, main character, illustration, setting
- Interesting words to describe book—for example, "colorful," "fun-filled," "exciting," and so on
- Who should read it

Next, we take the familiar book *Me and Neesie* by Eloise Greenfield and write a recommendation together on chart paper: "When Janell plays with her imaginary friend Neesie, she gets in trouble. Our favorite part was when Aunt Bea started to sit on Neesie, and Janell yelled, 'Don't sit on Neesie!' Read this book before it disappears!"

As guided practice, one student is then asked to begin writing her book review on large chart paper as the class looks on. Finally, students go back to their seats to work on their own reviews. (We first spend time talking with each student about their opening sentence to make sure that they are on target.) As students write at their desks, we ask them to share their openings aloud, so that there is constant modeling for other students.

Writing Endorsements

I wasn't particularly aware of book endorsements until I was asked to write one. Then, I immersed myself in the genre by reading dozens of these showcased remarks on front and back book covers and noticing the specifics of the messages, including length, word choice, sentence construction, and tone.

Because the requested endorsement was for one of my all-time favorite books, *Better Than Life*, by Daniel Pennac (Markham, ONT: Pembroke; York, ME: Stenhouse, 1999), I was delighted to take on the task. What I wrote appears on the front cover of the paperback edition:

> Anyone who loves to read and wants our young people to develop a similar passion will savor *Better Than Life*—an enchanting, beautifully written, and wise book.
> Regie Routman, teacher and author of *Invitations* and *Literacy at the Crossroads*

I was limited to twenty-five words, not counting the title. It took me three hours to write the above sentence. I share that struggle with students—how to decide what is absolutely essential in describing a book's impact, what words to use when you have severe length restrictions, and how to achieve a persuasive tone to lure the would-be reader.

Writing endorsements is a powerful exercise for students in distilling the essence of favorite books and conveying their message succinctly. Since the authors of endorsements are always credited, students must also decide what designation will appear following their names. Some students write, "student and writer." One fifth grader wrote, "aspiring writer and actress."

Creating Book Blurbs and Book Jackets

Most students are unaware that book blurbs, usually located on the back cover of books, are written by the author or publisher to sell books. Unlike the review, which may or may not be favorable, the blurb is always positive. It is helpful to examine book blurbs with students, noting the language and tone, and to write one together as a shared writing experience before expecting students to write their own. Use the blurbs to publicize favorite books for present and future students.

Making and writing book jackets (after studying how these look and are written) can be another way to review books and advertise favorites to peers. One of the only enjoyable reading activities I remember from my own school days is designing, illustrating, and writing a book jacket for a well-loved book.

CAPTURING A MOMENT: LEARNING TO WRITE WITH DESCRIPTION AND DETAIL

When I was reading the Pulitzer prize–winning novel *A Thousand Acres* by Jane Smiley, I felt like I was right there, on the farm and in the kitchen she rendered so vividly in her prose. The lines between book and reader blurred to the point where I felt intimately connected to the characters. When I finished *A Thousand Acres*, which I dearly loved, I went on to read everything else Smiley had written. With each of her books, I found myself completely taken up into the characters' lives, a benevolent intruder fortunate enough to witness events as they unfolded. Afterward, I kept thinking, what does Smiley do to give the reader that "right there" feeling? By setting down a momentary happening in acute detail, I decided, she creates a realistic moment that the reader is able to step right into. It is a moment in which all the senses are engaged, and the reader "feels" right along with the character on the page.

Here's an example from Smiley's short story "Ordinary Love," from her collection *Ordinary Love and Good Will* (1989). It is written in the voice of a mother of identical twins, one of whom has just returned home after a teaching stint in India.

> When Michael walks into the house, he is not Joe's twin, but a shadow of Joe, dressed all in white cotton and cadaverous. He greets me in a Michael-like way, "Hey, Ma! I'm back. Any calls?"—grinning, grabbing me around the waist, and kissing me on the lips, but his biceps are like strings, and his ribs press into me through his shirt. It is all I can do not to recoil in surprise. We try to maintain a light, ironic (though sometimes rueful) atmosphere around here, but I look at Joe, and see by his subdued smile that Michael's figure has pierced him, too. He sets down the bags. In the moment we wait for Michael to signal us what to do and how to act, I think an irresistible thought—that we have gotten back less than we sent out. (8)

Could I teach students how to "capture a moment"? My first attempt was with struggling high school sophomores and juniors whose enthusiasm for writing was not high. Colleague and friend Holly Burgess had invited me to work with her class. I knew that in teaching them how to capture a moment, the first thing I had to do was capture their attention. I began by telling them about my life, to connect with them on a human level and to gain their trust. I told them that I would work with them (I was giving up my lunch hour to do so) only if they made a serious effort to improve their writing. Several days later, I received an encouraging note from one of the students (see Figure 9-11).

When I returned the following week, I wrote in front of the students about a moment I'd had with my father, who had recently heard me speak at a conference for the first time. (See Figure 9-12 for final copy.) When I sent the piece to my dad for Father's Day, he responded that it was the best "card" I'd ever sent him. I asked the students to think of an adult in their lives who had had a strong impact on them and to reflect back on a moment they had shared with that person. I asked them to think about the following questions:

- What's happening?
- What do you see?
- What are you feeling?

Figure 9–11   A high school student's note

Dear Mrs. Routman,

Thank you for coming to our class. You gave a talk that made you and I almost one. As every word spilled out of your mouth I was grabing that word and trying to make a connection with my history. You told us something personal that was hurting you inside and I admire you as a hero for doing so.

You also tought me how to make writting fun. Like turning a job into pleasure. And you said somethings you have to write when you don't want to. But keep on going because you feel proud of yourself. I thought about that saying alot, I stills dislike writting alot, but I am going to do it to make myself proud.

Sincerely,
Jamar W.

P.S. I am looking forward to seeing you in my 6-6 period class again soon.

Figure 9–12   A Father's Day moment for my dad

The long, narrow room was dim. The huge shades on the tall windows were pulled almost all the way down. I was standing next to the overhead projector at the front of the room looking out at a sea of hundreds of faces. The only face I really saw completely, when I glanced to look at it, was my father's. Sitting in his impeccably groomed sport jacket, pants, and colorful tie, he was perched at the edge of his seat, leaning forward, staring intently at me.

I can still see him clearly. His hands were clasped together over his knees which were slightly apart. His short, silvery gray hair was well groomed as always except for the long piece to the right that swung gently over his forehead. His mouth was slightly open, showing the space between his two front teeth and a look of anticipation. But it was his awed expression and gaze that I will always remember, like a moment etched permanently in time.

It was a look I had not seen with such intensity ever before. There were tears welling up in his eyes. He seemed to be looking at me with such enormous pride, admiration, and joy. Yes, he had always been proud of me—for looking good, being kind, cooking well—but only in the last decade for what I had accomplished in my career.

Sometimes, when I drive down the street on my way home from work and I am thinking about my dad, I see him looking at me in that exact moment in time, and I feel very loved and cherished by him.

- What do you smell?
- What do you touch?
- What are you thinking?

I described a moment as being of short duration—a snap of the fingers, a few seconds, a flash. I asked students to use careful observation and description to slow the moment down in their writing, to take in the whole memory.

Cleo wrote about seeing his dead godmother at a funeral home (see Figure 9-13); Derrick wrote about falling in love. Because the exercise was concentrated and focused (a "moment" is a less intimidating concept to students than an "event" or a "situation") and concerned a person that meant a lot to the students, the end result was gratifying. Most of the students were proud of their writing and willing to read it aloud to their peers during sharing time.

Over the years, I have found that even second graders can learn to write descriptively if we teachers model, both by sharing our own personal moments with them, aloud and in writing, and by sharing student writing models.

I have used "capturing a moment" to improve fiction writing, to teach students to incorporate imagery into their work, for gift writing (see page 354), for quick writes, and as a technique for teaching students to expand or slow down their writing. To get started, use some of the student examples given here as models for your students. Then, save your students' exemplary writing pieces to use as models for future students.

I have included here the writing of several fourth graders (see Figures 9-14, 9-15, 9-16, and 9-17 on pages 350–352). "Christmas" was written as a quick write. So was Ted's piece about his grandfather, clearly influenced by Cleo's piece, which I had used as a model. Owen wrote about a moment with his grandpa, which he sent to him as a Christmas gift. His grandfather was said to have been delighted, because he didn't get to see Owen often. Alex's poignant moment with his dad at a baseball game was given as a Father's Day gift. Notice his willingness to revise without teacher prompting. Because this was a piece that mattered to him, he wanted it to be his best.

Conversations before writing is critical. As described on pages 250, 258, and 260, writing quality improves when you converse with one or more students in front of the class before students begin to write. I was working with a group of third graders on capturing a moment with their moms or a special person in their life as an alternative to the obligatory and usually boring Mother's Day cards kids create in school. I shared a familiar moment with my mom—coming home from elementary school to a plate piled high with freshly baked chocolate chip cookies. I also shared some student samples.

Before students began to write, I asked a few to tell me about their subjects. When Kendre, a struggling third-grade writer, talked about her mom making French toast for her, I capitalized on her memorable language by jotting it down for her on a Post-it. The act of writing down literary quotes validates what students have said, encourages students to use the phrases or sentences in their writing, jogs their memory while writing, and lets the student know what we consider memorable writing. Note how Kendre incorporated into her writing what had been noted for her on Post-its (see Figure 9-18 on page 353).

Fourth-grade teacher Julie Beers tried capturing-a-moment writing with her students as Mother's Day gifts. Notice how her own writing inspired her students' (see Figures 9-19 and 9-20 on page 354).

Figure 9–13   Cleo's moment at his godmother's funeral

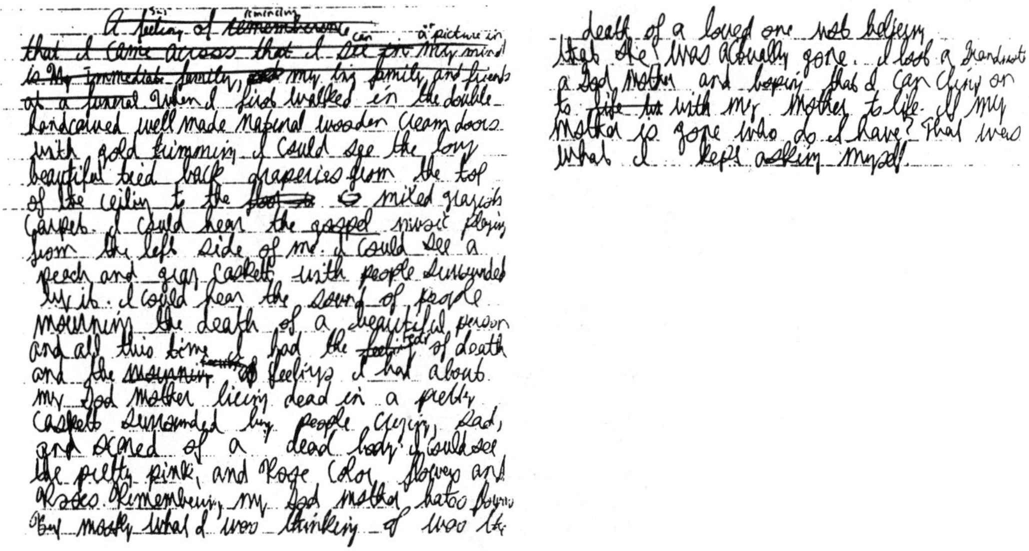

When I first walked in the double handcarved, well made, natural, wooden, cream doors with gold trimming, I could see the long, beautiful, tied-back draperies from the top of the ceiling to the mixed grayish carpet. I could hear the gospel music playing from the left side of me. I could see a peach and gray casket with people surrounded by it. I could hear the sound of people mourning the death of a beautiful person. And all this time I had the fear of death and the feelings I had about my godmother, lying dead in a pretty casket surrounded by people crying, sad, and scared of a dead body. I could see the pretty pink and rose colored flowers and roses, remembering my godmother hates flowers. But mostly what I was thinking of was the death of a loved one, not believing that she was actually gone. I lost a grandmother, a godmother, and hoping that I can cling on with my mother to life. If my mother is gone, who do I have? That was what I kept asking myself.

WRITING FICTION

Fiction is an important genre to teach because elements of good fiction—meaningful dialogue, interesting leads, lively descriptions—can be applied to other genres. Also, kids are eager to write fiction. They are naturally captivated by this genre and all its possibilities.

My experience with fiction writing is that many first and second graders write quite well by intuitively modeling their favorite stories. By the time kids get to third and fourth grade, however, great numbers of them write awful fiction. Kids of this age, generally unschooled in the elements of fiction writing, typically write rambling, episodic pieces without character development or coherent plot. Although I encourage these students to pursue fiction writing at home, I discourage it in the classroom until it has been specifically taught. Even when I make an exception, for a voracious reader who insists she is ready, I require a written plan before I give the go-ahead.

Interestingly enough, in intermediate-grade classrooms in which I have taught students how to write fiction and required them to try some aspects of it, not many students choose to complete their fictional stories. They understand that to write fiction

Figure 9–14
Capturing a moment

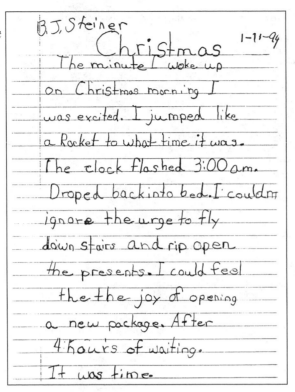

B.J. Steiner

Christmas   1-11-94

The minute I woke up
on Christmas morning I
was excited. I jumped like
a Rocket to what time it was.
The clock flashed 3:00 am.
Droped back into bed. I couldn't
ignore the urge to fly
down stairs and rip open
the presents. I could feel
the the joy of opening
a new package. After
4 hours of waiting.
It was time.

Figure 9–15
Capturing a moment

Ted Dole   1/11/94

I put my hand on the cold metcle
handel of the caskit looking
down opon the corps of my grand
father tears graguly driping down
my cheek wy him I said wy did
he leave me wy, all that we
did together the things I didn't
tell him. I refused to leave
my grand fathers body that
one moment was the absulut
sadist moment in my life.

Figure 9-16 Capturing a moment

1

by Owen Hearey

Owen 12-8-95

I was on my way back from an ice-cream shop with my grandfather. We were in his white Toyota. I was eating my vanilla frozen yogert with M+M's. He was huming his favorite song. The birds outside seamed to sing along with him. I could smell the air-freshner, and sent of his coffee. I was thinking how you don't get a lot of times like these with

2

your grandfather. Having a friendly talk. I could feel the extra seat conckeon under me. The soft warm fabric. The sweet New Jersy air floating through the window. My grandfather seemed so peaceful and kind. I only viseted him about once every 2 years. He was pushing easily on the gas pedal, gliding up and

3

down the tree covered lanes. I belived he was thinking the same thoughts I was. The fall leaves shined against the cloudy morning skies. My ice-cream was half melted, the M+Ms had lost some of there color into the vanilla soup. We were siting between the seat divider but our love was close and warm.

4

The pavement had loose gravel that crunched as we went over it. The engine was going chug, chug chug. That is a moment I will never forget.

351

Figure 9–17   Capturing a moment

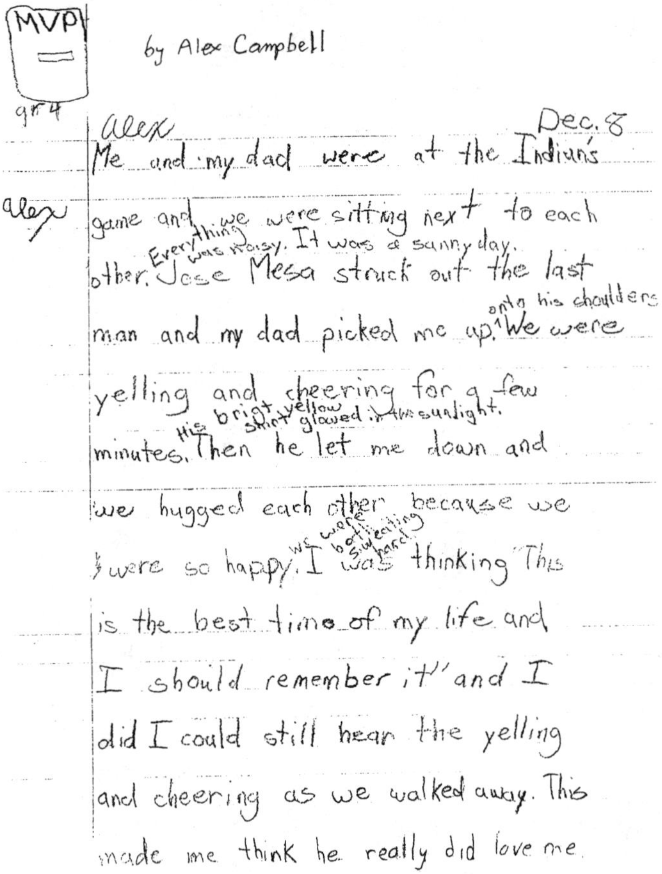

MVP
=
gr 4

by Alex Campbell

Alex →

Alex   Dec. 8
Me and my dad were at the Indians
game and we were sitting next to each
other. Jose Mesa struck out the last
man and my dad picked me up. We were
yelling and cheering for a few
minutes. Then he let me down and

we hugged each other because we
were so happy. I was thinking "This
is the best time of my life and
I should remember it" and I
did I could still hear the yelling
and cheering as we walked away. This
made me think he really did love me.

well requires hard work, careful observation, and much revision. However, their efforts are not wasted. On the contrary, students learn that elements of good fiction writing can be used in many other genres. When fourth graders who have been taught fiction writing later write nonfiction reports on famous people, their instruction in and practice with fiction is evident.

The Importance of Character

Lois Lowry (1996) notes that "in every book, the main character has to make a journey. Often it's an interior journey that involves the mind and heart, an interior quest."

When I am in a classroom of eager-to-be fiction writers, I begin by asking, "What makes good fiction?" Usually, students talk about detail, description, a problem to be solved, but "character," the essence of fiction, is rarely mentioned. We begin to make a list of qualities of good fiction. I write down what students say and probe for more with

Figure 9–18   Capturing a moment

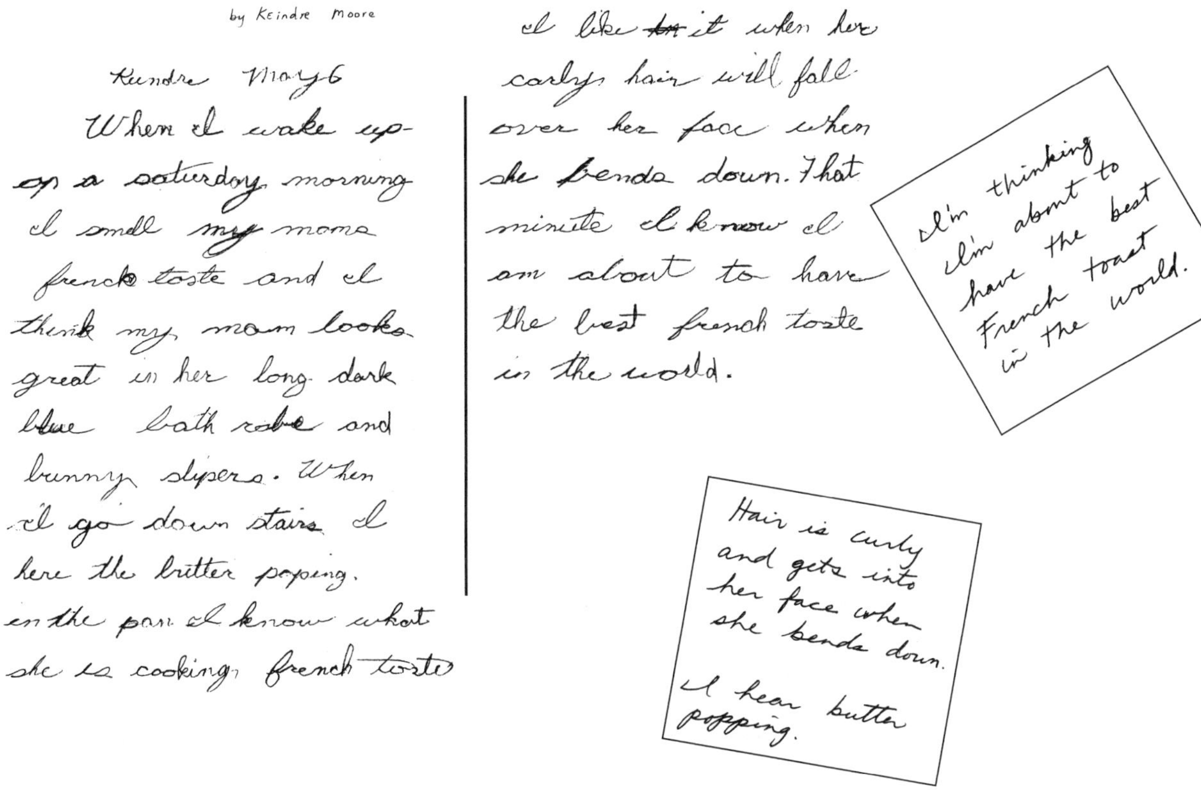

by Keindre Moore

Keindre May 6

When I wake up on a saturday morning I smell my moms frencs toste and I think my mom looks great in her long dark blue bath robe and bunny slipers. When I go down stairs I here the butter poping in the pan I know what she is cooking french toste

I like it when her carlys hair will fall over her face when she bends down. That minute I know I am about to have the best french toste in the world.

> I'm thinking I'm about to have the best French toast in the world.

> Hair is curly and gets into her face when she bends down. I hear butter popping.

statements such as, "What else is important to successful fiction? Think about a favorite book you have read." The following is a draft (which we will continue to revise) of typical responses from such a discussion:

- Realism—story must be believable
- Problem, trouble, suspense
- Detail, description, feelings
- Interesting words
- Plot
- Catchy beginning, strong ending
- Dialogue
- Parts, chapters
- Setting (or place)
- Character—wants something, has a problem to solve

Figure 9–19   Teacher Julie Beers' moment for a Mother's Day gift

No Words Needed

Spending an endless night at Lake West Hospital
wishing morning would come
Was that how you felt, mom?
Wondering if dad would live through the night or die in that cold, empty room
Did you wonder that too, mom?
Watching dad's eyes look at us filled with fear and pain.
Did you see those eyes, mom?
Wanting so desperately to take the pain away from dad and the worry from you.
Wouldn't you have liked that, mom?
Who would have thought an orange wooden chair just barely suitable for sitting would became my bed,
And for you - a warm, heated waterbed replaced for 10 days with a blue, hard plastic chair.
It was that night that I realized what an extraordinary woman you are.

Your life completely put on hold to stay
By the side of the one you so dearly love—
your partner, your soul-mate, my dad.
It was because of the way you live your life, always thinking of others first,
that made me cancel mine for days to be by your side.
A mother's love - is there anything more precious
a love so deep that it needs no words to express how we feel
Remember that night in the hospital? when things just got to be too much?
You were surrounded by friends, but feeling completely alone,
Everyone was giving you advice, and yet we were the only two who truly understood
I walked over to you and we embraced.
No words, just the warmth of your strong arms around me -
resting my head on your soft shoulder
I didn't want to let go. Not ever.
It is in those arms that I feel my best, my strongest, the safest.
It is because of you that I am who I am
Did you know that, mom?

Love Always, Julie

Figure 9–20   Inspired by her teacher's writing, a student's moment for a Mother's Day gift

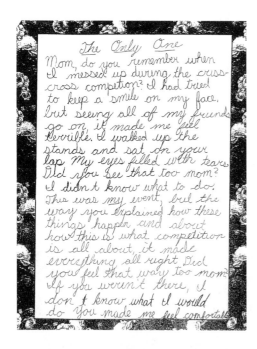

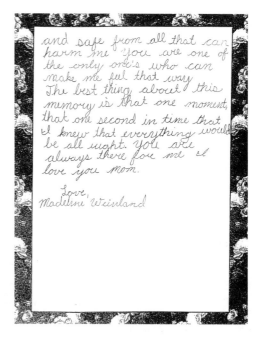

The Only One

Mom, do you remember when I messed up during the criss-cross competition? I had tried to keep a smile on my face, but seeing all of my friends go on, it made me feel terrible. I walked up the stands and sat on your lap. My eyes filled with tears. Did you see that too mom? I didn't know what to do. This was my event, but the way you explained how these things happen and about how this is what competition is all about, it made everything all right. Did you feel that way too mom? If you weren't there, I don't know what I would do. You made me feel comfortable and safe from all that can harm me. You are one of the only one's who can make me feel that way. The best thing about this memory is that one moment, that one second in time that I knew that everything would be all right. You are always there for me. I love you mom.

Love,
Madeline Weinland

I guide students in talking about how memorable fiction hinges on a well-developed, believable character. Together we brainstorm and create a realistic character. We talk about how most writers pull from their own experiences to make their characters believable, that fiction writers have a careful eye for observing the commonplace. Who is the character? What does he want? What is his problem? What kind of struggle will he have going after his goal? How will he succeed, or will he fail?

Even if you don't want to spend time getting into all the elements of fiction writing, focusing on characterization alone will improve students' writing. I began teaching character development years ago in a third-grade class in which the teacher was frustrated with her students' attempts at writing fiction. Specifically, many students were writing fast-paced, action-packed adventures with characters whose "development" consisted of being given a name. We began in that class by creating a realistic character together and discussing what her problem might be. (See pages 358–359 for a character created by another class.) Then we asked students to take that character and create a scene. Karen Horton, the classroom teacher, wrote along with the students and was amazed at the impact her own modeling had on students' writing. She said, "Everyone took a giant step forward. I saw the power of me writing, but it was so risky to write, for the first time, in front of my students." See Figure 9-21 on page 356 for Karen's writing and Figures 9-22 and 9-23 on page 357 for a student's first attempts.

Beginning Guidelines for Fiction Writing

For guidance in teaching students how to write fiction, I rely heavily on Marion Dane Bauer's *What's Your Story? A Young Person's Guide to Writing Fiction* (1992). I have also found "Trying on Fiction" by Donald Murray (in his *Crafting a Life in Essay, Story, Poem,* 77–100) extremely helpful for older students. Because I can be in any particular classroom only once a week, I divide our fiction writing unit into three one-hour lessons (see pages 362–364). You may want to spread these lessons out over longer periods to suit your own purposes and schedules.

As I do in almost everything I teach, I demonstrate for the students and work with them closely before I expect them to work on their own. On large chart paper, we do shared writings that focus on a main character, his problem and/or wants. (For procedures on shared writing, see pages 37–43.) Together we make several logical attempts to solve the character's problem. In doing so, we talk about how the protagonist's struggle must keep the story moving forward. For example, the character may have some initial success in getting what he wants, but larger obstacles will need to arise. If everything happens as predicted, there will be no tension or suspense, and the reader will lose interest. We develop a plot, write opening lines and dialogue, and discuss the importance of word choice. We also write an ending to the story. Published fiction writers have noted that they often know how their story will end before they put pen to paper.

We also post Bauer's statement, "Your story may come from your imagination, but it will always imitate life" (1992, 79), to remind us that the character and story we develop must be based on what we know.

Figure 9–21   A third-grade teacher writes aloud and creates a character

Mrs. Horton   4-23-93

"Hey, Barb, where are you
going?" called Sue in a teasing
voice. Barbara Friedman's oval
shaped face turned beet red as
~~her foot slipped~~   high
~~she fell off~~ the ˰balance beam.
It was unusual for her to slip,
but she was having difficulty
concentrating on this particular
Sat. morning in May. ~~She~~
          gymnastics
~~The~~ spring competitions were
taking place in two weeks
and she wanted her routines

to be flawless.
      Her green eyes started to fill
with tears. Her nose, & thin at
the bridge, and wider at the
nostrils, was filling up the way
it always does when she tried to
          her
hold back ˰tears. Her light brown
skin ~~was~~ began to be covered
with a thin layer of sweat.
Sweat, not from physical exertion
but from embarrassment.

Telling Details

"Telling details," the specific, particular, unique features and actions of an individual that give insight into personality, physical features, and lifestyle are a good place to begin when thinking about creating a character. Years ago, when Shelley Harwayne came to our district to conduct a summer writing workshop, she began by asking us to go around the room and divulge one "telling detail" about ourselves. I still remember what Shelley said about herself: that she did not own a pair of sneakers. A simple remark, but "telling" in its implications.

Once students have noted such details, we need to take the next step and show them how those details relate to their characters, especially how the character's wants are connected to or revealed by them.

When I initially teach kids how to do this, their responses are superficial. I find they need to be given many examples, such as, "coughs every time the teacher calls on him," "bites her fingernails all the way down to the skin," "twists her hair around her index finger when she is nervous." We begin to create a chart of telling details based on people they know:

- Habitually chews on the sleeve of his shirt
- Uses her shirt as a napkin
- Cheeks dimple when he smiles
- Hands blend into the light brown carpet
- Many necklaces look like snakes crawling around her neck
- Hair shines like black coffee

*Figure 9–22 A third-grade student's character
after a class shared writing and teacher modeling*

by Allison Waithe   4-23
            Barbra

"Oh, Barbra heradu herself say.
This paper on 'My Best Friend'
was so hard. It wouldn't be if she
had a best friend. Eaven if she
had One half of a friend.
But no. She looked to strage.
With short black hair, braces with
green rubber bands, fat cheeks,
little feet, of course she was weird
She looked over at Brandy. She's
my friend, thought Barbia. anybody
who talks to me. must like
me. But how do you spell 'My
Best Friend' L D class didn't go
over that. She raisd her hand.

"NO" she thought the wole class
would lagh at me. But it
was to late the teacer saw her
hand. "Yes, Barbra, said her teacer
"Nothing" said Barbra. "Barbra, said
her teacher. In this class we
say what we need to say." Barbra
was extremly sensitive she satrted crying.
The whole class looked at her.
This was enbaresing!

I ask the students to discreetly scrutinize a member of their family (without telling the subject he is being observed) and to note descriptive details about appearance and behavior. We begin listening for such details during read-alouds, marking them in books we are reading, sharing them with peers, and discussing how these details give us insight into character. It takes time, but after lots of modeling and discussion, sharing successful examples written by classmates and authors, and trial and error, students slowly begin to understand how telling details contribute to character development, and they begin to formulate some wonderful observations of their own (see Figure 9-24). Many students later incorporate these details into their fiction writing.

Figure 9–23 A third grader's beginning first attempt at fiction writing

OH NO Said Jayson as the
big dark figure came closer
and closer...

Jayson was Ten years old
and in foarth grad. Youshly he
had no trubols etsept sometimes
on fridday after school.

Figure 9–24 Telling details

Little Sisster Camille Ames

1. Sticks out tongue to the side when _thinking_.

2. Scrunches up her nose when smells something bad.

3. When gets frustrated she crunches her fists

4. Blushes when gets a complament from adult.

5. Cocks her head to the left when confused.

6. When excited she rubbs her hands toghether like shes cold or samthing.

7. Bits her lip when nervouse

8. Smiles and makes her eyebrows go up and down when up to somthing

Elizabeth Ames

Creating a Character: A Shared Writing

Once students understand detailed observations and character motivation, we word sketch a character together. After we have created one or more characters as a class, students go on to create their own characters. If they prefer, students can draw their characters. (See *Invitations*, 181–183.)

What follows is a first attempt by a fourth-grade class (word-processed from large, handwritten charts). You will want to try a similar exercise with your own students.

Character: *Stacy Allen, Ten Years Old*
She wants:

- To have friends and be popular
- Her new life to be like her old life
- Her brother to have friends so he will leave her alone

Problem:

- She just moved from Columbus, Ohio, to New York City, and she wants to make friends.
- Her new teacher is too strict.
- She gets blamed for a lot of things that she didn't do. She gets picked on.
- Her little brother, four years old, is a tattletale.

Telling details about Stacy (connect to wants):

- Bites bottom lip when she's nervous
- Twists her hair around her finger when she is about to cry
- Sucks her thumb when her brother tells on her
- Picks up her brother and threatens to drop him when he tells on her
- When she's bored, thinks about unanswered questions or how long bees live

Writing Dialogue

"Good dialogue moves the story forward by giving information and revealing character" (Bauer 1992, 80).

Typically, even avid readers and writers need demonstration and practice in order to write dialogue well. Even an excellent writer who knows how to write conversation may need help in using dialogue to illuminate character. (Also, see Figure 9-26 for a fourth grader's attempt at writing dialogue after instruction that included "capturing a moment.") An important point here is that our good students also need explicit instruction. A student with an excellent command of conventions and story structure can still produce a boring story. Without our expert guidance, many do.

Before I ask students to try their hand at dialogue, we create written conversation together. First, for students in grades four and above, we discuss how to write and punctuate conversation using the guidelines from *What's Your Story?* (Bauer 1992, 81–84). Students take notes in their writing notebooks, along with their other minilesson notes, so that these are available for easy reference.

Following is a shared writing of an opening conversation we wrote together on large chart paper. We tried several, based on the character we had started to create.

> "Do we have to move to New York?" Stacy was sulking.
> "Honey, it won't be as bad as you think," her mother said.
> "What if I hate it there? What if kids make fun of me again?" Stacy complained.
> "Sweetheart, please!"

> "Good morning class. We have a new student today. Her name is Stacy Allen."
> Stacy walked to the front of the sun-drenched classroom, biting her bottom lip.
> Lucas whispered to Adam, "What a loser." His whole table giggled softly.
> "Hi, I'm Stacy," she mumbled while twisting her hair around her right index finger. "I'm from Columbus, Ohio," she said, holding back the tears.
> Lucas whispered to Adam again.
> "Do you have a question to ask Stacy, Lucas?" Miss Leven asked sharply.

> "Umm, uh, yeah." He hesitated. "I heard that Columbus was a bad city, that a lot of people get killed there. Is that true?"

Afterward, students write dialogue for an opening scene with their own character (see Figures 9-25 and 9-26).

Concluding Thoughts on Writing Fiction

Because fiction writing is only one of several genres we teach, we must limit the time we spend teaching it. However, all students are expected to attempt writing some elements of fiction. For example, fourth-grade teacher Lisa Hardiman and I required students to complete and bring to final copy the following:

- A main character—name, problem, what does the character want?
- A page of telling details
- An opening scene
- A conversation that moves the story forward (see Figures 9-25 and 9-26)

Lisa was initially concerned about the time that would be necessary for completing the above components, given our emphasis on conferencing and the revision process.

Figure 9–25 An opening scene with dialogue, draft

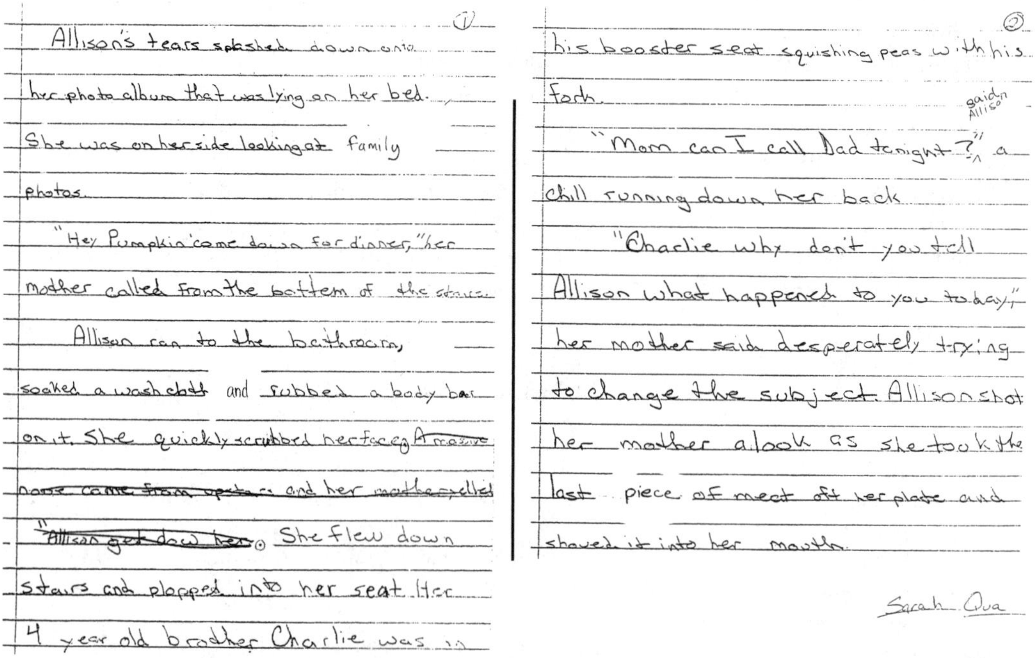
(1)
Allison's tears splashed down onto
her photo album that was lying on her bed.
She was on her side looking at family
photos.
"Hey Pumpkin come down for dinner," her
mother called from the bottom of the stairs.
Allison ran to the bathroom,
soaked a wash cloth and rubbed a body bar
on it. She quickly scrubbed her face. ~~A massive~~
~~noise came from upstairs and her mother yelled~~
~~"Allison get down here.~~ She flew down
stairs and plopped into her seat. Her
4 year old brother Charlie was in

(2)
his booster seat squishing peas with his
fork.
"Mom can I call Dad tonight?" said Allison a
chill running down her back.
"Charlie why don't you tell
Allison what happened to you today,"
her mother said desperately trying
to change the subject. Allison shot
her mother a look as she took the
last piece of meat off her plate and
shoved it into her mouth.

Sarah Qua

Figure 9–26   An opening scene with dialogue, edited draft

Life Beyond Anger
By, Elizabeth Ames

<u>Chapter One</u>

" It's to noisy here in New York, I wish that we never had moved here in the first place! " Complained Dawn.

" You'll get used to it honey," my mom replied for the tenth time.

" Wanna bet?" Dawn said solemnly.

" Dawn, chill, just lay off it," my mom replied frusterated.

" I liked California a whole lot better!" She exclaimed as she stomped upstairs.

Dawn was in her room on her bed thinking about her father and also wondering about school. It was the end of her life!

What if nobody likes me, what if I do something stupid, What if I don't make any friends?

While Dawn was worrying about school, her mom was a nervous wreck downstairs.

What if I go to the wrong building, what if I do badly at my job and get fired? Her mom wondered.

That night Dawn went to bed early to get her rest for school.

The next morning she got up at 7:00 to pick out her clothes.

As she rummaged through her clothes, school haunted her.

Finally she picked out a pair of cargo pants, a gray tank top, and black leather boots.

Dawn gave her long strawberry blond hair a quick brush, checked herself out in the mirror, and rushed downstairs, as not to be late for her first day at school.

All through Rugrats she bit her bottom lip.

Finally Rugrats was over, and it was time to go to school.

Dawn got into the car with hesitation.

By then her bottom lip had holes in them as deep as pot holes!

" Mom, I think I'm sick," Dawn faked.

" You can't pull that one on me," her mother replied.

Dawn sat back in her seat to try to think of more excuses.

When they got to the school, Dawn got out of the car slowly, and looked up at the tall brick building.

She took a deep breath, and opened the doors to her new school.

And though the time commitment is several weeks, the payoff for students is huge. For those who choose to take their fiction writing to completion, we note high quality, since expectations, demonstrations, practice, and guidance have been amply provided. Most important, what students have learned by writing fiction carries over into much of their other writing, such as interviews, nonfiction reports, responses to reading, and memoirs. As Lisa observed:

> Kids see that writing is not something you do quickly. With specific teaching of fiction and an emphasis on revising and editing, they see that good writing requires a lot of time and effort. I noticed that after our focus on fiction writing, all their writing improved, especially in the details they used. They were just more conscious of it. Sometimes while reading, a student would call out, "Hey, that's a telling detail."

Lastly, fiction can dramatically raise enthusiasm for writing among students, as seen in this excerpt from an article that Doug, a fourth grader, wrote for the monthly classroom newsletter to parents. His piece was called "Finally Fiction."

> The big news is that we are starting to write fiction! Finally, after a year and one month, we get to write about our wonderful dreams! The only "catch" is that it has to be realistic. A lot of kids think of fiction as aliens and space ships, but if we want to write fiction it must be realistic. The good part is we get to make a problem, tell what the character wants, and write telling details. . . .

Lesson Plans for Writing Fiction

Use the following sample lesson plans to guide your teaching. These plans were based on my work in one fourth-grade classroom three weeks in a row. Because fiction writing is one of many genres we teach, we limited our time and focus. You will want to adapt these plans to suit your own needs, purposes, and time frames.

Lesson 1

What Makes Good Fiction?
Show/discuss notable examples from literature (and, perhaps, the work of former students).

- Generate a chart together listing elements of quality fiction, supporting students in their inclusion of character and character's problem and/or wants. (Continue to add to and revise chart as you proceed with fiction lessons. Type when complete and add to writers' notebooks.)

Character
- Focus on characterization as you look at examples from literature. Ask the following questions:
  - What does character want?
  - What is his problem?
- Create a character together—include name, telling details, problem, wants.
- Give background on character's problem (include complexity of character). How will character face his problem? How will facing his problem change him? Have students use their own experience, what they know about themselves, and how they would feel when facing a problem to make character realistic.
- Have students create their own characters (suggested preparatory reading in Bauer 1992, 34–35), including
  - name
  - age
  - telling details
  - problem
  - what character wants
  - obstacles to success
  - how problem gets solved (ending)
- During the week, share these created characters in group share, and provide feedback. Students may need to create several characters before they devise a realistic one.

Homework Possibilities
Have students observe someone they know well for several days and record telling details. Or, have them pick a favorite character from a book they've read and discuss why

they like the character. Have them describe the character. Note and share telling details throughout the week.

Lesson 2

Plot

- Expand on character's attempt to deal with his or her obstacles and solve problem. Discuss interaction, how character meets or confronts other characters.
- Discuss narrative tension, why character must struggle; why character must make several attempts to solve problem; how protagonist's actions must both reveal character and drive the story forward. (Read Bauer, *What's Your Story?* 47–49.)
- Using character that was created together as a class, discuss/list three attempts to solve problem.
- Now have students create three situations to solve problem of their main character.

Opening Lines

- Discuss importance of opening lines. Read opening lines from memorable fiction:

    "Where's Papa going with that ax?"—*Charlotte's Web*

    "Walking back to camp through the swamp, Sam wondered whether to tell his father what he had seen."—*The Trumpet of the Swan*

- Discuss point of view and use of first ("I") or third person ("he"; "she").
- Have students write their openings. Emphasize importance of strong action or dialogue. Include basic facts about character—gender, age. Read aloud from Bauer, *What's Your Story?* 71–72.
- Share plot structure and opening lines, and provide feedback.

Homework Possibilities

Have students note leads, dialogue, character descriptions, and endings during WEB (see page 48) and read-alouds. Have them keep notes about their characters and jot down ideas about plot. Ask them to draw their character and one part of their setting in detail. (See "Visualizing the Main Character" in *Invitations*, 181–183.) Assign them several beginnings to complete.

Lesson 3

Writing Dialogue

- "Your story may come from your imagination, but it will always imitate life" (Bauer 1992, 79). Good dialogue moves the story forward by giving information and revealing character (Bauer 1992, 80). Only include dialogue that changes the story.

- Examine the use, form, and structure of dialogue written by well-known authors. Ask students, "What do you notice?"
- Guide students in creating dialogue together as a class (for character and part of plot class has created.)
- Write dialogue for an opening scene. (When possible, make use of tape recorders. Kids love it when they can "punctuate" what they hear. Then, have them transcribe the tapes.)
- Have students check their word choices:
  - *adjectives* (describing words). Are they interesting? (Have you avoided overly familiar words like "nice" and "pretty"? Are there too few? too many?)
  - *verbs* (action words). Are they strong and descriptive?
  - *nouns* (subjects, objects). Are they specific? (for example, "a blue jay" instead of "a bird.")
  - *imagery*. Is the language colorful? Are there similes (comparisons using *like* or *as*) and metaphors (direct comparisons of unlike things)?

Homework Possibilities

Have students copy favorite dialogue from books they are reading, or listen to conversations and write down dialogue that reveals the personality or character traits of the speakers. Notice word choices in independent reading and read-alouds. Record memorable words, similes, and metaphors. Practice writing similes and metaphors. Write several scenes with dialogue.

POETRY WRITING: A POWERFUL GENRE
FOR SPARKING QUALITY WRITING

Teaching kids of all ages to write poetry, and to love to write and read poetry, is probably my favorite teaching. It's sheer fun. It's exhilarating. Every child is successful. Each year, I am amazed at what kids can do, how insightful and clever they are, and what powerful poems they write.

Years ago, when Shelley Harwayne worked with our teachers in writing, she mentioned that she was collecting poems that sounded like a child could have written them, so that she could inspire children with possibilities. The following thought occurred to me: "Why not use poems that *children* have written, as models for other children?" For the past five years or so, I've been experiencing great success having kids write poetry, and I've been doing it by using poems written almost exclusively by kids. When a young writer sees an original draft of a poem written by a peer, in the student's own handwriting, the message is hopeful and encouraging to the emerging poet. I tell students: "These poems were written by students just like you. You can write like that too."

I focus on free verse—unrhymed poetry—which is what I write and what most contemporary poets write. While kids love to read rhyming poems, they are difficult to write. Students wind up so focused on finding the right rhyming word that poems often end up sounding contrived. When you take the emphasis off rhymes, kids are able to express themselves honestly and without restriction. They write poems about things that may not surface freely in a journal entry, such as the description of an object, deep feelings about something important to them, something that they're embarrassed about, something they dislike, and so on.

Most of these poems remain first-draft poems, even with older writers. Poetry is one writing genre where our emphasis is not on major revision. We stress having fun with language, form, punctuation, and ideas. I focus on students' ease in writing, in getting thoughts down quickly, in using strong voice. Then, after kids have written a bunch of poems, they choose one or more for publication and bring that to final copy. Because the poems are usually only a page in length, students are willing to work hard on the final spelling and editing for our classroom anthology. The anthology becomes a celebration of our work, part of our classroom library, and inspiration for other budding poets.

Advantages of Writing Poetry

Several months after we have completed a kindergarten poetry-writing focus, I talk with kindergarten teacher Christine Banks to get her feedback. Her first comment, which she repeated several times in our conversation, is, "Their writing had so much energy." This is a typical comment. Writing poetry, especially poetry that doesn't rhyme, is liberating for kids. Over and over I hear from teachers how excited students are about writing poetry and how much energy is contained in their verse.

The other comment Christine makes, and that other teachers often make, is, "Every child was successful." Poetry promotes ease of writing. Christine had four students in her class identified as special education: two were learning disabled, one was language delayed, and one was behavior disordered. Yet, from looking at the work of the class as a whole, I was unable to single out these students' work, as I might have been able to do with writing in another genre. Poetry seems to be a great equalizer.

Christine commented, "I loved how they had freedom, no rules, and could write just a few words or phrases rather than complete sentences." Second-grade teacher Jennifer Shoda concurred. "Because there was freedom built in to the process, all of a sudden I had kids writing that had never written before." And fourth-grade teacher Nancy Schubert, who had added free verse to her teaching of poetic forms such as haiku and cinquains, commented, "It frees kids up from the restrictions I grew up with in poetry. I never did free verse before because I didn't know how. These kids loved it, the boys as much as the girls. They were very serious about it. Poetry writing forced kids to pay close attention to language."

First-grade teacher Kevin Hill said that it was poetry that persuaded him that first graders could write with voice. He saw, for the first time, that kids who had trouble expressing thoughts in complete sentences could express language freely when they didn't have to worry about a formal structure. "I could actually *hear* individual students' voices," he explained. "Even without the child's name on the paper, I would have known who wrote the poem."

My favorite comment regarding poetry writing comes from Anne Topper, a parent of a first grader for whom writing was a challenge:

It was something of a surprise to me. I didn't think first graders could write poetry. Writing had been difficult for Kenneth, but poetry was different. The combination of not having to worry about spelling so he could use interesting words worked for him. He really got a sense of achievement from it. Also, seeing invented spelling in action, combined with traditional spelling, really sold me. Kenneth loved poetry. He came home saying he wanted to be a poet rather than a paleontologist, which is what he'd been saying for years that he wanted to be.

Writing poetry has many advantages and benefits for children. It:

- Inspires kids to move away from the conventional, boring language typical of early journal writing ("I like . . ."; I went . . ."; "It is fun to . . .") and toward interesting, colorful language and innovative word choice.
- Appeals to kids. Kids who dislike journal writing are often able to write poetry with pleasure and ease. "Every year, several students who don't like to write respond to poetry and take off with it," explains kindergarten teacher Kathy Wolfe.
- Encourages kids to write about things they love or are interested in. Gets kids looking outward, past themselves, beyond "I" and "me."
- Helps kids stay focused; less writing is necessary and there is less of a struggle to develop content.
- Accommodates kids' natural love of rhythm and song. Kids love to "clap poems," to feel the beat of the language.
- Focuses on oral language and expressive oral reading.
- Encourages kids to look closely at the world around them.
- Dovetails with reading. As we write poems together, we reread every time we add a line. This continuous rereading becomes a way to practice reading and do lots of shared reading. We also encourage students to reread their poetry on their own to be sure it's just the way they want it.
- Offers students immediate affirmation. With other genres, there isn't time for every student to share daily writing with the class, but all students can take part in poetry shares.
- Challenges gifted students. In journals, they write easily, but with poems, they have to think about the words they're using.
- Is open-ended. No requirements (even for mechanics), as in other genres.
- Is noncompetitive. Works as an equalizer. Sometimes, the best poems come from struggling students, and they really get to shine. Some kids who have had difficulty getting started writing get going right away.
- Presents an alternative, creative way to share knowledge in the content areas. (See pages 377–382 for "Writing Poetry in the Content Areas.")

Teaching Kids to Love Poetry Writing: Getting Started

Before we teach poetry writing, we gather dozens of favorite poetry books (from school and home libraries), establish a poetry corner, and immerse kids in listening to, reading, and enjoying all kinds of poems. While kids love rhyming poems and usually find these on their own, most of the poems I read are free verse, as that is what we will be writing. (See The Blue Pages, "Some Favorite Poetry Books for Inspiring Poetry Writing," page 35b.)

Some students copy favorite poems, and others memorize and recite poems, as well as raps, chants, and jump rope rhymes. Many classrooms also incorporate a "poet of the day" segment, in which students take turns leading a shared reading of a favorite poem (see page 37).

I like to have poetry reading and writing going on all year long in the classroom, not just for four weeks as a "unit." Except for kindergarten, where poetry writing works best after students have some letter/sound knowledge (unless dictation is used), it works well to introduce poetry writing at the beginning of the year. Everyone experiences early success with writing, and students have learned how to write in a genre they can choose to come back to again and again.

What Do We Already Know About Poetry?

When I introduce poetry writing, I start by saying something like, "I am so excited. Today, we're going to be writing poetry, and I know you're going to love it. I'll be showing you lots of poems written by kids just like you. But first, I want to find out what you think about writing poetry and what you know about it."

When I ask students in Tara Strachan's second-grade class, "How many of you like to write poetry?" only a few hands go up. When I probe, students give two main reasons for their lack of interest:

- Poems have to rhyme, and that's hard to do.
- I've never done it before.

The remarks of Tara's students are typical. But also typical is that, after just one hour of talking about poetry, listening to and seeing poems written by other students their age, and attempting to write their own poems, these students are wildly enthusiastic. When it is time to stop their writing and move on to gym class, there are protests and groans.

In Kevin Hill's first-grade class, we begin by brainstorming on large chart paper what students already know about poetry. They talk about the shape of poems, that they're all about one thing, and that they rhyme. We add to this list over the weeks as students notice and learn more about the poetry (see Figure 9-27). Next I show them an anthology of student writing from several years before, and we discuss what anthologies are. Students are always interested in this inclusive, varied publishing forum, and are eager to be included in something like it themselves.

Examining Poetry Anthologies

"Do you know what an anthology is?" I typically ask young students after we have talked about what students think and know about poetry. I begin by showing them three or four poetry anthologies, written and organized by students from previous years. (In the absence of these, you can use commercially published books.) With guidance, they

Figure 9–27   A first-grade shared writing: What we know about poetry

---

Notes on What We Know About Poetry

Words rhyme.
The shape is different than journal writing.
Neat, clear writing.
"You can get ideas from everything."
You can illustrate them.
Lots of words talking about the same thing.
Can be fiction or nonfiction or maybe partly both.
January 8, 1998

Words do not have to rhyme.
Writing can go down the page.
You don't have to have rhythm.
It doesn't have to be a song.
It could be about your "special thing."
Sometimes the sentences are long and stick out.
Uses describing words.
January 15, 1998

Use question marks and "interesting dots" to make it look like a poem.
Poems can change over time.
You take a breath when you come to a mark.
When you see . . . you slow down.
In one kind of poem, the first letter of each line tells a message (acrostic poem).
When you choose your words, they have to make sense.
Poems have white space.
Poems can start with one thing and jump to another thing.
February 19, 1998

By the smart first graders in Mr. Hill's class

---

come to see that an anthology is a collection of works by different authors. We talk about how a poetry anthology is a collection of poems by different poets. I tell them that we'll be creating one of these for the classroom library, to showcase and remember favorite poems we write. I flip through the student anthologies and we discuss how each is organized differently, comprising some or all of the following: title page, dedication, acknowledgments, contents, index, student-poet profiles, illustrations, end pages. I leave the anthologies in the class for a week or so and encourage students to browse through them—as well as other anthologies in the poetry corner—and think about how our anthology should be organized.

Sharing Poems by Other Students

After we have charted what we know about poetry and discussed what a poetry anthology is, I spend about fifteen minutes sharing and celebrating the poems of other students, on a wide range of subjects including sports, family, friends, objects, animals, thoughts, reading, loneliness, siblings, jealousy, longings, desires, and more.

The message the students receive, through hearing and seeing all these poems and from my comments as teacher, is very clear: "Poems can be about anything. They can be long or short, complex or simple, humorous or serious. These poems were written by kids just like you. You can write poetry too."

I put poems on transparencies on the overhead projector so that students can see the writing of each student poet. I do not share perfect, typed copies, but rather display poems in students' handwriting with their invented spelling. After I read each poem (I read many twice) I ask, "What did you notice?" or "What did you like?" or "What did the writer do really well?" (See Figures 9-28 through 9-32 on pages 370–373 for a variety of poems across grades K–4.)

Students often notice rhythm, and sometimes I reread the poem and ask them to clap along and "feel the beat." They often comment on the "repeating" of images and words in poems, the shape of the poem, how the words work to convey a feeling or idea. We note titles and last lines, how last lines are different, how you can tell the poem is over. With poems that make us smile or laugh, we talk about the humor and tone of poems. I note that poems can be brief or long, that they have a deliberate shape, and that they can be arranged exactly the way you want on the page. I help them to understand that poems look and sound different from other kinds of writing.

I used to begin slowly, making just a few major teaching points. For example, I'd note word choice and rhythm but leave line breaks and stanzas for another lesson. Over the years, I have learned that students can take in all the major points at once, that even kindergarten students can grasp the whole of writing poetry right from the start. Then, over the coming days and weeks, we work on the individual components as necessary. As we go along, we may have minilessons on such things as opening lines, use of stanzas, putting conversation into poems, writing in the first person, and using observation and vivid description. Once students have written a poem they like, we will focus on experimenting with line breaks (where each line ends) and white space (the deliberately chosen space that contains no print). (See Figures 9-29 and 9-30 on page 371 for a first grader's and a second grader's use of line breaks and white space.) Some teachers have found that examining black-and-white photos can help make the point of how white space creates shape and helps us see what's there more clearly.

With immersion in poetry, demonstrations, and especially sharing and discussing poems written by peers, all students can write memorable poetry. Until you have your own student collection of poems, or to supplement your collection with more poems and detailed guidelines, you may want to refer to *Kids' Poems: Teaching Children to Love Writing Poetry* (Routman 2000), available in four separate volumes for kindergarten, grade one, grade two, and grades three and four.

Writing a Poem Together

As in my teaching of all writing genres, I begin with a live demonstration. Either the class will write a poem together, or I will write a poem in front of them or share with them a poem or two that I have written. When we do a shared poetry writing, I want

Figure 9–28   Kindergartners' poems

Bumble
Bumble is a dead bee.
Bumble is a dead bee.
Bumble is a dead bee.
Bumble

by Bruce Kimmelfield

Knights
Armor
Castles
Weapons
Horses
by Teddy Cahill
written after a visit to the art museum

June
June
I Play
Baseball
June
My
Brother
Plays
Baseball
June
I
Wear
Shorts
June
I
Have
Fun

by Nate Bixenstine

Figure 9–29 ***A first grader's poem***

MY FRND
He moVD
HA WAS MY BEST
FRED LIV IS NOT
ESSE WITH OUT
HIM HES SAM

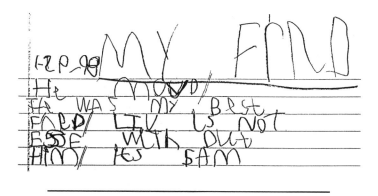

My Friend

He moved.
He was my best friend.
Life is not the same without him.
He's Sam.

by Max Wolff

Figure 9–30 ***A second grader's poem, with and without line breaks***

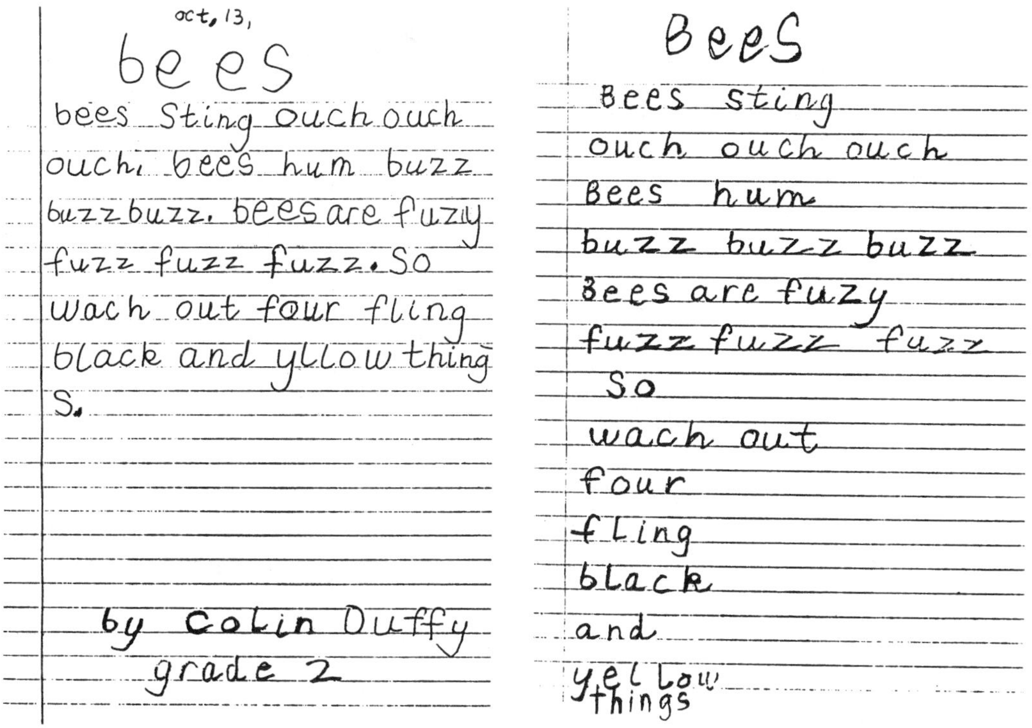

oct, 13,
bees
bees Sting ouch ouch
ouch, bees hum buzz
buzz buzz, bees are fuzy
fuzz fuzz fuzz. So
wach out four fling
black and yllow thing
s.
by Colin Duffy
grade 2
Bees
Bees sting
ouch ouch ouch
Bees hum
buzz buzz buzz
Bees are fuzy
fuzz fuzz fuzz
So
wach out
four
fling
black
and
yellow
things

Figure 9–31 A third grader's poem

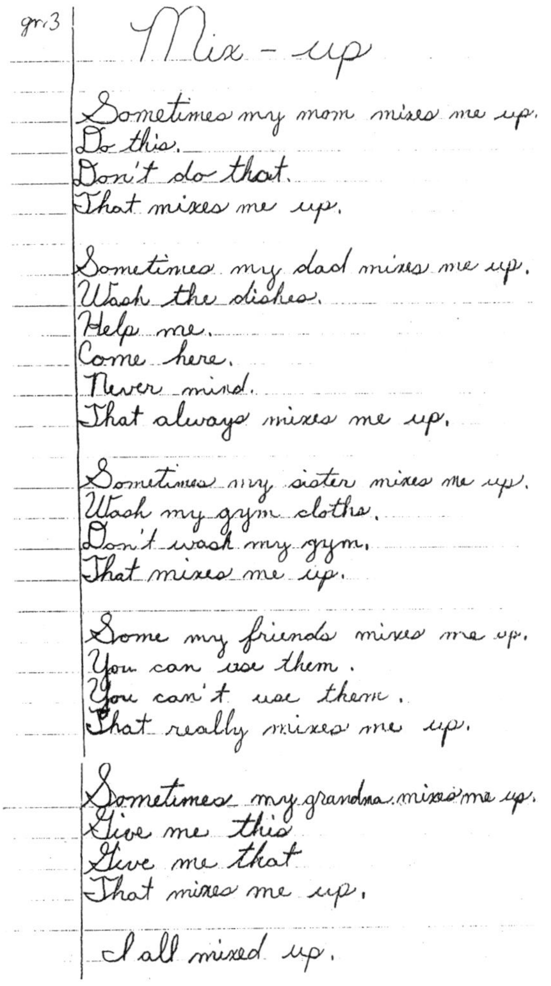

gr. 3

Mix-up

Sometimes my mom mixes me up.
Do this.
Don't do that.
That mixes me up.

Sometimes my dad mixes me up.
Wash the dishes.
Help me.
Come here.
Never mind.
That always mixes me up.

Sometimes my sister mixes me up.
Wash my gym cloths.
Don't wash my gym.
That mixes me up.

Some my friends mixes me up.
You can use them.
You can't use them.
That really mixes me up.

Sometimes my grandma mixes me up.
Give me this
Give me that
That mixes me up.

I all mixed up.

Mix-up

Sometimes my mom mixes me up.
Do this.
Don't do that.
That mixes me up.

Sometimes my dad mixes me up.
Wash the dishes.
Help me.
Come here.
Never mind.
That always mixes me up.

Sometimes my sister mixes me up.
Wash my gym cloths.
Don't wash my gym clothes.
That mixes me up.

Sometimes my friends mix me up.
You can use them.
You can't use them.
That really mixes me up.

Sometimes my grandma mixes me up.
Give me this.
Give me that.
That mixes me up.

I'm all mixed up.

by Andrea Martin

students to see that a poem can be about anything, and that it is important that we choose our words carefully. The subject of our shared writing can be a familiar classroom object, a season or the weather, a favorite book, a content area study, a feeling, or a shared experience (see Figure 9-33 on page 374 transcribed for students from a hand-written chart).

If you are uncomfortable writing in front of your students, write while they are writing, and share your efforts. Then, next time, write aloud in front of them and attempt to get over your fears. Our own writing, especially when we make our process visible, is a powerful model for students. See Figure 9-34 on page 375 for a fourth-grade teacher's first attempt at writing poetry.

Sometimes, with young students new to poetry, we will talk about the difference between a journal entry and a poem. I explain how the same topic looks and sounds different depending on whether it's being developed in poetry or prose. (See Figure 9-35 on

Figure 9–32   Fourth graders' poems

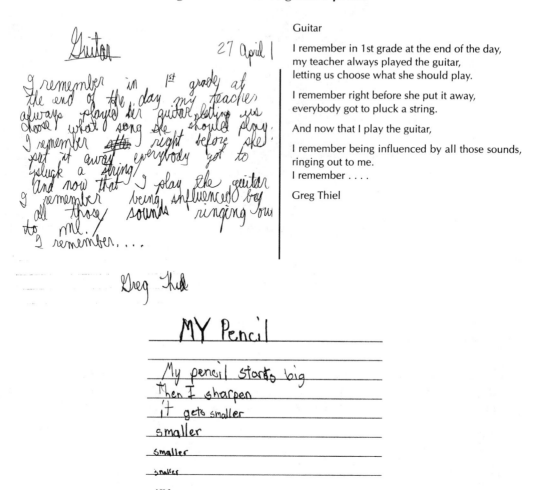

Guitar

I remember in 1st grade at the end of the day,
my teacher always played the guitar,
letting us choose what she should play.

I remember right before she put it away,
everybody got to pluck a string.

And now that I play the guitar,

I remember being influenced by all those sounds,
ringing out to me.
I remember . . . .

Greg Thiel

by Alex Stout

page 376 on Earth Day writing, done as a shared writing in both poem and journal form, with Kevin Hill's first graders.)

Focusing on the Language of Poetry

Before young writers are asked to write independently, it works well to have them focus on using simile, and sometimes metaphor, to help the reader get a picture of what the poet is writing about. We model this process to the whole class first. For example, in Karen Sher's kindergarten class, we brainstorm images together. When a student wants to write about rain, we ask, "How does it feel? Wet like what?" Or again, when a student is talking about how cold it is in winter, we ask "How cold is it? As cold as the inside of a freezer? Help me get a picture of how cold it was."

Figure 9–33   Shared poetry writing in kindergarten, written after student-led conferences

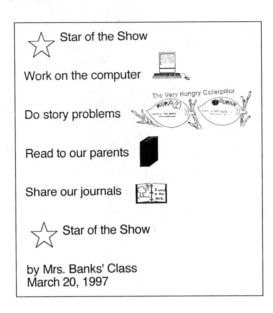

Dictation allows children to think and express themselves like poets without worrying about getting the words right on paper. Several years after we tried this process together, Karen called, "The results were wonderful. I still have all the poems that resulted from the exercise" (see Figure 9-36 on page 376 for a dictated poem).

Writing Poems Independently

As with all the writing genres introduced, students are expected to write poetry themselves during the teaching focus. And as with the other genres, students are given choice in what they want to write about.

When the introduction to poetry has been long (over thirty minutes) and we have talked about and viewed many poems, we may skip the usual oral brainstorming before writing and get right to composing. Before students go back to their seats to begin writing, I tell them that we'll have about twenty minutes of quiet writing time, and then those who want to can share their work. Students are instructed to put their name and date on every poem. I remind them to reread their poems to see if they want to make any changes and to start a new poem if they finish one before writing time is up. Almost everyone settles down and gets to work. Very few students have difficulty choosing a topic. For those few that do, we confer with students individually about possibilities.

As students are writing, the classroom teacher and I are moving about the room offering help and encouragement to students. I am continually amazed at the immediate quality of the poems. Additionally, there is always at least one student who has a history of struggling with writing who accomplishes in this first poetry session his best work to date. Often it is

Figure 9–34   Fourth-grade teacher Jennie Nader's first poem: Partial draft and final copy

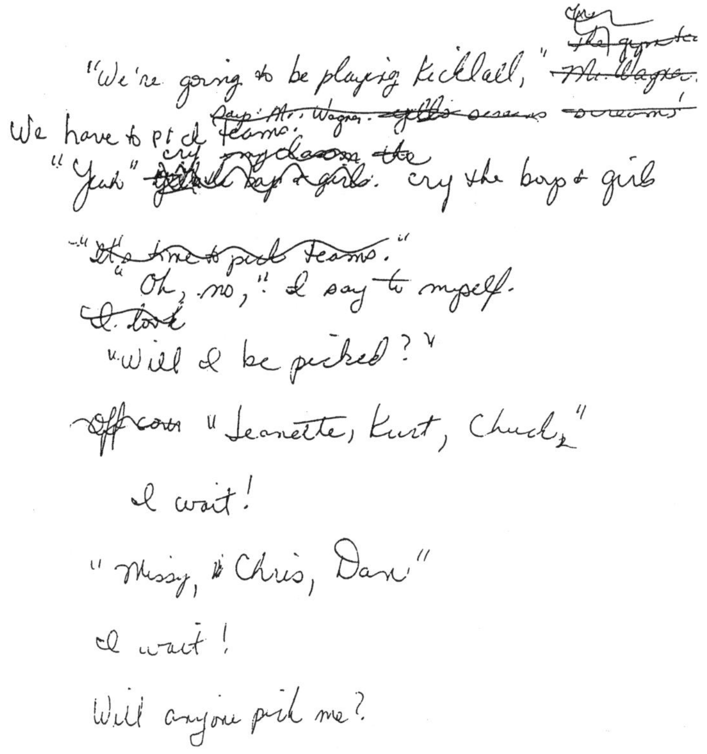

I Don't Want to be Last!

We're going to play kickball.
We have to pick teams.

Yeah! cry the boys and girls
Oh, no! I say to myself.
Will I be picked?

Jeanette, Kurt, Chuck,...
I wait!

Missy, Chris, Dan,...
I wait!

Will anyone pick me?

We're down to four students.
I don't want to be last!

Michelle, Julie, Jim,...
Two more left.
Will someone pick me?

The captain twists her face.
Begrudgingly she calls the
    next name.
I look down.
And silently wait.

She shouts across the field
I'll take...

My name is called.
I breathe a sign of relief.
Finally picked.
And not last.

both the content and the handwriting that are commendable. It always fascinates me that when kids care about their topic, they take more pride in the actual transcription.

Sharing and Celebrating Poems

Because I want students to hear good examples immediately, we do not wait until writing time is over to share notable work. Several times, we ask the kids to stop writing and to listen to and look at what a classmate has done well. This could be an entire poem or an individual element of the poem, such as the title, the beginning lines, the rhythm, a wonderful phrase or word choice. After a student stands up and reads his writing aloud, I may read it again and hold up the poem and comment on the shape, particular words, the topic. While such sharing does interrupt writing time, sharing while students are beginning a new genre serves several purposes:

*Figure 9–35   Difference between a journal
entry and a poem using the same topic and information*

> April 19, 1996
>
> Today half of the school went outside for a dedication ceremony. Our school raised enough money to plant two trees for Earth Day. The student council people talked, and the president thanked us all for contributing money to buy the trees.
>
> ---
>
> One Day Away From Earth Day
>
> Outside
> For a dedication ceremony
> Enough money raised
> To plant two trees
> Student council thanked us
> For all the money
> One day away from Earth Day
> Two new trees

Figure 9–36   A kindergartner's dictated poem

> MY MOM
>
> My mom is nice and soft
> Like a baby lamb that doesn't bite
> She tucks me in bed
> It feels warm like the summer sun
> She sings to me
> Like *the sound of music*
> Her brown hair is like cinnamon sticks
> She smiles as much as Sarah Stout
> I like her as much as I like to sing.
>
> by Alexander Boom

- It reinforces what the writer has done well and encourages him to continue.
- It shows the class what a good poem looks and sounds like.
- It gives students ideas for their own writing.
- It sets expectations for quality.

Once students are "on their way" with poetry writing, usually after a day or two, sharing during writing time is mostly discontinued so as not to disrupt the writing flow.

The sharing that takes place at the end of writing time usually involves only listening and celebrating. Because our main purpose has been to free kids up to write, to find joy and ease in writing, most students simply read their poems without a great deal of commentary from teachers or students. Sometimes, when a poem impacts students personally or they recognize superior quality, they spontaneously applaud.

Writing in the Style of Other Poets

Once students have had some initial success with writing poems, I encourage them to challenge themselves by trying out other voices or styles. We might listen to and look at Donald Graves' poems about growing up, *Baseball, Snakes, and Summer Squash*. I draw students' attention to what Graves is writing about: giggling in church, hating to eat a certain vegetable, being teased, getting a spanking, doing homework, and much more. "How many of you have had the same experiences?" Many hands are raised. I guide students to note that these poems are written in the first person, in stanzas, with conversation. After modeling, I ask the students to attempt to write in the style of Graves (see Figure 9-37).

We may also use *All the Small Poems and Fourteen More* by Valerie Worth to try our hand at writing short descriptive poems. Sometimes, weather permitting, we go outside with clipboards to closely observe an object in nature. Or, again, with upper elementary students, we may read and discuss *Cactus Poems* by Frank Asch and Ted Levin, first-person poems about desert creatures and plants. I will ask the students to try personification, beginning a poem with a question, and repeating certain lines for emphasis.

Use the poetry books and resources in The Blue Pages as well as your personal favorites, to explore and have fun with students writing various kinds of poems. Note that while students' first poems may imitate another poet—either a professional or student—this is often a necessary first step in finding their own styles and voices.

Sharing memorable students' poems can have a strong influence on peers. Notice how a second grader's poem about being nervous at a musical recital sparked another student to write about a similar experience (see Figure 9-38 on page 379).

Writing Poetry in the Content Areas

Writing poetry in the content areas offers another way to present information and to get the students to think about their knowledge in new ways. Near the end of a study about the Southwest, fourth-grade teacher Nancy Schubert and I experiment with poetry

Figure 9–37 Writing in the style of another poet, Donald Graves (student poem before adding line breaks)

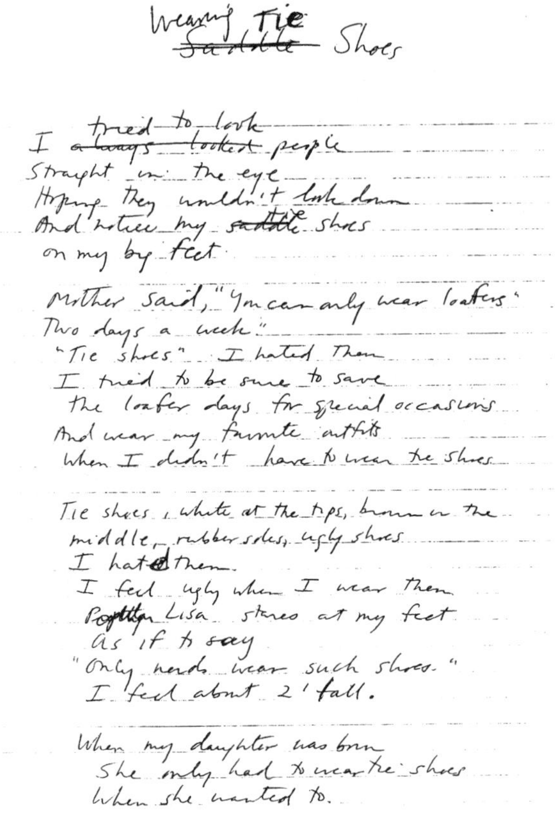
Wearing ~~Saddle~~ Tie Shoes

I ~~always looked~~ tried to look people
Straight in the eye
Hoping they wouldn't look down
And notice my ~~saddle~~ tie shoes
on my big feet

Mother said, "You can only wear loafers"
Two days a week."
"Tie shoes" I hated them
I tried to be sure to save
the loafer days for special occasions
And wear my favorite outfits
When I didn't have to wear tie shoes.

Tie shoes, white at the tips, brown in the
middle, rubber soles, ugly shoes.
I hated them.
I feel ugly when I wear them
Popular Lisa stares at my feet
as if to say
"Only nerds wear such shoes."
I feel about 2' tall.

When my daughter was born
She only had to wear tie shoes
When she wanted to.

Wearing Tie Shoes

I tried to look people
straight in the eye—
hoping they wouldn't look down
and notice my tie shoes
on my big feet.

Mother said, "You can only wear loafers
two days a week."
"Tie shoes!" I hated them.
I tried to be sure to save
the loafer days for special occasions
when I didn't have to wear tie shoes.

Tie shoes, white at the tips, brown in the
middle, rubber soles, ugly shoes
I hated them.
I feel ugly when I wear them.
Popular Lisa stares at my feet
as if to say
"Only nerds wear such shoes."
I feel about two feet tall.

When my daughter was born
she only had to wear tie shoes
when she wanted to.

by Regie Routman

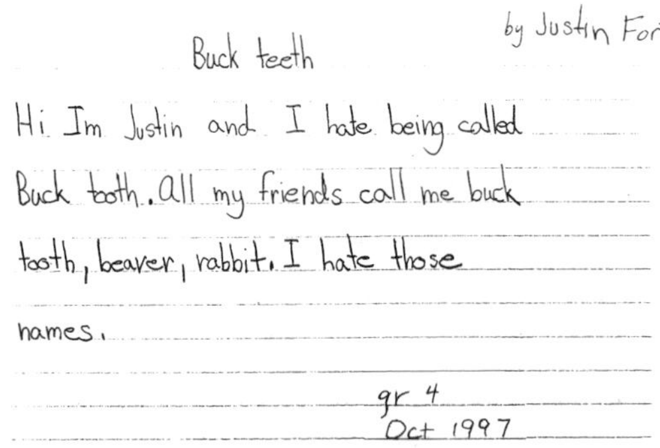
Buck teeth

by Justin Fort

Hi Im Justin and I hate being called
Buck toth. All my friends call me buck
tooth, beaver, rabbit. I hate those
names.

gr 4
Oct 1997

writing. First, we immersed students in lots of poems from relevant books such as *Cactus Poems,* by Frank Asch (1998), *Storm on the Desert,* by Carolyn Lesser (1997), and *This Big Sky,* by Pat Mora (1998).

I read and then reread several poems to the students, and then ask, "What did you notice?" We brainstorm the following list in a shared writing:

Figure 9–38 *One second-grade poet inspires another*

Violin
nexus

My   Violin   teacher

Saids   "your   up"/

no   not   me

I   wish   I   was

sick /   I'm   ^Hot pink

in   the   face /

But   I   do it!/

Hannah. T'Kindt

Piano Recitels   Jenna Stahl   May 14

I'm nervous   at piano recitels
when its   my   turn up,
I'm scared head to toe Like
a shark chasing after   me

I   go up to the   piano
sit on the   bench   and,

PLAY!

PLAY!

PLAY!

I'm not   scared   anymore

- Identical words are used at the beginning of each stanza.
- The poems are all about the same topic.
- Personification is used in many of the poems.
- The pattern changes at end.
- There is a lot of description.
- The first and last lines repeat.
- Metaphors are used in many of the poems.
- Some of the poems are humorous.
- Some of the poems pose questions.
- Sometimes the words are compatible with the poem's shape.

Nancy and I each struggle with writing a poem in front of the students before we ask the students themselves to write. Because there is sufficient modeling, they take to this writing easily and enthusiastically. See Figure 9-39 for an example of a student's poem resulting from this exercise. Note also Figure 9-40, a shared writing with first graders that presents interesting facts about animals the students had been researching. Students

Figure 9–39   A fourth grader's poem about the desert

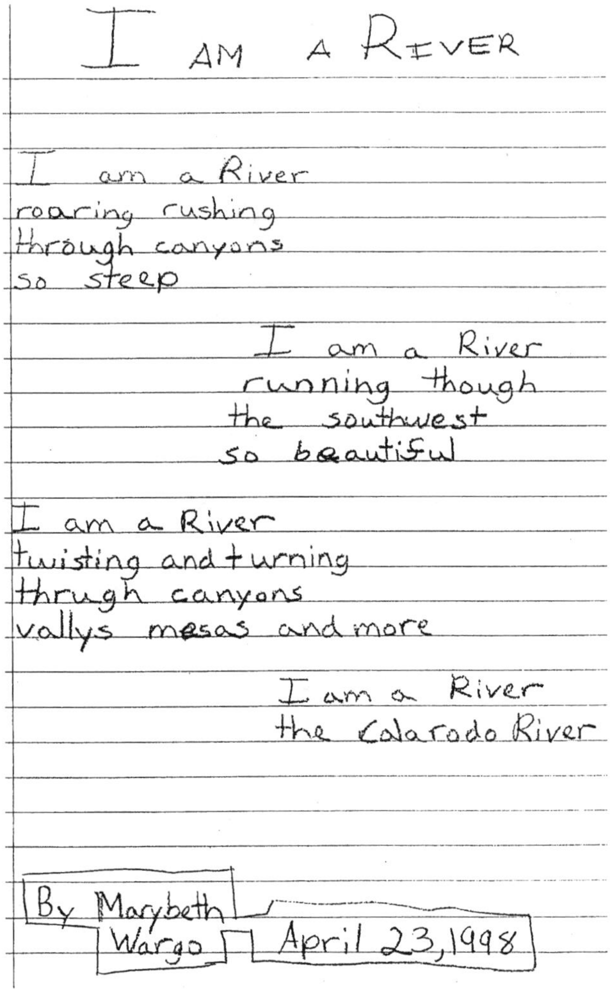

I AM A RIVER

I am a River
roaring rushing
through canyons
so steep

       I am a River
       running though
     the southwest
     so beautiful

I am a River
twisting and turning
thrugh canyons
vallys mesas and more

       I am a River
      the Colorado River

By Marybeth Wargo   April 23, 1998

loved writing and rereading this poem. Moreover, we found that because of their interest and involvement in creating the poem, they were able to better retain many of the facts that were incorporated in it.

Publishing Poetry

After students have written at least several poems, they are expected to bring their favorite one(s) to final copy. (In kindergarten and first grade, most teachers word process these for the students.) Because poems are rarely longer than a page and students have many choices for format and layout, they are typically quite willing to do minor revisions, check and correct their spelling and put their poem into a published, final form—handwritten or word-processed.

Figure 9–40   Shared poetry writing by a first-grade class, on facts learned about animals

---

Did You Know . . . ?

Did you know . . .
Koalas are often called teddy bears,
Not all black bears are black,
Penguins can make more noise than a football game,
Crocodiles were living when dinosaurs were?

Did you know . . .
A mother kangaroo's pouch has a bald baby inside,
The ostrich egg is as big as 24 chickens eggs,
There are more than 300 different kinds of parrots,
An alligator opens up its mouth to cool off?

Did you know . . .
When a baby wolf is born, the older wolves lick it,
Chimpanzees eat bugs off of each other,
The tiger's eyes glow bright red in the night,
A boa constrictor eats without chewing?

Did you know . . .
Polar bears have to teach their babies how to swim,
Sea lions are very noisy on the beach,
When pandas are first born, they are as long as from your thumb to your pinky,
The zebra's stripes look like they're painted?

Did you know . . .
The cougar is also called puma, mountain lion, and wild cat,
The cheetah has eye lines to protect its eyes from the sun,
A king cobra can't see you if you're not moving,
A hippo's leg is the same size as its teeth?

Did you know . . .
Some poeple use llama wool to knit sweaters,
Hyenas sound like they are laughing,
Buffaloes can drink up to 10 gallons of water a day,
Giraffes can hug with their necks?

Did you know . . .
Mrs. Johnston's class researched all these amazing facts?

May 1997

Student Anthologies

Publishing students' poems can be as simple or elaborate as you and the students decide. Some anthologies are a stapled booklet that includes one favorite poem, often illustrated, from each student. Others may be quite extensive with a specially designed cover and end pages, dedication page, table of contents, index, and about the poet pages. After noticing other anthologies, the teacher and students usually come up with a plan they can work with. Older students, used to extensive writing, can often manage the entire publishing project with minimal teacher guidance.

Students love receiving their own copy of the anthology, a "second edition" to take home and keep. The original, first edition, becomes a treasured part of the classroom library for the rest of the year and for years to come.

USING PICTURE BOOKS TO
INSPIRE PERSONAL NARRATIVE

When I am working in a school with students who don't like to write and who don't connect writing with their lives, I always use a great picture book as an ice breaker—to capture students' attention, engage their sensibilities, and get them thinking about their own personal narratives. Carefully chosen picture books with outstanding literary quality can be wonderful models for encouraging focused student writing. We always begin by savoring and enjoying the story as I read it aloud, with the students gathered close around me. I encourage the students to move beyond the story in our discussion of it, to connect it with their own lives, and then we focus on what the author and illustrator have done to hook us in, keep us interested, and inspire us.

For this purpose, I frequently read *Gettin' Through Thursday* (1998) by Melrose Cooper, illustrated by Nneka Bennett, as I recently did with one fourth-grade class. It is a poignant story of a close-knit family who are very resourceful in their attempts to make ends meet each week until Friday, when Mama gets paid. When Mama promises "a royal party" if one of her children makes the honor roll, Andre is jubilant—until he realizes that report card day is on Thursday, and there will be no money left over for a party. Mama creatively resolves the dilemma, and a new family tradition is happily put in place.

As we reread the story, I guide students in noticing how Cooper immediately sets the tone and draws readers in with his lead by using the character of Andre as storyteller. Looking closely at passages like the following, we focus on Andre's strong, distinctive voice:

> Mondays and Tuesdays amble by just fine. Wednesdays, we feel it comin', like an earthquake underground, makin' folks edgy before they even know why. And the next day, my family and I grit all we got toward gettin' through Thursday. That's because payday at Mama's school where she's a lunch lady doesn't come till Friday.

We look closely at the beautifully drawn illustrations that portray both the family's financial struggle and deep concern for one another. We notice how conversation keeps the story moving and helps us understand the characters—what they're thinking and feeling as well as experiencing. We talk about the many interesting verbs—*grumbled, whirled, stomped*—that zero right in on the action, and the many well-crafted lines, such as, "Every minute crept by, slow as a wounded snake." We reread the satisfying ending and talk about how it lends closure to the story, how the last paragraph connects with the second one (above) by repeating parts of it, and how the reader is left, with Andre and his family, feeling changed. We talk about how writers deliberately craft their words with an audience in mind.

Next, I give the students a homework assignment, in which I ask them to think about a family tradition that means a lot to them and come prepared to write about it the following day. We list some possibilities: birthdays, holidays, shopping, gift giving, meals. I describe the tradition that I plan to write about—going to the farmers' market every Saturday with my husband, Frank. I let them know that these traditions, once written, will be compiled into a class book, as a way to celebrate each other and to get to know each other better. I tell them that every class member will get a copy of our book of traditions.

Because the children I do this exercise with are typically students who are not used to choice in writing, I tightly structure the assignment. Each piece about family tradition must include:

- What the tradition is and how you participate in it
- Why it's important to you (why you love it)
- How it makes you feel

When I meet with students the next day, we review the writing assignment (which is posted on a chart in the classroom) and its purpose. Before I ask students to begin to write, I think aloud in front of them and begin to write my story on large chart paper. I make sure that they understand that my first attempt is a draft, that I am just getting my ideas down to be revised later. I am deliberate in trying to think of an interesting beginning, but emphasize that writers don't usually come up with a good lead on their very first attempt.

After I have modeled the exercise, I engage two students in conversation. This dialogue reinforces for students the expectations of the assignment: that they are expected to finish their drafts and check to be sure they have included all three required components of the assignment. As they begin to write, I circulate among them to answer any questions and offer encouragement. I spend time quietly conversing with students who still "don't know what to write." Once everyone is fully involved in their writing, I go back to my chart paper and continue my own story.

Over the next several days, we proceed in much the same way that we do with other writing projects. We have whole-class share at the end of each day's writing time. The teacher and I also conference one-on-one with students as they revise. We create an editing expectations list, and students are expected to peer edit before the teacher serves as final editor. I teach minilessons as needed. For this project, I focus on writing an interesting lead and choosing words carefully.

I ask each student to attempt at least two leads. First I demonstrate by writing two new leads to my piece. Using the big chart paper I am writing on, I cut and paste in front of them to add in two sentences (see Figure 9-41). Many students subsequently do similar cutting and pasting independently. Final copies reflect my teacher modeling. Note Johnny's piece on the Fourth of July and how he has improved his lead based on my model (see Figure 9-42 on page 385).

To complete this project, students work diligently and willingly. Their published pieces reflect their efforts and pride in writing a story that matters to them. Although the writing topic is assigned, students have a great deal of choice within the required framework, and they understand the purpose and audience. I am convinced that the high quality of their efforts is directly linked to the inspiration the literature provided.

*Figure 9–41   My beginning draft on going to the farmer's market
with a "cut and paste" addition*

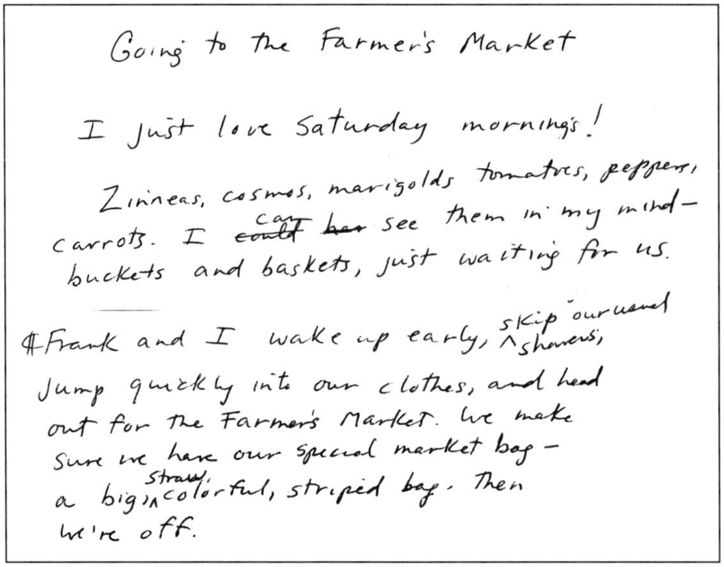

Going to the Farmer's Market

I just love Saturday mornings!

Zinneas, cosmos, marigolds tomatoes, peppers,
carrots. I ~~could her~~ *can* see them in my mind—
buckets and baskets, just waiting for us.

₰Frank and I wake up early, *skip our usual* ∧*showers,*
jump quickly into our clothes, and head
out for the Farmer's Market. We make
sure we have our special market bag —
a big∧*straw* colorful, striped bag. Then
we're off.

MORE AUTHENTIC WRITING

Autobiographies

Second-grade teacher Bev Sullivan ends each year with a wonderful autobiography-writing project. Each child writes and illustrates the story of his life, which is published in book form, complete with color photographs that have been scanned into a computer. Students and families love this special "keepsake."

Bev structures the project as follows:

- Birth
- Events I remember (significant happenings)
- Life right now (friends, school, house)
- Future (career goals, plans)

Students, who have been engaged in writing all year long, at this point respond knowledgeably and well to suggestions for revision. We teach many how to cut and paste to organize their material better and to add important details. Most do the final typing using the classroom computer and small, individual, portable word processors (see Figure 9-43 on page 386).

*Figure 9–42 Johnny's tradition piece, influenced by teacher modeling
(Note cut and paste)*

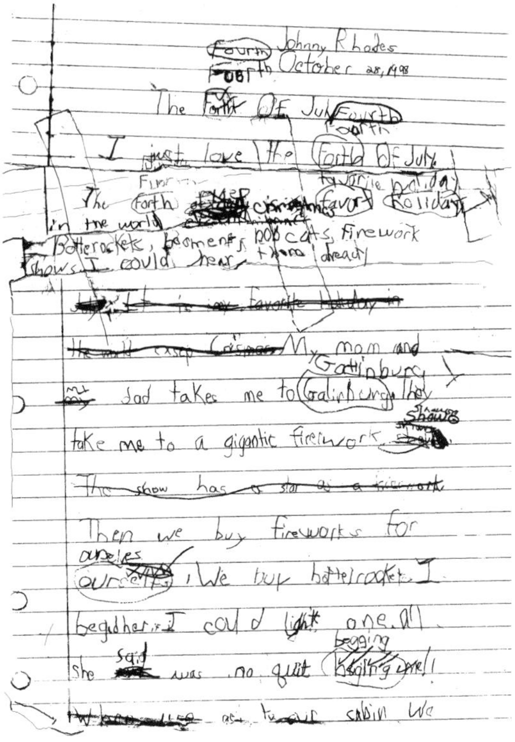

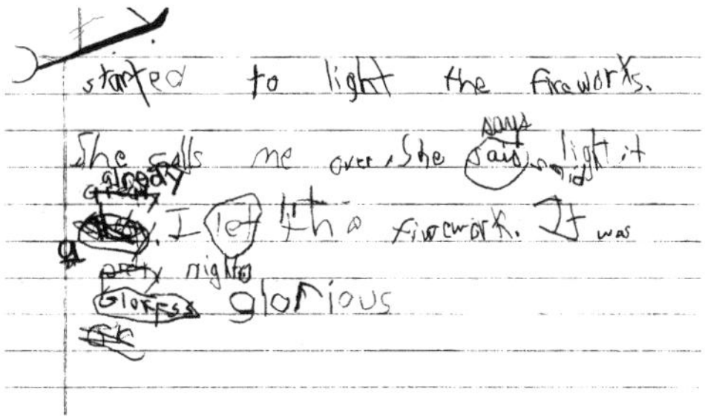

The Fourth of July

by Johnny Rhodes

I just love the Fourth of July. The Fourth is my favorite holiday in the world except Christmas. Bottle rockets, boomerangs, bobcats, firework shows. I could hear them already.

My mom and my dad take me to Gattinburg. They take me to a gigantic firework show. Then we buy fireworks for ourselves. We buy bottle rockets. I begged her if I could light one. All she said was, "No. Quit begging me."

When we got to our cabin, we started to light the fireworks. She calls me over. She says, "Light it." I light the fireworks. It was a glorious night.

Memoirs

While young students are comfortable writing about the factual happenings of their lives in autobiographies, memoirs present challenges because they are more sophisticated. Writers select particular life experiences and reveal something about themselves. Memoirs have a you-are-there immediacy and go beyond facts to include insights into personality and family and the writer's version of "the truth." Techniques of fiction writing, such as dialogue and descriptive detail, are usually incorporated into memoir, with the "I"—the author—developed as the main character.

I have not tried memoir writing before grade four. By age nine or ten, students are able to look back on their lives and choose particular incidents as revealing of who they are. I often have them start with a "life time line" to jog their memories of key happenings. I have found that the time line is a good way to brainstorm life story possibilities. For example, when I made my own time line, stories emerged that I had not anticipated or thought about recently: how jealousy over my newborn sister played out, memories of shyness with my first boyfriend, how much I enjoyed my grandmother's attention when I was in high school. Then I chose one of those stories and began to write in front of the students before expecting them to write.

Figure 9–43 Two pages from a second grader's autobiography

The question my parents asked my big brother Stephen, when I was born, was should we take her home. Stephen, fortunately said yes. If he didn't say yes, my parents probably would have taken me home anyway whether he liked it or not.   **3**

On my first birthday, when I was turning 1, I didn't know what to do with the candle. "Should I spit at it? Should I take it out and throw it? What should I do?" I thought. So Stephen (my big brother) blew it out for me!   **4**

Some of us have had great success using *When I Was Your Age: Original Stories About Growing Up (Vols. 1 and 2)*, edited by Amy Ehrlich, for models of "growing up" stories. (See The Blue Pages, "Writing in Multiple Genres.") For example, after reading and discussing the stories included in Ehrlich's text, Julie Beers modeled what it was like growing up with a wonderful father who was severely physically disabled, and students wrote their own personal stories.

See *Turning Memories into Memoirs* by Denis Ledoux for other ideas about writing memoirs.

Essays

The dictionary definition of *essay* is "a short literary composition on a particular theme or subject, usually in prose and generally analytic, speculative, or interpretative." An essay states an opinion and provides supporting evidence.

Donna Maxim began teaching essay writing to her third and fourth graders after a colleague loaned her *The Second Nature of Things*, a collection of well-written one-page essays about nature by Will Curtis. The essays were about topics her students were already familiar with—birds, trees, animals, insects—because of their long-term curriculum focus on woods and wildlife.

After reading the essays to and with the students, Donna and her class made a list of what they observed about them. For example, the essays were written in five to seven short paragraphs, directly quoted scientists, sometimes used metaphor and simile, did not necessarily give the main message in the first paragraph, gave facts and opinions, and occasionally included a poem or nursery rhyme.

Donna asked her students to think about five things having to do with nature that they might want to write their own essay about, and then she gave them a week to seek out resources, describe their messages, and make a final decision on their topic choice. In a writing minilesson she talked about how she chose a topic for her own essay, inspired by a recent newspaper article on right whales, and how she might start her essay with a fact, opinion, poem, or quote (perhaps from a newspaper article).

Other interrelated minilessons in science included recording in their science journals—setting up a resource page, how to list resources (title, author, and page numbers). Some minilessons in writing included choices for interesting leads (looking back at the Curtis possibilities), paragraph indenting, punctuating quotes, and essay organization.

Essay writing provided Donna's students with an opportunity to learn about a new genre while further exploring a topic they were already familiar with, woods and wildlife, and to broaden their learning through writing and by making presentations to peers. In addition, many of their essay-writing minilessons—such as picking a good title and creating a provocative lead—could be applied to other genres.

With Donna's guidance and Curtis' essays as models, the essays the students wrote were inspiring (see Figure 9-44). Donna noted the following about the experience:

> Because of my discovery of a new resource of age-level-appropriate literature that connected with a yearlong science study of woods and wildlife, I was able to create for my students a learning opportunity that crossed the curriculum. We researched and wrote together. In writing workshop, I demonstrated how I explored my choices and made my decisions in my own essay. We learned together about writing in a new genre. In reading and science workshop we read essays, investigated resources for the variety of woods and wildlife topics we had chosen to write about, and learned how to go about—and the importance of—recording information in our science journals.

For guidance in writing personal essays, see Don Murray's wonderful piece, "Trying on the Essay" (Murray 1996, 56–76), in which he states that "the most effective essays . . . are those that find a way for the writer to reveal a process of thought that invites the reader to think alongside the writer." See also *Essay Writing Made Easy* by Ann Birch in The Blue Pages.

Interviews

In beginning a new school year, teachers of all grades find interviews to be a great way for class members to get to know one another. In addition, interviews can be used to celebrate and show respect for individual and cultural similarities and differences. Such open, respectful talk—guided by teacher modeling and coaching—helps build community in the classroom.

Figure 9–44   A fourth grader's draft and finished essay

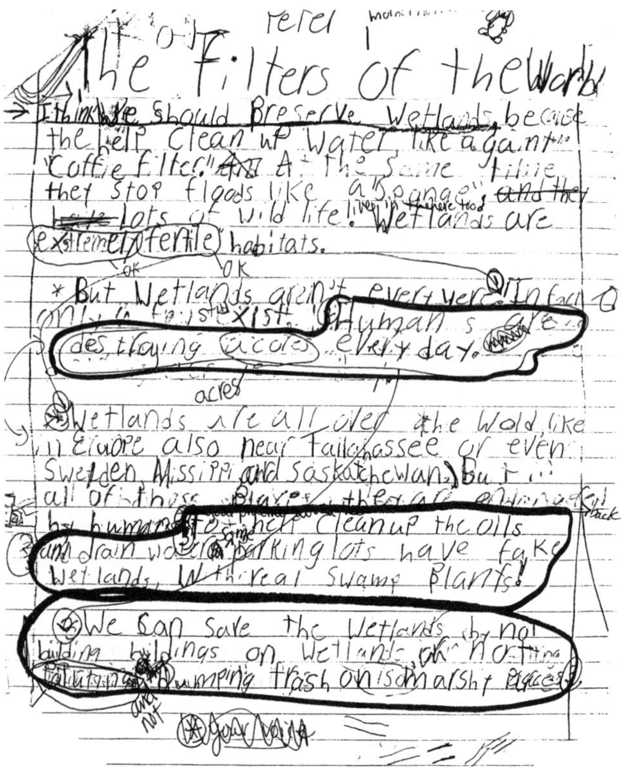

The Filters of the World

by Peter Hull

I think we should preserve wetlands, because they help clean up water like a giant coffee filter and they stop floods like a sponge. The plant roots keep the dirt in place and that helps clean the water. Wetlands are also home for a lot of wildlife including the great blue heron, Canada geese, the red-winged blackbird, dragonflies, muskrats, frogs, ducks, mosquitoes, and raccoons. Wetlands are extremely fertile habitats. There are minerals in the soil and the soil is very moist which attracts plants and insects.

Wetlands are all over the world—in Sweden, near Tallahassee, in Mississippi, and even in Saskatchewan. But wetlands aren't everywhere. In fact, only a few still exist today and these places are endangered by humans.

Humans are destroying acres of wetlands everyday. Some parking lots have fake wetlands in them with real swamp plants. We can save the wetlands by not building on the wetlands, not polluting the wetlands, and not dumping our trash on marshy places. We can help clean up the wetlands by cleaning up the oils that are spilled. We can also help save the wetlands by not draining the water.

In getting started with interviews, many teachers conduct a shared writing/brainstorming session to generate initial questions. Interesting questions promote engaging responses. Such questions might include the following:

- What do you like to do in your free time?
- What has been the best time in your life so far?
- What can you do very well?
- What's really hard for you?
- What person in your life do you most admire? Why?

- What is your favorite place? Explain.
- What are your likes and dislikes about school?
- What goals do you have for yourself—for now and for the future?

Often, the teacher will be interviewed first, as a model. Interviews can then be done as a whole-class shared writing—with one student at a time serving as the interview subject, as the "person of the day," perhaps—or in small groups with one person serving as scribe, or with partners.

Joan Servis and Julie Beers always start out their year by having students interview one another, and this becomes their first assigned writing project. Students continue to use their interviewing skills all year long, as they profile members of the school community for the monthly classroom magazine.

Kindergarten teacher Karen Sher has her class conduct interviews with guest visitors throughout the year; the interviews are then compiled in a book that includes Polaroid photos. Interview subjects are usually relatives (parents, grandparents, aunts, uncles, baby-sitters). Because Karen wants her students to focus first on oral language—listening to the speaker and posing relevant questions—no writing is done until after the guest leaves. At that time, the class reconstructs the interview by brainstorming what the speaker talked about. Karen notes, "I am always amazed by all they remember."

See *Classroom Interviews* by Paula Rogovin in "Multiple Genres" in The Blue Pages for using interviews across the curriculum.

Visitor's Guide to the Classroom

Individually, in small groups, or as a whole-class shared writing, students can be asked to create a written guide to inform visitors about their classroom or school. These guides can be a great help to teachers, as questions that are frequently asked by visitors can be answered in their pages.

When we had a local congressman visit, many teachers had their students write a guide for him, both so that he would know what to look for in our instruction of reading and writing, and so that he could see what we valued.

Writing a visitor's guide is also a good way to determine what your students believe is being taught in the classroom. For example, when a group of third graders wrote that good writers must spell every word correctly (even in drafts), the teacher realized that she had been overemphasizing this point.

Instructions, Directions, and "How To" Books

When students are asked to explain in writing the steps involved in playing a game, getting to a particular place, following a recipe, taking care of a pet, or constructing something from a kit, they learn how difficult it is to write in a sequential, organized fashion that the reader can easily understand. Writing directions and instructions is great practice for organizing ideas in a detailed, clear, logical fashion.

Authentic Writing Activities—
Quick, Easy, and Inspirational

Not all authentic writing has to be long or involved. Students love "short and sweet" writing because they can relate easily to the topic, and not much writing and editing are required. This type of writing has similar benefits for teachers.

Positive Comments About Fellow Students

Years ago I read a magazine article about a well-worn sheet of compliments that had been found tucked inside the wallet of a young man who had died. These statements, written by classmates during his early school years, had meant so much to the man that he had carried them around with him always. The story was resurrected in the 1993 book *Chicken Soup for the Soul: 101 Stories to Open the Heart and Rekindle the Spirit,* compiled by Jack Canfield and Mark Victor Hansen. I often thought it would be terrific for kids to give each other such a gift, and one year, after I had discussed the idea with Julie Beers, Julie decided to try it.

During one of the final weeks of the school year, Julie had her students write down a positive comment about each of their classmates. The writing was done in the classroom, so that students could think and write while looking at their subjects. Julie also wrote a compliment about each student. Then she compiled all the comments, which were written down on individual sheets for each student (see Figure 9-45 on page 391 for an excerpt), into a class booklet. The project was a huge success. The kids loved it and used the booklet, "Positive Comments About the Best Class in the World!" as a treasured fourth-grade memory book.

Advice

Everyone loves to give advice, and kids are no exception. In the 1994 book *Wit and Wisdom from the Peanut Butter Gang,* compiled by H. Jackson Brown, Jr., children of all ages give advice based on their life experiences. Using this book as a model, we have had students write their own advice—for families, classmates, and future students. What I love about having students write advice is that the writing is short, usually one sentence, and is often poignant and humorous (see Figure 9-46). Going to final copy is quick and easy. Kindergarten and first-grade teachers often turn these into big books, which students love to reread. Older students may write columns modeled on "Dear Abby." One group of fourth graders initiated a schoolwide advice column, complete with a drop-off box for questions and a monthly edition of the latest questions and responses. Other students like to include such a column as part of a classroom newspaper or magazine.

Figure 9–45   A fourth graders' positive comments

Madeline

Positive Comments About the Best Class in the World!

Laura: I love the way you are always by my side, and you have been a great friend the whole time you have been at Ohanay.

Xamira: I think your glasses make you look beautiful, I wish I could have your glass

Lindsay: I love your blue eyes and how they sparkle as you enter the room

Zoe: I love how you always are bringing up cows whenever there is co conversation yet!

Deante: I love your great smile and how you stick up for us girls.

Katie: I have always wanted your long brown hair. I think it looks so beautiful hanging down your back.

Kodak Moments

Many teachers photograph their students throughout the year and use these photos for writing in a variety of ways. Fourth-grade teacher Leslie Bakkila photographed classroom moments—such as science experiments, literature conversations, and field trips—that most parents didn't get to see, and compiled them into an ongoing class book for students, visitors, and families. Students volunteered to write captions describing the action of the photographs.

Loretta Martin takes pictures all year long of her students and keeps a photo envelope for each student. As she develops new film, she puts special photos in students' envelopes. Then as students update their portfolios, they choose snapshots that show them in a learning situation, and they write captions to go with the photos.

Lee Sattelemeyer and other teachers use their school's digital camera to photograph students. Then they put those photos onto the computer and students can print them out immediately and add them to their writing project or portfolio.

Figure 9–46 A kindergartner's advice

Don't mess with a big brother when he's angry.

Coming Attractions

Karen Lum's first graders have made brochures for incoming first graders to help orient them to the classroom (see Figure 9-47).

A principal I know gives a welcome booklet to every new entering student. Each page is headed with the name and job of an adult member of the school community—principal, classroom and special subject teachers, secretaries, custodians, nurse, and so on. Students are given time—with a veteran student as guide—to walk from room to room and meet each adult. Then, either the student guide or adult writes comments on the profile pages pertaining to each adult's role in the school. A brief welcome message is often included.

Captions, Labels, Signs, and Posters

Students can be encouraged to create and post useful environmental messages, such as school and classroom signs and posters championing school spirit, safety on the playground, decorum in the lunchroom, or proper use of the drinking fountain. Kindergarten students love to make labels and signs in their play areas. One kindergarten class made posters and tacked them up all around the school when their hamster was lost.

Figure 9–47   A first-grade Coming Attractions brochure

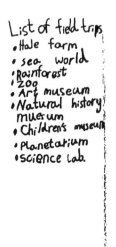

List of field trips
• Hale farm
• sea world
• Rainforest
• Zoo
• Art museum
• Natural history museum
• Children's museum
• Planetarium
• science lab.

The Best First grade

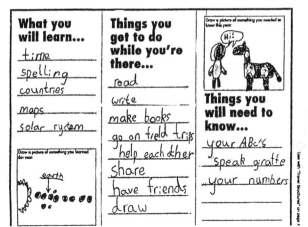

What you will learn...
time
spelling
countries
maps
solar system

Draw a picture of something you learned this year.
earth

Things you get to do while you're there...
read
write
make books
go on field trips
help each other
share
have friends
draw

Draw a picture of something you needed to know this year.
Hi!

Things you will need to know...
your ABc's
speak giraffe
your numbers

Students of all ages can label and write captions for snapshots depicting learning in progress that teachers or students have taken. (Some lucky teachers have been able to purchase disposable cameras for each student for special projects.) Photos and captions can be used for conducting science experiments; for portfolio documentation; for a classroom yearbook; or for informing families about classroom learning situations.

Announcements

Many classrooms have an announcement board where students and teachers post daily happenings, good news, and upcoming events.

Suggestions and Requests

Some teachers and principals have a suggestion box available for students. Students are invited to recommend changes in classroom procedures, the lunch program, and so on. For example, if a student wants to request a seat change, he may use the suggestion box to write to a teacher stating the reasons for his request.

Messages

Message boards can be used to facilitate in-class communication. Students write, post, and receive signed messages to other students and the teacher at a designated time.

Lists

List making is essential for most of us. Lists are a quick, efficient way to group items together for such purposes as recording, buying, organizing, recalling, saving, planning, and evaluating. Especially in the early grades, kids love making lists of all kinds.

At the end of each day, Maureen Landis and her students do a shared writing to recall major learning experiences. The daily list is posted on a Monday–Friday bulletin board. On Friday, when students write letters to their parents to inform them about their week, students use the bulletin board to jog their memory of the week's key learning events and experiences.

Bookmarks

Students can design their own bookmarks, which may include favorite quotes, original sayings about reading, or personal reading goals. Laminating bookmarks makes them durable.

Bookmarks can also be made for each guided reading book. Noting specific page numbers, students can jot down questions, words they don't understand, and/or key ideas for discussion (see page 121).

Calendars

Students—even secondary students—love to personalize their own monthly calendars and record important events, holidays, school functions, due dates for assignments, and personal reminders.

Create a template to reuse each month, a rectangular grid that has seven lines with boxes going across (for the days of the week) and five lines with boxes going down (for the numbered days of the month). With teacher guidance, students can record various messages and important happenings.

RETHINKING ASSUMPTIONS ABOUT WRITING IN KINDERGARTEN

Most writing genres can be taught successfully and usefully to very young children. In my experience, I have learned that kindergarten students, like all students, enjoy writing of all kinds: lists, cards, letters, invitations, recipes, memos, picture books, stories, poems, book reviews, and advice. Additionally, the issues that surface with writing in kindergarten apply across the grades.

One April, I asked Christine Hoegler which type of writing her kindergartners like best. "I don't know," she answered. "Let's ask them. We'll do a survey." Christine and the students brainstormed the different kinds of writing they'd done during the school year, and Christine wrote these down on a chart: journals, lists, research, letters, poems, book reviews, books. Then she gave each student a half sheet of $8^1/_2 \times 11$-inch paper, and each recorded what their favorite writing was. When this was done, Christine gathered the class together, arranged their papers on the floor according to the writing preferences they had listed, and asked the students the following questions (their responses follow in parentheses):

- What do you notice? ("Only one person picked journals.")
- Which category did most students pick? ("Research.")
- Which are tied for second place? ("Poems and book reviews.")
- What surprises you about these choices? ("No one chose writing books. Only one person chose lists.")

Christine then asked the six children who chose research to explain why they preferred that form. The responses were as follows:

- I love to go to the library and answer my questions.
- I like to ask questions and try to find the answers.
- I like looking up books.
- I like to find out mysteries.
- I like to read encyclopedias.
- I love to find out new information.

When we asked the students what they thought was the most difficult form, most said journals. Not surprisingly, the writing they found the easiest and most fun was also their favorite.

Given the amount of time most kindergarten teachers spend on weekly journal writing in our district, these results—which I duplicated informally with other kindergarten teachers I work with—are quite stunning. They raise some interesting questions:

- Why do journals at all? Or, should we refer to this segment as "diary writing" (a more child-friendly term) or call the journal a "writing book"?
- Why not model many genres and give students choice based on personal preference?

Even though journals can be helpful in giving teachers a formal record of student writing useful in documenting growth, we've discovered over the years that it's important for teachers of very young students to model many genres and authentic forms of writing, and to expect students to attempt to write in these genres.

Expanding Writing in Kindergarten

When I begin working with kindergarten students in Susan Mear's classroom, whose writing up to that point had been primarily in journals, I introduce myself as a person who loves to read and write and does lots of it. I begin by reading two favorite books, *Zoom* by Istvan Banyai (Viking, 1995), a marvelous wordless book that we have great fun discussing, and *So Much,* by Trish Cooke (Candlewick Press, 1994), a captivating family story that the children delight in acting out on the second reading. Next, I talk with the students about how I use writing in my own life.

I have brought to school the letters, stamped and addressed but not sealed, that I've written the night before: two thank-you letters (to friends who had invited me to dinner), a get-well card (for a teacher having surgery), a congratulations card (for a friend getting married), and a business letter (to my publisher). Except for the business letter, which is typed, the others are handwritten on beautiful blank cards. I read each card to the students, place it in the appropriate envelope, lick the envelope, and seal the contents. They understand that I will mail these letters today. I go on to show them some favorite blank cards from my collection, including postcards, which I intend to use for future writing. We discuss what they notice about my cards: that they are of different sizes, shapes, colors, and design, that they vary in layout, and that some open from top to bottom and others from side to side.

Together, we make a chart of the kinds of writing they might choose to do that day: notes, greeting cards, letters, birthday cards, letters to friends, get-well cards, as well as books, journal entries, and poems. Then we do a shared writing on chart paper and write a get-well note to a student who is in the hospital. We underline the words for the greeting and closing, *dear* and *love,* so that students can reference those words easily, and we talk about the format of a letter and how you have to be sure to sign your name. In preparation for today's writing, Susan has all kinds of interesting paper, cards, and envelopes available for the children to use.

Before students begin writing individually, we asked them what kind of writing they are going to do and what they want their message to be. We review all the things that they can do if they don't know how to write a word: ask a friend, stretch out the sounds, look at the laminated word card on the table (which includes several high-frequency words), check the posted word list (see Photo 9-2 on page 397), use books and messages in the room. Then they get to work. We get a variety of writing, such as get-well cards to grandparents, greetings to family members, lists, notes to friends, a letter to Santa, a

Photo 9–2   Getting ready to write notes and letters in kindergarten

thank-you card for a new dog, a letter to Mom telling her to have a happy day. (See Figure 9-48.) One student designs paper for others to use for writing. Interestingly, not one of the students chooses to do a journal entry. Toni Gibson, the special education aide, notes that students' engagement is high—higher than it is during their journal-writing sessions. Kids are attentive for over an hour—which includes time for sharing and celebrating. Although students will later hand deliver or send their letters and cards, for now, we collect them all. Susan and Toni want to make copies of some of the pieces for students' portfolios. They continue to make such copies throughout the year to demonstrate the students' growth.

Susan noted the following about the experience: "What impressed me the most was the depth of the writing and the growth that took place from children working on their own with just limited beginning sound knowledge. They had to learn phonics for their own purposes, and they did!"

Figure 9–48   Notes by kindergartners: Writing for relevant purposes and audiences

Dear Kyle's Mom,
  Thank you for letting me
run away to your house.

Susan and I continue to work together for several months. We demonstrate many kinds of writing and provide a variety of paper and writing utensils, whatever our imaginations, budget, art room supply, and family donations make possible. Susan devotes an entire wall in the classroom to reminding students of writing possibilities. While we are working together, a team from *Teaching K–8* visits to do a story (May 1995, 27–31). The morning they come, I am demonstrating how to write a book review, and that demonstration is ultimately featured on the magazine's cover.

Since that first time, going beyond journal writing with Susan, I have been invited to work with many kindergarten teachers to expand the types of writing very young children can do. Particularly amazing to me have been the wonderful poems kindergarten kids write so freely (see pages 364–382). Most noteworthy, however, is the increased level of engagement that students demonstrate when they are able to choose, not just a topic in an assigned journal, but from a wide range of real-world writing possibilities.

I love going into kindergarten classrooms and sharing my favorite books and life stories with students. Christine Banks notes, "Your natural enthusiasm when you visited my room created a great deal of energy for the students. 'Mrs. Routman's coming. Yeah! Look what I'm writing about!'"

Sometimes, after I have shown students how I always write on beautiful cards, the children design cards as part of an art project, and these personally designed cards can really motivate kids to write. For some students, designing their own paper is very important. In preparation for letter writing, Christine Banks has her students design beautiful blank cards with crayon-resist technique. Students first do a crayon design on white tag board. They then go over the crayon using watercolor paint, which sets the design. After they have completed this project, Christine notes how eager students were to write letters using their personally designed stationery.

Valuing Dictation

Dictation in kindergarten (or for any emerging writer) is a terrific way to show a child what it means to be a writer. Unburdened by transcription, the child is free to focus on his story or message. With teacher guidance and encouragement, the child is asked to verbally create a scenario, including characters, action, and a beginning, middle, and ending. Many kindergarten teachers now include dictation in their writing programs.

For years, dictation was discouraged and devalued because many felt that it gave children the message that they were not writers. However, the objective of dictation is to allow students to focus on creativity, use their imagination, and create stories—vital processes for all writers. Journal writing, or writing a message, serves a different purpose, which is to focus on the nuts and bolts of transferring thought to writing—producing a text by connecting letters with sounds and drawing a picture that matches the writing.

While dictation in itself does not particularly appeal to most young children, adding dramatization to it can. Renowned educator and writer Vivian Paley found that the success of dictation relied "on the promise of dramatization." When students dramatize their stories, the stories come to life for the whole class and can transform the classroom (Cooper 1993, 71).

Kindergarten teacher Karen Sher uses dictation several times a week. She is fortunate to have a few parent volunteers who she in-services in the process. Besides having students dictate stories that will be dramatized by the class (see Cooper 1993 for procedures), she also has them participate in a dictation writing center. Most children draw pictures at this time, and she tries to write down what they tell her during "free choice" time.

Continuing the Discussion About Writing in Kindergarten

Karen Sher asks about writing every day in kindergarten. She wants to know if anyone does it, not just the writing centers, but formal, daily writing with teacher guidance. One of her big questions is how much to push those kindergartners who do not choose to write. How much writing is a must for every kindergartner? While she and her colleagues have formal journal writing once a week, Karen is asking about daily writing because she has noticed that the same five children choose writing as a free choice activity. She is concerned that the rest of the class is only writing once a week during journal time.

Toni Gibson, a kindergarten aide, makes a similar observation. "The kids who are better readers and writers continuously choose to read and write," she explains:

They incorporate literate behaviors into their play. When given free choice, they choose literacy as opposed to playing with blocks or in the housekeeping area. Even when they do choose housekeeping or blocks, they use reading and writing as they participate in those activities. For example, in pretending they're in the doctor's office, they might read as they wait for the doctor. Or, as the doctor, they're writing prescriptions and notes saying whether or not the patient can go back to school.

Susan Mears shares that ever since she has introduced many kinds of writing into her classroom, most children do not choose journal writing—a strong indicator that journals are part of the teacher's agenda and not one that kids necessarily understand or value. Susan begins alternative writing early in the year with "Yes–No" surveys. She makes forms that have a student-generated question on top, such as "Have you lost a tooth yet?" and students go around the room and survey their classmates, checking "yes" or "no." Pretty soon, they are able to recognize these two words and copy them. Before long, they're writing them independently. Around December she moves to list writing and brings in toy catalogs. Kids make lists, which they are invited to take home with them, of what they want for their holiday gifts. Next come the "things to do" lists (lists very familiar to adults!), and initially these lists are made up of the names of the learning centers in the room. Still later, letter and card writing are introduced, followed by research, poetry, and book reviews.

How much writing is a "must" in kindergarten seems less important than making sure that the writing (and writing demonstration) is purposeful. For example, journal writing can be effective to kindergartners who see some purpose in the activity. Kindergartners who express dislike for journal writing typically have no idea why they are keeping journals. Karen Sher reinforces the purpose of journal writing with the following statement to her students: "When I see your journals, it helps me teach you better."

My observation has been that when the writing has significance for children—that is, when they understand its purpose and can connect it to its function in literacy—they seek to engage in the writing, not just fulfill an assignment. On a daily basis, it is our job as teachers to demonstrate and support how and why writers work, what they write, and how that writing impacts and enriches all aspects of people's lives—reading, thinking, communicating, creating, learning, and reflecting.

FINAL REFLECTIONS

Before we can expect students to write well in any genre, we need to apprentice them—and ourselves—to experts in the craft. We and our students need to first immerse ourselves in noteworthy, compelling literature of the chosen genre and then read it together, discuss it, and notice writers' techniques, personal styles, forms, word choices, leads, descriptions, power to persuade, ability to forge a connection with the reader, and more. Teaching writing is likely to be a superficial endeavor without such accompanying in-depth study and conversations.

Likewise, if our students are to see themselves as writers they need to see excellent examples of writing by students just like them—writing done for purposes and audiences that matter. Finally, we teachers need to find the courage to show students our own writing as well as to demonstrate writing by thinking and writing aloud in front of them. You and they will reap the benefits with inspired writers who do quality work.

CONTINUING THE CONVERSATION

• ***Come to agreement in your school on which writing genres will be taught at each grade level.*** Seek feedback from other teachers, administrators, and parents as well as courses of study and state and national guidelines. This is no easy task, but it is a vital one. Otherwise, what gets taught may be based on the whim or preference of a particular teacher. Then, upper-grade teachers rightly complain that they are receiving students who don't know how to write anything but journal entries and stories.

• ***Plan how you will teach particular genres to your students.*** Consult with a colleague you respect. Be sure you demonstrate writing in the genre before you expect your students to write. If possible, demonstrate your writing for students when your colleague has a planning period and can observe and give you feedback.

• ***Review how you are connecting literature and reading to writing.*** Even if you are working with older students, add reading and discussing picture books to your program. Guide students in observing what writers do. Read or revisit *Beyond Words: Picture Books for Older Readers and Writers* (Benedict and Carlisle 1992), *Picture Books: An Annotated Bibliography with Activities for Teaching Writing* (Culham and Spandel 1998; see annotation, page 28b), and *Lasting Impressions: Weaving Literature into the Writing Workshop* (Harwayne 1992).

CHAPTER 10

Spelling and Word Study in the Reading-Writing Classroom

Word work connected to reading in a first-grade guided reading group

> Word study becomes useful and instructive when it is based on students' levels of development and when appropriate words and patterns are explored through interesting and engaging activities.
>
> —*Donald Bear and Shane Templeton*

I don't know any teacher who doesn't struggle with how to teach spelling. Teachers worry they're not doing enough, that they're doing too much, and that they don't know what and how they should be teaching. Spelling remains as hot and confusing a topic as ever.

Because the teaching of spelling remains an area of uncertainty and concern for so many of us—and because learning to spell is part of becoming literate—we must become knowledgeable in this area. That means taking the time to study and consider how children learn to spell and translating that information—along with our classroom research and experiences—into a strong spelling program for our students. This is no easy matter. Not only are most of us overwhelmed by other curriculum demands, but sorting out and rethinking what we need to know about teaching spelling is time-consuming and challenging. This is why it is so important that as professionals we get together with our colleagues and share what we are doing, both what's working and what's not. As in teaching reading and writing, there is no one best way.

This chapter focuses on the interrelated topics of spelling and word study, which encompasses phonics. Some experts believe that invented spelling helps children explore phonics relationships (Wilde 1997, 75). I have also included a section on teaching vocabulary. Use the extensive, annotated spelling resources in The Blue Pages to educate yourself. See also "Integrating Spelling into the Reading-Writing Classroom" (*Invitations*) for additional, relevant content and resources. Think about organizing a spelling study group at your school to begin professional conversations about this important subject.

LEARNING TO SPELL

My experience has been that teachers who have the strongest reading-writing classrooms turn out the best spellers. That is, teachers who concentrate on spelling as part of the reading-writing-composing process and as a separate, focused word study based on students' needs, developmental levels, and interests are the most effective in terms of teaching students to spell.

Feedback from a Group of Fourth Graders

I interviewed Julie Beers' fourth graders at the end of a recent school year because they are some of the best spellers I know. Julie does not have a formal spelling program, but the students read and write all day long, in and out of school. She also does meaningful word work several times a week based on students' needs as demonstrated in their writing.

When I asked the students how they accounted for their success, they focused on several major points that, taken all together, helped them develop as spellers:

- Reading a lot
- Taking the time to proofread
- Caring about spelling

Students commented that having real reasons for writing, such as their class news magazine (page 450), made them care about spelling. Many said, "I want my work to look good." They credit their habit of "having-a-go" (having a try at a word) and then checking their spelling against the correct spelling of the word with helping them develop a spelling consciousness. Other helpful factors they noted include the following:

• ***Having minilessons to study words and patterns*** The notes that students took during minilessons and kept in their spelling folders served as important reminders about spelling strategies and generalizations.

• ***Learning spelling tricks/mnemonics*** Many students could still remember "tricks" teachers in earlier grades had taught them, such as "Never fry the end of a friend" and "Wed-nes-day." (Students put together a mnemonics booklet for a class reference.)

• ***Playing spelling games such as Scrabble and Boggle*** One student said that "Games help you remember words, because you're thinking about what letters go in which order, and to learn new words, because you're always thinking, 'Is that a word?'"

• ***Having dictionaries and spell checkers available*** Students spoke of all the editing work they do in connection with writing for real reasons.

• ***Not having boring workbooks and inappropriate tests*** Several students who had come to our district from other school districts spoke about how they disliked their old spelling program. As one student put it, "In my other school, no matter how much I studied for tests, I couldn't do well. I hated the tests. Now, I'm trying harder. Since I'm not bored, I work harder." Another student said, "Workbooks make everyone hate spelling, because they're so boring. People who were good at spelling said, 'This is too easy.' People who were bad at spelling said, 'This is too hard.'"

Considering the Research

Research on how children learn to spell yields much useful information for teachers. Some important points are listed below.

• ***Competent spellers are almost always competent readers.***   The remarks of Julie Beers' fourth graders, given in the above section, are fairly consistent with a recent longitudinal study that looked at how spellers develop through the elementary grades. Many good spellers attribute their spelling proficiency to reading and writing, not spelling lessons or tests. Likewise, these spellers are more likely to conceptualize how words look and think about what they mean (Hughes and Searle 1997).

Competency in reading and writing does not ensure spelling proficiency, however. A sizable group of kids who are competent readers and writers need extra support in spelling.

• ***Young writers move through predictable, developmental spelling stages*** (Henderson 1990; Gentry 1993).   While it can be very helpful to talk about stages of development, it is important to remember that such conceptions do not take into account the complexity of individual progress in spelling. See Figure 10-1 for "Stages of Spelling Development." For a similar classification of spelling stages using different terminology, see Henderson 1990.

• ***As students develop as writers and explore how language works, they invent spellings*** (National Research Council 1998).   Invented spellings (also referred to as temporary spelling, transitional spelling, developmental spelling, and phonetic spelling) are the reasoned approximations and strategies students use as they write words they don't automatically know how to spell. Based on what they know about letters, sounds, words, and language—including rules, patterns, visual configurations, meanings, and word origins—students make decisions about how to spell (Routman and Maxim 1996). These "errors" are actually developmentally appropriate and can tell us much about what students know, what strategies they are "using but confusing," and what they are ready to learn next.

In the early 1970s researchers such as Charles Read and Edmund Henderson conducted studies that demonstrated that the error patterns of young writers were logical and developmental. Carol Chomsky built on that research to realize that young children can write—using invented spellings—before they can read (Wilde 1999). In the 1980s Linda Clarke did a study that found that first graders who were encouraged to use invented spellings wrote many more words but had a lower percentage of correct spellings as compared with students in a traditional spelling program. Wilde then figured out that the inventive spellers actually had a higher total number of correctly spelled words per story (Wilde 1999, 178–179).

While generally we associate invented spellings with younger writers, such spellings

Figure 10–1   *Stages of Spelling Development*
(based largely on the research of Richard Gentry [1982])

---

1. ***Prephonemic spelling***   Children scribble, form letters, and string letters together but without the awareness that letters represent phonemes or speech sounds. Children do, however, create meaningful messages through their exploration. Prephonemic spelling is typical of preschoolers and beginning kindergartners.

2. ***Early phonemic spelling***   There is a limited attempt to represent phonemes with letters, for example, using one or two letters for a word ("m" for "my" and "nt" for "night"). Early phonemic spelling is typical of many kindergarten and beginning first-grade children.

3. ***Phonetic (or letter-name) spelling***   The child uses letters for phonemes—for example, "lik" for "like" and "brthr" for "brother." The child represents most phonemes, understands the concept of a word but is not quite reading yet. This is where we find many of our ending kindergartners and beginning first graders.

4. ***Transitional spelling***   In this stage, children are internalizing much information about spelling patterns, and the words they write look like English words. For example, the child may write "skool" for "school" and "happe" for "happy." Rules are employed, but not always correctly. With reading and writing practice, children integrate more spelling rules and patterns. This stage usually includes first through third-grade children.

5. ***Standard spelling***   At this stage, children spell most words correctly. We have found this stage occurs by the middle to end of third grade or in fourth grade. Children are now ready to learn to spell homonyms, contractions, and irregular spellings, as well as to begin to internalize the rules that govern more difficult vowel and consonant combinations, word endings, and prefixes and suffixes. (We have chosen to use the term "standard spelling" instead of "correct spelling." Even when children have not reached the highest level, they are inventing spelling that is "correct" for their developmental level.)

---

are also appropriate for older writers wanting to use sophisticated vocabulary. As fourth grader Caroline Krassen noted, "Invented spelling makes you feel that you have more than one hundred chests filled with words to choose from. You don't feel limited to only easier words."

• ***Attending to a student's overall literacy development before focusing on spelling results in more meaningful spelling work and greater overall achievement.***   A few years ago Sandra Wilde (1997) advocated attending first to the overall literacy development of poor spellers. Since reading and writing (and working out words through invented spellings) play such a major role in spelling development, common sense tells us that helping the child become a competent reader and writer must take priority over helping him to be a proficient speller. Once the child is a reader, he has a lot of information available to him to inform his understanding of spelling. That is, he can then potentially use what he knows about sounds, letter combinations, the way words look, and meaning and word derivations to write words as well as read them.

• ***Students learn more about words when word study is a conceptual inquiry process related to students' developmental levels as opposed to a one-size-fits-all memorization process*** (Zutell 1996).   Here is where the tension is for us teachers. While most of us recognize the necessity of teaching to students' needs in reading, we remain at the whole-class level for spelling instruction. This is due, I believe, as much to our limited knowledge of spelling development as to time constraints, curricular demands, and management issues.

- **_Only a handful of "rules" are worth teaching_**   Researchers generally agree that only a few spelling rules are so consistent as to be helpful to children:

  - Putting *i* before *e* (as well as the *ei* pattern)
  - Dropping *e* before adding a suffix
  - Changing *y* to *i* before adding a suffix
  - Doubling final consonants before adding a suffix (Wilde 1992, citing Wheat 1932)

Henderson (1990), however, urges caution with the teaching of any rules:

> It is not rules that children need but experiences. Their capacity as human learners will bring them to a feel for, or tacit knowledge of, words long before they will be able to understand rules. . . . literate adults do not use rules; they simply know. (59)

What Good Spellers Do

Based on wide research and practice, I have found that good spellers:

- Read a lot and enjoy reading
- Are committed writers
- Have a fascination with words
- Use what they already know about words to figure out new words
- View spelling as a mostly logical system that makes sense
- Integrate sound, visual, and meaning knowledge
- Use a variety of strategies, including utilizing relevant resources
- Care about correct spelling and self-monitor (are on the lookout for errors)
- Assume responsibility for proofreading and editing
- Take pride in doing their best work

If these are the characteristics of good spellers, the question then becomes, How do we teach so that our students exhibit these behaviors? In everything I have ever read and observed about spelling, being a good reader is the single most important factor for becoming a good speller. But again, proficiency in reading and writing does not necessarily transfer to spelling. While some good spellers are "naturals," most students require explicit instruction and word study in order to become competent spellers. However, such explicit instruction should not stand alone but be part of a comprehensive literacy program that includes many opportunities for authentic writing with real audiences. In order to teach spelling well, we must also use ongoing informal assessment to guide instruction and periodic formal assessment to document growth and guide teaching.

WHAT'S GONE WRONG IN
THE TEACHING OF SPELLING?

In order to do a better job teaching spelling—and all areas of the curriculum—we must reflect on our current practice. By becoming aware of typical problems and examining common pitfalls, we can become more knowledgeable and thoughtful as well as more effective in our literacy programs.

In my school district, we have spent many years dialoguing about and studying spelling research and practice in an effort to offer meaning-based spelling practices as part of a total literacy program. While some teachers, with their administrator's support, do not use a spelling textbook, others do. Most of us have moved beyond rote learning and the accompanying weekly tests on words that all contain the same pattern to words and patterns selected by teachers and students based on needs and interests. We view the teaching of spelling as part of purposeful writing as well as a separate, investigative word study. Even so, a decade after beginning our conversations about spelling, most of us still feel we are not teaching spelling adequately.

Overfocus on Personal Words

While fine in theory, the practice and management of this method, which has students select all or most of their spelling words from words they have trouble with in their own writing, is extremely time-consuming and difficult. Many teachers who incorporated weekly "Have-a-Go" sheets, on which students tried out alternate spellings (see *Invitations*), eventually confined their use to editing for publishing. Trying to meet with every student and go over their self-selected, weekly word lists was exhausting and, also, often allowed for only superficial instruction, as time constraints permitted teachers to spend only a few minutes with each student, unless they were fortunate enough to have trained parent volunteers on hand. Teachers experienced more success when they put limits on self-selection, having students choose only a few personal words a week as part of a larger spelling program.

In addition to being burdensome for teachers, overemphasis on student self-selection of spelling words can be an ineffective teaching strategy. Focusing on personal words encourages memorization, since self-chosen words often do not fit into any pattern. While memorization of words is an appropriate goal, in too many cases, there were no mini-lessons that encouraged inquiry and pattern finding, also necessary goals. As well, relying on student-selected words can be restricting, especially for those students who don't write much or who use limited vocabulary.

Inadequate Word Study

Too often, we teachers have taken a hit-or-miss approach to word study, with too little explicit teaching about how language works, that is, how knowing root words, prefixes, and suffixes can lead to both spelling competency and fuller understanding of words.

Often we fail to take into account developmental differences among students. High-frequency word lists, such as our core word lists (pages 426–427), are often the same for all students at a particular grade level. While these lists continue to be a powerful tool and benchmark, they do not address students' individual development as spellers.

Misuse or Misunderstanding of Invented Spelling

While invented spellings provide a window into a child's understanding and knowledge about how words work and can inform us about what to teach next, our encouragement of this method has sometimes gone too far. That is, we have accepted sloppy work and kept our spelling expectations too low (Routman 1996). However, it is through invented spellings that kids figure out how written language works. As Sandra Wilde (1997) notes, "When kids are inventing spellings, they are teaching themselves about phonics. Their invented spellings are a wonderful diagnostic tool for noting where kids are in their spelling development." We teachers must be sure, however, that our instruction is not "Spell it any way you want" but "Use all that you know about sounds, letters, patterns, and meaning to make your best attempt at spelling words."

Inadequate Communication with Parents

Our jargon, our talk that has sometimes devalued spelling, and our failure to clearly explain our spelling programs has made parents uneasy and kept them ill-informed. Most parents still do not understand the concept of writing as a process and the value of invented spelling for young writers. We must let parents know that invented spelling is not something we simply teach; it's what young writers have historically done on their own in the process of trying to figure out how written language works. Students who are encouraged to use invented spelling make generalizations about words and patterns, write more, and write with more interesting vocabulary, since they are not limited to words they know how to spell. At the same time, we need to let parents know that our standards are high and that students are expected to spell correctly a core of high-frequency words all the time. We must be clear about the value we place on correct spelling (certainly for publication), and that our eventual goal is for all students to be proficient spellers. We must also continue to show parents evidence of their child's growing spelling abilities.

Limited Teacher Knowledge Base

Too many teachers abandoned their textbook spelling programs without replacing them with systematic word study. Additionally, many of us gave too little attention to spelling as a logical system based on established language patterns and word derivations.

Our limited knowledge has led most of us to continue to approach spelling from a curricular perspective—usually scope and sequence, whole-class instruction—instead of a developmental perspective—usually needs-based, small-group instruction (Wallis 1999). To accelerate their spelling development, students need a developmental approach.

Lack of Meaningful Assessment and Monitoring

Often, we have failed to monitor and individualize the teaching of spelling. Even when teachers placed students on a developmental spelling continuum based on careful examination of students' writing, they did not always follow through with individual and small-group teaching and assessment.

Overreliance on Textbook Programs

While a good spelling textbook can be an excellent resource, it is not a total program. Teachers who use a spelling textbook—which provides a scope and sequence and whole-class instruction—generally follow the recommended activities very closely, even though some are of questionable value. Additionally, low-performing spellers are usually not well served by these programs—due to the fact that there are "too many new words to learn each week and a lack of the spelling pattern knowledge ('glue') that would allow the new words to adhere in memory" (Morris, Blanton, Blanton, and Perney 1995). This remains a troubling issue as some states continue to mandate the use of spelling textbooks.

Another common problem is that while many spelling textbooks are described by publishers as "integrated," often this integration is superficial. That is, words are chosen from literature or tied to a theme, but they do not particularly follow a common pattern or meet students' developmental needs.

Additionally, some spelling texts tend to overfocus on memorization. Many of us are all too familiar with the common problem of students who get a 100 percent on the weekly spelling test because they memorize the words and pattern of the week but then fail to apply what they've learned to their own writing. When students overrely on memorization, they focus on learning individual words, failing to view spelling as a conceptual language system with generalizations and patterns that can be applied to unfamiliar words.

Finally, spelling texts are organized around weekly word lists. In order that lists contain a designated number of words, some publishers use words not because they are high utility and useful for students to know, but because they bring the list to its proper word count.

DETERMINING YOUR SPELLING PROGRAM

What do we need to be teaching? Decide what you can manage responsibly, sensibly, and with integrity to demonstrate that your students are developing a spelling consciousness, getting to be better spellers, and writing with an audience in mind. Deciding what to do is no easy matter. There are many points of view and approaches to teaching spelling, and no shortcuts to take in teacher education.

In order to demystify the teaching of spelling and build your knowledge base, you will need to investigate how children develop in spelling, read professionally, converse with your colleagues, and pay close attention to what your students are doing in their writing. Learn and observe as much as you can through writing samples, assessments, and conferences. For example, look for evidence that kids are beginning to pay attention to patterns by trying them out in their own writing.

COMPONENTS OF A
COMPREHENSIVE SPELLING PROGRAM

I believe that spelling, like all areas of the curriculum, is best taught using an inquiry approach—investigating, questioning, problem solving, discovering, and forming generalizations about word patterns, concepts, and meanings. Explicit instruction must be part of a complete program that includes minilessons, shared reading and writing, formal and informal writing conferences, and word work enterprises such as word sorts and working with tiles (pages 428–431).

Be careful not to spend time on isolated activities that do not lead to increased understanding. Kids become spellers through writing for real reasons in which spelling matters and through explicit instruction, word study, and wide reading. Again, while a good spelling textbook can be a very useful resource for guiding instruction, carefully choose which lessons and activities will be most meaningful to your students without "covering" the text page by page.

In the description of the following components of effective spelling instruction, it is assumed that an excellent instructional reading program as well as daily, sustained independent-reading time are in place. It is also assumed that students are engaged in purposeful, daily writing. (See Chapters 6–9.) There is no reason to spell if kids don't write! Remember: a strong spelling program is not a separate entity but exists within the comprehensive literacy program.

- Assessment and evaluation
- Writing for authentic purposes and audiences
- Developing a spelling consciousness
- Learning and applying spelling strategies
- Word study and investigation
- Effective communication with parents

Assessment and Evaluation

The way children spell informs us about what they know, what strategies they are using and "using but confusing," and what they are ready to learn next. Unless kids misspell (just as they miscue in reading), we can't analyze their errors and make generalizations about them (Hughes and Searle 1997, 138).

To find out where children are in their spelling development and determine their instructional needs, you will want to do some assessment, and this can be formal or informal—through analyzing spellings in students' writing samples, spelling inventories, tests of high-frequency words, developmental spelling tests, and/or writing prompts (page 227).

Do connect children's spelling abilities with their overall literacy development. Keep in mind that if kids aren't reading much, they won't be good spellers. In fact, low-performing readers will usually be low-performing spellers (Wilde 1997). If they are poor spellers, focus on reading first.

Contexts for Assessing Students' Spelling

In order for students to progress in spelling, instruction must be geared to what they are ready for and can handle. Having a child focus on spelling words that are beyond his developmental level is inefficient. Similarly, having students spend time on words they already know how to spell makes no sense.

Some informal and formal contexts for examining students' spelling, determining needs and levels, selecting appropriate words for study, and guiding instruction include, but are not limited to:

- Students' writing
- Spelling inventories
- Spelling tests
- Dictations

Students' Writing

By examining students' daily, authentic writing, we can see what they know and can apply, what they are confused about, and what we need to teach them. From carefully examining their spellings, we can evaluate students':

- Knowledge and application of sound-letter relationships
- Knowledge and application of high-frequency words
- Knowledge of spelling patterns
- Knowledge of generalizations and rules
- Problem solving abilities
- Willingness to take risks
- Understanding of word meanings (ability to distinguish, for example, among *to, too,* and *two*)
- Use of proofreading strategies
- Misspelling patterns (for example, failing to drop the silent *e* when adding an ending) and common errors
- Instructional needs—or what we need to teach individually, in small groups, or with the whole class (Routman and Maxim 1996)

Spelling Inventories

Spelling inventories are quick assessments that are used to determine developmental spelling. Inventories contain lists of grade-level words (or lists of increasing difficulty), and a qualitative score is given for spelling accuracy. The highest grade level in which the child correctly spells between 50 percent and 75 percent of the words is considered the instructional level for teaching; above 90 percent is considered the independent level, and below 50 percent is the frustration level (Henderson 1990, 193, citing Emmett Betts 1946). Inventories can be used to note which spelling patterns students know, confuse, are close to knowing, and need to learn. Analyzing students' inventories is helpful with regard to planning instruction, for example, in forming groups based on what students know and are ready to learn. "If teachers . . . note pupils' errors at their instructional level on an informal spelling inventory, they are likely to find clear qualitative information about each child's tacit word knowledge" (Henderson 1990, 196).

Let children know why you are administering the inventories so that they understand the purpose of the activity and will be motivated to do their best work. Be sure to administer the inventories in a space where students cannot rely on resources. For younger children, you may want to administer the list in two sittings.

See Bear and Templeton (1998; 1996), Gentry (1997), Gentry and Gillet (1993), Gill and Scharer (1996), and Henderson (1990) for examples of inventories and guidelines for how to use them. One inventory, which many teachers find especially useful, is the QIWK (Qualitative Inventory of Word Knowledge), developed by Robert Schlagal (1989) for students in grades one through nine. This inventory is reproduced in Henderson (1990).

Whatever inventory you employ, be sure you also use students' writing samples when making judgments about their word knowledge. We use our core word lists as informal inventories but also examine students' writing for real purposes as evidence of their spelling knowledge.

Spelling Tests

Spelling tests can be weekly or periodical and can involve high-frequency words, core lists, and personal lists. Whether or not to test, how often to test, and how to test remains an area of concern.

Most teachers I know see little transfer from spelling tests to actual writing. So, while we may be pleased that spelling scores on tests are high, unless these words are also spelled correctly in daily writing, there have been no real gains. Neil Robinson, a second-grade teacher sums up: "I have a lot of kids do well on tests. Spelling tests mean nothing if kids don't apply the words in their writing. I have good readers who aren't good spellers. I need to learn how to help those kids—and all kids—make connections and become conventional spellers."

In addition, weekly spelling tests add undue pressure on young children and can have devastating effects on struggling spellers (see *Invitations*). Unless testing is done in an informal, nonthreatening manner, I'm against it. First-grade teacher Jim Henry went back to weekly spelling tests because he found parents expected and liked helping their child practice and learn spelling words (Henry 1999). However, he is careful to give clear guidelines to parents to keep this time stress free.

Chris Hayward, another first-grade teacher, stops me in the hall recently to ask what I think about first-grade teachers in another building who have reinstituted weekly spelling tests (after we had discontinued them). Since parents in our district often compare notes with one another, some first-grade parents in Chris' building are now requesting spelling tests. Chris asks me if I think testing is necessary. He himself feels that it's not, and wants confirmation. In the fall he had informed his parents that he would not be testing weekly. He told parents about research that supported his practice and gave them his own rationale—along with specifics on how he would be teaching and monitoring spelling, what parents could expect to see in their child's spelling development, and how he would be continually assessing (Hayward 1998). Chris holds his ground. He comments, "I need to do what I know is right for my students. Because I have continually communicated with my parents about how and why I teach spelling, they support the instruction I provide." (See Appendix A-12 for a newsletter citing research on spelling.)

Dictations

While there is a place for spelling dictations, we need to keep in mind that the spelling children do while the teacher dictates sentences to them is not the same as the spelling they do while composing. Dictation scores—of correctly spelled words—may be higher because the child is highly focused on spelling correctly. That is, she does not have to create meaningful content while spelling.

Some teachers use quick, weekly dictations of several sentences as a way to focus on proofreading and to demonstrate ongoing progress to parents. Students converse about spelling and punctuation as they peer edit with a partner.

Writing for Authentic Purposes and Audiences

Several years ago, spelling researcher Richard Gentry phoned me and asked if he could come visit our schools for a day. In particular, he wanted to see how our third and fourth graders were doing. He was concerned that while invented spelling was okay for the youngest writers, intermediate students needed to be spelling conventionally. He wasn't sure that this was happening in most places.

I took him into some of our best writing classrooms, where students were writing daily for real reasons and doing lots of publishing—mostly short pieces, but also a few big projects a year—with careful proofreading and accurate spelling a high priority. We were all quite nervous that we might not "measure up." While teachers were confident with their writing programs, they did not have formal spelling programs. They believed that their students were good spellers but they had no formal documentation to support this belief. Spelling was mostly taught in the context of extensive writing for real and authentic reasons. Students had a need to spell correctly when they published, and publishing for a chosen audience was important and valued. In addition, we had addressed word study in minilessons in which appropriate words and patterns were explored through interesting and relevant spelling activities.

Richard had planned to give a quick assessment test to the students to determine their spelling levels, but when he looked closely at their writing, he was so impressed with how well the students spelled, he felt that there was no need to administer the test. He commented that most students were spelling "above grade level." We expressed great relief. That visit confirmed for me the impact that meaningful writing has on children's spelling development. Richard later commented to me, "I was surprised that first through fourth graders were spelling so well. I was surprised to see teachers doing such a good job teaching spelling, because so many interpretations of holistic teaching leave spelling out."

These classrooms were not just excellent writing classrooms; they were also strong reading and language classrooms. It is, I believe, this combination that is so powerful with respect to spelling development. As Henderson (1990) asserts: "Ninety percent of an adult's spelling vocabulary is learned, if it is learned, by the application of word knowledge to texts written and read" (168).

The Impact of Writing on Spelling Development

Second-grade teacher Loretta Martin is an excellent spelling teacher, but she does not give weekly spelling tests. She has no complaints from parents, because she informs them exactly how she will be teaching and monitoring spelling—mostly through daily writing and conferencing, whole-class shared writing, and talking about and working with words in various contexts throughout the day. Loretta says that most of her spelling program is informal—mostly word study and word sorts based on what she observes in reading and writing contexts. Loretta is able to successfully teach without a formal program because she is highly knowledgeable about how children learn to spell, able to clearly articulate her beliefs and practices to parents and administrators, and careful to assess and monitor students' spellings and teach at the point of need. Perhaps most important, her students are reading and writing across the curriculum all day long. Publishing for real audiences is a big part of her literacy program. Early on in the school year, spelling and editing—including peer editing—are given high priority and students are expected to proofread and fix up most of their misspellings.

Developing a Spelling Consciousness

When I compliment Julie Beers' fourth graders on an early fall issue of their excellent monthly newsmagazine for parents (page 450), I also note that I found three spelling errors in the newsmagazine that interfered with fluent reading. When the next issue of the newsmagazine has no spelling errors, I congratulate the class on their superb work. Because the writing was authentic and mattered to them, many students assumed responsibility—along with the teacher—to read and reread the issue before it was printed in final form. For the rest of the school year, they hold to these rigorous standards for spelling accountability. Errors in spelling or mechanics on all future issues remain rare. Once students understand that correct spelling is a necessary convention for communicating with their audience—and not just the teacher's agenda—they take careful proofreading and correct spelling very seriously.

In order for kids to develop such a spelling consciousness, they need to care about their writing, assume accountability for their spelling, and recognize that not only do readers expect correct spelling, they are distracted from the content when there are misspellings in a text.

When I write, I reread as I go and I do so with a spelling consciousness. I am likely to fix up misspellings as I go along. I don't ignore them all until the end. We need to teach kids to do this for words they already know how to spell as well as for those they are close to knowing. Spelling researcher Sandra Wilde (1997) calls such words "one second words." These are words that students sometimes get right and that when misspelled are often off by just one letter (*thay* for *they*, for example). She recommends that students take just one extra second to check those words when writing and comments, "Adult writers do get most words right on their first drafts." Correcting as you go makes the process easier in the long run.

Cindy Marten shows her students how to fix one-minute words—"from your head" or "from the word wall"—and tells them her rationale for correcting these words: "I want you to spend a few extra minutes fixing up these words before we meet for a writing conference. Then we can spend our conferencing time working on what you're ready to learn, not what you already know but just forgot to do."

Spelling instruction and word awareness go on all day long—in shared reading, shared writing, in editing conferences, in rereading, publishing, noting features of words, posting words on word walls and charts.

I observe fourth-grade teacher Mark Austin transfer words from student writing on a social studies test to an overhead transparency. He asks kids why they think he's written these words down. Kids guess correctly that they are words that they misspelled on the test. He and the class divide the words into three columns:

- Words we know.
- Words we should know or can find easily.
- Words we don't know how to spell but that we can approximate better.

I love this activity for its effectiveness in heightening students' understanding of the importance of spelling and in raising their expectations. Even if students don't know how to spell a word, we can expect them to use their best approximations as well as available resources. For example, even a young writer approximating a multisyllable word should know that a long word will have many letters and that each syllable (or clap) requires a vowel (even if the student writes the wrong vowel).

Learning and Applying Spelling Strategies

I am always amazed that when I ask students what strategies they can use to spell a word, they usually stop after "Sound it out." I let them know that the strategy I use the most is, "Try writing it another way." In other words, "Does it look right to me?" Most students, even students with learning disabilities, can recognize misspelled words even if they cannot produce the correct spelling. Here is where the Have-a-Go sheet is very useful—for encouraging and teaching children to rely on the visual (how it looks) as well as the auditory (how it sounds)—for "fixing up" misspellings.

To assess what your students understand about spelling strategies, ask them this question: "What strategies can you use when you want to spell a word correctly?" Use their responses to guide your teaching.

The following is a list generated from a third-grade class that had been discussing and learning multiple spelling strategies:

- Circle the misspelled word and come back to it.
- Try writing the word another way until it looks right. (First note which parts of the word are correct by putting a check mark over those letters.)
- Use what you already know (spelling pattern or rule, small word within a bigger word, or word meaning).
- Stretch out the word slowly, and listen for all the sounds.
- Picture the word in your mind and think about the order of the letters.
- Ask a friend.
- Look around the room—in a book or on a chart or word wall—or anywhere you remember seeing the word.
- Check the dictionary (if you are sure about the first few letters).

Asking students to verbalize their spelling processes helps them to think about their spelling and to "move them toward new understandings." When they get words right ask them,

- How did you know that?
- Why do you think it works that way? (Hughes and Searle 1997, 135)

Utilizing Multiple Resources

We model how to use resources, some of which are co-constructed with students: word walls, charts, and dictionaries (commercial, personal, spelling big book). Other resources include thesauruses (occasional use), mnemonic devices, specialized dictionaries, quality spelling textbooks, family words, and peers (pages 422). Some teachers also provide handheld spell checkers for students who have difficulty spelling.

Word Walls

In my district, teachers of developing readers and writers all use word walls and/or charts that include high-frequency words (Cunningham 1995). Some posted words do not follow a rule or pattern, such as *was* and *said*, but many do. When a word follows a consistent pattern or rime, indicating that the word can be used by analogy to read and write other words, many teachers highlight the rime in some way. For example, because the word *day* might have "ay" highlighted, other "ay" words would not need to be listed. (See pages 274 and 276 for examples of word walls.)

To get the full benefit from your word wall, it is important that words that do not follow a pattern are distinguished from those that do. Reading specialist Cindy Marten puts a "helping hand" symbol next to those words that can help students spell many other words, and repeatedly tells and shows students, "If you know [this word], then you also know [that word]."

We let students know that once a word is on the word wall, they are expected to spell it correctly in all writing contexts. Some teachers will gently tell students to check the word wall when one of the listed, high-frequency words is misspelled in a student's writing. Other teachers, as they are circulating about the classroom during writing time, lightly pencil in a check mark or other symbol next to a misspelled word, which is a signal for the student to check the word wall and fix up the spelling.

Spelling Dictionaries

Be sure that you have a variety of accessible dictionaries for student use. Often classroom dictionaries are too advanced, and students spend a lot of time looking for words that they rarely locate. The following are some helpful resources. Also, you may want to check on-line dictionaries.

• ***Spelling "big book"***   Second-grade teacher Ellen Rubin puts all of her wall charts together in a "Big Book of Spells" that becomes a helpful classroom writing (and reading) reference. (See Figure 10-2 for sample page.)

• ***Personal student dictionaries***   Many publishers now distribute student dictionaries geared to particular age and grade levels. These are easier to use than commercial dictionaries and often include helpful lists such as months of the year, alternate ways to say common words like *said*, homonyms, and topic-related words, as well as high-frequency words arranged alphabetically. These booklets include space for students to add in their own personal words.

We have had much success with various student dictionaries published by Educator's Publishing (Cambridge, MA) (see *Invitations*, page 262), the "Quick-Word" handbooks offered by Curriculum Associates (North Billerica, MA), and the dictionaries published by Mondo (Greenvale, NY). Most of these are reasonably priced at about $2.00 (or less), with discounts for bulk purchase. Call or write for sample copies.

For young writers, I recommend waiting several months before bringing out the student dictionaries. Otherwise, some students will overrely on them and fail to take risks in their writing. That is, they will only write the words that they can spell or find spellings

Figure 10–2   A page from "Big Book of Spells"

Words spelled with <u>ea</u>			We learned that:

Words spelled with <u>ea</u>

b<u>ea</u>ch	a l<u>r</u>eady	<u>ear</u>th
b<u>ea</u>ds	br<u>ea</u>th	h<u>ea</u>rd
cheer l<u>ea</u>ders	d<u>ea</u>d	l<u>ear</u>n
cr<u>ea</u>m	El<u>ea</u>nor	s<u>ear</u>ch
dr<u>ea</u>m	h<u>ea</u>d	
<u>ea</u>ch	h<u>ea</u>ded	h<u>ea</u>r
<u>ea</u>ts	r<u>ea</u>dy	t<u>ea</u>rs
l<u>ea</u>f		y<u>ea</u>rs
m<u>ea</u>ns		
p<u>ea</u>ch		
pl<u>ea</u>se		br<u>ea</u>k
r<u>ea</u>ding	i<u>dea</u>	gr<u>ea</u>t
r<u>ea</u>lly		st<u>ea</u>k
scr<u>ea</u>med	b<u>ear</u>	
t<u>ea</u>		
t<u>ea</u>chers		oc<u>ea</u>n
t<u>ea</u>se		

We learned that:

1. There are at least 8 ways to say <u>ea</u>.

2. When we are reading, if we come to a word that has <u>ea</u> in it and we don't know the word, trying saying the long ē sound for the <u>ea</u> spelling. Why? Because we found more of that sound for the <u>ea</u> spelling pattern.

for. Then, because they're spending so much time worrying about spelling, they do little actual writing.

When you do bring out the dictionaries, be sure you demonstrate how to use them. Let students know that they are more likely to locate in dictionaries words that they can already read, and that the best use of the dictionary is for proofreading and checking spelling of questionable words after the draft is written. Dictionaries can also be an essential tool during word study time, especially for noting how meaning connects to spelling.

Word Study and Investigation

Think about calling your spelling program "word study." Students are fascinated with words. They love talking about words, hunting for words with similar patterns, discerning new meanings, and playing word games. Word study builds on their natural curiosity and is an opportunity to teach them about phonics, word patterns, meanings, origins, and spelling in an enjoyable, engaging manner. Besides providing an opportunity for explicit teaching, word study allows for discovery and investigation of words and patterns; that is, for making and testing hypotheses, problem solving, categorizing, coming to new generalizations and understandings, and applying knowledge to new words. "In word study, we do not just teach words—we teach students processes and strategies for examining and thinking about the words they read and write" (Bear and Templeton 1998, 223).

An inquiry approach to spelling meaningfully engages learners and encourages them to conceptualize and think about words, not memorize them. See *Invitations* (245–247), for an example of a minilesson that came about because of a confusion students had about when to double a final consonant. Students were encouraged to "discover" a spelling generalization, but direct teaching was also involved.

While some word work will be incidental, much of it is planned—in advance and in response to students' needs (based on formal and informal assessments) and interests. Again, it is our job to teach students what they will need to know. Reading Recovery now requires several minutes of word analysis, with the student "boxing" one word in every lesson. At first, boxes are used only for sounds, as in *h-o-m;* later, letter boxes are used, as in *h-o-m-e,* to connect sound to visual (see Figure 10-3).

Guiding Principles

• *Look for what students use but confuse.*   Students' error patterns and what they are experimenting with tell us what they are close to learning and ready to learn next.

• *A step backward is a step forward.*   So that students experience success, start with something known. For example, when introducing a new pattern, review a familiar one first, perhaps through a word sort.

• *Use words students can read.*   Choose words students can read in and out of context so that known pronunciation can aid spelling of letters.

• *Compare words "that do" a particular thing with words "that don't."*   For example, contrast words that double consonants with those that don't. Understanding how one word differs from another word helps define categories.

• *Sort by sight and sound.*   Have students read and sort words by how they are spelled and how they sound so that visual and sound patterns are integrated.

• *Begin with obvious contrasts first.*   For example, to avoid confusions when teaching different letters, begin with letters that look very distinct from each other.

• *Don't hide exceptions.*   Acknowledge and list the exceptions that don't fit the generalization or category.

• *Avoid rules.*   Guide students to discover generalizations about words through collaborative discussion and study.

• *Work for automaticity.*

Figure 10–3   Using boxes for visual word work

- *Return to meaningful texts.*
  (Slightly adapted from Bear, Invernizzi, Templeton, and Johnston 1996, 74–77.)

Also, I have found it helpful to keep in mind—and to share with parents—that word study includes the following increasingly complex focuses based on children's growing knowledge:

- Letters/sounds connection
- Word patterns
- Meaning connection

Henderson (1990) notes the above developmental sequence as follows:

1. Alphabet principle
2. Pattern principle
3. Pattern by meaning principle

"Only when children's sight vocabulary has expanded considerably will they have sufficient exemplars to realize the meaning connection" (65).

ORGANIZING FOR SPELLING AND WORD STUDY: COMBINING WHOLE-CLASS, SMALL-GROUP, AND INDIVIDUALIZED WORD STUDY

As already noted, a totally individualized spelling program is difficult and time-consuming to pull off. A combination focus on common patterns and generalizations (for whole-class and small cooperative groups) plus some individualization of words studied seems to make the most sense (Fresch and Wheaton 1997). Using this combination approach, organization is manageable; activities are planned around specific patterns; and students' developmental spelling levels are considered.

Many teachers I know expect students to master certain high-frequency words and patterns as well as words self-selected from their writing each week. In connection with helping students learn those words, teachers present minilessons and activities that promote inquiry, discovery, conversation, and interaction with respect to words and patterns. This information is also shared with parents (see Appendix G).

Some teachers have their students organize and save all spelling work—minilessons, completed word sorts, word hunts, personal word lists, spelling generalizations—in a spelling folder or word study notebook. This book not only serves as a record for students and teachers, it also lets parents and administrators see exactly what spelling work is taking place in the classroom.

Contexts for Teaching Spelling

The following contexts for teaching spelling occur throughout the day as part of a comprehensive literacy program. Some of these contexts are planned ahead, some are formed "on the run," but all are purposeful and in response to students' needs. In addition to the elements listed below, most teachers try to plan ten to fifteen minutes of word study—apart from reading and writing time—at least three times a week.

One-on-One Writing Conferences

Conferences are great forums for the demonstrations and direct teaching that are a hallmark of the effective teacher. Often, such lessons are conducted "in the margin" (Henry 1999) as teachers walk around individually conferencing with kids as they write. For example, I might notice as I circulate among students that a child is ready to spell a particular word, in which case I will stop and work through the spelling with the child on the page. I might say to a child, "I think you're ready to spell this word. I'll write it for you here so that next time you'll know where to find it." Some teachers highlight misspelled high-frequency words that students have been expected to spell correctly, reminding students that they need to "fix up" these words. Parents see these lessons "in the margin" as evidence that we are teaching spelling.

"Help Me"

First-grade teacher Jim Henry came up with the ingenious idea of organizing the incidental spelling instruction that was constantly occurring in his classroom. He used to write a word for a student who requested it on a scrap of paper, which the student would use and then throw away. Now he puts together small "Help Me" booklets, so that each student can save all those "scraps" for reuse and reference. (See Figure 10-4 for one page from a student's booklet.)

Before Jim will spell a word for a student, the student has to make his best attempt at spelling using all he knows. When a student approaches him for help, Jim does an interactive minilesson on the spot. He always has a small chalkboard handy, and begins by asking the student, "What do you know about this word?"

I was working in Jim's classroom one morning in early December when a student named Adam approached me for help with the word *breathe*, which he had written as *breeth*, a great invented spelling. Following Jim's model, I conversed with Adam. The whole lesson took but fifteen seconds and a lot of teaching and learning occurred.

Figure 10–4   A page from a first grader's "Help Me" booklet

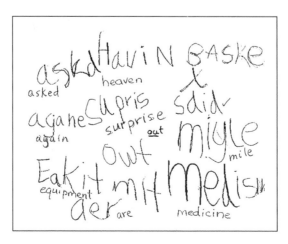

REGIE: You already know a lot about this word. What other two-letter combination could make the long *e* sound?

ADAM: *ea.*

REGIE: That's right. (*I write* breath *below his* breeth.) This says "breath." Can you think what one letter we need to add at the end to make it say "breathe"?

ADAM: *e.*

REGIE: Good. Now you have it.

Small Guided Reading Groups

Small-group guided reading is an excellent context for word work, since spelling and reading development go hand in hand. (See the photo at the beginning of this chapter of first graders working on *porch.*)

For example, when a first-grade teacher is introducing *Too Much Noise* by Ann McGovern to a small group, the teacher sets the purpose for reading the story and also goes over the tricky words *creak* and *squeak* while focusing on the sound of the "ea" vowel combination. For reinforcement, students do word hunts and sorts for long *e* words with "ea" and "ee" patterns using the familiar book *Over in the Meadow*. She then tells them to write *eat, meat*, and *beat* and other words that fit this pattern on their individual dry erase boards.

First-grade teacher Chris Hayward notes that such word work is "the backbone of my spelling program" and comments, "I think it's really important to integrate spelling into what kids are reading and writing."

Word Cards

I sometimes write down a book's high-frequency words on 3 × 5" cards, for use with developing readers. Using a magic marker, I print each word on a separate card. I keep cards grouped together according to book title. While at first I let students use the text in front of them for reference, later I expect students to know these words instantly in isolation and be able to read and write them. We can't be sure students truly know certain words until they use them in another context. This activity is effective because, although the words have been "isolated," they are introduced to students within a reading context.

Sentence Strips

Once students have read and understood a text, I sometimes use sentence strips for helping them look closely at words and their meaningful sequence. Sentence strips are made by copying onto paper a sentence (from a story or the child's own writing) and cutting it up, first in phrases and later in words and/or word parts depending on your purposes and the students' needs. Work can be done at the sentence, phrase, word, or letter(s) level.

I often use sentence strips in small-group or partner work, when students are not paying close enough attention to print—for example, when they are only looking at the first letter of a word and making a guess at it. I will cut up a sentence, and I will guide students in putting it together. I always ask students to match what we have done with the text in front of them, which encourages self-checking, an important reading strategy. Later, I will ask them to independently unscramble the pile of words to make a meaningful sentence.

Encourage self-monitoring through statements, such as,

- How do you know this word is ——— and not ———?
- Point to the word that starts with ——.
- Check with the book. Are you right?

Whole-Class Interactive Demonstrations

Using a student's writing, which has been photocopied (with student's permission) onto an overhead transparency, conduct a minilesson. Start by guiding students to notice what the writer has done well, then move to a line-by-line focus on spelling.

Such demonstrations can be based on teacher observations of students' reading and writing or on what you know students will need and are ready for. These minilessons are well planned and can be introduced to students with a statement such as, "I noticed today when we were reading that lots of you had trouble with ———, so let's examine ———." (Such interactive lessons can also take place in small groups.)

Shared Reading, Shared Writing, and Interactive Writing

Every time students read and write texts or make individual or class books can become an opportunity for word work, such as the following:

- Looking at and listening for particular letters, letter combinations, and words
- Noticing rimes
- Figuring out unfamiliar words
- Focusing attention on particular letters, patterns, or meanings that will be useful for reading and writing

See pages 41–43 and 123–124 for examples.

Partner Work and Peer Editing

Peers at comparable developmental levels, as well as older students paired with younger ones, can help each other while at the same time reinforcing important concepts. As an example, when a third grader was editing his writing, he circled *neighborhood* but couldn't find it in the dictionary because he was looking under the letters *na*. He turned to his partner and asked, "What are the first three letters of the word *neighborhood*?" His partner gave him the correct letters and the student was then able to easily find the word in the dictionary. (See page 316 for more on peer editing.)

When kids interact and talk with each other about words, they think harder about their points of view than when they talk only with the teacher. I have observed this in many contexts, for example, when students are manipulating tiles and letters to make words (pages 429–431) or doing word hunts. Note the following brief conversation between two third graders doing a word hunt for words with the long *a* sound:

EARL: Well, *they* has a long *a* sound.

AMY: Yes, but it doesn't have the patterns we're hunting for.

EARL: Well, let's put it on the board then.

The students add it to the board where they are listing "other ways long *a* is spelled." They continue hunting for "ay," "ai," and "a-e" words and find many more.

Finding Time to Teach Spelling

Try to set aside at least ten to fifteen minutes several days a week (or about fifty to seventy-five minutes a week) for focused spelling instruction and word study. Be sure that you also try to have sustained daily writing that includes writing on mostly self-selected—but some assigned—topics, often what has been teacher demonstrated. Such writing also involves conferencing, proofreading, editing, and taking some writing to final copy with correct spelling. See Chapters 6–9 on writing for specifics.

Some published spelling programs call for up to thirty minutes a day devoted to learning spelling words and doing spelling activities. Teachers rightly worry, however, that if they allow that much time for spelling, there's not enough time left for connected reading and writing.

Increasing curricular demands along with local and state instructional mandates can make it difficult to "fit" spelling in. On days when you cannot manage a separate spelling focus, be sure that spelling instruction is integrated into reading and writing through the various contexts discussed on preceding pages.

Working with Words

It is our job to teach kids how words work, that most words follow a pattern, that the "tricky" ones just have to be learned, and to provide the links they are missing. For example, we need to show them if they know a word in reading, they know it in writing and vice versa. It is not enough to just teach them words; we must also teach how to learn words.

Learning by Analogy

Meaningful pattern making is what the brain does innately. In fact, the brain's ability to make familiar connections is necessary to the formation of meaning (Jensen 1998, 95). Knowing and applying current brain research helps us teach in a way that makes sense to kids.

For example, while much "scientific research" champions sounding out one phoneme and letter at a time, in fact, my thirty years of teaching reading confirms that it is easier for students to use onsets and rimes, analyzing words by breaking them into meaningful chunks or patterns. A growing body of research confirms this assertion (Moustafa 1998). In a syllable, the onset is the letter(s) before the vowel; the rime is the vowel and the letter(s) that follows it. For example, in *that,* "th" is the onset and "at" is the rime. Knowing just thirty-seven rimes allows students to generate five hundred basic words (Adams 1990, citing Wylie and Durrell 1970). See Figure 10-5 on page 424.

Working with Low-Achieving Readers

I will pull students who do not have a core of at least twenty known words into a small group and teach basic vocabulary and rimes. For example, in a group of first graders who knew very few words, we practiced writing *we,* then erasing one letter to make *he, me,* and *be* while noticing that the *e* stays the same. When that was overlearned we worked on *went.* "Which letter do I have to change to make *rent*?" I asked. This was not automatic for kids. Then we made a pattern book together (see pages 123–124) in which each page began, "We went to ———." These kids could not effectively utilize journal writing time until they had a minimum, basic vocabulary.

Figure 10–5   37 basic rimes

ack	ank	eat	ill	ock	ump
ail	ap	ell	in	oke	unk
ain	ash	est	ine	op	
ake	at	ice	ing	ore	
ale	ate	ick	ink	ot	
ame	aw	ide	ip	uck	
an	ay	ight	it	ug	

In another example, a group of slow-achieving readers are reading *Danny and the Dinosaur* by Syd Hoff at the beginning of second grade. Page 41 reads:

"May we have a ride?"
asked the children.
"I'd be delighted,"
said the dinosaur.
"Hold on tight" said Danny.

When the children couldn't read *delighted* and *tight,* I wrote *right,* a word they did know, on my small chalkboard, and from there we isolated "ight" and transferred it to *delighted, tight, might,* and *fright.* I tell them, "If you know *right,* then you also know ————." Thinking of the next day's lesson, I make a note to begin by reviewing "ight." I give each member of our small group a dry erase board. We begin by writing *tight.* I ask them to check their spelling against page 41 of the book and ask them, "Are you right?"

While most kids are fascinated with words, learning words by analogy has to be demonstrated and scaffolded for students, especially for low-achieving readers. Just because students know *cat,* they do not automatically figure out words such as *that* and *mat* in reading and writing even if they know the separate parts. We have to teach students to think, "If I know 'ake' in *cake,* then I can quickly figure out words such as *lake, take,* and *stake.*" One way to promote such linking is to highlight common rimes on word walls, often by writing the rime in another color, underlining it, or placing a "helping hand" next to it (see page 416), which signals students that this is a pattern that can be applied to reading and writing other words. Another way is to do needed word work (as described above) and ask students questions, such as the following, to encourage them to use what is known to figure out a word that is unknown:

- What do you know?
- What do you notice?
- What do you hear?
- What stays the same?
- What letter(s) do you need to change to make a new word?
- How many words do you know that fit this pattern?
- If you know ————, what other words do you know?

Teaching students how to use rimes strategically is very different from our instruction of what we used to call word families, in which kids were presented with all the words that fit a pattern (through flash cards or a list) and were expected to memorize them after seeing the words over and over again. Teaching words by analogy is a thinking, meaning-making process.

Memorizing Words

For children to become competent spellers, a whole lot of words just have to be memorized. Then, as students write, they visualize and "call up" those learned spellings. For words that have not been committed to memory, students approximate as best they can by using their knowledge of letters and sounds, patterns, and meanings.

Even when students are memorizing words, it is helpful to combine memorization with discussion around the following questions:

- What do you already know about this word?
- What's the tricky part?
- How will you remember this word?

Memory alone is insufficient. The best word study combines memory with conceptualization and meaningful practice.

For example, noticing that many first graders are misspelling *house,* a word on our core spelling list for first grade (page 426), I conduct a quick lesson to help students memorize the word. I ask students to write "house" on their individual chalkboards. Then, working in their small groups of four to five (their seating arrangement), I ask each group to decide on what they think is the correct spelling. After two minutes of group discussion, during which I walk from group to group listening in on conversations and doing some prompting, I take the preferred spellings from each of the five groups, write each on the overhead or classroom chalkboard, and we talk about the spellings, asking the following questions:

- What do we all agree on? [I put a check over the letters common to all of the spellings, *h, o,* and *s.*]
- What do we already know that we can use? [We talk about how the "ou" sound can be spelled "ou" or "ow."]
- Which "ou" pattern looks right here?
- Is the silent *e* at the end of one group's spelling correct?
- How can we check our spelling?

Once we agree on the correct spelling, we quickly review the "tricky" parts—the "ou" and the silent *e*. Although students are memorizing the word, it is not memorization by writing the word over and over again (an ineffective practice) but memorization combined with scaffolded investigation and later, follow-up practice in connected reading and writing.

A Word Study Approach

Many teachers use the following well-accepted word study approach. Be sure you model the sequence first and engage kids in conversation so that word study is rich and interactive, not a dry and boring lockstep process.

- **Look**   Notice shape, patterns, visual features, and tricky or surprising parts of the word. Try to visualize the word. Ask, "What do you notice about this word?" "Does anything surprise you?" "Why?" Get discussion going. Investigate.
- **Say**   Say word to yourself. Say word slowly. Break it into syllables.

- **Cover** Visualize the word.

- **Write** Say sounds as you write the word.

- **Check** If your spelling is incorrect, note confusion. Repeat word study sequence until word is learned.

Word Lists

In theory, word lists should work like instructional reading texts; that is, there should be just enough challenge so that the learner can use what he already knows to problem solve and figure out words. In practice, this is difficult to do. Some teachers compromise by having students choose seven to eight words from a teacher-constructed list that has a specific pattern or meaning focus.

For example, a pretest is given to the whole class. For every word spelled correctly, students choose from an expanded list that includes more difficult words. Students who "consistently test at 80 percent or above on the pretest . . . create their own lists," but those lists must conform to the pattern being studied that week. "This procedure allows individualization of the words studied, yet maintains a common spelling pattern or rule for discussions, cooperative group activities, and peer assistance during writing" (Fresch and Wheaton 1997, 25; for examples and further explanation see 24–26).

When constructing weekly word lists, seven to ten words are plenty. Make sure that students can read all the words, that most words follow a pattern, and that the pattern being taught is appropriate with respect to the child's developmental spelling level. Words that don't follow a pattern must be learned by whatever means possible.

Core Word Lists

Lists are important. In one school's weekly language arts support group, several of us worked to create core spelling lists (see Appendixes G-1 and G-2) in response to parents' and teachers' questions about student spelling progress from grade to grade. We sat down by grade levels and asked ourselves, "What are the high-frequency words and patterns students are using and need to be using by the end of each grade level?" We cross-checked our lists with published lists, hashed them out across grade levels, and asked each other, "Do we expect most students at the end of this grade level to have mastered this word?" We tried the lists out with our students, shared them with parents, and continued to revise them until most of us were satisfied with the result. The process took about four years.

These lists have become part of our district assessment process in grades one through four. (See Appendixes I-4, I-5, and I-6.) Throughout the school year, teachers use them as a benchmark to determine where students are in their spelling. At the end of the school year, teachers send home the specific grade-level list with the student's final assessment on it. Recommendations for summer home study are noted as needed.

Our core spelling lists—and the high expectations they set—are taken seriously by teachers, and that has helped increase teacher respect between grade levels. Specifically, there is less blaming of previous grade-level teachers for what students don't know. For example, recently all of the second-grade teachers in one building complimented the first-grade teachers on how well the kids were spelling. And it was not just for the good spelling in students' daily writing. When second-grade teachers administered the first-grade core list at the beginning of the school year, they noted that the one hundred second graders had an average score of 85 percent accuracy. These same teachers also commented that every student capitalizes the word *I* in daily writing. Another second-grade teacher who observed excellent spelling of high-frequency words in a quickwrite (page 216) commented that this learned spelling was not based on memorization but was mostly a result of the real reading and writing students have done. Another teacher noted that at the end of first grade, all first-grade teachers had sent home words from the core list designating to parents the words that needed to be mastered over the summer. Apparently many parents took this task with their child seriously.

A word of caution here. Expectations for low-achieving readers will need to be adjusted. It is not a good use of these students' time to have them memorize words above their spelling readiness level. What they need are more language experiences, not isolated word work. Have them focus their energies first on extensive, meaningful reading and writing experiences.

While someone else's core lists can be used as a guide for creating your own, it is very important that teachers go through the process of list creation themselves. The most valuable part of creating core lists are the conversations about spelling that take place among teachers. Such conversations are vital for improving instruction and assessment.

High-Frequency Words

Students need to have a core of words that they can read and write automatically. Typically, many of these high-frequency words do not follow a pattern. Individual chalkboards or boards with dry erase markers are great for student word work, which can take place whole class or in a small group.

For developing readers and writers, it's a good idea to spend several minutes doing daily fast writes of several high-frequency words. Have students work together in a small group. Make sure all in the group agree on a word's spelling. If not, discuss the reasons for disagreement. Then, have kids repeatedly write the word and check themselves on proper spelling. We tell students, "Write it. Erase it. Write it again. Do it fast." Again, always connect word work to reading and writing, so kids know that this is not an isolated task.

Guard against encouraging even young students (first graders) to invent spellings of common words such as *went, come,* and *like.* It's not efficient for students to unlearn misspellings of words that they've been using over and over again. We need to keep our expectations for spelling of high-frequency words high, through emphasizing practice and use of word walls and other resources.

As a guide for choosing which words to study, use common high-frequency word lists, such as those provided by Pinnell and Fountas (1998) or Snowball and Bolton (1999) for words that are used a lot in reading and writing. One hundred high-frequency words make up 50 percent of all written material (Fry 1996; Snowball 1998). (See also Appendix G-1.)

Most of the words on our core lists are high-frequency words. Even though we do not have a core list of words for kindergarten, many kindergartners spell words such as *I, a, the, and, is, to, me, do, it, for, of,* and *mom* and *dad* by the end of the year. Some teachers post these words gradually on a "Words We Can Write" wall chart. Some, or all of these words, are also written on smaller charts that are available at tables during writing time.

Personal Words

When students are given the opportunity to choose their spelling words, they invariably select words that are relevant to their interests and needs. As a result, they are usually eager to learn how to spell these words.

If your students are selecting personal words from their own writing, teach them to:

- Select words that they will be using repeatedly.
- Note what they have already spelled right.
- Focus on the challenging or confusing part of the word.
- Use multiple strategies to remember the "tricky part."

Often students will have correctly written most of the letters in the word but may have confused the letter sequence, vowel pattern, or ending. When modeling, begin with what students already know.

It is our job to supplement students' personal words with words we know that they will need. For some students, choosing only from their writing is too limiting.

Word Sorts

I first learned about word sorts years ago when spelling researcher Jerry Zutell demonstrated their use at a reading conference. "A word sort is an activity that requires students to group words into different categories. They are called 'sorts' because they often involve sorting words written on individual cards into piles based on some criterion or contrast" (Zutell 1993). (Before sorting, students cut words on a page [as in Figure 10-6] into word cards.) Typical word sorts foster thinking and discussion about how words are alike or different and can be used to help students make generalizations about how words work.

Word sorts also focus students' visual attention on words. (Students have to be able to read the words in order to sort them.) As students sort, they have to look deeply at the word. As one first-grade teacher working with struggling readers told me, "After my kids have worked with a pattern in a sort, they really notice similar words in their reading and are excited every time they find something they know."

Figure 10–6   A closed word sort for teachers

beginning	protecting
sharpening	labeling
traveling	upsetting
bargaining	restructuring
forgetting	referring
happening	dismissing
alarming	remarking
allowing	discovering

Sorts can be open or closed; that is, students can decide how to categorize and sort the words (open sort) or teachers can determine how the words are to be categorized and sorted (closed sort). See Figure 10-6 for a closed sort I have used with teachers to promote understanding of why we double or do not double the final consonant at the end of certain words. Try this exercise by yourself or with colleagues. My experience has been that teachers can accurately sort but often cannot make the proper inference as to why.

Create sorts for rimes, patterns, and generalizations you want kids to know. Take words from familiar stories the students are reading or from published lists such as those created by Henderson (1990) and Phenix (1996). For guidelines on how to create and conduct sorts, see spelling resources in The Blue Pages, especially Bear and Templeton (1998), Bear, Invernizzi, Templeton, and Johnston (1996), Fresch and Wheaton (1997), Gentry and Gillet (1993), and Zutell (1996).

Word Hunts

Word hunts are a good activity for reinforcing phonics and spelling patterns. Select a pattern from a shared reading or writing you have done with students or from a guided reading group lesson. You might say something like, "I noticed that some of you struggled with this pattern today. Hunt for words with this pattern, and let's see what we can discover" (Wallis 1999). Be sure that students are using familiar books that they can easily read for this activity.

Working individually or with a partner, students record words that fit a pattern that has been studied, and notice how words are alike and different. Some teachers have students record their findings in a word study notebook that serves as an organized record of all word work. Students then bring their notebooks to guided reading group to discuss pattern words and check for accuracy.

Word hunts can also be whole-class activities. Note the chart (see Photo 10-1 on page 430) that second graders devised while hunting for words fitting particular patterns. Students first wrote their words on a Post-it. After the teacher checked it for accuracy, the word was written by the student on the chart. Some teachers prefer to write the words on the charts themselves, for handwriting consistency.

Word Work with Tiles

Several years ago I purchased hundreds of inexpensive one-by-one-inch white glazed tiles from a local ceramic and tile company for use in a word work adaptation of "making words" (Cunningham 1995). I was looking for a way to avoid the time-consuming process of cutting out lots of letters, distributing them, and collecting them.

Several times a month, as part of investigation and word study, I involve students for about ten minutes in whole-class word work. I also regularly use these tiles (with dry erase markers) in small guided reading groups because they are effective for focused word study, the management is quick and easy, and kids love using them. The conversations that take place, especially between students, help move their understanding forward.

Each group is supplied with a small tub of tiles, and each student is given a dry erase marker and a wiper—a Kleenex or old sock. I first ask students to take a few minutes to do some exploratory writing on the tiles and to become accustomed to manipulating them. (This free exploration helps them take our task more seriously when we are ready

Photo 10–1   Hunting for words to fit a pattern in a second-grade class

to begin.) Then, I choose a pattern or rule we have been working on and ask students to spell a word with that pattern. All members in a group have to come to agreement on spelling. I walk between groups guiding and prompting. For example, for a focus on "ar," we might start with *part* and move to *party, parting, partner*, and *apartment*. Kids love when we add challenge words such as *varnish* and *sardine*, and perhaps superchallenges such as *tarpaulin*. When groups disagree about spellings, we converse and use whatever resources are necessary to determine the correct spelling.

The tiles also work well with struggling readers. Having to write letters as well as manipulate them seems to facilitate word learning. At first, I supply all the tiles and letters and discuss the chunk I have provided. For example, my conversation goes something like, "Take three tiles. Watch me write *all*. This word says *all*. You make it. Now, let's make *tall*. That's right. We have to add a tile. What letter do we write? Okay, now erase one letter and make *hall*. Which letter did you need to change? Now, run your finger under the word *hall*. Say it." Connect the visual with the sounds. "Break the word apart. Make it again."

Kindergarten teacher Christine Hoegler uses tiles with lowercase letters already written on them (consonants in yellow and vowels in red). In small groups, for brief periods, she does letter and word work while other students are working independently. For example, for a group of children who still need help with letter recognition and letter sounds, she will give students several letters that they have been working on and call out a letter. "Find the *l*." The children will then point to the correct letter. She continues with each letter tile in the pile. Then she will say, "Find the letter that begins the word *lion.*" She may also, later, call out the letter sound in isolation and expect children to point to the letter.

For her students who already know their letters and sounds, she works with them in small groups and focuses on noticing beginning, middle, and ending sounds while forming one-syllable words. For example, using the letter tiles for *a*, *n*, and *d*, students make *and* and *dan*. Once successful, Christine asks them to trade the *d* for another letter, for example, *p*. She asks, "What word can you make now?" Once again, they focus on beginning, middle, and ending sounds but also talk about rhyming words and how knowing one pattern helps you figure out new words. As the children make a new word, Christine writes it on a dry erase board and, as a review, students read and reread the list of words made.

Wordplay

Since knowing nursery rhymes is a reliable indicator of success in learning to read, spend time with young children reciting, singing, clapping, and acting out such texts (Cunningham 1995, 39). Cunningham recommends using students' names, the alphabet, and alphabet books to teach letters, sounds, and concepts. Many teachers have had great success using children's names to teach phonemic awareness, phonics, and spelling. A chart of children's names (usually in alphabetical order) is posted in full view. One creative kindergarten teacher groups her children by the first letter of their first name, photographs each group, and makes a picture-name alphabet that the kids refer to all year.

Kids love wordplay. Kindergarten teacher Karen Sher plays a game she calls Guess My Word, a form of Hang Man, with her students. To highlight an important word or concept they have been studying, she might say, "I'm thinking of a word that has to do with the trip to the planetarium we just took." She draws four lines to show them the word has four letters (_ _ _ _). She supplies one letter and keeps giving them hints until students guess the word.

I use familiar poems to get students to play around with rhymes and words (page 36), clap syllables, and reinforce high-frequency words. For example, using a sliding mask to frame individual words (see *Invitations*, 190b), I gradually expose and highlight rimes and features of text. (Repeated readings of shared writing texts and familiar stories can be used in the same way.)

Teach students idioms, the hidden meanings of popular phrases, such as, "eat you out of house and home," "lead you by the nose," and "spill the beans." Students love collecting idioms and illustrating them. Marvin Terban's *Dictionary of Idioms* (New York: Scholastic, 1996) is a great resource that explains the meanings and origins of more than six hundred idioms. Mnemonic devices also enchant students.

See "Books That Encourage Children to Write" and "Word Play" in The Blue Pages, pages 126b and 130b, for excellent resources to play around with.

Word Derivations

Although much of what students learn about words is gleaned through their reading, we also need to directly teach them the origin of words, how word meanings can aid spelling, and how to utilize words derived from Greek and Latin word roots. For example, we teach homophones—words that sound the same but have different meanings, such as *bare* and *bear*. We also show them how to use base words to figure out new words—that by knowing *human,* for instance, you can figure out *humanistic, humanitarian, inhuman,* and *humane* in the context of the text.

Attention to meaning and grammar positively impacts spelling development. As students become more competent readers and writers, we need to teach spelling and meaning relationships—not just sounds and patterns—in learning to spell.

Effective Communication with Parents

Spelling is an area parents care deeply about. Our explanations about how, why, and what we teach in this area must be clear and explicit.

Informing Parents

Use your classroom newsletters as an opportunity to keep parents abreast of what you are teaching. (See examples in Appendixes A and G.) Many parents are relieved just to see spelling mentioned as part of classroom activity. Talk about what you're teaching, how you're teaching, general grade-level expectations, and how parents can help their child at home.

Even if you're not giving spelling tests, send home lists of high-frequency words for students to practice along with a letter of explanation. (See Figure 10-7.) Most parents expect to play some role in helping their children learn to spell. Also make sure that parents see writing samples, both edited and unedited. And be sure that parents are clear about what invented spelling is and what it isn't.

Figure 10–7   A letter to parents of high-frequency words to be studied

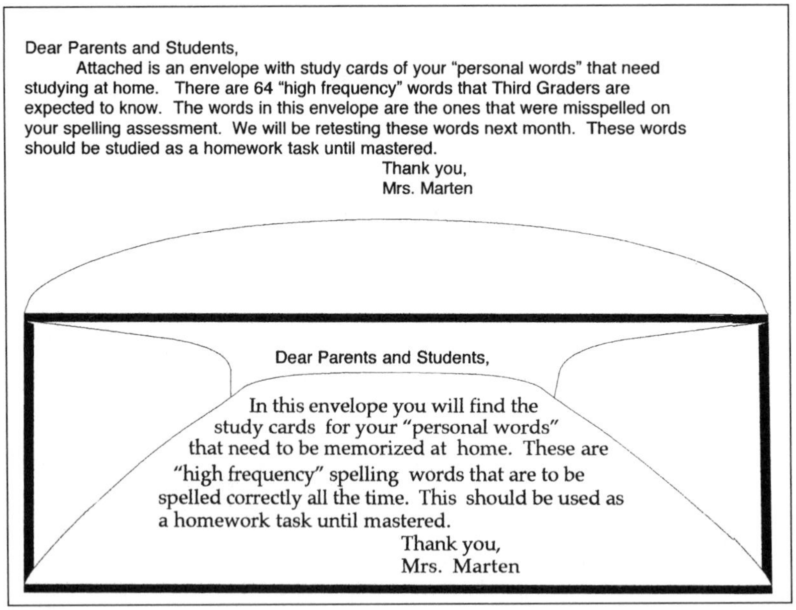

Dear Parents and Students,
     Attached is an envelope with study cards of your "personal words" that need studying at home.   There are 64 "high frequency" words that Third Graders are expected to know. The words in this envelope are the ones that were misspelled on your spelling assessment. We will be retesting these words next month. These words should be studied as a homework task until mastered.
          Thank you,
          Mrs. Marten

Dear Parents and Students,

     In this envelope you will find the study cards for your "personal words" that need to be memorized at home. These are "high frequency" spelling words that are to be spelled correctly all the time. This should be used as a homework task until mastered.
          Thank you,
          Mrs. Marten

Explaining Invented Spelling

Since many parents are new to the notion of invented spelling and how kids develop as writers, it's important to acquaint them with this important information. Since we have a new group of parents each year, our parent education must occur annually. Let parents know that our instruction to students is not "Don't worry about spelling," but "Use what you know and do the best you can." This sends a very different message to the child and parent and one that communicates that spelling does matter.

Every year, a conversation with a parent convinces me that we must do a better job educating parents. When I was seeking permission to share a wonderful piece written by a first grader with other teachers, an angry parent let me know that she did not appreciate her son's invented spellings. "No," she told me, "You cannot share the piece. Furthermore," she explained, "I sat my son down and drilled him on all those words." I felt awful that a piece of writing I believed should be celebrated wound up causing distress to the student. What the teacher and I had found charming and indicative of spelling knowledge and growth, the parent had found incorrect and inappropriate. We erroneously assumed that all parents understood the value and normalcy of invented spelling. While this story is atypical, it reminded us, once again, that we cannot assume that parents understand how young writers develop, and that it is our job to make spelling development explicit to parents.

One way to help parents understand is to invite them into the classroom during writing time. When Joanna Connors' child entered kindergarten, she was unfamiliar with invented spelling. She volunteered in kindergarten classes and saw it as "great" and became a strong parent advocate in our district. She commented, "As a writer, I was pleased to see concentration on content rather than on doing it perfectly, which is so inhibiting. Both of my kids are great spellers today."

Using a Published Program

Many of our teachers have gone back to a formal, published program because they feel more confident they are teaching phonics and rules that way. They also like the structure and guidelines such a program provides. Additionally, some say that they stay with a published program because parents relate to the traditional approach of seeing a workbook come home with their child. They get involved with helping with the activities and helping their child prepare for the weekly test. As one teacher told me, "I don't believe the workbook or tests help improve spelling, but parents think they do, so I stick with them."

There's no right answer here. The biggest concern I have with the approach is the time involved—time that could be spent more meaningfully. My experience has been that when we teachers are highly knowledgeable and articulate, parents trust our practices.

Having High Expectations for Conventional Spelling

Several years ago I read an article by Rebecca Sitton (1996) that greatly impacted our ongoing assessment in spelling. The article became the focus of discussion in our language arts support groups, and many of our teachers incorporated the author's recommendations. Sitton proposes doing away with Friday testing of words because of the emphasis on memorization and poor transfer to everyday writing. In its place, she suggests a different kind of test, an everyday test on "no excuses" words, those words that students are expected to spell correctly at all times.

Students know that each week a sample of their writing will be randomly collected for the purpose of assessing spelling, and one or more paragraphs will be bracketed and marked for spelling. (For younger students, perhaps only a few lines would be targeted.) Because students don't know when this will happen, each time they write they are more likely to proofread for spelling, especially for the high-frequency "no excuses" words. Because students may use—and, indeed, are encouraged to use—references to verify their spelling, all students have a chance to spell successfully. Students receive feedback on their progress and are expected to correct misspelled words. Weekly papers are filed as part of a student's ongoing record of spelling progress.

Parents love the no-excuses approach. It sends the message that invented spelling is only okay for words we wouldn't expect students to be able to spell. It invites parents to get involved and lets them know we value spelling and are holding students highly accountable. Instead of helping their child with a workbook page or preparing for the Friday test, parents' spelling involvement is connected to ongoing, authentic writing.

> The teacher sends home papers unmarked for "no excuses" words so that parents and children can work together toward the goal of spelling well in writing. This flexibility fits a busy family schedule much better than the Thursday night "cramming" ritual. (Sitton 1996, 7)

See Appendix G-4 for one teacher's letter explaining this approach to parents.

What Parents Can Do

There are many things that parents can do to further their child's spelling development. These include the following:

- Read aloud, perhaps having the child follow along looking at the print.
- Talk about words and demonstrate a fascination with words. One family I know has a "vocabulary night" once a week. Dinner conversation focuses on talk about interesting words, and a dictionary is present. Such discussion about words— meanings and spellings—has gone on for many years, and each of the children have excellent vocabularies.
- Praise your child's best invented spellings, and focus first on what the child knows.
- Reinforce the strategies being taught in school.
- Encourage writing at home for real reasons—letters, notes, memos, lists.
- Play word games.

See Appendix G-4 for many ideas for parents, based on their child's level of spelling development.

LEARNING AND USING NEW VOCABULARY

As teachers, we have long known that students with the best vocabularies are usually our strongest readers and comprehenders. I always share that information with students. I want them to know not just that words are fascinating, but that knowing and using interesting words appropriately is a hallmark of a smart person.

Applying Relevant Research

Students acquire many new words from reading widely, listening to stories, and talking about words (Smith and Elley 1994; Nagy 1988). While direct instruction has some impact on vocabulary growth, it is insufficient as the principal strategy for building an extensive vocabulary.

Doing lots of reading seems to be the surest way to build a broad vocabulary. Just twenty minutes of daily reading can potentially lead to learning at least one thousand words per year (Nagy, Anderson, and Herman 1987). Moreover, the more vocabulary words students know, the better able they are to infer unfamiliar words (Rupley, Logan, and Nichols 1998/1999, 336).

However, if students read only very easy books, that is, books "below the student's grade level of reading ability," vocabulary growth is likely to be minimal. Along these same lines, it has been suggested that listening to challenging material that builds a student's background knowledge may well be the most effective way to increase vocabulary (Carver and Leibert 1995).

This last statement points to the necessity of reading aloud stories for increasing the vocabulary of second-language learners and struggling readers. For all students—but especially for those who cannot read well enough to learn lots of new words from surrounding context—it is imperative that they listen to and participate in rich discussions involving all kinds of texts. A brief explanation of new words—in the context of the story—seems to help students remember new vocabulary (Brett, Rothlein, and Hurley 1996).

We also cannot assume that students automatically know how to figure out words in context. We have noticed in our one-on-one reading conferences (page 118) that many students—especially the struggling ones—just skip unfamiliar words. We need to show them, by thinking aloud as we read (pages 452–454), how good readers use surrounding context and background experience to deduce a word's meaning.

Teaching Vocabulary

While there is no one best way to ensure that students acquire a rich vocabulary, a combination approach that involves the following components seems to make the most sense:

- Reading extensively
- Hearing and discussing the rich language of texts
- Focusing on words through explicit instruction
- Actively participating in activities that lead to conceptualization of meaning— utilizing word study, word games, analogies, mental and visual associations, connecting to known words

Focusing on Interesting Words

We make it a priority for students to spend a lot of time talking about, looking up, and using interesting words. Such activities build on students' natural curiosity about words.

For instance, when I am working with a group of students in a small guided reading group or facilitating a literature conversation, we take time to focus on interesting words. My experience has been that we often ask students to learn too many new words from one book. Focusing on ten to fifteen words is plenty. Negotiate with students to choose words that are worth knowing because these words:

- Occur frequently
- Are necessary for understanding the text
- Can easily transfer to writing
- May not be easily defined by context
- Are particularly interesting

I make a vocabulary chart to go along with the book we're reading. When we decide a word is important enough or interesting enough to know, I write it on the chart. I find that talking about a new word only once is insufficient. I refer to the chart constantly, using the words both in conversations and in writing. Repeated use of these words makes an impact. Pretty soon, students are using the words too. When that happens, I make a point of bringing their usage to the attention of the class. For example, when Sarah, a fourth grader, wrote *reluctantly* in her fiction story and when Jason used *opinionated* in conversation, I made a big deal out of congratulating them. When words transfer to writing and speaking in a meaningful way, I know the student "owns" the word.

Sometimes, as part of responding to literature, students are asked to choose several words that they want to know that meet the criteria stated above. When Megan came to guided reading group, she could hardly contain her excitement. She and a group of second graders were discussing *The Dragonling* by Jackie Koller. "I got a word! I got a word!" she excitedly called out as she offered her words, *flattered* and *jostled,* for discussion. In addition to jotting words down, we instruct students to list the page number (to find the word again easily), at least several of the words surrounding it (to see if context is helpful), and to make an educated guess as to what the word means. Then, in group, if we can't figure the word out together, we look it up in the dictionary.

In an effort to focus on the importance of vocabulary, some teachers have students keep vocabulary notebooks. In one fourth-grade classroom, the teacher and students decided how this would be done and what strategies they would use to figure out new words. See Figure 10-8 for their guidelines created in a shared writing.

Many teachers still require students to look up lots of words in a dictionary in connection with reading a required text, and also to memorize definitions of words. Such work is often counterproductive as many students have difficulty figuring out which definition fits the context. "Definitions do not teach you how to *use* a new word" and "definitions do not effectively convey new concepts" (Nagy 1998, 6; italics in original). As in all areas of the curriculum, students need to be actively involved in vocabulary work for it to have relevance for them.

Also, as previously mentioned, attending to morphology or derivations of words (root words, prefixes, and suffixes) contributes to a student's understanding of the meanings of words. Finally, just as we seek to have students develop a spelling consciousness, we also want to make them more aware of words, word parts, syntax, and special language features so that they develop a word consciousness and adopt an inquisitive stance toward words.

Figure 10–8   A fourth-grade class' vocabulary guidelines

Strategies for Figuring Out New Vocabulary

- Read the rest of the sentence.
- Try to put in a different word that makes sense. See if it fits. If not, try another word.
- Think, "What could it mean?" Look at other parts of the text to help you.
- Use what you already know about the topic/word.
- Use the dictionary.

Choose at least 3 important words each week
that you want to know the meaning of.
Your words can come from any book you are reading.

Include the date, the title and author, the page number, the word, how it is used, and what you think the word means. Here's an example:

1-23-97   *The Lion, the Witch, and the Wardrobe* by C. S. Lewis
p. 40   probable
                 "Nothing is more probable . . ."
                 likely, very possible

Teaching Syllabication

I have made an overhead transparency of a high-interest newspaper article and am demonstrating my reading process as I think aloud in a third-grade classroom (pages 452–454). Each student receives a photocopy of "Even Sharks Unsafe When Killer Whales Show They Rule Seas" (from the *Cleveland Plain Dealer*), which describes the first known sighting of an orca whale killing a shark. In addition to focusing on understanding the article, I am using the article to teach syllabication.

Using two 5 × 7" index cards, I expose one line of print at a time as I move down the page. When I come to a difficult word, I pause. The first line reads, "Killer whales are kings of the sea—and now there's a videotape to prove it." I stop at the word *videotape* and highlight it with my sliding mask. Thinking aloud, I say, "v . . . tape. I know *tape,* so I'll draw a line before the *t*; the word must be *videotape* because that makes sense." As the students are following along on the overhead or on their individual copies, I show them that when I divide words into syllables, I use what I know about words and patterns and the meaning of the text to help me.

I divide *naturalist, apparently, electrified, encounter,* and *predator* into syllables. I teach them about open and closed syllables and also about how to skip the word, read on, and come back to it, and to substitute a word that makes sense (*swam* for *surged,* for example).

Regarding rules, I only teach the ones that work most all the time and are useful (page 406). I teach kids that syllables are either open or closed, and that sometimes you have to try reading a word several ways to see which way sounds right in the sentence.

Figure 10–9   A visual guide to help recall short vowels

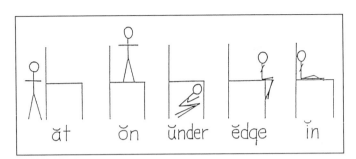

I tell the students that an open syllable ends with a vowel and is always long; it is "longing for protection." A closed syllable is protected by a consonant at the end of the syllable and is always short. So if you come across "tulip" and you can't read it, try pronouncing it "tul ip" and "tu lip" and see which sounds right in the context. Kids do need to know their short vowels cold, and if they don't, I offer them a "visual" short vowel sheet to help them remember. (See Figure 10-9.)

After we are about halfway through the shark story, I ask for a group of volunteers to join me in a small group. "I'd like to work with a group who wants to get better at figuring out hard words. That's something all good readers need to be able to do." I ask for volunteers because I don't want to stigmatize students. Eight students raise their hands. I have no way of knowing who the so-called good and poor readers are. I take whoever wants to come. I ask the remaining students to finish reading the article with a partner, divide hard words into syllables, circle any words that they can't figure out, and to write a one- or two-sentence summary of the article right on the photocopy. (We have previously worked on summary writing.) I guide my small group through these activities. My experience has been that repeated practice in such work transfers to problem solving multisyllable words independently.

It is not sufficient to teach kids rules of syllabication and strategies for "sounding out" difficult words in isolation. Readers must also learn how to put in a word that makes sense when they cannot decipher a word and how to use the text to help them properly pronounce words and figure out their meanings.

FINAL REFLECTIONS

Just as research recommends attending to the child's overall literacy development before focusing on spelling as a separate entity, so, too, we teachers will first want to focus on becoming excellent teachers of reading and writing. Then, just like our students, we will need opportunities for extended conversations about words, patterns, and meanings to increase our knowledge about the subject.

Start with what you can manage. In our district, that was a weekly study group (in our language arts support group) to talk about concerns about spelling, study the research, share ideas, and examine kids' writing for patterns and directions for teaching. From there, we moved to trying things out in our classrooms and sharing how teaching certain strategies, focused word study, or spelling activities were helpful or not. Most of all, we kept in mind that reading and writing for relevant purposes and audiences are an absolute necessity for developing good spellers who care about spelling. Once again, there is no reason to spell if you don't write.

CONTINUING THE CONVERSATION

• ***Form a study group with interested teachers.***   Become familiar with spelling research. Obtain copies of the articles annotated in The Blue Pages, "Spelling and Word Study." (Write, call, or use the Internet to contact the publishers of the respective journals.) Have one or two teachers read each article. Then, report and share information with the whole study group. Discuss implications for your teaching.

• ***Examine how you are incorporating meaningful word study.***   Keep track of patterns and meanings that you are exploring with your students. Share that information with parents and administrators.

• ***Use the spelling textbook judiciously.***   Try to find ways to use the textbook as an informative resource rather than as a total program. Give input into the text-selection process. Look for published programs that have a developmental approach and allow for some student choice rather than a one-size-fits-all approach. Do not abandon a textbook program unless you are highly knowledgeable and have a strong reading-writing classroom.

• ***Examine your communications to parents.***   Make sure you are briefly sharing relevant research, clearly describing your spelling program without jargon, explaining how you are assessing and monitoring spelling development, and providing meaningful ways for parents to support their child's spelling development.

CHAPTER 11

Reading Nonfiction

Reading the newspaper in a fourth-grade class

Nonfiction is more than information conveyed through words. It is a carefully crafted genre. It is a *literature of fact* that combines both verbal and visual texts.

—*Richard M. Kerper*

I'm as guilty as anyone of reading mostly stories to children and filling classroom libraries with great fiction and little else. For years I used the excuse—valid at the time—that you couldn't find quality nonfiction, especially in the paperback versions necessary to afford multiple copies. Happily, that's no longer the case. Since 1992, about half of all new books published for children are informational (Hepler 1998). Wonderful children's authors like Seymour Simon, Patricia Lauber, Gail Gibbons, Milton Meltzer, and many others inform and delight readers with engaging texts and eye-catching visual aids. Nonfiction is an increasingly explored art form.

Yet exemplary nonfiction—whether in the form of trade books or collected in language arts anthologies—remains far too uncommon in literacy classes (Moss et al. 1997, 419). This is ironic, because students naturally gravitate to nonfiction: any kindergarten or first-grade teacher will tell you about her students' keen interest in and partiality for informational books, to include reference books such as atlases. And this interest shows no age limits. Sales of nonfiction books equal sales of popular fiction (Carvajal 1997), and our nations' libraries report somewhat greater circulation for nonfiction. However, when we include all informational categories and formats, such as pamphlets, periodicals, microforms, mixed media, and software, nonfiction circulation is about double that of fiction (Boston Public Library fact sheet, Oct. 1998 fax, and County of Los Angeles Public Library fact sheet, Dec. 1998 fax).

More important, as students progress through our system of education, their subject-area classroom reading is primarily nonfiction: 85 percent of the reading done by middle school, high school, college, and postgraduate students is nonfiction (Snowball

1995). Nonfiction, which often includes specialized vocabulary and visual depiction of information, can be more complicated to read. Yet we have not been adequately preparing our students for this reading. Continuing to overfocus on fiction in language arts is unwarranted. Nonfiction books help students increase their knowledge about, and make connections with, the world around them. Well-written nonfiction provokes close observation, questioning, and investigation. Reading nonfiction affects the ease and skill with which students write nonfiction. Just as we expose students to narrative forms such as journals and stories, we must also expose them to nonfiction literary models. Without such exposure and modeling, students have great difficulty writing reports, explanations, and persuasive pieces.

WHAT IS NONFICTION?

Nonfiction is a sprawling genre that encompasses informational narratives (also called info-narratives or true stories), textbooks and reference books, newspapers and news-magazines. Included in the form are biographies and autobiographies, scientific findings and experiments, treatises on history and social studies, reports, directions and instructions, and much more.

Noted children's literature expert Susan Hepler defines nonfiction—or informational books—this way:

> Whatever we call the genre, it includes books about all of the sciences—natural, social, and physical; biography; history; sports; handicrafts; languages; geography; music; drama; and more. Surprisingly to some, informational books also include folktales and traditional literature because they bear information about the culture from which they come. (1998, 6)

Reading nonfiction also includes decoding and interpreting visual elements (graphs, charts, time lines, tables, maps, diagrams, photographs), which are increasingly being used in electronic information media (the Internet, CD-ROMs) as well as in the brochures, directories, and catalogues that have proliferated with the arrival of desktop publishing. Visual literacy is a necessity to function and communicate well in life (Moline 1996, 3).

Nonfiction, like all genres, is further delineated by writing style. Trade nonfiction, we hope, is written in graceful prose, stems from the author's passions and careful research, rings with a strong authorial voice, and appeals to a general audience. At the other end of the spectrum are textbooks and reference books, usually written by one or more authors with little or no personal voice and directed to a special-interest audience. In between are pieces that contain elements of both—elegant writing within a factual, sequential structure, for example (think of particularly moving eyewitness news accounts).

CHOOSING QUALITY NONFICTION FOR THE CLASSROOM

The nonfiction texts we use in the classroom must be of high quality. Students need to learn that facts are subject to interpretation, that two authors can take the same facts and interpret them differently, that nonfiction allows for point of view, that illustrations can carry as much meaning as print, and that critical readers always ask questions about what they read.

Additionally, in exploring notable nonfiction, we want to make students aware that the writer needs to know his topic well and that this usually requires a great deal of research. For students to write well in this genre, we also need to show them how the writer makes the topic appealing through engaging writing, clear and inviting visual aids, and logical organization.

Many nonfiction books used in classrooms today are informational narratives: real occurrences that read like a story (Saul 1999). Exemplary writers like Jennifer Owings Dewey, Lawrence Pringle, Seymour Simon, and Shelley Tanaka make true stories come alive with interesting characters and powerful imagery. But we do students a disservice if we do not also select books that emphasize other structural and organizational patterns, texts whose meaning resides as much in the visuals and illustrations as in the print (Carter and Abrahamson 1995).

Selection Guidelines

Good nonfiction is exciting! It is accurate, interesting, cohesive, clearly organized, and attractively laid out (Sudol and King 1996). It also uses the appropriate specialized vocabulary, summarizes important concepts, presents essential (and satisfying) details, offers valid generalizations, and includes illustrations or photos that support the text (see Bamford and Kristo 1998). However, the writing is paramount—without captivating leads, vivid imagery, and an engaging style, none of the above matters much. As a reader, I want to be fascinated and intrigued. This does not mean the text has to have a narrative structure. Beautifully designed texts that rely primarily on visual features supported by descriptive text, such as the Dorling-Kindersley books, can be equally superlative and appealing.

Perhaps most important, nonfiction has to have a "conceptual hook," as Wendy Saul wrote me recently. That is, we understand and remember key information in the text because it connects with concepts we already understand. Without these conceptual hooks, our learning is limited. For example, when Seymour Simon says (*Whales*, New York: HarperCollins, 1989), "The tongue of the blue whale weighs as much as an elephant," I am mesmerized by the creature's immensity. When Jennifer Owings Dewey tells her true story about being bitten by a snake (*Rattlesnake Dance*, 1997) and interweaves her narrative with facts and drawings about snakes, I pay attention and remember. When Laurence Pringle tells the fascinating story of one monarch butterfly's migration across a continent, in *The Story of a Monarch Butterfly* (1997), I am spellbound.

Features to Look For

When selecting books for classroom use, look for books and resources that have, at least, some of the following characteristics:

- Major concepts are clearly presented and developed.
- Sufficient background information is provided.
- Primary source materials such as letters, newspaper articles, and diaries are included so that the reader "hears" the voice of the people involved.

- Book organization is clear and logical.
- Information presented is accurate.
- Multiple perspectives are included.
- Readers are encouraged to think, interpret, and draw their own conclusions.
- Descriptions and visual aids are clear and enhance the text's meaning.
  Adapted from Zarnowski (1998, 104).

To help guide your selection of nonfiction, see "Literature Resources for Choosing Fiction and Nonfiction" in The Blue Pages, page 14b and "Criteria for Choosing Anchor Books," pages 66–67.

EXPLORING NONFICTION

Before we can expect students to read and write nonfiction competently on their own, they must be given the opportunity to listen to it being read aloud, discuss its attributes, observe as the techniques of reading it are demonstrated, and browse through a wide range of informational material. Our students need to be aware of the purposes for reading nonfiction and of how and why these books are researched, written, and organized.

Before Tara Strachan asks her second graders to do research reports on dinosaurs, she lets them explore books and resources she has gathered with the school librarian's assistance. First, she models browsing through a book. Then, in small groups or individually, students browse a number of books, reading parts here and there, and share some of their observations. Afterward, as a whole class, they talk about and record on a class chart what they noticed: voice, format, organization, leads, visuals, whatever.

Some teachers end browsing sessions by having students record in their journal what they remember and want to research (Robb 1994, 241). This is very much like what I do when I am getting ready to research and write. I consult many resources, make notes, put Post-its on pages and books to return to, and jot down questions I have. This gives me a good overview of my topic, lets me identify any number of possible subtopics, and makes me aware of different formats, organizational structures, and levels of investigation.

Browsing is a skill we need to model and teach all students in all genres. Our poorest readers try to read and remember every word and fail miserably. Browsing is like *relaxing* into a book (Saul 1999). Once you feel comfortable, reading and remembering are easier. A kindergarten teacher who models browsing every day told me, "My kids are now more observant of detail, have the vocabulary to talk about books, and are ferociously interested in books. They really know how to look at a book."

Guiding Questions

The following guiding questions—or ones like them—will help students think about how nonfiction books work. As with everything you teach, first demonstrate the process yourself by thinking aloud about the questions as you read a book to the class.

- Why did the author write this book? What do we expect to learn from reading it?
- What did the author need to know to write it?
- What sources did the author use to get information?

- How is this book organized?
- How will I need to read it (preview, use visuals, skim, take notes, skip certain sections, read difficult sections more slowly)?
- How does what I learn fit (or not fit) with what I already know?

Student conversations about nonfiction are critical. Rich talk that examines the evidence, poses hypotheses, and makes interpretations leads to understanding. We must let students experience what scientists, historians, and mathematicians do. We must give children "the opportunity to read and share observations, ask for clarification, test ideas among peers, and argue a position" (Zarnowski 1995, 188).

Regardless of the discipline, it is our job to guide students in reading, questioning, interpreting, and talking about the subject at hand. Furthermore, we need to monitor students' learning and check their understanding and conclusions. Otherwise, students will continue to have difficulty reading nonfiction, will fail to read it with a critical, questioning stance. High school English teacher Holly Burgess is emphatic on this point: "The importance of this kind of reading cannot be understated. Students who struggle are not just failing state proficiency tests; they are failing high school classes."

Exploring Science Books

With our guidance, students can learn to think like scientists, or at least to take on a scientific perspective when reading in this genre. Exemplary teacher/author Jeanne Reardon (1998) suggests the following prompts to help students think about the science in books they hear and read (similar questions could be adapted for other disciplines):

- What makes a book a science book?
- In what ways is this book a science book?
- What kind of science did the author need to know to write this book?
- What kind of science did the illustrator need to know to illustrate this book?
- How do the illustrations work?
- How does the author explain science in this book?
- What questions did the author have in her mind that she answered in this book?
- What does the author think is important? What does he want you to think about?
- How does the author think like a scientist? How does this book make you think like a scientist?
- Think about connections in this book. Did you make any connections to other things you know?

Exploring Books Related to History and Social Studies

Nonfiction promotes children's understanding of people, places, and past events and can lead to rich conversations about past and present life. History, one form of nonfiction, is essentially the story of often ordinary people (his-story, her-story) who act heroically because they believe strongly in something. History can demonstrate the power of courage in the face of danger, the possibility of making a difference, and therefore offer hope to readers.

Social studies specialist Myra Zarnowski (1998) believes that a powerful and important use of exemplary nonfiction must be to show how authors engage in "historical thinking": "Historical understanding requires historical thinking—taking a critical stance toward what is read and assuming a questioning attitude" (347). She recommends:

- Providing students with books that show authors engaged in historical thinking
- Showing and discussing how authors draw from and interpret multiple and perhaps conflicting sources. "Even young readers in the primary grades can begin to deal with contradictory versions of historical events" (350)
- Choosing books that include important historical concepts and generalizations, not just interesting events
- Focusing on connections between the past and the present

Additionally, Zarnowski (1995, 185) notes that in teaching social studies with literature, we must ensure that the selected literature is "good to learn from":

- Is this material interesting and comprehensible?
- Does it linger in the mind?
- Does it prompt original thoughts?
- Does it deal with major ideas related to the social sciences?
- Does it acknowledge dialogue, writing, and further learning?

Zarnowski also emphasizes that a writer of history "must be both a sifter and a shaper of information" (1998). That is, the writer interprets what he reads, views, and consults. Students need to know that nonfiction is interpreted truths, not just accumulated facts. Being able to think like a historian will influence the way students write.

With our guidance, students will see that writers of history (as well as science and other disciplines) do not just gather and copy information. They consult multiple sources, look for patterns, deal with conflicting historical accounts, hypothesize, combine information, make inferences, and form their own opinions. If students, supported by our demonstrations and scaffolds, write with such a historical (or scientific) perspective, we will be rid of the traditional boring reports and biographies that merely summarize facts.

One other point needs to be made here. Historical fiction cannot be used to teach social studies. Fiction is not fact and cannot be construed as such. At its best, though, historical fiction can give a feel for the period, a sense of time and place that is very helpful as background.

READING NONFICTION ALOUD

One of the best ways to show students how nonfiction texts are written and organized is to read aloud a variety of notable nonfiction, think aloud as we read, point out page layouts and provocative visuals, and prompt students to talk about what they notice. By studying well-known nonfiction authors and their writing styles, students become familiar with how scientists, historians, biographers, researchers, and inquirers think. As with fiction, the nonfiction we choose to read aloud often becomes a favorite and promotes further reading.

In that regard, it is important that we read aloud both expository and narrative texts so students read and write in multiples genres with ease, flexibility, and deep understanding. Top-notch nonfiction writers stir the imagination and write in a vivid, engaging style just as fiction writers do. The best nonfiction is aesthetically appealing while presenting information clearly and accurately and encouraging close observation of our world.

Like many other teachers, I spent many years focused on reading quality fiction aloud. It was only when I took a close look at my own reading—in the face of our students' poor showing on interpreting nonfiction texts—that I made nonfiction reading a priority. In spite of my love for fiction, the majority of my own reading (the daily newspaper, magazines, directions, instructions, cookbooks, "how to" manuals, professional books) and writing (articles and books about literacy) is nonfiction.

Tips for Reading Nonfiction Aloud

Reading nonfiction aloud is a perfect opportunity to show students how the genre works, how factual texts differ from fictional ones and need to be read differently. (Most of the tips that follow are true for fiction as well.)

• *Choose books (and magazines and newspaper articles) that capture your imagination (enthusiasm is contagious) and that will tap into students' interests.*

• *Choose a variety of types of nonfiction.*   Readers "must not limit nonfiction reading to a single structure any more than they should confine fictional reading to narrow genre offerings" (Carter and Abrahamson 1995, 320).

• *Always read the selection to yourself first* so you are familiar with the concepts, author, background, vocabulary, organizational structure, visual elements, writing style, and any points you may want to explain, clarify, and bring up for discussion.

• *Give a thoughtful introduction before you read aloud.*   Students need to be familiar enough with the vocabulary and the concepts to understand the text. This is where you can plant the "conceptual hooks" to help them. Without the proper background, students' learning will be limited regardless of how much effort they exert. (If additional background and experiences are necessary, introduce these resources and activities a day or two ahead of time.) You may want to talk about:

- The author
- The illustrations and other visual elements
- How the book is organized
- Why it was written
- How the research was conducted
- What types of information you expect to find
- Anything else that seems relevant to making the book easier to understand. (For example, you may also want to make some predictions about what you expect to learn from the book.)

• *Read only part of the book or read out of order,* depending on your purposes or the type of nonfiction. (Informational storybooks—info-narratives—and biographies can be read cover to cover, but most reference books can't be.) You may want to read all the headings of a chapter first to show students how to get a mental framework before reading. Or you may want to interpret a graphic or read only the section that pertains to a curriculum focus. Students need to know we can make choices about what and how to read.

• *Point out features of nonfiction text and explain their use:*
  • Organizational and location devices (headings and subheadings, index, table of contents, glossary, questions at end of sections)
  • Visual aids (illustrations, charts, graphs, diagrams, time lines, maps)
  • Writing style, structure, tone, and special vocabulary

• *Demonstrate asking the following questions about special features and formats:*
  • What do they tell us?
  • Why are they used?
  • What makes one format better than another for conveying information?

• *Verbalize your reading processes.* Your reading purposes determine how you read. Explain why you are reading slower, rereading a difficult or confusing passage, skipping certain sections, reading headings first; why and how you are consulting (and perhaps revisiting) the visual aids and captions; and how you are figuring out difficult vocabulary. For example, if you are savoring the language of part of an info-narrative, you may slow down as you do in fiction. If you are reading to learn and remember information, you may need to reread a passage several times. If you are reading for specific information, you may quickly skim to find it.

• *Encourage questions and lively discussion about topics, facts, concepts, generalizations, writing style, language, formats, and conclusions.* Discuss what the author has done to make the nonfiction interesting, what sources she has used, and how she has interpreted them.

• *Allow time to process the information.* You can't absorb twenty pages of information as quickly as you can a chapter of fiction.

• *Group or pair nonfiction books to elicit better observation.* Contrast and compare (this one has, this one doesn't) and help children discover how authors choose, slant, interpret, and infer similar information.

Confirming Nonfiction Attributes

Once students are familiar with nonfiction, recording what they know is a good way to confirm nonfiction attributes and keep that awareness visible and growing. Classroom teacher Loretta Martin reads lots of informational books with her second graders. After they have become familiar with this genre and learned that we read fiction differently from fiction, the class engages in shared writing to identify questions to think about when reading nonfiction. Here's what a recent class came up with:

How to Read Nonfiction

- Look at the cover or topic: Do I know something about this topic?
- Look at the title page: What is the copyright date?
- Read more slowly (if I need to): Did I understand what I read? Am I learning something new? Do I want to read other books on this topic?
- How can I show or tell what I've learned?

Another primary-grade class produced the following shared writing after their teacher had read many nonfiction titles aloud:

What We Have Noticed About Nonfiction

- There are lots of facts.
- Authors use drawings, graphs, and photographs.
- There is an index and sometimes a glossary.
- You can get new information by looking at the pictures and reading the captions.
- The author chooses words carefully. There's a good lead.
- The table of contents tells you how the book is organized.
- Drawings are labeled.
- There are headings that tell you what each part is about.
- You don't always have to read the whole book to get information.
- The author knows a lot about the subject.

LEARNING TO READ NONFICTION

Understanding nonfiction requires thorough background knowledge of the subject (Yochum 1991). For example, when I am reading the daily newspaper, I often skip or skim international articles. Without the political, historical, and cultural contexts (which I lack), my understanding is limited. I can get the facts of the piece but I can't interpret their significance or apply what I read to the "bigger picture." By contrast, when I read (or listen to) the national news, which I follow carefully, I feel capable of making informed judgments and offering my opinions (to my husband, family, and friends and, occasionally, to a newspaper's editors). Because I have the background information, the history—specialized vocabulary, some knowledge of the characters (politicians, authors, and other notables), area of the country, and past events—I am able to comprehend not only the facts but to place those facts in a rich context. That larger understanding makes it possible for me to integrate the facts with past happenings, grasp new concepts, make connections to broader related issues, and discuss possible implications and concerns.

Many students don't understand this difference, and we must be explicit in teaching them about it. What that means for the classroom is that we must be sure to check whether our students have adequate background knowledge and provide it for them when they don't. Only then can we expect them to understand what they read. Appendix D-1 is a checklist students can use to evaluate their approach to reading nonfiction.

Reading the News

Like millions of other people, I spend a portion of my day focused on the news. I am not much of a television watcher, so to stay informed I depend on the newspaper. For me, that means reading *The New York Times* every morning over breakfast and coffee with my husband. Frank reads a section, I read a section. We point out articles and editorials to each other, talk about what's happening, speculate about why, predict what may happen next, and puzzle over troubling occurrences.

While the volume of articles and features in a newspaper can be overwhelming, newsmagazines are selective in what they include. These newsmagazines are a primary source of news for a large segment of our population. I recently spoke with the subscription departments of the three major newsmagazines, *Time*, *Newsweek*, and *US News and World Report*. Total combined subscriptions are about ten million, with a readership of about fifty-eight million. Those of us who do not subscribe to a newsmagazine ourselves are part of the readership when we visit a doctor's office, travel by plane, or settle down in the reading room of the public library.

Being able to read, analyze, and interpret the news is part of being an informed and responsible citizen in a democracy. Our students need to acquire these skills. They need to know how current events—local, national, and international, political, economic, and scientific—affect our daily life. It is our job to teach them. News articles are an excellent model for nonfiction writing. Feature stories and editorials can be used to demonstrate and talk about leads, headlines, verbs, research, sources, explanations, photographs, captions, writing style. Some teachers and students begin one morning a week reading the newspaper. Students don't have to write anything. They read alone or with a partner, just the way we adults do. And they love it.

Reading the newspaper isn't always a cherished classroom activity, however. Sometimes teachers expect students to take notes and write a report. Then, instead of being the relaxing way many adults begin their morning, it becomes a chore. Think about how you read the newspaper—drinking a cup of coffee or tea, picking and choosing what you want to read, perhaps discussing interesting news with someone across the breakfast table. There is certainly no pressure to "report" on what you've read.

The teachers in my district have brought these real-world habits into the classroom. Now when students read the newspaper, they drink juice (often out of their own mugs they've brought from home), choose the articles they wish to read, and often chat with a classmate about what they discover. Each week several volunteers giving a brief oral talk about an interesting article. Even the reluctant readers read the newspaper with pleasure. (See the photo at the beginning of this chapter.)

Some classrooms become so enamored of reading the news that they write their own newspapers or newsmagazines, sometimes using desktop publishing to create the final editions. Fourth-grade teacher Julie Beers notes that of all the writing her students do, their monthly newsmagazine for parents—*WACK* (*Weird, Adventurous, Curious Kids*), modeled on *Time for Kids*—generates the most enthusiastic response and participation. The audience is "up close and personal." Students have lots of choice regarding topics, format, organization, and visual elements. Articles are short, so revision and editing are manageable. Students take this writing very seriously, and it shows. (After sending copies of their newsmagazine to the president of *Time for Kids*, she wrote the students, "As a connoisseur of classroom magazines, I can report that *WACK* is among the best I've seen.") Julie has capitalized on her students' interest by teaching most of her minilessons (on titles, leads, word choice, awareness of audience, endings) in connection with producing quality writing for the newsmagazine. (Figure 11-1 is a page from *WACK*. The cover photo for this book shows a conference around an upcoming issue.)

Of course, we first need to guide students in how to read and explore all sections of a newspaper or magazine—advertisements, editorials, comics, columns, feature stories—and take note of the message, format, style, and wording. Guided reading lessons using newsmagazines and newspapers can be a very powerful way to teach critical reading strategies—how to analyze, summarize, predict, figure out vocabulary, locate information, distinguish between fact and opinion, editorialize, read and interpret visual aids such as maps and tables, to name just some.

I keep my eyes peeled for interesting articles to use with third graders and older students. I look for short, timely, engaging articles about all aspects of life—science, history, social issues, current events—and I photocopy them to use in the classroom. When students have their own copy, they can underline, highlight, write in the margin, take notes, just as I do when I read nonfiction and want to remember salient points.

I also make an overhead transparency of the article, so as I am demonstrating, thinking aloud, and guiding, students can easily follow along. I show them how I underline or highlight key words and phrases, how I break multisyllable words apart, how I write notes or comments in the margin.

After my demonstration, small groups of students read the rest of the article or a new article, monitoring their group reading process on a worksheet (see Figure 11-2 and also reciprocal teaching, pages 137–140). I'll join one group to continue modeling and supporting, and after all groups have finished reading, we discuss and evaluate the experience as a class.

Newspapers are an excellent vehicle for encouraging responsible, thoughtful conversation about social issues. Steven Wolk (1998, 195–196) cuts out an interesting article and distributes copies to his class. After students have had a chance to look the article over, he reads it aloud with just enough explanation so that vocabulary and complex ideas are clear. Then he asks students to write a journal entry on their reactions. Initially, the entry may be in response to a prompt—for example, *If you were so-and-so, how would you have acted and why?* (Steven makes a point of writing his own response as well.)

A Guided Reading
Lesson with a Newsmagazine

Fourth-grade teacher Wendy Stafford has used literature in her reading program for over ten years, but always with the whole class. After our weekly language arts support group has focused on small-group guided reading for a month, she asks me to come in and model for her. She is concerned about managing multiple groups. The students are already seated at tables in mixed-ability groups of four or five, so we begin with these groupings.

Every week each child gets a copy of *Time for Kids,* an excellent newsmagazine for students this age. Wendy has been assigning independent reading in the magazine,

Figure 11–1 A page from
WACK, *a monthly newsmagazine for parents*

Beautiful Biomes

Did you know that the Banana tree is not a tree? Let me back up!

Ms. Beers' class is doing a biome study that we have been waiting to do. We read and take notes on the: Rain Forest, Woodlands, Alpine Tundra, Deserts and Grass Lands. It is great. We work in groups for each biome.

Each group made the 3-D plants in the biome that they worked on. Every biome has their own bulletin board to put their marvelous plants on.

Katy commented, " Biome work is hard but hard work pays off."

After all the research and plant models were completed, we did an exciting presentation that was extremely fun.

We are also researching vertebrates, invertebrates and the food chain.

Now you have been waiting to hear about... the Banana tree... which is not a tree... It is a plant with a trunk made up of hard leaves on top of hard leaves to make a base like a trunk!!!

By Andrew Wiedemann

Making A Difference:
Service Corps at Onaway School Helps Out!

Service Corps...
It may seem like some boring word, but actually it's a way for fourth graders at Onaway to help out their school, their community and most of all to make a difference. The leaders of Service Corps are Mrs. Shoda, a second grade teacher, and Mrs. Simpson, a fourth grade teacher. "I think Service Corps is a good way to help the community," says Mrs. Shoda.

One of the places Service Corps hopes to visit this year is the Kethley House nursing home. Other places Service Corps may go is a sight to clean up, and they hope to do a food drive. "It makes the people at the Kethley House so happy to see us." says Mrs. Shoda.

Service Corps may seem like a boring word, but it's a whole lot more!

By
Suzanne Arian

SGORR IS A BIG SUCCESS!

This is a fifty million dollar question! What does S.G.O.R.R. stand for? That's it, you said it! Ding, Ding, Ding, Ding... Student Group on Race Relations. We can't give you fifty million dollars, but we can promise you that your child is learning about life, having to trust people, and fairness in the world.

A group of high schoolers spend their valuable teen time teaching us about life. We see them a couple times a year. Our class enjoys the activities Sgorr does with us. It's so amazing how high schoolers bond with elementary kids so well!

By
Blair Kurit and Emily Krassen

Figure 11–2 A group reading
worksheet: reading a news article about sharks

Group Worksheet for Reading   Date 1/28/98

Title Even Sharks unsafe when killer whales show they rule seas.

Group members (underline scribe) Delishia-Arter-James Erica-Elizabeth

Predict Whales are killing sharks Whales will be the new boss of the sea Why did the female kill the shark?

Question Why did he race to the scene? Why did he put it on film?

Clarify Apparently "did do it" Thrashing - chopping apart

Summarize A female killed a 10-foot great white shark to feed her baby.

---

along with a worksheet of literal questions (*What is . . . ? Who is . . . ?*). Not surprisingly, the students dislike the activity, and there is little teaching going on. It's the typical "read the assignment and answer the questions." I want to demonstrate what good readers do *as* they read to understand. For many students, checking for understanding *after* they read is too late. (Figure 11-3 summarizes the following plan for reading nonfiction.)

Figure 11–3 A plan for a guided reading
lesson using a news article or other nonfiction piece

- Assessing what students know about what good readers do.
- Demonstrating how good readers think and problem solve: think aloud while reading a nonfiction article.
- Adding to what students know about what good readers do.
- Having students read together in small mixed-ability groups; asking them to raise questions, clarify, summarize, predict.
- Guiding one group as other groups collaborate independently.
- Checking for understanding and monitor group processes.

• <u>***Assessing What They Know About What Good Readers Do***</u>   (five minutes)

I begin by explaining what we will be doing together, saying something like: *Today we'll be working together in small groups and using strategies good readers use to understand what they are reading. I need to know what you know about what good readers do.* These fourth graders tell me the following, in the order listed:

- Read hard words.
- Break it up "in my head," sound it out, use the dictionary.
- Read ahead, figure out word from rest of sentence.
- Reread when something doesn't make sense.
- Use expression.
- Mouth the words.
- Notice punctuation and capitalization.

Focus on words, like this list, is typical. I ask for more, but this is the sum total of what they tell me, even with probing.

• <u>***Demonstrating How Good Readers Think and Problem Solve***</u>   (ten minutes)

I tell the students:

> This is a good beginning list, but we're missing some important strategies. I'm going to show you exactly what I do when I read. Follow along in your magazine as I read the first article, "A Huge New Dam Divides China."

I preview the visuals before I start to read and make some judgments regarding what the article will be about.

> Hmm. I'm wondering about the title. That could have a double meaning, such as the dam's not being only a structural divider, a wall to divert the water, but an issue that's dividing people. Maybe not everyone wants this dam to be built.
>
> I probably better look at the map the writer has included before I begin reading. I see the Yangtze River is in the south center of China, and there is a dam being constructed on it. Oh, and look at this photo on the next page, showing trucks and rocks and lots of people. Follow along as I read the caption, "Trucks dump rocks to stop the Yangtze's flow. A 370-mile lake formed by the dam will swallow thousands of villages." The people whose homes will be destroyed surely must be upset. I wonder why the dam is being built? I'll have to read to find out.

I begin to read the article aloud and think aloud as I am reading. I use what I know to say what I think a word means.

> "The Chinese have always dreamed of taming the mighty Yangtze (Yang-tsee) River." Hmm. I think "taming" must mean making it more gentle, because I know what it means to tame an animal. So that must mean the river is pretty rough. And I like how the writer helped me pronounce Yangtze by writing out the phonetic pronunciation in parentheses.

I continue reading the first paragraph and summarize to be sure I've understood it.

> "The world's third-longest waterway has inspired poems and paintings. But its fierce floods have also killed hundreds of thousands of people." I'm going to read that sentence again to be sure I've got the meaning. "The world's third-longest waterway has inspired poems and

Figure 11–4 "A Huge New Dam Divides China"

A Huge New Dam Divides China

The Chinese have always dreamed of taming the mighty Yangtze (Yang-tsee) River. The world's third longest waterway has inspired poems and paintings. But its fierce floods have also killed hundreds of thousands of people.

On November 8, trucks dumped boulders into a part of the river, finishing a key stage in building the world's biggest dam. The project, called Three Gorges Dam, will put a large area in central China underwater: farms, historical sites and three breathtaking canyons, or gorges.

The dam will be a huge wall across the Yangtze. Generators in the dam will harness the river's power, creating enough electricity to meet a tenth of China's energy needs. Just as important, it should prevent floods.

But environmentalists warn that sewage will back up and destroy the precious habitats of river dolphins, giant pandas and other rare animals. Some scientists

Trucks dump rocks to stop the Yangtze's flow. A 370-mile lake formed by the dam will swallow thousands of villages.

fear the dam will actually create more floods.

Three Gorges Dam won't be finished until 2009. But it's already affecting the stunning scenery and the 1.2 million people who must flee the area. Says truck driver Liu Zhucan, who had to leave his home: "They know that their homes will be flooded, and they're scared. You have to go, even if you don't want to."

---

paintings. But its fierce floods have also killed hundreds of thousands of people." Okay, it must be a very beautiful river if it inspires artistic expression. But it must be a dangerous river, too. The flooding must be pretty severe if so many people die. Maybe that's why people are divided about building the dam, because it will save lives but perhaps destroy some of the beauty of the river. What does the next paragraph say?

I read the second paragraph aloud. I visualize, try to work out my confusion by clarifying information and connecting to prior knowledge, and I summarize the paragraph.

So the project is underway. They've just dumped these huge rocks into the river. I get a picture in my mind of that, and I can see the rocks in the photograph. I'm confused about those boulders. Do they force the water to another spot after there's a huge pile of them? It says that a large area will be underwater, so that must mean that the water is displaced from one location to another. That would make the water higher in the other area and cause flooding. That's probably right, because I was at Hoover Dam once, and I remember how the dam raised the level of the water. Okay, so this paragraph says that this new dam will put a big area of China underwater and the work is underway with the dumping of boulders into the river.

I continue with the rest of article in this vein, reading and thinking aloud, stopping to clarify when something isn't clear to me, rereading when I'm not sure I've got the meaning, and summarizing as I go along. When I'm done with the entire article, I briefly summarize it: *Okay, now I'm going to summarize the whole article. I'm going to tell just the main points, the most important ones, not the details. Let's see. There's a huge new dam being built across the Yangtze River, in China, but it's a controversial project. While it's predicted to stop flooding and save human lives, it will destroy habitats of people and animals as well as some beautiful scenery.*

• ***Adding to What They Know About What Good Readers Do***   (five minutes)
After I finish reading the selection and demonstrating my thinking, I ask the students to tell me what I did while I was reading. With probing, students note that I cleared up confusions, used what I knew from my life, reread, asked questions, used the photograph and the map, stated the main points, hypothesized, and summarized. I add their comments to the ones they already made, and we delete the one about using the dictionary, since readers rarely stop to do this. I want them to become proficient at using the surrounding text first. We end up with the following list on a projected transparency:

Strategies Good Readers Use

Clarify
    Clear up confusions
    Put in a word that makes sense
    For a hard word, sound it out, break it up, read ahead, and come back to it

Connect to what you know
    Use what you've learned in your life

Reread to make sense

Visualize
    Make a picture in your mind
    Use title, map, picture, caption

Summarize
    Tell main parts

Ask questions

Predict
    Hypothesize; make a smart, educated guess

After the lesson, I format these strategies into a bookmark so students can refer to them while reading. (See Appendix D-3 for a bookmark that resulted from a similar lesson.)

• ***Students Reading Together in Small Mixed-Ability Groups***   (fifteen minutes)
Using another article (see Figure 11-5 and Photo 11-1) in the same newsmagazine, the students work in small groups to try out the process I have just demonstrated. Emphasis here is not on learning to read but reading to learn. Even students who cannot read all the words can follow along and join in the discussion. I give the following directions:

Work together to read the article "Bullies in the Park!" about some trouble between elephants and rhinos in Africa. Take turns reading, and help one another using the strategies we talked about and that you saw me use. If a student doesn't want to read out loud, that's okay. Be sure everyone follows along when someone is reading. I am going to give each group a worksheet on which to record your thinking, and I need someone in each group to serve as scribe. That person will write down the questions that come up, what needs to be

Figure 11–5 "Bullies in the Park"

At play, young elephants may lock tusks or toss sticks to rhinos. But without adult attention, some seem to turn violent.

Bullies in the Park!

Africa's orphan elephants turn against rhinos

THE TROUBLE STARTED ABOUT three years ago. Nearly every month, rangers in Pilanesberg National Park in northwestern South Africa would find an endangered white rhinoceros that had been killed. Then the same thing started happening at Hluhluwe-Umfolozi (Slush-*loo*-ey Oom-*fall*-o-zee) Park, in southeastern South Africa.

Rhinos are sometimes hunted for their valuable horns. But no one had touched the horns of these animals.

THE WRONG MOVE?
To ease crowding in Kruger Park, rangers moved young elephants to other parks. They should have moved whole families.

Their wounds hadn't come from guns.

The rangers who solved the crime were surprised to learn what was to blame. Young male elephants, which usually leave rhinos alone, had attacked and killed them.

ANGRY ORPHANS

Why would elephants murder rhinos? Experts guess the young elephants behaved badly because they had grown up without the attention of caring adults.

Several years ago, the population of elephants in South Africa's Kruger National Park was growing too large. Rangers tried to control the growth by slaughtering older elephants and then moving the young elephants to other parks and reserves. Since 1978, almost 1,500 orphans—600 of them males, or bulls—have been moved to unfamiliar locations, where they grew up without older elephants around them.

Moving the orphans helped preserve an endangered species. But it changed the elephants' social order.

"The whole thing has much to do with the setup of elephant society," says South African zoologist Marian Garai. Elephants normally live in tight-knit groups. Older males keep young bulls in line. But no such role models were provided for the orphans from Kruger. Garai believes this upset the young elephants and led them to lash out at rhinos.

"Elephants are complex and intelligent creatures," explains Garai. "They aren't immune to stress."

What can be done? Some rangers believe the elephant bullies need foster parents. When two adult female circus elephants were returned to Pilanesberg in 1979, soon after the first orphans arrived, the nervous youngsters quickly settled down.

Now officials hope a similar plan will work for the rhino-bashing bulls. Two years ago, Kruger Park began to move entire families of elephants to new homes instead of killing the elders and hauling away their young. Early next year, a few 40-year-old male elephants will be moved to Pilanesberg.

Preserving families may be the key to raising well-behaved elephants. Meanwhile, South Africa's white rhinos had better watch out. ∎

TIME FOR KIDS

clarified and how you do it, and a one-sentence summary about the article. Even though one person does the writing, you are all responsible for being able to tell me all these things. In other words, I should be able to call on anyone in the group to give me the summary. Are there any questions? Okay, start reading. In about fifteen minutes, we'll get back together and talk about the article and the strategies you used to understand it.

Figure 11-6 is one group's worksheet. (See page 139 for another group's worksheet. See Appendix D-7 for a blank form that can be used for fiction or nonfiction reading.)

• *Teacher Guiding One Group as Other Groups Collaborate Independently*
(simultaneous)

Wendy and I join a group. I continue to model and guide in this small group as students begin to read the article. I ask them to predict from the pictures and first paragraph. We sum-

Photo 11–1   Reading a newsmagazine article

*Figure 11–6   "Bullies in
the Park," group worksheet*

Kati Luca
David Mike
Dawn

T.F.K.
Connection - to people
bullies and elephant bullies.

Connections - to poachers
and white rhinos.

Clarify - that young
male elephants kill rhinos.

Connections - young male
adults need some care like
young male children.

marize together as we go along. Because I am with a group and this is a new process, I take the opportunity to do more teaching, demonstrating, and guiding—not just facilitating.

• **Checking for Understanding and Monitoring Group Processes**   (ten minutes)
After most of the groups have finished reading and discussing the article, I direct every-one's attention from group to group, asking: *What did your group need to clarify? How*

did you do it? What was your prediction? Did you raise any questions? Give us your summary for what you've read so far.

Considering that this is their first experience, the students have done extremely well. While all the groups other than the one Wendy and I led have had some difficulty clarifying points and summarizing, all of them have made credible predictions and raised thoughtful questions. Wendy is impressed. Some students who normally don't participate have blossomed in the small-group structure. Wendy comments,

> The students were better focused. Every student but one was really involved. I was surprised to see Joseph, who is often spaced out and silent, engaged and participating. And I got a better insight into Colin, who is bright but reluctant to put forth his best effort. I got a clearer idea of his thinking when I sat next to him in group. Also, Clarinda, who has difficulty writing, volunteered to be scribe for her group. That really surprised me.

This first guided reading lesson has taken forty-five minutes. For the second and third lessons, I model similarly and join a different group when students read collaboratively in their small groups. After students get better at reading nonfiction together, I only need to model strategies that continue to be difficult, as revealed in the previous "checking for understanding" session, and give sufficient background explanations so articles can be understood in a broader context. Once groups are effectively managing themselves and checking for understanding as they go, I join a group as silent observer and note taker just as I do with literature conversations (Chapter 5). In our "checking for understanding" sessions after reading, I only give evaluative feedback if the group does not provide it.

Typically, it takes students of all ages a while to be able to focus on reading for meaning. They usually are not able to monitor themselves well at first. While they can predict and ask questions, they usually have difficulty clarifying confusions, paying attention to words they don't know (they skip them), and summarizing the article's main points. They are not used to focusing on understanding *as* they read, as we teachers traditionally check for understanding *after* they read. With continued demonstrations, guidance, and practice, students become quite proficient in checking their understanding *as* they read, trying out the meaning of words they don't understand, and giving an adequate summary.

A Guided Reading Lesson with a Newspaper Article

For this lesson, I choose an article that tells how old boxes in a building in Washington, DC, slated for destruction contained, among other memorabilia from the 1860s, a sign reading "Missing Person's Office, Clara Barton." This is the first official documentation that Barton's role extended beyond nursing to locating missing soldiers and notifying their families.

Projecting a copy of the article on the overhead, I:

• ***Review the strategies good readers use while reading.***

• ***Preview the article by reading the title, looking at the picture and caption, predicting what I think it will be about.***

• ***Think aloud***—work through vocabulary, summarize as I go, ask questions—as I read the first half of the article.

• *Have the students read the rest of the article in small mixed-ability groups.* Read the rest of the article together. Help one another figure out words and what they mean.

> Ask questions and summarize as you go along. One person will write down what you discuss and need to clarify. Also, prepare a one-sentence summary of the most important information the writer is trying to give the reader. (Any one of you should be able to tell me this summary.) The last line says Barton was a humanitarian. See if you can figure out what that means. You have fifteen minutes to finish the article. Then I will ask you to tell me what your group's questions were and what strategies you used to figure words out.

• *Select one group to guide through the rest of the article and work with them while the other groups are working.*   First we review what's been read so far. They have difficulty remembering so we reread parts and discuss them.

• *Assess understanding by asking each group aloud:*   *What's something you needed to clarify? How did you do it? What's your summary?*

• *Project difficult words and questions on the overhead and work through them with students.*   Words that come up are *patent, occasionally, plaque,* and *administering.* I model how to figure out *administering* from the context of the sentence: "At 40, Barton joined the Union soldiers at war, administering good deeds and medical care to the wounded." I tell them to put in another word that makes sense, mentioning that it also needs to end in *ing.* The students suggest *giving, supplying, providing,* and *sending.* (Kids need lots of practice in this kind of work. Otherwise, they just skip the hard words and keep reading.) One student says she figured out *Union* because she knew it was a name (it's capitalized) and assumed it must be a group of people because a *family reunion* refers to a group of people.

Beginning Nonfiction Guided Reading in First Grade

Cathy Grieshop and I have been talking about the importance of teaching young children how to read nonfiction. She and I decide to conduct a guided reading of a nonfiction news article on wild kittens from *Your Big Backyard,* a science magazine published by the National Wildlife Federation (Vienna, VA).

We begin by asking the students what kind of writing this is. We talk about how the article is true, that the pictures are real photographs. We use the pictures and headings to predict: "This will be about kittens of tigers and cheetahs." We teach difficult vocabulary: *lynx, adventure, prey.* I ask students to read silently, circle unfamiliar words, and underline two new facts they learn. When Jason quickly finishes, I ask him to turn over his article and tell me what a *pride* is to be sure he has understood. He doesn't know. I ask him to reread the text and underline the part that explains what a pride is. The text reads, "Lion cubs belong to a pride. A pride is like a family where everyone takes turns babysitting." He underlines "A pride is like a family." Like any new genre we want students to learn to read thoughtfully, students will need repeated modeling, guidance, and practice before they become proficient. (See pages 157–160 for another lesson.)

USING TEXTBOOKS AND GUIDES

The business of school textbooks is booming (Manzo 1998). Since textbooks are required in most subject areas all through the grades, an understanding of their use and misuse is important.

All the years I was a student, and in the early years of my teaching, I relied on textbooks for my principal understanding of science and social studies. There may have been a hands-on experiment here and there, but mostly there were boring textbooks, whole-class round-robin oral reading, and right answers. I was a dutiful student, fulfilling assignments and doing well on tests. But opportunities for genuine questioning and exploration were rare. I never developed scientific or historical curiosity as a student, and for many years I failed to foster such thinking in my own students.

This does not mean I am antitextbook. It is only when they are the sole resource that I have a problem. There are a great many quality textbooks containing valuable information organized in a usable format. Textbooks can provide common background information and serve as supplemental resources. Textbooks, guides, and curriculum kits (for science and health) can provide an initial framework when we are planning for inquiry. "Sometimes we don't know enough about a topic to even begin asking questions. Guides can be a starting point. They provide ideas to react to and build upon. They can jump-start our thinking. What are the lessons in the guide about?" (Reardon 1996, 26).

Much of the information students will be expected to know in order to do well in school will come from textbooks. According to Gilbert Sewall, director of the American Textbook Council (an independent group that monitors history and social studies texts), textbooks still dominate the way history and most other subjects are taught: "Seventy to 90 percent of history teaching is 'textbook driven and derived'" (in Cohen 1995, 3). Reading textbooks is therefore a necessary literacy skill. However, students do not automatically know how to read a textbook with its headings, graphs, maps, and particular organizational structure. We need to teach students how to read a textbook in the same step-by-step, supported way we show them how to read other nonfiction.

Many commercial texts are bland, "politically correct," and "dumbed down," having been altered to meet the criteria for the huge statewide textbook adoptions that influence the way such material is written. According to Sewall, "Content is thinner and thinner" (1998, 14). In that regard, teachers need to take an active role in selecting textbooks. Several years ago, some of the teachers in my district made very vocal objections—in writing, to our director of curriculum—to a new social studies text that was about to be adopted: "high market appeal but little to no substance in content," "very poor writing style," "worksheets are too simple and deal with superficial concepts," "graphics look exciting but are difficult to understand," "little continuity and integration within units." As a direct result, a different, more cohesive series was finally purchased.

Even though carefully selected textbooks can help provide basic information that aligns with curriculum objectives, students always need the opportunity to examine multiple sources so they can ask important questions, form opinions, and come to thoughtful conclusions. At least some sources students consult should be primary documents—original letters, diaries, maps, interviews, speeches, and news accounts. Then, with teacher guidance, students can become critical readers making historical interpretations. (See Jackdaws in The Blue Pages, "Curriculum Inquiry: Social Studies/History," page 46b, for information on how to obtain facsimiles of historical documents.)

Introducing Students to a Science Textbook

To ensure that our students can read textbooks in a meaningful way, we first need to show students how textbooks work. When Linda Cooper introduced her fourth graders to the new science textbook, she guided them through its organization and special features. "What do you notice?" she asked. The students discussed differences between nonfiction and fiction, examined the text, and noted the following elements:

• *Table of contents*   Chapter titles grouped together in units, each unit concluding with the same sections: Science in Careers, People in Science, Developing Skills.

• *Text organization*   Chapters divided into sections, bold-print headings and subheadings, questions at the end of each chapter, additional information in boxes.

• *Visual aids*   Photographs, diagrams, maps, charts, and graphs.

• *Glossary*   For definitions of terms, arranged in alphabetical order, page numbers indicating where term is used in text.

• *Index*   In alphabetical order, some words have more page numbers after them than others, page numbers listed may not be sequential.

Linda and her students discussed how these elements related to finding information, how they didn't have to read the whole book or read it in a certain order, that they could go straight to the chapter or section that would answer their questions.

Using the Social Studies
Textbook as Part of Curriculum Inquiry

In her annual study of the Southwest, fourth-grade teacher Nancy Schubert uses her own collection of more than a hundred trade books (mostly nonfiction) but also acknowledges the usefulness of the textbook, *Regions Near and Far: Social Studies for a Changing World* (Banks et al. 1995).

Nancy has the students read the chapter on resources of the Southwest twice, first to get the overall idea and think of the big questions that are raised and the second time to generate and record their own important questions for discussion. The questions, summary and review, and activities the textbook's authors provide at the end of the chapter take up almost as much space as the preceding text. "Check Your Reading" includes the following questions, which can be answered in a few factual sentences:

1. Describe how any four resources of the Southwest are used.
2. How does a desert city like Phoenix get water?

3. Geography Skill: In which states are fuel resources found in the Southwest?

4. Thinking Skill: List three facts discussed in this lesson.

The students' own questions after reading the chapter are much more interesting and require more time and understanding to answer:

1. Would you want to live in a desert or where we live now? Explain.

2. How is the Southwest different from the Midwest (where we live)?

3. Explain how rivers help cities in the desert.

4. If less rain falls in the desert, why do you think people live there?

5. Do you think deserts are important? Why or why not?

6. If no irrigation was possible, what do you think would happen to land, crops, and people?

7. Discuss how you would use water if you lived in the Southwest.

Nancy tells the students that she is thinking of moving to the Southwest when she retires and would like their advice. Then, following the procedures for literature conversations (see pages 189 and 190), she lets the students disperse into small groups of three, four, or five to talk about their questions.

The discussion is spirited. Students refer to the maps and charts in the book as they talk. The students incorporate important facts in their responses but in relation to the "bigger picture."

After the students finish this unit in this vein—reading the text, discussing their questions, and consulting other resources, mostly exemplary trade books but some videos as well—Nancy administers the textbook publisher's unit test, five pages of multiple-choice and essay questions. With the exception of one student, everyone gets an A or a B. Nancy attributes the high marks to the engagement of the small groups and the high level of discussion: "I think it's because there was total involvement. There's no involvement when you tell a child to read a chapter and answer questions. When they're defending their own statements, they have ownership. Kids love to do this kind of discussion, but most of the time they haven't had enough experiences in school to feel confident."

This is not a textbook-based classroom, just the opposite. Nancy uses hundreds of trade books in the content areas but she recognizes the value of teaching students how to read a textbook as well as the useful knowledge such a resource can provide. Her goal is conceptual understanding of principles and synthesis of concepts. Her students' uniform success on the commercial test is proof that when you focus in depth on important concepts, the details and facts are also discussed and learned. When curriculum study is relevant to students and they can raise their own essential questions, they remember much more than when study is teacher and textbook driven.

FINAL REFLECTIONS

Increasingly, information is instantly available—through electronic media and the Internet—as well as through the printed page. Being able to skim, scan, interpret, summarize, visualize, compare, draw thoughtful conclusions, and understand nonfiction texts is critical to becoming a well educated, thoughtful citizen.

We must ensure that our students learn how to select and read all types of nonfiction. For them to be successful, we teachers must first learn how to make those selections ourselves, observe our own reading process, and teach our students the skills and strategies they will need to read and think scientifically, historically, mathematically, and so on. Nonfiction comprises the majority of reading that most of us do. Indeed, it's nothing short of a "life genre"—one we'll want to make sure our students understand, use, and enjoy to the fullest.

CONTINUING THE CONVERSATION

• *Take note of the books you read aloud to your students.* Are a good portion of them outstanding nonfiction? Have you checked them to be sure they meet the criteria for recommended nonfiction? Are you pointing out features of nonfiction as you read?

• *Compare two or more accounts of a famous person, event, or period in history.* Discuss how and why they differ. What sources have been used? Are both accounts credible? How does the author's point of view affect his or her interpretation of the facts?

• *Be on the watch for interesting articles in your local newspaper.* Make an overhead transparency of an article and think aloud about how you read the news. Make the strategies you use visible. When you photocopy an article for students (for classroom use only), leave "white space" on the page for students' jottings and notes.

• *Make sure your guided reading groups include nonfiction.* Do you have trade books that support study in the content areas? Are you specifically teaching students how to read and interpret these nonfiction books as well as news articles, instructions, graphs, tables, and maps?

• *Encourage students to add nonfiction genres to their voluntary reading.* Check students' reading records for some balance of genres. Share your own nonfiction reading. Be aware that students who report doing more nonfiction reading have higher reading achievement (Campbell and Ashworth 1995, 4).

• *Revisit your required textbooks.* Carefully examine the content and questions provided. Consult your librarian or subject specialist (if you are fortunate enough to have one) for trade books and other resources to support the required curriculum. Encourage students to write their own essential discussion questions.

• *Examine your own nonfiction reading process.* Review the lesson "Valuing Our Own Text-Solving Strategies," on pages 134–136. Jot down what you do when you read nonfiction. Are you teaching your students how to understand text *as* they read? Are you and they monitoring their understanding?

CHAPTER 12

Curriculum Inquiry

Developing a Questioning Stance Toward Learning

Inquiry in the classroom: Regie Routman working with two kindergarten students

■ Inquiry starts with one condition, and it simply will not lift off without it: wonder.

—*Stephanie Harvey*

I wonder about literacy all the time. Here are some things I've wondered about recently:

- Can students write well using the literature they read as a model even if their teacher doesn't write in front of them?
- How much of children's phonemic awareness is a consequence, a corollary, of learning to read?
- Can students become proficient spellers in excellent writing classrooms that do not have a formal spelling program?
- How can we teach for understanding *as* students are reading?
- How much can we influence the practice of teachers who remain resistant to change?

My wondering about things like this prompts investigations, which lead to reflections and conclusions, which change the way I teach. My inquiry is as much a questioning stance toward learning as it is a process of research. I don't just want to "find out." I want to understand various perspectives, grapple with conflicting information, challenge assumptions, pose new questions, and come to new understanding. Kids need to see their teachers as wonderers and inquirers the same way they need to see them as readers and writers.

463

WHAT IS INQUIRY? WHY IS IT IMPORTANT?

Inquiry-based teaching and learning begin with wonder about something. That wonder leads the teacher and her students to ask questions, browse, hypothesize, read, investigate, check many resources, collect data, consider various perspectives, solve problems, draw conclusions, revise, rethink, reformulate, and ask more questions. Work like this can only take place in a classroom in which there is lots of talk, exploration, and collaboration. The National Research Council and the National Academy of Sciences define inquiry as "a multifaceted activity that involves making observations; posing questions; examining books and other sources of information to see what is already known; planning investigations; reviewing what is already known in light of experimental evidence; using tools to gather, analyze, and interpret data; proposing answers, explanations, and predictions; and communicating the results" (1996, 23).

When students are inquirers, they explore issues and questions they care about and they understand what and why they are studying. They read, write, look, listen, speak, research, collaborate, interpret, experiment, share, report, explain, and ask new questions, always in connection with explicit teaching, opportunities to practice what they are being taught, and conferences that support their learning. The topic being explored may be determined by the teacher, the student, and/or curriculum requirements. Even when the topic or focus is predetermined, students still have the opportunity to negotiate some of their own questions.

An inquiry approach to science, social studies, any area of the curriculum, is far more likely to engage students than a textbook-bound approach. In fact, the first of the seven science content standards is "science as inquiry" (American Association for the Advancement of Science, 1993). Without the sustained engagement provided by genuine inquiry, there is no meaningful learning, no high-level thinking and reasoning.

When deciding whether an inquiry study qualifies as "good teaching," we need to evaluate:

- Its intellectual depth and breadth
- The quality of the questions it raises
- The number of opportunities it provides to explore, discover, and make meaningful connections
- Its coherence and relevance
- The number of excellent resources available and being used
- The major concepts being developed
- The learning taking place
- Whether the purposes for learning are clear
- Whether it includes explicit teaching to support learners
- Whether the reading, writing, viewing, listening, and speaking involved are authentic
- Whether it includes other forms of literacy like art, music, and drama
- Whether it produces evidence of understanding

Building on Our Natural Curiosity

These days, when I go into classrooms and introduce myself to students, I confess to being fascinated with literacy. I hold up and discuss the books and articles I am reading. I let the kids know I am a curious person always looking for information having to do with my questions and inquiries, that one of the ways I remember what I find out and discover what I think about what I find out is by jotting everything down in a notebook (I also show them my notebook). I tell them that eventually I organize my thoughts, conclusions, and opinions into published books and articles. I identify myself as a teacher-researcher, someone who is always raising questions and taking notes, and tell them they can be researchers too. I ask them what they are fascinated by and what they wonder about. I want students to know that inquiry results from questions driven by our own passions.

Developing a Questioning
Stance Toward Learning

Research as inquiry is something human beings of all ages love and seek out. We teachers need to model and support an inquiry stance toward learning. One of the best ways to encourage and model inquiry is through a writing workshop in which students explore their interests and passions by reading and writing. Time and time again, I am amazed at the striking improvement in effort and quality when students explore and write about that which they are curious and passionate. Look at the remarkable difference between Figure 12-1, a third grader's journal entry written to fulfill an assignment, and Figure 12-2, that same third grader's journal entry about something that fascinates him. (There are many other examples of engaged writing throughout this text.)

Thoughtful questioning must become central to all curriculum inquiry. We must nurture in our students (and in ourselves) the ability to inquire and problem solve throughout life. The questioning stance (challenging assumptions, clearing up confusions, raising new issues), not a head full of facts, is the mark of a well-educated person.

Teachers who ask probing, thoughtful questions and who teach and promote such questioning are giving their students the power to learn and go on learning. This is, in

Figure 12–1   A third grader's journal entries written to fulfill an assignment

1 – 11	1 – 19
I am happy because my Brothers are coming this Saterday I am very happy	Today I went to school to work I brot a crayola suet case I pat some stuff in it then I stated to work.

Figure 12–2   A third grader's journal entry about something that fascinates him

snake

1/20

My Gardner snake is cold blooded and it is a green Gardner snake and crals all around the places. My snake eats frogs and ather animals. My snake gos hunting far food or it stays and waits untit somthing come to the snake. My snake has to find a warm spot to keep warm somtimes my snake has to keep himself warm if it is cold. My snake dos'nt have arms or legs

and my snake has muscles to move it'self around and crale. My snake eats insects, worms, birds, frogs and other snakes, My snakes eggs are narrow and longl a deadly cobra has a hood and a bubble of poison in its mouth. My snake can swim over water. My snake lives in a hole. My snake well eat another snake. A deadly cobra can poisan my snake.

1/27

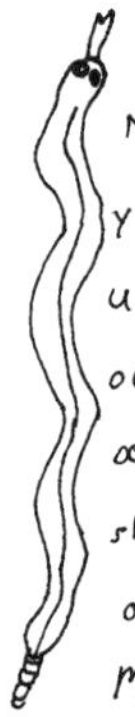

My snake sheds onse a year. My snake cat crall up a wall. My snake breths out of its tongue to get œsugen. When my snake sheds the skin comes off of ther face. My snake can see throth ther skin. A skull ofa snake has a fang hocked up to a poison sack.

fact, the essence of scientific thinking—being able to question independently, seek answers, and modify and extend what you know. Teachers who approach learning in this way are acknowledging that while they may indeed be experts, they are not experts in all fields and do not have all the "answers." When we question students, it is not so much to test their knowledge but to find out what they understand, are curious about, want to know, need to know. When we encourage and acknowledge students' questions, we respect and honor their interests and thinking. What I love about collaborative-group literature conversations (see Chapter 5) is that, with teacher guidance, students assume a questioning stance and structure that successfully transfers across the curriculum.

Writing about guiding students to become "infotectives" who use the Internet and other resources to problem solve puzzling information, technology expert Jamie McKenzie (1998) states, "The ability to frame good questions may be the most powerful technology ever invented, and we must pass it on to our students. Questions are the tools required for us to 'make up our minds' and develop meaning" (27).

Little kids are naturally curious: *Daddy, why does . . . ?* The questions go on forever, as any parent of a young child will tell you. It is only when kids get to school that they stop asking questions so freely. Nowhere is this more apparent than in secondary school, where students often feel "dumb" when they ask a question. It's not that kids lose their natural curiosity and fascination; it's just that what happens in school often doesn't relate to their lives or today's world, and they shut down. (The social aspect of not wanting to take the risk to ask plays a role here too.) Additionally, students are used to classrooms in which teachers ask most of the questions and already have the answers "in mind." When we encourage, support, and guide their natural inquiry and investigation, our students can set purposes for their learning, make connections across disciplines, and learn how to gather evidence and use it to confirm, revise, refute, extend, and construct learning.

Even kindergarten students can get involved in inquiry/research. For example, with the assistance of librarian Kathy O'Neal and trained volunteers, five-year-olds in my school district ask their burning questions and receive more than just answers. They quickly learn how and where to look for information as they observe Kathy or one of her volunteers modeling the process (see Figures 12-3 and 12-4). While an adult usually transcribes the information initially, eventually these five-year-olds begin to record—in pictures and/or writing—what they have learned and share that information with their classmates. (See page 498 for more on the role of the librarian in literacy classrooms.)

Figure 12–3   A kindergartner's research question and response

Figure 12–4   A kindergartner's research question and response

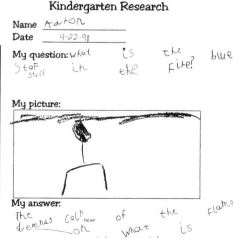

Kindergarten Research

Name Charur

Date   4-17-98

My question:

My picture: How do they Paint red and blue cps circles on ice (hockey rink)

My answer: It is Pointd ondr the Ice
painted   under

Kindergarten Research

Name Aaton

Date   4-22-98

My question: what is the blue stof stuff in the Fire?

My picture:

My answer: The derehas Colr color of the flame on what is Being broht and How Hot the burned Fire is.

Primary-grade teacher Carol Roberts begins each year with "wonder charts." Although she sets the topic for investigation so the whole class will be focusing on the same thing, she always begins by asking, *What do you wonder about magnets?* or whatever the topic happens to be (Saul and Reardon 1996, 36). Other teachers prefer to let each student study their own wonder topic. However, Jeanne Reardon notes, "The difficulty I find with children working on many different projects is that we lose the challenging comments and questions that come when the class has a common pursuit" (129). Personally, I like beginning with an overall topic (often directly related to the curriculum) but allowing students, within parameters that we have defined as a class, to choose which aspects to zero in on. A single, focused study is easier to manage and also builds community as students share resources and ideas and solve problems together.

Promoting Integrated Inquiry

"Integration, or integrated language arts, is an approach to learning and a way of thinking that respects the interrelationship of the language processes—reading, writing, speaking, and listening—as integral to meaningful teaching in any area. Integration refers to integration of the language arts as well as integration of the language arts across the curriculum" (*Invitations*, 276).

When inquiry is both genuine and integrated, then reading, writing, speaking, and listening are naturally part of the exploration or investigation. Interdisciplinary connections among math, science, social studies, art, and music occur in service to the concepts and topic being investigated. The arts and sciences come together seamlessly and purposefully as we explore topics, themes, and big ideas, at least some of which have been suggested by the students.

Integrated learning has been championed for over a decade, and "few innovations have been as widely accepted, or as poorly understood" (Shanahan 1997, 13). Unfortunately, in too many places "integration" has become a goal in itself without regard to whether the experiences are worthwhile or kids are becoming competent. When teachers try to fit as many subjects as they can into a unit of study, the links across the curriculum are forced and superficial.

Integrated curriculum that does not include students' interests and questions with respect to substantive "big ideas" is merely a teacher-directed thematic unit—an isolated unit on penguins, for example, rather than penguins as part of a study on adapting for survival, or a unit on seasons, rather than seasons as part of a study on how all things change.

I fussed for years over whether I was basing a focused study/unit on a theme or a concept or a topic and over whether I'd integrated enough subjects. I've at last concluded that it matters little what we call our study or how many disciplines are involved. It may well be that in some cases we can do a better job studying a single subject. What does matter is that what is being studied is worthwhile and challenging.

In particular, we need to be sure that we are teaching important concepts and principles—the "big ideas" (*living things adapt to their environment; some animals become extinct because of environmental changes caused by human interference and/or climatic shifts*)—and that the topic is relevant to students' lives as well as to required curricular objectives. The things we teach must deepen our students' understanding.

In too many cases, interdisciplinary study does not produce better instruction and learning. Too much time is been spent making trivial connections, too little time is spent reading. Shanahan (1997) notes that while "improved motivation is the one positive outcome for which there is convincing evidence" (and here we need to remember that motivation can be improved even by a very structured study if inquiry and student input are at its center), integration has not lead to increased understanding. "I have been able to identify no study, in any field with any age level, that has clearly demonstrated more coherent or deeper understandings, or better applicability of learning as a result of integration" (15).

This is important information to remember when we evaluate those proudly proclaimed "integrated language arts" textbooks (many of them basal readers). Too often, the connections are superficial: "Generally, the cross-curricular activities are not strongly related to the theme and are not anchored in the curricula of other subject areas" (Lipson et al. 1993, 258). A close look at the newest basals in the late 1990s confirms that the above statement is still true. So while a school district may well mandate a particular textbook in reading or a content area, we need to be sure we use it only as one resource and not as our total curriculum. A textbook continues to be but a single tool in the multifaceted process of inquiry, *not* the heart or the purpose of inquiry.

INQUIRY IN THE CLASSROOM: A REALITY CHECK

Much classroom inquiry is rooted in nonfiction and centers around reading, writing, and research. While the dictionary defines research as "systematic inquiry into a subject in order to discover or revise facts, theories, etc.," research in our classrooms seldom goes beyond collecting and regurgitating information. Often the work has no value to students beyond the grade received. And it's still rare for students to be allowed to present the results of their research in a speech or through a creative or visual arts project.

Genuine inquiry remains uncommon, both for students and for teacher-researchers, in part because our own education did not often ask us to pose questions, interpret, analyze, and rethink. It's hard to model inquiry for students if we don't live that model ourselves and if that way of looking at the world hasn't been modeled for us. Scientific inquirer Wendy Saul, writing to me earlier this year, put it this way: "For too long the mere collecting of information or artifacts has counted as substantive intellectual activity. The school question needs to become, 'What can we do to teach children how to think? How can we teach them the difference between thinking and simply collecting facts?'"

For too many students inquiry and research in the classroom remain teacher and textbook dominated, which causes them to disengage and underachieve. Most science programs, for example, have not provided students with "opportunities to *learn with understanding*" (Anderson and Lee 1997, italics theirs). Even when there is "hands-on" work, it frequently does not translate into meaningful inquiry and reflection. With no emphasis on interpreting, analyzing, and making inferences, collected information and data have only surface meaning.

A Cautionary Tale

When students have no choice with regard to the research reports imposed on them and when clear expectations about these reports have not been negotiated between students and teacher, the results can be disastrous—for children and for their families as well. Madelyn Peters is a sixth-grade teacher and the mother of fourth grader Sam. Sam's assignment to write a report "was a horrible experience," Madelyn recalls.

Every student was assigned a state to research, but neither the students nor their parents understood the point of the research. The guidelines were scant: students were required to answer twelve teacher-generated questions about their state, locate and use no fewer than ten and no more than twelve resources, draw a freehand map of the state, word process the final report on a computer, and include a handmade cover and a complete bibliography. They were on their own as far as finding information, taking notes, translating the notes into their own words, organizing the material, and completing the project, and most of the work was to be done at home.

Madelyn felt the assignment was unrealistic. For example, Sam had to choose where he would like to go to college in his assigned state. This was inappropriate given his age and not a real choice. As for drawing the map by hand, Sam simply hadn't the skill to do it, even though he tried. When Madelyn encouraged him to trace a map from one of his sources, Sam felt that was cheating. There were daily confrontations: there was never enough time to work on the project, it was difficult to find the information needed to answer all the required questions, Sam refused to include interesting information that was not required ("The teacher doesn't want it").

Nevertheless, the project was finally finished. Every day Madelyn asked her son, "Did you get to share your report today?" Every day she got the same reply, "No. The teacher says we're too busy." After all the hard work, the projects were never shared or displayed. Although they were numerically graded, there was never an explanation of how the grade was determined. Madelyn was angry but ultimately decided not to confront her son's teacher because she worried that the teacher would feel threatened by Madelyn's also being a teacher. She worries, though, whether she can "live through the experience" again when her youngest child reaches fourth grade.

What saddens me most about the preceding true story is that Sam's natural desire to learn and question was thwarted, perhaps irreparably. Two years later, Sam still shivers at the word *research*. His unpleasant memories of doing a lot of busy work without personal investment haunt him:

> Research is too hard. There's no point in doing it. The teacher made us do all the work, but we really didn't have to know that stuff! There were too many questions, and it was hard to find facts for all of them. I would have liked to have chosen the questions I was interested in. The only part I liked was drawing the cover.

Unfortunately, research-as-mandatory-report-writing remains common in many classrooms. While learning how to write a research report is a valuable skill—and students need to learn how to find resources, collect information, take notes, summarize—it is not inquiry unless it also engages the student and involves choosing which questions to pose, what investigations to conduct, and how to present the knowledge gained.

Also, parents need to be kept abreast of what's going on every step of the way and what the expectations are for them and their children. When most of the work winds up being done at home, students often have to compete with adult standards and wind up procrastinating. Teachers note that many parents make changes in their child's work so that it comes back to school looking quite different. By contrast, when all the work is done in the classroom in connection with sufficient time, materials, and teacher guidance, all students can be successful and student voice is kept intact.

PLANNING FOR CURRICULUM INQUIRY AND RESEARCH

For all curriculum areas—history, science, mathematics, whatever—we need to determine what is worth knowing. What is deemed worth knowing in schools is chiefly a matter of the district's course of study, state and national guidelines and standards, teacher preferences and beliefs, and societal factors. But equally worth knowing—in fact even more important—are the things students wonder about and question. Without student engagement, learning is limited. We must give students the time and the support they need to determine their questions and sort out their thinking. As much as possible, we need to put student inquiry at the center of the curriculum. Students need to be able to choose a topic in which they are interested, explore it by way of sustained, open-ended activities, and become experts on that topic. Teachers need to do this too. We can't simply read an article here, a book there. We must become actively engaged in study for meaningful purposes.

A collaborative curriculum is guided by two overriding questions (Breivik and Senn 1994, 21):

- What do I absolutely have to teach for students to understand this study?
- What can students discover on their own?

At the same time, we always need to ask:

- What is the purpose and relevance of this study?
- What are the goals for students?
- How will the students and I know we have accomplished those goals?

Such planning is in line with the *Curriculum Standards for Social Studies* (National Council for the Social Studies 1994), which states: "Social studies teaching and learning are powerful when they are meaningful, integrative, value-based, challenging and active." These principles "must undergird all social studies programs of excellence" (11–12).

Teaching for understanding must be at the heart of all our planning. In their provocative and thoughtful book *Understanding by Design* (1998), Grant Wiggins and Jay McTighe explain that "understanding involves the abstract and conceptual, not merely the concrete and discrete; concepts, generalizations, theories, and mental links between facts. And understanding also involves the ability to use knowledge and skill in context, as opposed to doing something routine and on cue in out-of-context assignments or assessment items" (24).

In teaching for understanding, the idea, topic, or process must (26):

- Have enduring value beyond the classroom
- Reside at the heart of the discipline and be encountered in context

- Need to be uncovered
- Engage students

While concepts and content standards are helpful in framing inquiry, what we teach—and help our students investigate—must be those things that "we want students to 'get inside of' and retain after they've forgotten many of the details" (10), that help them make connections to present and future learning. Only then does learning endure.

Activities, facts, questions, and research are all important, as long as they lead to an enduring understanding of what is worth knowing. For example, basic facts underpin all study, but factual knowledge is important only as it goes hand in hand with a focus on important and meaningful concepts and generalizations. Focusing on individual facts in isolation, on memorization without understanding, is not learning. "It is only when facts are the object of isolated, artificially constructed work that they have less to offer the learner. In real inquiry facts offer power and control" (Busching and Slesinger 1995, 44).

When students really understand something they can:

- Explain it
- Predict it
- Apply or adapt it to novel situations
- Demonstrate its importance
- Verify, defend, justify, or critique it
- Make qualified and precise judgments
- Make connections with other ideas and facts
- Avoid common misconceptions, biases, or simplistic views. (In ASCD 1997, 6–7)

Wiggins and McTighe (1998) also suggest using the following questions to probe for understanding:

- What should we make of this?
- What are the causes or reasons?
- From whose point of view?
- What is this an instance of?
- How should this be qualified?
- So what? What is the significance?

Planning is critical if curriculum inquiry and research are to be successful. Without planning, commitment, and collaboration, an inquiry curriculum is very difficult to achieve. Joining forces, teachers can share ideas, plans, and resources at and across grade levels. Unfortunately, far too much work with inquiry and research lacks understanding. We seldom devote the time, instruction, or evaluation needed to help students meaningfully use the wealth of information available to them. (See Chapter 4, "Teaching Children to Read," Chapter 11, "Reading Nonfiction," and The Blue Pages, "Critical Resources for Curriculum Inquiry," page 51b, for ideas about how to teach students to read and inquire with understanding.)

Questions to Guide Our Thinking and Planning

The questions that follow can guide our thinking as we plan and implement a curriculum inquiry. It's easy to skip over questions like these, but if we are to be thoughtful, responsive, and responsible in teaching our students, we need to think constantly about what we are doing and why. We also need to be sure to return to these (or similar) questions later and reflect on what we've learned. Rethinking what we do is important: if we don't practice it ourselves, we won't remember or be able to teach it to our students.

• *What is the purpose for this study?*   Is it required by the curriculum? Is it something students have expressed interest in? Is it relevant to life?

• *Do students understand the purpose of the inquiry?*

• *Have I communicated clearly with parents and administrators?*   Have I explained the "what" and "why" of the study? Will families be able to support their child in any related homework? Have I asked them whether they can provide resources, accompany a field trip, volunteer in the classroom, or share their expertise?

• *What are the important concepts, the big understanding, I want students to develop and learn?*   Have I determined this on the basis of the school district course of study? Local, state, or national standards? My and my students' questions and interests?

• *What knowledge do students need in order to understand these concepts?* What background information, prior knowledge, vocabulary, cultural beliefs, values, and perspectives impact the concepts? What connections, experiences, and activities need to be provided for understanding to occur?

• *How will I engage students in this study?*   Will I introduce it through activities and questions? Will I point out its relevance? Will I give them time to browse, explore, talk, formulate questions, rethink ideas?

• *Is this study, even if required, sufficiently open-ended?*   Can students raise their own questions, make their own discoveries, and follow their own interests?

• *At the same time, have I helped students narrow the study sufficiently so that it promotes in-depth learning?*

• *How will I know students have understood the major concepts?*   Have I set up evaluation procedures and rubrics? Will students provide oral or written explanations of their thinking? Will the study culminate in a major project? Will I use self-evaluations and/or peer evaluations? Will I be able to see students apply their knowledge to new areas?

• *How can I ensure that facts will not be used in isolation but as a means to understand concepts and make new connections?*   How can I frame the inquiry so that students are not merely reporting facts but are using those facts to make interpretations, inferences, and judgments and to come to new understanding?

• *What skills and strategies do I need to teach so students can learn these concepts and conduct their inquiries?*   Will I use minilessons to demonstrate (see Photo 12-1) how to observe? take notes? collect, delete, sort, categorize, and classify data? read nonfiction? summarize? problem solve? hypothesize? interpret?

• *What resources are necessary for students to be successful?* Will I be able to provide relevant, reliable, and appropriate resources, including printed matter, visual and electronic media, field trips, guest speakers?

• *Can all students read and access materials and information?* Who will help those with special needs? How? Through shared reading? dictation? collaborative note taking?

• *What physical and emotional climate do I need to set up?* Will students have enough time for initial explorations? Is there a strong tie-in with the library? Have I included the librarian in my planning? Will students be able to make choices? Will there be opportunities for collaboration, small-group work, and sharing? Will I demonstrate for my students, guide them, confer with them, support them, celebrate their achievements?

• *If I am integrating multiple disciplines, are the connections meaningful and natural rather than trivial and forced?*

• *What attitudes am I fostering?* Am I asking students to collaborate and work as effective group members, hone their curiosity, develop an interest in the topic, make discoveries, and make connections between school and the real world?

• *Will this study help develop higher-level thinking?* Are the students being challenged? Do the resources and planned activities encompass the complexity of learning and help clear up misconceptions? Will students, with my guidance, learn how to consider alternative viewpoints, interpret information, make comparisons, establish classifications, and draw conclusions?

• *Will students want to continue learning after the study is completed?* What will they need to be able to go on learning and answer lingering questions? More explanations? explicit instruction? additional resources?

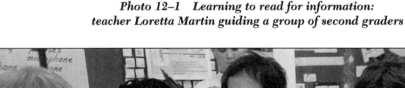

Photo 12–1 Learning to read for information:
teacher Loretta Martin guiding a group of second graders

• *How will students be evaluated?*   Have they participated in the evaluation plan? Do parents and administrators know ahead of time how students will be evaluated? Have I formulated a clear plan or rubric in advance? Will students be given a choice as to how they will present the knowledge they've acquired—a test, project, newscast, play, artwork, oral report?

Finding the Time

First, where do teachers find the time they need for the collaborative planning necessary for classroom inquiry? The lucky ones have meetings that are sanctioned by their administrators and are released from their classrooms to attend them. The others meet whenever they can, often on their own time, perhaps over dinner or on the weekend.

Finding time for inquiry in the classroom can also be a challenge. If children are answering their own research questions, a large chunk of time needs to be set aside for it each day. The only way to carve out the necessary time is to combine reading, writing, and science or social studies (and perhaps math) into one meaningful daily block, so that all guided reading and writing are centered around the research. Initially, this can be difficult to do.

Many teachers use their language arts block for curriculum inquiry, at least for several months of the school year. During these language arts periods, students read, write, inquire, and research. Because time is such a precious commodity, superficial themes and projects may need to give way to more substantial curriculum-related study involving less coverage and more depth. First-grade teacher Nancy Johnston says,

> The first year we did the research reports, I kept reading groups and journal writing going every day. I felt I had to. I was going crazy. Then I talked with you and my principal and became convinced that what we were doing in research was still meeting daily reading and writing requirements.

Nancy now sets aside at least a two-hour daily block for animal research as the year's culminating project (see pages 486–494), when her students are better able to read and write independently. She also integrates all her math teaching during this part of the year into the research project. Students study size, measurement, height, and weight; draw models of their animals; estimate; and write and solve word problems involving their animals.

During the daily research block, Nancy enlists any number of helpers. Parent volunteers read to children and help them find information; the Reading Recovery teacher and special education teacher work in the classroom with their designated students; and former students return as mentors. One year, six fourth graders, former students, came into the classroom for two hours each week (during their sustained silent reading time) and successfully guided their young apprentices through the research process.

Young researchers will usually require at least six weeks to complete a research project: a week for looking at books and resources to determine their questions, at least two weeks for researching and taking notes, at least a week to write their report, another week to illustrate and publish it, and a final week for sharing the finished report with their classmates.

Requirements Versus Choice

Teachers worry that promoting student inquiry means a free-for-all. Not so. It is our job as teachers to ensure that curricular objectives are met within the context of inquiry.

Even when students have choices, they require our guidance in reining in their inquiry so that it is feasible, manageable, and worth doing. A major challenge in planning for inquiry is negotiating parameters with students that establish a workable framework, meet curriculum requirements, maintain high expectations, and allow room for choice.

Many teachers begin with several broad, essential, overriding questions related to the topic of study and desired outcomes. Within this basic structure, students are then given the opportunity to ask their own questions and make their own choices. Student-initiated questions are engaging in a way that teacher-directed questions never can be. As long as a question is related to the study, it is valid. "Whether a question is about facts or concepts is less important than whether a question is a part of something significant. The outward form of the question may have little to do with the depth, or the importance of thinking that has occurred" (Busching and Slesinger 1995, 344).

There is always a place for requirements in curriculum inquiry, not just to meet local and state guidelines, but to ensure that students experience a variety of processes and projects that they may not otherwise encounter. For example, a teacher may require that all students research an assigned topic, consult multiple resources (including the Internet), present some information in the form of a pamphlet or brochure, or take notes in a particular manner. As in all good teaching, modeling and explicit instruction will be necessary throughout the inquiry process.

Taking Standards into Consideration

State and national standards that identify essential content and skills can be excellent teaching guides. "The only way to condense the breadth of the curriculum effectively and yet preserve the integrity of the disciplines is to ensure that the key concepts, principles, and generalizations become the focus for the selected topics of critical content" (Erickson 1998). The best standards do not prescribe how to teach but rather provide a framework for what is worth knowing within the particular discipline (see pages 584 and 588).

The *National Science Foundation Standards* (National Research Council and National Academy of Sciences 1996) is a worthy model for how standards can be used to guide instruction and can be used as such by any local school district that is identifying the essential concepts, processes, and skills in any of the content areas. These standards are not a curriculum or a set of procedures. Rather, they are designed to help us move toward teaching for understanding and inquiry. "This framework helps teachers bridge from facts to concepts and conceptual understandings" (Erickson 1998, 33).

Involving Students in Framing the Inquiry

Once a topic of study has been determined, whether on the basis of student interest, required curriculum and standards, teacher suggestion, or a combination thereof, students and teacher negotiate the parameters:

• ***What are the essential questions and big ideas?***   Have we made sure to take into account required curriculum and standards?

• ***What do we already know?***   Our prior knowledge, understanding, and misconceptions influence what we choose to study and how much background information we need.

• ***How can we find the information we need to answer our questions?***   What is our plan of action as a classroom unit that includes the students and the teacher?

• ***What kinds of resources and support will we need?***   Books? the library? demonstrations? teacher guidance? peer collaboration? the Internet and other technology? direct instruction in the skills and strategies for undertaking research?)

• ***How can we sort through all the resources,*** select the most relevant information, synthesize it, and draw conclusions?

• ***How has our thinking changed? How can we show what we know and have learned so others understand?***   Oral and written language? graphic arts? fine arts?

• ***What else do we still want to find out?***   Are there confusions that need clearing up? Have we raised new questions? Should we continue the study? conduct an independent study? (Appendix H is one framework for independent study.)

Two Models for Framing the Inquiry

Having established the topic of study, we need to provide lots of time to explore its various aspects and browse through relevant resources. Once children have acquired some background, they can begin to ask in-depth, thoughtful questions that lead to investigation and inquiry. "Yes, inquiry starts with exploration so that you know something about the topic first in order to ask meaningful questions. . . . The questions emerge from the initial exploration and immersion into the topic" (Kathy Short, in Siu-Runyan 1999, 6–7).

Questions can be posed and organized into meaningful categories by the whole class, in small groups, with a partner, or individually. My preference is to include at least some small-group work, because kids learn from the things other kids say and they feel supported by one another. (See pages 183–186 for ways to teach kids to ask thoughtful questions and an example of selecting the most significant questions through peer collaboration, and pages 27b–28b in The Blue Pages for selected teacher resources for learning how to ask better questions.) Lots of teachers make a big chart of the questions and, after the class has discussed them, help students categorize the questions and select the most significant ones. There are any number of ways to do this.

Many teachers organize students' questions using K-W-L (or an adaptation of it), a logical three-step procedure developed by Donna Ogle (1986) as a technique for getting students to read nonfiction with greater understanding. The three steps are:

1. K—What do I know?
2. W—What do I want to know?
3. L—What did I learn?

To put these three procedures into practice, Ogle recommends the following:

• *What do I know?*   Have your students brainstorm prior knowledge and categorize the resulting information.

• *What do I want to learn?*   Have your students (as a group, primarily) think about what they already know and develop questions before beginning to read.

• *What did I learn?*   Have students write down what they learned, check to see whether their questions have been answered, and read further if they still want to "know."

I also like the organization proposed by Jon Cook (Boomer et al. 1992, 21–25). Cook advises teachers and learners to ask four questions about a topic of study and together negotiate the answers:

1. *What do we know already?*
2. *What do we want, and need, to find out?*
3. *How will we go about finding out?*
4. *How will we know that we've found out when we've finished and how will we show it?*

Putting these four questions into practice involves four stages:

1. *The teacher and the learners agree on the topic.*
2. *The learners pool their ideas in small groups.*
3. *The groups come together as a class and, with the teacher as scribe, place their pooled notes and questions on the chalkboard or a flipchart.*
4. *The learners now reshape, on the basis of their collective considerations and their teacher's suggestions or requirements, their lists of "knowns" and "questions." Questions to be answered may be written up in three sections:*
   - Things all students must answer
   - Things to be considered in groups
   - Things of individual interest or concern

These stages are consistent with how questions for literature conversations are often considered and framed (see pages 183–186).

A SCIENCE INQUIRY IN FOURTH GRADE

A section of my school district's state science curriculum focuses on scientific methodology: conducting experiments, gathering information, interpreting information, and drawing conclusions. More specifically, students are expected to be able to design experiments or evaluate others' experiments keeping in mind that uncontrolled variables can influence results.

Science resource teacher Carol Hochman began questioning whether the predetermined experiments our teachers were using were truly scientific inquiry, because the teachers were already aware of the results. "As messy as it is, and as much time as it takes, students must begin to design their own experiments and determine what materials they will need to answer their own questions," she told me. So she teamed up with fourth-grade teacher Linda Cooper, and they attempted to teach students how to design experiments.

They began by modeling an experiment that Carol had deliberately designed to be unfair and that also did not answer the question originally asked. Carol challenged Linda to a contest to prove which one of them was the better athlete. They each had to throw balls into a container, but on her turns Carol changed the container, the balls, or the distance she stood from the container so that she always won. Students immediately recognized that an experiment, to be valid, needs to be fair. They were also introduced to the concepts that a variable is anything that can potentially change the results of an experiment (and perhaps make it unfair), that only one variable can be changed in any experiment, and that an experiment needs to be designed to answer the question being asked. With teacher guidance, they created a rubric made up of criteria for determining the quality of an experiment.

Next, Carol showed the students an advertisement for a scrubbing sponge she had purchased. The ad claimed food would not be trapped in the sponge, and Carol asked the students to design an experiment to determine whether or not this claim was true. While examining the box the sponge came in, the students discovered another claim, this one that the sponge would not scratch kitchen counters made of certain materials. The students decided to divide into two groups and devise two separate experiments, one to test one claim, one to test the other. Carol worked with one group, Linda worked with the other. (Figure 12-5 shows one group's experiment.)

After completing the experiments, the class checked their work against the criteria listed in the rubric they had created earlier during shared writing. They then revised the rubric—see Figure 12-6—based on their experience actually conducting an experiment.

Figure 12–5 A science experiment devised and recorded by students

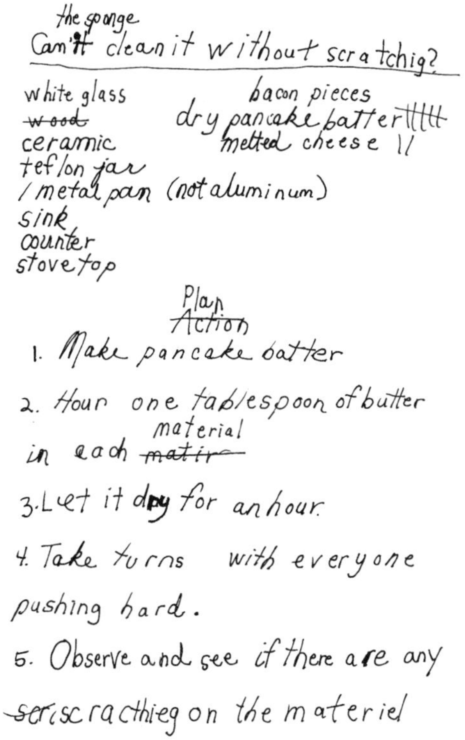

the sponge
Can't clean it without scratchig?

white glass   bacon pieces
~~wood~~   dry pancake batter ||||||
ceramic   melted cheese ||
teflon jar
/ metal pan (not aluminum)
sink
counter
stove top

Plan
Action
1. Make pancake batter

2. Hour one tablespoon of butter
   material
   in each ~~matir~~

3. Let it dry for an hour.

4. Take turns with everyone pushing hard.

5. Observe and see if there are any ~~ser~~ scra cthieg on the material

Figure 12–6 A class-created rubric for conducting an experiment

Experiment Rubric for Mrs. Cooper's Fourth-Grade Scientists

The experiment has a question.

There is a plan of action.

The experiment is fair.

The experiment could be done again under the same conditions.

Identified what the experiment can or can't do (show).

Did the experiment prove or disprove the advertisement?

Does the experiment answer the question?

As we made a plan of action, did we change anything when we needed to?

Did we use the right tools and take the right measurements?

The conclusion/results makes sense with what the data says.

Using the results of the experiments, the students, as a class, wrote a letter alerting the company of their findings (see Figure 12-7).

The benefits of this required inquiry were many. For one thing, the students received a thoughtful reply from the company explaining that "it is not uncommon for test results such as these to vary with the type of testing protocol used." The experiment also aroused the students' curiosity, and they learned what it means to conduct an experiment by controlling variables. They were ready to conduct additional experiments independently or in small groups.

MOVING TOWARD INQUIRY

Over the years, as I've worked with teachers to help students do research, write reports, and share what they have learned, I've found that many teachers are reluctant to relin-

Figure 12–7   A letter to a company supporting and questioning claims about a product

23325 Wimbledon Rd.
Shaker Heights, Ohio 44122

October 8, 1998

Household Products Division
Reckitt & Coleman Inc
1655 Valley Road
Wayne, N.J. 07470

Dear Sir or Madam,

Mrs. Cooper's fourth-grade class, along with Mrs. Hochman, our science teacher, bought your CHORE BOY LongLast scrubbing sponge because the advertisement caught our attention. As we were looking at the box, we got so absorbed in your advertisement that we decided to do some experiments of our own to see if the claims were right. The first claim that caught our eye was that the sponge would not trap food in the patented loop weave. Another claim that sounded fascinating was that the sponge would not scratch certain materials.

We planned two experiments to see if the claims were true. We split into two groups to test both claims. While designing our experiments, we tried to make it fair by keeping many of the variables the same.

In our first experiment we tried to see if the sponge scratched surfaces that you did not list. We put one tablespoon of pancake batter on each of these surfaces: porcelain sink, Formica counter, glass, plastic, stainless steel, ceramic, and Teflon. After letting the batter dry for one hour, we took the sponge and soaked it with water and cleaned the batter off of the surfaces. We observed the different surfaces to see if they were scratched. We are glad to report our conclusions matched yours and your claim was true.

The other experiment was to see if food would get trapped in the patented loop weave. To design this experiment we used different foods. We chose foods that people use a lot and we have found are hard to scrub. We tested dried ketchup, dried mustard, burned cheese, scrambled eggs, and cooked batter (with no oil). After scrubbing each of the different foods, we rinsed the sponge for fifteen seconds. We observed the sponge and all of the foods except burned cheese were trapped in the loop weave. We are not saying that you are wrong but maybe your experiment involved different foods, time for rinsing the sponge, different surfaces, stronger people, or rubbing the sponge while rinsing. Could you please share your experiments with us? We would appreciate hearing from you.

Thank you for taking your time to read this letter.

Sincerely,
Mrs. Cooper's class and Mrs. Hochman

quish their prearranged, teacher-designed research projects. And though perhaps the end products of these "canned" approaches may appear "impressive," they also all look and sound pretty much the same.

By contrast, when students have an integral role in deciding what the research process will entail and when the teacher is also a learner, the results are quite different. The students are not just writing a report. Rather, as they put information "in their own words," they are moving toward inquiry. They are asking and answering their own questions, noting and discussing questions that arise while browsing and reading, and recording "interesting ideas" that arise from their reading, writing, and thinking.

As a new teacher, Danny Young followed the same procedures for research reports that the other third-grade teachers at his school used. Even though he modeled the process every step of the way, he made all decisions regarding content and format. After several years, he began to have doubts about the process: "I could tell that kids weren't invested. Many of the final reports were boring. Kids had finished the project only because they had to. When I saw the quality writing I got in writing workshop when students had choice, I began to question the lack of choice in this project."

When Danny began negotiating the content and format of the reports with students, he discovered that student engagement was much higher. "I was shocked at how the kids came up with such good questions and a workable format," he says. Students worked for longer periods of time and worked more efficiently. Best of all, the final reports were rich with the students' own voice.

About five years ago, first-grade teacher Nancy Johnston and I had a conversation that changed how we both thought about research for young children. Nancy was frustrated with the animal research reports her students did each spring. Each year she planned for hours, sent home pages of elaborate instructions, and expected students to complete sophisticated projects. And those students who had parents who expended time and effort helping them complete the project did indeed turn in stunning reports. The reports of students without such parents looked quite different. Things hadn't changed much from when my own children were in elementary school, many years ago. I remember working for hours with them on assigned projects and thinking how unfair it was to the students who didn't have such support.

Nancy and I talked about having the kids do "child friendly" research that would produce reports that reflected what the children wondered and questioned and that looked and sounded like first graders did them. That meant we had to change the design of the report and our expectations of what kids could do. Especially, it meant we had to negotiate the content, format, and procedures with the students so that they had real choices and realistic expectations. It also meant the research project had to be done entirely at school; each day for weeks we set aside time for planning, thinking, researching, reading, taking notes, writing, publishing, and celebrating. It meant, in fact, putting curriculum inquiry into practice and deciding this project was important enough to warrant spending a large chunk of time on. (Each spring, we continue to modify our work from the year before.)

The results have been tremendously satisfying, especially for students and their families. Parents are excited about these reports and about how their children share information with them at home. Former students voluntarily come back every year, proud to talk to the new crop of researchers, read their treasured reports, answer questions, and give encouragement. It is noteworthy that these students all talk about how hard it was to do the report, but their pride at having done hard work successfully shines through. Nancy says that adding student choice and ownership to the reports made all the difference in students' enthusiasm: "I have kids begging to work on their reports. That never happened before. I integrate curriculum all year, but with these reports, I see the most authentic integration, because it all comes from the students. Everything is tied together—reading, writing, editing, scientific study."

Some Helpful Minilessons

If we want students to become researchers and inquirers and demonstrate what they know, we need to teach them the tools they will need. We need to show them how to do it. Some possible minilessons (see also Chapter 11, "Reading Nonfiction," pages 452–457) include, but are not limited to, showing our students how to:

- Browse through books and resources.
- Evaluate and choose useful and authoritative resources.
- Locate and use primary sources.
- Use the Internet to find information.
- Ask effective questions.
- Skim and scan information.
- Find facts.
- Notice and use pictures.
- Take notes.
- Organize information—order, headings, captions, visual aids.
- Write an interesting lead.
- Enhance information with drawings and photographs.
- Read, interpret, and construct graphs and diagrams.
- Use sidebars, graphs, and other visual elements to provide information.
- Use quotations effectively.
- Present a written report in an interesting format (see pages 326 and 327).
- Write nonfiction with a personal voice.
- Write, report, or present with your audience in mind.

Most of the minilessons above relate to finding out and inquiring through reading and reporting through writing, and this is a good place to begin. (See Figure 12-8, "Steps to doing research as inquiry.") To be fair to all students, however, relying solely on paper-and-pencil tasks and tests to gain and demonstrate understanding is too limiting. There are many other important ways to "find out" and show what you know, among them:

- Hands-on activities (science experiments and constructions, for example; see Egeland [1997] for a discussion of fifth graders who show what they know about science through constructions they design)
- Oral language formats (interviews, broadcasts, tapes)

Figure 12–8   Steps to doing research as inquiry: a brief summary

The steps below relate primarily to research through reading and reporting through writing. Always remember that students will be most engaged and successful when they have choices/input into topic, organization, and final presentation.

- Choose the overall topic and locate/gather resources. Resources can include, but are not limited to, informational books (may be picture books), the Internet, interviews, magazines, original sources such as diaries.
- Give students enough time to explore and browse these resources.
- Choose questions and subtopics to research (based on what you and your students know and what you want to find out).
- Read and take notes on questions, add new questions. Jot down phrases and big ideas.
- Organize the information—decide what to include and how to arrange.
- Write up what you've found out—capture the reader's attention with an inviting lead and an interesting format.
- Share/present what you now know, paying attention to your audience. Use a suitable format and include illustrations, a table of contents, an index, and a list of resources.
- Evaluate and reflect on the process.

- Musical scores
- Art (sketches, paintings, murals, sculptures)
- Drama (plays, skits)
- Interpretive dance
- Visual formats such as videos and interactive CD-ROMs

These formats also need to be demonstrated before we can expect students to use them successfully.

Helping Students Get Started

Many upper-grade teachers complain that kids can't do research writing and that more structure is needed. Here are a variety of ways to structure nonfiction writing when students are just learning this genre and learning about inquiry:

• ***A class big book***   After Ellen Battle's kindergarten students watched chicks hatch, they used interactive writing to create a big book about the experience. A first grader in Kevin Hill's class published a predictable nonfiction animal book for kindergartners after examining other models for format and language patterns.

• ***Shared writing***   The poem on page 381 was written by Nancy Johnston's first graders; each student contributed a favorite fact about the animal he was researching.

• ***Alternate pages in a book written by the teacher and the students***   First-grade teacher Kevin Hill had all students create a book, *I Like Bats! Do You?*, to culminate the class study on bats. Each student received a book in which Kevin had written one page of information followed by a blank page for students to follow his lead. Figure 12-9 shows several pages from one student's book.

• **_A simple sequential paragraph frame_** to help students organize their writing about what they learned. Here's one suggestion:

- The most important thing I learned was. . .
- I also learned. . .
- What I will remember most is. . .

Figure 12–9   The cover and beginning pages of an
information book, written by the teacher and a first grader

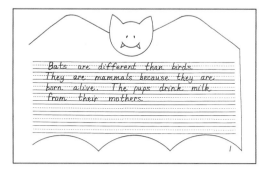
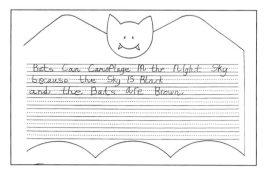

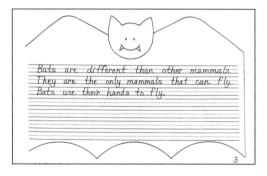
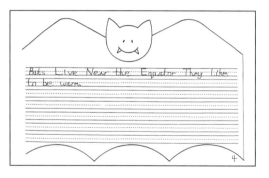

Here's another:
- First, I found out . . .
- Then, . . .
- Next, . . .
- Finally, . . .

Beginning with a Common Topic

When second-grade teacher Tara Strachan asked her students to complete a research report, she was worried she would be overwhelmed helping students find information if she let them choose their own topics without some parameters. Although she knew dinosaurs was a clichéd topic, she decided to begin with it nonetheless, because the study of dinosaurs is part of our district's second-grade curriculum as well as a topic all kids love. While Tara chose the overall topic, each child, after spending a lot of time browsing through resources (see page 443 on browsing nonfiction), chose a different dinosaur to research.

For teachers ready to give some choice but not total choice, beginning with a common topic (which sometimes is a curriculum requirement) makes the process manageable. Even when the teacher has selected the topic, very young students can, and should, choose the subtopics they want to study, the questions they will research, and the format and design of their final reports. Fourth-grade teacher Linda Cooper notes that selecting a common topic not only makes it easier to meet curriculum requirements but also encourages students to share information and thus enhances the classroom community.

Providing Resources

Students can't do research without lots of information at their fingertips. Yet many teachers assign research and provide few resources. Providing resources means not only demonstrating how to use school and public libraries and technology but also filling the classroom with a large number and variety of books and other quality resources that present information in different styles and formats. It is also important to find some way to organize these materials so students can access them easily. Some teachers invite former students back to help organize familiar books and resources in plastic tubs or crates.

If you're lucky, your school's library has a flexible schedule and is staffed by librarians who are eager to help students find information. Easy access encourages students to examine and peruse lots of books and resources before making final decisions about their research topic and questions. It's beneficial to set aside a substantial chunk of time every day for at least a week in which you read books on the topic aloud, let students browse and explore books and resources, and give students time to read on their own.

Nancy Johnston uses the school library, her own collection, books bought through school grants, books and magazines students bring in from home, animal posters, and lots of borrowed books from my and other teachers' collections to fill the classroom with nonfiction books and resources about animals. She also shows tapes from public television and takes her class on a trip to the Cleveland Zoo. And, since our district is computerized, information is also available through CD-ROMs and the Web.

For primary-grade teachers, the challenge remains finding enough easy material that students can read and interpret on their own (and/or have read to them). Keep in mind, even with easy material, that being able to read the words and use the information are two different skills. We need to teach both. Remember, too, that providing appropriate resources begins with giving students the background information they need. New information makes sense when we can integrate it into what we already know.

Using Former Students as Models and Mentors

Once a research project has been explained to the class, it is highly motivating to use former students' work as examples before negotiating expectations. Many teachers save "second editions" (photocopies) of former students' work and ask students what they notice about the work. Discussing criteria for quality work gives students standards to strive for (see pages 476–478). It is absolutely critical that we model and provide examples of what we expect our students to do.

In Nancy Johnston's first-grade class, as students become familiar with the animal they have chosen to research for a required project—by reading books and using the Internet—Nancy invites past students to come in and share their animal research reports. Each year eight or twelve students volunteer to come back to share their treasured books.

Maggie, now in grade three, proudly shares her "accordion" book about wolves, which she titled "Fang." She is clearly delighted to be back again (she also volunteered to share as a second grader). She tells the first graders that this book is her favorite published work to date and that she keeps it in a special drawer. She shares interesting facts, her author's page, and comments her dad wrote eighteen months later. I am struck by the voice in her writing. (See Figure 12-10.) Then the first graders ask questions:

- Were you frustrated?
- Was it hard to make the pictures?
- Was it hard to find facts?
- What did you like best about research?

DETERMINING THE QUESTIONS TO RESEARCH

When I am demonstrating how to begin a research project in the classroom, I start with whole-class or small-group brainstorming about possible topics to include. What questions do the students want answered? On big chart paper, through shared writing, we come up with possible topics as a class. The chart remains posted throughout the research study.

Then I ask the students, "What's a reasonable number of topics each of you should be responsible for?" After some discussion, most students in first and second grade agree three is minimum, six or seven is maximum. Tara Strachan's second-grade class decides that everyone should research what their particular dinosaur looks like and that other topics are optional. In Nancy Johnston's class, the nonnegotiable area has remained "amazing facts" or "interesting facts." (Figure 12-11 shows the decisions Nancy's first graders negotiated one year.)

Figure 12–10 *Excerpts from Fang, Maggie's book about wolves*

5

Did you know that the wolf can have up to fourteen babies and it usually only has six or seven, but I think that is amazing?!

6

When the wolf is born, it is as heavy as a loaf of bread. Wow!

7

Did you know that when lots of pups are born, it's called a litter? It's not like the litter in the recycling bin!

8

The male wolf can be six feet long. It can weigh 100 pounds. Two maggies would weigh about 100 pounds!

9

In zoos, wolves usually live to be 16 years old but in the wild, they can be older!

10

Figure 12–11 A first-grade animal research report: negotiated choices

You must choose to research at least three topics, including a section on most exciting facts!
Topic choices:

1. Animal babies—how long they develop inside the mother, how many babies are born at one time, how they grow, how long they live.
2. Where animal lives—home it makes, place in the world.
3. Food—what animal eats and how much, kind of teeth, how it gets its food.
4. Protection—what enemies it has, special body parts, does it fight or run, camouflage.
5. How it travels—alone or in a group, fast or slow.
6. Animal family—is it a mammal, reptile, etc.? cousins of your animal, names for mom, dad, baby?
7. Endangered—tell why or why not, ways to help.
8. What do the animals do all day?—"talk" to each other, spend time with "friends"

Taking Notes and Gathering Information

For our students to be able to do research well, we have to model the process every step of the way, showing students exactly what we do and how we do it. Each year, Nancy Johnston chooses an animal to research herself and takes her first graders through the same process of reading, thinking, taking notes, writing, and illustrating that she expects them to follow.

Teachers worry a lot about how to teach note taking. Keep in mind that there is no one best way. If you go through the process yourself and think about what you do, you will be on your way to teaching and supporting your students. However, young students just learning how to take notes probably need to be told to close the book before they write their notes, so they won't be tempted to copy directly from text.

One day I'm modeling note taking for Tara Strachan's second graders. I use photocopied pages of information about the dinosaur Tara is researching, which have been made into transparencies. I head blank transparencies with the four class-negotiated topics Tara has chosen to research: *Looks Like, Fascinating Facts, Defense,* and *Meals.*

Slowly, I read a page of information, think out loud as I am reading, underline significant words and phrases, reread when I am confused, skip parts that are hard or don't apply, and remove the page from the projector. Then, using the appropriate blank transparencies, and without looking at the original source, I model how I write down key phrases when taking notes—jotting down just enough information so that later I can incorporate the information into sentences. I repeat this process with two other pages, reading the information, thinking out loud, and then asking the students what they remember that they think is important to add to my notes. (See also *Invitations,* pages 281–284 for more specifics on teaching note taking.)

In Tara's classroom, as in Nancy's, students' names are posted in big print next to the topic they are researching. I tell them that if they come across facts specific to someone else's topic, they should consult this classroom chart and share what they have found with the appropriate researcher. I also suggest that it's nice to bring in books and resources for one another.

Afterward, as a review, I ask for volunteers to tell me what the students are to do:

1. Head blank papers with as many topics as they are researching.
2. Read for specific information.
3. Close the book and take notes on the appropriately headed page.
4. Share information that someone else in the class may need.

Nancy Johnston points out how important it is for the teacher to be a learner too, to be genuinely interested in every student's "Did you know . . . ?": "I always ask the child to show me that special fact in the book—it allows me to express my amazement at the fact as well and it is the perfect opportunity to check the accuracy of the fact and the child's comprehension."

The Importance of Conversation and Sharing

Wendy Saul realizes the importance of the classroom community as children strive to do a better job with inquiry: "The best teachers I know walk around the class listening like an editor for a remark or an insight or an approach that they want that student or group to share with the other children in class. Sharing like this often helps the entire class enjoy or poke around ideas in a new way." In Nancy Johnston's first grade and Tara Strachan's second grade, students are constantly sharing information with their classmates, helping one another find and interpret information and sift out what's most important and interesting, and reading information to and for each other.

As students are reading, thinking, questioning, and taking notes, we teachers need to walk around and find out what they are thinking so we can help clarify, challenge, and extend their thinking and pose new ideas and questions. The following questions encourage kids to articulate their thinking; they can be especially powerful for extending thinking when students are researching and inquiring in small groups:

- What are you doing?
- What are you thinking right now?
- How did you figure that out?
- What else did you do?
- Why did you do that?
- What's giving you trouble?
- What have you tried?
- What do you need to figure this out?

Choosing an Interesting Title

I've noticed that just about every book that makes it to *The New York Times Book Review* best-seller list has an intriguing title. People do judge books by their covers. So we spend a lot of time looking at and talking about titles and dedications in books published by both commercial and student authors and what wording makes them memorable.

Some former titles from Nancy Johnston's first graders have included "The Mighty Cat: The Lion," "Big One" (about the rhinoceros), "The Leaping Leopard," "Did You Know About the Baboon?," and " Black and White All Over: The Panda." Students have also been creative in their dedications, dedicating their books to "all the zebras in the world," "all living polar bears," and "every single rhino."

Writing the Report

The teachers in our school district spend a lot of time talking about and showing students nonfiction writing with voice and individual style. We read aloud nonfiction that has strong voice, pieces written both by professional authors and by students. We encourage students to read a paragraph or two, close their books, and in their own words tell another person what they've just read. We demonstrate how to take notes and turn them into interesting paragraphs. We teach all the elements of good writing, such as writing with engaging leads, details, and images (see Figure 12-12 for a third grader's beginning work on his introduction to his animal research report). Because we emphasize and model writing in a personal style, the reports sound like children wrote them. (The four chapters in this book on writing include detailed information on teaching writing.) Nancy Johnston's first graders developed the chart in Figure 12-13 to remind them of report writing's expectations and possibilities.

In first grade, many of the students choose to have the teacher or parent volunteer handwrite or word process their final copies. Revisions are mostly limited to the order of the information presented, but even first graders are expected to verify their facts. We often ask, "Show me where that information came from." In second grade and above, students do all the final work in revising, editing, and transcribing.

Students who finish their books first help others. From all the publishing and modeling that has gone on, they know how to help one another. One year a first grader said, "I know why we're doing this now and not at the beginning of the year. We couldn't have done it on our own then. Now we can do everything."

Showing What You Know

There are many ways for students to share the information they've learned. A brochure, pamphlet, chart, display, mural, newsmagazine, broadcast, video, comic book, are just a

Figure 12–12   First attempts at writing a lead for a report

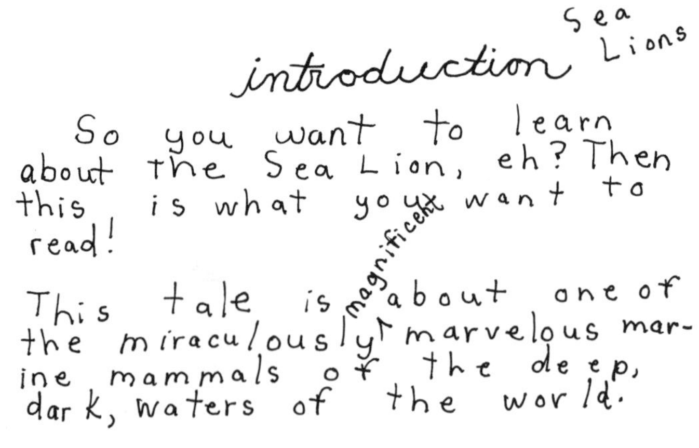

Figure 12–13   A first-grade animal research report: informal specification sheet

When you are writing your research facts, have you:

- made sure your facts are accurate?
- put your facts into your own words?
- written the information clearly?
- made the information sound exciting?

Have you thought about your writing style and format?

- interesting title
- table of contents ("look-up page")
- pictures on one page and writing on another, or both together
- question and answer
- writing as if you are the animal
- look back and find
- "Did you know?"
- writing as a scientist

few possibilities. My colleagues and I have found that students invest more energy in their research when they choose how to share what they've learned.

Kathy Short notes that a final presentation is critical to inquiry: "The presentation is where they figure out what they know and what they don't know. So I think some kind of presentation is essential to the process" (Siu-Runyan 1999, 12). However, she cautions that students need to concentrate on the important and compelling information they want to communicate before they think about how they can present that information. When students focus primarily on how they will present their information, presentations are often superficial.

In recent years students' choices for showing what they know have gone beyond typical book formats (see pages 326–328 in Chapter 8 for formatting ideas). One year fourth-grade teacher Lisa Hardiman and I worked with her students on a required research project. Each student chose a hero to investigate, a famous person who had realized a lifelong dream, and then performed multigenre research. Final presentations included first-person diaries (Figure 12-14, page 492), historical newspaper articles, radio broadcasts, dramatic speeches, interviews, a "live" Discovery channel biography with accompanying audiotape (Figure 12-15, page 493), and autobiographies.

Before students put what they learned and thought into their chosen form, they had to come up with a written plan for our approval and feedback. We supported them in becoming familiar with their chosen genre by providing and directing them to real-life examples and helping them note the specific criteria, organization, format, and visual elements involved.

When these fourth graders finished their famous-hero reports, each was also required to assume the role of the character and give an oral presentation. Their "performances" took place at a school assembly to which their parents were invited. (The event was videotaped for parents who could not attend.) Lisa showed the videotape in class the next day, a combination critique and celebration. I watched it with them. The kids were

Figure 12–14   A page draft from a complete diary of Elizabeth Stanton, by Leah Hitchens

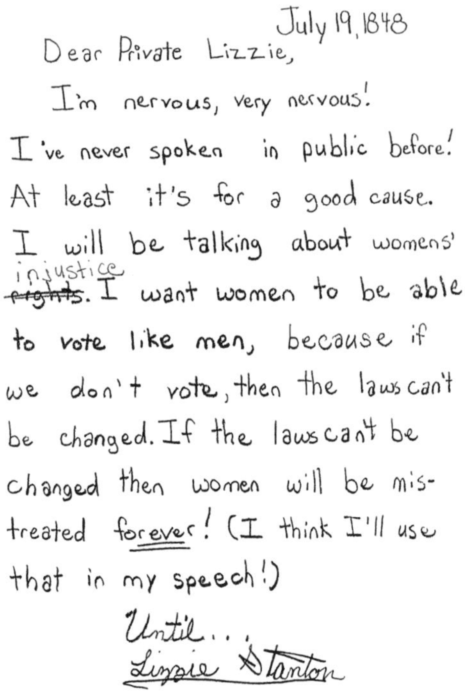

> July 19, 1848
>
> Dear Private Lizzie,
>
> I'm nervous, very nervous!
>
> I've never spoken in public before!
>
> At least it's for a good cause.
>
> I will be talking about womens'
> injustice
> ~~rights~~. I want women to be able
>
> to vote like men, because if
>
> we don't vote, then the laws can't
>
> be changed. If the laws can't be
>
> changed then women will be mis-
>
> treated forever! (I think I'll use
>
> that in my speech!)
>
> Until...,
> Lizzie Stanton

beaming. It was clear that they had learned a lot about their famous person. They had also realized firsthand that history is her-story and his-story.

In Nancy Johnston's first-grade class all students are expected to complete a small book, but each one chooses the book's format and organization. We spend a lot of time noticing and talking about different kinds of formats (lift-the-flap, pull-out-pages, accordion, traditional) and how these books are organized. (See page 130b in The Blue Pages for some books to use as models for different formats.) Because publishing is time-consuming, Nancy Johnston limits the options and has parent volunteers or former students help with the final writing and construction.

Other decisions include how the information will be presented (questions and answers, writing in the animal's voice, labeled diagrams), placement of print and illustrations, type of illustrations (freehand drawings, pictures clipped from magazines, photos printed off the Internet), cover design, and end pages.

Nancy's students assume the role of their animal or a scientist or zookeeper when they share their reports. Almost all dress in simple costumes that involve creative problem solving. No one ever says, *I don't know what to wear.* Students also share models of their animals made out of recycled materials. One student makes a crocodile using an egg carton to show the wide, open mouth, another makes a hippo from rocks and glue, and many rely on old socks to make animal puppets.

Families are invited for a specific day and time during the weeklong sharing. Nancy takes a photo of each child presenting and gives the photo to the family as a souvenir of this proud moment. Everyone listens respectfully and claps for the researcher when she

Figure 12–15   The opening paragraph from a "live" Discovery Channel biography

Mary Mcloed Bethune Introduction

Welcome to the Discovery Channel's biography of the day. Today's biography is about Mary Mcloed Bethune. Kind, loving, helpful, brave, determined, and most of all, a hero; that's Mary Mcloed Bethune. In 1875, a great woman was born, Mary Mcloed Bethune. She was the youngest child in her family and was born right after slavery had ended. Believe it or not, she was the only one out of her 13 brothers and sisters who went to school. Soon Mary got a school of her own. Many things happened, such as 50 Klan members came to her school. Much more happened. Mary Mcloed Bethune unfortunately died in 1955. It was a terrible day for many people. But, in her will she left a fabulous message.

Babyhood and early life were good for Mary. If only she knew she would leave her home forever. When Mary Mcloed Bethune was born in 1875 her family knew she would be a gifted child. Being born after the Civil War was better for Mary, since she was the first one in her family to be born free. Her family owned a plantation which they bought for freedom.

The one thing Mary wanted to do the most is read. Every day she would ask if she could go to school. One day a woman named Emma J. Wilson asked Mary's parents, Patsy and Samuel, if any of their kids would like to go to her African American School. They didn't have enough money to send all the kids, so they knew just to send Mary. When Mary heard she was going to school she thought it was the best day of her life. But when she heard she was going on a train to Maysville, she already felt homesick.

Mary was such a good student, before she knew it she was in college. Mary's college years were wonderful. Little did she know her present dreams would come true in the future. Her dream was to help young black children learn that they were as good as anyone else.

Mary was a great student. She got all A's, which is very hard, and she had a dream that she would run a school of her own. Soon her dream would come true.

by Amy Silver

is done. Peers give compliments and ask questions. The proud researcher enjoys the spotlight and answers all questions courteously and knowledgeably.

Evaluating Research Projects

Although letting young children own the research they do is very demanding for all involved, it is worth all the hard work. In one of Nancy's final newsletters to parents in June 1997, she wrote:

> I have been asked by a number of people, including myself (!), why we did this research, if
> I will do it again, and if it was worth all the time and energy it took the children (and me!),

and I would have to answer, "Yes!" I think the benefits far outweigh the hassles. If you were in for any of our presentations and really looked at your child's finished research book, I think you probably agree. The children's pride, their increased self-esteem, and their investment in "our animals" have been wonderfully rewarding for me. I am certain that by now you have become an "expert" on your child's research animal too!

Almost every year, the teachers I work with and I ask the students to evaluate the research process with us so we can continue to improve and refine what we do with upcoming classes, and we incorporate most of their suggestions. (Rubrics can also be developed with students, to use both as guides during the project and as evaluations after the project—see page 479.) One year Nancy Johnston's first graders made these suggestions:

- Sort books in the classroom—by animal families (reptiles, amphibians, birds, mammals), animal homes, animal babies, animal encyclopedia/atlas—so we can find them more easily.
- Let us come back to sort books for next year's class.
- Continue to use parents in the classroom. They helped us locate and read information.
- Continue to let students choose the format. Being able to create an accordion book, a pull-out-page book, or a lift-the-flap book was fun.
- Let students choose the color of paper they will use, or even alternate colors.

Students also made comments like these:

"I liked how we could all do a book in a different way."
"It was neat to know all about one animal and research it."
"I liked helping other people."
"I didn't want any help."
"We liked giving our reports in costume."
"It's wonderful because it's fun to learn about animals."
"Terrific. Two thumbs up, because it's fun to help people and fun to help people get done."
"I liked the reading better than the writing." (Many students said this.)

When we asked them what they thought the best part was, we got responses like these: "being done," "taking notes," "finishing illustrations," "drawing pictures," "getting my book all ready," "lifting the flaps," "starting the illustrations." Things they didn't like included: "would prefer oral report—not written," "illustrations, because I didn't like sharing the colored pencils," "I didn't like when books gave conflicting information, such as, one book said, 'The tiger sleeps in the day,' and another book said, 'Tigers sleep at night.'"

FINAL REFLECTIONS

As I was writing this book, the difference between simply reporting information and thinking about, analyzing, and interpreting information became apparent. For example, some of the things I struggled to understand were the issues surrounding standards. I began by reading, collecting facts, and summarizing, but as I thought more deeply about the topic and its relation to teaching and learning, I raised questions and sought answers.

I reread and rethought. I moved beyond reporting on standards to inquiring about standards. That is, I took the data and perspectives I had gathered, and then I thought about, questioned, and analyzed them until I understood the ideas and concepts well enough to draw my own conclusions.

This process is what we mean by inquiry. When we raise and attempt to answer questions like *What is significant here? Why is it this way? How does it work? Could it be otherwise?* we are not merely explaining and reporting. We are inquiring into—thinking about, analyzing, interpreting, evaluating—topics about which we feel strongly.

The challenge for us teachers is to move students beyond learning skills and facts to engaging in inquiry and investigation *using* those skills and facts—even within the sometimes constraining limits of mandated curriculum, state guidelines, and standards. We need to ask ourselves, *What is critical for students to know and be able to do to live successfully and thoughtfully in the twenty-first century?* not *What do I need to cover?*

CONTINUING THE CONVERSATION

• ***What do you wonder about?*** Share what you wonder with your students. If you are conducting teacher research in your classroom, even informally, tell your students what your questions are. Share some of your thoughts and notes in process.

• ***What is an area in which you are an inquirer or scientific thinker?*** Examine your own processes and thoughts. How can you use your own inquiry approach to enrich life in your classroom?

• ***Take a close look at a unit you teach.*** Are your interdisciplinary connections meaningful? Where are you building in students' interests and questions? Are you modeling the research process by going through it yourself and making your processes and thinking explicit to students? How are you teaching for understanding? What evidence do you have that students are gaining enduring understanding? How might your curriculum be more inquiry based?

• ***Examine your philosophy about student research reports.*** Do your students have enough choice and input about the topic, resources used, and final presentation? Are your expectations age appropriate? Is the research process humane, reasonable, interesting, and doable so that students will want to continue inquiring? Do students have a say in the evaluation process? Do they have an opportunity to share their work with peers and family?

CHAPTER 13

Critical Resources for Curriculum Inquiry

Librarians, School Libraries, and Technology

The Lomond lab was designed to be an integral part of the school library. Library resources for student use are only a step away.

■ We must teach students to be learners, because in their lifetimes so much new knowledge will be generated that they cannot expect to stop learning when they leave school. What are learners? They are people who inquire, who seek information, evaluate it, apply it to new problems, questions, or decisions, and assess how well the information has met their needs.

—*American Association of School Librarians and Association for Educational Communications and Technology (1998, 131)*

Today's information age requires that students become expert information seekers, users, sifters, and thinkers. For our students to become information literate, a strong partnership must be forged between librarians and teachers. Only then will technology, resources, and library use be maximized for the good of all students.

THE NEED FOR CURRICULUM INQUIRY

The amount of information available continues to grow at a dizzying rate. Since it's impossible to manage all the information in this information age, as teachers, we must help students learn the skills they need to find, evaluate, and utilize information. Some of these skills include questioning intelligently, hypothesizing and predicting; locating, reading, and comprehending; hypothesizing and problem solving; working collaboratively; and continuing the inquiry process.

Teaching students—and ourselves—how to probe, question, explore, investigate, and draw conclusions from information is necessary whether the subject is language arts, social studies, science, or mathematics. Information literacy refers to "the ability to acquire and evaluate whatever information is needed at any given moment" (Senn and Senn 1994, ix). The information-literate student, according to the first three of nine standards set forth by the American Association of School Librarians and Association for Educational Communications and Technology (1998):

- Accesses information efficiently and effectively
- Evaluates information critically and competently
- Uses information accurately and creatively (8–9)

Curriculum inquiry is a natural and excellent way to encourage the development of information-literate students who have the tools, strategies, and motivation for self-sustained curiosity and learning. (See Chapter 12, "Curriculum Inquiry: Developing a Questioning Stance Toward Learning.")

Information literacy demands teaching a research process that transcends current source formats such as books, CD-ROMs, and the World Wide Web, and can be used with future technologies. Information literacy is required in today's complex society.

THE SCHOOL LIBRARY: THE HEART OF CURRICULUM INQUIRY

The school library has the potential to be the information center of the school. As such, students and teachers would have frequent and comfortable access to texts and technology as well as the knowledge and support of the librarian for their selection and use. Unfortunately, the school library as inquiry center is still a rarity. Let's take a look at current reality and possibilities so that we educators can actively work toward a better system. Without free and easy access to knowledge, what we and students can learn and achieve remains sorely limited.

Today's Librarian

Despite the fact that library media specialists are trained as information specialists and instructional consultants, their principal role in too many schools remains that of glorified baby-sitters who read to kids and teach them the Dewey Decimal System. As they have done for decades, many teachers depend on library time as a student-free planning period. Students are deposited at the library door and picked up at the end of the thirty- or forty-minute period. Few teachers stay to assist students with book selection, despite the necessity of matching students with appropriate books and emphasizing the importance of reading. Instead of the library being an information-rich center of learning, in too many places the school library is merely a place to listen to stories and check out books.

This model persists in spite of research that demonstrates that librarians, teachers, and students need to work hand in hand planning and implementing an inquiry curriculum (Buchanan 1991; Lance, Welborn, and Hamilton-Pennell 1993). Although at its best the model introduces readers to books, one reader at a time, and demonstrates the power and possibilities of literature, its inflexible time constraints severely limit optimal library use and function.

An Exemplary Lesson in the Old Library Model

I sit in on librarian Kathy O'Neal's class at her request. She has asked me to observe her teaching and give her feedback, looking specifically at two questions: Is she trying to do too much? and How can she enrich her time with the students? Because of library cutbacks, she meets with seven classes every day, five days a week, for thirty-minute periods. I am amazed at what she accomplishes and balances in that short, rigid time frame and am filled with admiration for her skill and energy.

In the third-grade lesson I observe, she reads a new and unusual version of Rumpelstiltskin (*Rumpelstiltskin's Daughter*, by Diane Stanley) as the children are gathered on the rug in front of her. First, she sets the framework by talking about what the kids know about the Rumpelstiltskin tale. She confirms comments, adds to students' comments by scaffolding, and questions to get more information.

"Listen to see if this version sounds like the one you remember," Kathy comments before reading. A skilled story reader, Kathy holds the book wide open in front of her so that students can see the illustrations as she reads. She pauses occasionally to point out important features. "Isn't it odd that Rumpelstiltskin's name is already mentioned on page three? Usually, we don't learn it until the end." Later, "How is this Rumpelstiltskin different from other versions?" Although there is only time to read half of the book, she gets maximum participation from students. She then sets the purpose for the next lesson: "Next week we'll talk about how characters are alike and different in Rumpelstiltskin tales."

For the remaining ten minutes, Kathy guides students in signing out books. She points out a collection of other "fractured fairy tales" on a nearby table and encourages each student to sign out at least one chapter book. She zeros in on just the right book for several browsing students. When students have their books, they sit at tables and begin to read silently. Kathy often asks the students to "read me your first line," to be sure that the student can handle the book.

The marathon thirty minutes are over; the teacher is at the door, and Kathy has a five-minute break before the next class arrives. I don't see how she could do any more or any better than she has done, given the time and organizational constraints of this model.

The Changing Role of the Librarian

Every time I give a workshop for educators, I poll the audience for grade level and area of interest. When I ask how many librarians are present, only a few hands go up if any at all. I always make the point that this is a huge problem, that literacy—learning to read, write, and inquire across the curriculum—must be a shared responsibility. We simply cannot do our jobs well without the access to information that library media specialists can provide. Teachers and librarians form a natural and necessary partnership. Information literacy is a requirement in today's society, and the knowledgeable librarian can guide us in this vital collaboration.

A major roadblock to teachers and librarians collaborating in a new library model has been finding and providing teachers with the planning time that the old model provided. Another barrier has been that some administrators have not understood the transformative potential of a more flexible library system. As well, under pressure to provide much needed planning time for teachers, some administrators have backed off pushing for change. But not pushing for such change does us all a disservice.

The Need for Flexible Access

We should be able to use the library in school as we do in life, when we need to and want to, not based on a rigid schedule. Where flexible access exists in schools—that is, when the library functions on a schedule based on literacy needs—students see the library as the center of literature, information, and inquiry. In a flexible library program, teachers and librarians work as an integral team who plan, teach, and evaluate together. Students' and teachers' instructional needs drive how the library is used. (See Figure 13-1 for the difference between a traditional program and a flexible program as noted by elementary school librarian Kathy O'Neal.)

In such a plan, the librarian's role still includes assisting students with selecting books to read. Open checkout time several times each day allows students of all ages to select books individually or in small groups. However, the job is broadened to focus on collaborative planning with teachers across the curriculum, assisting teachers and students with topic exploration, helping students and teachers locate data and information, teaching hands-on research skills such as finding and using electronic information, and being available to support all aspects of curriculum inquiry. Literature studies and story times still continue—but are now relevant to and supportive of the curriculum. As well, some flexible library programs include regular weekly borrowing for the youngest students, which may well be the best way to help these students and their families establish a reading routine.

While many teachers initially resist open access because of lost planning time or not knowing how to work hand in hand with the teacher-librarian, eventually, most come to prefer this new structure, in which the teacher and librarian co-plan and co-teach. Administrators figure out alternative ways for teachers to have adequate release time, teachers feel supported in their instructional programs, students become more comfortable with using the library for research, librarians become teaching partners, and the school library becomes a natural extension of the classroom. (See Appendix C-4 for the current position statement on flexible scheduling from the American Association of School Librarians. See Figure 13-2 on page 500 for one teacher-librarian's framework for collaborative planning.)

At Lakeside Elementary School in Chattanooga, Tennessee, talented teacher-librarian Jo Ann Everett credits flexible scheduling and ongoing teacher/librarian collaboration with increased library usage and higher achievement-test scores. Specifically, students of teachers who had the highest library usage—in terms of both the amount of collaboration with the librarian and the number of materials checked out by teachers and students—had the highest test scores for reading comprehension and reference study as measured by a standardized test. Jo Ann comments, "In fact, most of the test scores fell into rank from the highest to the lowest based on library usage" (1998). These facts have held constant for the four years that flexible access has been in place.

Figure 13–1   What's a flexible library program?

What's a Flexible Library Program?

Flexible libraries are based on a fundamentally different understanding of the role of a library, and a librarian, in a school's instructional program.

Current Library Program	*Flexible Access Library Program*
Staff & students have **limited access** to the library	Staff & students have **flexible access** to the library
Librarian functions as **"support personnel"**	Librarian functions as a **team-teacher**
Library instruction is **separate** from classroom learning	Library instruction is **integrated** into classroom learning
Librarian and teachers teach from **separate curricula**	Librarian and teachers **share** design, teaching, and evaluation of curriculum units
Classroom teachers use library period for **planning time**	Teacher and librarian **teach together**; less planning time for both
Schedule driven	**Need** driven
Fixed schedule	**Flexible** schedule
Class limited to one library session per week @ 40 minutes (IF we have a 4/5 librarian)	Class' library time: 3 to 4 hours per month. Number & length of sessions according to need (with 4/5 librarian)
"Library Skills" taught **in isolation**	Skills modeled, practiced, & mastered **through actual use**
Emphasis on **skills**	Emphasis on **information literacy**, **research process**, and **inquiry**
"Library Day" pattern: Story & Checkout	Reading aloud & storytelling planned as needed
Personal reading selection on weekly "library day" in whole-class setting	Open Checkout Times daily for personal reading selection for individuals or small groups
Artificial patterns of library use	**Authentic** patterns of library use
Library program is **peripheral**	Library program is **integral**

by Kathy O'Neal

Figure 13–2   A flexible library program: A framework for collaborative planning for librarian and teachers

- Meet with teachers at each grade level to talk about changes or new directions for each classroom program in the following year.
- Review current units in social studies, science, and language arts.
- Begin to plan new units—look at existing resources, what is already being studied at other levels, developmental appropriateness of units.
- Agree on major curriculum units for the year.
- Establish a working calendar that includes research skills to be taught, schedule of book talks, schedule of research, etc.

by Ann Van Deusen

Jo Ann Everett acknowledges that the success and implementation of the school's flexible library program has stemmed from the leadership of her exemplary principal, Faye Kimsey Pharr. Jo Ann also notes, "My role has changed from that of a 'professional clerk' to that of a teacher-librarian. My knowledge of the curriculum is broader and more focused. I plan and help write units of study with the teachers, and I participate in the implementation of the units. Students see me in a totally different role and discipline is rarely needed in the library."

One of the big advantages of flexible access is that very young children learn how the research process works and how to conduct their own information searches. Both younger and older students relish independently using the library when they need to and want to. They like knowing that the teacher-librarian is available to help them when guidance is necessary. As well, students learn how to use and utilize all kinds of resources, at the point of need, in the process of curriculum inquiry. Perhaps best of all, students, teachers, and librarians all become more information literate while enjoying and appreciating the library as the center for information and literature.

Sixth-grade teacher Louis Matthias comments after one year of flexible library use:

> I have loved the instructional system we have used this year in the Woodbury Library. Instead of having a weekly class, I have used the library to enhance my instruction. The librarian, Mary Strouse, spends planning time with me, identifying what we want to teach. We then schedule my class at the times that fit my curriculum. Let's say my science unit has a lesson where my students need to research chemists. The librarian suggests we take part of the period reviewing how to use indexes in a number of scientific references before the students start their search. She presents the lesson, and I am there to work with the students when they are ready to do research. Another example is working on research papers. The entire process was so much better when it was taught by Mary and me. The papers I received this year are proof of that. One of the greatest opportunities with this type of scheduling came when I sent to the library those few students who were struggling to get their research papers completed. Mary would work with them individually on their papers as they continued the writing process. I would be very unhappy if we ever went back to the old system.

TECHNOLOGY AND LEARNING

Technology has ushered in a new information age. In record time, all kinds of data and reports are at our fingertips, enabling us access and links to sources and resources never before possible. While in the late 1990s technology such as computers, CD-ROM, and Internet on-line services dominate, new technologies will continue to enter the information marketplace.

The good news about technology is that students are highly motivated to read, write, publish, and inquire; information on any topic in the world is readily available and accessible; and students have the opportunity to grow in information literacy. As well, kids eager to operate a computer program are typically highly motivated to follow directions, pay close attention to what they have to do, and problem solve.

Yet, I'm worried that, with our increasing emphasis on technology, our "wired" schools are giving a loud and clear message that technology is the most important literacy medium. As more and more funds are allocated for technology, less money may be available for books and libraries. Spending for computer software continues to rise, one indication that "many schools are choosing technology over books" (Manzo 1997, 5). We teachers must be outspoken and proactive to make sure that school and classroom libraries are well stocked *before* investing heavily in more technology.

Concerns About Technology

Great numbers of us teachers, confused by all the new sources of information, are reluctant to change our traditional ways of accessing information. Moreover, most of us have not been properly trained to use the new technology. In fact, many teachers acknowledge that their students' skills and comfort levels exceed their own.

For most of us, the flood of information that continues to be easily available and accessible is a curse as well as a blessing. Unless we teach students how to evaluate the credibility and usefulness of sources, we may not be giving them an advantage. In fact, there is scant research that indicates that time spent with technology positively impacts learning and achievement. For example, while students who have more access to computers may write more, they don't necessarily write better (Trotter 1998).

The increasing use of the World Wide Web may be contributing to a decline in the quality and originality of research papers. Because it's so easy to insert information, quotes, and pictures, students are often not discriminating enough in deciding what to include in their papers. We need to teach students "how to assess sources to determine their credibility, as well as to trust their own ideas more than snippets of thought that materialize on a screen" (Rothenberg 1997). Because of an increase in "computer aided cheating," professors at universities (and high school teachers too, no doubt) are routinely searching the Internet when "electronic plagiarism" is suspected (Zack 1998, A26).

This relates to a problem a growing number of elementary teachers have complained about to me. Parents are word processing their students' reports at home, and the "enhanced" finished products often don't resemble the students' original work.

Perhaps most important, excessive exposure to electronic media and software is changing the way young children socialize and play, impacting their relationships, physical activity, and creativity in a troubling manner. Additionally, most software programs are of questionable quality and value (Healy 1998).

If a student can't read, I'm not sure how computers help. I'd rather buy ten paperback books for the classroom than one CD-ROM. So far, at least, most of the CD-ROMs I've looked at have more entertainment value than educational value. CD-ROMs have made books interactive for kids, with animation, sound, and other options. While electronic books can be enhanced and continually updated, paper books are more reliable. They don't crash, and they're more durable. Not to mention that much technology becomes obsolete within several years.

Still, I don't believe that we should choose between computers and books. Both are necessary for inquiry and learning.

> Reading for information and pleasure is our goal. Whether it is between two covers or on a screen, reading will become a matter of choice in the same way we choose television, radio, newspaper, or our neighbor to give us the news. Its format will vary according to our individual preferences, thus guaranteeing a place for books as we know them. (Morley and Russell 1995, 267).

The Enduring Value of the Book

I recently received an amusing but powerful e-mail from a friend introducing a "revolutionary breakthrough in technology." Trade named BOOK, "the new Bio-Optic Organized Knowledge device" is reported to be easy to use, compact, portable, affordable, and "powerful enough to hold as much information as a CD-ROM disk."

Thankfully, paper text print is here to stay, or so it seems. Even computer aficionados prefer to print out long texts rather than read them on a computer screen (Lewis 1998, 7). And I, for one, can't imagine reading the newspaper online every day. It's not cozy or relaxing. I like holding the paper in my hands and turning the pages. So it is with real books. As many have noted, you can't take the computer to bed with you. For me, there is nothing so comforting as curling up in bed with a favorite book, holding it in my hands, and savoring a wonderful story.

So far, at least, hardly anyone wants to read a book onscreen. We want the actual book, not the "virtual version." As best-selling author Anna Quindlen (1998) wrote,

> It is not simply that we need information, but that we want to savor it, carry it with us, feel the heft of it under our arm. We like the thing itself.
> It is not possible that the book is over. Too many people love it so. (68)

Confessions of a Technophobe

I know my age is showing when I say that technology baffles me. I live in fear of my computer crashing or my hard drive frying. I can read the words in the computer manuals, but they don't make sense to me. I hesitate to use computer support "hot lines," as past experience has shown that they can sometimes make my problem worse. (I once spent ninety minutes on the phone while a technician talked me through a problem. My computer-savvy son later told me, "Mom, just call me at work. I could have solved that problem for you in five minutes.") I don't find surfing the Internet particularly relaxing after a long day of teaching. I'd rather curl up with a book or talk with my husband. In fact, the amount of information available at my fingertips seems as much a blessing as a curse. There's just too much material and not enough time. I need my own personal information sifter, someone who would sort through the reams of material relevant to my life and work and give me only what's excellent and meaningful.

I know that my life was simpler before the days of e-mail, faxes, pagers, and cell phones. Today I use e-mail sparingly, preferring faxes and phone talks. I still prefer to write a letter by hand to someone I know and care about. I save all letters that I receive, and file them year by year, in personal and professional folders.

Still, I know technology is here to stay, and I need to "get with the program." I've talked with lots of other technophobes who feel the same way, while it seems that children are born "knowing" how to handle all this technology. However, our own processes in how we learn to use technology—or, in fact, how we learn to overcome any great learning challenge—can be instrumental in thinking about all teaching and learning. The following stories bring home some important principles about learning.

Learning from Technology Anxiety

One recent Saturday afternoon as I was logging online to check my e-mail, my computer froze. My son Peter had taught me how to get the machine offline by disconnecting the battery and wires, so I wasn't upset—yet. I disconnected the power, restarted the computer, and worked at writing this book. I waited a few hours for good measure, and then tried to log on to America Online. Everything worked for several seconds, but just when I should have been hearing the familiar welcome, "You've got mail," "Goodbye" from America Online appeared on my screen. So I tried to log on again. After several more attempts resulted in my being logged off immediately, I nervously called technical support. It took fifteen minutes of patient waiting, pushing certain numbers, and listening to various recorded messages before I reached a human voice.

After listening to my problem, my telephone technician, Ryan, helped me locate the proper file in my systems folder and change several settings he believed might be responsible for the problem. Like a soldier, I carefully followed orders, and I believed him when he said, "Your problem is fixed." We said our good-byes, and the problem recurred immediately as I attempted to log back on to the system. I redialed technical support. After fifteen minutes, I reached Sue, who had me check virtual memory, various megabytes and rams—some of which she had me increase in number. Next, she gave me instructions to rebuild my desktop (whatever that means), which she said was necessary because my program had gotten damaged. She told me what keys to hold down and press but said she couldn't stay on the line through the process. We hung up. I followed her directions verbatim. The computer went off and came on again, but nothing took place on my desktop. Once again, I called technical support, and after the customary long wait I reached Dennis, who quickly talked me through a different regimen to repair my America Online program. Then he had me test getting online. It was a go. Finally, he talked me through rebuilding the desktop, a procedure he recommended as normal and necessary monthly maintenance for my computer. I was dumbfounded.

"Never heard of that," I told him.

"Haven't you read your manual?

"Are you kidding? It's over nine hundred pages, and I don't understand the language."

"I know," he agreed. "It's like Greek." A kindred spirit who understood. I wanted this guy's number.

"How can I get you again?" I asked him.

"You can't," he told me. "In fact, I could lose my job for helping you rebuild your desktop. It's not part of my job. On rare occasions, people can lose files on their hard drive."

Luckily, my files survived intact, and I did too. Until the next breakdown. That came one summer morning when I was busily writing. When I went to print out my draft, I received the message on my screen that I could not use my printer because of internal error 8972. Several attempts brought up the same message. I was baffled and surprised. While I always write with the fear that some new computer problem may arise, I had assumed my fairly new (factory-rebuilt) laser printer would remain reliable. As I could feel my panic starting to build, I called the Hewlett Packard technical support number. After the usual long wait and transfer routine, I found myself talking to Daryl, a Mac technician who determined that my problem was due to my driver or operating system. More panic. That sounded major. A call to Peter, my computer-expert son. He predicted that I would need to reinstall the printer driver and if that didn't work, to reinstall the whole operating system. Did I have my disks to do that? After searching through drawers I found the disks and realized I'd better keep this stuff handy. I next called my dear colleague, computer maven Lee Sattelmeyer. Several hours later Lee was at my home. Sure enough, Peter was right. Reinstalling the printer driver had my computer and printer communicating again. Next time, I might even be able to troubleshoot that problem myself.

I thought a lot about why I get so fearful when technology fails, while Peter and Lee manage to stay so calm. They know, from knowledge and experience, that they are likely to be effective problem solvers and get the system working. On the other hand, lacking that background knowledge, experience, and success, I am helpless at independent problem solving. When something goes wrong, I haven't a clue as to how to fix it. Worse, I know I can't fix it myself. What I need is a lot of hand holding, observing, partnership experiences, and direct instruction to build my confidence and knowledge base. Then, gradually, I calm down as I come to realize that the problem is fixable and that, in the near future, I may even be able to figure it out by myself.

Implications for the Classroom

I imagine that kids who have difficulty with reading or any other subject experience the same kind of panic that I feel when confronting text and information beyond my level of understanding. Lacking a history of success in a subject or skill they are learning, they approach the task without confidence and without the knowledge that things will eventually make sense at the end, even it they don't at this moment.

What amazes me when I watch Peter and Lee work through a computer problem is that they often have no idea what has caused the problem or how they will fix it. Still, they approach the task with conviction. Because they have a strong base of computer knowledge and strategies, know what questions they need to ask themselves, and a track record of success solving past problems, they know they eventually will succeed. This is exactly the mindset and confidence we need to be instilling in our students.

We can't possibly teach our students all they need to know. But we can teach them the tools for problem solving. We can make sure—through effective teaching and guidance, opportunities for practice and feedback, and celebration of successes—that students become confident, independent problem solvers, continual questioners, and seekers of knowledge. For our struggling readers, this means providing shared reading, partner reading, lots of practice on easy texts, and lots of small-group and one-to-one instruction before we can expect them to read independently, problem solving with confidence as they go.

Because I recognize the necessity of being professional regarding technology but lack the knowledge we teachers need, I have asked Lee Sattelmeyer to write the following section. Lee has been an elementary school classroom teacher for twenty-five years. He also serves as his building's technology coordinator and sees himself as a teacher expert as well as a learner. In a recent letter to me he wrote the following:

> I believe you cannot be successful in integrating technology unless you have a vision. A vision cannot be developed without a philosophical basis for decision making and a sense of what is doable. A vision without some sense of connection to the rest of the school community is not very effective.

Lee's story, thoughts, and vision for getting involved with technology follow, in his own words.

TECHNOLOGY IN THE CLASSROOM:
THOUGHTS FROM A FELLOW TRAVELER
by Lee Sattelmeyer

Many of us in the teaching profession grew up without the benefits of modern technology available in today's classrooms. Because the technology is relatively new to us, we tend to be cautious in our acceptance of it as a valuable, integrated teaching tool. People who don't know me often see only my excitement; they don't know that a lot of thought has gone into my advocacy of the role technology can play in a child's learning environment. I struggle sometimes with how to implement this, but over the years I've developed a personal vision and some basic tenets when looking at how to use technology.

Several principles guide my thinking.

- *Technology is here to stay.* If you can't beat 'em, join 'em.

- *Know the technology basics.* You don't need all the latest doodads but should have a working knowledge of what is possible and what is available.

- *Technology does not replace the teacher.* Computers should not be seen as supplanting the teacher but as augmenting the way we do things, the way we teach, and the way that children learn.

- *Technology is fallible.* Often it is the human quality that makes the difference.

Technology Is Here to Stay

A number of years back, the tenth anniversary of the Apple computer was quietly celebrated. I remember the first Apple computer that went into our school library in the early 1980s. The machine did not come with much useful software. It featured an arcade game, Pong, an oversimplified version of Ping-Pong that didn't seem to have too much educational value at the time. Still, I thought the Apple was pretty amazing back then.

What I did notice was that the computer system consistently attracted my students when we went to the library. I didn't have much of an idea about how it could be used with kids at the time, just a lot of blind faith that at some point in the future, technology was going to impact my life and the lives of my students. It wasn't long before more useful software became available and changed the way I thought about teaching and learning with computers.

The "Aha!" came for me when I began thinking that word processors could be used to free up inhibitions in student writers. In addition to the motivational factor, I noticed that the reluctant writers were more willing to put thoughts down, knowing that to revise, they would not have to go through an endless series of rewriting their entire piece, only the parts that needed fixing. The next challenge was to convince my principal and especially parents that having a spell checker available to students was not going to mean the end of civilization as we know it. Gradually, opposition to the challenges of technology began to wane as more people accepted that spell checking helps the student writer identify spelling patterns and habitually misspelled words

Today's technology has become increasingly more complex and capable of enriching lives. It continues to offer us teachers challenges. Software exists now that allows the writer to dictate his or her ideas instead of typing them. This software can even read the project back to the writer. Might a mouseless and keyboardless world be in our future?

My point is that there is an ever increasing push to make technology better. Improvements in hardware and software lead to other improvements. More and more households and schools are acquiring this modern miracle. The industry is driven by demand for technology to work faster and do more. Since computers are not going to go away anytime soon, teachers need to become knowledgeable about technology and its impact on learning and instruction in the classroom.

The Teacher Is a Key Player

We weren't always sure, with those early machines, how their use was going to impact children's learning. We're not always sure today. One of the problems is that there isn't much in the way of hard empirical evidence that supports the premise that kids learn better with computers, the Internet, and such. We do have some information suggesting that the teacher (and teacher-librarian) are key players in whether children demonstrate increased understanding using technology. Part of the problem, I believe, is that we are at a transitional stage in our culture. We still tend to value statistical scores based on the ability to identify the correct answer to a series of isolated questions rather than the ability to integrate multiple sources of information to build the "big picture" or a gestalt.

Staff Development Is Crucial

If the teacher is a key player in whether students learn to use technology, then staff development is crucial. It is not surprising that a 1996 survey done by the U.S. Department of Education, *Advanced Telecommunications in U.S. Public Elementary and Secondary Schools*, indicated that 51 percent of efforts to educate staff in the integration and use of technology for instruction is left to teacher initiative. It is apparent that we have grabbed hold of the tiger's tail, but that much planning is required in order to tame the beast.

School districts seem to go through a similar pattern when adopting technology. The expensive equipment comes first, followed sometime later by the concern about how to use all the equipment effectively. Our district has gone through just such a process.

Over the years, I've been concerned with how to put technology into the hands of our students. I haven't always been successful and at times have even doubted my own vision. Seymour Papert, in *The Children's Machine: Rethinking School in the Age of the Computer*, suggests that there is an immunological response on the part of schools that seeks to protect existing practices and the status quo. Staff development is one area in which I see this occurring, for two reasons. One is, as Papert suggests, that we view teachers for the most part as technicians whose job it is to impart knowledge. As evidence of this, one has only to look to the growing number of states in which proficiency testing involves asking for a specific answer to an isolated problem. Inservice training is a realistic approach if this is how you view teaching—just train us in how to use technology and maybe our students will learn. The second reason we protect the status quo is that many of us are uncomfortable admitting that we don't know all the answers. Teachers in my building still have difficulty seeking my help when they don't know how to do something with technology, and many rarely share what approaches they're taking. It is more usual for me to hear that some piece of equipment or software isn't working. Both of the above viewpoints impact staff development plans because they severely limit the learning process.

It is crucial for staff development planning to be done on the district and building levels. A 1995 U.S. Congress report, *Teachers and Technology: Making the Connection*, issued by the now defunct congressional Office of Technology, suggests some guidelines. Foremost is the need for us teachers to have lots of hands-on experience with equipment and software and easy access to people who can explain how to effectively use technology in the classroom. The emphasis is away from what I call the "Let's put on a class" syndrome, in which we gather teachers together to teach them some skill like word processing. Instead we need to be showing teachers how to enhance the learning of their students, teaching them the skills that they need to be able do that. This means having people in each building who handle teacher requests for help in a timely fashion. That is a major paradigm shift for most of us. Unfortunately, it runs afoul of budgeting restraints that make school administrations reluctant to hire technology support personnel.

Rethinking a Traditional Computer Inservice

Last year, my building's technology team conducted a mandatory half-day staff development program during a teacher workday. Just a few months before, the district had added a Windows 95 computer to every classroom.

My building did not have a computer lab, only classroom computers. Traditional computer inservice meant going to the high school or middle school labs and being taught how to use an application program. Those classes were useful, but rarely addressed the classroom environment and our teaching of children.

I wanted to do something different, something that would have a relatively immediate impact on instruction and learning. I convinced our building technology team that we could put on a staff development program right in our own building by designing the content to meet our individual capacities and needs. The lack of a lab would not hinder us; we could use one of the classroom computer systems to conduct a short general meeting, and then move into additional classrooms for breakout groups. In the breakout groups, small groups of teachers would be able to explore what had been presented in the general meeting with support from the technology team members.

We sent out a list of what we called the "Minimum Competencies for Technology" to every teacher and requested that the teachers develop at least an awareness of each skill prior to the staff development program. Each teacher was assigned a tutor from the technology team to assist them in acquiring the skills before the program began.

There was the usual grumbling from a few people and even a query to the teachers' union as to whether we could really do this. I responded to the criticism with another question, asking why anyone would not want to acquire these skills, given that the equipment was already in the classrooms. It seems that what was really being challenged here was the ability of teachers on their own to remediate a perceived need in their building. Fortunately, my building administrator and the district administrator in charge of technology stood by us and supported the staff development program in every way they could.

The staff development program went off as scheduled. The theme for the day was using weather resources on the Internet to teach mathematical and science concepts. Embedded within the program were the technical skill components: how to use an Internet browser to visit Web sites; how to capture a picture from the Internet; and how to place a graphic within the body of a word-processing document. The development of the technological skills came during the breakout session, where they were incorporated naturally into the talk of developing math and science concepts. The focus on classroom application and the provision of technological support were the major differences between our staff development program and the typical technology inservice.

At the end of the half-day program, we had a debriefing session and gave the teachers an evaluation. I anxiously awaited criticism from my peers for daring to make a difference. To my surprise, there wasn't a single naysayer in the bunch, and I was encouraged by the conversations about our staff development program that continued throughout the year.

Examples of Teacher Leadership

I enjoy reading books about technology. In fact, I'm known in my building as a kind of "nut case" because I always read the computer and software manuals. Nothing, however, compares with the thrill I get watching teachers overcome obstacles in using technology with their students. I learn a lot from observing, talking with, and listening to teachers as they go about the business of using technology in their classrooms.

One first-grade teacher I know does a great job of cycling kids through the various computers in her room. The older Apple IIs are utilized just as often as the newer multimedia Macintosh and Windows 95 computers. Every time I visited the room last year, students would strike up a conversation about the software they were using or ask me about what I was planning to do to help fix some problem with their computers. Technology had obviously become an integral part of these students' lives.

I have a friend who is a second-grade teacher. He does some of the most creative and inspiring things with his students. I'm constantly amazed, because he is always pushing the limits of what I think kids can do. A few years back, he saw the HyperStudio (presentation software) stacks my students were creating. After he expressed interest in the program, I rustled up the resources to get him two copies. His students have been making their own programs ever since to express their understanding of a topic they've been exploring in class or to retell the story of a book they've read. His secret is to teach his students just enough about how the program works and then encourage them to go explore it on their own. Never are the students given an adult's preconceived idea as to what their limits are. There is one main expectation in that room regarding technology: students are expected to be self-motivated and to pass along to anyone asking for help the ideas and methods they have learned.

I have many other stories of how teachers have influenced my ideas about technology and teaching children. Not all of them are earthshaking, nor do all of the best ideas come from the techno-literate. I continue to learn from the teachers I come in contact with. What helps is to have an open mind and a sensitivity to even the most techno-phobic members of our staff.

Technology Is Changing Our Perceptions

In my lifetime, technology has created an explosion of information and new understandings about the universe we live in. Today it is becoming increasingly important to be able to quickly find and identify useful information to apply to real situations. With real-time video conferencing, e-mail, and the almost instantaneous retrieval of news, art, music, and other information from around the world, we are slowly having to rethink our perceptions about our world and our role in it.

Since technology isn't going to go away and it is changing how we look at ourselves and the world around us, I believe that it is important for schools to help students develop technological skills that will equip them for the future. Teachers are the ones who will have the responsibility to do that. Sooner or later some governmental body is going to dictate what technology use in a school means. Sometimes that works out okay, but often decisions are made not by the people who have an intimate working knowledge of how children learn but by policy makers who are far removed from the daily interactions of children in a learning environment. I'd much rather take a proactive stance in the integration of technology into my classroom than a reactive one.

Know the Technology Basics

If we accept the premise that technology is most effective when it is an integral part of the classroom instruction rather than an add-on to the instructional program, then teachers need to have a working knowledge of what is possible and what is available. (See "Basic Technology Terms," The Blue Pages, pages 54b–57b.) I strongly believe that teachers should also have a voice in deciding what comes into the classroom. What teachers want to do with technology should strongly determine the configuration of the equipment they acquire. I recommend doing some detective work to see what your school district's plans are. Contact the people involved in the process. Building-level and district-level technology leaders most often are very happy to talk to teachers about their vision for technology in the school and what decisions have been made regarding acquisition of equipment, development of a local area network, and software.

Global Access

It is the expressed goal of national and state initiatives to turn the stand-alone classroom computer into a global learning machine. Money is already trickling into the local school districts to help with the tremendous costs involved with transforming schools. More and more public schools are coming online and able to interact with others in the communication of ideas. Opening the door to the world also opens the potential for helping students construct an understanding of the world in a more dynamic way than previously possible.

The Internet

At first glance the Internet, with its multitude of Web pages, can seem daunting. It can be overwhelming to have all that choice at your fingertips. Understanding the way resources are located can be helpful. Every location is identified by a URL (uniform resource locator). URLs appear alien at first, with their strange abbreviations separated by slashes and periods. A URL is really only a pathway identifying the file you'd like to view that resides on a specific computer in a specific location of the world. I tell my students to think of the URL as an address much like their own home address. That seems to help them visualize what is taking place when they type in a location. I often overhear a student tell another not to forget the ".com" or ".org" affix, much like we would add "St." or "Blvd." to a conventional mailing address.

To tame the millions of available sites possible, there are professional newsletters, books, Web locations, and software products available to help bring some organization and peace of mind to the user. Top on my list of places that cater to children, parents, and teachers is Yahooligans, developed by the same people who run Yahoo. Yahooligans screens all Web sites for appropriate content and follows each site's hot links to make sure young users won't accidentally get into questionable content. Yahooligans is a full-featured site providing lots of opportunities for young learners to direct their own quest for information. See "Use of Technology and the Internet" and "Favorite Web Sites" in The Blue Pages, pages 52b–54b, for more on how to help make sense of the Internet's resources.

The Computer System

For classroom use, I recommend a computer system that includes a multimedia computer and a 15" or larger monitor. My personal preference is for a 17" monitor, because I find it easier to demonstrate software or computer use to a class gathered around the larger screen. In general, I suggest purchasing technology that was considered "new" six months ago. This provides for a more economical purchase and still allows for a suitable length of time that the system will be useful in the classroom. In general, I don't need the fastest processor or the latest equipment, because educational software doesn't require it and there are limits to how much and how fast information from the Internet can be pulled through the network wiring in our school buildings.

Portable Keyboards

If word processing is a major goal for your classroom or school, think about purchasing portable word-processing keyboards as an alternative to a full computer system. I am against using an expensive computer system primarily for word processing, which I see as overkill. Why purchase the power of a machine capable of creating and manipulating text, images, and sound only to do the relatively low-technical functions of a good typewriter?

For approximately three hundred dollars or less, a battery-operated keyboard can be purchased for use anywhere in the school or on field trips. These portable keyboards are a lower-cost alternative to expensive laptops. Interestingly enough, these lower-cost machines keep evolving and adding more and more features, such as a thesaurus and e-mail. Each of these portable keyboards may be connected to the classroom computer or a printer for printing text out. Because these are keyboarding input devices, text that is downloaded to the classroom computer goes right into the word processing program.

Printing Resources

Every student, and every teacher, likes to see their finished product printed out. Before networks were possible, a printer remained dedicated to the computer it was physically connected to. Today, it is possible for a printer to service multiple computers and multiple rooms over the network.

Most of us like the luxury of having our own printer in the classroom. Consider, however, sharing a printer with another classroom or two on the same network. Teachers will have reasonable access to printing capabilities while conserving money for other technology purchases, such as multiple digital cameras (cameras that allow you to directly import photos into the computer) or a minicomputer lab.

Software

Purchasing software can be a rather intimidating process. There are so many titles available, promising much and costing a lot. Your personal teaching philosophy as well as what you want to accomplish with the software should direct your purchases.

My personal preference is for programs that offer flexibility in their use with students. Drill and practice software provides the least flexibility in use because it was designed to do a specific job. Reference software allows for more flexibility. I can use it to teach many different types of lessons. I'm probably one of the few third-grade teachers who still uses William Steig's *Abel's Island* in my reading program. The main character, a mouse named Abel, describes the island he ends up on as being so many "mousetails" long and wide. After a lively debate about how big a mousetail is, some students use the reference software programs to research an answer to that question. Interesting math and science lessons evolve from that research and often spark further questions, such as how the dimensions of the island might change if Abel was a different species of mouse. So students head back to the reference programs to do more research on the different variables that might affect our understanding of Abel's surroundings.

By far my favorite software is open-ended in scope, allowing students to create records of their educational understandings. These programs can be simple programs that integrate word processing with some form of graphics capability. The more extensive presentation or authoring programs allow students the most flexibility by allowing them to control the look and feel of their work and how the information they've learned is presented to others.

Choosing Software

Our students' time for learning is precious, and no school system has unlimited financial resources. It is important that teachers choose software wisely. Over the years, I've developed a simple four-point strategy.

1. Identify needs
2. Gather information
3. Preview and pilot
4. Evaluate

I listen when teachers talk to me about their wish list for technology. Often they are looking for a better way to help their students understand a concept or develop a skill. I think about the adopted curriculum in our district and any changes coming from the state or national levels. These leads help me identify possible areas in which we could use some quality software, and I begin to develop a list.

Once I've identified the possible needs, I begin to gather information on possible software solutions. I look for software reviews in professional journals, such as *Science and Children* (The National Science Teachers Association) or *Teaching Children Mathematics* (National Council of Teachers of Mathematics) or in a trade magazine. Teachers who have gone to conferences are often willing to talk about software they've seen. I find it very helpful to get the advice of others who have used a piece of software, and I visit a number of Web sites dedicated to reviewing software. From these multiple sources I begin to develop a list of software that I would like us to have the opportunity to look at more closely.

Narrowing my list down to the best possible titles, I go about acquiring copies to examine. Software publishers are usually very willing to facilitate previewing their offerings. I find it most helpful to call their sales representatives. Be careful to follow their policies carefully, though, and communicate clearly that you are gathering information at this point, not making a commitment to purchase. I've found that it saves a lot of headaches later if both parties understand expectations.

Besides going directly to publishers, I've found visiting a teaching colleague, a library, or teachers college that has the software equally helpful. In these cases, I can get feedback from other people who have already used the software.

The best scenario involves using the software with the intended end users, our students. Watching student performance and evaluating outcomes gives me the most information about the suitability of the software in filling the identified need.

I prefer some type of formal evaluation when possible. That way, I can go over specific points later and make comparisons between similar pieces of software. You can download software evaluation protocols from a number of Internet sites and eventually develop your own by adapting the best from several models.

Once I've gotten to this stage, it is relatively easy to present a request to purchase software or write a minigrant requesting funding. The data yielded by the evaluation, in addition to positive student response, can make a strong case for the need for such a program.

Practical Possibilities for the Classroom: E-Mail and Presentation Software

Not every elementary teacher is as fortunate as I am to have several networked computers in the classroom. It isn't realistic to envision every student with an individual computer at his or her own desk any time in the near future. Obviously some strategy has to be utilized to maximize the potential of one or two computers in the classroom.

I mentioned before that I'm against the exclusive use of an expensive multimedia computer for word processing. Instead, I recommend that writing and word processing skills be developed in your students through the use of e-mail and presentation/authoring software. Both types of activities require students to learn to clearly communicate their ideas through the writing process.

The first year I was able to get a phone line installed in close proximity to my room, I purchased on my own an account to access the Internet through an Internet service provider. I ran a long extension phone line through my door to connect to an external modem. That brought e-mail capabilities into my classroom. Next I asked my students' parents whether they had e-mail capabilities, what knowledge or skills they'd acquired through their jobs or hobbies, and if they'd volunteer to answer student questions about their various areas of expertise. I developed a list of potential "experts" for my students to use to find answers to questions that arose during the learning process. Over the course of the year, the resource list was consulted whenever a question arose that could best be answered by one of our "specialists."

Some of the contacts developed an important relationship with the classroom community. The expert who perhaps had the most impact on my students was a child psychologist. His responses to student questions were always eagerly awaited, whether the questions were about "getting along" or one of the good doctor's hobbies.

After a while, our new e-mail friend began to pose questions to the class and asked them to provide him with answers. "How to handle a bully at recess" was the question that most stimulated conversations in the classroom. More than half a dozen responses were generated by individual students or student groups and sent to our resident expert. It wasn't so much the personal reply to each e-mail response but the way the children were made to feel that they had something of value to contribute that made an impact on my students.

I mentioned earlier that I use presentation/authoring software in my classroom. I like to have students present their understandings of the things they've learned and this kind of software allows students to be creative and work in small groups. I find the students who work on these multimedia projects are much more animated about their findings than if I'd assigned a traditional "research" paper, and they show evidence of incorporating higher-level thinking skills in their work. They learn the fine points of writing mechanics just as well as if I used a traditional teaching approach, and they tend to be less reluctant to do a report on paper.

Technology Does Not Replace the Teacher

Technology is not going to replace good teaching and teachers in general. It is only going to be able to do what the human mind has programmed it to do. There are skill-building programs that change the content based upon the student's performance. These programs are designed to move on to increasingly difficult content upon successful completion or to review/remediate material an individual learner is having difficulty with. These kinds of programs are frequently marketed as a whole-school or whole-district solution for raising test scores and are often very expensive. But even the best of these programs can not bring to bear the intuition, interaction, and empathy a teacher provides and that can make a significant difference in a child's life.

Technology isn't about to replace the printed text, despite visions of a "paperless society." I still prefer to print out my e-mail to read again later or snuggle up with a good book in my hand, and I continue to gain a great deal of insight into the creative mind of my students by examining the way they complete writing projects using "old fashioned" pencil and paper.

However, I have seen numerous examples over the years of the use of technology benefiting young writers. Word-processing programs have the ability to free a writer from the repetitive drudgery of handwritten drafts, enabling them to get down to the business of communicating ideas. The word-processing programs on the market now even provide immediate feedback to the writer about the mechanics of spelling and grammar. For the relatively small price of these programs, the classroom gains a tireless tutor, making students aware of improvements they can make to their writing.

Hypertext Links

After all these years, I have yet to master the art of scrolling down a screen full of text and not lose my place while reading. Because of this I find it harder to scan text on a monitor screen than to read printed text for the information I want. Others must have similar feelings about this, because today's research-oriented software programs, like the electronic encyclopedias and topical multimedia databases, are often indexed or provide hypertext links embedded in the text.

Hypertext links are areas of text that, if "clicked on" with the mouse, allow the reader to jump ahead to other information. The links are identified by different-color type. The reader can get to material of interest quickly, examine information related to the topic of inquiry, visit a Web site that pertains to the information, or get an explanation of a term or idea.

Hypertext links are similar to the "See also" statements in bound books. I was one of those children who loved cross-references in encyclopedias. I could browse happily for hours and often ended up with a pile of volumes laying around me. It was fun to read and learn that way, but terribly inefficient in completing a task-oriented project like a report. Now with hypertext links, that same inquisitiveness can be encouraged in children a little more efficiently.

Software Simulations

Software simulations, especially in math, science, and social studies, are becoming increasingly sophisticated. Simulations provide opportunities for children to develop understandings about a topic through role-play. Many of the topics, such as historical events, would be impossible or very difficult to reproduce in a school environment. Similarly, some of the science programs allow students to manipulate variables in a simulated experiment without costly equipment and sometimes difficult safety measures. Many quality simulations involve groups of students working together to accomplish a goal similar to what happens in the real world of work.

Software simulations provide students with valuable insights into the way the world works and how things are interconnected. These experiences augment the acquisition of knowledge in the content areas and can easily provide students with reasons to explore their understanding afterward through the writing process.

The Internet Is a Door to the World

Design features similar to the ones that make inquiry and report writing easier and more enjoyable in stand-alone software are also found in the latest versions of Web browsers (by Microsoft and NetScape). With Internet access, children's quest for knowledge can take on a global quality. (See page 53b for recommended Web sites.)

Repositories of cultural information, knowledge, and writing, such as the Library of Congress, are increasingly providing educational experiences for elementary-age learners. The congressional library in 1997 had a well-designed program to help students gain an understanding of how our nation was built upon the merging of a number of different cultures. My students became sleuths, examining original photographs, journal entries, and other pieces of information to determine what life was like in the past and how different groups of people were integrated into our society. Some of the more interesting writing for the year came out of their efforts to interpret photos we had looked at.

Webquests, a more formalized instructional model for integrating Internet Web experiences into the curriculum, was developed as a class at San Diego State University to show teachers how technology can be utilized to enhance student learning. Webquest combines research strategies, higher-level thinking skills, and the bounty of information found on the Internet to help develop student skills. The university's Web site is constructed to help interested parties get started developing their own Web experiences. Visitors to the site will not only find the how-tos of undertaking a Webquest but links to sample Webquests that the visitor may try out. (See page 54b.)

Technology Is Fallible

Technology is only as good as the people behind it. That includes the manufacturers of the hardware, the people who write the software, and the end users—us. Most of the time, everything works well together, but occasional problems are to be expected.

A Model for Understanding How Programs Work

I like to help children understand on a simplistic level how computer programs function by having them build a chain of dominoes. After the chain is built, I remove a section of it and ask them to predict what will happen when we knock over the first domino. Without hesitation they always tell me that the chain reaction of the falling dominoes will stop when it hits the gap. With this simple display, children begin to understand how things can go wrong with computers and software.

It is important to teach children how to properly handle software. A small damaged area of recorded media on a floppy disk program or a CD-ROM can end the useful life of a software program. The damage wipes out a part of the program's instructions and, like the domino chain, at some point the program stops functioning. While the bound encyclopedia volume with a missing or torn page still has a useful life, that damaged software program has gone to "electronic heaven." Because of this, changing a CD-ROM disk or a floppy at a computer station in my classroom is a privilege students acquire based upon their demonstration of responsible use.

Similarly, some electronic bit of information can get corrupted on the computer's hard drive or lost once it is loaded into the CPU. The effect is the same. The computer stops functioning, often just when you need it the most. Many times, fortunately for us, restarting the computer can often restore functionality.

Back Up Important Files

I tell our staff to be sure that they back up important data files. I frequently make multiple copies on floppies of curricular materials I design. Unfortunately, I often find myself pressed for time with my duties as a classroom teacher and my duties as a building and district technology leader. On occasion, I've failed to take my own advice when it comes to backing up my hard drive. That is usually when the worst happens. I recently suffered through hard drive crashes on both the Macintosh and Windows 95 machines I use. Gone for good is the electronic portfolio I was building to show my growth as a teacher, many of the curriculum items I'd created since the last backup, and many examples of my students' writing and research presentations.

With multimedia projects becoming increasingly large because of sound bites, digital pictures, and even motion pictures, it makes sense to spend a couple of hundred dollars on a removable media hard drive for teachers to share. Similar in concept to the floppy disk, these drives store much more information (100 megabytes to more than a gigabyte) at the speed of a hard drive. Student work or your own personal files can easily be backed up on the removable cartridges. These cartridges are relatively inexpensive and can be used to restore important work after cataclysmic events like a hard drive crash.

Reinstalling Troublesome Software

You are at the mercy of the software programmers. Well-designed word-processing and presentation software programs have most of the features you'll want. They are pretty good neighbors in your computer, too. Every once in a while, I run into some program that contains an element of poor programming that makes it a difficult resident on your machine. When this is the case, unpredictable error messages can pop up at inconvenient times. When this happens you might be able to save whatever you or your students are working on but often you'll lose everything done since the last time the work was saved. A reinstallation of the afflicted software will sometimes clear up the problem. If it reoccurs, you may want to contact the software publisher unless you have a local computer guru that likes the challenge of detective work (which can often take hours) to find the problem.

Record Troublesome Behavior

I frequently share with teachers one of the best pieces of advice I was ever given with respect to technology: keep a log of inexplicable events that disrupt normal use. Patterns of misbehavior by the computer often point the way to a solution. I keep a record on paper of recurrent problems showing what occurred, when it happened, what I did when it happened, and any error messages that appeared on the screen.

This strategy is especially helpful for intermittent problems. As one of the teacher leaders in our district, I got a Windows machine about six months before the rest of them were installed. Being a Macintosh lover who could argue very passionately about why Macs were the way to go, I'd never seen such a problematic computer in my whole life.

No one, not even the repair technician from the computer company, would believe me because the problems couldn't always be duplicated. I kept being told that I didn't know what I was talking about.

I think it was my passion for Macs that got in the way of people believing that something was really wrong with my machine. I took the advice of keeping a log seriously. Over a period of two weeks the log began to show a pattern that pointed to a problem with the random access memory (RAM) of the machine. A simple repair restored the computer to life, and we've been happily together ever since.

A FINAL THOUGHT

Living with technology isn't always easy. Over the years, I've learned to question how I use it with children and made changes in the way I use it in my classroom. I've had to struggle with my beliefs about how children learn and the role technology can play versus the reality of a world that still wants to rank children based upon how well they can recall information out of context on a test. I continue to struggle with the time constraints of school and the fact that there is not enough equipment to go around. But it is my students who keep me going. They are the ones who approach technology with a different viewpoint that stimulates the learner in me. As they did many years ago with the first Apple computer, the students I come in contact with continue to instill in me a wonderment and belief that technology has potential in helping kids learn.—*Lee Sattelmeyer*

FINAL REFLECTIONS

At its best, technology can be a great tool for learning and obtaining information. In partnership with teacher-librarians, we can teach our students how to access, evaluate, and use information wisely and well. However, technology will not revolutionize education. Effective teachers, thoughtful students, and an involved citizenry are needed for that. It is not technology that teaches our students how to read and write, reason, think creatively and logically, collaborate, or synthesize information. As knowledgeable professionals, that remains our job. I close with a favorite quote from author E. L. Konigsburg (1995):

> The best possible tool of my line of work is the word processor that lies not in the middle of my desk but in the left side of my brain, for it is the brain and not the IBM PC that processes words into language.

CONTINUING THE CONVERSATION

• *Examine your school's library program and your relationship with the librarian*. Take a leadership role in getting conversations going about establishing a flexible library program in your school. Check out the resources in The Blue Pages for support and ideas. Reflect upon what you can do to make the library program a collaborative part of curriculum inquiry.

• *Take stock of your technology literacy and how you are utilizing technology*. What are you doing to increase your skills? Are you using technology in your classroom wisely? Is the time students are spending involved with technology worth their time? Would they sometimes be better served reading or engaged in another activity?

• *Read a good book on the use of technology in the classroom*. You may want to start with books that deal with the basics. Once you have become more comfortable with terminology and tried out some of the suggested activities found in those types of books, include other books that provide more philosophy on learning, teaching, and the integration of technology into the curriculum. Establishing an understanding and a personal belief in the benefits of technology will help sustain your personal efforts to reform instruction in your classroom. (See recommended resources, pages 52b–53b.)

• *Identify the technology leaders within your building*. Teaching can be isolating and teachers are often reluctant to talk about things they are unsure of, such as using technology in their classrooms. Talk to the teachers you perceive as being comfortable with technology. They are usually very interested in sharing how their students are using technology and are often interested in working together with others in the development of curriculum using technology. Ask if you could observe what is being done in their classrooms and if they have any advice for you on promoting the use of technology in your room. Ask if you could "borrow" some of their students to help you develop the same skills in your students.

• *Meet regularly with a group of teachers to support the use of technology in instruction*. The group can compile personal experiences, share lessons, and suggest books, articles, and Web sites that promote the use of technology. Don't just leave the activities on a cognitive level, but plan time for actual hands-on use of technology. Working through the same projects/experiences that you will be asking your students to do will make you more comfortable with the process.

• *Attend a workshop or college class on using technology*. Be an active participant—don't just sit there taking notes. Ask the difficult questions, such as, How can what you are learning translate into instructional practices and learning outcomes for your class? and How does the inclusion of technology improve conventional practice?

CHAPTER 14

Developing Collaborative Communities

Creation, Organization, and Sustenance

Collaboration in the classroom: Regie Routman and second-grade teacher Neal Robinson debriefing and planning after a demonstrtation lesson

> They get bullied, they get scapegoated, they get targeted for criticism by every right-wing demagogue in the United States. But I don't know any group of professionals who come to their work with so much genuine love and basic decency and generosity of spirit as school teachers.
>
> —*Jonathon Kozol (Flanagan 1998)*

I am doing a chat session after a keynote talk at a state reading conference. A teacher comments, "I notice that you said 'we' throughout your talk. In my school, everything is 'I.' Teachers don't work together." I tell her that I hadn't realized I was doing that, but that I'm not surprised. Collaboration is part of my living, breathing teaching life. Even though I pen the words for this book, the text is the work of many colleagues. I couldn't know what I know by myself. Without rich, professional conversations, we remain isolated and limited in our practices and our effectiveness.

Our profession is a demanding one. It is only through collaboration and collegiality that we grow and thrive. Teacher collegiality directly impacts both student achievement and the tone and morale of our classrooms and our schools. When collegiality exists in a school, adults:

1. Talk with one another about practice.
2. Observe one another engaged in practice.
3. Work on curriculum together.
4. Teach one another what they know.

As Roland S. Barth states, "The quality of adult relationships within a school has more to do with the quality and character of the school and with the accomplishments of students than any other factor" (Barth 1991, 163).

520

Before we can establish community in our classrooms, before our classrooms can be spaces in which students feel valued, respected, challenged, and engaged in meaningful work, we need to be part of such a community ourselves. Collaboration, collegiality, and community are best taught to our students through our own example. When we teachers are part of a strong professional community, student achievement and engagement are higher. Effective teaching goes hand in hand with teacher collegiality.

This chapter begins with a discussion of professional development—including in-school language arts support groups and my job as a language arts coach—and moves to an examination of community, including ways of establishing and maintaining classrooms and schools that are inviting, well-organized, and collaborative, and where students, teachers, and parents feel welcome and valued. Where community coexists with meaningful tasks, problems related to student behavior are few.

MAKING PROFESSIONAL DEVELOPMENT A PRIORITY

In spite of the fact that research has shown again and again that teachers are the single most important factor in student achievement, we do not put our money into making educators as professional and knowledgeable as possible.

I am reminded of how little value we place on the professional development of teachers when I read about the great sums of money being spent on other resources. Two examples. When a wealthy foundation generously awarded $110 million in grants to public schools in Idaho in 1998, $28 million was immediately earmarked for computer hardware and software, despite the fact that little documentation supports the fact that money poured into technology raises achievement ("Foundation Pledges $110 Million for Public Schools in Idaho." *The New York Times Education*, August 19, 1998, A26).

The America Reads Challenge Act of 1997 proposed an astounding $2.75 billion, with the majority of those funds allocated for one million volunteers to tutor students in reading. Yet there is very little research documenting the effectiveness of one-to-one tutoring by adult volunteers (Wasik 1998, 266; 282).

Why does the public continue to believe that resources and experts outside of the profession can teach our students? And why are we not more outspoken in this regard?

Taking Charge of Our Own Professional Development

I believe the most effective professional development is teachers sharing, talking, and working together, face to face, on a regular basis. The best a school district can do is to provide time and funds for such collaboration and sharing. We teachers are desperate for time to talk with each other about our teaching beliefs and practices as well as our concerns and questions. Every time we have had release time in our district where teachers meet to talk and plan, the overwhelming benefit has not been the final plan or product created, but the conversations that take place at and across grade levels. Curriculum tasks are easier to accomplish when they are shared.

Meaningful change cannot take place without effective, informed teachers. In fact, where school reform is most successful, the staff acts "as a team of professionals working together toward improvement of the entire school" (Shields and Knapp 1997, 292). Ongoing and long-term professional development will always be a necessity, and we teachers need to lead the way.

We can:

- Plan our own professional development and see ourselves as experts.
- Invite other colleagues to openly dialogue on a regular basis.
- Share information, resources, and ideas.
- Lobby for release time to collaborate with our colleagues.
- Attend noteworthy professional conferences and share what we learn.
- Expand our network to include mentors, school/community/university partnerships.
- Read professionally.
- Stay abreast of important research.
- Take responsibility for being a learner. (See *Invitations* and *Literacy at the Crossroads*, pages 171–185, for more suggestions.)

We can be mentors to our students only if we are fully literate—readers, writers, and thinkers in the fullest sense. And we alone are responsible for getting ourselves to that state. As Neal Robinson commented at the end of his second year of teaching: "I realized the teachers around me that I admired and that were innovative were always reading professionally. I've waited for people to hand me stuff. I know I have to take the initiative and read on my own. I can't believe I've been so passive so long, but I was so overwhelmed."

Concerns About Staff Development

If we are not part of a professional community, our effectiveness as teachers is limited. An educator from out of state wrote the following in a letter to me: "Staff development has not been a priority. Teachers have been expected to write their own curriculum and conduct their own training. Things are very splintered throughout the district. . . ."

I immediately identify with the concerns of this writer. Her note could have been written by any number of teachers in districts across the country. Unfortunately, little or no professional development in reading and writing is the norm rather than the exception. Often a district mandates a practice, yet teachers are given little information and resources on how to implement it. Everything is expected to simply fall into place.

Even when staff development exists, it can be a disappointment. We all have upsetting stories of imposed "training" sessions that turn out to be irrelevant and a waste of our time. We have also learned that even good staff development is no guarantee that anything will change. In general, we move too fast, neglect to make our purposes clear, and fail to involve the whole community in the change process. Additionally, we overrely on "experts" from out of town while failing to utilize and pool our own talents and resources.

Lack of funding also impacts staff development. Most teachers have to pay their own way to conferences; sometimes they must even pay for substitutes to fill in for them back in the classroom. In one district, teachers told me they had to pay for subs even if they didn't need one (because of "fairness"), a union issue.

The best professional development is ongoing and teacher driven, builds on teachers' strengths, and meets the needs of both educators and students. Most often, it seeks to include teachers across grade levels, as well as the school principal. Drawing on the latest and most relevant research, educators are helped to explore and articulate their own philosophies and practices.

The best professional development also shows respect for teachers, in both large ways and small. When I am invited to do a workshop in an organized, pleasing space in which participants are served coffee in real cups and the food looks and tastes wonderful, the message is that teachers are appreciated. Conversely, when teachers have to buy their own coffee and the bare minimum is provided, the message is quite different. I have nothing against serving teachers pizza on paper plates when they are giving their time to after-school professional development or curriculum writing. But when central office administrators are served catered food on real china for their meetings, teachers feel slighted. We are all professionals and should be treated equally. Like our students, we learn best when we feel valued.

One way some schools begin ongoing staff development is to create literacy teams to plan professional opportunities for staff. In Alief, Texas, committees of teachers, specialist teachers, and administrators have been formed in various elementary buildings. These literacy teams get input from the entire staff on the creation of schoolwide plans that focus on improving instruction and implementing instructional strategies. Team members provide weekly (mostly after-school) staff development through such educational vehicles as viewing and discussing videos, developing book study groups, discussing current professional journal articles, offering university-level literacy courses within the district, modeling literacy lessons in classrooms, and coordinating visits with outside consultants, as well as with colleagues, to work with teachers. The literacy team's focus has also extended to families, with parent literacy nights helping family members work more effectively with their children at home.

Charee Cantrell, a teacher who is a literacy specialist at Alexander Elementary, commented on the program:

> The benefits of developing a school literacy team were numerous. We saw an increase in the quality of instructional decisions made by our staff. There was a significant increase in our primary reading scores, and our state-mandated test scores were also impressive. Timely diagnostic interventions increased for struggling students. The efforts of our literacy team also contributed to teachers being viewed in a much more professional light by parents, administrators, and colleagues. Perhaps the strongest indicator of our success became evident when teachers stopped blaming and complaining about previous instruction, thus emphasizing a deficit model, and started celebrating and praising students' strengths upon which they could build.

Two other examples of teachers taking charge of their professional development follow. The first describes the importance of schoolwide language arts support groups; the second deals with the role of the language arts coach. Both of these contexts have been a major part of my job.

Language Arts Support Groups

We have been meeting weekly for over a decade (*Invitations*; *Literacy at the Cross-roads*). Our support groups are basically safe arenas to converse about our teaching, reflect on what we are doing and thinking, to problem solve together, and to set new directions for teaching and learning. We support each other to strive for excellence. We dialogue, listen to each other, and often learn that our situations and struggles are similar. We read and discuss related research. We converse about such issues as how to teach spelling, how to move to student-led conferences and portfolios, and how to communicate more effectively with parents. As one visiting principal noted, "I came for answers and I came away with interesting conversations."

It is difficult to make time and space for serious conversation. Many of us feel overwhelmed, exhausted, and strained from dealing with too few resources and too many demands on our time. Because days reserved exclusively for staff development are few, our voluntary, before-school meetings (8:30 A.M.–9:00 A.M.) have been critical to our continuing growth as effective teachers. Not only are teachers—and administrators, who usually attend—well informed, they are connected to each other, because they are given the opportunity to share ideas and information in a safe, friendly, predictable setting each week. In many cases, it has taken years to build solid trust and respect for each other, but these caring and sharing communities have been our best and most efficient form of professional development.

Recently I received a letter from a frustrated teacher who found the courage to begin a group in her school. She wrote that the following passage from Maya Angelou's *Wouldn't Take Nothing for My Journey Now* had inspired her:

> I looked up the road I was going and back the way I come,
> and since I wasn't satisfied, I decided to step
> off the road and cut me a new path.

Then she wrote me the following:

> I knew it was time to "cut me a new path." Last Monday I began inviting the teachers in my building to my room on Thursday afternoons for a get-together. I asked them to spread the word and come with a story of something that just wasn't working well in their rooms. The staff seemed really eager to do something like this.
>
> We had our first meeting. One colleague was so grateful to have a forum where she felt "safe" that she cried. And the next morning in my mailbox at school there was a note: "Thank you for bringing us together. This just might be the only way I get through this year!" We had shared some behavior plans we had in place in our rooms, talked about how to deal with parents, and talked some of how to handle the spelling issue. We agreed that we would meet for forty-five minutes each Thursday. This week we're going to come with some ideas on spelling and how we might do a better job of dealing with spelling in our classrooms. I was relieved because that's where I need some help right now!

Cut your own path—start your own professional group. In *Invitations*, I described procedures for beginning and maintaining a support group, and in *Literacy at the Cross-roads*, I wrote about the change process and urged teachers to become political and step outside of their classrooms.

Setting the Year's Agenda

During our first meeting of the school year, we share noteworthy professional books that we have read over the summer and brainstorm areas of focus for the year. We never run out of topics. In fact, the longer we meet, the more in depth each focus becomes. Some topics have included reading professional articles and books, staying informed on the politics of literacy, sharing ideas and resources, studying an area of the curriculum, and relationship building. (See Figure 14-1 for one year's agenda.)

We also brainstorm ways to maintain staff development/support in the face of insufficient funding:

- Utilize common planning times.
- Take part in weekly support group.
- Circulate journal articles we discuss to everyone in the building.
- Videotape lessons and share/discuss them.
- Observe a colleague teaching.

Figure 14–1   An agenda from a language arts support group

September 20, 1996

Dear colleagues,
Many staff members attended our language arts support group last week where we discussed possible topics for this school year. The following topics were suggested for our agenda:

- ***Parent education***
  - Create a resource(s) for parents that explains steps for reading, writing, and spelling. First, research what's out there. Examine existing resources such as *Parents as Partners* (First Steps handbook) and other books/articles written for parents.
  - Set up a professional library for parents.
  - Discuss ways for positive parent involvement.
- ***Sharing from recent professional workshops/experiences***
  - multiage
  - authentic assessment
  - phonics (workshop by OH Dept. of Ed., word study video)
  - visit to Nancie Atwell's school
- ***Reading and discussing a professional book***
- ***Communicating spelling and phonics to parents***
- ***Understanding the change from core to anchor books***
- ***Teaching writing/writing workshop***
  - Decide what genres will be taught at each grade level.
- ***What works and what doesn't***

Regie Routman
Regie Routman

With respect to the last item, we have several ways of freeing up teachers:

- A kindergarten teacher agrees to take a fourth-grade class (which will be trained to help the younger children with journal writing).
- A floating sub, administrator, or student teacher covers the class.
- We combine two classes.
- Teachers observe during a planning time.

"I Thought I Was the Only One."

A first-year teacher approaches me after a support group in which I spoke about and modeled guided silent reading. "I got so much out of that meeting," she told me. "It was great to hear another teacher say he has difficulty choosing the 'right' book for guided reading. I thought I was the only one."

The opportunity to share our frustrations and concerns, as well as new ideas and successes, builds community by humanizing us. So many of us still work in isolation, closely guarding our failures and successes. Hearing about the struggles of others, especially teachers we think have it all together, makes us realize that everyone is a learner.

One morning when we were discussing how to get writing workshop going, Susannah expresses her frustration with writing workshop as I had modeled it. In fact she abandoned the writing workshop model that I had presented to her one month after working with me. Later she commented, "You can't run a marathon before you can walk. Last year, I couldn't do writing workshop four to five times a week. I can do it three times a week, but only if I assign the topic. I'm not comfortable starting with choice. I've made it manageable by taking 'baby steps.'"

I am forced, hearing these comments, to take a look at my assumptions about choice and daily writing. If the teacher can't manage it, isn't it still better to have kids writing than not? Susannah's remarks humble me because she is a strong, dedicated teacher and a wonderful writer. I have failed to recognize her individual needs and comfort level. I admire her courage in saying, "This didn't work for me," which opened up the conversation about writing.

Our support groups provide a safe haven for "coming out" about our problems and for working them through together. It does, however, take years for some teachers to feel safe enough to risk sharing what's not working in their classrooms.

Taking a Political Stance

How can we show the public the power of excellent teaching of reading and writing? How can we make our voices heard?

We need to become proactive, not just reactive. We invite a state representative, Peter Lawson Jones, to visit one morning. In preparation, many teachers do a shared writing with their respective classes, which will be given to Mr. Jones to explain to him what he will be seeing in the reading/writing program in their classrooms. If questions about the teaching of reading came up at the state level, we want him to be able to advocate and say, "Wait a minute. I visited a local school and observed kids learning to read. Here's what I saw." When he visited, one of the things he commented on was that he saw a lot of phonics teaching taking place in various literacy contexts.

We teachers need to see that being political is a necessary part of our job as responsible professionals. (See "Teacher as Political Activist," page 6, and "Resources and Support for Political Action" in The Blue Pages for specific suggestions.)

Building Community and Collegiality

Melissa approaches me one day and says that she is depressed over the lack of community in her school: the staff are not working together as a team, teachers are competitive, and kids show a lack of respect for the school by habitually tearing down hallway displays. We agree to set aside our next language arts support group to discuss ways to build community. In the meeting, teachers speak about the lack of consideration students show one another. One teacher expresses concern at seeing a child yelling at a teacher. We decide to start the community-building process with ourselves. Louise suggests that we read a book and discuss it together as a staff. I recommend *The Dreamkeepers: Successful Teachers of African American Children,* by Gloria Ladson-Billings.

After the meeting, Sandy Endling, an aide who works in the library where we meet, stops me and says, "That was an interesting meeting. I couldn't help listening to the conversation. I wrote down the title of that book." I ask her if she would like to join our book discussion, and she is delighted. I then go door to door telling staff members about our planned discussion, and almost everyone in the building signs up, including the speech therapist, psychologist, and school secretary. Excitement is high. That same day, I place an order at the local bookstore for multiple copies of *The Dreamkeepers*. I ask the school secretary to post an announcement of our upcoming book talks.

For the first three weeks that we meet, everyone wants a total group discussion. Teachers resist small groups, afraid that they will miss something. Twenty-eight teachers attend each week! Remarkable! Several tell me that these support group conversations continue all day—in the hallways, on the playground, in the lunch room. While many of these conversations are uncomfortable and black teachers share more openly than white teachers, the ongoing talk does help improve the climate of the building. Feelings that have been festering about discipline, prejudice, and teaching are out in the open in a respectful, nonconfrontational manner. The end result is a more comfortable, trusting, collegial tone in the building. (See pages 189–190 for guidelines we established for book discussion.)

Some other ways our support group meetings have been used to build community have included:

- Sharing favorite adult literature
- Sharing favorite children's literature and how we use it in the classroom
- Writing schoolwide book reviews of favorite books and posting them in the hallways
- Starting our meeting with a breakfast to celebrate a birthday or special achievement

The Role of the Language Arts Coach

A teacher in another state calls me to chat about my role as a language arts coach. He is clearly frustrated with his job, which is similar to mine. "How do you deal with the people who don't change?" he asks. An interesting question. I tell him truthfully that I see my role as supporting teachers, not changing them. Teachers themselves are responsible for whatever changes do or do not take place.

Because so many teachers have written or asked about what my role as language arts coach involves and because such a position can be important for promoting professional development, I have chosen to write about my job with the hope that other educators and administrators will see its value and create similar support positions in their own districts. However, much of what I do could be done by teachers and administrators working collaboratively, as long as the school or district shows that they value such collaboration by providing time, resources, and support for it.

Although my job title is language arts resource teacher, I see myself primarily as a language arts coach. In this capacity, I try to help my colleagues think about what they are doing in their classrooms and to learn from their—and our—experiences. I work side by side with teachers, demonstrating and hand holding, coaching and cheerleading, observing and gently critiquing, planning and problem solving, nudging them forward, encouraging risk taking, and supporting all their efforts. As teachers, we know the benefit of using these behaviors in our work with students. It is crucial that we are also supported this way ourselves.

In the fall of 1987, when our district moved from basals and workbooks to a literature and writing process approach, I was asked to assist teachers in the transition process. Through June 1998 I taught language arts across the curriculum one morning a week in each of our five K–4 buildings, occasionally also working in our 5–6 building and high school. In the afternoons I was based at Mercer School, where I worked for four years as a Reading Recovery teacher. Most other years, I worked as a reading specialist for slower-achieving readers in second-grade classrooms (see page 147). Presently, my work as a coach has expanded to other schools and districts around the country.

Supporting Teachers

The first thing I ask teachers each year is, "How can I support you?" My offer is meant to be an invitation to all teachers. Then, for those I do work with, I try to support their goals, not create goals for them, unless they request it. I let teachers know right away that I am not an evaluator. I am a peer working with peers. I tell them, "My job is to support you. I will keep what goes on in your classroom between us. However, I will brag about you to your principal when I see something wonderful."

The stance I take (or try to take) is nonthreatening. I assure teachers that I don't have all the answers, that we'll be learning together as we go along, working hand in hand. I build on teachers' strengths and focus on what they're doing well. This is a deliberate, necessary stance. Otherwise, I couldn't work with my colleagues. They must feel that I trust and respect them before they can trust and respect me. We cannot work together successfully until this trust takes hold.

I work with new teachers, established teachers who request to work with me, and teachers whose principals request and encourage our working together. Upon teachers' request, I conference with them, plan with them, observe their teaching, and provide feedback. I do demonstration teaching, provide relevant resources, and make suggestions to optimize classroom management, physical room setup, the classroom library, and independent work possibilities.

I no longer actively seek to work with teachers who are disinterested or negative. I learned the hard way that it is not a good use of my time or effort to work with a teacher who is resistant to change and growth. My husband, Frank, helped me make that choice by reminding me about eating pistachio nuts (which we both love). Either you can eat the nuts that open easily and set aside the ones that are really hard to open, or you can spend most of your time trying to crack open those few tough nuts. Or, put another way by Jan Turbill and Brian Cambourne: "Go with the goers."

Supporting Principals

Principals tell me that my job as a language arts coach has made their job as instructional leader far more effective. I guide their new teachers and continuing teachers, conduct individual reading assessments as requested, promote staff development opportunities, keep them informed about upcoming workshops, make recommendations of noteworthy professional books for the library, share relevant research, make specific professional recommendations for the building, share pertinent information from literature and conferences, and sometimes serve as a liaison with parents.

I meet regularly with principals in each K–4 building and keep them abreast of who I am working with, discuss what our goals are, and seek their input and recommendations. Sometimes, our meeting is a scheduled weekly time. More often than not, our meeting is arranged on the particular morning based on when we both have time available.

Several times a year, I also attend a district-level meeting with all the elementary principals and our executive director of elementary education. At that time, I informally share how I think we're doing in the teaching and assessing of reading and writing, where I think we need to be heading, and what staff development is necessary. I also provide information that may help administrators in their roles. For example, I have given principals some guidelines on what to look for in the reading/writing program when they are in classrooms (see Figure 14-2 on page 530). I have also made a presentation to our district Administrative Council on what's happening politically on the national level and what the local implications are.

In the past, I have made recommendations that led to the development of a standardized district wide writing prompt, a standardized district wide authentic reading assessment, and a weekly course for our reading tutors that sought to impact achievement by aligning their efforts with what was happening in the classroom. Putting these recommendations into practice involved my working closely with all teachers and principals. In the case of the reading assessment, for example, my role included teaching all K–4 teachers how to do retellings with students, since retellings were to be a component of the assessment (see pages 595–598).

Hosting Visitors

Some of the support that other teachers, administrators, and I provide extends to teachers outside of our immediate school community. We have hosted hundreds of visitors to our schools, including educators at all levels and students from local universities. To keep these visits from creating overwhelming demands on our time, we often designate one day a month for visitors. That way, when educators call to inquire, they can also sign up

Figure 14–2   What to look for in a reading-writing classroom

Some Guidelines for Teaching Reading and Writing

What to look for in the reading program

- reading aloud daily
- sustained time daily for free choice reading with appropriate book match
- students' reading records: titles, authors, genres
- shared reading: teacher reading while students follow along
- teacher conference notes on each student
- most time spent reading, not responding to reading
- small group guided reading: mostly silent guided reading, not round robin oral reading (includes small groups for explicit skills instruction, as needed), and literature discussion groups (heterogenous)
- partner reading
- evidence of teaching vocabulary
- well-stocked and organized classroom library and reading corner

What to look for in the writing program

- writing in various genres
- teacher modeling: various genres and how to respond to writing
- shared writing: teacher scribing while composing with students
- students' writing records: topics, genres, publishing information
- teacher conference notes on each student
- spelling lessons: connected to writing
- most writing topics chosen by students
- editing/proofreading expectations
- evidence of revision and editing
- teaching of conventions: not through exercises, but in process of writing
- a short piece going to final copy at least once a month: grades two and up

Regie Routman
Written for principals in my school district.

with the school secretary for a specific morning, and teachers know in advance when we may have guests. When visitors do arrive, we provide them with a packet that includes guidelines for visiting classrooms, a map of the building, and our philosophy of teaching.

We encourage visitors to arrive early so that they can join our language arts support group. Following our support group, I meet with visitors, explain what they are likely to see in our reading-writing classrooms, answer any questions they have, and orient them to the building. I encourage them to talk to the children and look at their work, as well as to look for the "why" of what's happening in the classroom and not overfocus on "activities" and bulletin boards. When possible, the principal and a classroom teacher also join this brief meeting.

I set aside time at the end of the morning to follow up with visitors. Often the principal and a teacher who may be free will join us. This debriefing time helps me to learn what impressions the visitors are carrying away, to clear up misconceptions, and to answer any remaining questions. Often, the main comments that visiting teachers make relate to feeling validated for what they are already doing.

Facilitating Language Arts Support Groups

This is the part of my job of which I am most proud. Since 1987, teachers have been meeting voluntarily on a weekly basis to collaborate, talk, share, stretch their thinking, and learn more about teaching. The day that I am in a K–4 building is the day that our support group meets, so I typically have five meetings a week. Either I or another teacher or pair of teachers serve as facilitator for the group. (See pages 524–527 for operating details of the language arts support group, including how we use this time to demonstrate strategies and take teachers through the process of guided reading and writing.)

In these meetings, I work hard at responding to teacher needs, listening to concerns, and nudging teachers forward where it seems appropriate. For example, I have suggested a focus on nonfiction guided reading (after our district's poor showing in science on Ohio's fourth-grade proficiency test) and a focus on writing (after teachers raised numerous questions about the management and processes of teaching writing).

I encourage teachers to stay up-to-date on the latest research, to institute "best practice," and to seek out and attend excellent conferences. I carry a folder with me of relevant articles and materials that I know teachers may ask for, such as information on spelling and phonics, or specifics on upcoming conferences. After a group of teachers attended the annual meeting of the National Conference of Teachers of English in November 1997, there was a surge of interest in becoming better informed and more political. To save teachers time, I talked them through a long article that summarized the research on phonemic awareness, informed them about informational Web sites, and shared current information from *Education Week*. Regularly, I also share relevant journal articles and new and excellent professional books. Often, a journal article will become the focus of discussion for a week. Occasionally, we all agree to purchase and read a professional book and discuss it together over a period of several weeks.

Providing Demonstrations

Before I start working with a teacher, we take some time to talk and plan together. Hardest for me, I try to listen well without interrupting. We schedule this time together, which may be ten minutes to thirty minutes, during a teacher's planning time or class time while the students are engaged in an independent activity. I have no set or hidden agenda before we begin. I sincerely want to know how I can best meet the needs of that teacher: What should be our first focus? How can I be most helpful? Are there any resources I can provide? What demonstrations would be instructive? During our planning time together, I explain the "why" as well as the "how" and "what" of what I'll be demonstrating. All teaching practice is based on the theory and beliefs we hold, whether we articulate them or not. I try to make my beliefs explicit and align them with my practice.

I have found that I usually need to work for at least several weeks with a teacher to accomplish any particular goal. Since my sessions with teachers, including demonstrations and follow-up time, typically last about one hour, I can usually work with three teachers, and sometimes four, each morning that I am in any particular building. Weekly, I also try to work with, or at least touch base with, all new teachers. (Principals deliberately schedule a planning time for new teachers on the morning I am in their building to facilitate our meeting together.) Because my time in each building is limited to one morning a week, sometimes several teachers at a grade level will be freed up to observe a demonstration.

After a teacher and I have talked and planned, I take the initiative. For example, depending on the teachers' needs, I might demonstrate how to get journal writing going or teach kids to write with voice or think aloud in reading nonfiction or establish successful literature conversations. My demonstrations include the management of the class as well as the curriculum focus. For example, I will need to model how to teach students to work collaboratively in small groups before we can effectively establish literature conversation groups in the classroom. Especially for new teachers, the modeling of successful management strategies is critical to effective teaching.

Following any demonstration, I try to make time for follow up—to answer the teacher's questions, to discuss what went well or not so well, to talk about concerns and/or expectations, to plan the next steps. (See the photo on the opening page of this chapter.) Because of time constraints, this part of our meeting is usually conducted "on the run"; that is, it is most often an informal conversation that takes place before I leave for my next scheduled classroom. However, I always try to give the teacher sufficient opportunity to respond to significant issues arising from our time together.

While most demonstrations involve the whole class, demonstrations are also done in small groups for guided reading lessons and with individual students for a reading or writing conference. After I demonstrate, I expect the teacher to be willing to try a similar lesson. (See Photo 14-1.) I might say something like, "I've been modeling journal writing [or questioning strategies or literature conversation groups] for you for several weeks now. How about if next week you try it? I'll coach you, cheer you on, and give you feedback." A third-grade teacher commented about this challenge: "This is the most significant thing I remember about our early relationship. Your invitation empowered me to try a new behavior."

When I coach on the next visit, I learn what the teacher has internalized and how effective my demonstrations have been, where the confusions are, and what I need to demonstrate again. When a lesson a teacher does goes badly, it is likely that I wasn't clear enough in setting expectations, or that what I thought was being modeled or understood was not. I try not to put the teacher on the defensive when I have questions about his lesson. I might say, "I notice you were doing such and such. Tell me about this."

A lot of what I do in classrooms is trial and error. My attitude is, "Let's try this." I am willing to experiment if I believe that what we are about to do may improve teaching and learning and the school lives of children. For example, while working with kindergarten classes, several teachers shared the children's frustration, as well as their own, with journal writing. I decided to see if kindergartners could write poetry and book reviews. To everyone's delight, the children did wonderfully well (see pages 364–382).

Despite the fact that I am viewed as an expert, I often feel that I do not know enough. I am always seeking to know more and to do a better job. I still fly by the seat of my pants at times, but as my experience grows, I trust myself more. I allow myself to fail, knowing that errors are a necessary part of all learning. Not surprisingly, I often learn the most from lessons that don't go well. Then I'm forced to scrutinize my practice and modify it. I never take the stance that the students failed. If my lesson failed, it's because I didn't set it up so that the kids could be successful, which is my job as a teacher.

Photo 14–1   Coaching first-grade teacher Chris Hayward in a guided reading group lesson

I demonstrate by example that I am a lifelong learner. Fellow teachers see my commitment to learning through my ongoing professional reading, my constant efforts to solicit their ideas and feedback, my frequent attendance at conferences, and my classroom practice. Many teachers know that I keep a notebook in which I record reflections and observations, raise questions, set goals, and jot down important learning experiences so that I can revisit them.

Modeling Collaboration

This is perhaps my most important role and greatest challenge. I strive to be a good and open-minded listener, to promote continuing dialogue, to respect each learner, and to carefully nurture growing trust. Collaboration must become a natural part of our teaching, and we need to constantly model it for our students.

Ongoing professional collaboration is our most effective staff development. Our job is such a difficult one; it is only by sharing that it becomes manageable. But more than manageable, we all become far more effective instructionally. I believe that most of us are at our best when we can bounce our thoughts, beliefs, and ideas off of others. As one teacher said to me, "My most effective and fulfilling curriculum lessons have been the ones where I've worked collaboratively."

Encouraging Sharing

My experience has been that teachers are reluctant to share with their colleagues and need to be pushed to do so. Many tell me that they feel that they are "showing off" or "bragging" when they discuss those elements of their practice that they feel have worked well. We teachers are a pretty insecure bunch. So, to facilitate communication in our language arts support group, I will say something like, "I was in Joyce's room last week, and she's doing some wonderful stuff with writing. I asked her to bring some student work and share it with you."

Sometimes teachers are discouraged from opening up to colleagues based on their past experiences. One teacher confided in me that he became discouraged after sharing his practice with colleagues who did not reciprocate. More than that, he was upset when colleagues failed to give him feedback on how his ideas were used or adapted. He is now very reluctant to share with other staff members, and there is nothing I can say to change his mind.

I think part of the problem here is that we teachers receive so little outside recognition for our ideas, we want to hold on tightly to what we've created. I used to feel the same way. Finally, after many years, I was able to be generous with my knowledge and experience, without the expectation of getting anything in return. I realized that new ideas are plentiful and that I could "afford" to give them away. Also, I saw part of my job as a professional as being willing to support other teachers in their growth.

High school teacher Holly Burgess believes that it may be just plain "busyness" that keeps teachers from following up with colleagues who have shared their practice. Now, she comes right out and asks teachers for their response to her ideas. She comments, "Sometimes my best student sample will be one elicited from another teacher's use of 'my idea.' And I let them know that."

I try to encourage teachers to be outspoken about their efforts in the larger educational arena and to let them know that their voice matters. I have encouraged and supported teachers to present at local and national conferences (with me and on their own) and to write for publication. Some have written journal articles; several have written professional books for teachers.

Fostering Professional Development

Although staff development is not part of my officially designated role, I see it as my most important job. I continually seek to organize and promote staff development opportunities in addition to our weekly language arts support groups. While most of our professional development is "in house," I have initiated bringing in workshop speakers such as Andrea Butler, Jerry Harste, Shelley Harwayne, Don Holdaway, Rob Tierney, and Sheila Valencia, to name a few. These speakers challenged our thinking and nudged us forward in our professional growth.

Over the years, as I read about new research or attended a conference session that demonstrated "best practice," I have brought that information back to our district, usually to our language arts support groups. That information helped us to get started with portfolios, student-led conferences, and other authentic assessment practices that, in turn, had ramifications for instructional practices in the district. In our support groups, we looked at what other districts were attempting, read professionally, and discussed the implications for our district of new practice and research.

For several years, as co-chair of our K–12 Language Arts Committee, I served as a resource for creating a new language arts course of study for our district (*Literacy at the Crossroads*, 54–62). Part of my role in this effort included fostering connections and conversations between high school and elementary teachers, some of which continue to this day. Most recently, discussing the latest national political happenings has spurred us to become more politically active. We have communicated more explicitly with parents in newsletters, published letters to the editor in local newspapers, and invited politicians and journalists into our schools.

Facilitating Summer Writing and Committee Process

Each year, I have worked with colleagues the week after school ends in June. This summer session has been our only extended time period in which teachers can work together across grade levels on the language arts. Over the years, we have developed author studies, selected the latest and best culturally diverse literature for guided reading, written guidelines for using the literature, created meaningful enterprises to accompany the books, and most recently, developed and refined both standardized and informal authentic assessment tools for reading and writing. (See Appendix I.)

I am always nervous and uneasy the first day we convene. Every group takes a while to gel, and I am never quite sure how the various personalities of the newly formed group will work together. Some grade-level groups have many members, while others seem underrepresented. Some teachers have many concerns, which they freely "vent," while others are silent. It is very important, in the course of facilitating a process such as this, to make sure that all participants are heard and that all voices are respected.

This past summer, we began by introducing ourselves by name, building, and grade level or position. Even in our small district, not everyone knows everybody else. Although these sessions have usually comprised teachers of grades one, two, and three, kindergarten and grade four teachers are now present to extend our work. Several Reading Recovery teachers join our first-grade teachers. Some teachers who have tutored students or worked with small groups of students also join us. In an effort to validate our work as teachers and to begin the process of building community, I read aloud from Patricia Polacco's *Thank You Mr. Falker* (New York: Philomel, 1998), an autobiographical story of a woman whose life was greatly impacted by a fifth-grade teacher who taught her how to read. I suggest we begin each day with a read aloud, and we do. Each day someone brings a new and wonderful book to share.

We begin our work by brainstorming an agenda of the general and specific topics and tasks we will cover as a group. This initial agenda for creating assessment tools in reading and writing is only a starting point to get the conversations going. We spend the first hour sharing together as a whole group: Are these the main tasks and areas of concern? What do we need to discuss across grade levels and with respect to specific grade levels? What's missing? How much time should we spend on each task? Our whole-group discussion focuses largely on our writing prompts and reading assessment, and as comments and topics are discussed, a teacher records them on a projected transparency. This serves to acknowledge everyone's contribution and to organize our work.

In midmorning, we break up into grade-level groups. Several teachers take me aside to express their concerns about a few teachers dominating the discussion. By the second day, however, these concerns vanish. We have learned that when we listen respectfully to each other, we teachers feel valued and validated, and we find that we have much to learn from each other. We learn to compromise, to understand different points of view, and to work through difficulties—all skills we seek to teach our students. By the end of the second day, we are rolling along. We have defined the tasks we need to accomplish both in grade-level groups and across grade levels, and teachers sign up for small groups dealing with issues of their choice.

I make sure we reconvene as a whole group one or more times each day. Whole-group share serves several purposes. It validates the work and thinking of each group; it encourages cross-grade-level sharing and continuity of thinking; it allows time for questions to be raised and clarified; and it helps set future directions. Mostly, I have found that whole-group discussion helps us to maintain the big picture for our district while recognizing the needs and expectations of our colleagues who teach the grade levels that come before and after ours.

For example, when our fourth-grade teachers share how they have changed the directions for administering our district's standardized writing prompt, other grade levels adopt or adapt some of these changes. There is a real spirit of collaboration. Daily, each group records their work on a computer disk, and when we can, we print out copies for all.

At the end of the week, I am amazed at what we have accomplished. On the morning of the last day, I look around and am overcome with enormous pride. Everyone is working so hard. The room is filled with meaningful activity. I see collaboration at its best. I am so privileged to be working with such dedicated and talented teachers.

My role has been to affirm, coax, celebrate, lead, guide, provide resources, give my opinion, and, ultimately, to trust the group decision even when it is has been different from my own. I feel proud of the work we have accomplished but even more pleased with the spirit engendered. As one teacher summed up, "Everyone's voice was heard; everyone was respected."

CREATING AN INVITING CLASSROOM

In classrooms in which students are thriving academically and socially, teachers are not just knowledgeable about the content they are teaching. They know their students well and value and respect their culture, language, and families. Teachers deliberately work with students to set up the classroom as a community—both physically and emotionally—so that students can have meaningful choices, engage in interesting and challenging enterprises, and have lots of opportunities for collaborative talk and small-group work.

Classrooms that are "genial," high-functioning environments share five characteristics that guide the learning that takes place there:

1. Freedom to choose
2. Open-ended exploration
3. Freedom from judgment

4. Honoring every student's experience
5. Belief in every student's genius; genius is defined as "giving birth to joy" (Armstrong 1998, 1)

The classroom environment should be a space that nurtures individual inquiry and creativity.

The characteristics listed above also contribute to the raising of good citizens. Susan Ohanian (1999) reminds us that "the basics" must encompass much more than reading, writing, and arithmetic.

> Helping students acquire skills that will enable them to be productive members of tomorrow's workforce should be only one very small mission of our schools. More importantly, we need to help students acquire the habits of mind to become good human beings: good parents, good friends, and good citizens of our democracy. (150–151)

We need to set up our classrooms so that students are able to achieve both academically and socially and also acquire the life skills necessary to become thoughtful, contributing members of our democratic society.

Promoting High Engagement and Achievement

Students are more likely to be engaged in their work when they understand its purpose, find it relevant, receive helpful feedback, and have some choice in structuring instructional tasks. Students are also most motivated when tasks are "moderately challenging" and lead them to "make new discoveries and to reorganize their understandings" (Turner and Paris 1995, 666). Additionally, successful collaboration and conversations with peers in a relaxed community setting contribute to motivation and achievement.

The role of choice is important here. Students invest more in a task when they are given some say in how they will perform it—when, for example, they are asked to choose one of several questions to respond to or decide on the format for a final report. Again, a student's freedom to choose does not mean that anything goes. For me, choice must be accompanied by parameters, high and specific expectations, and rigor.

> Choices are carefully designed within safe and clear structures so that kids can experience the delight of having a limited number of choices to make. . . . The important point is that students feel empowered when they make choices. (Armstrong 1998, 61)

High academic engagement in the classroom and high achievement go hand in hand. In language arts classrooms in which there is high engagement in literacy activities, more than 90 percent of the children remain productively involved more than 90 percent of the time, even when the teacher has to leave the room momentarily (Pressley et al. 1999, 23).

When classrooms are set up for inquiry, open-ended tasks, and challenging work, children become high achievers. "If their brains are asking questions relevant to the task, hypothesizing about outcomes, generating theories, collecting data, disagreeing about facts, searching out genuine answers, and recording them for public scrutiny, then learning is taking place at a high-challenge level" (Caine and Caine 1997, 163).

By contrast, when students are expected to be compliant in their completion of simple and "closed" teacher-directed tasks, achievement gains are often short term. Students may function as "good technicians" in the early grades but as tasks become increasingly complex and require more understanding, they experience great difficulty (Healy 1994, 50).

High academic engagement cannot exist until students understand, support, and are able to self-monitor the procedures, routines, and behaviors that have been negotiated between themselves and the teacher. As well, students need to feel safe and comfortable in the learning environment. While negative emotions impair learning, positive emotions enhance learning and achievement (Coles 1998, 75).

Establishing the Social and Emotional Climate

Kids can't learn much if they're not socially and emotionally comfortable in their classrooms. Although we cannot combat societal problems such as poverty, violence, and fractured families, we can, at least, do our best to make sure that when our students are in school, they are able to experience emotional and social stability as well as academic excellence. Knowing our students well, caring about them, and valuing them is as important as knowing the subject matter we teach.

First-grade teacher Elisabeth Tuttle says that teachers must fall in love with each and every one of their students before they can properly teach them. "The ones I had difficulty responding to at the beginning, I love the most now. They need me the most." She credits her cooperating teacher with showing her the way: "She just loved each one of her students. She loved being there. They loved being there. They greeted her with a hug in the morning and ended each day with a hug. There were hugs all day long."

Karen Sher, who teaches kindergarten, concurs: "You have to care about students before you can get students to care." Karen notes how important a strong sense of classroom community is to the learning process. Some years community is easy to attain; other years it is a challenge. But it needs to happen. At the very least, students must feel valued equally. Fourth-grade teacher Julie Beers notes that when she finds the good qualities in a "difficult" student, all the kids begin to see the good in him too.

Children also need to feel emotionally safe in their classrooms. When I walk into a fourth-grade classroom, returning to teach writing, a student quickly approaches me. The look on his face is pure fear. "She [the teacher] is going to get me," he said, pointing to his name written in block letters on the board. "I didn't do the homework you assigned. I forgot to ask my parents how they use writing at work and in their life."

"Don't worry about it," I tell him. "Ask them tonight. That will be fine." No learning would take place with this child until he could relax and feel safe. Until then, no risking or true problem solving would occur, only behaviors to avoid the teacher's wrath. While of course we need to hold students accountable for their work, such accountability must not include bullying and/or threats.

Fourth-grade teacher Jennie Nader expresses her view of the kind of environment conducive to student learning: "I think that when the teacher is open with students, shares personal issues, and models risk taking, this helps students to be risk takers. When they feel safe in the face of new challenges, children learn not to fear making mistakes. Fear of mistakes limits their learning; they must feel that they are in a safe environment that values them for being themselves."

One way to set an inviting, accepting, and caring tone in the classroom is to write a letter to students before school begins. In your letter, tell students about yourself, your interests, hobbies, what you wonder about. You might include photocopies of photos that show what you like to do, and of your family, pets, and friends. Encourage students to come to school with similar photos, or letters expressing their own interests, thoughts, and ideas. (See pages 60b–62b for ways to connect home and school literacy.)

Students' Emotions and Learning: Incorporating Brain Research

Studies have shown that the emotional states of students impact how well they learn. When students feel safe, well cared for, free to express themselves and make mistakes, and part of a classroom community, they are more likely to be academically successful (Elias et al. 1997).

Less than a decade ago, teachers who conducted classroom meetings to encourage students to talk to one another were sometimes accused of "feel good" teaching. The implication was that such activities were a waste of time. Today, we know that taking the time to get to know each other and build community in the classroom is one of the best ways to get the mind working well. Providing children time to connect with peers and teachers through opportunities to collaborate and dialogue builds trust and reduces discipline problems. The brain functions best when there is adequate challenge, specific feedback, and no threat. "Brain research has validated the importance of creating a learning community" (Jensen 1999).

For optimal learning and student engagement in the classroom, Jensen (1998) recommends combining ritual with novelty. The predictable structures of daily rituals (for example, routines for class openings, dismissals, getting the teacher's attention, visitors) help build community, help keep the classroom running smoothly, and reduce stress. At the same time, novelty activities (for example, suddenly changing the tone and tempo of the classroom by adding music, group movement, or clapping) help keep students' attention. The trick is to find the right balance of predictable routine and novelty.

Veteran fourth-grade teacher Joan Servis comments: "I spent many years in boring classrooms as a student, and I try to make sure that doesn't happen to my students. I tend to keep things moving along at a pretty quick pace, interspersing humor, new choices, and opportunities for movement."

Setting Up Classroom Procedures

I've been thinking a lot about classroom management. I'd never thought much about the actual term until I read Alfie Kohn's book *Beyond Discipline* (1996), which made me realize that *management* is a terrible word. We're really talking about student compliance when we say "management," but what we actually want is students who self-monitor and assume responsibility for the congenial, productive functioning of the classroom. We teachers still assume most of the responsibility for the running of the classroom. That works fine until we leave the room or have a substitute. It is only when students negotiate acceptable behaviors and routines with the teacher and assume responsibility for putting them into practice that we can effectively teach. Of course, for very young children and for some older ones, self-monitoring is difficult even after acceptable behaviors are negotiated and agreed on.

Establish Routines with Students Early

How we arrive at the procedures that make the classroom run smoothly and fairly tells a lot about the tone and power structure in the classroom. When students have a say in how the classroom is organized and managed, they take more responsibility for putting rules and routines into practice. All of us work harder to achieve a goal when we have been part of the decision making process that has gone into attaining it, as opposed to being told what to do. (See Figure 14-3 for class-created rules by first graders.)

Joan Servis does not assign jobs. Just as she voluntarily pitches in to help the school community run well, she expects students to help her determine and assume responsibility for the tasks necessary for the classroom community to function well. On a weekly rotation basis, students volunteer for such tasks as watering plants, board washing, and writing the daily schedule each morning. Joan notes that she has never had a job go unfilled (Servis 1999).

I have learned that we have to model all the behaviors we expect from students; that is, we have to show them what particular behaviors look like and sound like. Otherwise, a simple activity like leaving the classroom to go to a special class (such as art or physical education) can become a disruptive, energy-draining experience.

The following are among the classroom behaviors and routines that you will probably want to discuss, model, practice, and revisit with your students:

- Entering the room
- Getting settled
- Sharpening pencils
- Leaving the room
- Collaborating in a small group
- Whispering
- Using the bathroom
- Walking in the hallway
- Getting materials
- Requesting help

Figure 14–3   Class-created rules: grade one

A Shared Writing of Class Expectations in First Grade

1. Keep hands and feet to yourself.

2. Listen when others are talking.

3. Use kind words.

4. Use a "six-inch" voice.

5. Clean up materials when finished.

6. Be the best you can be!

Hallie Stewart's first-grade class
Written during the first month of school and posted all year.

- Actively listening
- Working when visitors are present
- Following through on routines when the teacher is absent.

Any of these routines can become problematic if expectations have not been agreed upon and modeled. When Brendan Tiller's second graders commandeer the classroom first thing each morning, Brendan holds a class meeting to restore order. Now, when I walk into Brendan's room just before the school day begins, I am amazed at the prevailing calm. Everyone is quiet and engaged in reading a book. Previously, the noise level was high and much time had to be spent quieting kids down. When I ask Brendan about the change, he explains that he has done away with traditional "bell work," the before-school, on-the-board-assignment that many teachers employ. Brendan became frustrated with these types of assignments because they did not easily transfer into reading and the work didn't engage the students. Another distraction that Brendan faced in the morning was "coat room havoc." Having kids put their things away unsupervised usually led to problems. Brendan's solution: "The kids come in and read now." Immediately upon arriving in the classroom, kids sit down with a book. Brendan then calls a few kids at a time into the coat room to put away their lunches and personal items. When the class moves into small guided reading groups after the school's morning announcements, students are focused and ready.

Teachers who initially take sufficient time to establish a classroom community with predictable routines, clear expectations, warm personal relationships, and a climate of respect reap the benefits all year long and, ultimately, wind up with more time for teaching. While it sounds easy to set up a classroom for success, it requires skill and experience—and firmness and patience. Nowhere is this more apparent than with new teachers.

Dealing with Typical Problems

Nathan was new to our district, a second-grade teacher full of the promise of just having completed an exceptional college career. It was something of a shock to him, therefore, to be struggling daily with students' off-task behaviors. Observing his class, I noticed the following: Nathan was such a conscientious teacher, he felt he had to monitor everything, and since he had taken all the responsibility for running the class upon himself, the kids didn't feel that they needed to share this responsibility with him. Nathan had to constantly interrupt his lessons to tell someone to sit down, be quiet, behave better, and so on. The rules that the classroom had composed together were useless, because Nathan assumed full responsibility for enforcing them.

One morning I was modeling one-on-one reading conferences for Nathan. We needed the class to work quietly for thirty minutes, something they hadn't been able to do up to that point. I told the class why we needed the quiet work time without interruptions and that they would all want to have that quiet conference time with the teacher. Then I appointed a "facilitator" at each table of four to five kids, and we modeled how the facilitator could courteously and respectfully help keep the group quiet and on task. For fifteen minutes they worked well, but then kids started getting noisy and leaving their seats. I interrupted the individual conferencing and went around to each table, asking the kids, beginning with the facilitators, what had gone well and what was a problem in keeping order, and how that problem could be solved. One girl who had interrupted the teacher to ask a question finally admitted that a group member could have answered her question (it was not an emergency). In the next fifteen minutes the noise level dropped, but several students were distracting the class by walking around, one to get a book, one to ask another student a question, one to throw something away. So, at the end of the morning we reevaluated one of our rules— "No walking around"— and amended it to, "Leave your seat only when necessary." We also added a box that students could use to write to the teacher about problems, possible solutions, and requests for help.

Laura Farragon is a first-year teacher with high expectations. She had set up a disciplinary system in her classroom in which children accumulated or lost "points" depending on their positive or negative behaviors. When I began working with her second-grade class in the fall, we had to stop what we were doing every few minutes so that Laura could discipline them, taking off points when the kids were off task or noisy. After the interruption, they would be quiet for a short time, and then the whole process would begin again. Each day, Laura went home feeling exhausted and burned out because of all the time and energy she spent handing out and taking away privileges.

I knew from experience that before we could teach anything effectively, she had to create a climate of respect and model the routines and behaviors she expected, such as walking down the hall in an orderly fashion, taking pencils out of desks, returning to the class after art or music, sitting down quietly. Her primary concern was with maintaining an acceptable noise level. I modeled for her ways to achieve this goal. We asked the students, "What does quiet look like and sound like?" Student responses included the following: "whispering," and "heads close together." Next, we had one group of students model "huddling" in front of the whole class. Then we had the rest of the class form small groups and we circulated among these, acting as coaches as each group modeled the behavior.

In retrospect, Laura noted that she always felt that she had to be in front of the class, which meant that she taught everything whole class. She admits that she couldn't really experience everyone's potential until she worked in small groups with students. But she couldn't work successfully in small groups until students took responsibility for working and behaving appropriately.

> At first, I took responsibility for telling the students everything they were doing wrong. I felt like an overseer rather than a facilitator. Now they hold themselves accountable. They tell other group members to be quiet, and they take responsibility for the behavior of the entire class as well as for self-management. So I spend less time managing kids who are off task. No points at all now. I used to take minutes away from free time, as a disciplinary measure. Kids used to keep a tally of minutes on their desk. If I said, "You lose two minutes," they had to record it on a note card. That took a lot of time. At first, with the new system, they asked, "Do I gain or lose minutes?" I would answer, "Neither. You just act appropriately." It took a month for them to get used to not having a reward system. It's much easier for me now.

Even parents appreciated the change. One parent who had accompanied the class on a field trip in the fall commented on how much better kids' self-control was at a holiday party months later. Laura said, "The kids settle themselves down more quickly. It used to be like a circus in here just before the bell at the end of school. I'm so much happier now. I get more done. I feel confident now that I can work with a group. Before, I always had to be in front of the class leading the way."

When we teachers learn to share responsibilities with students and problem solve difficulties together, the classroom climate improves. One effective way to accomplish this is through class meetings specifically called for this purpose. At the end of a recent school year, I interviewed second-grade teacher Neal Robinson, asking him how he accounted for efficient organization and commendable student behavior in his classroom, when it was such a struggle the first year. He commented:

> Last year I told them what I expected. We made a chart. I thought they would just do what we agreed upon. But it didn't work out that way. I wound up negative and always on their case. I was so busy being the police officer. I was afraid to give them responsibility. I didn't really believe they could handle it.
>
> Now, when things don't go well, we talk about it as a class. I help them to be accountable. I ask, "How can we do better?" We discuss our problem and solve it together. Then if things start to get out of hand, the kids remind each other of what to do.

Self-Evaluating the Tone of the Classroom

Our genuine interest in students as people is necessary in order for them to thrive. As a way to self-assess her sensitivity to her students, Maggie Donovan (1997) gathers her first graders together every week and asks them the same question: "What do you remember me saying to you this week?" She learned that the children's work, behavior, attitudes, and home life cannot be separated, and that our responses in the classroom are connected to our power as teachers to approve, welcome, give permission, and so on. She was reminded how crucial it is to speak in a caring manner and to actively listen.

> Everyone could quote me with certainty even after days or weeks had passed. Perhaps we need to stand conventional wisdom on its head and ask not, "Are they listening to me?" but "Am I really listening to them?" (34–36)

One way to examine the tone of your classroom is to ask yourself: "What would it be like to be a student in this classroom?"

- Would I feel like a valued member of the classroom community?
- Would my voice be heard and respected?
- Would I find the work meaningful and engaging?
- Would I have enough choices?
- Would I be comfortable with the physical setup?
- Are there ample opportunities for dialogue and negotiation?
- What are my opportunities for learning?
- How much listening to "teacher talk" is there?
- Is it a cheerful, upbeat place?
- Are there ample opportunities for dialogue and negotiation?
- Are there sufficient interesting books and reading materials in genres of my choice?
- Would I be academically and socially successful?
- Would I like the way problems are handled?
- Would I get the help, support, and nurturing I need to succeed?
- Would I want to spend a day as a student in this classroom?

Organizing the Classroom

The way our classrooms are set up and organized speaks volumes about what we value and believe. I can tell almost immediately upon walking into a classroom what the philosophy of the teacher is, just by viewing the way the room is organized (or not) for student access, attractiveness and comfort, and utilization of space and materials. The following are some items that I particularly notice:

- Library corner (size, location, appeal, quality of collection, ease of access)
- Open area where the class gathers (shared reading and writing, reading and writing aloud, class meetings)
- Teacher's desk (or lack of it; whether it is the focal point of the room or not)
- Blocks, easels, play corners (imaginative play and artistic expression)
- Bulletin boards (teacher- and student-created; connected to curriculum)
- Children's work (display, accessibility, quality)
- Charts (teacher- and student-created, related to curriculum and students' needs and interests)
- Comfortable living space (soft seating, curtains, lamps, plants, carpeted areas)
- Desks clustered (or big tables to promote small-group work)
- Furniture arrangement (collaboration, increased display space, and small work areas)
- Tone of classroom rules (negative or positive)
- Noise level (silence vs. engaged "hum")
- Who is doing most of the talking

Some teachers set up literacy "centers"—separate areas in the classroom for reading, writing, listening, word play, science, and other activities. These centers, when they exist, need to be consistent with our beliefs about learning, that is, that a center can be physically present and be—or not be—an opportunity for fostering strategic, independent learning. Literacy center purposes must be worthwhile, and routines for their use must be firmly established.

Teachers that have well-organized classrooms also have predictable schedules (see pages 291–292) and well thought out plans (see *Invitations*, 430–436).

Seating That Supports Group Work

Just about all of our students work in groups, because social participation in authentic tasks maximizes learning. Either students sit with their desks pushed together, or we use large round or rectangular tables to accommodate four to five students. Four seems to be the ideal number, and in our seating arrangements we try to maintain a balance of race, gender, and personalities. Varying the group members throughout the school year ensures that all class members get to work with one another. (See Figures 14-4, 14-5, and 14-6 on pages 545–547 for various room plans.)

Group skills build language and thinking, not just social skills. In business we bring together people who know different things so that they can talk and problem solve to-

Figure 14–4   Room plan for Karen Sher's kindergarten class

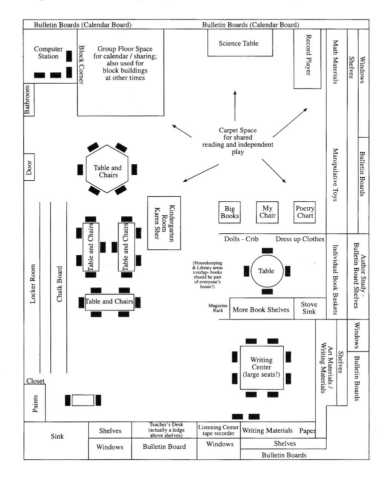

gether. Group members raise questions and seek clarification. Being able to work well with others is an important life skill that we need to teach our students.

Once kids know how to work in groups, everything goes easier. Group work helps keep the lower-achieving students on task by providing support within the group. Highly functioning groups also make it possible for the teacher to work with one student or group without worrying about discipline. Moreover, "Groupwork will usually produce more active, engaged task oriented behavior than seatwork" (Cohen 1994, 19–21).

A sixth-grade teacher comments: "Sometimes I think it's just noise and idle talk, but when I sit down and join the group, they're always on task." Our science resource teacher notes, "I don't have any discipline problems because the kids are doing something and collaborating." See Chapter 5, "Literature Conversations," for teaching students to work and self-manage small groups across the curriculum.

Chair Pockets

For organization purposes, especially when teachers have replaced desks with large ta-bles, we use "chair pockets," fabric sacks that attach to the backs of chairs, to hold

Figure 14–5   Room plan for Elisabeth Tuttle's first-grade class

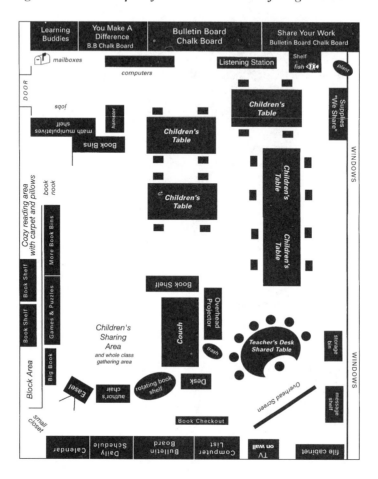

students' materials and supplies and to keep tabletops free for work in process. (See Photo 14-2.)

Kindergarten teacher Susan Mears first introduced chair pockets over a decade ago after seeing them in photographs of classrooms in New Zealand. My father, who was in the fabric business, donated the fabric for the first batch, and Susan figured out how to construct them. They were an immediate hit, and as more and more teachers got rid of desks to allow more flexible space in the classroom, chair pockets served as terrific organizers. Susan and other teachers initially paid for these pockets themselves, at a cost of five dollars each, or over one hundred dollars per class. Depending on the sturdiness of the fabric, they lasted one to three years.

After several years, the PTO (Parent-Teacher Organization) picked up the making of the pockets as a schoolwide project and bought the fabric (usually upholstery quality) and other necessary materials in bulk. When made of sturdy material, the pockets can last up to four years. Susan puts hers in the washer (on a gentle cycle) and drier twice a year. Chair pockets are now available to all K–4 teachers, who wind up loving them. See Figure 14-7 on page 548 for directions on how to construct chair pockets.

Figure 14–6   Room plan for Julie Beers' fourth-grade class

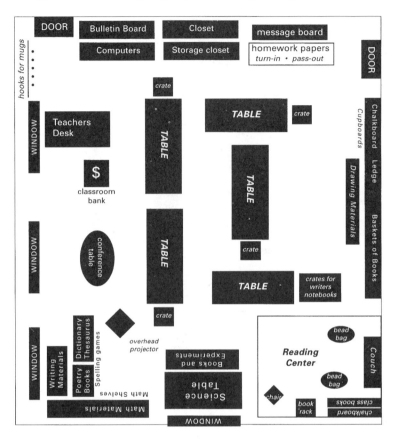

Photo 14–2   The chair pocket

Figure 14–7   Directions for making a chair pocket

Each pocket requires:

- A piece of fabric 18" wide by 62" long. The fabric should be cut with the bias (stretch) running across the short side of the fabric as shown below.
- 44" bias tape cut into two 22" pieces.
- pins.
- heavy duty sewing machine and needle (depending on thickness of fabric).

Directions:

1. Cut fabric.
2. Mark folds.
3. Fold and iron folds in the direction indicated by the curved arrows. (Curving to the right means fold over right side of fabric; curving to the left means fold under.)
4. Sew both hems using two rows of stitching.
5. Pin edges. (If using thick fabric, hand baste where several folds meet.)
6. Machine baste edges 1/2".
7. Pin bias tape over the raw edges, folding 1" under on each end (top and bottom of pocket).
8. Stitch two rows of seam along binding on each side of the pocket.

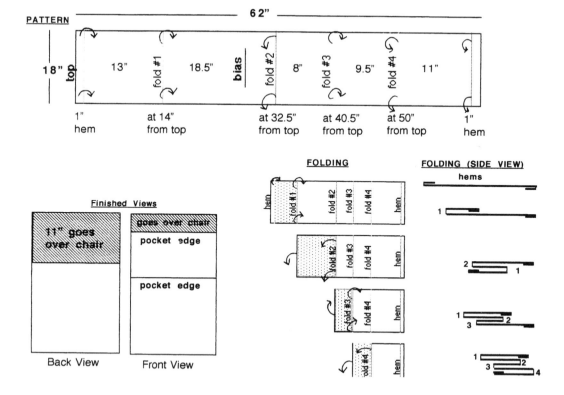

Aesthetics Matter

The way the room looks influences the feeling of friendliness and sense of community in the classroom. A homelike setting that includes such items as live plants, comfortable furniture arrangements, and attractive displays positively impacts student behavior and achievement (Foster-Harrison and Adams-Bullock 1998). As well, students in classrooms with excellent lighting have better attendance records and better moods (Jensen 1998, 54, quoting Edelston 1995).

An inviting library space is critical. Young children use the classroom library more when it is a separate, bright, carpeted space with pillows and comfortable chairs (Morrow 1983, noted in Krashen 1993, 36). See pages 84–90 for classroom library organization that meets the needs and interests of students, and note the photo on page 85.

See Figures 14-4, 14-5, 14-6 for examples of room arrangements in kindergarten, grade one, and grade four that promote access to literacy as the highest priority. Note that there is an open area where the whole class can gather for demonstrations and shared activities, that desks or tables are arranged for collaboration, and that there are areas for conferencing, small-group work, and for individual or paired reading. Messages, schedules, and announcements are clearly posted. Exhibits and bulletin boards feature mostly children's work and are clearly and prominently displayed, and explained by the children and teacher. Materials such as markers, pens, crayons, pencils, paper, and envelopes are organized and available and their use and care has been modeled by the teacher. Books, reading and reference materials, computers, and play areas are easily accessible, and the children know the routines for their use.

Again, be sure that students have some say in how the classroom is organized and arranged. When we teachers make all these decisions, we give students the message that the classroom belongs exclusively to us. By contrast, when we share and negotiate decisions about the room's appearance and layout, organization and use of the library corner, and appearance of bulletin boards, we are giving the message that the classroom belongs to all of us.

If you must have your classroom "ready to go" for the start of school, do reserve the content and creation of at least one bulletin board (preferably more) for your students. And, instead of commercial borders, consider having students design their own. Not only do these borders change the look of the room from commercial to child-centered, they provide an opportunity to teach the use of patterns in design.

ESTABLISHING SCHOOLWIDE COMMUNITIES

Learning communities are not limited to our classrooms but must expand to include the whole school—other teachers, administrators, parents, and the wider community. When I visited the Manhattan New School in New York City, founded by Shelley Harwayne and other teachers, I wrote down a comment Shelley made so that I wouldn't forget it: "You don't belong to a class; you belong to a school."

For over a decade I have been teaching daily in five schools. The culture of each is totally different, not visible on the first visit because each school looks beautiful—clean and well kept and full of children's meaningful work proudly displayed everywhere. But once inside for a while, the differences surface, and they have mostly to do with a feeling of community. In the schools in which administrators support teachers and teachers share materials and ideas freely, teachers have more energy. In schools in which everyone works together for the common good, there are high spirits and little divisiveness. On the other hand, where teachers do not regularly meet, share ideas, and collaborate, factions exist as teachers harbor resentments and feel isolated from the whole.

Fostering Teacher/Administrator Collaboration

A school community depends on the effective partnership of administrators and teachers. Each needs to articulate their expectations in order to achieve honest, open communication. The following suggestions have proven helpful in the promotion of teacher/administrator collaboration:

- Create a building support group or literacy team facilitated by teacher leadership (see pages 524–527).
- Establish professional libraries. Some administrators will buy professional books for teachers to discuss at study groups, support groups, and/or faculty meetings.
- Determine the master schedule together, to ensure creating language arts blocks and grade-level planning times that work for all involved.
- Allow some choice in how the budget is allocated.
- Save faculty meetings for professional development and sharing. Use grade-level representatives, meeting at regularly scheduled intervals with the principal, as liaisons for communicating building business.
- Attend conferences together. Too often, teachers who attend conferences alone have difficulty, when they return, convincing their principal of changes they want to make. (A few well-known speakers will now host teacher groups only when administrators are also in attendance.)
- Share research, such as recent articles supporting alternative assessments.
- Set classrooms up to facilitate teacher/administrator collaboration.
- Work together to maximize instructional time and relieve time pressures.
- Freely share ideas and materials.

Relieving Time Pressures

On the first day of school several years ago, principal Pat Heilbron suspended the usual morning faculty meeting after a few brief remarks by stating, "I know that the best thing I can give you is the gift of time." Her actions showed great respect to us as teachers. She also arranged common planning times for each grade level and told the staff that they could negotiate changes in the master schedule with one another.

We teachers never have enough time. Most of us are exhausted from "donating" countless hours beyond contract time. The following are some ways to rearrange school time in order to reduce pressure on teachers and administrators and promote more effective teaching.

• *Hire a roving substitute.*   Several principals in our district initiated this thoughtful action, which made it possible for teachers to conference one-on-one with students when teachers were learning how to manage the portfolio process. In another district, a floating substitute one day a week has enabled support specialists and classroom teachers to plan collaboratively.

• *Add additional, paid days to the school calendar.*   This is an optimal way to achieve pupil-free days for the whole district, to ensure ongoing professional development.

• *Consider an early dismissal for students (or a scheduled late morning start) once or twice a month.*   Some districts have been able to secure state waivers that allow teachers uninterrupted time to write curriculum, plan together, share ideas, and attend professional development meetings in the district.

• *Provide release time daily.*   Build in a planning period each day.

• *Provide large, uninterrupted, daily blocks of time for language arts.*   Work as a building team to ensure efficient and fair scheduling.

• *Reduce interruptions.*   I am always amazed at the number of interruptions that occur during teaching time. Well-meaning secretaries call up to ask for attendance, to have someone come to the office, to remind a student about an appointment, or to make a request. Be strict about keeping public address (PA) announcements to the bare essentials. As possible alternatives, consider written notes and e-mail. One way fourth-grade teacher Joan Servis deals with phone messages from the office is to delegate "phone duty" to students. Students are happy to take turns answering the phone and relaying messages, and Joan's teaching is not interrupted.

Educating Community Members

Brian Malley, assistant superintendent of curriculum for Regina Public Schools in Saskatchewan, Canada, makes sure that his board of education is informed about what's going on in classrooms. "It's hard to make decisions without information," he notes.

Some weekly board meetings in Regina begin with a thirty minute (or more) focus reserved for what's going on in classrooms. This is, happily, a far cry from the way most meetings of other boards are conducted. Teachers explicitly show how they teach reading. For example, using students they have brought along, teachers have demonstrated how they teach reading strategies and how students apply those strategies to their reading. As well, board members have been shown baskets of leveled books with explanations of how and why they are leveled.

Fourth-grade teacher Julie Beers makes sure that the packet of information she hands out each year to parents at our open curriculum night in the fall clearly and explicitly states how, why, and what she teaches. (See Appendix A-7.)

As stated previously, inviting politicians into our schools and showing them what and how we are teaching, as well as writing informative newsletters to parents, are other activities that help keep the school community informed.

Extending Community Beyond the Classroom

When I wrote *Literacy at the Crossroads,* the single most important thing I learned from my research was that in every case where parents became dissatisfied with the schools, communication had broken down and trust and respect had diminished. In most cases, parents were not part of the change process from the beginning but were informed after changes were already in place. We must continually work to earn and keep the trust of our students' families.

Fostering Parent Support: Suggestions and Commentary

What follows are several ideas that teachers and administrators have successfully put into practice. (See *Literacy at the Crossroads,* 64–73, for more specific examples. See also pages 263–266 in this text.) In all cases, we need to value parents and treat them with respect and also make our teacher voices clear, rational, and strong.

• *Make it easy for children new to the neighborhood to meet other children.*
Former principal Rosemary Weltman gave all families who had moved into her school community over the summer a student directory that listed the names, grade levels, addresses, and phone numbers of students from the previous school year. Parents could easily locate kids on their street or in nearby neighborhoods to introduce to their children, often easing their child's transition into a new school.

• *Prepare informative newsletters that parents can easily access and understand.*
In addition to their written newsletters, kindergarten teachers Kathy Wolfe and Rob Fellinger leave newsletters on voice mail. Second-grade teacher Loretta Martin uses large-size type for her newsletters, to make them easier and more enjoyable for parents to read. One parent wrote her the following note in response: "Thank you. My husband is legally blind. This is the first time he can read the newsletter." Each week, first-grade teacher Chris Hayward includes in the class newsletter a paragraph about relevant research that supports the way he teaches (see Appendix A-11). Parents tell him they are clearer now about why he teaches as he does and better able to deal with conflicting reports in the media.

First-grade teacher Kevin Hill uses shared writing to jointly compose the weekly newsletter with his students, and he asks parents and students to read and discuss it together (see Appendix A-8). Fourth-grade teachers Julie Beers and Joan Servis send parents monthly newsletters written by the students, using the newsletters as an opportunity to teach journalism and quality writing (see page 449). Another fourth-grade teacher, Linda Cooper, occasionally uses multiple small groups to do shared writings of weekly happenings. Other teachers make sure that their newsletters are jargon-free and that literacy terms, when they do employ them, are clearly defined.

Use your newsletters to talk about curriculum, classroom procedures and expectations, and class happenings. Include the "what," "why," and "how" of your teaching so that parents understand your approach. Keep the tone upbeat and the content brief—no more than one page, if possible. Celebrate what your students are accomplishing, and thank parents for their role in their child's education. See Appendix A for a sampling of excellent newsletters.

• ***Look for alternative ways to communicate with parents.*** In place of phone calls and notes, Jessica Morton uses e-mail to communicate with those families that have Internet access at home. She finds e-mail useful for noting a child's progress and for quickly addressing significant issues or concerns (Morton 1998, 74).

Before school starts or in early September each year, fourth-grade teacher Joan Servis asks the parents of her students to write her a letter explaining anything about their children that might be helpful to her in ensuring that they have a successful year. Second-grade teacher Stephanie Eagleton does the same and comments that one of her parents concluded the informational letter by writing, "Thank you. This is the first time any teacher has ever asked me for input on my child." Parents always appreciate teachers who seek their feedback. As one parent noted, "It sends an immediate signal that the teacher cares about my child as an individual—and about me as the parent."

First-grade teacher Hallie Stewart lets parents know exactly what she is doing in reading group each day. Each child has a weekly bookmark that includes the days of the week and a place to insert book titles and page numbers. At the end of each reading group, on each child's bookmark Hallie writes the pages that were read and discussed in group that day. Then, each child takes the book and bookmark home and continues reading with their parents.

I make a bookmark listing the strategies that the student is working on to remind the reader of this helpful information (see page 121). Extras are made for use at home; parents then know what is being taught and can reinforce these same strategies.

• ***Make learning events visible to families.*** Loretta Martin takes photos of her students in learning situations throughout the year. While she takes the photos with her own camera, she uses classroom supply money to pay for the film and processing. In the spring, when students put together profiles of their learning, students are asked to choose and include eight to ten photos from a large collection and write captions that describe what the pictures depict.

Throughout the school year, first-grade teacher Hallie Stewart (formerly Hallie Butze) takes photos of her students involved in various activities. In the spring, she compiles a selection of photos with added captions into a class photo book. Each night the book goes home with a different student and the family fills out a comment sheet which is added to the photo book (see Figure 14-8 on page 554). No student has ever forgotten the book or brought it back late.

These are powerful ways to include parents in the life of the classroom. They are able to see pictures of Readers Theatre, field trips, science experiments, special classroom visitors, small group work, and much more. Students learn to write meaningful captions, and highlights of their school year are permanently preserved. Additionally, some teachers, including special subject teachers, also make videos so that parents can see activities in art, music, and physical education, as well as other learning that takes place in the classroom.

• ***Assume that all parents want the very best education for their children, and keep communication open.*** It can be exasperating when parents do not respond to our communications and conference invitations. There are rare exceptions, of course, but I have learned that parents who do not respond often feel helpless, overwhelmed, and afraid to hear what they perceive will be more bad news about their child's progress. The following story brings home this point.

Figure 14–8   Family comments on class photo book

Child's Name Rebecca Semel
Family Member/s Alan Semel

Comments from the child: The winter party was grat.
I loved when we went to the
art museum. I liked the pupet show
at sea world because I love pupets.
Comments from the family member: All of the pictures
are wonderful! It will be terrific to have these
memories for all to see. Rebecca has had an excellent
year with her class and especially with Ms. Butze. Thank
you.

Our favorite picture is petting the sting rays
Because They are slimy. And it was fun
to see them.

I am having a conference with the mother of a student named Ronnie. Ronnie's mother, Mrs. Trillion, failed to come to fall conference despite several phone calls and notes from Ronnie's teacher. Ronnie is one of the students I work with as a pull-in support teacher in a second-grade classroom (see page 528). Not only is he one of the poorest readers in second grade, he is one of the most demanding. He sulks when I don't call on him first and seeks attention throughout our reading sessions by speaking out of turn and repeatedly getting out of his seat.

After winter break, I am particularly concerned, since Ronnie has clearly lost ground in reading, an indication that he has not read the books we sent home over vacation. When I call his mom, I emphasize the importance of us working together to maximize Ronnie's potential. She agrees to meet with me, the classroom teacher, and Ronnie. I want her son to be present, since Ronnie is obviously central to any improvement plan that we devise.

As we talk and get to know each other, I learn—for the first time—that Mrs. Trillion is raising her three children herself, and that she works two consecutive jobs. Ronnie attends a church after-school program daily (where he does his nightly at-home reading) and doesn't get home until 7:30 P.M. His mom tells us, with tears in her eyes, that she rarely gets a chance to look at Ronnie's school work or help him with his reading.

We problem solve together to build in fifteen minutes every day when Ronnie and his mom can read together. There is no available time early in the morning, so we settle on 8:00 P.M. I give Ronnie the choice of either reading to his mom or having his mom read to him. After some discussion, we agree that Ronnie will take several minutes to read to his mom and talk about the book. In the time remaining, she will read to him.

Our conference has been both eye opening and humbling for me. For the first time, I truly understand Ronnie's constant need for attention. I also understand the difficulty Mrs. Trillion faces in participating fully in the life of our school. How often have I and other teachers made false assumptions about lack of parental response? This family has lots of books in the home and a mother with a complicated life who wants to do right by her children. With our support, she does. By the end of the school year, Ronnie is reading close to grade level and making sure that he and his mom keep their nightly appointment.

- ***Be sure that parents understand the importance of their role in their child's reading attitudes and achievement.*** Fathers, grandfathers, and other significant male role models need to know how important it is that they get involved in children's reading at an early age. Donald Pottorff of Grand Valley State University in Allendale, Michigan, found that boys tend to see reading as a female-dominated activity. When he and his colleagues surveyed a wide cross-section of students in grades two, four, six, and eight, they found that the students perceived girls as being better at reading and writing. When they asked which of their parents was more likely to read to them, almost all picked mothers. Fathers were most often associated with the reading of newspapers. "If reading and writing are seen by boys as gender-inappropriate, then boys may well avoid these activities as much as possible, or at best simply tolerate them" (Pottorff, Phelps-Zientarski, and Skovera 1997).

This study has particular significance because, outside of the United States, young girls do not outperform boys in reading. In the United States, however, boys typically score lower on standardized tests and are referred for special help in disproportionate numbers.

This is important information to share with parents. We need to strongly encourage fathers to read aloud, discuss books and other reading materials, and read and talk about books in front of their children. The study cited confirms what I find out every time I ask students, "Who knows someone who belongs to a book club?" I ask this question when I am introducing literature conversations, to let students know that this is a real-life activity. But apparently, it is a real-life activity for women only. Rarely does a student say that their dad, uncle, or grandfather reads and discusses books with others.

FINAL REFLECTIONS

The emotional, social, and intellectual factors of learning must all work in tandem in order for students to feel successful and valued. When any one of these areas is out of alignment, students may experience difficulty and discomfort in the learning environment. Taking the time to carefully and respectfully set up the classroom physically, socially, emotionally, and academically—with lots of student input—pays big dividends all year long.

The aforementioned priorities are true for us educators too. When students, teachers, and families feel cared for, appreciated, and trusted—and when language, culture, and talents are honored—community develops as all participants feel free to question, disagree, make choices, and set goals while living and learning together.

CONTINUING THE CONVERSATION

• *Assess the collegiality quotient in your school.*   What are you doing to improve it or make sure it stays viable?

• *Evaluate the structures and strategies that enable time for professional development in your school and district.*   Explore creative solutions that increase time for professional opportunities.

• *Take a close look at the physical setup of your classroom.*   Are there areas for small-group work and free reading? Are the spaces attractive and inviting? Do displays show child collaboration and/or involvement? Does the classroom arrangement foster collaboration? Are you inviting student suggestions?

• *Incorporate recent research on learning and the brain for brain-compatible teaching.*   See related resources on brain research in The Blue Pages. For example, since the body needs liquid replenishment (eight to twelve glasses of water a day) in order for the brain to function optimally (Jensen 1998, 10), consider allowing students to have water bottles with them at all times to avoid dehydration and reduce stress. Also, since music and art education promote creativity, thinking, and problem solving, these disciplines should be required for all students (Jensen 1998, 36). Jensen notes, "Two rules come from the field of brain research and enrichment. One is to eliminate threat, and the other is to enrich like crazy" (1998, 40).

• *Make a plan for your continuing professional development.*   Decide what you will do this year, whether it's subscribing to a professional journal, reading one or more titles recommended in this text, being instrumental in starting a teacher support group in your school, and/or attending a state or national conference.

• *Review how you are communicating with families.*   Do parents really understand what is going on in the classroom and why and how you teach as you do? What are you doing, or what could you do, to make sure families feel welcome and valued in your classroom and school?

CHAPTER 15

Evaluation as Part of Teaching

A second-grade student-led conference: a student proudly explains her work to her dad

■ No single test can accurately measure what a child knows or a community needs to know. An array of assessments needs to be available for multiple purposes—accountability, school evaluation, reporting to parents, and instructional improvement.

—Anne C. Lewis

I once heard a principal say, "Parents don't test their children; they observe them and interact with them." When we say to parents, *Tell me about your child,* and they do, we don't then ask, *What test did you give to get that information?* We accept the parents' observations. We know that they have had ongoing experiences with the child, that they know and love their child well, and that they therefore have valuable information to share.

So, too, as teachers, we have ongoing experiences with our students, know them well, care about them. As we carefully observe them and talk with them each day, analyze records and notes taken in various contexts, and support them in their work and self-assessments, we obtain valuable information for teaching and goal setting. Then, as their parents do, we use those meaningful assessments to guide our teaching. Such classroom-based assessment does not mean that we do not use standardized measures, which can be appropriate and necessary. It does mean, however, that the overwhelming majority of our assessments and evaluations occur in the day-to-day work of the rich literacy classroom.

It is interesting that while the usual meaning of *assessment* has to do with the collection of data, the term is a derivative of *assidere,* a Latin word meaning to sit beside someone. And therein lies its essence. By sitting right next to the child, we observe his strengths and weaknesses, how he thinks and solves problems, how he performs simple and complex tasks. But observation is not enough. Unless we summarize and interpret these data, use them to make professional judgments, and take actions that improve teaching and learning, assessment is not especially useful. It is the analysis of data—our notes, our observations, the results of various day-to-day assessments—that bring meaning to assessment and make it rise to the level of evaluation. Assessment without evaluation is pointless.

When assessment becomes evaluation, assessment and instruction go hand in hand. Through our daily teaching we observe what the child is doing and attempting to do, and we determine what it is we need to do to help the child move forward. We accomplish this in our comprehensive literacy program through effective teaching that uses various approaches and strategies across the disciplines (see Chapter 2).

In *Invitations*, I wrote extensively about assessment and evaluation—beliefs and goals, processes and products, standardized tests, anecdotal records, interviews and surveys, checklists, report cards and grading, self-evaluation, my early thoughts on portfolios. I stand by what I wrote in 1991. Here, I want to:

- Connect important beliefs about evaluation to effective practices
- Relook at portfolios
- Look at self-assessment as a way to improve instruction and learning
- Investigate reporting to parents
- Deal with standards
- Discuss how mandated assessment can be used to improve instruction

As professionals we need to have continuing conversations with our colleagues and members of the larger educational community, collaborating with them on understanding, interpreting, explaining, changing, and designing assessment tools. Our continuing professional development is the best resource we have for improving assessment and instruction. This chapter can be a framework for your thinking. You may also want to form a study group to examine some of the useful assessment and evaluation resources in The Blue Pages (pages 62b–64b). And remember to approach assessment from a wide perspective. Many examples in this chapter come from kindergarten: if we can teach a kindergartner to assess her own learning, lead her own conference, any age student can be successfully taught to do the same.

BELIEFS ABOUT ASSESSMENT AND EVALUATION

One of the problems with "meaningful" assessment and evaluation is that it's easy to have the pieces look like they are in place without their having any impact on instruction and learning. Unless we match our beliefs with useful and developmentally appropriate practices, we are just going through the motions. For example, a portfolio that is kept because it is required but that does not include student choice and reflection will do little to improve learning. Or a spelling inventory that is given and scored but never analyzed and used to achieve specific teaching and learning outcomes will do nothing to help students become better spellers. Yet again, a running record given to an older, fluent reader yields no information on that reader's comprehension. So it's important for us to examine our beliefs and align them with meaningful practices. Once again, I share my beliefs and practices as a catalyst for you to think about your own beliefs and start your own conversations.

Assessment Must Serve the Learner

This is of utmost importance. Assessment must promote learning, not just measure it. That is, when learners are well served, assessment becomes a learning experience that supports and improves instruction. The learners are not just the students but also the teachers, who learn something about their students. (See the informal reading evaluation on page 120 for an example).

Assessments like this are realistic, relevant, and connected to meaningful literacy tasks in the daily life of the classroom. They are fair to the learner and show the learner's true strengths as well as weaknesses. Purposeful assessment tasks promote high-level thinking, problem solving, and performance both "on the spot" and over time. The experience is participatory and useful to the learner as well as the evaluator. The process matters as much as the product; that is, how the learner strategizes and approaches the task is as important as the end result. Goals are set for future learning. Assessment and evaluation procedures are constantly reviewed and revised as necessary.

Meaningful Assessment Interacts and Aligns with Instruction and Has Value for the Student, Teacher, Parent

This belief is closely connected to the first one. Evaluation and assessment are worthwhile for the learner and part of the ongoing meaningful life of the classroom. Assessment like this is often called *authentic;* that is, it connects to the learners' experiences, interests, and strengths in a real context. Students experience tasks and questions as they typically occur in life and have access to the resources that are usually available in their attempt to demonstrate their understanding. (And it's important to remember that this can be true even of a standardized measure.)

For example, when we originally developed a standardized writing prompt in our district (page 227), we failed to allow time for revising and editing. Rather than constructing the task to align with the way we teach writing (Chapters 6–9), we created a one-shot deal. When we changed the task to match the way we teach and allowed time on separate days for revising and editing, the results were much more meaningful. Another example? Our state-mandated reading assessment for grades 1–3 is standardized, but we designed it to match how we teach and administer it in the normal context of daily teaching (see pages 593–599).

A lot of meaningful assessment will be informal and occur in multiple literacy contexts. Some of it is planned, but much happens "on the spot" in response to a student's actions. It can take the form of observations, anecdotal records, informal reading conferences (page 114), one-on-one writing conferences (page 317), whole-class sharing (page 310), verbal comments made on the run (page 420). Assessments like these are the first steps in the evaluation process. For assessment to become evaluation, we teachers (often with our students) need to analyze our observations and data and set new teaching directions. When teachers take the time to carefully examine their observations, they are able to take "critically influential" actions with both individuals and the whole class (Paratore and McCormick 1997, 227).

Assessment information can be obtained though a variety of reading, writing, and speaking contexts experienced as a class, in a small group, with a partner, or individually:

book reviews	journals	reading logs
displays	listening activities	retellings
dramatizations	literature conversations	shared reading
essays	oral reading	shared writing
guided reading	poems	storytelling
illustrations	Readers Theatre	videos
		writing samples

The list is endless; any meaningful enterprise that goes on in the classroom is a potential context for assessment.

Teachers, Parents, Students, and Other Stakeholders Need to Understand and Value the Process

So much of assessment remains a mystery, not just to students and parents but to teachers as well. Too few of us understand how "standards" are determined, how standardized tests are constructed, and what the scores mean. We work hard to prepare our students for standardized tests, but we never get to see the test and determine whether our preparation was helpful.

Likewise, students don't understand why they are taking these tests, and few of us can explain the results in a way that makes sense to parents or students. Students rarely find out how they did; their parents simply receive a score a few months later.

For true understanding to occur, all stakeholders (students, teachers, parents, community members) need to know the criteria in advance. That's why we develop rubrics and seek input from students in developing the criteria (pages 573–574). Meaningful assessments help teachers, students, parents, and other stakeholders make informed decisions. That is, in order to improve instruction, the assessment must give detailed and specific feedback. The language we use must be clear and jargon-free.

Formal, Standardized Assessment Provides the Big Picture

Different audiences—self, teacher, family, school, district, state, nation—need different types of feedback. We do need to know how a program is working, how students are doing nationally, or whether a student qualifies for a special program. Combined with other assessments, formal, standardized measures are appropriate for accountability, monitoring, selection, and placement *as long as* they are supplemented with other assessments. Only when a standardized test—or any assessment—is given complete and total weight and treated as an end in itself do I strenuously object: one test cannot give an accurate picture of what the child knows, how the child is doing, and what the child needs to learn next.

Self-Assessment Is Critical

Self-assessments include but are not limited to carefully selecting work for portfolios, noting reading strategies (page 130), comparing present writing with an earlier writing sample and/or editing or rewriting that sample (pages 278–281), rating books read (pages 52–54), completing interviews and attitude surveys (*Invitations*, pages 317–321), evaluating work against a rubric, writing a report card on yourself (*Invitations*, page 350) or a narrative of your progress (*Literacy at the Crossroads*, pages 159–163), reflecting on daily learning, and setting goals. Even very young children can self-assess. (See Figure 15-1.)

There is no guarantee that when we ask kids to evaluate themselves, they will do so in a reflective way or that their learning will improve as a result. In many cases, students dutifully fill out a checklist that reflects our agenda, not theirs. Because the task has no meaning for them, nothing changes. Unfortunately, this problem is a common one with regard to portfolios. Students may look at their work and select pieces to include, but they will not make thoughtful judgments about their work until we demonstrate how to do it and get them to value the process. Self-evaluation, if it is to impact learning, must be taught and modeled and must include an action plan, not just reflections and goals.

Our goal for all learners is that in the course of our teaching them reading, writing,

Figure 15–1 A kindergarten end-of-year oral self-assessment, administered by kindergarten teacher Karen Sher

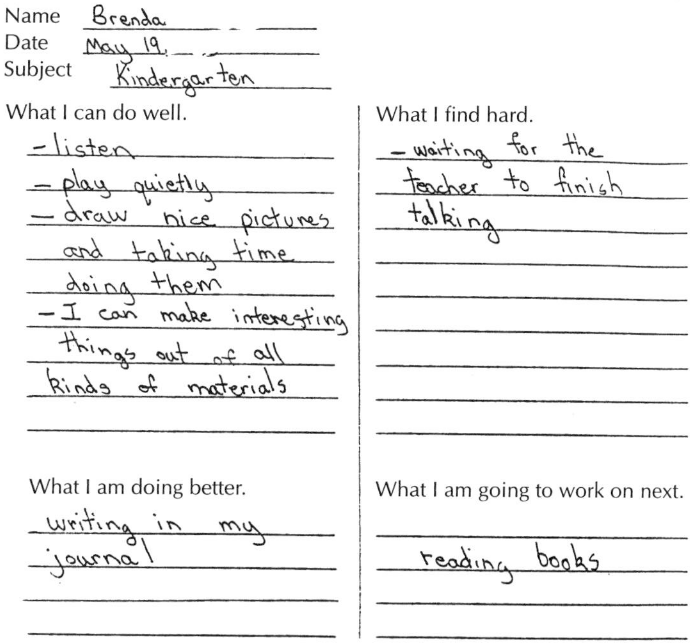

thinking, viewing, listening, problem solving, they will eventually ask their own questions, monitor their own understanding, and take responsibility for moving their learning forward. Ongoing self-evaluation will thus have become part of who they are as learners.

In writing this book, I have became a stronger self-evaluator. That is, by writing every day, showing that writing to editors and colleagues, and listening to what these readers had to say, I got better at assessing what was missing, what wasn't clear, what was redundant. The chapter drafts I wrote later in the process were clearer than the earlier chapter drafts had been. Also, even though my editors and readers gave me valuable suggestions, the final responsibility for assessing how a chapter is organized and what it contains remains with me. For example, even though my editor felt a lead for a certain chapter was fine (and it was), I knew it didn't fit with my intended message and I rewrote it. We need to teach our students that our suggestions and opinions are not the final say—rather they need to use what we tell them to ask their own questions, become self-assessors who continually monitor their own learning.

Students need lots of opportunities and purposeful learning "encounters" to self-question, pose questions, and take an inquiry stance toward learning. A philosophy of education course stands out for me because of the opportunity for self-assessment. In addition to several required essay questions, we students were given the option of writing and answering our own essay question. It was the first time I can ever remember being asked to raise my own important question as part of the evaluation process. I loved the challenge of wrestling with a question that focused on what I deemed worthwhile and critical, and I loved being trusted to determine what an essential question was. My voice and point of view were being encouraged along with my knowledge and evidence of learning. I felt exhilarated from the experience and have never forgotten it. The final test of knowledge is, after all, being able to decide what's important and not needing the teacher to determine it.

If we've taught students to ask important questions (see Chapters 5 and 12), why can't students also demonstrate what they know by creating and answering their own important question(s)?

REVISITING PORTFOLIOS: WHERE ARE WE NOW?

My definition of a portfolio has evolved to this: a reflective selection of artifacts, work samples, and records that demonstrate who we are as literate beings (readers, writers, thinkers, and learners) and how we have developed over time. (*Artifacts* refers to significant objects or keepsakes such as photos, letters, or awards.)

I first wrote about portfolios in late 1990. At the time, portfolio assessment was the new kid on the evaluation block, and little had been written about it. Many teachers were trying out the process and experiencing difficulties: where do we find the time, what criteria will students use to decide what to include, what happens to the portfolio from year to year? We vacillated between excitement at the inherent self-reflection and self-evaluation and frustration at the enormous amount of time and energy the whole process took. As one colleague honestly put it, "Portfolios are killing me."

Almost a decade later, there is so much information on portfolios it's hard to sift through it all. Most of us have stayed with the process because we see the enormous positive impact it has on documenting, analyzing, and understanding growth over time.

Through trial and error, professional reading, and collaboration with our colleagues, we've become better informed and better able to manage the process. Still, the difficulties, confusions, and feelings of being overwhelmed persist:

- Is it worth all the work to assemble a portfolio that is passed on to the student's next teacher only to sit in a closet?
- Do collections of best work really represent the student as learner?
- If the student makes all the choices, how can we get depth and balance?
- What about the role of parents? Is it fair to leave them out and not allow them to contribute home literacy artifacts?
- What about the enormous investment of time? Where does this time comes from?
- Without ongoing portfolio conferences with kids, how meaningful is the process?

In too many cases, portfolios have become the new buzzword, "the thing to do"—collections assembled without much regard for beliefs about teaching and learning, tedious collections used like worksheets. For portfolios to work well, teachers have to be grounded in how students learn and view the portfolio as documentation of growth over time across multiple contexts.

In our school district, whenever portfolios were integrated into the fabric of the classroom—which was rare—teachers and administrators were highly knowledgeable, committed to the process, and willing to take the extra time and effort to communicate effectively with students and parents. In those classrooms, students understood the "what," "why," and "how" of portfolios. They were always thinking and reflecting about their work in process and continually reevaluating and setting goals for themselves. Parents valued and appreciated portfolios because they could finally "see" what their child was doing and learning. This was the best of portfolios, a collaborative process that helped students think and talk about their work and showcase their learning.

I had the privilege of working for several years in two such classrooms, with two excellent teachers: second-grade teacher Loretta Martin and fourth-grade teacher Joan Servis. When I wanted to know whether the kids valued portfolios and understood the process, I asked them:

- What is a portfolio?
- Who's it for?
- What goes in and who decides?

In both these classes, this writing/thinking exercise was done first in small groups working collaboratively. Then we came together as a whole class and decided which responses to include. Note the thoughtful responses of Joan Servis's fourth graders (see Figure 15-2 on pages 564–565) and Loretta Martin's second graders (see Figure 15-3 on page 565).

These responses stand in stark contrast to those I've received from students who are "doing" portfolios: "It's for the teacher." "It's a waste of time." Or, most typical, "It's a safe place to keep special stuff." The notion of self-evaluation is usually absent.

A group of literacy educators asked to discuss portfolio practices agreed that learner-centered portfolios are important not only for noting and evaluating literacy development in a rich and broad way but also for promoting many aspects of learning, some of

Figure 15–2   Fourth graders' responses to
"What's a Portfolio?"; "What Goes In?"; "Who Decides?"

What Is a Portfolio?

- A showcase of your work and growth
- Something to keep things you've done well on for your future teachers to see
- *Your personal keepsake—things you're proud of that you might want to share with others
- Work that you put in so you can reflect on it
- *Shows your ability as a student
- A place where you can keep your work for future reference
- A collection of work that shows your growth and past

Who's It For?

- It's for us, because it's work we're proud of and we want to keep—and for our teachers so they know what we've done.
- It's also to show our parents what we've done in school and our growth.
- A model to share with younger students to show them things they might be doing later on.
- Mostly for you and your parents—teachers mostly know where you are. It's a good way to show parents what you've been doing.
- In answer to the question, "Should the state mandate portfolios?": A portfolio is personal for child, parent, and student—not for the state. The state wouldn't understand what everything was, so what could they do with it? What would they get out of it—not self-explanatory.

What Goes in and Who Decides?

- We decide because it's our work, and we should be able to decide what's good about it.
- If we're not proud of some work, we shouldn't have to put it in if we don't want to.
- *It should be a good balance of all subjects, including strengths and weaknesses.
- Teacher should say what subjects, but not the exact pieces. Parents shouldn't have input because they're not here—don't know the work you're doing.
- Teachers should limit what goes in—provide boundaries.
- Parents should have some input—not require, but give suggestions.
- Should be mainly children's decisions.
- "If you just put in everything you're completely proud of, you might leave something out that's important." Teacher can help here.
- Parents should not decide; parents are there to see what you're doing, not to tell you what to do.
- Parents should have some input.
- You share your portfolio at a triangular conference so they see it then, so they don't need to have a say in what goes in.
- Parents and teachers can make suggestions but kids are the only ones who know what we've done well on. Should be our decision.
- Parents shouldn't have anything to say about it. Picking things out to put in is a skill you need in order to do a portfolio.
- Parents and teachers should only be able to give suggestions.
- Everybody should be able to make suggestions but student has final say.

*Three out of the four groups agreed on this.

Figure 15–2, continued

What Goes In?

- Include something from all the different subjects—a good balance, including strengths and weaknesses, a combination of papers and ideas you are and aren't proud of.
- Include a piece from every subject that you're proud of and a piece you're not proud of but that shows your growth.
- For math, we should do a demonstration to show how we're doing.
- For spelling, we should do "Have-a-Go."
- We should include the authors we read to show our growth in writing.
- For writing, we should show a piece that's descriptive and has good vocabulary.
- For science, we should write up our favorite experiment.
- A math homework sheet from the beginning of the year and one from the end.
- Mapping packets, writing folders, writing records, self-evaluation of all subjects, WEB sheets, specific papers from all subjects, experiment sheets, short story you wrote/poem, favorite book, a sheet of questions you wrote for reading discussion.

Figure 15–3   Second graders' responses to "What's a Portfolio?": a shared writing

About Portfolios, Draft

- Describes things about you
- Tells things about you that are important
- Lets you look back on your learning
- LETS YOU KNOW ABOUT YOURSELF: You can look back and see what you've learned and what you can do even better
- Tells how you're doing in school and what you're learning
- Shows how you've improved
- Has important or special papers or things you might need
- Lets teacher, family, classmates, principal, visitors know more about you and see how much you've learned
- Could include report card
- Has some of your writing: "If you would look from one piece to another you could see I did something better"
  final draft or final copy
  first draft
  best piece

How we will use the portfolio:

- What you're working on
- What you've learned
- What more we want to learn

Written by Mrs. Martin's second-grade class.

which include reasoning, self-reflecting, planning, examining evidence, questioning assumptions, and taking greater responsibility for learning (Tierney et al. 1998).

I see the strength of portfolios as supporting assessment, promoting student learning, and enabling all the stakeholders—students, parents, teachers, administrators, community members—to see and talk about student work. What is essential is that portfolios bring together a wide range of work over diverse contexts that represents the journey of a student's learning and thinking. In addition, an "ability to look carefully and describe thoughtfully is central to the utility of portfolios. After all, what is the point of collecting work if you don't know how to look at it? Or if does not help to keep the child at the center of your focus?" (Jervis 1996, 98–99).

Getting Started

One easy and powerful way to get started with portfolios is with a selection of personal reflective pieces that represent the learner. Many teachers start the year off by putting together a "Me Box" of their own as a model. The conversations that emerge when the things in a "Me Box" are shared help build community and respect as classroom members learn what their teacher and peers excel at, value, and cherish. As well, such an activity connects home-school literacy. Figure 15-4 is a letter to families of second graders explaining a "Me Box," Figure 15-5 is a suggested list based on what I included in mine. When second graders in Loretta Martin's classroom later wrote written reflections about what they learned, the following were typical comments: "I learned more about the other people in my class," "I learned that there is no such thing as girl stuff or boy stuff," "I learned not to be shy. I learned to share things."

One of the biggest advantages in beginning with your own valued selections is that students new to the portfolio concept "get it." The students in one fourth-grade classroom originally saw portfolios as "something to put all your work in." After I shared my living portfolio, they quickly understood a portfolio to be "about you and mostly for yourself," a mechanism "to show how you've changed," "to show how much you've learned."

The Teacher Portfolio: Possibilities, Perspectives, and Implications for Teaching

I have had a portfolio for years. I share it with students when I go into classrooms, and I share it with teachers in buildings where I work and when I speak at conferences. I put my portfolio together for three reasons:

1. I believe we teachers need to experience what we are requiring our students to do so we know firsthand what the process involves.
2. I like having a model to share with students and teachers to show possibilities ("Here's what one looks like").
3. I want to become more reflective about my learning and to share more of who I am with students and teachers.

These are important reasons to keep a portfolio, and the container—a large folder, a notebook, a box—is the least of it. Whereas before I used to keep everything in an oversized

Figure 15–4 A letter to families explaining a "Me Box"

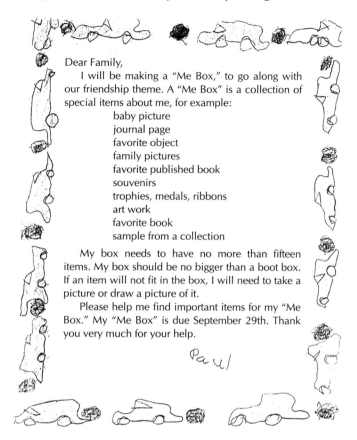

Dear Family,
I will be making a "Me Box," to go along with our friendship theme. A "Me Box" is a collection of special items about me, for example:

      baby picture
      journal page
      favorite object
      family pictures
      favorite published book
      souvenirs
      trophies, medals, ribbons
      art work
      favorite book
      sample from a collection

My box needs to have no more than fifteen items. My box should be no bigger than a boot box. If an item will not fit in the box, I will need to take a picture or draw a picture of it.
Please help me find important items for my "Me Box." My "Me Box" is due September 29th. Thank you very much for your help.

                    Paul

Figure 15–5 Suggestions for what to include in my "Me Box"/personal portfolio

Portfolio Components
Personal

favorite book, author

favorite magazine

pictures of family
   grandparents
   parents
   sisters, brothers, cousins

picture of best friend

picture of pet

special object or thing(s) you collect

letters, cards

writing pieces

Include why each is important to you.

Regie Routman

folder, now I am more likely to gather what I want to share when I need it. My portfolio is a living one; it is part of my life and needs to be "out" so I can use it easily. The portfolio as a container of work and artifacts has no authenticity. It is only when the contents make a statement about who we are as people and as learners—as well as document and encourage growth—that the portfolio has value. My portfolio is an approach and process to learning, not just a place for me to keep significant items and materials. I believe the same needs to be true for our students.

The most valuable aspect of putting together a portfolio is going through the process and experiencing the procedures and problems firsthand. It influences what we ask our students to do. I *never* give my portfolio to someone to examine without being present to talk about it. I know that only I can explain why certain pieces are there and what they mean to me. For me, unless the owner of the portfolio is present to explain it, it's not a portfolio. It's a collection of work. Only the rightful owner of the portfolio can bring it to life and make it a portfolio—reflective, meaningful, personal, responsive—by having conversations with the teacher, with peers, with family members, and with administrators and other educational stakeholders.

Looking at portfolios in this way, I realized that scoring them is inauthentic and has no meaning for me or for students. I also began to question the common practice of having students write brief comments—often called "entry slips"—on why pieces have been included (what one student in our district referred to as "all that Post-it stuff"). I have never done this, nor felt the need to do it. However, if teachers have demonstrated reflection and shown they value it, an entry slip explaining why a piece is in the portfolio may sometimes be helpful. In fact, some teachers note that such reflections help students "jump start" their portfolio conversations when talking to their parents and teacher.

Here's what I now include in my portfolio: my reading record, my writing notebooks, significant pieces of writing in process or completed, and important life stories. These things are a natural part of my life and are in keeping with what I do in the course of living as a reader, writer, thinker, and explorer. My living portfolio is part of who I am, not a separate entity.

There is no one right way to work with portfolios. However, when we go through the process ourselves, we gain a greater understanding of what it is we are asking our students to do. Having experienced the possibilities and pitfalls firsthand, we are better able to make informed decisions on portfolio use. Also, doing professional reading and discussing what's working and not working with portfolios—as the teachers in our district did over many years—is very helpful. (See "Portfolios" in The Blue Pages for recommended resources.)

USING SELF-ASSESSMENT TO IMPROVE INSTRUCTION AND LEARNING

Students can perform a self-assessment alone, in connection with their teacher, or as a class. Whole-class assessments can tell us what messages we have been giving to students and what they understand about literacy processes and practices. Figure 15-6, "What a Good Reader Does," and Figure 15-7 on page 570, "What a Good Writer Does," are the result of whole-class shared writing in Loretta Martin's second-grade class. Note that Figure 15-7 reveals small group work on the whole-class draft before the class gathered to determine a fi-

Figure 15–6   What a Good Reader Does: a shared writing by a second-grade class

What a Good Reader Does

READ!
Reads books and gets ideas for writing
Usually keeps a reading log
Reads books to get information
Reads to learn
Reads every day
Reads to somebody or gets read to
Asks other people to recommend books
Rereads to learn more
Can talk about what s/he has read and learned
Reads at the rate he/she can understand
Doesn't race when reading
Does lots of things (strategies) to figure out a word:
    skips it, goes on, and comes back to it
    breaks word into syllables
    stretches word
    uses pictures
    sounds it out
Goes back and rereads when something doesn't make sense
Tries to read books that mostly he/she can understand
Reads easy, medium, and hard books
Doesn't skip pages
Reads all kinds of things: books (fiction/nonfiction), magazines, newspapers, signs, comics, mail, instructions, labels, clothing, cards, posters
Practices reading
Writes
Writes about the book
Reads over what s/he has written

by Mrs. Martin's second-grade class, December

---

nal draft. (See Appendixes B-3 and B-4 for responses from a fourth-grade class.) Try such an exercise with your students. Besides revealing what your students value and understand, shared writing like this is an excellent reference and reminder for students.

How Am I Doing? Teacher Evaluation

Several years ago, I suggested to exemplary kindergarten teacher Karen Sher that she ask her students and their parents to tell her how well they thought she was doing her job. She resisted at first, because she believed—as most of us do—that she wasn't quite "measuring up." But Karen is a learner and risk taker, so she decided to go

Figure 15–7 What a Good Writer Does: a revision of a working draft

What A Good Writer Does

WRITES!

Writes all kinds of things: stories, poems, songs, words fiction, non-fiction, science fiction, not always books but pieces, reports, fairy tales, biographies, instructions auto-biographies, comics (comic books), magazines, games, cards, music, newspapers, letters — Parts of — move lower

Reads

Reads to find out different styles of writing

Reads other books for information

edits Spelling capitelieing punchuation marks

Publishes as much as posible.

Sounds out words

Rereads/

Proofreads

Thinks before writing/problem solves

Uses good handwriting especily when doing final copy.

Reads over and makes sure it makes sense and sounds right

Shares writing

Conferences with classmates and teacher, or Parent

~~Fixes up misspelled words~~

Uses "sloppy copy" to write final draft

Crosses out when Makes changes

Writes action words

Puts in a good lead

Revises & Cuts & Pads to make more sence

Files Writing

DRAFT 1-5-94

keeps a Writing folder

Tipes

ahead. Now every year she asks her students and their parents to evaluate her as she evaluates the students, with "three pluses and a wish" (Mills 1990). (See Figure 15-8 for the letter she sends to parents and Figure 15-9 for the narrative section of one report card.)

Here's what her students told her when she gathered them around at the end of one school year and asked them, *How am I doing as a teacher?*

Pluses

1. You give us long play times and extra recess.
2. I like when you read to us. It's relaxing.
3. I like how you set up snack.
4. I like when you read with expression.
5. I like how you help us with our reading so we don't make lots of mistakes.
6. You let us draw during rest time.
7. I like sharing in circle time.

Figure 15–8   Karen Sher's letter to parents: "Three pluses and a wish"

SHAKER HEIGHTS CITY SCHOOL DISTRICT

ONAWAY SCHOOL
3115 Woodbury Road
Shaker Heights, Ohio 44120
(216) 295-4082

ROSEMARY WELTMAN
Principal

Dear Parents,

As the school year draws to a close, I find myself assessing my own strengths and weaknesses as well as those of the children. I, too, have to always be vigilant about understanding WHAT I KNOW and WHAT I'M WORKING ON.

The purpose of this letter is to request your feedback/assessment of the job I've done as your child's kindergarten teacher. It is critical for teachers to be aware of parental thoughts and feelings regarding what is valuable during their child's school experiences. Furthermore, I can only continue to grow in my profession if I set clear goals for the future.

Please find attached a questionnaire entitled, How Am I Doing As A Teacher? Three Pluses and a Wish. This is the same format I will use for your child's final report card narrative. Please take a few minutes to jot down three teacher pluses that your child benefited from this year and one 'wish' to help me work on my future growth. I've appreciated the affirmation, honesty and sincerity that you have given me this year. I've enjoyed your children immensely, and thank you for the large part that you've played in making this a successful year.

Sincerely,

Karen Sher

Figure 15–9   A narrative on the kindergarten report card: "Three pluses and a wish"

November

Three pluses and a wish

+ Asha is a deeply caring child. She is quick to provide support and empathy when another child is in need.

+ Asha has strong oral and language skills. She is also very musical—often making up songs—and humming when she works!

+ Asha has a good understanding of how books work as well as a solid understanding of phonics connections. I will be encouraging Asha to pay closer attention to the text when she reads, helping her to firmly establish 1-1 correspondence. At the present time, she mostly relies on text memory when "reading" to me.

A wish or two . . .

In math, Asha will benefit from more counting (both by rote and using objects) experiences as well as more opportunities to sort and classify everyday objects.

An area I'd like to help Asha grow in this year is WORK HABITS. I often need to repeat directions a number of times. Also, Asha doesn't always wait for directions before beginning. I want to encourage Asha to take her time to do careful work that she can be proud of. Attending to directions as well as to fine motor details will continue to improve with time—she is so very young!

Wishes

1. Read with more expression.
2. When people are talking when you're reading, don't put the book down. Leave it up and tell the person to stop talking.
3. Don't play the guessing game every day.
4. Give more rest time.
5. Give more outdoor recess and more fresh air.
6. Not to sit so long like now.

Figure 15-10 on page 572 is a typical appreciative response Karen has received from parents. For Karen, the most rewarding response—and also the most surprising—came from the mother of one of her most challenging students. Karen had worried that the response might be negative, because she often had to contact this mother about her child's inappropriate behavior. Here's what Derrick's mother wrote:

> You knew and understood Derrick so well and were so in tune with his needs. You were able to give him the special attention he needed so he could grow and learn in "his way" in your class. Your flexibility in his case was well beyond what I would have expected from any teacher. . . .
>
> Communication with you was great. You were always available to talk to—even spontaneously. Although I often said, "Oh, no!" when you'd call at my work or home, I

Figure 15–10   A response from a parent: "Three pluses and wish"

How Am I Doing As A Teacher
Three Pluses and a Wish

+ The plus I appreciate most is that
you have helped Zoë to feel good about
herself — through listening carefully to
her, using positive messages, and encouraging
independence. And let's not forget hugs + affection !!
+ I love seeing how the class works
together, using the compassionate
communication model (most of the time!).
From a disorganized group of pre-schoolers, you've
produced a happy, organized group of elementary
+ students.
    I'm impressed with your focus on
your own education — the seminars and
committees that keep you on the cutting
edge of education in elementary schools
(Example: the wonderful 3-way conferences).

A Wish:
    That you had been able to
do the K–1st grade experiment you
and Rosemary were discussing * It's a
worthy idea, and though I wish we
could have taken part in it, I hope
you have the opportunity to try it
in the future.
      —Joanna Connors

* taking Kindergartners to first grade

didn't really feel that way. I was glad you did not withhold your concerns and that you took action when the incident occurred rather than much later when Derrick would not even recall what happened!

When we sincerely ask our students and parents how we are doing as teachers, we are being courageous and are demonstrating that we want to improve our teaching. Like Karen, we may also be richly rewarded.

Questions to Guide Our Self-Assessment

The following questions can guide our own assessment of our teaching, especially when we keep them uppermost in our minds:

• <u>**Why do I teach the way I do?**</u>   Do my beliefs align with my instruction? Are my beliefs grounded by relevant research, classroom experiences, and careful reflection?

• <u>**Am I making decisions based on what kids do and can do?**</u>   Am I using observations and multiple assessments to get an accurate portrait of each student's learning? Am I then using those assessments and evaluative measures to guide instruction?

• ***How do I know when kids are getting better?*** One curriculum director told me that when he asked his teachers how they assessed their students, several said they relied on "gut-level feel." While our intuition can support our findings, a "gut-level feel" is not a responsible assessment. We must have data, work samples, and multiple assessments to support and share with students, parents, and the school community.

• ***So what? What difference does it make?*** I ask myself this all the time. Perhaps a lesson has gone really well. The kids enjoyed it and were engaged. Still, so what? What really happened that was—or was not—significant for moving instruction and learning forward? Or again, students write an entry slip saying why they selected a piece for their portfolio. So what? If the students are merely fulfilling the teacher's request without much thought, the activity is a waste of time. Or yet again, a thematic unit has been fun and the students have enjoyed it. So what? If it wasn't related to important concepts, it has been of questionable value.

Questions to Help Students with Their Own Evaluation

Think about developing questions with your students that will support their reflection on their own learning. (You will want to adapt these questions to the age of your students.) Here are some suggestions:

Reading

- How much time am I setting aside each day for reading?
- Am I reading in a variety of genres?
- Am I choosing mostly "just right" books?
- When I don't understand, what strategies do I use to be sure I am comprehending as I read?
- Am I setting goals for myself? How do I know I am accomplishing them?

Writing

- Am I writing every day?
- Am I revising for clarity and interest when necessary?
- Am I learning to rely on myself as final editor?
- Does my writing have a distinctive voice?
- Am I "reading like a writer"—noticing what authors do and how and when they do it?
- Am I carefully examining writing in a genre before I attempt to write in that genre?
- Am I setting goals for myself? How do I know I am accomplishing them?

See *Invitations*, 342–364 for many practical example of self-evaluations.

Rubrics

When Bena Kallick and Marian Liebowitz led an assessment workshop in our school district in January, 1997, they emphasized, "If we want kids to do quality work, they have to know what quality is." They have to see and experience what "quality" looks like or sounds like. Well-constructed rubrics are one way to help kids (and parents and teachers too) understand what we mean by quality and guide learners to assess and improve their work. Rubrics list and describe criteria for determining the quality of specific tasks and projects and can be used as scoring guides. (Pages 227–228 describe how rubrics can be used to improve writing quality.) Rubrics should be developed jointly by teachers and students so that everyone is clear on the criteria for excellent work and everyone has an opportunity to be successful.

However, a rubric does not improve the quality of student work or performance unless it aptly describes the qualities we are seeking, contains worthwhile descriptors, and is understood and valued by those who use it. Using a rubric effectively also assumes that the criteria are established before the work is undertaken so students (and parents) understand the goal they are working toward and can evaluate their work in process, not just when it is completed. Additionally, when students have some say in constructing the rubric, they take it and their work more seriously.

Thoughtful rubrics can help improve the quality of student work. The written indicators need to be very clear and specific, students need to see and discuss examples of exactly how excellent work demonstrates these criteria, and they need to try the task themselves with the criteria in hand. In keeping with the model for effective teaching and learning on pages 22 and 23, rubrics need to be demonstrated and worked with as a class before students are sent off to use them on their own.

I like rubrics best when students, with our guidance, determine the criteria for outstanding work. An excellent way to help students do this is to label some examples: *Here is where the writer has done such and such.* To that end, students routinely need to examine samples of excellent work as well as samples of average and poor work. (You can save work samples from previous students or trade samples with a teacher in another building. Be sure to remove students' names unless you have their permission to use the work.) By talking together in small groups about actual work samples of differing quality, students begin to see that a particular piece has certain qualities while another piece is missing such qualities. They see firsthand what they need to add or change to make their own work in progress better. (See Figure 5-13 on page 203 for one example of a rubric, as well as *Invitations*, pages 334–338).

A caution about rubrics. They can be overused. Save them for important projects, processes, and products. It is neither necessary nor desirable for students to list criteria and score every piece of work against those criteria, especially after they have internalized what we mean by "quality." Sometimes, an informal sheet listing specifications for an assignment or project is advantageous; with a "spec sheet" like this, the focus is on the work, not the score. Even very young children can develop "spec sheets" (see Figure 15-11).

REPORTING TO PARENTS: REFINING THE SYSTEM

Several years ago, a group of dedicated teachers in our district began pilot-testing different reporting forms and procedures—including student-led conferences—in an effort to improve our reporting system and align it with our new language arts course of study (see *Literacy at the Crossroads*, pages 157–158). As a result, a parent with several children in the same K–4 elementary school might receive a different reporting form for each child.

*Figure 15–11   Informal criteria for choosing a favorite published book
for the portfolio: a shared writing in February in Nancy Johnston's first-grade class*

My Favorite Published Book   DRAFT

- The illustrations go with the words and the story.
- The illustrations are neat and colorful and fill up the page.
- My published book means the most to me because

  1. I put the most throught into it.
  2. It has adventures.
  3. It's about sports or animals.
  4. I had a trip in it.
  5. It's my first published book.

- It's the first book I could read.
- The sentences make sense.
- I used great words.
- People's comments (at the back of the book) are special to me.

After about five years of this experimentation, many parents were totally confused (as were some teachers), and it was clear we needed consensus and consistency.

In addition to meeting with teachers (at grade levels and across grade levels) to determine a common reporting system, we also sought comments from parents. Under the leadership of principal Rosemary Weltman, the language arts support group at one of the district schools held an hour-long meeting before school one day at which parents were asked, *What would you like to see in a reporting system?* Fifty concerned parents showed up.

We learned that most of these parents loved and valued student-led conferences. Most felt they had never before learned so much about what was going on in their child's school life. They commented on the pride, confidence, and enthusiasm with which their son or daughter talked knowledgeably about his or her own learning. They spoke of the rapport they witnessed between their child and the teacher. They spoke of the value of the portfolio for understanding what students were actually doing and learning. Several parents of kindergartners mentioned how impressed they were that their child not only could set learning goals but also understood goal setting.

One parent aptly stated, "I always thought of assessment as a way for the teacher and parent to improve learning. Now, I'm seeing that student-led conferences help students understand the 'why' of learning and assessment. I used to ask, 'Why did you get a C?' and my son would answer, 'I don't know.' Now he can talk about his own learning."

We also learned how important it is not only to set goals at a conference but to have an action plan. As one parent put it, "My fourth grader has figured out what he needs to say to make everyone happy, and his teacher will go away smiling. Kids learn to play the game and say, 'I'll work harder.' But, often, that means nothing."

We discovered parents still wanted a traditional checklist of grade-level benchmarks.

As one parent said, "I use the checklist as a road map so I can fill in the gaps at home." And most still wanted grades "so you know how your child is doing in the district."

So, finally, after years of reading, studying, discussing, brainstorming, struggling, and debating, we came to a reporting system that currently includes:

- A checklist of "key indicators" that align with our course of study in each subject area
- Narrative comments by the teacher that support the checklist
- A portfolio of required "common tools" (see below) and student-selected work that provides evidence that supports the checklist and narrative

We moved from reporting to parents four times a year to trimesters and from optional student participation in a parent-teacher conference to required student participation in at least one conference. It has taken almost a decade to get our present system in place, and there are still many glitches—far too many indicators, language that confuses parents, too much teacher time required, the never ending "grades" issue. As is true for all teaching, we are still "in process."

Common Tools for Reading and Writing

Several years ago, portfolio expert Sheila Valencia spent several days working with a group of K–4 teachers in our district. Her description of "common tools" fit well with our desire to have student portfolios include district requirements as well as student selections: "Common tools are specific, agreed-upon assessment tasks and techniques designed to assess specific student learning outcomes. They are intended to add consistency and focus to the portfolio, and, as such, they help teachers with instructional decisions and student evaluation" (Valencia 1998, 43–44). Common tools are used on a predictable schedule and are common to all students at a grade level.

Common tools addressed our problem of inconsistency with portfolios and assessment. Because we lacked common tools as well as district guidelines, portfolios and assessment varied from teacher to teacher. With common tools, the uniform use of portfolios in grades K–4 finally became a districtwide reality, to the great relief of teachers, parents, and administrators. Now everyone can count on seeing certain common anchors, which are linked to categories on our report card. Perhaps most important, the common tools are closely aligned with our language arts course of study. And we can also use them to meet state assessment requirements.

To develop our common tools, grade-level representatives met for an entire school year, and a larger committee then refined these suggestions during a weeklong work session the following summer (see pages 535–536). Our common tools include assessments in phonics, spelling, reading, and writing. While all common tools are required, only some are standardized. Each K–4 teacher has a complete assessment notebook that includes the common tools for each of the grade levels. (See Appendix I for some explanations, directions, and examples.) Notice how one first-grade teacher expanded on the required phonics assessment (a dictated sentence containing thirty-seven "sounds" [Clay 1993]) and created an opportunity to effectively communicate with parents on their child's progress. See Figure 15-12.

Photo 15–1   Teachers reviewing common tools work at a language arts support group

Figure 15–12   A first grader's fall and spring dictation: "Hearing and recording sounds and words"; a "spec sheet" for parents on what to look for

September dictation:

The bus is coming it will stop ere to let me get on
Thebs kershtlmti

April dictation:

The busiscomeing itlllwlle
stopher tolatme gaton
Peter
4/11/96

Writing Checklist for Parents

As you compare your child's sentence dictation from the beginning of the year to the current sample, please look for changes in the following areas:

- Spacing between words
- Neatness of printing
- Use of lowercase letters
- Matching beginning sounds to letters
- Matching ending sounds to letters
- Use of vowels
- Capitalization
- Use of periods
- Number of conventionally spelled words

  Praise your child on the areas s/he has developed and look to see where your child may need more guidance and practice.

Nancy Johnston 1995–96

A Brief Summary of Our Common Tools

Kindergarten

- A *self-portrait and name sample* in the fall
- *Unassisted journal writing sample* in the winter and spring

Grades 1–4

- *Letter identification and phonics assessment* (grade one only)
- A *writing prompt* (see pages 227–229) in the fall and spring
- A *record of books read and a reading reflection* in the fall and spring (grades two, three, and four only)
- A *benchmark book assessment* (see Appendix I-8) and an oral retelling (see page 595)
- A *spelling inventory* selected from our core words lists (see page 426) in the fall and spring
- A *letter to next year's teacher* (see page 335)

All of the common tools, plus samples the student chooses from across the curriculum, become part of the student's portfolio.

You will want to have your own conversations to determine what is needed and appropriate for students in your school and district. There is no definitive list of assessments and benchmarks to use. (A benchmark, by the way, is an agreed-on reference point whereby the student demonstrates acquisition of the achievement objective. It is a standard of performance that is accessible to students and parents.)

The conversations in our district continue. We are still very much in process and consider our document a "working draft." For example, while we have selected several benchmark books for each grade level, they are all fiction. We need to add other genres such as nonfiction and poetry as well as new fiction with which students are unfamiliar.

Writing Narratives for the Report Card

When narratives became part of our report cards, Bernice Stokes, our director of elementary education, scheduled a professional development meeting so teachers could learn how to write quality narratives. Mostly, we collaborated at grade levels to write meaningful, pertinent comments that described the particular learner as opposed to general comments like "making good progress in reading." We referred to a literacy profile (Griffin, Smith, and Burrill 1995) and suggestions from Tara Azwell and Kathy Egawa (in Azwell and Schmarr 1995) to guide us. In writing these narratives, teachers worked hard to base their comments on anecdotal records, student performance, writing samples, reading records, running records, and retellings (to name several assessment contexts).

However, in spite of continuing efforts to do better, we're still failing to communicate what parents say they need to know. Kindergarten teacher Karen Sher tells how she sent home a five-page narrative the night before a parent-student-teacher conference only to be asked first thing the next day, "So, exactly what is Terry doing?" Other teachers spend entire weekends and weeks of weekday evenings writing report cards. That enormous time expenditure is of questionable value, especially when a conference is also held. As one exhausted teacher said, "I feel like I'm always out of breath. There needs to be two of me. It takes one hour to do each report card, and it still doesn't match the way we teach."

Student-Led Conferences

Many teachers in our district began holding student-led conferences after a group of teachers had been pilot-testing them for a number of years (*Literacy at the Crossroads,* pages 153–163). While such conferences are not required in our district, triangular conferences are. That is, all students in grades K–4 must be present at least one conference during the school year even if the teacher leads it.

The biggest advantage of student-led conferences as part of the reporting process is that parents understand what their child is learning because the child can explain it, supported by the portfolio. These conferences demonstrate what understanding looks like, especially if students "perform"—by working out a math problem or writing and then explaining the work and process, for example. At their best, student-led conferences connect curriculum, instruction, and assessment. Parents see the relationship between the teacher and student (by the same token, the teacher sees the interactions between parent and student), witness the child's ability to verbalize and explain his or her learning, and participate (with the teacher and their child) in jointly establishing workable goals and an action plan (see Figure 15-13 on page 580). See the resources for "Student-Led Conferencing" in The Blue Pages for guidelines for using such conferences with your own students.

So, if student-led conferences are so terrific, why isn't everyone doing them? They take a lot of time (most teachers find that a quality conference takes at least forty-five minutes), planning, and work on the part of students and teachers. They require a committed administrator and a flexible teachers union that allows teachers to "trade time."

Student-led conferences also need to be clearly explained to parents, since they cut down on the "alone time" parents have with their child's teacher. Some parents object when the teacher relinquishes control; they still want to know what the teacher thinks. Some teachers also feel uncomfortable using student-led conferences exclusively. They want a separate conference with parents in which to forge a true partnership.

Nonetheless, in my experience, when teachers abandon student-led conferences, it isn't because they don't value them. In most cases, they just get tired of volunteering so much extra time. Some teachers have tried to reduce the time involved by:

- *Scheduling a number of conferences at the same time,* then moving from conference to conference to see how they're going, assisting as necessary.

- *Setting up "stations"* and having families move from one activity to another (see Figure 15-14 on page 581 and Photo 15-2 on page 582).

- *Scheduling four conferences every hour,* meeting with each student-parent group for fifteen minutes to discuss the student's progress and set goals together.

- *Sending home the portfolio before the conference* Teachers that do this include guidelines for viewing and responding to the portfolio.

- *Scheduling spring "open house" as a portfolio evening* Students come with their families and share their portfolios.

Figure 15–13   An action plan from a fourth-grade student-led conference

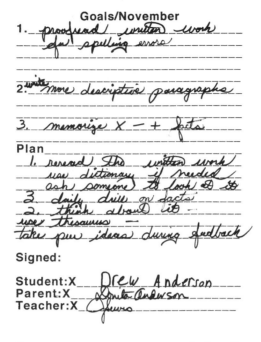

Having students and parents come twenty minutes before their scheduled
conference Parents, with their child, preview the portfolio ahead of time and jot down
questions.

- *Meeting ahead of time with those parents who have concerns* Then the parent is
ready for a "celebration of learning" and goal-setting conference with his child.

As many as six families might be in the room at the same time during these conferences. Students share portfolios and explain their work. Usually, there is a preset agenda
(see Figure 15-15 on page 582). The teacher moves around the room and gently monitors what's going on, sometimes joining a conference to listen in or add comments. Second-grade teacher Loretta Martin conducts this kind of conference in the fall, then she
meets with the parents in the spring. But what I love best about Loretta's approach to reporting is her written and verbal invitation to parents to come see their child's learning as
part of the everyday life of the literacy classroom.

Student-Led Conferences in Kindergarten

It is March and I sit in on a group of student-led conferences in Christine Hoegler's
kindergarten class. It is 8:00 A.M. and four families have arrived. There are four stations
in the room—journal writing, math, reading aloud, and teacher conference. The child
and parents move from station to station every fifteen minutes (Christine sounds a gentle
bell). Each station has enlarged-print directions for parents in full view as students show
their parents what they know (see Figure 15-14).

Figure 15–14 Kindergarten stations for student-led conferences

Station One: Read Aloud

At this station, your child will share class big books and some of our class-made big book variations. Things to look for at this station:

- Does you child attend to the print or is s/he focused on the picture as s/he shares the story?
- Is your child using their reading finger to point to words as s/he shares the text?
- Does the spoken word match the text or is your child telling the story in his/her own words?
- Notice the strategies that your child is using to decode unknown words: Does s/he look at the picture, initiate beginning sounds, self-correct, and reread for meaning?

Remember your role is not to correct your child's reading but to recognize and praise some of the beginning literacy strategies that you see your child using.

Station Two: Math: Concept of Number

At this station, your child will teach you how to play two games that develop an understanding of number combinations of a given quantity. The first game involves shaking beans out of a cup and comparing color combinations. The second game involves making designs with pattern blocks using two shapes. Your child will look for number arrangements within their design. Things to look for at this station:

- Can your child verbalize the number combination s/he has made from beans or the pattern block design?
- Does your child stick with the given quantity?

Your role at this station is to learn how to play these games. Take turns with your child with each game. Your child should be the one to verbalize the number combinations.

If you finish with time left, have your child teach you to play the shape game called "Trapezoid Cover-Up."

Station Three: Journal

At this station, your child will write in his/her journal. Things to look for at this station:

- Listen to hear your child associate sounds with letters while s/he writes.
- Watch if your child is using their spacer and how s/he uses it.
- Does your child's writing make sense?
- Does your child use words found in the environment to help spell words correctly?
- Does the picture match the text?

Your role at this station is to observe your child in the act of independent writing. Please do not help your child with sounds or to spell words correctly.

The reading aloud station contains piles of books—familiar favorites (such as *Brown Bear, Brown Bear* and *Mrs. Wishy-Washy*), class-made books, and big books. I observe Kenesha read to her mother proudly and listen as Kenesha's mother prompts and praises her.

At the journal writing station, Keith rereads former journal entries to his parents, pointing to each word as they proudly look on. Then Keith writes a new entry in front of them. Using the posted directions, his parents give him the same kind of support his

Photo 15–2   Parents and student at a kindergarten journal writing station

Figure 15–15   Agenda from a second-grade student-led conference

Isabel

My Conference

Reading:
① Share assessment folder.
② Reading Log.
③ Read.

Writing:
① Writing folder
②. Journal
③ Weekend News.

Spelling:
① Spelling folder
② Have-a-go pad.

Math:
① Math Journal
② Math assessment
③ Geoboard
Science/Social Studies/Health
① Chemistry folder
② Healthy snack

teacher does: "Where could you find the word *tomorrow*?" Keith looks up at the word board, walks over to it, removes the *tomorrow* word card, and copies the word correctly into his journal.

Kara and her parents are at the conference station. Christine notes Kara's strengths and what's going well. Then they all look at the new entry Kara has just written at the journal writing station and at a book review of *I Know an Old Lady Who Swallowed a Fly* (1997) she wrote recently. Afterward Christine suggests that Kara draw a picture in her journal while Christine meets with Kara's parents privately. Parents and kids alike value these conferences highly (see Figure 15–16).

Figure 15–16   Parent's evaluation of a kindergarten student-led conference

> I always find it so helpful in improving my instruction and assessment practices, to hear your reactions to our conferences. Please take a few minutes to complete the question below. Thank you in advance for taking the time to help me improve my teaching.

The spring Student Led Conference was . . . Great!

It was really wonderful to see Michael in action. He has learned a great deal.

During the conference my child was . . .

Excited – confident and proud of his accomplishments. He was eager to show me everything

What did you gain from the student led conference?

The process – all they go through to learn reading and writing and math

What changes would you make to the student led conference, if any?

I wouldn't make any changes. You were very organized and it showed the parents how much their children have learned.

Thank you –

Lisa Henry

Framework for a Student-Led Conference

While many kindergarten, grade one, and grade two teachers like having simultaneous conferences, many teachers of older grades prefer one conference at a time. The success of student-led conferences depends on doing a number of things:

• *__Plan ahead.__* Set a time line into motion a few months before that itemizes what you and your students need to do to prepare (complete reading and writing assessments and self-evaluations, select and organize work for the portfolio, send a letter to parents notifying them of the upcoming conference and their role in it).

• *__Set a tentative agenda.__*   With your students, negotiate what will take place at the conference.

• *__Prepare for the conference.__*   Show students a videotape of a conference and discuss it, or choose a student and role-play one. Give each student an opportunity to rehearse with and receive feedback from a peer. Coach the students who need more assistance.

• ***Follow the agenda during the conference.*** Often, students have a separate folder of work for each area of the curriculum. While the student leads the conference and explains his or her work and progress, parents ask questions for clarification and converse with their child. The teacher mostly listens and prompts but, because most parents want this, often gives some input after each subject area.

• ***Set goals.*** Use the last ten minutes of the conference to review what has been accomplished and jointly set goals.

• At the conference, or in school the next day, ***make an action plan*** to achieve these goals. The student, the teacher, and the parents all sign this action plan.

In preparation for the student-led conference, Joan Servis' fourth graders write tentative goals and an action plan. Joan guides her students to be sure their goals and plan are realistic. Quite often, parents want to add to or change the goals and plan. Joan writes the agreed upon revised goals and plan of action right in front of the student and parents at the conference, and everyone signs it. (See Figure 15-13 on page 580.)

DEALING WITH STANDARDS

Many of us are confused by the standards movement and with good reason. We've been bombarded by so much information, jargon, and rhetoric that it's very difficult to make sense of it all. I admit to being as confused as anyone else. In fact, it was only through writing this section based on the preparatory reading I did that I worked out many of my misunderstandings.

Standards are here to stay, so we need to understand what they are, what their potential is, and how best to deal with them. As we do with all important issues in education, we need to be knowledgeable—for our own sake, for the sake of our students, and (very important) to be able to communicate intelligently and effectively with parents and the public.

What Are Standards?

Standards define and describe the knowledge we expect *all* students to learn and the skills at which they need to be proficient. High-quality knowledge and performance standards deal with things that are important for students to learn, are meaningful for today's world, are specific and clear, and are attainable by all students (National Education Goals Panel 1996, 11).

In principle, quality standards promote higher expectations, deeper understanding, better performance, equity, and accountability—all noble goals. We cannot continue our present course in which great numbers of students achieve only minimum competence. Our democracy is founded on the belief that all students deserve and require a quality education. Furthermore, to compete in today's global economy requires a fully educated citizenry—one that knows how to find and use information and is able to solve problems independently, work collaboratively, and think critically. And parents and society have the right to know how students are performing and how they measure up.

Presently, just about every state has developed or is developing standards in a effort to raise the educational bar. In addition, voluntary national standards now exist in almost all disciplines. While these standards specify *what* is to be learned, *how* content is implemented and taught is meant to be left up to local school districts. Schools and districts use state and national standards as a guide for designing curriculum and determining what processes, skills, and strategies students will need to understand content.

What Do We Hope Standards Will Achieve?

"The true measure of whether or not standards are any good is whether or not kids are learning more" (Pimentel and Arsht 1998, 40). This is ultimately what standards are all about: How can we ensure that all students are learning? Does their demonstration of their learning measure up? In other words, based on the standards we set, are they doing well enough?

Academic standards (when rigorous and well written) have the following benefits (Joftus and Whitney 1998, 28, 32):

- They set clear, high expectations for student achievement.
- They provide a basis for holding students, educators, schools, and districts accountable.
- They promote educational equity by demanding that all students achieve at high levels.
- They guide efforts to measure student achievement, improve teacher training, develop more effective curricula and instructional strategies, and design school systems most conducive to learning.

I see other potential benefits. Thoughtfully conceived and constructed standards:

- Start conversations in schools, districts, and communities about what is worth knowing, understanding, and doing
- Can be used to set common, agreed-on learning outcomes and "benchmarks for success" that support a coherent program of instruction (For example, the way my school district's common tools set our standards for reading and writing.)
- Provide specific criteria for excellent work, along with sample papers, projects, and demonstrations (videos, for example) that meet those criteria
- Let students and families clearly understand what it is they are to write, perform, do, master
- Provide supports and resources so students can produce or perform to the standard(s)
- Provide resources to support and promote professional development
- Talk about learning and assessment in a common language that is clear to students, parents, teachers, administrators, and community members
- Help us monitor and analyze student progress

- Help low achievers meet success
- Make all of us work harder to ensure that all students receive whatever it takes for them to meet success at the grade level—early intervention, longer school days, summer school, adequate and well-educated support staff, multidimensional teaching and assessment strategies

The Standards Downfall

Unfortunately, we have a long way to go before present standards have a major impact on student achievement. Much of what's happening at present is cosmetic. That is, while there are lots of standards documents in place, there's little evidence that standards themselves are raising student performance levels in ways that involve deep and enduring understanding.

The Standards Are Not Equitable

While current standards are written for all students, equity is a major problem. All kids are expected to meet the standards. Yet all kids are not created equal, nor do they have equal access to the opportunities that enable school success.

If we truly espouse high standards for all, then our country must be willing to spend large sums of money to that end. Most poor and urban districts, which typically have large numbers of low-performing students, do not have equal access to the resources and quality teachers needed to provide the learning experiences the standards demand (Joftus and Whitney 1998, 28). And students who struggle with English as a second language are automatically penalized for their lack of fluency. Unless we as a nation provide the school and the district with the necessary resources (adequate funding, excellent books and libraries, quality textbooks and instructional materials, attractive and well-maintained physical spaces, up-to-date technology, small class sizes, qualified teachers, professional development for teachers) needed to ensure that all students receive an education that meets the standards, we are punishing many schools and students by holding them accountable for higher standards while failing to support them. "For tens of thousands of urban youngsters, it's a kind of double jeopardy: The system failed to educate them adequately, and now it punishes them for not being educated" (Wolk 1998, 48).

The Standards Are Not Rigorous

Also, most standards today are not strong enough, clear enough, or rigorous enough for their benefits to materialize. They don't make sense to teachers, parents, or students. When a group of experts from the fields of English, history, geography, mathematics, and science examined state standards recently, their main conclusion was that most state standards are not strong enough academically "to bear the considerable burden now being placed on them." One major problem is that instead of focusing on the knowledge and understanding that is most important in each discipline, there is an overfocus on skills and facts in isolation. Another big concern is the erroneous push for specific methodology. "Many states wrote standards of teaching rather than standards of learning." That is, states emphasized the how of teaching rather than designing standards that are broad enough to leave specific curriculum and instructional decisions at the local level. "Standards, if done right, should not standardize what happens within schools. Rather, they should free the schools from top-down dictates while obliging them to focus on results" (Finn, Petrilli, and Vanourek 1998, 39 and 56.)

The Standards Are Difficult to Use

Besides being vague and incomplete, most state standards are also difficult to use. They are mostly content standards, not performance standards. That is, they may spell out what it is students should know, but there is little guidance on how to assess whether or not a student meets the standard. In a performance assessment, students create or do something that demonstrates their understanding (as opposed to selecting a right answer on a commercial test). It is performance standards that "enable teachers, students, and parents to judge whether a particular piece of student work actually meets the standard" (Tucker and Codding 1998, 56).

Performance standards include:

- A succinct description of what students must know and be able to do (that's the content standard)
- Samples of student work to create a vivid image of what kind of work meets the standards
- Commentaries on those samples that explain the features that cause them to meet the standards

So, while the best state standards may be helpful, they are not really usable in a productive way until all the stakeholders—students, teachers, parents, community members—not only understand what students need to learn and do but also can determine how they are progressing and what concepts, skills, and strategies they still need to learn to meet the standards. "Including samples of student work is the key to making the standard usable by teachers, children, and parents. Any student should be able to look at a performance standard and say, 'I understand now. I can learn how to do that'" (Tucker and Codding 1998, 56).

The Standards Don't Lead to an Inquiry Curriculum

Another major roadblock is that "standards and newer assessments assume that students will demonstrate complex thinking, deeper understanding, and sophisticated performance" (Erickson 1998, vii). Yet such worthy outcomes require educators who know how to design and implement a concept-based inquiry curriculum that leads to achievement of the standards. Students cannot be expected to test well in problem solving, responding to open-ended questions, and reading and writing analytically until we teachers demonstrate and teach for such in-depth analysis and understanding. "Only by framing our teaching around valued questions and worthy performances can we overcome activity-based and coverage-oriented instruction" (Wiggins and McTighe 1998, 27).

TESTING AND STANDARDS

Standards have led to an enormous investment of time and materials devoted to testing. And in too many cases, this translates to a fixation on "skills." It is now the norm in schools across the country for teachers to focus not on teaching and learning essential concepts but on having students pass tests designed to measure whether standards are being met. Yet "there is no evidence that testing and preparation for tests helps to develop literacy" (Krashen 1998, 444).

Using Standardized Tests: Mixed Messages

Some second- and third-grade teachers in our district say they are very upset at being required to administer standardized tests in the fall. Parents overvalue these scores, and the tests measure kids in a totally different way from how we teach them. One teacher unhappily notes that some of her proficient second-grade readers don't do well on the test.

Testing drives instruction, no doubt about it. I walk into a second-grade classroom and see students correcting punctuation on a worksheet. The classroom is that of a strong writing teacher whose students do lots of editing in the course of daily writing and regular publishing. But she has been sobered by the disappointing results of some of her former students on the standardized test given in third grade in the fall, so she is preparing her students for a task they need to be able to perform in order to do well on the test. We don't teach skills in isolation, but we use an assessment that asks kids to be proficient on skills exercises. What a mixed message we send to parents. On the one hand, we say, *Don't worry about the test. We don't teach that way.* On the other hand, we use the test to identify low-performing students.

High-Stakes Testing: Major Concerns

The mania for test results is understandable. The stakes are perilously high. Test scores are routinely published in newspapers and impact real estate values as well as school standing. School district reputations rise and fall on the basis of test scores. Schools can be put on probation by a state for poor scores. In some cases, poor test results can lead to state monitoring and the removal of principals and teachers (Hartocollis 1998). In other states, if scores don't go up, the district doesn't get funding.

No wonder teachers and students panic about not being able to "measure up." In my state, Ohio, the first state "proficiency" testing comes each school year in the spring of fourth grade. Teachers and schools devote months to test preparation, so much time, in fact, that some teachers complain that they are not teaching much else. Teachers everywhere know firsthand that what gets tested is what gets taught. "If a test measures some things in a broad subject area, and the teacher teaches to the test, rather than to the broad domain, you end up with high scores on the test rather than if there was a fair representation of their knowledge of the domain" (Monty Neill, director of the National Center for Fair and Open Testing, in Henry 1998).

Testing is appealing because it looks objective to the public and appears to provide answers to how students are doing in our schools. However, it is still true that income and family background have more to do with high test scores than any other factors.

> The S.A.T.'s ability to predict success in college is questionable. At best, the scores are 25 percent accurate when it comes to predicting the variation in first-year college grades, and they have not been shown to predict whether someone will graduate from college. The test does correlate highly to parents' income and educational level. (Garcia 1997)

Thus, test scores reflect the opportunities and learning experiences students have had, making it critical that low-achieving students also receive equal and excellent opportunities, not the isolated skills instruction that is so typical of their education (Coles 1998).

Additionally, test results are often misinterpreted and overgeneralized. For example, long-term NAEP data show that the average scores on reading achievement in the United States for nine-, thirteen-, and seventeen-year-olds have changed little between 1971 and 1996. Over 90 percent of our students can read at the literal level. Yet many people in politics and the media say that 40 percent "can't read." These 40 percent *can* read at basic levels, but they—and the great majority of students—are not meeting higher standards that indicate a command of challenging subject matter and high-level thinking. Most educators and the public are unaware that NAEP ratings of "basic" and "proficient" are arbitrarily set. There is no clear description or agreement on what constitutes "basic" in terms of skills. Rather, it's a cutoff score improperly equated with an array of skills. (For useful information on "high-stakes assessments in reading," contact the International Reading Association for its position statement.)

Even when tests are constructed to include higher-level thinking, we must be cautious about the conclusions we draw and how we use the scores. For one thing, the level of test anxiety greatly impacts performance. For another, problem solving on a test cannot be equated with problem-solving ability. *"There is virtually no systematic evidence that the quality and level of problem solving in test situations is at all highly correlated with level and quality of problem solving in naturally occurring (that is, noncontrived) situations"* (Sarason 1998, 79, italics the author's.)

The Hope of Standardized Tests

Standardized tests, if they are well constructed to assess what is truly worth knowing and understanding, can improve instruction and learning. For example, Ohio's state proficiency test in science tests concepts rather than facts. This focus provided the impetus for learning how to teach science in depth and for understanding—and aligning our curriculum with—those standards. Or again, our district's teacher-designed standardized reading assessments (for grades 1–4) have improved instruction and learning (see pages 593–599).

Teaching to such a test can be a positive thing *as long as* we continually provide all students the demonstrations, strategies, resources, support, and specific feedback they need to gain that knowledge and understanding. Standardized tests—when we do employ them—need to be supported by portfolios, performance-based assessments, open-ended questions, teacher observations, and self-assessments based not only on work samples but also on interests, motivation, and attitudes about learning.

We need to keep test scores in perspective. Even when tests deemphasize multiple-choice responses, they are only a single, limited indicator of ability. A standardized test does not measure performance over time, perseverance, motivation to succeed, leadership skills, imaginativeness, curiosity, effort, interpersonal skills, or maturity—all necessary attributes that may, in fact, be a far better predictor for success in school, work, and life. "Conventional test scores have long been known to be uninformative about cognitive and personality variables (interests, motivations, hobbies, idiosyncrasies)" (Sarason 1998, 77).

Once again—but important enough to be restated—since test scores mostly reflect the opportunities students have had, we need to level the playing field. As all teachers and parents know, test results can be used unfairly to judge the quality of a school, to label and sort kids, and to plan programs of remediation. Only high-quality education for all students and multiple methods of assessment yield fair information of what students know and are able to do.

Looking Carefully at Tests

American students are the most tested students in the world, and it doesn't look like that distinction is going change any time soon. Our testing mania is ironic, because if testing were the means to higher achievement, we'd be the top-achieving country. Since we live in a culture where testing is highly valued, we need to be proactive and vocal in being sure that the tests being used are good ones.

Noted professor, educator, and writer Howard Gardner (1998) says that with any proposed test, he always asks four questions:

- Does the test focus on something that is indisputably important?
- Does it test the desired skill directly, or does it use other methods as an index of the student's proficiency (for example, testing students' "writing ability" by asking them to choose the best-written of four sample passages)?
- Are teachers prepared to help students acquire the required skills, and do they have the necessary resources?
- Could students who do well on this test do well on a different sort of exam that presumably tests the same skill?

The first question is especially important. Is the test sampling a meaningful component of the curriculum, something essential for students to be learning? If not, we are wasting a lot of time in schools preparing students for a test instead of preparing them for lifetime literacy.

Smart Ways to Deal with Standards and Testing

Below are some practical ways to deal intelligently and realistically with standards and testing. All of them depend on ongoing professional development and strong, well-informed teachers and administrators. There is no shortcut; we must be willing to take the time to bring standards to life in a way that respects the needs and interests of students while promoting inquiry and high-level learning. Otherwise, the best-conceived standards will have little impact. "Standards—and the curricula tied to them—take on life only when teachers work with them through judging student work, debating what meeting the standards looks like, and hardest of all, figuring out what to do to get students to meet the standards" (David and Shields 1999).

• ***Start Conversations in Your Own School and District.*** A good starting point with state and national standards is to begin local conversations about what we want students to know and do. Set aside time to read, meet, and discuss and then write standards that match your beliefs and fit within national and state guidelines. In my school district, state standards and requirements led us to form a K–12 language arts committee that met over five years to develop a language arts framework that supported our district's and community's beliefs and goals and that aligned with state standards. Those districtwide conversations with teachers across all grade levels were a first and led to a cohesive, workable curriculum. We determined a logical progression of knowledge and skills that builds on a foundation of standards and benchmarks established in the early grades. (See *Literacy at the Crossroads*, pages 55–62, for a description of our committee/change process.)

We were fortunate that our state standards for language arts were rigorous, developmentally appropriate, and an excellent model for thinking about learning and teaching. The state standards helped us focus on curriculum objectives and materials and to match assessment with our new framework. One of our goals was to be specific enough to guide learning for understanding, but not so specific and detailed that instruction would be reduced to a narrow focus on discrete skills. However, determining the standards was just the beginning. The translation of standards into rigorous classroom practice followed by improved student outcomes continues to be a long, slow process.

Frankly, we didn't always know how well the kids were learning in our district—an important goal of well-thought-out standards—until we designed relevant assessments that aligned with our language arts framework. Pages 593–599 tell how we developed assessments that aligned with what we expected students to know and do and matched the way we were teaching.

• ***Make Sure You Understand, Can Explain, and Put into Practice What You Mean by Good Standards.*** This is just good teaching. Basically, three factors intersect:

- What do we want students to know and be able to do?
- What resources and support will they need?
- How will we/they know when and what they know?

It's very important to ensure that all necessary resources are available to help all students learn. While we develop one set of standards for all students, some students will need lots of support to meet those standards.

• ***Do Some Professional Reading to Increase Your Understanding of Standards and Testing.*** It's hard to create good standards and tests until you understand what good ones look like and how they can be used to improve instruction and learning. See the assessment and evaluation resources listed in The Blue Pages. Select one or more to read and discuss with colleagues.

• ***Write Standards That Have the Potential to Improve Instruction and Learning.*** As stated earlier, Tucker and Codding (1998, 49–50) provide a useful format for creating exemplary standards:

1. *Performance descriptions*   A performance description is a succinct narrative statement of what students are expected to know and be able to do that describes what is most essential to learn in each discipline.
2. *Samples of student work*   Examples of actual student work are matched to the performance descriptions to provide a vivid image of what it actually takes to meet the standard.
3. *Commentaries on the student work*   These commentaries draw attention to the features of the student work that meet the standard and state why the expert graders made that judgment. In this way, the reader comes to understand exactly what it takes to meet the standard.

• ***Communicate Clearly with Families and Community Members.***   The growing trend of publishing test scores in newspapers and ranking and rating districts by those scores is appalling. Such scores reflect a community's affluence (or lack of it) and parents' educational background far more than what's been taught in school. Be sure to read Popham's "Why Standardized Tests Don't Measure Educational Quality" and other standardized testing resources (see The Blue Pages) so you can explain—without being defensive—exactly what test scores do and do not mean.

• ***Design Standardized Assessments That Align with Your Beliefs, Curriculum, and Standards.***   Such assessments require a commitment from administrators who will provide release time for teachers to work together across a school district. Such work cannot be an add-on to our overloaded days but must be a regular part of them. In-house assessments that match our standards and the way we teach offer the best hope for connecting teaching, learning, and assessment. The conversations about teaching and learning that take place during this challenging work are as valuable, or more valuable, than the assessment documents that result.

• ***Connect Standards to Authentic Assessment in the Classroom.***   All standards (whether at the classroom level or mandated by the state) need to be interconnected with assessment. While most of us have little or no say about national and state standards, we can and must set relevant and challenging standards for our students in our schools and classrooms. While we may have no choice about giving a standardized test, we can make sure that our classroom-based assessment is meaningful. Additionally, we need to establish external benchmarks to determine whether or not students are meeting the standards as well as to ensure that these standards are rigorous enough—that is, that our students can perform as well as their counterparts elsewhere. Those performance benchmarks need not be represented on a commercial publisher's standardized test but they need to be clear, usable, and aligned with district standards.

Students, teachers, and parents need to know the criteria for a successful product or process up front, and they need to see examples of work that meets (and doesn't meet) the criteria. Rubrics, checklists, and samples of work that serve as exemplars can be helpful for setting realistic expectations and standards. We need to ensure that ongoing, authentic assessment is part of engaging, daily instruction that focuses on students' meaningful work.

According to Joan Herman (1997) meaningful alternative assessments:

- Ask students to create, design, produce, perform, or do something
- Tap complex thinking and/or problem solving
- Use tasks that are instructionally meaningful
- Invoke authentic real-world applications
- Are scored by people exercising judgment, rather than by machines

Moreover, students need to actively monitor, evaluate, and reflect on their work. Such self-assessment—tied to exemplars and criteria established prior to beginning a task—fosters independent learners who continually set new goals for learning. Because self-assessment is necessary for students to take control of their learning, much of this chapter has dealt with authentic assessment through portfolios, student-led conferences, and self-evaluations.

However, self-assessment is only effective if students clearly know and understand:

- What their goals are
- How to attain those goals—a workable plan with support as needed
- The skills and strategies needed to attain the goals
- How to check to see that they've reached the goals
- What to do if the goals have not been met

USING MANDATED READING
ASSESSMENT TO IMPROVE INSTRUCTION

Two years ago, my state, Ohio, required that school districts test all primary-grade students in reading at the end of grades one, two, and three, and furthermore, identify those students reading below grade level. The state also required school districts to notify parents of struggling students and to offer intervention services. While this Ohio state assessment mandate requires a standardized test, it does not dictate that we use a commercially published one. *Standardized* simply means that all students must receive the same assessment, under the same conditions, at the same time. Procedures and scoring are standardized; that is, directions must be scripted to ensure they are exactly the same for everyone, and criteria for passing must be clear, explicit, and known ahead of time.

Accordingly, rather than respond with dismay to this new testing mandate, my colleagues and I seize it as an opportunity to improve assessment, instruction, and learning. In a school system where teachers are used to "doing their own thing," the mandate enables us to implement appropriate standardized testing, provide some consistency with assessment, and impose needed professional development. Indeed some teachers are relieved at this requirement because, as several note with frustration, "Nobody holds us accountable." Finally, we will have consistency. Others recognize another key advantage: at the end of each grade, parents will now receive clear documentation of their child's reading record and ability. Such documentation will eliminate the devastating surprise some parents receive when, after years of being told their children are "doing fine," eventually discover otherwise. The state assessment will enable parents and teachers to work together to identify struggling readers early on and offer the thoughtful, substantive instructional support that enable all children to become successful readers.

The state mandate offers yet another advantage: teachers are already devoting much time to the standards requirements—collecting and documenting the benchmarks that each child is expected to meet. While such monitoring is laudatory, it consumes critical teaching and learning time. Now, as teachers respond to the new state assessment requirement, this time will be much better spent as a viable part of instruction and learning.

I approach Bernice Stokes, our director of elementary education, and offer to work with teachers to create our own standardized reading test that aligns with our teaching philosophy and practice. Years ago, we teachers devoted extraordinary time and effort to do away with standardized reading tests in first and second grades. There is no way we can go back to decontextualized assessment that does so little to inform our teaching and is unrelated to everything we know about how children learn to read and how best to teach them. We want an assessment that serves our multiple professional needs:

- Matches our curriculum and instruction
- Improves our teaching and learning
- Provides our various audiences with specific, detailed information about our reading instruction and its record of success—clear documentation that our teaching is helping our students become capable readers

Providing Staff Development

At the same time that we begin to develop standardized assessments and common tools (see Appendix I), we also institute professional development. Because our reading assessments (see Appendix I-8) will involve knowing how to administer and analyze running records and retellings, all K–4 teachers need to receive training and practice sessions in these techniques. (Up to this point, the training has been voluntary.) We offer a course consisting of three dinner sessions lasting from 4 to 7 P.M., which is taken by more than fifty K–4 teachers. Reading Recovery teacher leader Libby Larabee does two sessions on taking and analyzing running records (see page 112), then Libby and I do a joint session on retellings and taking an informal reading evaluation (see page 114). We spend part of this session listening to two taped retellings (while following the written transcript) and deciding whether or not the students "passed." Then the teachers, working in small groups by grade level, use a retelling worksheet to list the most important elements of a retelling on one or two of our benchmark book excerpts and to determine what the prompted questions might be. (See Appendix I-10.)

Learning How to Take Running Records

It has taken almost ten years for teachers to say they are ready and willing to learn how to take running records. In one of our buildings, Liz Schutter, the Reading Recovery teacher, spends six weeks demonstrating and coaching in our thirty-minute weekly support group. She uses the first two weeks to explain how to take a running record and the next two weeks to teach how to analyze a running record. The second to the last week she has teachers work in small groups analyzing and scoring a running record. For the final week teachers are asked to try a running record on a student and come back with questions and concerns. (Later in the year, our district also offers a course in how to take and analyze running records.)

Learning How to Use Retellings

In a retelling, the reader or listener tells orally or in writing what he remembers from a story or text. Librarians retell stories all the time, especially folktales and stories handed down through the oral tradition. Retelling is an excellent strategy for both evaluation and instruction. Before students can retell, they need to know how stories work and the main elements of a story. We cannot expect students to retell a story until we have taught them how and they have had lots of practice.

We start with oral retellings to emphasize speaking and listening and because written ones are more difficult, especially for students below grade three.

During a required staff meeting, I demonstrate how to do a retelling. The week before we had discussed an excellent chapter on retellings by Lesley Mandel Morrow (in Gambrell and Almasi 1996.) Morrow defines retellings and gives the research supporting their use for improving reading comprehension, especially for struggling readers. To follow up, I pass out handouts that give options for doing retellings. (See Figure 15-17 on page 596.) Then I do one myself, in front of about thirty teachers, much as I expect my colleagues to demonstrate to their students in their classrooms.

I use *Just Me and My Dad*, by Mercer Mayer (1977), which I found by browsing through the shelves in one of our school's book rooms. The book is entertaining, as well as short and predictable. I thought it would be easy to retell the story. It isn't. I had to read the book six or seven times before I could be confident I could retell it without forgetting anything. Interestingly enough, with each rereading I understand more. I especially notice details in the pictures that add to and change the meaning. I look and think about the expressions on the characters' faces. I focus more carefully on sequence. I practice out loud a few times and then check myself by looking quickly through the text and illustrations. After first sharing how difficult it was for me to retell this simple story and how much preparation had been involved, I read the book aloud to my colleagues and, in an expressive voice and in my own words, retell the story. After our discussion of retelling and my demonstration, I notice immediate and direct application to classrooms.

Practicing Retellings in the Classroom

When I work with students on retellings, I explain why we are learning how to retell—that it is an excellent way to become actively involved with a story and to increase our understanding. With very young students, taking the part of the character and role-playing with props aids retelling. A retelling done as a shared writing also helps students recall and understand stories. These retellings often become favorite texts for shared reading.

One day in Jennifer Shoda's second-grade classroom, she and I model retellings. First we talk about what a retelling is. Then I retell *Just Me and My Dad*, by Mercer

Figure 15–17   Some possible ways to involve students in retellings

Notes: Some Possible Ways to Involve Students in Retellings

Whole Class

- Listen to repeated readings of a story over several days. Use illustrations to point to key details. Create story map together first—list characters, settings, events. Do retelling as an interactive writing on chart paper. Use retold version as shared reading/big book/student book(s).
- After students are familiar with retellings, do a shared writing of possible prompts. Post in classroom.

Small Group

- Read story together several times in group. Retell story with support of pictures in book. Create a written retelling of familiar story. (Or, students tape their retelling, and teacher transcribes onto large chart paper with slight editing.)

Partner

- Interactive—retell story together taking turns and supporting each other.
- One retells; one prompts and assesses.

Drama

- Students do a Readers Theatre with a story or story part. "Perform" story several times reading text/script. When students are very familiar with story, they retell story orally without scripts.
- Use simple puppets or props to help retell story.

Tape Recording

- Use teacher tape as model.
- Have student tape self and assess by going through book while listening to self retelling.

Self-Assessment

- Students self-evaluate using agreed upon criteria or rubric.

Regie Routman, February 1998

Mayer, after reading it to them first. Then Jennifer retells *The Frog Price Revisited,* by Jon Sciezska, which she has read to the class four or five times over several weeks. The students prompt her when she has difficulty recalling. Afterward we construct a chart together (a "spec sheet," see page 577) that lists what we agree are the essential parts of a retelling:

- You need to speak clearly and expressively.
- You need to state the title and author.
- You need to give an introduction that includes the characters and setting.
- You need to list the important events in order.
- You need to include some important details.
- You need to say how the story ends.

We also agree that prompts like the following can be used and list them on another chart:

- What happened when/after . . . ?
- What else happened?
- Why did . . . ?
- Where . . . ?
- Who . . . ?

Next the students choose a partner to whom to retell *The Frog Prince Revisited*. First we talk about how being a careful listener is necessary and that you should let your partner finish the retelling without interruption unless he or she requests a prompt.

When I am in the classroom a few weeks later, Jennifer Shoda has just completed multiple readings of *Popcorn*, by Frank Asch. Each student is working with a partner, and each pair has a copy of the book. We review the charts we made earlier, and then the pairs take turns retelling the story. The listening partner pages through the book as the retelling partner speaks. We notice that because students know the story very well, they speak with expression and often quote certain words and phrases verbatim. The students say that their expressive voice "came later," after they got going and were more relaxed.

When I notice that some students are not using the language of storytelling, I guide the students in using familiar language to sequence and organize their retelling:

- Introduction—once upon a time . . . , one fall night. . . , once . . .
- What happened?—and then . . . , then . . . , next . . . , after that . . .
- Ending—finally . . . , the last thing that happened was . . .

The following week, students work with partners on a book both have chosen to retell. (See Photo 15-3.) Before they begin, we give them five minutes to review the book. We go over the evaluation form that each student will fill out. (See Appendix I-10.) After a student has finished retelling, his or her partner says what he or she did well and then notes areas for improvement. Clipboard in hand, each student fills out an evaluation for how his or her partner has done, and they set goals together. (See Figure 15-18 on page 598.)

Even first graders can retell, prompt each other, and evaluate themselves. In Joyce Pope's first-grade class, we read *Amazing Grace*, which the children know well, and we retell the story using shared writing. Then with a partner, students reread a familiar book and retell it to each other. First I coach a pair in front of the class and post guidelines:

- Tell what the story is about and who is in it.
- Tell the problem.
- What happens in the story?
- What happens next? after that?
- How does the story end?

Joyce makes and laminates bookmarks for each child with these guidelines on them, as a reference. With demonstrations and practice sessions, these students—like all our students—become proficient at retelling a story.

Now, when students are asked to retell as part of their standardized reading assessment, they are confidently doing a familiar task that has become integral to ongoing reading work in the classroom. Instruction and assessment go hand in hand.

Photo 15–3   Practicing retelling with a partner

Figure 15–18   A second-grade retelling evaluation by partner

Self-Evaluation of Retelling for Fiction

Name __Ralph_____ Date __4/20/98__

Name of Story _____Bully Trouble_____

___✓___ I gave the title and author.

___✓___ I began with the introduction.

___✓___ I told when and where the story took place.

___X___ I told the story in order.

___X___ I remembered all the important events.

___✓___ I told about all the important characters.

___✓___ I told some important details.

___✓___ I told how the story ended.

___X___ I used an expressive voice.

Goals: 1. Use expressive voice.
2. Rember important events
3. Tell the story in order.

By: Rob

Putting Mandated Assessment into Practice

Mandated assessments and standardized tests are facts of life in our schools. However, our experience in Ohio demonstrates that such mandates don't necessarily dictate the testing instruments. You may have a choice! Like us, you may be able to design your own assessment tools. Check with your state department of education, find out exactly what is required, and do whatever is legal and feasible to ensure testing that is fair, relevant, and useful to students and teachers.

Our development of common tools in reading—which includes standardized measures—would not have become a reality in our district without the Ohio state standardized testing mandate. While it took a year of hard work to create a satisfactory working draft, my colleagues and I found this work tremendously satisfying and significant. It was the first time we managed to align standardized testing with our beliefs and practices.

At first teachers complained about "all the time on assessment" they were spending. Eventually, most found that they could easily weave the reading assessment into the ongoing learning life of their classrooms. Assessment and evaluation as part of teaching—that enable teachers and children to learn more—make good sense and save time in the long run.

FINAL REFLECTIONS

Fostering a love of learning and desire to continue learning must not be hampered by testing. In the context of the rich, literacy classroom, it is possible and necessary to use assessment and evaluation so the learner and other important stake holders are well served. As professionals, we must be vigilant and outspoken to ensure that assessment practices are developmentally appropriate, humane, and meaningful. Use the recent NCTE resolution on "Testing and Equitable Treatment of Students" (see Appendix C-1) to support your beliefs and practices and to ensure that testing does not drive instruction.

With ongoing learning as our overarching goal, continuous self-assessment is necessary, not just for our students but for us teachers too. While the terms "assessment" and "evaluation" still make many of us uncomfortable, it is only by being well informed and engaging in continual professional conversations that we can boost our knowledge and improve teaching and learning.

CONTINUING THE CONVERSATION

- ***Write down your beliefs about assessment and evaluation.*** Do it without referring to this text or any other. Then, ask yourself,

  - If this is what I believe, how am I putting these beliefs into practice?
  - What can I change to make my evaluation process more effective, humane, and workable?
  - What are some ways I will know that my practices are effective for improving instruction and learning?

• *Work to ensure that your school and district testing practices are developmentally appropriate and fair to children.* This is no easy matter. With so much pressure for high test scores, inappropriate practices are rampant. Get together with your colleagues. Use the resources on pages 62b–65b to help you state your case.

• *Take a hard look at how your prepare students for high-stakes testing.* While it's absolutely necessary to prepare your students for tests, is your focus and time spent reasonable? Do students understand why and what they are being prepared for? See the test-taking resources on pages 62b–65b to increase your knowledge, guide your instruction, and help you communicate more intelligently with parents in this highly charged area.

• *Decide how you can adjust your daily teaching so that assessment is part of instruction and not separate from it.* The traditional school structure does not build in time for assessment or stress the importance of ongoing assessment. As we did, you may want to start a study group. (Many of us met for months through our language arts support group. Without those conversations, student-led conferences would never have become a reality.)

• *Make sure authentic classroom-based assessments are guiding your instruction and that such assessments have priority over standardized tests.* Be sure you are clearly communicating how and why you assess to the families of your students and how you use that assessment to inform instruction. Teacher assessment has been deemphasized and devalued in the media, so we need to be outspoken on the importance and value of classroom-based assessment.

• *Ask yourself, "Can students apply what they have learned to new contexts?"* Before students can apply what they have learned, they have to be able to problem solve, make judgments, recall and transfer information, and be aware of their thinking processes so that knowledge in one situation can be used to create new learning in another. Our instruction and assessment must encompass this high level of thinking if we are to equip our students to become lifelong learners.

Final
Reflections

Asking questions and inquiring lie at the heart of what it means to be a professional. One never "arrives" at a destination of "all knowing." Along with our successes and growing knowledge, we continue to observe, learn, collaborate and self-reflect as we extend and refine our knowledge and insights. Being fully professional means taking responsibility for such growth and change. My hope is that *Conversations* has become a part of your professional conversation; that it has inspired you to try things out and question, to consider and reconsider your own teaching and learning and to realize what is possible in your own school with your students. Only through becoming professional in every sense, not just in how we teach in the classroom but in how we lead our literacy lives, can we hope to reach all students and make a difference in our society.

Recently a teacher asked me, "Is this a political book?" While I did not set out to write a political book, education *is* political. Furthermore, we need to understand that *being political* means transcending the confines of the classroom and reaching out to the larger community as literacy leaders; it means writing and sending helpful newsletters to families, taking charge of your own professional development, knowing important current research about language learning, sharing what you know with your colleagues, understanding standards and standardized testing so you can make them work for students in your district and explain them to parents. It means speaking out and standing up for what you believe. So, yes, in that sense *Conversations* is a political book.

The pressures on us teachers have never been greater. The challenges of our diverse society are mirrored in our classrooms and demand we be as informed, compassionate, and knowledgeable as possible. As public expectations for more accountability and

601

tougher standards continue to grow, many of us feel constricted by standardized curriculums that increasingly demand test preparation as the number one priority. Only by being fully professional and informed can we surmount these difficult challenges. And again, building our professional knowledge base begins with conversation and personal inquiry.

It is human nature to dwell on our inadequacies and failures. Teaching is tough work. Focus on what's going well, what you admire and value, what you can improve upon and change. Have a positive mindset. This can be particularly difficult for new and inexperienced teachers. Watch specifically for positive interactions and events—shield yourself from the naysayers in your school. If you are feeling overwhelmed, start with what seems doable for you—such as shared reading and shared writing. Do less but in more depth. And don't forget to have some fun—don't forget your love of teaching, learning, and working with young minds that drew you to our profession in the first place.

When I was working with one earnest new teacher, he was so intent on getting the lesson "right" that he often failed to notice the eager young children in front of him. "Don't forget to breathe," I used to tease him. Teaching *is* serious business but it is about the joyful business of learning.

All offerings in *Conversations* are invitational. Just as I respect families and their cultures and firmly believe all kids can learn, I respect you as a learner and trust you to go on learning. Being a lifelong learner is not just about becoming a more effective teacher. My best loved teachers were also fascinating people with wide-ranging interests and stirring stories.

There is no formula for effective teaching. Continue to develop, observe, reflect upon and refine your own theory and practice. Make time for thinking, on your own and with your colleagues. Question everything—and relish the learning that results. Have the courage of your well-informed convictions. I wish you abundant success on your own professional learning journey.

WORKS CITED

Adams, Marilyn J. 1990. *Beginning to Read: Thinking and Learning About Print*. Cambridge, MA: MIT Press.

Allen, Janet, and Kyle Gonzalez. 1998. *There's Room for Me Here: Literacy Workshop in the Middle School*. York, ME: Stenhouse.

Allen, Linda. 1998. "An Integrated Strategies Approach: Making Word Identification Instruction Work for Beginning Readers." *The Reading Teacher* (November).

Allington, Richard. 1997. Balanced Reading Instruction. Speech given at the annual meeting of the International Reading Association, Atlanta, Georgia.

———. 1997. In *Building a Knowledge Base in Reading* by Jane Braunger and Jan Patricia Lewis. Portland, OR: Northwest Regional Educational Laboratory; Newark, DE: International Reading Association.

———. 1997. Speech given at the annual conference of the New England Reading Association. Hartford, Connecticut.

———. November 1998. personal communication.

Allington, Richard, and Haley Woodside-Jiron. 1997. "Thirty Years of Research . . . : When Is a Research Summary Not a Research Summary?" Albany, NY: National Research Center on English Learning and Achievement, SUNY–Albany.

———. 1998. "Decodable Text in Beginning Reading: Are Mandates and Policy Based on Research?" *ERS Spectrum: Journal of Research and Information* (Spring): 3–29.

Allington, Richard, et al. 1996. *The First R: Every Child's Right to Read*, edited by Michael F. Graves, Paul van den Broek, and Barbara M. Taylor. New York: Teachers College Press.

American Association for the Advancement of Science. 1993. *Benchmarks for Science Literacy. Project 2061*. New York: Oxford University Press.

American Association of School Librarians and Association for Educational Communications and Technology. 1998. *Information Power: Building Partnerships for Learning*. Chicago: American Library Association.

Anderson, Charles W., and Okhee Lee. 1997. "Will Students Take Advantage of Opportunities for Meaningful Science Learning?" *Phi Delta Kappan* (May): 720–724.

Anderson, Richard C., Paul T. Wilson, and Linda G. Fielding. 1988. "Growth in Reading and How Children Spend Their Time Outside of School." *Reading Research Quarterly* (Summer): 285–303.

Applebee, Arthur N. 1996. *Curriculum as Conversation: Transforming Traditions of Teaching and Learning*. Chicago: The University of Chicago Press.

Armstrong, Thomas. 1998. *Awakening Genius in the Classroom*. Alexandria, VA: Association for Supervision and Curriculum Development.

Association of American Medical Colleges, reported in *The Plain Dealer*, Cleveland, OH, December 1, 1996

Association for Supervision and Curriculum Development. 1997. *Education Update*. Alexandria, VA: Association for Supervision and Curriculum Development.

Atwell, Nancie. May 1997. New Bridges to Literacy. Conference session, Cleveland, Ohio.

———. 1998. *In the Middle: New Understandings About Writing, Reading, and Learning*. Portsmouth, NH: Boynton/Cook.

Ayres, Linda R. 1995. "Phonological Awareness Training of Kindergarten Children: Three Treatments and Their Effects." In *Reconsidering a Balanced Approach to Reading*, edited by Constance Weaver. Urbana, IL: National Council of Teachers of English. (1995 Ph.D. dissertation.)

Azwell, Tara, and Elizabeth Schmar. 1995. *Report Card on Report Cards: Alternatives to Consider*. Portsmouth, NH: Heinemann.

Babbitt, Natalie. 1990. "Protecting Children's Literature." *Horn Book Magazine* (November/December): 703.

Bamford, Rosemary A., and Janice V. Kristo, eds. 1998. *Making Facts Come Alive: Choosing Quality Nonfiction Literature K–8*. Norwood, MA: Christopher-Gordon.

Banks, James, et al. 1995. *Regions Near and Far: Social Studies for a Changing World.* New York: Macmillan/McGraw-Hill School Publishing.

Barth, Roland S. 1991. *Improving Schools from Within: Teachers, Parents, and Principals Can Make the Difference*. San Francisco: Jossey-Bass.

Bauer, Marion Dane. 1992. *What's Your Story? A Young Person's Guide to Writing Fiction*. New York: Clarion.

Baumann, James F., James V. Hoffman, Jennifer Moon, and Ann M. Duffy-Hester. 1998. "Where Are Teachers' Voices in the Phonics/Whole Language Debate? Results from a Survey of U.S. Elementary Classroom Teachers." *The Reading Teacher* (May): 636–650.

Bear, Donald R., and Shane Templeton. 1998. "Explorations in Developmental Spelling: Foundations for Learning and Teaching Phonics, Spelling, and Vocabulary." *The Reading Teacher* (November): 222–242.

Bear, Donald R., Marcia Invernizzi, Shane Templeton, and Francine Johnston. 1996. *Words Their Way: Word Study for Phonics, Vocabulary, and Spelling Instruction*. Upper Saddle River, NJ: Merrill.

Benedict, Susan, and Lenore Carlisle. 1992. *Beyond Words: Picture Books for Older Readers and Writers*. Portsmouth, NH: Heinemann.

Betts, Emmett. 1946. *Foundations of Reading Instruction with Emphasis on Differentiated Guidance*. New York: New York American Book Company.

Bissex, Glenda. 1996. *Partial Truths: A Memoir and Essays on Reading, Writing, and Researching*. Portsmouth, NH: Heinemann.

Bond, Guy, and Robert Dykstra. 1997. "The Cooperative Research Program in First-Grade Reading Instruction." *Reading Research Quarterly* (October/November/December): 348–417.

Boomer, Garth, Nancy Lester, Cynthia Onore, and Jon Cook, eds. 1992. *Negotiating the Curriculum: Educating for the 21st Century*. London: The Falmer Press. First published in Australia in 1982.

Bradley, Ann. 1997. "Panel Reports Ample Action on Teaching." *Education Week* (November 26): 9.

Braunger, Jane, and Jan Patricia Lewis. 1997. *Building a Knowledge Base in Reading*. Portland, OR: Northwest Regional Educational Laboratory; Newark, DE: International Reading Association.

Breivik, Patricia Senn, and J. A. Senn. 1994. *Information Literacy: Educating Children for the Twenty-First Century*. New York: Scholastic.

Brent, Rebecca, and Patricia Anderson. 1993. "Developing Children's Classroom Listening Strategies." *The Reading Teacher* (October): 122–126.

Brett, Arlene, Liz Rothlein, and Michael Hurley. 1996. "Vocabulary Acquisition from Listening to Stories and Explanations of Target Words." *Elementary School Journal* (March): 415–422.

Brick, Madeline. 1993. "When Students Write Home." *Educational Leadership* (April): 62–63.

Buchanan, Jan. 1991. *Flexible Access Library Media Programs*. Englewood, CO: Libraries Unlimited.

Busching, B. A., and B. A. Slesinger. 1995. "Authentic Questions: What Do They Look Like? Where Do They Lead?" *Language Arts* (September): 341–343.

Button, K., M. J. Johnson, and P. Furgeson. 1996. "Interactive Writing in a Primary Classroom." *The Reading Teacher* (March): 446–454.

Caine, Renate Nummela, and Geoffrey Caine. 1997. *Unleashing the Power of Perceptual Change: The Potential of Brain-Based Teaching*. Alexandria, VA: Association for Supervision and Curriculum Development.

California Department of Education. 1999. *Reading/Language Arts Framework for California Public Schools: Kindergarten Through Grade 12*. Sacramento: California Department of Education.

Calkins, Lucy M. 1994. *The Art of Teaching Writing*. Portsmouth, NH: Heinemann.

Campbell, Bebe Moore. 1994. *Brothers and Sisters*. New York: G. P. Putnam's Sons.

Campbell, J. R., and K. P. Ashworth, eds. 1995. *Report in Brief: A Synthesis of Data from NAEP's Integrated Reading Performance Record at Grade 4*. Washington, DC: National Center for Educational Statistics.

Carter, Betty, and Richard Abrahamson. 1995. "Castles to Colin Powell: The Truth About Nonfiction." In *Into Focus: Understanding and Creating Middle School Readers*, edited by Eylene Beers and Barbara Samuels. Norwood, MA: Christopher-Gordon.

Carter, Carolyn. 1997. "Why Reciprocal Teaching?" *Educational Leadership* (March): 64–68.

Carvajal, Doreen. 1997. "You Can't Read Books Fast Enough." *The New York Times*, The News of the Week in Review, August 24, 3.

Carver, Ronald P., and Leibert, Robert E. 1995. "The Effect of Reading Library Books at Different Levels of Difficulty upon Gain in Reading Ability." *Reading Research Quarterly* (January/February/March): 26–47.

Cassidy, Jack, and Drew Cassidy. 1998/1999. "What's Hot, What's Not for 1999." *Reading Today* (December/January): 1, 28.

Caswell, Linda, and Nell K. Duke. 1998. "Non-Narrative as a Catalyst for Literacy Development." *Language Arts* (February): 108–117.

Clay, Marie. 1985. *The Early Detection of Reading Difficulties: A Diagnostic Survey with Recovery Procedures*. 3d ed. Auckland, NZ: Heinemann.

———. 1991. *Becoming Literate: The Construction of Inner Control*. Portsmouth, NH: Heinemann.

———. 1993. *An Observation Survey of Early Literacy Achievement*. Portsmouth, NH: Heinemann.

———. 1998. "Introducing Storybooks to Young Readers." In *By Different Paths to Common Outcomes*. York, ME: Stenhouse. (Originally published in *The Reading Teacher* [December 1991]: 264–273.)

Clay, Marie, and Peter Johnston. 1997. "Interpreting Oral Reading Records." In *Knowing Literacy: Constructive Literacy Assessment*. York, ME: Stenhouse.

Cohen, Elizabeth G. 1994. *Designing Groupwork. Strategies for the Heterogeneous Classroom*. 2d ed. New York: Teachers College Press.

Cohen, Philip. 1995. "Challenging History: The Past Remains a Battleground for Schools." *ASCD Curriculum Update*. Alexandria, VA: Association for Supervision and Curriculum Development.

Coles, Adrienne D. 1998. "Students Nationwide Learn to Lobby for Education." *Education Week* (April 1): 22, 28.

Coles, Gerald. 1998. "Commentary: No End to the Reading Wars." *Education Week* (December 2): 38, 52.

———. 1998. *Reading Lessons: The Debate over Literacy*. New York: Hill and Wang.

Cooper, Patsy. 1993. *When Stories Come to School: Telling, Writing, and Performing Stories in the Early Childhood Classroom*. New York: Teachers & Writers Collaborative.

Culham, Ruth, and Vicki Spandel. 1998. *Picture Books: An Annotated Bibliography with Activities for Teaching Writing*. Portland, OR: Northwest Regional Educational Laboratory.

Cummings, Pat. 1992. *Talking with Artists*. Vol. 1. New York: Bradbury Press.

———. 1995. *Talking with Artists*. Vol. 2. New York: Simon and Schuster.

———. 1999. *Talking with Artists*. Vol. 3. New York: Clarion.

Cunningham, Patricia. 1995. *Phonics We Use*. New York: HarperCollins.

Cunningham, Patricia, and Richard L. Allington. 1999. *Classrooms That Work: They Can All Read and Write*. 2d ed. New York: Longman.

Curtis, Will. 1992. *The Second Nature of Things*. Hopewell, NJ: Ecco Press.

Darling-Hammond, Linda. 1997. *The Right to Learn: A Blueprint for Creating Schools That Work*. San Francisco: Jossey-Bass.

David, Jane L., and Patrick M. Shields. 1999. "Commentary: Standards Are Not Magic." *Education Week* (April 14): 40, 42.

Dickinson, David K., and Lori Lyman DiGisi. 1998. "The Many Rewards of a Literacy-Rich Classroom." *Educational Leadership* (March): 23–26.

Donovan, Maggie. 1997. "Shine Up Your Face: First Graders Evaluate Their Teacher's Responses." *Primary Voices K–6* (November).

Dudley-Marling, Curt, and Dennis Searle. 1995. *Who Owns Learning: Questions of Autonomy, Choice, and Control*. Portsmouth, NH: Heinemann.

Duffy, Gerald G. 1993. "Rethinking Strategy Instruction: Four Teachers' Development and Their Low Achievers' Understandings." *The Elementary School Journal* (January): 244.

Eeds, Maryann, and Ralph Peterson. 1997. "Literature Studies Revisited: Some Thoughts on Talking with Children About Books." *The New Advocate* (Winter): 49–59.

Egeland, P. 1996/1997. "Pulley, Planes, and Student Performance." *Educational Leadership* (December/January): 41–45.

Elbaum, Batya E., Jeanne Shay Schumm, and Sharon Vaughn. 1997. "Urban Middle-Elementary Students' Perceptions of Grouping Formats for Reading Instruction." *Elementary School Journal* (May): 475–500.

Elbow, Peter. 1998. *Writing with Power*. 2d ed. New York: Oxford University Press.

Elias, Maurice, et al. 1997. *Promoting Social and Emotional Learning: Guidelines for Educators*. Alexandria, VA: Association for Supervision and Curriculum Development.

Elley, Warwick. 1998. *Raising Literacy Levels in Third World Countries: A Method That Works*. Culver City, CA: Language Education Associates.

Erickson, H. Lynn. 1998. *Concept-Based Curriculum and Instruction*. Thousand Oaks, CA: Corwin Press.

Ernst, Karen. 1994. *Picturing Learning: Artists and Writers in the Classroom*. Portsmouth, NH: Heinemann.

Everett, Jo Ann. December 1998. Personal communication.

Falk, Beverly. 1998. "Focus on Research. Testing the Way Children Learn: Principles for Valid Literacy Assessments." *Language Arts* (September): 57–66.

Fink, Rosalie. 1998. "Successful Dyslexics: A Constructivist Study of Passionate Interest in Reading." In *Reconsidering a Balanced Approach to Reading*, edited by Constance Weaver. Urbana, IL: National Council of Teachers of English.

Finn, Chester E. Jr., Michael J. Petrilli, and Gregg Vanourek. 1998. "Commentary: The State of State Standards. Four Reasons Why Most 'Don't Cut the Mustard.'" *Education Week* (November 11): 39, 56.

Flanagan, Anna. 1998. "Inner City Curriculum 'Parched,' Kozol Says." *The Council Chronicle* (September): 3.

Fletcher, Ralph. 1993. *What a Writer Needs*. Portsmouth, NH: Heinemann.

Foster-Harrison, Elizabeth S., and Ann Adams-Bullock. 1998. "Fastback: Creating an Inviting Classroom Environment." Bloomington, IN: Phi Delta Kappa Educational Foundation.

Fountas, Irene C. and Gay Su Pinnell. 1996. *Guided Reading: Good First Teaching for All Children*. Portsmouth, NH: Heinemann.

Fox, Mem. 1993. *Radical Reflections*. New York: Harcourt Brace.

Fractor, Jann S., Marjorie C. Woodruff, Miriam G. Martinez, and William H. Teale. 1993. "Let's Not Miss Opportunities to Promote Voluntary Reading: Classroom Libraries in the Elementary School." *The Reading Teacher* (March): 476–484.

Fresch, Mary Jo, and Aileen Wheaton. 1997. "Sort, Search, and Discover: Spelling in the Child-Centered Classroom." *The Reading Teacher* (September): 20–31.

Fry, Edward. 1996. Spelling in Isolation. Presentation at "Reading Hall of Fame" at the annual meeting of the International Reading Association, April, New Orleans, Louisiana.

Galda, Lee. 1998. Presentation at the Colorado Council of the International Reading Association, February, Denver, Colorado.

Garcia, Eugene E. 1997. "Where's the Merit in the S.A.T.?" *The New York Times*, OP-ED, December 26, A 39.

Gardner, Howard. 1998. "What Do Tests Test?" *The New York Times*, OP-ED, December 4, A29.

Gentry, J. Richard. 1982. "An Analysis of Developmental Spelling in GYNS AT WORK." *The Reading Teacher* (November): 192–200.

———. 1997. *My Kid Can't Spell! Understanding and Assisting Your Child's Literacy Development*. Portsmouth, NH: Heinemann.

Gentry, J. Richard, and Jean Wallace Gillet. 1993. *Teaching Kids to Spell*. Portsmouth, NH: Heinemann.

Gill, Charlene Hillal, and Patricia L. Scharer. 1996. "'Why Do They Get It on Friday and Misspell it on Monday?' Teachers Inquiring About Their Students as Spellers." *Language Arts* (February): 89–96.

Goodman, Ken. 1970. "Behind the Eye: What Happens in Reading." In *Reading: Process and Program*, edited by K. Goodman and O. Niles. Urbana, IL: National Council of Teachers of English.

———. 1995. In "Miscue Analysis for Classroom Teachers" by Prisca Martens, Yetta Goodman, and Alan D. Flurkey. *Primary Voices K–6* (November): 3.

Goodman, Yetta. 1995. "Miscue Analysis for Classroom Teachers" by Prisca Martens, Yetta Goodman, and Alan D. Flurkey. *Primary Voices K–6* (November).

Gornick, Vivian. 1998. "Apostles of the Truth That Books Matter." *New York Times*, Feb. 20.

Graves, Donald H. 1994. *A Fresh Look at Writing*. Portsmouth, NH: Heinemann.

———. 1997. A Critical Historical Look at the Relationship Between Reading and Writing. Whole Language Umbrella Conference, July, Bellevue, Washington.

———. July 1998. Personal communication.

Griffin, Patrick, Patricia G. Smith, and Lois E. Burrill. 1995. *The American Literacy Profile Scales: A Framework for Authentic Assessment*. Portsmouth, NH: Heinemann.

Gunning, Thomas G. 1995. "Word Building: A Strategic Approach to the Teaching of Phonics." *The Reading Teacher* (March): 484–488.

Hanseen, Evelyn. 1998. "They Gotta Do It Themselves: Students Raising Questions for Literature Discussion." *The New Advocate* (Fall): 357.

Hartocollis, Anemona. 1998. "New York Report: New Test for 4th Graders Sows Alarm Across State." *The New York Times*, November 30, A23.

Harvey, Stephanie. 1998. *Nonfiction Matters: Reading, Writing, and Reserach in Grades 3–8*. York, ME: Stenhouse.

Harwayne, Shelley. 1992. *Lasting Impressions: Weaving Literature into the Writing Workshop*. Portsmouth, NH: Heinemann.

———. 1999. *Going Public: Priorities and Practice at the Manhattan New School*. Portsmouth, NH: Heinemann.

Hayward, Christopher. 1998. "Monitoring Spelling Development." *The Reading Teacher* (February): 444–445.

Healy, Jane. 1994. *Your Child's Growing Mind*. New York: Doubleday.

———. 1998. "The 'Meme' That Ate Childhood." *Education Week* (October 7): 36–37.

Heaviside, Sheila, Riggins, Toija, and Farris, Elizabeth. 1996. *Advanced Telecommunications in U.S. Elementary and Secondary Schools*. *http://nces.ed.gov/pubs/97944.html*.

Henderson, Ed. 1990. *Teaching Spelling*. 2d ed. Boston: Houghton Mifflin.

Henry, Jim. 1999. *Fresh Takes on Using Journals to Teach Beginning Writers*. New York: Scholastic Professional.

Henry, Tamara. 1998. "Efforts to Improve School Standards Come at a Price." *USA Today*, July 14, 2A.

Hepler, Susan. 1998. "Nonfiction Books for Children: New Directions, New Challenges." In *Making Facts Come Alive: Choosing Quality Nonfiction Literature K–8*, edited by Rosemary A. Bamford and Janice V. Kristo. Norwood, MA: Christopher-Gordon.

Herman, Joan. 1997. "Assessing New Assessments: How Do They Measure Up?" *Theory into Practice* (Autumn): 198.

Hill, Bonnie Campbell, Nancy J. Johnson, and Katherine L. Schlick-Noe, eds. 1995. *Literature Circles and Response*. Norwood, MA: Christopher-Gordon.

Hindley, Joanne. 1997. Writing Workshop Minilessons: Resources and Teaching Strategies. Session at annual conference of the National Council of Teachers of English, November, Detroit, Michigan.

Ho, Minfong. 1995. *The Art of Writing: An Illustrated Journal*. Philadelphia, PA: Running Press.

Holdaway, Don. 1979. *The Foundations of Literacy*. New York: Scholastic, and Portsmouth, NH: Heinemann.

———. 1980. *Independence in Reading*. Portsmouth, NH: Heinemann.

Huck, Charlotte S., Susan Hepler, Janet Hickman, and Barbara Z. Kiefer. 1997. *Children's Literature in the Elementary School*. 6th ed. New York: McGraw-Hill.

Hughes, Margaret, and Dennis Searle. 1997. *The Violent E and Other Tricky Sounds: Learning to Spell from Kindergarten Through Grade 6*. York, ME: Stenhouse; Markham, ONT: Pembroke.

International Association for the Evaluation of Educational Achievement. July 1992. *How in the World Do Students Read? IEA Study of Reading Literacy*. The Hague, The Netherlands.

Jaeger, Richard M., and John A. Hattie. 1995. "Detracking America's Schools: Should We Really Care?" *Phi Delta Kappan* (November): 219.

Jenkins, Carol Brennan. 1999. *The Allure of Authors: Author Studies in the Elementary Classroom*. Portsmouth, NH: Heinemann.

Jenkins, Christine. 1997. "The Baby-Sitters Club and Cultural Diversity: or, Book #X: Jessi and Claudia Get Lost." In *Using Multiethnic Literature in the K–8 Classroom*, edited by Violet J. Harris. Norwood, MA: Christopher-Gordon.

Jensen, Eric. 1998. *Introduction to Brain-Compatible Learning*. San Diego, CA: The Brain Store, Inc.

———. 1998. *Teaching with the Brain in Mind*. Alexandria, VA: Association for Supervision and Curriculum Development.

———. 1999. Insights on Better Classroom Management from Brain Research. Session at annual meeting of Association for Supervision and Curriculum Development, March, San Francisco, California.

Jervis, Kathe. 1996. *Eyes on the Child: Three Portfolio Stories*. New York: Teachers College Press.

Joftus, Scott, and Terry Whitney. 1998. "Commentary. High Standards Without Big Lawsuits." *Education Week* (November 18): 28, 32.

Keene, Ellin Oliver, and Susan Zimmermann. 1997. *Mosaic of Thought: Teaching Comprehension in a Reader's Workshop*. Portsmouth, NH: Heinemann.

Kerper, Richard M. 1998. "Choosing Quality Nonfiction Literature: Features for Accessing and Visualizing Information." In *Making Facts Come Alive: Choosing Quality Nonfiction Literature K–8*, edited by Rosemary A. Bamford and Janice V. Kristo. Norwood, MA: Christopher-Gordon.

Knapp, Michael S., Patrick M. Shields, and Brenda J. Turnbull. 1995. "Academic Challenge in High-Poverty Classrooms." *Phi Delta Kappan* (June).

Kohn, Alfie. 1996. *Beyond Discipline: From Compliance to Community*. Alexandria, VA: Association for Supervision and Curriculum Development.

Konigsburg, E. L. 1995. *TalkTalk: A Children's Book Author Speaks to Grown-Ups*. New York: Atheneum.

Krashen, Stephen. 1993. *The Power of Reading: Insights from the Research*. Englewood, CO: Libraries Unlimited.

———. 1998. "Bridging Inequity with Books." *Educational Leadership* (January): 18–21.

———. 1998. "Every Person a Reader: An Alternative to the California Task Force Report on Reading." In *Reconsidering a Balanced Approach to Reading*, edited by Constance Weaver. Urbana, IL: National Council of Teachers of English. (Published as a monograph in 1995 by Language Education Associates, Culver City, CA.)

———. 1999. *Three Arguments Against Whole Language and Why They Are Wrong*. Portsmouth, NH: Heinemann.

Krashen, Stephen, and Jeff McQuillan. 1998. "The Case for Late Intervention: Once a Good Reader, Always a Good Reader." In *Reconsidering a Balanced Approach to Reading*, edited by Constance Weaver. Urbana, IL: National Council of Teachers of English. (Published as a monograph in 1996 by Language Education Associates, Culver City, CA.)

Kraus, Robert. 1971. *Leo the Late Bloomer*. New York: Windmill Books.

Lance, Keith Curry, Lynda Welborn, and Christine Hamilton-Pennell. 1997. *The Impact of School Library Media Centers on Academic Achievement*. Castle Rock, CO: Hi Willow.

Leonhardt, Mary. 1997. "Racial Gap in Testing Is Really a Reading Gap." *The New York Times*, Editorials/Letters, November 10, A24.

Lewis, Anne C. 1997. "Washington Commentary: National Tests Ignite Scorching Debate." *Phi Delta Kappan* (December): 259.

Lewis, Peter H. 1998. "Taking on New Forms, Electronic Books Turn a Page." *New York Times* (July 2): 7.

Lipson, Marjorie, Sheila Valencia, Karen Wixson, and Charles Peters. 1993. "Integration and Thematic Teaching: Integration to Improve Teaching and Learning." *Language Arts* (April).

Lowry, Lois. 1996. Featured talk at the Annual Convention of the National Council of Teachers of English, November 24.

Manzo, Kathleen Kennedy. 1997. "School Library Budgets Decline, Study Shows." *Education Week* (October 1): 5.

———. 1998. "Drilling in Texas." *Education Week* (June 10): 32–37.

———. 1998. "More Dollars for Textbooks Draws Sellers." *Education Week* (September 30): 1, 12.

Martens, Prisca, Yetta Goodman, and Alan D. Flurkey. 1995. "Miscue Analysis for Classroom Teachers." *Primary Voices K–6* (November).

Maurice, Elias, et al. 1997. *Promoting Social and Emotional Learning: Guidelines for Educators*. Alexandria, VA: Association for Supervision and Curriculum Development.

McIntyre, Ellen. 1995. "Teaching and Learning Writing Skills in a Low-SES, Urban Primary Classroom." *Journal of Reading Behavior* 27 (2).

McKenzie, Jamie. 1998. "Grazing the Net: Raising a Generation of Free-Range Students." *Phi Delta Kappan* (September): 26–31.

McQuillan, Jeff. 1998. *The Literacy Crisis: False Claims, Real Solutions.* Portsmouth, NH: Heinemann.

Meier, Deborah. 1995. *The Power of Their Ideas: Lessons for America from a Small School in Harlem.* Boston: Beacon Press.

Mills, Heidi. 1990. "Teachers and Children: Partners in Learning." In *Portraits of Whole Language Classrooms,* edited by Heidi Mills and Jean Ann Clyde. Portsmouth, NH: Heinemann.

Moline, Steve. 1995. *I See What You Mean: Children at Work with Visual Information.* York, ME: Stenhouse.

Morley, Judith, and Sandra Russell. 1995. "Making Literature Meaningful: A Classroom/Library Partnership." In *Battling Dragons: Issues and Controversy in Children's Literature,* edited by Susan Lehr. Portsmouth, NH: Heinemann.

Morris, Darrell, Lina Blanton, William E. Blanton, and Jan Perney. 1995. "Spelling Instruction and Achievement in Six Classrooms." *The Elementary School Journal* (November): 145–160.

Morrison, T., J. Jacobs, and W. Swinyard. 1999. "Do Teachers Who Read Personally Use Recommended Literacy Practices in Their Classrooms?" *Reading Research and Instruction* (February): 81–100.

Morton, Jessica. 1996. *Kids on the 'Net: Conducting Internet Research in K–5 Classrooms.* Portsmouth, NH: Heinemann.

Moss, Barbara, Susan Leone, and Mary Lou Dipillo. 1997. "Exploring the Literature of Fact: Linking Reading and Writing Through Information Trade Books." *Language Arts* (October): 418–429.

Moustafa, Margaret. June 1997. Personal communication.

———. 1998. "Whole-to-Part Phonics Instruction." In *Practicing What We Know,* edited by Constance Weaver. Urbana, IL: National Council of Teachers of English.

Murray, Donald M. 1990. *Shoptalk: Learning to Write with Writers.* Portsmouth, NH: Heinemann.

———. 1996. *Crafting a Life in Essay, Story, Poem.* Portsmouth, NH: Heinemann.

Nagy, William. 1998. *Teaching Vocabulary to Improve Reading Comprehension.* Urbana, IL: National Council of Teachers of English; Newark, DE: International Reading Association.

Nagy, W., R. C. Anderson, and P. Herman. 1987. "Learning Word Meanings from Context During Normal Reading." *American Educational Research Journal* 24: 237–270.

National Academy of Sciences. 1998. *Preventing Reading Difficulties in Young Children.* Report published by the National Academy of Sciences, Washington, DC.

National Center for Education Statistics. 1999. *Executive Summary: NAEP 1998 Reading Report Card for the Nation and the States.* Washington, DC: National Center for Education Statistics, U.S. Department of Education.

National Council for the Social Studies. 1994. *Curriculum Standards for Social Studies: Expectations of Excellence.* Washington, DC: National Council for the Social Studies.

National Education Goals Panel. 1996. *Executive Summary: Commonly Asked Questions About Standards and Assessments.* Washington, DC: National Education Goals Panel.

National Research Council. 1998. *Preventing Reading Difficulties in Young Children.* Washington, DC: National Academy Press.

National Research Council and the National Academy of Sciences. 1996. *National Science Foundation Standards.* Washington, DC: National Academy Press.

Nia, Isoke Titilayo. 1998. "Commentary: Story Matters." *The Council Chronicle* (April): 16.

Norton, Donna E. 1993. "Webbing and Historical Fiction." *The Reading Teacher* (February): 432–436.

Ogle, Donna. 1986. "K-W-L: A Teaching Model That Develops Active Reading of Expository Text." *The Reading Teacher* (February): 564–570.

Ohanian, Susan. 1999. *One Size Fits Few: The Folly of Educational Standards.* Portsmouth, NH: Heinemann.

Optiz, Michael F., and Timothy V. Rasinski. 1998. *Good-Bye Round Robin: Twenty-Five Effective Oral Reading Strategies.* Portsmouth, NH: Heinemann.

Palincsar, Annemarie Sullivan. 1986. "The Role of Dialogue in Providing Scaffolded Instruction." *Educational Psychologist* 21 (1, 2): 73–98.

Papert, Seymour. 1993. *The Children's Machine: Rethinking School in the Age of the Computer.* New York: Basic Books.

Paratore, Jeanne R., and Rachel L. McCormick, eds. 1997. *Peer Talk in the Classroom: Learning from the Research.* Newark, DE: International Reading Association.

Parker, Diane. 1997. *Jamie: A Literacy Story.* York, ME: Stenhouse.

Pearson, David. 1993. "Focus on Research: Teaching and Learning Reading, A Research Perspective." *Language Arts* (October): 505.

Pennac, Daniel. 1999. *Better Than Life.* Markham, ONT: Pembroke; York, ME: Stenhouse.

Phenix, Jo. 1996. *The Spelling Teacher's Book of Lists: Words to Illustrate Spelling Patterns . . . and Tips for Teaching Them.* Markham, ONT: Pembroke; York, ME: Stenhouse.

Pikulski, John. 1994. "Five Successful Reading Programs for At-Risk Students." *The Reading Teacher* (October).

Pimentel, Susan, and Leslye A. Arsht. 1998. "Commentary: The State of State Standards. Don't Be Confused by the Rankings; Focus on Results." *Education Week* (November 11): 40, 56.

Pinkney, Jerry. 1996. Speech given at the Georgia Council of the International Reading Association, March 29, Atlanta, Georgia.

Pinnell, Gay Su, and Irene C. Fountas. 1998. *Word Matters: Teaching Phonics and Spelling in the Reading/Writing Classroom.* Portsmouth, NH: Heinemann.

Pinnell, Gay Su, and Andrea McCarrier. 1994. "Interactive Writing: A Transition Tool for Assisting Children in Learning to Read and Write." In *Getting Reading Right from the Start: Effective Early Literacy Interventions,* edited by E. Hiebert and B. Taylor. Needham Heights, MA: Allyn and Bacon.

Pottorff, Donald, Deborah Phelps-Zientarski, and Michele Skovera. 1997. *Journal of Research and Development in Education.*

Pradl, G. W. 1996. "Reading and Democracy: The Enduring Influence of Louise Rosenblatt." *The New Advocate* (Winter): 9–22.

Pressley, Michael, Joan Rankin, and Linda Yokoi. 1996. "A Survey of Instructional Practices of Primary Teachers Nominated as Effective in Promoting Literacy." *The Elementary School Journal* (March): 375.

Pressley, Michael, Richard Allington, Lesley Morrow, et al. 1999. *The Nature of Effective First Grade Literacy Instruction.* CELA tech report.

Quindlen, Anna. 1998. *How Reading Changed My Life.* New York: Ballantine.

Raphael, Taffy E., and Susan I. McMahon. 1994. "Book Club: An Alternative Framework for Reading Instruction." *The Reading Teacher* (October): 102–116.

Reardon, Jeanne. 1998. Children, Science, and . . . Books. Presentation at the International Reading Association annual convention, May, Orlando, Florida. A segment of *The Neglected Genre: An Inquiry-Based Exploration of the Science/Literature Connection,* Science Trade Books for Young Readers.

Rees, Nina Shokraii. 1998. "The Real Divide on Education." *The New York Times,* OP-ED, October 8, A31.

Richgels, Donald J. 1995. "Invented Spelling Ability and Printed Word Learning in Kindergarten." *Reading Research Quarterly* (January/February/March): 107.

Richgels, Donald J., Darla J. Poremba, and Lea M. McGee. 1996. "Kindergartners Talk About Print: Phonemic Awareness in Meaningful Contexts." *The Reading Teacher* (May): 632–642.

Robb, Laura. 1994. "Second Graders Read Nonfiction: Investigating Natural Phenomena and Disasters." *The New Advocate* (Fall): 239–252.

Rosenblatt, Louise. 1995. *Literature as Exploration.* 5th ed. New York: The Modern Language Association of America.

Rothenberg, David. 1997. "Point of View: How the Web Destroys the Quality of Students' Research Papers." *Chronicle of Higher Education* (August 15).

Routman, Regie. 1991, 1994. *Invitations: Changing as Teachers and Learners K–12.* Portsmouth, NH: Heinemann.

———. 1995. "Donald Graves: Outstanding Educator in the Language Arts." *Language Arts* (November): 524, 525.

———. 1996. *Literacy at the Crossroads: Crucial Talk About Reading, Writing, and Other Teaching Dilemmas*. Portsmouth, NH: Heinemann.

———. 1997. "Ready to Read." *Parents* (October): 78–86.

———. 1998. "Selected Reading-Writing Strategies for L.D. and Other At-Risk Students" in *Practicing What We Know: Informed Reading Instruction*, edited by Constance Weaver, pp. 377–393. Urbana, IL: National Council of Teachers of English.

———. 2000. *Kids' Poems.* New York: Scholastic.

Routman, Regie, and Donna Maxim. 1996. "Invented Spelling: What It Is and What It Isn't." *School Talk* (April). Urbana, IL: National Council of Teachers of English.

Rubenstein, Susanne. 1998. *Go Public! Encouraging Student Writers to Publish*. Urbana, IL: National Council of Teachers of English.

Ruddell, Martha Rapp. 1998. "Research Base Lacking, Says NRC." *Reading Today: News of the Profession* (October/November): 4.

Ruenzel, David. 1997. "AVID Learners: What Happens When Students Normally Dumped into Remedial Classes Get the Chance to Shoot for College?" *Teacher Magazine* (January): 19.

Rupley, William H., John W. Logan, and William D. Nichols. 1998/1999. "Vocabulary Instruction in a Balanced Reading Program." *The Reading Teacher* (December/January): 336–346.

Samway, Katharine Davies, and Gail Whang. 1996. *Literature Study Circles in a Multicultural Classroom.* York, ME: Stenhouse.

Sarason, Seymour. 1998. *Political Leadership and Educational Failure.* San Francisco: Jossey-Bass.

Saul, Wendy. 1999. Personal communication.

Saul, Wendy, and Jeanne Reardon, eds. 1996. *Beyond the Science Kit: Inquiry in Action*. Portsmouth, NH: Heinemann.

Schlagal, Robert. 1989. "Constancy and Change in Spelling Development." *Reading Psychology* 10 (3): 207–232.

Schmoker, Mike. 1996. *Results: The Key to Continuous School Improvement*. Alexandria, VA: Association for Supervision and Curriculum Development.

Servis, Joan. 1999. *Celebrating the Fourth: Ideas and Inspiration for Teachers of Grade 4.* Portsmouth, NH: Heinemann.

Sewall, Gilbert. 1998. "Teaching and Learning: Report Assails New Social Studies Texts." *Education Week* (June 17): 14.

Shanahan, Timothy. 1997. "Reading-Writing Relationships, Thematic Units, Inquiry Learning…In Pursuit of Effective Integrated Literacy Instruction." *The Reading Teacher* (September): 12–19.

Shields, Patrick M., and Michael S. Knapp. 1997. "The Promise and Limits of School-Based Reform: A National Snapshot." *Phi Delta Kappan* (December): 292.

Silva, Cecilia, and Esther L. Delgado-Larocco. 1993. "Facilitating Learning Through Interconnections: A Concept Approach to Core Literature Units." Language Arts (October): 469–474.

Sipe, Lawrence. 1998. "First- and Second-Grade Literary Critics: Understanding Children's Rich Responses to Literature." In *Literature-Based Instruction: Reshaping the Curriculum,* edited by Taffy Raphael and Kathryn Au. Norwood, MA: Christopher-Gordon.

Sitton, Rebecca. 1996. "Achieving Spelling Literacy: A No-Excuses Approach." *California Reader* (Fall): 7.

Siu-Runyan, Yvonne. 1999. "Inquiry, Curriculum, and Standards: A Conversation with Kathy Short." *The Colorado Communicator* (February): 4–17.

Sloan, Megan S. 1996. "Encouraging Young Students to Use Interesting Words in Their Writing." *The Reading Teacher* (November): 268–269.

Smith, Dinitia. 1998. "Secret of the Eternally Young Sleuths." *The New York Times*, July 11, A11, A13.

Smith John W., and Warwick B. Elley. 1994. *Learning to Read in New Zealand.* Katonah, NY: Richard C. Owen.

Snow, Catherine E., M. Susan Burns, and Peg Griffin, eds. 1998. *Preventing Reading Difficulties in Young Children*. Washington, DC: National Academy Press.

Snowball, Diane. 1995. "Building Literacy Skills Through Nonfiction: Some Tips on How You Can Help Children Become Better Readers and Writers of Nonfiction." *Teaching K–8* (May): 62–63.

———. 1998. An Inquiry Approach to Spelling. Annual meeting of the International Reading Association, May, Orlando, Florida.

Snowball, Diane, and Faye Bolton. 1999. *Spelling K–8: Planning and Teaching*. York, ME: Stenhouse.

Sudol, Peg, and Caryn M. King. 1996. "A Checklist for Choosing Nonfiction Trade Books." *The Reading Teacher* (February): 422–424.

Stahl, Steven A., Ann M. Duffy-Hester, and Katherine Anne Dougherty Stahl. 1998. "Theory and Research into Practice: Everything You Wanted to Know About Phonics (But Were Afraid to Ask)." *Reading Research Quarterly* (Summer): 344.

Taberski, Sharon. 2000. *On Solid Ground: Strategies for Teaching Reading, K–3*. Portsmouth, NH: Heinemann.

Tancock, Susan. 1994. "A Literacy Lesson Framework for Children with Reading Problems." *The Reading Teacher* (October): 135.

Terban, Marvin. 1996. *Dictionary of Idioms*. New York: Scholastic.

Tierney, Robert J., and Timothy Shanahan. 1991. "Research on the Reading-Writing Relationship: Interactions, Transactions, and Outcomes." In *Handbook of Reading Research*, 2d ed., edited by R. Barr, M. L. Kamil, P. Mosenthal, and P. D. Pearson. New York: Longman.

Tierney, Robert J., and Carolyn Clark, with Linda Fenner, Roberta J. Herter, Carolyn Staunton Simpson, and Burt Wiser. 1998. "Theory and Research into Practice. Portfolios: Assumptions, Tensions, and Possibilities." *Reading Research Quarterly* (Oct./Nov./Dec.): 474–486.

Trotter, Andrew. 1998. "A Question of Effectiveness." *Education Week* (October).

Tucker, Marc, and Judy B. Codding. 1998. "Commentary: Raising Our Standards for the Standards Movement." *Education Week* (February 18): 56.

Turner, Julianne, and Scott G. Paris. 1995. "How Literacy Tasks Influence Children's Motivation for Literacy." *The Reading Teacher* (May): 662–673.

United States Congress Office of Technology Assessment. 1995. *Teachers and Technology: Making the Connection*. Washington, DC: U.S. Government Printing Office. *http://www.wws.princeton .edu/~ota/disk1/1995/9541.html*.

United States Department of Education. 1996. *Advanced Telecommunications in U.S. Public Elementary and Secondary Schools*. Survey. Washington, DC: United States Department of Education.

United States Department of Education. September 1997. *NAEP Trends in Academic Progress Report*. Washington, DC: United States Department of Education.

Valencia, Sheila W. 1998. *Literacy Portfolios in Action*. Fort Worth, TX: Harcourt Brace.

Van Lann, Nancy. 1990. *Possum Come A-Knockin*. New York: Knopf.

Vygotsky, Lev. 1978. *Mind in Society*. Cambridge, MA: Harvard University Press.

Wagstaff, Janiel. 1994. *Phonics That Work*. New York: Scholastic Professional Books.

Wallis, Judy. January 1999. Personal communication.

Wasik, Barbara. 1998. "Volunteer Tutoring Programs in Reading: A Review." *Reading Research Quarterly* (July/August/September): 266, 282.

Weaver, Constance. 1994. *Reading Process and Practice*. 2d ed. Portsmouth, NH: Heinemann.

———, ed. 1998. *Practicing What We Know: Informed Reading Instruction*. Urbana, IL: National Council of Teachers of English.

———, ed. 1998. *Reconsidering a Balanced Approach to Reading*. Urbana, IL: National Council of Teachers of English.

Weikart, David P. 1998. "High/Scope Study Raises Direct-Instruction Questions." *Education Week* (July 8).

Wells, Gordon. 1998. "Some Questions About Direct Instruction: Why? To Whom? How? And When?" *Language Arts* (September): 28.

Wheat, Leonard. 1932. "Four Spelling Rules." *Elementary School Journal* 32: 697–706.

Wiggins, Grant, and Jay McTighe. 1998. *Understanding by Design*. Alexandria, VA: Association for Supervision and Curriculum Development.

Wilde, Sandra. 1992. *You Kan Red This! Spelling and Punctuation for Whole Language Classrooms,* Portsmouth, NH: Heinemann.

———. 1997. *What's a Schwa Sound, Anyway? A Holistic Guide to Phonetics, Phonics, and Spelling.* Portsmouth, NH: Heinemann.

———. 1997. Session on teaching and learning spelling at the annual meeting of the Oregon Reading Association, February, Portland, OR.

———. 1999. "How Children Learn to Spell: Evidence from Decades of Research." In *Voices on Word Matters,* edited by Irene C. Fountas and Gay Su Pinnell. Portsmouth, NH: Heinemann.

Wolk, Ronald A. 1998. "Commentary: Education's High-Stakes Gamble." *Education Week* (December 9): 48.

Wolk, Steven. 1998. *A Democratic Classroom.* Portsmouth, NH: Heinemann.

Worthy, Jo. 1996. "A Matter of Interest: Literature That Hooks Reluctant Readers and Keeps Them Reading." *The Reading Teacher* (November): 204–212.

Worthy, Jo, Megan Moorman, and Margo Turner. 1999. "What Johnny Likes to Read Is Hard to Find in School." *Reading Research Quarterly* (Jan./Feb./Mar.): 12–27.

Wylie, R. E., and D. D. Durrell. 1970. *Elementary English* 47: 787–791.

Yochum, Nina. 1991. "Children's Learning from Informational Text: The Relationship Between Prior Knowledge and Text Structure." *Journal of Reading Behavior* 23 (1): 87–103.

Yopp, Hallie Kay. 1995. "A Test for Assessing Phonemic Awareness in Young Children." *The Reading Teacher* (September): 20–29.

Zack, Ian. 1998. "Universities Finding a Sharp Rise in Computer-Aided Cheating." *New York Times Education* (September 23).

Zarnowski, Myra. 1995. "Learning History with Informational Storybooks: A Social Studies Educator's Perspective." *The New Advocate* (Summer): 188.

———. 1998. "It's More Than Dates and Places: How Nonfiction Contributes to Understanding Social Studies." In *Making Facts Come Alive: Choosing Quality Nonfiction Literature K–8,* edited by Rosemary A. Bamford and Janice V. Kristo. Norwood, MA: Christopher-Gordon.

Zutell, Jerome. 1993. Session at International Reading Association, April, San Antonio, Texas.

———. 1996. "The Directed Spelling Thinking Activity (DSTA): Providing an Effective Balance in Word Study Instruction." *The Reading Teacher* (October): 98–108.

The Blue Pages

RESOURCES FOR TEACHERS

Regie Routman

with

Judy Wallis

Houston, TX
Spring Branch Independent School District
K–12 Language Arts Director

and

Susan Hepler

Alexandria, VA
Children's Literature Specialist

and with contributions by

Annie Gordon
San Francisco, CA
Grades Four and Five Teacher

Libby Larrabee
Cleveland, OH
Reading Recovery
Teacher Leader

Danny Miller
Los Angeles, CA
Editor, Heinemann

Kathy O'Neal
Shaker Heights, OH
Children's Librarian

Lee Sattelmeyer
Shaker Heights, OH
Grade Three Teacher

Wendy Saul
Baltimore, MD
Professor of Education, UMBC
Director, NSF-Funded Elementary
  Science Integration Project

Professional Resources for Teachers

Annotations with Judy Wallis

The Blue Pages comprise carefully selected resources—primarily professional books but also journal articles and Web sites—to support you in your continuing professional development. Knowing firsthand that the role of reading and reflecting is vital to our professional health, Judy Wallis and I have selected those resources that are worth teachers' limited time. Resources that are bulleted (•) are our personal favorites, titles we consider to be particularly outstanding. Resources annotated by Judy Wallis have *J.W.* at the end. We suggest you begin by perusing through the titles and annotations of topics that interest you and selecting several to read and, perhaps, discuss with your colleagues.

Use the table of contents for The Blue Pages (at the front of this book)—organized to go along with chapters and topics in *Conversations*—to locate areas of particular interest. Placing resources in particular chapters and categories, admittedly, was often arbitrary. When a book fit easily within several domains, we chose the placement that seemed most logical to us. More importantly, all of the resources connect to what it means to be a professional. That is, these resources will inform you on the latest research, theory, and practice and are excellent for rethinking, reflecting upon, and improving your own teaching and learning. We recognize that there is a wealth of existing professional literature, and we have, no doubt, overlooked terrific resources that you will want to add.

Just about all of the included professional resources in The Blue Pages are new to this edition and have publication dates after 1994. The exceptions are a few previously overlooked titles and an occasional, formerly cited title. Most are available in paperback. For resources up to and including 1994, see *The Blue Pages* or *Invitations*.

Reading Professionally

Both Judy Wallis and I make time in our busy lives to read widely and talk with other educators about our reading. Indeed, Judy calls it "engaging in the professional conversation." She comments:

"Reading professionally has always been a priority in my life as an educator. Sometimes my reading re-

sulted in answers to classroom questions I had; at other times I heard the voice of another educator halfway across the country puzzling over issues similar to mine. In both cases, I found my teaching life enriched; I seemed less alone in my classroom each day."

My professional reading is the mainstay of my teaching-learning life as it is for every excellent teacher I know. Reading, thinking, reflecting, discussing, inquiring, reconsidering, and taking new action are an integral part of what it means to be a teacher. I wrote *Conversations* to move our professional-teaching-learning lives forward. While the text is full of practical ideas, it is the personal and collegial in-depth study, deliberation, and rethinking of specific topics that will most impact your teaching. Use the professional resources in The Blue Pages to begin and continue your own conversations.

Chapter 1: Teacher as Professional

While all of the books and resources in The Blue Pages deal with "teacher as professional," the ones that follow deal exclusively with this topic or do not fit easily into a special category.

Teacher as Professional

Bredekamp, Sue, and C. Copple, eds. 1998. *Developmentally Appropriate Practice in Early Childhood Programs*. Rev. ed. Washington, DC: National Association for the Education of Young Children.

This position statement (91 pages) has become a highly acknowledged document for looking at appropriate and inappropriate practices for infants, toddlers, preschoolers, and primary-grade students. It is an outstanding reference for all teachers, administrators, parents, and policymakers who want to ensure the development of favorable early childhood practices in language and literacy learning. Be sure your school library has a copy of this publication.

• Burns, M. Susan, Peg Griffin, and Catherine E. Snow, eds. 1999. *Starting Out Right: A Guide to Promoting Children's Reading Success*. Washington, DC: National Academy Press.

This book is a set of recommendations about the acquisition of literacy and is primarily written for parents, but it is also important reading for teachers. It outlines the kinds of language and literacy experiences to look for in preschool programs, how initial reading instruction should look in the early grades, the questions parents should ask school board members, policy makers, and principals, and how parents can assess progress in acquiring skills in early reading. The book grew out of an earlier report, Preventing Reading Difficulties, *which includes recommendations made about instructional methods and materials. These two publications and their recommendations will likely have future policy implications.* (J.W.)

Darling-Hammond, Linda. 1997. *The Right to Learn: A Blueprint for Creating Schools That Work.* San Francisco: Jossey-Bass.

A highly regarded, national educator discusses policies and practices that are needed to make learner-centered schools work for all students. Darling-Hammond brings clarity to such issues as standards and standardized testing, teaching and learning for understanding, grouping, using text books, and what it means to be professional.

Graves, Donald H. 1998. *How to Catch a Shark: And Other Stories About Teaching and Learning.* Portsmouth, NH: Heinemann.

Donald Graves tells us fascinating life stories about teaching and learning in and out of the classroom. In sharing these powerful stories, he illustrates the power of stories, and encourages us to tell our own.

Hubbard, Ruth S., and Brenda M. Power. 1999. *Living the Question: A Guide for Teacher-Researchers.* York, ME: Stenhouse.

This eloquently written book offers a wealth of support to educators interested in using teacher research to answer questions about teaching and learning. Not only do the authors provide a brief historical perspective of teacher-as-researcher, they suggest practical procedures and suggestions for identifying research questions, collecting data, and interpreting and sharing findings. However, the real beauty of this book is in the many teacher-researchers' experiences Hubbard and Power have included. (J.W.)

Kohn, Alfie. 1998. *What to Look for in a Classroom... and Other Essays.* San Francisco, CA: Jossey-Bass.

Alfie Kohn challenges educators to reconsider some of our assumptions about education and children. His writings in a variety of publications have sparked debate for more than a decade. This collection of writings packages Kohn's most thought-provoking ideas and insights for educators and parents. In the nineteen essays that have previously appeared in Phi Delta Kappan, Educational Leadership, Education Week, *and other publications, the author discusses topics such as classroom management, grading, incentive programs, self-esteem, and children's role in classroom decisions.* (J.W.)

Paley, Vivian Gussin. 1997. *The Girl with the Brown Crayon.* Cambridge, MA: Harvard University Press.

Written in her final year of teaching, exemplary kindergarten teacher Vivian Paley challenges our assumptions about what is possible in a literature and child-centered classroom when all the children's voices are valued. We learn much about Paley's classroom—and teaching and learning—through the eyes of Reeny, an African American student, and her peers. This book was awarded Harvard University's annual prize for an outstanding text about education and society.

Pressley, Michael, Richard Allington, Lesley Morrow, et al. 1999. "The Nature of Effective First-Grade Literacy Instruction." *cela.albany.edu /1stgradelit/literacy.html.*

This interesting and very useful report discusses [cela.albany.edu/ 1stgradelit/index.html] *in th̲e̲ ̲rst-grade p̲ort for b̲ iate the d̲ the autho̲ e of such lent class̲ itive and ̲ be-tween skills and literature, and ̲ ding provided learners in these successful teachers' classrooms. The report is currently available online, but it will be published.* (J.W.)

- Weaver, Constance. 1994. *Reading Process and Practice: From Socio-Psycholinguistics to Whole Language.* 2d ed. Portsmouth, NH: Heinemann.

  For all educators who want the latest tie-in between theory and practice on all aspects of language learning, this comprehensive (731 pages) and readable text offers a wealth of information in an integrated, useful manner. In addition to detailed discussions of the reading process (including phonics, miscue analysis, research studies supporting whole language practices, Reading Recovery) and extensive, current resources and activities, this new edition also includes two informative chapters on whole language that address whole language principles, common misconceptions, and whole language teaching as a continuing process of development. The chapter "Reading, Literature, and the Dramatic Language Arts" by Ruth Beall Heinig is full of suggestions for combining the dramatic language arts with whole language. "Whole Language Learning and Teaching for Second Language Learners" by Yvonne Freeman and David Freeman addresses approaches to teaching and supporting second-language students. An amazing resource!

- Weaver, Constance, ed. 1998. *Practicing What We Know: Informed Reading Instruction.* Urbana, IL: National Council of Teachers of English.

  Literacy instruction has become a hotly debated topic and it often produces teaching dilemmas for classroom teachers. This practical book helps translate theory into practice and provides insight into issues such as phonics, word skills, and strategy instruction. This book builds on the companion volume, Reconsidering a Balanced Approach to Reading *(1998). Both beginning and experienced teachers wanting sound perspectives on reading instruction will find this text a useful resource to have on their bookshelf. (J.W.)*

Weaver, Constance, Lorraine Gillmeister-Krause, and Grace Vento-Zogby. 1996. *Creating Support for Effective Literacy Education.* Portsmouth, NH: Heinemann.

  The excellent resource contains most of the necessary materials to present effective and convincing workshops for administrators, teachers, parents, and policymakers. The authors offer suggestions and lists of sources and resources to use in communicating research on creating effective literacy programs. The ready-to-copy materials, supported by pertinent information, provide educators with transparencies and handouts to use in presentations. (J.W.)

Support for Political Action

Through the research cited, incidents described, information listed, and practical suggestions offered, the following resources and organizations can aid your political efforts in your own school, district, and community.

Allington, Richard. 1997. "Overselling Phonics." *Reading Today* (August/September): 15–16.

  This article was reprinted in Classrooms That Work: They Can *All* Read and Write. *2d ed. by Patricia Cunningham and Richard Allington (Longman, 1999), and can also be accessed on the University of Albany's Web site:* www.albany.edu/reading/allington.htm.

  Allington, a well-r____ ____rcher, de-____ ____that there ____tle phon-____ that "di-____s" is the ____ids need ____nd dis-____

[handwritten note: www.albany.edu/tree-tops/reading/allington.html]

Berger, ____ ____ading for the Pu____ ____ *Reading Teacher* (September): 7–10.

  Excellent suggestions on how educators can successfully respond to and write for the public media.

Berliner, David C., and Bruce J. Biddle. 1995. *The Manufactured Crisis: Myths, Fraud, and the Attack on American's Public Schools.* Reading, MA: Addison-Wesley.

  Berliner and Biddle provide a counterattack to address a growing chorus of critics who report an array of data intended to support the demise of public schools. The authors unravel myths created to unsettle the public and garner support for special interest groups' agendas. These myths, such as declining SAT scores and increased illiteracy, are answered with facts and proposals for real solutions to the dilemmas public schools face. Educators owe it to themselves to read this thoughtful book for two reasons: to consider many of the present myths and to remember the important work we must continue. (J.W.)

- Braunger, Jane, and Jan Patricia Lewis. October 1997. *Building a Knowledge Base in Reading.* Portland, OR: Northwest Regional Educational Laboratory; Urbana, IL: National Council of Teachers of English; Newark, DE: International Reading Association.

    A synthesis of key findings from research on learning to read. Core understandings with sample classroom applications are clearly presented along with supporting research that considers classroom contexts. Be sure you and your school have a copy of this landmark publication. Very supportive for teaching reading as a meaning-getting process.

Brinkley, Ellen H., with Connie Weaver, et al. 1997. "Believing in What's Possible: Taking Action to Make a Difference." *Language Arts* (November): 537–544.

    This excellent article tells the story of educators who joined together in a grassroots effort to counter attacks on the curriculum. They offer specific suggestions to help others interested in forming similar alliances created to support and strengthen public education. (J.W.)

Center for the Improvement of Early Reading Achievement (CIERA). Elfrieda Hiebert, director. University of Michigan School of Education, 610 E. University Ave., Ann Arbor, MI, 48109. See also pages 6b and 22b.

    To get beyond narrow, "scientific research" on beginning reading, see summaries of CIERA research reports. Full reports can be downloaded at www.ciera.org.

The Center on Education Policy. 1001 Connecticut Avenue N.W., Suite 619, Washington, DC, 20036. *www.ctredpol.org*

    Founded in 1995, this independent organization, in support of public schools, advocates for more effective pubic school education by pro-

ducing publications, convening meetings, making presentations, and providing expert advice upon request.

Goodman, Kenneth, ed. 1998. *In Defense of Good Teaching: What Teachers Need to Know About the "Reading Wars."* York, ME: Stenhouse.

    Important, disturbing, carefully documented information about how extreme political and religious groups, the media, and "disinformation groups" have been responsible for mandating "back to basics" and intensive, systematic phonics instruction across the country. Specific suggestions for political action.

Keresty, Barbara, Susan O'Leary, and Dale Wortley. 1998. *You Can Make a Difference: A Teacher's Guide to Political Action.* Portsmouth, NH: Heinemann.

    Three teachers describe how their political actions saved a school district program. Practical suggestions for how teachers can get involved at their own local levels.

Kernan-Schloss, Adam, and Andy Plattner. 1998. "Talking to the Public About Public Schools." *Educational Leadership* (October): 18–22.

    The authors argue that it is more important for schools "to listen well than to listen to everyone." They propose some important communication suggestions that focus on ways to assure the public that schools are doing a better job of educating students. (J.W.)

Krashen, Stephen. 1999. *Three Arguments Against Whole Language and Why They Are Wrong.* Portsmouth, NH: Heinemann.

    Educators will appreciate Stephen Krashen's concise discussion of the arguments opponents of whole language use in the reading wars. He reviews research on eye fixation studies, the role of context in learning to read, and methodologies related to whole language and a skills approach to explain or refute the claims made by critics. The final chapters in this short, five-chapter book offer some real solutions and provide perspective about the reading wars. (J.W.)

- McQuillan, Jeff. 1998. *The Literacy Crisis: False Claims, Real Solutions.* Portsmouth, NH: Heinemann.

Through careful analysis of a wide body of current research, McQuillan calls into question the current overfocus on isolated skills and phonics and demonstrates that access to print and the amount of reading students do are the best predictors of reading achievement. He documents that states that have the best library systems and print access have the highest reading scores on the NAEP (National Association of Educational Progress). Conversely, states with the poorest print access have the lowest reading achievement. An eye-opening book for making well-stocked classroom and school libraries—and lots of time for voluntary reading—absolute necessities for improving reading achievement for all students.

Moustafa, Margaret. 1997. *Beyond Traditional Phonics: Research Discoveries and Reading Instruction.* Portsmouth, NH: Heinemann. See page 25b.

Novick, Rebecca. 1998. *Learning to Read and Write: A Place to Start.* Portland, OR: Northwest Regional Educational Laboratory. See page 9b.

Routman, Regie. 1996. *Literacy at the Crossroads: Crucial Talk About Reading, Writing and Other Teaching Dilemmas.* Portsmouth, NH: Heinemann.

The author clarifies "good" reading and writing practices, whole language and phonics, and how the push for "back to basics" is influencing educational policy. Lots of specific suggestions for how educators can become politically savvy and more effective communicators with the public.

Weaver, Constance, Lorraine Gillmeister-Krause, and Grace Vento-Zogby. 1996. *Creating Support for Effective Literacy Education.* Portsmouth, NH: Heinemann. See page 26b.

Weaver, Constance, ed. 1998. *Reconsidering a Balanced Approach to Reading.* Urbana, IL: National Council of Teachers of English. See page 24b.

Web Sites and Pages for Legislative News and Information Related to Reading, Professional Development, and Political Action

American Library Association, 50 East Huron, Chicago, IL 60611. *www.ala.org*

CATENet: *jburke5@ix.netcom.com*

An electronic roundtable created and moderated by English teacher Jim Burke for the California Association of Teachers of English. Designed to keep California teachers, and teachers of all grade levels across the nation, talking and informed about the profession.

http://www.toread.com

A Web page created by CATENet member John Nemes to serve as a clearinghouse for the dissemination of reading research through conferences, journals, and other publications.

Center for Improvement of Early Reading Achievement: *www.ciera.org*

See pages 5b and 22b.

Education Week: www/edweek.org

A weekly publication devoted to news and views related to all aspects of education.

International Reading Association, 800 Barksdale Road, P.O. Box 8139, Newark, DE, 19714. *www.reading.org*

Click on advocacy.

The League of Women Voters, 1730 M Street N.W., Washington, DC, 20036. *www.lwv.org*

National Association for Education of Young Children: *www.naeyc.org*

Click on public policy.

National Council of Teachers of English, 1111 West Kenyon Road, Urbana, IL, 61801. *http://www.ncte.org/action*

National Education Association: *www.nea.org*

Click on legislative action.

http://readingonline.org

Articles on research and practice, online discussion forums, and analysis of issues related to reading.

U.S. Senate: *http://www.senate.gov*

Chapter 2:
A Comprehensive Literacy
Program: Essential Elements

Comprehensive Literacy Resources

- Beers, Kylene, and Barbara G. Samuels, eds. 1998. *IntoFocus: Understanding and Creating Middle School Readers*. Norwood, MA: Christopher-Gordon.

  This comprehensive text covers most of the aspects a teacher needs to consider in order to create a literacy program for middle-school readers. Contributions from twenty-seven educators address topics such as characteristics of the middle-school reader, how to encourage and support reading and literature discussion, and ways to reach struggling readers through comprehension and strategy instruction. This text provides practical suggestions and annotated book lists as well as many examples of students' work. (J.W.)

Bodrova, Elena, and Deborah J. Leong. 1996. *Tools of the Mind: The Vygotskian Approach to Early Childhood Education*. Englewood Cliffs, NJ: Prentice-Hall.

  Lev Vygotsky, a Russian psychologist who wrote about human development and learning, has had a powerful influence on current teaching practices. This excellent resource includes an initial concise and informative overview of Vygotskian principles and compares them to other theories of child development. The remainder of the book discusses how to apply Vygotsky's theory to promote development and suggests ways to structure learning experiences to encourage learning. Chapter 4 provides an in-depth discussion of the Zone of Proximal Development (ZPD), a concept incorporated into the work of many current language arts researchers and practitioners. Educators interested in learning more about Vygotsky may want to read Vygotsky in the Classroom: Mediated Literacy Instruction and Assessment *by Lisbeth Dixon-Krauss (Longman, 1996). (J.W.)*

Button, Kathryn, Margaret J. Johnson, and Paige Furgeson. 1996. "Interactive Writing in a Primary Classroom." *The Reading Teacher* (March): 446–454.

  An excellent, detailed article for understanding and applying interactive writing principles and procedures with lots of examples from a kindergarten classroom.

Cambourne, Brian. 1995. "Toward an Educationally Relevant Theory of Literacy Learning: Twenty Years of Inquiry." *The Reading Teacher* (November): 182–190.

  If you are not familiar with Cambourne's conditions of learning (Invitations, pages 12–14) and how to apply them to the literacy classroom, you will want to read and discuss this "distinguished educator" article. Excellent for thinking about and determining your own theory of learning.

Cooper, Patsy. 1993. *When Stories Come to School. Telling, Writing, and Performing Stories in the Early Childhood Classroom*. New York: Teachers & Writers Collaborative.

  In a one-on-one setting, the teacher writes down the child's oral story while clarifying the child's intentions through questioning and conversation. Afterward, the story is acted out by the teller and other classmates. Great for improving children's narrative and dramatization skills.

- Cunningham, Patricia M., and Richard L. Allington. 1999. *Classrooms That Work: They Can All Read and Write*. 2d ed. New York: Longman.

  The authors have updated and expanded their comprehensive and powerful first edition. In the first chapters, they address the current debate about the role of phonics instruction. In Chapters two through six, they discuss the components of a balanced reading program, adding in many examples from teachers across the country. Chapters eight through ten suggest ways to organize and manage good instruction, providing sample schedules for different grade levels. School-wide literacy issues and "things worth fighting for" are included in the final chapter. Photographs and boxed suggestions help make the book practical and informative. Both experi-

enced and new teachers will find they can read straight through the book or selectively. Educators interested in school-wide change may also want to read Schools That Work (1996) by the same authors. (J.W.)

Edwards, Carolyn, Lella Gandini, and George Forman, eds. 1998. *The Hundred Languages of Children: The Reggio Emilia Approach: Advanced Reflections, Second Edition.* Greenwich, CT: Ablex.

> *Educators will find interesting information about the schools that have evolved over the past 40 years in Reggio Emilia, an area in northern Italy. This remarkable system is anchored in constructivist theory and based upon the philosophies of Froebel, Montessori, Dewey, Vygotsky, and others. Administrators and primary teachers will find the essays by a number of respected early childhood educators reassuring, enlightening, and thought-provoking. This text will be especially helpful to those refining and restructuring programs for young children.* (J.W.)

● Fisher, Bobbi. 1998. *Joyful Learning in Kindergarten.* Rev. ed. Portsmouth, NH: Heinemann.

> *This book describes what an observant, knowledgeable kindergarten teacher does in her classroom in a typical day and why she does it. It is a remarkably clear and pragmatic explanation of a classroom based on Don Holdaway's Natural Learning Model. Each chapter highlights a specific aspect of the classroom. The chapters on assessment, dramatic play, and questions teachers ask are especially strong. Although the book is focused on the kindergarten level, teachers from prekindergarten through grade two will find many ideas, routines, themes, and record-keeping suggestions that will directly apply to their whole language classrooms.* (J.W.)

Hindley, Joanne. 1996. *In the Company of Children.* York, ME: Stenhouse.

> *This remarkable text is written in the strong voice of an exceptional teacher. Hindley uses many student examples and photographs to enhance her clear descriptions of how she creates a comprehensive literacy program for her third-*grade class. She discusses management issues, using children's literature, incorporating genre study, teaching through minilessons in the reading/writing workshop, and holding student conferences. Both new and experienced teachers will appreciate this practical book filled with specific suggestions. (J.W.)

International Reading Association and the National Association for the Education of the Young Child (NAEYC). *Learning to Read and Write: Developmentally Appropriate Practices for Young Children.* 1998. Newark, DE: International Reading Association.

> *This document provides guidelines and recommendations for teaching young children to read and write. The document provides an excellent overview of issues facing early childhood educators and policy makers and summarizes research to guide instruction for three age ranges: birth through preschool, kindergarten, and primary children. It also includes a continuum of early reading and writing development and suggested classroom practices that teachers will find helpful. (This position statement also appears in* Young Children *[July 1998, 53 (4): 30–46].)* (J.W.)

● Mallow, Frances, and Leslie Patterson. 1999. *Framing Literacy: Teaching and Learning in K–8 Classrooms.* Norwood, MA: Christopher-Gordon.

> *Teachers will find this comprehensive text an excellent resource in creating and refining a comprehensive literacy program. Written in a conversational voice, the many samples of students' work and strategy suggestions enhance this text. Because of its organization, a reader may select one of two ways to read: going first to the parts that answer immediate questions or reading straight through the book, moving through the sections: theory building, informed action, inquiry, and planning. Educators committed to the goal of matching beliefs and classroom practice will appreciate the unique way the authors approach the theory that undergirds teaching decisions. The book is filled with practical suggestions and classroom vignettes that are sure to answer many questions elementary and middle school teachers will have. Particularly helpful chapters include Chapter 8, which de-*

tails excellent assessment options; and Chapters 9 and 12, which outline a variety of instructional options related to classroom planning. (J.W.)

Manning, Deborah A., and Jean W. Fennacy. 1993. "Bringing Children to Literacy Through Shared Reading." In *Bringing Children to Literacy*, edited by Bill Harp, 45–64. Needham, MA: Christopher-Gordon.

An outstanding chapter that demonstrates how shared reading is used throughout the day in a second-grade classroom to engage children in reading and literacy.

McGee, Lea M., and Donald J. Richels. 1996. *Literacy's Beginnings: Supporting Young Readers and Writers*. 2d ed. Boston, MA: Allyn and Bacon.

Teachers who work with young children will find this a helpful resource. Not only do the authors provide an emergent literacy perspective, they also present classroom vignettes, suggested teaching practices, and a comprehensive guide to quality early literacy programs. Chapters contain a four-part design: discussion of key terms, an illustrative case study to make real-life connections, application of the chapters' key information, and a chapter summary with references. Most helpful is the book's specific focus on the emergent reader and writer. (J.W.)

● Novick, Rebecca. 1998. *Learning to Read and Write: A Place to Start*. Portland, OR: Northwest Regional Educational Laboratory.

The author closely examines research on how oral and written language develops and connects that research to specific recommended preschool and primary-grade classroom practices. Includes related profiles of five schools in the Northwest as well as about forty pages of informative handouts for educators and parents. An invaluable resource for teaching reading and writing as meaning-centered processes.

Payne, Carleen daCrux, and Mary Browning Schulman. 1998. *Getting the Most out of Morning Message and Other Shared Writing Lessons*. New York: Scholastic Professional.

Detailed, explicit text and visuals for meaningfully incorporating shared writing into your primary-grade literacy program. Lots of wonderful, practical examples.

Phenix, Jo. 1994. *Teaching the Skills*. Markham, ONT: Pembroke; York, ME: Stenhouse.

A terrific, commonsense text for teaching skills in the reading-writing classroom. Combines traditional and holistic approaches.

● Robb, Laura. 1998. *Easy-to-Manage Reading and Writing Conferences*. New York: Scholastic.

This text explores the art of conferencing so essential in a balanced literacy program. After a brief introduction that discusses the benefits and basic tenets of conferences, the author guides the reader by suggesting a conference menu for "just beginning" and "experienced" teachers in order to increase success in incorporating this approach. The remainder of the book is organized around different types of conferences such as whole and small-group conferences, conferences that monitor and improve reading, and conferences that monitor and improve writing. While the book is intended for intermediate-grade teachers, many of the suggestions transfer to all grade levels. (J.W.)

● Rhodes, Lynn K., and Curt Darling-Marling. 1996. *Readers and Writers with a Difference: A Holistic Approach to Teaching Struggling Readers and Writers*. 2d ed. Portsmouth, NH: Heinemann.

The second edition of this comprehensive text addresses the needs of students who struggle. The authors have broadened the audience to include classroom teachers as well as those who work with students in resource rooms. Updated and expanded chapters include recent theory and research in reading and writing. (See also 64b) (J.W.)

● Short, Kathy G., Jerome C. Harste, and Carolyn Burke. 1996. *Creating Classrooms for Authors and Inquirers*. 2d ed. Portsmouth, NH: Heinemann.

Experienced teachers will appreciate this in-depth text that presents curriculum as inquiry and the authoring cycle framework as the vehicle for organizing study. Much of the information from the first edition is included along with the authors' current thinking. The second section of the book is expanded. Along with the activities included in the first edition, this book includes some new, well-described strategies teachers will want to integrate into their own classroom practices. (J.W.)

Worthy, Jo. 1996. "Removing Barriers to Voluntary Reading for Reluctant Readers: The Role of School and Classroom Libraries." *Language Arts* (November): 483–492.

The author found that when reluctant readers have access to materials that interest them, they do choose to read. Teachers and librarians are the vital team for maximizing that access. An excellent article for promoting voluntary reading for all students.

Reading Aloud

See page 39b for reading nonfiction.

Lesesne, Teri S. 1998. "Reading Aloud to Build Success in Reading." In *IntoFocus: Understanding and Creating Middle School Readers*, edited by Kylene Beers and Barbara G. Samuels. Norwood, MA: Christopher-Gordon.

This well-written chapter highlights important aspects of read-aloud and discusses different approaches for incorporating it into the language arts program. For example, Lesense explains how to use read aloud to "read and tease," to introduce genre or units of study, and to share an entire book. While the suggested literature included is more appropriate for middle school students, teachers of all grades will find helpful suggestions and guidelines. (J.W.)

Moss, Barabara. 1995. "Using Children's Nonfiction Tradebooks as Read-Alouds." *Language Arts* (February): 122–125.

Very helpful for how to select, read aloud, and respond to nonfiction texts.

- Trelease, Jim. *The Read-Aloud Handbook*. 4th ed. New York: Penguin Books, 1995.

Updated periodically, this classic text for parents and teachers gives rationale and guidelines for reading aloud as well as a "giant treasury" of annotated recommendations for all grade levels. An excellent resource for choosing books and promoting reading for pleasure.

Vardell, Sylvia M. 1998. "Using Read-Aloud to Explore the Layers of Nonfiction." In *Making*

Facts Come Alive: Choosing Quality Nonfiction Literature K–8, edited by Rosemary A. Bamford and Janice V. Kristo, 151–157. Norwood, MA: Christopher-Gordon.

Provides lots of ways to read nonfiction aloud. "Cover-to-cover read-alouds, participatory read-alouds, chapter read-alouds, caption read-alouds, browsing, believe-it-or-not sharing, and introducing structural elements through reading aloud" (154).

Brain-Based Learning

Bransford, John D., Ann L. Brown, and Rodney R. Cocking, eds. 1999. *How People Learn: Brain, Mind, Experience, and School*. Washington, DC: National Academy Press.

This report, prepared by a distinguished panel, offers perspectives to teachers, administrators, and policymakers on the current research about the mind, the brain, and the processes of learning. The book is organized into four parts: "Introduction," "Learners and Learning," "Teachers and Teaching," and "Future Directions for the Science of Learning." Educators involved in school renewal and restructuring will find the specific conclusions and recommendations especially helpful. (J.W.)

Caine, Renate Nummela, and Geoffrey Caine. 1997. *Education on the Edge of Possibility*. Alexandria, VA: Association for Supervision and Curriculum Development.

Caine and Caine package brain research in accessible ways for educators. If you only have time for one book, read their book, Making Connections: Teaching and the Human Brain *(ASCD 1994). It impacted many teachers' perceptions of how students learn. In this more recent text and its companion,* Unleashing the Power of Perceptual Change: The Potential of Brain-Based Teaching *(1997), the authors update and expand upon their earlier work. Teachers and administrators will find the book useful when considering school restructuring. The research, case studies, and discussion of the obstacles and challenges are both interesting and thought-provoking.* (J.W.)

Caine, Renate Nummela, and Geoffrey Caine. 1997. *Unleashing the Power of Perceptual Change: The Potential of Brain-Based Teaching*. Alexandria, VA: Association for Supervision and Curriculum Development.

The authors describe how their research on learning and the brain has been translated into transforming teachers' perceptions and practices in two schools. A fascinating, thoughtful text for realizing new possibilities and opportunities for teacher and student learning.

Jensen, Eric. 1998. *Introduction to Brain-Compatible Learning*. San Diego, CA: The Brain Store, Inc.

This practical book compares and contrasts traditional learning with the brain-compatible approach and provides an introduction to 12 key principles of brain-compatible learning. In 102 pages, educators will find an easy-to-read overview of why applying the new information about the brain is critical. (J.W.)

Jensen, Eric. 1998. *Teaching with the Brain in Mind*. Alexandria, VA: Association for Supervision and Curriculum Development.

Jensen provides research on theories of the brain and emotions and gives practical tips and techniques for using that information to enhance learning in the classroom. Important research to know about and discuss.

Smith, Frank. 1998. *The Book of Learning and Forgetting*. New York: Teachers College Press.

Over the past three decades, Frank Smith has contributed and influenced thinking about how one learns to read and write. In this book, he contrasts the "official theory" of learning with a correct, but suppressed "classic view" in which learning occurs every moment of our lives. This provocative book provides Smith's perspectives as a cognitive psychologist and warns that the "official view" has produced damage to the educational system. He suggests our option is to "acknowledge and work with the natural strengths of the human brain" (viii). (J.W.)

Chapter 3:
The Literature Program

For recommended literature and literature extension resources published up to and including 1994, see *Invitations* and *The Blue Pages*.

The Literature Program (Fiction and Nonfiction)

American Library Association. 50 East Huron Street, Chicago, IL 60611.

Publishes many professional books for teachers and librarians and Book Links *(see page 70b). Also publishes the Newbery and Caldecott Award. Check the ALA home page for links to useful information:* http://www.ala.org/.

Association for Library Service to Children (ALSC), A Division of the American Library Association. 50 East Huron Street, Chicago, IL 60611.

Publishes many useful brochures designed to support a literature and library program, for example, "The Newbery and Caldecott Awards: A Guide to the Medal and Honor Books," and "Programming Author Visits." Check the ALSC homepage for a complete publications list: www.ala.org/alsc/publication.html.

The Children's Book Council, Inc. 568 Broadway, New York, NY 10012. *www.cbcbooks.org*

Publishes a newsletter with information about children's books, book publishers, and inexpensive publishers' materials. Sells pamphlets, posters, and bookmarks that support reading and writing; sponsors National Children's Book Week in November and Young People's Poetry Week in April. Distributes annually: "Children's Choices" (a yearly selection of newly published books that children prefer), "Outstanding Science Tradebooks for Children" (first published in spring issue of Science and Children*), and "Notable Children's Trade Books in the Field of Social Studies" (first published in spring issue of* Social Education*).*

Cole, Ardith Davis. 1998. *Literacy Activities for Building Classroom Communities*. Scarborough, ONT: Pippin.

Lots of suggestions for meaningful reading/writing activities (in place of "seat work") in the literature classroom. Assumes that a cooperative classroom community is already in place.

Fractor, Jann S., Marjorie C. Woodruff, Miriam G. Martinez, and William H. Teale. 1993. "Let's Not Miss Opportunities to Promote Voluntary Reading: Classroom Libraries in the Elementary School." *The Reading Teacher* (March): 476–484.

Very useful for the rationale, research, and specifics for setting up a high-quality classroom library.

Heald-Taylor, B. Gail. 1996. "Three Paradigms for Literature Instruction in Grades 3 to 6." *The Reading Teacher* (March): 456–466.

Presents three ways of viewing literature instruction: "curriculum as fact, curriculum as activity, and curriculum as inquiry." Excellent for discussion and rethinking your teaching.

Hoffbauer, Diane. 1998. "The Web of Life." In *United in Diversity: Using Multicultural Young Adult Literature in the Classroom.* Urbana, IL: National Council of Teachers of English.

Describes four related YA books that represent different cultures and gives strategies for in-depth study through such activities as developing perspectives, conceptual webbing, and creating alternative endings.

Huck, Charlotte S., Susan Hepler, Janet Hickman, and Barbara Z. Kiefer. 1997. *Children's Literature in the Elementary School.* 6th ed. New York: McGraw-Hill.

You will want to have access to this updated edition (783 pages) of the "classic" children's literature textbook. The text encompasses three parts: "Learning About Books and Children," "Exploring Children's Literature," and "Developing a Literature Program." Comprehensive and outstanding. Numerous, specific examples and visuals to guide your teaching.

International Reading Association. 1997. *More Teachers' Favorite Books for Kids: Teachers' Choices 1994–1996.* Newark, DE: International Reading Association.

Teachers' Choices are the U.S. trade books published for children and adolescents that teachers have selected to be exceptional for use across the curriculum. Books are grouped by suggested reading levels. Annotations and bibliographic information are provided for each title, and indexes list books by title, author, and illustrator. (IRA also publishes Children's Choices *and* Young Adults' Choices.)

Jenkins, Esther C., and Mary C. Austin. 1987. *Literature for Children About Asians and Asian Americans: Analysis and Annotated Bibliography,*

with Additional Readings for Adults. Westport, CT: Greenwood.

Although this text has not been updated, it is still the most comprehensive resource for books by and about Asians (as of 1994), and therefore, it is included. In addition to recommended literature, the book includes criteria for selecting books for a cross-cultural curriculum.

Krashen, Stephen. 1998. "Bridging Inequity with Books." *Educational Leadership* (January): 18–21.

A research-based article that confirms that access to books and "the number of books per student in the school library" is one of the best predictors of reading achievement.

Kruse, Ginny Moore, Kathleen T. Horning, and Megan Schliesman. 1997. *Multicultural Literature for Children and Young Adults, Volume 2: 1991–1996.* University of Wisconsin-Madison: Cooperative Children's Book Center.

Both this volume and the first volume (1980–1990) provide a fully annotated listing of carefully selected literature by and about people of color. Both are arranged in sixteen thematic and genre-related categories, including "Seasons and Celebrations," "Issues in Today's World," "Historical People, Places, and Events," "Contemporary People, Places, and Events," "Picture Books," "Fiction for Children," and "Fiction for Teenagers." Appendices include authors and illustrators of color, a listing of the titles categorized by ethnic or cultural groups, and an annotated list of recommended resources.

• Lukens, Rebecca J. 1999. *A Critical Handbook of Children's Literature.* 6th ed. New York: Longman.

Teachers using a reading and writing workshop approach will find this book an excellent source for planning minilessons and literature study. The author organizes the book by briefly discussing the different genres found in children's literature. The rest of the book is devoted to in-depth discussions of literary elements such as plot, theme, and characterization. Poetry, rhyme, and nonfiction are also discussed. (J.W.)

Norton, Donna E. 1993. "Webbing and Historical Fiction." *The Reading Teacher* (February): 432–436.

> *An excellent article for implementing webbing, described here as "a method for graphically and visually displaying relationships among ideas and concepts" (432). Presents vocabulary webs, literary webs, and instructional unit webs. Keep in mind that webbing requires much teacher guidance and scaffolding.*

Norton, Donna E., with Saundra E. Norton. 1999. *Through the Eyes of a Child: An Introduction to Children's Literature.* 5th ed. Columbus, OH: Merrill.

> *Norton's comprehensive text is an excellent resource for teachers. One of the major differences in this and other children's literature texts is its two-part chapter design. After several introductory chapters, the remaining chapters are each divided into two sections. The first presents characteristics of each genre along with classic titles. The second part lists practical, field-tested teaching tips and strategies. An additional feature is the inclusion of issue-related discussions that mirror many of the daily dilemmas teachers using a literature-based reading program face. The text is accompanied by a CD-ROM that includes 3000 titles. (J.W.)*

• Raphael, Taffy E., and Kathryn H. Au, eds. 1998 *Literature-Based Instruction: Reshaping the Curriculum.* Norwood, MA: Christopher-Gordon.

> *This edited book includes chapters by many respected literacy educators. The topics span a wide variety of issues related to the theory and practice of literature-based instruction. Larry Sipe's chapter, "First- and Second-Grade Literacy Critics: Understanding Children's Rich Responses to Literature," is especially helpful to those interested in forging a stronger link between literacy criticism and literacy. Other chapters address the role of culture and second language learners, thematic studies, and assessment issues in literature-based programs. Both new and experienced teachers will find this book useful. (J.W.)*

Samway, Katherine Davies, Gail Whang, and Mary Pippitt. 1995. *Buddy Reading: Cross-Age Tutoring in a Multicultural School.* Portsmouth, NH: Heinemann.

> *Lots of practical plans and workable suggestions for partner reading with peers, older and younger students, and volunteers.*

Silva, Cecilia, and Esther L. Delgado-Larocco. 1993. "Facilitating Learning Through Interconnections: A Concept Approach to Core Literature Units." *Language Arts* (October): 469–474.

> *Great ideas and theoretical underpinning for developing "conceptually related units of study" and not just "using authentic literature." Very helpful for transitioning to appropriate use of literature and going beyond "core book" concept.*

Sorenson, Marilou, and Barbara Lehman, eds. 1995. *Teaching with Children's Books: Paths to Literature.* Urbana, IL: National Council of Teachers of English.

> *Teachers, administrators, and teacher educators give insightful perspectives on using literature in the classroom. Many thoughtful and practical ideas.*

• Tunnell, Michael O., and James J. Jacobs. 2000. *Children's Literature, Briefly.* 2d ed. Columbus, OH: Merrill.

> *This text differs from more extensive children's literature texts. Since the topics are arranged in three sections, information is easy to access. The first section serves as an overview and frames the brief discussions of each genre in the second section. Each of those chapters includes an annotated list of ten favorites, a list of twenty more titles, and another five "easier to read" book suggestions. The third section features teaching issues such as teacher as reader, reading motivation, and building classroom libraries. A CD-ROM with more than 8000 titles adds a fourth list of books from which teachers may select. (J.W.)*

Worthy, Jo. 1996. "A Matter of Interest: Literature That Hooks Reluctant Readers and Keeps Them Reading." *The Reading Teacher* (November): 204–212.

> *Noting that, for struggling readers, "far more important than readability is interest" (205), the author provides recommendations for series books, sophisticated picture books, performance texts, poetry and verse, popular texts, and much more.*

Literature Resources for Choosing Fiction and Nonfiction

American Library Association. 50 East Huron Street, Chicago, IL 60611.

Publishes annual lists of notable books for children and young adult readers in its journal, Booklist. Copies can be secured by sending a self-addressed, stamped business envelope.

Appraisal: Science Books for Young People. A quarterly. Boston: MA: The Children's Science Book Review Committee. Northeastern University, 403 Richards Hall, Boston, MA 02215.

A children's librarian and a subject specialist each write a detailed review for many new science trade books. The varying perspectives are helpful for determining the books' quality and usefulness.

- Bamford, Rosemary A., and Janice V. Kristo, eds. 1998. *Making Facts Come Alive: Choosing Quality Nonfiction Literature K–8.* Norwood, MA: Christopher-Gordon.

Annotates the Orbis Pictus Award winners (annual award from the National Council of Teachers of English for an outstanding nonfiction book) as well as honor books and notable nonfiction. Includes a very brief summary and distinguishing features, such as historical photographs, first person narrative, labeled diagrams, detailed drawings. Also contains excellent chapters for choosing and using nonfiction in the classroom.

Bamford, Rosemary A., and Janice V. Kristo, eds. 1998. "Response Guides to Nonfiction Children's Literature." In *Making Facts Come Alive: Choosing Quality Nonfiction Literature K–8,* 233–267. Norwood, MA: Christopher-Gordon.

Eleven guides to notable nonfiction titles such as The Magic School Bus Inside a Beehive *by Joanna Cole,* The Librarian Who Measured the Earth *by Kathryn Lasky, and* The Great Fire *by Jim Murphy. Each book guide includes distinguished features, a synopsis, response suggestions, connecting books, and an interview with the author. A good model for determining appropriate response to nonfiction.*

Barrera, Rosalinda B., Verlinda D. Thompson, and Mark Dressman, eds. and the Committee to Re-

vise the Multicultural Booklist. 1997. *Kaleidoscope: A Multicultural Booklist for Grades K–8.* 2d ed. Urbana, IL: National Council of Teachers of English.

"An annotated bibliography of selected books about or related to African Americans, Asian Americans, Latinos or Hispanic Americans, and Native Americans" (xi), published from 1993–1995. Grouped by genre or theme (rather than by cultural group) with topics such as "People and Places," "Understanding the Past: History," "Individuals to Know: Biography and Autobiography," "Picture Books: Primary and Beyond," "Folktales, Myths, and Legends," and "Fiction for Intermediate Readers." A terrific resource for knowing and choosing quality multicultural literature.

Book Links

Bimonthly magazine for teachers and librarians. Chunks books together and gives valuable suggestions for teaching themes and content studies. See page 70b for complete information.

Horn Book, Inc. 1999. *The Horn Book Guide Interactive.* (CD-ROM) Portsmouth, NH: Heinemann.

This database of 2,000 books features ranked reviews, Outstanding (1) to Unacceptable (6), which allow for easy access to titles published since 1990. Periodically updated, this is a valuable resource for curriculum designers, teachers, and librarians. Entries may be summoned by title, author, genre, subject, age level, or ranking.

International Reading Association. 800 Barksdale Road, P.O. Box 8139, Newark, DE 19714. *http://www.ira.org/*

Publishes annual lists of best books (chosen by votes) each November in The Reading Teacher *(children and teachers' lists) and in the* Journal of Reading *(young adult list). Obtainable for $1.00 per list by writing to the International Reading Association.*

Kobrin, Beverly. 1995. *Eyeopeners II: Children's Books to Answer Children's Questions About the World Around Them.* New York: Scholastic.

Readers may recall Kobrin's first resource, Eyeopeners!, *in which she reviewed more than 500 imaginative and enriching nonfiction books. In this second volume, she reviews more* than 800 new books sure to inspire and increase teachers' use of nonfiction books, grouped by categories to ease locating the needed topics and titles. This valuable resource book is designed to be used by teachers, parents, and librarians. (J.W.)

Krey, DeAn M. 1998. *Children's Literature in Social Studies: Teaching to the Standards.* Washington, DC: National Council for the Social Studies.

Carefully selected and annotated children's books published in the 1990s offer support for complying with the national standards in social studies. An excellent resource.

Muse, Daphne, ed. 1997. *The New Press Guide to Multicultural Resources for Young Readers.* New York: The New Press.

An annotated bibliography that includes a detailed synopsis of more than 1,000 multicultural books arranged by themes or topics (such as "The Family," Cultural Traditions," "Community/Friendship," and "Newcomers Establishing Roots") and organized by grade levels K–3, 4–6, and 7–8. Includes essays on multicultural education and an extensive appendix of resources. A unique, quality reference and resource for K–8.

National Council for the Social Studies. *Notable Children's Trade Books in the Field of Social Studies.*

Publishes an annual list of notable books (K–8) that appears in the April/May issue of Social Education. *Write to the Children's Book Council, 568 Broadway, Suite 404, New York, NY 10012 to obtain your free copy. Include a self-addressed, business size, stamped envelope.*

National Council of Teachers of English. 1111 West Kenyon Road, Urbana, IL 61801–1096. *http://www.ncte.org/*

Publishes an annotated list of award winning books each October in Language Arts. *Obtainable by writing to the NCTE at the address above.*

National Science Teachers Association. *Outstanding Science Trade Books for Children.*

Publishes an annual list of outstanding science books in the March issue of Science and Children.

Phelan, Patricia, ed. 1996. *High Interest-Easy Reading: An Annotated Booklist for Middle School and Senior High, Seventh Edition.* Urbana, IL: National Council of Teachers of English.

This annotated bibliography is part of the NCTE series. It includes both fiction and nonfiction titles for students who typically do not enjoy reading. The book is organized in chapters that group the titles into genre-related themes such as "Adventure," "How-to Books," "Folklore and Legends," and "Issues of Our Time." More than three hundred titles are included. To help teachers use the book, three indexes arrange the books by title, author, and subject. Educators will also appreciate the information about award-winning books and the directory of publishers. (J.W.)

Samuels, Barbara G., and Kylene G. Beers, eds. 1996. *Your Reading: An Annotated Booklist for Middle School and Junior High, 1995–1996 Edition.* Urbana, IL: National Council of Teachers of English.

Part of an on-going set of resources that support literature-based reading programs, this volume contains more than 1,100 annotations of the highest quality books published between 1992 and 1996. This resource is intended to assist intermediate and middle school teachers in selecting books for classroom use. Arranged thematically and with an extensive subject index, teachers may choose from sections such as "Growing Up," "Imagined Lands," and "Science All Around You." In addition, the authors and contributors include a list entitled "100 Books from 25 Years of Young Adult Literature: 1967–1992." See the 1999 edition, edited by Ben Nelms. (J.W.)

Sudol, Peg, and Caryn King. 1996. "A Checklist for Choosing Nonfiction Trade Books." *The Reading Teacher* (February): 422–424.

"Tips and guidelines" for reviewing and selecting quality nonfiction trade books. Includes a helpful checklist with the following delineated sections: accuracy, organization and layout, cohesion of ideas, specialized vocabulary, reader interest.

● Susag, Dorothea M. 1998. *Roots and Branches: A Resource of Native American Literature—Themes, Lessons, and Bibliographies.* Urbana, IL: National Council of Teachers of English.

An outstanding, comprehensive resource for using and honoring oral and written Native American literature. Also intended "to support each student's search for his or her cultural ties to ancient and contemporary writers and story-tellers" (7), to help us confront stereotypes, and to understand the multiple contexts of American Indian lives. For intermediate and secondary grades.

Sutton, Wendy K., ed. 1997. *Adventuring with Books: A Booklist for Pre–K through Grade 6.* Urbana, IL: National Council of Teachers of English.

More than 1,200 annotations were selected from the 10,000 books reviewed for this latest edition of Adventuring with Books. *Designed to help educators select the best in children's litera-ture, this resource is arranged first by genres or topics such as books for young children, poetry, traditional literature, fantasy, social studies, and science, then further divided by categories such as nursery rhymes, folk songs, animal fantasy, and astronomy, and handicrafts. Several types of indexes make locating just the right book un-complicated. Additional appendices include a list of children's literature prizes, awards, and lists and a directory of publishers. Be sure to also consult the 1999 edition, edited by Kathryn Pierce Mitchell. (J.W.)*

Response to Literature

Bamford, Rosemary A., and Janice V. Kristo, eds. 1998. "Response Guides to Nonfiction Chil-dren's Literature." In *Making Facts Come Alive: Choosing Quality Nonfiction Literature K–8,* 233–267. Norwood, MA: Christopher-Gordon. See page 14b.

Cole, Ardith Davis. 1998. *Literacy Activities for Building Classroom Communities.* Scarborough, ONT: Pippin. See page 11b.

Hill, Suan, and Jane O'Loughlin. 1995. *Book Talk: Collaborative Responses to Literature.* Ar-madale, Australia: Eleanor Curtain; Winnipeg, MAN: Peguis.

Using a "cooperative structure" to talk about books, the authors present many enterprises for combining meaningful literature extensions with discussion about books.

Hoffbauer, Diane. 1998. "The Web of Life." In *United in Diversity: Using Multicultural Young Adult Literature in the Classroom.* Urbana, IL: National Council of Teachers of English. See page 12b.

Hoyt, Linda. 1998. *Revisit, Reflect, Retell: Strategies for Improving Reading Comprehension.* Portsmouth, NH: Heinemann.

More than ninety strategies and ideas to choose from for responding to literature. Repro-ducibles for teacher-guided and independent work.

Norton, Donna E. 1993. "Webbing and Historical Fiction." *The Reading Teacher* (February): 432–436. See page 13b.

Turner, Julianne, and Scott G. Paris. 1995. "How Lit-eracy Tasks Influence Children's Motivation for Literacy." *The Reading Teacher* (May): 662–673.

An important article for noting the impact of classroom tasks (such as response to literature) on students' motivation for and understanding of literacy. The study found that authentic, chal-lenging reading and writing tasks that led stu-dents to construct new understandings were more important for student motivation than the type of reading program in place.

Readers Theatre

Dixon, Neill, Anne Davies, and Colleen Politano. 1996. *Learning with Readers Theatre: Building Connections.* Winnipeg, MAN: Peguis.

Everything you need to know to be successful with Readers Theatre—beginning and plan-ning, reading and performing with expression, practicing storytelling, writing scripts, staging, incorporating Readers Theatre across the cur-riculum, evaluating, and communicating with families. A first-rate resource.

Martinez, Miriam, Nancy L. Roser, and Susan Strecker. 1998–1999. "'I Never Thought I Could Be a Star': A Readers Theatre Ticket to Fluency." *The Reading Teacher* (December–January): 326–334.

An excellent article for describing the proce-dures and benefits of Readers Theatre. A five-day instructional plan is included.

Resources That Support Author/Illustrator Study

For recommended resources published through 1994, see pages 97b–100b in either *Invitations* or *The Blue Pages*. Also, check with your librarian for authors' memoirs, addresses, Web sites, specific information, and additional resources.

Many authors and illustrators now have "official" Web sites, which you can locate (as well as links to related sites) by entering the author's name on any major search engine.

Author Cards International, Inc. 1996. *Author Cards*. Seattle: School Art Materials.

    One hundred small laminated cards, each with a photo and name of an author and/or illustrator on the front and with biographical information and published works on reverse side. Educational and fun to read and collect.

Commire, Anne, ed. 1999. Updated annually since 1972. *Something About the Author*. Detroit: Gale Research (hardbound).

    Written for teachers and students, this is a comprehensive resource containing detailed information about children's authors' and illustrators' personal and professional lives, published works and works in progress, and fascinating "Sidelights." If your school district does not own this outstanding reference series, check with your local public library.

Copeland, Jeffery S., and Vicky L. Copeland. 1994. *Speaking of Poets 2*. Urbana, IL: National Council of Teachers of English.

    In interview format, twenty distinguished poets share their hopes about writing for children as well as their lives, writing styles, and specific works.

Cummings, Pat, ed. 1995. *Talking with Artists*. Vol. 2. New York: Simon and Schuster Books for Young Readers.

    Excellent resource for artists' backgrounds, family lives, source of ideas, and work habits. Includes such illustrators as Floyd Cooper, Denise Fleming, Kevin Henkes, Brian Pinkney, and Vera B. Williams. Interview format supported by illustrations. A good writing model for our students. See also Volume 1 (New York: Bradbury Press, 1992) and Volume 3 (New York: Clarion, 1999).

Holtze, Sally Holmes. 1996. *Seventh Book of Junior Authors and Illustrators*. New York: H. W. Wilson.

    This teacher reference, the sixth in the series, offers complete and interesting autobiographical and biographical sketches of about 250 noted children's authors and illustrators. A new volume is published every five to six years.

Jenkins, Carol B. 1999. *The Allure of Authors: Author Studies in the Elementary Classroom*. Portsmouth, NH: Heinemann.

    Set within the history of literature study, this valuable guide helps teachers develop a rationale and procedure for studying authors in the K–8 classroom. The author worked with children and teachers studying nonfiction author Joanna Cole (grade three), novel author Avi (grade five), and picture-book author Mem Fox (grade three) and presents three sample author studies. Using Cynthia Rylant and Carolyn Coman as other examples, Jenkins explores principles of author studies and presents ways of weaving strands of author information, exploring literary elements, and personal response into an author study.

Kotch, Laura, and Leslie Zackman. 1995. *The Author Studies Handbook: Helping Students Build Powerful Connections to Literature*. New York: Scholastic Professional.

    Wonderful suggestions and meaningful activities for author study in the classroom. Helpful visuals included. For grades K–8.

Kovacs, Deborah. 1995. *Meet the Authors: Twenty-Five Writers of Upper Elementary and Middle School Books Talk About Their Work*. New York: Scholastic.

    Each lively profile includes background and insight into the authors' writing life as well as a suggested writing activity supplied by the author.

Krull, Kathleen. 1994 and 1995 respectively. *Lives of the Writers: Comedies, Tragedies (And What the Neighbors Thought)* and *Lives of the Artists: Masterpieces, Messes (And What the Neighbors Thought)*. San Diego, CA: Harcourt Brace.

    These volumes are geared to upper-intermediate through high school students. They contain fascinating biographical narratives followed by "Bookmarks" that detail interesting facts. Great model for writing biographies—leads, conclusions, word choices, voice, and varied sentence structure. Also available in this series are Lives of the Musicians: Good Times, Bad Times (And What the Neighbors Thought) *(1993)*; Lives of the Athletes: Thrills, Spills (And What the Neighbors Thought) *(1997); and* Lives of Presidents: Fame and Shame (And What the Neighbors Thought) *(1998)*.

Madura, Sandra. 1995. "The Line and Texture of Aesthetic Response: Primary Children Study Authors and Illustrators." *The Reading Teacher* (October): 110–118.

Wonderful specifics for initiating author/illustrator studies with picture books. Sensitizes educators to "aesthetic response and expression through the visual arts." Describes a unit study of author-illustrator Eric Carle.

McClure Amy A., and Janice V. Kristo, eds. 1996. "Author's Voices: Perspectives of Notable Authors on Wordcrafting." In *Books That Invite Talk, Wonder, and Play,* 207–307. Urbana, IL: National Council of Teachers of English.

In short-essay format, thirty-eight popular children's authors give insight into how they write and craft their literary language. A wonderful accompaniment to book and author study as well as to writing workshop for noting how and what writers compose.

Meet the Author Collection. 1994–1999. Katonah, NY: Richard C. Owen.

This hardback series offers appealing autobiographies of famous authors and illustrators. Written in first person, each book establishes a link between those who write books and poems and the children who read them by providing interesting insights on the authors' writing processes. Notable authors and poets such as Eve Bunting, Patricia McKissack, Lois Ehlert, Jean Fritz, Karla Kuskin, and Jane Yolen are among those featured in delightful photographs and anecdotes recalled by the writers themselves. Written for readers in grades two through five, these 32-page hardbound books offer motivation for reading and writing. (J.W.)

Silvey, Anita, ed. 1995. *Children's Books and Their Creators.* Boston: Houghton Mifflin.

Focuses on memorable twentieth-century literature in multiple genres (preschool through high school). Comprehensive volume is organized alphabetically by children's literature topics/issues, authors, and illustrators. A wealth of information for anyone interested in children's books.

Turner, Robyn Montana. 1992. *Georgia O'Keeffe (Portraits of Women Artists for Children)*. New York: Little, Brown.

This is but one in an excellent series of biographies of prominent women artists including Rosa Bonheur, Mary Cassatt, Frida Kahlo, Georgia O'Keeffe, and Faith Ringgold. The books are distinctive for the informative, carefully researched text, photographs related to each artist's life, and beautiful color reproductions of the artist's work. Use as a read aloud for the early grades. Intermediate-grade students can read them on their own. Reaffirming to young women (and young men) who are interested in art and becoming artists. Fills a need for more books on famous women.

Venezia, Mike. 1990–1999. *Getting to Know the World's Greatest Artists*. Chicago, IL: Children's Press.

A great series for introducing young children to art and artists. Written in enlarged, clear text, the book presents the artist as a real person. Color reproductions of the artist's work plus fanciful illustrations open up the world of art to students in grades K–4. Some of the celebrated artists in the series include: Botticelli, Leonardo da Vinci, Hopper, Goya, Cassatt, Monet, Picasso, Gauguin, Rembrandt, and Van Gogh.

Leveling Books

Brooks, Ellen. 1996. *Just-Right Books for Beginning Readers: Leveled Booklists and Reading Strategies.* New York: Scholastic Professional.

Guidelines and strategies for choosing and using literature. Includes annotated book lists organized by reading stages. Helpful and practical.

Fountas, Irene, and Gay Su Pinnell. 1999. *Matching Books to Readers: A Leveled Book List for Guided Reading, K–3.* Portsmouth, NH: Heinemann.

A comprehensive theory and practice guide to book leveling—what it is, why it's important, and what primary teachers should understand about choosing the most effective texts for children. Includes a leveled book list of 7,500 titles. See also Fountas and Pinnell 1996, page 23b.

Gunning, Thomas G. 1998. *Best Books for Beginning Readers*. Boston: Allyn and Bacon.

An extensive, annotated listing of more than 1,000 leveled beginning reading books, along with strategies for using them.

Hart-Hewins, Linda, and Jan Wells. 1999. *Better Books! Better Readers! How to Choose, Use and Level Books for Children in the Primary Grades*. York, ME: Stenhouse; Markham, ONT: Pembroke.

Provides helpful guidelines for choosing and using books and a bibliography of leveled books for organizing the classroom collection.

Hiebert, Elfrieda H. 1998. "Selecting Texts for Beginning Reading Instruction." In *Literature-Based Instruction: Reshaping the Curriculum*, edited by Taffy E. Raphael and Kathryn H. Au, 195–218. Norwood, MA: Christopher-Gordon.

Lays out a useful framework that can serve as guide for both selecting texts and making decisions about leveling them.

Moore, Paula. 1998. "Choosing Quality Nonfiction Literature: Aspects of Selection for Emergent Readers." In *Making Facts Come Alive: Choosing Quality Nonfiction Literature K–8*, edited by Rosemary A. Bamford and Janice V. Kristo, 75–89. Norwood, MA: Christopher-Gordon.

Most leveled book lists are heavily fiction. Moore presents specific guidance for leveling nonfiction. Particularly helpful.

Peterson, Barbara. 1991. "Selecting Books for Beginning Readers." In *Bridges to Literacy: Learning from Reading Recovery*, by Diane DeFord, Carol Lyons, and Gay Su Pinnell, 119–147. Portsmouth, NH: Heinemann.

Detailed guidelines and specific criteria for organizing beginning reading books into levels of difficulty and learning how to do so. Includes a leveled bibliography of storybooks.

Children's Magazines for the Classroom Library

The following magazines have been carefully selected for use within the reading program. While the list contains publications that include a variety of genres, many of the magazines listed contain primarily nonfiction material. We have included Web sites when available to assist teachers and librarians in obtaining additional information.

American Girl. Published by Pleasant Company Publications, 8400 Fairway Place, Middleton, WI 53562. *www.americangirl.com*

This full-color magazine is published bimonthly and contains a variety of articles, features, and stories. Characters from the popular American Girl series appear regularly along with other selections that focus on items of interest for girls from eight to fourteen. Issue features include: "Amelia's Notebook," "Cooking," "Heart to Heart," and "Letters to You." (J.W.)

Cobblestone Publications. Published by Cobblestone Publishing Company, 30 Grove Street, Suite C, Peterborough, NH 03458. *www.cobblestonepub.com*

Cobblestone produces several high quality nonfiction student magazines for different purposes and age levels. Appleseeds, designed for grades two through four, features a variety of topics that relate to social studies and science and includes interviews and biographical sketches. Other publications extend classroom content studies and are designed for grades four through nine. Faces includes information on people, places, and cultures; Cobblestone highlights American history topics; Calliope explores world history themes; and Odyssey investigates the world of science. Footsteps is designed to celebrate the heritage of African Americans; it explores themes such as courage, perseverance, freedom, and equality. Each is affordable and published nine times a year. (J.W.)

Cricket Magazine Group. Published by Carus Publishing Company, Cricket Magazine Group, 315 Fifth Street, Peru, IL 61354. *www.cricketmag.com*

Cricket publishes seven high-quality magazines: Babybug, Ladybug, Cricket, Spider, Cicada, Muse, and Click. Babybug, designed for the very young child, looks more like a small book than a magazine. The publisher suggests that it is suitable for ages six months to two years. However, prekindergarten and kindergarten teachers will find their students eager to read it. Ladybug, for ages two through six, is a collection of stories, poems, games, and songs— all beautifully illustrated. First- and second-grade teachers enjoy using these with students. Click, designed for ages three through seven and Muse, for ages eight through fourteen, feature the arts, science, cultures, history, nature, and the environment. Spider, for ages six through nine, is similar to Ladybug. Cricket, for ages nine through fourteen, and Cicada, a literary magazine for ages fourteen and up, contain a variety of genres and topics. All are published ten to twelve times a year. Some of the publications include parent resources. (J.W.)

Dragon Fly: A Magazine for Investigators. Published by the National Science Teachers Association and edited by Miami University. 1840 Wilson Blvd., Arlington, VA 22201–3000. *www.nsta.org*

This exceptional, bimonthly magazine contains a variety of articles and essays that emphasize an inquiry approach to science. In addition, the magazine lists interesting Web sites, publication opportunities, and interviews designed to appeal to the ages eight through thirteen. Educators will appreciate the Dragonfly Teacher's Companion, *which is also available. It features science-related articles and information and contains suggested units of study and instructional ideas.* (J.W.)

Kids Discover. Published by Kids Discover, 170 Fifth Avenue, New York, NY 10010.

Kids Discover *is an excellent resource for classroom use. This high-quality periodical covers a variety of topics such as pyramids, explorers, knights and castles, endangered species, and many others. Issues contain engaging full-color pictures, photographs, and graphics that promote nonfiction reading. Subscriptions for this monthly publication are affordable and back orders are available in bulk. Some schools order multiple copies to use for small literature study groups and inquiry projects.* (J.W.)

National Geographic World. Published by National Geographic Society. Washington, DC 20036. *www.nationalgeographic.com/world*

National Geographic World *is published twelve times yearly and contains articles, facts, and activities about animals, sports, science, and other cultures. Formats vary from a typical article style with full-color photographs to a comic-strip presentation. Students enjoy the variety of subjects and activities that are included.* (J.W.)

Owl. Published by Bayard Press, 25 Boxwood Lane, Buffalo, NY 14225. *www.owl.on.ca*

Owl, *for ages eight and up, and two other related magazines offer full-color articles about math, science, and nature in nine yearly issues. The other magazines are* Chirp *for preschoolers through age six and* Chickadee *for ages eight and up. In addition to the informational articles, all three magazines contain stories and activities for young readers.* (J.W.)

Ranger Rick. Published by the National Wildlife Federation, 8925 Leesburg Pike, Vienna, VA 22184. *www.nwf.org/nwf*

Ranger Rick, *for ages seven through twelve, and* Your Big Backyard, *for ages three through six, are published twelve times yearly. Both of these high-quality magazines contain a variety of interesting articles, facts, stories, and full color photographs about animals and their habitats.* (J.W.)

Sports Illustrated for Kids. Published by Time, Inc., Time & Life Building, Rockefeller Center, New York, NY 10020–1393. *www.sikids.com*

Students interested in sports will enjoy this monthly magazine. It contains a variety of interesting information that includes articles about sports, sports trivia and facts, and in-depth coverage of famous sports figures and athletes. (J.W.)

Stone Soup: The Magazine by Young Writers and Artists. Published by the Children's Art Foundation, 765 Cedar Street, Suite 201, Santa Cruz, CA 95069. *www.stonesoup.com*

Featuring the works of young writers and artists through age thirteen, Stone Soup *has invited student submissions for more than 25 years. It is published bimonthly, six times each year. Features include "The Mail Box," stories, poems, artwork, and reviews. Photographs of the young artist or author often accompany the students' works. This high-quality, affordable publication is sure to increase authentic reasons for students to read and write.* (J.W.)

Time for Kids. Published by Time, Inc., Time & Life Building, Rockefeller Center, New York, NY 10020–1393. *www.timeforkids.com*

This magazine, a version of Time, *contains up-to-date news and photographs. The 26 yearly issues are published weekly during from September to May. Two editions are available: a four-page primary edition for grades two and three and an eight-page intermediate edition for grades four through six. A teacher's guide and supplementary teaching materials are included and also available at the Web site. (To save money, some teachers share a subscription and rotate magazines each week.)*

Zillions. Published by Consumer Union of U.S. Inc., 101 Truman Ave., Yonkers, NY 10703–1057.

Zillions is published bimonthly and mirrors the adult companion magazine, Consumer Reports. *It features consumer information of interest to young people. It is most appropriate for ages eight through fourteen. Regular features include "Testing Stuff," which often features consumer toy testing information, "Ads and Fads," and "Money Smarts." Some information is presented in a comic strip style. (J.W.)*

Zoobooks. Published by Wildlife Education. Ltd., 12233 Thatcher Court, Poway, CA 92064–6880. *www.zoobooks.com*

Zoobooks have long offered elementary students opportunities to explore and build scientific concepts. Especially helpful in classrooms where teachers encourage inquiry, these reasonably-priced magazines are published monthly, twelve times yearly. They include beautifully colored photographs and interesting informational texts. (J.W.)

Some Excellent K–6 Language Arts Web Sites (Selected and annotated by Kathy O'Neal)

Amazon.com. *http://www.amazon.com*

How did I ever get along without this? While I rarely actually order books here, I use it constantly for reviews, bibliographic data, related titles, subject searches, and author information. Find out what's in print and what's available in paperback, and for how much. The kids' department is great, too.

Association for Library Service to Children: Cool Sites for Kids. American Library Association. *http://www.ala.org/alsc/children_links.html*

Cool sums it up. Dozens of the sites that kids and their teachers will love, all organized so you can actually find them when you need them.

Children's Book Council Online. *http://www.cbc.org/navigation/teaindex.htm*

This association of children's book publishers has a unique wealth of information and promotional material gathered here that you won't find anywhere else.

Children's Literature Ring. *http://www.webring.org/cgi-bin/webring?ring=kidlit&list*

Ninety-five sites, all related to children's books, connected in a huge ring so we can jump in anywhere and browse to our hearts' content. A book lover's paradise.

The Children's Literature Web Guide (CLWG). *http://www.acs.ucalgary.ca/~dkbrown/*

Thorough and well-designed, this site will connect you to nearly all the essential literature Web sites. Lots of author links, too.

Indian Hills, Ohio, Primary School Library. *http://www.ih.k12.oh.us/pslibrary/media.htm*

This Ohio school library has created a Web site that reflects the vitality and quality of its language arts curriculum. Check out the librarian's links to "Great Sites for Librarians and others interested in the teaching of children's literature."

Internet Public Library Youth Division: Reading Zone—Resources for Teachers and Parents. *http://www.ipl.org/cgi-bin/youth/youth.out.pl?sub=rzn9800*

Irresistible. Well-annotated links to a wide variety of reading and writing sites for children as well as educators.

Internet School Library Media Center: Literature & Language Arts Resources. *http://falcon.jmu.edu/~ramseyil/childlit.htm*

Teachers will find education-oriented links organized in useful categories here: "General Children's Literature Sites," "Want to Talk?," "Book Awards," "Book & Media Reviews," "The Genres," "Bibliotherapy," "Enrichment Activities," etc.

Kathy Schrock's Guide for Educators. *http://www
.capecod.net/schrockguide/*

> *Everything you'll ever need to know about
> curriculum. Don't miss the "Additional Informa-
> tion" section at the end.*

Reading Online. International Reading Association.
http://www.readingonline.org

> *This is the International Reading Association's
> electronic journal, a forum for communication,
> dialogue, and participation in literacy issues.*

Chapter 4:
Teaching Children to Read

Teaching Reading

Allen, Janet, and Kyle Gonzalez. 1998. *There's Room
for Me Here: Literacy Workshop in the Middle
School.* York, ME: Stenhouse.

> *A middle school teacher and university pro-
> fessor describe their collaboration in Literacy
> Project, an assisted reading program for strug-
> gling readers aged eleven through fifteen.
> Demonstrates how shared reading can be the
> foundation for moving resistant readers and
> writers toward independence. Lots of classroom-
> based ideas for all ages.*

● Allen, Linda. 1998. "An Integrated Strategies Ap-
proach: Making Word Identification Instruction
Work for Beginning Readers." *The Reading
Teacher* (November): 254–268.

> *The author combines ongoing research and
> practice to demonstrate that direct, systematic in-
> struction in word identification is best developed
> from the quality children's literature teachers are
> using in the curriculum. The recommended teach-
> ing program includes "understanding rhyme,
> learning key words and their spelling patterns
> (rimes), learning to use the cross-checking strat-
> egy, and learning to spell and read a core of high
> frequency words." Don't miss reading and dis-
> cussing this significant article—specific and prac-
> tical with a strong research base.*

Booth, David. 1998. *Guiding the Reading Process:
Techniques and Strategies for Successful In-
struction in K–8 Classrooms.* Markham, ONT:
Pembroke; York, ME: Stenhouse.

> *More than seventy teaching strategies and
> ideas for all aspects of reading are described. A
> useful resource.*

● Braunger, Jane, and Jan Patricia Lewis. 1997.
Building a Knowledge Base in Reading. Port-
land, OR: Northwest Regional Educational Lab-
oratory; Urbana, IL: National Council of
Teachers of English; Newark, DE: International
Reading Association. See page 5b.

● Butler, Dorothy. 1998. *Babies Need Books: Sharing
the Joy of Books with Children from Birth to Six.*
Rev. ed. Portsmouth, NH: Heinemann.

> *The author writes convincingly of how and
> why to get babies, toddlers, and young children
> involved with books. Selected, annotated books
> "which will involve them deeply" are included in
> separate chapters for each age level from birth
> through age six. A wonderful resource and gift
> for parents, teachers, and anyone involved with
> young children.*

Center for the Improvement of Early Reading
Achievement (CIERA). Elfrieda Hiebert, director. University of Michigan School of Education,
610 E. University Ave., Ann Arbor, MI, 48109.

> *Established in collaboration with five other dis-
> tinguished universities to address problems in
> reading instruction and to disseminate informa-
> tion on solutions to persistent reading problems,
> CIERA has published quarterly summaries of re-
> search reports related to reading since 1997. Full
> reports can be downloaded at www.ciera.org.*

Chambers, Aidan. 1996. *The Reading Environment:
How Adults Help Children Enjoy Books.* York,
ME: Stenhouse.

> *A short, terrific book that focuses on support-
> ing children to become lifelong readers by pro-
> viding them with daily time to read and
> opportunities to respond to books in an attrac-
> tive classroom setting. Emphasizes a "well-cho-
> sen book stock," reading aloud, browsing,
> storytelling, book owning, and more. Very help-
> ful for setting up a successful reading classroom.*

● Clay, Marie M. 1998. *By Different Paths to Common Outcomes.* York, ME: Stenhouse.

> *Experienced primary teachers will find this
> book a vehicle for examining and evaluating
> current understandings and classroom prac-
> tices. The book, a collection of previously un-
> published articles and some of Clay's seminal
> papers, is divided into three sections that ex-
> plore early literacy development, observing
> what children know, and the challenges educa-*

tors face in helping children become literate. As always, Clay provides thoughtful perspectives that promote personal reflection on teaching and learning. (J.W.)

Clay, Marie. 1998. "Introducing Storybooks to Young Readers." In *By Different Paths to Common Outcomes*. York, ME: Stenhouse. (Originally published in *The Reading Teacher* [December 1991]: 264–273.)

Discusses and models how to make a text more accessible through a rich, interactive story introduction.

● Fountas, Irene C., and Gay Su Pinnell. 1996. *Guided Reading: Good First Teaching for All Children*. Portsmouth, NH: Heinemann.

This comprehensive text about creating a classroom literacy program is a valuable resource for primary teachers. While the focus is on guided reading, this book provides extensive information about designing and organizing a balanced literacy program. The authors provide chapters that address assessment, book leveling, strategy instruction, and flexible grouping. The extensive book list, arranged both by title and level, is a good place to begin thinking about how to select books appropriate for leveled instruction. However, teachers will also want to add quality children's literature. (J.W.)

Iversen, Sandra. 1997. *A Blueprint for Literacy Success: Building a Foundation for Beginning Readers and Writers*. Bothell, WA: The Wright Group.

A practical guide for new teachers or teachers new to the early grades, this text is filled with photographs of classrooms and practical teaching suggestions. In addition to a brief introduction to literacy terms, the book discusses how to help emergent readers and writers develop important skills and strategies. An additional bonus is the collection of large-print blackline masters with simple texts, songs, and sight words ready for classroom use. (J.W.)

Jobe, Ron, and Mary Dayton-Sakar. 1999. *Reluctant Readers: Connecting Students and Books for Successful Reading Experiences*. Markham, ONT: Pembroke; York, ME: Stenhouse.

In addition to a multitude of ingenious strategies and activities to motivate and engage reluctant readers, the authors annotate lists of

reading materials kids love, such as alphabet books, sophisticated picture books, sports books, information books, audio books, books with strong girl characters, humorous books, survival books, and much more. A wonderful resource.

Johnston, Peter, and Marie Clay. 1997. "Recording Oral Reading" and "Interpreting Oral Reading Records." In *Knowing Literacy: Constructive Literacy Assessment* by Peter Johnston. York, ME: Stenhouse.

If you don't have a Reading Recovery teacher in your building who can teach you how to take running records, these pages and accompanying tape will be very helpful.

● Keene, Ellin Oliver, and Susan Zimmermann. 1997. *Mosaic of Thought: Teaching Comprehension in a Readers Workshop*. Portsmouth, NH: Heinemann.

This text is terrific for understanding and teaching the strategies proficient readers use during the act of reading in order to comprehend. Strategies that are discussed and demonstrated include: activating prior knowledge, determining the most important ideas, asking questions, creating mental images while reading, making inferences, retelling or synthesizing, using a variety of "fix-up" strategies when meaning becomes unclear. This book takes effort to read because of the way it is organized—lots of vignettes, long chapters, no index—but it is worth the commitment.

● Krashen, Stephen. 1993. *The Power of Reading: Insights from the Research*. Englewood, CO: Libraries Unlimited.

In an easy-to-read format, the author describes the research that supports access to books and free, voluntary reading as the best predictors of reading achievement. Don't miss reading and discussing this powerful book.

Martens, Prisca, Yetta Goodman, and Alan D. Flurkey. 1995. "Miscue Analysis for Classroom Teachers." *Primary Voices K–6* (November).

Procedures, explanations, and examples for notating and analyzing miscues, which are "anything a reader reads that differs from the expected response to a written text" (1). Excellent for informing your teaching. Those interested will find this themed issue of Primary Voices on miscue analysis helpful.

- Ministry of Education, Wellington, New Zealand. 1997. *Reading for Life: The Learner as a Reader.* Katonah, NY: Richard C. Owen.

  A new edition of the classic Reading in Junior Classes *(1993), this text is invaluable to primary teachers desirous of establishing a balanced and comprehensive reading program. Specific and practical for all aspects of the reading process. Excellent visuals and photos support the text.*

Optiz, Michael F., and Timothy V. Rasinski. 1998. *Good-Bye Round Robin: Twenty-Five Effective Oral Reading Strategies.* Portsmouth, NH: Heinemann.

  While acknowledging that most of the reading students do should be silent, the authors discuss how, why, and where oral reading fits into the reading program. Many helpful techniques for appropriate and effective use of oral reading in the classroom.

- Phinney, Margaret Yatsevitch. 1988. *Reading with the Troubled Reader.* Portsmouth, NH: Heinemann.

  In this outstanding resource, which I had overlooked in previous publications, Phinney presents five types of troubled readers. For each, she describes their problems and explicitly shares a wealth of strategies for working with them successfully.

Rasinski, Timothy, and Nancy Padak. 1996. *Holistic Reading Strategies: Teaching Children Who Find Reading Difficult.* Englewood Cliffs, NJ: Prentice-Hall.

  Describes numerous techniques and strategies for working with struggling readers. Applicable to working with all readers.

Rhodes, Lynn K., and Curt Dudley-Marling. 1996. *Readers and Writers with a Difference: A Holistic Approach to Teaching Struggling Readers and Writers.* 2d ed. Portsmouth, NH: Heinemann. See page 64b.

Routman, Regie, and Andrea Butler. February 1996. "How Do I Actually *Teach* Reading Now That I Am Using Literature?" *School Talk* (February). Urbana, IL: National Council of Teachers of English. (Reprinted in *Practicing What We Know: Informed Reading Instruction*, edited by Constance Weaver. Urbana, IL: National Council of Teachers of English, 1998, 175–183.)

  Discusses how to develop important reading strategies and foster independence in the context of authentic literacy events.

- Smith, John W. A., and W. B. Elley. 1994. *Learning to Read in New Zealand.* Katonah, NY: Richard C. Owen.

  This was a breakthrough book for some of our teachers, because it moved us into guided silent reading and away from "round robin" reading of literature. A powerful theory-into-practice book with lots of specifics for teaching reading effectively. For all grade levels.

- Taberski, Sharon. 2000. *On Solid Ground: Strategies for Teaching Reading, K–3.* Portsmouth, NH: Heinemann.

  A master teacher describes how she skillfully assesses children's reading, demonstrates effective reading strategies, uses a variety of contexts for teaching reading and word study, and organizes lots of books, time, and opportunities for children to read and reflect upon their reading. A major strength of this book is its specificity on using ongoing assessment to transform instruction and learning. Research-based, practical, and wonderfully explicit.

Weaver, Constance, ed. 1998. *Practicing What We Know: Informed Reading Instruction.* Urbana, IL: National Council of Teachers of English. See page 4b.

Weaver, Constance, ed. 1998. *Reconsidering a Balanced Approach to Reading.* Urbana, IL: National Council of Teachers of English.

  Weaver informs our instruction by sharing significant research studies and summaries related to phonemic awareness and phonics, interest as a factor in learning to read, working with disabled readers, and teaching with "real books." Going beyond the narrow body of "scientific research" overfocused on skills in isolation, these studies broaden our vision and encourage us to practice effective reading instruction.

Phonemic Awareness and Phonics

Allington, Richard. "Overselling Phonics." 1997. *Reading Today* (Aug./Sept.): 15–16. See page 4b.

Clymer, T. 1996. "The Utility of Phonic Generalizations in the Primary Grades." *The Reading Teacher* (November): 182–187.

The author contends that the phonics generalizations we teach need to be valid 75 percent of the time; that is, "If the pupil applied the generalization to 20 words, it should aid her/him in getting the correct pronunciation in 15 out of the 20 words" (186). The utility of forty-five common phonic generalizations is presented (with only half of these meeting the 75 percent criteria). A reprint of the classic article originally published in The Reading Teacher *in 1963.*

Cunningham, Patricia M. 2000. *Phonics They Use: Words for Reading and Writing*. 3d ed. New York: Addison-Wesley Longman.

Educators eager to find ways to include word study and phonics into their daily instruction will find many useful suggestions in this text. While the author's approach is a curricular one, teachers may match activities and investigations to students' developmental needs. Word walls are carefully explained, and Cunningham offers a variety of ways to study and sort words. However, teachers should exercise caution and choose carefully from the many activities included. Be sure to read the last chapter first; the historical and theoretical information will assist you in keeping phonics instruction and activities in proper perspective. (J.W.)

Dombey, Henrietta, Margaret Moustafa, and the staff of the Centre for Language in Primary Education. 1998. *W(hole) to Part Phon' ics: How Children Learn to Read and Spell*. London: CLPE; Portsmouth, NH: Heinemann.

Just forty-four pages, this thoughtful guide draws together the most helpful information about learning and the teaching of reading—especially in relation to graphophonics—and explains how to translate it into effective classroom practice. Especially helpful is a developmental guide to appropriate classroom activities that foster successful reading.

Gunning, Thomas G. 1995. "Word Building: A Strategic Approach to the Teaching of Phonics." *The Reading Teacher* (March): 484–488.

Documents studies that reveal novice readers' "preference for the use of pronounceable word parts as a decoding strategy" (484) as compared with letter-by-letter decoding. Also demonstrates "word building" for teaching students how to decode difficult words through known onsets and

rimes and an analogy strategy. Very useful for thoughtful and meaningful decoding work.

International Reading Association. 1997. "The Role of Phonics in Reading Instruction: A Position Statement of the International Reading Association." Newark, DE: International Reading Association.

A sane and helpful pamphlet to share with parents, board members and policy makers. (Free copy with a self-addressed stamped envelope.)

● Moustafa, Margaret. 1997. *Beyond Traditional Phonics*. Portsmouth, NH: Heinemann.

A wonderfully readable, slim book that details breakthrough discoveries about how children learn to read. Readers will discover how children analyze sound-letter correspondences through onsets and rimes and why it makes good instructional sense to teach phonics in a way that honors and embraces children's natural, savvy learning strategies.

Phenix, Jo. 1996. *The Spelling Teacher's Book of Lists: Words to Illustrate Spelling Patterns... and Tips for Teaching Them*. Markham, ONT: Pembroke; York, ME: Stenhouse.

Useful for teaching common patterns, with corresponding examples of words. See spelling resources for full annotation.

Richgels, Donald J., Darla J. Poremba, and Lea M. McGee. 1996. "Kindergartners Talk About Print: Phonemic Awareness in Meaningful Contexts." *The Reading Teacher* (May): 632–642.

Suggests meaningful activities for developing phonemic awareness in the context of a reading/writing classroom (as opposed to isolated, direct instruction). Specific, research-based, and supportive.

Routman, Regie, and Andrea Butler. 1995. "Phonics Fuss: Facts, Fiction, Phonemes, and Fun." *School Talk* (November). (See page 71b for how to obtain a back issue.)

Clarifies phonics issues and offers practical suggestions for meaningful teaching of phonics in a whole literacy context.

● Stahl, Steven A., Ann M. Duffy-Hester, and Katherine Anne Dougherty Stahl. 1998. "Theory and Research into Practice: Everything You Wanted to Know About Phonics (But Were Afraid to

Ask)." *Reading Research Quarterly* (July/August/September): 338–355.

I breathed a sigh of relief when I completed this sane, comprehensive article that specifically details various approaches to phonics instruction. While stating the necessity for phonological awareness and early, explicit phonics instruction and practice, the authors conclude that as long as we provide students with the information, "it may not matter exactly how the instruction occurs" (351). Read and discuss this important article with your colleagues.

Troia, Gary A. 1999. "Phonological Awareness Intervention Research: A Critical Review of the Experimental Methodology." *Reading Research Quarterly* (January/February/March): 28–52.

If you are feeling pressured by requests to incorporate an excessive amount of phonemic awareness into your instruction, you will find this article helpful. The author reviews 39 studies of phonological intervention and finds that there is inconclusive evidence to support such practice. For quick reading, start with the introduction and then skip to the discussion. (J.W.)

● Wagstaff, Janiel. 1994. *Phonics That Work.* New York: Scholastic Professional.

In just over 100 pages, Wagstaff takes current research on phonics and shows us how to incorporate it in the classroom in a meaningful way. Practical and easy to understand and use.

Weaver, Constance, Lorraine Gillmeister-Krause, and Grace Vento-Zogby. 1996. "How to Help Your Child Learn Phonics" and "Facts on the Teaching of Phonics." In *Creating Support for Effective Literacy Education.* Portsmouth, NH: Heinemann.

A helpful brochure and fact sheet to share with colleagues, parents, administrators, and community members.

Wilde, Sandra. 1997. *What's a Schwa Sound Anyway: A Holistic Guide to Phonetics, Phonics, and Spelling.* Portsmouth, NH: Heinemann.

Discussion of topics such as phonics, spelling rule, skills, and the phonics debate—along with definitions of terms—helps teachers better understand the role phonemic awareness, phonics, and spelling play in the language arts curriculum. A comprehensive chapter entitled "What Does Invented Spelling Tell Us About Kids'

Knowledge of Phonics?" suggests ways teachers can analyze students' writing to plan future instruction. Read the book once quickly, and then keep it on the shelf as a helpful resource. (J.W.)

Yopp, Hallie Kay. 1995. "A Test for Assessing Phonemic Awareness in Young Children." *The Reading Teacher* (September): 20–29.

Presents the "Yopp-Singer Test of Phoneme Segmentation" to measure "a child's ability to separately articulate the sounds of a spoken word in order" (21). Recommends and describes activities related to stories, songs, and games that can be easily incorporated in the preschool, kindergarten, and grade-one meaning-based classroom to develop phonemic awareness.

Chapter 5:
Literature Conversations

Literature Conversations

Use the following excellent resources (as well as those in *Invitations* and *The Blue Pages* [1994]) to help shape your literature conversations. There is no one right or best way.

Eeds, Maryann, and Ralph Peterson. 1995. "What Teachers Need to Know About the Literary Craft." In *Book Talk and Beyond: Children and Teachers Respond to Literature,* edited by Nancy Roser and Miriam Martinez, 24–31. Newark, DE: International Reading Association.

Discusses how teachers can guide students to incorporate elements of literary craft, such as structure, character, and point of view, into literature study to raise it to "that deeper level of noticing and insight that we call dialogue." *Includes excerpts from classroom transcripts.*

● Eeds, Maryann, and Ralph Peterson. 1997. "Literature Studies Revisited: Some Thoughts on Talking with Children About Books." *The New Advocate* (Winter): 49–59.

Discusses the beliefs that underpin literature study and how those beliefs have been misinterpreted since their superb, groundbreaking book, Grand Conversations *(1990), was published. An outstanding article for understanding literature study at its finest. Those unfamiliar with* Grand Conversations *should not miss reading this still relevant book.*

Egawa, Kathy. 1998. "Eliciting Quality Responses to Literature in Spite of Limited Resources." *The New Advocate* (Spring): 153–164.

Describes how literature study can work with limited copies of a book through a combination of strategies such as reading aloud, shared reading, and buddy reading. Detailed suggestions for Shiloh, *by Phyllis Naylor and* A Taste of Blackberries, *by Doris Buchanan Smith.*

Gambrell, Linda B., and Janice F. Almasi, eds. 1996. *Lively Discussions! Fostering Engaged Reading.* Newark, DE: International Reading Association.

Many solid perspectives and ideas—both theoretical and practical—for establishing, sustaining, and evaluating small-group literature discussions that focus on collaborating, interpreting, asking questions, and sharing responses to literature. Has an excellent chapter on story retelling by Lesley Mandel Morrow.

Hill, Bonnie Campbell, Nancy J. Johnson, and Katherine L. Schlick-Noe, eds. 1995. *Literature Circles and Response.* Norwood, MA: Christopher-Gordon.

A great book for establishing literature discussions in the elementary classroom. Detailed guidelines and suggestions for all aspects of the process.

Jewell, Terry A., and Donna Pratt. 1999. "Literature Discussions in the Primary Grades: Children's Thoughtful Discourse About Books and What Teachers Can Do to Make it Happen." *The Reading Teacher* (May): 842–850.

Two teachers describe how they modeled a structure for interactive "response-driven" discussions with student-raised questions in second-grade classrooms. Jewell and Pratt analyzed their transcripts of the discussions and found comments they made as teachers—"procedural reinforcements"—played an essential role. Excellent for learning how specific teacher actions foster lively, effective literature discussions.

Paratore, Jeanne R., and Rachel L. McCormack, eds. 1997. *Peer Talk in the Classroom: Learning from the Research.* Newark, DE: International Reading Association.

This important volume examines peer-led discussions and shows how teachers can use their careful observations as teacher researchers to teach and support students more effectively. Fascinating reading for educators interested in understanding and promoting opportunities for quality peer talk in the classroom.

Pradl, G. W. 1996. "Reading and Democracy: The Enduring Influence of Louise Rosenblatt." *The New Advocate* (Winter): 9–22.

Read this exceptionally thoughtful article (if you don't have time to read Louise Rosenblatt's groundbreaking, now classic Literature as Exploration, *first published in 1938 and recently reissued in 1995) to appreciate literature study as central to the life of a democracy and to foster rich reader/text "transactions" in the classroom.*

Raphael, Taffy E., and Susan I. McMahon. 1994. "Book Club: An Alternative Framework for Reading Instruction." *The Reading Teacher* (October): 102–116.

Details one effective model for literature-based reading instruction that supports student-led discussion groups.

Samway, Katharine Davies, and Gail Whang. 1996. *Literature Study Circles in a Multicultural Classroom.* York, ME: Stenhouse.

Discusses literature study circles (LSCs) in a fifth/sixth-grade classroom. Applicable and useful K–8.

Schlick-Noe, Katherine, and Nancy Johnson. 1999. *Getting Started with Literature Circles.* Norwood, MA: Christopher-Gordon.

Written for teachers in grades 1–6 who want to get started and keep going with literature circles. The authors give helpful and specific guidelines for establishing the classroom climate, choosing books, forming groups, discussing books, and implementing focus lessons, response journals, and extension projects.

Wiencek, Joyce, and John F. O'Flahavan. 1994. "From Teacher-Led to Peer Discussions About Literature: Suggestions for Making the Shift." *Language Arts* (November): 488–498.

Answers teachers' most frequently asked questions as they implement student-led discussion groups. Specific and helpful.

Resources That Teach How to Question More Effectively

Busching, Beverly A., and Betty Ann Slesinger. 1995. "Authentic Questions: What Do They Look

Like? Where Do They Lead?" *Language Arts* (September): 341–343.

Strategies for teaching students how to ask important questions related to fiction and non-fiction. "Whether a question is about facts or concepts is less important than whether a question is a part of something significant" (344).

Cecil, Nancy Lee. 1995. *The Art of Inquiry: Questioning Strategies for K–6 Classrooms.* Winnipeg, MAN: Peguis.

Discusses different types of questions and provides many useful questioning strategies and activities related to both fiction and nonfiction.

Commeyras, Michell, and Georgiana Sumner (Jamie Metsala, ed.). 1996. "Literature Discussions Based on Student-Posed Questions." *The Reading Teacher* (November): 262–265.

Offers a rationale, based on research, for using and valuing student-generated questions.

Morgan, Norah, and Julianna Saxton. 1994. *Asking Better Questions: Models, Techniques, and Classroom Activities for Engaging Students in Learning.* Markham, ONT: Pembroke; York, ME: Stenhouse.

Specific ways to give students more opportunities to develop questioning skills across the curriculum.

Saul, E. Wendy. 1995. "'What Did Leo Feed the Turtle?' and Other Nonliterary Questions." In *Book Talk and Beyond: Children and Teachers Respond to Literature*, edited by Nancy Roser and Miriam Martinez. Newark, DE: International Reading Association.

Terrific for understanding the difference between skills-related questions and literary questions. Specific examples given.

Chapters 6, 7, 8, 9: Teaching Writing

Teaching Writing

For recommended writing resources published up to and including 1994, see *The Blue Pages*, pages 2b–42b.

Areglado, Nancy, and Mary Dill. 1997. *Let's Write: A Practical Guide to Teaching Writing in the Early Grades.* New York: Scholastic Professional Books.

Writing and revising strategies, lesson plans, and a wealth of photographs and student samples offer good advice to teachers just implementing a writing workshop approach. This practical book assists educators of young children consider many aspects of a successful writing program. (J.W.)

• Atwell, Nancie. 1998. *In the Middle: New Understandings About Writing, Reading, and Learning.* Portsmouth, NH: Boynton-Cook.

Educators who were influenced by Atwell's 1987 edition of In the Middle *will be equally affected and inspired by this second edition. In it, Atwell draws from her own experiences at the Center for Teaching and Learning in Edgecomb, Maine in advocating that teachers take a more explicit instructional stance. She assumes a similar perspective by including an array of suggested minilessons, actual scripts from her teaching, and numerous examples to assist others in refining their own teaching and learning. The six new chapters offer practical and important ideas about genre study, evaluation, and procedures for using a reading/writing workshop approach.* (J.W.)

Culham, Ruth and Vicki Spandel. 1998. *Picture Books: An Annotated Bibliography with Activities for Teaching Writing.* 5th ed. Portland, OR: Northwest Regional Educational Laboratory.

More than one hundred notable picture books are organized according to writing traits—ideas, organization, voice, word choice, and sentence fluency—to provide strong writing models and to suggest specific possibilities for writing.

Fletcher, Ralph, and Joann Portalupi. 1998. *Craft Lessons: Teaching Writing K–8.* York, ME: Stenhouse.

A variety of one-page minilessons in the craft of writing—such as surprise endings, using stronger verbs, narrowing the time focus—that discuss the technique, show how to teach the lesson, and list supportive literature resources.

Hindley, Joanne. 1996. *In the Company of Children.* York, ME: Stenhouse. See page 8b.

• Murray, Donald. 1996. *Crafting a Life in Essay, Story, Poem.* Portsmouth, NH: Heinemann.

Murray, a master craftsman, shows us how and why he writes and gives us a close-up view of his process and thinking. One of my all time fa-

vorite books for learning to write ourselves and teaching our students how to write well. Specific, helpful, and inspiring for writers of all ages.

Routman, Regie, and Donna Maxim, eds. 1996. "How Do We Get *Quality* in Writing, Not Just Quantity?" *School Talk* (September).

Key practices supporting teacher as writer, the use of quality literature, and purposeful teacher intervention are described along with visuals of student record keeping. Resource bibliography included.

Spandel, Vicki. 1996. *Seeing with New Eyes: A Guidebook on Teaching and Assessing Beginning Writers*. 3d ed. Portland, OR: Northwest Regional Educational Laboratory.

This collection of student writings and drawings along with practical teaching ideas provide opportunities for teachers to rethink and expand their writing programs. Teachers will find the sample rubrics, discussion about portfolio use, and question-answer section useful. (J.W.)

Spandel, Vicki, and Richard J. Stiggins. 1997. *Creating Writers: Linking Writing Assessment and Instruction*. 2d ed. New York: Longman.

This book answers a variety of questions teachers ask as they create and strengthen classroom writing programs. The authors effectively weave together instruction and assessment by considering the two in tandem. One chapter, "Troubleshooting, or What Can Go Wrong and What to Do About It," is especially useful. The authors view writing as problem solving and suggest strategies that offer instructional assistance for both novice and experienced teachers. (J.W.)

Journal Writing

Chancer, Joni, and Gina Rester-Zodrow. 1997. *Moon Journals: Writing, Art, and Inquiry Through Focused Nature Study*. Portsmouth, NH: Heinemann.

Beginning with an inquiry observing the lunar cycle of the moon, two teachers ably demonstrate how students can use Nature Journals, "sketch pad-notebooks," to record observations and facts by drawing and writing—stories, poems, and reflections. Applicable to all grades.

Cooper, Patsy. 1993. *When Stories Come to School: Telling, Writing, and Performing Stories in the Early Childhood Classroom*. New York: Teachers and Writers Collaborative. See page 7b.

Henry, Jim. 1999. *Fresh Takes on Using Journals to Teach Beginning Writers*. New York: Scholastic Professional.

A talented first-grade teacher clearly demonstrates how he uses journals as the mainstay of his literacy program. Lots of great ideas for meaningful journal writing, word work, and skills teaching. Explicit, practical, and inspiring.

Parker, Diane. 1997. *Jamie: A Literacy Story*. York, ME: Stenhouse.

A remarkable story about an amazing kindergartner and her supportive parents and teachers. An interactive journal that the parents and child keep together—with emphasis on reader response to literature—plays a critical role in expanding literacy development.

Sketch Journals

Ernst, Karen. 1994. *Picturing Learning. Artists & Writers in the Classroom*. Portsmouth, NH: Heinemann, 1994.

Ernst masterfully demonstrates how students can effectively combine words with drawings to see and explore their world. In A Teacher's Sketch Journal (1998) she provides a window into her own thinking-writing-sketching process.

Rief, Linda. 1999. "Picturing Possibilities." In *Vision and Voice*, 32–65. Portsmouth, NH: Heinemann.

An exemplary middle school teacher and her students demonstrate journaling across the curriculum through sketching and through cartoons.

Robinson, Gilllian. 1996. *Sketch-Books: Explore and Store*. Portsmouth, NH: Heinemann.

Explores the value and use of sketch-books for a record of a child's "visual, manipulative, and creative development." Includes how to design and make sketch-books.

Minilessons

Atwell, Nancie. 1998. "Minilessons." In *In the Middle: New Understandings About Writing, Reading, and Learning*, 148–216. Portsmouth, NH: Heinemann.

A wealth of detailed examples for four broad categories of minilessons for writing and reading: procedures (rules and routines), literary craft (what authors do), conventions of written language (what readers need), and strategies. Invaluable for upper elementary through high school.

Avery, Carol. 1993. "The Minilesson." In *And With a Light Touch: Learning About Reading, Writing, and Teaching with First Graders*, 117–139. Portsmouth, NH: Heinemann.

Lots of ideas and sample minilessons for the primary grades including many "Possible Minilesson Topics."

Brent, Rebecca, and Patricia Anderson. 1993. "Developing Children's Classroom Listening Strategies." *The Reading Teacher* (October): 122–126.

The authors provide specific strategies for teaching children to listen effectively when classmates share their writing and at other times throughout the day.

Fletcher, Ralph, and Joann Portalupi. 1998. *Craft Lessons: Teaching Writing K–8*. York, ME: Stenhouse. See page 28b.

Lunsford, Susan H. 1997. "'And They Wrote Happily Ever After': Literature-Based Minilessons in Writing." *Language Arts* (January): 42–48.

Explains how to use children's literature to teach story beginnings, descriptive language, and story structure to greatly impact writing quality in the primary grades. See also Lunsford's excellent detailed resource, Literature Based Minilessons to Teach Writing: 15 Engaging Lessons That Help Your Students Write Happily Ever After *(New York: Scholastic Professional, 1998).*

Selected Writing Resources for Students

Bauer, Marion Dane. 1992. *What's Your Story?: A Young Person's Guide to Writing Fiction*. New York: Clarion Books.

Wonderful for helping aspiring writers to plan and focus their stories, develop realistic characters and dialogue, and create a satisfying plot and conclusion. Best for grades four and above and also an excellent teacher resource. Also works as a read-aloud. See also Our Stories: A Fiction Workshop for Young Authors.

Bauer, Marion Dane. 1996. *Our Stories: A Fiction Workshop for Young Authors*. New York: Clarion Books.

A valuable follow-up to Bauer's What's Your Story?, *this text showcases excerpts from notable fiction of students in grades 4–12. Helpful for students ready to learn how to evaluate and revise their writing in a workshop setting.*

Christelow, Eileen. 1995. *What Do Authors Do?* New York: Clarion Books.

An author-illustrator discusses how authors get ideas, develop stories, deal with writer's block and rejection, work with publishers, and celebrate successes. A picture book for K–4.

Cowley, Joy. 1995. *A Guide for Young Authors*. Bothell, WA: The Wright Group.

A well-known New Zealand author discusses what stories are and how to write them. A thirty-page picture book for K–3 students.

Fletcher, Ralph. 1996. *A Writer's Notebook: Unlocking the Writer Within You*. New York: Avon Books.

Written to guide young writers, this conversational handbook by a distinguished writer encourages elementary-grade students to pay close attention to the world around them by recording moments, conversations, happenings, details, images, thoughts, lists, secrets, memories, and more.

Fletcher, Ralph. 1999. *Live Writing: Breathing Life into Your Words*. New York: Avon Books.

Fletcher shares many terrific strategies for improving writing quality, especially in fiction writing. He writes both as a reading-writing teacher and as an author for middle-grade students.

Giff, Patricia Riley. 1993. *Write Up a Storm with the Polk Street School*. New York: Bantam.

The author of the Kids of the Polk Street School series takes young writers through the steps she uses to write her stories, in the belief that "anyone can write a story." Delightful and encouraging—a good read. Recommended for grades 1–4.

Granfield, Linda, and Mark Thurman, illustrator. 1998. *Postcards Talk*. Markham, ONT: Pembroke.

Gives the history of postcards along with lots of ways to use old ones and create unique new ones.

• Heller, Ruth. 1997. *Mine, All Mine*. New York: Grossett & Dunlap.

This seventh book in Ruth Heller's best-selling language series serves as a springboard for teach-

ing parts of speech. All the books are available in both hard cover and paperback. As colorful as it is beautifully written, this text, like the others in the series, entertains and teaches students to appreciate the building blocks of language. Teachers enjoy weaving these Heller books about nouns, verbs, adjectives, adverbs, and prepositions into reading and writing minilessons. An eighth book about interjections and conjunctions entitled Fantastic, Wow, and Unreal *completes this popular parts-of-speech series. Once modeled instructionally, students will use these books independently as a resource for their own writing.* (J.W.)

Johnson, Paul. 1997. *Pictures and Words Together: Children Illustrating and Writing Their Own Books.* Portsmouth, NH: Heinemann.

Filled with practical suggestions and samples of children's work, this book provides comprehensive information on how to help children lay out, write, and illustrate their own books. Teachers will find lots of guidance in this text about ways to develop students' visual literacy through bookmaking. (See also The Blue Pages *for Johnson's earlier texts on bookmaking.)* (J.W.)

Leedy, Loreen. 1991. *Messages in the Mailbox: How to Write a Letter.* New York: Holiday House.

Tips and formats for writing letters and greeting cards. Engaging picture book format. Great for children in grades K–4.

Lester, Helen. 1997. *Author: A True Story.* Boston: Houghton Mifflin.

In picture-book format, a children's author humorously explains how she evolved from a struggling writer to a published author. Kids love her honesty and appreciate her ideas.

Levine, Michael. 1994. *The Kid's Address Book: Over 2,000 Addresses of Celebrities, Athletes, Entertainers, and More... Just for Kids!* New York: Berkley Publishing.

A collection of names and addresses of famous people and organizations. Can be used to encourage letter writing.

Stevens, Janet. 1995. *From Pictures to Words: A Book About Making a Book.* New York: Holiday House.

Illustrator Janet Stevens humorously and explicitly details her process of creating a picture-book story.

Stinson, Kathy. 1994. *Writing Your Best Picture Book Ever.* Markham, ONT: Pembroke.

A thirty-two-page picture book describes how to get ideas, draft a story, revise it, and put the finishing touches on your very own picture book.

Weekly Reader's Read Magazine. 1995. *Dear Author. Students Write About the Books That Changed Their Lives.* CA: Conari Press.

Written to authors both living and dead, students in grades 6–12 poignantly express how a particular book affected them. Also a good model to use to encourage upper elementary students to write to favorite authors.

Favorite Resources for Publishing

Gayolord, Suan Kapuscinski. 1994. *Multicultural Books to Make and Share.* New York: Scholastic Professional.

Book forms from various cultures are described—including historical overviews, techniques, and clear directions for constructing and writing, and specific projects. Includes helpful visuals. Teachers and students find this a terrific resource.

Henderson, Kathy. 1996. *The Market Guide for Young Writers. Where and How to Sell What You Write.* 5th ed. Cincinnati: Writer's Digest Books.

Detailed basics and specifics about how to get published. Includes manuscript preparation, online opportunities, inspiring essays by published young writers and editors, and an extensive "market list" of publishing opportunities. For writers ages 8–18.

Johnson, Cynthia. 1998. *Think Big! Creating Big Books with Children.* Bothell, WA: The Wright Group.

Written by a multiage primary teacher, this colorful "big book" is full of specific guidelines, suggestions, and colorful visuals for having students use a story, song, or poem to create quality big books for classroom use.

Johnson, Paul. 1997. *Pictures and Words Together: Children Illustrating and Writing Their Own Books.* Portsmouth, NH: Heinemann.

Advice and guidelines on how young children can create interrelated texts and illustrations. Lots of specific suggestions, visuals, and samples of children's work for planning, sketching, drawing, illustrating, laying out pages, and making all kinds of books. (See also Johnson's earlier texts on bookmaking in The Blue Pages.*)*

King, Laurie, and Dennis Stovall. 1992. *Classroom Publishing: A Practical Guide to Enhancing Student Literacy*. Hillsboro, OR: Blue Heron Publishing.

    This outstanding, comprehensive resource describes innovative publishing projects across the curriculum with lots of examples and details. Includes valuable annotated sections, such as "Markets for Young Writers" and "Contests," which include submission guidelines for quality publications that publish student writing. Great for students, teachers, and parents.

Rubenstein, Susanne. 1998. *Go Public! Encouraging Student Writers to Publish*. Urbana, IL: National Council of Teachers of English.

    In this powerful text, the author convincingly argues—with numerous practical suggestions and ways to overcome obstacles—that writing for publication dramatically improves students' writing. Comprehensive appendix of nearly 150 publishing opportunities includes sources that publish student writing, submissions guidelines, formats for cover letters and manuscripts, and writing contests. Intended for middle and high school teachers but applicable to elementary grades as well.

Treetop Publishing, P.O. Box 085567, Racine, WI.

    While many teachers know and use Treetop's bound, blank books that are available in assorted sizes, the sturdy, dark-lined templates in various sizes and formats are particularly useful. Writers of all ages use these templates under blank, unlined paper when they are handwriting final copies for projects, letters, and greeting cards. The templates contribute to neatness and evenly spaced lines on the page.

Good Books with Interesting Formats: A Beginning List

Be sure students focus on content before they concern themselves with how to present their information. See pages 326–328 for discussion of format in writing and publishing. See also "Nonfiction with Interesting Formats," page 130b.

Armstrong, Bev. 1994. *Reptiles: Creative Drawing Fun for Artists of All Ages*. New York: The Learning Works and Scholastic.

    Every page of this thirty-two-page book includes instructions (step-by-step illustrations) for learning how to draw different reptiles as well as an interesting fact about each animal. Part of the Superdoodles nonfiction series. Kids who prefer illustrating to writing love this model.

Brooks, Bruce. 1997. *NBA by the Numbers*. New York: Scholastic.

    Each facing set of pages in this photo-picture book contains a large, bold number and a heading followed by an informational paragraph in large print. Some examples of headings include: "1: Alert Dribbler," "2. Tricky Passes," and "9: Slammin' Dunkers." An inviting and easy organizational format for kids who like to write about sports and other topics.

Cole, Henry. 1998. *I Took a Walk*. New York: Greenwillow.

    A young child takes a walk in the woods, where she sees and hears nature all around her. Pages ending with "I saw..." require the reader to open up a fold-out page for the list of answers. An easy-to-create, engaging format for young writers.

Cole, Joanna, and Stephanie Calmenson, eds. 1996. *Give a Dog a Bone: Stories, Poems, Jokes, and Riddles About Dogs*. New York: Scholastic.

    As the title indicates, multiple genres are combined in a delightful book about dogs that also includes factual information. Inspired some of our students to incorporate their factual reports about an animal or sport into stories, poems, jokes, and riddles.

Dewey, Jennifer Owings, with Don MacCarter, photographer. *Wildlife Rescue: The Work of Dr. Kathleen Ramsay*. 1994. Honesdale, PA: Boyds Mills Press.

    We have used this beautifully written story of a veterinarian who cares for sick and injured birds and animals as both a model for good nonfiction writing and for using photographs to help tell a story.

Dorling Kindersley books, published in Great Britain and wildly enjoyed by students and teachers.

    Beautiful books on every subject feature detailed illustrations and labeled parts. No matter where you open the book, the two pages facing each other are complete. Great model for kids who prefer to give most of their information through detailed illustrations with explanations and who don't want to worry about exact sequence. DK books can also be used as a model to show that books come in all sizes and shapes, from pocket-size to oversize, that formats and fonts can differ— even within the same text, and that illustrations and diagrams can dominate a text.

Epstein, Diana. 1996. *The Button Book*. Philadelphia: Running Press.

Fascinating facts about buttons in a miniature book (2 3/4" × 3 1/4") with an attached, string bookmark that has a small button on the end of it.

Fox, Peter, photographer. 1997. *Classic Outdoor Games*. Palo Alto, CA: Klutz.

A twelve-page, laminated, foldout informational booklet/brochure with color photos. Colorful game headings on each page (in various fonts) are followed by rules and descriptions. An engaging, alternative format for presenting information.

Klutz publishes other instruction books with interesting formats, including The Buck Book: All Sorts of Things to Do with a Dollar Bill—Besides Spend It *by Anne Akers Johnson (1993).*

French, Vivian. Illustrated by Alison Wisenfeld. 1995. *Spider Watching*. Cambridge, MA: Candlewick Press.

Part of the Read and Wonder series that features, side by side, in each two-page spread, interesting, true facts about spiders (or other creatures) as well as a continuing fiction story that incorporates facts.

Gordon, Lynn. 1996. *Fifty-Two Fun Party Activities for Kids*. San Francisco: Chronicle Books.

Fifty-two laminated cards (3 1/2" × 2 1/4") with labeled pictures on one side and a description of an activity on the reverse side. An interesting nonbook format for presenting information to kids.

Grutman, Jewel H., and Gay Matthaei. 1994. *The Ledgerbook of Thomas Blue Eagle*. New York: Lickle Publishing.

A first-person, fictional account of a Dakota Indian that appears handwritten in cursive accompanied by charming, colorful pen-and-ink drawings. Book opens and is read top to bottom.

The handmade, handwritten quality of this book, which looks like an old ledgerbook, inspires students to use this beautiful writing and artistic model.

Jones, George. 1995. *My First Book of How Things Are Made: Crayons, Jeans, Peanut Butter, Guitars, and More*. New York: Scholastic.

Teachers and students love this book, both for the fascinating information it contains and its interesting format. For each topic, for example, "How Crayons Are Made" and "How Orange Juice Is Made," photographs accompany numbered procedures. Each number is highlighted in color and followed by a descriptive paragraph. A useable model for organizing "how to" books, directions, explanations, and instructions.

Mayers, Florence Cassen. 1994. *Baseball ABC*. New York: Harry N. Abrams.

Baseball information, memorabilia, and color photographs accompany each letter of the alphabet. A good model for students who want to organize their information in an alphabet book.

Maynard, Christopher. 1997. *Informania: Sharks*. Cambridge, MA: Candlewick Press.

Fascinating facts about sharks are cleverly presented in a hard cover, spiral-bound book with tab dividers for inventive chapter headings. Uses a variety of writing genres such as news reports, letters, cartoons, memos, profiles, FBI guide, a pull-out map, and homework assignment—all in one book!

Rosen, Michael J., ed. 1996. *Purr... Children's Book Illustrators Brag About Their Cats*. San Diego: Harcourt Brace.

More than forty authors and illustrators contribute delightful stories about their cats (and, also, their dogs, in the 1993 Speak! Children's Book Illustrators Brag About Their Dogs). A fine model for brief, engaging, first-person accounts about pets. Some students use this as a model for soliciting student writing contributions for their own publications.

Singer, Beth W., and Jack Kelly, illustrator. 1996. *The Hairy Book: The (Uncut) Truth About the Weirdness of Hair*. Reading, MA: Addison-Wesley Longman.

Julie Beers' third and fourth graders' all-time favorite book for format. Spiral bound with a "hairy" (fake fur) slip-on cover that includes a re-movable comb labeled The Hairy Book. *A zany book with multiple fonts, headings, fanciful drawings, and snippets of information on each page.*

Young, Ed. 1997. *Mouse Match: A Chinese Folktale.* San Diego: Harcourt Brace.

Charming telling of Chinese mouse bride story "about looking within the uniqueness and greatness of oneself, and really seeing" (Author's Note). Accordion-pleated pullout book, tied together with ribbon. Story with pastel and watercolor collages on one side and Chinese characters in black and white on reverse side.

Writing in Multiple Genres

Birch, Ann. 1993. *Essay Writing Made Easy: Presenting Ideas in All Subject Areas.* Markham, ONT: Pembroke; York, ME: Stenhouse.

Birch provides a concise, useable guide on essay writing across the curriculum, including information on choosing topics, planning, and finding and utilizing information. The book also contains writing tips and sample essays by students.

Ehrlich, Amy, ed. 1996. *When I Was Your Age: Original Stories About Growing Up.* Cambridge, MA: Candlewick Press.

A helpful volume for enjoying and writing life stories. Distinguished children's authors, such as Katherine Paterson, Walter Dean Myers, Avi, and Laurence Yep, were invited to write life stories for this volume. "The story you might choose to tell doesn't have to be literally true in every detail but should be located in time and space in your own childhood. It can be dramatic or serious or funny—whatever tone is right for the characters and plot" (Introduction, page 6). Before each story, the author's notes give background on the particular piece. James Howe noted, "while I can't swear that every moment of this story really happened, I know that every feeling is true" (49). See also Volume 2 (1999).

Ledoux, Denis. 1993. *Turning Memories into Memoirs.* Lisbon Falls, ME: Soleil Press.

Lots of detailed ideas and activities for writing life stories. Includes such topics as "memory jogs," interviewing, researching, "telling the truth," and organizing the writing.

● Murray, Donald. 1996. *Crafting a Life in Essay, Story, Poem.* Portsmouth, NH: Heinemann. See page 28b.

Rogovin, Paula. 1998. *Classroom Interviews: A World of Learning.* Portsmouth, NH: Heinemann.

A first-grade teacher demonstrates how she makes interviews with her students' families central to teaching reading, writing, researching, collaborating, and making connections across the curriculum. Outstanding for all elementary grades.

Poetry

Glover, Mary Kenner. 1999. *A Garden of Poets: Poetry Writing in the Elementary Classroom.* Urbana, IL: National Council of Teachers of English.

A classroom teacher writes eloquently about how to teach poetry writing to children. Through her own example, she demonstrates how to create a classroom where children write all kinds of thoughtful poems with interesting and engaging content, titles, imagery, voice, and form. Includes useful bibliographies of recommended poetry books. A terrific resource.

Heard, Georgia. 1999. *Awakening the Heart: Exploring Poetry in Elementary and Middle School.* Portsmouth, NH: Heinemann.

Chock full of wonderful suggestions for introducing poetry, establishing poetry centers in the classroom, reading poetry, incorporating "tools to help craft poetry," and poetry projects. Be sure to revisit Heard's classic, For the Good of the Earth and the Sun: Teaching Poetry *(Portsmouth, NH: Heinemann, 1989).*

Routman, Regie. 2000. *Kids' Poems: Teaching Children to Love Writing Poetry.* New York: Scholastic.

All children—even kindergarten students—enjoy writing poetry when they are immersed in hearing and reading poems, examine poems written by kids like themselves, and are encouraged to write free verse (poems that don't rhyme) on a topic of their choice. In four separate volumes—kindergarten, grade one, grade two, and grades three and four—Routman demonstrates how to inspire and teach poetry writing. Each book begins with practical guidelines that are followed by twenty poems written by different students. Each poem is shown in a two-page spread that includes the handwritten form on one side (the student's draft with invented spellings) and the typed, published form on the adjacent page.

Struthers, Betsy, and Sarah Klassen, eds. 1995. *Poets in the Classroom.* Markham, ONT: Pembroke; York, ME: Stenhouse.

Great suggestions and strategies for introducing students to poetry writing.

Some Favorite Poetry Books for Inspiring Poetry Writing (mostly free verse)

See page 120b for "More Poetry" (includes rhyming poems).

Adoff, Arnold, ed. 1994. *My Black Me. A Beginning Book of Black Poetry.* New York: Dutton.

Asch, Frank. 1996. *Sawgrass Poems. A View of the Everglades.* San Diego: Harcourt Brace.

Asch, Frank, and Ted Levin. 1998. *Cactus Poems.* San Diego: Harcourt Brace.

Chandra, Deborah. 1993. *Rich Lizard and Other Poems.* New York: Farrar Straus & Giroux.

Esbensen, Barbara. 1996. *Echoes for the Eye: Poems to Celebrate Patterns in Nature.* New York: HarperCollins.

Fletcher, Ralph. 1997. *Ordinary Things. Poems from a Walk in Early Spring.* New York: Atheneum.

Florian, Douglas. 1996. *On the Wing.* San Diego: Harcourt Brace.

Graves, Donald. 1996. *Baseball, Snakes, and Summer Squash. Poems About Growing Up.* Honesdale, PA: Boyds Mills Press.

Hopkins, Lee Bennett, ed. *Small Talk. A Book of Short Poems.* San Diego: Harcourt Brace.

Hudson, Wade, ed. 1993. *Pass It On. African-American Poetry for Children.* New York: Scholastic.

Lesser, Carolyn. 1997. *Storm on the Desert.* San Diego: Harcourt Brace.

Lyne, Sandford, ed. 1996. *Ten-Second Rainshowers: Poems by Young People.* New York: Simon & Schuster.

Merriam, Eve. 1993. *Quiet, Please.* New York: Simon & Schuster.

Mora, Pat. 1998. *This Big Sky.* New York: Scholastic.

Otten, Charlotte F. *January Rides the Wind. A Book of Months.* New York: Lothrop, Lee & Shepard.

Stevenson, James. 1998. *Popcorn: Poems by James Stevenson.* New York: Greenwillow.

Swanson, Susan Marie. 1997. *Getting Used to the Dark. 26 Night Poems.* New York: Dorling Kindersley.

Turner, Ann. 1993. *Grass Songs: Poems of Women's Journey West.* New York: Harcourt Brace Jovanovich.

Turner, Ann. 1998. *Mississippi Mud. Three Prairie Journals.* New York: HarperCollins.

Wood, Nancy. 1995. *Dancing Moons.* New York: Doubleday.

Worth, Valerie. 1987 *All the Small Poems.* New York: Farrar Straus & Giroux.

Chapter 10: Spelling and Word Study in the Reading-Writing Classroom

See also the Phonics resources, page 24b.

Spelling and Word Study

Barney, Linda A., and Robert G. Forest. 1996. *Spell Smart: A Spelling Resource Book for Classroom Teachers.* North Billerica, MA: Curriculum Associates.

This helpful ninety-page handbook provides an overview of spelling research, recommended practices, and lots of useful information and ideas for setting up a comprehensive spelling program.

• Bean, Wendy, and Chrys Bouffler. 1997. *Read, Write, Spell.* York, ME: Stenhouse.

This practical and accessible book emphasizes the links between reading, writing, and spelling. In the introduction and first two chapters, the authors address three myths about spelling, briefly explain some of the theoretical connections among reading, writing, spelling, and outline Brian Cambourne's conditions of learning. The rest of the book is devoted to practical strategies that incorporate reading and writing and assessment and evaluation procedures. Both new and experienced elementary teachers will find the ninety pages of this book packed with good ideas and strategies about the relationship of spelling to reading and writing. (J.W.)

• Bear, Donald R., and Shane Templeton. 1998. "Explorations in Developmental Spelling: Foundations for Learning and Teaching Phonics, Spelling, and Vocabulary." *The Reading Teacher* (November): 222–242.

The authors of this comprehensive article address why and how we need to understand and teach spelling as a developmental process. Each developmental spelling stage is described with implications and suggestions for word study instruction that integrates spelling, phonics, and vocabulary. A terrific discussion article for increasing our knowledge and planning appropriate word study.

• Bear, Donald R., Marcia Invernizzi, Shane Templeton, and Francine Johnston. 2000. *Words Their Way: Word Study for Phonics, Vocabulary, and Spelling Instruction.* 2d ed. Upper Saddle River, NJ: Merrill.

This book offers an excellent road map for educators interested in organizing their spelling and word study curriculum developmentally. The first four chapters present a theoretical foundation and explain how to use the spelling inventory to assess spelling development. The remaining chapters outline characteristics of each developmental stage and suggest appropriate word study activities. The book includes helpful blackline masters that can be used for picture and word sorts along with word lists grouped by spelling patterns. The word study activities may be embedded in guided reading as well as incorporated into students' independent work. (J.W.)

Cramer, Ronald L. 1998. *The Spelling Connection: Integrating Reading, Writing, Spelling Instruction.* New York: Guilford Press.

For more experienced educators interested in

reading a variety of texts on spelling instruction and its connection to the other language arts, this book will provide one more perspective on the subject. The author organizes the book in seven chapters that discuss the foundations of spelling knowledge, the beginnings of writing, the role of invented spelling, links to reading and writing, approaches for planning systematic instruction, assessing growth, and common questions and answers. While useful suggestions are made throughout the book, the first three chapters, and especially the chapter on invented spelling, seem most helpful to those trying to clarify their own thinking. (J.W.)

Dombey, Henrietta, Margaret Moustafa, and the staff of the Centre for Language in Primary Education (CLPE). 1998. *W(hole) to Part Phon' ics: How Children Learn to Read and Spell.* London: CLPE; Portsmouth, NH: Heinemann. See page 25b.

Fox, Barabara J. 1996. *Strategies for Word Identification: Phonics from a New Perspective.* Englewood Cliffs, NJ: Merrill.

Perhaps the most helpful feature of this book is found in the activities suggested to initiate and reinforce word study. Charts, photographs, and examples help busy educators access many excellent strategies to incorporate into either explicit or embedded instruction. (J.W.)

• Fresch, Mary Jo, and Aileen Wheaton. 1997. "Sort, Search, and Discover: Spelling in the Child-Centered Classroom." *The Reading Teacher* (September): 20–31.

The authors describe a weekly spelling instructional plan based on both observations of children's writing and results from a developmental spelling inventory. Activities include pretest/word selection, word sorts and word hunts, words in context, flexible activities, and peer post-testing. An outstanding resource for organizing a meaningful spelling program that combines whole-class and small-group study of common patterns and rules with individualized word study.

• Gentry, Richard. 1997. *My Kid Can't Spell! Understanding and Assisting Your Child's Literacy Development.* Portsmouth, NH: Heinemann.

This ninety-page guide, written for parents to

support their child's spelling development, is also excellent for teachers. Gentry describes the developmental spelling stages all children go through. As well, for each grade level from grades two through eight, he includes a grade-level placement test and the kinds of patterns students should be mastering. Includes useful guidelines and strategies for helping kids become competent spellers.

Gill, Charlene Hillal, and Patricia L. Scharer. 1996. "'Why Do They Get It on Friday and Misspell It on Monday?' Teachers Inquiring About Their Students as Spellers." *Language Arts* (February): 89–96.

A group of teachers who are uncomfortable with their spelling program begin to change and improve their instruction by questioning and discussing their practices, administering and analyzing spelling inventories (graded word lists), utilizing word study activities, and developing a rubric to inform grading decisions. A helpful article for rethinking your spelling practices.

Golick, Margie, and Jane Church (illus.). 1995. *Wacky Word Games*. York, ME: Stenhouse; Markham, ONT: Pembroke.

Students will enjoy engaging in word play with this thirty-two-page picture book of word games, puzzles, and picture clues.

Hayward, Christopher. 1998. "Monitoring Spelling Development." *The Reading Teacher* (February): 444–445.

A first-grade teacher describes how he incorporates a simple table (a spreadsheet that lists the same thirty high-frequency words under each student's name) to monitor and inform spelling instruction.

• Henderson, Ed. 1990. *Teaching Spelling*. 2d ed. Boston: Houghton Mifflin.

A well-known and respected spelling researcher describes children's developmental spelling stages and connects them with observations of students and suggested formal and informal teaching activities by grade levels. Appendix 1 contains grade-level words grouped by spelling pattern, very useful for word study. Appendix 2 provides the QUIK (Qualitative Inventory of Word Knowledge), a well-known spelling inven-

tory of word lists. This is a very specific, helpful text for increasing your knowledge and planning a comprehensive spelling program.

Hughes, Margaret, and Dennis Searle. 1997. *The Violent E and Other Tricky Sounds: Learning to Spell from Kindergarten Through Grade 6*. York, ME: Stenhouse; Markham, ONT: Pembroke.

The authors describe a longitudinal study that examined good and poor spellers from two elementary schools that "put language and literacy development at the center of their programs" (13). The study began with fifty-seven children and ended with thirty-five children. Explicitly shares links between reading, spelling, and vocabulary. Very useful for a study group on how good spellers develop.

• Phenix, Jo. 1996. *The Spelling Teacher's Book of Lists: Words to Illustrate Spelling Patterns... and Tips for Teaching Them*. Markham, ONT: Pembroke; York, ME: Stenhouse.

This is a terrific resource for teachers of all grades who embrace an investigative, problem-solving approach to spelling and word study. The extensive lists of words that share common patterns and meanings are a good starting point for class- and student-created lists. Extremely useful for increasing your knowledge about words and organizing a meaningful spelling program.

Pinnell, Gay Su, and Irene C. Fountas. 1998. *Word Matters: Teaching Phonics and Spelling in the Reading/Writing Classroom*. Portsmouth, NH: Heinemann.

A companion to their earlier book, Guided Reading, this text offers the same helpful format and practical information for designing and incorporating word study into a comprehensive literacy program. Pinnell and Fountas urge educators to assist students in becoming "word solvers" and emphasize a variety of activities. The book includes such topics as systematically planned word study and applied word study in writing and reading. One of the strongest chapters, written by master teacher Mary Ellen Giacobbe, provides guidance on how to support word study within writing workshop. As in Guided Reading, there are many charts, students' examples, and photographs to support classroom implementation. A companion volume, Voices on Word Matters (1999), contains *reflections and additional suggestions for word study.* (J.W.)

Routman, Regie, and Donna Maxim. 1996. "Invented Spelling: What It Is and What It Isn't." *School Talk* (April).

In the context of a "good spelling program," the authors explain students' "invented spellings," tell what we can learn from them, and suggest specific teaching points.

Snowball, Diane, and Faye Bolton. 1999. *Spelling K–8: Planning and Teaching.* York, ME: Stenhouse.

This text is extremely helpful for planning a schoolwide spelling program based on spelling investigations and rich discussions about spelling strategies. The text begins by exploring and developing knowledge of letters, sounds ("We look for letters and listen for sounds"), letter-sound relationships, and spelling patterns. Topics such as the following are each detailed in separate chapters: onsets and rimes, contractions, compound words, homophones, plurals, prefixes and suffixes, and derivations and origins of English words.

Wagstaff, Janiel. 1999. *Teaching and Writing with Word Walls.* New York: Scholastic Professional.

The author describes useful principles, procedures, and activities for building and using various types of word walls in daily reading and writing contexts in the primary grades. She details the following word walls as references for learning: ABC wall (for alphabet and letter-sound correspondences), Chunking wall (for making analogies from known to unknown words), Words-we-know wall (for irregular high frequency words), and Help walls (for language conventions).

Wilde, Sandra, ed. 1996. "Teaching Writers to Spell." *Primary Voices* (November).

This themed issue is very helpful for examining the specifics of a spelling program grounded in the writing process. Wilde provides a framework for teaching spelling and "A Speller's Bill of Rights" as a foundation tool for planning and assessing instruction. As well, several classroom teachers describe their meaning-based spelling programs and reflect on their practices.

• Wilde, Sandra. 1999. "How Children Learn to Spell: Evidence from Decades of Research." In

Voices on Word Matters, edited by Irene C. Fountas and Gay Su Pinnell. Portsmouth, NH: Heinemann.

An outstanding historical summation of research and practice on how children develop as spellers. Use and share the detailed information explaining invented spelling to increase your own knowledge and to communicate with parents.

Zutell, Jerry. 1996. "The Directed Spelling Thinking Activity (DSTA): Providing an Effective Balance in Word Study Instruction." *The Reading Teacher* (October): 98–108.

For teachers who want to involve their students in thoughtful word study, Zutell clearly describes an interactive, problem-solving, concept-forming technique in which "students and teachers work collaboratively to discover patterns of relationships" (100). Includes specifics for planning, choosing words and patterns to study, and carrying out related activities such as word sorts.

Vocabulary

Allen, Janet. 1999. *Words, Words, Words. Teaching Vocabulary in Grades 4–12.* York, ME: Stenhouse.

With rich literature at the center of the curriculum, Allen helps us plan vocabulary instruction that is explicit and concept-based. Lots of useful activities, strategies, graphic organizers and appendices.

Nagy, William E. 1988. *Teaching Vocabulary to Improve Reading Comprehension.* Urbana, IL: National Council of Teachers of English; Newark, DE: International Reading Association.

The "classic" text (forty pages) contains useful research and practice on teaching vocabulary.

Robb, Laura. 1999. *Easy Minilessons for Building Vocabulary: Practical Strategies That Boost Word Knowledge and Reading Comprehension.* New York: Scholastic.

Robb includes principles and guidelines for vocabulary instruction along with practical strategies and activities for meaningful vocabulary study. A useful appendix of Greek and Latin Roots is accompanied by examples of related words. Applicable K–12.

Rupley, William H., John W. Logan, and William D. Nichols. 1998/1999. "Vocabulary Instruction in a Balanced Reading Program." *The Reading Teacher* (December/January): 336–346.

> Recommends and discusses specific strategies for promoting vocabulary growth through both direct instruction and wide reading. Very helpful for implementing meaningful vocabulary instruction.

Chapter 11: Nonfiction Reading

See also these closely related resources: *Reading Aloud*, page 10b, *Literature Resources for Choosing Fiction and Nonfiction*, page 14b, and *Curriculum Inquiry*, below.

Nonfiction Reading

- Bamford, Rosemary A., and Janice V. Kristo, eds. 1998. *Making Facts Come Alive: Choosing Quality Nonfiction Literature K–8*. Norwood, MA: Christopher-Gordon.

  > Notable educators describe how they choose and use nonfiction in the literacy program. Full of excellent theory and practice regarding reading aloud, reading, discussing, and writing nonfiction. See page 14b.

Moss, Barbara, Susan Leone, and Mary Lou Dipillo. 1997. "Exploring the Literature of Fact: Linking Reading and Writing Through Information Trade Books." *Language Arts* (October): 418–429. See page 41b.

Newspapers in Education. Torrance, CA.

> More than 700 daily newspapers in the United States are ready to help elementary teachers use newspapers effectively in the classroom. Contact the NIE (Newspapers in Education) department at your local newspaper.

Snowball, Diane. 1995. "Building Literacy Skills Through Nonfiction: Some Tips on How You Can Help Children Become Better Readers and Writers of Nonfiction." *Teaching K–8* (May): 62–63. See page 42b.

Zarnowski, Myra. 1998. "Coming Out from Under the Spell of Stories: Critiquing Historical Narratives." *The New Advocate* (Fall): 345–356.

> A marvelous article for understanding and teaching students (and ourselves) how to read and interpret outstanding historical nonfiction. Noting that students do not have strategies for reading history, Zarnowski highlights the problems and gives ways to help students read with a historical and critical perspective.

Choosing Nonfiction

Appraisal: Science Books for Young People. A quarterly. Boston: MA: The Children's Science Book Review Committee. Northeastern University, 403 Richards Hall, Boston, MA 02215. Subscription rate /$46.00 (U.S.). See page 14b.

Bamford, Rosemary A., and Janice V. Kristo, eds. 1998. *Making Facts Come Alive: Choosing Quality Nonfiction Literature K–8*. Norwood, MA: Christopher-Gordon. See page 14b.

Krey, DeAn M. 1998. *Children's Literature in Social Studies: Teaching to the Standards*. Washington, DC: National Council for the Social Studies. See page 15b.

Moss, Barbara. 1995. "Using Children's Nonfiction Trade Books as Read-Alouds." *Language Arts* (February): 122–125. See page 10b.

Sudol, Peg, and Caryn King. 1996. "A Checklist for Choosing Nonfiction Trade Books." *The Reading Teacher* (February): 422–424. See page 15b.

Vardell, Sylvia M. 1998. "Using Read-Aloud to Explore the Layers of Nonfiction." In *Making Facts Come Alive: Choosing Quality Nonfiction Literature K–8*, edited by Rosemary A. Bamford and Janice V. Kristo, 151–157. Norwood, MA: Christopher-Gordon. See page 10b.

Chapter 12: Curriculum Inquiry: Developing a Questioning Stance Toward Learning

Curriculum Inquiry

We have found the following resources especially helpful for planning, supporting, and implementing curriculum inquiry in the classroom, for promoting nonfiction writing (and reading), and for teaching for understanding. See also resources for related chapters: Chapter 13, Critical Resources for Curriculum Inquiry: Librarians, School Libraries, and Technology, and Chapter 11, Nonfiction Reading. For useful science, social studies, and math resources published up to and including 1994, see *Invitations* or *The Blue Pages*.

● Blythe, Tina, and the teachers and researchers of the Teaching for Understanding Project. 1998. *The Teaching for Understanding Guide*. San Francisco: Jossey-Bass.

Written as *"a practical tool for making understanding a more achievable goal in classrooms" (xii), this thoughtful guide and framework helps us teach so students acquire understanding. "Understanding is being able to carry out a variety of actions or 'performances' that show one's grasp of a topic and at the same time advance it. It is being able to take knowledge and use it in new ways" (13). An excellent resource.*

● Boomer, Garth, Nancy Lester, Cynthia Onore, and Jon Cook, eds. 1992. *Negotiating the Curriculum: Educating for the 21st Century*. London and Bristol, PA: The Falmer Press.

Because this is still the single most helpful book I have read for understanding and implementing curriculum inquiry, I am including it again, even though it was listed in The Blue Pages (1994). The authors provide terrific information for planning, questioning, and negotiating meaningful curriculum. Very provocative reading for coming to grips with sharing power in the classroom, giving students real choice, and learning collaboratively. Terrific for discussion and rethinking your teaching.

Chase, Penelle, and Jane Doan. 1996. *Choosing to Learn*. Portsmouth, NH: Heinemann.

Two chapters are particularly helpful for primary teachers considering purposeful thematic studies: "Envisioning Curriculum" and "The Responsibility of Choice." In the former, the authors outline how a new theme unfolds in the classroom. The latter explores the other side of choice—the learners' responsibility. This book follows and explores issues connected to a previous one by the authors entitled Full Circle: A New Look at Multiage Education. (J.W.)

Dickinson, David K., and Lori Lyman DiGisi. 1998. "The Many Rewards of a Literacy-Rich Classroom." *Educational Leadership* (March): 23–26.

A study that found that the amount of writing students did in first grade, especially informational writing, positively influenced reading achievement. Important research to discuss and apply.

● Duthie, Christine. 1996. *True Stories: Nonfiction Literacy in the Primary Classroom*. York, ME: Stenhouse.

A first-grade teacher describes nonfiction genre study in reading and writing workshop, including such topics as procedures and supports, author study, characteristics of nonfiction books, writing formats, how to get information, and biographies and autobiographies. Includes an extensive bibliography of outstanding nonfiction. Each book annotation includes the topic, teaching features (such as poetic text, cross-sectional drawings, format), and a short description of the book's content and purposes. A gem.

Erickson, H. Lynn. 1998. *Concept-Based Curriculum and Instruction: Teaching Beyond the Facts*. Thousand Oaks, CA: Corwin Press.

Very helpful for identifying and writing about essential understanding, questions, processes, and skills to create meaningful, coherent curriculum. Informative for K–12 educators for developing concept/process curriculum that aligns with local, state, and national standards.

Fisher, Bobbi, and Pat Cordeiro, eds. 1994. "Generative Curriculum." *Primary Voices K–6* (August).

Inquiry generated by the interests of children, teachers, and the prescribed curriculum is highlighted in this themed issue. Great ideas for engaging students in authentic questioning and learning.

Five, Cora Lee, and Marie Dionisio. 1996. *Bridging the Gap: Integrating Curriculum in Upper Elementary and Middle Schools*. Portsmouth, NH: Heinemann.

An upper elementary grades teacher and a seventh-grade middle school teacher describe how they collaborate and use inquiry and a workshop approach for thematic learning and questioning across the curriculum. Lots of usable ideas and resources.

Hall, Jody S., with Carol Callahan, Helen Kitchel, Patricia Pierce, and Pedie O'Brien. 1998. *Organizing Wonder: Making Inquiry Science*

Work in the Elementary School. Portsmouth, NH: Heinemann. See page 42b.

- Harvey, Stephanie. 1998. *Nonfiction Matters: Reading, Writing, and Research in Grades 3–8.* York, ME: Stenhouse.

  The author thoughtfully outlines the necessary ingredients for creating classrooms where inquiry is both encouraged and experienced by students. Divided into three sections, the first section develops important principles for establishing inquiry-based classrooms. The second section is devoted to the elements of the research/inquiry process. In the third section, the author shares ideas and strategies for finalizing, presenting, and assessing student projects and performances. Appendices include sample forms to use as is or adapt. (J.W.)

Kobrin, Beverly. 1995. *Eyeopeners II: Children's Books to Answer Children's Questions About the World Around Them.* New York: Scholastic.

  Annotations and teaching ideas for hundreds of quality nonfiction books.

Meinbach, Anita Meyer, Liz Rothlein, and Anthony D. Fredericks. 1995. *The Complete Guide to Thematic Units: Creating the Integrated Curriculum.* Norwood, MA: Christopher-Gordon.

  The authors offer practical approaches for designing and evaluating thematic studies. They suggest strategies to promote student success and offer several sample units for primary and intermediate students complete with teacher suggestions and student activities. For example, primary units include "Growing Up" and "Folktales from Around the World," while the intermediate units are entitled "Space: The Final Frontier," "The Wild, Wild, West," and "Geometry." The book includes forms for planning and classroom use. (J.W.)

Moline, Steve. 1996. *I See What You Mean: Children at Work with Visual Information.* York, ME: Stenhouse.

  Discusses and demonstrates how and why to read and write visual texts for thinking, problem solving, and communicating. Lots of strategies and samples of children's work for using all types of visual texts, such as time lines, diagrams, maps, tables, glossaries. A great resource for all grades. An accompanying video is also available.

Moss, Barbara, Susan Leone, and Mary Lou Dipillo. 1997. "Exploring the Literature of Fact: Linking Reading and Writing Through Information Trade Books." *Language Arts* (October): 418–429.

  A terrific article for increasing understanding on the use and importance of nonfiction books. Excellent suggestions for reading and writing informational texts.

Moss, Joy F. 1996. *Teaching Literature in the Elementary School: A Thematic Approach.* Norwood, MA: Christopher-Gordon.

  This excellent resource includes a variety of well-planned thematic units that feature children's literature, include learning objectives, and offer a variety of teaching suggestions. The model units included are designed for use at grade levels ranging from one through six. Teachers will appreciate the thoroughness of each unit. (J.W.)

Ogle, Donna M. 1986. "K-W-L: A Teaching Model That Develops Active Reading of Expository Text." *The Reading Teacher* (February): 564–570.

  If you haven't yet read this "classic" article, you will want to do so and discuss it with your colleagues. You'll to learn how to interactively guide a group of children in reading "expository material." Can easily be adapted to an investigation of any topic.

Rief, Linda. 1999. *Vision and Voice: Extending the Literacy Spectrum.* Portsmouth, NH: Heinemann.

  Master teacher Linda Rief demonstrates how she honors voice in her seventh and eighth graders by guiding them through in-depth research and exploration. Students write and perform an original musical drama as a response to Lyddie, by Katherine Paterson; create a rain forest in a school hallway; and use sketching, cartooning, songwriting, interviews, storytelling, and more to expand the parameters of language arts. An accompanying multimedia CD makes it all come beautifully to life.

Robb, Laura. 1994. "Second Graders Read Nonfiction: Investigating Natural Phenomena and Disasters." *The New Advocate* (Fall): 239–252.

A very helpful article on how to implement and manage meaningful inquiry and research in a primary classroom. Includes examples and suggestions for reading, writing, discussing, informing parents, presenting information, and evaluating.

Ross, Elinor Parry. 1998. *Pathways to Thinking: Strategies for Developing Independent Learners K–8*. Norwood, MA: Christopher-Gordon.

The author suggests a number of ways educators can embed real opportunities for thinking into any content-area study. The author includes introductory chapters that review learning theories and then suggests strategies for stimulating and encouraging thinking and problem solving. A particular strength is a review of the theories of many respected researchers, including Piaget, Vygotsky, Bloom, and Gardner. (J.W.)

Shanahan, Timothy. 1997. "Reading-Writing Relationships, Thematic Units, Inquiry Learning... In Pursuit of Effective Integrated Literacy Instruction." *The Reading Teacher* (September): 12–19.

A particularly insightful article that explores optimal reading-writing connections and "integration," not as an end in itself but "as a way to effect particular educational outcomes" (15). Terrific for discussing and understanding successful integrated instruction.

• Short Kathy G., Jean Schroeder, and others. 1996. *Learning Together Through Inquiry: From Columbus to Integrated Curriculum*. York, ME: Stenhouse.

This text builds on the premise of "curriculum as inquiry." It describes how to apply an inquiry cycle of study to broad-based concepts and topics. Suggestions are offered for planning and supporting students' pursuit of their questions. The authors provide tips for organizing content-area studies. (J.W.)

Snowball, Diane. 1995. "Building Literacy Skills Through Nonfiction: Some Tips on How You Can Help Children Become Better Readers and Writers of Nonfiction." *Teaching K–8* (May): 62–63.

Specific suggestions for helping students read and write nonfiction purposefully and effectively.

Wiggins, Grant, and Jay McTighe. 1998. *Understanding by Design*. Alexandria, VA: Association for Supervision and Curriculum Development.

Believing that knowledge, skills, and facts do not automatically lead to in-depth understanding, the authors provide a conceptual framework and curriculum design process for making student understanding (including engagement, interest, and self-evaluation) more likely. They describe a "backward design process" that starts at the end with goals or standards (including the evidence we could accept that shows students understand) and then asks, "What kinds of lessons and practices are needed to master key performances?" (8). Don't miss reading this ground breaking, thought-provoking text. An accompanying video (see page 72b) is also outstanding.

Science

Find It!: Science CD ROM. Designed by Wendy Saul and available through The Learning Team, 84 Business Park Drive, Armonk, NY 10504. Yearly update.

Imagine having your very own science librarian. "I'd like books on electricity for my third graders. Please include both fiction and nonfiction. Have any of them won awards? Do any include African American characters?" This is the kind of search that Find It! will allow K–8 educators to undertake in minutes. More than 3,300 annotated books are reviewed, and author bios as well as cover scans are provided. A graphically exciting and satisfying resource for teachers, librarians, and students.

Hall, Jody S., et al. 1998. *Organizing Wonder: Making Inquiry Science Work in the Elementary School*. Portsmouth, NH: Heinemann.

This practical guide offers lots of suggestions about initiating an inquiry-based science program in elementary classrooms. The book includes case studies and strategies for guiding and supporting students through investigations. Samples of children's work are included to show how students reflect on and record their learning. While Hall and her colleagues highlight the inquiry process, they also suggest a teaching approach that is aligned with the concepts and strategies outlined in the national science standards. (J.W.)

National Research Council and the National Academy of Sciences. 1996. *National Science Foundation Standards*. Washington, DC: National Academy Press.

    These national science education standards guide the achievement of scientific literacy and include the "fundamental concepts and principles that underlie the standards." Inquiry-based learning is recommended as one major way to teach science.

Saul, Wendy, and Jeanne Reardon, eds. 1996. *Beyond the Science Kit: Inquiry in Action*. Portsmouth, NH: Heinemann.

    A terrific resource for learning how to become scientific inquirers ourselves and translating our own excitement and scientific engagement to the classroom. Elementary teachers explain how they use science kits, field trips, questions (teachers' and students'), observations, collaborative thinking, projects, and much more to make research and science lively and relevant to students' lives.

Children's Science Trade Books and Authors (Selected and annotated by Wendy Saul)

Children's science trade books should be considered a necessary part of any robust reading program. Sources below help users identify excellent selections. It might also be useful to check out a few authors (listed alphabetically) who have consistently produced works of distinction. Each of these folks continue to write noteworthy books.

Aliki, a science writer whose folk artist-like illustrations bring both clarity and humor to her work, often takes on topics where chronology and a sense of procedure really matter.

James Arnosky brings an artist's eye and a naturelover's sensibility to his books about wandering and looking carefully at the world around us.

Vicki Cobb is as brash in style as Aronosky is gentle, but she keys into young people's fascination with dirt and grime and goo and provides readers with a clear sense that science has many voices."

Joanna Cole, now almost a household name because of her Magic School Bus books, is also a master of expository prose. Look at any of her nonfiction books next to the chapter on writing nonfiction in her book *On the Bus with Joanna Cole* (Heinemann 1996). See, also, the Scholastic video that tells the story of how the Magic School Bus books came to be.

Jennifer Owings Dewey's personal narratives are woven seamlessly with lots and lots of information. I love her for her adventures as well as her grace as a writer.

Robert Gardner has for years managed to create original experiment books, characterized by both interesting, coherent activities, and clear, deliberate examples of procedural writing. Take a look at his new one, *Science Project Ideas About Rain* (Enslow 1997) as a good example.

Jean Craighead George has probably done as much as anyone in the world to help children understand that as humans we are at once animals *on* the planet and custodians *of* the planet. She does this through fact and imagination and heart, and each time she writes my hope for all of us is renewed.

Laurence Pringle's willingness to explore controversial and difficult topics, for example, death, pollution, and addiction, make him a natural for anyone looking to help children recognize what convincing evidence looks like.

Seymour Simon brings a schooled yet youthful enthusiasm to his many books about animal behavior, astronomy, and now, the human body (see his new series from Morrow). For teaching kids about the relationship between text and illustration, or about the use of metaphor in writing exposition, these books are a must.

But here's where the plan to focus on authors breaks down. Everyone should know about the publisher HarperCollins' longstanding commitment to the Let's Read and Find Out Science series. Originally conceived by reading specialist Roma Gans and scientist Franklyn Branley, this series has succeeded in bringing limited content and carefully chosen, gentle illustrations to central concepts in science. Most include a hands-on activity as well.

And how does one stop herself from talking about just a few extraordinary titles like Walter Wick's *A Drop of Water* (Scholastic 1997) whose photographs do as much to inspire question-posing as any book I've ever read. And what about Barbara Lehn's charming *What Is a Scientist?* (Millbrook 1999) featuring photographs of children in her first-grade class engaged in the most basic processes of collecting information and measuring. Add photos of your own students to her collection for a further celebration of children's scientific efforts. And for those seeking to interest an older group, try Rebecca L. Johnson's *Braving the Frozen Frontier* (Lerner 1997), an actual account of women working in Antarctica.

For information on all of these authors, these books, and many more, try the following:

Once upon a Gems Guide: Connecting Young People's Literature to Great Explorations in Math and Science (University of California, Berkeley: Lawrence Hall of Science, 1996).

Although this nearly 400-page volume complements the GEMS hands-on science units, the information provided is useful for most K–8 teachers. In many cases the books are not particularly current, but the ideas for using them are timeless. Do you remember E. Nesbit's fairy tale Milisande *(Harcourt 1989) in which she says, "I wish I had a golden hair a yard long, and that it would grow an inch every day, and grow twice as fast every time it was cut?" It's a math problem for literature lovers.*

Outstanding Science Tradebooks for Children.

This award-winning list of the year's best science books (all nonfiction and biography) is published each year in the March issue of Science and Children. *It (along with back issues) can be also be obtained by contacting the Children's Book Council (67 Irving Place, New York 10003), which, along with the National Science Teachers' Association, sponsors the award and takes responsibility for writing the annotations.*

Science Books and Films. A.A.A.S., 1776 Massachusetts Avenue, Washington, DC 20036.

This magazine, published six times a year by the American Association for the Advancement of Science, has working scientists review children's books as well as other media. Although the journal doesn't review quite as many titles as, for instance, School Library Journal, *the approach is an important one for teachers and children to study. This is also an excellent place to keep up with science-related videos, films, CDs, and so on.*

To encourage authentic science-related reading and writing we need to understand science as activity, either our own, the work of others, or the kind of activity where we observe and try to make sense of the activity nature provides.

Here are several books that promote science activity, giving children something to read about, write about, and do.

San Francisco's Exploratorium, a museum that knows the ins and outs of science activity, has recently produced several excellent books. "The Exploratorium Snackbooks," written by Paul Doherty et al., are as original in their ideas as in their titles: *The Cool Hot Rod and Other Electrifying Experiments on Energy and Matter* (1996) or *The Spinning Blackboard and Other Dynamic Experiments on Force and Motion* (1996).

In 1996 Pat Murphy created *The Science Explorer: Family Experiments from the World's Favorite Hands-on Science Museum.* That book together with its sequel, *The Science Explorer Out and About* (both from Henry Holt), enable schools or students' homes to become lively sites for doing and thinking about how the world works.

Favorite Science Web Sites (Selected and annotated by Wendy Saul and Donna Neutze)

Web sites are particularly good places to check out what's new in science, probably because people within that community are less afraid of technology than many of us. The following are worth your time:

American Association for the Advancement of Science. *http://www.AAAS.org*

If teachers want to understand more about the "big picture" or figure out where to go next in their planning AAAS is there at your side. All of their publications, the now classic Science for All Americans *and* Benchmarks *are being supplemented with conceptual maps, curricular materials, and lists of tradebooks keyed to the science concepts identified in* Benchmarks. *The best place to find out the latest information on AAAS is to check out their Web site under Project 2061.*

National Academy Press. *http://www.nap.edu/*

This site is designed for teachers who want to review publications describing what's new in science curricula. "The reading room" at this site itself contains more than 1000 science and technology books, intended primarily for adult readers.

The remaining sites are places with lots of links to other sites. With a quick click you can fly from place to place.

www.ornith.cornell.edu

A cache of participatory data and scientific sharing, this site receives and distributes information from all over the world and offers visitors a chance to participate by looking outside their own classroom walls. You can join the "Nest Box Network," track bluebirds, listen to sounds of various species (and send in your own tapes), or gather information for the warbler watch.

The Exploratorium: the Museum of Science, Art, and Human Perception. *http://www.exploratorium .com/*

This Web site is chock full of various exhibits, activities, and information, much of which is presented in interactive format. A visitor might learn how to throw a curve ball, listen to the sounds of the rain forest, play memory games, or explore the nature of sunspots. Highlights include the monthly listing of "Ten Cool Sites" and the Cool Sites searchable archives, "The Exploratorium Science Snacks," and "The Digital Library."

The Franklin Institute Science Museum Homepage. *http://www.fi.edu/*

Visitors to this site might choose to see what is in the Franklin Institute Spotlight, visit online exhibits, or tap into the Educational Hotlists. The inQuiry Almanac is a monthly online magazine with searchable archives. Musing with Mac is yet another monthly regular. Features such as "Flights of Inspiration" provide educator resources in the Teachers' Zone. If you're up for a challenge, you might try to solve one of the Puzzlers.

NASA Homepage. *http://www.nasa.gov/NASA_home page.html/*

The homepage for the National Aeronautics and Space Administration provides links to the many NASA internet offerings. With a click, one can obtain information about the NASA Education Program, access NASA's latest available information, view the latest Hubble images, visit video galleries, and read about the most recent space science news. The Earth Science Enterprise will be of special interest to both students and educators.

National Geographic. *http://www.nationalgeograph ic.com/*

Visit the Caspian Sea. "Dive into an interactive kelp forest." Join the Kids Talk Board. Read what's "In the News." Maybe you'd like to meet real pirates or see the solar system in 3D. There's something for everyone, including Explorers Hall, Collector's Corner, the Map Machine, and Kids: Features and Fun.

The Nine Planets. *http://seds.lpl.arizona.edu/unine planets/nineplanets/nineplanets.html*

Take a multimedia tour of the solar system at The Nine Planets Web site. Visitors may choose between a full tour or an "Express Tour." The site utilizes text, graphics, sound, and movies in its tour. The data is plentiful, and easy to read and comprehend. Much of the data links to addition sources of information. The site could easily be used to accompany books on the solar system, such as those by Seymour Simon.

The Virtual Field Trip Site. *http://www.field guides.com/*

Go on a field trip without leaving your classroom. This site currently features virtual field trips to deserts, oceans and salt marshes, as well as visits with sharks and other fierce creatures. In the Teacher's Lounge, educators can submit ideas for their own tours, or link to other resources. Teacher's resources are available for each of the site's virtual field trips.

Social Studies/History (Selected and annotated by Danny Miller)

1998. *Eyewitness Activity Files*. New York: Dorling Kindersley.

Facsimile documents such as photographs, booklets, posters, pictures, charts, and letters to make historical periods come to life. These activity files are useful for students to learn what primary sources look like and how to use them in the inquiry process.

1997. *Families of the World Series*. Winnipeg, MAN: Peguis.

This series offers books that contain teaching opportunities and curricular support designed to make social studies come alive for students. Teacher materials accompany the student materials and assist in planning. Written for students in grades four through six, the books feature families from countries such as China, Mexico,

Germany, Zimbabwe, and Columbia and include a table of contents, maps, colored photographs, and a glossary. Teacher materials (1998) offer teaching suggestions and pertinent background information. (J.W.)

Graves, Donald. 1999. *Bring Life into Learning: Create a Lasting Literacy*. Portsmouth, NH: Heinemann.

History, art, science—indeed, all disciplines are created by people. Donald Graves shows us how to explore and develop curriculum through a focus on and study of people. In so doing, he maintains that we discover and understand the world through the lives of those who had a role in shaping and creating it. An innovative book to enliven your curriculum and teaching.

Hakim, Joy. 1993–1995. A History of U.S. Series. New York: Oxford University Press.

These comprehensive history books are well researched, detailed, and entertaining to read. The series provide excellent coverage of U.S. history from the Constitution through the twentieth century. The titles in this series include: From Colonies to Country; The New Nation; Liberty for All?; War, Terrible War; Reconstruction and Reform; An Age of Extremes; War, Peace, and All that Jazz; All the People. (D.M.)

Hoose, Phillip. 1993. *It's Our World, Too! Stories of Young People Who Are Making a Difference.* Boston: Little, Brown.

This inspiring book tells stories of courageous young people who've taken steps to move their world in a more positive direction—from saving rain forests to distributing food to the homeless to building an international statue for peace. It sends a strong message that students don't have to wait until they're adults to take action about issues that concern them: they have the power to change some things now. (D.M.)

Jackdaws. Amawalk, NY: Jackdaw Publications.

Facsimiles of historical documents organized in portfolios and photo collections. A terrific source for integrating primary source materials, such as photos, letters, diaries, newspaper articles, and maps, into your study of U.S. and world history. Geared to older students, upper elementary through high school.

National Council for the Social Studies, 3501 Newark Street NW, Washington, DC, 20016–3167, 202-966-7840.

NCSS holds an annual national conference and publishes two journals devoted to the teaching of social studies. Curriculum Standards for Social Studies: Expectations of Excellence, *published in 1994, is a useful framework and guide for connecting your curriculum to national standards.*

Percoco, James A. 1998. *A Passion for the Past: Creative Teaching of U.S. History.* Portsmouth, NH: Heinemann.

History comes to life when we step beyond the narrow bounds of the history textbook and experience historical research firsthand. Percoco shows us how. By taking advantage of the many resources in our own communities, we can travel to historic sites and exhibits, examine archives and other primary source documents, analyze movies and documentaries, conduct interviews and much more. And, an engagement with the past helps students understand and think critically about the present.

Sobel, David. 1998. *Mapmaking with Children: Sense of Place Education for the Elementary Years.* Portsmouth, NH: Heinemann.

This engaging text will open new possibilities that extend far beyond the boundaries of traditional geography education. Because this text ties mapmaking to all content areas and offers many instructional suggestions, students learn to see mapmaking as a relevant and necessary skill for life. Many photographs, drawings, and examples enrich the book. (J.W.)

Steffey, Stephanie, and Wendy J. Hood, eds. 1994. *If This Is Social Studies, Why Isn't It Boring?* York, ME: Stenhouse.

This edited collection of essays written by classroom teachers details successful strategies for teaching social studies at elementary, middle, and high school levels. The chapters describe creative ways to introduce point of view, theme cycles, exploring historical perspectives through inquiry, connecting to history through storytelling, and other approaches to social studies that take into account the ways children learn best. (D.M.)

Weitzman, David. 1975. *My Backyard History Book.* Boston: Little, Brown.

> *Though older than others listed, this text is a classic because it invites children and teachers to discover the wonders and pleasures of history right in their own backyards. It introduces kids to the idea that they have a family history that can be studied just as one studies Columbus or George Washington. Kids learn to think of themselves as detectives—tracking down clues and hints in the study of their own history. Fun activities include creating personal and family time lines and maps, and uncovering the meanings behind family and place names.* (D.M.)

Zarnowsi, Myra. 1995. "Learning History with Informational Storybooks: A Social Studies Educator's Perspective." *The New Advocate* (Summer): 183–196.

> *Discusses the possibilities and pitfalls in using nonfiction trade books to teach social studies. Notes that "For the purpose of learning history, quality nonfiction makes better reading material than informational storybooks" (189), but that "writing original informational storybooks promotes children's understanding of social studies" (190).*

- Zarnowski, Myra, and Arlene F. Gallagher, eds. 1993. *Children's Literature & Social Studies: Selecting and Using Notable Books in the Classroom.* Washington, DC: National Council for the Social Studies.

> *This treasure of a resource for K–8 teachers gives a wealth of practical information for using excellent trade books in the social studies program. Part 1 of the book examines the selection of books; Part 2 addresses ways to purposefully use these books. In-depth information is given for choosing and using nonfiction to read aloud, picture books, biographies, autobiographies, and historical novels. Suggested ways to use these books in discussion and writing about significant social issues are included. Excellent bibliographies, some of which are annotated, abound throughout this terrific eighty-page book.*

Favorite Social Studies/History Web Sites

The National Archives and Records Administration. *http://www.nara.gov*

> *An excellent resource for teachers and students that provides background information on the National Archives' extensive holdings. An online exhibit hall features exhibits ranging from the Declaration of Independence, Constitution, and Bill of Rights, to World War II posters and "When Nixon Met Elvis." The Digital Classroom section offers guidelines for creating a school archives, and cross-curricular connections involving primary documents.*

National Center for History in the Schools. *http://www.sscnet.ucla.edu/nchs/*

> *The Center publishes its National History Standards both online and in print form. Their Web site contains information about the Standards and Curriculum Guides, and an extensive catalog of teaching materials and resources.*

National History Day. *http://thehistorynet.com/NationalHistoryDay/*

> *The yearlong National History Day competition is an exciting way for students to study and learn about historical issues, ideas, people, and events. The Web site includes teacher and student guides, topic ideas, and related links.*

National Park Service. *http://www.cr.nps.gov/*

> *"Links to the Past" examines the cultures, historic places, and structures and objects that make up the vast American landscape. The National Park Service is responsible for preserving and protecting many of these important legacies. Its Web site provides helpful tools for researching different periods in American history, cultural trends, archaeology, ethnography, and important historical sites in the United States. Teachers and students can pose online questions to National Park Service historians.*

Smithsonian Institution. *http://www.si.edu*

> *This terrific resource contains links to all of the Smithsonian museums, including the National Museum of American History, the National Portrait Gallery, the National Museum of the American Indian, the Anacostia Museum and Center for African American History and Culture, and many other Smithsonian organizations, research centers, and libraries around the country. Most of the museum Web sites have education and outreach sections, virtual exhibitions, and online resources for kids. Additional links for kids include Muse (http://www.musemag.com) and Kids' Castle (http://www.kidscas*

tle.si.edu/), *an interactive Web site for children ages eight to sixteen.*

Statue of Liberty National Monument & Ellis Island Immigration Museum. *http://www.nps.gov /stli/*

    This Web site from the National Park Service provides a wealth of information about the history, restorations, and research collections of the Statue of Liberty National Monument and the Ellis Island Immigration Museum. Information is also available on the Ellis Island Oral History Project, the oldest and largest oral history project dedicated to preserving the first-hand recollections of immigrants coming to America during the years Ellis Island was in operation—from 1892 to 1954. The 1,500 interviews include an extensive examination of everyday life in the country of origin, family history, reasons for coming to America, the journey to the port, experiences on the ship, arrival and processing at the Ellis Island facility, and an in-depth look at the adjustment to living in the United States.

United States Holocaust Museum. *http://www .ushmm.org/*

    In addition to providing extensive background on the Holocaust, the Web site of this Washington, DC museum includes online exhibitions of current human rights issues around the world and a collection of teaching resources, bibliographies, and guidelines for teaching the Holocaust to elementary, middle, and high school children.

Mathematics (Selected and annotated by Annie Gordon)

Curriculum Inquiry in Mathematics

• Math By All Means Series. 1991–1997. Math Solutions Publications, Sausalito, CA, 94965.

    This is a series of mathematical replacement units written by various authors and published by Math Solutions Publications, a division of Marilyn Burns Education Associates. These indispensable units are key companions for both the new or veteran math teacher who wants to adopt a problem-solving approach in the math classroom. The units

span grades one through six and offer thoughtful and engaging explorations into such topics as Place Value, Money, Probability and Geometry (Grades 1–2); Multiplication (Grade 3); Probability, Geometry, and Division (Grades 3–4); and Area and Perimeter (Grades 5–6). The units are formatted to include whole class, small group, and independent activities and games. A feature I particularly like is the "From the Classroom" section that illustrates the lessons through vignettes filled with authentic teacher-student dialogue. These vignettes have helped me to think in advance about questions or problems that might arise, and how best to approach them. (A.G.)

Investigations in Number, Data, and Space. 1998. Dale Seymour Publications, Palo Alto, CA, 94303.

    This is a curriculum package (K–5) that was written and developed by various authors at TERC, funded in part by the National Science Foundation, and published by Dale Seymour Publications. The goals of the Investigations units are to present students with math problems that are meaningful, to expose children to mathematical ideas in depth, and to help teachers deepen their own mathematical thinking and teaching practices. Investigations should be strongly considered by teachers and administrators who are looking to adopt a comprehensive and enriching math curriculum. While the complete package consists of several units at each grade level, individual units can be purchased separately. Even if a school has not adopted this curriculum, teachers should consider utilizing one or more units to augment the math program at their grade level. My school has implemented this program, and while I do not use all of the Investigations units at my grade level, I have found several that form the core of my math curriculum. There are some very engaging activities and games here, as well as some solid homework assignments. The "Teacher Note" section is wonderful as it provides interesting explanations about the math concept being taught as well as insight into how children may think or learn.

Trafton, Paul R., and Diane Thiessen. 1999. *Learning Through Problems: Number Sense and Com-*

putational *Strategies*. Portsmouth, NH: Heinemann.

This book, a primary source for teachers, is easy to read, accessible, and most helpful to the teacher just beginning to teach math through a problem-solving approach. The book is divided into three sections: "Problem-Centered Learning," "Developing Number Sense and Computational Strategies," and "In the Classroom: Guidelines, Reflections and Ideas," all offering teachers classroom examples where developing number sense and computational skill are a central focus of the activities.

Connecting Math and Literature

Whitin, David J., and Sandra Wilde. 1992. *Read Any Good Math Lately?* Children's Books for Mathematical Learning, K–6. Portsmouth, NH: Heinemann.

This book is an educational as well as practical guide for bringing children's literature, fiction and nonfiction, into the classroom. The chapters are organized by mathematical topic, for example, classification, subtraction, multiplication, or big numbers. Each chapter, which begins with a concise summary of the mathematical content of the topic under discussion, refreshed my own thinking about familiar mathematical ideas. Every chapter then offers suggestions for children's literature at specific grade levels and offers stories about how various teachers have used the books in their own classrooms. The first-grade teacher who wants to teach estimation through a children's book can do so with ease and efficiency, and so can the fifth-grade teacher who wants to use literature to explore fractions. While the book is excellent as a whole, it is a good "pick and choose" book; teachers can find what they need when they need it. Helpful bibliographies are listed at the end of each chapter.

Burns, Marilyn. 1992. *Math and Literature (K–3): Book One*. Sausalito, CA: Math Solutions Publications.

Bresser, Rusty. 1995. *Math and Literature (4–6)*. Sausalito, CA: Math Solutions Publications.

Sheffield, Stephanie. 1995. *Math and Literature (K–3): Book Two*. Sausalito, CA: Math Solutions Publications.

These books are valuable resources for teachers who want to integrate children's literature into the math classroom. They provide synopses of the selected stories and give detailed descriptions of how they can be used to link math and literature in the classroom. The lessons clarify the mathematical concepts within each story and then offer concrete suggestions about how to work with them in the math classroom. Every year, after I have introduced a couple of these literature-related lessons to my class, I hear my fourth-grade students looking for and pondering potential mathematical moments in other pieces of literature. I particularly like the excerpts of classroom discussions that are written up. The examples of children's work that are included also provide a good baseline for assessment.

Home-School Connections in Mathematics

Teachers who adopt a problem-solving approach to math education need to address concerns that parents have about a "nontraditional" math program. Regardless of whether parents found their own mathematical education adequate or inadequate, exciting or painful, a pedagogical approach that is different stimulates questions and arouses concern. Listed here are two excellent books (Litton and Mokros) that support teachers, and likewise help teachers take a proactive approach to include and educate the parents of their students.

Burns, Marilyn. 1998. Math: *Facing an American Phobia*. Sausalito, CA: Math Solutions Publications.

This book is at the top of the list. It is an engaging, entertaining book that thoroughly examines why so many people in our country are fearful of—and actively avoid—mathematics. Captivating in both its message and tone, this book describes ways in which traditional math programs have failed (resulting in a nation of math phobics) and how we—teachers and parents—can reverse this historic trend. The book invites the reader to thoughtfully entertain ideas about what children truly need to become skilled, confident, and prepared for the math needs of today's world. It is quite persuasive in its call for change and is an essential read for math enthusiasts and phobics alike.

● Litton, Nancy. 1998. *Getting Your Math Message out to Parents: A K–6 Resource*. Sausalito, CA: Math Solutions Publications.

This is an excellent resource for all K–6 teachers. It provides an easy-to-read, practical and proactive approach for communicating with parents. The central idea is that once parents understand and support their child's math program, students benefit and become successful learners. The book details a variety of ways that teachers can effectively inform parents about their children's math education. The author is sensitive to both teacher responsibilities and parent concerns, and deals effectively with each by discussing the topics of: math newsletters, back-to-school nights, parent conferences, homework, using volunteers in the classroom, and hosting family math nights. Helpful examples are included from primary and upper elementary grades. This book is a "must read" for every teacher.

Mokros, Jan. 1996. *Beyond Facts and Flashcards: Exploring Math with Your Kids*. Portsmouth, NH: Heinemann.

This book suggests practical, age-appropriate mathematical games, activities, and questions that stem from everyday situations. It is a very good resource for parents of elementary students who care about their child's math education and want to participate in it more fully. This is also an entertaining book that teachers can use themselves, as well as recommend to parents. By looking more closely at grocery coupons, recycling, gardening, and traveling, for example, the author explores settings and situations that can enrich a child's understanding of math in daily life. I think parents will appreciate the "Where Is the Math?" section, as it offers a quick summary of the main mathematical ideas of each chapter.

Writing and Mathematics

Burns, Marilyn. 1995. *Writing in Math Class: A Resource Guide for Grades 2–8*. Sausalito, CA: Math Solutions Publications.

This is a useful and accessible resource for teachers who want to integrate writing into their math curriculum. For those who doubt the book's premise, the text begins by making a persuasive case for why students should write in math class. It then illustrates how teachers can use writing assignments to support their students' learning and assess their understanding, help students solve math problems and explain their mathematical thoughts and ideas. There is also a clever chapter on how to blend math and creative writing. The book offers many quality suggestions for math-related writing assignments and gives teachers tips for helping students with their mathematical writing. Many fine examples of student work are included.

Mathematics Education Reform

● National Council of Teachers of Mathematics. October 1998. Principles and Standards for School Mathematics: Discussion Draft. Reston, VA: National Council of Teachers of Mathematics.

This extensive draft document, from which the final publication—Standards 2000—will be produced, is an outgrowth of the three NCTM Standards documents that were published within the last ten years. Those documents, The Curriculum and Evaluation Standards for School Mathematics *(1989), the* Professional Standards for Teaching Mathematics *(1991), and the* Assessment Standards for School Mathematics *(1995), provided a visionary approach for school mathematics programs. The* Principles and Standards for School Mathematics *intends to "build on the foundations of the original NCTM Standards." This document further intends to combine and make more accessible "the classroom aspects of all three documents." The* Principles and Standards for School Mathematics *presents ten mathematical standards that should be addressed throughout the various grade levels. This document describes five content standards: Number and Operations; Patterns Functions and Algebra; Geometry and Spatial Sense; Measurement; Data Analysis, Statistics and Probability; and five process standards: Problem Solving; Reasoning and Proof; Communication; Mathematical Connections and Representation. New grade-level groupings are presented, and after an overview of all of the standards is provided, each standard is then discussed in some detail according to the grade level grouping (pre-K–2; 3–5; 6–8; and 9–12). Rather than being highly prescriptive as to how to teach and evaluate the standards, the document discusses what students should know and be able do in math. Sample questions and examples of student work are supplied throughout. This document can also be viewed on the World Wide Web at:* http://standards-e.nctm.org.

Teaching Children Mathematics. Reston, VA: National Council of Teachers of Mathematics.

Teaching Children Mathematics (TCM) *is the NCTM's monthly professional journal published for educators who are teaching at the pre-K–6 grade levels. The journal is easy to read and each issue provides a thoughtful balance of lessons and teaching tips, dialogue and reflection, as well as research findings. This is a good resource for preservice and inservice teachers who want to stay current on developments in mathematical education.* .

Mathematics Teaching in the Middle School. Reston, VA: National Council of Teachers of Mathematics.

Mathematics Teaching in the Middle School (MTMS) *is NCTM's monthly professional journal for middle-school teachers and teacher educators. Like* TCM, *this journal offers a mix of lesson ideas, editorials, and opinions, mathematical connections with other subject areas and research results. This journal is accessible and a valuable resource for educators teaching at the middle school level.*

Chapter 13: Critical Resources for Curriculum Inquiry: Librarians, School Libraries, and Technology

Use of the Library

American Association of School Librarians, and Association for Educational Communications and Technology. 1998. *Information Power: Building Partnerships for Learning.* Chicago and London: American Association of School Librarians; Association for Educational Communications and Technology.

"The library media program is the keystone in a school's efforts to promote efficient and effective self-directed inquiry" (69). *In coordination with national school library standards for information literacy, this guide is written to promote improvement in school library media programs. Part 1 includes the philosophy statement for the standards and the goals of the school library media program. Part 2 describes the principles that undergird an excellent school library media program and how they might be applied.*

Breivik, Patricia Senn, and J. A. Senn. 1994. *Information Literacy: Educating Children for the 21st Century.* New York: Scholastic.

Techniques for giving students in your school the tools and processes necessary to become information literate and lifelong, independent learners. Describes how and why to institute collaborative planning, resource-based learning, and flexible libraries with librarians as information specialists.

• Buchanan, Jan. 1991. *Flexible Access Library Media Programs.* Englewood, CO: Libraries Unlimited.

Explains the concepts and research behind flexible access and gives guidelines for designing, cooperative planning, implementing, and evaluating a flexible access library media program. Extremely helpful and specific for librarians, teachers, and administrators desiring to make the school library the hub for information literacy.

Giorgis, Cindy, and Barbara Peterson. 1996. "Teachers and Librarians Collaborate to Create a Community of Learners." *Language Arts* (November): 477–482.

Describes one school's change process toward greater collaboration between teachers and librarians. Can be used as a discussion starter to foster similar change in your school.

Heiligman, Deborah. 1998. *The New York Public Library Kid's Guide to Research.* New York: Scholastic and The New York Public Library.

Written for intermediate students and older, this is a useful, reader-friendly guide for using the library and researching a topic. Includes such topics as how to find references, take notes, judge the reliability of sources, use the

Internet, interview people, and conduct surveys.

Use of Technology and the Internet (Selected and annotated by Lee Sattelmeyer)

Bix, Cynthia Overbeck. 1996. *Kids Do the Web*. San Jose, CA: Adobe Press.

While promoting Adobe software solutions to Web publishing, this book is useful to anyone thinking of putting up a Web site. The book examines twenty-eight Web sites written by or for children. There is a helpful critique of design and format of each Web site.

Carter, Gene R., Project Director, and Sawatzky, Jamie, ed. 1998. *Only the Best: The Annual Guide to the Highest-Rated Educational Software and Multimedia*. Alexandria, VA: Association for Supervision and Curriculum Development.

An annual compilation of the top-rated software programs published during the year that will help educators begin to identify potential software purchases for their classrooms, schools, or district. Programs listed in this book are included based on multiple assessments by evaluators that may include professional, public, and private organizations. Includes an interdisciplinary list.

Classroom Connect. www.classroom.com

Published monthly September through June, this magazine provides helpful guidance for educators looking for ways to meaningfully incorporate technology into classroom instruction. In addition to listing Web sites and Web resources, this publication contains lesson plans, projects, informative articles, and details about a variety of Quest experiences such as GalapogosQuest, AfricaQuest, and AsiaQuest. (J.W.)

Dede, Chris, ed. 1998. *ASCD Yearbook 1998: Learning with Technology*. Alexandria, VA: Association for Supervision and Curriculum Development.

This book is a compilation of nine stories about projects that were designed to enhance student learning through the use of technology.

The authors of these projects share a common belief in the promise of technology integration into the curriculum. Readers will gain valuable insight into the role technology can play in supporting educational reform and empowering student learners.

Heide, Ann, and Linda Stilborne. 1999. *The Teacher's Complete and Easy Guide to the Internet*. 2d ed. Toronto, ONT: Trilfolium Books; New York: Teachers College Press; Newark, DE: International Reading Association.

Heide and Stilborne provide teachers with a terrific, easily accessible resource that is chock full of valuable information and practical activities for integrating the Internet into the classroom. Along with an accompanying CD, the text includes extensive information on how to search and use the Web and describes numerous excellent Web sites. A great guide for anyone interested in using the Internet to enhance student learning.

Jody, Marilyn, and Saccardi, Marianne. 1996. *Computer Conversations: Readers and Books Online*. Urbana, IL: National Council of Teachers of English.

This book suggests multiple ways that educators can integrate the use of technology into the language arts curriculum through electronic dialogues about books students read, e-mail, and student research.

Leu, Donald J., and Leu, Deborah Diadiun. 1998. *Teaching with the Internet: Lessons from the Classroom*. Norwood, MA: Christopher-Gordon.

The authors share stories from other educators, suggest how to keep online activities simple and focused, and recommend Internet resources. A well-organized book useful to teachers wanting to get started with integrating Internet activities into the curriculum.

McKenzie, Jamie. 1998. "Grazing the Net: Raising a Generation of Free-Range Students." *Phi Delta Kappan* (September): 26–31.

A thoughtful article for understanding how to connect research on the Internet with essential questions that lead to inquiry. Terrific for discussion.

Milner, Anna, and Burrows, Terry. 1996. *The Internet*. New York: Dorling Kindersley.

A general guide to using the Internet that covers a broad range of topics including e-mail, FTP, and the Web. The general information in the guide will be helpful to both new users of the Internet and those more familiar with it. The appendix contains a useful glossary of Internet related terms.

Miller, Elizabeth B. 1998. *The Internet Resource Directory for K–12 Teachers and Librarians, 98/99 Edition*. Englewood, CO: Libraries Unlimited.

This book includes the URL and an annotation for 14,400 sites on the Internet that will be of interest to educators and librarians working with K–12 students. Sites are organized into eleven different areas of the K–12 curriculum. The annotations for each site are especially helpful in determining which sites to examine for potential inclusion in curriculum use. An "update" Web site is associated with the book.

Morton, Jessica. 1996. *Kids on the 'Net: Conducting Internet Research in K–5 Classrooms*. Portsmouth, NH: Heinemann.

A primary teacher describes how she and her students conduct yearlong research on a topic largely by asking questions of experts around the world via e-mail. Useful for getting familiar with how to use the Internet as a classroom resource.

Owston, Ron. 1998. *Making the Link: Teacher Professional Development on the Internet*. Portsmouth, NH: Heinemann.

Based upon the premise that staff development needs to be personalized for individual needs, this book offers some concrete examples on how to effectively utilize the Internet and its resources.

• Papert, Seymour. 1993. *The Children's Machine: Rethinking School in the Age of the Computer*. New York: Basic Books.

A thought-provoking book that looks at the role of computers in children's learning, the social agency of School, and the profound affect technology will have on both. Papert provides the reader with a vision for integrating technology.

Rouk, Ullik, ed. 1996. *Plugging In: Choosing and Using Educational Technology*. Washington, DC: Council for Educational Development and Research.

Part of the EdTalk series published by the Council for Educational Development and Research, Plugging In *provides some guidelines for evaluating the use of technology in instruction. Blank tables, graphs, and charts that educators may use to plan and evaluate instructional programs that utilize technology are included.*

U.S. Congress. Office of Technology Assessment. 1995. *Teachers and Technology: Making the Connection*. Washington, DC: U.S. Government Printing Office. *http://www.wws.princeton.edu/~ota/disk1/1995/9541.html*

Favorite Web Sites
(Selected and annotated by Lee Sattelmeyer)

In the rapidly changing neighborhood of the Internet, it is not unusual for Web sites to frequently change addresses or go off-line. The following Web sites were chosen based upon their stability and potential use to educators. Many of them have additional links to other sites outside their own Web pages.

American Association of School Librarians.
http:// www.ala.org/aasl
On this useful Web page, you can access the most recent draft of Information Literacy Standards for Student Learning.

Berit's Best Sites for Kids.
http://db.cochran.com/li_toc:PBSPage.db
A very friendly and child-oriented Web site designed for children up to age twelve, parents, and teachers. Hotlinks to 700 child-friendly Web sites are organized into categories. Each link is annotated and rated by Berit to help the user.

The Children's Literature Web Guide.
http://www.acs.ucalgary.ca/~dkbrown
One of the most complete Web sites dedicated to children's literature and language arts. The site offers current information on books, conferences, and authors' Web pages. There are resources for parents, teachers, and writers.

Education Weekly On-Line.
http://www.edweek.org
   Professional site with information useful to planning strategies for classroom instruction or school district initiatives.

Educators Technology Center of Indiana.
http://etc.iupui.edu
   This site is run by the School of Education at Indiana University Purdue University Indianapolis. It is an organized list of links to other sites useful to children, teachers, and administrators. Teachers can quickly find sites that deal with various topics such as staff development in technology, copyright laws, lesson plans, and technology magazines online.

The Eisenhower National Clearinghouse for Mathematics and Science Education.
http://www.enc.org
   A national resource site for information on mathematics and science instruction, instructional materials, and technology. The site hosts a teacher-led evaluation of computer software that is part of Ohio's SchoolNet project.

Global SchoolNet Foundation. *http://www.gsn.org*
   Information and support for teachers wanting to involve their classes in telecommunications.

The Internet Public Library. *http://www.ipl.org/*
   A wonderful location on the Web for locating sites for students. This Web page is organized into curriculum categories. Navigating to a particular category opens a Web page with annotated entries for each posted Web site.

Library of Congress. *http://www.loc.gov/*
   A primary source index for locating historical resources such as cookbooks, journals, news articles, land surveys, advertisements, audio recordings of famous speeches, photos, movies, and fine art. The Library of Congress develops a number of educationally designed resources for classroom teachers, such as "The American Experience" and "On This Date." Math, science, and social studies activities can be easily designed around the resources located at this site. This is a site that all teachers should be aware of.

The National Geographic.
http://www.nationalgeographic.com/
   Plenty to see and do at this site. This site includes a lot of Web pages useful for the classroom teacher in teaching geography, social studies, and science. Students can get additional information on projects the organization has worked on and can learn more about the world they live in.

700+ Great Sites. *http://www.ala.org/parentspage/ greatsites/amazing.html*
   A great place for finding useful Web sites for children. The annotated URL listings were compiled and organized by the American Library Association. Visitors to this Web site will find it very helpful for identifying potential sites for classroom or home use.

Webquest.
http://edweb.sdsu.edu/webquest/wbquest.html
   The home page describing what the elements of an effective webquest is, how to get started, and sample webquests to use in the classroom. See page 516 for webquest description.

Yahooligans. *http://www.yahooligans.com*
   One of the best resources for teachers and children using the Internet. This search engine/Web directory includes only Web sites safe for children to use. A very useful feature, but often unknown by teachers, is its "The Big Picture" page. This Web page is a reference source for Web sites that deal with topical issues that are currently in the news.

Basic Technology Terms

Computer System

The computer system is made up of various components. Some desktop units are composed of add-on units; others are self-contained. There are also portable laptop models. Common elements of computer systems include:

CD-ROM drive: Allows the computer system to run programs formatted on CD-ROM disks. CD-ROM stands for compact disk read-only memory. This format has become the favored format for software programs because of its large storage capacity of approximately 600 megs (an abbreviation for *megabyte*, a unit of measurement that equals one million characters).

Computer case: The computer case houses the CPU and other hardware. A desktop case lays flat, or horizontally, on the desktop, with the monitor on top of it. A minitower case sits upright or vertically on the desktop, shelf, or floor. The monitor for this type of system sits comfortably at eye level in front of the user. A self-contained system conveniently holds all components in one reasonably sized box. The advantage of having this type of system is that it requires a minimum amount of setup and generally takes up less desktop space. The disadvantage is that these computers typically do not allow for significant upgrading of hardware.

CPU: Abbreviation for *central processing unit*, the number-crunching brains of the computer.

Disk drive: Allows storage of data files to a floppy disk. The floppy gets its name from the "floppy" Mylar material that holds the magnetic media inside the rigid plastic case. The internal three-and-a-half-inch 1.4-meg floppy is the standard format for computer systems, although fewer computer programs use this format anymore because of its limited storage capacity.

Hard drive: A large storage device that contains the code for the computer's operating system, applications, and other programs. It is usually the default location for the storage of data files. The hard drive gets its name from the rigid metal platters that hold the magnetic media.

Keyboard: Standard device for the input of information. The QWERTY format is the keyboard arrangement held over from the days of mechanical type. (The letters *QWERTY* appear in that order on the top row of the letters keyboard.)

Modem: Because many school systems are developing their own networks, modems are found less often in school computer systems. Modems are still very popular for connecting home computing systems to the Internet. A modem is a piece of hardware that allows one computer to talk to another computer over telephone lines.

Monitor: A video screen that may be of the cathode-ray tube variety, similar to a TV screen, or a liquid crystal display most often found in laptop computers.

Mouse: An input device that allows the user to point and click on icons or options displayed on the monitor screen. A Macintosh mouse has only one button that manages the various mouse functions. A PC mouse splits the mouse functions between two buttons.

RAM: Random-access memory is memory that the computer uses to run programs. The operating system, programs, and data are stored in RAM for as long as the information is needed and the computer is turned on. All information in RAM disappears when the electricity is turned off. Today, RAM comes in different flavors, such as DRAM, which stands for dynamic RAM, but the function remains the same. If you have a choice, get as much RAM as you can afford when purchasing a computer system. The additional RAM allows for growth. New software programs tend to have larger memory needs than programs that have been around for a while.

Removable media drives: These drives are not yet standard on computer systems but are becoming increasingly popular. Expect to see different formats that are not compatible with other types and makes of removable drives. They combine the benefits of the large storage capacity found in hard drives with the facility and portability of the floppy disk drive.

Internet

The Internet is a worldwide network of interconnected computers. Individual computer systems connect to the Internet through a host system such as a university's mainframe computer or an individual Internet service provider (ISP).

FTP: File Transfer Protocol provides a method for downloading files to an individual computer from some other location on the Internet. This is usually handled transparently by a Web browser but may be done with an individual FTP application such as Fetch.

HTML: HyperText Markup Language is the programming language of the Web page. The abbreviation is often found as an affix (.html) at the end of a URL.

HTTP: HyperText Transfer Protocol is used to transfer Web pages across the Internet. http:// is typed before a URL in the address section of a Web browser.

Hypertext: Hypertext is text on a monitor screen (either in a software program or on a Web site) that points to information somewhere else. Clicking on hypertext with the mouse cursor tells the computer to request that that information be sent to it.

ISP: An Internet service provider provides access to the Internet for individual computer systems, usually for a monthly fee. ISPs are often local companies that provide users with basic services such as e-mail and Internet access.

Online service provider: An online service provider (OSP) provides, in addition to Internet access, access to online services such as informational databases and chat areas. OSPs tend to have dial-in access numbers for cities nationwide. This is especially handy for frequent travelers since access is usually only a local phone call away. America Online (AOL) and CompuServe are examples of this type of service.

Search engines and Web directories: To the average user, search engines and Web directories seem very similar. Both allow users to locate topical resources on the Web using some form of keyword or Boolean search. There is a major difference between these two, however. Search engines, such as Excite or InfoSeek, send out software "robots" to "crawl" through the Web, tirelessly indexing the words found on individual Web pages. They are more likely to provide the most up-to-date listing of resources, but they can also return a number of useless URLs. Web directories, such as Yahoo and Ask Jeeves, which feature human intervention, often provide better results, since Web sites are reviewed and then categorized for the user.

URL: The URL, or uniform resource locator, is the "address" that is typed in a Web browser to locate Web sites and files on the Internet. Knowing the most common affixes found on the server names of a URL can help you understand what information might be found at that sight (*.com* designates a commercial sight, *.org* a nonprofit organization, *.gov* a government site, *.edu* a site run by an educational establishment, and *.mil* a military-related site).

Web browser: A Web browser is an application program that is used to navigate the World Wide Web.

The two most common Web browsers used are NetScape Navigator and Microsoft's Internet Explorer.

Web page: Web pages come in all different "flavors," from plain text to rather ingenious creations that incorporate video clips, sound bites, hypertext links, and more. The "page" is what appears on the monitor screen after the Web browser retrieves the information found at the Internet address defined by the URL.

Web site: A Web site is a location on the Internet that consists of a home page (the main Web page for a site that is identified by the URL) with additional linked pages (pages associated with the site, which have additional information on a topic). A typical Web site may contain text, graphics, pictures, movies, and sounds. A Web browser is used to view these pages.

WWW: The World Wide Web is the portion of the Internet that contains Web pages.

Network

A network connects multiple computers in different locations and allows the computers to communicate with one another. Network functions are managed by a main server or multiple servers. Network functions may include Internet access, mail services, printing services, and the provision of software programs for use at individual computer stations.

LAN: A LAN, or local area net, is comprised of networked computers in one general location such as a school building.

Network card: Network cards allow individual computers in a network to communicate with one another.

WAN: A WAN, or wide area net, is comprised of all the networked computers and servers spread out over several locations, such as the school buildings for a school district.

Software

Application: A program designed to help do a task. Word processing, spreadsheet, and database programs are examples of this type of software.

Drill and practice: A program designed to help the user practice a specific skill or memorize specific facts. The skill is usually not practiced in the context that it would naturally be found.

Multimedia: A multimedia software program combines multiple visual and auditory components, such as text, motion pictures, pictures, and/or sound.

Operating system: The software program loaded when the computer is turned on. The operating system contains the commands that allow the user to interface with the computer hardware. It defines the "look and feel" of the computer. Windows 98 and the Mac OS are examples of operating systems.

Presentation or authoring software: These are software programs that allow the user to design a program to present ideas to an audience using multimedia components. This type of program is usually in a card or slide format. Microsoft's PowerPoint and Roger Wagner's HyperStudio are examples of these kinds of programs.

Simulation: A software simulation program is a program that allows the user to experience an event that might be impossible to experience in "real life." Software simulations may provide insight into historical events, allow experimentation in science without risk of injury or use of specimens, or participation in decision making or politics. These programs engage the learner by having him or her participate in the experience through role playing.

Chapter 14: Creating Collaborative Communities: Creation, Organization, and Sustenance

Developing Collaborative Communities

Armstrong, Thomas. 1998. *Awakening Genius in the Classroom*. Alexandria, VA: Association for Supervision and Curriculum Development.

This book offers inspiration and a host of practical ideas. In just eighty pages, the author urges educators to look at each student as a ge-

nius. He outlines and describes twelve qualities of genius, which include curiosity, joy, imagination, inventiveness, and sensitivity. After identifying factors in the home, school, and popular media that shut down genius, educators will find wonderful, easy-to-implement suggestions for awakening genius in the classroom and in themselves. (J.W.)

Birchak, Barb, Clay Connor, Kathleen Marie Crawford, Leslie H. Kahn, Sandy Kaser, Susan Turner, and Kathy G. Short. 1998. *Teacher Study Groups: Building Community Through Dialogue and Reflection*. Urbana, IL: National Council of Teachers of English.

For educators who are interested in establishing productive, school-based study groups (professional support groups), this helpful text describes how to start, organize, facilitate, set agendas, deal with problematic issues, and more.

Cameron, Caren, Betty Tate, Daphne MacNaughton, and Colleen Politano. 1997. *Recognition Without Rewards: Building Connections*. Winnipeg, MAN: Peguis.

Lots of ideas, activities, and examples for creating a classroom in which students "develop the internal desire and skills to be lifelong learners" without the use of rewards. Very practical, specific, and thought-provoking.

Diller, Debbie. 1999. "Opening the Dialogue: Using Culture as a Tool in Teaching Young African American Children." *The Reading Teacher* (May): 820–828.

A first-grade teacher poignantly shares how she learned to teach and reach her African American students once she understood and respected their rich culture and language. An excellent, insightful article for learning how to successfully meet the needs of students of diverse cultures. Great for discussion.

Fullan, Michael, and Andy Hargreaves. 1996. *What's Worth Fighting for in Your School?* 2d ed. New York: Teachers College Press.

Fullan and Hargreaves encourage teachers and administrators to demonstrate leadership and take action so that collegiality and collaboration become the norm in a school. Practical and inspirational for how to change and improve the culture and climate of our schools.

Garmston, Robert, and Bruce Wellman. April 1998. "Teacher Talk That Makes a Difference." *Educational Leadership* (April): 30–34.

 The authors explain the difference between "discussion" and "dialogue" and provide guidelines for developing these skills to transform professional talk. An excellent article for learning how to effectively communicate with colleagues and improve learning.

Harwayne, Shelley. 1999. *Going Public: Priorities and Practice at the Manhattan New School.* 1999. Portsmouth, NH: Heinemann.

 At the end of her comprehensive book, Shelley Harwayne writes, "I am hopeful Going Public *serves as a compliment to the profession as well as a very personal staff development tool." Indeed it does. Through stories, letters, anecdotes, artwork, and demonstrations, Harwayne—as author, school founder, principal-teacher, and colleague—describes how to create a "stunning school environment" where literature, literacy, and living are interwoven into a "literary landscape." See also the companion volume,* Lifetime Guarantees: Literacy Lessons from the Manhattan New School.

Iverseen, Sandra, and Tracey Reeder. 1998. *Organizing for a Literacy Hour: Quality Learning and Teaching Time.* Bothell, WA: The Wright Group.

 This book contains many tips for organizing literacy instruction. The strength of the book is the colored photographs of classrooms that accompany related discussions about grouping, planning instruction, arranging the learning environment, and assessing student progress. Primary teachers will find this book a helpful resource to consult for classroom management suggestions. (J.W.)

Kohn, Alfie. 1996. *Beyond Discipline: From Compliance to Community.* Alexandria, VA: Association for Supervision and Curriculum Development.

 *A thought-provoking book about how to cre-*ate high-functioning classrooms in which teachers and students share decision making and responsibilities and students feel valued, respected, and connected to a caring community.

Koshewa, Allen. 1999. *Discipline and Democracy: Teachers on Trial.* Portsmouth, NH: Heinemann.

 Sometimes, even experienced teachers can find themselves face to face with an unruly class. Koshewa provides a deeply thoughtful and sensitive account of one such class and the teacher who struggled to uphold her democratic, community-oriented ideals while meeting the challenges of disruptive students. Experienced teacher and initiate alike will find this moving and often riveting account helpful and provocative.

Morrow, Lesley Mandel. 1997. *The Literacy Center: Contexts for Reading and Writing.* York, ME: Stenhouse.

 Elementary teachers interested in learning more about designing learning environments that promote student choice, social collaboration, and meaningful literacy tasks will find this practical guide useful. Divided into two sections, the first explores many of the issues related to literacy centers. The second and more extensive section contains many resources for organizing and managing the literacy center. (J.W.)

Pervil, Sunny, George Wood, Terry Anderson, Deanna Siller, Kathy Collier Paul, and Mary Waskow. 1998. *Democracy in the Classroom: Primary Voices K–6* (October).

 Authors of this themed issue share helpful ideas for creating community in the classroom by fostering collaboration, shared decision making, and respect. Includes recommended professional readings and classroom materials.

• Servis, Joan, 1999. *Celebrating the Fourth: Ideas and Inspiration for Teachers of Grade 4.* Portsmouth, NH: Heinemann.

 Veteran teacher Joan Servis describes how she develops and sustains a caring learning community of students, teachers, and parents. Joan demonstrates how she sets up her classroom so that all students feel important and respected as well as academically successful. In separate chapters, she details how she teaches and as-

sesses reading, writing, math, social studies, and science. Written with humor, energy, and passion, this outstanding text is a gift to all intermediate teachers.

Turner, Julianne, and Scott G. Paris. 1995. "How Literacy Tasks Influence Children's Motivation for Literacy. *The Reading Teacher* (May): 662–673. See page 16b.

Professional Development Opportunities

BEL (Balanced Early Literacy) Project. Mondo Professional Development Services. Mark Vineis, President; Maggy Thurston, Director of Professional Development, 1 Plaza Road, Greenvale, NY, 11548. 800-242-3650.

The BEL Project offers educators a comprehensive model for school reform aimed at ensuring that every child is underway in reading and writing in the early grades. The professional development plan is carried out over four years. Teachers participate in both off-site and on-site ongoing professional learning opportunities throughout the school year. Teachers learn to use ongoing assessment, flexible instructional groups, and guided reading. A Reading Recovery program must be in place to meet the needs of first-grade children still at risk despite good first teaching and sites are required to appoint a full-time, school-based literacy coordinator.

Costa, Arthur L. and Robert J. Garmston. 1994. *Cognitive Coaching*. Norwood, MA: Christopher-Gordon.

The authors present a thoughtful approach to staff development in this book. They draw from their own research and work in clinical supervision to provide effective principles for encouraging reflective practice and professional growth. The book includes a thorough discussion of cognitive coaching and also contains several useful appendices. One in particular, "The Language of Coaching: Questioning," provides practical suggestions for those interested in fostering this approach. The authors also conduct seminars; information is available

through The Institute for Intelligent Behavior, 2896 Knollwood Drive, Cameron Park, CA 95682. (J.W.)

ELIC (Early Literacy Inservice Course). Rigby Professional Development, Ann Van Horn, Director, 1350 E. Touhy Avenue, Des Plaines, IL, 60018. 800-795-9086; fax 847-390-2860.

Based on the staff development program that has trained the majority of teachers in Australia since 1983, this literacy course for groups of up to twelve teachers in grades K–3 offers school districts a model for effective teacher change. The course includes looking closely at language learning, reading and writing processes and strategies, evaluation, and more. Teachers meet weekly for twelve weeks with a trained facilitator for one two-hour interactive session, usually after school.

First Steps®. Kevlynn Annandale, Heinemann, 361 Hanover Street, Portsmouth, NH 03801.

First Steps® is a schoolwide professional development model designed to improve student outcomes in literacy. This educational resource comprises courses and materials researched and developed by the Education Department of Western Australia. Through the use of Developmental Continua, First Steps enables teachers to assess and monitor their students' literacy progress and provides links to developmentally appropriate teaching strategies and leaning activities in the areas of reading writing, spelling, and oral language. First Steps offers schools and districts a planning and professional development model that builds the school's capacity to provide for ongoing professional growth. In addition, principal workshops provide strategies to support schoolwide implementation of the program.

Garmston, Robert. 1997. *The Presenter's Fieldbook: A Practical Guide*. Norwood, MA: Christopher-Gordon.

Educators are often asked to share their own or others' good ideas with fellow teachers. This book offers a plethora of suggestions on how to design, deliver, and use resources to create effective presentations. (J.W.)

LLIFE (Literacy and Learning Inservice: Four–Eight). Rigby Professional Development, Ann Van Horn, Director, 1350 E. Touhy Avenue, Des Plaines, IL, 60018. 800-795-9086; fax 847-390-2860.

A partner course to ELIC, LLIFE is aimed at grades 4–8. LLIFE emphasizes the need for teachers in every curriculum area to develop their students' literacy potential. By focusing on strategies that help students use reading and writing to learn in all subjects, LLIFE prepares teachers to help students meet the content-area reading challenges of grades 4–8. In addition, LLIFE encourages communication among elementary, middle school, and junior high school teachers.

L4L (Leadership for Literacy). Rigby Professional Development, Ann Van Horn, Director, 1350 E. Touhy Avenue, Des Plaines, IL, 60018. 800-795-9086; fax 847-390-2860.

L4L is a two-day seminar designed specifically for elementary and middle-school administrators interested in supporting a balanced literacy program in their schools. This seminar addresses the importance of administrators' support, involvement, and basic understandings of the strategies and techniques observed in classrooms.

Mondo Professional Development Services. Mark Vineis, President; Maggy Thurston, Director of Professional Development, 1 Plaza Road, Greenvale, NY, 11548. 800-242-3650.

Mondo provides a range of professional development services for schools, districts, and counties in any area related to language learning and the reading and writing processes. Educational speakers have extensive classroom experience and continue to work with teachers and children in schools on a regular basis. Custom professional development is available to schools and school districts.

• Roller, Cathy M. 1998. *So... What's a Tutor to Do?* Newark, DE: International Reading Association.

This text serves as an excellent support for adults assisting students in tutorial settings. The author synthesizes past research in reading and writing and describes activities that are essential in tutoring sessions. Each of these activities is thoroughly described in a separate chapter. The
book serves as a reminder for experienced teachers and outlines best practice strategies for those less experienced. (J.W.)

Weaver, Constance, Lorraine Gillmeister-Krause, and Grace Vento-Zogby. 1996. *Creating Support for Effective Literacy Education.* Portsmouth, NH: Heinemann. See page 4b.

Home-School Connections

Beisel, Roberta, et al. 1997. *HomeLink: Home Activities for the Emergent Reader.* Carlsbad, CA: Dominie.

This excellent resource is designed to encourage parent participation in students' literacy development through enjoyable literacy activities. The program includes a binder that is divided into five resource sections that include: Early Literacy Learning, Learning the Alphabet, Learning Words and How They Work, Supporting Reading at Home, and Supporting Writing at Home. Educators will find that this comprehensive program includes simply written parent letters, suggestions for reading and writing activities accompanied by uncomplicated directions, enjoyable games, and puzzles. Perhaps the most outstanding feature is the set of blacklines for attractive little books that tell a story and include simple illustrations. Because of the popularity of the small books, the publisher has added supplemental sets of books schools may purchase to expand the program. Even though the program is expensive, schools and teachers will find these quality materials attractive and easy to use. (J.W.)

Education Department of Western Australia. 1995. *Parents as Partners: Helping Your Child's Literacy and Language Development.* Melbourne: Longman; Portsmouth, NH: Heinemann.

This forty-four-page booklet is packed with information, activities, and strategies for parents to support their children's learning. The concise explanations of developmental stages, practical strategies, and the many resource pages/parent handouts on how parents can help their children with reading, writing, speaking, and listening make this a valuable resource.

- Hydrick, Janie. 1996. *Parents Guide to Literacy for the 21st Century: Pre-K Through Grade 5*. Urbana, IL: National Council of Teachers of English.

  Hydrick answers many questions parents have about literacy and literacy education in a clear and concise voice. Topics such as authentic assessment, the kinds of books included in a literacy program, supporting children's reading and writing, and spelling are covered in an easy-to-read format. This guide is useful to educators in two ways: it can be recommended to parents to answer questions about school and literacy learning, and it can also serve as a model for the kind of language educators can use as they attempt to answer parents' and community member's questions. This book is one to keep handy to loan to parents. (J.W.)

- KEEP BOOKS. Published by The Ohio State University Literacy Collaborative.

  KEEP BOOKS, inexpensive take-home books, offer schools a way to provide continuing reading opportunities for students. This take-home book program is made up of a wide range of simple texts that invite an interactive reading experience. The books are small, approximately four by five inches, and contain simple black and white line drawings. Children are encouraged to write their names in the back of the book, to color illustrations, and to keep them as a collection in a special place. While the books do not replace quality children's literature, schools can make these attractive little books available for young readers to own. For more information on this excellent resource, contact: KEEP BOOKS, OSU-Literacy Collaborative, 200 Ramseyer Hall, 29 W. Woodruff Ave., Columbus, Ohio 43210. (J.W.)

National Children's Book and Literacy Alliance, Mary B. Barrett, President and Executive Director, P.O. Box 634, Franklin, MA 02038–0634. phone/fax 508-533-5851. *www.ncbla.org*

  NCBLA is a national, nonprofit coalition that serves as an information and education center to publicize critical children's literacy issues and provide workshops and information to individuals and organizations who have a direct impact on children and their families. Founded in 1997 by award-winning authors and illustrators to promote children's literacy and reading through literature.

Parkes, Brenda, Judy Nayer, Barbara Shook Hazen, and Lisa Trumbauer. 1998. *Discovery Links*, Emergent level. New York: Newbridge Educational Publishing.

  Thirty-two beautiful, reproducible, easy-to-assemble, nonfiction little books. Appealing phototexts with high interest science topics. Great take-home books for enjoying and practicing reading.

The Partners Literacy Kit. 1997. Columbus, OH: Seeding Publications.

  This excellent kit contains materials designed to encourage and support parent involvement. In addition to a twenty-five-minute video in which adults demonstrate supportive strategies to use with beginning readers, there are handbooks, question and answer booklets for parents, bookmarks with reminders about reading with children, and small books to use in demonstrations. The consumable materials included with the program are reasonable and may be ordered in large quantities. (J.W.)

Power, Brenda. 1999. *Parent Power: Energizing Home-School Communication*. Portsmouth, NH: Heinemann.

  Parent Power is a unique, comprehensive resource kit that fosters home-school communication. It includes forty-one one-page reproducible essays for parents—in both Spanish and English—that cover a range of topics of greatest concern to parents: learning to read, monitoring television, coping with homework, and the like. It also includes a CD-ROM that enables teachers to customize the essays as well as plan for a comprehensive parent-outreach program. Additional offerings include a list of award-winning Web sites for parents, bibliographies of parent resources, and ideas for creative outreach events such as art fairs, family math nights, ethnic celebrations, and more.

Reach Out and Read, Reach Out and Read National Center, Boston Medical Center, One BMC Place, 5th Floor High Rise, Boston, MA 02118. 617-414-5701; fax 617-414-7557.

This national literacy readiness program was founded in 1989 by three Boston doctors (including Perri Klass, who is the current medical director) to link medical care with early literacy. Health clinics serving needy families provide books for children along with materials to parents on how to read to and with their infants and toddlers. More than 100 sites in thirty-four states. Make sure qualifying families in your area know about this exemplary program.

Zrna, Julie, Anne Robinson, and Kim Falkenberg. 1996. *Partners in Print: A Parent-Involvement Program for Beginning Readers*. Cypress, CA: Creative Teaching.

Designed by former primary teachers who have had extensive experience in staff development and literacy instruction, this kit includes all the materials necessary to conduct twelve parent workshops designed to familiarize parents with ways to assist emergent readers. The program includes a comprehensive loose-leaf binder that contains workshop outlines and handouts, a video to assist the leadership team in planning the workshops, overhead transparencies, activity posters, and take-home activity sheets. A variety of additional resources are available including big and little books and Spanish materials. Because the program is expensive, it may be more reasonable for several schools or a district to purchase the kit. (J.W.)

Chapter 15: Evaluation as Part of Teaching

Assessment and Evaluation

● Azwell, Tara, and Elizabeth Schmar. 1995. *Report Card on Report Cards: Alternatives to Consider*. Portsmouth, NH: Heinemann.

Don't miss this outstanding text for gaining perspectives, information, and support for reporting to parents. Lots of useful information for understanding and creating narrative reports, rubrics, report cards, parent-teacher-student conferences, self-assessments, and alternatives to letter grades.

Barr, Mary A., Dana A. Craig, Dolores Fisette, and Margaret A. Syverson, eds. 1999. *Assessing Lit-*

eracy with the Learning Record: A Handbook for Teachers, Grades K–6. Portsmouth, NH: Heinemann.

The Learning Record Assessment System is an expanded form of the Primary Language Record, originally developed in London. The instrument is designed to record the progress of students from kindergarten through grade twelve, to inform instruction, and to provide a portfolio of information for administrators, teachers, students, and parents. Student performance is measured by a variety of authentic language and literacy tasks and by consultations with students and parents. A companion handbook is also available for teachers of grades six through twelve. Additional information on this document may be obtained from Center for Language in Learning, 10610 Quail Canyon, El Cajon, CA 92021. www.learning record.org/lrorg. (J.W.)

● Beaver, Joetta. 1997. *Developmental Reading Assessment*. Glenview, IL: Celebration Press.

Educators will find these materials especially useful for placing students in appropriate instructional texts and for assessing students' progress in reading. Designed to be used in kindergarten through third grade, this framework includes leveled texts, observation forms for recording data, and a developmental continuum. A resource guide accompanies the materials and outlines how to use the assessment and plan subsequent instruction. A training video and facilitator's guide is also available. (J.W.)

Bridges, Lois. 1995. *Assessment: Continuous Learning*. York, ME: Stenhouse; Los Angeles, CA: Galef Institute.

Based upon six defining principles of authentic assessment, this text suggests a variety of resources for teachers to inform their assessment practices and expand their knowledge of skilled classroom observation. Perhaps the most useful aspects of the book are the examples of forms and checklists and suggestions for implementing portfolios drawn from Bridges' work with twenty-two teachers and administrators. (J.W.)

Costa, Arthur L., and Bena Kallick, eds. 1995. *Assessment in the Learning Organization: Shifting the Paradigm*. Alexandria, VA: Association for Supervision and Curriculum Development.

This theory-into-practice text offers lots of useful information for examining, clarifying, changing, and improving assessment practices. Knowledgeable educators write insightfully about communicating with parents, standardized testing, authentic assessment, giving up old mental models, developing writing prompts in science, performance-based assessment, portfolios, and much more. Chapter 4, "Self-Evaluation: Making It Matter" by Alison Preece, pages 30–55, is especially helpful and practical.

Early Literacy Profile. (Draft 1999). Albany, NY: State Education Department.

Consisting of a set of standardized tasks that are designed to be completed in a classroom context and evaluated according to developmental scales, this assessment is organized around the New York State Learning Standards. The various tasks capture evidence used to evaluate students' proficiency in reading, writing, listening, and speaking. The document includes rubrics, and forms that might serve as models for teachers and school districts interested in developing more thoughtful language arts assessments. (J.W.)

Educators in Connecticut's Pomperaug Regional School District 15. 1996. *A Teacher's Guide to Performance-Based Learning and Assessment*. Alexandria, VA: Association for Supervision and Curriculum Development.

Filled with actual examples of rubrics, checklists, and assessment lists used with primary through high school students, this resource contains practical and thoughtful suggestions for implementing a range of authentic assessment practices. Teachers will find the models included helpful. Though many are designed for language arts, the book also contains samples from other content areas such as science and mathematics. (J.W.)

• Egeland, Paul. 1996/1997. "Pulley, Planes, and Student Performance." *Educational Leadership* (December/January): 41–45.

A wonderful article for looking beyond paper and pencil assessment to a variety of authentic ways for students to demonstrate their learning—for example, through sketching, constructing, and hands-on activities that align with learning tasks.

• Falk, Beverly. 1998. "Focus on Research. Testing the Way Children Learn: Principles for Valid Literacy Assessments." *Language Arts* (September): 57–66.

An outstanding article for moving toward "standards-referenced" authentic assessment that is useful for learning and teaching and that gives students opportunities to problem solve and apply knowledge to real world contexts. Also terrific for discussion.

Fiderer, Adele. 1995. *Practical Assessments for Literature-Based Reading Classrooms*. New York: Scholastic.

A plethora and range of assessment forms are included and helpfully arranged into chapters that include reader profiles, reading ability assessments, comprehension assessments, daily reading activities, and portfolios. A final chapter includes a variety of suggestions for home-school connections. While the accompanying text is minimal, it is informative. Kindergarten to grade six teachers familiar with authentic assessments and those just getting started will find this resource invaluable! (J.W.)

Fiderer, Adele. 1995. *35 Rubrics and Checklists to Assess Reading and Writing*. New York: Scholastic.

Designed for use in grades K–2, this resource couples assessment suggestions and tips with actual forms. While most forms will not be new to teachers who are currently using authentic assessments, they are formatted nicely for primary students and will provide models that can be customized or used as models to design others. (J.W.)

Glazer, Susan M. 1998. *Assessment Is Instruction*. Norwood, MA: Christopher-Gordon.

Glazer writes that "this book is about managing and balancing the merging of literacy assessment and instruction in classrooms." Educators new to teaching and those ready to make a shift to bring assessment and instruction closer together will find this book useful. Topics such as organization, comprehension, composition, and reporting to parents are just a few the author addresses. In creating a rationale, the book begins with an interesting overview of past assessment practices. (J.W.)

Griffin, Patrick, Patricia G. Smith, and Lois E. Burrill. 1995. *The American Literacy Profile Scales: A Framework for Authentic Assessment.* Portsmouth, NH: Heinemann.

Profile bands describe, not prescribe, "what is normal development for average students." Many of our teachers found this resource particularly useful for learning the language that describes learners' strategies and responses—and using that language in writing narratives on report cards and in other assessment/learning contexts.

Hill, Bonnie Campbell, Cynthia Ruptic, and Lisa Norwick. 1998. *Classroom Based Assessment.* Norwood, MA: Christopher-Gordon.

Presents extensive, possible tools for assessment and details the use of anecdotal records, checklists, rubrics, and much more. Includes professional growth opportunities, recommended readings, assessment forms, and an accompanying CD-ROM so forms can be easily reproduced and modified. The first of four "Corner Pieces" in an assessment series.

Rhodes, Lynn K., and Curt Darling-Marling. 1996. *Readers and Writers with a Difference: A Holistic Approach to Teaching Struggling Readers and Writers.* 2d ed. Portsmouth, NH: Heinemann.

The excellent assessment chapter offers teachers many practical suggestions for evaluating student performance. (See also 9b.) (J.W.)

Routman, Regie, and Donna Maxim, eds. 1996. "What Do I Do About Report Cards Now That I've Changed My Teaching?" *School Talk: Changing Report Cards* (November).

Several teachers describe and demonstrate how report cards have evolved in their schools to be more congruent with their teaching beliefs and practices.

Schmoker, Mike. 1996. *Results: The Key to Continuous School Improvement.* Alexandria, VA: Association for Supervision and Curriculum Development.

This book was instrumental for me in realizing—and acting on that realization—that while we had goals and teamwork in place in our district, we were missing the "regular collection and analysis of performance data" that is essential for improving achievement.

Wiggins, Grant. 1998. *Educative Assessment.* San Francisco: Jossey-Bass.

Wiggins asserts "the aim of assessment is primarily to educate and improve student performance, not merely to audit it" (7; emphasis is the author's). To that aim, he informs our thinking on such issues as authentic tasks, ongoing feedback, rubrics, standards, portfolios, self-evaluation, letter grades, accountability, and much more. Excellent for discussing and rethinking theory and practice related to assessment.

Standards and Testing

Anderson, Susan R. 1998. "The Trouble with Testing." *Young Children* (July): 25–29.

Discusses the negative effects of standardized tests on young children and urges us educators to use and design more authentic assessments. "For many parents their child's score does not measure just one day, or even a week, of their child's work; it mirrors the family's success, the parents' affluence, and the child's future" (27).

Calkins, Lucy, Kate Montgomery, and Donna Santman, with Beverly Falk. 1998. *A Teacher's Guide to Standardized Reading Tests: Knowledge Is Power.* Portsmouth, NH: Heinemann.

In addition to explaining how standardized tests are constructed, scored, and interpreted, the authors provide useful test-taking strategies. Helpful for increasing your own knowledge, preparing students for test taking, and communicating with parents.

Fair Test: National Center for Fair and Open Testing, 342 Broadway, Cambridge, MA. *www.fairtest.org*

A nonprofit public education and advocacy organization that provides resources, publications, guidelines, and support on issues related to assessment reform. "Fairtest works to end the abuses, misuse, and flaws of standardized testing and to make certain that evaluation of students and workers is fair, open, accurate, relevant, accountable, and educationally sound" (goal statement). The organization publishes a quarterly, Fair Test Examiner, available for $30.00/year (individual) or $45.00/year (institutions).

National Center on Education and the Economy. *New Standards.* 700 11th Street NW, Suite 750, Washington, DC. *www.ncee.org*

NCEE is "*organized to provide resources to schools, districts and states interested in standards-based reform.*" *New Standards committees have developed a system of performance standards for many content areas. In 1999, they published primary literacy standards for kindergarten through third grade. These primary grades standards for the language arts are accompanied by a CD-ROM that shows examples of student performances and work samples that meet the standards. Helpful for understanding "How good is good enough?" when developing local and state standards.*

- Popham, W. James. 1999. "Why Standardized Tests Don't Measure Educational Quality." *Educational Leadership* (March): 8–15.

  A terrific article for understanding (and explaining to parents and other stake holders) what standardized tests do and do not measure. Presents a strong argument that high scores are less a matter of what's been taught in school and more a matter of intellectual background outside of school (which is closely related to socioeconomic status).

Taylor, Kathe, and Sherry Walton. 1999. *Children at the Center: A Workshop Approach to Standardized Test Preparation, K–8.* Portsmouth, NH: Heinemann.

  The authors provide useful, clear information (which many of us lack) for understanding common test terms, preparing students for test taking, and talking with parents. An invaluable resource for responsibly using assessment "in the service of children and learning."

- Tucker, Marc S., and Judy B. Codding. 1998. *Standards for Our Schools: How to Set Them, Measure Them, and Reach Them.* San Francisco: Jossey-Bass.

  For all of us who are confused by standards, this text sheds light on how to improve school performance through establishing high standards, analyzing student performance against those standards, and instituting practices that help students meet the standards. Useful for developing exemplary standards and for understanding what's needed for standards to work.

Zemelman, Steven, Harvey Daniels, and Arthur Hyde. 1998. *Best Practice: New Standards for Teaching and Learning in America's Schools.* 2d ed. Portsmouth, NH: Heinemann.

The authors describe best practices in reading, writing, mathematics, science, social studies, and the arts; examine issues and connections related to national standards projects and documents; and provide descriptions of exemplary "best practice" programs. A definitive text for administrators, teachers, and policy makers dedicated to school renewal and reform.

Standards: Some Useful Web Sites

For helpful information on putting standards into practice, see:

Achieve, Inc. *www.achieve.org*

  Provides state standards for most states and also presents these standards in a searchable database. Provides some examples of states' graded student work. Links to other education organizations and Web sites.

McREL Foundation.
www.mcrel.org/standards-benchmarks/
  Provides a database and lots of detailed information for understanding and implementing K–12 standards and benchmarks in many curriculum areas.

The New York Times Learning Network.
www.nytimes.com/
  Teachers, parents, and students of grade 6–12 can access news stories, detailed lesson plans, activities, and links that make connections to national standards in American history, science, social studies, language arts, and other areas.

The following are several organizations that present their national standards:

American Association for the Advancement of Science. *www.aaas.org/*

National Council for the Social Studies. *www.ncss.org/standards/home.html*

National Council of Teachers of English. *www.ncte.org*

National Council of Teachers of Mathematics. *www.NCTM.org*

National Standards for History. *www.ssnet.ucla.edu/nchs/standards.html*

Portfolios

Courtney, Ann M., and Theresa L. Abodeeb. 1999. "Diagnostic-Reflective Portfolios." *The Reading Teacher* (April): 708–714.

With guidance and support from their teacher, second graders learn how to use their portfolios to self-assess, to continually set and monitor appropriate learning goals, and to reflect on their learning.

Danielson, Charlotte, and Leslye Abrutyn. 1997. *An Introduction to Using Portfolios in the Classroom.* Alexandria, VA: Association for Supervision and Curriculum Development.

The title of this book aptly describes it; it is indeed an introduction for those implementing portfolios. Covering the basics, the types of portfolios, their development, the benefits, and the management, this seventy-five-page book packages good suggestions and will answer initial questions educators at all levels might ask. (J.W.)

• Hebert, Elizabeth A. 1998. "Lessons Learned About Student Portfolios." Phi Delta Kappan (April): 583–585.

A principal shares insights from a decade of experiences with portfolios. Helpful and specific for all educators interested in meaningful involvement with portfolios. Excellent for discussion.

Hurst, Beth, Cindy Wilson, and Genny Cramer. 1998. "Professional Teaching Portfolios: Tools for Reflection, Growth, and Advancement." *Phi Delta Kappan* (April): 578–582.

The authors present the rationale for having a professional teaching portfolio and provide excellent suggestions for creating, presenting, and using one in the job market and in the classroom.

• Jervis, Kathe. 1996. *Eyes on the Child: Three Portfolio Stories.* New York: Teachers College Press.

Classroom-based stories make portfolio implementation come to life. A wonderful book for understanding and realizing the possibilities for using portfolios in a realistic, meaningful way.

Lenski, Susan Davis, Marsha Riss, and Gayle Flickinger. 1996. "Honoring Student Self-Evaluation in the Classroom Community." "Establishing Patterns of Communities Through Language." *Primary Voices K–6* (April, Themed Issue): 24–32.

The authors describe the purposes and benefits of student-led parent conferences in a fifth-grade classroom and include guidelines for preparation, implementation, and evaluation. A very thoughtful article.

Lyons, Nona, ed. 1998. *With Portfolio in Hand: Validating the New Teacher Professionalism.* New York: Teachers College Press.

The authors of this book present a range of perceptions about professionals creating and maintaining portfolios. As a professional who has struggled with creating a portfolio, I found that the chapters reflected the power, potential, and pitfalls portfolios present. The book will be particularly useful to teachers trying to put their classroom assessment practices to work in their own lives. Learning by doing is clearly a more authentic way of gaining insights, and readers will better understand the complexities and inherent value of portfolios by reading all or selected chapters of this book. (J.W.)

• Martin, Giselle O., with Dianne Cunningham and Diana Muxworthy Feige. 1998. *Why Am I Doing This? Purposeful Teaching through Portfolio Assessment.* Portsmouth, NH: Heinemann.

The introductory chapters explain the history of the Hudson Valley Portfolio Assessment Project. However, of most interest to teachers will likely be the latter chapters—a collection of stories that represent primary and intermediate teachers' experiences with authentic assessment. Two particularly interesting chapters are "Helping Children Monitor Their Own Learning," which contains examples of tools developed to promote self-reflection, and "Authentic Assessment at Work in a Self-Contained Classroom of Learning-Disabled Students," which explains the use of authentic assessment practices in a middle-school classroom. The book is thoughtfully written and will be useful to teachers at all levels striving to refine their assessment practices. (J.W.)

Routman, Regie, and Donna Maxim. 1997. "So You Want to Use Portfolios: Perspectives, Possibilities, and Pitfalls." *School Talk: Using Portfolios* (February).

Two teachers share their beliefs about portfolios, along with practical information on getting started, deciding what goes in, and dealing with the portfolio process in the classroom. Includes an extensive resource bibliography.

Sunstein, Bonnie S. 1996. "Assessing Portfolio Assessment: Three Encounters of a Close Kind." *Voices from the Middle* (November): 13–22.

Sunstein asserts, "A portfolio-keeping process

must be at once reflective and reflexive... A student looks first internally, at her self and her work as she reflects. But then she must look outside herself to understand the external standards that her institutions expect" (17). An excellent, provocative article for thinking about meaningful portfolio assessment and "reflexive inquiry" as well as the teacher's role as mediator in the process.

Tierney, Robert J., and Carolyn Clark, with Linda Fenner, Roberta J. Herter, Carolyn Staunton Simpson, and Burt Wiser. 1998. "Theory and Research into Practice: Portfolios: Assumptions, Tensions, and Possibilities." *Reading Research Quarterly* (Oct./Nov./Dec.): 474–486.

An excellent article for offering perspectives, multiple viewpoints, and useful information on effectively using learner-centered portfolios in the classroom.

• Valencia, Sheila W. 1998. *Literacy Portfolios in Action.* Fort Worth, TX: Harcourt Brace College.

Perhaps the most comprehensive portfolio text to date, this book, written by an expert in portfolio use, offers educators detailed information about how to design, implement, and maintain a portfolio system customized to fit the needs of a district, school, or individual teachers. The book is filled with excellent discussions about how to engage students in the self-reflection, goal setting, self-evaluation involved in portfolio use. Teachers will appreciate the numerous student samples, photographs of actual student portfolios, and the charts that help explain options and clarify the process. The final chapter links portfolio use to grading practices and report cards. Educators serious about portfolio use will find that this thoughtfully written book will serve as an excellent resource for implementing and refining an assessment system using portfolios. (J.W.)

Vizyak, Lindy. 1996. *Student Portfolios: A Practical Guide to Evaluation.* Bothell, WA: The Wright Group.

Written by a first-grade teacher, this guide is packed with useful information and reproducibles.

Wolf, Kenneth, and Yvonne Siu-Runyan. 1996. "Portfolio Purposes and Possibilities." *Journal of Adolescent & Adult Literacy* (September): 30–36.

An excellent article for clarifying the purposes for keeping a portfolio and making decisions about portfolio form, content, process, and use.

Student-Led Conferences

Cleland, JoAnn. 1999. "We Can Charts: Building Blocks for Student-Led Conferences." *The Reading Teacher* (March): 588–595.

Provides useful preparation guidelines for teachers and students interested in implementing student-led conferences.

Countryman, Lyn Le, and Merrie Schroder. 1996. "When Students Lead Parent-Teacher Conferences." *Educational Leadership* (April): 63–68.

Centering on student portfolios, the authors describe the benefits and procedures for student-led conferences with sixth and seventh graders at a middle school.

Grant, Janet Millar, Barbara Heffler, and Kadri Mereweather. 1995. *Student-Led Conferences: Using Portfolios to Share Learning with Parents.* Markham, ONT: Pembroke; York, ME: Stenhouse.

This book helped many K–4 teachers in our district implement student-led conferences. We discussed it in our language arts support group and adapted many of the suggested procedures and practices.

Picciotto, Linda. 1996. *Student-Led Parent Conferences.* New York: Scholastic.

Includes the basics for planning, managing, and launching student-led conferences. Helpful and practical.

Servis, Joan. 1999. "The Power of Self-Assessment and Student-Led Conferencing." In *Celebrating the Fourth: Ideas and Inspiration for Teachers of Grade 4.* Portsmouth, NH: Heinemann.

In considerable detail, Servis describes how she guides students in organization, preparation, rehearsal, performance, and goal setting for student-led conferences. Very useful.

Professional Journals, Newsletters, and Other Periodicals

Journals

It is costly to pay for subscriptions to multiple journals. See if your school district, school, or library will order one subscription for the faculty to share and rotate.

To help me do my job, our district's library media office sent me the table of contents for many journals (at my request). Then, I requested to see copies of specific articles based on the titles. When I came across an outstanding article, I let my colleagues know about it.

Accessing Journal Articles

Teachers whose schools do not subscribe to educational journals should take advantage of their local public libraries since they often carry these journals. University as well as local libraries are wonderful resources for teachers as they search for the many articles mentioned herein. Also, many schools now have access to the Internet, a tremendous source of information for teachers in search of articles about education. The home pages of many of the educational associations such as IRA (International Reading Association) and NCTE (National Council of Teachers of English) include information about the articles that are published in their journals. Teachers can search for particular journal articles on the World Wide Web and call the appropriate association to order the issue that contains the journal article that they want. Some organizations such as IRA have instituded online journals.

Democracy & Education
4 issues per year/subscription $35 membership
The Institute for Democracy and Education
College of Education
McCracken Hall
Athens, OH 45701–2979
740-593-4531

> *A quality journal written by and for teachers that focuses on issues related to democratic practice. For example, recent themed issues have addressed tracking and ability grouping, democratic management alternatives to standardized testing, classroom and community building, and project-centered learning. The In-*

> *stitute sponsors a conference in Athens, Ohio, every fall.*

Educational Leadership
8 issues per year/subscription $36
Association for Supervision and Curriculum Development (ASCD)
1703 N. Beauregard Street
Alexandria, VA 22311–1714

> *A journal for elementary, middle-school, and secondary teachers and administrators interested in being on the cutting edge of current educational theory and practice. For anyone interested in being well informed about good ideas regarding today's educational practices. ASCD offers many excellent professional development opportunities through an annual conference, continuing professional development workshops and conferences, and many publications and resources for administrators and teachers.*

Elementary School Journal
5 issues per year/subscription $36 (individual); $86 (institutions); $26 (NAESP); $23 (students)
University of Chicago Press
Journals Division
5720 South Woodlawn
PO Box 37005
Chicago, IL 60637

> *Geared toward a more scholarly audience, this journal contains studies, research reviews, and analyses of ideas for elementary teachers, administrators, teacher educators, and researchers.*

English Journal
6 issues per year/subscription $20 (individual); $60 (institutions). Membership in NCTE is a prerequisite for all individual subscriptions.
National Council of Teachers of English
1111 W. Kenyon Road
Urbana, IL 61801–1906
877-369-6283
www.ncte.org

> *For middle-school and junior and senior high school English teachers. This journal presents the latest developments in teaching composition, reading skills, oral language, literature, and the uses of varied media.*

68b

Language Arts
6 issues per year/subscription $20 (individual); $60
(institutions). Membership in NCTE is a
prerequisite for all individual subscriptions.
National Council of Teachers of English
1111 W. Kenyon Road
Urbana, IL 61801–1096
877-369-6283
www.ncte.org

    *This journal is for elementary teachers and
teacher educators who want to stimulate and
encourage children to discover language—reading, writing, listening, and speaking—as a
means of learning about the world and about
themselves. Each issue provides classroom
strategies, methods, reports of research, and
opinions.*

The New Advocate
4 issues per year/subscription $30 prepaid; $45
purchase order
Christopher-Gordon Publishers, Inc.
1502 Providence Highway, Suite 12
Norwood, MA 02062

    *Noted authors, illustrators, and educators
share their perspectives on children's literature
and related issues in this outstanding literary
journal. Book and media reviews are included.*

Phi Delta Kappan
10 issues per year/subscription $39
408 N. Union Street
PO Box 789
Bloomington, IN 47402–0789

    *Concerned with issues relating to leadership,
research, trends, and policy, Phi Delta Kappan
(named for the educational fraternity) is a must
for those truly interested in what's happening in
our schools today. Contains an annual Gallup
poll of this country's attitude toward public
schools.*

Primary Voices K–6
4 issues per year/subscription $15 (individual); $30
(institutions). Membership in NCTE is a
prerequisite for all individual subscriptions.
National Council of Teachers of English
1111 W. Kenyon Road
Urbana, IL 61801–1096
877-369-6283
www.ncte.org

    *This journal works from a unique editorial
concept: each issue is conceived and written by
different teams of elementary educators. Drawing on their interest in a common topic, they
take readers into their classrooms—showing
samples of their students' work, providing rich
descriptions of classrooms, and suggesting helpful resources.*

Reading Research Quarterly
4 issues per year/subscription $45.00
Reading Research Quarterly
800 Barksdale Road
PO Box 8139
Newark, DE 19714–8139
www.reading.org

    *A scholarly journal of mostly quantitative re-
search related to the language arts, especially
reading. Recent issues dealt with volunteer tutoring programs, phonics. Try to have a subscription in your school district, and pick and
choose what's relevant.*

The Reading Teacher
8 issues per year/subscription $45 (individual); $90
(institutions). Includes annual membership.
International Reading Association (IRA)
800 Barksdale Road
PO Box 8139
Newark, DE 19714–8139

    *This practical journal for preschool and ele-
mentary teachers focuses on teaching approaches and techniques and also includes
reviews of children's books, tests, and other
teacher resources. Subscription includes "Reading Today," a bimonthly newspaper on news of
the profession.*

    *Note that IRA sponsors an annual conference, a
World Congress, as well as state and local conferences; publishes professional publications and
brochures for teachers and parents; and identifies
and distributes "Children's Choices"—a yearly
list of books children vote as their favorites.*

Teaching K–8
8 issues per year/subscription $23.97
PO Box 54805
Boulder, CO 80328–4808
800-678-8793

    *This publication, subtitled "The professional
magazine for teachers," carries columns on read-*

ing, math, science, technology, professional growth, assessment, school and classroom libraries, parenting—all written by well-known educators. It carries ten reader exchange networks, such as Art Pals, Whole Language Network, Substitute Teachers Network, and Paraprofessionals Exchange. Each issue includes reports on innovative schools and teachers throughout the country, which the editors have personally visited. It also features a monthly personal interview with well-known authors and illustrators of children's books. Editorial content includes emphasis on multiage, whole language, integrated curriculum, and professional growth.

Voices from the Middle
4 issues per year/subscription $15
(individual); $30 (institutions). Membership in NCTE is a prerequisite for all individual subscriptions.
National Council of Teachers of English
1111 W. Kenyon Road
Urbana, IL 61801–1096
877-369-6283
www.ncte.org

This journal is based on the premise that middle-school teachers face a unique set of circumstances and challenges, and that hearing from other middle school teachers about their successes, solutions, or concerns begins an ongoing process of conversation and reflection. Each issue is themed, with one article that addresses the theoretical background of the theme, and three articles that provide specific, rich descriptions of grades 6–8 classroom practices.

Young Children
6 issues per year/subscription $30
National Association for the Education of Young Children
1509 16th Street, NW
Washington, DC 20036–1426

Early childhood educators will find this journal to be thought-provoking, informative, and supportive in the area of professional growth. Major issues and ideas in the field are discussed. Contains such items as a calendar of conferences, book reviews, Washington public policy updates, and a section of reader commentary.

Newsletters/Other Periodicals

Book Links
bimonthly magazine/subscription $24.95
Booklist Publications
The American Library Association
50 E. Huron St.
Chicago, IL 60611

Aptly described by its subtitle, Connecting Books, Libraries, and Classrooms, *this bimonthly magazine is for teachers, librarians, parents, and anyone else who works with books and children. Each issue explores the connections between literature and the learning experience for children and young adults, and contains articles, recommended reading lists, and interviews that provide strategies for using books effectively in teaching.*

Education Week
43 issues per year/subscription $37.97
Education Week
6935 Arlington Road, Suite 100
Bethesda, MD 20814
www.edweek.org

An education newspaper that will keep you up to date on the latest happenings around the country. Important for being a fully informed and politically active educator. Several of us split a subscription. None of us read it all. Price quoted is bargain rate that is usually available, at least for new subscribers.

The Kobrin Letter. Concerning Children's Books About Real People, Places and Things
Pro Bono/Send SASE
The Kobrin Letter
732 Greer Road
Palo Alto, CA 94303

This is the only periodical devoted exclusively to the review and recommendation of children's nonfiction books. Two or three themes or topics are dealt with in each issue, and information from six to ten books per topic is included. For example, one issue dealt with "Trees" and "Habitats" and "Multicultural Celebrations."

Rethinking Schools
4 issues per year/subscription $12.50
Rethinking Schools Limited
1001 East Keefe Avenue

Milwaukee, WI 53212
800-669-4192
www.rethinkingschools.org

　　Rethinking Schools is a nonprofit, activist, independent newspaper published by Milwaukee-area teachers. This provocative, thoughtful publication focuses on local and national reform in urban elementary and secondary schools. Articles and issues connect classroom practice with broad policy issues and are written by educators from all over the country. Recent issues dealt with such topics as teaching for social justice, school choice in education, charter schools, the role of teachers' unions, multicultural videos and audiotapes, and funding education. This is an important publication for dealing with equity and social-justice issues in a forthright, constructive manner. Back issues, books, and free catalog are also available.

School Talk
4 issues per year/subscription $10.00 per year ($14.00 CAN). Membership in NCTE is a prerequisite for all subscriptions.
Back issues/$2.50, single copy; $17.00, 20 copies of a single issue
National Council of Teachers of English
1111 W. Kenyon Road
Urbana, IL 61801–1906
877-369-6283
www.ncte.org

　　A quality, eight-page newsletter for elementary classroom teachers from the Elementary Section Steering Committee of NCTE. Some popular past issues include: "Phonics Fuss: Facts, Fiction, Phonemes, and Fun," "Using Portfolios," "Invented Spelling: What It Is and What It Isn't," and "Using the Internet in Reading and Writing Workshop." Practical ideas and a resource bibliography included with each issue.

Study Group Materials

ASCD, IRA, and NCTE feature inquiry kits and study group packages from time to time on topics of interest to educators. Watch for information in journals on home pages, and flyers about these professional organizations' offerings.

Book Clubs

Because book clubs have become a major supplier of trade books to elementary classrooms in the U.S. and because they offer a wide range of interesting books across all genres, information about the two major book clubs is included. Within each club, there are different clubs for different grade levels and prices are discounted. Note that many of the books on the literature lists may first be available exclusively through book clubs but later will be available through trade publishers. Check with your local bookstore or book distributor. For information regarding the nature and use of school book clubs and how they contribute to children's literacy development, see "School Book Clubs and Literacy Development: A Descriptive Study" by Dorothy S. Strickland and Sean A. Walmsley, 1994 (available from the National Research Center on Literature Teaching and Learning, State University of New York at Albany).

Scholastic Book Clubs
PO Box 7503
Jefferson City, MO 65102–9966
800-724-2424

　　Scholastic has eleven book clubs, including Firefly (pre-K), See Saw (K–grade 1), Lucky (grades 2–3), Arrow (grades 4–6), Carnival (K–grade 2), Carnival Intermediate (grades 3–6), TAB (grades 7 and up), Trumpet Early Years (pre-K–K), Trumpet Primary (grades 1–3), Trumpet Intermediate (grades 4–6), and Club de Lectura (preschool–grade 5). Monthly brochures offer titles from the eleven clubs and include award-winning books. Also offers books to teachers grouped by theme and special offers for specific curriculum areas.

Troll Book Clubs
2 Lethbridge Plaza
Mahwah, NJ 07430
800-541-1097

　　Troll has five clubs, Troll Pre-K/K (preschool and K), Troll 1 (grades K–1), Troll 2 (grades 2–3), Troll 3 (grades 4–6), and Troll 4 High Tops (grades 6–9). Each month about forty-five titles are offered as well as different teacher specials, such as award-winning books and theme sets that can be used in the classroom.

Favorite Videos

There are many fine videos and video series available to provide educators with ideas and models of classroom practice. We have included only a few; some because they are classics, others because the topic is particularly relevant at this time. While videos are expensive to own, many can be rented or the costs shared among several schools. In spite of their expense, they are a powerful staff development tool and provide access to experts and visits into teachers' classrooms across the country.

We are also aware of the growing number of CD-ROMs and their potential role in staff development and teacher support. However, as this book went to press, there were so few that we did not list them. As more become available, they will be reviewed and listed in future editions.

Book Club: A Literature-Based Curriculum. 1997. Littleton, MA: Small Planet Communications.

Teachers interested in using Book Club, a small, student-led discussion group approach developed by Taffy Raphael, will enjoy this practical guidebook and video. The video, which captures many classroom examples of intermediate students interacting within the Book Club framework, can help teachers take the first step in using a literature-based program. A guide with practical teaching tips offers suggestions and lesson plans for multibook units that connect to science and social studies. One caution: use the framework as a guide and avoid making it an activities approach to literature study. (J.W.)

The Brain and Learning. 1998. Alexandria, VA: Association for Supervision and Curriculum Development.

This series of four 20- to 30-minute videos will provide educators with current information from leading neuroscientists and education experts about how to apply the burgeoning body of brain research in the classroom. Among the topics covered in this excellent series are how learning actually occurs in the brain, the influence of environment on the brain, and what parents need to know about these new insights. (J.W.)

A Close-up Look at Teaching Reading: Focusing on Children and Our Goals. 1996. Portsmouth, NH: Heinemann.

This set of videos is perfect for providing professionals in a school or school district with meaningful staff development. In the four-part series on teaching reading, master teacher Sharon Taberski shares her classroom organization and demonstrates how teachers can use authentic assessment, provide meaningful strategy instruction, and create a responsive and literate environment for students. Elementary teachers will find immediate application for these 20-minute video demonstrations of instructional routines essential in a comprehensive reading program. A User's Guide accompanies the set of four videos, which are entitled: "Independent Reading and "Reading Share;" "Read Aloud and Shared Reading;" "Reading Conferences;" and "Guided Reading." (J.W.)

- *Learning by Design.* 1998. Alexandria, VA: Association for Supervision and Curriculum Development.

This excellent video is a companion to Understanding by Design (see page 42b). In it, the six facets of understanding are demonstrated in a variety of classroom vignettes. Both elementary and secondary educators will find this video useful in sparking thoughtful discussions among administrations, teachers, and parents. (J.W.)

- *One Classroom: A Child's View.* 1994. Portsmouth, NH: Heinemann.

In this classic video hosted by Don Graves, second-grade Johanna leads a tour of her classroom at Mastway School in New Hampshire. In explaining how the classroom works, she stops to engage with classmates, inviting them to comment, read their writing, or share their reading. The importance of ownership is powerfully demonstrated in this short video. Both new and experienced teachers will find it helpful in thinking and rethinking the importance of student responsibility, the nature of the classroom environment, and how learners' perceptions of their role as decision makers influences their learning. (J.W.)

- *The Reading/Writing Connection.* 1991. Champaign, IL: Center for the Study of Reading.

  This classic video shows the power of a literate teacher! Educators will see exceptional teacher Dawn Martine at work with her second-grade students in Harlem, New York and learning along with other colleagues in her writing group. Watching this 50-minute video will provide both new and experienced educators with many practical ideas to incorporate in their own teaching. Dawn, a master teacher, demonstrates how to involve students in meaningful literacy events that are interwoven throughout the day. The video concludes with a lively discussion between Dawn and well-known educator Dorothy Strickland. A viewers' guide that includes background information and suggested discussion topics is included. (J.W.)

Solving the Classroom Management Puzzle. 1998. Bothell, WA: The Wright Group.

Teachers looking for sound advice on how to organize an effective literacy environment will find this video immensely helpful. Rather than treating management and instruction as two separate entities, they are woven together to show the reciprocal relationship. The 31-minute video successfully combines a lecture format along with video from actual classrooms to extend and demonstrate suggested principles. Part of a series entitled Classroom Impact, this video along with others covers an array of topics pertinent to language arts educators. (J.W.)

Recommended Literature by Grade Level, K–8, and Supplemental Lists

Annotations by Susan Hepler

About These Lists

Literature is the heart of our literacy programs. Whether you use a total literature program that relies exclusively on trade books or a basal textbook program that is supplemented with trade books, you will want to be familiar with exemplary children's literature. Inspiring literature can be used to read aloud, teach reading, promote rich literature conversations, and encourage a lifelong love of reading.

The following K–8 literature lists have been carefully composed to reflect a wide variety of outstanding literary and artistic literature—picture books, poetry, folktales, realistic fiction, historical fiction, science fiction, humor, and nonfiction. These lists are meant to be used as a reference and starting point for conversations about what literature will work best in your own school or district.

The literature lists are totally new, that is, with few exceptions, the titles are not repeats of previous lists in *Invitations* or the stand-alone *The Blue Pages* (1994). However, be sure to revisit our former lists that serve as a foundation for these lists. While we set our task as selecting the best from recently published literature, remember that "old favorites" such as *The Little Red Hen*, *Strega Nona*, *The Stories Julian Tells*, *Tuck Everlasting*, and *Hatchet*, are still strong teaching choices. However, because many children are widely read, it is also necessary to keep ahead of their reading so they don't endlessly read *Hatchet*, *Charlotte's Web*, or some other classic at one grade level and then again at a later grade level.

The supplemental lists include author/illustrator studies as skeleton organizers for your own preparation of other author studies. Many authors and most publishers now have web pages where you can find additional information. Recognizing the important influence of reading on writing, we have also included an extensive section, "Books That Encourage Children to Write," as part of the supplemental lists.

Grade-level literature lists are organized alphabetically by title. Each book annotation includes a brief summary, noteworthy characteristics about the literary and artistic quality, and possible suggestions for discussion and response. "Series" after an annotation means that there are either sequels or other titles featuring the same characters. Key features of each grade-level list precede the list of books, and each list also includes suggested authors and illustrators for in depth study.

So that books can be used for small-group guided reading and literature conversations, we recommend purchasing six to ten copies of each selected title. To make the literature affordable in multiple copies, we have chosen titles, most of which are available in paperback. The parenthesis following the publishing information indicates the paperback publisher. An empty parentheses means that there was no paperback publisher when this book went to press. However, paperback books regularly go in and out of print, so you will want to periodically check availability. Also, to help you locate all recommended books on the lists easily, all literature is included in the index of *Conversations* by title, author and illustrator.

Balancing the Collection

We have made a big effort to include more nonfiction and culturally diverse titles than on previous lists. Much more quality nonfiction is now available, and at least 25 percent of all included titles are nonfiction. We selected these titles because of the relevance of the content, the way the narrative works, the organizational patterns of the text, and the way illustrations point readers to traditional nonfiction visual conventions such as graphs, sidebars, and glossaries. (See pages 441–443 for specific guidelines for choosing nonfiction.)

At least 40 percent of the all titles on the lists are "culturally diverse." We believe that the books children read—and the books in our school and classroom libraries—must represent every ethnic group and culture. However, while the number of children's books published in the last ten years has doubled from the previous decade, less than 5 percent of new books being published are "culturally diverse." So finding excellent literature to include is a challenge. Looking at current literature, the good news is that African Americans are now presented most frequently and with fewer stereotypes than any other cultural group. However, while some strong Asian characters are portrayed, there is meager coverage of Latino culture and an appalling lack of literature related to Native American culture. Regarding the latter, the literature that exists is mostly folktales; there are few books on Native American history or their lives today (Galda 1998).

We prefer the term *culturally diverse* to the common term *multicultural,* which has taken on varying—and often confusing—meanings. By "culturally diverse" children's literature, we mean quality texts and illustrations that accurately and respectfully portray the different people, cultures, and perspectives of our society. When students engage with the characters in these books, they have the potential for serious and thought-provoking discussion about such issues as bias, freedom, justice, and equality. Additionally, culturally diverse literature has the power to humanize us and increase our sensitivity, tolerance, and compassion for people and other cultures. (Take a careful look at the texts and illustrations in your classroom and school collections. Some old books may have to go.)

Using These Books in Your Reading Program

With the exception of the kindergarten list in which books are meant to be read *to* the child, all books in the grade level lists are meant to be read *by* and *with* children in the guided reading program. While the lists are organized by grade levels for your teaching convenience, many books work on multiple levels. For example, a book that works well for guided reading and literature conversations at one grade level could be a wonderful read aloud at a previous grade level or a terrific book for cementing reading strategies at a higher grade level.

Because developing readers need daily practice on easy books, we have included lots of information and recommendations in "Little Books for Developing Readers," in a section placed between the kindergarten and grade one lists. You may also want to check the information and resources on leveling books on pages 18b–19b. There is also information and extensive recommendations for "Books in Series." As well as being terrific for turning kids on to reading, a number of these series books are also appropriate for guided reading.

Books in Series

Introduction

Because series books are important for turning many students on to reading, we have deliberately included a separate category for them. Many inexperienced readers have become "hooked" on series fiction and then, eventually, moved on to more sophisticated materials. Not only are series books wildly popular with students, they perform an important function in increasing students' comprehension. As readers become more familiar with the common elements of each book in the series—characters, author's style and tone, language, content, predictable format, and concept demands—they can focus more on meaning, and their confidence and competence grows. Then, it becomes our job to help readers expand their reading preferences to include the full range of rich literature in various genres.

As children, both Susan Hepler and I became avid readers through series books. We read every title in a series, proudly owned many of them, and often reread favorites. Susan read "Biographies of Famous Americans." We both read Nancy Drew books, a series that, along with Hardy Boy books, dates back to 1927. The rules in the series never varied: "No serious violence: a character could be knocked unconscious only once in every book. Each chapter must end with a cliffhanger." And while characters have evolved "from fearless Nancy" in the first book to "Flirtatious Nancy" in the late 1980s, those rules have held (Smith 1998).

Books in a fiction series have "common elements of characters and/or setting," "formulaic plots," and "end with loose ends tied up, questions answered, and the satisfaction of a happy ending, at least for the protagonists." Series books are designed to appeal as a total concept rather than on a book's individual merits. In addition, because children choose these books and enjoy reading them, they provide "a valuable incentive for the reading practice that young readers need." Not only does such reading improve fluency; it also provides social connections for communities of readers who enjoy, discuss, and interpret these books (Jenkins 1997).

The following series books have proven popular with readers over the years. Check the grade-level lists for other series books, as well, and be sure to include your students' favorite series in your classroom library.

Most series books noted are fiction but we have included quality nonfiction series when we could find them. While not all books in a series are equally of high quality, useful in the classroom, or appealing, the series on this list provide consistent and reliable reader support. However, many of the series on this list feature excellent writing and some single titles would support guided reading. Just be sure to read individual titles before you purchase. Some series books appear only in paperback, not hardbound. Note that we have not included mass market series such as Nancy Drew, Babysitter's Club, Goosebumps, or sports series as these are books that kids will easily find and read on their own.

Easy Reader Format (Grades 1–2)

Most titles feature easy-reader format of three or four short chapters, six to ten lines of text, plenty of illustrations, and approximately thirty-two to forty pages long. Several series here are picture storybooks, as well.

Amelia Bedelia stories by Peggy Parrish, illustrated variously. HarperCollins. Classic misadventures of a maid who misunderstands.

Arthur series by Marc Brown. Little, Brown. Animals-as-humans, picture book (also see next list).

Clifford stories by Norman Bridwell. Scholastic. Large red dog and his neighborhood friends.

Eyewitness readers. Level 1 and 2. Dorling Kindersley. Nonfiction.

Frog and Toad series by Arnold Lobel. HarperCollins. Classic friendship stories.

Grandpa and Uncle Wainey series by James Stevenson. Greenwillow. Family tall tales.

Gus and Grandpa series by Claudia Mills, illustrated by Catherine Stock. Farrar Straus & Giroux. Boy and grandfather.

Henry and Mudge series by Cynthia Rylant, illustrated by Suçie Stevenson. Simon & Schuster. Boy and dog.

Lionel stories by Stephen Krensky. Dial. Boy at school and at home.

Little Bear stories by Else Homelund Minarik, illustrated by Maurice Sendak. HarperCollins. The series that started the genre.

Let's-Read-and-Find-Out science series. HarperCollins. Nonfiction on many topics.

Little Bill series by Bill Cosby, illustrated by Varnette P. Honeywood. Scholastic. Brothers in family dilemmas.

Mr. Putter and Tabby series by Cynthia Rylant, illustrated by Arthur Howard. Harcourt. Older man and friendly cat.

Mud Flat series by James Stevenson. Greenwillow. Humorous animal friendships.

Nate the Great by Marjorie Sharmat. Putnam. Boy detective in the neighborhood.

Oliver Pig; Amanda Pig series by Jean Van Leeuwen. Dial. Pig family life.

Pinky and Rex series by James Howe. Simon & Schuster. Girl-boy realistic friendship.

Poppleton series by Cynthia Rylant, illustrated by Mark Teague. Blue Sky/Scholastic. Pig and his friends.

Willy stories by Anthony Browne. Candlewick. Gorilla boy experiences dreams, bullies, etc.

Zelda and Ivy stories by Laura McGee Kvasnovky. Candlewick. Fox sisters humorous rivalry.

Easy Chapter Book Series (Grades 2–3)

These short novels feature more text than the previous category, usually more than sixty pages in length, illustrations every few pages, and stronger or more complex literary elements (plot, character, theme, language, etc.).

Adam Joshua series by Janice Lee Smith, illustrated by Dick Gackenback. HarperCollins. School life.

Arthur series by Marc Brown. Little, Brown. Animals-as-humans, chapter format.

Aunt Eater series by Doug Cushman. HarperCollins. Anteater detective stories.

Best Enemies series by Katherine Leverich. Morrow. Girl rivalry and friendships.

Cam Jansen series by David A. Adler. Viking. Girl detective, short chapters.

Catwings series by Ursula LeGuin, illustrated by S. D. Schindler. Orchard. Flying cat adventures.

Junie B. Moon series by Barbara Park, illustrated by Denise Brunkus. Random House. Precocious kindergartner.

Magic Tree House series by Mary Pope Osborne, illustrated by Sal Murdocca. Random House. Boy and girl time-slip adventures.

Mary Marony; Horrible Harry; Song Lee; Marvin Higgins series by Suzy Kline. Penguin. Realistic family and school settings.

Poetry selected by Lee Bennett Hopkins. HarperCollins. Poems on a variety of topics.

See also nonfiction series by:

Gail Gibbons. HarperCollins and Holiday House. Interesting formats and visuals.

David A. Adler biographies. Holiday House. Easy picturebook format.

All About... series by Jim Arnosky. Scholastic. Nonfiction nature observation sketchbooks.

Transitional Books in Series (Grades 2–5)

Books in this category feature varying lengths, relevant themes, longer chapters, and a few illustrations. Some upper elementary age readers do not seek the solace of series books, preferring instead to read books in one genre or by one author. However, these series provide continued support to reader growth.

Amber Brown series by Paula Danziger. Putnam. Girl with issues of friendship, family, divorce, and daily life.

Amelia's Notebook series by Marissa Moss. Tricycle. Inviting journal format.

Angel series by Judy Delton. Houghton Mifflin. New stepfather in family series.

Boxcar Children mysteries by Gertrude Chandler Warner. Whitman. Orphan family adventure stories.

Dear America series. Scholastic. Girls in history as seen through their fictitious diaries.

Dimwood series by Avi, illustrated by Brian Floca. Orchard. Mouse bravery.

Einstein Anderson series by Seymour Simon. Viking. Short story science mysteries.

Encyclopedia Brown series by Donald Sobol. Dutton. Boy detective short mysteries.

Eyewitness readers. Level 3 and 4. Dorling Kindersley. Nonfiction.

Gator Girls series by Stephanie Calmenson and Joanna Cole, illustrated by Lynn Munsinger. Morrow. Ups and downs of alligator friendships.

Julian, Huey, and Gloria stories by Ann Cameron, illustrated variously. Knopf. Neighborhood stories of two brothers and girl.

Lives of the... series. Kathleen Krull, illustrated by Kathryn Hewitt. Harcourt. Short biographies of writers, artists, athletes, explorers, etc.

Magic School Bus series by Joanna Cole and Bruce Degen. Scholastic. Science and humor on field trips.

Marvin Redpost series by Louis Sachar. Random House. Humorous family and school situations.

Mr. Tucket series by Gary Paulsen. Delacorte. Orphaned boy on the Oregon Trail.

One Day in the... series. Jean Craighead George. HarperCollins. Informational stories in an ecosystem.

Ramona series by Beverly Cleary. Morrow. Neighborhood and family stories.

Skinnybones series by Barbara Park. Knopf. Humorous boy stories.

Sports story series by Matt Christopher. Little, Brown. Contemporary boy sport stories.

Stories of the States books. Silver Moon Press. Geography and information.

Time Warp Trio series by Jon Sciezska, illustrated by Lane Smith. Viking. Humorous and hip time-slip fantasies.

Wayside School series by Louis Sachar. Knopf. Wacky doings in thirty-story high school.

Wolfbay Wings series by Bruce Brooks. Harper-Collins. Hockey team.

Woodland Mysteries by Irene Schultz. Wright Group. High interest/low vocabulary. Multicultural adoptees in family solve mysteries.

Yang Family series by Lensey Namioka. Little, Brown. Chinese American family's assimilation.

Young Merlin series by Jane Yolen. Scholastic. Medieval Merlin's rise in Arthur's time.

Zack Files by Dan Greenburg, illustrated by Jack E. Davis. Grosset & Dunlap. Supernatural adventures of New York fifth-grade boy.

Nonfiction by Vicki Cobb, Joanna Cole, Kathleen Krull, Patricia Lauber, Laurence Pringle, and Seymour Simon.

More Challenging Series for Older Readers (Grades 4–7)

While series are still important to many middle school readers, others graduate to YA authors such as William Sleator, Gary Paulsen, Lois Duncan, and Richard Peck. Others gravitate to adult authors such as Danielle Steele, John Grisham, and Stephen King, or genres such as science fiction or romance. Nonetheless, these series have proved popular with older readers.

Alice series by Phyllis Reynolds Naylor. Atheneum. Humorous and poignant stories of motherless girl growing up.

Anastasia Krupnik series by Lois Lowry. Houghton Mifflin. Girl growing up from age nine to middle school.

Bingo Brown series by Betsy Byars. Viking. Humorous view of middle-school boy's life.

Contender series by Robert Lipsyte. HarperCollins. Serious themes, boy sport stories.

Dinah stories by Claudia Mills. Macmillan. Thoughtful and dramatic girl in middle school.

Face on the Milk Carton mysteries by Caroline Cooney. Delacorte. Contemporary girl.

Friendship Ring series by Rachel Vail. Scholastic. How it feels to be a girl in seventh grade.

Harry Potter series by J. K. Rowling. Scholastic. Popular, inventive British school fantasy.

He-Man Club series by Chris Lynch. HarperCollins. Middle-school boys avoid girls.

Herculeah Jones mysteries by Betsy Byars. Viking. Friends solve mysteries.

Here There Be... series by Jane Yolen. Harcourt Brace. Short fantasy stories.

Homecoming series by Cynthia Voigt. Atheneum. Extended Maryland family saga.

Orp series. Suzy Kline. Putnam. Middle school boy school and family stories.

Orphan Train series by Joan Lowery Nixon. Dell. Prairie America in late 1850s.

Petticoat Party series by Kathleen Karr. Harper-Collins. Humor with girls on the Oregon Trail.

Quilt series by Ann Rinaldi. Scholastic. Girl in early 1800s Massachusetts.

Redwall series by Robin Jacques. Putnam. Animal adventure fantasy.

Roll of Thunder, Hear My Cry series by Mildred Taylor. Dial. African American family saga, 1900s onward.

Soup series by Robert Newton Peck. Knopf. Turn-of-the-century boy antics.

Tomorrow When the War Began adventures by John Marsden. Houghton Mifflin. Resourceful band of teens save Australia.

"Un..." series and other collections by Paul Jennings. Penguin/Puffin. Hilarious, gross, weird, and crowd-pleasing short stories for read aloud.

Vesper Holly mysteries by Lloyd Alexander. Dutton. Female adventurer in fantasy historical settings.

Young Merlin series by T. A. Barron. Philomel. Merlin's youth and young adulthood.

Nonfiction by Rhoda Blumberg, Russell Freedman, Joy Hakim, Jim Giblin, Jim Haskins, Jim Murphy, and Jerry Stanley.

Kindergarten

This list features excellent titles with strong story lines and themes powerful to five- and six-year-olds. They engage the soon-to-be reader with humor, rhyme, visually challenging pictures, and experience among genres such as folktales, picture storybooks, nonfiction, and poetry. While a few kindergartners may be able to read some of these books, most titles in this list are intended to be read aloud and then discussed and perhaps extended with classroom projects. Many have predictable and repetitive text, large print, and few sentences to assist children in noticing features of print.

Books may be grouped into themes such as being a kindergartner/going to school; mouse stories; family life; beloved toys and possessions; aspects of curriculum including counting, money, alphabet, seasons, planting; and cultural diversity both in the classroom and in the world. Some key ideas in this collection include what happens in families, growing in competence, solving problems, making things, and observing the neighborhood. See previous lists for additional titles.

Suggestions for kindergarten author studies include Frank Asch, Byron Barton, Eric Carle, Donald Crews, Lois Ehlert, Denise Fleming, Pat Hutchins, and Bill Martin.

Bunny Money by Rosemary Wells. New York: Dial, 1997. (   )
   Ruby and Max spend all of their money to buy Grandma a birthday present, but not without the usual mishaps. Endpapers decorated with bunny money may be blown up and photocopied to use as currency in a class store or to replay the story in this picture storybook. See also Bunny Cakes *(Dial, 1997). (Series)*

Can I Help? by Marilyn Janovitz. New York: North-South Books, 1996. (North-South)
   Crisp rhymed text, patterned question and response, and a cumulative review of the jobs a small dog performs to help his father plant the garden invite children to read. (Series)

"Charlie Needs a Cloak" by Tomie de Paola. New York: Simon & Schuster, 1982. (S & S)
   The perfect informational picture storybook for discussing with children how an informational picture storybook "works." Note the story begins before the title page, the humor of the nibbling sheep and the thieving mouse, the process within pictures and across the text with careful "directions" for making a cloak from fleece to sewing, and the ending glossary of words and pictures. This book rewards the close looker.

Cleversticks by Bernard Ashley, illustrated by Derek Brazell. New York: Crown, 1991. (Dragonfly)
   Ling Sung doesn't seem to be able to do anything that the other kindergartners can do until he shares his prowess with chopsticks. Good for talking about growing competencies, this pairs well with Amy Schwartz's Annabelle Swift, Kindergartner *(New York: Orchard, 1988) and* Kindergarten Kids *by Ellen Senisi (New York: Scholastic, 1994).*

Elizabeti's Doll by Stephanie Stuve-Bodeen, illustrated by Cristy Hale. New York: Lee and Low, 1998. (   )
   In this beautifully illustrated celebration of imagination, Elizabeti creates Eva, a doll, out of a huggable rock and carries it on her back until it is lost in a fire pit but recovered. Talk about making play things from found objects, share dolls, or compare Elizabeti's daily life in a Tanzanian village with that of children in your area. Another excellent book about a handmade African toy is Karen Lynn Williams' Galimoto, *illustrated by Catherine Stock (New York: Lothrop, 1990).*

Feast for 10 by Cathryn Falwell. New York: Clarion, 1993. (Clarion)
   An African American family shops for items, one to ten, and then counts down to supper as they prepare dinner together. Consider how families help each other or how meals are prepared; talk about numbers in daily life, or compare it to her Christmas for 10 *(1998).*

How Teddy Bears Are Made: A Visit to the Vermont Teddy Bear Factory by Ann Morris, photographs by Ken Heyman. New York: Scholastic, 1994. (Scholastic)
   Three children see a product made from start to finish by a factory of diverse workers. Talk about the special equipment needed, machine versus handwork, the steps in making these bears, and compare this to the process of making other toys. Ask children to bring in a favorite toy or stuffed animal and discuss where it comes from or how it was made.

It Begins with an A by Stephanie Calmenson, illustrated by Marisabina Russo. New York: Hyperion, 1994. (Scholastic)

    Four rhyming verbal and pictorial clues ask children to guess a word. Beginning sounds are natural clues and while words such as camera, icing, soft g-giraffe, and quarter may be difficult for some, children are eager to play the game. Large gray letters at each page's end invite readers to repeat "What is it/she/he?"

The Kissing Hand by Audrey Penn, illustrated by Ruth E. Harper and Nancy M. Leak. Washington, DC: Child Welfare, 1993. (   )

    Perfect for allaying (both child and adult) kindergarten anxiety, this sentimental little book shows an initially nervous raccoon going to school with his mother's kiss planted squarely on his palm. He gives her one, too, and each can pat a cheek and think reassuringly of how they love each other when they are apart.

Mama Cat Has Three Kittens by Denise Fleming. New York: Holt, 1998. (   )

    Colorful poured paper pulp illustrations and minimal text show a cat family at play while one sleeps. However, night falls and the sleeping kitten is now ready to play. Note the small animals tucked in and encourage listeners to chime in. Pair with Lois Ehlert's Top Cat *(San Diego: Harcourt Brace, 1998) for another funny cat relationship or with the similarly patterned text by Minfong Ho,* Hush! A Thai Lullaby, *illustrated with cut paper and ink by Holly Meade (New York: Orchard, 1996).*

Minerva Louise at School by Janet Morgan Stoeke. New York: Dutton, 1997. (Dutton)

    A silly chicken ventures into school and mistakes cubbies for nestboxes, jump ropes for hay, and so forth. Children with insider knowledge of school appreciate the humor. Some may recognize in Minerva Louise aspects of the famous Rosie from Pat Hutchins' Rosie's Walk *(New York: Macmillan, 1968) or even Peggy Parrish's* Amelia Bedelia *books (HarperCollins). (Series)*

Miss Bindergarten Gets Ready for Kindergarten by Joseph Slate, illustrated by Ashley Wolff. New York: Dutton, 1996. (Dutton)

    Anxious or hungry, scared or excited, animal children anticipating the first day of school are introduced alphabetically while Miss Bindergarten, a bear, calmly prepares the classroom. The text of the rhyming story is useful for talking about first-day school jitters, noticing the alphabet, comparing this classroom to your own, and thinking about others' points of view. Later in the school year, revisit this class in Miss Bindergarten Celebrates the 100th Day *(New York: Dutton, 1998), a virtual manual in how to celebrate this now-traditional kindergarten "holiday." (Series)*

Ann Morris' books. Photographs by Ken Heyman. New York: Lothrop. (Lothrop)

    Morris and Heyman involve young readers in a particular aspect across world cultures with such titles as Play *(1998) or* Work *(1998). The books invite cultural comparisons but also send a message about being human across cultures: everyone makes and plays with toys, work is worldwide, and we all live someplace. Point out the index, a key to the culture or place of the photo, and read aloud further information about some of the pictures. (Series)*

Mouse Mess by Linnea Riley. New York: Blue Sky Press, 1997. (Scholastic)

    Rhyming text and glowing collage illustrations show the havoc a small mouse wreaks in a human kitchen. "Now that mouse is clean and fed / he leaves the mess and goes... / to bed." Another adventurous mouse can also be found in Laura Numeroff's popular If You Give a Mouse a Cookie *(New York: HarperCollins, 1985).*

Mouse TV by Matt Novak. New York: Orchard Books. 1994 (Orchard).

    Each member of the mouse family argues over what to watch on TV. The solution is no TV and instead playing games, singing, making faces, doing science experiments, and reading. Discuss what happens when one turns off the TV, have a TV-free night and find out, or celebrate "Turn off the TV Month" in April. There are many pro-reading picture storybooks, but another funny take on the no-TV theme is David McPhail's Fix-It *(New York: Dutton, 1984).*

Mouse Views: What the Class Pet Saw by Bruce McMillan. New York: Holiday, 1993. (Holiday)

    A class pet explores the classroom and is viewed in clear, close-up photos sitting on unobvious but typical objects such as chalk or stacked paper. A guess is confirmed by turning the page.

An end map encourages readers to map their own school corridors or classroom, or to draw a mouse-eye view of something. Don't miss McMillan's explanatory end note. Other part-to-whole photograph guessing games may be found in Tana Hoban's clever "look" series, such as Look Book (*New York: Greenwillow, 1997*).

My Very First Mother Goose, edited by Iona Opie, illustrated by Rosemary Wells. Cambridge, MA: Candlewick, 1996. (   )

Mother Goose helps children increase phonemic awareness as they match known text with words and the ink-and-watercolor illustrations make this oversize collection especially winning. Flood the class with other versions by well-known illustrators such as Tomie de Paola, Brian Wildsmith, Arnold Lobel, Richard Scarry, and James Marshall and ask children to discuss their favorites.

Noisy Nora by Rosemary Wells. New York: Dial, 1997. (   )

With full-color illustrations and larger-sized than the 1973 edition, this classic story resonates anew with children who are jealous of their parents' attention to siblings. Nora's mouse family seems to ignore her until she reminds them with a "monumental crash" that she is still there. For other sibling rivalry stories, see the hand-lettered, splashy color of Lucy Cousin's Zsa Zsa's Baby Brother (*Cambridge: Candlewick, 1995*), Zelda and Ivy (*see page 76b*) or the tongue-in-cheek Darcy and Gran Don't Like Babies by Jane Cutler, illustrated by Susannah Ryan (*New York: Scholastic, 1993*).

Night at the Fair by Donald Crews. New York: Greenwillow, 1998. (   )

The colorful joys of going to the fair in the night (rides, treats, games) invite children to talk about their own experiences at fairs and carnivals. Typical Crews patterns include contrasting words (top/bottom, where we've been/where we're going) and a self-portrait, plus the date when he finished the manuscript ('97, but you'll have to look carefully!). Use, along with his autobiographical Bigmama's (*Greenwillow, 1991*), to introduce Crews' many other books as an author study.

Sam and the Tigers by Julius Lester, illustrated by Jerry Pinkney. New York: Dial, 1996. (Dial)

Set in a time when animals and people lived together and everyone was named Sam, Lester's story is a version of the original Indian story in which tigers vie for clothes before turning themselves to butter. Lester's unique voice, Pinkney's snappy illustrations, and the large format make for a great read aloud.

Snow by Uri Shulevitz. New York: Farrar Straus & Giroux, 1998. (   )

While everyone else relies on the weather report, a young boy predicts from a single snowflake the major snowstorm that will eventually blanket the city. Fanciful illustrations and humorous touches such as bending buildings and the characters coming to life in a bookstore window mirror a child's excitement.

Snowballs by Lois Ehlert. San Diego: Harcourt Brace, 1995. (Harcourt)

Rhyming text and innovative collages illustrate all sorts of snowpeople that could be made in the snow. Brightly decorated figures invite children to make their own in creative ways. A recipe for popcorn "snowballs" and winter facts are included. Pair with Nina Crews' photocollage Snow Ball (*New York: Greenwillow, 1997*) in which an urban African American girl anticipates the season's first snowstorm. Or, read about a snowman contest in Henry and Mudge and the Snowman Plan by Cynthia Rylant (*New York: Simon & Schuster, 1999*).

So Many Circles, So Many Squares by Tana Hoban. New York: Greenwillow, 1998. (   )

Brilliant color photographs are cropped so that children notice geometric shapes in the environment. Hoban's many books explore spirals, shadows, reflections, color, and construction, among others. See also Steve Johnson's Alphabet City (*New York: Viking, 1995*), which discovers alphabetic shapes in the city; then walk around the school with a Polaroid or digital camera and capture other letters, colors, or shapes in the environment.

So Much by Trish Cooke, illustrated by Helen Oxenbury. Cambridge, MA: Candlewick, 1994. (Candlewick)

Kindergartners love participatory reading of this cumulative family gathering to celebrate Dad's birthday as each "Ding, dong" is followed by "Yoo, hoo" or "Pow, pow." Everyone wants to hug, squeeze, or wrestle with the baby because they love him "SO MUCH" printed in large type. The happy extended family and the large exuberant paintings practically surround listeners in the warmth.

The Surprise Garden by Zoe Hall. New York: Scholastic, 1998. (   )

In simple language and bold collage illustrations, three children celebrate the joys of planting a garden. Pair with other planting books and start your own garden either in paper cups or in a corner of the schoolyard. Or make a class collage garden from seed catalogs and magazine pictures with labels for each row.

The Teeny Tiny Woman by Arthur Robins. Cambridge, MA: Candlewick, 1998. (Candlewick)

This traditional tale of the theft of a teeny tiny bone is one of the first "scary" stories children remember. Older or more sophisticated readers will appreciate Calmenson's variation, The Teeny Tiny Teacher *(see page 91b).*

There Was an Old Lady Who Swallowed a Fly retold and illustrated by Simms Taback. New York: Viking, 1997. (   )

This rollicking visual interpretation of the traditional song invites children to sing, chant, or read along as the old lady consumes a fly, spider, bird, and so on, until the horse does her in. To help children discover that there are other versions of common songs, encourage comparisons to Alison Jackson's Thanksgiving parody I Know an Old Lady Who Swallowed a Pie *(New York: Dutton, 1997)* or Teri Sloat's Pacific Northwest version, There Was an Old Lady Who Swallowed a Trout! *illustrated by Reynold Ruffins (New York: Holt, 1998). Also see the more traditional version by G. Brian Karas,* I Know an Old Lady *(New York: Scholastic, 1995).*

The "Very" books by Eric Carle. New York: Philomel. (Philomel)

Carle's quartet of books about a hungry caterpillar, busy spider, lonely firefly, and quiet cricket all have teaching points, patterns to discover, and classroom extensions, making his books perfect for author study. Read or retell selectively from his autobiographical book for

older readers The Art of Eric Carle *(New York: Putnam, 1996)* and be sure to sample his many other titles during read aloud.

What Mommies Do Best/What Daddies Do Best by Laura Numeroff. New York: Simon & Schuster, 1998. (   )

Two halves mirror each other as animal mom and child bake, sew on buttons, watch a sunset or read a book and then in nonsexist manner, dad and child do the same thing. Perfect for helping children modify their ideas of who "owns" certain jobs, this book also invites a class to write about things they do with a parent.

Yo! Yes? by Chris Raschka. New York: Orchard, 1994. (Orchard)

Two boy strangers meet; one is bold, the other shy. One is white, the other brown. They chat, become friends, and go off together. Eloquent pictures and minimal hand-lettered text of one or two words per page invite children to notice print. While this is not a predictable text, many children are so taken with the message that they memorize and "read" the story to each other. Compare with Leon and Bob, *page 90b.*

Little Books That Support Developing Readers

Recognizing that developing readers need frequent practice on easy and familiar books in order to become independent, in *The Blue Pages* (1994), I devoted careful attention to "Books Which Invite Readers into Print" and "Developing Early Reading Strategies." (See pages 110b–119b for characteristics of these books as well as annotated choices.) Since that time, more publishers have recognized the importance of providing "little books" that are supportive of young readers, especially in kindergarten and grade one. Because such books are not available in sufficient quantity from well-known children's authors, supplemental program books become necessary. However, once children are readers, the wealth of excellent children's literature available renders such purchases unnecessary.

The focus of this section is to help you build a classroom library and early reading program that contains lots of appropriate and easy books. These books are meant to support developing readers in kindergarten and grade one as well as struggling readers in the primary grades. Unless otherwise stated, many of these books can be used for guided reading. In particular, where an entire collection has been recommended, we feel titles are good choices for guided reading. Therefore, for small-group guided reading, you may want to consider purchasing multiples of some titles. If you are primarily looking to build a classroom library, you may prefer to order only one copy per title to ensure your developing readers have many books to choose from.

Selecting Supplemental Books

Even if you are using a basal text in grade one and the literature included is noteworthy, selections are necessarily limited in number, variety, and levels. There are simply not enough stories in the basal text to give students sufficient opportunities for the massive practice needed to become readers. While basal publishers now offer supplementary "little books," these are often bland and homogenized with many titles in a series looking and sounding the same. Therefore, be sure you carefully examine options before purchasing.

As a viable alternative, consider examining and purchasing quality supplemental books from a variety of publishers. Use the information presented in this section to help create your own balanced collection. There is no short cut to this process. Knowing what's in the marketplace is part of being professional and informed. Form a small book-selection committee of teachers in your school who are willing to review books. Contact publishers' representatives. Most will send samples or bring books on site for examination. Be choosy. Note that these little books are often accompanied by consumables and teacher resources. Our recommendation is to buy the books first. While teacher resources can be helpful for thinking about extensions, remember that students become readers by practicing what they have learned through guided and voluntary reading and not through activities about reading. Purchase books from multiple publishers as well those written by award-winning authors and illustrators. (For some suggestions, see kindergarten and grade one literature lists in this text, pages 79b–82b and 88b–92b.)

We also recommend—that for diversity in texts, genres, and illustrations—you spend your budget on a variety of reading materials. It is important to note that many nonfiction little books are now available. For some students, these are more appealing and easier to read than narratives (Caswell and Duke 1998).

A Caution About Phonics Readers

Phonics readers—also known as decodable texts—are proliferating everywhere, and business is booming. Now that phonics instruction is required in many states, that mandate has been misinterpreted to mean students must have special materials to learn phonics.

While there has been some attempt to write these phonics books as stories, they are still mostly contrived and stilted. They may be fine for some students for practicing a particular sound, but decodable texts are not storybooks. Even if you only buy the readers, they cost as much as any publisher's "little book" whose average cost is $4.00 to $5.00. In addition, phonics readers are often elaborately packaged with big books, sentence strips, take-home materials, games, tests, and expensive teacher guides. Put your money into real books. For most students, you can effectively teach how the code works in the context of well-written texts.

Recommended "Little Books" (Selected and annotated by Libby Larrabee)

Benchmark Education Company
629 Fifth Avenue
Pelham, NY 10803
877-236-2465

> *Early Connections* (72 titles)
> *These books are part of an integrated nonfiction literacy program with many components. The collection is divided into social studies, science, and math titles. All are highly recommended. Texts inform and support the strategic development of the developing reader. Titles have real-life photographs with cultural diversity. There is a reproducible take-home version for all the titles, and a helpful teacher resource manual is available. Packaged in a variety of ways.*

Capstone Press
151 Good Counsel Drive
PO Box 669
Mankato, MN 56002–0669
800-747-4992
http.//www.capstone-press.com

Pebble Books (64 titles)

This nonfiction collection provides good supplemental reading material. It has sixteen topics (four titles each). The texts range from very simple to more complex sentence structures. The photographs used are beautiful and support the text. Each text has a table of contents and some resource information in the back of the book. Expensive.

Creative Teaching Press, Inc.
PO Box 6017
Cypress, CA 90630–0017
800-444-4287

Learn to Read Series (144 titles)

There are four components in the *Learn to Read Series*: Science, Math, Social Studies, and Fun and Fantasy. Each component has three levels ranging from simple to more complex text. There is some repetition of characters across the levels. The overall quality of this series varies greatly so teachers need to choose carefully. The science set is the best and would be good for a classroom library. Packaged in a variety of ways.

Curriculum Associates, Inc.
PO Box 2001
North Billerica, MA 01862–0901
978-667-8000
www.curriculumassociates.com

Think About Series (45 titles; will be 90 titles by fall 1999)

This series provides fine supplemental reading material for content area instruction and is highly recommended. It contains content-area nonfiction and fiction. Topics in Math, Science, and Social Studies have a general focus and are presented in three stages. Stages 1 and 2 contain five nonfiction titles in each subject area. The subjects covered gradually introduce developing readers to content area language and concepts. Beautiful photographs support stories ranging in difficulty from simple phrases to more complex sentences.

Fictional stories covering content area concepts learned earlier are introduced at Stage 3. Colorful illustrations support the text and the same characters appear in all three subject areas. Teacher guides are provided for each subject area at each level. Packaged in a variety of ways.

Dominie Press, Inc.
1949 Kellogg Avenue
Carlsbad, CA 92008
800-232-4570
www.dominie.com

Joy Readers (80 titles)

The *Joy Readers* are written by noted New Zealand author, Joy Cowley. The series is divided into eight sets of ten books apiece. Texts range from caption books to stories with more extended text. Most of the stories are engaging with colorful, supportive illustrations. Basic vocabulary is reinforced across the series. Some of the characters are revisited at different levels. The books are reasonably priced and a teacher guide is available.

Carousel Readers (132 titles)

Carousel Readers are good supplementary reading material. They provide a range of reading experiences from simple caption books to stories with more complex text. The stories are interesting with colorful, culturally diverse illustrations that support the text. Titles are divided into the Carousel Earlybird Readers (four sets of eleven titles) and the Carousel Readers (eight sets of eleven titles). Twelve big books of selected titles and a teacher guide are available.

Teacher's Choice Series (100 titles)

This series features stories that have been written by classroom teachers and reading specialists familiar with the needs of developing readers. It provides good supplementary reading material. Cultural diversity is represented. Stories are predictable and colorful illustrations support the text. The series is divided into ten sets.

Many titles in the collections above have been written by Reading Recovery personnel, literacy specialists, and classroom teachers. All are available in Spanish. This publisher has many other collections for the developing reader. All are packaged in a variety of ways. While many of these series would be good additions to a classroom collection, teachers should preview them in order to choose an appropriate variety.

Talk-About Books (8 titles). Please see description in *The Blue Pages* (1994), page 118b.

Read More Books (16 titles). Please see description in *The Blue Pages* (1994), page 118b.

Reading Corners (30 titles). Please see description in *The Blue Pages* (1994), page 113b. Additional titles have been added since 1994.

Kaeden Books
PO Box 16190
Rocky River, OH 44116
800-890-READ

Literature Series (48 titles)

This series provides wonderful supplementary reading material. The stories are engaging with a high level of predictability and excellent picture support. The Literature Series is divided into twelve sets of four books each. Series A contains six-packs of sixteen titles appropriate for developing readers. Series B contains six-packs of twelve titles that have more text and are appropriate for more independent readers. The books are also presented in two packages as the Reading Success Series that can be used for guided reading.

Math Sets (8 titles)

Simple math concepts are covered in easy to read stories. The texts are repetitive and predictable. The picture support is good. Teachers may want to preview these for content appropriate to their programs.

World of Discovery (22 titles)

Titles are appropriate for developing to independent readers. The stories are engaging and the colorful illustrations offer excellent support of the text. More titles will be added to this collection.

One of the strengths of the titles in the collections above is that many of them are written by Reading Recovery personnel. Cultural diversity is represented. Collections are packaged in a variety of ways. Teachers should preview them to make appropriate choices.

Mondo Publishing
One Plaza Road
Greenvale, NY 11548
888-88-MONDO
www.mondopub.com

Bookshop Literacy Program

This literacy program has many components, such as big books, charts, audio cassettes, student consumables, etc. The books provide young readers with fiction and nonfiction titles presented in a variety of formats. Some titles have special features such as pull-outs and lift-up flaps. A diversity of cultures is represented in beautifully illustrated stories. Many of these books would be an excellent addition to a classroom library.

The books most appropriate for the developing reader are those in the Beanbag Series, Level 1, and some of Level 2. Texts range from simple captions to more complex sentences. Four of the titles at each level are available in Spanish. Teacher resource guides for each level are available. Packaged in a variety of ways.

Newbridge Educational Publishing
PO Box 6002
Delran, NJ 08370–6002
800-867-0307

Discovery Links (88 titles)

This outstanding nonfiction series was developed for use in guided reading and the entire collection is highly recommended. Science concepts are introduced through text that engages and informs the reader. Beautiful photographs are the hallmark of this series. A diversity of cultures is represented. Careful consideration has been given to the needs of the developing reader. Text increases in complexity across the sets within each of the levels. Emergent and early levels each have thirty-two titles. The fluent level has twenty-four titles. All titles are available in Spanish. Teacher guides provide strategies for teaching nonfiction reading and writing in science. Home/school connection books at emergent and early levels contain reproducible mini books for all sixty-four titles. Strategies for Informational Thinking, Reading, and Writing *is the take-home component for the fluent level. Books reasonably priced and packaged in a variety of ways.*

outside the box, inc.
A Sage Publications Company
2455 Teller Road
Thousand Oaks, CA 91320
800-808-4199
www.sagepub.com/otb

Science for Emergent Readers (45 titles)

These readers explore science topics familiar to young children. The stories have predictable texts with beautiful, supportive illustrations. Set A includes twenty-five titles arranged into the following topics: Animals from Nose to Tail, Cycles of

Life, The Ground Beneath My Feet, Taking Care of Me, and *Wonderful Water.* Set B includes twenty titles arranged under these topics: *Look and Listen, Mini-Beasts, Planet Earth,* and *A World of Weather.* Ten big book versions and teacher guides are available. The entire series is good for a classroom collection. Books are reasonably priced and packaged in a variety of ways.

Harry's Math Books (25 titles)

These books reinforce number learning, introduce basic math concepts, and initiate early operations. The titles are divided into two sets. Set A (fifteen titles) includes texts that deal with numbers and number concepts in story form. Set B (ten titles) includes texts that help children learn about comparing and ordering, sorting and classifying, early operations, and geometric shapes. Ten big book versions and teacher guides are available. Packaged in a variety of ways.

Oxford University Press Education
PO Box 1550
Woodstock, IL 60098
888-551-5454

Oxford Reading Tree (55 titles and 8 wordless titles)

These titles are especially appropriate for the developing reader and excellent for guided reading. The entire set is recommended. The characters are first introduced in eight wordless titles. These engaging characters then reappear in a variety of real-life stories. Language ranges from easy, repetitive sentences to more complex sentence structures. Colorful, culturally diverse illustrations support the texts at all levels. Packaged in a variety of ways.

Cat on the Mat Series (21 titles)

The titles in this "classic" series represent six different categories of text structures; wordless, one-word sentences, one/two changes sentences, cumulative sentences, and limited predictable. Beautiful illustrations support the stories. The concern with this set is that the illustrations cover the complete page and some of the text may be difficult to read for some developing readers. Helpful teacher's notes are included.

Peguis Publishers
100–318 McDermot Ave.
Winnipeg, MAN, Canada R3A 0A2
800-667-9673

Tiger Cub Series (32 titles)

This series provides good supplementary reading material. The size of the books is smaller than many little books and is very appealing. Text is highly predictable using rhythm, rhyme, and repetition. Titles are grouped in four packs of eight titles each: *Tiger Cub Readers, Tiger Cub Stories, Tiger Cub Chants and Poems,* and *Tiger Cub Songs.* Five packs of each title are available. Teachers should review titles as some of them in each set are more appropriate for independent readers.

Richard C. Owen Publishers, Inc.
PO Box 585
Katonah, NY 10536
800-336-5588

Books for Young Learners (41 titles)

These are beautiful books! The entire collection would be a wonderful addition to any classroom. The titles are divided into three sets; emergent (fourteen titles), early (twenty titles), and fluent (seven titles). Photographs and beautifully drawn illustrations support these fiction and nonfiction texts. The publisher provides a leveling bar on the back of the books suggesting approximate levels for shared, guided, and independent readings of each book. Concepts, story lines, and language structures range from simple to more complex. Texts have culturally diverse themes and twenty-two titles are available in Spanish. Packaged in a variety of ways.

Rigby
PO Box 797
Crystal Lake, IL 60039–0797
800-822-8661
http://www.Rigby.com

PM Collection (250 titles)

This collection is highly recommended for guided reading. Engaging titles have been carefully leveled to support the development of strategic reading behaviors. The stories are based on children's oral language and offer practice with basic vocabulary. Illustrations are colorful and several characters are revisited across the levels. Text in *PM Starters* (forty titles) ranges from caption to simple repetitive sentences. Text in the *PM Story Books* (168 titles) ranges from simple to more complex sentence structures and storylines. Recently, *PM Nonfic-*

tion titles have been added to this collection. *Teacher guides are available.*

Discovery World (40 titles)

Discovery World provides the developing reader with many kinds of nonfiction experiences. These titles would be excellent supplementary reading material. Colorful texts have been leveled to progress in difficulty and cover most primary grade topics. Texts introduce children to many features common in nonfiction texts. Teacher notes are included with each level and big books are available.

Windmill Books (82 titles)

This collection will provide good supplementary reading material. The collection is divided into three series: Concept Readers, Early Readers, and Early Fluent Readers. Carefully leveled stories have interesting topics and supportive illustrations.

Literacy 2000 Series. Please see description in *The Blue Pages* (1994), page 117b.

Tadpole Readers (20 titles). Please see description in *The Blue Pages* (1994), page 118b.

This publisher has many other collections for the developing reader. Cultural diversity is represented in the collections. Teachers should preview collections to choose an appropriate variety. Packaged in a variety of ways.

Scholastic, Inc.
2931 E. McCarty Street
Jefferson City, MO 65101
800-724-6527
www.scholastic.com

Shoebox Library and Shoebox Library Extenders (128 titles)

Scholastic trade books are conveniently leveled and packaged with the needs of the developing reader in mind. The resource manual gives teaching suggestions and other titles that can be added to the library. Each level includes four copies of eight titles. The Library Extenders add an additional four copies of four titles. Teachers should preview this series since it is packaged by leveled sets and in larger collections.

Reading Discovery (129 titles)

This series from Australia offers a wide variety of fiction and nonfiction titles packaged in six

levels, each level having a range of difficulty. *Colorful illustrations, photographs, and a variety of text layouts are used to support the developing reader. Some titles would be very appropriate for guided reading. Many would provide good supplementary reading material. Teacher notes and supplemental materials are available. Packaged in a variety of ways. Take time to preview.*

Science and Social Studies Literacy Centers (60 titles)

These science readers have simple informational text supported by beautiful photographs. Titles (five each) are grouped in a variety of interesting topics. The social studies readers provide culturally diverse texts on themes of interest to developing readers. The text is simple and the photographs are supportive. Excellent supplementary nonfiction material. Teachers should preview.

Seedling Publications, Inc.
4079 Overlook Drive
East Columbus, OH 43214–2931
614-451-2412 or 614-792-0796
http://www.SeedlingPub.com

Seedling Collection (41 titles)

The stories in this collection have diverse topics in a range of levels to support the developing reader. The texts offer predicable language patterns and supportive illustrations. Some nonfiction topics are presented in storylike settings. Some titles are in Spanish and a resource guide is available. Titles are reasonably priced and sold for the single copy price.

Shortland Publications, Inc.
50 S. Steele St. Suite 755
Denver, CO 80209–9927
800-775-9995

Storyteller (96 titles)

These narrative and nonfiction titles are very suitable for guided reading. Colorful texts support the developing reader. The beautiful photographs and illustrations are culturally diverse. Special features such as die-cuts and cut-away pages are found in some of the titles. The teacher resource book includes oral reading record forms. Available in Spanish. Packaged in a variety of ways.

Sundance Publishing
234 Taylor Street
PO Box 1326
Littleton, MA 01460–4326
800-343-8204

Book Project Beginner Books (48 titles)

The same characters appear throughout all the titles in this colorful series. Texts are repetitive and predictable. The characters can be introduced with stories that are teacher read alouds. These books would provide good supplementary reading material. Teacher guide with reproducibles available. Take time to preview.

Little Red Readers (80 titles)

These fiction and nonfiction readers are divided into five graduated levels. The language patterns are predictable, and colorful photographs and illustrations provide familiarity and support. Cultural diversity is represented. The print is rather large. Teacher guide sheets come with each book. Take time to preview.

Little Blue Readers (40 titles)

These nonfiction readers are also divided into five graduated levels. They are similar to Little Red Readers but with more text and photographs. The print gets smaller in Level 3 but is still rather large. Teacher guide sheets are included. Preview materials.

The Wright Group
19201 120th Avenue NE
Bothell, WA 98011
800-523-2371
www.wrightgroup.com

The Story Box (120+ titles). Please see description in *The Blue Pages* (1994), pages 113b and 118b.

Sunshine Series (300+ titles). Please see description in *The Blue Pages* (1994), page 118b.

Twig Books (144 titles). Please see description in *The Blue Pages* (1994), page 112b.

These three collections have had many titles added to them since reviewed in 1994. Some are sequels to those in the original collections. More nonfiction titles have been added. Spanish editions, big books, and teacher guides are available. Teachers will want to preview these collections. Many titles are excellent and very appropriate for guided reading as well as for independent practice.

Visions (120 titles)

In this collection, African American children are portrayed in authentic stories depicted in three themes: Me and My Family, My Neighborhood and Community, and My World. Text describing day-to-day experiences is repetitive and predictable. Illustrations are colorful and well done. Big books and teacher's guide are available.

Wonder World (200 titles)

This collection of fiction and nonfiction titles (about 112 appropriate for the developing reader) provides a variety of genres and diverse themes. These fact-based stories have wonderful illustrations and photographs and are leveled into sets. They would be a good addition to a classroom collection. Teacher guide available.

Foundations (237 titles)

This collection is appropriate for guided reading and is suggested as an intervention program by the publisher. The collection includes fiction and nonfiction titles. Stories are engaging and offer appropriate support to the developing reader. Cultural diversity is represented. Big books, teacher guides, and records of reading behavior are available.

This publisher has many other collections for the developing reader. Titles are packaged in a variety of ways. Preview collections to choose an appropriate variety.

Grade 1

Books on this list include many titles that first graders will be able to read on their own but not, perhaps, in the early months of school. Teachers should consider some titles as read alouds and eventually as shared or guided reading as the year progresses. New readers need many books with predictable text, clear print consistently placed on the page, and familiar language structure and story lines. When students are firming up their reading strategies, newness of the book is less important than the suitability of the book for guided or independent reading. Refer to The Blue Pages (1994), "Books Which Invite Readers into Print" and "Developing Early Reading Strategies" (pages 110b–119b). Also refer to "Little Books That Support Developing Readers" for books to choose for guided reading and practice, and to "Books in Series " (see page 75b) for a selection of excellent early reader books to have on hand in the classroom.

Titles on this list may be grouped in themes that include trickster characters in traditional literature; pattern and variations in folktales; universality of family life situations; qualities of friendship; finding the marvelous in the ordinary; and making a difference by doing something. Nonfiction selections encourage close observation of nature and the outdoors, plus learning about ponds, forests, and water life.

Suggestions for first-grade author studies include Jim Arnosky, Tomie de Paola, Mem Fox, Kevin Henkes (see page 122b), Arnold Lobel, Bruce McMillan, Audrey and Don Wood plus others such as Martin, Ehlert, Crews, and Fleming from the kindergarten list.

Nonfiction by Jim Arnosky. Various publishers.
>
> *Featuring wild animals found broadly in the United States, Arnosky's books make fine introductions to nonfiction. Short sentences, one to two to a page, repeated text patterns, and sketchbook illustrations assist in shared reading. See* Otters Under Water *(New York: Putnam, 1995),* Raccoons and Ripe Corn *(1991), and* Deer at the Brook *(both New York: Lothrop, 1986).*

Anansi and the Talking Melon by Eric A. Kimmel, illustrated by Janet Stevens. New York: Holiday, 1994. (Holiday)
>
> *Anansi hides in a cantaloupe and fools an elephant and other animals into thinking fruit can talk. See other stories of this Caribbean or African trickster by Kimmel as well as Verna Aardema's* Anansi Does the Impossible!: An Ashanti Tale *(New York: Simon & Schuster, 1997). (Series)*

Around the Pond: Who's Been Here? by Lindsay Barrett George. New York: Greenwillow, 1996. (Morrow)
>
> *A girl and boy walk around a pond and see signs that readers are invited to speculate about: Who's been here? Bits of shell, gnawed wood, feathers, and so forth reveal their sources on the next page—beaver chewings, painted terrapin eggs, and a wood duck nest. More animal infor-*

mation is appended. Talk about signs of animal life in the neighborhood and become a sharp-eyed neighborhood observer. Follow up with Denise Fleming's In the Small, Small Pond *(New York: Holt, 1993). (Series)*

At the Edge of the Forest by Jonathan London, illustrated by Barbara Firth. Cambridge, MA: Candlewick Press, 1998. (   )
>
> *A sheep rancher and his son set out to kill a sheep-stealing coyote but at the last moment, the boy prevails when the coyote and his family interact. A better alternative, they decide, is to find a dog to patrol the fences and keep the sheep safe. Discuss solving problems with alternatives. Beautiful watercolor illustrations of winter and spring settings inspire young painters, as well.*

Chato's Kitchen by Gary Soto, illustrated by Susan Guevara. New York: G. P. Putnam, 1995. (Paper Star)
>
> *Bold illustrations match the gutsy telling of this story set in the barrio. Chato the cat and his buddy Novio Boy prepare frijoles, fajitas, salsa—"the works" for a dinner for his new mouse neighbors but the neighbors will be the main dish! When the mice bring along their friend, Chorizo the dog, they trick the tricksters. Note and discuss the menu glossary of Spanish words also easily defined in context.*

The Giant Carrot by Jan Peck, illustrated by Barry Root. New York: Dial, 1998. (   )
>
> *This variation on Tolstoy's folktale "The Enormous Turnip" features a family who raises a giant carrot. The youngest child's song helps the cumulative chain of people finally pull it up. Perfect for read aloud and also to be dramatized. There's even a recipe for carrot pudding. Pair with Aubrey Davis' version of* The Enormous Potato, *illustrated by Dusan Petricic (Toronto: Kids Can Press, 1998).*

Ginger by Charlotte Voake. Cambridge, MA: Candlewick Press, 1997. (Candlewick)
>
> *Large print in one or two sentences per page tell of a large ginger cat who, like many siblings, resents the arrival of a new kitten. Voake's leisure story illustrated with scratchy line and watercolor is in large enough format for several readers to pore over at once. Compare to Rosemary Well's* Noisy Nora *(see page 81b).*

The Gingerbread Boy by Richard Egielski. New York: HarperCollins, 1997. (   )

The familiar story, refrains and all, is elegantly reillustrated in an urban setting with the cookie escaping from construction workers, street musicians, and a rat before meeting his demise in the tricky fox's mouth. Compare to Paul Galdone's classic version (New York: Clarion, 1975) or Jim Aylesworth's The Gingerbread Man, *illustrated by Barbara McClintock (New York: Scholastic, 1998) with boldface chants to help children chime in. Barbara Baumgartner's* The Gingerbread Man, *illustrated by Norman Messenger (New York: DK Ink, 1998), features predictable text, large print, plus plenty of white space to help new readers.*

Greetings, Sun by Phillis and David Gershator. New York: DK Ink, 1998. (   )

Two children on a tropical island greet what they encounter during the day in short rhymes celebrating the commonplace. Beach, classroom, home, and outdoor settings are noted in a form inspired by African praise songs. Make up couplet rhymes that celebrate your classroom and neighborhood.

Henry and Mudge and the Best Day of All by Cynthia Rylant, illustrated by Suçie Stevenson. New York: Macmillan, 1995. (Aladdin)

Henry's birthday is complete with party, presents, and favors including crackers for his big dog Mudge. Discuss favorite days, design your own best birthday party, or hold a class unbirthday party and do things Henry did on his best day. Introduce readers to this warm and humorous series of some twenty titles. For a multigenerational birthday party, see Loretta Lopez's bilingual Birthday Swap/ ¡Que Sorpresa de Cumpleaños! *(New York: Lee & Low, 1997) This extensive series develops first graders' love of reading while providing plenty of volumes to practice on. (Series)*

Leon and Bob by Simon James. Cambridge, MA: Candlewick, 1997. (Candlewick)

While in his new apartment, Leon plays with his imaginary friend Bob and sees a possible new friend from his window. However, Leon's plans to make friends almost fail when Bob "disappears" along with Leon's courage. Left to his own resources, Leon finds the courage make a new friend—whose name is Bob. Discuss the many ways we make friends or use our imaginations. Pair with Chris Raschka's Yo! Yes? *(see page 82b).*

Lilly's Purple Plastic Purse by Kevin Henkes. New York: Greenwillow, 1996. (Greenwillow)

When overeager Lilly shows off her weekend acquisitions, her teacher (the wonderful Mr. Slinger) confiscates them for the day thus earning her anger and retaliation. But Lily writes and thinks her way out of her dilemma in this continuation of her stories told in Chester's Way *(1988) and* Julius, Baby of the World *(1990, both New York: Greenwillow). Discuss problem solving in this story and notice the many unballooned conversation words in the pictures. (See "Planning an Author/Illustrator Study: Kevin Henkes," see page 122b).*

Mr. Putter and Tabby Pour the Tea by Cynthia Rylant, illustrated by Arthur Howard. San Diego: Harcourt, 1994. (Harcourt)

An old man adopts a pet that, like him, is not cute or peppy, and they become the best of friends in this easy-reading series. Gentle humor, likeable and active older characters, worthwhile themes, and a feel for today's idioms make Rylant's stories readable, contemporary, and meaningful. See also Rylant's humorous "Poppleton" and "Henry and Mudge" series. (Series)

Mud by Mary Lyn Ray, illustrated by Lauren Stringer. San Diego: Harcourt Brace, 1996. (   )

This free-verse hymn to before-spring-comes-mud evokes sights, sounds, and actions associated with this common phenomena. Share the silly Pigs in the Mud in the Middle of the Rud *by Lynn Plourde, illustrated by John Schoenherr (Scholastic, 1997). Start a class writing with the opening words, "One night it happened."*

My Best Friend by Pat Hutchins. New York: Greenwillow, 1993. (   )

Two friends, with different strengths, help each other at a sleepover when one overcomes her fright at billowing curtains. Discuss friendships, differences in competencies, and self-confidence. See also Juanita Havill's Jamaica stories, such as Jamaica and the Substitute Teacher *(Boston: Houghton Mifflin, 1999) or Kevin Henkes' friendship trio story,* Chester's Way *(New York: Greenwillow, 1988).*

Nuts to You! by Lois Ehlert. San Diego: Harcourt Brace, 1993. (   )

In glorious collage illustrations a hungry squirrel raids the flower beds and sneaks into an apartment until the friendly teller of the story tempts it back outside by tossing peanuts on the sidewalk. Augment the four ending pages of squirrel information with Brian Wildsmith's cheery Squirrels *(New York: Oxford, 1987)* or photographer Bianca Lavies' Tree Trunk Traffic *(New York: Dutton, 1989)*. Set up a squirrel feeder nearby and watch what happens.

Officer Buckle and Gloria by Peggy Rathmann. New York: Putnam, 1995. (   )

Officer Buckle's numerous safety tips at school assemblies are made more palatable by the antics of his dog Gloria. That is, until the Officer quits when he's convinced audiences are ignoring him in favor of his funny dog. A disaster returns the two friends to their duties. Endpapers of safety tips invite similar displays but what appeals to readers are the humorous details in the background, including many child-written letters to the duo.

Something Beautiful by Sharon Dennis Wyeth, illustrated by Chris K. Soentpiet. New York: Doubleday, 1998. (   )

In the city, an African American girl notes trash, a homeless person, and a word sprayed on her door and vows to find something beautiful. Friends in her multicultural neighborhood suggest the many things, qualities, and behaviors that are beautiful. The girl's final gesture is to do something to make the world more beautiful: clean up some trash and scrub the word off her door. Simple and moving, the story asks us to cherish beautiful acts and do something, as well.

Something from Nothing by Phoebe Gilman. New York: Scholastic, 1993. (Scholastic)

What can you do with your best blanket when it begins to get shabby? Let Grandpa make something out of it. Note the parallel story of the mice below the floor of the cutaway house and the use of repetitive language. Compare Joseph's solution for using an old blanket with the one in Kevin Henkes' Owen *(New York: Greenwillow, 1993)*.

Tale of a Tadpole by Barbara Ann Porte, illustrated by Annie Cannon. New York: Orchard, 1997. (   )

Solid science framed in a story tells how Francine and her family observe the metamorphosis of Fred the tadpole but into a toad, not a frog. Patience, family interaction, careful observation, and setting a wild pet free are all valued here. Pair with other books about pond life such as Wendy Pfeffer's easier nonfiction From Tadpole to Frog, *illustrated by Holly Keller (HarperCollins, 1994)* or take a trip to the pond in spring.

The Teeny Tiny Teacher: A Teeny Tiny Ghost Story, Adapted a Teeny Tiny Bit by Stephanie Calmenson, illustrated by Denis Toche. New York: Scholastic, 1998. (   )

A teacher and her students discover a bone on a walk in the forest and the ensuing classroom unrest, the teacher's very funny statements, and children who know the familiar pattern make the variant a hit. See Robins' original version, The Teeny Tiny Woman *(see page 82b)* or The Teeny Tiny Ghost *by Kay Winters, illustrated by Lynn Munsinger (New York: HarperCollins, 1997)*. Rewrite another favorite folktale using a classroom setting.

Three Little Pigs by Steven Kellogg. New York: Greenwillow, 1997. (Greenwillow)

In this contemporary retelling, the pigs' waffle business is threatened by a thug wolf Tempesto. Mom returns from retirement to vanquish the wolf and send him to the Gulf of Pasta to mellow out. Introduce "double meanings" and look for all of the puns tucked into the text. Children who know the original tale will also enjoy other take-offs such as Susan Lowell's southwest version, The Three Little Javelinas, *illustrated by Jim Harris (Flagstaff, AZ: Northland, 1992)*, or Eugene Trivizas' pacifist The Three Little Wolves and the Big Bad Pig, *illustrated by Helen Oxenbury (New York: McElderry, 1993)*. Good read alouds to introduce the idea of variants in folktales.

Tom by Tomie de Paola. New York: Putnam, 1993. (Paper Star)

In this autobiographical picture storybook, young Tomie and his butcher grandfather share a love of mischief that gets Tomie momentarily into trouble at school. For more insight into Tomie's childhood and Italian upbringing, see his other autobiographical stories such as The

Art Lesson *(Putnam, 1989), his updated* Nana Upstairs, Nana Downstairs *(Putnam, 1998), and the beginning chapter book* 26 Fairmont Avenue *(Putnam, 1999).*

Too Many Tamales by Gary Soto, illustrated by Ed Martinez. Putnam, 1993. (Paper Star)

Maria loses her mother's wedding ring while helping make the holiday tamales. So she convinces her cousins to eat the whole plate of food before discovering the truth. Rich paintings depict the extended Hispanic family gathering and their joint efforts to replace the eaten tamales. Share family stories, holiday customs, or explore other books about making food.

Where Once There Was a Wood by Denise Fleming. New York: Henry Holt, 1996. (   )

In this environmental picture book lush textured paper pulp illustrations portray the wild creatures and plants that thrive in a wooded area before a housing development changes the habitat. End matter suggests ways to create neighborhood habitats more conducive to wildlife. Pair with books such as Eve Bunting's Butterfly House, *illustrated by Greg Shed (New York: Scholastic, 1999) and George's* Around the Pond *(see page 89b) and make the schoolyard a more environmentally friendly place.*

Whoever You Are by Mem Fox, illustrated by Leslie Staub. New York: Harcourt Brace, 1997. (   )

Journey around the world, no matter where you are, we look different, eat different foods, or speak different languages, but we all share the same joys and pains. An excellent discussion starter about our own strengths and different abilities. Many other books such as Ann Morris/Ken Heyman's photo collections (see page 80b) or the Mary D. Lankford/Karen Dugan collaborations about games played around the world (New York: Morrow) also make the same points.

Grade 2

Books on this list reflect a second grader's desire for increasing knowledge of the world, its animals, people, geography, and ecology. Included, too, are picture storybooks with good discussion possibilities and worthwhile shorter novels that move children into more challenging reading and thinking.

These titles may be grouped according to a unifying idea or pattern such as: the importance of family stories; the life cycle pattern both in biography and in nature; biographies of people who make a difference locally, regionally, and nationally; biodiversity and interdependence; the values of work; and the celebration of individual differences. Novels feature children or animals overcoming problems by individual and group actions; humor; an exposure to different genres; and an introduction to several series. Since children need to practice new skills and build up speed, the need for series books is strong in these years. Introduce series books into the classroom and encourage children to read widely. (See "Books in Series," page 75b.)

New readers at this grade may need to return to previous lists to build fluency and confidence. Support all readers by revisiting books on the previous lists that are thematically related as a way of helping children see how patterns in idea, genre, or structure continue and endure.

Suggestions for second-grade author or author/illustrator studies include Verna Aardema, Marc Brown, Gail Gibbons, Steven Kellogg, Bill Peet, Brian Pinkney, Cynthia Rylant, James Stevenson, and Vera B. Williams, plus others on previous lists such as de Paola, Henkes, and McMillan.

David A. Adler's biographies. New York: Holiday House. (Holiday)

This series encapsulates an entire lifetime in a few words with well-chosen anecdotes and frequent illustrations. "Important Dates" or timelines of each subject are included for such people as Frederick Douglass, Simon Bolivar, Sitting Bull, Louis Braille, Eleanor Roosevelt, Thurgood Marshall, and Florence Nightingale. Set up a timeline of some agreed-upon length and let children enter their discoveries along the proper decades to make history visual.

Adam Joshua series by Janice Lee Smith, illustrated by Dick Gackenback. New York: HarperCollins. (Harper)

Five to seven short illustrated chapters portray the dilemmas, fun, and daily occurrences in a typical suburban second- or third-grade classroom. Adam's dog comes to school; the science fair poses problems; show-and-tell gets out of hand. Once children have read one book, the rest seem easy. The latest, Baby Blues *(1995), discusses sibling arrivals. Lengths vary from 76 to 176 pages.*

Shorter titles are really repackaged from longer originals to invite new readers. (Series)

All About Deer by Jim Arnosky. New York: Scholastic, 1996. (Scholastic)

Lively page design and informational text with labeled drawings make this a good shared reading text to help children understand how nonfiction works. Look at labels; note how the text proceeds from wholes to parts, details, close-ups, etc. See too his "all about" books on alligators, owls, and other animals. (See also "Nonfiction by Jim Arnosky," page 89b.) Research another animal and create a class all-about book in the manner of Arnosky. (Series)

Amazing Grace by Mary Hoffman, illustrated by Caroline Binch. New York: Dial, 1991. (   )

When Grace's classmates tell her she can't play Peter Pan because she is a girl and black, her grandmother takes her to see a famous Trinidadan ballerina. Grace's exploration of her identity continues in Boundless Grace *(New York: Dial, 1995) when she visits her father's new family in The Gambia. (Series)*

Amelia's Road by Linda Jacobs Altman, illustrated by Enrique O. Sanchez. New York: Lee & Low, 1993. (Lee & Low)

As a child of migrant workers, Amelia is tired of moving and wishes for a place of her own, which she creates by burying a box of memorabilia before they move on. Talk about special items, things, and actions that comfort us, and moving.

Beany (Not Beanhead) and the Magic Crystal by Susan Wojciechowski, illustrated by Susanna Natti. Cambridge, MA: Candlewick Press, 1997. (Candlewick)

In five medium-length chapters Beany decides how to use the wish she thinks her "magic crystal" holds. Problems with a school contest, a lost class pet, and a less-than-helpful friend all tempt Beany to use her wish before an elderly, lonesome neighbor brings out Beany's best. Good realistic fiction with typical problems, gentle humor, frequent illustrations, and a kind view of the classroom are all strengths of the book. (Series)

Cactus Hotel by Brenda Z. Guiberson, illustrated by Megan Lloyd. New York: Henry Holt, 1991. (Owlet)

The life cycle of a saguaro cactus from seed to compost is viewed as a complete ecosystem of dependent desert life. Consider what interdependent environments surround your school or exist in the neighborhood. Add to the discussion of biodiversity by comparing with Denise Fleming's Where Once There Was a Wood *(see page 92b) or Lynne Cherry's hopeful pair* A River Runs Wild *(1992) and* The Great Kapok Tree *(1990; both San Diego: Harcourt Brace).*

Cherry Pies and Lullabies by Lynn Reiser. New York: Greenwillow, 1998. (   )

Four generations baked pies, picked flowers, made quilts, or sang lullabies. "Every time it was the same, but different." While text is simple, the change in the way busy mothers do things makes an interesting discussion topic. Discuss, too, other aspects of daily life that used to be one way but are now another or interview grandparents around the neighborhood for their perspective. See also her similarly patterned bilingual Tortillas and Lullabies *(1998) lovingly illustrated by a group of women, "Corazones Valientes."*

Chirping Crickets by Melvin Berger, illustrated by Megan Lloyd. New York: HarperCollins, 1998. (HarperTrophy)

Clear concise information on crickets is accompanied by vibrant illustrations in this "Let's Read and Find Out" series book. Call attention to labels, close-up details, cross sections of cricket egg-laying, and several little pictures within the big pictures. End matter includes advice on keeping a pet cricket and telling temperature from chirps. Pair with Barbara Ann Porte's story of a contemporary Chinese American family, Leave That Cricket Be, Alan Lee, *illustrated by Donna Ruff (New York: Greenwillow, 1993).*

Cocoa Ice by Diana Appelbaum, illustrated by Holly Meade. New York: Orchard, 1998. (   )

A love for cocoa links a girl from Maine and one from Santa Domingo as each imagines what life is like to live in a far-off country. One narrator explains how her family harvests and dries the cocoa beans and trades them to schooner captains bound for New England. The other describes how her family harvests ice—which her father trades for cocoa. Think about what we eat each day and where it comes from. Locate food origins on a map.

Come on, Rain by Karen Hesse, illustrated by Jon J. Muth. New York: Scholastic, 1999. (   )

A celebration in poetic prose of the relief rain brings to a city girl and her neighborhood. Note what is observed and the author's specific word usage that appeals to our senses.

A Dragon in the Family by Jackie French Koller, illustrated by Judith Mitchell. New York: Little, Brown, 1996. (Minstrel)

In the Middle Ages, a boy brings a dragon he's befriended into a mistrustful village, which results in the eventual arrest of his father. Action, believable characters, good discussion possibilities about doing the right thing and about the character of dragons, plus short exciting chapters make this short novel a good read. (Series)

Good-Bye, Charles Lindbergh by Louise Borden. New York: McElderry, 1998. (   )

Based on a true story. Gil sees a small biplane land in the neighbor's field and gets to meet the famous aviator. The self-effacing hero merely wants to put up his tent and stay with his plane for the night. But he gives Gil and his friend a pamphlet about his famous flight. Follow this book with Robert Burleigh's Flight, illustrated by Mike Wimmer (New York: Philomel, 1991), which introduces readers to Lindbergh in poetic prose. Explore family stories about meeting or seeing a famous person. See Family Stories/Memoirs, page 128b.

Grace's Letter to Lincoln by Peter and Connie Roop, illustrated by Stacey Schuett. New York: Hyperion, 1998. (Hyperion)

To help elect Lincoln as president, Grace's family organizes a rally and Grace writes to Lincoln that perhaps he'd win more votes if he grew a beard. When Lincoln's victory train passes through on his way to Washington, he singles Grace out as the girl who gave him good advice. Based on a true story, this sixty-three-page story reads smoothly but children may need help in organizing the many family members in the opening chapters and understanding the historical context. The same incident is also the subject of Karen Winnick's picturebook Mr. Lincoln's Whiskers (Honesdale, PA: Boyds Mills Press, 1996.

Grandmother Bryant's Pocket by Jacqueline Briggs Martin, illustrated by Petra Mathers. Boston: Houghton Mifflin, 1996. (   )

In Maine in 1787, eight-year-old Sarah has been plagued by nightmares after her barn burns and her dog dies in the fire so her parents send her to stay with her grandmother. Gifts of a pocket in which to keep medicinal herbs and the arrival of a one-eyed cat help heal Sarah of her bad dreams. Like Barbara Cooney's strong illustrations for Donald Hall's Ox-Cart Man (New York: Viking, 1979) the pictures show life on a New England farm. But the discussion of the story will no doubt center on overcoming one's fears.

Horrible Harry series by Suzy Kline, illustrated by Frank Remkiewicz. New York: Viking. (Puffin)

In four or five easy chapters with many illustrations, Kline explores classroom issues around the hapless Harry, his best friend and narrator Doug, and others in the class including Song Lee who has her own series. The first book, Horrible Harry in 2B (1988) introduces the classroom while successive titles such as Horrible Harry and the Dungeon (1996) introduce Harry to the "time out" room for discipline problems. Good series and great author with which to lure children into reading up from the "I Can Read" format. (Series)

I Am Rosa Parks by Rosa Parks with Jim Haskins, illustrated by Wil Clay. New York: Dial, 1997. (Puffin)

In easy-reader format, Rosa Parks tells her own story as a child of landowners in rural Alabama in the 1920s to her eventual involvement in civil rights struggles. While the text does not state the year (1955) of her famous sit-down in the Montgomery bus and the beginnings of the bus boycott, students can find out more about this era in biographies of Dr. Martin Luther King. See also I Am Rosa Parks by Eloise Greenfield (New York: HarperCollins, 1995). Read about another Civil Rights hero in the integration of New Orleans schools five years later in The Story of Ruby Bridges by Robert Coles, illustrated by George Ford (New York: Scholastic, 1995).

Junie B. Jones Is Not a Crook by Barbara Park. New York: Random House, 1997. (Random)

Kindergartner Junie, a brattier Ramona Quimby, is funny, opinionated, and irrepressible with a five-year-old's view of the world. Junie's situations such as her struggle with the morality of "finders, keepers; losers, weepers," her funny definitions, and her view of others appeal to older children because, while text looks easy, it takes some sophistication to appreciate the humor in Junie's point of view. (Series)

Keepers by Jeri Watts, illustrated by Felicia Marshall. New York: Lee and Low, 1997. (   )

Kenyon's African American grandmother is a Keeper, the family member who passes on the stories to the next generation. Kenyon wants to buy her a ninetieth birthday present but instead spends his money on a baseball glove. But as he grapples with his conscience, he finds a new present for her—a handmade book of her stories and his grandmother decides he can be the next Keeper. Obvious extensions include discussing and writing family stories and making books, but exploring the role of stories in our lives would be interesting, as well.

A Log's Life by Wendy Pfeffer, illustrated by Robin Brickman. New York: Simon & Schuster, 1997. (   )

Stunning collage illustrations involve readers instantly in the life cycle of an oak tree while presenting the number of animals, fungi, insects, birds, and microscopic living things that depend on the tree in its life and decomposition. Pair with Jane Bosveld's more ambitions sequoia life cycle book, While a Tree Was Growing, *illustrated by Daniel O'Leary (New York: Workman, 1997).*

Marianthe's Story: Painted Words/Spoken Memories by Aliki. New York: Greenwillow, 1998. (   )

Everyone has a life story and this picture book tells a double story of an immigrant girl's first days in an American school where she understands no one but a sympathetic male teacher gives her a paintbrush. Over time, she paints her life. In the second story, when she has learned English, she tells the class the story of her pictures. A sympathetic portrayal of support at home and support at school, the book is sure to evoke discussion.

My Brother Ant by Betsy Byars. New York: Viking, 1996. (Puffin)

Timid Anthony (or Ant) is lucky to have a big brother who can scare away monsters from under the bed, read to him, and write a letter to Santa in July for him. While the brother, known only as "I," writes in script, he looks about eight or nine

in this easy-to-read series. This story is a catalyst for talking or writing about ways siblings or other family members show they care for each other. See also Ant Plays Bear *(Viking, 1997). (Series)*

My Rotten Red-Headed Older Brother by Patricia Polacco. New York: Simon & Schuster, 1994. (Aladdin)

Patricia's brother Richie is gross, a freckle-faced pest and a tease—until she really needs him when she faints from too much merry-go-round. Polacco's family provides endless material for her picture storybooks and this well-designed book features photo-album endpapers that validate the characters while contrasting nicely with the marking pens and penciled illustrations.

An Octopus Is Amazing by Patricia Lauber, illustrated by Holly Keller. New York: Crowell, 1990. (HarperCollins)

This brilliantly clear nonfiction title in an easy-reader format follows the general life cycle of an octopus while leaving readers with a sense of wonder about this intelligent, playful animal. A model for the way life cycle books are written, it also features well-organized, very purposeful illustrations that deserve extra attention for how they complement the text.

The Paperboy by Dav Pilkey. New York: Orchard, 1996. (Orchard)

What is it like to have a real Saturday morning job, to get up in the dark and visit the neighborhood? A brown boy and his corgi dog in a country setting lead readers through his early morning delivery of the paper in which he thinks about Big Things, notices small changes and familiar sights, and returns to bed just as his family is rising. Notice Pilkey's paintings from various perspectives of the hours just before dawn to sunrise. Talk about the rewards of doing a job well.

Penguins! by Gail Gibbons. New York: Holiday, 1998. (Holiday)

A model of efficient text and illustration, this book provides readers with information, contrasting various penguins, and introducing physical characteristics. Help children notice how nonfiction works: split pictures, labels, maps, cross sections, and so forth, and invite them to use these techniques in their own nonfiction projects. See Antarctic Antics: A Book of Penguin Poems *by Judy Sierra, illustrated by Jose Aruego and Ariane Dewey (San Diego: Gulliver/Harcourt Brace, 1998) for poetry and word play that is based on the factual material Gibbons covers.*

Piggie Pie by Margie Palatini, illustrated by Howard Fine. New York: Clarion, 1995. (Clarion)
Grinch the witch goes looking for plump piggies at Old MacDonald's farm but the piggies disguise themselves and trick her into going away in this humorous story. Together make a list of other books in which cleverness conquers force, or tricky characters get out of sticky situations, or the usual winners don't win. Those are long lists. Extend the discussion by comparing Gary Soto's Chato's Kitchen *(see 89b) or read the sequel,* Zoom Broom *(Hyperion, 1998).*

Poetry selected by Lee Bennett Hopkins. New York: HarperCollins. (HarperCollins)
A poet in his own right, Hopkins selects poems and presents them in easy reader format. See such appealing titles as Blast Off! Poems About Space, *illustrated by Melissa Sweet (1995);* Good Rhymes, Good Times, *illustrated by Frané Lessac (1995);* Marvelous Math, *illustrated by Karen Barbour (1997); and* Sports! Sports! Sports!, *illustrated by Brian Floca (1999) (all New York: HarperCollins).*

Potato: A Tale from the Depression by Kate Lied, illustrated by Lisa Campbell Ernst. Washington, DC: National Geographic Society, 1997. (   )
Written by a real child, this shard of Dust Bowl memoir tells how a family picked potatoes for the summer and sold culls back home. Compare with Michael O. Tunnell's Mailing May *(illustrated by Ted Rand; New York: Greenwillow, 1997), a true story of a girl who was shipped in 1914 to her grandmother's as train baggage. Gloria Rand's* Baby in a Basket, *illustrated by Ted Rand (Dutton, 1997), is a true family story of a baby nearly lost floating downstream when a family leaves Fairbanks, Alaska, to catch a boat for Seattle in 1917. See writing Family Stories/Memoirs, page 128b.*

Raven: A Trickster Tale from the Pacific Northwest by Gerald McDermott. San Diego: Harcourt Brace, 1993. (   )

The trickster steals fire from the sky gods to give it to humans in this traditional tale. Pair with other trickster tales across cultures, such as Janet Stevens' Tops and Bottoms *(San Diego: Harcourt Brace, 1995), Natalie Babbitt's* Ouch! A Tale from Grimm, *illustrated by Fred Marcellino (New York: HarperCollins, 1998), Paul Goble's stories about the Plains Indian trickster Iktomi, or Steven Kellogg's raucous* Three Little Pigs *(see page 91b).*

See You Around, Sam by Lois Lowry. Boston: Houghton Mifflin, 1996. (Houghton Mifflin)
Standing on its own, the third humorous chapter book about Sam presents a preschooler who, forbidden to wear his plastic vampire fangs in the house, decides to run away but he works out his anger with neighborhood support. Good read aloud choice later in the year to introduce a new series for readers ready for more challenging books, and an excellent shared reading for its many extension possibilities (neighborhood map of the action; interviews with those helping Sam; a bag with additions as he journeys; "museum" of things from the story; etc.). (Series)

She's Wearing a Dead Bird on Her Head by Kathryn Lasky, illustrated by David Catrow. New York: Hyperion, 1995. (Disney)
With an afterword to confirm the truth, Lasky presents a picture storybook version of how the Audubon Society began when two women became appalled by the number of birds being destroyed to make hats before the turn of the century. A theme on birds is easy to assemble from the many fine fiction, nonfiction, and folktale books available.

The Smallest Cow in the World by Katherine Paterson, illustrated by Jane Clark Brown. New York: HarperCollins, 1991. (Harper)
Marvin creates an imaginary cow to comfort him in his family's move to caretake another Vermont farm but is ridiculed by new schoolmates until his family helps him. With easy reader format, a sixty-four-page text, and eloquent illustrations, this makes a good choice for starting the year as it invites readers to talk about adapting to new situations. Marvin, however, continues to resist change in Marvin's Best Christmas Present Ever *(1997), which begins in winter but ends with a surprise in spring. (Series)*

Three Cheers for Tacky by Helen Lester. Boston: Houghton Mifflin, 1994. (Houghton Mifflin)

   In this picture book, an endearing penguin tries to make the team for the Penguin Cheering Contest but is less than perfect. However, the message about difference and individuality shines through as it did in the popular Tacky the Penguin *(Houghton Mifflin, 1988). See also Lester's picture book autobiography,* Author: A True Story *(Houghton Mifflin, 1997), for charming and revealing comparisons of her writing as a child and as an adult. (Series)*

Tornado by Betsy Byars, illustrated by Doron Ben-Ami. New York: HarperCollins, 1996. (Harper)

   When a tornado appears, the family gathers in the root cellar while the farmhand Pete tells stories of his childhood pet dog who got blown to him in another tornado and almost had to be returned to his former owners. Things don't seem quite so scary when you have good stories to listen to is the theme of this good guided reading choice of seven episodic chapters (forty-nine pages). See also Wild Weather: Tornadoes, *page 102b.*

Vejigante Masquerader by Lulu Delacre. New York: Scholastic, 1993. (Scholastic)

   A Puerto Rican boy makes his own costume with adult help so that he can join the older boys in Carnival mischief. When a goat eats part of his costume, it seems a disaster until his understanding mother helps. Look for the lizard in most pictures; discuss neighborhood relationships.

Wild Willie and King Kyle, Detectives by Barbara Joosee, illustrated by Sue Truesdell. New York: Clarion, 1993. (Dell)

   Friends and neighbors Willie and Kyle do everything together until Kyle moves to Cleveland and a girl moves into his old house. In successive books in the series, Kyle returns, the three form a prickly friendship and a detective agency. Fast-paced, funny, and surprising, this series is a hit with both boys and girls. The problems of a three-way friendship has many echoes in literature; a picture storybook on this theme is Keven Henkes' Chester's Way *(New York: Greenwillow, 1988). (Series)*

Grade 3

Literature selected for this list reflects children's growing interest in the world: other cultures; diverse American culture; family and local history; people who made a difference; plus the rewards of work and the joy of creating something. Novels are selected from a variety of genres that introduce themes such as overcoming fears and difficulties, family support as a character changes, doing the right thing, and accepting change. Refer to "Books in Series" on page 75b to select and introduce these popular works into the classroom to support children's developing facility with text and sustain their interest in becoming self-sufficient readers.

Picture storybooks have been selected for their outstanding use of language and illustration as well as discussible and relevant themes. Some introduce literary devices such as letters, which help develop children inferential abilities, first-person narratives, or literary language such as metaphor and simile, which teachers will want to help children appreciate. The traditional literature genre of tall tales is also introduced here as well as a snappy retelling of familiar tales. Refer to previous lists for other related or classic titles.

Nonfiction selections include many types from photo essays and life cycle books to biography with an increasingly sophisticated use of graphics that convey information: captions, indexes, glossaries, sidebars, labels, diagrams, charts, graphs, close-ups, and maps, which all need to be "read" and understood. To demonstrate how information may undergird good literature, books on the subjects of mummies and insects are selected from several genres. Photoessays challenge old stereotypes by presenting contemporary people who blend the old traditional ways with the modern.

Suggestions for a third-grade author study include Aliki, Eve Bunting (see 123b–124b), Beverly Cleary, Barbara Cooney, Demi, Dick King-Smith, Karla Kuskin, Ted Lewin, Giulio and Betsy Maestro, Margaret Mahy, Jerry Pinkney, Patricia Polacco, and William Steig, plus others such as Gibbons and Arnosky from previous lists.

Amber Brown Is Not a Crayon by Paula Danziger, illustrated by Tony Ross. New York: Putnam, 1994. (Scholastic)

   In nine chapters Danziger creates a real third grader who is angry over her best friend Justin's move to another town. Told in present tense with plenty of dialogue, the book's ample white space and frequent illustrations tease readers into tackling longer text. The series has more emotional depth than the "Adam Joshua" series making it slightly more challenging cognitively without raising reading levels significantly. In other books in the series, Amber deals with chicken pox, divorce, school, and stepparent challenges. (Series)

Boss of the Plains: The Hat That Won the West by Laurie Carlson, illustrated by Holly Meade. New York: DK Ink, 1998. (   )

This lively picture book biography tells how hat-maker John Stetson made the thick fur felt hat a western staple in the mid-1800s. Pair with other biographies of famous pioneer Americans or group with a theme on careers or inventors.

Bugs and Other Insects by Bobbie Kalman & Tammy Everts. New York: Crabtree, 1994. (Crabtree)

Illustrated with stunning photos, text introduces readers to insect qualities and family divisions. Each class: flies, wasps and bees, butterflies and moths, ants, termites, crickets and grasshoppers, and finally beetles are differentiated. Useful to introduce a unit on insects because it categorizes tidily, introduces terminology, and interests readers in further study. Among classroom references include James K. Wangberg's question-and-answer resource, Do Bees Sneeze? (Golden, CO: Fulcrum Publishing, 1997). (Series)

Butterfly House by Eve Bunting, illustrated by Greg Shed. New York: Scholastic, 1999. (   )

With help from her grandfather, a girl makes a house for the Painted Lady larvae and releases the butterfly that develops. Lyrical language evokes emotion and thought and "How to Raise a Butterfly" encourages classes to find caterpillars to raise and release. (See Author Study, page 123b).

Chicken Sunday by Patricia Polacco. New York: Philomel, 1992. (Paper Star)

In this story based on Polacco's childhood, three children earn money to buy Miss Eula an Easter hat from a Russian Jewish shopkeeper by selling Ukrainian Easter eggs. Themes of understanding and friendship across cultures and generations are illuminated by glorious artwork by this prolific author. See Thank You, Mr. Falker (page 106b) and Pink and Say (page 105b).

The Discovery of the Americas by Betsy Maestro, illustrated by Giulio Maestro. New York: Lothrop, Lee and Shepard, 1991. (Mulberry)

The Maestros are magicians at explaining eons of history in simple text. From the landbridge to the peopling of North America to the Europeans who explored here, children are led to discover how the continent has changed. See also the next book in the series, Exploration and Conquest: The Americas After Columbus, 1500–1620 (page 108b). (Series)

Eleanor by Barbara Cooney. New York: Viking Penguin, 1996. (Puffin)

This meticulously researched biographical segment of Eleanor Roosevelt's life covers her lonely childhood and her schooling near the turn of the century. An afterword mentions all that she was able to accomplish in later years. Group with other biographies to talk about what qualities make strong character; conduct research to learn more about Roosevelt's contributions; construct a timeline of people and eras the class discovers in a year's worth of study.

The Gardener by Sarah Stewart, illustrated by David Small. New York: Farrar Straus & Giroux, 1997. (   )

In 1935, Lydia is sent from the country to the city to live with her uncle because her family can't find work. Told in letters, this rich and rewarding story reveals how Lydia brightens her dour uncle's bakery with her cheer and a suitcase full of seeds. Discuss symbols or metaphors surrounding gardening, seeds, and growth and let children draw parallels. Discuss how people cope in difficult times and note the setting, the Depression Era.

A Handful of Beans: Six Fairy Tales Retold by Jeanne Steig, illustrated by William Steig. New York: HarperCollins, 1998. (   )

Six well-known tales are told in such stylish and humorous language, with lively dialogue and frequent verse, that they make excellent Readers Theatre possibilities. Let children de-

cide how to break up the narrative into parts and present the tales to each other or to another class. Examine other retellings of the same tale, as well.

Diane Hoyt-Goldsmith's cultural biography series. Photographs by Lawrence Migdale. New York: Holiday. (Holiday)

Titles in these photo essays each reveal details of a modern child within his or her family and culture in the United States. Lacrosse: The National Game of the Iroquois *(1998) features an Onondaga boy playing the game and making traditional sticks.* Migrant Worker *(1996) shows a Latino family living along the Mexican border while* Celebrating Chinese New Year *(1998) is set in San Francisco's Chinatown. Many earlier titles are useful in Native American studies and all warmly present the rich cultural diversity of the United States. Note author's sources, headings, glossary, index, and excellent picture captions. (Series)*

I Am the Mummy Heb-Nefert by Eve Bunting, illustrated by David Christiana. San Diego: Harcourt Brace, 1997. (   )

An Egyptian princess tells of her life in the first two-thirds of this poetic text, and the final third explains how she was mummified. Pair with the more challenging Cat Mummies *by Kelly Trumble, illustrated by Laszlo Kubinyi (New York: Clarion, 1996) to learn more about the ancient civilization of Egypt and the practice of mummifying. Another Egyptian title is* The Librarian Who Measured the Earth *(see page 104b). See also the Author Study of Eve Bunting, page 123b.*

I Have Heard of a Land by Joyce Carol Thomas, illustrated by Floyd Cooper. New York: Harper-Collins, 1998. (   )

This lyrical picture storybook of free black homesteaders is told from the point of view of a strong woman whose determination builds a community for her family in the Oklahoma Territory. Cooper's illustrations show people joyously making a home on the prairie and provoke a good discussion of the ways in which we help ourselves make better lives.

In My Family/En mi familia by Carmen Lomas Garza. San Francisco: Children's Book Press, 1996. (Children's)

This dual language Spanish/English book features glowing paintings celebrating the author's Mexican American upbringing family life. Making empanadas, curing earaches, making food from cactus, or celebrating special days are some of the activities depicted in each double-page spread. Invite bilingual contributions and celebrate children's own family outings, work, food preparation, gatherings, and important moments in a class or individual books. See also her Family Pictures *(1990).*

Insectlopedia by Douglas Florian. San Diego: Harcourt Brace, 1998. (   )

Short, inventive poems about arthropods (mayfly, praying mantis, hornet, black widow spider, termites, beetles) ask readers to see how fact undergirds good poetry while illustrations of watercolor on brown paper bags with collage added invite young artists to experiment. Good complementary read aloud with Bugs and Other Insects *(see 98b).*

John Henry by Julius Lester, illustrated by Jerry Pinkney. New York: Dial, 1995. (   )

Lester's exuberant read-aloud prose and Jerry Pinkney's lovingly researched illustrations bring the African American tall tale railroad hero to life. Introduce him and encourage research into the tall tale tradition: Febold Feboldson, Sally Ann Thunder Ann Whirlwind Crockett, Gib Morgan, and Pecos Bill, Paul Bunyan and Johnny Appleseed in versions by Ariane Dewey and Steven Kellogg, among others. A literary or "made-up" tall tale is Anne Issac's Swamp Angel, *illustrated by Paul Zelinsky (New York: Dutton, 1994). Enrich units of United States social studies with this most American of genres.*

Nights of the Pufflings by Bruce McMillan. Boston: Houghton Mifflin, 1995. (Houghton Mifflin)

This excellent photo essay with interesting author notes follows an Icelandic girl and her friends as they assist the puffins in making it to the ocean from their birthplaces. A good example of how humans are increasingly alert to the effect of urbanization on habitats, this book pairs well with Stephen W. Kress' Puffin Project (Gardiner, ME: Tilbury, 1997) or Gail Gibbons' The Puffins Are Back *(New York: Harper-Collins, 1991) as evidence of how people are making an ecological difference.*

One Grain of Rice by Demi. New York: Scholastic, 1997. (   )

Brilliant and stylish paintings reminiscent of Indian art illustrate the traditional tale of mathematical choice: would you rather have one grain of rice doubled each day for a month or other riches? The visuals reinforce the nonfiction mathematical concept and invite children to confirm how quickly the doubling piles increase, especially when readers see the fold-out spread of elephants carrying the astounding number of rice grains.

Piñata Maker/El Piñatero by George Ancona. San Diego: Harcourt Brace, 1994. (Harcourt)

In both Spanish and English text, Ancona follows a Mexican man who runs his own piñata business in a small village. Full-color photos show how a piñata is assembled for various festivals and make the process inviting as an art project. Use as a model of directions for making something or in culture studies units. See also Barrio: José's Neighborhood *and other books by this fine photo-essayist.*

Poppy by Avi, illustrated by Brian Floca. New York: Orchard, 1996. (Dell)

Told in snappy, crisp prose, this twenty-chapter tale of mouse courage introduces the Dimwood series. It features Poppy who dares to question the idea that an evil owl is actually protecting her extended family from porcupines. Avi's well-developed characters, dialogue, fast plot and theme of true courage plus Floca's warm drawings make this an excellent shared reading. Pair with other books about brave but small creatures such those in Dick King-Smith's novels or the more challenging Mrs. Frisby and the Rats of NIMH *by Robert C. O'Brien (New York: Atheneum, 1971). (Series)*

Premlata and the Festival of Lights by Rumer Godden, illustrated by Ian Andrew. New York: Greenwillow, 1996. (HarperTrophy)

In Bengal, India, Premlata's mother is too poor to celebrate Diwali, the Festival of Lights. But when a kindly landowner gives her money for the lights, Prem spends it on treats for her family. Scared as evening approaches, Prem is saved and the true cause of her family's poverty is revealed. Themes of courage and self-help plus an Indian setting make this short book a good discussion choice. While most Indian words are defined in context, others such as tap are not, so as a sort of glossary, readers may contribute entries to be organized later into a word wall display.

The Puppy Sister by S. E. Hinton, illustrated by Jacqueline Rogers. New York: Delacorte, 1995. (Dell)

Nick would have preferred a sister to a puppy but Aleasha wants to play human games, eat human food, and understand human talk. The charm of this book is that the author makes us believe a dog could turn into a human. Readers will note how dog emotions are interpreted in a humanlike way, the friendly but reserved personality of the other pet, a cat, and the clues that Aleasha is finally human.

Safe Return by Catherine Dexter. Cambridge, MA: Candlewick, 1996. (Candlewick)

In this true story from Sweden in the 1800s, Ursula lives with relatives since her parents have died. While the island economy is based in hand-knit sweaters, Ursula's hated last attempt lies tangled in a corner. When her aunt and the ship carrying the year's knitting to market do not return, Ursula keeps up her hope by really learning to knit. Spare prose, strong setting, and memorable characters invite children to consider how we deal with fear and how community helps. Both women and men knit on this island and children may want to master the craft.

School Mouse by Dick King-Smith, illustrated by Cynthia Fisher. New York: Hyperion, 1995. (Hyperion)

The mouse Flora learns to read by listening to the children in the one-room school where she lives. Reading saves her family when she reads the word "poison." Some nuance and lengthy sentence structure invite discussion but frequent illustrations and plenty of dialogue keep readers moving. Use to introduce this reliable author of animal fantasy (along with Poppy, this page). See also Three Terrible Trins (1994), the much more challenging Babe the Gallant Pig (1983), and its sequel, Pigs Might Fly (1990) (all New York: Crown).

The Shaman's Apprentice: A Tale of the Amazon Rain Forest by Lynne Cherry and Mark J.

Plotkin. San Diego: Harcourt/Gulliver Green, 1998. (   )

In the rain forest accurately illustrated by Cherry, a boy describes how the shaman cures with leaves, roots, and bark. When the shaman can't cure malaria naturally, he loses favor with the Tirio tribe until an ethnobotanist learns about forest medicine from the shaman and writes of it, bringing new respect for this nearly lost wisdom. It is based on a true story.

The Silver Balloon by Susan Bonners. New York: Farrar Straus & Giroux, 1997. (Farrar)

Fourth-grader Gregory releases a helium balloon with name and address attached and it nets him a new friend, an old man. The two exchange treasures, ones which send Gregory to the library, to maps, and to a fossil expert to identify. Gregory's experiences strengthen him in many ways and send the message that the world is a fascinating place if you have the curiosity to see. The author warns children, however, that helium balloons are hazardous to animals that may swallow them.

So Far from the Sea by Eve Bunting, illustrated by Chris K. Soentpiet. New York: Clarion, 1998. (   )

Bunting's spare story is told by Laura Iwasaki who has come to visit her grandfather's grave at Manzanar for the last time before moving east. Scenes from Laura's father's memory alternate with the four family members walking through the dusty remains of the camp. This piece of family history introduces many children to a part of World War II, but it also celebrates families. (See also the Author Study of Eve Bunting, page 123b and the bibliography of Family Stories/Memoirs, page 128b.)

The Stories Huey Tells by Ann Cameron, illustrated by Roberta Smith. New York: Knopf, 1995. (Knopf)

Five short stories warm all readers—this African American family listens to, takes care of, and does things with each other. Themes include overcoming fears with help, obeying family rules, and being inventive and experimental. More Stories Huey Tells, *illustrated by Lis Toft (New York: Farrar Straus & Giroux, 1997), is slightly more serious but humorous as Huey tries to rejuvenate his August sunflowers with* food and get his father to stop smoking. Each five-chapter book, at a little over 100 pages, makes a good small-group discussion choice as well as an entertaining read. (Series)

The Storytellers by Ted Lewin. New York: Lothrop, Lee & Shepard, 1998. (   )

In this picture storybook, Lewin's glorious praise of storytelling is set against the souks of Fez, Morocco, where Lewin watercolors reflect photographs he took there. Abdul and his grandfather visit the market, passing by dyers, rug weavers, brass workers, the tannery, and other stalls to set up their own rug. There they release a white pigeon to fly into the heavens and bring back a story for the townspeople now gathered. Lewin's many well-illustrated books help children explore aspects of different cultures with wonder and respect.

Uncle Jed's Barbershop by Margaree King Mitchell, illustrated by James Ransome. New York: Simon & Schuster, 1993. (Aladdin)

An African American traveling barber postpones opening his own shop, helping his neighbors in crisis. The neighborhood helps him celebrate his life of work when he finally realizes his dream. What is the value of work? Why do we work? See, too, a boy with a job in The Paperboy *(page 95b) and a book about honor in the workplace,* Eve Bunting's A Day's Work *(New York: Clarion, 1994).*

Volcanoes and Other Natural Disasters by Harriet Griffey. New York: Dorling Kindersley/Eyewitness Readers, 1998. (Dorling Kindersley)

Covered are natural disasters (volcanoes, tidal waves, earthquakes, hurricanes, and the like) through the ages. Sidebars include small photographs, and imaginative drawings enliven the accounts of the eruption of Vesuvius, earthquakes in Lisbon, the Great San Francisco fires and Australian bushfires, and the famous east coast hurricane of 1938. A useful group discussion choice for weather studies, it would pair well with selections from Patricia Lauber's well-written and more challenging Hurricanes: Earth's Biggest Storms *(New York: Scholastic, 1996) and* Volcano: The Eruption and Healing of Mount St. Helens *(New York: Simon & Schuster, 1986).* (Series)

When Jesse Came Across the Sea by Amy Hest, illustrated by P. J. Lynch. Cambridge, MA: Candlewick, 1997. (   )

In immigrating to America from Eastern Europe in the late 1800s, Jessie leaves behind her beloved grandmother but makes a life in the new land which finally includes her as well. Invite children to discover how their own families arrived here (see Family Stories/Memoirs, page 128b). Pair with Elisa Bartone's immigrant story Peppe the Lamplighter *with Ted Lewin's luminous illustrations (New York: Lothrop, 1993), or family stories such as* Potato *(see page 96b), or* Grandfather's Journey *(see page 104b).*

When the Whippoorwill Calls by Candace Ransom, illustrated by Kimberley Bulcken Root. New York: Morrow, 1995. (   )

When land for Shendandoah National Park was appropriated in the 1930s, the government forced people to leave but bought their land and moved them to new homes. The abandoned homesites discovered years later by a girl cause her to wonder who lived here. What are the clues? Compare with the clues hikers discover in Crescent Dragonwagon's Homeplace, *illustrated by Jerry Pinkney (New York: Macmillan, 1990). Ask children to consider local inhabited or uninhabited places and discover or imagine their history.*

Wild Weather: Tornadoes by Lorraine Jean Hopping, illustrated by Jody Wheeler. New York: Scholastic, 1993. (Scholastic)

In this well-designed, easy-reading concept book, six short chapters in both narrative and informative text discuss tornadoes across America. In shared reading note the conventions of nonfiction such as tables, flow diagrams, charts, and maps and discuss how text and pictures work together. Using the "Total Tornadoes" chart, develop a color key in increments of ten, and place findings on your own blank U.S. map. What else can be discovered from this chart?

Wilma Unlimited: How Wilma Rudolph Became the World's Fastest Woman by Kathleen Krull, illustrated by David Diaz. San Diego: Harcourt Brace, 1996. (Harcourt)

This picture book biography tells how a determined Rudolph overcame polio, was noticed as a basketball player, and later became a world-class runner. Stunning illustrations and a spare, smooth text make this a good shared reading experience. See, too, David Adler's* Lou Gehrig: The Luckiest Man Alive *(San Diego: Gulliver Books, 1997), which traces the short career and struggles of this much loved athlete.*

Wolf! by Becky Bloom, illustrated by Pascal Biet. New York: Orchard, 1999. (   )

A humorous story that speaks to overcoming the difficulties in learning to read eloquently, with expression, and well. Discuss children's former and current challenges in learning to read. Ask children what other stories this reminds them of as there are many wolf stories, and books with themes of pro-reading books or overcoming difficulties. Compare to a version of "The Bremen Town Musicians," as well.

Grade 4

Books on this list include an increasing sense of form and complexity and demand from the reader a greater knowledge of the world. Some novels are set in key United States historical periods: the Civil War, Oregon Trail, immigration, and settlement. Texts also feature various narrative devices, more complex stories and characters, and language of greater depth. Readers of this age need to develop speed, and series books as well as helpful book talks or appropriate booklists guide them to more satisfying choices with literary quality. See "Books in Series," page 75b, for suggestions to have on hand.

Themes include the power of ideas, developing values, making good choices and the consequences of bad ones, the resilience of the human spirit in the face of hardship, and the struggle for some to become readers and writers. Picture storybooks have been chosen for their literary and artistic quality plus their ability to generate discussion.

Nonfiction examines biography in short form and in picture storybook format while the subjects of water and of bats are explored in different kinds of text—informational and fantasy. Help children notice the many conventions of nonfiction: glossaries, picture captions, headings, graphs, charts, and text organization. Help them see, too, that nonfiction writing can be lively and involving when it uses examples, vivid description, anecdotes, and a variety of other writing techniques. Authors of nonfiction about bats and mud explore their respective topics creatively and surprisingly.

Suggestions for fourth-grade author studies include Joanna Cole, Sid Fleischman, Jean Craighead George (see 124b–126b), Paul Goble, Eloise Greenfield, Patricia McKissack, Phyllis Reynolds Naylor, Jack Prelutsky, Jon Scieszka, Chris Van Allsburg, and Jane Yolen plus authors on previous lists such as Bunting, Cleary, King-Smith, Polacco, and Steig.

Angela Weaves a Dream: The Story of a Young Mayan Artist by Michele Sola, photographs by Jeffrey Jay Foxx. New York: Hyperion, 1997. (   )

In this photo essay, Angela, a young Mayan girl in Mexico, learns to weave the symbolic and sacred designs of her culture from the expert village weavers. Help readers note nonfiction conventions of glossary, author and illustrator notes, and the many sidebars. Respect for both modern and ancient Mayan culture is also found in George Ancona's personal and photographic essay, Mayeros: A Yucatec Maya Family *(New York: Morrow, 1997), in which a family prepares for the town's fiesta.*

Bats: Shadows in the Night by Diane Ackerman, photographs by Merlin Tuttle. New York: Crown, 1997. (   )

In lyrical text, the author recounts a trip she made to explore bat diversity with the famous expert, Merlin Tuttle. An example of fine writing, the text imparts both the author's excitement in discovery and plenty of bat information. To study bats and note how nonfiction works, group with Laurence Pringle's moving account of Merlin Tuttle's evolution toward a career as Batman: Exploring the World of Bats *(New York: Scribners, 1991); Betsy and Giulio Maestro's nonfiction* Bats: Night Fliers *(New York: Scholastic, 1994); and Carolyn Arnold's informational* Bats, *with photographs by Ronald Hewett (New York: Morrow, 1996).*

Christmas in the Big House, Christmas in the Quarters by Patricia C. McKissack and Fredrick L. McKissack, illustrated by John Thompson. New York: Scholastic, 1994. (   )

Using a seasonal setting, the authors contrast slave quarters and big house family life on a tidewater Virginia plantation in 1859. The book is suffused with the readers' knowledge that this time is about to come to an end as text foreshadows the Civil War (Frederick Douglass, William

Lloyd Garrison, and John Brown, runaway or spying slaves, attitudes in the north, freedom songs, etc.). A model for nonfiction writing, fine research, and excellent documentation in endnotes and foreword, this read aloud also features accurate illustrations that convey and contrast emotions as well as document the times. See also the Civil War-set Pink and Say *(page 105b).*

Dear Levi by Elvira Woodruff, illustrated by Beth Peck. New York: Knopf, 1994. (Knopf)

Twelve-year-old Austin writes letters to his brother in Pennsylvania as he journeys to Oregon over six months time in 1851. Enduring hardship, hard choices, and incredible changes, Austin arrives on the family claim near the Columbia River only to find it has been sold by his dead father's unscrupulous partner. Kristiana Gregory's Across the Wide and Lonesome Prairie: The Oregon Trail Diary of Hattie Campbell *(New York: Scholastic, 1997) covers some of the same distance from a girl's perspective. Research lends authenticity to these fictional accounts and readers may want to read excerpts from several of the primary resources cited in references. See too* The Barn *(page 107b) and Gold Rush-set books such as* The Ballad of Lucy Whipple *(page 112b) and* Mr. Tucket *(page 109b).*

A Drop of Water by Walter Wick. New York: Scholastic, 1997. (   )

Using exciting photographic close-ups, Wick invites readers to marvel over the properties of water with short readable explanations of terms such as surface tension and refraction. Note Wick's inspirational sources (preface and afterword) and his ability to convey excitement as he researched his subject matter. Each double-page spread has a corresponding experiment, such as bubble-making, succinctly explained in the end matter. Let small groups work out a demonstration of each of these for an in-class activity. See also Snowflake Bentley *(page 106b).*

Frindle by Andrew Clements. New York: Simon & Schuster, 1996. (Aladdin)

Clever fifth-grader Nick invents a new word much to the exasperation of his teacher. The legendary and strict Mrs. Granger maintains that frindle *is not an acceptable substitute for* pen. *But when Nick enlists the help of his classmates, what began innocently turns into a local uproar as the media take notice and the story (and word) spread across the country. Where do words come from? How do fads start? Are school rules fair or arbitrary? What constitutes great teaching? Is Nick a classroom threat or an asset? Clements raises some good discussion points and provides a surprising and satisfying ending in this short, easy book.*

Gettin' Through Thursday by Melrose Cooper, illustrated by Nneka Bennett. New York: Lee & Low, 1998. (   )

In this picture storybook, Andre gets on the honor roll only to have to postpone his African American family's celebration until payday. He pouts until the family throws him a dress-rehearsal party before the real one on payday. Told with dropped gs, the colloquial text sounds like a boy's voice as he learns to delay gratification. Write about family celebrations or things you've had to anticipate. (See page 128b for more discussion.)

Grandfather's Journey by Allan Say. Boston: Houghton Mifflin, 1993. (Houghton Mifflin)

This picture storybook for older readers is based on Say's grandfather who immigrated to America from Japan at the turn of the century. Themes include knowing and understanding grandparents, immigration, the feelings one has on being a part of two cultures, and longing to be where you are not. See sequels Tree of Cranes *(1991) and* Tea with Milk *(1999, both Houghton Mifflin), as well.*

Just Juice by Karen Hesse. New York: Scholastic, 1998. (Scholastic)

Nine-year-old Juice can't read and must decide whether to stay at home with her mother and out-of-work and illiterate father or return to school in order to learn to read. Told by Juice in a rural dialect, this powerful story quickly involves readers in the plight of this poor family, their independence but need for the social worker's help, and their gradual success. Preview Chapter 16 in which Juice helps her mother give birth before reading this aloud.

Keepers by Alice Schertle, illustrated by Ted Rand. New York: Lothrop, 1996. (   )

"Keepers" are the items, insights, thoughts,

and bits that we remember with significance. In various kinds of poetry, Schertle captures moments—such as carousel rides, seeing an insect or lizard in a new way, or considering an old ukulele no one plays. This collection might inspire writers to view objects, ideas, and feelings from a different point in concise language—or to appreciate this ability in some of the finer books they read.

The Librarian Who Measured the Earth by Kathryn Lasky, illustrated by Kevin Hawkes. Boston: Little, Brown, 1994. (   )

Eratosthenes asked so many questions as a youth in Greece and later as a scholar in Egypt that he eventually figured out how to measure the earth's circumference. His work was accurate to within 200 miles. While most fourth graders may not understand the math without help, the book presents clearly a person whose desire to know galvanized his life and transcended his times. Use in studies of ancient civilizations, as augmentation to math and science curriculums, or as a good example of picture book biographies.

Lives of the... series by Kathleen Krull, illustrated by Kathryn Hewitt. San Diego: Harcourt. (   )

Each volume manages to encapsulate a life in three pages with biographical highlights, interesting anecdotes, scandals, and influences of some twenty famous people. Sections of Lives of the Athletes: Thrills, Spills (and What the Neighbors Thought) *(1997) not only read aloud well, but also intrigue readers to discover more by reading longer biographies or autobiographies. Krull and Hewitt have also written about presidents, explorers, composers, authors, and artists, as well. Use to introduce a biography theme or to demonstrate how the lively anecdote can enrich student-written family stories. (Series)*

The Magic Squad and the Dog of Great Potential, illustrated by Frank Remkiewicz. New York: Delacorte, 1997. (Dell)

Ten-year-old Calvin, a middling sort of student, decides to take care of a "foster dog" from the Humane Society but the dog has an uncertain future. Calvin demonstrates persistence, responsibility, and finally a passion for his school project when it involves animals he loves. Themes of focus and responsibility, a family daycare setting in an urban environment, intergenerational friendships, and believable characters make this a good (and fast) read. See also the first Calvin story, Jazz, Pizzazz, and the Silver Threads (New York: Bantam Doubleday Dell, 1996). (Series)

Mary Anning: The Fossil Hunter by Dennis Fradin, illustrated by Tom Newsom. Parsippany, NJ: Silver Press, 1998. (Silver Press)

This short biography of the eleven-year-old who discovered the first complete fossil of an ichthyosaur in the crumbling cliffs of Lyme Regis, England, recalls when the world was just beginning to "discover" evidence of the natural past. Read aloud parts of Charles Wilson Peale's 1801 first uncovering of a mastodon in James Giblin's The Mystery of the Mammoth Bones *(New York: HarperCollins, 1999). See, too, Catherine Brighton's* The Fossil Girl *(Brookfield, CT: Millbrook, 1999) and Jeannine Atkins'* Mary Anning and the Sea Dragon *(New York: Farrar Straus & Giroux). (Series)*

Mud Matters by Jennifer Owings, illustrated by the author and photographed by Stephen Trimble. New York: Miles Cavendish, 1998. (   )

Who'd think you could make mud interesting and personal? But this beautifully illustrated and creative book takes us from Dewey's Southwest childhood fascination with mud and making things such as a horno (outdoor oven) to her encounters with Zuni Mudheads, mud wasps, and coil pots without missing a beat—or a reader. Write your own mud (or rain or snow or tree branch) story.

On the Bus with Joanna Cole: A Creative Autobiography by Joanna Cole with Wendy Saul. Portsmouth, NH: Heinemann, 1996. (   )

This excellent read aloud provides a window into how and why a writer writes and builds on children's loving familiarity with the Magic School Bus series. Cole discusses where she gets her ideas, the roots of her lifelong love of informational books, how to organize information, the process of developing topics, the art of collaboration, and the nuts and bolts of dummies, sketches, drafts, and book production. See Carol Jenkins' The Allure of Authors *(Portsmouth, NH: Heinemann, 1999) for an excellent plan for an author study of Cole. (Series)*

Out of Darkness: The Story of Louis Braille by Russell Freedman, illustrated by Kate Kiesler. New York: Clarion, 1997. (   )

Blinded at the age of four, Louis Braille was sent to a school for blind boys and there developed a writing and reading system of punched dots that was to change the sightless world. However, he and his system had to struggle against the embossed letter system that the French government had approved. A good short (eighty pages) introduction to Freedman's readable and lively biographies, this is illustrated with watercolors and includes a chart of Braille letters.

Pink and Say by Patricia Polacco. New York: Philomel, 1994. (   )

In this extremely moving story, two Union soldiers in Confederate territory form a brief friendship. Two weeks later both are captured and the black Pink dies at Andersonville prison while the white Say survives to tell this Polacco family story. Children will need some historical background to see this book in its historical context. For other books that celebrate family, see Family Stories/Memoirs, page 128b.

Ruth Heller's World of Language series. New York: Grosset and Dunlap. (Paper Star)

Heller's witty series in rhymed text with bright illustrations entertains as it teaches parts of speech by giving examples of, for instance, interjections and conjunctions and their uses in Fantastic! Wow! and Unreal! *(1998), which completes the series. See other titles, too, such as* Behind the Mask *(1995) (prepositions) and* Mine, All Mine *(1997) (pronouns), and many earlier titles. See, too, her autobiography,* Fine Lines *(Katonah, NY: Richard C. Owen, 1996).*

Shiloh by Phyllis Reynolds Naylor. New York: Atheneum, 1991. (Dell)

Told in West Virginian regional dialect, this modern classic invites discussions about lying, honor, character, and the nature of rural life when Marty shelters a dog from an abusive owner. Sequels cover Marty's relationship with his family and with the increasingly drunk Judd Travers in Shiloh Season *(1996) and his rehabilitation in* Saving Shiloh *(1997, both Atheneum). Cynthia Rylant evokes the setting of this trilogy in her poetic* Appalachia: Voices of Sleeping Birds, *illustrated by Barry Mosers (San Diego: Harcourt Brace, 1991). (Series)*

Silverwing by Kenneth Oppel. New York: Simon & Schuster, 1997. (Aladdin)

An excellent read aloud fantasy, this story in-cludes enough sympathetic information about bats to convince all readers of their importance to our ecosystems. Shade, a runty Silverwing bat, becomes separated from his migrating flock and is pursued by evil owls because he has dared to see the sun in the daylight world. The author has created a bat mythology (based on world bat myths), imagined a bat civilization complete with predator bats, and borrowed the age-old theme of the least leading the rest. Pair with good nonfiction about bats to check fact against fantasy, such as Bats: Shadows in the Night *(page 103b). (Series)*

Smoky Night by Eve Bunting, illustrated by David Diaz. San Diego: Harcourt Brace, 1995. (Har-court)

In this thoughtful picture storybook, Daniel and his mother must leave their apartment building for shelter during an urban riot. Mis-trust of neighbors prevails until a friendly fire-fighter reunites not one but two missing cats to their owners. Striking illustrations are framed in a variety of found materials, each appropriate to the page of text it illustrates and each a part of the whole. See Author Study, page 123b, as well as other Bunting titles that raise complex social issues.

Snowflake Bentley by Jacqueline Briggs Martin, illus-trated by Mary Azarian. Boston: Houghton Mif-flin, 1998. (   )

A Vermont boy followed his passionate inter-est in snowflakes with a career that included documenting them in drawing and photography. This picture book biography of a self-made sci-entist features informational sidebars and a short epilogue. Snowflake Bentley also makes an appearance in Johanna Hurwitz's Faraway Sum-mer *(New York: Morrow, 1998)*.

The Story of Money by Betsy Maestro, illustrated by Giulio Maestro. New York: Clarion, 1993. (Mul-berry)

The informational history of our money sys-tem, from trade and barter to gold coins and dol-lars, is traced. Useful end matter presents foreign money, unusual facts, and other data. Since making and having money is a preoccupa-tion of this age group, you may want to pair this with books about entrepreneurs, or start a school store or class money-making venture.

The Tarantula in My Purse and 172 Other Wild Pets by Jean Craighead George. New York: Harper-Collins, 1996. (HarperCollins)

Nearly two dozen autobiographical short sto-ries about raising a house full of children and wild pets (skunks, raccoons, crows, owls, etc.) give readers the true-life fact behind George's fiction. Each chapter invites further animal re-search or locating a George title to see how she works the facts into narrative. See also her en-capsulated stories of famous animals such as the Alaskan life-saver dog Balto or the real Smokey Bear told in Animals Who Have Won Our Hearts, *illustrated by Christine Merrill (New York: HarperCollins, 1994). See Author Study, page 124b.*

Thank You, Mr. Falker by Patricia Polacco. New York: Philomel, 1998. (   )

At first fifth-grader Tricia loves her new school but her challenges in learning to read nearly overcome her until her new teacher helps her. Words have power—to hurt like bullies use them, or to open the world, like Mr. Falker did for Tricia. Like most of her work, this book is emotional and autobiographical and would pair well with The Bee Tree *(1993)*, My Rotten Red-Headed Older Brother *(Page 95b), and others. For more on literacy and its values, see* Just Juice *(page 104b)*.

Yang the Third and Her Impossible Family by Lensey Namioka, illustrated by Kees de Kiefte. Boston: Little, Brown, 1995. (Dell)

Yingmei Yang changes her name to Mary, tries to make friends with the girls in her school, and hides a cat from her family of musicians because she is afraid they can't afford a pet. While this easy-to-read book provides many examples of cultural clashes, it also features worthwhile themes of valuing both your own family and in-dividual differences. A pat but satisfactory end-ing for young readers, humor, the value of individual talents, and making friends provide discussion material. (Series)

Your Move by Eve Bunting, illustrated by James Ran-some. San Diego: Harcourt Brace, 1998. (   )

Ten-year-old James wants to go out with a street gang even though he has to take his six-year-old brother Issac along. When the gang attempts to spray paint over the marker of an older rival gang, his brother is nearly injured and James makes an important choice. Like many of Bunting's picture storybooks, this one examines decision making in spite of peer or other pressures, and provides good discussion material as well. See the Author Study on Eve Bunting, page 123b.

Grade 5

More of the world, its people, and the challenge of being human are included in the books on this list. Several books have historical settings in addition to survival themes as children of this age typically think that they could survive if they needed to. Check lists in previous Blue Pages for classic survival stories and other notable fiction. Titles selected include more complex relationships among families and friends but with hopeful conclusions as fifth graders still want happy endings. Fantasy selections intertwine with folklore and information that builds on prior knowledge of how fantasy works. The genre of biography is explored in various formats such as picture book, short vignette, partial, and complete.

Nonfiction introduces a variety of formats to would-be report writers and centers on topics of oceans, money, animals, and children of other cultures. Inventors and scientists who thought creatively are explored both in illustrated biographies and in collections of short biographies. A theme centers on how scientists learn to "read" evidence and reconstruct what has happened in the past. Refer to the fourth-grade list as well for books students may have missed or want to reread.

Suggestions for fifth-grade author study includes Avi, Natalie Babbitt, Betsy Byars, Karen Hesse, Johanna Hurwitz, Lois Lowry, Lawrence Pringle, Katherine Paterson, and Yoshiko Uchida as well as those from the fourth-grade list.

Accidents May Happen: Fifty Inventions Discovered by Mistake by Charlotte Foltz Jones, illustrated by John O'Brien. New York: Delacorte, 1996. (Bantam)

Interesting and informative short stories, illustrated in cartoons, about the invention or discovery of such household items as cellophane, *liquid paper, yo-yos, plus ice-cream sodas, Worcestershire sauce, and dynamite pique reader's curiosity while inviting them to wonder about the origins of other everyday things. Good short read alouds, research starters, or let readers inform each other by reading different selections and retelling them to the class. See also her* Mistakes That Worked *(1991).*

The Barn by Avi. New York: Orchard Books, 1994. (Camelot)

This deceptively simple book artfully presents motherless nine-year-old Ben's attempts to keep his father alive by promising to build a barn. Felled by a stroke (a "fit"), Father must be propped up, fed, cleaned, and cared for by each of his three children in 1855 Oregon territory. In order to keep the land they are homesteading, they must improve it and remain for three years. Each of the three face different issues but in completing the task as Father dies, the narrator Ben shows his mettle. Readers will argue over what exactly Father's gift was and how it might be that Ben continued to remain on the land.

Chi-Hoon: A Korean Girl by Patricia McMahon, photographs by Michael F. O. Brien. Honesdale, PA: Boyds Mills Press, 1993. (Boyds Mills)

Color photographs and a narrative of the life of an eight-year-old Korean girl give children insight into modern-day Korean life. See, too, Ted Lewin's beautiful watercolor-illustrated Ali, Child of the Desert *(New York: Lothrop, 1997),* I. Onyefulu's Ogbu: Sharing Life in an African Village *(San Diego: Harcourt Brace, 1996), and Laurie Dolphin's photo essay chronicling Tibetan flight to India to escape religious persecution,* Our Journey from Tibet *(New York: Dutton, 1997). These excellent nonfiction titles about contemporary children halfway around the world help nurture global understanding.*

Dealing with Dragons by Patricia Wrede. San Diego: Harcourt Brace, 1990. (Point)

The immensely popular series begins with this story of Cimorene, a princess tired of passive castle life who apprentices herself to a dragon. Humorous references to folktale conventions and content let children read as insiders. Introduce this by discussing the connections between fantasy and folklore, asking children what they know about princesses, wizards, magic, and dragons. (Series)

Discovering the Iceman by Shelley Tanaka, illustrated by Laurie McGaw. New York: Hyperion, 1997. (　　)

　　Uncovering a mystery, readers see how a 5,300-year-old frozen man was discovered in an Alpine glacier and brought to the laboratory where forensic scientists interpreted the remains. Pair with Don Lessem's The Iceman *(New York: Crown, 1994) for the same content. Also consider Johan Reinhard's* Discovering the Inca Ice Maiden *(Washington: National Geographic, 1998) and Donna M. Jackson's* The Bone Detectives, *illustrated by Charlie Fellenbaum (Boston: Little, Brown, 1996), for straightforward and well-documented accounts of how forensic anthropologists interpret evidence.*

Dolphin Man: Exploring the World of Dolphins by Laurence Pringle, photographs by Randall S. Wells & Dolphin Biology Research Institute. New York: Atheneum, 1995. (　　)

　　Pringle's nonfiction account of one man's work in a career he loves also illuminates the dolphin's behavior in family pods as observed in Sarasota Bay, Florida. See, too, his Elephant Woman *(1996), another in this series that inspires readers to consider a career in natural science. (Series)*

The Dragon's Pearl by Julie Lawson, illustrated by Paul Morin. New York: Clarion, 1993. (　　)

　　The traditional eastern dragon offers an interesting comparison with the usually better-known western one. In an effort to save a valuable dragon's pearl from robbers, a boy swallows it, transforming himself into a dragon. For another presentation of Chinese dragon transformation, see Laurence Yep's The Dragon Prince, *illustrated by Kam Mak (New York: HarperCollins, 1997). The quintessential western dragon may be found in Margaret Hodge's* Saint George and the Dragon, *illustrated stunningly and symbolically by Trina Schart Hyman (Boston: Little, Brown, 1984).*

Duke Ellington: The Piano Prince and His Orchestra by Andrea Davis Pinkney, illustrated by Brian Pinkney. New York: Hyperion, 1998. (　　)

　　Rhythmic prose and bold scratchboard artwork that seems to dance portray the life story of this well-known composer and band leader. Read aloud or mark for Readers Theatre so children can hear the musicality of the words. Then listen to Ellington's music.

Exploration and Conquest: The Americas After Columbus 1500–1620 by Betsy and Giulio Maestro. New York: Lothrop, 1994. (Mulberry)

　　Pictures and text involve readers in exploration of North and South America and the problems it caused indigenous peoples. Maps, detailed weaponry, birdseye views plus dramatic depictions of displaced people and lost ships help readers understand the next century after Columbus. Cartier, Magellan, Columbus, and Pizarro also appear in the newspaper-formatted The History News Explorers *by Michael Johnstone (Cambridge, MA: Candlewick Press, 1997).*

Family Tree by Katherine Ayres. New York: Delacorte, 1996. (Yearling)

　　Eleven-year-old Tyler starts sixth grade with a project doomed to failure, a family tree. Hers is chopped down: her mother died when she was born and her carpenter father is angry over questions about his Amish past. But as she begins to ask questions, she discovers an extended family ready for reconciliation. Research "the plain people" (Raymond Bial's Amish Home, *New York: Houghton Mifflin, 1993 is a good beginning), talk about Tyler's and her father's changing attitudes, the apt metaphor the teacher poses for immigrants to this country, and families in general.*

Fig Pudding by Ralph Fletcher. Boston: Houghton Mifflin, 1995. (Dell)

　　Eleven-year-old Cliff is the oldest of six kids in one hilarious, warm, and happy family— playing, laughing, arguing, telling stories, celebrating. So the death of his brother in a freak bicycle accident seven chapters into the book comes as a shock and a tragedy for both the family and the reader. Incredibly, by the end of the book we are once again laughing as the family pulls together even as they face their grief honestly. A moving, funny book worth small-group discussion and sure to evoke some interesting journal writing.

I Am the Iceworm by MaryAnn Easley. Honesdale, PA: Boyds Mills Press, 1996. (Dell)

Fourteen-year-old Allison's plane crashes while she is on her way to live with her mother in Alaska. With the pilot killed, Allison is forced to survive not alone in the wild as in Gary Paulsen's Hatchet (New York: Bradbury, 1987) but in an Inupiat village with a culture she has never experienced before. Soon the outsider, or "ice worm," begins to appreciate this world and her own, through observation, participation, and finally a courageous act, before she is reunited with her mother. Readers may see parallels with other survival novels or stories in which two cultures meet.

Jonah the Whale by Susan Shreve. New York: Scholastic, 1998. (   )

New to the school, overweight sixth-grader Jonah Morrison imaginatively invents a career for himself when his classmates call him "the whale." He decides he will be a host of a kid's cable TV show and interview celebrities. Jonah's other problems include a working mother, absent father figure, and a baby brother. With humor, lively dialogue, and believable characters, Shreve creates a fast-paced story with a character who triumphs over everything and realizes his dream,. An easier read for less-able readers and a quick read for others. (See also Frindle, page 103b.)

The Life and Times of the Peanut by Charles Micucci. Boston: Houghton Mifflin, 1997. (Houghton)

Each busy double-page spread discusses some aspect of the peanut: growth, uses, making peanut butter, George Washington Carver, peanut jokes, and history, for instance. Facts are represented in a variety of nonfiction conventions. Call attention to flow diagrams, charts, headings and subheadings, or timelines so that children can begin to notice and use these techniques in their own nonfiction writing. Other books by Micucci cover apples and honeybees. (Series)

Mary on Horseback: Three Mountain Stories by Rosemary Wells. New York: Dial, 1998. (   )

In spare prose, three short vignettes chronicle the beginnings of health services to Appalachia. Each short story presents a different point of view—one of Mary herself as she realizes what she will have to do in order to help poor families scattered throughout the mountains, a second of a Scottish nurse who leaves home to do something to make a difference, and the third of a mute young girl who follows Mary around giving new overalls to girls so that their dresses won't catch fire as they tend stoves all day. Link this with other books about occupational choices or biographies of people who have made a difference.

Mr. Tucket by Gary Paulsen. New York: Delacorte, 1994. (Dell)

Fourteen-year-old Francis Tucket is captured by Pawnees when he doesn't pay attention while practicing with his new rifle at the rear of his Oregon-bound wagon train. Freed by a one-armed mountain trapper, Tucket begins to learn the skills that will enable him to grow up. A fast plot, cliff-hanger chapters, and vibrant characters pique interest in the pre-Gold Rush days in 1848. This book is the first in a popular series which appeals to both girls and boys. (Series)

The Music of Dolphins by Karen Hesse. New York: Scholastic, 1996. (Apple)

Her spirit shaped by the dolphins who raised her, a feral child now called Mila observes her human captors from a dolphin standpoint. Spare in the telling, this book asks readers to contrast dolphin behaviors with those of people and the result is a challenge to what we think it means to be human. See also Laurence Pringle's Dolphin Man (page 108b).

The Octopus: Phantom of the Sea by Mary M. Cerullo, photographs by Jeffrey L. Rotman. New York: Dutton, 1997. (   )

An excellent nonfiction read aloud choice, this lively and anecdote-wealthy account of the intelligent cephalopod involves readers in biodiversity, scientific methods, and ecology. Introduce a unit on ocean life or compare this treatment of octopuses to information found in Lauber's An Octopus Is Amazing (see page 95b) or James Martin's Tentacles: The Amazing World of Octopus, Squid, and Their Relatives (New York: Crown, 1993) before asking children to research and write about another animal.

Popcorn by James Stevenson. New York: Greenwillow, 1998. (   )

Thirty-two free verse poems provide both text and interesting page and typeface design to inspire readers to reflect on nature, family life, and small moments, while the book suggests young writers use the format as a springboard. See also Stevenson's Sweet Corn *(1995). (Series)*

The Prince of the Pond by Donna Jo Napoli, illustrated by New York: Dutton, 1992. (Puffin)

This humorous novel begins the moment a frog discovers himself sitting in a pile of prince clothes and tries to make sense of his new life as Pin the frog. Jimmy, the Pickpocket of the Palace *(1995)* follows Pin's son as he is turned into a human and saves the family pond from a curse. Strong descriptive powers, biological accuracy, and a story based on familiar folklore components are strengths of this novel pair. Compare Ellen Conford's funny The Frog Princess of Pelham *(Boston: Little, Brown, 1997).*

Randall's Wall by Carol Fenner. New York: McElderry Books, 1991. (Skylark)

An artistically talented but social outcast fifth grader, Randall has build a defensive wall around himself but friendship with the imaginative Jean causes him to take some risks. Believable characters, a humorous scene where Randall takes a bath fully clothed, and touching moments of caring exhibited by both children and adults provide discussion points for why people are excluded and how humans create a community of concern.

Robin's Country by Monica Furlong. New York: Knopf, 1995. (Knopf)

A supposedly mute and starving boy stumbles into Robin Hood's forest stronghold, having escaped from brutal treatment in a nearby household. Marian mistakes him for a spy but eventually warms to the boy and teaches him archery. While the 139-page novel covers major legendary events in a well-realized medieval setting, the story is more about overcoming difficulty in tough times. Traditional versions of Robin Hood may be found in short books by Jane Louise Curry or Robert Leeson and in the challenging but complete novel of Roger Lancellyn Green.

Run Away Home by Patricia McKissack. New York; Scholastic, 1997. (Scholastic)

In 1886 in Alabama, an eleven-year-old African American girl named Sarah Crossman and her land-owning family befriend and give refuge to Sky, a runaway Apache boy. When the family stands to lose its land for owed taxes, Booker T. Washington provides carpenter employment but the family must face down Klan riders. Suspense, textured characters, and strong research ground this story. Race relations at the end of the century foreshadow events to come, which are chronicled by other authors such as Mildred Taylor.

Running Out of Time by Margaret Peterson Haddix. New York: Simon & Schuster, 1995. (Aladdin)

Jessie thinks she is living in an Indiana village in 1840 until a diphtheria epidemic forces her mother to confide that it's actually 1996 and this village is really a tourist site in trouble. The shocked girl must escape into the outside to get help before the evil experiment can do any more damage. Readers will enjoy watching the author create believability and then will be absorbed in Jessie's discovery of toilets, television, telephones, and other amazing aspects of modern life. See also The Apprenticeship of Lukas Whittaker *(page 111b),* a more challenging book also set before the general discovery of germs.

Biographies by Diane Stanley and Peter Vennema. New York: Morrow. (Mulberry)

Using primary sources and documenting the research, the authors present large-format biographies that look like picture books. However, the information load, and the concepts, as well as the subject matter, make these biographies perfectly suited to fifth grade. Subjects include Cleopatra, Shakespeare, Joan of Arc, Shaka: King of Zulus, and Charles Dickens, among others. Be sure to read the author's note, and other front and back matter, plus observe the way the illustrations reflect the period in which the subject lived. *(Series)*

Starry Messenger: Galileo Galilei by Peter Sis. New York: Farrar Straus & Giroux, 1996. (   )

It is only with multiple readings that the reader sees how Sis has created this spare and symbol-laden picture-book biography of the man who maintained that the world moved around the sun and that observation was key to scientific thought. Readers will need some context to understand how and why Galileo was imprisoned and to notice the many well-planned illustrations. But the rewards make the work worth it.

Sticks by Joan Bauer. New York: Delacorte, 1996. (Dell)

> *In this lively first-person narrative, fifth-grader Mickey Vernon wants to become a pool champ but must overcome his anger and receptivity to bullying. By paying attention to geometry and vectors and with the help of a mentor who once knew his dead father, Mickey wins, in more ways than one. Subthemes include dealing with an older bully, achieving balance after the death of a parent, and the value of practice and perseverance in perfecting a sport or skill. The story also shows math principles in action, a rarity in intermediate fiction.*

Yolanda's Genius by Carol Fenner. New York: Simon & Schuster, 1995. (Aladdin)

> *Yolanda, a formidable African American fifth grader, defends her younger learning-disabled brother against playground bullies, drugs, and their new school. Convinced that the first-grader brother has hidden harmonica talents, even though he has trouble learning to read, Yolanda mounts a campaign to help her mother understand and support her brother's strengths. By discussing the joys of both urban and suburban life, astute readers will see that the problems can be similar in either setting.*

Grade 6

Patterns in this list include a more sophisticated treatment of American history with emphasis on the Oregon Trail and the California Gold Rush, early 1800s, treatment of disease in the last century, and the sorry history of slavery. Themes include self-knowledge, knowing what's important, the consequences of decisions, and humanity's imperfect nature.

Nonfiction introduces a variety of topics while asking readers to understand the scientific process and to examine evidence in forming hypotheses about the world. In addition, biographies in a variety of formats introduce adventurers, explorers, and people who saw the world as a fascinating place, a strand from previous grade's lists. These short biographies read as short stories and also serve as language arts and science topics.

Many novels on lists from previous editions of The Blue Pages still make good group reads and should be considered as additional excellent titles. Given the limited number of longer books a teacher can select for guided reading or reading aloud, a teacher will want to choose carefully. Children arrive in sixth grade collectively having read widely and teachers need to be aware of previous reading patterns before they choose small-group and whole-class books.

Check "Books in Series" (page 75b) to add titles to the class collection so that readers who enjoy series can find good ones. Middle school is traditionally the beginning of the end of free reading for many children as well as the beginning of reading adult popular fiction (such as romance novels and Stephen King) and it is a particular challenge to keep the reading flame alive.

Suggestions for sixth-grade author studies include Cynthia DeFelice, James Cross Giblin, Mary Downing Hahn, Scott O'Dell, Gary Paulsen, Richard Peck, Louis Sachar, Jerry Spinelli, Mildred Taylor, and Cynthia Voigt and those on the fifth-grade list for other possibilities.

Anastasia's Album by Shelley Tanaka. New York: Hyperion, 1996. (   )

> *This nonfiction read aloud illuminates the early 1900s life of the Russian princess as shown in her own photographs. Be sure to set Anastasia in historical context. The photos and the eloquent text make the Russian life of this privileged family personal and immediate. "Read" the pictures to discuss how they reveal personality and the times, a practice useful in any social studies curriculum that uses primary source material such as old photographs.*

The Apprenticeship of Lucas Whitaker by Cynthia DeFelice. New York: Farrar Straus & Giroux, 1996. (Avon)

> *In 1849, there was yet no cure for tuberculosis or "consumption" as it was known. Twelve-year-old Lucas Whitaker loses his whole family to the disease, tries believing in superstitious cures, and finally apprentices himself to a doctor in his struggle to understand what has happened. Excellent discussion of understanding by scientific proof rather than by superstition and a graphic depiction of medicine at the mid-century point. See Paul Fleischman's more challenging* Path of the Horse *(New York: HarperCollins, 1983), which is set in the great yellow fever epidemics of 1793 as well as* Time for Andrew, *page 115b.*

The Ballad of Lucy Whipple by Karen Cushman. New York: Clarion, 1996. (Clarion)

Following the death of her father in Massachusetts, Lucy and her mother move the family to a rough-and-tumble California Gold Rush mining town. Longing for her former life, Lucy writes plaintive letters to her grandparents, dreams over the few books she has, and bakes pies to earn money for her passage home. Unusual friendships, a fire that destroys the town's buildings but not its spirit, and her mother's impending marriage cause Lucy to consider what she really wants. Well-detailed history, a compelling cast of characters, and a crisp plot make a good read while supporting the social studies curriculum. Pair with Paulsen's much easier Mr. Tucket *(see page 109b).*

Bandit's Moon by Sid Fleischman, illustrations by Joseph A. Smith. New York: Greenwillow, 1998. (   )

Outlaw Joaquin Murieta, the "terror of the roads," rescues the orphaned Annyrose and helps her find her brother. She repays his kindness by teaching him how to read in this robust adventure set in the California Gold Rush in the mid 1800s. Short chapters, colorful characters, a plot that twists and turns, dialogue, and illustrations invite reluctant readers.

Belle Prater's Boy by Ruth White. New York: Farrar Straus & Giroux, 1996. (Dell)

In a Virginia coal-mining town in the fifties, Gypsy and her eccentric cousin Woodrow form a friendship when he comes to live with their grandparents next door. Throughout their sixth-grade year, the two support each other in discovering and dealing with how Gypsy's father died and why Woodrow's mother has simply walked away from her family. Exploring the territory "where two worlds touch" and what or who is beautiful, this also shows a child taking the first steps toward self-discovery. The author's Sweet Creek Holler *(Farrar Straus & Giroux, 1988)* shares the same setting.

Brian's Winter by Gary Paulsen. New York: Delacorte, 1996. (Dell)

In this sequel to Hatchet *(New York: Bradbury, 1987)*, Paulsen asks "What if Brian hadn't been rescued and had to survive the Canadian winter?" Illustrating the themes of man's struggle against the environment and himself, Paulsen's narrative is suspenseful and fast-paced. Also see The River *(New York: Doubleday, 1991)* and Brian's Return *(New York: Delacorte, 1999)* in which Paulsen continues to play with alternative sequels. Group with other survival stories or introduce Paulsen and his many novels to readers.

Children of the Dust Bowl: The True Story of the School at Weedpatch Camp by Jerry Stanley, illustrated with photographs. New York: Crown, 1992. (Crown)

Ostrasized by Californians as "dumb Okies," children arriving from the Oklahoma Dust Bowl were denied an education until one group created their own school. From two derelict buildings it grew into classrooms, a shop, science lab, and a full curriculum. Children raised money by selling produce and helped hammer the nails to build the school. The school still exists and is a tribute to hardship and prejudice overcome. Excellent nonfiction writing and compelling period photographs introduce children to a period they may know only through the movie "The Wizard of Oz." See Out of the Dust *(page 114b).*

Crocodiles, Camels and Dugout Canoes: Adventures Episodes by Bo Zaunders, illustrated by Roxie Munro. New York: Dutton, 1998. (   )

Eight short biographical essays invite armchair explorers to go along with Ernest Shackleton, Charles Waterton, Richard Burton, Mary Kingsley, and Antoine de Saint-Exupery among others. Fast-paced narrative, gripping opening sentences, and compelling stories make good discussion material as well as pithy models for writing. Pair with Linda Cummings and Pat Cummings' shorter sketches, Talking with Adventurers *(page 114b).*

Ella Enchanted by Gail Carson Levine. New York: HarperCollins, 1997. (HarperCollins)

Cursed by a fairy at her birth, Ella must obey any order given her but is protected by the gentle magic of her fairy godmother, the castle cook. When her conniving father marries a rich widow, the usual bad luck follows but Ella tries to overcome the obedience curse in as number of unique ways that help her mature. Strengths include a cleverly imagined kingdom of elves, ogres, and centaurs, comforts in the face of cruelty such as worthwhile friendships, reading, and perseverance, and frequent humor. More challenging than Wrede's Dealing with Dragons *(see page 107b)*, this story is another example of how fantasy leans on traditional literature.

Flying Solo by Ralph Fletcher. New York: Clarion, 1998. (   )

Rachel, who has chosen to be mute following the death of a classmate, joins other sixth graders in running the class when the substitute teacher doesn't show up. The results of this experiment are mixed but no one in the class remains unaffected. A quick read, lively and believable dialogue, journal entries that reveal or confirm emotions, and a cast of recognizable sixth graders make this book a good small-group discussion novel.

The Friend by Kazumi Yumoto, translated by Cathy Hirano. New York: Farrar Straus & Giroux, 1996. (Dell)

Kiyama and his two sixth-grader friends decide to spy on an old man to see if they can learn about death. But in befriending him, they learn a different lesson from the one they had expected. Readers may need support initially in keeping characters and details straight, but the picture of contemporary Japanese life, the candid way the author presents middle-school friendships and emotions, and her portrayal of unsentimental, intergenerational relationships make this book full of discussion possibilities.

Holes by Louis Sachar. New York: Farrar Straus & Giroux, 1998. (   )

A wonderfully complex plot rewards readers who pay attention. Nothing is wasted and all clues are relevant to solving the mystery. Why is Stanley Yelnats digging holes in the desert? Sentenced to "camp" for supposedly stealing a pair of tennis shoes, Stanley discovers that his family history is tied up in the story of the bandit Kissing Kate Barlow's lost treasure. Short chapters, a winning and easily delineated cast of characters, and Stanley's friendship with the at-first illiterate Zero lend appeal to middle-school readers.

Jip: His Story by Katherine Paterson. New York: Lodestar/Penguin, 1996. (Puffin)

Jip falls from a Vermont wagon in the 1850s, is thought to be a gypsy's child, and is raised in more-or-less servitude at the town poorhouse. There he befriends an elderly man who, because of his intermittent periods of madness, is kept in a cage. A widow and her children provide support for Jip's schooling and a subsequent lifesaving friendship with his teacher. Education, treatment of the poor and mentally ill, the Quakers' role in underground railway, the emergence of new roles for women, and a surprise ending give readers many things to discuss in this intense novel. See also her Lyddie *(New York: Dutton, 1991)*.

Leon's Story by Leon Walter Tillage, illustrated by Susan Roth. New York: Farrar Straus & Giroux, 1997. (   )

In this riveting memoir, this African American sharecropper's son in North Carolina tells anecdotes from his life from the late 1930s through the 1960s. This very personal account of Tillage's involvement with segregation and the beginnings of Civil Rights is like listening to an old friend talk about his life. Sure to provoke discussion, the book provides first-hand testimony that supports a study of this period.

Letters from a Slave Girl: The Story of Harriet Jacobs by Mary E. Lyons. New York: Macmillan, 1992. (Aladdin)

The fictionalized account of Harriet Jacobs, born a slave in North Carolina in 1813, presents a girl who runs away from her three-year-old mistress to hide in her grandmother's attic for seven years. Her observations, written in dialect based on Jacobs' own writing, give readers a remarkable picture of this historical period. See also Many Thousand Gone *(page 114b)*.

A Long Way from Chicago: A Novel in Stories by Richard Peck. New York: Dial, 1998. (   )

For seven years Joey and his sister spend summers with Grandma starting in 1929. Grandma runs things her way, is entirely unsentimental and indefatigable—a true original. Peck's timing and understatement create humor, his characters are memorable, and his pacing is sure. Each chapter stands on its own but the book as a whole reveals a boy's understanding as he grows from nine to sixteen.

Many Thousand Gone by Virginia Hamilton, illustrated by Leo and Diane Dillon. New York: Knopf, 1993. (Knopf)

   Short biographical vignettes of famous protesters of slavery, well-known figures such as Harriet Tubman, Frederick Douglass, Sojourner Truth, and Dred Scott, African Americans and others, trace part of the history of slavery in the United States. A good introduction to well-known and lesser-known activists in human rights for African Americans.

Mick Harte Was Here by Barbara Park. New York: Knopf, 1995. (Bullseye)

   Looking back, eighth-grader Phoebe Harte tells in this short novel (89 pages) about her seventh-grade brother's death, helmetless, in a bicycle crash. She fleshes out her funny brother's short life, the ways in which she and her grieving family cope, and the way Mick begins to be remembered in school and at home. Ralph Fletcher's Fig Pudding *(see page 108b) deals with the same event from the viewpoint of an eleven-year-old boy whose younger brother dies in the same manner. Discuss family support, death and grief, the value of humor, and the ways each author reveals character (actions, dialogue, thoughts, what others say, etc.).*

The Most Beautiful Roof in the World by Kathryn Lasky, photographs by Christopher Knight. San Diego: Gulliver, 1998. (Gulliver)

   Biologist Meg Lowman takes her two young sons to the cloud forest in Belize to observe insects and plants in the rain forest canopy. Lasky relates facts through narrative and the fresh photographs help readers capture the excitement this biologist feels as she studies this rich ecosystem. Pair with Jean Craighead George's easy novella One Day in the Tropical Rainforest *(New York: HarperCollins, 1990) or other books about this important and biologically diverse area.*

Out of the Dust by Karen Hesse. New York: Scholastic, 1997. (Scholastic)

   In spare free-verse narrative, Billie Jo tells her own story of life on the Dust Bowl prairie—her piano-playing hands scarred and gnarled by a fiery accident with kerosene and a wood stove, mother dead from the same accident, and her father withdrawn and unable to work. Billie Jo

must decide what to do with her life in the mid 1930s—as little by little, hope returns to her and to her father. Hesse's research into the times undergirds the story but readers must infer much and pay attention to the background Hesse reveals in each vignette. For pictures of the era see the biography Restless Spirit: The Life and Work of Dorothea Lange *by Elizabeth Partridge (New York: Viking, 1998), as well as Woody Guthrie's* This Land Is Your Land *(below), for more about the Dust Bowl era and its legacy.*

Painters of the Caves by Patricia Lauber. Washington, DC: National Geographic, 1998. (   )

   Lauber presents a panorama of prehistoric people in Europe by examining ancient artifacts and rock paintings. By blending facts and photographs with an enthusiastic text she conveys her love of her subject and interests readers in how scientists make sense of the past by using evidence to construct a plausible reality.

Talking with Adventurers by Pat and Linda Cummings, eds. Washington, DC: National Geographic, 1998. (   )

   Conversations with twelve scientists include answers to ten interview questions asked by children: How did you get started? What is the scariest thing you've encountered? (At least four said "snakes.") What was your biggest discovery? What expeditions are you currently involved in? Since scientists including Jane Goodall, Robert Ballard, and others are still contributing to the field, these short pieces inspire further research on the Internet and at the library.

This Land Is Your Land by Woody Guthrie, illustrated by Kathy Jakobsen. Boston: Little, Brown, 1998. (   )

   While most children know the first two verses, few know the last two, which are more typical of Guthrie's pointed "subversive" politics of the 1930s. Illustrations draw on icons from all fifty states, and frame the verses and chorus in a sort of postcard design typical of the Dust Bowl era. The more you know about Guthrie and the times, the more visual references you can discover. An appreciation by Pete Seeger, a three-page panorama of the country, and a short biography of Guthrie round out this majestic treatment of the song.

Time for Andrew: A Ghost Story by Mary Downing Hahn. New York: Clarion, 1994. (Avon)

In a riveting ghost story, Andrew from the present trades places with his namesake at the turn of the century so that the ancestor may recover from diphtheria for which there was no cure at this time. But the cured boy refuses to return to the past. Hahn's well-researched period detail plus a satisfying ending not typical of most time-slip fantasies makes this a good introduction to studies of the genre and the importance of its themes as well as to historical units.

Twelve Impossible Things Before Breakfast by Jane Yolen. San Diego: Harcourt, 1997. (   )

This collection of Yolen's short stories introduces readers to various types of fantasy: scary, fanciful, thoughtful, or gross. Some rework classics or put new twists on well-known folktales while others slip into the past or visit the future. The middle grades are a prime time to nurture fantasy readers with the breadth and depth of the genre. Introduce readers to Vivian Alcock, Peter Dickinson, T. A. Barron, Patricia Wrede, William Sleator, J. R. R. Tolkien, Lloyd Alexander, Brian Jacques, and Ursula LeGuin, for starters.

The Watsons Go to Birmingham—1963 by Christopher Paul Curtis. New York: Delacorte, 1995. (Dell)

Ten-year-old Kenny tells of his African American Michigan family: loving but exasperated parents, little sister, and edgy older brother Byron, "an official juvenile delinquent." Amidst the humorous and sometimes cruel incidents, readers see a working family determined to keep Byron from succumbing to the streets. A trip to Grandma's in Alabama to straighten Byron out culminates in Kenny's witnessing the events of the Birmingham church bombing, which killed four girls. Glorious writing and a winning main character make this a good discussion or read-aloud choice.

"What Do Fish Have to Do with Anything?" And Other Stories by Avi, illustrated by Tracy Mitchell. Cambridge, MA: Candlewick, 1997. (Candlewick)

Seven powerful short stories explore ways middle schoolers change in their ability to relate to each other and to adults. Several first-person narratives sound like ten- to fourteen-year olds everywhere and the issues they deal with—parents who don't understand you or listen, the disappearance of an angry older brother, what it means to be an adult, standing up for yourself, becoming a person—Young Adult universals. Use several stories as discussion possibilities and let readers choose among the others and react in response journals. See Carol Jenkins' The Allure of Authors (Heinemann, 1999) for an author study of Avi.

Wringer by Jerry Spinelli. New York: HarperCollins, 1997. (HarperCollins)

Each boy who reaches age ten gets to become a wringer in the annual town pigeon shoot—that is, he gets to wring the necks of still living but wounded pigeons. Palmer LaRue is nearly sick with the prospect as he struggles with his conscience, a pigeon that becomes his pet, his peers, and his relationship with a neighbor girl. Going against expectations and speaking up for beliefs are the themes of this spare story. Sure to elicit passionate discussion, the book shares some of the same allegorical features Spinelli explored in Maniac Magee (Boston: Little, Brown, 1990).

Grades 7–8

Books on the seventh- and eighth-grade list include more sophisticated literary patterns, more complex themes and characters, and ambiguous endings. Themes reflect the developmental tasks of this age level: finding out who you are, breaking away from family toward independence, living in a complex society, discovering how to work, and the nature of friendships. Topics include American history, biographies, autobiographies of authors, and a variety of genres including short stories. Layered fantasy is about larger ideas and is built upon certain conventions of the genre, which readers will want to talk about. As on the previous lists, many of the authors of books on this list have written extensively for middle-school readers and once readers are familiar with these authors, they tend to want to read more of their work. Teachers should introduce as many authors and their works as is possible. Middle school traditionally is the age at which children, because of school and extracurricular demands, often cease recreational reading and do not return until after adolescence—or perhaps ever. Reward recreational reading in the classroom (discussion time, extra credit, praise) as often as possible and encourage the reading habit over school holidays. Suggestions for seventh- and eighth-grade author studies include Patricia Beatty, Peter Dickinson, Paul Fleischman, Sid Fleischman, Russell Freedman, Virginia Hamilton, Jim Murphy, William Sleator, Gary Soto, and Lawrence Yep, plus those on the previous two grade lists.

The Abracadabra Kid: A Writer's Life by Sid Fleischman. New York: Greenwillow, 1996. (Beech Tree)

The author of light, tightly plotted, popular middle-grade fiction writes with the same wit and good pacing about his life growing up in California where he taught himself to be a magician, traveled in vaudeville, and became interested in little-known and curious facts as well as the vagaries of the English language. Group with other novel-length autobiographies, such as Richard Peck's Anonymously Yours *(New York: Morrow, 1995) or Ted Lewin's* I Was a Teenage Professional Wrestler *(New York: Orchard, 1993). Ask readers to pair novels by an author with the author's autobiography to see how writers make use of their own lives in their books. See "Being a Real Author or Illustrator," page 127b.*

Bat 6 by Virginia Euwer Wolff. New York: Scholastic, 1998. (   )

In 1949, sixth-grade girls from two rival Oregon farm towns meet to play for the softball championship. But when the deeply troubled Shazam, whose father was killed at Pearl Harbor, sees Aki, whose parents are newly returned after seven years in an internment camp, she violently attacks her. Themes of courage, responsibility, and peaceful reconciliation plus Wolff's unerring sense of place and period give readers much to discuss. Each chapter told by one of the girls from either team is initially distracting but contributes to the whole narrative's power. See also Michael O. Tunnell's nonfiction The Children of Topaz: The Story of a Japanese American Internment Camp Based on a Classroom Diary *(New York: Holiday, 1996), Eve Bunting's picture storybook,* So Far from the Sea *(see page 101b) and Jerry Stanley's nonfiction* I Am an American: A True Story of Japanese Internment *(New York: Crown, 1994).*

Biographies by Russell Freedman. New York: Clarion; Holiday. (   )

Freedman is a pioneer in the area of lively and fair biographies (as well as other nonfiction) mightily fortified with strong illustrations selected from contemporary documents and photographs. Choices range from the painter of the Prairie Indians, Karl Bodmer, told in An Indian Winter *(Holiday, 1992),* The Wright Brothers: How They Invented the Airplane *(Holiday, 1991),* Lincoln: A Photobiography *(Clarion, 1987) and* Eleanor Roosevelt: A Life of Discovery *(Clarion, 1993) to* Martha Graham: A Dancer's Life *(Clarion, 1998) and* Out of Darkness: The Story of Louis Braille *(see page 105b). Guide readers to appreciate Freedman's documentation and sources as well as his way with anecdote and word.*

Bull Run by Paul Fleischman, illustrated by David Frampton. New York: HarperCollins, 1993. (HarperCollins)

This innovative author introduces aspects of this famous opening Civil War battle in sixteen short first-person vignettes. People include a horse lover, a former slave, a sketch artist, a slave woman, a landowner, and other whose stories often fold into each other. Seeing an event from multiple perspectives lets readers consider how our expectations and our experiences color what we understand. See, too, his other historical and narratively experimental books such as Whirligig *(Henry Holt, 1998),* Dateline: Troy *(Cambridge, MA: Candlewick, 1996), and* Seedfolks *(see page 118b).*

Catherine, Called Birdy by Karen Cushman. New York: Clarion, 1994. (HarperCollins)

Fourteen-year-old Catherine keeps a journal of her observations, frustrations, and daily doings in England in the Middle Ages. Detail, humor, and nuanced implications make readers work to understand the deep well of research Cushman drew upon to write this story. Help readers notice what choices a writer makes when using the limited viewpoint of the journal writer. Pair with Cushman's The Midwife's Apprentice *(Clarion, 1995) or Frances Temple's* The Ramsay Scallop *(New York: Orchard, 1994) for a study of life in medieval times.*

Discovering the Ice Maiden: My Adventures on Ampato by Johan Reinhard. Washington, DC: National Geographic, 1998. (   )

This anthropologist uses a compelling narrative and excellent photographs to show readers first how and where the frozen girl from the Inca Empire was discovered in Southern Peru. Secondly, he shows how work in the laboratory revealed the wonder, excitement, and importance of this find. Fields of archaeology, anthropology, and forensics as well as scientific investigation are explored here, too. See also Discovering the Iceman *(page 108b).*

Dragon's Gate by Lawrence Yep. New York: Harper-Collins, 1993. (Harper)

Otter flees China to build the railroad on Golden Mountain, the Sierra Nevadas of California, only to find that he has been misinformed about life there. Disillusioned, he becomes involved in the first strike of Chinese railworkers in a little-known period in American history. The title has a literal as well as symbolic meaning for Otter.

The Ear, the Eye and the Arm by Nancy Farmer. New York: Orchard, 1994. (Puffin)

Three children escape from the family military compound to an adventurous survival in a future science fiction setting of Zimbabwe. Farmer's ability to mix survival and fantasy conventions with traditional African beliefs, legends, and geography, plus a collection of memorable characters and a fast-paced plot make this a book worth enjoying as well as studying.

An Extraordinary Life: The Story of a Monarch Butterfly by Laurence Pringle, paintings by Bob Marstall. New York: Orchard, 1997. (   )

From the acknowledgments through the excellent and chronologically organized text to the end matter that includes an index, further readings, directions for raising monarchs, and a call to action to save butterfly habitats, this book is a well-designed masterpiece. By following an individual butterfly, Pringle takes readers from a Massachusetts hayfield to a winter refuge in Mexico. Sidebars, captions, and plenty of information in Marstall's detailed paintings provide further information.

Full Steam Ahead: The Race to Build a Transcontinental Railroad by Rhoda Blumberg. Washington, DC: National Geographic, 1996. (   )

Using primary sources and documentation, the author focuses on the people and the times in the race to build a railroad across the country. Con men, Indian raids, the role of Chinese laborers, visionaries, and the details of moving men and materials are all covered in an extremely readable fashion. See also her other well-written nonfiction such as Commodore Perry in the Land of the Shogun *(New York: Lothrop, 1985) and* What's the Big Deal? Jefferson, Napoleon, and the Louisiana Purchase *(National Geographic, 1998).*

The Giver by Lois Lowry. Boston: Houghton Mifflin, 1993. (Laurel Leaf)

In a future utopia, children are given their occupational training beginning at age twelve. Jonas' occupation will be to receive the memories of this society's pleasures, annoyances (snowstorms), or horrors (wars). It is only when he discovers that euthanasia will kill his adopted baby brother that Jonas rebels. An enigmatic ending, powerful themes of choice and free will, the nature of dystopias, and a believable protagonist make this book eminently discussible.

Grab Hands and Run by Frances Temple. New York: Orchard, 1993. (HarperTrophy)

Felipe, his mother, and his five-year-old sister flee from a city in El Salvador after his father disappears. Memories of his father (who he learns has died), his grandparents in the country, and his dog pull him back even as they sustain the fleeing family. The book hints at the massacres and atrocities that have propelled so many Central Americans northward, and presents background for a discussion of why people immigrate. See also her Central America-set books, Tonight by Sea *(1995) and* A Taste of Salt *(1992; both Orchard).*

Habibi by Naomi Shihab Nye. New York: Simon & Schuster, 1997. (Aladdin)

Fourteen-year-old Arab American Liyana Aboud has moved from St. Louis back to her father's homeland, Palestine or Jerusalem. In short, poetic diary entries Liyana considers her feelings about displacement, an avalanche of new relatives, new customs, age-old enmity, and friendships across cultures when she meets Omer, a Jewish settler. Sections read aloud beautifully and Liyana's gradual steps to become herself in a more restrictive culture are worth noting.

Help Wanted: Short Stories About Young People Working edited by Anita Silvey. Boston: Little, Brown, 1997. (Little)

A solid and varied collection of a dozen stories presents teenagers working in such venues as fast food or community service and helps readers explore why people work, as well as satisfactions and frustrations of working.

I Am Wings: Poems About Love by Ralph Fletcher. New York: Bradbury, 1994. (Apple)

Singly, each free verse poem is about some aspect of adolescent love. But read as a narrative, the collection chronicles a relationship from first glance to final break-up from a boy's standpoint. Good inspiration for writers to try their own hands at unrhymed poems about feelings. For a two-sided view of love, see Naomi Shihab Nye and Paul B. Janeczko's collection titled I Feel a Little Jumpy Around You: A Book of Her Poems & His Poems Collected in Pairs. New York: Simon & Schuster, 1996.

Jayhawker by Patricia Beatty. New York: Morrow, 1991. (Mulberry)

Stealing slaves from neighboring Missouri to the free state of Kansas, Lije is part of events stemming from Lincoln's Emancipation Proclamation. Readers also meet other historical figures such as Jesse James, Jim Hickok, and John Brown. Useful as an introduction to the Civil War period, the book also is typical of Beatty's many other well-researched United States historical novels. (Series)

Join In: Multicultural Short Stories by Outstanding Writers for Young Adults, edited by Donald Gallo. New York: Doubleday, 1993. (Laurel Leaf)

This powerful collection reveals the troubles and challenges of teenagers from various cultures living in the United States: new traditions and values, a smothering grandmother, a beached whale, jobs, the offer of marriage, peers, and school. But many of the struggles are universal. See other collections edited by Gallo, as well.

My Life in Dog Years by Gary Paulsen. New York: Delacorte, 1998. (Random House)

Short stories introduce readers to Paulsen's many dog companions—some from his youth, others working dogs or sled dogs. His clever turn of phrase and his ability to personalize dogs without personification make his writing shine for animal lovers while arousing curiosity about Paulsen's life in general. Paulsen's many novels appeal to a wide range of readers making him an ideal author study for this age group and above.

Petty Crimes by Gary Soto. San Diego: Harcourt, 1998. (   )

Ten short stories portray reflective as well as self-centered Hispanic teenagers who learn valuable lessons as they cope, scam, jive, make friends, and try to get along with their families and neighbors. Rich language, Spanish phrases understood in context, and a sure sense of what it takes to grow up make these good discussion stories. See Soto's many other story collections, as well.

Seedfolks by Paul Fleishman. New York: HarperCollins, 1996. (HarperTrophy)

In a very short story in multiple viewpoints a disparate group of city dwellers turn a vacant lot into a garden and themselves into a neighborhood community. The advantage of this concise story is that it raises many discussion points of how we are to survive in an urban setting that seems increasingly more violent and dangerous. See, too, his Whirligigs (New York: Holt, 1998) for a well-designed coming-of-age novel about a boy whose penance for killing a girl in an automobile accident is to place four whirligigs in four "corners" of the country.

Soldier's Heart by Gary Paulsen. New York: Delacorte, 1998. (   )

Fifteen-year-old Charlie Goddard leaves Minnesota excited to fight in the Civil War and sure that he'll be home by fall. Paulsen's riveting narrative spares readers little and his use of detail— Charlie's positioning a rifle so a dying boy can shoot himself; the results of bartering with the enemy; the fear—make this a powerful read and a strong indictment of war. The title comes from the period's term for post-traumatic stress or shell shock from former generations. See also Bull Run, *page 116b.*

Step by Wicked Step by Anne Fine. Boston: Little, Brown, 1996. (Bantam)

    In an old mansion, five children on a class trip find a diary written by a boy who left home because he could not exist with his stepfather. Each in turn describes his or her own stepfamily existence and complicated family emotions, and feelings of loss or acceptance. The diary device is frequently found in middle-grade fiction. Discuss how diaries function for the reader of a book, for the character in the book, and how they focus our attention on what is not being said.

Tangerine by Edward Bloor. San Diego: Harcourt Brace, 1997. (Apple)

    A legally blind seventh grader with clear vision about himself navigates a move with his family to the disaster-ridden Tangerine, Florida, while his self-absorbed older brother destructs in an absorbing, fast-paced (if lengthy) plot with vividly drawn characters. Paul's determination in playing goalie on a soccer team and his brother's obsession with football make this extra appealing to boys.

Tomorrow When the War Began by John Marsden. Boston: Houghton Mifflin, 1995. (Dell)

    When Ellie and six of her high school students return from a campout in an Australian bush gorge, they discover that their town and perhaps country has been overrun by foreign invaders and form cunning and courageous plans to subvert the enemy. Marsden's respect for adolescent intelligence and gender equity plus his ability to tell a riveting story make this seven volume series shine but this title stands on its own mainly because of the characters' developing competencies, the emergence of individual strengths, and the believable relationships among the four girls and three boys. (Series)

What Jamie Saw by Carolyn Coman. New York: Front Street, 1995. (Puffin)

    Nine-year-old Jamie witnesses violence from his mother's boyfriend and the family flees to a rural trailer. He finally faces his fears with the help of his courageous mother. Powerful themes of the consequences of child abuse, parental love and determination, the nature of fear and bravery move readers in this short (125 pages), powerful, award winner. See Carol Jenkins (1999) for an excellent chapter on engaging middle-school readers with this novel.

While No One Was Watching by Jane Conly. New York: Holt, 1998 ( )

    Three children are left on their own while their father works on Maryland's eastern shore and an irresponsible aunt goes on a drinking binge. Eleven-year-old Earl tries to help feed the other two by reluctantly joining his cousin, a bike thief. Feisty Angela copes by inventing a rich imaginary life, and lonely Fat Frankie steals a pet rabbit that eventually proves the key to help for the three. Urban poverty and the network of neighborhood caring that supports the working poor play a part and contrast with the lives of the two suburban children who set out to reclaim the rabbit. A survival story that is both tough and hopeful. See also her Crazy Lady *(New York: HarperCollins, 1993).*

White Lilacs by Carolyn Meyer. San Diego: Harcourt, 1993. (Harcourt)

    Based on an incident in Texas in 1921, the story concerns teenager Rose Lee Jefferson as she witnesses the eviction of "coloreds" from their land because "whites" in the city wants to build a park. Concrete issues, a clear sense of time and place, and those who fight against racism are strengths of this book. See other related titles by Mildred Taylor, such as The Well: David's Story *(New York: Dial, 1995) and* Leon's Story *(see page 113b), as well as the sequel to this story told 75 years later,* Jubilee Journey *(Harcourt, 1998).*

Who Do You Think You Are? Stories of Friends and Enemies selected by Hazel Rochman and Darlene X. McCampbell. New York: Joy Street, 1993. (Little, Brown)

    Seventeen stories by a culturally diverse group of authors stretch the definition of a friend: one who lures you to new experiences or lets you down, one who transforms or exposes you. Be sure to begin with the preface to set up the discussions of the stories you choose.

Woman in the Wall by Patrice Kindl. Boston: Houghton Mifflin, 1997. (Puffin)

    An extremely shy child withdraws into herself and disappears behind the nooks and crannies of the family's rambling old house. Anna literally walls herself off in this almost-fantasy until she becomes a teenager, full of self-involvement, anxiety, physical changes, and isolation—that is, until she emerges. The symbolic and metaphoric nature of this book asks readers to consider the way the author has created belief in the very real theme of finding yourself. See also her curious and compelling Owl in Love *(Houghton Mifflin, 1993).*

More Poetry

No classroom should be without poetry but it is difficult to place a grade level on poetry. Therefore, we have chosen from among recent years some volumes of poetry to become familiar with. National Poetry Month is in April but don't hesitate to put poetry in your classroom all year long.

Antarctic Antics: A Book of Penguin Poems by Judy Sierra, illustrated by Jose Aruego and Ariane Dewey. San Diego: Gulliver, 1998. (   )

Baseball, Snakes, and Summer Squash by Donald Graves, illustrated by Paul Birling. Honesdale, PA: Boyds Mill Press, 1996. (Boyds Mill)

Cactus Poems by Frank Asch, illustrated by Ted Levin. San Diego: Harcourt Brace, 1998. (   )

Can I Help?, see page 79b.

Come on, Rain, see page 94b.

Cool Melons—Turn to Frogs: The Life and Poems of Issa by Matthew Golub, illustrated by Kazuko G. Stone. New York: Lee & Low, 1998. (   )

The Dream Keeper by Langston Hughes, illustrated by Brian Pinkney. New York: Knopf, 1994. (Knopf)

Echoes for the Eye: Poems to Celebrate Patterns in Nature by Barbara Esbensen, illustrated by Helen K. Davie. New York: HarperCollins, 1996. (   )

Getting Used to the Dark: 26 Poems by Susan Marie Swanson, illustrated by Peter Catalanatto. New York: Dorling Kindersley, 1997. (   )

The Goof Who Invented Homework: And Other School Poems by Kalli Dakos, illustrated by Denise Brunkus. New York: Dial, 1996.

Grass Sandals: The Travels of Basho by Dawnine Spivak, illustrated by Demi. New York: Atheneum, 1997. (   ).

Greetings, Sun, see page 90b.

Hurry, Hurry, Mary, Dear illustrated by Erik Blegvad. New York: McElderry, 1998.

I Am Wings: Poems About Love, see page 118b.

Insectlopedia by Douglas Florian, see page 99b.

It Begins with an A, see page 80b.

Maples in the Mist translated by Minfong Ho, illustrated by Jean and Mou-sien Tseng. New York: Lothrop, 1996. (   ).

Mud, see page 90b.

My Very First Mother Goose, see page 81b.

Navajo: Visions and Voices Across the Mesa by Shonto Begay. New York: Scholastic, 1995. (Scholastic)

Old Elm Speaks: Tree Poems by Kristine O'Connell George, illustrated by Kate Kiesler. Boston: Houghton Mifflin, 1998. (   ).

Ordinary Things: Poems from a Walk in Early Spring by Ralph Fletcher, illustrated by Walter Lyon Krudop. New York: Atheneum, 1997. (   )

Poetry selected by Lee Bennett Hopkins, see page 96b.

Popcorn, see page 109b.

Riddle-Lightful: Oodles of Little Riddle Poems by J. Patrick Leurs. New York: Knopf, 1998. (   ).

Sawgrass Poems: A View of the Everglades by Frank Ash, San Diego: Harcourt Brace, 1996. (   ).

Secret Places selected by Charlotte S. Huck, illustrated by Lindsay George. New York: Greenwillow, 1993. (   ).

The Sky Is Always in the Sky by Karla Kuskin, illustrated by Isabelle Dervaux. New York: HarperCollins, 1998. (   ).

A Song of Colors by Judy Hindley, illustrated by Mike Bostock. Cambridge: Candlewick, 1998. (   ).

Ten-Second Rainshowers: Poems by Young People compiled by Sandford Lyne, illustrated by Virginia Halstead. New York: Simon & Schuster, 1996. (   )

That Secret Diamond: Baseball Poems by Paul Janeczko, illustrated by Carol Katchen. New York: Atheneum, 1998. (   ).

This Big Sky by Pat Mora. New York: Scholastic, 1998. (Scholastic)

This Land Is Your Land, see page 114b.

This Same Sky by Naomi Shihab Nye. New York: Four Winds, 1992. (Aladdin)

Supplemental Literature

Planning an Author Study

The following author studies are suggestions for teachers as they plan curriculum. The bare bones framework implies that teachers have read widely in the author's work and have weighted and grouped the books for classroom ideas. While it is a good idea to have on hand as many of the author's books as possible, the teacher may concentrate the attention of the whole class on only several in a particular category. Some books may make good guided reading choices for small groups while individuals become experts on other titles and share their discoveries with the class in discussion. (See Carol Jenkins' well-organized discussion of preparing author studies in *The Allure of Authors*, 1999.)

The purpose of any author study should be close observation of some part of the author's work so that readers may enjoy, understand, and generalize about the author's typical subject matter, patterns, and style in the art of writing, typical themes, types of characters, usual settings, etc. In each of the studies that follow, we have proposed an anchor book chosen to reveal in class discussion some important information about the kind of books each author writes. Supplementary titles compare well with the core book, either because they follow similar themes and patterns, or because they extend and enrich the patterns that the core book follows. By constructing curriculum this way, teachers empower readers to understand a small piece of the literary world and to know one creator very well.

We have pointed the way to background reading for the teacher in "Author Insights." However, there are many sources for author information and the librarian should be the central resource for this. Several reliable sources for author information referred to in this section are listed in "Resources That Support Author/Illustrator Study" on page 17b. Many authors and illustrators have their own Web sites or maintain one at their publishers' Web sites. Check "Children's Literature Web Guide," page 21b, for sources of up-to-date information. Be sure to write to publishers in the publicity or school and library marketing departments for author biographical handouts, as well.

Author/Illustrator Study: Kevin Henkes (Grades K–3)

About the Author
Kevin Henkes (born in 1960) has written picture storybooks for primary children as well as novels for middle-grade readers. He has also illustrated the writings of other authors. This study concentrates on his picture books about the spunky mouse character Lilly and her friends in school or neighborhood settings. Henkes' stories are true picture books—a seamless blend of pictures and text—and his secure and comforting universe populated with real emotions make his books perfect for young children. Patterns in Henkes' work include mice characters, family and school dilemmas and settings, cartoonish artwork with small print asides, a child who acts to solve his own problems but with adult assistance, use of favorite words such as "wow," and lists of closely observed details.

Author Insight
Cummings (1995), page 46–51.

Mandel, Ellen. 1996. "The Books of Kevin Henkes," *Book Links* (July): 21–23.

Silvey (1995), page 303–304.

Anchor Book
Lilly's Purple Plastic Purse. New York: Greenwillow, 1996. (Mulberry)

> *Lilly loves school and her teacher. Exuberantly, she brings movie star glasses, a necklace, and a purse that plays music to school and can't resist showing it around during story time. Her teacher confiscates everything and Lilly writes him a nasty note. On the way home, Lilly once again examines her prizes and discovers a wonderful note from Mr. Slinger that makes her feel guilty and awful until she thinks of a way to make everything all right.*

Read and discuss the story, letting children notice pictures and comment on Lilly's actions and their consequences. The following questions lead children deeper into Henkes' work.

1. What kind of person is Lilly? How do you know? Help children see how Lilly's actions reveal her character. Encourage lively adjectives, such as *adventurous* and *angry*, above the bland *nice* and *good*.

2. What does she like about school? This makes a good numbered vertical list. Leave room for a parallel list of what children in the class like about their

school. Note Lilly likes sights, smells, foods, and settings, as well as things, and encourage children to think widely and personally.

3. Is Mr. Slinger a good teacher? Let children sort out his quirks and unique features as well as the fairness of his treatment of Lilly.

4. What do you notice about the pictures? Help children notice the way Henkes uses little picture sequences to reveal changing emotion and build to a climax, for instance, when Lilly is cross with the teacher. Note the many symbols (music notes for happiness, puffs of smoke for action, etc.), the little print for comments, how some pictures are framed and the frame is broken when emotions run high, and many other Henkes conventions.

5. Notice what the mouse classroom is studying and compare it to your curriculum. Mr. Slinger values writing. As a reflection, set up a "Lightbulb Lab— Where Great Ideas Are Born" and let children write like Lilly's class does.

Supplementary Books
Julius, The Baby of the World (1990); *Chester's Way* (1988); and *Chrysanthemum* (1991). All New York: Greenwillow (Mulberry).

> *The two earlier stories work well after the core selection to further round out Lilly's character. In* Julius, *she is jealous of her new brother until a cousin oversteps Lilly's limits; in* Chester's Way, *Lilly arrives on the scene of a two-person friendship and changes it forever—until a fourth friend arrives. Ask children to see parallels and patterns over the three books.* Chrysanthemum *is another school story without Lilly. Share this to remind readers that Henkes also writes other books but that the patterns are similar. Note the background map in the mouse class—the shape of Wisconsin, Henkes' home state.*

> *At the conclusion of this study, be sure to make a chart of "What we notice about Kevin Henkes' books" as the story and illustrative patterns are so strong. If you have paused for author information, make a chart or Web of "What we know about Kevin Henkes," as well.*

Author Study: Eve Bunting (Grades 3–6)

About the Author
Eve Bunting (born in 1928) is a prolific author of picture books, middle-grade novels, and young adult novels. This study concentrates on her picture storybooks that deal with complex social issues. Bunting believes that the truth will not hurt children but will help them ask better questions and begin to form better answers to unfair situations. Patterns to notice in Bunting's stories include a child at the center of an emotion-packed situation, a measure of hope as people make decisions and continue to behave honorably, the tacit assumption that the adult world is trying to help, and the inclusion of a culturally diverse characters facing human dilemmas.

While many of Bunting's books would appeal to early elementary-aged children, we have chosen her more complex picture storybooks that raise issues children of third grade through middle school would discuss. In rare instances, a mature second-grade class might work with this author study, as well.

Author Insight
Silvey, page 101–102.

Bunting, Eve. 1995. *Once upon a Time.* Katonah, NY: Richard C. Owen.

Phinney, Margaret Yatsevitch. 1997. "Eve Bunting: A 'Wonderful Happenstance'." *The New Advocate* (Summer): 10, 3.

Anchor Book
Smoky Night, illustrated by David Diaz. San Diego: Harcourt Brace, 1994. (Harcourt)

> *Inspired to write about people caught in the Los Angeles riots, Eve Bunting presents Daniel, his mother, and their cat Jasmine watching from their apartment window as looters in the street below race through damaged stores. When fire threatens their building, Daniel and his mother, along with others, make their way to a public shelter but in the chaos, Jasmine can't be found. Daniel's mother has indicated prior to this that she does not shop at Mrs. Kim's grocery because it is "better to buy from our own people." (In David Diaz's bold illustrations, Daniel's and his mother's race is not defined.) But when a kindly fireman brings back not only Jasmine but Mrs. Kim's cat as well, and the two formerly warring cats are friends, Daniel suggests that when you know someone, you can like them.*

> *David Diaz won the Caldecott award for his collage illustrations. (See the July/August 1995 issue of* Horn Book *for his acceptance speech and insight into his artwork.)*

1. Intermediate-aged children (grades 3–5) have some ideas of riots and unrest. If you do not want to "scoop" the book's content, begin by asking readers to talk about the cover, the endpapers, and title page. Then read the dedication and ask what readers predict from this additional information. Then discuss what a riot is so that you do not have to stop reading when the term is introduced.

2. Why is Daniel scared? This allows readers to discuss the very real incidents, to notice that unpredictable happenings can be terrifying, and to see Daniel reacting in honest ways.

3. Who helps? And how do they help? The reassurance amidst this chaos is that so many people are caring for each other—his mother who keeps Daniel in bed against the wall with her, the man who warns them about the hot railings, and the people at the shelter all reach out. It is important for children to know that even in the roughest times, there are some adults who can and will help. But Daniel helps, too, as it is his observation that moves to heal the neighborhood rift.

4. Look closely at the photographed backgrounds. What has Diaz included and why does he chose those materials for his collage? How do the colors of the paintings change as the story goes along? By changing color, what does Diaz indicate? Help children notice how our viewpoint of the action is far away or close-up, depending on the events and emotion the story conveys.

5. While it is often difficult for young readers to put a theme into words, intermediate readers can ask themselves what Bunting hoped readers would think about after finishing this book.

6. You might share the story with children that, when this book came out, some librarians refused to put it on the shelves of the elementary school because they thought it was not suitable for children. (See Routman 1996, page 148–151.) Ask them what they think about the suitability of this book.

Supplementary Books

Bunting has written movingly about many contemporary social issues. While each book stands on its own, older elementary age children may investigate the background against which each book is set and decide whether there is anything society needs to do about these issues. *Your Move* (see page 106b) presents a boy with a choice to join a street gang or be a role model for a younger brother. *The Blue and Gray*, illustrated by Ned Bittinger (New York: Scholastic, 1996) is set on an old Civil War battlefield among new housing developments and asks readers to consider how far black and white friendships have come.

Earlier books all illustrated by Ronald Himler (New York: Clarion) focus on different social issues: Mexican immigrant labor in *A Day's Work* (1994), homeless people sleeping in public places in *Fly Away Home* (1991), the Vietnam War's legacy in *The Wall* (1990). See also *So Far from the Sea* (1998) (see page 101b).

At the end of this study, be sure to create a chart of generalizations, "Things We Notice about Eve Bunting's Books." Preceding this might be constructing a comparison chart with titles going down the left hand side, and categories across the top to be filled in beneath, grid style. Useful categories would include title, illustrator, setting, something about the child in the book, the problem, the helping adults, possible solutions, big idea or theme, and a catch-all category of "interesting observations."

Author Study: Jean Craighead George (Grades 4–8)

About the Author

Jean Craighead George (born in 1919) always includes accurately observed natural science in her many books and series. Her concern for the interrelatedness of all living things, her awareness of ecological systems, and her well-researched inclusion of animal facts make her popular with children who want the truth about the environment. George's One Day in the... series present a child in a different ecosystem who solves a small problem while observing all that goes on in that area: rain forest, desert, woodland, prairie, or tundra. Other series books, subtitled *An Ecological Mystery*, are novels that stand on their own merits but are related in that a middle-school-aged child must make important decisions about preservation of some part of the wild. Many other books by George, in the form of nonfiction, picture storybooks, and the "moon" series that traces twelve regions in the Native American landscape over twelve months' time, make wonderful use of closely observed nature.

George lives in Chappaqua, New York, and estimates that at some time during their childhood times, the family had raised, helped, and released some 173 wild pets. Therefore, the anchor book begins the study and the supplementary books intend that the reader read other books to see how George uses her animal knowledge in real life to inform her fiction.

Author Insight
Silvey, 268–269.

George, Twig. 1996. "Writing Eco-Mysteries." In *Beyond the Science Kit: Inquiry in Action*, edited by Wendy Saul and Jeannie Reardon, pages 144–166.

George, Jean Craighead. 1982. *Journey Inward*. New York: Dutton. (Adult content and tone)

Before beginning the anchor book, ask readers to generate a list of books by Jean Craighead George that someone in the class has read. Put tally marks or a child's name by the title so that you can see where your readers are. As someone reads another book by George, use a different color so that you can see "before" and "after" reading, a good way to measure the impact of this unit on the reading choices of your class and publicly acknowledge individual reading efforts.

Start with one book in common, the anchor book. Then let children choose another George title from a limited shelf, assign sets of a title to small groups, or offer free choice (any George book) to readers. Her books divide loosely into "One Day in the..." series, "Moon" series, "Eco-Mysteries" series, novels, the "Julie" trilogy, straight nonfiction, and informational picture storybooks. George's vast work includes some forty books for children in print and all make use of accurate science, closely observed nature, a respect for an animal in its natural habitat, and a passion for responsible stewardship. Most put a child at the center, an occasional knowledgeable adult at the edge, descriptive passages detailing biodiversity or animal behavior, and a positive outcome.

Anchor Book
The Tarantula in My Purse and 172 Other Wild Pets, with illustrations by Jean Craighead George. New York: HarperCollins, 1996. (HarperCollins)

Jean George's family brought home a large assortment of wild pets—several crows, skunk, box turtles, kestrels, a goose and duck who were nearly arrested, a raccoon, and owls were among them. It was the closely observed habits of these animals that intrigued George to learn more. For instance, several stories about crows including one who used a tin plate to slide down the children's slide, are included in this book. The same anecdotes appear in her novel, The Cry of the Crow *(HarperCollins, 1980).*

1. The first chapter sets the scene. How did George come to be a nature observer? A writer? Discuss how her life and interests prepared her for an occupation later.

2. In each succeeding chapter, a pet is introduced and its relationship with the family is described. You may wish to record the animal names since some are quite apt (a crow named Bituminous) while others come from the Latin names for the species (a skunk named Meph).

3. If George wrote a short nonfiction paragraph about each animal, she'd have a different book. Small groups might pull out this nonfiction information and augment it by reading other sources. They might survey the library and Internet sources, for instance, on information about crows.

4. Note George's watercolor illustrations and invite children to render an animal chosen from a photograph or a pet modeled from real life.

5. Keep track of George's attitude toward wild animals as pets. She is squarely on the side of nature and often tells the reader how she feels about pets, about exploitation, about habitat changes, and about returning wild pets to the woods.

Supplementary Books
When the class has read a variety of other books, pull the content together by grouping readers who have read similar books in a series (see introductory paragraph). Ask them to talk within the group about their books. Then seek generalizations about content, characters, themes, values, settings, and so forth.

Some series make elegant charts. For instance, compare the "One Day in the..." series using the following categories. Give each book group a nine-box strip of paper (1" × 9") marked off evenly. (Note that the categories themselves should be lightly written across the box top but that the entries in the box should be bold. Titles will be aligned one under the other at the end. Categories below may then appear on their own strip in bold above the assembled chart.)

- Book Title and Year Published

- Setting (encourage detail: global location, descriptive words)

- Kinds of Animals Found (may be useful to categorize as insects, reptiles, birds, etc.)

- Names of Plants Found (may be useful to categorize as grasses, trees, flowering plants, etc.)

- Main Character (age, physical description, attitude)

- The Problem

- What Action/Outcome to Solve Problem

- Theme(s)

- Five Index Words with the Most Entries

When each group completes its chart, align them one under the other and see what patterns you can discover by reading down. This is an excellent activity to help children return to the book for specifics while working on the chart. Later, when the children compare their work to that of others, they are more easily able to build generalizations such as:

- "All of the books in this series are about..."

- "An index shows where in the book a topic is covered. In these books, topics with the most entries are ... because..."

- "All of the main characters are about age... and they are curious, determined, concerned..."

- "When Jean Craighead George writes a book in this series, she wants us to think about..."

Other series may be charted in this way as well. Examine the books for patterns and suggest categories to groups but let them develop their own as the discussion progresses. George's characters often face consequences of their well-intentioned actions and discover painful truths about themselves and life in general. Be sure to investigate characters and their thoughts, actions, and changes.

Additional activities include:

1. Note and read aloud some of George's evocative descriptions of habitat. Try describing some local habitat beautifully.

2. On a map of the Americas, locate each of George's books that someone in class has read. Add to the map as readers discover other book settings. What do you notice about George's choice of setting?

3. Discover more about George in biographical or autobiographical books. View a video of her and make connections among her books and between her books and her life. Chart your findings.

4. Many of George's books are organized chronologically, or at least as months pass. Take some part of your local environment and keep track of it on a regular basis. What changes? What endures? Write about the class discoveries as "Nine months in the life of..." or develop a character and put him or her into this environment.

5. Generate a list of further research possibilities and investigate a topic relevant to your school curriculum. If a report is called for, use some device that George has used to interest readers in the content (chronological organization, a first-person observer, lyrical prose, evocative description of setting, etc.).

Books That Encourage Children to Write

The following categories suggest ways teachers can group books to help children notice aspects of text that might help or inspire them in their own writing. Some books are models, of either style, form, or content. Others suggest the difficulties and rewards of being a writer. Still others ask readers to notice what the author did and see if this idea can be recast in another way. This list re-sorts many books mentioned previously while adding a few titles too good to be missed but not mentioned elsewhere in these lists. For a more thorough treatment of the topic, check *Book Links* magazine (Chicago: American Library Association) subject indices, *Subject Guide to Books in Print* (New York: Bowker), and other resources that group books by content and theme. Also, check annotations of the books referred to as many other related titles are often "tucked into" an annotated selection.

Alphabet Books

Numerous alphabet books suggest ways for children to organize writing. Examples include topically themed ones for older children, such as *G Is for Googol: A*

Math Alphabet Book by David M. Schwartz, illustrated by Marissa Moss (San Francisco: Tricycle Press, 1998) or a look at Japanese culture in *A to Zen* by Ruth Wells, illustrated by Yoshi (New York: Simon & Schuster, 1992). Nikki Grimes' *C Is for City*, illustrated by Pat Cummings (New York: Lothrop, 1995) plays with alliteration to create a simple alphabetic narrative. Examine other ABC books to discover whether they teach the alphabet to preschoolers or operate on a more challenging plane. Themed alphabet books make good content reviews for older elementary students.

ABC I Like Me! by Nancy Carlson. New York: Viking, 1997. (Puffin)

Alice and Aldo by Alison Lester. Boston: Houghton Mifflin, 1998. (　　)

The Disappearing Alphabet by Richard Wilbur, illustrated by David Diaz. San Diego: Harcourt, 1998. (　　)

The Hullabaloo ABC by Beverly Cleary. New York: Morrow, 1998. (　　)

It Begins with an A, see page 80b.

Miss Bindergarten Gets Ready for Kindergarten, see page 80b.

Navajo ABC: A Diné Alphabet Book by Luci Tapahonso, illustrated by Eleanor Schick. Boston: Little, Brown, 1995. (Aladdin)

Tomorrow's Alphabet by George Shannon. New York: Greenwillow, 1996. (Mulberry)

V for Vanishing: An Alphabet of Endangered Animals by Patricia Mullins. New York: HarperCollins, 1993. (HarperTrophy)

The Wacky Wedding by Pamela Edwards, illustrated by Henry Cole. New York: Hyperion, 1999. (　　)

Being a Writer

Picture storybooks and novels often feature someone who struggles with writing. (See the section on Diaries and Journals in which young authors write to work through some problematic time.) What to write, for what audience, organization, and revision are problems all writers face. The following books each deal specifically with some aspect of the writerly craft.

Arthur Writes a Story by Marc Brown. Boston: Little, Brown, 1996. (Little, Brown)

Family Tree, see page 108b.

Nothing Ever Happens on 90th Street by Roni Schotter, illustrated by Krysten Brooker. New York: Orchard, 1997. (Orchard)

What Do Authors Do? by Eileen Christelow. New York: Clarion, 1995. (Clarion)

Being a Real Author or Illustrator

Many authors and illustrators have written eloquently about their lives. This small listing doesn't begin to reflect the many authors who have explored their roots and resources but it is a start.

The Abracadabra Kid, see page 116b.

Author, A True Story by Helen Lester. Boston: Houghton Mifflin, 1997. (　　)

But I'll Be Back Again by Cynthia Rylant. New York: Orchard, 1989. (Beech Tree)

A Caldecott Celebration by Leonard Marcus. New York: Walker, 1998. (　　)

The Invisible Thread by Yoshiko Uchida. New York: Beech Tree, 1995. (Beech Tree)

It Came from Ohio: My Life as a Writer by R. L. Stine. New York: Scholastic, 1997. (Apple)

Knots on My Yo-Yo String: The Autobiography of a Kid by Jerry Spinelli. New York: Knopf, 1998. (Knopf)

Meet the Author series. Katonah, NY: Richard C. Owen.

On the Bus with Joanna Cole, see page 105b.

Talking with Artists, Vols 1–3, by Pat Cummings. Various publishers. (　　)

The Tarantula in My Purse, see page 106b.

Three: An Emberly Family Sketchbook by Ed, Rebecca, and Michael Emberly. Boston: Little, Brown, 1998. (　　)

The World of William Joyce Scrapbook by William Joyce. New York: HarperCollins, 1994. (HarperCollins)

Diaries and Journals

A travel journal organizes information in a chronological order as someone journeys. Some nonfiction ones like *Amazon Diary* by Mark Grenberg and Hudson Talbott (New York: Putnam, 1996) convey information about a particular area or country, while fictional others such as *Amelia Hits the Road* by Marisa Moss (Berkeley, CA: Tricycle, 1997) chronicle a person's changes as he or she passes through time and place.

Amelia's Notebook by Marisa Moss. Berkeley, CA: Tricycle, 1995. (Tricycle) (Pleasant Company)

Anni's Diary of France by Anni Axworthy. Dallas, TX: Whispering Coyote, 1994. (   )

The Diary of Latoya Hunter: My First Year in Junior High by Latoya Hunter. New York: Crown, 1992. (Crown)

Learning to Swim in Swaziland by Nila K. Leigh. New York: Scholastic, 1993. (Scholastic)

Mississippi Mud: Three Prairie Journals by Ann Turner, illustrated by Robert J. Blake. New York: HarperCollins, 1997. (   )

The Private Notebooks of Katie Roberts, Age 11 by Amy Hest. Cambridge, MA: Candlewick, 1995. (Candlewick)

Rachel's Journal: The Story of a Pioneer Girl by Marisa Moss. San Diego: Harcourt Brace, 1998. (   )

Speaking of Journals: Children's Book Writers Talk About Their Diaries, Notebooks, and Sketchbooks by Paula W. Graham. Honesdale, PA: Boyds Mills Press, 1999. (Boyds Mills)

Step by Wicked Step, see page 119b.

The Top Secret Journal of Fiona Claire Jardin by Robin Cruise. San Diego: Harcourt Brace, 1998. (   )

Wish You Were Here by Kathleen Krull, illustrated by Amy Schwartz. New York: Doubleday, 1997. (   )

Family Stories/Memoirs

Many books are based on some modest but powerfully shaped vignette from family history. Kathryn Lasky's *Marven of the Great North Woods*, glowingly illustrated by Kevin Hawkes (San Diego: Harcourt, 1997), tells how her father Marven was sent at age ten North from Duluth to be a bookkeeper in a lumber camp to avoid the influenza outbreaks of 1918. Such books as Patricia Polacco's many titles, including *Pink and Say* (see page 108b) let children see that an incident may be framed as just that—not a whole life story but a part of it well and completely told. Encourage children to tell a small story very well, rather than a whole life blandly.

Cherry Pies and Lullabies, see page 93b.

Family Tree, see page 108b.

Gettin' Through Thursday, see page 104b.

I Have Heard of a Land, see page 99b.

In My Family/En mi familia, see page 99b.

A Long Way from Chicago, see page 113b.

Keepers, see page 95b.

Marianthe's Story, see page 95b.

My Rotten Red-Headed Older Brother, see page 95b.

Pete's a Pizza by William Steig. New York: HarperCollins, 1998. (   )

The Piano Man by Debbi Chocolate. New York: Walker, 1998. (   )

Potato, see page 96b.

Seven Brave Women by Betsy Hearne, illustrated by Bethanne Anderson. New York: Greenwillow, 1997. (   )

So Far from the Sea, see page 101b.

The Well: David's Story by Mildred Taylor. New York: Dial, 1995. (   )

When I Was Your Age: Original Stories About Growing Up, edited by Amy Ehrlich. Cambridge, MA: Candlewick, 1996; Volume II, 1999. (   )

When Jesse Came Across the Sea, see page 102b.

Fooling with Folktales

Folktale variations proliferate in children's books. Cinderella variants alone would fill a page. Among the best are such recent titles as Tony Johnston's regional *Bigfoot Cinderrrrrella* (New York: Putnam, 1998), Frances Minters' urban rap *Cinder-Elly*, illustrated by Brian Karas (Puffin, 1997), and Deborah Nourse Lattimore's witch reworking, *Cinderhazel* (New York: Blue Sky Press, 1997). Select a group of variants and decide what has been changed: characters, setting, time frame ("what happened next"), or point of view ("what really happened as told by___"). Older children or a class of children are entirely capable of writing their own versions of another tale if given some models for starters. Books on this list are variants or combinations of commonly known traditional tales but there are many others and the genre is so popular that there are new titles published each year. Ask your librarian. For developing a folk- and fairy tale unit, see *Invitations* (pages 170b–185b) for a unit plan.

Cinder Edna by Ellen Jackson, illustrated by Kevin O'Malley. New York: Lothrop, 1994. (Lothrop)

Dealing with Dragons, see page 107b.

Dinorella: A Prehistoric Fairy Tale by Pamela Edwards, illustrated by Henry Cole. New York: Hyperion, 1997. (   )

Ella Enchanted, see page 112b.

Fanny's Dream by Caralyn Buehner, illustrated by Mark Buehner. New York: Dial, 1996. (   )

The Giant Carrot, see page 89b.

The Gingerbread Boy, see page 90b.

A Handful of Beans, see page 98b.

Piggie Pie, see page 96b.

The Prince of the Pond, see page 110b.

The Prog Frince: A Mixed-Up Tale by C. Drew Lamm, illustrated by Barbara McClintock. New York: Orchard, 1999. (   )

Rapunzel: A Happenin' Rap by David Vozar, illustrated by Betsy Lewin. New York Doubleday, 1998. (   )

Rumpelstiltskin's Daughter by Diane Stanley. New York: Morrow, 1997. (   )

The Teeny Tiny Teacher, see page 91b.

Three Little Pigs, see page 91b.

Wolf!, see page 102b.

Letters

An increasing number of stories are told in a series of letters. Stories such as Mary Lyons' *Letters from a Slave Girl* (see page 117b) let the reader in on the thoughts of a character as the plot unwinds. Others such as Michelle Cartlidge's Mouse Letter series (New York: Dutton, 1993) invite children to create their own letters. A third category deals with the joys, dilemmas, or consequences of letter-writing.

Dear Peter Rabbit (1994) and *Yours Truly, Goldilocks* (1998) by Alma Flor Ada, illustrated by Leslie Tryon. New York: Atheneum. (Aladdin)

Dear Annie by Judith Caseley. New York: Greenwillow, 1991. (Mulberry)

Dear Bear by Joanna Harrison. Minneapolis: Carolrhoda, 1994. (Lerner)

Dear Levi, see page 103b.

Don't Forget to Write by Martina Selway. Nashville: Ideals, 1992. (Ideals)

The Gardener, see page 98b.

Grace's Letter to Lincoln, see page 94b.

The Long, Long Letter by Elizabeth Spurr, illustrated by David Catrow. New York: Hyperion, 1996. (Disney)

The Silver Balloon, see page 101b.

Memories of My Youth

In the voice of a young child, the books on this list offer a backward look to a younger time, perhaps of two or three years ago, or even last year. These stories are often especially humorous to one as old or older than the remembering child. Help writers frame their recollections with phrases such as "I used to/But now I" structures or help them select categories such as changes in their favorite foods, toys, spare time activities, bedtimes, and so forth.

Tell Me Again About the Night I Was Born by Jamie Lee Curtis. New York: HarperCollins, 1996. (HarperCollins)

When I Was Little by Toyomi Igus, Illustrated by Higgins Bond. Orange, NJ: Just Us Books, 1992. (Just Us)

When I Was Little: A Four-Year-Old's Memoir of Her Youth by Jamie Lee Curtis, illustrated by Laura Cornell. New York: HarperCollins, 1993. (HarperCollins)

When I Was Five by Arthur Howard. San Diego: Harcourt, 1997. (Voyager)

Models

Books that have a powerful format or strong organizational structure practically beg to be played with by children. The following books invite readers or classes to create an alternative version or to play with words in the manner of the author. (See "Popular Press Sayings," 131b).

The Best Thing About a Puppy by Judy Hindley. Cambridge, MA: Candlewick, 1998. (   )

The Character in the Book by Kathe Zemach. New York: HarperCollins, 1998. (   )

Feast for 10, see page 79b.

Fun, No Fun by James Stevenson. New York: Greenwillow, 1994. (   )

If by Sarah Perry. Malibu, CA: J. Paul Getty Museum and Venice, CA: Children's Library Press, 1995. (   )

Meanwhile... by Jules Feiffer. New York: HarperCollins, 1997. (HarperCollins)

Meet My Staff by Patricia Marx, illustrated by Roz Chast. New York: HarperCollins, 1998. (   )

Squids Will Be Squids: Fresh Morals/Beastly Fables by Jon Sciezska and Lane Smith. New York: Viking, 1998. (   )

Today I Feel Silly & Other Moods That Make My Day by Jamie Lee Curtis, illustrated by Laura Cornell. New York: HarperCollins, 1998. (   )

The Top Secret Knowledge of Grown-Ups by David Wisnieski. New York: Morrow, 1998. (   )

Things That Are Most in the World by Judi Barrett. New York: Atheneum, 1998. (   )

Willy the Dreamer by Anthony Browne. Cambridge, MA: Candlewick, 1998. (   )

Nonfiction with Interesting Formats

Nonfiction formats make use of many techniques: sidebars, pictures with captions, labeled drawings, cross sections, time lines, and other visual conventions. In addition, many life cycle books and process books organize text very specifically from parts to whole. The books on this list barely scratch the surface of models children could use in their own informational writing. Be sure to notice how nonfiction text and pictures convey information along with the more obvious noting of what the book conveys. See also page 32b for annotations on good books with interesting formats.

All About... series by Jim Arnosky, see page 93b.

Bugs and Other Insects, see page 98b.

Chirping Crickets, see page 93b.

Duke Ellington, see page 108b.

The Life and Times of the Peanut, see page 109b.

Penguins!, see page 95b.

Snowflake Bentley, see page 106b.

So Many Circles, So Many Squares, see page 81b.

Volcanoes and Other Natural Disasters, see page 101b.

Wild Weather, see page 102b.

Word Play

Some books invite readers to try a hand at making their own versions of word play. Pamela Edwards Duncan creates a "D-lightful tale" about a dazzling dinosaur jewel in *Dinorella: A Prehistoric Fairy Tale*, illustrated by Henry Cole (New York: Hyperion, 1997). Children can work in small groups to tell their own letter-dominated stories as they exercise their alliterative skills with dictionaries and vocabulary. Yet others are so strongly patterned that children can reconstitute the form with their own stories if teachers help them extract the form's markers.

Add It, Dip It, Fix It: A Book of Verbs by R. M. Schneider. Boston: Houghton Mifflin, 1995. (   )

Bug Off! by Cathi Hepworth. New York: Putnam, 1998. (   )

Donovan's Word Jar by Monalisa DeGross. New York: HarperCollins, 1994. (Harper)

Four Famished Foxes and Fosdyke by Pamela Edwards Duncan. New York: HarperCollins, 1995. (Harper)

Frindle, see page 103b.

One Sun by Bruce McMillan. New York: Holiday, 1990. (   )

Play Day: A Book of Terse Verse by Bruce McMillan. New York: Holiday, 1991. (Holiday)

Ruth Heller's World of Language series, see page 105b.

Sit on a Potato Pan, Otis! More Palindromes by Jon Agee. New York: Farrar Straus & Giroux, 1999. (   )

Some Smug Slug by Pamela Edwards Duncan. New York: HarperCollins, 1995. (Harper)

Spring: An Alphabet Acrostic by Steven Schnur, illustrated by Leslie Evans. New York: Clarion, 1999. (   )

Who Ordered the Jumbo Shrimp? and Other Oxymorons by Jon Agee. New York: HarperCollins, 1999. (   )

Word Wizard by Cathryn Falwell. New York: Clarion, 1998. (   )

Popular Press Sayings

Another powerful model is the category of sayings. The paperback titles on this list, while aimed at adults, elicit children's responses quickly. They may also be brought to final form easily and a collection of them make good "class books."

Kid's Random Acts of Kindness by Dawna Markova. Emeryville, CA: Conari, 1994. (   )

Life's Little Frustrations Book by G. Gaylord McTigue. New York: St. Martin's, 1994. (   )

"Please Don't Kiss Me at the Bus Stop": Over 700 Things Parents Do That Drive Their Kids Crazy by Merry Bloch Jones. Kansas City, MO: Andrews McMeel, 1997. (   )

Really Important Stuff My Kids Have Taught Me by Cynthia C. Lewis. New York: Workman, 1994. (   )

Wit & Wisdom from the Peanut Butter Gang by H. Jackson Brown Jr. Nashville: Rutledge Hill Press, 1994. (   )

Wordless Books

Stories without words provide children with a chance to get a complete story in mind and consider what to pay attention to in the illustrations. Allow children to work together to explain the story before they start to write. Encourage some to tell the story from the point of view of one of the characters. Help writers determine whether they will use conversation and provide a minilesson on how this looks in print. See also "Wordless Books" lists in *Invitations*.

Carl the Dog series by Alexandra Day. New York: Farrar Straus & Giroux, various dates.

Magpie Magic: A Tale of Colorful Mischief by April Wilson. New York: Dial, 1999. (   )

Mouse books by Emily Arnold McCully (*Picnic; School; The New Baby*). HarperCollins, various dates. (HarperCollins)

Re-Zoom by Istvan Banyai. New York: Penguin, 1995. (Puffin)

Tabby: A Story in Pictures by Aliki. New York: HarperCollins, 1995. (   )

Time Flies by Eric Rohmann. New York: Crown, 1994. (Dragonfly)

The Tooth Fairy by Peter Collington. New York: Knopf, 1995. (   )

A Small Miracle by Peter Collington. New York: Knopf, 1997. (   )

You Can't Take a Balloon into the Metropolitan Museum by Jacqueline Preiss Weitzman, illustrated by Robin Preiss Glasser. New York: Dial, 1998. (   )

Zoom by Istvan Banyai. New York: Penguin, 1995. (Puffin)

Books I Have Loved

by Regie Routman

I decided to add this personal list because often at conferences when I share my reading log, teachers ask me for a copy of my leisure reading, what I read in summer "for fun." I have included my favorites since 1993 when I first began keeping a reading log. These are books that I have found exceptionally literary, engaging, thoughtful, and beautifully written. Several of these are professional books.

Amy and Isabelle by Elizabeth Strout (fiction)

Angela's Ashes by Frank McCourt (memoir)

Are You Somebody? The Accidental Memoir of a Dublin Woman by Nuala O'Faolain (memoir)

Beloved by Toni Morrison (fiction)

Better Than Life by Daniel Pennac (nonfiction/professional)

Bird by Bird: Some Instructions on Writing and Life by Anne Lamott (nonfiction)

Cat's Eye by Margaret Atwood (fiction)

Charming Billy by Alice McDermott (fiction)

Cold Mountain by Charles Frazier (historical fiction)

Crossing to Safety by Wallace Stegner (fiction)

Dance of the Happy Shades and Other Stories by Alice Munro

Dancing After Hours by Andre Dubus (short stories)

The Diving Bell and the Butterfly by Jean-Dominique Bauby (memoir)

Durable Goods by Elizabeth Berg (fiction)

Fall on Your Knees by Ann-Marie MacDonald (fiction)

Fugitive Pieces by Anne Michaels (fiction)

The Girl with the Brown Crayon by Vivian Gussin Paley (professional)

The God of Small Things by Arundhati Roy (fiction)

High Tide in Tucson by Barbara Kingsolver (nonfiction essays)

I Know Why the Caged Bird Sings by Maya Angelou (fiction)

The Liar's Club by Mary Karr (memoir)

Like Water for Chocolate by Laura Esquivel (fiction)

Love and Good Will by Jane Smiley (short stories)

Love in the Time of Cholera by Gabriel García Márquez (fiction)

Madame Bovary by Gustave Flaubert (fiction)

Missing May by Cynthia Rylant (YA fiction)

9 Highland Road by Michael Winerip (nonfiction)

Out of the Dust by Karen Hesse (historical fiction, prose poem)

Paula by Isabel Allende (memoir)

Pigs in Heaven by Barbara Kingsolver (fiction)

The Power of Their Ideas by Deborah Meier (professional)

Radical Reflections: Passionate Opinions on Teaching, Learning and Living by Mem Fox (professional)

Schools of Thought by Rexford Brown (professional)

The Shipping News by Annie Proulx (fiction)

A Slender Thread: Rediscovering Hope at the Heart of Crisis by Diane Ackerman (nonfiction)

The Stone Diaries by Carol Shields (fiction)

A Stone in My Shoe: Teaching Literacy in Times of Change by Lori Neilson (professional)

Stones from the River by Ursula Hegi (fiction)

A Thousand Acres by Jane Smiley (fiction)

What Jamie Saw by Carolyn Coman (YA fiction)

When She Was Good by Norma Fox Mazer (YA fiction)

Without by Donald Hall (poetry)

Writing Down the Bones by Natalie Goldberg (nonfiction)

Appendix A:
Communicating with Parents

A-1: Why I Read Aloud to My Children

Why I Read to My Children

By Christopher de Vinck

Most nights I read aloud to my children before they sleep: "Mr. Popper's Penguins," "My Father's Dragon," "Treasure Island" and "James and the Giant Peach" have been some of their favorites over the years. I have been doing this since my eldest son was small, and my reasons are many.

Oh, I believe the psychologist Jean Piaget when he speaks about assimilation, children picking up information that fits in with what they already know. My children have heard thousands of different sentence patterns over and over again as they sat beside me during those many nights.

To be sure, my children have picked up new words along the way. When my oldest son, David, was four years old, he walked around the house stating he felt soporific after he heard about the soporific effects lettuce had on Beatrix Potter's slothful rabbits. Karen learned what a bungalow was as she listened to how Uncle Wiggily crawled out from his home at the beginning of each new adventure.

Of course, it is true that a rich reading background adds to a child's intellectual baggage. I have been an English teacher for the past 16 years and I have had, for the most part, two types of students: those who have rich personal background and those who have this personal experience *and* a wide reading experience.

All children come to schools with a wide diversity of personal experiences. I would say only 10% also come with a wide reading background. The child with the widest personal and reading background seems to carry the most intellectual baggage into my class-room year after year. This is the child, who, eventually, scores the highest on the verbal section of the SATs, who is able to make sudden and clear connections between books and life, who has the strongest sense of what it means to live a life of reflection, who is the strongest writer. The SAT *is* a very biased test. It is biased against those who do not read.

Thinking is looking at experiences and making conclusions. Writing is the physical evidence of our thinking. The more we experience, the more information we have inside our minds and our

hearts. The more information we have, the better conclusions we can make about our own lives.

But I read aloud to my children each night for reasons that go beyond Piaget, vocabulary, writing and information retrieval.

I want eight-year-old Michael to taste the chocolate as Willie Wonka guides the children on a grand tour of his factory. I want Karen to smell the flowers Francie Nolan's father bought for her in "A Tree Grows in Brooklyn." I want my children to feel the hunger Richard Wright endured in "Black Boy." I want my son David to smack his hand, someday, against Boo Radley's house in "To Kill a Mockingbird." I want my daughter to feel the moonlight against her bare breasts as did Annie in Jamaica Kinkaid's glorious little book "Annie John."

I read aloud to my children be-cause I want them to feel the hand of Ivan Illyich against their cheek just before he dies. I want my children to someday receive the blessing of Father Zosima in "Brothers Karamazov." I want my children to believe that it can, indeed, rain flowers as it did in "One Hundred Years of Solitude." I want my children to watch Sydney Carton Walk up the steps to the guillotine. I want them to carry Addie's coffin along with Faulkner in "As I Lay Dying." I want my children to listen to Reb Saunders in "The Chosen." I want the water from the pump in "The Miracle Worker" to run against the small hands of David, Karen and Michael.

"Mrs. Keller!' Annie Sullivan screams out with joy to Helen's mother. "Mrs. Keller! Mrs. Keller! She knows!" Helen Keller finally learned that these funny little symbols—"A," "B," "C," "D"—mean words, sentences, language, life, freedom. "She knows!"

Reading makes possible the connection between our minds and the near magical notions drawn up from our impossible hearts. I also read to my children because I like the feel of their warmth against my arms and the sound of their quiet breaths as they listen to my voice circling around them night after night.

Reading aloud to children every day gives them the widest entry to that place we call freedom. Reading aloud to children begins the slow process of education that ends in parents and teachers celebrating: "They know! They know! Their hearts and minds have made the connections. Our children are free. They know!"

Mr. de Vinck is the author of "Augusta and Trab" a children's novel just published by Four Winds.

From The Wall Street Journal *November 1993 reprinted by permission*

A-2: Learning to Read and Write: A Brochure for Parents

Learning to Read and Write

The Mercer School staff recognizes and builds upon the rich language experiences that all children bring to school. These prior experiences lay the foundation for formal reading and writing instruction. We strive to provide the children with extensive language opportunities that will develop lifelong reading and writing behaviors. Our beliefs about reading and writing instruction stem from current research and from our experiences with and knowledge about how children learn to read and write. Guided by the Shaker Heights Language Arts Course of Study, teachers instruct using literature to create a balanced language arts program. Activities that encourage the use of critical thinking skills are an integral part of instruction. Teachers organize literacy instruction using multiple approaches depending on the purpose and the objective of a particular lesson.

MERCER READS!

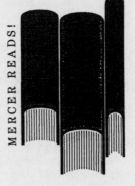

Reading and Writing at Mercer School

How do good readers read?

Parents play a critical role in developing children's language/life experiences. Successful readers read for both meaning and enjoyment by using:

- knowledge and past experiences (knowledge cues)
- the text and illustrations (semantic cues)
- the sentence structure and grammar (syntactic cues)
- letter-sound relationships (phonetic cues)

Successful readers integrate multiple cueing systems while struggling readers tend to over rely on just one or two of them.

How will my child be taught to read and write at Mercer?

Most important, your child will be immersed in a rich literature and language environment as he or she listens, talks, writes, and reads using whole, meaningful texts throughout the school day. Your child will be taught how to use all cueing systems effectively through teacher demonstrations, peer modeling, discussion, small group instruction, and daily reading and writing opportunities.

Reading and Writing in Kindergarten

The kindergarten program focuses on early literacy activities that promote language development, vocabulary growth, listening comprehension, and a beginning understanding of how print works (e.g. directionality of print, letter-sound relationships, space between words, etc.). Kindergarten children become writers and authors as they express their ideas through drawing, dictating stories, and experimenting with their own writing and spelling.

Mercer students are expected to read and/or be read to each day at school and at home. Mercer students are expected to write on a daily basis.

What can I expect to find each day in every Mercer Classroom?

Reading aloud:

A competent reader, usually the teacher, reads aloud to the children, promoting story enjoyment and literature appreciation.

Shared reading/shared writing:

In an enjoyable reading situation, the students follow the text and are invited to read along while observing the teacher reading. Similarly, the whole class generates a writing piece as the teacher records and contributes to their words/thoughts.

Guided reading/writing:

This is the core of our instructional program. The teacher develops lessons based on the needs and interests of children. These lessons are used to teach reading/writing strategies and skills that will enable the children to read and write independently.

Independent reading/writing:

Students select books to read or topics to write about and they are in charge of their own reading and writing, both at home and in school. Although we provide explicit instruction, guidance, and support, research confirms our beliefs that children learn to read by reading often and to write by writing often just as children learn to play a musical instrument or sport by practicing these skills.

You will see students taking responsibility for daily reading and writing and record keeping of their work. In every classroom, you can view a well organized collection of quality literature (a wide variety of picture books and chapter books, fiction and non-fiction, poetry, and other resources). The literature collection will be located in an attractive and inviting reading area that is accessible to all students.

A-3: What Is a "Just Right" Book?

Shaker Heights City School District
Shaker Heights, Ohio

What is a "just right" book?

Your child will be reading many books this year. A "just right" book is a book that your child can read independently; books should be neither too difficult nor too easy in order for your child to grow as a reader.

The "five finger rule" is one way for your child to choose a "just right" book.

Once your child has chosen a book, ask him or her to read the first page aloud. As your child reads, he/she should count on one hand any unknown words. If there are five or more unknown words on a full page of text, this book is too difficult! If your child knows all the words, it may be too easy.

When reading a "just right" book:

- reading should be fairly fluent (not too choppy sounding)
- your child should be able to tell you about what he/she has read
- your child should be interested in the topic

Children enjoy and benefit from rereading familiar text, but in order to grow as a reader, your child needs to read books which are "just right." If your child chooses a book that is too difficult, this would be a great choice for reading together.

Remember: Reading aloud to your child is valuable at any grade level!

Shaker Heights City School District
8/18/98

A-4: Inviting Parents to Read Aloud in the Classroom

January 26, 1998

Dear Families,

On February 2, 1998 our class will be participating in the African American Read-In sponsored by the National Council of Teachers of English and endorsed by the International Reading Association. The children will be reading materials selected from works authored by African Americans.

I would like to invite you to come in and read aloud to the students on this day. We will stop our activities to meet your time and work schedules. The only time during our day that is not open is 1:30–2:00 P.M. (gym). You may read one of your favorite books or I will have one ready for you. If you would like to read to the class on this day, please fill out the form below. Thank you.

Sincerely,

L. Martin

_____

Name _____   Phone # _____

I will need a book.   Yes _____   No _____

A-5: Weekly Review

Name *Jenna Lowry*   Date *November 29/98*

Here are some things I've done this week:
* used the geoboard to learn about geometry
* practiced for my conference
* prepared my portfolio for my conference
* made a Thanksgiving turkey
* made a list of things I am thankful for
* discussed playground safety

I've learned about:
* 's (shows possession or a contraction)
* an agenda
* sides, angels, parallel lines
* more about lines of symmetry
* muscles, bones, and joints

I've been working on these skills:
* following written and oral directions
* working cooperatively
* spelling-should, would, could-"These words must be spelled correctly every time I use them."
* telling time

I have been reading *Ginger Brown: The Nobody Boy*

It's about *a girl who finds a Boy in her yard.*

They become friends. They play with each other.

Next week I will *learn about solid shapes.*

Student Comments: *I felt like a grown up when I had my conference because my handwriting has improved.*

Teacher comments:
Jenna, you did an excellent job sharing your portfolio yesterday.

Parent comments:
We also feel that Jenna did a great job sharing at her conference, we are very proud.

I have read this review with my child and added my comments. *Jenna B.*
Parent Signature and Date

A-6: Blank Weekly Review

WEEKLY REVIEW

Name

Here are some things I've done this week:

Here are the things I've learned:

1.

2.

3.

I've worked on these skills _____

_____

_____

I have been reading _____

It is about _____

_____

_____

_____

My goal for next week is _____

_____

Student comments:

Teacher comments:

Family comments:

I have read this review with my child and added my comments.

(date)_____

Adapted by Loretta Martin

*A-7: Curriculum Information to Parents: Philosophy,
Reading, and Writing Components*

My Philosophy

Focusing on Children's **STRENGTHS** must come first when looking at learners.

Children learn best through **REAL** reading and writing, not through **EXERCISES** in reading and writing.

The classroom environment is tied into the **REAL WORLD**. The activities have a purpose. **RISK TAKING** is encouraged.

The classroom would be **MULTI MODAL** in nature (incorporating music, art, dance, drama, etc.)

The children should be encouraged to **REFLECT** (teachers also).

Students are **CAPABLE** and can be **TRUSTED** to learn.

I believe in **CHOICES** for learners.

The student and teacher **COLLABORATE** in planning.

The focus is on **PROCESS** and **PRODUCT**.

The classroom should be "**LEARNER-CENTERED**," which empowers both teacher and student.

Goals

1. I want your child to have the lifetime "**HABIT**" of reading and writing.
2. I want your child to be "**JOYFULLY LITERATE**."
3. I want your child to be a "**PROBLEM SOLVER**" and a "**RESPONSIBLE DECISION MAKER**."
4. I want your child to be part of a "**COMMUNITY OF LEARNERS**," cooperating and collaborating with his or her peers.
5. I want your child to have "**HIGH SELF-ESTEEM**" both in and out of the classroom.
6. I want your child to learn how to resolve his or her own problems through "**CONFLICT RESOLUTION**."

The Curriculum

Reading Components

1. *W.E.B. (Wonderful Exciting Books)*

Self-selected fiction and nonfiction books are read for a minimum of 30 minutes every evening. The students record finished books in a notebook. They are interviewed on the books by me or their peers.

2. *Guided Reading*

We read books I have selected that are worthy of in-depth discussion. We respond to what we read in the form of notes and questions in our reading spirals. Students generate questions worth discussing.

3. *Read Aloud*

We listen to good literature daily for predicting outcomes, discussing, and enjoying.

4. *D.I.R.T. (Daily Individual Reading Time)*

The class loves this time of the day, which is usually after lunch. They are allowed to sit or recline anywhere in the room. Have you heard about the theme song?

5. *Poetry*

We have a class poet job that consists of selecting poetry to be read aloud to the class. The poet practices reading the poems before reading them to the class. I also read poetry aloud frequently.

6. *Time Magazine for Kids*

Every Wednesday morning we read *Time Magazine* and drink juice from our favorite mugs. This is the "real world" of reading. It bridges the gap between the real world and school and gives us the opportunity to discuss the events of the world.

7. *Care Partners*

Every Friday we meet with our care partners in Mrs. Mauser's class. We focus on reading, writing, drama, and math.

Writing Components

1. *Writing*

The students have a notebook divided into different genres where they write every day about topics that interest them. We do not take every piece to final copy but I do expect each student to publish one piece per month and two projects a year.

The format of writing always begins with a minilesson where the children are expected to take notes and keep their notes in their notebooks. The students have 20–30 minutes to write and then time to share with the class.

Genres include poetry, fiction, nonfiction, essay writing, letters, book reviews, and newspapers. We also do a lot of writing in the content areas of science and social studies.

2. *Spelling*

The purpose of learning to spell is to be able to write. Standard spelling is taught through strategies that focus children's attention on words in their writing.

The students find some of their spelling words within their writing or within the content area we are researching. I assign spelling words from the content areas or frequently used words.

We have a structured spelling time daily. During that period of time we focus on spelling rules, spelling activities that reinforce skills, and "Give It a Go."

Frequently, I dictate sentences to the students. They are required to proofread and correct the sentences. Then the sentences are rewritten without errors. We call this "golf."

Dictionaries are in frequent use, as we strive for standard spelling in all our work.

Speaking

I believe students should have many opportunities to practice their speaking skills. We have daily sharing, poet of the week, and presentations. Students are also encouraged to participate in class as much as possible.

by Julie Beers, Grade 4 teacher

A-8: A Shared Writing of a First-Grade Class Newsletter

ALL IN ONE
December 2, 1997
<u>What's New This Week in Grade One, Room One?</u>

There's something fishy going on in first grade!

This morning Mrs. Hochman brought the Science Lab to our school. She helped launch our study of ocean creatures with a fin-tastic lesson about fish. Here's our collaborative news report so you can talk with us about our learning. (Notice how well we included details to tell who did what, where, when and why.)

The first graders of Room One on Tuesday morning, December 2nd, used the Art Room as a Science Lab to learn more about fish. We observed a goldfish to draw scientific details on a fish diagram. Mrs. Hochman dissected a white bass to show us the body parts inside a fish. We thought it was cool because we have never looked inside a fish before. Our favorite part was when the fish was cut open because that was very interesting.

Please let Mr. Hill know if you are willing to donate any of the following items for upcoming class projects:

blue or green crepe paper streamers	blue or green-colored juice
rolls of pennies, nickels, or dimes	cupcake baking papers
sugar cookie dough	fish-shaped cookie cutters
frosting and sprinkles to decorate cookies	gummy fish or gummy worms

A-9: A Newsletter for Parents of Kindergartners About Learning to Read

Let's Read!

Room 9

1-20-98

Dear Families,

Reading is an important part of the kindergarten curriculum. Each day, children listen to and discuss several stories. We read together enlarged versions of books and poems. While reading the story, I often use a pointer or my "reading finger" to point to each individual word. Familiar stories are read and reread until many children know them by heart. As children use pictures to help them remember a story and start to point to individual words, they are beginning to make sense of print and to use letters and sounds within the context of a familiar story. Research has shown that teaching skills in context helps students to use these skills as they read. (See the attached fact sheet "On Teaching Skills in Context"). We have at least one "booktime" each day. Here, children look at books independently or with a friend. Many times, children discuss the story, the pictures or read the words together. This is a time when children practice and extend the reading strategies they are learning. Most children are very focused and interested at booktime.

Children are permitted to borrow classroom books. Some children enjoy signing out books which they can read themselves and some prefer borrowing books for parents to read aloud. Please respect your child's preferences. It is very important that your child enjoy your shared book time. This will help him/her to develop a love of books and reading. Please be sure that books are returned after a day or two so that other students will have access to them. Please help your child to remember his/her book borrowing responsibilities.

Be sure to ask your child about our "Book Buddies" program. Each week, we work with the students in Mrs. Schubert's fourth grade. Every kindergartener has a special "book buddy" who reads with/to him/her. Sometimes, we work on projects together. We recently worked with book buddies to write and illustrate stories about the toys brought in for "Marvelous Toy Day". Having an older teacher/friend is an exciting experience for "teachers" and "learners" alike.

Next week, your child will be bringing home a reading homework sheet. I'm sure that you have been reading to your child every day. The reading homework sheet is the recording of that reading. Please read to your child, record the title of the book and a simple explanation. Record what your child says. Do not expect him/her to do the writing unless he/she requests it. The child should then draw a face in the "opinion" column to express his/her opinion. This is meant to be a relaxed pleasant experience for all of you. It is not meant to be stressful. However, it IS important that the sheet be returned to school in your child's folder each Friday. This is the beginning of the responsibility of homework and the type of work that will continue in first grade. Please check to make sure that your child's homework folder is in good repair and that he/she sees the job of returning it as his/her responsibility. If the folder needs to be replaced, please provide a new one and write your child's name and cubby number in permanent marker.

Thank you.

Sincerely,
Peg Rimedio

***NOTE:
The Nature Center at Shaker Lakes will present Native American music and storytelling on Saturday, January 24 and Wednesday, February 11. Call 321-5935 for information. Thanks to Chris' mom for letting me know.

A-10: A Newsletter for Parents of Kindergartners About Learning to Write

WE CAN WRITE!

Room 9
April 13, 1998

Dear Families,

There has recentlly been an explosion of writing in our classroom. Children are writing stories, sentences, copying from books and writing notes and letters. Some choose use the computer to write stories at worktime.

We are in the process of publishing a big book of our writing. I typed work on the computer, using conventional spelling and the children's own language. This helps children to see the connection between their writing and printed text.

For your information, I have attached a copy of the stages of beginning writing as well as my rules of writing for helping kindergartens when they write. I hope these will be helpful as you supervise your child's writing at home.

When children move on to first grade, they will be expected to use logical invented spelling when writing. If your child is still using random letters to write stories, please help him/her start to notice the beginning sounds in words. You might say, "I am thinking of something you can ride and it starts with B like ball." Then encourage him/her to use the beginning sounds to stand for words. Help the child to stretch out the words to hear beginning and ending sounds. If your child is freely using sounds in writing, you could make a list of common words (family names, the, me, my, I, a, like) and encourage him/her to remember the spelling.

At all levels, it is helpful to publish your child's story by typing or writing it in conventional spelling. Then you can read the story together.

I hope you are enjoying this exciting time of beginning writing as much as I am.

Happy Spring,
Peg Rimedio

***NOTE:
On Thursday we will visit Madroo's Farm in the morning. Be sure children dress for the weather. Friday a.m. is the Art Museum trip.

A-11: Beginning of School Welcome and Information Letter to Parents of Fourth Graders

September 8, 1998

> *"Education is not filling of a pail, but the lighting of a fire."*
> —William Butler Yeats
> (Irish poet)

Dear Family,

I hope all of you had a relaxing Labor Day weekend. I am so fortunate to have such a wonderful class. It is going to be a great year. I am looking forward to sharing the curriculum, goals, and plans with you at Open House on September 17th. I hope all of you can come. It makes such a difference in your child's education when we work together and we are all on the same page.

There are a few things I did not think could wait until Open House:

• **WEB** is our nightly reading program. WEB stands for *Wonderful Exciting Books*. The students are required to read a book at their level for at least 30 minutes each night (Sunday—Saturday). I will monitor their book selection. I would appreciate it if you could reinforce how important it is to read every night and make sure your child is reading. The students are required to have their WEB book in school each day.

• **Science Experiments** will be presented by two students every Friday afternoon. Each child will do his/her own experiment. I have books at school that the students may use to choose an experiment or they can find one on their own.

I modeled an experiment in school so the students would know what to do. We also took notes in our science notebooks on how to present their experiment. The schedule is attached so you can be aware of your child's date for the experiment.

• **Things to Do** sheets are used daily so your child can record the homework and other things to remember for the next day. Please check the things to do nightly and make sure your child is doing the homework.

• **End of the day meetings** are held each day to record the day's events and what we learned. We will use this information for a class newspaper we will publish bimonthly. I am also hoping these meetings help your child communicate what is going on in school each day with you.

What's going on in school . . . (in case the meetings are not serving their purpose!)

• **Math:** geometry, reviewing facts, math alphabet

• **Science:** meal worms, scientific method, biomes

• **Reading:** Books by Jean Craighead George, researching biomes

• **Writing:** We will be decorating our writer's notebook. *Students will need pictures, special ribbons, stickers,* anything that may inspire writing ideas, write school supply poems.

• **Social Studies:** Mapping

• **And . . .** Sketching, self-portraits, and care partners!

See you at the Fall Social Wednesday Night!!!
J. Beers

A-12: A Weekly Newsletter to Parents of First Graders, Citing Spelling Research

The Parent Connection
A Weekly Newsletter for Parents
CHRISTOPHER HAYWARD

APRIL 12, 1996
Listening to the children talk about their spring break makes it sound as if everyone really relaxed and enjoyed themselves.

This week in math we continued exploring the concept of fractions. Before children can understand the concept of fractions, they must first think of fractions as parts of a whole which can be separated and reassembled to form the same whole. They must also understand that these fractional parts must be *equal* in size. A knowledge of fractions extends children's understanding of numbers and helps them accurately describe numerical situations. Just as children need to see models of whole numerals to understand them, they must see models of fractions in order to understand their relative value. In first grade, work with fractions is best done with everyday objects and concepts that children can relate to their lives. This week we used food to help us understand fractions. We learned the fractions 1/2, 1/3, and 1/4 by cutting up bananas, apples, potatoes, and a red pepper. We used an orange and grapefruit to explore the fractions of 1/8, and 1/10. After cutting the fruit and vegetables into fractional pieces, the children used the pieces and some paint to create their own fraction books. Not only did we use nutritional food to explore fractions, but we also used some "junk" food as well. We used peanuts, Hershey Bars, Reeses Cups, a Symphony Bar, and a Butterfinger to explore fractional pieces. Using manipulatives to explore this difficult concept makes the study more interesting and easier to understand, especially if the manipulatives are edible. Be sure to ask your child about these exciting lessons.

Next Tuesday, April 16, our class will be taking a field trip to Hale Farm and Village. The children are required to pay a $4.50 fee. The entire first grade will be leaving the school at 9:30 A.M. and will be returning at 2:00 P.M. Please have your child return his/her permission slip and fee on Monday. Children not returning the permission slip or fee will not be allowed to attend this exciting trip.

Our class would appreciate any coupons you could send to school next week. We will be using the coupons as part of a math lesson involving the counting of money.

I look forward to seeing you next Thursday, April 18, at the Onaway School Spring Open House at 7:00 P.M. Come and celebrate the achievements your child has accomplished this year.

Facts: On the Teaching of Spelling

Background

For decades, more people seem to have considered themselves poor spellers than good spellers, despite the fact that most of us spell correctly the vast majority of the words we write. With spelling, we seem to expect that all of us should spell one hundred percent correctly, even on first drafts, and even as young children. Perhaps it is this unrealistic expectation that leads some parents and others to object when teachers use newer methods of helping children learn to spell, such as encouraging children to "use invented spelling" in their early attempts to write. Such critics mistakenly assume that children who initially use invented spelling will never become good spellers, or that if the time-honored method of memorizing spelling lists were used instead, *every* child would become a perfect speller. Neither observed experience nor research supports these assumptions.

What research demonstrates
- Young children using invented spelling employ a considerably greater variety of words in their writing than those encouraged to use only the words they can spell correctly (Gunderson & Shapiro 1987, 1988; Clark 1988; Stice & Bertrand 1990).

- Young children encouraged to use invented spellings seem to develop word recognition and phonics skills sooner than those not encouraged to spell the sounds they hear in words (Clarke 1988).

References and Resources

Gunderson, L., & Shapiro, J. 1987. Some findings on whole language instruction. *Reading-Canada-Lecture* 5 (1): 22–26.

Gunderson, L., & Shapiro, J. 1988. Whole language instruction: Writing in 1st grade. *The Reading Teacher* 41: 430–437.

Clarke, L.K. 1988. Invented versus traditional spelling in first graders' writings: Effects on learning to spell and read. *Research in the Teaching of English* 22:281–309.

Stice, C.F., & Bertrand, N.P. 1990. *Whole language and the emergent literacy of at-risk children: A two-year comparative study.* Nashville: Tennessee State University. Center of Excellence: Basic Skills, ED 324 636.

Appendix B:
Comprehensive Literacy Program

B-1: *Working Explanations for a Comprehensive Reading and Writing Program*

Working Explanations for a Comprehensive Reading and Writing Program

Reading Program	*Writing Program*
Reading Aloud	Writing Aloud
Shared Reading	Shared Writing
Guided Reading	Guided Writing
Independent Reading	Independent Writing

Opportunities to Respond to Text

Comprehensive Reading Program

Reading Aloud
A competent reader (usually the teacher) reads aloud to children. To be most effective reading aloud is done daily in classrooms and goes across the curriculum. Reading aloud, which has been proven the most influential factor in children becoming readers, promotes story enjoyment and literature appreciation.

Shared Reading
Shared reading is any enjoyable reading situation in which the student follows the text (on the overhead, chart paper, or in personal copies) while observing an expert (usually the teacher) reading it with fluency and expression. Students are invited to read along. Shared reading is one way to immerse students in rich literature without worrying about reading level or performance. Learning occurs naturally as students/teacher observe, explore, evaluate all aspects of the story and content.

Guided Reading
Guided reading (whole group, small group, or individualized) is the core of the instructional reading program. Guided reading depends on the teacher to be the instructional leader in designing learning experiences built upon the needs of each child. Reading strategies are taught within the context of the literature. Guided reading is done in small heterogeneous groups with emphasis on discussion and personal response to literature. Small groups on the student's instructional level meet regularly to develop and apply reading strategies and skills.

Independent Reading

Students self-select books and are in charge of their own reading. Independent reading occurs daily at school and at home. Monitoring may be done by the students, teacher and/or parent/s through the use of reading records (which means written records of books read) and conferences.

Comprehensive Writing Program

Writing Aloud

Writing on chart paper, the overhead projector, or the chalkboard, the teacher demonstrates by writing in front of the students. The teacher says out loud what she/he is doing—the actual thinking and rethinking that goes on mentally. The teacher is also demonstrating and talking about the format, spacing, handwriting, spelling, punctuation, and vocabulary choices in the process of writing. These demonstrations go across the curriculum.

Shared Writing

In a relaxed atmosphere the teacher and the students compose collaboratively, negotiating topics, meanings, and choice of words with the teacher acting as scribe. This strategy promotes the development of writing by encouraging all students to participate orally while the teacher is demonstrating the conventions of writing. The teacher's questioning and direction allows the students to write what they might not be able to write independently. Shared writing may include brainstorming, drafting, revising, editing, and final copy.

Guided Writing

Guided writing (whole class, small group, or individualized) is the core of the writing program. The student holds the pen and does the writing while the teacher guides, responds, and extends the student's ideas and skills. Students choose their own topics most of the time. Minilessons occur in response to students' needs. Conferences, peer response, and sharing are essential. Writing pieces might include responses to literature, letters, poems, and reports. Ideally, spelling and handwriting are taught within the context of guided writing.

Independent Writing

Students select topics and are in charge of their own writing. Independent writing occurs daily and is monitored by the child and teacher through the use of journals, logs, and free writing.

Teacher/expert holds the text or the pen in the following components: Reading Aloud, Writing Aloud, Shared Reading, Shared Writing.

In moving toward independence the student holds the text or the pen in the following components: Guided Reading, Guided Writing, Independent Reading, Independent Writing.

Responding to literature (through listening, speaking, writing, further reading, art, drama, music, dance) and daily opportunities to share are integral for balancing a reading and writing program.

See also Figure 2-1 on p. 23

B-2: Some Guidelines for Teaching Reading and Writing

What to look for in the reading program

daily reading aloud of quality literature

sustained time daily for free choice reading with appropriate book match

students' reading records: titles, authors, genres

shared reading: teacher reading while students follow along

teacher conference/assessment notes on each student

most time spent reading, not responding to reading

small-group guided reading: mostly silent guided reading, not round robin oral reading (includes small groups for explicit skills instruction, as needed), and literature discussion groups (heterogeneous)

partner reading

evidence of teaching vocabulary

well-stocked, organized, attractive classroom library and reading corner

What to look for in the writing program

writing in various genres

teacher modeling: various genres and how to respond to writing

teaching of craft of writing

shared writing: teacher scribing while composing with students

students' writing records: topics, genres, publishing information

teacher conference/assessment notes on each student

spelling lessons: connected to writing

most writing topics chosen by students

editing/proofreading expectations

evidence of revision and editing

teaching of conventions: not through exercises, but in process of writing a short piece going to final copy at least once a month: grades two and up

writing/publishing for real audiences

Regie Routman, Shaker Heights, OH, City Schools
(written for principals in my school district)

B-3: What a Good Reader Does

What Does a Good Reader Do?
(Whole-Class Brainstorming Session)

1. Can't stop reading
2. Reads at own pace
3. Oral reading—reads slower so others can understand
4. Reads a variety of books
5. Reads anything if it looks interesting, even the back of a cereal box!
6. Chooses "quality" books
7. Reads good literature
8. When stuck on word:
   sounds out
   figures out by rest of sentence
9. Reads back of book or first chapter to see if wants to read book
10. Reads silently (to himself/ herself)
11. Desires/wants to read
12. Reads a little bit to see if can read it

13. Doesn't always judge a book by a cover (especially chapter books)
14. Takes recommendations
15. Sometimes chooses challenging books
16. Finds series and authors they like and reads all their books
17. Recommends books to friends
18. Talks about books
19. Reads book reviews to see if interested
20. Reads while eating
21. Reads at bedtime
22. Tries to read even when they're not supposed to:
    When teacher is talking to students
    While eating
    While doing homework
23. Talks about books

Joan Servis' Fourth-Grade Class
March, 1998

B-4: What a Good Writer Does

What a Good Writer Does

1. Rereads what is written
2. Spells most words correctly
3. Picks interesting topics
4. Sticks to the topic
5. Uses descriptive vocabulary
6. Someone is able to read the writing (legible)
7. Doesn't bore the reader
8. Uses catchy leads
9. Uses thesaurus
10. Revise and edit
11. Has closure
12. Good books give ideas and better vocabulary
13. Uses punctuation and capitalization correctly
14. Relates to life
15. Has title, beginning, and ending in stories
16. Write about what she/he knows
17. Has a plot (story)
18. Uses points of view
19. Writes with a voice
20. Sounds real
21. Uses dialogue well
22. Pulls reader into story
23. Can write in several genres
24. Uses details to flesh out story or article
25. Asks for feedback

Joan Servis' Fourth-Grade Class
March, 1998

B-5: *Reading Record/Monthly Recording*

Monthly Recording

Month/Year_____

Title	Author	Genre	Rating

1.

2.

3.

4.

5.

6.

7.

8.

Favorite authors for the month: _____

_____

Favorite books (I'll be sure to reread):

_____

_____

B-6: Self-Assessment for Sustained Silent Reading

Reading Any Place

Self-Assessment

Name: _____ Date: _____

How much time do you spend reading?

   a lot   a little   not much

If you did not read, why not?

What do you read during RAP?

What will help you next time during RAP?

My goal for RAP is

Teacher comments:

by Julie Beers

Appendix C:
Position Statements

C-1: NCTE Resolution: On Testing and Equitable Treatment of Students

1998 NCTE Resolutions
On Testing and Equitable Treatment of Students

Background

The use of systematically administered standardized tests continues to escalate. In many countries, states, and provinces, the results of those tests are being increasingly used to accredit schools, affirm the ongoing certification of teachers, reward schools and school districts monetarily, and determine individual student grade promotion and retention. Historically, NCTE has viewed such large-scale, high-stakes standardized testing with serious reservations. Resolutions from 1971, 1976, 1977, 1985, and 1989 all address the limitations of standardized testing with regard to authentic assessment of the English language arts classroom. In previous resolutions, the Council has opposed "over-simplified and narrowly conceived tests of isolated skills and decontextualized knowledge," contrasting the "tension between the breadth of the English language arts curriculum and the restrictive influence of standardized means of assessing student learning" (Resolution On Testing, 1995). Concerned about the distortion and reduction of . . . curriculum" and the "unwise expenditure of public funds " (Resolution On Testing, 1995) on the development and administration of these tests, NCTE has also supported alternative forms of assessment, holding that "nationally normed standardized tests are a barrier to student opportunity, to the professional development of school staff, and to sound curriculm" (Resolution On the Development and Dissemination of Alternative Forms of Assessment, 1990). The "lack of fit between what the schools do to test student learning and what researchers know about students' language development" (Resolution On Assessment, 1991) continues to be a concern today.

Today's widely administered standardized tests are single measure and largely multiple choice; more to the point, often they do not reflect student learning. Further, such tests become disproportionately crucial regarding student grade-level progress in school. In addition, many school districts provide neither reasonable instruction regarding appropriate test-taking practices nor effective assistance for students who do not achieve the requisite scores. Finally, many testing programs do not account for differently-abled learners (through the use of multiple assessment beyond standardized, multiple choice, paper-and-pencil measures) or for learners for whom English is not their first language. Be it therefore

Resolution

Resolved, that the National Council of Teachers of English affirm that no student be retained because of the results of standardized test scores alone;

> that NCTE condemn the wholesale usurpation of the English language arts curriculum by excessive attention to test preparation;
> that NCTE condemn the use of assessment instruments in English with students who are not sufficiently proficient in English;
> that NCTE support ongoing teacher and student critique of test making and test taking;
> that NCTE continue to support the use of alternative forms of assessment in order to ensure equitable treatment of all students;
> that NCTE support teacher-developed, contextualized, and reasonable classroom instruction regarding test-taking practices for students; and
> that NCTE distribute this resolution to federal and state education agencies, professional education associations, teacher unions, the media, parent groups, and appropriate organizations, and urge them to voice their support of this resolution.

Reprinted with permission of NCTE. May be reprinted for educational purposes. See Web site *www.ncte.org/resolution/* for other resolutions on topics of interest to teachers of English and language arts.

C-2: NCTE Resolution: On Phonics as a Part of Reading Instruction

On Phonics as a Part of Reading Instruction

Background

Reading is a complex act of constructing meaning. Research has shown that successful readers bring to this act a rich background of personal experiences, a repertoire of strategies and skills, and a knowledge of how language and text work. Although beginning readers have less experience with written text, the same basic processes underlie their reading. When the press, legislators, and policy makers ignore this research, the definition of reading is often reduced to nothing more than successfully sounding out words. The impact of this limited view has been decisions which reduce the ability of teachers to make instructional decisions, as evidenced by California currently allocating more than $300,000,000 to phonics-based readers. Such a decision seriously constrains teachers' and childrne's access to a full range of literacy resources. Instead of phonics as one important strategy used by all readers, it has been elevated to represent reading itself, especially for beginning readers. Be it therefore:

Resolution

Resolved, that the National Council of Teachers of English declare that reading is a complex process of constructing meaning;

that phonics for beginning as well as experienced readers is only one part of the complex, socially constructed, and cognitively demanding process called reading;

that all readers need to learn a range of reading strategies, including phonics;

that it is the professional responsibility of teachers to develop extensive knowledge of reading and a repertoire of teaching strategies to adapt to the needs of individual children in order to ensure success;

that NCTE urge policy makers and legislators to affirm that decisions about reading instruction are primarily the responsibility of professional educators; and

that NCTE establish a continuous dialogue with other professional literacy organizations on reading and reading instruction.

C-3: NCTE Resolution: On the Importance of a Print-Rich Classroom

On the Importance of a Print-Rich Classroom Environment

Background

There is a general agreement among English language arts educators that a rich literate environment is foundational to literacy development. Children need many opportunities to be read to, to read with others, and to read by themselves materials that have content that is relevant to their lives and language that is predictable and familiar. Children should be encouraged to explore print through their reading and writing. When children have opportunities to write their own stories, to read their own and others' stories, and to write in response to reading, they are able to employ much of their knowledge of reading in meaningful ways.

And yet, curricular guides from state departments of education suggest narrowing the scope of reading materials used for beginning reading instruction. Writing instruction for children in these guides focuses on the forms of writing (correct spelling and letter formation) rather than on composing meaningful messages.

These documents stipulate that materials purchased with state funds must include a strong emphasis on skills; spelling; and systematic, explicit phonics instruction. They indicate that the materials should provide practice in accurate and fluent reading in decodable stories and that such texts include only words that contain the letter-sound relationships that children have been explicitly taught. Some teachers and administrators are translating these statements into mandates that decodable texts are the only materials that can be read by young children until they have achieved a certain level of proficiency.

It is necessary to make a clear statement to those involved in the development of language arts instruction and curriculum that NCTE believes that in all types of instructional programs teachers must involve all students, from the beginning of their schooling, in daily writing and daily reading of a wide variety of literature and other print materials. Be it therefore:

Resolution

Resolved, that the National Council of Teachers of English urge professionals developing language arts instruction and curriculum for young children to assert the necessity of a print-rich classroom environment that includes a variety of children's literature, such as information books, stories, nursery rhymes, song charts, poems, and books with predictable language and themes familiar to children;

that NCTE advocate that such texts be a major component of literacy instruction and that children be permitted and encouraged to read and write such texts by themselves and with their peers and teachers and to have such materials read to them daily;

that NCTE recommend sufficient time be allocated daily to engage children in a range of purposeful writing experiences in early childhood programs, and

that NCTE distribute this resolution to appropriate members of state education agencies, curriculum directors, language arts and reading specialists, classroom teachers, and editors of publications for teachers and for parents.

C-4: American Library Association: Position Statement On Flexible Scheduling

Position Statement On Flexible Scheduling

Schools must adopt the educational philosophy that the library media program is fully integrated into the educational program. This integration strengthens the teaching/learning process so that students can develop the vital skills necessary to locate, analyze, evaluate, interpret, and communicate information and ideas. When the library media program is fully integrated into the instructional program of the school, students, teachers, and library media specialists become partners in learning. The library program is an extension of the classroom. Information skills are taught and learned within the context of the classroom curriculum. The wide range of resources, technologies, and services needed to meet students learning and information needs are readily available in a cost-effective manner.

The integrated library media program philosophy requires that an open schedule must be maintained. Classes cannot be scheduled in the library media center to provide teacher release or preparation time. Students and teachers must be able to come to the center throughout the day to use information sources, to read for pleasure, and to meet and work with other students and teachers.

Planning between the library media specialist and the classroom teacher, which encourages both scheduled and informal visits, is the catalyst that makes this integrated library program work. The teacher brings to the planning process a knowledge of subject content and student needs. The library media specialist contributes a broad knowledge of resources and technology, an understanding of teaching methods, and a wide range of strategies that may be employed to help students learn information skills. Cooperative planning by the teacher and library media specialist integrates information skills and materials into the classroom curriculum and results in the development of assignments that encourage open inquiry.

The responsibility for flexibly scheduled library media programs must be shared by the entire school community.

THE BOARD OF EDUCATION endorses the philosophy that the library program is an integral part of the districts educational program and ensures that flexible scheduling for library media centers is maintained in all buildings and at all levels.

THE DISTRICT ADMINISTRATION supports this philosophy and monitors staff assignments to ensure appropriate staffing levels so that all teachers, including the library media specialists, can fulfill their professional responsibilities.

THE PRINCIPAL creates the appropriate climate within the school by advocating the benefits of flexible scheduling to the faculty, by monitoring scheduling, by ensuring appropriate staffing levels, and by providing joint planning time for classroom teachers and library media specialists.

THE TEACHER uses resource-based instruction and views the library media program as an integral part of that instruction.

THE LIBRARY MEDIA SPECIALIST is knowledgeable about curriculum and classroom activities, and works cooperatively with the classroom teacher to integrate information skills into the curriculum.

At the time of this printing, all AASL position statements were under review to determine their alignment with the latest edition of *Information Power* (*Information Power: Building Partnerships for Learning*; Chicago: American Library Association, 1998). The most current version of this position statement is available via the AASL Web site at *http://www.ala.org/aasl* or from the AASL office at 800-545-2433, ext. 4386.

Appendix D:
Reading

D-1: A Self-Evaluation Checklist for Reading Nonfiction

❏ What do I already know about the topic?

❏ What are my questions?

❏ Do I need to read slowly? Do I need to reread?

❏ Will skimming the piece help me get an overall picture of the author's purpose and point of view?

❏ Am I noticing headings and subheadings to frame my thinking?

❏ Am I reading the captions, graphs, charts, and other visual aids and connecting what I learn to the text?

❏ Do I understand what I am reading?

❏ What do I do when I don't understand? Reread? Circle words? Write in the margin? Highlight key phrases and sentences? Study the visuals provided? Take notes?

❏ What have I learned?

❏ Have my questions been answered?

❏ How will I show what I have learned?

❏ What questions do I still have?

D-2: Strategies for Understanding **When You Read**

Summarize

Tell most important things that happened.

Clarify

Ask questions.

Reread.

Skip difficult word(s), read ahead, and come back to it. "Blank it."

Put in a word (or name) or synonym that makes sense.

Break word into syllables or chunks.

Sound word out.

Try to figure out word from other words around it.

Write down the word. Look at it again later.

Stop at the word; think about what you know.

Go back to an earlier part and reread.

Look in other parts of the book—index, cover, pictures, headings.

Write down the word several different ways (breaking into syllables).

Ask questions
Connect to what you know

Think of other words that resemble the hard word.

Think about what you already know about the topic.

Predict

Make an educated guess ("You're hypothesizing") based on what you know.

Use what you already read and learned.

Use chapter headings, the cover, information on the inside flaps and back cover.

Visualize

Make a picture in your mind.

Mrs. Cooper's Fourth-Grade Class, December 1997

D-3: Bookmark for Reciprocal Teaching

Ask questions
Ask questions about
the story as you
are reading.

Summarize
Tell the most
important ideas.

Predict
Tell what you
think will
happen next.

Clarify
Clear up confusions;
for example,
what does a
word mean?

Use as a bookmark for "reciprocal teaching." Adapted from Annemarie Sullivan Palinscar, 1986, "The Role of Dialogue in Providing Scaffolded Instruction," *Educational Psychologist* 21 (1 & 2): 73–98.

D-4: Letter and Form to Teachers on Leveling Books

Dear Lomond Staff,

We have attempted to level the books in the Owl's Nest using the system in *Guided Reading*. When a book was not listed, we leveled the book using the following criteria: story content, print size and amount, vocabulary, and comparison to known leveled book. Five staff members from varied grade levels participated.

We see our efforts as "work in progress." You all are the experts. You are knowledgeable about how difficult or easy a book is, because you are using these books with children. So, as you continue to use the books will you please compare the books within the levels, and if you find big discrepancies, use the following form to let us know and we will review the leveling. This form can be used as well to recommend books to purchase and add to our collection. Thanks so much for your help.

Sincerely,

Cathy and Liz

Evaluation Response for Text Leveling

Name _____ Grade _____

Book evaluated:

  Book title: _____

  Book level: _____

  Book author: _____

  Is the book appropriately placed on the level? (Explain.)_____

_____

_____

  To what level should it be moved? _____

  Are there points of difficulty that make it harder than it seems? _____

_____

Requesting books to be ordered

  I recommend that the following book be ordered for the Owl's Nest. (Explain.)

_____

_____

_____

D-5: An Informal Reading Conference with a Third Grader

INFORMAL READING CONFERENCE

NAME: Abby G.   DATE: Feb. 23, 1998

- Bring me a book that you can read pretty well.
TITLE OF BOOK: Runaway Ralph   GENRE: fiction

- Why did you choose this book? saw movie first & then wanted to read book

- What is the reading level of this book for you? _ hard _ easy ✓ just right "Some words are easy, some are hard." "It's inbetween medium & hard." didn't mention understanding

- Tell me what the book is about so far.
has read to p.19, retells with detail with some teacher prompting

- Read this part of the book for me. (Take notes as the child reads aloud.)
prefers to read pp.19-20 silently, moves lips as reads, reads slowly
difficult vocabulary to check after reading:
    p.19 perilously - "really." I went back to it to figure the word out.
        ventured - "came"
        exhilarated - "scared"
    p.20 - scurried - pronounced it secured - "ran fast"
    Mostly, she can figure out approximate meanings, had some difficulty pronouncing "perilously," "exhilarated," & "scurried."

- Tell me what you remember about what you just read.
excellent retelling in sequence, some exact words from text, lots of detail

- Let's discuss your strengths and what you need to work on.
Strengths:
understands what she reads, can figure out unknown vocabulary

Goals:
write down words you don't understand, ask someone. Reread if you don't understand.

- How long do you think it will take you to complete this book?
we decided together on 5 days (based on 150 pages and 30 pages a day - to take about 1 hour, each day, reading)

Regie Routman

D-6: *Informal Reading Conference Form*

INFORMAL READING CONFERENCE

NAME: DATE:

- *Bring me a book that you can read pretty well.*

TITLE OF BOOK:_____ GENRE:_____

- *Why did you choose this book?*

- *What is the reading level of this book for you?   __hard __easy __just right*

- *Tell me what the book is about so far.*

- *Read this part of the book for me. (Take notes as the child reads—aloud or silently.)*

- *Tell me what you remember about what you just read.*

- *Let's discuss your strengths and what you need to work on.*

Strengths:

Goals:

- *How long do you think it will take you to complete this book?*

D-7: *Group Worksheet for Reading*

Date _____

Title _____

Group members (underline scribe) _____

_____

Predict

Question

Clarify

Summarize

D-8: Self-Evaluation Form for Retelling Fiction

Name_____ Date _____

Name of story_____

_____

_____I gave the title and author.

_____I began with an introduction.

_____I told when and where the story took place.

_____I told the story in order.

_____I remembered all the important events.

_____I told about the important characters.

_____I told some important details.

_____I told how the story ended.

_____I used an expressive voice.

Goals:

Retelling partner: _____

Appendix E: Literature Conversations

E-1: Teachers as Readers

Guidelines for Organizing a Teachers as Readers Book Group

- Organize a group of approximately 10 members, one of whom ideally should be a school administrator, parent, community member, or school board member.
- Select a group leader or discussion facilitator for each meeting.
- Determine meeting dates.
- Establish a regular meeting place and time.
- Set norms and expectations for meetings.
- Encourage participants to maintain reading response journals.
- Decide who will provide refreshments.

Determine Reading Material

- Consult your local librarian or visit your local bookstore for suggestions.
- Study book reviews.
- Check recommended reading lists (see list of resources in this brochure).
- Consider books by theme, several books by the same author, literature about or from a particular culture, local writers, short stories, or award-winning books.

What Are They?

Teachers as Readers Book Groups consist of teachers who meet regularly to talk about the children's books, young adult literature, professional books, and adult fiction and nonfiction they've read. Teachers use the knowledge and ideas they've shared to create richly literate classrooms where students read with confidence and pleasure.

Why Form a Teachers as Readers Book Group?

- Share quality literature with colleagues.
- Gain experience and confidence in talking about books.
- Learn from the ideas and experiences of others.
- Realize that everyone brings a different meaning to text.
- Become familiar with a wider range of children's and young adult literature, professional books, and adult fiction and nonfiction.
- Learn strategies, through personal experience, for guiding students to become lifelong readers.

For further information on starting a Teachers as Readers Book Group, contact

Gerald Casey
Field Services Coordinator
International Reading Association
800 Barksdale Road
PO Box 8139
Newark, Delaware 19714-8139, USA
Telephone: 302-731-1600, ext. 281

E-2: Role of Facilitator and Group Member

Role of Facilitator in Conversation Groups

- Checks to see that team members are prepared
- Helps keep conversation going
- Gives ideas for others to add to, when needed
- Encourages everyone to speak
- Stays with literary questions
- Treats everyone with respect
- Encourages eye contact
- Makes statements (not questions) to guide the conversation, such as,

  "Let's discuss why . . ."
  "Tell us what you mean by . . ."
  "Tell us why you agree . . ."
  "Let's talk about . . ."
  "So you're saying . . ."
  "I'm wondering . . ."
  "Explain what you mean."
  "Let's look in the book."
  "Tell us about that."

Role of Group Member

- Reads book carefully and prepares notes
- Refers to notes, goes back to book
- Expresses how and why they feel the way they do
- Stays with the topic/question
- Adds on to speaker and gives examples, piggybacks
- Asks questions for clarification
- Doesn't raise hand
- Makes eye contact with speakers
- Uses polite language
- Gets in the conversation with comments such as,

  "I think . . ."
  "I agree . . ."
  "I disagree . . ."
  "I'd like to add . . ."
  "I'm confused about . . ."

Some Advice on Literature Conversations

- Be prepared by reading the book twice and thinking about it.

- When you read the book the second time, take good notes. This will affect good conversation. The better your notes, the better the conversation.

- Focus on literary questions. Literary questions are questions that do not have a right or wrong answer and can be discussed.

- To make sure you have good questions, have a mock discussion with yourself on the question. Start discussion group with "What's your opinion . . . ?"

- If you like one idea and the rest of the group likes another, don't be afraid to argue for what you believe. If you want to add something, say it. Don't keep it to yourself.

- Listen to what each person has to say about the topic. If a person has a good thought, don't let it go. Piggyback on it, or tell why you think it's good. When you are discussing, try to stay on the topic. Give other people a chance to say something.

- Compare the story with your life.

- Help group members with words they don't understand.

- Enter the conversation at least two or three times.

- Sit up straight and lean into the conversation.

- Always have the book with you. Refer back to the book for proof.

- Make eye contact with the person you're talking or listening to.

- No put-downs. Respect other people.

E-4: Self-Evaluation Form for Literature Conversations

Self-Evaluation
Literature Conversation Group

Name _____ Date _____

Book/story_____

1. What did I do well today (and/or improve on) during group discussion?

2. What do I still need to improve on during group discussion?

3. What questions do I still have?

Appendix F: Writing

WRITING RECORD

WHAT DID I WORK ON TODAY?
Be descriptive and specific.

Name: _____

Week of _____	Week of _____
Monday	Monday
Tuesday	Tuesday
Wednesday	Wednesday
Thursday	Thursday
Friday	Friday
I want to publish:	

WRITING WORKSHOP
WHAT DID I WORK ON TODAY?

NAME: _____

Monday:_____

_____

_____

_____

Tuesday:_____

_____

_____

_____

Wednesday:_____

_____

_____

_____

Thursday:_____

_____

_____

_____

Friday:_____

_____

_____

_____

F-2: Cumulative Writing Record

W R I T I N G   R E C O R D

Title/Topic	Audience	Genre	Date Started	Date Ended	What Happened to the piece?

F-4: Family Feedback Form for Writing Notebook

Feedback on _____**Writing Notebook**

Family member(s) who reviewed the notebook_____

What did you notice that impressed you? (Include strengths and weaknesses.)

What are your goals for your child in writing?

Do you have any questions or comments about the writing program?

F-5: Teacher's Response to Parents' Questions About Writing

January 22, 1998

"A writer's night is not night enough."
A class favorite quote

Dear Parents,

Thank you for taking the time to respond to the writing notebook form. It was helpful for me to read your comments. I read each form carefully and compiled a list of questions you had about the writing program. I decided to type my comments so everyone could benefit and would have a better understanding of the writing program and my expectations.

How often can each child publish?

I require one published piece a month. This includes *WACK* articles, friendly letters I assign, business letters I assign, book or movie reviews, essays, poetry, and projects. Each month we focus on a different genre and then I ask the kids to publish something so I know that they understand that style of writing. This also gives them opportunities to use editing skills, the computer, and/or their best handwriting. The students know that a good project (which are ongoing throughout the year) should take a few months. (See attached "How to do a project" form.)

Why are some sections empty?

At the beginning of the year we talked about the different things each child "could" write about and then they labeled dividers according to those topics. It is possible their interests have changed and they have decided not to work on a certain section at this time. I required an attempt at fiction. They each had to develop a character, make a plan, and use telling details. It was then up to each child if they wanted to publish that fiction story. Some children are publishing them for their project this year. Other children chose a different topic for their project. The important thing is that they feel passion about their project so they will *want* to write. This also explains why some pieces are incomplete. The students may have decided to work on something else. Each child was told, however, that at this point, they must know what their project is and work on it every day. They are accountable for their time and must use it wisely. I have started writing on their writing record if I noticed them wasting their writing time. I also started checking them daily.

Why do I see misspelled words? Why is my child not writing neater?

When a piece goes to final copy, their spelling must be impeccable. I also require "no excuse" words to be spelled correctly in their daily writing. These are words fourth-grade students should know how to spell. Of course, the focus while writing is getting ideas down on paper not spelling and neatness. I do, however, tell the students they should be proud of all their work (even rough drafts!). I have tried to give five minutes at the end of each writing time for the students to check "no excuse" words, proper punctuation, capitalization, and grammar but I have not always been consistent. I will try harder to provide that time!

When do children get individualized instruction to correct their mistakes?

Every day at the beginning of writing I spend the first 10 minutes looking at each child's writing and asking what they need from me. I make notes on things I notice that I need to teach for minilessons or things I need to work on individually with students. During writing, I conference with students who need help with ideas, revision, and editing. I keep track of who I conference with each day so I am sure to meet with every one at least every other week even if the student did not request a conference.

Is the focus on creative writing?

It is my goal to expose the children to all kinds of writing. In my year plan, I mapped out a different genre for each month including poetry, reviews, fiction, report writing, essays, friendly letters, business letters, and articles. The students are responsible for trying each genre and in most cases publishing that particular genre. (See the attached writing record to see what your child has published so far this year.) We even invited Mrs. Connors and Mrs. Kurit in to teach our minilessons on writing reviews. Mrs. Connors gave each child a reporter's notebook to take to restaurants, movies, on interviews for taking notes!

Should my child be writing in cursive?

Question of the day!!! I require cursive on everything except in the writer's notebook. In the notebook the students use whatever they are most comfortable using so their ideas can flow. We work on cursive papers three times a week as well as write our grammar lesson and spelling dictation in cursive each week. At the end of the cursive unit, the children who are still not comfortable will be part of a lunch time cursive club. Since the writing of choice seems to be printing, the students sometimes forget to write in cursive. You can help reinforce this.

Why are some pieces not very long?

This issue varies with each notebook. If you noticed pieces that seemed incomplete or you think they could be longer, talk to your child about it. It could be because they did not want to publish it and it was not a required piece or they plan to complete it at another time or it could be because their writing time is not always used wisely. A trip to Borders to look at models for writing or just talking about what your child is working on in school at night might be the motivation your child needs to write their heart out each day. We discussed in school that when you select a project, immerse yourself with materials about that project. For example, if you are writing about dogs, bring in pictures of dogs, stuffed animals, books about dogs, dog quotes . . . and lay them all around you as you write for motivation and ideas.

I have also attached a copy of the fourth-grade writing rubric as well as the rubric the children used for evaluating their story and letter they wrote for the practice proficiency test. I hope this was helpful. If you have any other questions or would like to come "write" with us some day, please call!

Thanks,
J. Beers

F-6: Editing Expectations: Second-Grade Shared Writing

Editing Expectations

1. **Reread**
   - Did you leave any words out?

2. **Spelling**
   - Circle *most* misspelled words.
   - Correct at least *five* of them.
        Look at the word and spell it again another way.
        Sound it out.
        Use your dictionary.
        Ask a neighbor.
        Look around the room for the word.

3. **Neatness**
   - Use good handwriting.
   - Space between words.
   - Be sure there are no capital letters in the middle of words.

4. **Proper Punctuation**
   - Put a **.** , **?** , **!** at the end of every sentence.

5. **Capitalization**
   - Start every sentence with a capital letter.
   - Always capitalize the work "I."
   - Capitalize important names and places, days of the week, months, book titles.

6. **Reread**
   - Is your story *exactly* the way you want it?

Mr. Robinson's Second-Grade Class
Mercer School in Shaker Heights, OH
November 18, 1998

F-7: Editing Expectations: Third-Grade Shared Writing

EDITING

CHECK YOUR PAPER OVER!!!

1. Look for misspelled words and circle them.
   - Look them up in your dictionary.
     - Cross out the misspelled words and try to write the correct spelling on top of it.
   - Ask a friend.
   - Look around the room for the word.
   - Ask an adult.

2. Go back and put in punctuation.
   - Put periods, question marks, or exclamation marks at the end of each sentence.
   - Put commas between words when you pause, and to separate words such as "My friend, John, Nathan, and I."
   - Examples of sentences with punctuation:
        The teacher said, "No talking!"
        John mowed the lawn.
        What is your name?
   - Use apostrophes: It's (it is) a nice day.
   - When you start a new paragraph indent.

3. Use capitals:
   - at the beginning of every sentence
   - with important names
   - with *I*
   - with states, cities, important places, countries, and streets
   - with titles of books, authors, and illustrators (also underline book titles)

4. Put in a better word for one that doesn't sound right. Try to have your piece as good as it can be.

5. CHECK IT OVER!

6. Conference with a friend.

7. READ IT OVER AGAIN VERY CAREFULLY!

Mr. Young's Third-Grade Class, Second Draft, January 13, 1994

Appendix G: Spelling

G-1: *Most Frequent Words in Writing*

100 Most Frequent Words in Writing

a	friends	lot	their
about	from	make	them
after	fun	me	then
all	get	more	there
and	go	my	they
are	good	no	things
as	got	not	this
at	had	of	time
back	has	on	to
be	have	one	too
because	he	or	up
big	her	other	us
but	him	our	very
by	his	out	want
came	home	people	was
can	house	play	we
could	I	said	went
day	if	saw	were
did	in	school	what
didn't	is	see	when
do	it	she	will
don't	just	so	with
down	know	some	would
every	like	that	you
for	little	the	your

G-2: *Guidelines for the Use of Core Spelling Words Lists*

Core Spelling Words
by grade level

Children will not become proficient spellers unless they are reading and writing daily in meaningful contexts.

Words chosen for spelling study should be appropriate to the child's developmental spelling level and should represent words the child uses in reading and writing. (However, it is not appropriate to pull words out of literature that are not part of the child's writing vocabulary, for example, pulling "radiant" out of *Charlotte's Web* in grade two.)

It is expected that the majority of students will have mastered the appropriate grade-level list by the end of the school year, that is, those words are to be spelled correctly in daily writing.

High-frequency words, from other lists or experiences, should be included for study.

Explicit instruction—focus lessons, demonstrations—is necessary and is expected. By explicit instruction, we mean guiding children in working out the rules and patterns of our language, for example, when to double final consonants and forming plurals.

It is expected that word families—onsets and rimes—will be taught. For example, along with *right* on the grade two list is the expectation that other *ight* words be taught. (See page 53 of the Language Arts Course of Study for lists of rimes.)

It is expected that previous grade-level lists are to be revisited. Additionally, words such as "they're," "there," and "their," and "two," "to," and "too" need to be revisited each year.

Just because a word is not on a core list does not mean it should not be taught.

Teachers will also expect certain content area words to be mastered.

Developed by Mercer School Language Arts Support Group Spring, 1993
Revised February, 1994, June, 1995, May, 1996
Lists are meant to be shared with students, teachers, and parents.

G-3: A Second-Grade Core Spelling Words List

Core Spelling Words
to be mastered by the end of the grade level

about	girl	one	think
another	gone	other	this
any	grandfather	our	those
are	grandmother	outside	throw
because	happy	people	together
been	help	put	too
better	how	read	two
boy	hurt	right	under
brother	I'm	school	use
catch	knew	seen	very
child	know	should	walk
children	leave	sister	want
color	made	story	were
could	many	street	what
dear	mother	take	when
down	much	teacher	where
each	myself	thank	which
eat	never	that	while
every	new	their	who
everybody	nice	there	would
father	now	these	write
friend	off	they	yard
			yesterday

Days of the Week

Sunday
Monday
Tuesday
Wednesday
Thursday
Friday
Saturday

Months of the Year

January	July
February	August
March	September
April	October
May	November
June	December

Color Words: red, orange, blue, green, yellow, purple, black, white

Number Words: one, two, three, four, five, six, seven, eight, nine, ten, eleven, twelve, thirteen, fourteen, fifteen, sixteen, seventeen, eighteen, nineteen, twenty

Developed by Mercer School Language Arts Support Group Spring, 1993
Revised February, 1994, June, 1995, May, 1996
Lists are meant to be shared with students, teacher, and parents.

G-4: Letter to Parents Explaining "No Excuses" Spelling List

OUR WEEK IN REVIEW

March 17–21

On Monday, your child was given an ordered list of the first forty-three words (see attached list) from a list of the 100 highest-frequency words used in writing. Within our writing framework, the words on this "no excuses" list must be spelled accurately every day, all day long, in every subject. No exceptions. Like adults in the real world, the children can "look up" these words by referring to this list whenever they write and are expected to look if there is a question about the spelling of any word on the list. This list will be expanded slowly. The class will be informed ahead of time that on a predetermined date, word forty-four will be added to the "no excuse" list. About once every one to two weeks, I will randomly select one of your child's writings in which to assess spelling. The "no excuse" words in the selected sample will be expected to be spelled correctly. The children can refer to their "no excuse" list as often as they need to in order to spell with accuracy in their everyday writing. Hopefully, this random selection sends the message that "I'm looking, I care, and, most importantly, I want to see if you care."

Have a peaceful weekend!

Ellen Rubin

"No Excuses"! List

the	of	and	a	to
in	is	you	that	it
he	for	was	on	are
as	with	his	they	at
be	this	from	I	have
or	by	one	had	not
but	what	all	were	when
we	there	can	an	your
	there are			your pencil
their	said	which		
their pencils				

G-5: *Letter to Parents Explaining Goals and Curriculum for Word Study*

Dear Parents,

You will hear us talk about Word Study in third grade. Mr. Sandstrom and I are working together to teach your child far more about spelling than basic memorization. As you will see, memorizing words is just one part of our Word Study in third grade. We are studying about letters, sounds, patterns, and meanings of words. I have four goals for our Word Study program:

1. *Students will learn spelling strategies to assist in spelling unknown or unfamiliar words.* I want your child to be able to rely on "sounding it out" as ONE of several strategies to use when writing a challenging or new word. Some of the other strategies I will teach are: using references, asking a more expert speller, Three Tries, Sounds Like, and Looks Like.

2. *Students will learn how to memorize words. I will teach them which words should be memorized.* Expecting students to memorize every word just does not work. However, there are key words that we call "Accountability Words." These words are very common words that are used in writing. You have received a list of our Accountability Words. We will continue to send regular updates about your child's progress in memorizing these words. These words can be studied like the multiplication tables; they just need to be memorized and spelled correctly all the time. Even if your child has not yet learned all of these words, the words still must always be spelled correctly. Resources can be used: our class Word Wall, class Word Plus dictionary, Portable Work Wall all can be consulted. After studying and correcting the spelling of these words enough times your child will learn them!

3. *Students will learn common patterns used in spelling.* Third graders typically are ready to learn the various long vowel patterns. Much of our word study will begin with examination of the various long vowel patterns. For example, when we do a Word Study about long "a" patterns we will explore and discover the following long "a" patterns: **same, pain, play, eight**.

4. *Students will develop a spelling consciousness*. I expect your child to become a word expert. As we explore words through spelling and meaning your child will begin to develop a curiosity and interest in words that will carry over into reading and other academic areas. We will become more aware of words and patterns and students will begin to find "spelling bloopers" in newspapers, menus, advertisements, school publications (we hope not, but it happens!) They have already developed a "Spelling Ticket" to issue to anyone who is "caught" making a spelling mistake.

If you have any questions about our Word Study lessons in third grade do not hesitate to call me. Also, feel free to stop by our class during Word Study time. It is usually every day from 1:15–2:00. Just check with Mr. Sandstrom in the morning to be sure there hasn't been a change in the schedule.

Sincerely,

Cindy Marten
Reading Specialist

G-6: Suggestions for Parents on Word Study (for Working with Their Children)

Letter Sounds Connection

1. Stay after a movie is over and watch the credits roll. Have your child find all the letters in his or her name. Or look for all of the Cs.

2. Go through a magazine with your child looking for pictures of things that begin with a certain letter. Connect it to something meaningful. If your child's name begins with a B, for pictures of things that start with B. Make a page that has a big B on the top. Have your child cut out all the pictures that start with B and paste them on the page.

3. Encourage writing at home by having a "Writing Table" stocked with:
   - Many kinds of writing instruments: pencils, pens, crayons, markers
   - Many kinds of paper: cards, envelopes, construction paper, different colors of paper, lined paper, plain paper, graph paper, Post-it Notes, business cards, stationery
   - Scissors
   - Glue
   - Tape

   Write letters to your child and leave your notes on his "Writing Table" or in his lunchbox. Encourage him to write back to you.

4. When you are preparing to go to the grocery store invite your child to help you with the shopping list. If your child needs more apple juice for his lunch box have him look at the words *apple juice* on the box and tell you how to spell the words. He will read the letters to you as you write them on the list. When you are at the store, in the juice section, have your child find the apple juice and match the words to your list.

5. Cut out letters from magazines so your child can see all of the different ways a letter can look: G g **g G**

Developing: Word Patterns

When students are at this stage of development they are becoming aware of their spelling errors and often want to spell everything "the right way."

1. If the word they are attempting is one of our "Accountability Words" then have your child first try to write the word three times and then circle the one that "Looks Right" and then check the word on his portable word wall. This activity will accomplish three of our spelling goals: raising spelling consciousness, developing use of references, building stronger visual memory.

2. If the word they are attempting is a new word then have your child write it. In school we say, "Use all that you know about letters, sounds, and patterns and work out the best spelling you can of the word." Then after the first attempt, we write the word two other ways—our best attempts. We then look at the three attempts and circle the one that looks right. After going through this process students often come up with the correct spelling.

3. Play spelling games using common patterns. For example, if your child is practicing the common pattern, "ai," you can make up a game. Make up letter cards that have common beginnings: b, c, d, m, p, sh, str, pl, dr, etc. and cards that have common endings: t, nt, l, m, st, n, r, etc. Have your child match up the card to the common "ai" vowel combination to make up new words.

Secure: Meaning Connection

1. Explore common suffixes and prefixes. Have your child begin a word collection of words that start with any of the following prefixes:

anti	de	mis
auto	en	pre
bi	em	sub
circum	ex	tele
co	micro	trans

Also collect words with common suffixes:

age	ish	ment
ary	ist	ness
ceed	ive	ship
er	ize	th
ful	less	y
ion		

2. Students at this stage can be challenged in word games such as Scrabble and Boggle. Be sure to have a good dictionary nearby.

3. On-line resources that explore words and spelling are invaluable if you have on-line access. Here are three excellent web sites for spelling at this stage:

- **http://www.mcdougallittell.com/lit/liactspe.htm**
  Has engaging activities for advanced spellers to explore in word study.
- **http://www.spellingbee.com/cctoc.htm**
  Exciting activities provided weekly. All previous lessons are available. This site is a required site for any student who participates in the National Spelling Bee competition. But even if your child isn't participating, the site has excellent resources and high-level activities and discussions about word explorations.
- **http://www.m–w.com/netdict.htm**
  Webster's dictionary site with links to word study activities. It's a perfect tool for looking up spelling and meaning on-line. It also has excellent word study activities including vocabulary challenges.

Cindy Marten

G-7: Personal Word Wall Form

A	B	C	D	E	F
G	H	I	J	K	L
MN	OP	QR	S	T	UV
W	X	Y	Z	Other	Other

REVISION CONFERENCE

What did I do? Where do I need suggestions?

Reread several times.
Go back to the beginning—or the part you're working on—and read it again. Look carefully at your writing.

Should I add something?
interesting vocabulary, a capturing beginning, strong ending, capitalization and punctuation

Should I take something out?
things that don't make sense, confusing words, boring words or words that are used too much, something that's already been said, misspelled words

Should I move things around?
to make more sense, to sound clearer and better

_____

Suggestions/Goals   date _____

Appendix H:
Curriculum Inquiry

H-1: Independent Study Guidelines

Independent Study Guidelines: Worksheet 1

Name: _____

The topic for my study is: _____

Follow these steps and dues dates

1. *Prepare* for Your Independent Study   Due _____

You should complete worksheets 1 and 2 and hand them in to your teacher. Remember, you are exploring what you already know about your topic and should use your own knowledge first. Once you've written all the I know and I wonder statements you can think of, get a book or article about your topic, look it over, and you'll come up with even more!! Now you're ready to do some research.

2. Gather Information: READ and THINK and READ and THINK

Use the fact-finding sheets or some other form of note taking to record the facts you find, the answers to your "I wonder" questions, and your own thoughts and reflections about the topic that your research makes you think about.

3. Organize Your Information/Write a Rough Draft   Due _____

The sheet called "Organize Your Information" is VERY IMPORTANT. You need to carefully go over that sheet **and then** write your rough draft. Once a rough draft has been completed it should be handed in to your teacher for editing.

4. Your Final Project—Finally!   Due _____

You should write the final copy of your report once your draft has been edited and returned to you.

The page called "Your Project" is the final step. Complete the page and have it checked by your teacher **BEFORE** beginning to make a project. Once it has been checked, you can make your project.

Finally, you should practice telling about (presenting) your project based on the new information you've learned and recorded in the report. By now, you should know your topic well enough so you do not have to refer to or read from the report at all—you have to be able to talk about your topic in your own words.

Developed by Jeannine Perry and other teachers at Mercer School, Shaker Heights, OH.

Independent Study Guidelines: Worksheet 2

I Wonder . . . .

What would you like to know about your topic?

Write down some of the questions that you wonder about.

When you run out of questions, it's time to start gathering information about your topic. Once you start reading about it, you'll come up with even more "I wonder" questions.

Fact-Finding Sheet

Your Name:_____

Complete a sheet for EACH different resource you use to find your facts and information.

My facts have been collected from . . .

☐ a book   ☐ a magazine   ☐ a video   ☐ a filmstrip

☐ an interview   ☐ the Internet   ☐ a computer program

☐ class discussion ☐ somewhere else _____

Title/Name of Resource_____

Author_____

Facts I found out

What are some new questions this resource made me think of?

Organize Your Information

Once you have gathered information, organize your information by:

- rereading your notes from your fact-finding sheets

- organizing the information into categories

- writing a rough draft that includes your thoughts about what you've learned during your research; *these questions will help you reflect on your learning:*

  1. What did you think about when you were learning about your topic?

  2. How does your topic make you feel?

  3. What's exciting about your topic?

  4. Have you answered your questions?

  5. What do you still wonder about?

- editing your rough draft and writing a final copy

Before you try to write a minireport or create a project, think about these questions:

- ☐ Have you investigated enough to put your information into your own words?
- ☐ Could you tell someone information about your topic?
- ☐ Have you answered your questions?
- ☐ Do you really know several new and interesting things about your topic?

If you answered "no" to any of these questions, it's not time for you to write a report or create a project. Keep reading and researching about your topic until you can say "yes" to each of these questions.

Your Project

*Name:*_____

Your Project: I will show others what I learned by. . . .

    ☐ a poster or chart   ☐ a mobile

    ☐ an oral or written "report"   ☐ a puzzle

    ☐ a poem, song, or play   ☐ a model

    ☐ a labeled diagram   ☐ a collage

    ☐ a picture book   ☐ a map

Plan Ahead:

My project will show/teach . . .

The supplies I will need to find are . . .

Draw a sketch of your project or make an outline of the steps you will need to do for your project.

Have your teacher check this paper BEFORE you do your project.

Appendix I:
Evaluation: Common Tools

I-1: A Kindergarten Portrait and Name Sample

First Trimester
November

Portrait and Name Sample

Teacher Preparation

- Obtain 9" x 12" white construction paper for each student.
- Copy Name Sample sheets for each student.
- *Regina's Big Mistake* by Marissa Moss and picture exemplars.
- Familiarize yourself with this script.

Script

Directions to children. Say:

"Today, I'm going to ask you to draw a picture of yourself. Artists call that a self-portrait. Before you start to draw, I'm going to read you a story called Regina's Big Mistake *by Marissa Moss. It's about a little girl named Regina who has a hard time drawing pictures. She can never get them to look exactly the way she wants them to. Let's read the book and find out what happens. I'd like you to notice the colors and details that Regina and the illustrator use."*

Read the book and solicit discussion. Draw attention to the author's illustrations in the book. Say:

"Look at how the author drew Regina." (on page 5)

"What are some of the details that the illustrator used?" (eyes, nose, mouth, lips, bangs and individual braids, hair beads, neck, shoulders, etc.)

Say:

"Now, I would like you to draw a picture of yourself. Put in as much color and detail as you can. Here are some pictures that kindergarten students have done in the past."

Show picture exemplars to students.

Remember, this is a picture of you, so just draw you and no one else!"

Have the students write their name sample on the line on the form provided and staple it to the front of the child's self-portrait.

I-2: *A First-Grade Standardized Writing Assessment: Purposes and Teacher Notes*

Shaker Heights City School District
Shaker Heights, Ohio
Standardized Writing Assessment
Grades 1–4

Purposes of Standardized Writing Assessment

The standardized writing assessment has been designed by Shaker educators to:

- use personal narrative to assess student progress in writing at the district level, classroom level, and student level to:
- set goals and objectives for instruction,
- set district goals and objectives for professional development,
- share data with all members of school community,
- report proficiency to the state of Ohio.

Teacher Notes

- Administer fall prompt for the third week of September.
  Administer spring prompt the first week of May.
- Administer the writing prompt in the morning.
- Use the paper that is provided. Please remind students to skip lines.
- Be sure papers have no names on them and are coded so you will know to whom the paper belongs. In the upper right-hand corner of each paper, it is coded to note school, the date, **your initials**, and grade level followed by the number you've assigned to each student. Keep a record of the numbers and corresponding names for yourself.
  Recommendations: Complete the first four lines to be coded before xeroxing the writing page—leaving only the student number to be filled in at the time of the assessment.
- Identify the students (as noted) in the upper left-hand corner of their paper by placing a check on the appropriate line:
  I.E.P. All students with an I.E.P. containing language arts sections.
  NS New student (entered Shaker school during the current year).
  ESL English as a second language students.
- For students with I.E.P.s for language arts, follow testing procedures as outlined in the I.E.P.
- You are encouraged to use prompts of your own choosing from time to time throughout the year so children have experience writing from a common prompt. Do not rehearse or use this exact prompt at any other time.

I-3: A First-Grade Fall Writing Assessment

Fall Writing Assessment
Grade One

Administration of Writing Prompt

To administer the prompt, follow directions and script exactly as written. Directions are in bold print, verbal script is in italics. In order for results to be standardized, we all need to follow the same procedures.

Begin by saying to students:

"I'm going to read a story about John and his friend, called My Friend John. *While I'm reading, I want you to be thinking about one of your own friends. Then we'll talk about favorite times with your friends. We will write our own stories about our friends. We will use the* What Good Writers Do *checklist to help us."*

Note to teacher.

After reading the book to students, take about ten minutes to brainstorm the favorite time students spent with their friends. The teacher should record the students' ideas on a chart, overhead, chalkboard, etc., as is the teacher's practice.

Put the checklist on the overhead and distribute the checklist and writing paper to each student. Review the checklist of *What Good Writers Do*. Remind the students to write a story—*not* a list—about their friend that includes a beginning, middle, and end.

Say to students,

"You will have twenty minutes to write. If you are finished before I say "stop," read your writing over. See if you want to add or change anything in your story." **(Teacher puts start time on chalkboard.)** *"You may begin writing now."*

After twenty minutes say,

"Stop writing. You have five minutes to read over your paper and use the checklist to check your writing."

Collect all papers after five minutes.

Shaker Heights City School District
8/23/99 Grade 1

I-4: A First-Grade Reading/Writing Overview

Shaker Heights City School District
Shaker Heights, Ohio

Common Tools
Grade One Reading/Writing Overview

Fall Assessment
(First two weeks of school)

- *Letter Identification:* Name upper and lowercase letters.
- *Phonics Assessment:* Students write a dictated sentence.
- *Spelling Words:* Write the list of twenty words selected from the core spelling words.

(Administer second week in September)

- *Full writing assessment: My Friend John* by Charlotte Zolotow.

(Administered by the Fall Conference)

- *Reading Assessment:* Informal reading conference or administer the benchmark (if student can meet the standard).

Spring Assessment
(First week of May)

- *Spring Writing Assessment: Chester's Way* by Kevin Henkes.

(To be completed by the third week of May)

- *Letter Identification:* Name upper and lower case letters. (Optional)
- *Phonics Assessment:* Students write a dictated sentence.
- *Spelling Words:* Write the list of twenty words selected from the core spelling words.
- *Reading Assessment:* Running record/retelling on benchmark book to meet state and district requirement (if the student has demonstrated proficiency at first-grade level earlier in the year, use the informal reading conference and attach a photocopy of text used).

(May/June)

- Letter to next year's teacher.

Letter identification and phonics assessment are adapted from Marie Clay's *Observation Survey*, 1993. Portsmouth, NH: Heinemann

I-5: A Second-Grade Reading/Writing Overview

Shaker Heights City School District
Shaker Heights, Ohio

Common Tools
Grade Two Reading/Writing Overview

Fall Assessment
(First two weeks of school)

- *Spelling Words*: Write the list of twenty-five words selected from core spelling words.

(Administered second week in September)

- *Fall Writing Assessment: Rosie & Michael* by Judith Viorst

(Administered by the first Friday in October)

- *Reading Assessment:* Administer the benchmark for first grade for those students scoring 94% or below; administer the second grade benchmark for those students who scored 95% or above.

Spring Assessment
(Second week of May)

- *Spring Writing Assessment: Wednesday Surprise* by Eve Bunting

(To be completed by the third week of May)

- *Spelling Words:* Write the list of twenty-five words selected from core spelling words.

- *Reading Assessment:* Running record/retelling on benchmark book to meet state and district requirement. If the student has demonstrated proficiency at second-grade level earlier in the year, hold an informal reading conference with that student.

(May/June)

- Letter to next year's teacher.

I-6: A Fourth-Grade Reading/Writing Overview

Shaker Heights City School District
Shaker Heights, Ohio

Common Tools
Grade Four Reading/Writing Overview

Fall Assessment

(First two weeks of school)

- *Spelling Words:* Write the list of thirty words selected from core spelling words.

(Administer second week in September)

- *Fall Writing Assessment: When I Was Young in the Mountains* by Cynthia Rylant

(Administered by the first Friday in October)

- *Reading Assessment:* Administer the benchmark (if student can meet the standard). If student doesn't pass, use the third-grade benchmark assessment.

Spring Assessment

(Second week of May)

- *Spring Writing Assessment: The Tarantula in My Purse* by Jean Craighead George

(To be completed by the third week of May)

- *Spelling Words:* Write the list of thirty words selected from core spelling words.

- *Reading Assessment:* Retelling on benchmark book to meet state and district requirement. This is not necessary if the student has demonstrated proficiency earlier in the year. An informal reading conference can be used for students who have met the standard.

- (Letter to next year's teacher has been replaced by the fifth-grade student letter, as requested by Woodbury.)

I-7: Thinking About Your Reading

Thinking About Your Reading

Date _____   Name _____

1. How often did you read during this two-week sweep?

    ❏ everyday   ❏ most days   ❏ not often

2. List the different kinds (genres) of books that you read.

3. When you look at your log/record, what do you notice about the kinds (levels) of books you are reading? Are most of them:

    ❏ easy (familiar or you knew all the words)
    ❏ medium (just right)
    ❏ hard (needed some help or difficult to understand)

4. What was your favorite book to read? Tell why.

5. What would you like to read next?

Adapted from S. Valencia 6/97
Shaker Heights City School District
8/23/99 Grade 2

Attach to two-week sweep for fall and spring

I-8: *Informal Reading Conference and Benchmark Book Assessment*

—Informal Reading Conference—
—Benchmark Book—

Important Notes to the Teacher

The purpose of the reading assessment is twofold. One is to fulfill the state requirement to identify children who are not meeting the grade-level standard. The other is to improve instruction and learning. Use this one-on-one time to guide instruction, to diagnose, and to teach. When this reading assessment is administered throughout the year, the task becomes manageable.

These assessments can be given at any time of the year when you feel the child will be successful at reaching the benchmark, but no later than the third week in May. Every student must be assessed **at least** twice per year. These two assessments will become part of the student's permanent portfolio.

If the benchmark is reached during the first or second trimester, the child must be reassessed during the third trimester, no later than the third week of May. However, the second assessment will be an individual informal reading conference using the student's self-selected independent reading book.

If a student passes the grade-level assessment do *not* give a reading assessment at a higher grade level. For both teacher information and for the student to feel successful, it is strongly suggested that students who do not meet the benchmark be given the assessment for the grade level immediately preceding or given an informal reading evaluation. **No student should be given an assessment at a higher grade level at any time**.

At the end of May, even if a teacher believes a student cannot meet the grade-level benchmark, the student must be given the opportunity so that the assessment results that are reported to the state reflect objectivity and not subjective teacher judgment.

Both the running record and the retelling must be given together, on the same day. For example, the student reads the *Henry and Mudge* passage, and the teacher then *immediately* administers the retelling.

If a teacher feels a student is ready to pass the benchmark assessment but the student fails to pass, the assessment cannot be administered again for at least one month.

I-9: A First-Grade Reading Assessment Procedure

Reading Assessment Procedure

Meet with each student one-on-one. Have all three benchmark books on a table.

Benchmark Books—Grade 1

"Puddle Trouble" in *Henry and Mudge* by Cynthia Rylant
"The Garden" in *Mr. Putter and Tabby Row the Boat* by Cynthia Rylant
"Bedtime" in *More Tales of Oliver Pig* by Jean Van Leeuwen

Say to the student:

"Look through the books on the table. Choose a book that looks interesting to you and that you haven't read before."

If the child is having difficulty, the teacher may select one of the books for the student.

Follow directions on the retelling sheet for the particular book. Say to your student:

"I am going to ask you to read part of this book out loud to me and then retell what you have just read. If you want to read the passage again before you retell it, you may reread it either silently or out loud."

Administer the running record. Then have student retell what they read. Use any of the attached generic prompts to help students do a complete retelling.

To have met the benchmark for proficiency in reading, the student will need to have passed both the running record (90% accuracy) and the retelling as directed on the attached worksheets.

I-10: A First-Grade Story Retelling (Narrative)

Retelling: _____ Passed
_____ Not Passed

Story Retelling (Narrative)
Summary Worksheet—*Mr. Putter and Tabby Row the Boat*

Name: _____ Grade 1

Teacher: _____

Date: _____

NO PROMPTING/NEEDS PROMPTING

BENCHMARK TITLE: "Sweaty" in *Mr. Putter and Tabby Row the Boat* by Cynthia Rylant

> **GENERIC RETELLING PROMPTS**
>
> The teacher may wish to probe responses with further generic questions:
>
> What else can you tell me?
> Who else was in the story besides the characters you've mentioned?
> What else happened in the story?
> What happened after such-and-such?
> Where/when did the story take place?
> What comes next?
> When did the story happen?
> Then what happened?
>
> from Connie Weaver's
> *Reading Process and Practice,* Heinemann, 1994

What happened to Mr. Putter and his cat Tabby?

LITERAL QUESTIONS:

_____ 1. It was a hot summer day.

_____ 2. Mr. Putter and his cat lay around and sweated.

_____ 3. They decided to go to the big pond.

_____ 4. They talked to their neighbor Mrs. Teaberry.

_____ 5. Mrs. Teaberry said she would make food to eat.

_____ 6. Mr. Putter liked Mrs. Teaberry's funny food.

_____ 7. Mr. Putter went home to get ready to go to the big pond.

INFERENTIAL QUESTION:

_____ 8. What do you think will happen at the pond?

EVALUATION QUESTION:

_____ 9. How do you know that Mrs. Teaberry and Mr. Putter were friends?

----

*6 OUT OF 9 FOR PASSING

INDEX

Page numbers in boldface indicate pages on which full publishing information and/or a full annotation or description is given.